Encyclopedia of World Cultures

Volume II

OCEANIA

ENCYCLOPEDIA OF WORLD CULTURES

David Levinson
Editor in Chief

North America
Oceania
South Asia
Europe and the Middle East
East and Southeast Asia
Soviet Union and China
South America
Middle America and the Caribbean
Africa
Bibliography

The Encyclopedia of World Cultures was prepared under the auspices and with the support of the Human Relations Area Files at Yale University. HRAF, the foremost international research organization in the field of cultural anthropology, is a not-for-profit consortium of twenty-three sponsoring members and 300 participating member institutions in twenty-five countries. The HRAF archive, established in 1949, contains nearly one million pages of information on the cultures of the world.

Encyclopedia of World Cultures

Volume II

Oceania

Terence E. Hays
Volume Editor

G.K. Hall & Co.
Boston, Massachusetts

MEASUREMENT CONVERSIONS

When You Know	Multiply By	To Find
LENGTH		
inches	2.54	centimeters
feet	30	centimeters
yards	0.9	meters
miles	1.6	kilometers
millimeters	0.04	inches
centimeters	0.4	inches
meters	3.3	feet
meters	1.1	yards
kilometers	0.6	miles
AREA		
square feet	0.09	square meters
square yards	0.8	square meters
square miles	2.6	square kilometers
acres	0.4	hectares
hectares	2.5	acres
square meters	1.2	square yards
square kilometers	0.4	square miles

TEMPERATURE

°C = (°F − 32) × .555

°F = (°C × 1.8) + 32

First published 1991
by G.K. Hall & Co.
70 Lincoln Street
Boston, Massachusetts 02111

10 9 8 7 6 5 4 3 2 1

Library of Congress Cataloging-in-Publication Data

(Revised for vol. 2)
Encyclopedia of world cultures.

Includes bibliographical references and index.
Filmography: p.
Contents: v. 1. North America / Timothy J. O'Leary, David Levinson, volume editors. v.2. Oceania / Terence E. Hays, volume ed.
1. Ethnology—North America—Encyclopedias.
I. Levinson, David. 1947- .
GN307.E53 1991
306'.097 90-49123
CIP

ISBN 0-8161-1808-6 (v. 1)
ISBN 0-8161-1809-4 (v. 2)

The paper used in this publication meets the minimum requirements of American National Standard for Information Sciences—Permanence of Paper for Printed Library Materials. ANSI Z39.48-1984. ∞™
MANUFACTURED IN THE UNITED STATES OF AMERICA

Contents

Project Staff

Research
Christopher Latham
Nancy Gratton

Editorial and Production
Eva Kitsos
Abraham Maramba
Victoria Crocco
Elizabeth Holthaus
Ara Salibian
John Amburg
Nancy Priest

Cartography
Robert Sullivan
Rhode Island College

Editorial Board

Contributors

Steven M. Albert
Philadelphia Geriatric Center
Philadelphia, Pennsylvania
United States

Lak

William H. Alkire
Department of Anthropology
University of Victoria
Victoria, British Columbia
Canada

Woleai

Thomas Bargatzky
Institut für Völkerkunde und Afrikanistik
Universität München
Munich
Germany

Samoa

John Barker
Department of Anthropology and Sociology
University of British Columbia
Vancouver, British Columbia
Canada

Maisin

Kathleen Barlow
Department of Sociology and Anthropology
Gustavus Adolphus College
Saint Peter, Minnesota
United States

Murik

Robert Borofsky
Department of Anthropology
Hawaii Loa College
Kaneohe, Oahu, Hawaii
United States

Pukapuka

Ross Bowden
Department of Sociology
La Trobe University
Bundoora, Victoria
Australia

Kwoma

David J. Boyd
Department of Anthropology
University of California, Davis
Davis, California
United States

Fore

Paula Brown
Department of Anthropology
State University of New York at Stony Brook
Stony Brook, New York
United States

Chimbu

Mark Busse
Papua New Guinea National Museum
Boroko, National Capital District
Papua New Guinea

Boazi; Kiwai

James G. Carrier
Department of Anthropology
University of Virginia
Charlottesville, Virginia
United States

Manus

Laurence M. Carucci
Department of Sociology
Montana State University
Bozeman, Montana
United States

Marshall Islands

Ann Chowning
Department of Anthropology
Victoria University of Wellington
Wellington
New Zealand

Lakalai; Sengseng

Brenda J. Clay
Department of Anthropology
University of Kentucky
Lexington, Kentucky
United States

Mandak

John Connell
Department of Geography
University of Sydney
Sydney
Australia

Siwai

Leslie Conton
Fairhaven College
Western Washington University
Bellingham, Washington
United States

Usino

Marjorie Tuainekore Crocombe
University of the South Pacific
Suva
Fiji

Cook Islands

Ron Crocombe
University of the South Pacific
Suva
Fiji

Cook Islands

William H. Davenport
University Museum of Archaeology/Anthropology
University of Pennsylvania
Philadelphia, Pennsylvania
United States

Santa Cruz

William W. Donner
Department of Anthropology
Kutztown State University
Kutztown, Pennsylvania
United States

Ontong Java

A. L. Epstein
Department of Social Anthropology
University of Sussex
Brighton, Sussex
England

Tolai

Ellen E. Facey
Department of Sociology and Anthropology
Mount Allison University
Sackville, New Brunswick
Canada

Nguna

Richard Feinberg
Department of Sociology and Anthropology
Kent State University
Kent, Ohio
United States

Anuta

Edwin N. Ferdon, Jr.
Arizona State Museum
University of Arizona
Tucson, Arizona
United States

Tahiti

Raymond Firth
London
England

Tikopia

James G. Flanagan
Department of Sociology and Anthropology
University of Southern Mississippi
Hattiesburg, Mississippi
United States

Wovan

Karl J. Franklin
Summer Institute of Linguistics
Ukarumpa via Lae
Papua New Guinea

Kewa

Deborah Gewertz
Department of Anthropology-Sociology
Amherst College
Amherst, Massachusetts
United States

Chambri

Michael Goldsmith
Department of Politics
University of Waikato
Hamilton
New Zealand

Tuvalu

Jane C. Goodale
Department of Anthropology
Bryn Mawr College
Bryn Mawr, Pennsylvania
United States

Tiwi

Ward H. Goodenough
Department of Anthropology
University of Pennsylvania
Philadelphia, Pennsylvania
United States

Truk

Richard A. Gould
Department of Anthropology
Brown University
Providence, Rhode Island
United States

Ngatatjara

Murray Groves
Department of Sociology
University of Hong Kong
Hong Kong

Motu

C. R. Hallpike
Department of Anthropology
McMaster University
Hamilton, Ontario
Canada

Tauade

David Hanlon
Department of History
University of Hawaii at Manoa
Honolulu, Hawaii
United States

Pohnpei

F. Allan Hanson
Department of Anthropology
University of Kansas
Lawrence, Kansas
United States

Rapa

Thomas G. Harding
Department of Anthropology
University of California, Santa Barbara
Santa Barbara, California
United States

Sio

Brigitta Hauser-Schäublin
Institute of Ethnology
University of Basel
Basel
Switzerland

Abelam; Iatmul

Terence E. Hays
Department of Anthropology
Rhode Island College
Providence, Rhode Island
United States

Gahuku-Gama; Garia; Gogodala; Tairora; Tor

Karl G. Heider
Department of Anthropology
University of South Carolina
Columbia, South Carolina
United States

Dani

Gilbert Herdt
Committee on Human Development
University of Chicago
Chicago, Illinois
United States

Sambia

Antony Hooper
Department of Anthropology
University of Auckland
Auckland
New Zealand

Tokelau

Alan Howard
Department of Anthropology
University of Hawaii at Manoa
Honolulu, Hawaii
United States

Rotuma

Judith Huntsman
Department of Anthropology
University of Auckland
Auckland
New Zealand

Tokelau

Patricia L. Johnson
Department of Anthropology
Pennsylvania State University
University Park, Pennsylvania
United States

Gainj

Margaret Jolly
Department of Anthropology
Macquarie University
North Ryde, New South Wales
Australia

Pentecost

Dan Jorgensen
Department of Anthropology
University of Western Ontario
London, Ontario
Canada

Telefolmin

Miriam Kahn
Department of Anthropology
University of Washington
Seattle, Washington
United States

Wamira

Roger Keesing
Department of Anthropology
McGill University
Montreal, Quebec
Canada

Malaita

Bruce M. Knauft
Department of Anthropology
Emory University
Atlanta, Georgia
United States

Gebusi

Bernd Lambert
Department of Anthropology
Cornell University
Ithaca, New York
United States

Kiribati

Joan C. Larcom
Agency for International Development
Washington, D.C.
United States

Malekula

Rena Lederman
Department of Anthropology
Princeton University
Princeton, New Jersey
United States

Mendi

William A. Lessa
Department of Anthropology
University of California, Los Angeles
Los Angeles, California
United States

Ulithi

David Levinson
Human Relations Area Files
New Haven, Connecticut
United States

Easter Island; Tasmanians

Michael Lieber
Department of Anthropology
University of Illinois at Chicago
Chicago, Illinois
United States

Kapingamarangi

John Liep
Institute of Anthropology
University of Copenhagen
Copenhagen
Denmark

Rossel Island

Lamont Lindstrom
Department of Anthropology
University of Tulsa
Tulsa, Oklahoma
United States

Tanna

Sherwood G. Lingenfelter
Biola University
La Mirada, California
United States

Yap

Jocelyn Linnekin
Department of Anthropology
University of Hawaii at Manoa
Honolulu, Hawaii
United States

Hawaiians

Nancy C. Lutkehaus
Department of Anthropology
University of Southern California
Los Angeles, California
United States

Manam

Nancy McDowell
Department of Anthropology
Franklin and Marshall College
Lancaster, Pennsylvania
United States

Mundugumor

Kenneth McElhanon
Asbury Theological Seminary
Wilmore, Kentucky
United States

Selepet; Wantoat

William H. McKellin
Department of Anthropology and Sociology
University of British Columbia
Vancouver, British Columbia
Canada

Mafulu

David F. Martin
Department of Prehistory and Anthropology
Australian National University
Canberra, Australian Capital Territory
Australia

Wik Mungkan

Mervyn Meggitt
Department of Anthropology
Queens College
Flushing, New York
United States

Mae Enga

William E. Mitchell
Department of Anthropology
University of Vermont
Burlington, Vermont
United States

Wape

George E. B. Morren, Jr.
Department of Human Ecology
Cook College, Rutgers University
New Brunswick, New Jersey
United States

Miyanmin

John Morton
Department of Sociology
La Trobe University
Bundoora, Victoria
Australia

Aranda

Mark S. Mosko
Department of Anthropology
Hartwick College
Oneonta, New York
United States

Mekeo

Steven Nachman
Department of Sociology, Anthropology, Social Work
Edinboro University of Pennsylvania
Edinboro, Pennsylvania
United States

Nissan

Philip L. Newman
Department of Anthropology
University of California, Los Angeles
Los Angeles, California
United States

Gururumba

Eugene Ogan
Department of Anthropology
University of Minnesota
Minneapolis, Minnesota
United States

Kurtatchi; Nasioi

Richard J. Parmentier
Department of Anthropology
Brandeis University
Waltham, Massachussetts
United States

Belau

James G. Peoples
Department of Sociology and Anthropology
Ohio Wesleyan University
Delaware, Ohio
United States

Kosrae

Nicolas Peterson
Department of Prehistory and Anthropology
Australian National University
Canberra, Australian Capital Territory
Australia

Warlpiri

Nancy J. Pollock
Department of Anthropology
Victoria University of Wellington
Wellington
New Zealand

Futuna; Nauru

Jan Pouwer
Rhenen
The Netherlands

Mimika

Karl Rambo
Norman, Oklahoma
United States

Chimbu

Margaret Rodman
Department of Anthropology
McMaster University
Hamilton, Ontario
Canada

Ambae

William Rodman
Department of Anthropology
McMaster University
Hamilton, Ontario
Canada

Ambae

Paul Roscoe
Department of Anthropology
University of Maine
Orono, Maine
United States

Mountain Arapesh; Tongareva; Yangoru Boiken

David Routledge
University of the South Pacific
Suva
Fiji

Bau

Richard Scaglion
Department of Anthropology
University of Pittsburgh
Pittsburgh, Pennsylvania
United States

Keraki; Orokolo; Tangu

Harold W. Scheffler
Department of Anthropology
Yale University
New Haven, Connecticut
United States

Choiseul Island

Wulf Schiefenhövel
Forschungsstelle für Humanethologie
Max-Planck-Gesellschaft
Andechs
Germany

Eipo

J. W. Schoorl
Institute of Cultural Anthropology
Free University
Amsterdam
The Netherlands

Muyu

Andrew Strathern
Department of Anthropology
University of Pittsburgh
Pittsburgh, Pennsylvania
United States

Melpa

Nicholas Thomas
Department of Prehistory and Anthropology
Australian National University
Canberra, Australian Capital Territory
Australia

Marquesas Islands

Robert Tonkinson
Department of Anthropology
University of Western Australia
Nedlands, Perth, Western Australia
Australia

Mardudjara

Charles F. Urbanowicz
Department of Anthropology
California State University, Chico
Chico, California
United States

Tonga

Kathleen Van Arsdale
Englewood, Colorado
United States

Asmat

Peter Van Arsdale
Graduate School of International Studies
University of Denver
Denver, Colorado
United States

Asmat

J. Van Baal
Doorn
The Netherlands

Marind-anim

Roy Wagner
Department of Anthropology
University of Virginia
Charlottesville, Virginia
United States

Daribi

Annette B. Weiner
Department of Anthropology
New York University
New York, New York
United States

Trobriand Islands

James F. Weiner
Department of Social Anthropology
Manchester University
Manchester
England

Foi

Robert L. Welsch
Department of Anthropology
Field Museum of Natural History
Chicago, Illinois
United States

Ningerum

Nancy M. Williams
Department of Anthropology and Sociology
University of Queensland
Saint Lucia, Queensland
Australia

Murngin

Donna Winslow
Département d'anthropologie
Université de Montréal
Montréal, Québec
Canada

Ajië

James W. Wood
Department of Anthropology
Pennsylvania State University
University Park, Pennsylvania
United States

Gainj

Michael Young
Department of Anthropology
Research School of Pacific Studies
Australian National University
Canberra, Australian Capital Territory
Australia

Dobu; Goodenough Island

Marty Zelenietz
Dartmouth, Nova Scotia
Canada

Kilenge

Preface

This project began in 1987 with the goal of assembling a basic reference source that provides accurate, clear, and concise descriptions of the cultures of the world. We wanted to be as comprehensive and authoritative as possible: comprehensive, by providing descriptions of all the cultures of each region of the world or by describing a representative sample of cultures for regions where full coverage is impossible, and authoritative by providing accurate descriptions of the cultures for both the past and the present.

The publication of the *Encyclopedia of World Cultures* in the last decade of the twentieth century is especially timely. The political, economic, and social changes of the past fifty years have produced a world more complex and fluid than at any time in human history. Three sweeping transformations of the worldwide cultural landscape are especially significant.

First is what some social scientists are calling the "New Diaspora"—the dispersal of cultural groups to new locations across the world. This dispersal affects all nations and takes a wide variety of forms: in East African nations, the formation of new towns inhabited by people from dozens of different ethnic groups; in Micronesia and Polynesia, the movement of islanders to cities in New Zealand and the United States; in North America, the replacement by Asians and Latin Americans of Europeans as the most numerous immigrants; in Europe, the increased reliance on workers from the Middle East and North Africa; and so on.

Second, and related to this dispersal, is the internal division of what were once single, unified cultural groups into two or more relatively distinct groups. This pattern of internal division is most dramatic among indigenous or third or fourth world cultures whose traditional ways of life have been altered by contact with the outside world. Underlying this division are both the population dispersion mentioned above and sustained contact with the economically developed world. The result is that groups who at one time saw themselves and were seen by others as single cultural groups have been transformed into two or more distinct groups. Thus, in many cultural groups, we find deep and probably permanent divisions between those who live in the country and those who live in cities, those who follow the traditional religion and those who have converted to Christianity, those who live inland and those who live on the seacoast, and those who live by means of a subsistence economy and those now enmeshed in a cash economy.

The third important transformation of the worldwide cultural landscape is the revival of ethnic nationalism, with many peoples claiming and fighting for political freedom and territorial integrity on the basis of ethnic solidarity and ethnic-based claims to their traditional homeland. Although most attention has focused recently on ethnic nationalism in Eastern Europe and the Soviet Union, the trend is nonetheless a worldwide phenomenon involving, for example, American Indian cultures in North and South America, the Basques in Spain and France, the Tamil and Sinhalese in Sri Lanka, and the Tutsi and Hutu in Burundi, among others.

To be informed citizens of our rapidly changing multicultural world we must understand the ways of life of people from cultures different from our own. "We" is used here in the broadest sense, to include not just scholars who study the cultures of the world and businesspeople and government officials who work in the world community but also the average citizen who reads or hears about multicultural events in the news every day and young people who are growing up in this complex cultural world. For all of these people—which means all of us—there is a pressing need for information on the cultures of the world. This encyclopedia provides this information in two ways. First, its descriptions of the traditional ways of life of the world's cultures can serve as a baseline against which cultural change can be measured and understood. Second, it acquaints the reader with the contemporary ways of life throughout the world.

We are able to provide this information largely through the efforts of the volume editors and the nearly one thousand contributors who wrote the cultural summaries that are the heart of the book. The contributors are social scientists (anthropologists, sociologists, historians, and geographers) as well as educators, government officials, and missionaries who usually have firsthand research-based knowledge of the cultures they write about. In many cases they are the major expert or one of the leading experts on the culture, and some are themselves members of the cultures. As experts, they are able to provide accurate, up-to-date information. This is crucial for many parts of the world where indigenous cultures may be overlooked by official information seekers such as government census takers. These experts have often lived among the people they write about, conducting participant-observations with them and speaking their language. Thus they are able to provide integrated, holistic descriptions of the cultures, not just a list of facts. Their portraits of the cultures leave the reader with a real sense of what it means to be a "Taos" or a "Rom" or a "Sicilian."

Those summaries not written by an expert on the culture have usually been written by a researcher at the Human Relations Area Files, Inc., working from primary source materials.

The Human Relations Area Files, an international educational and research institute, is recognized by professionals in the social and behavioral sciences, humanities, and medical sciences as a major source of information on the cultures of the world.

Uses of the Encyclopedia

This encyclopedia is meant to be used by a variety of people for a variety of purposes. It can be used both to gain a general understanding of a culture and to find a specific piece of information by looking it up under the relevant subheading in a summary. It can also be used to learn about a particular region or subregion of the world and the social, economic, and political forces that have shaped the cultures in that region. The encyclopedia is also a resource guide that leads readers who want a deeper understanding of particular cultures to additional sources of information. Resource guides in the encyclopedia include ethnonyms listed in each summary, which can be used as entry points into the social science literature where the culture may sometimes be identified by a different name; a bibliography at the end of each summary, which lists books and articles about the culture; and a filmography at the end of each volume, which lists films and videos on many of the cultures.

Beyond being a basic reference resource, the encyclopedia also serves readers with more focused needs. For researchers interested in comparing cultures, the encyclopedia serves as the most complete and up-to-date sampling frame from which to select cultures for further study. For those interested in international studies, the encyclopedia leads one quickly into the relevant social science literature as well as providing a state-of-the-art assessment of our knowledge of the cultures of a particular region. For curriculum developers and teachers seeking to internationalize their curriculum, the encyclopedia is itself a basic reference and educational resource as well as a directory to other materials. For government officials, it is a repository of information not likely to be available in any other single publication or, in some cases, not available at all. For students, from high school through graduate school, it provides background and bibliographic information for term papers and class projects. And for travelers, it provides an introduction into the ways of life of the indigenous peoples in the area of the world they will be visiting.

Format of the Encyclopedia

The encyclopedia comprises ten volumes, ordered by geographical regions of the world. The order of publication is not meant to represent any sort of priority. Volumes 1 through 9 contain a total of about fifteen hundred summaries along with maps, glossaries, and indexes of alternate names for the cultural groups. The tenth and final volume contains cumulative lists of the cultures of the world, their alternate names, and a bibliography of selected publications pertaining to those groups.

North America covers the cultures of Canada, Greenland, and the United States of America.

Oceania covers the cultures of Australia, New Zealand, Melanesia, Micronesia, and Polynesia.

South Asia covers the cultures of Afghanistan, Bangladesh, Burma, India, Pakistan, Sri Lanka, and the Himalayan states.

Europe and the Middle East covers the cultures of Europe, North Africa, the Middle East, and the Near East.

East and Southeast Asia covers the cultures of Japan, Korea, mainland and insular Southeast Asia, and Taiwan.

Soviet Union and China covers the cultures of Mongolia, the People's Republic of China, and the Union of Soviet Socialist Republics.

South America covers the cultures of South America.

Middle America and the Caribbean covers the cultures of Central America, Mexico, and the Caribbean islands.

Africa covers the cultures of Madagascar and sub-Saharan Africa.

Format of the Volumes

Each volume contains this preface, an introductory essay by the volume editor, the cultural summaries ranging from a few lines to several pages each, maps pinpointing the location of the cultures, a filmography, an ethnonym index of alternate names for the cultures, and a glossary of scientific and technical terms. All entries are listed in alphabetical order and are extensively cross-referenced.

Cultures Covered

A central issue in selecting cultures for coverage in the encyclopedia has been how to define what we mean by a cultural group. The questions of what a culture is and what criteria can be used to classify a particular social group (such as a religious group, ethnic group, nationality, or territorial group) as a cultural group have long perplexed social scientists and have yet to be answered to everyone's satisfaction. Two realities account for why the questions cannot be answered definitively. First, a wide variety of different types of cultures exist around the world. Among common types are national cultures, regional cultures, ethnic groups, indigenous societies, religious groups, and unassimilated immigrant groups. No single criterion or marker of cultural uniqueness can consistently distinguish among the hundreds of cultures that fit into these general types. Second, as noted above, single cultures or what were at one time identified as single cultures can and do vary internally over time and place. Thus a marker that may identify a specific group as a culture in one location or at one time may not work for that culture in another place or at another time. For example, use of the Yiddish language would have been a marker of Jewish cultural identity in Eastern Europe in the nineteenth century, but it would not serve as a marker for Jews in the twentieth-century United States, where most speak English. Similarly, residence on one of the Cook Islands in Polynesia would have been a marker of Cook Islander identity in the eighteenth century, but not in the twentieth century when two-thirds of Cook Islanders live in New Zealand and elsewhere.

Given these considerations, no attempt has been made to develop and use a single definition of a cultural unit or to develop and use a fixed list of criteria for identifying cultural units. Instead, the task of selecting cultures was left to the volume editors, and the criteria and procedures they used are discussed in their introductory essays. In general, however, six criteria were used, sometimes alone and sometimes in combination to classify social groups as cultural groups: (1) geographical localization, (2) identification in the social science literature as a distinct group, (3) distinct language, (4) shared traditions, religion, folklore, or values, (5) maintenance of group identity in the face of strong assimilative pressures, and (6) previous listing in an inventory of the world's cultures such as *Ethnographic Atlas* (Murdock 1967) or the *Outline of World Cultures* (Murdock 1983).

In general, we have been "lumpers" rather than "splitters" in writing the summaries. That is, if there is some question about whether a particular group is really one culture or two related cultures, we have more often than not treated it as a single culture, with internal differences noted in the summary. Similarly, we have sometimes chosen to describe a number of very similar cultures in a single summary rather than in a series of summaries that would be mostly redundant. There is, however, some variation from one region to another in this approach, and the rationale for each region is discussed in the volume editor's essay.

Two categories of cultures are usually not covered in the encyclopedia. First, extinct cultures, especially those that have not existed as distinct cultural units for some time, are usually not described. Cultural extinction is often, though certainly not always, indicated by the disappearance of the culture's language. So, for example, the Aztec are not covered, although living descendants of the Aztec, the Nahuat-speakers of central Mexico, are described.

Second, the ways of life of immigrant groups are usually not described in much detail, unless there is a long history of resistance to assimilation and the group has maintained its distinct identity, as have the Amish in North America. These cultures are, however, described in the location where they traditionally lived and, for the most part, continue to live, and migration patterns are noted. For example, the Hmong in Laos are described in the Southeast Asia volume, but the refugee communities in the United States and Canada are covered only in the general summaries on Southeast Asians in those two countries in the North America volume. Although it would be ideal to provide descriptions of all the immigrant cultures or communities of the world, that is an undertaking well beyond the scope of this encyclopedia, for there are probably more than five thousand such communities in the world.

Finally, it should be noted that not all nationalities are covered, only those that are also distinct cultures as well as political entities. For example, the Vietnamese and Burmese are included but Indians (citizens of the Republic of India) are not, because the latter is a political entity made up of a great mix of cultural groups. In the case of nations whose populations include a number of different, relatively unassimilated groups or cultural regions, each of the groups is described separately. For example, there is no summary for Italians as such in the Europe volume, but there are summaries for the regional cultures of Italy, such as the Tuscans, Sicilians, and Tyrolians, and other cultures such as the Sinti Piedmontese.

Cultural Summaries

The heart of this encyclopedia is the descriptive summaries of the cultures, which range from a few lines to five or six pages in length. They provide a mix of demographic, historical, social, economic, political, and religious information on the cultures. Their emphasis or flavor is cultural; that is, they focus on the ways of life of the people—both past and present—and the factors that have caused the culture to change over time and place.

A key issue has been how to decide which cultures should be described by longer summaries and which by shorter ones. This decision was made by the volume editors, who had to balance a number of intellectual and practical considerations. Again, the rationale for these decisions is discussed in their essays. But among the factors that were considered by all the editors were the total number of cultures in their region, the availability of experts to write summaries, the availability of information on the cultures, the degree of similarity between cultures, and the importance of a culture in a scientific or political sense.

The summary authors followed a standardized outline so that each summary provides information on a core list of topics. The authors, however, had some leeway in deciding how much attention was to be given each topic and whether additional information should be included. Summaries usually provide information on the following topics:

CULTURE NAME: The name used most often in the social science literature to refer to the culture or the name the group uses for itself.

ETHNONYMS: Alternate names for the culture including names used by outsiders, the self-name, and alternate spellings, within reasonable limits.

ORIENTATION

Identification. Location of the culture and the derivation of its name and ethnonyms.

Location. Where the culture is located and a description of the physical environment.

Demography. Population history and the most recent reliable population figures or estimates.

Linguistic Affiliation. The name of the language spoken and/or written by the culture, its place in an international language classification system, and internal variation in language use.

HISTORY AND CULTURAL RELATIONS: A tracing of the origins and history of the culture and the past and current nature of relationships with other groups.

SETTLEMENTS: The location of settlements, types of settlements, types of structures, housing design and materials.

ECONOMY

Subsistence and Commercial Activities. The primary methods of obtaining, consuming, and distributing money, food, and other necessities.

Industrial Arts. Implements and objects produced by the culture either for its own use or for sale or trade.

Trade. Products traded and patterns of trade with other groups.

Division of Labor. How basic economic tasks are assigned by age, sex, ability, occupational specialization, or status.

Land Tenure. Rules and practices concerning the allocation of land and land-use rights to members of the culture and to outsiders.

KINSHIP

Kin Groups and Descent. Rules and practices concerning kin-based features of social organization such as lineages and clans and alliances between these groups.

Kinship Terminology. Classification of the kinship terminological system on the basis of either cousin terms or genera-

tion, and information about any unique aspects of kinship terminology.
MARRIAGE AND FAMILY
Marriage. Rules and practices concerning reasons for marriage, types of marriage, economic aspects of marriage, postmarital residence, divorce, and remarriage.
Domestic Unit. Description of the basic household unit including type, size, and composition.
Inheritance. Rules and practices concerning the inheritance of property.
Socialization. Rules and practices concerning child rearing including caretakers, values inculcated, child-rearing methods, initiation rites, and education.
SOCIOPOLITICAL ORGANIZATION
Social Organization. Rules and practices concerning the internal organization of the culture, including social status, primary and secondary groups, and social stratification.
Political Organization. Rules and practices concerning leadership, politics, governmental organizations, and decision making.
Social Control. The sources of conflict within the culture and informal and formal social control mechanisms.
Conflict. The sources of conflict with other groups and informal and formal means of resolving conflicts.
RELIGION AND EXPRESSIVE CULTURE
Religious Beliefs. The nature of religious beliefs including beliefs in supernatural entities, traditional beliefs, and the effects of major religions.
Religious Practitioners. The types, sources of power, and activities of religious specialists such as shamans and priests.
Ceremonies. The nature, type, and frequency of religious and other ceremonies and rites.
Arts. The nature, types, and characteristics of artistic activities including literature, music, dance, carving, and so on.
Medicine. The nature of traditional medical beliefs and practices and the influence of scientific medicine.
Death and Afterlife. The nature of beliefs and practices concerning death, the deceased, funerals, and the afterlife.
BIBLIOGRAPHY: A selected list of publications about the culture. The list usually includes publications that describe both the traditional and the contemporary culture.
AUTHOR'S NAME: The name of the summary author.

Maps

Each regional volume contains maps pinpointing the current location of the cultures described in that volume. The first map in each volume is usually an overview, showing the countries in that region. The other maps provide more detail by marking the locations of the cultures in four or five subregions.

Filmography

Each volume contains a list of films and videos about cultures covered in that volume. This list is provided as a service and in no way indicates an endorsement by the editor, volume editor, or the summary authors. Addresses of distributors are provided so that information about availability and prices can be readily obtained.

Ethnonym Index

Each volume contains an ethnonym index for the cultures covered in that volume. As mentioned above, ethnonyms are alternative names for the culture—that is, names different from those used here as the summary headings. Ethnonyms may be alternative spellings of the culture name, a totally different name used by outsiders, a name used in the past but no longer used, or the name in another language. It is not unusual that some ethnonyms are considered degrading and insulting by the people to whom they refer. These names may nevertheless be included here because they do identify the group and may help some users locate the summary or additional information on the culture in other sources. Ethnonyms are cross-referenced to the culture name in the index.

Glossary

Each volume contains a glossary of technical and scientific terms found in the summaries. Both general social science terms and region-specific terms are included.

Special Considerations

In a project of this magnitude, decisions had to be made about the handling of some information that cannot easily be standardized for all areas of the world. The two most troublesome matters concerned population figures and units of measure.

Population Figures

We have tried to be as up-to-date and as accurate as possible in reporting population figures. This is no easy task, as some groups are not counted in official government censuses, some groups are very likely undercounted, and in some cases the definition of a cultural group used by the census takers differs from the definition we have used. In general, we have relied on population figures supplied by the summary authors. When other population data sources have been used in a volume, they are so noted by the volume editor. If the reported figure is from an earlier date—say, the 1970s—it is usually because it is the most accurate figure that could be found.

Units of Measure

In an international encyclopedia, editors encounter the problem of how to report distances, units of space, and temperature. In much of the world, the metric system is used, but scientists prefer the International System of Units (similar to the metric system), and in Great Britain and North America the English system is usually used. We decided to use English measures in the North America volume and metric measures in the other volumes. Each volume contains a conversion table.

Acknowledgments

In a project of this size, there are many people to acknowledge and thank for their contributions. In its planning stages, members of the research staff of the Human Relations Area Files provided many useful ideas. These included Timothy J. O'Leary, Marlene Martin, John Beierle, Gerald Reid, Delores Walters, Richard Wagner, and Christopher Latham. The advisory editors, of course, also played a major role in planning the project, and not just for their own volumes but also for the project as a whole. Timothy O'Leary, Terence Hays, and Paul Hockings deserve special thanks for their comments on this preface and the glossary, as does Melvin Ember, president of the Human Relations Area Files. Members of the office and technical staff also must be thanked for so quickly and carefully attending to the many tasks a project of this size inevitably generates. They are Erlinda Maramba, Abraham Maramba, Victoria Crocco, Nancy Gratton, and Douglas Black. At G. K. Hall, the encyclopedia has benefited from the wise and careful editorial management of Elizabeth Kubik and Elizabeth Holthaus, the editorial and production management of Michael Sims and Ara Salibian, and the marketing skills of Linda May and Lisa Pemstein. Finally, I would like to thank Melvin Ember and the board of directors of the Human Relations Area Files for their administrative and intellectual support for this project.

DAVID LEVINSON

References

Murdock, George Peter (1967). *Ethnographic Atlas.* Pittsburgh, Penn., University of Pittsburgh Press.

Murdock, George Peter (1983). *Outline of World Cultures.* 6th rev. ed. New Haven, Conn. Human Relations Area Files.

Introduction

If you turn a globe just so, all you can see is the Pacific Ocean, the earth's largest geographic feature. Its estimated area of some 181 million square kilometers is greater than that of all of the world's land areas combined; however, even when Australia is included, the Pacific contains only about 9 million square kilometers of dry land. The rest consists of more than half of the world's volume of free water, with an average depth of over 4,000 meters and reaching depths over 10,600 meters in the Mariana Trench, just south of Guam. From the Bering Strait in the north to the Antarctic Circle is a distance of more than 14,700 kilometers, and to cross the Pacific at its greatest width, between Singapore and Panama, one must travel about 19,700 kilometers. A first impression of Oceania, then, is one of vast size and distances.

Perhaps not surprising in the face of such immensity (especially to the modern air traveler), the most characteristic feature of the Pacific Ocean is emptiness. Although it contains more islands than are found in all other oceans combined, the overwhelming majority of the tens of thousands of islands of Oceania are in the southwestern quadrant of the Pacific. But this is still a very large area, and it includes some island groups that will not be considered in this volume. Japan, the Philippines, and most of Indonesia are covered in a later volume of this encyclopedia that deals with East and Southeast Asia. Here we will be concerned with the island continent of Australia, New Guinea, and the islands of Melanesia, Micronesia, and Polynesia (see map 1). Thus the scope of this volume is limited, but it still encompasses a huge area that is astoundingly diverse.

The Physical Environment

The diversity of Oceania begins with the physical environment of its islands. A geologist might begin to portray this environment by drawing on a map of the Pacific what is called the "Andesite Line," which follows deep trenches in the ocean floor in a southerly direction from Japan to New Guinea, then veers eastward almost to Western Samoa, where it turns southwest and passes New Zealand. West of this line is the great Continental Australasiatic Platform, composed of metamorphic, granitic, and andesitic rock, and to the east is the Pacific Basin, formed mainly of basalt. Over millions of years the heavier basaltic basin gradually has sunk until only the peaks of its mountain ranges currently breach the ocean's surface in the form of *oceanic islands*; the relatively lighter platform west of the Andesite Line correspondingly has risen. This general process, together with regional upfoldings and upliftings of the ancient continental rock, erosion, and changes in sea level with the advance and retreat of glaciers elsewhere in the world, has resulted in the current appearance of *continental islands* and, of course, the continent of Australia itself. Generally speaking, the islands to the west of the line are larger and closer together than are those to the east. Still, Australia (with an area of 7.7 million square kilometers) and New Guinea (800,000 square kilometers) are exceptional in size, as the average Pacific island covers only 60 square kilometers and many of the islands are much smaller than that.

While initially useful, a simple contrast between *continental* and *oceanic* islands does not indicate adequately the diversity of island types and its consequences for those who inhabit them. Geographers usually recognize three main types of islands in the Pacific: *continental islands, volcanic islands*, and *coral islands*.

Examples of the first type include such islands as New Guinea, the Bismarck Archipelago, Bougainville, New Caledonia, New Zealand, and Viti Levu in the Fiji group (see map 1). These islands represent some of the portions of the Continental Australasiatic Platform that currently are above sea level, and they are the products of millions of years of uplift, folding, faulting, erosion, and sedimentation. Elevations can reach over 4,000 meters on a number of peaks in the central cordillera that runs the length of New Guinea, and about 3,700 meters on Mount Cook in New Zealand. In the mountains of continental islands one finds the headwaters of great river systems, such as the Fly and Sepik rivers of New Guinea. The landscapes of continental islands are highly diverse, ranging from the vast deserts that cover much of Australia to bare mountain peaks, high plateaus, and lowland alluvial plains, all of which can be found on any given island. In addition, most of the continental islands nearer the equator are fringed with coral reefs, the most extensive of which is the Great Barrier Reef of Australia.

Volcanic islands are found throughout much of the Pacific, where they have been formed through volcanic intrusion from the continental platform or directly from the ocean floor. The Andesite Line marks the most unstable part of the Earth's crust, with thousands of volcanoes forming what is sometimes called a "ring of fire" encircling the Pacific Basin. These volcanoes tend to be of the *explosive* type, and their eruptions can be spectacular, as in the case of Krakatoa in Indonesia. When it last erupted in 1883, the sound of the explosion was heard in Australia and its ash eventually circled the Earth. Others, such as Manam off the northeastern coast of New Guinea, can be locally destructive yet still provide habitable environments for people (see the Manam summary in this volume). Volcanoes in the Pacific Basin are of the *flow* type, capable of erupting dramatically, as occasionally happens on the island of Hawaii, but they are also *island-building,* with their flows of basalt gradually creating or extending the land area, as has occurred in the creation over millions of years of the whole Hawaiian chain, Tahiti, Kosrae, and Pohnpei. Volcanic islands are often called "high" islands because they can include mountains of considerable elevation (e.g., Mauna Kea at 3,900 meters in Hawaii), and precipitous cliffs plunging into the sea or bordering large, deep valleys. Most volcanic islands are also fringed by coral reefs.

The third main type of island is formed from coral. The hard, rough coral one might find in a shop that sells rocks or seashells is actually the exoskeleton of fleshy polyps that live in colonies protected by the lime they extract from sea water and then secrete. The animals can only live in water that is saline, clear, warm (18–22° C), and shallow (no deeper than about 36–45 meters). When the top of an undersea mountain or an offshore submerged portion of an island provides these required conditions, colonies of living coral can form and grow (affording dazzling sights for scuba divers). If their base then sinks too much, or rises to break the surface of the ocean, the animals die, leaving behind their coral exoskeleton. When this happens in areas that are exposed to the air, algae gradually encrust the coral and fill its pores, and wind-blown sand or sediment helps to create reefs, islets, and islands.

Reefs or islands based on coral are called elevated reefs when they extend 8 meters or more above sea level; an example is the island of Guam, whose limestone cliffs reach 180 meters above the ocean's surface. Most coral islands are much lower than that, with atolls averaging only 3–4 meters at their highest points, although they can still provide living space for resourceful people. Coral islands occur in a variety of types, based primarily on their shapes and structures, such as fringing reefs (Rarotonga), barrier reefs (Belau), and atolls (Truk). Even within these types, however, there is diversity. Atolls consist of coral reefs embracing a lagoon, or sheltered body of sea water. Most are small and have a simple structure, such as Ulithi with its reef and thirty tiny islets, totaling only a few square kilometers of land, and channels leading into its central lagoon of about 470 square kilometers. Truk, on the other hand, is more complex, consisting of about forty low coral islets enclosing a lagoon up to 64 kilometers in diameter, inside of which are another seventeen high islands of volcanic origin. The enormous size of Truk's lagoon made it an ideal berthing place, first for the Japanese fleet and then that of the Allied forces, during World War II. Thus, while coral islands can generally be contrasted with continental or volcanic islands in terms of their lower topography, smaller land area, poorer soils, and frequent scarcity of fresh water (with the only source, rainfall, readily percolating through the limestone), they still provide widely diverse habitats for living organisms, including human beings.

Popular images of Pacific islands seldom reflect the range of physical forms they actually manifest, and the same is true of Oceanic climates. With the major exceptions of Easter Island, New Zealand, and the southern two-thirds of Australia, nearly all of the inhabited islands of Oceania are located within the tropics, with average temperatures of 18° C in the coldest month. But climate is a function of more complicated factors, such as elevation, topography, and wind patterns. In addition, large islands are physically complex enough to create their own weather systems. Thus one can find in Australia steamy, tropical zones in the far north, "Mediterranean climates" in the southeast, and a largely arid interior where extremely high daytime temperatures can plunge to −10° C near the ground at night. New Guinea, too, is a land of contrasts, ranging from hot and humid lowlands to temperate highlands and even glaciers and permanent snow on the highest mountain peaks.

The climates of most of the smaller islands of the Pacific are largely a result of their positions within five major atmospheric circulation regions. Only a few islands, but with New Zealand prominent among them, are subject to the cold waves, general rains, cyclones, and cold-front storms associated with the *midlatitude westerlies,* strong year-round winds that predominate north of 25° N and south of 27° S. Virtually no islands are located within the large *doldrums* area, with its low winds, high humidity, and nearly constant high temperatures, found just south of the equator in the western Pacific. Most of the islands with which we are concerned here are influenced by the remaining three circulation systems.

In the eastern Pacific, *trade winds* dominate, blowing from the northeast north of the equator and from the southeast in the south. In addition to their importance to sailors (who gave them their name), the trade winds dramatically affect local climates. Typically the windward side of affected islands is cloudy and wet during most of the year, while the leeward side is relatively cloudless and drier. (This effect can be witnessed clearly on the island of Hawaii, where 254 and 51 centimeters of rain might fall on opposite sides of the island in a typical year.) In the western Pacific, the seasonal *monsoons* replace the trade winds, generated largely by the periodic heating and cooling of the great landmasses of Asia and Australia. A rainy season is brought with the monsoons from Asia in the northern winter and spring, with a dry season prevailing when the wind direction reverses during the northern summer and autumn. Finally, the *typhoon* zone must be mentioned. While typhoons (or hurricanes) can occur in most regions of Oceania, they are most common in the northwest (especially on Belau and the Caroline Islands) and the southwest (from Vanuatu to Samoa). These storms, with winds exceeding 120 kilometers per hour and torrential rains, can be devastating to islands and their populations, and low atolls can easily be swamped by temporary rises in sea level of 5 or 6 meters.

It should be clear from the preceding discussion that Oceanic landforms, soils, and climates are too diverse to allow a generalized description, and one should expect that the differences among them have had important and variable consequences for the plants and animals (including human beings) that have been able to colonize the islands. An additional crucial factor has been the previously mentioned one of distances, especially the relative proximity to the great continental landmasses, with the corresponding factor of isolation.

Most of the plants on Pacific islands, apart from those more recently introduced by people, derive from the Asian continent, with seeds, spores, and fruits carried to them by wind, waves, and animals such as birds. This process has not been simply a transference, however, since evolutionary events (such as genetic drift and selective reproduction) and competition in new ecological niches has resulted over the millennia in the development of countless new species. In general, the farther one goes out into the Pacific away from Asia, the fewer families, genera, and species of plants are found and the more the local flora (until modern times) is endemic (i.e., the product of localized evolution from ancestral stocks). In Australia, 50 percent of the native plant species are endemic; in New Zealand, the figure rises to 68 percent; in New Caledonia, 80 percent; and in the Hawaiian chain, 95 percent. Additional factors determining the richness and complexity of island floras include the size and topography of a given island.

On atolls and other low islands, natural vegetation resembles what one would typically find on an ocean beach; given continual exposure to sea air and tides, any plants must be both water-resistant and salt-resistant. Thus *seacoast or strand* vegetation consists largely of grasses, sedges, woody vines and shrubs, and a few palms. On larger islands, whether volcanic or continental, a wider range of vegetation communities can exist. If rivers deposit mud along the shore, there may be stands of mangroves lining the shore and river estuaries, and backwaters can create large swampy regions filled with grasses, sedges, cane, and palms. Farther inland there might be grassy savannas or drained alluvial areas associated with larger rivers, with large, buttressed trees, lianas (woody vines), canes, and palms. On the largest and highest islands a succession of vegetation communities will be found at varying elevations. Typically, *lowland hill forest* occurs up to about 1,000 meters above sea level on continental islands; transitions occur at about one-half the elevations indicated on volcanic islands in the Pacific Basin. This zone usually contains many different tree and palm species, but little ground vegetation. Above this, and up to about 2,200 to 2,700 meters, one finds the *lower montane rain forest,* where palms give way to tree ferns, oaks, and pines and eventually to beech, wild bamboo, and pandanus trees. In this elevation zone, too, especially where human forest clearance has occurred, there can be extensive grasslands, dominated by sword grass and with few trees. From about 2,700 meters to 3,000 meters one enters the *montane cloud forest,* a low-canopied, permanently wet and cold forest dominated by tree ferns, with a dense floor consisting of rotting vegetation. Finally, on the highest islands, an *alpine region* may be identified above 3,000 meters; usually dry and sunny, this region will contain conifers, shrubs, and heaths, as well as occasional grassy areas up to the snow line.

As far as animals are concerned, the same factors are important as with plants, but the problems of original dispersal are greater. As with the flora, the native fauna of Oceania is derived mostly from Asia; until modern times and with the help of people, no American land vertebrates were able to cross the vast open areas of the eastern Pacific. But even in the west, an imaginary line (called "Wallace's Line" or, somewhat modified, "Huxley's Line," after the two great naturalists Alfred Wallace and Thomas Huxley) drawn roughly between the Celebes and New Guinea divides the world's richest from the world's poorest vertebrate faunas. Despite the extension of the continental platform far out into the western Pacific, sea levels have never been low enough to connect Asia completely with Oceania. Thus none of the larger Asian and Indonesian land mammals, such as tigers, monkeys, and squirrels, were able to cross the intervening stretches of deep sea, and indeed few vertebrates at all have been able to reach Oceania without human assistance.

In general, as with plants, as one proceeds from west to east in the Pacific, the fauna becomes more impoverished; for example, on the island of New Guinea there are at least 550 species of land birds, while on remote Henderson Island (near Pitcairn Island, far to the east), there are only four. In the western Pacific, the natural fauna includes bats, rodents, monotremes (egg-laying mammals), and marsupials as the only mammals, although sea birds and land birds abound. In the central and eastern Pacific, prior to the intervention of people, one would have found only bats, rodents, sea birds, and some land birds. One effect, then, of distances in the Pacific has been reduction of faunal diversity, well illustrated by the Hawaiian chain where there were no indigenous land mammals, snakes, lizards, frogs, or freshwater fish. A contrasting effect, though, and one related to isolation, has been the evolution of many unusual forms of animal life. The monotremes (e.g., platypus) and marsupials (e.g., kangaroos, koalas, etc.) of the Australia and New Guinea regions are good examples, as are the many species of flightless birds, such as the cassowaries and emus of New Guinea and Australia and the kiwis and now-extinct moas of New Zealand. In the absence of natural predators (and people), these birds proliferated (with over seventeen species endemic to Hawaii) and sometimes grew to enormous size, as with the moa, which reached a height of over three meters. In contrast to the land, of course, the seas of Oceania have always been abundantly stocked, with fish, turtles, shellfish, and other marine animals.

The physical environment of Oceania has been described here in some detail for two reasons: first, to counteract the stereotypical image of Pacific islands conveyed by travel posters to beach-loving vacationers; and second, to provide some general context for understanding the degree to which Oceanic peoples have been constrained—often severely—by the physical settings to which they have had to adapt. In the absence of large, domesticable land mammals, pastoralism has never been a viable option in the Pacific, and hunting and gathering could only be a significant subsistence base in Australia and on the largest continental islands. While many wild food plants continue to be utilized in Oceania, as is clear from the cultural summaries in this volume, horticulture has been feasible on many islands only for people who brought with them or subsequently obtained at least most of their staple crops from elsewhere. With at least some general appreciation of the nature of the island environments, we can better understand both the original human settlement of the Pacific and the world of Oceanic islanders today.

The Settlement of Oceania

When Europeans first entered the Pacific in the sixteenth century, nearly all of the islands of Oceania had already been discovered by the aboriginal islanders. Although the size of the indigenous population at the time of European contact is impossible to know with precision, current estimates by anthropologists suggest that perhaps as many as 3.5 million people were settled on 1,000 or fewer of the islands by that time. Over the centuries since then, Western Europeans have speculated regarding the origin (or origins) of the peoples of Oceania, proposing canoeloads of Native Americans, or "lost tribes of Israel," or fleeing refugees from the sinking mythical continent of Mu as their ancestors. Few scholars today would give credence to any such proposals. While systematic archaeological research has only been undertaken intensively in the past few decades, the general outlines of the human settlement of Oceania have now emerged, and for some areas at least we know a great deal about Pacific prehistory.

There are no human fossils or any other kind of evidence that would suggest that human beings in the Pacific evolved there from some prehuman ancestor. Indeed, the most liberal estimates of how long any of Oceania (as defined in this volume) has been inhabited do not exceed 50,000 years; that is, they fall within the time period when modern forms of *Homo sapiens* have existed on earth. Obviously, then, Pacific islanders are derived from people who originally went into Oceania from someplace else. All responsible scholars today would say that, as for so much of the native flora and fauna, the initial source was Asia, including insular southeast Asia.

To get a general idea of how this occurred, we might follow some scholars and divide the Pacific into *Near Oceania* and *Remote Oceania*. Near Oceania includes the islands of the western Pacific from Australia and New Guinea eastward to the end of the Solomon Islands. As mentioned previously, these islands tend to be relatively large and are fairly close together, often grouped in clusters (or archipelagoes) within which at least some islands are mutually visible under clear conditions. In the remainder of the Pacific, the islands of Remote Oceania are separated from Near Oceania by at least 350-kilometer gaps of open ocean, and many archipelagoes are 1,000 kilometers or more from their nearest inhabited neighbors. All available evidence indicates that Near Oceania was initially settled by people tens of thousands of years before anyone ventured into Remote Oceania, or at least before they left behind any evidence of their presence there.

Relative nearness to Asia and its large southeastern islands—where the human lineage goes back in time at least a million years—is only one of the conditions that favored the earlier settlement of Near Oceania. Another has to do with global physical and climatic changes during the Pleistocene epoch, beginning over 2 million years ago. During that long period, major drops in worldwide atmospheric temperatures resulted in the formation of enormous ice caps in the Northern Hemisphere and ice fields in the Southern Hemisphere. This impoundment of much of the Earth's water resulted in significant lowering of sea levels and shorelines around the world. Conversely, warming periods resulted in partial melting of these ice caps and consequent raising of sea levels.

During the later stages of this epoch, with one climax about 53,000 years B.P. (before the present) and another about 20,000 B.P., sea levels in the southwestern Pacific dropped to such an extent (by about 120 to 140 meters from their present levels) and for such long periods that two massive land units were created called the "Sunda (or Asian) Shelf" and the "Sahul (or Australian) Shelf." The former connected Sumatra, Borneo, Java, and Bali to mainland Asia, and the latter joined Australia to New Guinea and many of its nearby islands. These dry-land connections facilitated the dispersal of Asian plants, animals, and peoples to Near Oceania, although Sunda and Sahul were themselves still separated by deep ocean troughs no narrower than the 90-kilometer-wide gap then existing between Timor and Australia. While sea levels were lowered in Remote Oceania as well, of course, its islands remained relatively isolated because of their still-vast distances from both Sunda and Sahul.

Given these conditions, then, it is not surprising that diverse types of evidence now indicate the earliest presence of Oceanic peoples in "Greater Australia," with generally-agreed-upon dates such as: eastern New Guinea's Huon Peninsula by 40,000 B.P. and the interior of the island from 30,000 to 25,000 B.P.; New Ireland, 32,000 B.P.; Buka, in the Solomon Islands, 28,000 B.P.; Lake Mungo, in the western part of New South Wales in Australia, 32,000 to 24,000 B.P.; Keilor, near Melbourne in southeastern Australia, 45,000 to 36,000 B.P.; various sites in the state of Western Australia, 38,000 to 35,000 B.P.; and Tasmania, then joined to the rest of Australia, about 30,000 B.P.

We do not know a great deal about these pioneer settlers apart from their mainly stone and wooden tool kit and the fact that they all apparently subsisted by hunting, gathering, and fishing. They were certainly highly mobile, as can be seen by their rapid colonization of the whole continent of Australia, and at least the initial arrivals must have possessed viable watercraft. While prehistorians debate many of the details of early settlement, all would agree that it was a gradual process, undoubtedly involving numerous separate landfalls and many different small groups. The apparent lack of any clear relationship between Australian Aboriginal languages and those of New Guinea or the rest of Oceania is but one indication that the diversity of the native peoples of the Pacific began a very long time ago.

New arrivals of human groups in Near Oceania (and local diversification within it) unquestionably continued to occur over thousands of years, perhaps slowing with the final major rise in sea levels at about 7,000 B.P. In any case, the next large-scale human incursions into the Pacific, as well as expansion into Remote Oceania, seem to have begun about 4,000 B.P.

During a period lasting for 1,000 to 1,500 years, new groups of people colonized Oceania, initially sailing from the islands of eastern Indonesia along the northern coast of New Guinea into Near Oceania, where they settled on the seacoasts and offshore islands amid the descendants of the earlier arrivals. By about 3,500 B.P. they were established in the Bismarck Archipelago and had expanded to the Santa Cruz Islands, the New Hebrides (Vanuatu), and New Caledonia (see map 1). Soon afterward some of their representatives moved on to become the first settlers of Fiji, Tonga, and Samoa (by about 3,000 B.P.) and smaller islands such as Futuna and Uvea.

These new Oceanians are considered by most prehistorians to have been the bearers of the "Lapita Culture" (so named after a site in New Caledonia), and archaeologists have been able to trace their influence and probable movements thanks to discoveries on numerous islands of a relatively sudden and widespread appearance of their trademark: a distinctive kind of pottery, characterized by small dentate (toothlike) patterns stamped into the clay and simple line incisions, often in complex geometric designs. The people who made this pottery appear to have been village-dwelling horticulturalists with a tool kit that, like their ornamentation, emphasized the use of shells. They clearly had impressive navigational and sailing skills, enabling them to engage in extensive interisland trade and to spread out well into the central Pacific. By about 500 B.C. (or 1,500 B.P.) the distinctive Lapita pottery largely disappears from archaeological sites in the western Pacific. Rather than seeing this disappearance as the result of massive extinctions or some other cataclysm, most scholars interpret it simply as a reflection of local change, coinciding with the development of what would become the classic "Polynesian" way of life (see below).

Both during and after the Lapita period, further expansion into Remote Oceania continued, with the Pacific serving less as a barrier than as a highway. The Cook Islands, the Society Islands, and the Tuamotu Archipelago were settled by about 2,500 B.P.; the Marquesas Islands and remote volcanic islands such as Rapa, within the next 500 years; and, remotest of all, Easter Island, by 1,500 B.P. Not all movements were in a simple easterly direction, however. By 1,500 B.P., people (probably from the Marquesas) had settled in the Hawaiian chain and it is likely that the Fiji-Samoa-Tonga "triangle" was a major staging area for movements to the southwest (reaching New Zealand by about 1,000 B.P.) and northwestward into the Ellice Islands (Tuvalu), the Gilbert Islands, the Marshalls, and the Carolines during the period from 2,000 to 1,500 B.P. New immigrants also continued to enter Oceania, with groups originating in Indonesia and the Philippines first settling areas such as Belau and Yap.

Many of the details of the settlement of Oceania are not yet known, and most of those we do know cannot be included in a brief outline such as that offered here. Moreover, there is much that we will never be able to know for sure since the original inhabitants of the Pacific islands—like their descendants today—were the agents of tremendous changes in the islands themselves, thereby complicating the tasks of historical reconstruction. The introduction of new plants and animals, deforestation through fire and land-clearing activities, and the depletion and extinction of many natural species began to alter the Pacific landscapes from the beginning. What we can say with some certainty is that the Pacific was colonized over a long period of time, at many different periods in time (with some places settled much more recently than others), probably for many different reasons (including both accidental and purposeful ventures), and by many different groups of people, who varied among themselves in physical types, languages, and cultures. Much of this diversity has been subsequently enhanced and redirected through both mixing and isolating of populations and as a result of local adaptations to circumstances that were themselves highly diverse.

Languages and Cultures of Oceania

To appreciate better the linguistic and cultural diversity of Oceania, both in the past and the present, it will be useful once again to divide this immense field of interest into more manageable regions. Since the early nineteenth century, geographers, anthropologists, and others have divided Oceania into major "ethnic regions" or "culture areas" in terms of perceived physical and cultural similarities and contrasts among its peoples. The most commonly used categorization is based on one proposed in 1831 by the French navigator Jules S-C Dumont d'Urville, and is represented in general on map 1 and in more detail on maps 2–6.

Australia (from the Latin *australis*, or "southern") is singular in both its vast size (nearly 7.7 million square kilometers) and its Aboriginal population, whose cultures developed in ways largely isolated from the rest of Oceania. North of Australia is *New Guinea*, which, with its land area of more than 800,000 square kilometers, is the second-largest island in the world (after Greenland). New Guinea is usually considered a part of *Melanesia* (from the Greek *melas*, or "black," and *nesos*, "island"), but on the maps in this volume (see maps 3 and 4) what may be called "Island Melanesia" is presented separately, encompassing the Bismarck Archipelago, the Solomon Islands, Vanuatu (formerly the New Hebrides), and New Caledonia. The 5 million square kilometers of ocean in the northern Pacific demarcated as *Micronesia* (from the Greek *mikros*, meaning "small") includes only about 2,800 square kilometers of land, with approximately 2,000 islands (many of which are indeed tiny) in four main groups: the Mariana, Caroline, Marshall, and Gilbert islands (see map 5). Finally, there is the great "triangle" of *Polynesia* (from the Greek *polys*, meaning "many"), which includes the Hawaiian group, Easter Island, and New Zealand at its corners and over 39 million square kilometers of ocean. Scattered over that large area of water are such major archipelagoes as the Marquesas Islands, the Tuamotu Archipelago, the Society Islands, the Cook Islands, Samoa, Tonga, and the Fiji Islands, totaling only some 8,260 square kilometers of land (see map 6).

These demarcations, while useful for purposes of orientation, must be understood as artificial constructs rather than reflections of natural, discrete groupings of peoples. Indeed, some anthropologists today would recommend abandoning them altogether, in part because they vastly oversimplify reality, but also because from the beginning they have been associated with ethnocentric and racist assumptions. For example, when d'Urville published his division of Oceania into "Malaysia" (including what is now called Indonesia), "Polynesia," "Micronesia," and "Melanesia" (which for him included Australia), his classification was as much evaluative as it was descriptive. Thus, he speculated that the Pacific had been settled by two distinct human "stocks," one giving rise to Malaysians, Polynesians, and Micronesians, the other producing the Melanesians. He noted, approvingly, the "yellow to copper" skin color often found in the inhabitants of the former regions and considered their bodies "well-proportioned"; these "traits," together with the widespread occurrence of rigid social stratification and institutionalized chieftainship, led him to regard these peoples as relatively "civilized." Certainly, to him, they differed strikingly from the "dark-skinned" and "uncouth" Melanesians, who he suspected were of "low intelligence."

Physical traits have played an important part in shaping the images of Pacific islanders held both by early travelers and by the modern general public. One example concerns the island of New Guinea, named "Nueva Guinea" in the sixteenth century by the Spanish voyager Ynigo Ortiz de Retes because he thought the people he saw there physically resembled those he knew from the "Guinea Coast" of West Africa. We now know from blood-group data and other genetic studies that any resemblances between Africans and New Guineans (or any other Pacific islanders) are the result of common adaptive responses and not recent common ancestry. In fact, modern scholars find little basis for any "racial" classification of the peoples of Oceania. It is undeniable that a traveler landing on Truk (in Micronesia) or Tahiti (in Polynesia) will tend to see many people with light brown skin and straight or wavy hair, just as in Papua New Guinea or Vanuatu (in Melanesia) a person is likely to see many darker-skinned people with "frizzy" hair. However, such traits, as well as body build and stature, vary enormously in the Pacific (as they do elsewhere in the world) and are not distributed neatly by island, island group, or region. Moreover, many physical traits (such as apparent skin color, hair color or form, and body build) are influenced by nongenetic, cultural factors and practices. When we use terms like "Melanesia," "Micronesia," and "Polynesia," then, we must be careful not to presume or imply that these refer to different "races" in the Pacific; nor, as we shall see below, do they refer in any simple way to homogeneous "culture areas." We have already seen that the Pacific was settled over a very long period of time and by many different groups of people; the legacy is one of human diversity in all respects—physically, culturally, and linguistically.

Before considering further the major "culture areas" of Oceania, it will be useful to outline briefly the linguistic diversity found in the islands, which have been home to about one-fourth of the world's total languages. Most Pacific languages have not yet been studied systematically, and classifications based on their presumed genetic relationships (i.e., connections through common ancestral languages) are continually being modified as we learn more about them. (In the cultural summaries for this volume, a degree of standardization has been attempted by following in most cases the groupings shown in the *Language Atlas of the Pacific Area,* edited by S. A. Wurm and S. Hattori.) Virtually all linguists agree, however, that the languages of Oceania can be assigned to three major groups, each of which is unrelated to the others: *Australian, Austronesian,* and *Papuan.*

The smallest of these groups consists of about 200 languages that were spoken by Aboriginal Australians. Perhaps 50, or one-fourth, of these are now considered to be extinct and many more are on the path to extinction as increasing numbers of Aborigines adopt English and fail to pass on their traditional languages to their children. Virtually all of the Australian languages are thought to be genetically related to each other, but their classification into language families and other groupings is still debated. At present, no clear linkages have been demonstrated between any Australian language and others in the Pacific or elsewhere in the world.

The second-largest group consists of the Austronesian (formerly called "Malayo-Polynesian") languages. After the Indo-European Family, Austronesian languages are the most numerous and most widely dispersed in the world, with more than 800 languages spread across two-thirds of the Earth's circumference, from Madagascar to southeast Asia, Taiwan, the Philippines, and throughout most of the Pacific. Perhaps as many as 450 of these are found in Oceania as defined in this volume. Nearly 250,000 people speak Fijian, and Samoan has about 200,000 speakers; however, most Austronesian languages in Oceania currently have fewer than 10,000 speakers. Most linguists consider these languages to be derived from a language (called Proto-Oceanic) associated with the Lapita culture discussed earlier. Over time, it is thought, this single ancestral language community dispersed and diverged; now members of the Oceanic Subgroup of Austronesian languages are found along the northern and eastern coasts of New Guinea and throughout most of Melanesia, Polynesia, and all of Micronesia, except for Palauan, Yapese, and the language of the Chamorros of Guam (these being affiliated with Southeast Asian Austronesian languages). The Austronesian languages of the Pacific are in continual evolution, influenced in part by dynamic interaction with speakers of Papuan languages, and there is much controversy among linguists regarding lower-level groupings, especially for those Austronesian languages spoken in Melanesia.

The largest and most complex major group of languages in Oceania consists of the Papuan languages. There are over 700 distinct Papuan languages (with uncounted dialects), but fewer than 50 of these are adequately documented. More than 60 language families have been proposed to bring order to this diversity, but current evidence suggests that not all of the Papuan languages are genetically related to each other. Indeed, until recently, they were designated simply as "Non-Austronesian languages," a label still used by many scholars, to indicate this fact; that is, it was clear from their grammatical structures and other features that they were not related to Austronesian languages or to those of Australia, but it was doubted that they formed a single higher-level group. Some Papuan languages are found in eastern Indonesia, but most are spoken by the peoples of New Guinea, the Bismarck Archipelago, and the island of Bougainville. Given their distribution, and especially their predominance in the interiors of Melanesian islands, most scholars suppose that the first settlers of Near Oceania (see above) were speakers of a language (or languages) ancestral to Papuan languages, with the current diversity and complexity developing subsequently within the region. While a few languages, such as Chimbu and Enga in the highlands of Papua New Guinea, have nearly 200,000 speakers each, most Papuan languages are spoken by only a few hundreds or thousands of people. Extensive borrowing from Austronesian-speaking neighbors and the influence of lingua francas and intrusive languages such as English and Indonesian make the situation even more dynamic and complex today.

Indeed, as if the linguistic picture in Oceania were not complex enough, one result of that very complexity has been the creation of numerous pidgin languages, with some arising among Pacific islanders themselves as they traded and otherwise interacted across language boundaries, and others occurring in the context of the colonial period when islanders vastly expanded their contacts with others, especially through plantation labor (see below). A partial list would include Micronesian Pidgin English, Hawaiian Pidgin, Samoan Plantation Pidgin, Queensland Plantation Pidgin, Chinese Pidgin English, Sandalwood English, Macassarese Pidgin, Torres Strait Broken, Hiri Motu, Bahasa Indonesia, and Melanesian Pidgin English, the last with three main dialects: Tok Pisin (in Papua New Guinea), Solomons Pijin, and Bislama (or Bichelemar, in Vanuatu).

Oceania's linguistic diversity, with about 1,500 distinct

languages traditionally spoken and probably most islanders fluent in at least one of the pidgins just mentioned, parallels at least as much diversity in cultures. A few cultural traits could be said to have been shared throughout the traditional Pacific (e.g., subsistence-based life in domestic households, land typically owned by kinship-based units, and the absence of draft animals and the wheel). But differences far outnumber similarities, and the "culture areas" into which Oceania is conventionally divided must themselves be appreciated as broad regions possessing some general shared characteristics but also much diversity, as is evident from the 151 cultural summaries included in this volume. These cultures have been selected for inclusion on the basis of their representativeness of this range as well as for their prominence in the literature on the Pacific.

When they first met Europeans there were perhaps as many as 300,000 Aborigines, divided into about 600 tribes, living in Australia. Tribes varied considerably in size (averaging about 450 members) and consisted of intermarrying "hordes," each of which claimed a common territory and shared a language, name, and certain cultural practices. A horde comprised the members of a clan (based on either matrilineal or patrilineal descent) and their in-married spouses; the clan was considered to be the collective owner of an area identified by the presence of sacred places, established by ancestral beings during "the Dreamtime" (or "the Dreaming"), when they gave form to the Earth and established traditional customs. Throughout Aboriginal Australia, subsistence was based on hunting and gathering and tribal boundaries were ecologically based. Vast and intricate networks of tracks and paths crisscrossed the continent, through which intertribal trade was conducted and joint ceremonial undertakings were facilitated. While coastal regions offered somewhat richer and more various food resources than did the deserts of the interior, wild game and plant food in general were seasonal and scattered, requiring frequent travel. In the desert areas, people engaged in what has been called "restricted wandering" within a prescribed, though often huge, area; some coastal peoples practiced "centrally based wandering," periodically fanning out from semipermanent home bases. In this volume, the diversity of Aboriginal cultures is well represented by seventeen summaries (see map 2), including the major desert peoples (e.g., Aranda, Mardudjara, Ngatatjara, Pintupi, and Warlpiri), those of the more varied northern regions (e.g., Murngin, Tiwi, and Wik Mungkan), and island dwellers as different from each other as the Torres Strait Islanders and the Tasmanians.

The island of New Guinea is home to speakers of more than 700 languages and its environmental and cultural diversity defy easy generalization. Perhaps 2 million people lived there at the time of first contact with Europeans (which for a few groups in the interior occurred as recently as the 1960s), and the variety of their traditional ways of life is conveyed by sixty-nine cultural summaries in this volume (see map 3). Occupying the high valleys of the central cordillera of mountains running like a spine almost the length of New Guinea are the "highlanders," represented here by nineteen summaries. These peoples still tend to live in either densely settled villages or scattered homesteads or hamlets, mostly organized in terms of patrilineal descent with clans and tribes as major political units and the "big-man" style of leadership (as is generally true for New Guinea, with exceptions such as Mekeo, the Trobriand Islands, and Wogeo). Most highlanders continue to be sweet-potato cultivators, with domestic pigs being of central importance in ceremonial exchange systems and other intergroup transactions. The Sepik River is another major geographical feature of the island, and on its banks and tributaries are found numerous groups who depend on riverine resources, sago, and yams as primary food sources. Both matrilineally and patrilineally organized societies are found here and across the northern part of the island, and the region is justifiably world-famous for its massive traditional ceremonial houses and elaborate art styles. Sepik and northern lowland peoples are extremely diverse, however, as can be appreciated through the seventeen cultural summaries from this region. The southern lowland and coastal areas are also diverse, with yams, taro, or sago usually complementing hunting and fishing as food sources. Patrilineal descent is the most common basis for social organization, and settlements ranged traditionally from large riverine or coastal villages in the southwest and southeast to enormous communal longhouses in the Papuan Gulf region and the interior, with the coastal gulf peoples rivaling those of the Sepik in their stunning artwork and ceremonial structures. Another major region for art production is the Massim, consisting of a number of islands and island groups off the southeastern tip of New Guinea. The peoples of the Massim, most of whom are organized in terms of matrilineal descent, are also well known for their participation in the *kula* system, which links numerous islands in a complex network of ceremonial exchange, trade, and political alliance.

Apart from New Guinea, Melanesia (see map 4) had perhaps one-half million inhabitants when European contact began. Twenty-nine cultural summaries in this volume make it clear that there are no traits that are universal in the region or that are uniquely "Melanesian." Indeed, in the Solomon Islands area are found several "Polynesian outliers" (including Anuta, Ontong Java, Rennell Island, and Tikopia), where Polynesian languages are spoken and basically Polynesian cultures (see below) are found in the midst of quite different peoples. As is true of the rest of Oceania, nowhere were Melanesians dependent on cereal crops; rather, tree and root crops were the traditional staples, with taro (*Colocasia esculenta*) being the most widespread of these. Communities of varying sizes are still organized either matrilineally or patrilineally, and, except on the Polynesian outliers, leadership and status in general are largely acquired rather than hereditary. Ceremonial exchange and prestige displays of garden produce continue to be generally important facets of intercommunity relations, and secret societies and cults were traditionally something of a Melanesian hallmark. Associated with these latter groups were highly developed plastic and graphic arts (now largely devoted to the tourist trade), especially in New Britain, New Ireland, and the New Hebrides (now called Vanuatu). Despite these general features, there was and still is considerable cultural diversity in Melanesia, as one can readily see from the cultural summaries for Vanuatu societies alone (Ambae, Malekula, Nguna, Pentecost, and Tanna).

The range of societies found in Micronesia is well represented by fourteen cultural summaries in this volume (see map 5). Perhaps 180,000 people lived on Nauru and in the Mariana, Caroline, Marshall, and Gilbert islands when Europeans first entered the region. Most of these people lived in small hamlets on small islands or atolls, with sociopolitical organization based on the control of land, which was usually vested in matrilineal descent groups. Systems of hereditary ranking and stratification were universal, and some island groups were linked in extensive empires. Overseas trading, using single-outrigger canoes, was also a feature that connected the far-flung islands in this region. As well as serving as a "highway," the sea also was and still is a storehouse of food for Micronesian peoples, whose island homes have always had a very limited land fauna. Staple crops traditionally included taro, yams, breadfruit, pandanus fruits, and coconuts. Underlying these broad similarities is diversity, with three main regions often distinguished: the *Western* groups of the Marianas (see Chamorros summary), Palau (Belau), and Yap; *Central,* including Kosrae, Pohnpei, Truk, and the Polynesian outlier of Kapingamarangi; and *Eastern* Micronesia, consisting of Nauru, the Marshall Islands, and the Gilbert Islands (Kiribati).

Polynesia, with perhaps 500,000 inhabitants at first contact with Europeans, displayed general cultural unity, although the Society Islands (Tahiti) and the rest of Eastern Polynesia differed somewhat from Western archipelagoes such as Samoa, and even more from Fiji (see map 6). These broad differences, as well as other particulars, can be ascertained from the twenty-two cultural summaries of Polynesian groups in this volume. In general, scholars consider what they call the "classical" Polynesian culture to have derived from the Lapita Culture (see above section on the settling of Oceania), taking its major shape around 500 B.C. This classical form consisted of settlements in large villages, with kin groups tracing descent cognatically. Everywhere political authority was hereditary, and elaborate religions, with priests and multitudes of gods, were also highly organized. Taro and breadfruit were major staples obtained through shifting cultivation, and fishing was of major importance, as it is today. Polynesians are famous for their navigational and sailing skills, ornate body decoration (especially tattooing), and wood-carving. However, as the summaries in this volume make clear (especially those for the Cook Islands, Futuna, and Rapa), the past two centuries have brought enormous changes to Polynesia, as they have to the rest of Oceania.

Oceania in the Modern World

According to archaeological and other evidence, insular southeast Asian traders, slavers, trepang collectors, and bird of paradise plume hunters regularly sailed the waters and visited the coasts of western New Guinea and northern Australia for centuries before the first Europeans arrived there. While their impact on the native peoples of the southwestern Pacific was doubtless significant, they left little in the way of written documentation of the cultures they encountered or of their dealings with the people. The historical record, and Oceania's emergence into the modern world, effectively began in the early sixteenth century.

Starting in the late thirteenth century, "the East" (i.e., Asia and the islands of modern Malaysia and Indonesia) lured Europeans seeking spices and continuing the long search for *Terra Australis Incognita,* the "southern continent" that many thought must exist to balance the known land masses of the northern hemisphere. In the late fifteenth century, land routes to the East were dominated by the Turks and no longer open to Europeans, so the latter looked to the sea. The Catholic church, through the Agreement of Tordesillas in 1491, divided the world (arrogantly) at a line 370 leagues west of the Cape Verde Islands; all to the west "belonged to" Spain, with Portugal's domain encompassing that half of the globe east of the line. Thus was set in motion Spain's voyages to the Western Hemisphere in search of spices and gold and its discovery of the New World in the process.

The first Spaniard to see the Pacific Ocean was Vasco Núñez de Balboa, who viewed it looking south from what is now Panama and named it, accordingly, the "South Sea." Throughout the sixteenth century Spanish explorers sailed southwest from Europe, rounding Cape Horn and scouring the Pacific seeking riches. The first of these was Ferdinand Magellan, who named the ocean "Pacific" because it seemed so calm compared to his stormy passage through what would later be called the Straits of Magellan. It is yet another indication of the emptiness of the Pacific, referred to at the beginning of this essay, that Magellan sailed across the entire ocean before touching land in the Mariana Islands of western Micronesia in 1521. Contemporaneous with the Spanish voyagers, Portuguese ships sailed to the southeast, around the Cape of Good Hope in Africa, and entered the Pacific from the west, landing at Yap in the 1520s and New Guinea in the 1540s. Iberians continued to explore the ocean for another half-century, "discovering" such island groups as the Solomon Islands (named in 1568 by Alvaro de Mendaña, who hoped he had found the fabled source of the gold of King Solomon), the Marshall Islands, the Ellice Islands, the Marquesas Islands, and the northern Cook Islands. Their quest for material riches was largely unfulfilled, but they sought the glory of God as well as of kings, and Catholicism was established early, especially in Micronesia.

Following the defeat of the Spanish Armada in 1588 and other political changes in Europe, the hegemony of the Spanish and Portuguese in the Pacific was drastically reduced. Such explorers as Pedro de Quirós and Luis Váez de Torres continued to make important "discoveries" (e.g., the New Hebrides, the Gilbert Islands, and the Torres Strait, all in 1606) but, apart from western Micronesia, the Pacific in the seventeenth century was largely the province of the Dutch. Their primary motivation was business, particularly in spices, and in 1602 they established the Dutch United East India Company. From their bases in the "Dutch East Indies" (Malaysia and Indonesia), Dutch ships probed to the east, with Willem Schouten and Jacob le Maire sailing along the northern coast of New Guinea and eastward to Futuna and Tonga in 1616, and Abel Tasman exploring much of the southern coast of Australia as well as Tasmania, which now bears his name, and as far east as Fiji in 1643. Little of what the Dutch found was made public due to their concern with secrecy for purposes of trade monopoly, but sketchy reports trickled back to Europe and inspired such fanciful works of literature as *Gulliver's Travels.*

Further power struggles in Europe in the eighteenth century resulted in significant new presences in Oceania. Occasional Dutch explorers still made new "discoveries," such as Jacob Roggeveen, who sighted Samoa and Easter Island in 1722, but it was the French and English ship captains who came to dominate the Pacific in the 1700s. Some were buccaneers, preying on the Spanish galleons that by then regularly sailed between the Philippines and South America, but others were in search of colonies or scientific knowledge. French navigators such as Philip Carteret and Louis Antoine de Bougainville explored the Solomon Islands, and the Englishman Samuel Wallis visited the Marshall Islands, Tahiti, and other parts of Micronesia and Polynesia. But *the* major European figure in the Pacific from 1768 to 1779 was the great British navigator Captain James Cook.

Cook's first voyage, from 1768 to 1771, was undertaken primarily for scientific knowledge (although British colonial ambitions were a significant factor as well). He was commissioned to observe the transit of Venus before the sun, with Tahiti identified as the best location for the necessary astronomical measurements, and to find Terra Australis. He returned with detailed charts and new information regarding Tahiti and New Zealand, as well as other islands, but no news of a southern continent. From 1772 to 1775, he covered almost the whole of the Pacific, including the coast of Antarctica, and established that Australia was large, but not the continent that had been imagined, and indeed that Terra Australis was only imaginary. On a final voyage, from 1776 to 1779, his goal was another illusion—to find the "Northwest Passage" that would connect the North Atlantic and North Pacific oceans. What he found included the Hawaiian Islands (which he named the Sandwich Islands after his friend and patron, the Earl of Sandwich), where he was killed by native Hawaiians in 1779. The list of islands and island groups "discovered" or "rediscovered" by Cook is long, including the Hawaiian group, Christmas Island, New Caledonia, the Cook Islands, the Gilbert Islands, Fiji, Tonga, the Solomon Islands, Easter Island, and part of the Tuamotu Archipelago. In addition, his carefully drawn charts proved finally that New Guinea, New Zealand, and Australia were not joined together, as many had supposed. Cook's accomplishments, including a vast quantity of scientific specimens and observations, have never been equaled, in the Pacific or elsewhere in the world. By the conclusion of Cook's voyages, the main outlines of the island groups of Oceania were charted, and only locally systematic exploration would be undertaken in the future. From the Europeans' point of view, now was the time for exploitation of the resources and people of this vast new realm.

The War of 1812 effectively disrupted the American whaling industry in the Atlantic Ocean, but worldwide demand for whale oil for lamps and whalebone for corsets and other uses continued unabated. Until markets changed and whale populations dwindled in the 1850s, hundreds of whaling ships prowled the central Pacific, introducing Western goods and Western diseases in the process. The continuing trade in spices had created increasing demands by Asians for furs, pearl shells, trepang, and sandalwood, the last being an aromatic wood taken from trees that, as was soon discovered, covered vast tracts of the islands of the New Hebrides, Fiji, and much of the rest of Polynesia. During the heyday of the whalers and traders (1780–1850) there was virtually no official European colonial presence in Oceania, and reports of atrocities in the islands fanned the flames of evangelical movements then popular in Europe and the United States. Missionaries were quick to see a need for their influence, and few parts of the Pacific were left untouched by them. The London Missionary Society sent the first wave, in 1797, to Tahiti, Tonga, and the Marquesas Islands, and additional groups to Fiji in 1835 and the New Hebrides in 1839. Congregationalists from the United States arrived in the Hawaiian Islands in 1820, and other Protestant groups fanned out into the Cook Islands (1821), Tonga (1822), Fiji and Samoa (1830), the Caroline Islands (1852), and the Gilberts and Marshalls (1857). In addition to other, smaller, mission groups, Catholic missionaries soon were established in Tahiti (1836), New Caledonia (1840), and Fiji (1844). To this day, new groups of missionaries are arriving and expanding throughout Oceania, but those early representatives were especially significant, not only in terms of their effects on the customs and beliefs of Pacific islanders but also because their presence constituted a major factor in the development of commerce and accompanying demands for the establishment of colonial governments and services.

From the middle of the 1840s to the beginning of the First World War, newcomers began systematically to strip Oceania of its resources, both natural and human. In 1847 the first laborers were "recruited" from the New Hebrides and the Loyalty Islands, and soon blackbirders were scouring the Pacific, offering trinkets and often-false promises of good pay and prompt repatriation after a term of service on Australian sugar plantations, in the guano mines of Peru, or wherever cheap labor was needed. Thousands of male Pacific islanders were thus shipped off to distant places, often under coercion and treated as virtual slaves. Many died of diseases or other causes, and countless individuals were never returned to their homes, sometimes simply being dropped off at whatever port was convenient for the labor recruiters. In part due to pressure from Pacific missionaries, Great Britain passed an anti-blackbirding act in 1872, which largely, but not completely, ended this traffic in human cargo.

As if in reciprocity for those who were removed, European powers also came to regard Oceania as a dumping ground for their "undesirables," with New Caledonia chosen in 1864 by the French as a place to get rid of convicts from home just as Australia had been founded as a colony by the British in 1788 for the same purpose. Asians began to pour into the Pacific, with Chinese and Japanese laborers (in 1865 and 1878, respectively) being brought to work on plantations in Hawaii. People were also brought from India to work in the burgeoning sugar industry of Fiji; the first group arrived in 1879, and today their descendants constitute the majority population in the Fiji Islands.

The demand for labor on Pacific islands was nearly limitless as European-owned plantations began to occupy vast tracts of land. While sugarcane was the major plantation crop in Queensland, Australia, and Fiji, the copra trade had a broader and longer-lasting influence. The dried meat of the coconut (copra) was highly valued as a source of oil for cooking, soaps, cosmetics, and other products in worldwide demand, and millions of coconut palms were planted and managed throughout the Pacific. Missionaries saw copra as a limitless source of cash, and commercial firms obtained rights to countless hectares of coastal and island land. For example, from 1884 to 1899, the Neu Guinea Kompagnie turned most of the coastline of northeastern New Guinea into plantations for copra, as well as tobacco and other crops, and, beginning in 1905, the firm of Lever Brothers established Lever's Pacific

Plantations, Ltd., in much of Fiji and the Solomon Islands. Copra continues to be the major commercial export of many islanders.

American, Australian, British, French, and German business interests also came to dominate the mercantile trade that blossomed throughout Oceania to supply plantation managers, itinerant traders, and small storekeepers, who now seemed to be everywhere. Prominent among these were such companies as the German-owned Godeffroy and Son, which established its headquarters in Apia (Western Samoa) in 1856 and soon monopolized Micronesia and spread out to New Britain. Another company, and still a major presence throughout the Pacific, was the British firm Burns Philp (South Seas) Company, Ltd., which soon after the beginning of the twentieth century controlled much of the shipping business and countless trade stores in locations ranging from port towns to tiny islands. Such prospects, combined with the strategic importance of Pacific islands as coaling depots and naval stations and the discovery of mineral resources (e.g., nickel in New Caledonia in 1863, gold in New Guinea in 1889, and phosphate on Nauru in 1899), made Oceania an increasingly desirable part of the world for European colonies in the latter half of the nineteenth century. Australia had been established as a colony of the British in 1788, and long before, in 1565, Spain had claimed part of the Mariana Islands and extended its influence in Micronesia. But it was in the middle and late 1800s that the European colonial powers rushed to expand their empires.

The Dutch, formalizing their long-standing hegemony in the "East Indies," claimed the western half of New Guinea in 1848, and in 1884 Germany annexed the northeastern quadrant of the island (plus Manus, New Britain, New Hanover, New Ireland, and Bougainville), to which Great Britain responded in the same year with the proclamation that the southeastern quarter was British New Guinea (later renamed Papua and transferred to Australian control as the Territory of Papua in 1906). Elsewhere in Melanesia, France seized New Caledonia in 1853 and the New Hebrides in 1882, only to reach a compromise with Great Britain in 1906 by forming the jointly administered Anglo-French Condominium of the New Hebrides. During this period the French also annexed, in Polynesia, the Marquesas Islands, Tahiti, the Wallis Islands, and the Austral Islands. Fiji was ceded to Great Britain in 1875, and in 1892 the latter established the Gilbert and Ellice Islands Protectorate. At the very close of the century, the United States annexed the Hawaiian Islands and New Zealand acquired the Cook Islands. In Micronesia, the United States seized Guam in 1898, and in the following year the rest of Spain's interests were dissolved with their sale of the northern Marianas, the Carolines, and the Marshalls to Germany.

In the midst of all these maneuvers, Pacific islanders were little more than pawns. Guamanians had revolted against their Jesuit missionaries in 1670, and the Spanish-Chamorros War lasted from 1672 to 1700, but Spain, predictably, won. New Caledonians staged an uprising against the French in 1878, as did Caroline Islanders opposed to their overlords in 1887 and Western Samoans in 1908. But there could be little hope for success against the nineteenth-century superpowers, and none would be achieved until global politics changed with two world wars.

While World War I was fought far from the Pacific islands, it brought about major realignments of the colonial powers' positions in Melanesia and Micronesia. Germany lost its colonies immediately in 1914 at the outbreak of the war, with Japan taking over the Mariana Islands (except Guam), the Carolines, and the Marshalls and with Australia seizing German New Guinea and Nauru. Following the war, the new shufflings were formalized, with the League of Nations awarding the Mandated Territory of New Guinea to Australia and a comparable mandate in Micronesia to Japan.

The next big political changes came with World War II. In 1941 Japan seized Guam from the United States, but at the end of the war it lost all of its Micronesian holdings, as all of those islands became the Trust Territory of the Pacific Islands, administered for the United Nations by the United States. Australia's mandate became the United Nations Trust Territory of New Guinea, which merged in 1949 with Papua to become the Territory of Papua and New Guinea, and New Caledonia became an overseas territory of France. To be sure, World War II brought many other changes as well, as the Pacific became a battleground, with fierce fighting devastating New Guinea and the islands of Melanesia and Micronesia, in the course of which military forces also introduced vast quantities of Western goods and influences. In New Guinea and Melanesia, one of the manifestations of this impact was the flowering, during the war and in the postwar years, of numerous "cargo cults," nativistic movements focusing on prophecies of the magical arrival of vast amounts of material goods ("cargo") and natives taking control over their own affairs.

While independence from colonial rule was not as imminent as the prophets had hoped, the postwar period has indeed seen a "new Pacific" emerge; today, France remains the only major colonial power in Oceania. Contributors of the individual cultural summaries in this volume have ably charted these political changes, as well as providing localized examples of the broad social and cultural changes that could only be sketched here. I close this introductory essay with a brief survey of the current status of the islands of Oceania as political entities (see map 1) and some basic demographic information. By organizing that survey by "culture areas," I show that these distinctions, whatever qualified value they may have in subdividing "traditional" Oceania, are poor guidelines in understanding the complexity that characterizes the peoples of the Pacific today.

Australia is an independent state and a member of the British Commonwealth, federated in 1901, with its capital in Canberra (see map 2). Its nearly 7.7 million square kilometers had a population of a little over 16 million in 1986, only about 1 percent of whom were Aborigines. Australian Aborigines are represented by sixteen cultural summaries in this volume, in addition to the Torres Strait Islanders, who numbered about 6,100 in 1980; the islands of the *Torres Strait*, with a capital on Thursday Island, are an Australian possession.

The island of *New Guinea* is divided into two political entities (see map 3). The western half, with an area of about 422,000 square kilometers, was Dutch New Guinea until 1963, when it was awarded by the United Nations to Indonesia and became Irian Barat, or West Irian. In 1969, it became *Irian Jaya*, a province of Indonesia, with its capital in Jayapura and a population of about 1.2 million people in 1980. In this volume, the peoples of Irian Jaya, who have not been studied as extensively as have their eastern neighbors, are represented by ten cultural summaries. The eastern half of the island constitutes the main portion of *Papua New Guinea* (capital, Port Moresby), an independent state and member of the British Commonwealth since 1975 with a total land area of about 462,000 square kilometers (see maps 3 and 4). In 1984, a national census estimated a population of 3,350,000, which included the inhabitants of the "mainland" (represented in this volume by fifty-nine summaries) and the islands of Bougainville (two summaries), Buka (Kurtatchi), Manus (one), New Britain (four), and New Ireland (three).

Elsewhere in Melanesia (see map 4), the *Territory of New Caledonia and Dependencies* has been an overseas territory of France since 1946, with Noumea as the capital city. Its land area of about 19,000 square kilometers was home to 145,400 people in 1984 on New Caledonia itself and the Loyalty Islands (see Ajië and Loyalty Islands summaries in this volume). The *Solomon Islands* became an independent state and member of the British Commonwealth in 1978. Its 1984 population of 251,000 (represented by ten cultural summaries) was distributed across about 30,000 square kilometers of land, including such major islands as Choiseul, Guadalcanal (where the capital, Honiara, is located), Malaita, New Georgia, San Cristobal, the Santa Cruz Islands, and Santa Isabel. Finally, the former New Hebrides became the *Republic of Vanuatu*, an independent state, in 1980. It consists of about eighty islands and islets, totaling about 13,000 square kilometers of land and including most prominently Ambrym, Aoba (Ambae), the Banks Islands, Efate (home of the capital, Port-Vila), Erromanga, Espiritu Santo, Malekula, Pentecost, Tanna, and the Torres Islands. The 132,000 ni-Vanuatu (indigenous citizens of Vanuatu) censused in 1984 are represented in this volume by six cultural summaries.

In December 1990 the United Nations Security Council officially terminated the Trust Territory of the Pacific Islands established under U.S. administration at the end of World War II. That former region now consists of five political entities (see map 5). The *Commonwealth of the Northern Marianas*, with its capital on Saipan, became an American commonwealth in 1975. Its 1980 population of about 18,000 people lived on 471 square kilometers of land. At the southern end of the Mariana Islands, *Guam* is an unincorporated territory of the United States, with a land area of about 550 square kilometers. Most of its inhabitants live in or near the capital city of Agana, and a cultural summary of its native Chamorros people is provided in this volume. The *Federated States of Micronesia*, established as an independent state in free association with the United States in 1979, includes most of the Caroline Islands. It consists of four states—Kosrae; Ponape (or Pohnpei), site of the capital, Kolonia; Truk; and Yap—totaling about 1,200 square kilometers of land. Its population was estimated at a little more than 77,000 in 1980, and it is represented by eight cultural summaries in this volume. The *Republic of the Marshall Islands* (with two cultural summaries, Bikini and Marshall Islands) has been an independent state in free association with the United States since 1979, and the 1980 census enumerated about 32,400 residents. Its capital is on Majuro Atoll, one of thirty-four major islands in the group, which total only 181 square kilometers of land spread over more than 1,100 islands and islets. The *Republic of Palau* (*Belau*) was established in 1981, but it is still negotiating its free-association status. Its six major islands, with the capital town of Koror on Babelthuap, total 461 square kilometers of land and had a population of about 14,800 in 1980. Apart from the former trust territory, Micronesia includes two more political entities, each of which has a cultural summary in this volume. The *Republic of Kiribati*, with its capital on Tarawa, has been an independent state and member of the British Commonwealth since 1979, and includes Banaba, the Gilbert Islands, Line Islands, and Phoenix Islands. Its 1984 population of 61,400 lived on thirty-three tiny islands with a total land area of only 690 square kilometers, but claiming 3.5–5 million square kilometers of the sea. The *Republic of Nauru*, an independent state and member of the British Commonwealth since 1968, has only about 21 square kilometers of land, but includes 320,000 square kilometers of ocean. Most of its population of 8,600 in 1984 resided in or near the capital city of Yaren.

Finally, although Polynesia presented perhaps the least cultural diversity in traditional Oceania, today it includes the widest range of political entities to be found there (see map 6). *American Samoa* (combined with Western Samoa for a cultural summary in this volume), with its capital city of Pago Pago, is an unincorporated United States territory. It consists of seven major islands with 36,400 people living in 1984 on about 200 square kilometers of land and exploiting a 390,000-square-kilometer area of the sea. The political state of *Cook Islands* has been self-governing, in free association with New Zealand, since 1965. In 1984 its estimated 16,000 people (represented by four cultural summaries) lived on 240 square kilometers of land spread over numerous small islands, such as Mangaia, Manihiki, Pukapuka, Rarotonga (with the capital town of Avarua), and Tongareva.

Easter Island is a province of Chile; the 180-square-kilometer island's population was counted as 1,867 in 1981, with most people living in or near the capital town of Hanga Roa. *Fiji*, which is as often considered a part of Melanesia as it is of Polynesia, has been an independent state and member of the British Commonwealth since 1970. Administered from the capital city of Suva on the island of Viti Levu, Fiji's area of over 18,000 square kilometers of land is scattered over more than 300 islands. Indians now constitute a majority of the population, estimated at 680,000 in 1984; traditional Fijian groups, including Rotumans, are represented in three cultural summaries in this volume. Over 5 million square kilometers of the Pacific are occupied by *French Polynesia*, an overseas territory of France granted internal autonomy in 1977, with its capital in Pape'ete on Tahiti in the Society Islands. In 1984, 159,000 residents were counted on about 130 islands, totaling about 4,000 square kilometers of land. Five cultural summaries are included here, representing major island groups such as the Society Islands (Tahiti), the Marquesas Islands, the Australs (Rapa), and the Tuamotu Archipelago (Mangareva and Raroia). *Hawaii* has been a state of the United States since 1959, with its capital city of Honolulu located on Oahu, one of eight major islands, with a total land area of almost 17,000 square kilometers. The 1980 census included 964,691 residents, only a minority of whom are of native Hawaiian descent.

New Zealand, an independent state and member of the

British Commonwealth, consists of two major islands, with the capital city of Wellington located on the North Island. The total land area is almost 270,000 square kilometers, and its 1981 population of a little more than 3 million was estimated to be about 9 percent Maori, 2 percent other Pacific islanders, and the rest of European descent. The small island of *Niue,* having only 258 square kilometers of land but claiming 390,000 square kilometers of sea, is a self-governing state in affiliation with New Zealand since 1974, with fewer than 3,000 inhabitants (mostly in the capital town of Alofi) in 1984. While not represented by a cultural summary in this volume, *Pitcairn Island* is well known to the general public as the refuge of the mutineers from Captain William Bligh's ship, H.M.S. *Bounty.* It is a British colony with only 45 residents in 1983, descendants of the mutineers and Tahitians; Adamstown is the capital of this tiny (5 square kilometers), remote island. *Tokelau* is a territory of New Zealand, administered from Apia in Western Samoa. Its 1981 population of about 1,500 lived on three atolls totaling only 10 square kilometers of land. Nuku'alofa is the capital of the *Kingdom of Tonga,* a member of the British Commonwealth since 1970. Tonga consists of about 170 islands, with a total land area of 670 square kilometers within 700,000 square kilometers of ocean, which were home to about 104,000 people in 1984. *Tuvalu* (formerly the Ellice Islands), with its capital on the small atoll of Funafuti, became an independent state and member of the British Commonwealth in 1978. Its 1984 population of 8,200 lived on 26 square kilometers of land and claimed 900,000 square kilometers of sea. The *Territory of the Wallis and Futuna Islands* has been a French overseas territory since 1959, with Mata Uta as its capital (see Futuna cultural summary). In 1983, about 11,800 people lived on its twenty-five islands totaling 255 square kilometers of land. Last is the *Independent State of Western Samoa,* an independent state and member of the British Commonwealth since 1962. Its eight islands, with the capital of Apia on the island of Upolu, comprise almost 3,000 square kilometers of land, and the 1983 population was estimated at 159,000.

Reference Resources

The vastness of the literature on Oceania is proportional to that of the ocean itself. The following suggestions and references, including the sources on which this essay is based, are intended to direct the reader to the major sources, which will lead in turn to the rest.

General Works

The most comprehensive scholarly survey of Oceania for the general reader is Oliver's *The Pacific Islands* (1989b). A good nonnarrative collection of entries by specialists covering the whole of the Pacific is the *Historical Dictionary of Oceania* (Craig and King 1981). Good, up-to-date atlases of Oceania do not exist, but a helpful recent guide is Motteler (1986). The only attempt at a comprehensive bibliography of the older scholarly literature is Taylor's *A Pacific Bibliography* (1965). For a useful listing of more specialized bibliographies, see Fry and Mauricio (1987). Many excellent films on the Pacific are now available for classroom use, a partial listing of which is found at the end of this volume. More extensive lists and ordering information can be found in Hamnett (1986) and Heider (1983).

The Physical Environment

No general works on the Pacific as a whole are available, but the first chapter in Oliver (1988) is very useful as an overview, and Barrau's monographs (1958, 1961) on subsistence agriculture survey the economically important plants of Oceania. Brookfield with Hart (1973) are thorough with respect to Melanesia and New Guinea, and Brookfield's (1973) and Ward's (1972) edited collections include good treatments of specific cases of geographic change. For a modern, somewhat pessimistic, account of ecological devastation in the contemporary Pacific, see Mitchell (1989).

The Settlement of Oceania

Reconstructions of Pacific prehistory are continually changing with new data and new perspectives. Good general overviews can be found in Bellwood (1978), Irwin (1990), and Terrell (1986). Fascinating studies of the navigational skills involved in settlement of the Pacific have been written by Lewis (1972, 1978). More regionally focused recent studies include J. Allen (1989) and Jones (1989) for Australia; White and O'Connell (1982) for Sahul; Jennings (1979) on Polynesia and Melanesia; and Allen and White (1989) on the Lapita Culture.

Languages and Cultures of Oceania

A good overview of Pacific islanders from the viewpoint of a physical anthropologist is the book by Howells (1973); more recent genetic studies are collected in Hill and Serjeantson (1989). The *Language Atlas of the Pacific Area* (Wurm and Hattori 1981) has been used as a common reference for the cultural summaries in this volume. More specialized studies include Dixon (1980) on Australian languages; Foley (1986) on Papuan languages; Pawley (1981) on Austronesian languages; and Keesing (1988) and Mühlhäusler (1986, 1988) on pidgins and creoles.

Oliver's (1988) comprehensive survey of Oceanic cultures has been issued (1989a) in an abridged form. General collections of articles by specialists on particular cultures include Harding and Wallace (1970) and Vayda (1968). Thomas (1989) critically examines the notion of "culture areas," especially for Melanesia and Polynesia. Australian Aboriginal cultures are surveyed in Berndt and Berndt (1985) and Tindale (1974); the Tasmanians are the subject of a book for the general audience by Davies (1974). No comprehensive survey of the cultures of New Guinea is available, but a collection edited by Hastings (1971) is useful, and Souter (1963) provides a highly readable overview. Chowning (1977) usefully surveys Melanesia, and collections of articles by specialists include Langness and Weschler (1971) and May and Nelson (1982). Alkire's books (1972, 1978) on Micronesia are excellent general works, as are those by Goldman (1970), Howard (1971), Howard and Borofsky (1989), and Kirch (1984) for Polynesia. More sources on particular cultures will be found at the end of each cultural summary.

Oceania in the Modern World

The history of Pacific exploration and settlement by Europeans has been the subject of countless books for the general reader. Among the best of these are Daws (1980), Furnas (1946), Michener and Day (1957), Moorehead (1966), and

Snow (1979). Scholarly analyses of exploration include Beaglehole (1966), Dodge (1976), Fisher and Johnston (1979), Friis (1967), Grattan (1963a, 1963b), Howe (1984), Maude (1968), and Spate's authoritative trilogy (1979, 1983, 1988). More specialized but still readable studies include Hughes (1986) on Australia and Smith (1989) on Polynesia. Recent studies by scholars on missionaries in the Pacific include Boutilier et al. (1978), Gunson (1978), and Whiteman (1983).

World War II as seen by Pacific islanders is presented in a fascinating collection by White and Lindstrom (1989). An excellent reference work on modern Oceania is the area handbook edited by Bunge and Cooke (1984).

Acknowledgments

The contributors, who include more than 100 anthropologists, historians, and other scholars, as well as members of the Human Relations Area Files (HRAF) research staff, cannot be thanked enough for sharing their knowledge in the cultural summaries in this volume. For assistance and advice (but not final responsibility) in selecting the cultures to be included and the authorities to write the summaries, I am grateful to Renée Heyum, Mac Marshall, Douglas Newton, William Rodman, Paul Roscoe, Richard Scaglion, and Robert Tonkinson. Patricia Hurley Hays made valuable suggestions regarding this introductory essay.

References

Alkire, William (1972). An *Introduction to the Peoples and Cultures of Micronesia.* McCaleb Module in Anthropology no. 18. Reading, Mass.: Addison-Wesley.

Alkire, William (1978). *Coral Islanders.* Arlington Heights, Ill.: AHM.

Allen, Jim (1989). "When Did Humans First Colonize Australia?" *Search* 20:149–154.

Allen, Jim, and J. Peter White (1989). "The Lapita Homeland: Some New Data and an Interpretation." *Journal of the Polynesian Society* 98:129–146.

Barrau, Jacques (1958). *Subsistence Agriculture in Melanesia.* Bernice P. Bishop Museum Bulletin no. 219. Honolulu.

Barrau, Jacques (1961). *Subsistence Agriculture in Polynesia and Micronesia.* Bernice P. Bishop Museum Bulletin no. 223. Honolulu.

Beaglehole, J. C. (1966). *The Exploration of the Pacific.* 3rd ed. Stanford: Stanford University Press.

Bellwood, Peter S. (1978). *Man's Conquest of the Pacific.* Auckland, N.Z.: William Collins.

Berndt, Ronald M., and Catherine H. Berndt (1985). *The World of the First Australians: Aboriginal Traditional Life Past and Present.* Rev. ed. Canberra: Australian Institute for Aboriginal Studies.

Boutilier, James, et al., eds. (1978). *Mission, Church, and Sect in Oceania.* Lanham, Md.: University Press of America.

Brookfield, Harold C., ed. (1973). *The Pacific in Transition: Geographical Perspectives on Adaptation and Change.* New York: St. Martin's Press.

Brookfield, Harold C., with Doreen Hart (1971). *Melanesia: A Geographical Interpretation of an Island World.* London: Methuen.

Bunge, Frederica M., and Melinda W. Cooke, eds. (1984). *Oceania: A Regional Study.* Area Handbook Series. Washington, D.C.: American University, Foreign Area Studies.

Chowning, Ann (1977). *An Introduction to the Peoples and Cultures of Melanesia.* 2nd ed. Menlo Park, Calif.: Cummings.

Craig, Robert D., and Frank P. King, eds. (1981). *Historical Dictionary of Oceania.* Westport, Conn.: Greenwood Press.

Davies, David (1974). *The Last of the Tasmanians.* New York: Harper & Row.

Daws, Gavan (1980). *A Dream of Islands: Voyages of Self-Discovery in the South Seas.* New York: W. W. Norton.

Dixon, R. M. W. (1980). *The Languages of Australia.* Cambridge: Cambridge University Press.

Dodge, Ernest (1976). *Islands and Empires: Western Impact on the Pacific and East Asia.* Minneapolis: University of Minnesota Press.

Fisher, Robin, and Hugh Johnston, eds. (1979). *Captain James Cook and His Times.* Seattle: University of Washington Press.

Foley, William A. (1986). *The Papuan Languages of New Guinea.* Cambridge: Cambridge University Press.

Friis, H. R., ed. (1967). *The Pacific Basin: A History of Its Geographical Exploration.* Special Publication no. 38. Washington, D.C.: American Geographical Society.

Fry, Gerald W., and Rufino Mauricio, comps. (1987). *Pacific Basin and Oceania.* World Bibliographical Series, vol. 70. Oxford: Clio Press.

Furnas, J. C. (1946). *Anatomy of Paradise: Hawaii and the Islands of the South Seas.* New York: William Sloane.

Goldman, Irving (1970). *Ancient Polynesian Society.* Chicago: University of Chicago Press.

Grattan, C. Hartley (1963a). *The Southwest Pacific since 1900: A Modern History.* Ann Arbor: University of Michigan Press.

Grattan, C. Hartley (1963b). *The Southwest Pacific to 1900: A Modern History*. Ann Arbor: University of Michigan Press.

Gunson, Neil (1978). *Messengers of Grace: Evangelical Missionaries in the South Seas, 1797–1860*. New York: Oxford University Press.

Hamnett, Judith D. (1986). *A Guide to Films about the Pacific Islands*. Working Paper Series. Honolulu: University of Hawaii, Center for Asian and Pacific Studies, Pacific Islands Studies Program.

Harding, Thomas G., and Ben J. Wallace, eds. (1970). *Cultures of the Pacific: Selected Readings*. New York: Free Press.

Hastings, Peter, ed. (1971). *Papua/New Guinea: Prospero's Other Island*. Sydney: Angus & Robertson.

Heider, Karl G. (1983). *Films for Anthropological Teaching*. Special Publication no. 16. Washington, D.C.: American Anthropological Association.

Hill, Adrian V. S., and Susan W. Serjeantson, eds. (1989). *The Colonization of the Pacific: A Genetic Trail*. Oxford: Clarendon Press.

Howard, Alan, ed. (1971). *Polynesia: Readings on a Culture Area*. Scranton, Pa.: Chandler.

Howard, Alan, and Robert Borofsky, eds. (1989). *Developments in Polynesian Ethnology*. Honolulu: University of Hawaii Press.

Howe, K. R. (1984). *Where the Waves Fall: A New South Sea Islands History from First Settlement to Colonial Rule*. Honolulu: University of Hawaii Press.

Howells, William (1973). *The Pacific Islanders*. New York: Charles Scribner's Sons.

Hughes, Robert (1986). *The Fatal Shore*. New York: Alfred A. Knopf.

Irwin, Geoffrey (1990). "Human Colonisation and Change in the Remote Pacific." *Current Anthropology* 31:90–94.

Jennings, J. D., ed. (1979). *The Prehistory of Polynesia*. Cambridge, Mass.: Harvard University Press.

Jones, Rhys (1989). "East of Wallace's Line: Issues and Problems in the Colonisation of the Australian Continent." In *The Human Revolution: Behavioural and Biological Perspectives on the Origins of Modern Humans*, edited by Paul Mellars and Chris Stringer, 743–782. Princeton: Princeton University Press.

Keesing, Roger M. (1988). *Melanesian Pidgin and the Oceanic Substrate*. Stanford: Stanford University Press.

Kirch, Patrick V. (1984). *The Evolution of the Polynesian Chiefdoms*. New York: Cambridge University Press.

Langness, L. L., and John C. Weschler, eds. (1971). *Melanesia: Readings on a Culture Area*. Scranton, Pa.: Chandler.

Lewis, David (1972). *We, the Navigators: The Ancient Art of Landfinding in the Pacific*. Wellington, N.Z.: A. H. & A. W. Reed.

Lewis, David (1978). *The Voyaging Stars*. Sydney: William Collins.

Maude, H. E. (1968). *Of Islands and Men: Studies in Pacific History*. New York: Oxford University Press.

May, R. J., and H. Nelson, eds. (1982). *Melanesia: Beyond Diversity*. 3 vols. Canberra: The Australian National University, Research School of Pacific Studies.

Michener, James A., and A. Grove Day (1957). *Rascals in Paradise*. New York: Random House.

Mitchell, Andrew (1989). *A Fragile Paradise: Nature and Man in the Pacific*. London: Collins.

Moorehead, Alan (1966). *The Fatal Impact: An Account of the Invasion of the South Pacific, 1767–1840*. New York: Harper & Row.

Motteler, Lee S. (1986). *Pacific Island Names: A Map and Name Guide to the New Pacific*. Honolulu: Bishop Museum Press.

Mühlhäusler, Peter (1986). *Pidgin and Creole Linguistics*. London: Basil Blackwell.

Mühlhäusler, Peter (1988). "Towards an Atlas of the Pidgins and Creoles of the Pacific Area." *International Journal of the Sociology of Language* 71:37–49.

Oliver, Douglas (1988). *Oceania: The Native Cultures of Australia and the Pacific Islands*. 2 vols. Honolulu: University of Hawaii Press.

Oliver, Douglas (1989a). *Native Cultures of the Pacific Islands*. Honolulu: University of Hawaii Press.

Oliver, Douglas (1989b). *The Pacific Islands*. 3rd ed. Honolulu: University of Hawaii Press.

Pawley, Andrew (1981). "Melanesian Diversity and Polynesian Homogeneity: A Unified Explanation for Language." In *Studies in Pacific Languages and Cultures in Honour of Bruce Biggs*, edited by Jim Hollyman and Andrew Pawley, 269–309. Auckland: Linguistic Society of New Zealand.

Smith, Bernard (1969). *European Vision and the South Pacific, 1768–1850: A Study in the History of Art and Ideas*. New York: Oxford University Press. 2nd ed. New Haven, Conn.: Yale University Press, 1985.

Snow, Philip, and Stefanie Waine (1979). *The People from the*

Horizon: An Illustrated History of the Europeans among the South Sea Islanders. Oxford: Phaidon.

Souter, Gavin (1963). *New Guinea: The Last Unknown.* Sydney: Angus & Robertson.

Spate, Oskar H. K. (1979). *The Pacific since Magellan,* Vol. 1, *The Spanish Lake.* Canberra: Australian National University Press.

Spate, Oskar H. K. (1983). *The Pacific since Magellan,* Vol. 2, *Monopolists and Freebooters.* Canberra: Australian National University Press.

Spate, Oskar H. K. (1988). *The Pacific since Magellan,* Vol. 3, *Paradise Found and Lost.* Minneapolis: University of Minnesota Press.

Taylor, Clyde R. H. (1951). *A Pacific Bibliography: Printed Matter Relating to the Native Peoples of Polynesia, Melanesia and Micronesia.* Wellington, N.Z.: Polynesian Society. 2nd ed. Oxford: Clarendon Press, 1965.

Terrell, John (1986). *Prehistory in the Pacific Islands: A Study of Variation in Language, Customs, and Human Biology.* Cambridge: Cambridge University Press.

Thomas, Nicholas (1989). "The Force of Ethnology: Origins and Significance of the Melanesia/Polynesia Division." *Current Anthropology* 30:27–42.

Tindale, Norman B. (1974). *Aboriginal Tribes of Australia: Their Terrain, Environmental Controls, Distribution, Limits, and Proper Names.* 2 vols. Berkeley: University of California Press.

Vayda, Andrew P., ed. (1968). *Peoples and Cultures of the Pacific: An Anthropological Reader.* Garden City, N.Y.: Natural History Press.

Ward, R. Gerard, ed. (1972). *Man in the Pacific Islands: Essays on Geographical Change in the Pacific Islands.* Oxford: Clarendon Press.

White, Geoffrey M., and Lamont Lindstrom, eds. (1989). *The Pacific Theater: Island Representations of World War II.* Honolulu: University of Hawaii Press.

White, J. Peter, and James F. O'Connell (1982). *A Prehistory of Australia, New Guinea, and Sahul.* New York: Academic Press.

Whiteman, Darrell L. (1983). *Melanesians and Missionaries: An Ethnohistorical Study of Social and Religious Change in the Southwest Pacific.* Pasadena, Calif.: William Carey Library.

Wurm, S. A., and Shîro Hattori, gen. eds. (1981). *Language Atlas of the Pacific Area: Part I, New Guinea Area, Oceania, Australia.* Pacific Linguistics, Series C, no. 66. Canberra: Australian National University.

TERENCE E. HAYS

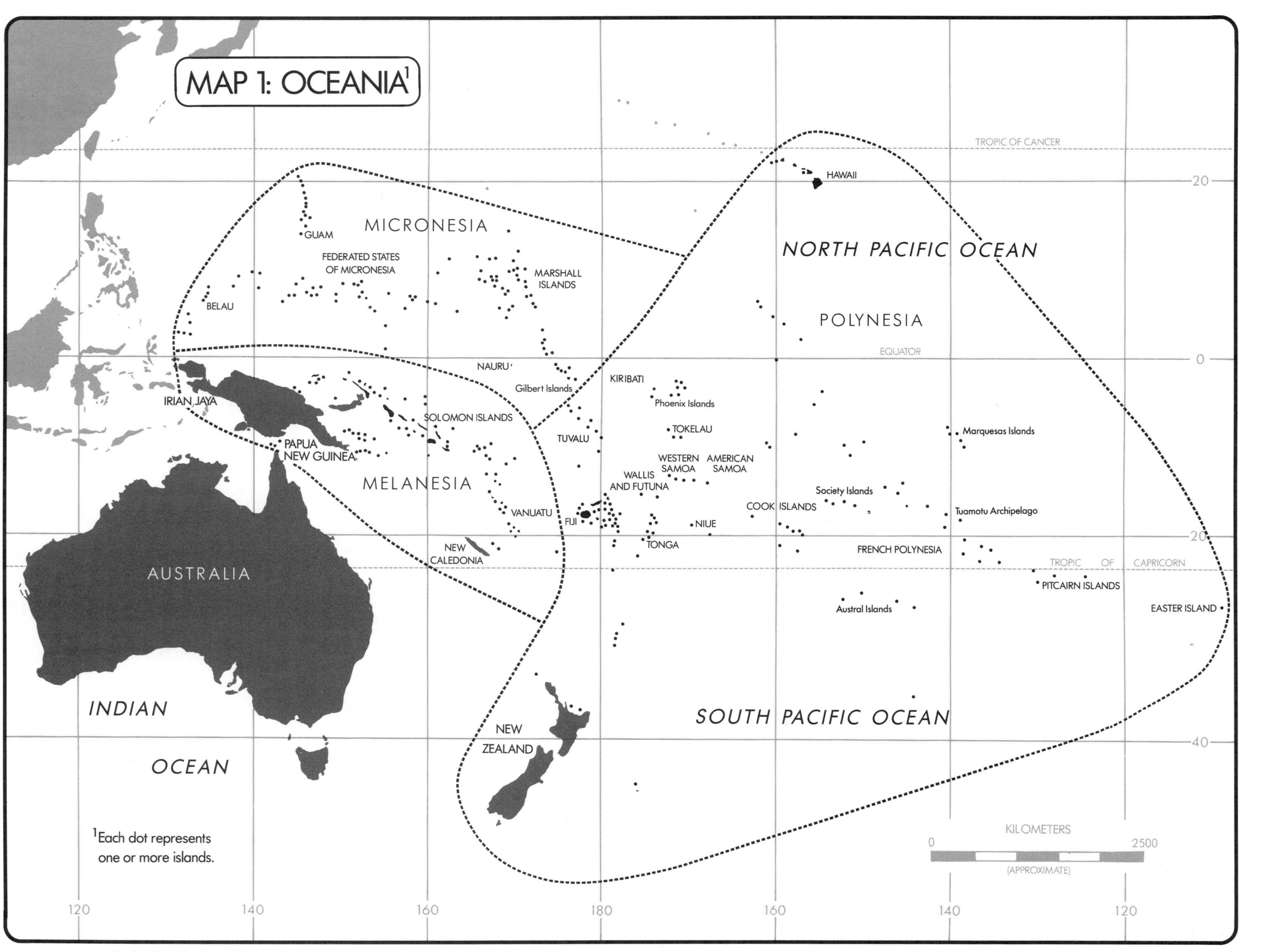

[1]Each dot represents one or more islands.

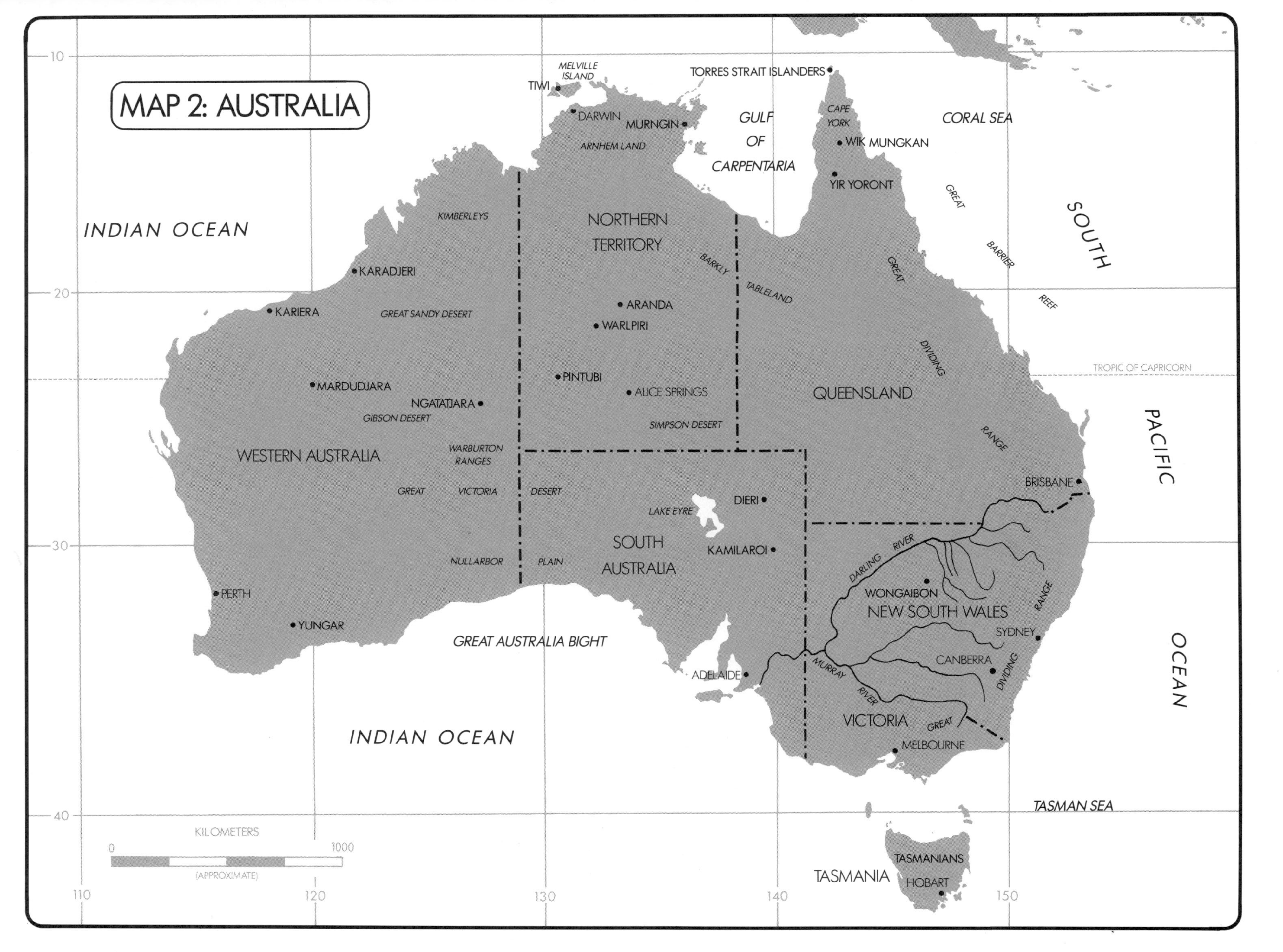

MAP 2: AUSTRALIA
INDIAN OCEAN
INDIAN OCEAN
SOUTH PACIFIC OCEAN
CORAL SEA
TASMAN SEA
GULF OF CARPENTARIA
GREAT AUSTRALIA BIGHT
TROPIC OF CAPRICORN
WESTERN AUSTRALIA
NORTHERN TERRITORY
SOUTH AUSTRALIA
QUEENSLAND
NEW SOUTH WALES
VICTORIA
TASMANIA
MELVILLE ISLAND
TIWI
DARWIN
MURNGIN
ARNHEM LAND
TORRES STRAIT ISLANDERS
CAPE YORK
WIK MUNGKAN
YIR YORONT
KIMBERLEYS
KARADJERI
KARIERA
GREAT SANDY DESERT
MARDUDJARA
NGATATJARA
GIBSON DESERT
WARBURTON RANGES
GREAT VICTORIA DESERT
NULLARBOR PLAIN
PERTH
YUNGAR
BARKLY TABLELAND
ARANDA
WARLPIRI
PINTUBI
ALICE SPRINGS
SIMPSON DESERT
LAKE EYRE
DIERI
KAMILAROI
ADELAIDE
GREAT BARRIER REEF
GREAT DIVIDING RANGE
BRISBANE
DARLING RIVER
WONGAIBON
SYDNEY
CANBERRA
MURRAY RIVER
MELBOURNE
TASMANIANS
HOBART
KILOMETERS
0
1000
(APPROXIMATE)
10
20
30
40
110
120
130
140
150

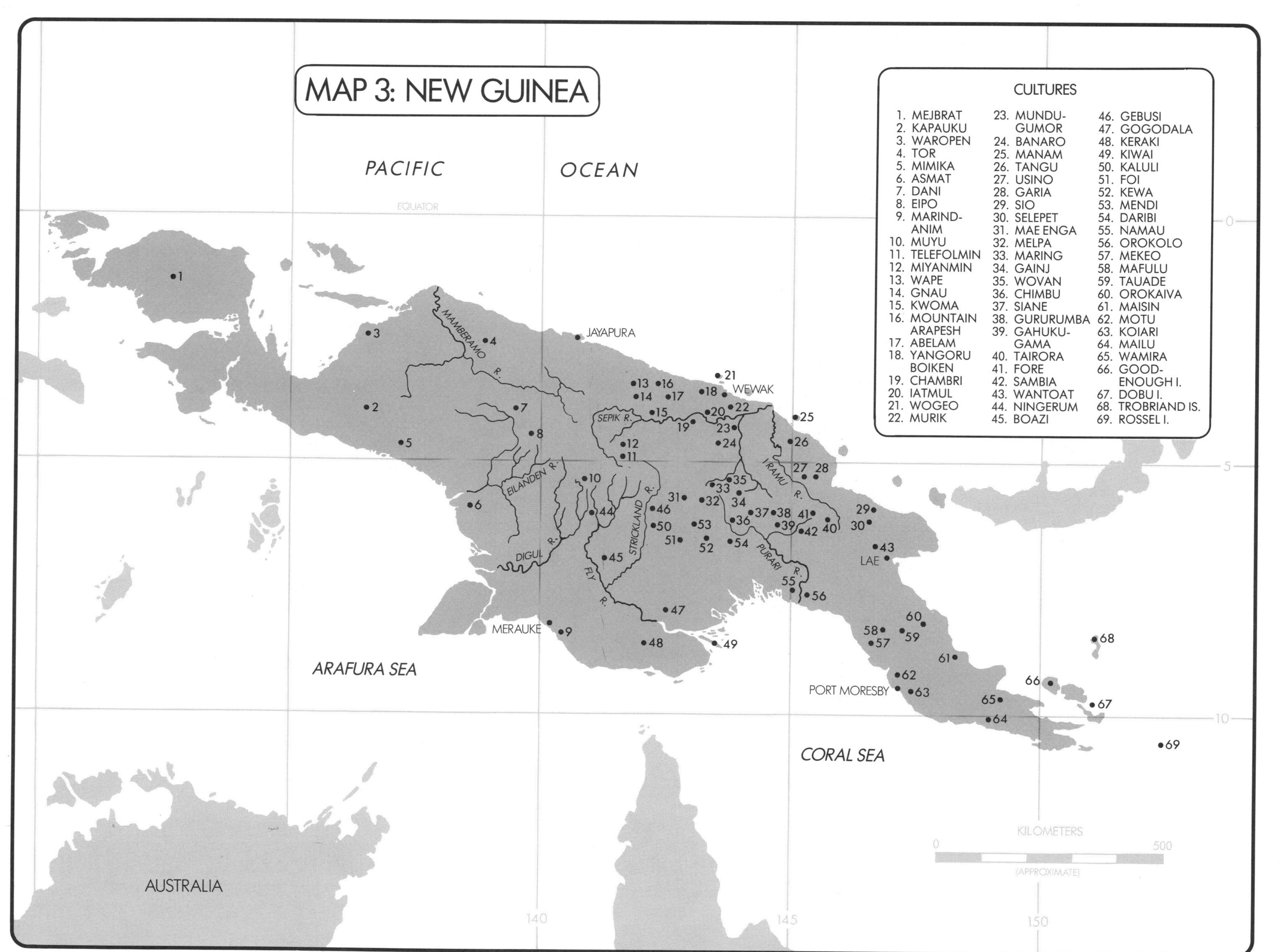
MAP 3: NEW GUINEA
PACIFIC
OCEAN
EQUATOR
CULTURES
1. MEJBRAT
2. KAPAUKU
3. WAROPEN
4. TOR
5. MIMIKA
6. ASMAT
7. DANI
8. EIPO
9. MARIND-ANIM
10. MUYU
11. TELEFOLMIN
12. MIYANMIN
13. WAPE
14. GNAU
15. KWOMA
16. MOUNTAIN ARAPESH
17. ABELAM
18. YANGORU BOIKEN
19. CHAMBRI
20. IATMUL
21. WOGEO
22. MURIK
23. MUNDU-GUMOR
24. BANARO
25. MANAM
26. TANGU
27. USINO
28. GARIA
29. SIO
30. SELEPET
31. MAE ENGA
32. MELPA
33. MARING
34. GAINJ
35. WOVAN
36. CHIMBU
37. SIANE
38. GURURUMBA
39. GAHUKU-GAMA
40. TAIRORA
41. FORE
42. SAMBIA
43. WANTOAT
44. NINGERUM
45. BOAZI
46. GEBUSI
47. GOGODALA
48. KERAKI
49. KIWAI
50. KALULI
51. FOI
52. KEWA
53. MENDI
54. DARIBI
55. NAMAU
56. OROKOLO
57. MEKEO
58. MAFULU
59. TAUADE
60. OROKAIVA
61. MAISIN
62. MOTU
63. KOIARI
64. MAILU
65. WAMIRA
66. GOOD-ENOUGH I.
67. DOBU I.
68. TROBRIAND IS.
69. ROSSEL I.
JAYAPURA
WEWAK
MAMBERAMO R.
SEPIK R.
RAMU R.
EILANDEN R.
DIGUL R.
STRICKLAND R.
FLY R.
PURARI R.
LAE
MERAUKE
PORT MORESBY
ARAFURA SEA
CORAL SEA
AUSTRALIA
KILOMETERS
0
500
(APPROXIMATE)
140
145
150
0
5
10

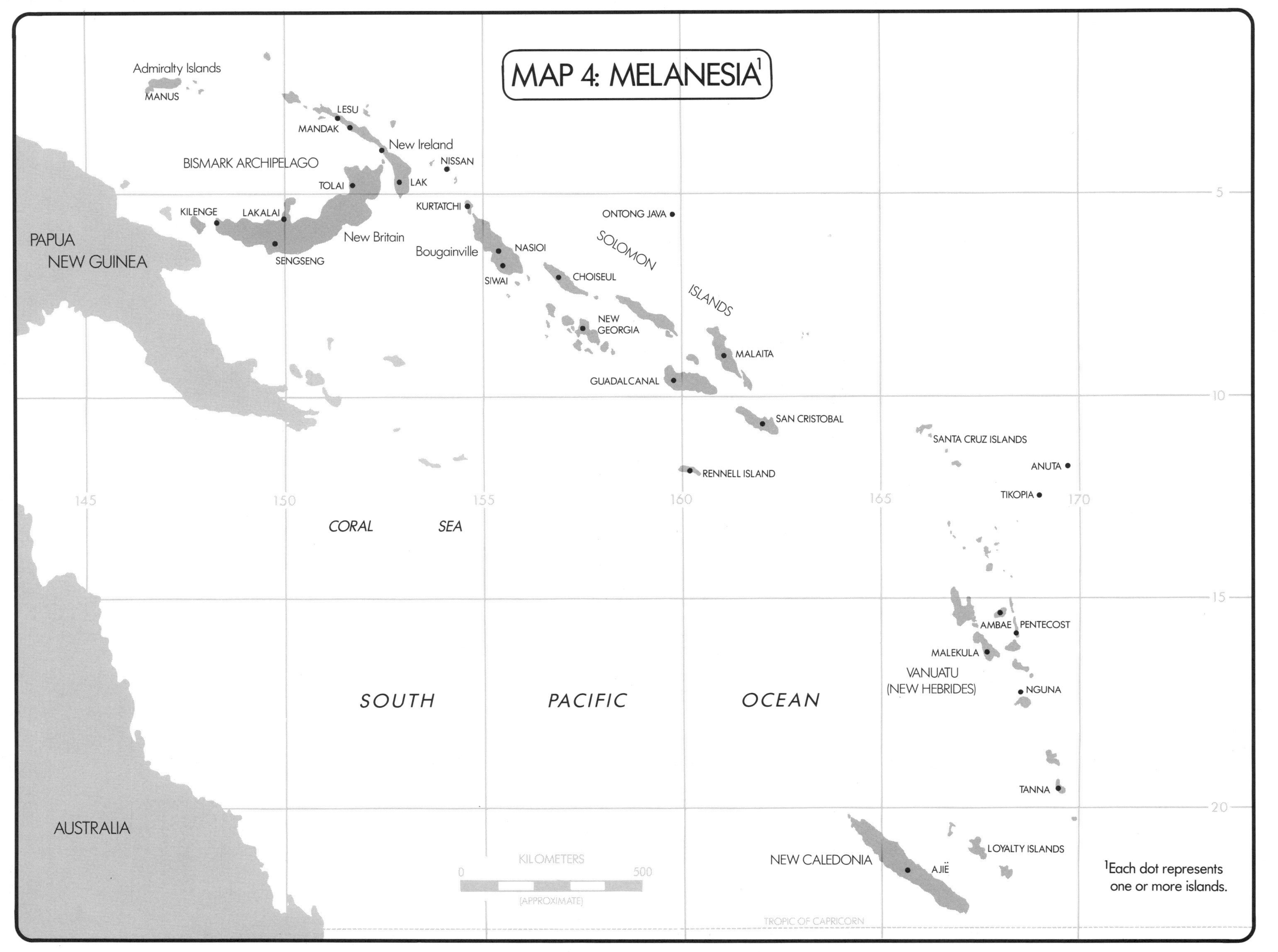

MAP 4: MELANESIA[1]
Admiralty Islands
MANUS
LESU
MANDAK
New Ireland
BISMARK ARCHIPELAGO
NISSAN
TOLAI
LAK
KURTATCHI
ONTONG JAVA
KILENGE
LAKALAI
PAPUA
NEW GUINEA
New Britain
SENGSENG
Bougainville
NASIOI
SIWAI
SOLOMON
CHOISEUL
ISLANDS
NEW
GEORGIA
MALAITA
GUADALCANAL
SAN CRISTOBAL
SANTA CRUZ ISLANDS
RENNELL ISLAND
ANUTA
TIKOPIA
145
150
155
160
165
170
5
10
15
20
CORAL
SEA
AMBAE
PENTECOST
MALEKULA
VANUATU
(NEW HEBRIDES)
NGUNA
SOUTH
PACIFIC
OCEAN
TANNA
AUSTRALIA
KILOMETERS
0
500
(APPROXIMATE)
NEW CALEDONIA
AJIË
LOYALTY ISLANDS
TROPIC OF CAPRICORN
[1]Each dot represents one or more islands.

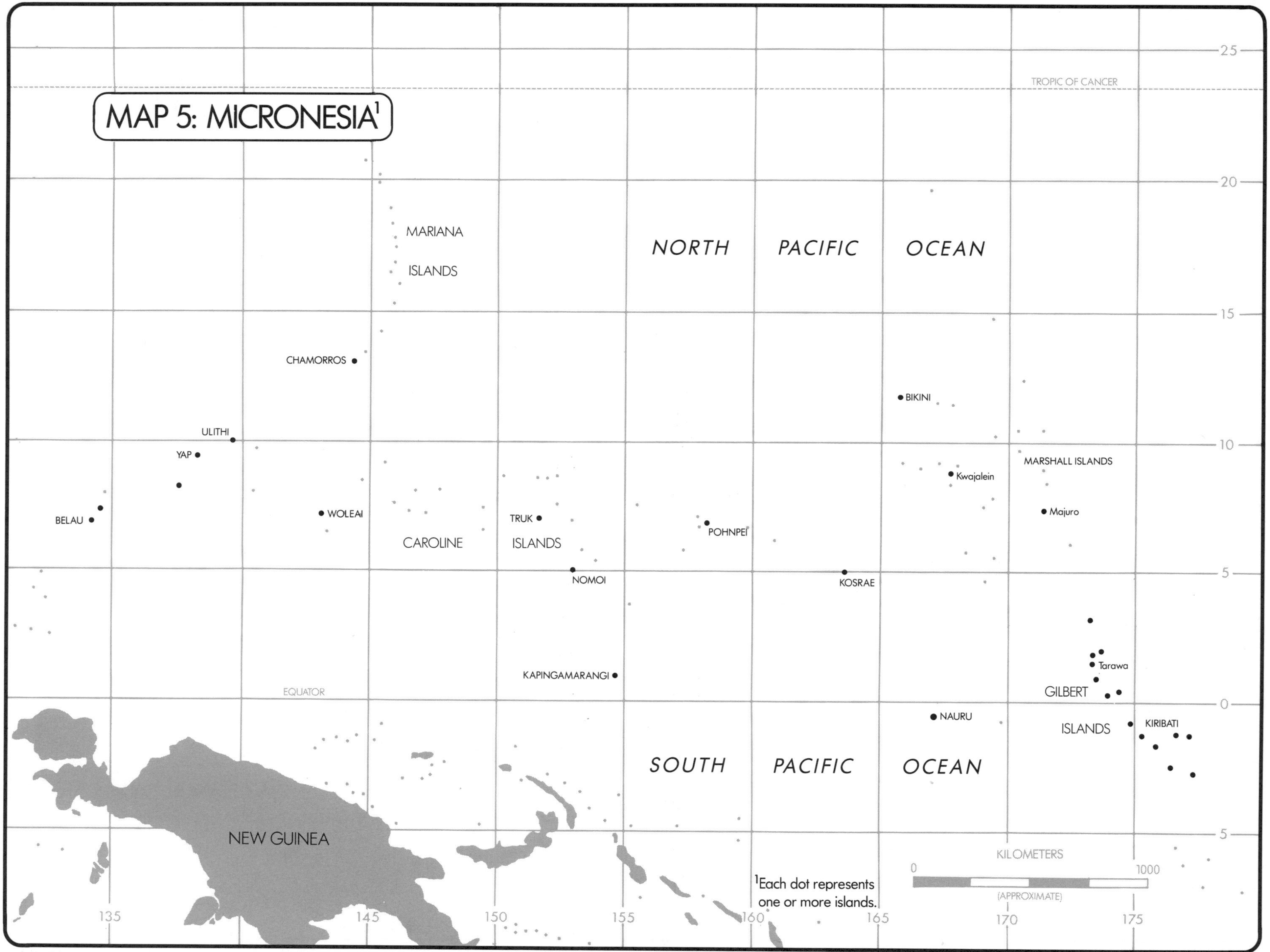

MAP 5: MICRONESIA[1]

[1]Each dot represents one or more islands.

MAP 6: POLYNESIA[1]

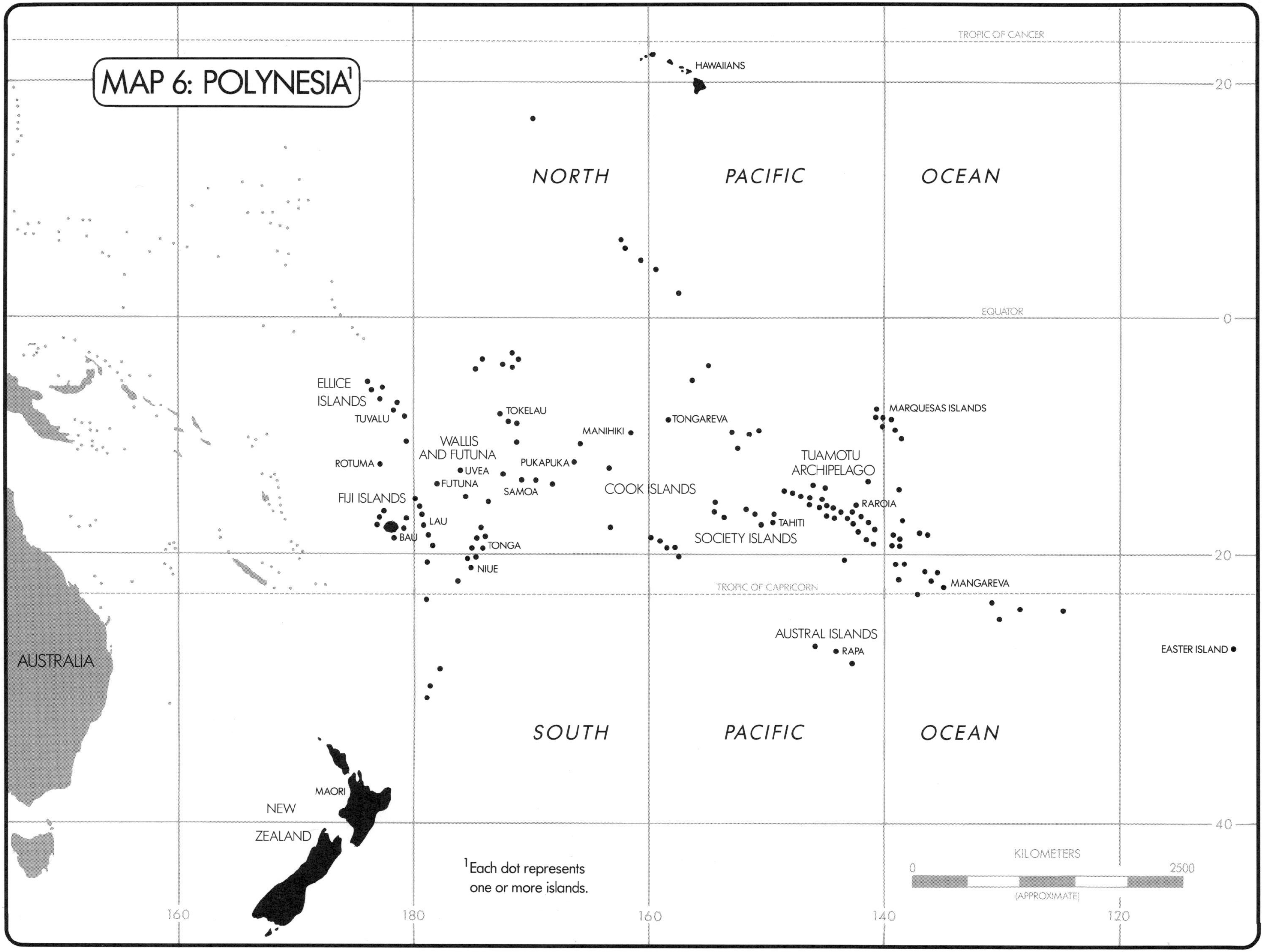

TROPIC OF CANCER
HAWAIIANS
NORTH PACIFIC OCEAN
EQUATOR
ELLICE ISLANDS
TUVALU
TOKELAU
MANIHIKI
TONGAREVA
MARQUESAS ISLANDS
WALLIS AND FUTUNA
ROTUMA
UVEA
FUTUNA
PUKAPUKA
SAMOA
COOK ISLANDS
TUAMOTU ARCHIPELAGO
RAROIA
FIJI ISLANDS
LAU
BAU
TONGA
NIUE
TAHITI
SOCIETY ISLANDS
TROPIC OF CAPRICORN
MANGAREVA
AUSTRAL ISLANDS
RAPA
EASTER ISLAND
AUSTRALIA
SOUTH PACIFIC OCEAN
MAORI
NEW ZEALAND
KILOMETERS
0
2500
(APPROXIMATE)
20
0
20
40
160
180
160
140
120

[1]Each dot represents one or more islands.

Encyclopedia of World Cultures

Volume II

OCEANIA

Abelam

ETHNONYMS: Abulas, Ambelam, Ambelas, Ambulas

Orientation

Identification. The Abelam live in the East Sepik Province of Papua New Guinea and are divided into several subgroups; the most prominent is the Wosera, who are so named after the area they inhabit. This is the southernmost group of the Abelam. The other groups are named for geographic direction: northern, eastern, etc. The whole region is called Maprik, named after the Australian administrative post established in 1937 in the heart of Abelam territory.

Location. From the Sepik floodplains in the south the Abelam extend to the foothills of the Prince Alexander Mountains (coastal range) in the north. The Plains Arapesh living there call their neighbors in the south Abelam. The Abelam live in two ecological zones, the hills (up to about 600 to 700 meters above sea level) and the relict alluvial plains. These zones are characterized by different landforms, altitudes, annual rainfall, and soil types. In the north, the foothills are covered with thick secondary vegetation; virgin forest has almost completely disappeared due to shifting cultivation and to the high population density that was also responsible in former days for many fights and wars over land.

Demography. The Abelam number over 40,000. Parts of the Abelam territory range, with 70 persons per square kilometer, are among the most densely populated areas in Papua New Guinea.

Linguistic Affiliation. Linguistically, Abelam forms, together with the Iatmul, Sawos, Boiken, and Manambu, the Ndu Family of the Sepik Subphylum, which is classified as part of the Middle Sepik Stock, Sepik-Ramu Phylum. All of these language groups are located within the Sepik Basin, except for the Boiken who have spread over the coastal range to the north coast.

History and Cultural Relations

In prehistoric times, the Sepik-Ramu Basin was flooded with salt water; this inland sea probably reached its maximum extent 5,000 to 6,000 years ago when it reached as far westward as Ambunti. The sea then began to drop gradually until it attained its present level around 1,000 years ago. During that span of time the Sepik Basin with its young floodplains began to develop and became separated from the Ramu Basin by the Bosman Plateau. Linguists point out that the Ndu Family of languages had a common ancestry, which suggests a common settlement history. Linguistic evidence also suggests that the Ndu speakers moved into the Sepik Plains from the south of the river. The Abelam evidently migrated northward during the last few centuries until after World War II, although there is much debate about where the Abelam came from and when they began moving north. Except for sporadic contacts with hunting parties from Indonesia, the first direct contact with the outside world occurred immediately before World War I, when the Abelam were discovered by the German ethnologist Richard Thurnwald who was traveling through Abelam territory on his way over the Alexander Mountains to the north coast. Before long, European goods (and also diseases) had reached the Maprik area. Soon missionaries arrived as well, and by 1937 an Australian patrol post (Maprik) was established, land was cleared for an airstrip, and a road to the coastal town of Wewak was built. World War II brought drastic changes to the Abelam way of life; thousands of Japanese, Australian, and American soldiers fought bloody battles on Abelam territory using technology unknown to the Abelam. The establishment of further patrol posts, missionary stations, trade stores, and schools, the substitution of a cash economy based on wage labor for the indigenous subsistence economy, and the development of flourishing towns led Abelam life in new directions. In precolonial times the Abelam—not as a whole group but as many individual villages—had already had continuous relations with neighboring groups. Those with the Plains Arapesh were the most highly esteemed because the Arapesh villages supplied them with valuables, shell rings, and other shell ornaments in exchange for pigs. Relations with the Boiken in the east, the Sawos in the south, and different groups in the west were restricted more or less to border villages.

Settlements

Throughout the Maprik area there were continuous population movements, not only the general south-to-north pattern but also minor movements within the region. These movements generally involved small kin groups who affiliated themselves with an already existing settlement or who formed new settlements elsewhere. Only after warfare ceased and peace was imposed did these movements stop and villages become relatively permanent. In the north, the Abelam probably absorbed many Arapesh people—or, rather, killed them or chased them off and took their territory. This high mobility is still reflected in the alliances of small groups in hamlets with other groups in other hamlets. Abelam villages vary in size. They are much smaller in the south with only 50 to 80 people. In the north, they now number up to 1,000 people. In the south, settlements are basically hamlets; in the north they are villages, preferably situated on a hill ridge, consisting of forty to fifty hamlets. Each is autonomous, at least concerning their relations with other settlements. Villages are structured as an association of hamlets who have formed something like a localized league. The village territory is generally divided into "upper" and "lower" topographical units. The structure of villages in the north is complex. Through rituals for different root crops, yam festivals, and initiation, the different major hamlets—each of which has a special role within this network of rituals—are bound together. Buildings such as storehouses, sleeping and dwelling houses, menstruation huts, and the towering ceremonial houses are built on the ground in a triangular plan. They consist more or less of a roof with a ridgepole gently sloping down from the front towards the back. Most spectacular are the ceremonial houses (*korambo*) with a large ceremonial ground (*amei*) in front of it. Only major hamlets have a korambo, which may be up to 25 meters tall, with a painted facade. The korambo and amei are considered the village center but larger villages may have up to ten or fifteen such centers. The building material is timber and bamboo for the inner structure; sago palm fronds are used for the thatch. Lashing techniques are elaborate.

Economy

Subsistence and Commercial Activities. The Abelam are horticulturalists living mainly on yams, taro, and sweet potatoes. The soils in the area, as well as the Abelams' skills in gardening, yield considerable harvests of different varieties of yam and taro. In the north they are cultivated mostly in hillside gardens. In the south, in the Sepik Plains, vegetation is sparse and consists mostly of *Imperata* grasslands. There yields are much smaller. The Abelam depend also on sago palms, which they exploit only seasonally, and on coconuts, bananas, and a large variety of vegetables and fruits. The Abelam practice slash-and-burn cultivation, allowing fallow periods of only a few years compared to as many as twenty years in the past. Today coffee and cocoa are grown as cash crops and are a major cause of the shorter fallow periods. Apart from *asakua* yams which grow in the poorly drained soils in the plains, there are dozens of other varieties of yam. In special ritual gardens men cultivate long yams that may grow up to 2 meters long. These are not grown for immediate consumption but for ritual yam exchange. After being harvested, they are decorated with plaited or wooden masks and with various ornaments for display at yam festivals where competition between the yam growers is important. These yam exchanges are held either between hamlets of the same village whose residents are members of different moieties or—in a much more dramatic form—between enemy villages. The growing and exchanging of yams has pervaded almost all aspects of Abelam life, and all male initiations are closely linked with it. Everything connected with women is inimical to long yams. Sexual intercourse during the planting season is avoided. This seems to have resulted in seasonal births in such villages. The production of a long tuber is, in a symbolic way, equated with the procreation of a child but with the emphasis that the long tuber is a creation of men only. The relation between men and women has been described as that of complementary opposition. Whereas yams and taro are grown primarily for daily consumption, the raising of pigs is done for exchange only. At each major yam exchange pigs must be contributed, too. Pigs, like long yams, may not be eaten by their owners.

Industrial Arts. All art objects such as elaborately patterned plaits for the ceremonial house, carvings, and paintings, as well as decorated pots and bone daggers, are made by men for their ceremonial life. The Abelam artist, though esteemed as a gifted specialist, is a yam grower like every other adult male. Meshwork used as boar-tusk ornaments and worn by men during fights and ceremonies, featherwork, and various body ornaments are produced by men who otherwise are not artists. Today the most important personal items of both men and women are net bags. (In former times both sexes were almost completely naked in everyday life.) The Wosera are among the most prolific makers of net bags. The production of net bags is known and performed by all women, though the knowledge of dyeing is limited to a few. Some women are renowned for their artistic skill.

Division of Labor. In subsistence activities there exists a more or less strict division of labor. Men fell the trees and clear the land for new gardens. Then they fence it off, sometimes assisted by women. Men plant all varieties of yams; later women plant taro between the yam mounds. Weeding the gardens as many as six times before harvest—is done exclusively by women. Men put up sticks for the yam vines and later they dig out the tubers, which women then clean of dirt and excessive roots. During all male communal affairs (with few exceptions during initiations) they are provided with food by women.

Trade. Piglets are reared only by women, who invest much labor in the production of pigs. In former times this was the only means to obtain wealth in the form of shell rings received from the Arapesh in exchange for pigs. Occasionally men from northern villages made trading expeditions not only to Arapesh settlements in the mountains (for shell rings, yellow paint, and magical substances) but sometimes even to the north coast. There they filled long bamboo tubes with salt water and carried them back to their villages. They used carvings and net bags—as trading goods and as gifts for their partners who provided them with shelter and food along the track. The large and beautifully patterned net bags (which are used also as marriage payments) were much more important as trading goods in the Wosera than they were in the north. Ceremonial earthen bowls, decorated elaborately, were mostly produced in southern villages and traded to northern villages. In general, however, each community was self-sufficient. Nevertheless, there were networks of cooperation between villages concerning the promotion of fertility, tubers, fruits, and men. Sometimes fertility was not promoted but instead inhibited—often by illness and death, believed to be caused by the witchcraft and sorcery for which some villages were well known.

Land Tenure. All land is owned by lineages and clans (*kim*). The wealthiest clans, if they have enough members, are the most powerful within a settlement as they will own, at least in part, the historically and thus ritually most important ceremonial grounds. A lineage's claim on land is demonstrated by their regularly using land for gardens. The individual plots owned by different lineages are marked by perennial plants; these are often overgrown by shrubs but are quickly rediscovered by old men when disputes over land arise. If a man clears land for a new garden or plants trees on ground not used by him before and nobody protests against it, he is regarded as the rightful owner.

Kinship

Kin Groups and Descent. Most clans are split into lineages, members of which often live together as a local unit. In a hamlet generally two or three clans (or rather lineages) are represented. This arrangement means that, within a lineage, a man with his brothers and their sons, as well as most of the in-marrying wives of their children, live together. Relations between siblings are close, expressing themselves also in continuous mutual assistance in all kinds of matters, with such assistance also extended to the children of brothers. The elder brother has some authority over the younger who pays him respect. Each nuclear family has several houses: a sleeping house for the father, a dwelling house for the mother and her children, and one or several storehouses for the root crop. In polygamous marriages not all in-marrying cowives live together in the same hamlet—where they live depends on the relationship between cowives. But a man wants his wives to live on his own land. Otherwise, if his children are born on another clan's land, his claim over his children may be challenged. Although, ideally, Abelam clans are said to be patrilineal, affiliations with other lineages and clans are very flexible. Continuous relations with one's mother's relatives (living on the land of the mother's brother), fosterage, and adoption give many opportunities for temporary and/or permanent association. This flexibility also leads to many disputes over landownership, rights of land use, etc. And because of this associational flexibility and also the absence of elaborate genealogies, clans as social organizational units are only predominant in questions of landownership. Clans are associated with the names of spirits, specific water holes where the spirits are temporarily found, magical leaves, and emblems (mostly birds). Most of these attributes become relevant only in ritual context but even then they are not applied systematically but rather casually or in a flexible manner. Sometimes they are used as attributes for moieties rather than clans.

Kinship Terminology. Kin terms are used mostly on special occasions such as during a dispute when somebody wants to express how closely related he or she is with somebody else. In mortuary ceremonies, during the wake, and before the corpse is buried, the deceased is addressed in kin terms only. In everyday life mostly proper names are used. Cousin terms follow the Iroquois system.

Marriage and Family

Marriage. Lineages are said to be exogamous and marriages within them are frowned upon. Marriages take place within a village. In some parts of Maprik region endogamy within the ceremonial moieties (*ara*) prevail in order to prevent competition between father and son-in-law. Sister exchange is a preferred form of marriage. In general, considerable freedom of choice is acknowledged to women in cases where the parents had not arranged intermarriage of their children. In former days marriage took place soon after first menstruation. In marriage transactions shell rings (nowadays supplemented by money) play an important role. Marriage payments can be substituted by giving at least one child back to the wife's clan. Sometimes, if no marriage payment at all is given, a man with his family has to live on his father-in-law's land and assist him, as a member of that household, in all communal subsistence activities such as clearing brush, planting, and harvesting. Divorce is not uncommon and usually occurs with the wife's return to her own family; in such cases the bride-wealth is returned by her kin or by her new husband upon remarriage.

Domestic Unit. The smallest domestic unit consists of a man with one or more wives and their children if they all live in the same hamlet. But for most activities in the gardens, brothers and their wives cooperate, often assisted by brothers-in-law. Within a common garden owned mostly by male relatives of a lineage, each family has its own plot. Each woman owns her own pigs and chickens and plans her daily work independently from others. She has to be asked permission if her husband wants to sell one of her pigs. Even in polygynous households, cooking is done by each woman separately.

Inheritance. Ideally, inheritance is patrilineally organized. This concerns mainly landownership and clan membership though there are many exceptions which give rise to disputes.

Socialization. The pattern of adult roles is transmitted to children at a very early age through their being actively motivated to participate in everyday activities. If left back in the village, they are put under the supervision of older children who form playing groups. At the same time they are entrusted with social responsibility. Through various stages of initiation, boys and young men attain manhood, which is connected with ritual knowledge. The most prominent ritual event in a girl's life is the first-menstruation ceremony, which is acted out communally by all women of a village.

Sociopolitical Organization

Social Organization. Apart from households, lineages, and clans within the village, the nonlocalized moiety system provides the structure for male initiations as well as for yam festivals. Members of one moiety (*ara*) have their personal yam exchange partners, and each ara initiates the sons of their exchange partners. Thus, all ceremonial activity is balanced between ara. Although membership is primarily inherited from one's father, the equality of the two aras' membership may be maintained by occasionally transferring members from one ara to the other.

Political Organization. Within the ara but also within assemblies held by hamlets or larger parts of the villages (as in disputes) the role of "big men" (*nemandu*) as the actual leaders becomes apparent. Apart from ritual knowledge (often transmitted to the first-born son), which is used as religious legitimation for political actions, oratorical skill is an important qualification for becoming a nemandu or an influential man.

Social Control. Nemandu are mostly conflict resolvers, settling disputes by stressing the importance of solidarity and cooperation. Disputes (which are quite frequent) are held on the ceremonial ground. They become settled under the guidance of influential men through the singing of conciliatory ritual songs, by the exchange of shell rings, or by fighting.

Religion and Expressive Culture

Religious Beliefs. Ceremonial houses (korambo) and ceremonial grounds (amei) are the focus of most rituals connected with the life-cycle events for men and women. For a girl parts of the first-menstruation ritual as well as the presentation of shell rings as marriage payments take place in front of the korambo. During the death ritual, the corpse is left there for one night. The korambo is also important for its mere presence and does not really serve as a meetingplace. It is mainly for housing those spirits (*ngwalndu*) who visit the living temporarily before going back to another world. In a ceremonial building the huge carved ngwalndu figures may be stored until they are used for an initiation. The large painted facade of a korambo is visually dominated by big faces associated with ngwalndu spirits. Although ngwalndu are to some extent ancestral spirits, no genealogy is reported linking the living with these powerful beings who influence the life of men, plants, and animals. The soul of a man (that soul which is associated with clan membership) is thought to live after death with a ngwalndu. While ngwalndu seem to be the most important supernaturals, there are nevertheless many others as well, both male and female.

Ceremonies. Initiations of boys and men into the secrets of Abelam religion are divided into many stages, the first taking place when the boy is 5 or 6 years old, the last between 30 and 50. In each initiation boys are acquainted with one category of spiritual beings. This begins at an early age with the least important, and as adults they learn, after they have seen ngwalndu, the last secret beyond which there is only a boundless void. Important parts of initiation ceremonies take place in the ceremonial house where artists arrange elaborate compositions of carved, painted, or plaited figures, decorated with shell rings, feathers, flowers, and leaves. No explanation is given to the initiates. The aim of these rituals is to show them the secrets rather than to verbalize a meaning. For each display of artifacts in a ceremonial house there is an associated dance. In these dances men are painted and decorated all over—thus they are transformed into beings from another world.

Arts. Abelam art is rich, with the emphasis on painting. Paint is seen as a magical substance that gives life to a piece of wood (carving). Only then do the figures become powerful and active. Paint is a metaphor for a magical substance used in sorcery, which in this case is not life-giving but life-taking. Throughout Abelam territory different art styles can be recognized, although there are also many commonalities. Abelam artists are highly respected but only rarely do they serve as political leaders.

Medicine. The Abelam have a large body of knowledge concerning herbs and plants in the bush that were traditionally used as remedies for various diseases. A few old men and women were considered experts and were consulted regularly. Under the influence of Western medicine the traditional knowledge is vanishing rapidly. Apart from diseases for which Abelam knew effective cures, they also recognized others which they traced back to magic and sorcery. For these no remedies except ritual and the supernatural could be of help.

Death and Afterlife. There is almost no "natural" death recognized, apart from those old people who had been sitting already for a long time "at the ashes of a fire." All other deaths are attributed to magic and sorcery mostly performed in other villages. Symbols of people's life souls are kept in specialized villages. As soon as a lethal illness is suspected these are checked in order to find the cause and origin of the sorcery performed. After death the corpse is displayed in front of the ceremonial house and a wake is held. The body is buried the following morning. There are many rituals held over several years until the soul is eternally freed from its bond to life. There are different souls, one associated with blood, one with bones. The latter is considered the eternal one, who becomes visible during the night as a shining star.

See also Iatmul, Yangoru Boiken

Bibliography

Forge, Anthony (1966). "Art and Environment in the Sepik." Royal Anthropological Institute, *Proceedings for 1965*, pp. 23–31. London.

Kaberry, Phyllis M. (1941). "The Abelam Tribe, Sepik District, New Guinea: A Preliminary Report." *Oceania* 11:233–258, 345–367.

Kaberry, Phyllis M. (1971). "Political Organization among the Northern Abelam." In *Politics in New Guinea*, edited by Ronald M. Berndt and Peter Lawrence, 35–73. Seattle: University of Washington Press.

Lea, David A. M. (1969). "Access to Land among Swidden Cultivators: An Example from New Guinea." *Australian Geographical Studies* 7:137–152.

Scaglion, Richard (1981). "Samukundi Abelam Conflict Management: Implications for Legal Planning in Papua New Guinea." *Oceania* 52:23–38.

Scaglion, Richard. (1983). "The 'Coming' of Independence in Papua New Guinea: An Abelam View." *Journal of the Polynesian Society* 92:463–486.

BRIGITTA HAUSER-SCHÄUBLIN

Ajië

ETHNONYMS: Canaque, Houaïlou, Kanak, Kanaka

Orientation

Identification. Ajië is one of the major southern languages found in New Caledonia. Today, Ajië speakers call themselves "Kanak," which has deep political meaning for them, because along with the vast majority of the other native peoples in New Caledonia, they are asking for independence from France. "Canaque" was introduced to the territory by Polynesian sailors, and in the local context it had a pejorative meaning. In the early 1970s the native peoples of New Caledonia changed the spelling to "Kanak" and this marked the birth of a Black-power type of consciousness. If they are successful in their quest for independence, their new country will be named "Kanaky."

Location. Ajië is spoken primarily on the east coast of New Caledonia's main island, La Grande Terre, from Monéo to Kouaoua in the Houaïlou Valley, but it has spread as far as Poya. Ajië is also spoken or understood by other western and southern language groups in New Caledonia, particularly those on the Ajië's border. Rainfall distribution reflects the classical opposition between windward and leeward slopes, and this feature is accentuated by the mountainous character of the main island. Average local rainfall may exceed 400 centimeters in the east and may be less than 100 centimeters in the west. Seasonal distribution is marked by maximum rainfall during the first three months of the year, although heavy daily rainfall is rare. The average temperature falls between 22° C and 24° C, with February being the hottest period and July–August the coolest.

Demography. In 1774, Captain Cook estimated that there were 60,000 natives on La Grande Terre and other sources guess that there were another 20,000 in the Loyalty Islands at that time. Regardless of the actual numbers, it is clear that every part of the islands was claimed or occupied by the local population. In 1989 the total population of New Caledonia was 164,173, of which 73,598 were Kanak. The Kanaks are the largest ethnic group in the territory (44.8 percent of the total population), followed by the Europeans (33.6 percent), Wallisians (8.6 percent), Indonesians (3.2 percent), Tahitians (2.9 percent), Vietnamese (1.5 percent), and Ni-Vanuatu (1 percent). The Ajië are approximately 3,600 or 5 percent of the native population. They can be found in the commune of Houaïlou and in the territorial capital of Noumea.

Linguistic Affiliation. New Caledonian languages belong to the Eastern Subdivision of the Austronesian languages. There are thirty-two native languages in New Caledonia, of which twenty-eight are still spoken. Ajië is one of the nine major languages of the southern language group. It is from the same proto-Melanesian root language as all the other languages in New Caledonia with the exception of Faga Uvea, which is spoken in the north and south of the island of Ouvea and has Polynesian origins.

History and Cultural Relations

According to the archaeological record, the earliest ancestors of the Kanaks came to New Caledonia from southeast Asia between 6,000 and 5,000 years ago. They brought with them slash-and-burn agriculture, irrigation techniques, a polished-stone tool complex, pottery, and double-pontoon sailing craft. There was also settlement from within Melanesia, especially from the Solomon Islands and Vanuatu. After 1840 there was regular contact with European and American whalers, merchants, and sandalwood traders in addition to British and French missionaries. After New Caledonia was annexed by France in 1853, tribal lands were expropriated for the establishment of a penal colony, settler colonialism, and nickel mining. This systematic and radical reduction of Kanak lands meant that the culturally cohesive and contiguous clan territories of the past were reduced to a shattered collection of isolated communities. By the end of the nineteenth century, Kanaks were confined to native reserves and compelled to do corvée (forced labor) for the settlers and on public works. After World War II, colonial policy was liberalized, forced labor was abolished, and the Kanaks were accorded the right to vote. However, in spite of increased political participation, the Kanaks continued to be economically marginalized as the financial gap between the Kanaks and the rest of the New Caledonian population continued to widen. The early 1970s was a boom period for New Caledonia because of the rise in world nickel prices (the territory has one-fourth of the world's nickel deposits). Urbanization increased as the rural areas were drained of labor. The collapse of the nickel boom in the mid-1970s led to unemployment and economic recession. Kanak youths returned to overcrowded native reserves only to find that there was little place for them. At this time Kanak demands for participation in economic and political decision making increased and the Kanak independence movement grew. In 1984 the Kanaks boycotted territorial elections, set up a provisional government, and demanded freedom from French rule and a "Kanak socialist independence." A settlement known as the Matignon Accords was negotiated in 1988 between Kanaks, the settlers, and the French government. This agreement heralds a ten-year "peace period" during which the French government will attempt to redress the socioeconomic inequalities in the territory, particularly by promoting development and training programs in Kanak communities. In 1998, at the end of this ten-year period, New Caledonians will be asked to choose between independence and staying within the French republic.

Settlements

Ancient settlements were collections of round men's and women's huts, rectangular collective kitchens, oblong meetinghouses, and variously shaped ateliers. Each woman had a hut where she raised her small children. These structures were built alongside one large dwelling known as *bweamwa* in Ajië, which was the symbol of the clan. This large central dwelling, used by the chief and adult males, was erected on a raised mound with a central alleyway lined with coconut palms and tropical pines leading up to it and two smaller alleyways flanking it. The central alleyway served as a collective ceremonial ground for activities such as public speeches and yam redistribution while the smaller alleyways were used for more intimate rituals such as ceremonial exchanges of shell money. Around inland settlements were yam mounds and irrigated taro gardens on hillsides. It was this social space of family residences, agricultural lands, water channels, and hunting and gathering territories that formed the basis for ritual, economic, political, and social action in traditional times.

Economy

Subsistence and Commercial Activities. Inland settlements cultivated several varieties of bananas, yams, and taro using elaborate irrigation methods. Yams were, and still are, considered "noble" and were used in ceremonial exchanges in the past. It was the yam's annual cycle that established the rhythm of the Kanak year. Fishing was a regular activity for settlements by the sea and on riverbanks. In the forest Kanaks gathered fruit, nuts, and palm-tree buds. Captain Cook introduced pigs and dogs to the islands and other Europeans introduced a variety of plant and animal species including deer, which the Ajië now hunt in the forest. Colonization affected Kanak agriculture dramatically. Lands were confiscated by settlers, gardens were ravaged by marauding cattle, and irrigation networks were destroyed by miners. The fallow period was shortened, which led to erosion and a diminished productive capacity. Subsistence crops gave way to cash crops such as coffee, which the Ajië began producing as early as 1900 and which remains an important source of income. Yams are the only crop that has offered some resistance to the overall regression of Kanak subsistence agriculture. A powerful mining and metallurgical industry coexists with agriculture in New Caledonia. In addition, tertiary activities have expanded quickly in keeping with the territory's highly developed private and public sectors. One of the major nickel and cobalt centers on the east coast was opened near the Ajië's territory in 1901, and although agriculture, fishing, and forestry are still the major employers, mining is a close second, followed by public service.

Industrial Arts. Kanaks manufactured various tools, weapons, and ceremonial objects out of serpentine, which was collected at the base of mountains and in riverbeds by men. Ceremonial axes were the most important, measuring as much as 30 centimeters in diameter. These items were produced for ceremonial exchange in Houaïlou up until 1908. Women produced fiber skirts, capes, baskets, mats, and shell jewelry. There is evidence to support the idea that the women had their own circuit of exchange.

Trade. Traditionally, each local community was integrated into a larger political and geographical system of alliance and exchange. In addition to ceremonial exchanges, trade occurred between villages on the coast and those in the interior mountain chain. Seafood (including fresh, salted, and smoked fish) was traded in a ritualized fashion for tubers (taro and yams) and wild plants from the mountains.

Division of Labor. The nuclear and extended families were the basic production unit with neighbors and allies being called in to help according to the size of the task. The division of labor occurred according to gender and age, and work was organized according to a ritual, seasonal calendar overseen by clan elders. Both men and women hunted seafood individually and collectively using spears, fishing lines, and nets. Men hunted what little game there was—birds, bats, and rats—with spears, built huts and boats, and looked after yam production, irrigation works, and heavy agricultural duties. The women collected wood and water, looked after children, and did the repetitive agricultural chores such as weeding. Men worked with stone and wood, constructing tools and weapons, and women worked with clay and plant fibers, making pots, mats, baskets, and fiber skirts. Today, families continue to cooperate in agriculture.

Land Tenure. In traditional times Kanaks maintained individual rights to land. They were of four types:
(1) First occupation rights—land belonged to the family that first cleared and occupied the land.
(2) Inheritance rights—a man inherited land from his father and through his father the right to cultivate land in any of the successive sites occupied by his paternal ancestors. Succession was usually masculine. However, if a woman was the last in her line, she inherited access to her family's land until her son (who then took the name of his maternal grandfather) was old enough to inherit it.
(3) Acquired rights—through marriage a man established a relationship with his brothers-in-law who could then give him some of their land. A man could also give land to his allies if he was unable to give a sister or daughter in marriage exchange.
(4) Ceded rights—even though the first cultivators of the soil always had rights over that land, they could welcome newcomers or harbor refugees on that land and give them the right to settle there on a temporary or permanent basis.
Land claims have been a central issue in the independence struggle and the French government has set up a series of land development agencies to deal with the problem but the population pressure in the Kanak reserves continues to mount. Although the Ajië are approximately 80 percent of the population in the commune of Houaïlou, the native reserves cover only 20 percent of the land.

Kinship

Kin Groups and Descent. The nuclear family was the basic unit of Kanak society. The family was incorporated into an extended family (usually three generations deep), lineage, and clan that did not represent territorial groups but rather successively larger patrilineal units sharing the same rites and symbols and the same marriage customs. Extended families were assembled into wider groups of affiliation by reference to a common place (homestead mound) of origin. Genealogy was spatially manifested by routes marked by a succession of occupied sites or mounds, and within each clan the lineages were positioned hierarchically according to the antiquity of their first residence in the genealogical itinerary. During the colonial period, clans were arbitrarily associated with a territory so that previously social groupings became geographic groupings on reserves.

Kinship Terminology. On La Grande Terre there were at least two distinct kinship systems. In the first system, in Hienghène, Balade, Pouebo, and Voh, all sisters and female cross and parallel cousins were called by the same term. The unique attribute of this system was its asymmetry, as a father's sister's husband was called maternal uncle even though his wife (father's sister) was called mother. In the second system, a distinction was made between consanguines and affines, that is, between sisters and female cross and parallel cousins.

Marriage and Family

Marriage. Each man and woman had a series of obligatory and optional social actions in terms of residence and marriage. Marriage traditionally was exogamous, patrilineal, and between cross cousins. However, the system was flexible. Distant cousins married and sometimes it was sufficient just to be symbolic cross cousins. Residence was usually virilocal; however, uxorilocal residence was always an option. Marriages were negotiated by families of similar rank through a series of ceremonial exchanges, and although there are "love" marriages occurring today, many young people, particularly those of chiefly rank, still have arranged marriages. Polygamy was sometimes practiced, but because of the influence of

Christianity monogamy is now the rule and divorce is not common, although couples sometimes separate and take up common-law relationships with other partners.

Domestic Unit. The nuclear family is the basic social unit. Children move around frequently among relatives and it is not uncommon for a childless family to receive children to raise as their own. Older parents will live with one of their children.

Inheritance. Under the current system reserve land is inalienable and is owned collectively, and therefore one inherits the right of access to land in the reserve rather than the land itself. Homes and movable property are inherited by the spouse and children.

Socialization. Children are raised by both parents, siblings, and other relatives. Children are taught to respect clan elders and it is the elders who will collectively discipline a wayward youth. Boys are brought up through a series of initiation rites and girls receive instruction during menstrual seclusion.

Sociopolitical Organization

New Caledonia is an overseas territory of France and it is ruled through the office of the high commissioner. The territory has some autonomy over regional matters, but France controls all areas of education, defense, law and order, justice, etc. Today, everyone in New Caledonia is considered a French citizen.

Social Organization. The traditional social structure was closely related to a set of spatial reference points such as homestead mounds, inhabited places, and various other natural features, all of which were carefully inventoried and delimited the rights of the human population over its lands and waters. Those people descended from the first homestead mounds occupied by the clan were considered clan elders and they were consulted on all moral issues (e.g., land disputes) and matrimonial matters. Ceremonial exchanges reinforced families' social and political identity vis-à-vis one another. For example, maternal and paternal kin-group relations were defined by the ceremonial exchanges surrounding birth, marriage, and death.

Political Organization. Heads of lineages were seen as the guardians of the social and symbolic relations that united families into communal and regional political alliances. These "chiefs" were also focal points in a redistribution network. They received a part of the first yam harvest and a certain portion of all the land animals and fish caught. Some have seen these offerings as a type of tribute but in fact the chief quickly redistributed these offerings and sometimes even supplemented the redistribution with food from his own garden. Chiefs were reduced by colonial civil service into labor-recruitment officers and tax-collection agents. The territory is now divided into thirty-two districts known as *communes* and organized into three provinces that send elected officials to a territorial congress. A large number of traditional chiefs have entered the modern political arena.

Social Control. The structural model for Kanak society was the family where the junior family members were under the authority of the senior members. Similarly, junior lineages traditionally owed "service" to elder ones and conversely the elders had responsibilities toward the cadet lineages, just as adults were responsible for the well-being of the children who owed them obedience.

Conflict. Prior to French occupation, Kanak men engaged in clan warfare. The Kanaks also strongly resisted French occupation, killing settlers and missionaries. The largest rebellion against French presence took place in 1878 when the Kanaks almost regained control of their islands. In the twentieth century, the clash of Kanak nationalism against the mass of entrenched settlers has catapulted the territory into world headlines.

Religion and Expressive Culture

Religious Beliefs. The majority of Ajië were converted to Christianity in the early 1900s by the famous French Protestant missionary and ethnologist, Maurice Leenhardt, who built his church and school in the heart of Ajië territory. Prior to that, the Ajië had a number of important totems such as the shark, the caterpillar, the lizard, and thunder. In the traditional religion the gods inhabited all important geographical features of the Kanak landscape—mountain summits, river sources, grottos, etc. Each clan had its own gods that had given birth to the clan ancestors or with whom the clan ancestors had formed alliances. It was these gods who gave power to human rituals and symbols. Gods were worshipped on clan altars, and each time a clan changed location the clan gods were moved to the new site. Spirits of the dead also were believed to roam the Kanak landscape and to be dangerous to human activities.

Religious Practitioners. Each clan had a special magic knowledge that they specialized in. Within the clan there were also specialists who dealt with specific magic and rituals such as preparing the gardens for planting or the warriors for battle. Sorcery existed but it was not practiced by specialists; rather, it was available to all who cared to use it since it was occult power and not the person that was the source of the ill will.

Ceremonies. The most elaborate ceremony was the *pilou pilou,* which could take three to four years of preparation and last several weeks. It was the culmination of Kanak social life, expressing the vitality of the host clan and its alliances through orations, collective feasting, dancing, and a distribution of ceremonial objects and food.

Arts. Petroglyphs have been found in New Caledonia; however, their origins remain uncertain. Kanak sculpture was primarily part of the architecture of the large central dwelling: carved support posts, ridgeposts, and doorways. Elaborate arrowheads were the main art form and representation of the clan ancestors was the principal theme. The male artists were specialists and recognized as such. The reputation of a well-known artist would continue after his death. Kanaks also possessed a rich oral tradition of historical tales, myths, humorous and moral stories, poetry, and proverbs. Kanak music consisted of songs and percussion music. Dances were often narrative, a choreographed version of a traditional activity such as fishing or yam production. Men and women both participated in the collective dances that accompanied all ceremonial events and were part of the preparations for battle.

Medicine. Illness was associated with a totem: for example, weight loss with the lizard, hysteria with the caterpillar, swelling with the shark, anemia with the rat. Each illness could be cured by a specific herb that would be chewed or chopped and then sucked on. The herb acted on the totem, not the illness. Plants from the forest, fish and plants from the sea, and some taro species were also used for medicinal purposes in poultices, infusions, etc.

Death and Afterlife. The spirits of the dead inhabited an underworld and could surface at times. In order to ensure that they did not take up residence in their former bodies, the Kanaks bound corpses in fetal positions. Mothers were buried with a wooden stick so that they would think that they had a child in their arms and would not come looking for their offspring. Geographical features that were traditionally believed to be the gateways to the underworld remain known and respected and are still the object of offerings and prayer. This practice is part of the Ajië's unique bond with the land.

See also Loyalty Islands

Bibliography

Clifford, J. (1982). *Person and Myth: Maurice Leenhardt in the Melanesian World.* Berkeley: University of California Press.

Connell, J. (1987). *New Caledonia or Kanaky? The Political History of a French Colony.* Australia: National Center for Development Studies, Australian National University.

Leenhardt, M. (1979). *Do Kamo: Person and Myth in the Melanesian World.* Chicago: University of Chicago Press.

Thompson, V., and R. Adloff (1971). *The French Pacific Islands: French Polynesia and New Caledonia.* Berkeley: University of California Press.

Ward, A. (1982). *Land and Politics in New Caledonia.* Australia: Research School of Pacific Studies, Australian National University.

DONNA WINSLOW

Ambae

ETHNONYMS: a Bai, Angai Tagaro, Aoba, Butona, Leper's Island, Lombaha, Longana, Nduindui, Oba, Omba, Opa, Waluriki

Orientation

Identification. Ambae is an island that has had many names. The earliest European who wrote on the region adopted the explorer Bougainville's designation of the island as Ile de Lepreux or Leper's Isle; after 1880, most European writers used one of five variant spellings of Aoba, usually pronounced Omba. People on the island insist that Aoba is a name of nonindigenous origin, possibly a European misappropriation of the local word for "seabird." In 1980, near the time of Vanuatu's Independence, the Aoba Council of Chiefs officially renamed the island Ambae. Acrimonious debate between customary chiefs and Western-educated young leaders preceded the council's decision to give the island a new name. On Ambae, as in many parts of Vanuatu, knowledge of a place's "true" name is a vital aspect of establishing control over the place itself.

Location. Ambae is situated in northern Vanuatu between 167°40' and 167°46' E and between 15°13' and 15°24' S. It has a total land area of 399 square kilometers and is one of the largest islands in northern Vanuatu. Its volcano (which is dormant rather than extinct) has a central caldera that rises to 1,300 meters with cloud cover above 450 meters. Eruptions have occurred in small craters along the NE-SW spine of the island. The most recent spilled down the northeast coast in the early 1900s. There are no permanent rivers on Ambae but lack of water seldom is a problem, even during the dry season from April to October: parts of the island receive up to 400 centimeters of rainfall per year. Dark volcanic loam carpets much of the island, and in most years Ambaeans enjoy a rich harvest of root crops, green vegetables, fruit, and nuts. Two shoulders of the central mountain separate the eastern and western sides of the island. The mountainous terrain makes foot travel between East and West Ambae difficult, and there is little trade or intermarriage between people living on the two sides of the island.

Demography. In 1885, a British colonial official estimated the population of Ambae to be between 10,000 and 12,000; however, a 1919 census recorded only 4,000 people living on the island. According to the last official census in 1979, the island's population of 7,754 resides in 306 separate localities. The two halves of the island have roughly equal numbers of inhabitants, but two-thirds of the population of West Ambae live in Nduindui, a densely settled area of 18.2 square kilometers over which households are more or less evenly distributed. Throughout the rest of the island, clustered households form hamlets. Typically, these include three or four nuclear families. For example, in Longana in 1982, hamlet size averaged 16 people. Occasional hamlet clusters, such as develop around a church, may have populations that approach 100. Hamlets are scattered along the coast and in the hills, up to a maximum of about 3 kilometers inland.

Linguistic Affiliation. There are two languages spoken on the island, Nduindui (West Ambae) and Northeast Aoban (East Ambae). Both are multidialectal: on the eastern portion of the island alone, linguists have found over fifteen dialects. People from East and West Ambae understand each other's native language only with difficulty and usually communicate with each other in Bislama, the lingua franca of Vanuatu.

History and Cultural Relations

On 23 May 1768, Louis de Bougainville became the first European to lead a landing party to the rocky shores of Ambae. He was dispatched back to his vessels with a volley of stones and arrows. Almost a century elapsed before other Europeans visited the island and, from first contact until independence in 1980, whites in the archipelago stereotyped Ambaeans as intractable and sometimes violent. Conversion to Christianity reached a peak in the 1930s. Most West Ambaeans joined the Church of Christ, a denomination that encouraged copra production but prohibited rank taking, kava drinking, and traditional forms of marriage and burial. Christianity and cash cropping coexist with customary practices in East Ambae, where Anglicans tolerant of many elements of the indigenous culture gained a majority of converts.

Settlements

Prior to the 1930s, most settlements in East Ambae were in the hills where residents were nearer their gardens and safer from attack than on the coast. In times of warfare, some settlements were fortified with log palisades. Each married woman, including cowives, had her own house in which she slept with her daughters and young sons. Older boys and adult men slept in the men's clubhouse *na gamal*. Christianity changed the structure of hamlets and encouraged relocation to the coast. Churches became spatial and social centers of hamlets. Women's houses became family homes in which husbands and sons might also sleep. Most na gamals ceased to be forbidden to women. But men's activities still take place in and around the na gamal, the largest traditional building in a hamlet. About two-thirds of the houses still have thatched roofs and bamboo walls. The need to rebuild makes hamlet mobility possible. Moves often reflect concerns with land tenure, although ill health attributed to magic and sorcery also can be an important reason for leaving a particular place. Cement and corrugated iron are increasingly used in house construction, which is reducing hamlet mobility. Rural water development projects have constructed village cisterns to catch rainwater; these also encourage permanent settlement. Two towns are beginning to develop on the island, one at the old Anglican mission station on Lolowai Bay at the eastern tip of the island, the other at Nduindui in West Ambae. Dirt roads link these settlements with grass airstrips at Longana, Walaha, and Red Cliff and with many outlying hamlets. A handful of resident white traders lived on the island in the early to mid-1900s. The last such trader/planter left prior to independence.

Economy

Subsistence and Commercial Activities. Swidden horticulture provides Ambaeans with subsistence crops. Gardens are maintained under a seven-year fallow cycle. Yams, taro, and bananas are the staple crops. Sweet potatoes, manioc, and island cabbages are also important. A variety of other indigenous and exotic fruits and vegetables supplement these crops. Kava (*Piper methysticum*) is grown in quantity for its roots. These are ground to produce an infusion that men drink to produce a state of relaxation. Men and women use kava medicinally. Some hunting of birds, fruit bats, and feral pigs takes place. Fishing plays a minor role in subsistence as fish poisoning is feared to be common among predatory fish species and smaller reef-feeding fish. Development projects have introduced some commercial deep-water hand lining for snappers. There is some cash cropping of cocoa. Coconuts, however, have been the major cash crop since the 1930s. The practice of planting coconut palms in gardens has taken much of the arable land out of the swidden cycle. Households make copra in small smoke driers. Production time is approximately nine person-days per ton and yields are about two tons per hectare annually. In 1978, per capita income from copra was $387 in the Longana district. Differential control of coconut plantation land has led to considerable income inequality.

Industrial Arts. Ambaeans once built sailing canoes with mat sails. Today, men continue to make kava bowls, ceremonial war clubs, and a few items of regalia for use in graded society (*hungwe*) activities. Women weave pandanus mats in a variety of lengths, widths, and degrees of fineness. Imported dyes have largely replaced indigenous vegetable dyes, but turmeric is still used to color mat fringes.

Trade. Trade in pigs occurs between Pentecost and East Ambae. In the past, there were trade links between East Ambae and Ambrym. West Ambaeans traded widely throughout the northern islands.

Division of Labor. The household is the basic unit of production in subsistence gardening and cash cropping coconuts. Men fish and hunt, whereas women weave mats. Child care is a cooperative effort on the part of mothers, fathers, and siblings, with mothers being the primary care givers for infants. Male hamlet residents generally work together in house building.

Land Tenure. In West Ambae, there are concepts of village and patrilineage land, but in both parts of the island individuals rather than kinship groups are now the primary landholding units. Coresident brothers, however, often own and use land together. In the past, leaders were able to acquire their followers' land through intimidation as well as through customary exchange payments. Land use is important in establishing land rights, but residential and garden use are not sufficient in themselves to determine ownership. Usufruct rights are available to any adult. Ownership, with rights of disposal and the right to plant coconut palms, is acquired primarily through contributions to funerary feasts (*bongi*) and occasionally through cash purchase. Landowners are primarily male but women can and do own land in both East and West Ambae. A few landholders in East Ambae have been able to acquire plantation landholdings that are much larger than the 2.5-hectare average through inheritance, purchase, and contributions made at bongi ceremonies of poorer families. Inequality of landholding in Longana is such that in the late 1970s, 24 percent of the population controlled more than 70 percent of available plantation land. Conflict over land is frequent and is often provoked by planting coconuts or undertaking other income-producing activities.

Kinship

Kin Groups and Descent. Everyone in East Ambae belongs to an exogamous matrilineal moiety ("Tagaro" or "Mwerambuto"). Children also acquire their mother's clan membership, but clans are neither corporate nor very important in social organization. Moiety affiliation is crucial in defining roles on ceremonial occasions. In West Ambae, there is a legend that people lost their knowledge of matrilineal moiety and clan membership in a great flood. Today they have a cognatic kinship system.

Kinship Terminology. Both East and West Ambae use a Crow-type cousin terminology. Mother's brother and father's sister are more strongly marked in the East.

Marriage and Family

Marriage. Before conversion, men of high rank on both sides of the island often practiced polygyny. Such men aspired to have ten wives. One would be a member of his own moiety with whom he could not have sexual intercourse. Child betrothal also was common. Churches discouraged both polygyny and arranged marriage. Today young people have considerable freedom to choose a marriage partner, so long as (in East Ambae) moiety exogamy is followed. Bridewealth exchanges customarily involved tusked pigs and mats. Nowadays, cloth, household goods and/or money are included. Postmarital residence tends to be virilocal. All missions on the island discourage or prohibit divorce, and legal separation of marriage partners is very rare.

Domestic Unit. The household composed of the nuclear family is now the basic domestic unit. Prior to conversion to Christianity, settlement patterns were such that the domestic unit was the extended family.

Inheritance. In West Ambae, land inheritance is patrilineal. In East Ambae, land inheritance is said traditionally to have been bilateral, but the pattern of funerary obligations suggest the priority of matrilineal land transmission. Children must make funerary gifts to the father's matrilineal kin to secure ownership of his land. Matrilineal heirs need make no such payment. Land inheritance is often contentious.

Socialization. Parents share duties as primary caretakers, and grandparents, father's sisters, and the mother's brothers also play important roles in socialization. Children learn primarily through imitation rather than verbal instruction. Both wives and children may be subject to beatings, although legal sanctions may be imposed in cases of severe physical abuse. A national system of education has replaced many (but not all) church schools. Most children can walk to school through grade six. Boarding schools on the island provide education through high school.

Sociopolitical Organization

Social Organization. Locality, politics, and, to a lesser extent, kinship determine group membership. Moieties and clans are dispersed and noncorporate; affiliation in kinship groups larger than the extended family assumes most importance in the context of the mat displays and exchanges that accompany marriages and funerary feasts. In everyday life, the hamlet is the basic unit of cooperation. Hamlets join together into long-standing, largely endogamous alliance networks formed on the basis of affiliation with Christian denominations. Alliance networks, in turn, are subdivisions of named territorial units. There are ten such "districts" on Ambae, each of which claims a measure of cultural and linguistic distinctness. Residents of each district share an identity based on a sense of place and common culture. Districts are the electoral unit used to determine membership in the state-sponsored island government.

Political Organization. Big men on East Ambae are men of rank, titleholders in an elaborate social hierarchy consisting of grades scaled in terms of relative prestige. Prestige in the graded society or hungwe is allocated to individuals on the basis of their ability to accumulate and dispose of boars with tusks in particular stages of development. The man of highest rank in the community often serves as its designated leader on ceremonial occasions. Within groups of allied hamlets, high-ranking men compete with each other for authority, prestige, and privilege. The alliance network is the largest political unit on East Ambae within which a leader can exercise authority on a regular basis. Similarly, on West Ambae, hamlets and groups of allied hamlets are the most important political divisions but there the church rather than the rank association controls processes of recruitment to positions of political authority.

Social Control. High-ranking chiefs on Ambae at the turn of the century possessed the legitimate right to order an offender's execution. When the Anglo-French Condominium of the New Hebrides "pacified" the island in the 1930s, chiefs lost the power of life or death over their followers; however, the central government exercised little control over the internal political and legal affairs of the island throughout the colonial era. Today, Ambae remains largely autonomous in conducting its legal affairs. Ambaeans process most disputes and a broad range of offenses in village and district courts. These courts use written legal codes that local people themselves devised. The courts impose fines that offenders pay in cash or in traditional valuables, specifically pigs and pandanus mats.

Conflict. The introduction of firearms almost certainly increased levels of violence on the island, although the true extent of conflict before contact is hard to judge with accuracy. However, all sources—European and indigenous alike—agree that 1870 to 1930 on East Ambae was an era of endemic raiding, "days of never-ending revenge," in which the political reputation of chiefs depended as much on their prowess in warfare as on their abilities in the graded society.

Religion and Expressive Culture

Religious Beliefs. Except for two people, everyone on the island identified themselves as a Christian on the 1979 census. Within living memory, however, most people believed in a high god—Tagaro Lawo (or Tagivui)—who made the earth, and in two culture heros—Tagaro Biti and Mwerambuto—who created humans and many elements of customary culture.

Religious Practitioners. The main practitioners who deal in magic and the supernatural are diviners, clairvoyants (who find lost objects), and weather magicians. Other practitioners are specialists in customary medicine, which is still widely practiced. People sometimes accuse each other of sorcery, a serious breach of local law.

Ceremonies. Major ceremonial occasions include rank takings, betrothals, weddings, funerals, Christmas, Easter, and saints' days honoring the patron saints of local churches. Kava, drumming, singing, and traditional dancing are important elements of many ceremonies, especially on the eastern half of the island.

Arts. Unlike the people of Ambrym and Malekula, Ambaeans are not well known in Vanuatu as carvers and artisans. The artists in an Ambaean community are the community's best singers, dancers, storytellers, speech makers, weavers of pandanus mats, and makers of a highly regarded feast food (generically called *laplap* in Bislama) made of grated root crops steamed in an earth oven and decorated with coconut cream.

Medicine. In the people's view, traditional and Western medicine complement each other. Despite the existence of a small hospital on each end of the island, well-respected specialists in traditional "leaf medicine" still exist on Ambae. Patients usually pay for the spells and herbal compounds these experts provide with pandanus mats and pigs rather than money.

Death and Afterlife. A dead person's closest relatives hold a series of funerary feasts in his or her honor. They arrange small feasts every ten days until the hundredth day of mourning, when a major feast is held. During this time, the spirit of the deceased is believed to linger near his or her community. A final feast is held 1,000 days after a death. This feast signals the end of mourning and the complete separation of the spirit of the dead person from the world of the living. According to custom, spirits then go to the crater lakes on the top of the Ambae volcano. There they join their ancestors in a shadow world similar to the world of living people.

See also Pentecost

Bibliography

Allen, M. R. (1968). "The Establishment of Christianity and Cash-Cropping in a New Hebridean Community." *Journal of Pacific History* 3:25–46.

Blackwood, Peter (1981). "Rank, Exchange and Leadership in Four Vanuatu Societies." In *Vanuatu: Politics, Economics, and Ritual in Island Melanesia,* edited by Michael Allen. New York: Academic Press.

Rodman, Margaret Critchlow (1987). *Masters of Tradition: Consequences of Customary Land Tenure in Longana, Vanuatu.* Vancouver: University of British Columbia Press.

Rodman, William L. (1985) "'A Law unto Themselves'": Legal Innovation in Ambae, Vanuatu." *American Ethnologist* 12:603–624.

Rodman, William L., and Margaret C. Rodman (1990). "To Die on Ambae: On the Possibility of Doing Fieldwork Forever." In *The Humbled Anthropologist: Tales from the Pacific,* edited by Philip DeVita. Belmont, Calif.: Wadsworth Publishing Co.

WILLIAM L. RODMAN AND MARGARET C. RODMAN

Anuta

ETHNONYMS: Cherry Island, Nukumairaro

Orientation

Identification. Anuta is a volcanic island in the eastern Solomon Islands. Its inhabitants are physically, linguistically, and culturally Polynesian. The island's European name was bestowed in honor of a Mr. Cherry, who first sighted it from the HMS *Pandora* in 1791 while searching for the *Bounty* mutineers. Nukumairaro, meaning "land from below," is said to be an archaic name deriving from the fact that Anuta is "below" (i.e., to the east of) Tikopia, its nearest populated neighbor, about 112 kilometers distant.

Location. Anuta is at approximately 169°50' E and 11°40' S. It is a small volcanic island, roughly circular, and three-quarters of a kilometer in diameter. Its southern portion is coastal flat; the northern part is covered by a hill, rising to a maximum altitude of 78 meters. The climate is tropical and may be divided into two seasons. The trade-wind season (*tonga*) lasts from mid-April to mid-October. It is relatively cool and dry, although the sky is frequently overcast, and a brisk wind blows constantly from the southeast quadrant. Weather during the monsoon season, or *raki*—mid-October through mid-April—is more variable. Periods of hot sun alternate with drenching rains. Winds may be calm for days at a time, but during this season Anutans also experience occasional devastating hurricanes.

Demography. The population at the time of European contact is unknown. In the early twentieth century, the population numbered between 100 and 150 people. In March 1972 there were 162 people living on Anuta and 42 Anutans residing overseas, mostly on Tikopia and in the central Solomons. People return and depart with every ship. However, if one takes the resident population to be 160, population density is on the order of 1,000 persons per square kilometer, making Anuta one of the most densely populated islands in the Pacific. Between 1972 and 1988, the resident population rose to more than 200 people, with another 50 or so living overseas.

Linguistic Affiliation. Linguists have classified Anutan (Anu) as a Nuclear Polynesian language, within the vast group of Austronesian languages. However, in contrast with the languages of other western Polynesian "outliers," Anu includes many words of Tongic origin. The extent to which this is due to direct Tongan contact as opposed to indirect borrowing via East Uvea is a matter for debate.

History and Cultural Relations

Archaeological remains show Anuta to have been inhabited by humans for almost 3,000 years. According to Anutan oral traditions, however, the island's present population arrived much more recently—about 300 to 350 years ago—from Tonga and Uvea (most likely East Uvea or Wallis Island). The first chief was the Tongan leader known as Pu Kaurave. The Uvean leader was named Pu Taupare. When Pu Kaurave's son, Ruokimata, left no heir, the chieftainship passed to the Uvean line. Later there were immigrants from Samoa and Rotuma, as well as extensive contact and exchange with Tikopia. Visitors from Tuvalu (formerly the Ellice Islands) and Taumako in the Santa Cruz group made little lasting impact.

Settlements

Dwellings are distributed in a somewhat ragged line along the island's southern shoreline. The closest the Anutans have to a term for "village" is *noporanga,* which literally means "dwelling place." Villages are not demarcated by any physical boundary. Anuta has two distinct naming systems for the villages. Initially there were two noporanga: Mua or "Front" to the east, and Muri or "Back" to the west. The first church house was constructed to the west of Muri, and a number of houses were subsequently erected near the church. These houses took on the church's name, St. John, and came to be designated as a third noporanga. According to the newer system, Mua and Muri are grouped together under the name Rotoapi and contrasted with houses to the west, known as Vatiana in this system. Houses have a rectangular floor plan and are built low to the ground, with steep roofs. Frames are made from coconut and other durable woods; the walls are thatched with sago leaves and roofs with coconut fronds. Doors are less than a meter high, so that entry and exit is by crawling on hands and knees.

Economy

Subsistence and Commercial Activities. The economy emphasizes subsistence agriculture and fishing. Major crops include manioc, *Colocasia* and *Cyrtosperma* taro, coconuts, papayas, bananas, and tobacco. Less important foodstuffs include sweet potatoes, yams, pumpkins, watermelons, and a host of minor crops. Tools include digging sticks, poles for harvesting fruits and nuts, and (in postcontact times) steel bush knives. Anuta's intensive agricultural system involves crop rotation, terracing, weeding, and mulching. Fishing is done on the fringing reef, with nets and spears, and on the open sea, mostly with hook and line. Ocean fishing is usually done from a canoe. Techniques include bottom fishing over an inshore reef, trolling, and night fishing for flying fish with a light and long-handled net. Shellfish are sometimes collected and birds hunted. Chickens are raised and occasionally eaten.

Industrial Arts. Anuta has no full-time specialists. However, some specially skilled people devote inordinate amounts of time to canoe building, house construction, carving bowls, bailers, and paddles, and plaiting mats and baskets.

Trade. As of the early 1970s, there was no trade store on the island. Therefore, trade was confined to passing ships or was conducted by relatives visiting other islands—especially Guadalcanal, site of the Solomon Islands' capital. In addition, regular exchange with Tikopia—the nearest populated island—has occurred for many generations.

Division of Labor. Men do most of the fishing, including all fishing on the open sea. Both men and women garden and cook food, with women putting somewhat more time than men into these activities. Carpentry is performed by men. Mat making is almost entirely a female occupation.

Land Tenure. Land is owned and worked collectively by the elementary domestic unit, known as the *patongia.* This consists ideally of a group of brothers, their wives and children, their sons' wives and children, and assorted adoptees. If members of a domestic unit cannot get along, they divide their land and become separate units. Most crops are under the jurisdiction of the domestic unit on whose land they are growing. A few, like coconuts and papayas, however, are regarded as collective property of the community regardless of where they are found. In addition, chiefs may overrule domestic units' decisions regarding what, when, where, and how to plant, cultivate, and harvest.

Kinship

Kin Groups and Descent. Anuta has three types of corporate groups. In increasing order of inclusiveness, these are the patongia, *kainanga* (clans), and *kanopenua.* Members are recruited to these units on the basis of patrilineal descent and *aropa,* or positive feelings as expressed through economic support and cooperation. The patongia is the elementary domestic unit (see above). There are four kainanga, each of which consists of a group of patongia that trace descent through a line of males to a founder about nine generations ago. The kanopenua is the entire population, including all persons born to Anutan fathers and any long-term visitors who have been incorporated into one of the patongia. The term *pare,* or "house," may denote a patongia or a group of related patongia. *Kano a paito* can be synonymous with pare, or it may refer to a "kindred." If unqualified, kano a paito refers to paternal kin; the maternal kindred is *te kano a paito i te paai o te papine,* "the kindred on the woman's side."

Kinship Terminology. Anutans use an Iroquois-type system of nomenclature for kin in the parent's generation. Hawaiian-type cousin terms are used. The system emphasizes generation rather than relative seniority.

Marriage and Family

Marriage. Genealogies show a few particularly important chiefs to have practiced polygyny. Otherwise, monogamy has been the universal practice. Divorce has always been a rare occurrence, and since missionization it has been entirely prohibited. One must marry outside of one's domestic unit, and sibling marriage is forbidden. Otherwise, there are no absolute prohibitions. Normally one marries cousins, and the more distant the connection, the more appropriate the marriage. A married woman joins her husband's domestic unit and moves into his household.

Domestic Unit. The domestic unit, or patongia, approximates a patrilateral extended family. A married couple and their children may live in a separate house, but members of the same patongia share ownership of garden land, crops, buildings, canoes, and all other forms of property. They harvest and prepare food collectively, and normally they eat together as a single unit.

Inheritance. Since property is owned collectively by the domestic unit, how to dispose of it upon a person's death is rarely an issue. Occasionally, garden land is transferred upon marriage from a woman's natal unit to that of her husband; and at the time of a funeral, it may be transferred to the unit of the deceased's mother's brother. Should a patongia die out, its property may pass to units of the leader's close collateral kin or units with whom the extinct patongia has been in a close cooperative relationship.

Socialization. Children are cared for by all adults and older siblings in the domestic unit. In addition, adoption is common and children spend much of their time with members of their adoptive patongia. Training emphasizes respect for rank and for property belonging to other domestic units. Children may be scolded and restrained from getting into trouble, but physical punishment is unusual and rarely severe.

Sociopolitical Organization

Social Organization. Anuta is a small-scale Polynesian chiefdom. Anutan society is hierarchically organized on the basis of age, sex, and proximity to a chiefly line. In addition, Anutans admire strength, intelligence, and skill at navigation, storytelling, carpentry, gardening, and other crafts. This provides a degree of social mobility in a system that otherwise seems rigidly stratified on the basis of genealogical criteria.

Political Organization. Anuta is divided into four ranked "clans" (kainanga). The two senior kainanga are led by chiefs (*ariki*); the remaining two are not. The senior chief is known as Te Ariki i Mua ("The Chief in Front") or Tui Anuta; the junior chief is Te Ariki i Muri ("The Chief in Back") or Tui Kainanga. The two ariki trace their ancestry to a pair of chiefly brothers who lived about nine generations ago. A chief is normally succeeded by his eldest son. In the 1890s, Anuta was incorporated into the British Solomon Islands Protectorate. In 1978 the Solomon Islands became an independent nation and claimed sovereignty over Anuta as well as neighboring islands. The national and provincial governments provide some shipping, medical care, and schooling. Anutans, however, continue to assert local autonomy by refusing to pay taxes, run for government office, or vote in elections.

Social Control. Under normal circumstances, social control is maintained by the high value placed on traditional custom and an appreciation of the importance of such custom. In addition, it is encouraged by a belief that disrespect or disobedience directed toward a person of superior rank is certain to produce disease or other misfortune. In extreme cases, a chief has the authority to have an offender flogged or exiled to the ocean. At present, government or church authorities might also be called upon to intercede. This action is unusual, however, because it compromises local sovereignty.

Conflict. Anutans relate several tales of visitors from other islands being killed or driven off. Internal conflicts have arisen over control of the chieftainship and access to garden land during times of famine. In recent years, external political and economic pressures have led to development of factions and ongoing conflict.

Religion and Expressive Culture

Religious Beliefs. Precontact Anutan religion involved a form of ancestor worship. For most of this century, the island has been Christian. Since about 1916, the entire population has been affiliated with the Anglican church. Still, belief in the power of ancestral spirits and the presence of malicious ghosts continues. The major pagan deities were ghosts of deceased chiefs. Other ancestors were sometimes asked for help with household problems. Spirits who had never been human (*tupua penua,* or "spirits of the land") were powerful and dangerous, although at times they might help people who had shown them respect. Ordinary ghosts (*atua*), on the other hand, were normally malicious and rarely helped the living. Anutans continue to believe in pagan spirits. By far the most important spiritual being, however, is now the Christian God, followed by assorted saints.

Religious Practitioners. Traditionally, chiefs also were high priests. Assisted by "ritual elders" known as *mataapure,* they performed sacred *kava* rites to keep the gods favorably disposed. Spirit mediums, called *vakaatua,* facilitated two-way communication with the spirit world. In contrast with chiefly status, there were no genealogical requirements for spirit mediumship. Since missionization, the community's religious leader has been a trained catechist. This person is appointed by the chiefs in consultation with a council of advisors (*nga maru*), on the basis of character, oratorical skill, and scriptural knowledge. The catechist, in turn, appoints a number of assistants to aid in performance of services. The Companions of the Brotherhood of Melanesia and the Mothers' Union are voluntary associations established to assist in the conduct of church business.

Ceremonies. Life-crisis rites surrounding birth, marriage, and death continue to be practiced. Other major ceremonies are performed when a young child eats his first fish and when he is taken to the hilltop for the first time. These ceremonies occur when the child is about a year of age. Sometime prior to adolescence, a major ceremony is held to honor the first boy and the first girl in each "house." Male initiation, at the time of puberty, involves ritual circumcision. Christian celebrations of Christmas, Easter, a number of saints' days, baptism, and confirmation have been added to the ceremonial calendar.

Arts. Visual arts include tattooing and designs carved into canoes, clubs, and dance paddles. Performing arts include storytelling, song, and dance. Traditionally, the only musical instruments were sounding boards and human voice and body. Today, these are augmented by a few guitars and ukuleles.

Medicine. Most illnesses are attributed to the activity of spirits or taboo violation. Effective treatment requires confession of the misdeed and forgiveness by the offended party, accompanied by prayer. Some Western medicines are available via the Solomon Islands government.

Death and Afterlife. When someone dies, the population divides into several groups to wail funeral dirges (*puatanga*) in the house of the deceased. This is followed by an exchange of goods between the deceased's closest kin and every other household. A funeral service is held in church, and the corpse is buried by the deceased's mother's brother or members of the mother's brother's "house." Anutans take Christian ideas about the afterlife quite literally, believing that one goes to Hell or Heaven depending on one's moral virtue while alive.

See also Santa Cruz, Tikopia, Tonga, Tuvalu, Uvea

Bibliography

Feinberg, Richard (1977). *The Anutan Language Reconsidered: Lexicon and Grammar of a Polynesian Outlier.* New Haven, Conn.: Human Relations Area Files.

Feinberg, Richard (1981). *Anuta: Social Structure of a Polynesian Island.* Laie, Hawaii, and Copenhagen: Institute for Polynesian Studies and the National Museum of Denmark.

Feinberg, Richard (1988). *Polynesian Seafaring and Navigation: Ocean Travel in Anutan Culture and Society.* Kent, Ohio: Kent State University Press.

Yen, Douglas E., and Janet Gordon, eds. (1973). *Anuta: A Polynesian Outlier in the Solomon Islands.* Pacific Anthropological Records, no. 21. Honolulu: Bernice P. Bishop Museum, Department of Anthropology.

RICHARD FEINBERG

Aranda

ETHNONYMS: Arrernte, Arunta

Orientation

Identification. Aranda refers first of all to a language group. There have been at least eleven dialects in this group, each spoken by a different cultural bloc living in the desert areas of central Australia. The most northerly of these groups, the Anmatjera, Kaititj, Iliaura (or Alyawarra), Jaroinga, and Andakerebina, are not usually known as Aranda, even though they are Aranda speakers. Aranda is a postcontact denomination, now commonly accepted. It normally refers only to the following groups, some of which have died out by now or lost their distinct identities: Western Aranda, Northern Aranda, Eastern Aranda, Central Aranda, Upper Southern Aranda (or Pertame), and Lower Southern Aranda (or Alenyentharrpe).

Location. Arandic groups have been distributed throughout the area of the Northern Territory, Queensland, and South Australia between 132° and 139° S and 20° and 27° E. They have mainly occupied the relatively well-watered mountainous areas of this desert region, although several groups, particularly around the northern, eastern, and southern fringes of the Aranda-speaking area, have very extensive sandhill regions within their territories.

Demography. The total population of Aranda speakers in precontact times probably did not exceed 3,000. The population fell very sharply after the coming of Whites, mainly through the introduction of new diseases. At the present time the total population figure is comparable to that of the precontact era and is rising, although the spatial and cultural distribution of that figure has shifted dramatically. Major settlements at or near Hermannsburg, Alice Springs, and Santa Teresa account for the bulk of the Aranda population.

Linguistic Affiliation. Australian Aboriginal languages, of which there are some 250, form a distinct family. Of the Arandic dialects, the most commonly heard today are Western Aranda (Hermannsburg / Alice Springs district) and Eastern Aranda (Alice Springs / Santa Teresa district). The total number of Aranda speakers probably does not exceed 3,000, one-half of whom would be speakers of Western Aranda. Most people are competent in more than one dialect and many are fluent in second and third languages, including various forms of English. Loan words, largely from Western Desert and Warlpiri neighbors, are commonly used and integrated into Aranda. Arandic languages now have a number of literary forms for use in publishing and bilingual education.

History and Cultural Relations

Aborigines have lived in central Australia for at least 20,000 years, although few details of their history are known. The Aranda were nomadic hunters and gatherers when Whites first came to Central Australia in the 1860s, but from the 1870s onward they steadily moved into a more sedentary (though still mobile) way of life on missions, pastoral stations, and government settlements. Relations between Aranda groups and between Aranda groups and their neighbors (mostly Western Desert people) have varied from friendship, alliance, and intermarriage, on the one hand, to enmity and hostility on the other. Relations with European interests have also varied greatly over the years, ranging from guerrilla warfare and cattle stealing to enforced or voluntary settlement and work on missions and cattle stations. European attitudes and practices towards Aranda people have also varied greatly—from tolerance to bigotry, from laissez-faire to paternalism, and from protectionism to murder. Since World War II, when development in central Australia greatly increased, the Aranda have lived through the official government policy of assimilation. They are now experiencing the effects of the relatively new policy of self-determination, which has caused their lives to be increasingly affected by Aboriginal bureaucracies.

Settlements

Although the Aranda used to be nomadic hunters and gatherers, they had very clear notions of homelands. Within these territories there were well-trodden circuits that people would use during the yearly round. Camps were normally made at named places, well watered, and usually very closely associated with mythological beings. The size of these camps changed dramatically from time to time as members left in order to visit relatives or new people joined. Sometimes a camp might consist of no more than a single extended family, while at other times it might be occupied by some 200 people gathered together for lengthy ceremonies. People spent much of their time in the open air, although temporary shelters and windbreaks were commonly built to protect them from sun, wind, and rain. Since contact with Whites, these same shelters and windbreaks have been used on missions and pastoral stations, although many of the materials used to build them have been new (e.g., tarpaulin and corrugated iron). In recent decades there has been an increasing use of houses built of more durable materials (like cement and brick) and the provision of electricity and reticulated water. These houses and facilities may be found in large settlement areas like Alice Springs, Hermannsburg, and Santa Teresa, or at outstations, which are relatively new settlements occupied by small extended-family groups at places of personal and mythological significance.

Economy

Subsistence and Commercial Activities. The Aranda were originally hunters and gatherers. Large game animals included red kangaroos, euros (wallaroos), and emus; smaller game animals included various marsupials, reptiles, and birds. Many insects, fruits, and vegetables were gathered, including grass seeds that were ground into a flour to make bread. Dingoes were sometimes domesticated and would occasionally act as hunting dogs. As White settlement increasingly restricted traditional hunting and gathering grounds, the Aranda became increasingly reliant on Western foodstuffs, particularly white flour, sugar, and tea. Today, some hunting and a little gathering take place, but people mainly rely on the meat, jam, bread, etc. that can be bought from supermarkets and local stores. Government funding of social security payments and community development projects is now of considerable economic importance.

Industrial Arts. In their hunting and gathering days the Aranda, like all Aborigines, had a fairly simple tool kit, consisting mainly of spears, spear throwers, carrying trays, grinding stones, and digging sticks. There were no specialist professions, and any man or woman could make equipment to hunt and gather. Many men and women have now acquired European-style professional skills.

Trade. In one sense, trade was, and still is, endemic to Aranda social life, since family members and groups are bound to each other through various kinds of gift and service exchange. In precontact times, long-distance trade extending far outside the Aranda-speaking area was carried out for certain specialty goods, like ochers and *pituri* (native tobacco). Today the Aranda produce arts and crafts for the local and national tourist and art markets.

Division of Labor. Adult men are the main hunters of large game, while women and children, sometimes with men, hunt smaller game and gather fruits and vegetables. Women are the primary care givers to children up to adolescence, but men tend to take a good deal of interest in the training of adolescent boys. In the contemporary environment women tend to take care of most domestic work, while men often seek work on pastoral stations and the like. Many educated Aranda now live and work in bureaucratic organizations and some are beginning to question the ideology of the sexual division of labor.

Land Tenure. As individuals, Aranda people have rights in land through all four grandparents and may acquire rights by other means as well. There is a strong belief that one belongs to or owns the country of one's paternal grandfather and that one has a very strong connection to the country of one's maternal grandfather. Ultimately, land is managed and owned by rights to ritual property and this property is distributed through a complexly negotiable political framework. In precontact times, bands would wander over the territories of a local alliance network and be more or less economically self-sufficient. Today, these territorial alliance networks still exist, but the extent to which Aranda people can dispose of their own countries is made problematic by White settlement. The bulk of Aranda territory is occupied by White pastoralists, although a small amount is owned and managed (as recognized in Australian law) by Aranda people.

Kinship

Kin Groups and Descent. In hunting and gathering times the Aranda were organized into nomadic bands of bilateral kindred. The size and composition of these bands fluctuated greatly over time. Today, small settlements are organized along similar lines and mobility is very high. Larger settlements tend to be organized as neighborhoods, again reflecting the importance of extended family structures. In certain respects, descent is cognatic; in others it is ambilineal, but with a patrilineal bias. People regard themselves as part of a single, territorially based, cognatic group, descended from one or more common ancestors, but for certain purposes they also recognize separate lines of inheritance through males and females, often affording a kind of priority to agnation.

Kinship Terminology. The Aranda have given their own name to a kinship type in which marriage is enjoined with a classificatory mother's mother's brother's daughter's daughter. At the time of contact some Aranda groups employed a subsection system (with eight marriage classes), while most employed a section or Kariera system (with only four classes). Today the subsection is used by the majority of Aranda groups. Moieties are recognized but not named.

Marriage and Family

Marriage. Marriages were originally arranged between families on a promise system, although this system has been increasingly eroded up to the present time. Today, people are just as likely to marry "sweethearts" as they are to marry into the "correct" families. The prescribed marriage category for a man is mother's mother's brother's daughter's daughter, but other categories have always been allowed. There has probably been a general increase in "wrong" marriages since contact with Whites. In precontact times, bride-service was normal, with a man often remaining with his parents-in-law for some time before his promised wife matured to marriageable age. Polygyny was permissible, but it was not the norm; today it is extremely rare. Divorce and broken marriage promises have probably always been current. Marriage between dialect groups or between Aranda and non-Arandic Aborigines is common, and there is also a certain amount of marriage between Aborigines and Whites, usually between Aboriginal women and White men.

Domestic Unit. A hearth group might consist of an elder man, his wife, and their unmarried children, together with a number of other relatives, such as parents, unmarried siblings, and sons-in-law working bride-service. But because of the flexibility of hearth groups, both in terms of size and composition, it is difficult to say that even this unit would be typical.

Inheritance. The main heritable property, until recently, was land, together with the myths, ritual acts, and paraphernalia that still effectively act as title deeds to land. Rights in land and ritual property are open to intense politicking within the framework of ambilineal descent, although descent is not the only criterion used to qualify a person's claims. Historically, one's place of conception (or, less frequently, place of birth) has been important.

Socialization. Infants and children are heavily indulged by their parents until adolescence, when they tend to be disciplined for the first time. In childhood development the emphasis is on the fostering of independence and autonomy; hence deprivation and physical punishment are often frowned upon. A great many Aranda children now attend schools. Some of these schools cater to their peculiar needs and are bilingual.

Sociopolitical Organization

Social Organization. The major sources of social differentiation are sex and age. Outside of this there is very little specialization, although some individuals might be recognized as being more skillful than others in certain respects, such as traditional healing, and thus would be accorded more prestige. There is a strong egalitarian ethic, with an emphasis on individual autonomy relative to sex and age. Some kindred groups can become more powerful or expand at the expense of others over time. Racial and ethnic differences can sometimes be very important in the organization of social life in the wider context.

Political Organization. Insofar as the Aranda have been and are politically autonomous, they are governed by elder men and to a lesser or less public extent by elder women. This authority tends to be land-based. Territories are first of all agnatically defined, although one can inherit rights in them through women. An elder's jurisdiction relates to ritual property belonging to the places in which he has acquired rights and to younger relatives who might handle that property. Male initiation was and still is an important disciplinary procedure in which elder men over many years exercise power and influence over younger men. Initiation is also the channel by which juniors may themselves become respected elders. Political organization as a whole is coextensive with the organization of kinship and marriage, with territorial groupings or dialect groups (or "tribes") being more or less synonymous with local alliance areas. This system now meshes with local and federal government systems in the Australian state.

Social Control. Learning to behave correctly is largely a matter of kinship obligations and these are learned throughout a person's lifetime. In early childhood one learns an ethic of generosity and compassion for one's fellows, which leads to a generalized sense of family identity. As a person grows older, he or she learns that certain relationships should be marked by respect or shame and that he or she has different responsibilities. Many infringements of law, usually to do with ritual property or marriage and access to women, are solved by mobility and asylum, but there are also different types of violent punishment (which have historically included the death penalty, the spearing of limbs, and rape).

Conflict. Conflict usually arises over sexual relations and access to ritual property, land, and locally generated wealth. It may manifest itself in sorcery accusations and violent feuding or "payback" killings. In many areas, particularly where populations are relatively dense, conflict has increased, partly because of the indiscriminate placing together of different tribal peoples and partly because of access to alcohol.

Religion and Expressive Culture

Religious Beliefs. Cosmology is marked by a division between sky and earth, with the latter being the focus of close attention. There are a great many myths (or "dreamings") which tell of totemic ancestors who originally created the universe and everything within it. Some of these myths are secret and known only by a restricted group of men or women. There are also many noncreationist, nonesoteric stories suitable for children and public narration. Nowadays, much of this mythology operates in conjunction with Christian beliefs, stories, and hymns. The borrowing and trading of religious knowledge across ethnic boundaries has always been common in central Australia. The totemic ancestors are regarded as being embodied in the ground and their spiritual essences pervade the land. The environment is also populated by various types of bad spirit beings and ghosts.

Religious Practitioners. There are no religious specialists as such, although the most senior men in local groups are often singled out as being religious "bosses." There have been many different types of ritual practice, though only some are vigorously carried out today. All adult men and women traditionally had the right to act out or sing or to supervise the acting and singing of certain "dreamings" in ritual. A few men are now Christian priests.

Ceremonies. Men and women used to have their own ritual spheres and to a certain extent still do. One historically important ceremony, which has become less significant recently, is the "increase ritual"—a rite guaranteeing the fertility of a local area associated with particular totemic beings. Initiation ceremonies included circumcision and subincision (slitting the ventral surface) for boys and introcision (ritual defloration) for girls. Male initiation still takes place and remains very important. A third male initiation ceremony, which would last for several months, was the *inkgura* festival, held as a gathering of the clans whenever the local area could sustain a large group for a long time.

Arts. Largely, though not exclusively, restricted to ritual contexts, the arts include body decoration, ground paintings, incised sacred boards, singing and chanting, dramatic acting, and storytelling. Favored mediums for artistic expression include feathers and down; red, yellow, black, and white paints; clap sticks; and small drone pipes. In the 1930s many Western Aranda very successfully took up watercolors and that tradition remains strong. Today many Aranda are connoisseurs of country and western music, as well as adventure movies. Quite a few play guitar and some are learning to make their own videos.

Medicine. Traditional healers, who may be male or female, rely almost exclusively on shamanic arts, although there are a great many local medicines that are known and generally used. Today, the traditional system of healing operates in tandem with the provision of Western medicines and healing techniques. Most women now give birth in hospitals.

Death and Afterlife. Traditionally, death was followed by burial and this still occurs, usually with Christian ceremony. At death one aspect of the spirit can be completely annihilated, although it may first wander about as a ghost. Others say that this spirit ascends to the sky, sometimes to be with God, but sometimes to be banished to an evil place. Another part of one's spirit, which originally came from a totemic ancestor, goes back into the ground to become the land. This spirit may be reincarnated in another human being, but this is not regarded as personal survival or immortality.

See also Dieri, Mardudjara, Ngatatjara, Pintupi, Warlpiri

Bibliography

Spencer, Baldwin, and Frank Gillen (1927). *The Arunta: a Study of a Stone Age People.* London: Macmillan.

Strehlow, Carl (1907–1920). *Die Aranda- und Loritja-*

Stämme in Zentral-Australien. 5 vols. 7 pts. Frankfurt am Main: Joseph Baer.

Strehlow, T. G. H. (1947). *Aranda Traditions.* Melbourne: Melbourne University Press.

Strehlow, T. G. H. (1971). *Songs of Central Australia.* Sydney: Angus and Robertson.

JOHN MORTON

Asmat

ETHNONYMS: Asmat-ow, Samot

Orientation

Identification. The Asmat are hunting, fishing, and gathering people who inhabit an area which they refer to as *Asmat capinmi,* the Asmat world. The term "Asmat" (or "As-amat") means "we the tree people." In anthropological usage, the term Asmat labels the people (collectively), the language, and the geographic area. A single individual is referred to as an "Asmatter."

Location. The Asmat live within the Indonesian province of Irian Jaya (previously known as West Irian), which in turn occupies the western half of the island of New Guinea. Scattered over an area of some 25,000 square kilometers, these people inhabit a tropical lowland, alluvial swamp, and rainforest zone. The geographic coordinates are approximately 6° S and 138° E. Irian Jaya is located at the periphery of the monsoon region, with the most prevalent winds in Asmat blowing from November through April. The hottest month is December, the coolest June. Rainfall regularly exceeds 450 centimeters annually.

Demography. It is estimated that there are approximately 50,000 Asmat people. Village size currently ranges from about 300 to 2,000. While extremely variable, the estimated average rate of growth has been about 1 percent during the past thirty years. There is very little migration into or out of the area. Demographic factors of importance in the pre- and early-contact eras included the practice of infanticide, *papis* (ritual wife exchange), intra- and intervillage adoption of children and widows of war, and deaths associated with warfare. During the contact era, diseases such as cholera, influenza, and yaws have impacted growth.

Linguistic Affiliation. The determination of which scattered groups constitute the Asmat is, in part, an artifact of outside intervention and classification processes dating to the pre-1963 era of Dutch occupation. Five dialects are spoken in the Asmat language, which is a member of the Asmat-Kamoro Family of Non-Austronesian languages. Bahasa Indonesia, the national lingua franca of the country, also is spoken by many.

History and Cultural Relations

As an indigenous Papuan people, the Asmat are descended from groups of lowland, swamp-dwelling people whose still-earlier ancestors likely settled portions of New Guinea as far back as 30,000 years ago. Owing to accurate accounts kept by explorers and traders, virtually all of the earliest contacts made with the Asmat by Europeans are known. The first was made by the Dutch trader, Jan Carstensz, on 10 March 1623. Next to arrive, almost 150 years later on 3 September 1770, was Captain James Cook. Occasional contacts were made during the next 150 years, but it was not until 1938 that a Dutch government post called Agats was opened. Permanent contact has been maintained since the early 1950s. Agats has grown into Asmat's central administrative, trading, and mission town.

Settlements

Villages (in the strictest sense of the term) have arisen during the contact era. There has been a trend toward the spatial consolidation of traditionally more disparate *yew* (the maximal social/kin unit, each centered around a men's house and based on principles of patriambilineal descent). Settlements usually are located either along outer perimeters of sweeping river bends, or along small tributaries near points where they join large rivers. These locations afford both strategic and resource advantages. Mission and government posts are based near some villages.

Economy

Subsistence and Commercial Activities. The Asmat traditionally were subsistence-based, relying upon a combination of hunting, fishing, and gathering activities, which continue today. Horticultural activity first was introduced in the late 1950s. Processed stipe of the sago palm remains the dietary staple. First under Dutch and then Indonesian auspices, a partial wage-based economy has been introduced. Exportable hardwoods and crocodile hides are among the most valued items, reaching Singaporean and Japanese markets.

Industrial Arts. Traditionally the craft emphasis was upon wood carving. The *wowipits,* "master carver," was renowned for his technical skill and creativity. *Perindustrian,* the Indonesian term for "cottage industry," has been introduced to aid production and marketing activities. Asmat carvings are sought by collectors worldwide.

Trade. During the precontact era most trade was intraregional, with the primary items being of ritual value (e.g., triton shells). One exception was stone for use in axes. This was obtained through an extended network reaching to the foothills of the central highlands. Current trade patterns now include manufactured items as well and also involve merchants (primarily Indonesians of Javanese and Chinese heritage), missionaries, and the occasional tourist.

Division of Labor. This largely is based on gender. Women are responsible for net fishing, gathering (assisted by children), the transport of firewood, and most domestic tasks. Men are responsible for line and weir fishing, hunting, most horticultural activities, the felling of trees, and construction projects. Both sexes assist with sago processing.

Land Tenure. Local, autonomous sociopolitical aggregates of equal status are associated with more or less defined tracts of land. Rivers and river junctions constitute key points of demarcation. Boundaries are not rigid, changing as intervillage alliances and resources fluctuate. Sago palm groves, as well as individual hardwood trees, constitute inheritable and rigidly controlled resources. In recent decades major disputes have arisen with the government owing to differing conceptions of land tenure.

Kinship

Kin Groups and Descent. The yew is the nexus of Asmat kin and social/ritual organization. It is complemented by a complex yet flexible patriambilineal descent system (i.e., one wherein male lines predominate but female lines also are traced and actively recognized). Strong residential/spatial and dual organizational features are found. The tracing of actual and putative genealogical relationships beyond the great-grandfather is perceived to be superfluous and rather dysfunctional. Being a member of a domiciled core constitutes sufficient proof of being a relative.

Kinship Terminology. Each yew is divided into named halves or moieties, termed *aypim.* These moieties are reflected in the positioning of fireplaces within the men's houses. The kinship system is classificatory, with certain terms crosscutting generational lines. What the authors have termed "residential override" is operative, in that (despite an essentially bilateral recognition and naming of kin) once a young man enters the men's house he progressively has less to do with his mother and her consanguineal relatives. The terms *cemen* (literally, "penis") and *cen* (literally, "vagina") are used to clarify certain male and female kin relations, respectively.

Marriage and Family

Marriage. In principle, marriage is yew-endogamous and aypim-exogamous. Strict incest prohibitions only cover the nuclear family. Bride-price, provided by the groom in installments, traditionally consisted of such items as stone axes, bird of paradise feathers, and triton shells. Tobacco and small Western goods now are being included. Polygamy continues to be practiced by a few of the most prestigious males, although governmental and mission pressure against it has been intense. Similar pressure has been exerted against the practice of papis. While not a common occurrence, divorce does take place. Occasionally it is precipitated (in polygamous households) by interwife tensions, but more often it is caused (in monogamous as well as polygamous households) by problems between husband and wife. Some wives cite physical abuse as the primary cause. Some husbands cite inadequate cooking skills. A woman's return to her original yew and aypim signifies divorce; there is no formal ritual.

Domestic Unit. At marriage a woman becomes more closely affiliated with her husband's aypim, and takes up residence there. Individual houses are built, occupied, and maintained by extended families in the vicinity of the men's house. The informal adoption of children, even those whose parents remain viable members of the same village, is relatively common. This is perceived to be a means of maintaining "yew balance."

Inheritance. Certain important ritual items, such as *bipane* "shell nosepieces," are heritable. Principles of primogeniture do not pertain. Of primary importance are songs and song cycles, which can be inherited by a *soarmacipits* a "male song leader," a *soarmacuwut*, a "female song leader," or other yew leaders. Leadership positions per se are not heritable, but they tend to run in families.

Socialization. The primary responsibility for child rearing rests with female members of the extended family. Apart from socialization occurring through government- or mission-run school programs, most takes place through informal extended family and yew contexts.

Sociopolitical Organization

Social Organization. Traditionally, social organization (often involving ritual) revolved around activities of the yew and its associated men's house. The yew was the largest stable unit of social organization. Since the 1950s this focus has diminished somewhat. Some men's houses have been replaced by community houses, open to all.

Political Organization. For this traditionally egalitarian society, political organization was based upon the interplay of yew-prescribed activity (including warfare and ritual) and the dictates of the *tesmaypits,* ascribed charismatic leaders. Ascribed leadership, based on a combination of skill, generosity, and charisma (*tes*), is still important today; but the government's appointment of an Asmatter who does not possess tes to a local post can create a great deal of friction. The ability of tesmaypits to develop flexible intersettlement alliances and confederations, once so important to the waging of war and peace, has been curtailed.

Social Control. Traditionally, social control largely was exerted by the various tesmaypits and was tied to allegiances that they had developed over time. While attenuated, this practice continues. Strong processes of peer sanction are operative, including gossip and the open berating of husbands by their wives. Wife beating occurs and is implicitly condoned.

Conflict. Ritualized warfare, head-hunting, and cannibalism were distinctive features of Asmat life through the early 1950s. Strikes, ambushes, and skirmishes still occur occasionally, and—as with ritual warfare in the past—they are aimed at revenge. The latent function is seen to be the rectification of cosmic and also population balance.

Religion and Expressive Culture

Religious Beliefs. Traditionally an animistic society, the Asmat have developed an intricate pattern of rituals that pervades village life. Various Catholic, Protestant, Islamic, and government programs (introduced since 1953) have attenuated but not erased beliefs in a complex spiritual system based on the conception of a dualistic, balanced cosmos. Spirit entities are thought to inhabit trees, earth, and water. The spirits of deceased ancestors mingle among the living, at times aiding or hindering activities and bringing sickness. Cyclical rituals—such as those involving the carving of elaborate ancestor (*bis*) poles—and rituals that accompanied head-hunting raids, the death of great warriors, and ceremonies of peace and reconciliation can be related to the appeasement of the ancestral spirits.

Practitioners. Sorcerers and shamans (*namer-o*) mediate between humans and the spirit world. These statuses represent visionary callings requiring long apprenticeships. Practitioners perform magic, exorcisms, and healing. Tesmaypits organize and supervise rituals, employing head singers and providing food for ceremonies. In recent years, cargo-cult leaders also have emerged.

Ceremonies. Villages celebrate major rituals on a two-to four-year cycle. Ritual warfare (and the activities that preceded and followed each battle) traditionally was understood as integral to the cosmology of dualism, reciprocity, and checks and balances. Feasting, dancing, the carving of artworks, and lengthy song cycles continue to reflect this perspective. Mythological, legendary, and historical heroes are extolled in epic song-poems lasting several days. Initiation, papis, adult adoption, and men's house construction are also accompanied by ceremonies.

Arts. Asmat art, music, and oral literature are closely bound to ceremonial and socioeconomic cycles. The master carvers (wowipits) have been recognized as among the best of the preliterate world. Exuberance of form, shape, and color characterize ancestor (bis) poles, war shields, and canoe prows. Drums and head-hunting horns are considered to be sacred objects, although only singing is viewed as "music." Music serves as a vehicle of possession, social bonding, political oratory, therapy, cultural transmission, and recreation.

Medicine. Most curers also are religious practitioners. They employ herbal remedies (including tobacco), sorcery, and magic. The introduction of Western medicine has been systematically promoted by missionaries but only erratically promoted by the Indonesian government. Earlier Dutch programs were deemed superior.

Death and Afterlife. Virtually all sickness and death is attributed to spiritual intervention or cosmic imbalance. Such imbalance leads to vulnerability. Upon death, family and close friends grieve openly and intensively for several hours, flinging themselves down and rolling in the mud of the riverbank. Mud is believed to mask the scent of the living from the capricious spirit of the dead. The body traditionally was bound in pandanus leaves, placed on a platform, and left to decay. Relatives retrieved certain bones; the skull of one's mother often was worn on a string around the neck or used as a pillow. The spirits of the dead enter *safan*, "the other side." Most Asmat now rely upon burial, with some deaths accompanied by Christian funerals.

See also Mimika

Bibliography

Amelsvoort, V. F. P. M. (1964). *Culture, Stone Age, and Modern Medicine.* Assen, The Netherlands: Van Gorcum.

Van Arsdale, Kathleen O. (1981). *Music and Culture of the Bismam Asmat of New Guinea: a Preliminary Investigation.* Hastings, Nebr.: Crosier Press, Asmat Museum.

Van Arsdale, Peter W., and Carol L. Radetsky (1983–1984). "Life and Death in New Guinea." *Omega* 14:155–169.

Voorhoeve, C. L. (1965). *The Flamingo Bay Dialect of the Asmat Language.* The Hague: Martinus Nijhoff.

PETER VAN ARSDALE AND KATHLEEN VAN ARSDALE

Banaro

ETHNONYMS: Banar, Banara

The Banaro are a group numbering about 2,500 located along the middle course of the Keram River, a tributary of the Sepik River in Madang and East Sepik provinces, Papua New Guinea. Banaro is a Papuan language isolate belonging to the Sepik-Ramu Phylum. The Banaro are today concentrated in two villages. Formerly, they lived in four villages, two on either side of the Keram. Each village consists of from three to six hamlets, which in turn have from three to eight multifamily houses. Each hamlet also includes one communal structure, sometimes referred to as the "goblin hall." Subsistence is based on sago processing, the cultivation of taro, yams, bananas and sugarcane, fishing, and the exploitation of wild and domestic pigs. Sibs are the landholding group among the Banaro. The Banaro produce their own pottery and use bows and arrows.

The Banaro are organized into several patriclans, each of which is further divided into two subclans. Affiliated with each subclan are several localized patrilineages. Marriage among the Banaro is an exchange of women between exogamous patriclans. Sister exchange is the ideal, although the actual choice of a husband is generally in the hands of the girl and her mother. Bride-price is required. The domestic unit is a group of coresident brothers, along with their wives and children. The families live in a communal house, divided into apartments for each nuclear family. Each Banaro hamlet consists of a single patriclan. The communal houses are divided in two, each half belonging to each of that clan's subclans. The latter are totemic, unilineal, exogamous groups. Each subclan is allied with several other subsibs in wife exchanges. The alliances are effectively self-perpetuating and new alliances are established by the old and influential men among the Banaro. These leading men also have the responsibility of settling disputes and making economic and military decisions. The headmen lead by persuasion, not by command, and their power base is secured through a monopoly on magic.

The Banaro place great faith in magic. Magic is regarded as the primary means of manipulating the natural and supernatural worlds. Boys and girls both undergo initiation, with the girls marrying shortly thereafter. The most important supernaturals are the ghosts of the ancestors and the mischievous goblins, or minor spirit beings.

Bibliography

Thurnwald, Richard (1916). *Banaro Society.* American Anthropological Association Memoirs 3 (4).Menasha, Wis.

Bau

ETHNONYMS: Kubuna, Mbau, Tui Kaba

Orientation

Identification. The name "Bau" was originally that of a house site (*yavu*) at Kubuna on the Wainibuka River in the interior of Viti Levu, the main island of Fiji, but today "Bau" usually refers to the small offshore islet, home of the paramount chiefs, and "Kubuna" to those who claim kinship with the chiefly families, or those who "go with" Bau in the wider politics of all Fiji.

Location. The Kubuna moved down the Wainibuka and then the Wailevu (Rewa) river valleys to occupy the northeastern coast of the Rewa Delta and the Kaba Peninsula before making a home for their chiefs on the small islet of Bau, at 17°58' S, 178°37' E. This islet is no more than 8 hectares in extent and 15 meters above sea level at the highest point.

Demography. When Bau was at the height of its power, the population on the islet is said to have been 4,000. The paucity of available data permits no more than a guess as to the number of its supporters. Mid-nineteenth-century estimates varied between 100,000 and 300,000 for all of Fiji, of whom perhaps half supported Bau, but traditions tell of disastrous epidemics—associated with the earlier arrival of Europeans—ravaging the population by as much as 40 percent. The 1986 census revealed Fijians in the provinces that "go with" Bau totaling 175,000.

Linguistic Affiliation. The language is one of 300 "communalects" (dialects largely confined to one community) that exist among the contemporary population of 300,000 Fijians. In the early nineteenth century, a lingua franca based on the communalects of Bau and Rewa was used by Fijians from different parts of the islands when they wished to communicate, and European missionaries chose Bau for translation of the Bible. Europeanized Bauan, sometimes also called Old High Bauan, has now become the basis for Standard Fijian, which is in the Oceanic Branch of Austronesian languages.

History and Cultural Relations

Although Fiji has been inhabited for at least 3,500 years, much intervening history has been lost to memory. All of the great chiefdoms of eastern Viti Levu trace their founding ancestors to the Nakauvadra Mountains near the north coast, but existing genealogical information cannot be held to relate to earlier than the sixteenth century. The Bau had two great chiefly lines, that of the Rokotui Bau, the sacred chiefs, and the Vunivalu, war chiefs and executive chiefs. After moving to the islet, the Bau began extending their influence. The Vunivalu Naulivou exploited musket-bearing European beachcombers to such effect that at the time of his death in 1829, Bau seemed well on the way to establishing a Fiji-wide hegemony. Rebellion in 1832 halted this inexorable rise, and as the century advanced, relationships between Bau and other chiefdoms, and between Fijians and Europeans, became increasingly complex. Missionaries arrived at Bau in 1839. Their progress was limited during the early stages of the war between Bau and Rewa, which dominated Fiji's politics during the middle years of the century, but in 1854, the Vunivalu Cakobau converted to Christianity, and the climactic battle of Kaba, in 1855, took on the character of a struggle between pagan and Christian power in Fiji. Thereafter, European influence increased. Fiji was ceded to Great Britain in 1874, with Cakobau signing the deed as King of Fiji. The British colonial administration adopted a fairly benign paternalism towards all Fijians. Alienation of land was stopped, but evolution of Fijian society and adaptation to change were severely limited. The old chiefdoms such as Bau became relatively insignificant, although some of the chiefs were involved in administration. With independence in 1970, and even more so after the military coups of 1987, however, the chiefly confederations have once again come to the fore.

Settlements

Although the focus of the chiefdom was Bau Island, there were many tributary towns and villages, each with their own territory up and down the Tailevu coast, along the north coast of the delta, and on nearby islands in the Koro Sea. During the period of greatest turbulence, villages were elaborately defended. Those in the swamplands of the delta, in particular, were surrounded with impenetrable barriers of fences and ditches strengthened with concealed and upraised spikes. Special structures included the temple to the ancestral god of the paramount chiefs, the house sites of the most important families, which were built on rock-stepped platforms, and the stone-bordered canoe docks, representing political supremacy. In order to provide more land, terraces were leveled and foreshore reclaimed, and a bridge was built to connect the islet with the mainland more than a kilometer away. During the time of friendship with Rewa, a 2-kilometer canal was dug linking adjacent channels of the great river to provide easier access between the two centers of power.

Economy

Subsistence and Commercial Activities. Bauan Fijians were subsistence horticulturists, raising root crops such as taro and cassava on a swidden basis on the drier Tailevu coastal lands, but planting swamp taro in carefully mounded and ditched plots in the Rewa Delta. Fishing and collecting the resources of mangroves and the nearby reefs provided important additional food. Trading with Europeans began when the latter discovered stands of sandalwood on the northern island of Vanua Levu in the first decade of the nineteenth century, and it greatly intensified when the technology associated with the drying of sea slugs (trepang) was brought to Fiji from China in the 1820s. The chiefs of Bau deployed their supporters in order to acquire the cash they needed to buy guns, ammunition, and, in the case of the Vunivalu Cakobau of Bau, a schooner for his personal use. Today, 60 percent of the total population lives in villages, largely still with a subsistence economy and the continued obligations of communal life, but rural-urban drift is creating problems. More Fijians work for wages and seek employment in towns, resulting in a lack of housing, employment, and education opportunities and a weakening of the resources of the villages. Since the coups of 1987, the Fijian-dominated government has sought to redress imbalances that it perceives between Fijians and Indians, originally brought to the country by the colonial administration in 1878 to work in the plantation sugar industry that eventually became the basis of the colonial economy.

Industrial Arts. Traditional crafts of Fiji included the making of pots, woven mats, and fine bark cloth by the women, and, by the men, the carving of whalebone ivory (sometimes inlaid with pearl shell) and a wide variety of wooden artifacts, including spears and clubs, bowls for the ceremonial drinking of kava, and the great seagoing double-hulled canoes that permitted speedy passage between the islands of Fiji and to Samoa and Tonga to the east.

Trade. Bauan power rested on the ability to maintain a wide network of tributary relationships that involved the supplying to it of all the resources of the land and sea, including the crafts mentioned above. Europeans were integrated into the system whenever possible, particularly in the first half of the nineteenth century.

Division of Labor. In traditional times, family units spread widely over the land, cultivating and collecting. The division of labor was acccording to both age and sex. Men produced a far greater proportion of the family's food, for agriculture was and remains the domain of men. Young girls might collect taro leaves, but otherwise they would not go to the gardens. Fishing by line or net and the collection of molluscs and other products of the reef are women's work, as is the fetching of water, most cooking, and the care of house and children. Young children of 8 or 9 might help their parents, but lack of responsibility usually lasts until 14 or so. The heavier tasks fall on the younger men and women. The domestic seniority system serves to organize household production; this arrangement was especially true of the traditional extended family.

Land Tenure. Land was held by the "family," which was defined more or less inclusively in different parts of Fiji. During the period of its rise to power, Bau struggled with Rewa for control of the delta and sought to impose a tributary relationship on those they conquered. The colonial government defined principles of land tenure retrospectively, creating homogeneity in place of a system built on dynamism and change. They based their system at least in part on Bauan norms.

Kinship

Kin Groups and Descent. Fijian society is organized into a hierarchy of kinship groups of increasing orders of inclusiveness. At Bau, the chiefly *yavusa* was divided into four patriclans: the two chiefly *mataqali,* a warrior clan, and a herald clan divided into two subclans associated with each of the chiefly lines. With the rise to political importance of the chiefly confederations since the 1987 coups, clan relationships at the individual level are becoming more important once again.

Kinship Terminology. The system is of the Iroquois type, with some special features. There is the usual sharp distinction between cross and parallel relatives, but bifurcate merging occurs in all but the second descending generation, in which kinship reckoning is simply generational. Among the chiefly families of Bau, the *vasu* relationship, between ego and mother's brother, was used to cement ties with other chiefdoms. The vasu was able to make particular demands on the material wealth of his maternal uncle's kin group, frequently doing so in the interests of his own chiefdom.

Marriage and Family

Marriage. Traditionally, the preferred marriage alliance was between cross cousins; marriage between tribes was possible only after formal request. Nonsororal polygyny was practiced, and a man's status was defined by the number of his wives. The great chiefs married many times, usually in the interests of extending political power. This meant that all of the chiefly families of Fiji were closely related, often many times over in succeeding generations. In such situations, the status of the first wife was distinctly superior. The title of the principal wife of the Rokotui Bau was "Radi ni Bau," and his second wife was titled "Radi Kaba." The principal wife of the Vunivalu was called "Radi Levuka." Marriage ceremonial was more or less elaborate depending on the rank of the participants. Patrilocal residence was the norm, and divorce could be effected easily by either party.

Domestic Unit. The traditional extended family consisted of several married pairs and their children, inhabiting separate dwellings but sharing and cooperating in one cook house. Typically, men of the family would be closely related to the paternal line, but a daughter and her husband might also belong. The senior male would use the ancestral house site (yavu).

Inheritance. Dwelling houses are allocated by the family head and remain under his control, as do garden plots and other family property such as canoes. At his death, his surviving senior sibling determines the disposition of the house if the deceased has no mature sons. In the case of the great chiefs, the council of the whole tribe (yavusa) would determine succession and with it all rights to property.

Socialization. The rigor and principles of family ranking are a microcosm of larger kin groups and communities. Children are subordinate to their parents, but they are also ranked relative to each other by birth order. Aboriginally, they were ranked first by order of marriage of their mothers and then between full siblings by birth order. The first child (*ulumatua*) has a special status. Obedience and respect are demanded of the child by the father; after infancy the child is constantly taking orders. Punishment by the father is the main disciplinary mechanism, and the mother is more indulgent than the father, particularly towards boys and young men of the family.

Sociopolitical Organization

Social Organization. The social organization of the chiefdom was extraordinarily complex, with all aspects of its existence ringed with ceremony. Each individual identified with a hierarchy of increasingly inclusive groups: extended family, subclan, clan (yavusa), federation of clans (*vanua*), and political confederation (*matanitu*). The focus of the chiefdom was the chiefly clan, which was supported and defended by two groups of hereditary fishers, who also had the role of defending the chiefs from attack by land or sea.

Political Organization. As head of the political confederation, the chiefly clan of Bau sought to maintain a network of tributary relationships through its subclans. This arrangement implied a degree of political instability, and, indeed, the history of the first half of the nineteenth century was one of a ceaseless struggle for power. Warrior subclans were spread as a shield along the north coast of the Rewa Delta and at the base of the

Kaba Peninsula, separating Bau and Rewa. More distant ties were based on acknowledged ancestral kin relationships. As such, they required to be constantly reinforced within the contemporary play of political forces. The colonial administrative system and that of the immediate postindependence period divided the old chiefdom of Bau between several new administrative units, but in postcoup Fiji the chiefly confederations are again assuming political significance.

Social Control. Reflecting a preference for avoiding direct confrontation, gossip, ostracism, and social withdrawal have always been important forms of social control. Fear of divine retribution was and remains a powerful sanction at both the individual and the community level. The colonial government made Fijians subject to its judicial system, but since the 1987 coups there has been an attempt to reincorporate traditional principles into the legal system.

Conflict. There were ceremonial ways of asking forgiveness where there was a wish for reconciliation, ending with the drinking of kava. The vasu could also defuse potential conflict, being able effectively to represent the female side in a patrilineal society.

Religion and Expressive Culture

Religious Beliefs. In traditional times, religious belief centered on the deified founders of clans, frequently worshipped in animal form. In addition, each group had its own set of animal and plant totems, deemed to be inhabited by ancestral spirits. The missionaries succeeded in driving ancient beliefs underground, but they surfaced several times at the end of the nineteenth century, usually in the form of atavistic cults as vehicles for anticolonial opposition. Today, Methodism claims the support of most Fijians, although there is an important Roman Catholic minority.

Religious Practitioners. Traditionally, priests formed hereditary clans, exercising important divinatory and healing roles and acting as the voice of the ancestral gods.

Ceremonies. These were mainly associated with life cycles and with intergroup relationships. In ancient times, there was a ceremony of first fruits, when the various tributaries of Bau brought offerings of food to the Rokotui Bau and later to the Vunivalu, these usually being in the form of delicacies for which particular groups were well known. This ceremony was conducted according to the traditional calendar.

Arts. Singing and chanting, dancing, and joke telling were the traditional arts. The sexes never danced together and had quite different dances. Both danced standing and sitting. The women used delicate hand movements, while the men often danced with fan and spear or club, or with sticks.

Medicine. Disease was understood as deriving from malevolence of the spirits, particularly after the violation of taboos. Women collected and compounded herbal cures, while men applied them—a reflection of the belief that men possessed heavenly power (mana) whereas the strength of women came from the earth. Massage was also an important healing technique, but women massaged only women, and men only men.

Death and Afterlife. The ceremony associated with death was extremely elaborate, particularly when the status of the deceased was high, reflecting its importance in traditional belief. Tributary groups would come to pay homage to the corpse and to the bereaved family, cementing ties in the process. After the burial of a high chief, a taboo was laid on the waters around Bau, and the women, having kept vigil over the corpse for four to ten days, would cut their hair; only after 100 nights of mourning would the taboos be lifted. Wives were strangled to go with their husbands into the spirit world, for on the way lurked Ravuyalo, who killed the spirits of those who failed to accompany their spouses. The unmarried were buried with a club for their own defense.

See also Lau

Bibliography

Nayacakalou, R. R. (1975). *Leadership in Fiji*. Melbourne: Oxford University Press.

Ravuvu, Asesela D. (1988). *Development or Dependence: The Pattern of Change in a Fijian Village*. Suva, Fiji: University of the South Pacific.

Thomson, Basil (1908). *The Fijians: A Study of the Decay of Custom*. London: Heinemann. Reprint. 1968. London: Dawsons.

Williams, Thomas (1858). *Fiji and the Fijians*. Vol. 1, *The Islands and Their Inhabitants*. London: Alexander Heylin. Reprint. 1982. Suva: Fiji Museum.

DAVID ROUTLEDGE

Belau

ETHNOMYMS: Palau, Pelew

Orientation

Identification. Hearing the word *beluu*, "village homeland", early British explorers of the western Pacific mistakenly referred to the Belau Islands as "Pelew"; the spelling "Palau" became standardized in nineteenth-century German scientific writings. The form "Belau" more accurately reflects contemporary pronunciation and has become a symbol of national unity.

Location. Belau, an archipelago in the western Pacific Ocean, is located between 6° and 8° N and 134° and 135° E. The islands form the westernmost group of the Caroline Islands of Micronesia. Belau includes over 200 geologically and ecologically diverse islands; the largest, Babeldaob, is a volcanic island of 362 square kilometers. Other island types include high limestone and platform limestone islands, small reef islands, and one true atoll. A coral reef encircling most of the archipelago creates lagoons rich in marine resources and permits relatively smooth intervillage sailing. The climate is tropical, with constantly high humidity, a mean temperature of 27° C, and rainfall ranging from 320 centimeters per year in the south to 425 centimeters per year on Babeldaob. A yearly wind shift from westerly monsoons in the summer to easterly trades in the winter is interrupted only by typhoons, which periodically destroy homes, harbors, and farms.

Demography. The population in 1988 was approximately 14,000, about half of whom live on the island of Koror. Estimates of precontact population range from 20,000 to 40,000. From the late eighteenth century on Belauans were subject to decimation by introduced diseases and by the intensification of warfare caused by imported firearms. The Japanese began a massive colonial resettlement program in the 1930s, resulting in a foreign population of over 24,000 in Koror by 1940. Since World War II the local population has risen dramatically, and many Belauans have moved to Guam, Hawaii, and California.

Linguistic Affiliation. Belauan, an Austronesian language, is spoken uniformly throughout the archipelago; only minor differences in accent and idiomatic expressions indicate a speaker's home village. Most Belauans over the age of fifty are also fluent in Japanese, and those younger than fifty speak English. Belauan is referred to as a Nonnuclear Micronesian language, since it has closer genetic affinity with languages spoken in eastern Indonesia, Taiwan, and the Philippines than with those spoken in the rest of Micronesia. The language is noted for its complex system of verbal inflections, the presence of a phonemic glottal stop, and an archaic set of lexical items found in chants and myths.

History and Cultural Relations

The archipelago was discovered more than 2,000 years ago by Austronesian voyagers sailing from insular Southeast Asia. These early settlers occupied both low-lying islands, where fishing was the primary subsistence activity, and high volcanic and limestone islands, where extensive taro cultivation was possible. Perhaps as late as the twelfth century A.D., the islanders constructed monumental terraced earthworks and built inland villages on elaborate stone foundations. There is a strong possibility that prior to European contact Belau had interaction with the Chinese, whose ships could have been the source of the ceramic and glass beads still functioning as exchange valuables. Sir Francis Drake visited briefly in 1579; extensive relations between Belau and the West began in 1783 when the East India Company packet *Antelope* wrecked on the reef. The islands have been subject to successive claims by colonial powers: Spain (1885–1899), Germany (1899–1914), and Japan (1914–1944). In 1947 Belau became part of the Trust Territory of the Pacific Islands, a United Nations "strategic trusteeship" under the administration of the United States. Constitutional self-government was proclaimed in 1981 when the Republic of Belau seated its first government, while the islands continued to be subject to the trusteeship. After decades of bitter factional and legal disputes, Belau is currently negotiating a Compact of Free Association with the United States. The first president of Belau, Haruo Remeliik, was assassinated in 1985; the second president, Lazarus Salii, died of gunshot wounds in 1988.

Settlements

There are two types of settlements, relatively "rural" villages located on Babeldaob, Ngcheangel, Beliliou, and Ngeeur, and the relatively "urban" town of Koror. Starting in the nineteenth century, Belauans abandoned their inland villages and built new settlements closer to coastal harbors and alluvial streams. Koror was the center for nineteenth-century colonial trading operations, was later the headquarters of the Japanese-mandated Pacific islands, and is presently the home of most government offices, schools, retail shops, restaurants, and tourist facilities. Many Belauans maintain dual residences in Koror and in their home villages, and some even commute by motorboat on a daily basis. Formerly, villages consisted of residential and meeting houses constructed of closely joined lumber, with thatched roofs, and elevated bamboo floors; today, tin roofs and concrete block foundations are favored in new construction. In many places on Babeldaob one can still detect the typical village layout, with meeting houses located on a central paved square, canoe houses and men's clubhouses standing near the shore or river, and residential houses fanning out along elevated stone walkways.

Economy

Subsistence and Commercial Activities. Fish and taro have long been the staple foods of Belau. Fishing by spear gun, line, hand net, and trap is carried out in the coastal lagoons; high-powered speedboats are used for trawling outside the reef. The catch is pooled by local cooperative associations for retail sale in Koror. In preparation for funerals and festivals, men work the lagoon with huge nets. Women take pride in taro cultivation on "dry" upland slopes and in "wet" irrigated swamps; the backbreaking labor required has led many younger women to substitute cassava and imported rice. Young men raise pigs for slaughter at ceremonial events. Increasingly vast amounts of imported commercial goods are replacing locally produced items. In Koror the government is the largest employer, and little locally owned industry has flourished. Belau is completely dependent upon U.S. government funds and upon payments from other countries for access to Belau's marine, strategic, and recreational resources.

Industrial Arts. Skills such as wood carving, meeting-house construction, and tortoiseshell-ornament production are becoming rare; basket weaving, however, is widely practiced by women. Most able-bodied men are expert fishermen, and individuals win renown by developing specialized techniques and by possessing expert knowledge of tides and spawning cycles. Young people strive to obtain advanced educational and business training at stateside schools. In the villages, wage earners include schoolteachers, nurses, magistrates, land registrars, and religious officials.

Trade. Interdistrict trade in the traditional context involved not only daily necessities such as lamp oil, pottery, wooden implements, palm syrup, and canoe sails but also specialized prestige goods such as turmeric powder, tortoiseshell ornaments, women's shirts, red-ocher dye, and dugong bracelets. In the nineteenth century, European settlers established trading centers for the commercial extraction of trepang, pearl shell, and copra. Now, a few families in each village run small retail stores. A complex system of social exchange, involving the presentation of food and service in return for cash and valuables across the affinal bond, is the principal focus of daily economic life. U.S. currency is used in financial transactions; Belauan valuables supplement cash in customary exchanges.

Division of Labor. The most important division of labor is between fishing, emblematic of male virtue, and taro cultivation, symbolic of female productiveness. This split parallels the duel system of exchange values, women using locally produced hammered turtleshell trays and men using beads and cylinders of foreign origin. Women take charge of domestic activities, such as food preparation, child care, and laundry, and they also carry heavy responsibility in selecting holders of male and female chiefly titles.

Land Tenure. Prior to changes imposed by colonial powers, land was either "public land of the village" (*chutem buai er a beluu*), subject to the local chiefly council, or "land of the principal houses" (*chetemel a kebliil*), controlled by chiefly titleholders and senior matrilineal relatives. Residential sites and taro patches were assigned to affiliated family segments rather than being passed down to offspring. These lands reverted to chiefly control for redistribution. German officials instituted patrilineal land inheritance and encouraged nuclear families to move their houses and to plant coconut trees on unused village land. Today, land is divided into "public land" controlled by the national government, "clan land" controlled by chiefly houses, "village land" governed by village councils, and private property owned in fee simple. The national government is forbidden by the constitution to use eminent domain for the purpose of helping a foreign country.

Kinship

Kin Groups and Descent. The basic kin unit is the "house" (*blai*), which is composed of individuals linked by strong matrilateral bonds (*ochell*, or "offspring of women") and of individuals associated by weaker patrilateral ties (*ulechell*, or "offspring of men"). Each house controls a residential site, taro patches, a chiefly title, exchange valuables, and ceremonial prerogatives. Houses form wider affiliative networks (*kebliil*) both within the village and between villages, which function to channel social cooperation, exchange, and inheritance. The complexity of Belauan kinship lies in the lateral breadth of relationships rather than in the depth of remembered genealogies.

Kinship Terminology. Distinctive characteristics of the system of kin terms include: the overriding of generation (offspring of women label offspring of men as "children"); the importance of sibling rank reflected in senior and junior terms for both males and females; a reciprocal term for cross-sex siblings signaling the solidarity of the brother-sister pair; the existence of a special term for mother's brother; and the generalization of the respectful kin terms "mother" and "father" in polite address to all elders. With respect to the generational stratification of sibling and cousin terms, the system could be labeled Hawaiian; with respect to the skewing of generations due to the importance of matrilineal ties, it could be labeled Crow. Titleholders are never addressed by their personal names.

Marriage and Family

Marriage. Marriage is fundamentally an economic institution. Traditionally, high-ranking women were prohibited from "falling," that is, marrying a man of lower rank. The prohibition was based on economic considerations—if the husband were of low rank his relatives would be unable to make a sufficient financial contribution and the couple's male child would lack the financial assets needed to maintain his chiefly authority. Today, individuals are free to select spouses, but social rank and wealth are critical considerations. Fragile marital ties are subordinate to enduring kinship ties: while the former are severed at death or divorce, the latter are a "bridge forever." High-ranking individuals tend to marry outside of the village, and there is still considerable rank endogamy. Newly married couples establish independent houses on land near the husband's father's house; men who receive a chiefly title can move back to their matrilineal home. Divorce is frequent and remarriage is the norm.

Domestic Unit. The residential family (*ongalek*) often includes grandparents and other extended kin. Adoption of children within the network of kin is common.

Inheritance. Property belonging to the house is controlled by senior "offspring of women" members, who select the heirs to land and valuables. Much private property passes in the patriline. Women give turtleshell heirlooms to their daughters.

Socialization. Mothers play a greater role in child raising than fathers; children have a more relaxed, affectionate relationship with fathers than with mother's brothers. Older siblings take on child-care responsibilities. Young men's clubs act as powerful peer reference groups.

Sociopolitical Organization

Social Organization. The principles of democratic egalitarianism and inherited hierarchical rank conflict in contemporary Belau. Rank pertains to relations between siblings, between houses in a village, between titles in a political council, and between villages within the state. According to myth, four villages were regarded as preeminent: Imeiong, Melekeok, Imeliik, and Koror. Financial wealth, elected political office, and esoteric knowledge are other sources of social power.

Political Organization. Prior to the indoctrination into democratic values and practices, Belau was governed by chiefs, whose titles were ranked according to the social hierarchy of local land parcels. Called *dui,* the word for "coconut palm frond," titles possess sacredness and demand respect apart from the person who carries the title. The highest titleholders from Melekeok village (the Reklai title) and Koror village (the Ibedul title) have emerged as "paramount chiefs" of the archipelago. Today, Belau is a self-governing constitutional republic, headed by an elected president and a national legislature. Traditional chiefs play an advisory role at the national level. Each state is headed by an elected governor and sends two senators to the national legislature. At the village level, a council of chiefs parallels a council of elected officials, headed by a magistrate. The central role of multivillage confederacies, once factions for intervillage warfare, has vanished.

Social Control. Traditional sanctions, including fines and banishment, applied by the local council of chiefs are supplemented by the legislated civil code, which in turn is subject to the laws of the Trust Territory.

Conflict. In the absence of interdistrict political councils in the precolonial period, intervillage hostility functioned as a primary means of political integration and as a mechanism for the financial enrichment of chiefs. Warfare took the form of either swift head-hunting raids or massive sieges aimed at the devastation of the enemy village. Also, rivalry among chiefs and competition over title inheritance created powerful motives for political assassination.

Religion and Expressive Culture

Religious Beliefs. Belau has been heavily missionized by Catholics, Seventh-Day Adventists, and Mormons. A nativistic movement, Modekngei, or "Let Us Go Forth Together," is a powerful religious and educational force. Except for some village gods (represented in stone monuments), the traditional pantheon has been replaced by the Christian trinity. Christianity and Modekngei provide the primary religious dogmas; the latter stresses purification rites and trances.

Religious Practitioners. Traditional male and female religious specialists performed offerings to local gods (*chelid*) and, while in trance, spoke the messages and prophecies of the gods. Male titleholders served as ritual specialists in the domestic cult, focusing on manipulating ancestral spirits (*bladek*) through offerings of burnt coconut and small pieces of money. Today, Belauans can serve as Christian deacons, ministers, and priests; Modekngei utilizes ritual specialists.

Ceremonies. Important traditional ceremonies include interdistrict dancing festivals (*ruk*) and competitive feasts between local fishermen's clubs (*onged*). Protestants and Catholics observe the principal festivals of the Christian calendar; followers of Modekngei assemble weekly at the ritual center in Ibobang.

Arts. Skills such as canoe building and decorative wood carving are currently being revived as folk art. "Storyboard" carvings depicting events from folklore are a major tourist item. Local dance teams perform at festivals; older women sing archaic funeral chants and songs. Storytelling is a highly respected form of verbal art.

Medicine. Western medicine is available at the central hospital in Koror and in village clinics; villages place a high value on public health and sanitation. Traditional curing employs herbal medicines applied on the side of the body opposite the affected part.

Death and Afterlife. Funerals are costly, elaborate rituals. The deceased's female relatives maintain a mourning period, and male relatives collect financial contributions to be distributed to heirs at a subsequent ceremonial occasion called "death settlement talks." Burial takes place in community graveyards, although formerly burial was under the house platform. A week after burial, close relatives meet again to pave the grave and to send the spirit to its final resting place in the southern part of the archipelago.

See also Woleai

Bibliography

Barnett, H. G. (1949). *Palauan Society: A Study of Contemporary Native Life in the Palau Islands.* Eugene: University of Oregon Publications.

Force, Roland, and Maryanne Force (1972). *Just One House: A Description and Analysis of Kinship in the Palau Islands.* Bernice P. Bishop Museum Bulletin no. 235. Honolulu.

Krämer, Augustin (1917–1929). "Palau." In *Ergebnisse der Südsee-Expedition, 1908–1910,* edited by Georg Thilenius, B. Melanesien, vol. 1. Hamburg: Friederichsen.

Parmentier, Richard J. (1987). *The Sacred Remains: Myth, History, and Polity in Belau.* Chicago: University of Chicago Press.

RICHARD J. PARMENTIER

Bikini

ETHNONYMS: Escholtz Islands

Bikini is the largest of the twenty-six islands in the Bikini Atoll in the Marshall Islands. Bikini is the northernmost atoll in the Ratak chain of atolls and islands and is located at 11° 31' N and 165° 34' E. The twenty-six islands have a total land area of 7.6 square kilometers and surround a large lagoon some 641 square kilometers in area. Bikini has drawn considerable attention since the relocation of the 161 resident Bikinians in 1946 so that the atoll could be used as a test site for atomic and nuclear weapons by the U.S. government. Because of radiation contamination from the tests, Bikini is uninhabitated today and will probably remain so for some years. Bikinians today number over 400 and live elsewhere in the Marshall Islands, mainly on Kili. Bikinian identity is based on rights to ownership of land on Bikini that are inherited from ancestors.

Bikini was settled before 1800 possibly by people migrating from Wotje Atoll. Because of the island's relative isolation, Bikinians had little contact with other peoples in the Marshalls. First contact with Europeans was evidently in 1824 with the Russian explorer Otto von Kotzebue, although no European actually settled on Bikini until after 1900. The first American missionary arrived in 1908 and Bikinians were drawn into the copra trade during the German colonial period, which ended with World War I. The Japanese ruled the Marshalls from World War I to World War II, and they established a base on Bikini during World War II. After the war, the Marshalls became a Trust Territory of the U.S. and achieved independence in 1986.

Because of its isolation and the large lagoon, Bikini Atoll was selected by the U.S. government as the site for testing the effects of atomic bombs on naval vessels. This decision led to negotiations with the Bikinians and their agreeing to relocate to Rongerik Island in 1946. When this site proved inadequate, they relocated again to Kwajalein Island in 1948 and then Kili later in 1948, where most remained, although some also settled on Kwajalein and Jaluit. An organized attempt was made by the Department of the Interior to develop the Kili community economically, an effort that met with limited success.

From 1946 to 1957, twenty-three atomic and nuclear tests were conducted at Bikini. In 1968, Bikini was declared habitable by the U.S. government and 100 Bikinians had returned by 1974, though the island was now barren of much of the vegetation that had existed when they left in 1946. When tests in 1978 showed unacceptably high levels of strontium 90 radiation in Bikinians on the island, the island was declared uninhabitable and the people relocated again to Kili. As compensation for the loss of their land, the Bikinians were awarded hundreds of thousands of dollars in 1956 by the United States. Some payments went to individuals while others were used to establish a trust fund for the entire community. These payments have made Bikinians, along with people from Enewetak, Rongelap, Utirik, and Kwajalein who also received compensation, wealthier than other Marshall Islanders. The payments also made the Bikinians economically dependent on income from the trust fund and contributed to an erosion of participation in prerelocation economic pursuits such as taro and copra production. Relocation also changed traditional patterns of social and political organization. On Bikini, rights to land and landownership were the major factor in social and political organization and leadership. Also, the Bikinians, as Marshall Islanders, were under the nominal control of the Paramount Chief of the islands, though actual contact with other islands was minimal. After relocation and settlement on Kili, a dual system of land tenure emerged, with disbursements of interest from the trust fund linked to landownership on Bikini and a separate system reflecting current land tenure on Kili influencing current political alliances and leadership. Regular contact with the U.S. government led the Bikinians to reject the primacy of the Paramount Chief and instead to look to U. S. government officials for support and assistance.

See also Marshall Islands

Bibliography

Kiste, Robert C. (1974). *The Bikinians: A Study in Forced Migration.* Menlo Park, Calif.: Cummings Publishing Co.

Mason, Leonard (1954). "Relocation of the Bikini Marshalese: A Study in Group Migration." Unpublished Ph.D. dissertation, Yale University.

Boazi

ETHNONYMS: Boadzi, Suki

Orientation

Identification. Boazi is the name of a language spoken by approximately 2,500 people who live along the middle reaches of the Fly River and along the central and northern shores of Lake Murray in the southern lowlands of New Guinea. Boazi speakers use the name "Boazi" to refer to their language, but their names for themselves are the names of the eight territorial groups into which they are divided. The use of the name "Boazi" (both by Boazi speakers and others) to refer to all Boazi speakers (or in some cases to refer to those who live along the Fly River as opposed to those who live around Lake Murray) is the result of the recent colonial and current postcolonial context in which Boazi speakers live. Prior to the colonial period, there does not seem to have been any conception of group membership beyond the territorial group. Nonetheless, the eight Boazi-speaking territorial groups share a common history, culture, and social structure. Early colonial documents also refer to Boazi speakers as "Suki," a name now reserved for culturally similar people living farther down the Fly River.

Location. The Lake Murray–Middle Fly area is located between 6°30' and 8° S, and 141° and 141°5' E. The dominant geographical features of the area are the Fly River, with its 10-kilometer-wide floodplain, and Lake Murray, which is 60 kilometers long and 15 kilometers wide at its widest point. Away from the river and lake are low ridges covered with open forest or closed canopy rain forest. In the marginally lower areas between these ridges are extensive sago swamps from which Boazi speakers get most of their food. The area receives 250 centimeters of rain per year, over half of which falls during the northwest monsoon, which lasts from late December to mid-April.

Demography. In 1980 there were approximately 2,500 Boazi speakers. The population density of the Lake Murray–Middle Fly area is about 0.3 person per square kilometer. There is no reliable information on population growth or decline.

Linguistic Affiliation. According to C. L. Voorhoeve (1970), Boazi is spoken in three dialects: Kuni at Lake Murray, and North Boazi and South Boazi along the Fly River. The Boazi language is one of two languages in the Boazi Language Family, the other being Zimakani which is spoken around the southern part of Lake Murray and the confluence of the Fly and Strickland rivers. The Boazi Language Family is the easternmost of the three language families in the Marind Stock, which is part of the Trans–New Guinea Phylum.

History and Cultural Relations

Boazi speakers are culturally similar to groups to the south and west of the Lake Murray–Middle Fly area, including the Suki, Yéi-nan, Marind-anim, Bian Marind, and the tribes of the Trans–Fly, but they are culturally very different from the peoples who live to the north of the Lake Murray–Middle Fly area such as the Yonggom, Aekyom (or Awin), and the Pare speakers. To date no archaeological research has been done in the Lake Murray–Middle Fly area. It is therefore impossible to say with any certainty how long people have been in the area or where the ancestors of the present-day Boazi speakers came from. Boazi speakers claim that their ancestors originated in the Lake Murray–Middle Fly area itself, and Boazi oral history records various military conquests and subsequent movements of people within the Lake Murray–Middle Fly area prior to the arrival of Europeans. The first contact between Boazi speakers and Europeans took place in June 1876 during d'Albertis's exploration of the Fly River. d'Albertis had brief hostile encounters with people along the middle reaches of the river both during his ascent and during his descent later that year. For the fifty years following d'Albertis's visit, Boazi speakers both along the Fly River and at Lake

Murray had only brief and sporadic contacts with Europeans. In the late 1920s, in response to head-hunting raids by Boazi speakers on peoples close to Australian and Dutch government stations, the colonial administrations both of the Australian Territory of Papua and of Dutch New Guinea began trying to pacify the Boazi speakers of the Middle Fly. This led to a period of Dutch control and proselytization by Dutch Catholic missionaries in the Middle Fly from 1930 to 1956. Dutch control did not, however, extend to the Lake Murray area where traditional warfare continued into the late 1940s. In 1956, Boazi speakers became citizens of the Independent State of Papua New Guinea.

Settlements

Villages range in population from about 50 to 600 persons. Families alternate between living in a village and living in small camps near their sago swamps and hunting grounds. Both villages and camps are usually built on low islands or peninsulas in the swamps and marshes of the Fly River floodplain. All villages have a separate house for unmarried men. This house is physically removed from the rest of the village and serves as the married men's clubhouse and the repository of the central objects of the men's secret cult. Traditionally, houses were simple, open-sided structures with dirt floors, sleeping platforms of split *Areca* palm, and roofs of sago leaves or *Melaleuca* bark. Today, however, houses have raised floors of split palm and walls of sago palm frond stems in addition to their sago-thatch roofs.

Economy

Subsistence and Commercial Activities. Boazi speakers are primarily hunters, fishermen, and sago makers. The Lake Murray–Middle Fly area is extraordinarily rich in wildlife. Wild pigs, cassowaries, wallabies, and deer abound. The forests and marshlands are home to many types of birds, including goura pigeons, bush fowl, ducks, and geese, and the rivers and lakes contain a great variety of fish as well as turtles and crocodiles. Hunting is done with bows and arrows, using a variety of hunting techniques, including stalking, blinds, and driving game toward hunters with fire or noise. Dogs are often used in hunting larger game. Boazi speakers fish with traps, spears, hooks, and commercially made nylon nets. The most important food item, however, is sago, a starch extracted from the pith of the sago palm (*Metroxylon sagu*), which grows naturally in the extensive freshwater swamps of the area. Boazi speakers also plant coconut palms, bananas, and some tubers, but gardening plays only a minor role in their adaptation to the environment.

Industrial Arts. Boazi speakers are preindustrial and, prior to the arrival of White men, used only stone tools. Any adult can produce virtually all of the implements necessary for day-to-day living from materials found in the local environment.

Trade. Prior to pacification, Boazi speakers raided their neighbors for the few things which they could not produce themselves—most importantly, stone for tools, since the Lake Murray–Middle Fly area has no stone. Today, they are able to buy steel tools, metal pots, Western clothes, and some European foods from small, indigenously owned trade stores in the area. Money is obtained primarily from the sale of crocodile skins or from contract labor outside the Lake Murray–Middle Fly area.

Division of Labor. Boazi speakers have a loosely defined sexual division of labor. Hunting, making bows and arrows, carving paddles, cutting canoes, and building houses are considered men's work, although some aspects of house building, such as making roof panels from sago palm leaves, may be done by either men or women. Women's work includes making sago, gathering firewood, cooking, and weaving baskets and mats. Most other tasks may be done by either sex. In Durkheim's terms, the Boazi exhibit a high degree of mechanical solidarity with little interdependence of tasks and virtually no specialization of labor. The nuclear family is the maximum unit of production.

Land Tenure. Within the territory of a territorial group, individual tracts of land are owned communally by totemic groups or, in some cases, patrilineages. Individuals can obtain access to forest products (e.g., trees for canoes) or the right to hunt in a particular area through matrilateral or affinal ties as well as through membership in the totemic group that owns a tract of land. Within the landholdings of a totemic group, sago swamps are owned by individual members of that group. Coconut palms, banana stands, and other garden plants are owned by the people who planted them.

Kinship

Kin Groups. Each Boazi speaker is a member of a lineage, a totemic group, and a moiety. Lineages are named for their apical ancestors, and totemic groups have animals such as the pig, cassowary, crocodile, and various types of fish as their totems. Totemic groups are divided into moieties, one consisting of groups with land-animal totems and the other consisting of groups with water-animal totems. While Boazi speakers talk about lineages, totemic groups, and moieties as if they all recruit members through patrilineal descent and are hierarchically organized, there are important differences in the recruitment of members between lineages on the one hand and totemic groups and moieties on the other. An individual always belongs to the same lineage as his or her father, but in the recruitment of individuals to totemic groups and moieties, patrilineal descent is subordinated to the principles governing marriage exchanges: a man gives a woman to a man in the opposite moiety from whom he receives a wife; and a man should belong to the same lineage, and therefore the same totemic group and moiety, as the woman he gives in exchange for his wife. In cases in which a man gives his uterine sister, or another woman from his totemic group, in exchange for his wife, the marriage-exchange principle and the principle of patrilineal descent have the same result—that is, the man will continue to belong to his father's totemic group and moiety. But when a man gives a woman from a lineage that is part of another totemic group, he will change his totemic group, and in some instances his moiety, to that of the woman whom he has given in exchange for his wife.

Kinship Terminology. While descent is patrilineal, kinship is reckoned bilaterally. Boazi kinship terms distinguish between cross cousins and parallel cousins, and separate terms are used for father's older brother, father's younger brother, father's sister, mother's older sister, mother's younger sister, and mother's brother. Both father's older brother and mother's older sister are addressed and referred to as though they were members of the grandparental generation. In addition to their use with actual kinsmen and kinswomen, kinship terms (denoting relative age and membership in the same or opposite moiety as the speaker) are used both in addressing and in referring to all Boazi speakers.

Marriage and Family

Marriage. Marriage is by the exchange of women, preferably uterine sisters, between men of opposite moieties. In addition to a rule of moiety exogamy, there are restrictions on marriages between individuals who are closely related matrilaterally. Marriages are usually between members of the same territorial group, although there is no rule of group endogamy. Marriages are usually arranged by the fathers and the mothers' brothers of the men and women involved. Following marriage, a man is expected to help his wife's father with hunting and heavy labor. This is facilitated by a pattern of uxorilocal postmarital residence, which usually continues at least until a couple has two or three children. While polygyny was a part of the traditional culture of Boazi speakers, today, under the increasing influence of Christianity, most marriages are monogamous.

Domestic Unit. The nuclear family is the typical domestic unit, although the people living in the same house may include parents or widowed sisters of the husband or wife, and married daughters and their husbands and children. In some instances, pairs of brothers and their families may live in the same house. As mentioned earlier, unmarried men sleep in a separate house although they regularly visit their natal families or married siblings.

Inheritance. Boazi speakers have few inheritable artifacts or wealth objects. An individual's few personal effects are either buried with the person or distributed to his or her children. A man's sago swamps and coconut palms are divided among his sons, and in some cases among his sons and daughters.

Socialization. Infants and children are raised primarily by their mothers or their oldest sisters. Children are encouraged to be independent and physically competent, and they are discouraged from showing pain and ridiculed if they fall down or hurt themselves. For boys, the freedom of childhood continues, with only slight restrictions, until they marry. Girls, however, are increasingly pressured to accept responsibility and to be productive from about the age of 9 or 10.

Sociopolitical Organization

Social Organization. While social relations among Boazi-speaking men are egalitarian, social relations between the sexes are unequal, with men having more power than women. Traditionally, the only leadership position was that of war leader (*kamok-anem*). This position was generally occupied by married men between 30 and 45 years of age who earned the position by demonstrating courage and cunning in warfare. Today, each Boazi village has an elected representative to the local government council which is the lowest level of representative government in Papua New Guinea.

Political Organization. The maximal political units are the territorial groups, which range in population from 50 to 1,000 people. In Boazi, these territorial groups are called *mangge izwam* or "land people." Traditionally, each territorial group lived in a constant state of war with its neighbors, and even today relations between territorial groups are often tense and occasionally hostile, and the borders between groups are under almost constant dispute. A person belongs to the territorial group into which he or she is born. Each territorial group has two types of members: *miavek* and *bwiatak*. The former are patrilineal descendents of one of the original members of the territorial group. The latter are individuals who have come to live with the territorial group, either through their own migration or through the migration of one of their patrilineal ancestors. Because they are descended from the original members of the territorial group, *miavek* members have somewhat stronger claims to land and sago swamps.

Social Control. Social control is maintained through threats of physical retaliation and sorcery. Both forms of social control have been seriously undermined, however, by the colonial and postcolonial governments and by Christian missionaries. The government has made both physical retaliation and sorcery criminal offenses, and the teachings of missionaries have led many young Boazi speakers to question the efficacy of sorcery.

Conflict. Warfare was an important part of traditional Boazi culture. Boazi speakers were fierce headhunters and cannibals who were feared by many groups in the southern lowlands of New Guinea. Even today, conflicts between territorial groups are continual, with most conflicts stemming from disputes over women or land. There is also considerable strife within territorial groups, but in these cases individuals have the option of moving to another camp or village.

Religion and Expressive Culture

Religious Beliefs. Most Boazi speakers believe in a combination of Christianity and traditional beliefs in ghosts, spirits, sorcery, and the power of magical objects. Elements of Christian mythology are often mixed with Boazi mythology. Boazi speakers believe in a variety of supernatural beings including ghosts, spirits associated with particular locations, and forest and marsh spirits. Many forest and marsh spirits play only minor roles in day-to-day life, but ghosts and the spirits associated with particular locations are believed to be the source of both benevolent and malevolent magical power. Beliefs in traditional supernatural beings are often mixed with beliefs in Christian supernatural beings.

Religious Practitioners. Although some Boazi speakers are recognized as having greater knowledge of sorcery and greater magical powers than others, sorcery and magic can, according to Boazi tradition, be learned by any man and by some women.

Ceremonies. Many traditional ceremonies, including male initiation, were closely tied to head-hunting and therefore are no longer performed. Tame-pig feasts, which include appeals to spirits and which traditionally preceded a head-hunting raid, are still occasionally held.

Arts. Boazi speakers produce little representational or abstract art. Traditionally, they made elaborate trophies from the heads of their head-hunting victims, but these are no longer produced. Musical instruments include large hourglass drums and bullroarers. Dances to the accompaniment of drums are held to celebrate marriages, national and Christian religious holidays, and the end of the traditional period of mourning.

Medicine. Illness is attributed to spirits, sorcery, the breaking of postpartum taboos, excessive amounts of impure blood in the body, and (for men) contact with menstrual blood. A variety of traditional medical techniques are used; prominent among these are bleeding to remove the impure blood and burning to relieve pain.

Death and Afterlife. Death is the most important life-cycle event. Mourning consists of one or two days of wailing and dirges before the body is buried. After the burial, a formal period of mourning is observed which usually lasts about forty days. During this time, people are supposed to speak in low voices and are not permitted to beat their drums. At the end of the mourning period, a large feast is held for the community, but the spirit of the dead person is believed to frequent the village or camp until his or her death has been avenged.

See also Marind-anim

Bibliography

Busse, Mark (1987). "Sister Exchange among the Wamek of the Middle Fly." Ph.D. dissertation, Department of Anthropology, University of California, San Diego.

Voorhoeve, C. L. (1970). "The Languages of the Lake Murray Area." In *Papers in New Guinea Linguistics,* edited by S. Wurm, no. 10. Pacific Linguistics, Series A, no. 25. Canberra: Australian National University.

MARK BUSSE

Chambri

ETHNONYMS: Chambuli, Tchambuli

Orientation

Identification. The Chambri (called Tchambuli by Margaret Mead) live south of the Sepik River on an island mountain in Chambri Lake in East Sepik Province of Papua New Guinea.

Location. Chambri Lake is approximately 143°10' E and 4°7' S. The lake is created by the overflow of two of the Sepik's tributaries. This overflow occurs during the northwest monsoon season, from September to March, when rainfall nearly doubles in intensity from a dry-season average of 2.07 centimeters to an average of 3.72 centimeters per month.

Demography. In 1933, Mead reported that the Chambri population was approximately 500 people, but it is likely that this estimate was too low. It may well have excluded some 250 people: migrant laborers away on plantations, as well as their wives and children remaining on Chambri Island. In 1987, the total number of Chambri living on Chambri Island, and elsewhere in Papua New Guinea and beyond, was about 1,500. Of these, approximately one-half were living in the three contiguous home villages of Kilimbit, Indingai, and Wombun. The next-largest cluster of Chambri live in a settlement on the outskirts of the provincial capital of Wewak.

Linguistic Affiliation. The Chambri language is a member of the Nor Pondo Family of Non-Austronesian languages and is related to Yimas, Karawari, Angoram, Murik, and Kopar.

History and Cultural Relations

Because the Chambri were a preliterate people, one can only speculate about their history. It is likely that their distant ancestors lived in small, semisedentary hunting and gathering bands. Perhaps in response to the intrusion of those Ndu speakers who became the Iatmul, the bands of early Chambri coalesced about 1,000 years ago and eventually formed what are now the three Chambri villages on the shores of the fish-rich lake. The Chambri were contacted first by Australians in the early 1920s, and by 1924 relations between them were well established. Extensive labor migration to distant plantations began in 1927. In 1933, Mead and Reo Fortune worked for six months as anthropologists among the Chambri, and in 1959 Catholic missionaries completed construction at Indingai village of the most elaborate church in the Middle Sepik. The peoples of the Sepik River, those living along its northern and southern tributaries and those further south in the Sepik Hills, are united in a regional trading system based on interpenetrating ecological zones. This system links the Chambri with their neighbors—particularly the Mali and Bisis speakers of the Sepik Hills and the Iatmul of the Sepik River—in an exchange network that includes not only subsistence goods but ceremonial complexes.

Settlements

The three Chambri villages stretch along the shore of Chambri Island and range in population from 250 to 350.

Each village has five men's houses, although at any given time some of them may be house sites only. In its ideal form, a Chambri men's house is an impressive two-story structure with high gable ends, surmounted with carved finials, large oval second-story windows, and elaborately carved and painted interior posts and other heavy timbers. Membership in a men's house is patrilineally inherited and includes men from several patriclans. Formerly, and to some extent still, women marrying into a clan lived in a large multifamily clan house. Those Chambri currently residing in Wewak live in a crowded squatters' settlement, as large as a Chambri village, composed of small houses made of a variety of scavenged or bush materials. The residential pattern at the camp in Wewak replicates that on Chambri Island, with migrants from Kilimbit, Indingai, and Wombun living in their own respective sections.

Economy

Subsistence and Commercial Activities. The Chambri subsist primarily on fish they catch and on sago they either barter for with surplus fish—as they had done prior to European contact—or purchase with money. In 1987, the Chambri acquired 15 percent of their sago through barter. Principal sources of income now come from the sale of smoked fish to migrant laborers in the towns and the sale of carvings and other artifacts to art dealers and to tourists. The Chambri supplement their diet of fish and sago with greens and fruits from the forest; some also grow watermelons, yams, beans, and other vegetables during the dry season on the exposed lake bottom. Chickens and ducks are common, far more so than pigs.

Industrial Arts. Prior to European contact, the Chambri were producers and purveyors of specialized commodities used throughout the Middle Sepik region. Women wove large mosquito bags from rattan and reeds; men made tools from stone quarried on Chambri Mountain. Today, both men and women produce for the tourist trade with women weaving baskets from reeds and men carving wooden artifacts, based on traditional designs of ritual figures.

Trade. Fish-for-sago barter markets are still regularly held in the Sepik Hills between Chambri and Sepik Hills women. In addition, there is a market held twice a week on Chambri where foodstuffs are available for purchase with money.

Division of Labor. Chambri women are responsible for fishing, marketing, and food preparation. Chambri men, in addition to their ritual responsibilities, build houses, canoes, and carve artifacts. Formerly, warfare and production and trade in stone tools were also important male activities.

Land Tenure. Land is patrilineally inherited as are fishing areas. Women use the fishing areas of their husbands. It is not uncommon, in addition, for individuals to gain temporary access to the resources of their matrilateral kin.

Kinship

Kin Groups and Descent. The Chambri divide themselves into over thirty exogamous patriclans and into two sets—one affinal and the other initiatory—of partially cross-cutting patrimoieties. The patriclans are landowning, residential, and ceremonial groups named for their founders; members refer to each other as the people of the same totems, indicating the common inheritance of numerous totemic names and powers. Together, all clan members assume responsibility for paying, and receiving payment on, affinal debts.

Kinship Terminology. Chambri kinship terminology is of the Omaha type, using the criterion of mother's brother's daughter equals mother's sister.

Marriage and Family

Marriage. Polygyny has become increasingly rare since the early 1960s when the Catholic mission became fully established in the area. Mother's brother's daughter marriage is the most commonly stated preference; 30 percent of Chambri marriages do take place with a member of the matrilateral cross cousin's clan. Although subject to some recent change, most marriages are still within the village and virtually all are with other Chambri. Given that Chambri settlements are both dense and contiguous, when a woman leaves her clan land to move to that of her husband, she still remains close to her natal kin. Marriage involves prestations of bride-wealth, traditionally in shells and now in money. Prestations by wife takers are of great political importance and provide the context for a clan to demonstrate its wealth and importance. In their turn, wife givers reciprocate with food. Among non-Catholics, divorce may be initiated by either husband or wife, frequently for reasons of incompatibility or infertility. However, divorce is discouraged by kin on both sides since it should involve a return of affinal payments. In cases of divorce, young children remain with their mothers until they are old enough to assume patrilineal responsibilities.

Domestic Unit. Formerly all women lived in large multifamily clan houses, which functioned as maps of family solidarity and affinal interdependence. Each of a man's wives would situate her cooking hearth in the portion of the house allocated to her husband and fasten there the carved hook bearing the totemic insignia of her own patriclan. From this hook, she would hang the basket containing a portion of her patrimony of shell valuables. Today, under the influence of the Catholic church and a cash economy, these houses have been largely replaced by smaller, single-family dwellings. Clan members often prefer living in these smaller dwellings because they can better protect private purchased goods, such as radios, from agnatic claims.

Inheritance. Property including land, fishing rights, and valuables, as well as ritual prerogatives, implements, and powers, are inherited by male and, to a lesser extent, by female patriclan members.

Socialization. Mothers take responsibility for primary socialization; nonetheless, they frequently leave their children with their sisters or with other women when they have work to do, particularly when they go out to fish. Young children are rarely left with men who, although affectionate and indulgent, regard excrement and urine as polluting. A bond of great importance to Chambri children is with their mothers' brothers. Frequently, if disgruntled, children will seek solace from these matrilateral kinsmen. Moreover, mothers' brothers have an essential role as nurturers in the initiation, through scarification, of their sisters' sons.

Sociopolitical Organization

Social Organization. Chambri society is largely egalitarian with all patriclans, except those linked through marriage, considered potential equals. For affinally related clans, wife givers are regarded as superior to wife takers. Gender relations are also of relative equality, with men and women operating in largely autonomous spheres. The Chambri never developed a strong male-oriented military organization in large part because, as valued providers of specialized commodities, they were left in relative peace. Relations of trade mitigated also against the development of male dominance because Chambri men could not have appreciably increased the flow of valuables to themselves through the control of women and their products.

Political Organization. Through his own marriage(s) and those of his junior agnates, a Chambri man becomes immersed in complex obligations that provide him with the opportunity of achieving political eminence. The struggle to make impressive affinal payments generates widespread competition in which men try to show that they are at least the equal of all others in their capacity to compensate wife givers. Those individuals and patriclans unable to compete in the politics of affinal exchange are likely to become subsumed as clients of those who are more successful. In addition, since 1975 when Papua New Guinea became a nation, the Chambri have voted in, and have often provided candidates for, local, regional, provincial, and national elections.

Social Control. In the past, and still to a limited extent, internal and external social control was maintained through violence or threats of violence focusing on sorcery and raiding. Conflicts were and are resolved through debates in men's houses; today, as well, the Chambri have recourse to the judicial procedures of the state, such as local and regional courts. For Chambri living in Wewak, the police are often called in when conflict threatens to get out of control. In most of these cases when police help is sought, the dispute is subsequently settled with payment of damages, determined during a community meeting, followed by a ceremony of reconciliation.

Conflict. Although, as mentioned, the Chambri lived in relative peace with their neighbors, they were, on occasion, both perpetrators and victims of the head-hunting raids that were both sources and indicators of ritual power.

Religion and Expressive Culture

Religious Beliefs. Since the early 1960s the Chambri have considered themselves to be staunch Catholics. They are, at the same time, convinced that all power, whether social or natural, is ancestral power. Religion—as well as politics and, indeed, all activities of importance—focuses on evoking and embodying ancestral power through the recitation of (usually secret) ancestral names. In addition to the spirits of the dead are a variety of autochthonous powers that dwell in stones, whirlpools, trees, and, most importantly, crocodiles. All are thought to act not only on their own volition but under the control of those Chambri who know the relevant rituals.

Religious Practitioners. All adult persons have some knowledge of efficacious names; by definition, powerful men are the most knowledgeable about these names. Anyone who knows secret names—that is, who has power—has the capacity for sorcery. Some men and women have the special capacity to be possessed by spirits from their maternal line in order to diagnose illness, misfortune, and the causes of death. Others contact paternal spirits in dreams for the same purposes.

Ceremonies. Many Chambri ceremonies are rites of passage during which persons are increasingly incorporated into their patriclans. At the same time, matrilateral kin are presented with affinal payments to compensate them for the corresponding diminution of their maternal portion of these persons. The most elaborate of these ceremonies is initiation during which young men receive the hundreds of incisions on their backs, arms, and upper thighs that release the maternal blood that contributed to their fetal development. Other ceremonies, requiring the evocation of the powers of particular patriclans, are believed to ensure that, for instance, the wet season will come, particular species of fish will reproduce, and fruits of the forest will be plentiful. Through the performance of such clan-held ceremonial prerogatives and obligations, a totemic division of labor emerges in which, through the efforts of all, the universe is regulated.

Arts. Whether in the form of drums, masks, carved or painted men's house timbers, or decorated hooks, art for the Chambri embodies ancestral powers and/or refers to clan-based claims to those powers. The art now made for the tourist trade is largely derived from these forms, but it is not invested with ancestral power.

Medicine. Since it is believed that people succumb to disease only when they are depleted of power—sometimes as the result of sorcery—indigenous curing practices attempt to restore that lost power. This kind of cure can be done through several, frequently combined, means: offended ancestors are compensated, often through animal sacrifice; medicines, bespelled so as to become imbued with ancestral power, are applied to, or consumed by, the sick person. Today, the Chambri have access to a local aid post and to mission and provincial hospitals. Western medicine, although eagerly used, has not replaced traditional diagnoses and treatments.

Death and Afterlife. Chambri ideas about the destination of spirits are, by their own acknowledgment, inconsistent: spirits are variously believed to go to the Christian heaven, to remain in ancestral ground, and to travel to a remote place no living being has visited. Regardless of any particular view, however, Chambri also insist that the dead are never very distant. They believe that the living and the dead readily engage in each other's affairs.

See also Iatmul

Bibliography

Errington, Frederick, and Deborah Gewertz (1986). "A Confluence of Powers: Entropy and Importation among the Chambri." *Oceania* 57:99–113.

Errington, Frederick, and Deborah Gewertz (1987). *Cultural Alternatives and a Feminist Anthropology.* Cambridge: Cambridge University Press.

Gewertz, Deborah (1983). *Sepik River Societies: A Historical Ethnography of the Chambri and Their Neighbors.* New Haven: Yale University Press.

Gewertz, Deborah, and Frederick Errington (1991). *Twisted Histories, Altered Contexts: Representing the Chambri in a World System.* Cambridge: Cambridge University Press.

Mead, Margaret (1935). *Sex and Temperament.* New York: Morrow.

DEBORAH GEWERTZ

Chamorros

ETHNONYM: Tjamoro

The Chamorro are the indigenous inhabitants of the island of Guam and the surrounding Southern Mariana Islands. The present-day descendants of the precontact Chamorros have a syncretic culture, greatly influenced by Spanish, Filipino, Japanese, and especially American culture. The Chamorro language is classified as an Austronesian language. Guam is now a U.S. territory. The Chamorro occupied the five southernmost islands of the Marianas in Micronesia. In 1978 the Chamorros numbered 75,000, with 52,000 in Guam and 13,500 in the Northern Marianas. Some communities were located inland, but most were near the shore with most houses made of plant material. Dwellings of high-status families, however, often had stone foundation columns (*latte*).

Subsistence was based primarily on fish, aroids, yams, breadfruit, and coconuts. Rice was also grown and eaten on Guam, the only place the grain was found in precontact Oceania. Chickens were the only domestic animals present when Europeans arrived. Men did most of the gardening as well as deep-sea fishing while women gathered littoral sea resources and cooked. There was a division of labor by class. From the upper classes came the sailors, carpenters, fishers, and warriors, and the highest class owned most of the land and controlled the production of shell money and canoes. Wood and stoneworking were highly developed crafts, as was pottery making. The Chamorros did not produce tapa cloth, nor did they have any woven fabrics.

The Chamorros organized themselves into matrilineal sibs and lineages. Descent was matrilineal. The traditional rule of residence is unknown, but it was probably matrilocal. Marriages were usually monogamous, and there was considerable premarital sexual freedom. Following the wedding, the bridegroom owed a period of bride-service to his wife's parents. Intermarriage between social classes was restricted, as the highest class did not marry down, and members of the lowest class were not permitted to marry up. The Chamorros were organized into households, lineages, and clans. The highest level of integration was the district, which was composed of one or more neighboring villages. Each large island had more than one district. Chamorro society was evidently characterized by a high degree of social stratification, consisting of three classes: the *matua* or *chamorri*, which included the highest-ranking nobles and chiefs; the *atchaot* or middle class; and the *mangatchang*, which was the class of commoners. There was a complicated economic specialization according to class, and social intercourse between classes was regulated by strict rules of etiquette.

The districts were the largest politically autonomous units. Rivalry and warfare among the districts was common, and they were probably hierarchically ordered. The district chief (*maga-lahe*, which means "leader" or "firstborn") was the highest-ranking male relative within the clan. Succession was through younger brothers and then through male parallel cousins and nephews, according to order of seniority.

The deceased ancestors (*anite*) of the Chamorros were believed to inhabit an underworld paradise. These personages were also worshipped in an ancestor cult for, as the people's guardians, the ancestors were feared and venerated. Shamans (*makana*) invoked the anite to bring success in warfare, cure illness, bring rain, and aid fishing expeditions. Certain specialists called *kakahnas* could both cause and cure illness in individuals. Native doctors (*surnhana*) used mainly herbs in their treatments; these doctors were most often old women. In addition to the ancestral souls, the Chamorros recognized various other spirits but evidently no powerful deities.

Bibliography

Carano, Paul, and Pedro C. Sanchez (1964). *A Complete History of Guam.* Rutland, Vt.: Charles E. Tuttle.

Thompson, Laura (1945). *The Native Culture of the Marianas Islands.* Bernice P. Bishop Museum Bulletin no. 185. Honolulu.

Chimbu

ETHNONYMS: Kuman, Simbu

Orientation

Identification. The Chimbu live in the Chimbu, Koro, and Wahgi valleys in the mountainous central highlands of Papua New Guinea. An ethnic and linguistic group, not traditionally a political entity, the Chimbu are speakers of Kuman and related dialects. Most people living in the Chimbu homeland identify themselves first and foremost as members of particular clans and tribes—identification as "Chimbus" is restricted primarily to occasions of interaction with nonethnically Chimbus. The term Chimbu was given to the people by the first Australian explorers (in the early 1930s) who heard the word *simbu* (an expression of pleased surprise in the Kuman language) exclaimed by the people at first meetings with the explorers.

Location. The Chimbu homeland is in the northern part of Simbu Province, in the central Cordillera Mountains of New Guinea, around the coordinates 6° S and 145° E. They live in rugged mountain valleys between 1,400 and 2,400 meters above sea level, where the climate is temperate, with precipitation averaging between 250 and 320 centimeters per year. To the east live the Chuave and Siane, and to the north live the Bundi of the upper Jimi Valley. In many ways culturally very similar to the Chimbu are the Kuma (Middle Wahgi) people living to the west. South of the Chimbu in the lower Wahgi and Marigl valleys are Gumine peoples, and farther south are lower altitude areas, lightly settled by Pawaia and Mikaru (Daribi) speakers.

Demography. Approximately 180,000 people live in the 6,500 square kilometers of Simbu Province. Of those, more than one-third live in the traditional homeland areas of the Kuman-speaking Chimbu. In most of the northern areas of the province, population densities exceed 150 persons per square kilometer, and in some census divisions population densities exceed 300 persons per square kilometer.

Linguistic Affiliation. Kuman and related languages (SinaSina, Chuave, Gumine) are part of the Central Family of the East New Guinea Highlands Stock of Papuan languages.

History and Cultural Relations

Little archaeological evidence exists for the Chimbu area proper, but data from other highland areas suggest occupation as long as 30,000 years ago, possibly with agriculture developing 8,000 years before the present. It is believed that the introduction of the sweet potato (*Ipomoea batatas*) about 300 years ago allowed for the cultivation of this staple food at higher altitudes with a subsequent increase in the population of the area. Oral traditions place the origin of the Chimbu at Womkama in the Chimbu Valley, where a supernatural man chased away the husband of the original couple living in the area and fathered the ancestors of the current Chimbu tribal groups. First Western contact occurred in 1934 when an expedition, led by gold miner Michael Leahy and Australian patrol officer James Taylor, passed through the area, and soon afterward an Australian government patrol post and Roman Catholic and Lutheran missions were established. The initial years of colonial administration were marked by efforts to curtail tribal fighting and establish administrative control in the area. Limited government resources and staff made this goal difficult, and by the beginning of World War II only a tenuous peace had been imposed in parts of Simbu. Following the war, Australian efforts to extend and solidify administrative control continued, local men were recruited as laborers for coastal plantations, and coffee was introduced as a cash crop. Establishment of elected local government councils after 1959 was followed by representation of the area in a territorial (later national) legislative body and by the creation of a provincial legislature. Local tribal politics remain important and tribal affiliation greatly influences the participation in these new political bodies.

Settlements

In contrast to highland areas to the east, Kuman Chimbu do not arrange their houses into villages but rather have a dispersed settlement pattern. Traditionally, men lived in large men's houses set on ridges for purposes of defense, apart from women, girls, and young boys. Each married woman and her unmarried daughters, young sons, and the family's pigs lived in a house that was situated some distance from the men's house and in or near the family's gardens. By situating their houses near the gardens, women were able to remain close to their work and better manage their pigs, a family's greatest economic asset. Although this housing pattern still exists to some extent, reduction in the segregation of the sexes, reduction in tribal fighting, and economic development have resulted in more men living with their families in houses that are located near coffee gardens and roads. Most Chimbu houses are oval or rectangular, with dirt floors, low thatched roofs, and walls woven from flattened reeds.

Economy

Subsistence and Commercial Activities. The primary subsistence crop in Simbu is the sweet potato. Grown in fenced and tilled gardens, sometimes on slopes as steep as 45°, sweet potatoes provide food for both people and pigs. Sweet potatoes are the main food at every meal, comprising about 75 percent of the diet. Over 130 sweet potato cultivars, or varieties, are grown in different microenvironments and for different purposes. Sweet potato gardens are usually made in grass or forest fallow areas by digging ditches in a gridwork pattern to form a checkerboardlike pattern of mounds 3 to 4 square meters in size on which vine cuttings are planted. Gardens are planted throughout the year, with impending requirements for food, such as the need for more sweet potatoes for upcoming food exchanges and increased pig herds, influencing planting as much as climate seasonality. In addition to sweet potatoes, other crops grown for consumption include sugarcane, greens, beans, bananas, taro, and nut and fruit varieties of pandanus. Pigs are by far the most important domesticated animal to the Chimbu and are the supreme valuable, sacrificed to the ancestors in pre-Christian times and blessed before slaughter today. Pigs, killed and cooked, are the main item used in the many ceremonial exchanges that are crucial to creating and cementing the many social relationships between individuals. By giving partners pork, vegetables, money, and purchased items (such as beer) the contributors create a debt that the receivers must repay in the future in order not to lose valued prestige. These exchanges occur at various times, for various reasons—for example, to celebrate marriage, to compensate for injury or death, or to thank a wife's natal kin group for the children born into the husband's clan. By far the largest of these exchange ceremonies is the pig ceremony (*bugla ingu*), at which hundreds or even thousands of pigs are slaughtered, cooked, and distributed to friends and affines at the final climax of events. Money has become an increasingly important item exchanged in these ceremonies. For most rural people, money is primarily earned through the growing of coffee in small, individually controlled gardens. In addition to coffee, money is acquired through the selling of vegetables in local markets and, for a small minority, through wage employment.

Industrial Arts and Trade. Crafts of clothing and tool making are now largely abandoned, their products replaced with items manufactured beyond the local communities and purchased in stores. All subsistence work, before contact, relied upon the skillful use of local woods, fibers, canes, stone and bone materials, and a few trade items. In general, men made the wooden tools and weapons and constructed fences and houses; they also made artifacts of cane, bamboo, and bark.

Division of Labor. As in precolonial times, the division of labor remains based primarily upon gender. Men fell trees, till the soil, dig ditches, and build fences and houses; women do the bulk of the garden planting, weeding, and harvesting, care for the children, cook, and care for pigs. Men are also responsible for political activities and, in time of tribal warfare, defense of the territory. The production of coffee is primarily the responsibility of men, and the few Chimbus with wage employment are almost exclusively men. Predominantly, women sell items (mostly fresh vegetables) in the local markets.

Land Tenure. Each family's land is divided among a number of different plots, often on different types of soil at different altitudes. Land tenure in Chimbu is marked by relative fluidity. Most commonly land is jointly inherited from a father to his sons. But it is not unusual for associations with more distant agnates and with kin or affines in other clans to result in rights to use their land. Rights to land in fallow remain in the hands of the previous user so long as those rights are defended. Despite the high population densities in most parts of Chimbu, absolute landlessness is unknown because of the ability of individuals to acquire land through any of a number of different contacts. But the advent of cash cropping has led to a lack of land suitable for growing coffee and other tree crops. Therefore, although land for food is available to all, access to the means to earn money through commodity production has become limited. This lack of land suitable for cash crops has led to a large number of Chimbus, over 30 percent in some higher altitude areas, to migrate away from their home territories to towns and lower, less crowded rural lands.

Kinship

Kin Groups and Descent. Chimbu view their kin groups as consisting of patrilineal segments, "brother" groups, which have descended from a common patrilineal "father" ancestor. The clan, with an average population of 600–800, is the usual unit of exogamy. Clan names are often taken from the ancestral founder's name combined with a suffix meaning "rope." Clans are further divided into subclans, kin groups with between 50 and 250 persons. The subclan group is often the main organizing unit at ceremonial events, such as marriages and funerals, and subclan members undertake some joint agricultural activities. Smaller groups are sometimes identified within the subclan. These "one blood" or men's house groups consist of close agnates or lineage mates.

Kinship Terminology. Kinship terms are classificatory by generation and bifurcate merging, distinguishing sex and relative age among siblings and father's siblings.

Marriage and Family

Marriage. Marriage in Chimbu, as in many parts of the world, represents a social and economic link between the groom's kin group and the bride's kin group. The ceremony reflects this with a large number of valuables, primarily pigs and money, negotiated and arranged by senior members of clan segments and given as bride-price. Men are usually in their early twenties when they are first married, women are usually aged 15 to 18. Residence after marriage is usually patrivirilocal. Polygyny is still common, although the influence of Christian missions has reduced its occurrence. Having more than one wife is economically advantageous for men because women are the primary laborers in the gardens. Until the birth of children, marriages are very unstable, but divorce occurs sometimes years after children are born.

Domestic Unit. Until recently, men always lived separately from their wives in communal men's houses, joining their wives and children most often in the late afternoon at mealtime. Coresidence of a married couple in a single house is becoming more common. If a man has more than one wife, each wife lives in a separate house and has her own gardens. An individual man and his wife or wives are the primary productive unit. Often closely related men will cooperate in the fencing and tilling or adjacent garden plots. Households commonly join others during short visits.

Inheritance. Brothers jointly inherit their father's land in crops as well as rights to fallow and forest land. Usually most of the land is distributed to sons after they are married, when the father gets older and becomes less active. Other valuables are distributed to other kin after a man dies. Land of childless men is redistributed by senior men of the clan segment.

Socialization. Infants and children of both sexes are cared for primarily by their mothers and other sisters. At about the age of 6 or 7, boys move in with their fathers if they live in a separate men's house. Starting at about age 7, about half of Chimbu children begin to attend school. Up to adolescence Chimbu girls spend large amounts of time with their mothers, helping in daily work. Boys form play sets with others of similar age from the same area, and these sets of related boys form relationships that last through adulthood. The initiation ritual for males, held during the preparation for the pig ceremony, involved the seclusion and instruction of boys and young men at the ceremonial ground in the meaning of the *koa* flutes and other ritual questions and proper behavior. Since the festivals were held at intervals of seven to ten years, and all youths who had not previously participated were taken, it was a men's group rite rather than a puberty ceremony. The initiates were subject to bloodletting and painful ordeals. These ceremonies have ceased, except for revealing the flutes to young people at the time of the feast. At first menstruation, girls were secluded and for a few days (or weeks) instructed in proper behavior, and then their passage was celebrated with a family feast including members of the local subclan and kinsmen. Some girls are still secluded and celebrated in a family rite.

Sociopolitical Organization

Social Organization. Chimbu society is organized around membership in agnatic kin groups with small groups at the lower level combining with other groups to form larger inclusive memberships, much like a segmentary lineage system. Individual loyalties and associations are generally strongest at the smallest, least inclusive level associated with common residence areas and shared resources. The clan, the largest exogamous group, commonly acts as a unit in large ceremonial activities and does have a common territory. The largest indigenous sociopolitical organization is the tribe. The tribe, numbering up to 5,000 people, acts as a defensive unit in times of tribal fights with people from other tribes. The marriages contracted between members of different clans and tribes are fundamental in establishing political and economic relationships beyond the local level.

Political Organization. In traditional times the tribe was the largest political unit, but parliamentary democracy, begun in the late 1950s and early 1960s, created constituencies much larger than the traditional kin-based political units, but the influence of small local groups centered on leaders, called "big-men," has not diminished. These men are influential in organizing ceremonial exchanges of food and money, as well as rallying support for the candidacies of those standing for election. Typically more than one man from each tribal group stands in elections, fracturing support among many local candidates and allowing the successful candidate to win with often less than 10 percent of the total votes. In many ways modern parliamentary politics has not increased the scale of Chimbu political groups—even national-level politicians can gain office with a following not much larger than those supporting some traditional leaders in the past.

Social Control and Conflict. Although the possibility of violence, between family members as well as between large tribal groups, serves to control people's actions, mediation by third parties, often politically important men, is more often used to prevent or resolve disputes. Accusations of witchcraft are also levied against those who are perceived to be threatening agnatic group strength, usually against women, who marry into the group and are seen sometimes to have divided loyalties. Warfare occurs between different tribes and occasionally between clans within a tribe. Traditionally, the relations between tribes were characterized by a permanent state of enmity, which served as an important contributing factor to the unity of a tribe. In the decades following colonial contact warfare at first diminished, only to reappear in the 1970s. Although the incidence of warfare is related to competition over scarce land, often the incident that precipitates fighting is a dispute over women, pigs, or unpaid debts.

Religion and Expressive Culture

Religious Beliefs. The indigenous Chimbu religion had no organized priesthood or worship. The sun was seen as a major spirit of fertility. Supernatural belief and ceremonies concentrated on appealing to ancestral spirits who, if placated through the sacrifice of pigs, were believed to protect group members and contribute to the general welfare of the living. Although many traditional supernatural beliefs still exist, various Christian sects claim the majority of Chimbus as members.

Ceremonies. Of the most important traditional ceremonies, initiation of boys into the men's cult is no longer practiced (having been actively discouraged by missionaries); the large pig-killing ceremonies (bugla ingu) are still held but with less emphasis on the sacrificing of pigs to ancestral spirits.

Arts. The visual arts are concentrated on body decoration with shells, feathers, wigs, and face paint being worn at times of ceremonial importance. Songs, poetry, drama, and stories are important as forms of entertainment and education. Musical instruments include two types of bamboo flutes, wooden and skin-covered drums, and bamboo Jew's harps.

Medicine. Illness and sudden death are attributed to witchcraft, sorcery, and transgression of supernatural sanctions. There was a very limited traditional herbal medical technology, but for most illnesses the people now make use of the government medical aid posts and hospitals.

Death and Afterlife. Although Christian beliefs have modified traditional beliefs, it is still thought by many that after death one's spirit lingers near the place of burial. Deaths caused by sorcery or war that are not revenged result in a dangerous, discontented spirit that can cause great harm to the living. Chimbu stories are replete with accounts of deceiving ghosts.

See also Daribi, Gururumba, Melpa, Siane

Bibliography

Bergmann, W. (1971). *The Kamanuku.* 4 vols. Mutdapilly, Australia: The Author.

Brookfield, Harold, and Paula Brown (1963). *Struggle for Land: Agriculture and Group Territories among the Chimbu of the New Guinea Highlands.* Melbourne: Oxford University Press.

Brown, Paula (1972). *The Chimbu: A Study of Change in the New Guinea Highlands.* Cambridge, Mass.: Schenkman.

Nilles, J. (1943–1944; 1944–1945). "Natives of the Bismarck Mountains, New Guinea." *Oceania* 14:104–123; 15:1–18.

Nilles, J. (1950–1951). "The Kuman of the Chimbu Region, Central Highlands, New Guinea." *Oceania* 21:25–65.

Nilles, J. (1953–1954). "The Kuman People: A Study of Cultural Change in a Primitive Society in the Central Highlands of New Guinea." *Oceania* 24:1–27; 119–131.

Ross, J. (1965). "The Puberty Ceremony of the Chimbu Girl in the Eastern Highlands of New Guinea." *Anthropos* 60:423–432.

KARL RAMBO AND PAULA BROWN

Choiseul Island

ETHNONYMS: Lauru, Rauru

Orientation

Identification. Choiseul Island is the northwesternmost island in the Solomon Islands chain of the western South Pacific, lying between Bougainville Island and Papua New Guinea to the west, Santa Isabel to the east, and Vella Lavella and New Georgia to the south, all of which are 40 to 80 kilometers distant.

Location. Choiseul covers an area of 2,100 square kilometers, is about 130 kilometers long and 12.8 to 32.2 kilometers across, and is generally a mass of deep valleys and sharp, jungle-clad ridges, mostly between 243 to 606 meters in elevation (maximum elevation 160 meters). Average daytime coastal temperature is 26° to 32° C, and rainfall averages 254 to 508 centimeters per year.

Demography. In 1956 the native Melanesian population was about 5,700; in the early 1980s it was estimated to be 7,900. It seems to be growing rapidly because of decreased infant mortality and increased longevity, both attributable to improved health care.

Linguistic Affiliation. The peoples of Choiseul speak four different Melanesian languages, all more similar to one another than to those spoken on adjacent islands. Dialectal variation is small except for the central-eastern language, which has the most speakers and the widest distribution. Ultimately, the languages of Choiseul, of Santa Isabel, and of New Georgia and its neighbors form one set that is related most closely to the languages of Bougainville and, through them, to the languages of the Central and Southern Solomons.

History and Cultural Relations

No archaeological work has been done on Choiseul, but based on the linguistic variation, it has been estimated that the island has been occupied for about 3,500 years. It was sighted by European explorers in 1568 and in 1768 but it was not until the late 1800s that the people had significant contact with persons other than the inhabitants of the neighboring islands, and their interactions with the latter were typically hostile and violent. A major effect of contact with the outside world was uneven access to firearms, and that development increased the deadliness of the intergroup conflict that was endemic on and between the islands of the Western Solomons. Choiseul and other islands were transferred from the German to the British colonial sphere in 1899. Christian missionaries then began to work the area, and they found its peoples ready and more or less willing to be pacified and Christianized. On Choiseul, intergroup warfare continued here and there into the 1920s, but well before the beginning of World War II the island was fully pacified and Christianized (in different areas by Methodists, Catholics, and Seventh-Day Adventists). Other forms of European penetration such as coconut plantations have been very limited and sporadic. Few Japanese or Allied troops set foot on Choiseul, so it was only indirectly affected by the World War II. The Solomons became an independent nation in 1978, but that had little effect on Choiseul, which remains isolated and severely underdeveloped.

Settlements

Prior to pacification and Christianization, the bulk of the population lived inland on ridge tops, either in compact and sometimes fortified villages of up to fifty houses, or in small hamlets of a few houses each located closer to gardens. Large canoes and canoe houses were hidden in the coastal flats, which were too vulnerable to attack for permanent residence. The government and missions encouraged compact settlement on the coastal flats where health and educational services could be provided; by the beginning of World War II few inland villages remained, and today there are none. Most villages are now rows of houses strung out along a flat of coastline and flanked with the coconut plantations owned and worked by some inhabitants. Houses, now as before, are made from palm and vine materials; most families now maintain a sleeping house (which may feature prestigious corrugated-iron roofing) raised off the sandy surface by stilts 1.2 to 1.5 meters high; behind it there is usually an on-the-ground cookhouse in which older people sleep to keep warm. Most villages have a houselike church that is used also as a school, and some have a dispensary stocked with minor medical supplies.

Economy

Subsistence and Commercial Activities. Prior to colonization, subsistence was mainly by shifting, slash-and-burn horticulture; the principal food crops were taro, yams, and bananas. Also seasonally and ritually important was the *ngari* nut or *Canarium* almond, groves of which were privately owned. Meat sources included opossums and wild pigs; some domestic pigs were kept for ceremonial feasts. Sea fishing was not a major source of food, and the Choiseulese do not think of themselves as a sea people but as a bush people who now happen to live on the beach. Because there is a blight that attacks most forms of taro, the principal food (introduced by the missions) is now the sweet potato; it is supplemented by white rice acquired from Chinese traders and, again, by bananas, papayas, and wild but edible flora and fauna. Aside from working off the island as wage laborers, which only young men do, the only source of cash income is the sale of copra to Chinese traders. Ownership of coconut plantations is unevenly distributed and so also are cash incomes and desired commodities (tobacco, tea, pots and pans, tools, rice, tinned meat). The local economy is severely dependent on fluctuations in the world market for copra.

Industrial Arts and Trade. Ground stone and shell tools were replaced early on by metal axes and saws. A distinctive form of shell "money" known as *kesa* was attributed a mythical origin, but other shell rings and disks used as money or as ornaments were manufactured locally or were imported from the Roviana region to the south.

Division of Labor. Most domestic labor was and still is done by women and girls who do also much of the planting, weeding, and harvesting of the crops and the gathering of firewood. Men and boys do most of the work of preparing the land for planting, gather materials for houses, and occasionally hunt and fish. Men occupy all positions of public significance—village headman, preacher-teacher, officer of the local court.

Land Tenure. Ownership of land is by kin groups known as *sinangge,* but ownership of trees is by single persons. Because only flatter strips along the shoreline suitable for coconut plantations are really valuable and because such land is in very short supply, land-tenure disputes are common and difficult to settle.

Kinship

Kin Groups. The term sinangge (Varisi language) designates both the egocentric personal kindred and the cognatic stock consisting of all descendants of a married pair, whether through males or females. Named units of the latter kind, some seven to twelve generations in depth, are associated with large areas of land, some of it said to have been first cleared by the founding ancestor; in some instances that area is divided between different branches of the major sinangge. Any member of a sinangge—and each person is a member of more than one—has a right to use of some of its land for subsistence purposes but cannot alienate it from the group. Usually a subset of the members of such a cognatic stock reside together at some place on its land and form a cohesive political, economic, and ceremonial unit via common allegiance to a big-man leader; the local group centering on such a sinangge may include not only the spouses and relatives of spouses of sinangge members, but also long- or short-term visitors, some of whom (in the past) may have been enjoying the protection of its big-man or leader. In principle membership in the "little sinangge" is always open to members of its more inclusive sinangge, and any individual may freely choose to affiliate himself or herself with any local sinangge within any large sinangge of which he or she is a member. In practice, each local sinangge effectively controls who is allowed admission to its ranks; although it cannot admit to its ranks persons not descended from the relevant apical ancestor, it can exclude persons who are such descendants.

Descent. Descendants of a sinangge founder are divided into those related to him solely through men (i.e., his patrilineal descendants) and those related to him through at least one female tie (i.e., his nonpatrilineal descendants). This distinction is relevant only in internal affairs; it has no bearing on membership status per se.

Kinship Terminology. This system departs from being simply "generational" or Hawaiian-like only in having a distinct term for a mother's brother (not "father") and in designating a man's sister's child as "grandchild."

Marriage and Family

Marriage. Kin groups were and are neither exogamous nor endogamous in principle, and kinship beyond first- or second-cousin range is not a bar. The most prestigious form is via payment of bride-wealth in the form of kesa, in which case postmarital residence is in the community of the husband and his family. When bride-wealth is not given the husband is expected to reside with the bride and her natal family, and their offspring are expected to remain active members of the wife's little sinangge.

Domestic Unit. In the early years of marriage a couple usually resides in the same house as the parents of one of them. As they acquire children they expand into a house and gardens of their own, usually located in the same village; subsequent residence might be in virtually any village in which either spouse has kin, though there is of course a strong preference for residence with close kin such as parents or siblings.

Inheritance and Succession. Heritable forms of property includes kesa and groves of valuable trees, both of which devolve equally on a man's sons, though it seems likely that, in the case of a big-man, the eldest son or likely successor would attempt to acquire all the shell money. A big-man's eldest son was entitled to succeed him, but only if the son was an able leader.

Sociopolitical Organization

Political Organization. In the precolonial era law and politics were dominated by competition, and often violent conflict, between big-men who were at the centers of factions focused on their own little sinangge. These men were expected to protect their followers from external violence and to assist them in getting revenge or compensation; they sought military support from other big-men to whom they had to promise compensation in kesa presented ceremonially at a feast. A big-man's followers supported him in defensive and offensive action and by contributing to his ceremonial feasts.

Social Control. Aside from contractual relations established between big-men, and between big-men and some of their followers, the rights and duties of persons vis-à-vis one another were (and still are) mainly those entailed by kinship, and they were (and are) enforced mainly by expectations of reciprocity. Otherwise the only recourse was to self-help (in the extreme instance to take by stealth the life of the offending party) or to securing the aid or protection of a big-man.

Conflict. The precolonial history of Choiseul was dominated by violent conflict between big-men, or between contractual alliances of big-men, and their factions. This conflict often took the form of a group making a surprise attack at dawn on a village, burning its houses and killing all of its inhabitants who did not manage to escape. There was no taking of land or captives, though raiders from New Georgia to the south took heads for religious purposes.

Religion and Expressive Culture

Religious Beliefs. Present-day Choiseulese are all Christians and church services are a daily routine in all villages of sufficient size to have a resident preacher-teacher; the aboriginal religion has not been practiced (openly at least) for several decades. The aboriginal cosmology included various *bangara* or "gods" and "spirits" of the bush, some good, some evil, as well as ghosts of the dead. Some little sinangge kept shrines dedicated to particular gods or bangara and one member of the group regularly made offerings of food there in order to secure the god's blessings for the group; usually that god is reputed to have presented itself to the group. The ghosts of greatest significance and alleged power were those of former big-men; their sinangge might propitiate them but their influence for good or ill was not restricted to that group, and their kin who were not members of the group could propitiate them at that shrine. Anyone could maintain a shrine for and give offerings of food to recently deceased parents or grandparents.

Religious Practitioners. Some men were thought to have the special skill of being able to communicate with gods, spirits, or ghosts and to discern whether personal misfortune arose from sorcery or the displeasure of such a being.

Death and Afterlife. The corpse was usually disposed of by cremation, but in some areas interment and later exhumation of the bones were preferred. Ashes and bones were put in a clay pot and often placed in a shrine somewhere in the nearby forest or, in the case of a big-man, in a larger shrine maintained by the sinangge of which he was once the leader. The spirit of the deceased might remain around the village for a while and occasionally reveal itself (an ominous sign of dis-

satisfaction); but eventually it departed to the land of the dead, Ungana, somewhere high on Bougainville Island. Life there was much the same as among the living, though with little work and much happiness.
See also New Georgia

Bibliography

Bennett, Judith A. (1987). *Wealth of the Solomons: A History of a Pacific Archipelago, 1800–1978*. Honolulu: University of Hawaii Press.

Scheffler, Harold W. (1965). *Choiseul Island Social Structure*. Berkeley: University of California Press.

HAROLD W. SCHEFFLER

Cook Islands

ETHNONYMS: Cook Islanders, Cook Islands Maoris

Orientation

Identification. The Cook Islands is an independent state in an associated-state relationship with New Zealand. It has its own parliament and government and its own laws and judiciary, but defense matters and foreign policy should be handled, according to the relationship, in consultation with New Zealand. In practice the Cook Islands has taken radically different policies on some issues from New Zealand without consultation (e.g., New Zealand forbids visits by nuclear warships whereas the Cook Islands permits them), and the Cook Islands has its own minister and ministry of foreign affairs that operate independently of those of New Zealand. The designation "Cook Islanders" includes all persons tracing genetic ancestry to one (or more) of the twelve inhabited islands of the Cook group. This is not exclusive, however, as probably all Cook Islanders also have some non-Polynesian blood. Significant European genetic and cultural influence began about 150 years ago and has continued to the present. A relatively small African genetic but not cultural influence began not long after, but it ceased with the whaling industry in the last century. Chinese genetic influence occurred in the late nineteenth century, and a recent minor input of diverse Asian peoples is occurring. Residence within the Cook Islands is far from a necessary criterion for identity as about two-thirds of all people who consider themselves Cook Islanders live in New Zealand, Australia, or elsewhere overseas.

Location. The Cook Islands stretch from 156 to 167° W and 3 to 23° S. The total land area is only 240 square kilometers, but the sea area is nearly a thousand times larger, at 2.2 million square kilometers.

Demography. The 1986 resident population of the Cook Islands was 16,425. The population is static as the high natural growth rate is balanced by the rate of emigration to New Zealand and Australia, to both of which Cook Islanders have automatic right of entry. About 87 percent of the population live in the southern group, which are high islands, and the remainder in the northern atolls. Residents with no indigenous blood ties number in the several hundreds, most of whom are Europeans living on the capital island of Rarotonga.

Linguistic Affiliation. Each island, and in the case of Mangaia, each village had some minor linguistic differences from the others. In all cases except Pukapuka and Nassau, however, these were dialects of a basically common Eastern Polynesian Austronesian language, whose closest relatives are found in French Polynesia and New Zealand. The language of Pukapuka and Nassau is Western Polynesian, as is the culture. Today Cook Islands Maori is the language of government and the church, and all Cook Islanders learn English in school.

History and Cultural Relations

Almost every island culture has a unique origin or origins outside the Cook Islands. The only exceptions are Manihiki and Rakahanga, which trace a common origin from Rarotonga, and it is possible that the first of many migrations into Mangaia was also from Rarotonga. Rarotonga itself traces its earliest settlers to the Marquesas early in the Christian era, but these peoples were dominated by a migration perhaps 800 years ago from Raiatea in the Society Islands. A migration from Manu'a in Samoa, led by the defeated chief Tui Manu'a, had a significant but not dominant influence on Rarotongan history, though not on its culture. Later migrants from various islands of Polynesia were absorbed but seem not to have had any cultural impact. The other islands trace their origins mainly to the Society Islands, excepting Pukapuka's diverse origins from the west and occasional later incursions, such as that of Tongans to Mangaia long after settlement by Eastern Polynesians. It is also possible that Tongareva, the northernmost atoll, was settled very early by Western Polynesians, with Eastern Polynesian influence following later. Settlement by Europeans and others was never extensive, but it was very influential in bringing radical change to the religion, technology, economy, political system, and some values.

Settlements

Most Cook Islanders traditionally lived in hamlets (of perhaps fifty people) which were accessible to their agricultural lands. The London Missionary Society, beginning its work in the Cook Islands in 1821, persuaded the people to resettle in villages in groups of a few hundred or, in some cases, more than a thousand people. This policy soon coincided with commercial convenience, as the people came to value imported commodities and to export their own products, and with administrative convenience: initially that of their own chiefs, then from 1888 that of the British Protectorate, and from 1901 that of the New Zealand Dependency. On Rarotonga, due mainly to its greater size, the advent of motor vehicles (of which most families own at least one) has led in the past twenty years to resettlement in individual homes on the land being farmed.

Economy

Subsistence and Commercial Activities. Almost all Cook Islanders derive some sustenance from the land, lagoon, or ocean. But whereas these areas provided total sustenance in the past, they are now of relatively minor importance. Agriculture, formerly the main economic activity, now has a lesser role. Most households keep a few chickens, pigs, and/or goats for domestic consumption more than for sale. The main income today is from salaries, wages, or business profits. Government is the largest single employer, with about 21 percent of those aged 15–64 being its full-time salaried employees. If we add those in the casual employ of the central government and the permanent or casual employ of local government, and those who are still full-time students, more than one-third of working-age Cook Islanders are in government employ or education. The next-largest category is employed in the travel industry. Others work in the international finance center (now the largest in the Pacific islands), in clothing and shoe factories, for the churches, or in services. The highest incomes are those of the more successful business and professional people, of whom a considerable proportion are Europeans, but in comparison with most countries there are no major concentrations of wealth. A high proportion of assets is owned by the government (including the majority shareholding in the largest hotel). The small market and system of landholding facilitate distribution of assets and incomes.

Industrial Arts. Traditional arts are maintained mainly by women because fewer of them have salaried employment, the arts can be done at home, and there is both a domestic use for them and a commercial market (mainly to tourists or for export). These crafts are mainly items of fiber (mats, baskets, hats, etc.) or cloth (especially embroidered quilts). Traditional men's industrial arts are now confined mainly to factories making wooden or shell items of traditional design for the tourist market. In every village there are men who maintain vehicle and small boat engines or who specialize in building construction.

Trade. Small stores, mainly locally owned, are found in every village; bakeries are also common. There is a small market for fresh produce in Rarotonga, but prices are high as turnover is small and most stores are overcapitalized (e.g., they own and operate their own vehicles despite low utilization). Most people produce some of their own food and both give and receive some from relatives and friends, as well as buying some privately. Small businesses are dominated by women. Medium-sized businesses are operated mainly by Cook Islanders or Europeans, though a number of them are run by Cook Islanders married to or in partnership with Europeans. The largest businesses, including the larger airlines, some of the larger hotels, and the banks, are generally owned overseas.

Division of Labor. The traditional division of labor is much modified, though deep-sea fishing and other marine employment is still almost exclusively male, as are construction and most forms of heavy labor. Senior management, both government and private, was exclusively male until recent years.

Land Tenure. Land cannot be bought or sold, except to the government for public purposes, and even leases are generally restricted to indigenous Cook Islanders or the small percentage of nonindigenous permanent residents. Traditionally land was held for practical purposes by small, localized kin groups, with succession mainly in the male line except in the event of no male issue, illegitimacy, uxorilocal residence, or adoption. From 1902 the Land Court has registered most land in the name of its "traditional" holders at the time of the court investigation, and it has allowed bilateral inheritance thereafter. With minimal use of provisions for consolidation and exchange, the average of three or four landholders originally registered per unit of land has now become dozens and in many cases hundreds. For housing or other intensive usage it is now usual for individuals to obtain a lease or "occupation right" from their co-owners. Thus while every Cook Islander is a landowner, the fraction of right that many of them hold is insignificant. If most of them did not live in other countries, there would be major problems of shortage and allocation. Political parties promise to reform the system but do not do so, because the public supports land-rights reform in theory but opposes it in practice, as individuals fear that they will be worse off after any change. Disputes within groups of owners in common are frequent.

Kinship

Kin Groups and Descent. Descent is now traced bilaterally with equal weight given to both sides. Every major kin group is now spread out not only over many of the Cook Islands but even more so throughout New Zealand, Australia, French Polynesia, and in many cases other countries. Interaction by mail, telephone, and personal messages on government-broadcast radio is reinforced by the sending of money and/or goods and relatively frequent visits, especially for weddings, funerals, laying of memorial stones, or family reunions. These reunions can involve 20–150 people coming together, often from several countries.

Kinship Terminology. A classificatory system, with Hawaiian-type cousin terms, is used. Seniority is generally indicated in the kinship terms.

Marriage and Family

Marriage. Since the acceptance of Christianity in the nineteenth century all marriage has been monogamous. In the past polygamy was theoretically allowed, but in practice it was only possible for those of outstanding rank or strength. Trial marriage has long been common. Arranged marriages no longer occur. Separation and divorce are relatively common, as is common-law marriage. Postmarital residence is neolocal as a matter of preference, but for convenience couples often reside with either set of parents-in-law until separate housing can be arranged.

Domestic Unit. The 1986 census showed an average of just under five persons per dwelling. The nuclear family is the preferred unit, but many children stay with relatives for higher schooling or as a result of illegitimacy or broken marriages. Grandparents usually like to have one grandchild live with them. These and other causes, including work transfers, lead to many short-term domestic arrangements.

Inheritance. Landownership rights are distributed equally among descendants, but leases and occupation rights are generally allocated to individuals on the basis of occupation, need, or personal preference. Other property is ideally shared equally among the children, but this is not practicable with consumer goods such as automobiles and refrigerators, which are allocated to individuals.

Socialization. Children are raised by the older members of the household they are in at the time. Infants are treated with great indulgence. Respect for others is highly valued. Christian teachings constitute a significant element of training.

Sociopolitical Organization

Social Organization. Traditionally each district of each island had its own hierarchy of rank titles, ideally based on male primogeniture, but today rank titles are equally often held by women. This structure still exists but its main significance is in relation to organizing meetings of landowners and ceremonial activities. Elective status, occupation, education, and wealth are today much more important organizing principles. The clergy are much respected and have relatively high levels of personal consumption. There is considerable social and geographical mobility and no clear social classes.

Political Organization. The central government, which provides a very extensive range of services, is comprised of a parliament of twenty-four members elected every five years. Parliament elects the prime minister from among its members, and he selects a cabinet of seven ministers to govern the country. Local government is by island and comprises a majority of elected members plus the *ariki* (highest-level chiefs) ex officio. These island councils derive almost all their funds from the central government and have limited powers and functions. There is a "House of Ariki" to which all ariki belong, but it usually meets only once a year and sometimes not for several years. Its functions are advisory and ceremonial, and it has almost no powers.

Social Control. At a formal level this is maintained by a central government police force, which has increased greatly in size in the last decade. But social control at the community level is maintained largely by the fact that in such small communities most people have a network of ties by blood, marriage, and common activities and by the high value given to compromise and the avoidance of direct conflict. Senior relatives and religious leaders also play a significant role in social control.

Conflict. Warfare was endemic on many islands until the establishment of Christian missions in the nineteenth century. But war was rare on some of the small islands. With the exception of three islands in close proximity (Atiu, Mauke, and Mitiaro), distances between islands were generally too great to allow interisland conflict. Since Christianity was adopted there has been no overt conflict. There is no army and the police force is unarmed.

Religion and Expressive Culture

Religious Beliefs. There are fourteen different Christian denominations active in the islands, with about seventy churches, or about one church per 250 people. The Baha'i faith, the only non-Christian faith with an organized community, has less than 1 percent of the population as members. There are a few Hindus and Muslims among the nonindigenous transient population. While the Christian God is paramount, the traditional deities are often referred to, often in jest but often not, and a compromise that allows a place for both is not uncommon, though not publicly acknowledged.

Religious Practitioners. Only the Cook Islands Christian Church (to which over 60 percent of the population belong) trains some of its ministers in the country, but it too sends most of them to New Zealand, Fiji, Australia, or the United States. All other denominations train their clergy in those countries. The clergy have a respected status and participate in all community activities of any significance. There are also some faith healers and dispensers of herbal and other remedies who use a combination of Christian and traditional pre-Christian techniques.

Ceremonies. Only the traditional Christian ceremonies are observed, though with some adaptations (e.g., the *nuku*, or pageants, at which dramatic performances are accompanied by feasting at the time of a Christian rite). Ritualized hair cutting ideally marks the puberty of selected boys, and involves substantial gift giving as well as feasting.

Arts. Tattooing was abandoned in the nineteenth century and has not been resumed. Secular expressive arts are highly developed, with literally dozens of dance troupes (all part-time and mostly unpaid) and dozens of composers of music and song in the tiny population.

Medicine. Government doctors, nurses, and hospitals are located on all of the larger islands but, particularly if their treatment is not successful, people often turn to traditional healers who use herbal and supernatural methods.

Death and Afterlife. Government regulations used to require burial within twenty-four hours of death owing to the hot climate and absence of preservation facilities. This rule curtailed the traditional death ceremonies, which otherwise would last for months. On the main island (Rarotonga), however, facilities for preservation now exist. This development is leading to a practice of holding the body until relatives from other countries arrive. As most Cook Islanders now live in other countries, it is also becoming increasingly common for bodies to be returned to the island of birth, together with accompanying relatives—another very expensive procedure. A year or more after the death it is customary to hold a major ceremony to lay the headstone over the grave. The stone is always purchased overseas at considerable cost, and relatives from several countries may attend the ceremony. Belief in the afterlife follows the Christian tradition.

See also Manihiki, Pukapuka, Tongareva

Bibliography

Baddeley, Josephine (1978). *Rarotongan Society: The Creation of Tradition.* Unpublished Ph.D. dissertation, University of Auckland.

Buck, Peter H. (1932). *Ethnology of Manihiki and Rakahanga.* Bernice P. Bishop Museum Bulletin no. 99. Honolulu.

Buck, Peter H. (1934). *Mangaian Society.* Bernice P. Bishop Museum Bulletin no. 122. Honolulu.

Crocombe, R. G. (1964). *Land Tenure in the Cook Islands.* Melbourne: Oxford University Press.

Rare, Raira (1967). *E Au Akonoanga na te Iti Tangata o te Kuki Airani.* Wellington, N.Z.: Government Printer.

RON CROCOMBE AND MARJORIE TUAINEKORE CROCOMBE

Dani

ETHNONYMS: Akhuni, Konda, Ndani, Pesegem

Orientation

Identification. Dani is a general term used by outsiders for peoples speaking closely related Papuan (Non-Austronesian) languages in the central highlands of Irian Jaya, Indonesia (formerly Netherlands New Guinea, West New Guinea, Irian Barat).

Location. The various Dani groups live in and around the Balim River, approximately 4° S, 138° to 139° E. The greatest concentration of Dani is in the Grand Valley of the Balim. To the north and west of the Grand Valley, in the upper Balim and adjacent drainage areas, live the Western Dani. This is generally a rugged, mountainous country, with a temperate climate. Because of the high altitude and the sheltering ranges, the Dani area is temperate and unaffected by monsoon cycles. In the Grand Valley, the mean range of temperature is from 26° C to 15° C. Rainfall in the Grand Valley is about 208 centimeters per year, but wet and dry periods occur irregularly. For all practical purposes, the Grand Valley Dani do not recognize any yearly seasonal cycles, nor do they shape their behavior around them.

Demography. The broad floor of the Grand Valley, at 1,500 meters, has about 50,000 people, or about half of the entire estimated Dani population. It is densely populated, one of several such broad valleys found across the central ranges of the island. The other Dani are scattered across the rough mountain terrain from about 900 meters to about 1,800 meters above sea level. The major concentration of non-Dani in the area is in Wamena, the Indonesian administrative center, a town of some 5,000 people at the southern end of the Grand Valley.

Linguistic Affiliation. The half-dozen languages and dialects of the Great Dani Family are related to other Non-Austronesian language families of the Irian Jaya Highlands Stock, which belongs to the Trans-New Guinea Phylum.

History and Cultural Relations

The western half of the island of New Guinea, where the Dani live, was part of the Netherlands East Indies until 1949. With the independence of the rest of Indonesia, the Dutch held on to Netherlands New Guinea until it was transferred to Indonesia in 1963 via a United Nations Temporary Executive Authority. It is now the Indonesian province of Irian Jaya. Even as the Javanese component of the population is being increased through the resettlement program (*Transmigrasi*), a small Free Papua movement continues to demand independence from Indonesia. But neither the new settlements nor the insurgents have had any direct effect on the Dani. No archaeology has been done in the Dani area. Some Dani groups were contacted briefly by expeditions prior to World War II, but the first permanent outside settlements were established by Western Christian missionaries in the 1950s. By 1960, the Dutch government was carrying out its program of pacification and development in the Grand Valley. This has been continued and intensified by the Indonesian government since 1962.

Settlements

Dani compounds are scattered across the floor of the Grand Valley. The basic compound is one round men's house, a smaller round women's house, a rectangular common cook house, and a rectangular pig sty. The largest compounds may have up to half a dozen more women's houses. The structures are linked together by fences and open onto a common courtyard. Behind the houses, and enclosed by an outer fence, are casual household gardens. The houses are built of wood and thatched with grass. Compounds vary greatly in size. They may contain just a single nuclear family or many families and assorted others. A compound may stand by itself or it may be physically attached to several other compounds. The compound itself is a social unit, at least in terms of intensity of social interaction. These largest compound clusters may house well over 100 people, but they do not form social units. The population of the compound is fairly unstable, as people often move about from one place to another, usually in the same general area, for a variety of reasons. Although a few Dani now live at the government centers in houses with sawn-lumber walls and corrugated-zinc roofs, most settlements in the Grand Valley have changed little in forty years.

Economy

Subsistence and Commercial Activities. About 90 percent of the Dani diet is sweet potatoes. They are grown in the complex, ditched field systems surrounding the compounds. The men prepare the fields with fire-hardened digging sticks, and women do most of the planting, weeding, and harvesting. The ditch systems capture streams and run the water through the garden beds. In wet periods, the ditches drain off excess water. These gardens usually go through a fallow cycle, and when they are again cleared, the rich ditch mud is plastered on the garden beds. Dani living near the edges of the Grand Valley may also practice slash and burn horticulture on the flanking slopes. Because of the absence of marked growing seasons, the sweet potatoes are harvested daily throughout the year. In addition to sweet potatoes, Grand Valley Dani grow small amounts of taro, yams, sugar cane, bananas, cucumbers, a thick succulent grass, ginger, and tobacco. Pandanus, both the kind with brown nuts and the kind with red fruit, is harvested in the high forests, and now the trees are increasingly planted around the valley floor compounds. Although the Western Dani had adopted many Western fruits and vegetables, especially maize, before actual contact, the Grand Valley Dani are more conservative and even by the 1980s only minor amounts of a few Western foods were grown there. Domestic pigs are an important part of the Dani diet, as well as being major items in the exchanges at every ceremony. The pigs live on household garbage, and forage in forests and fallow gardens. Pigs are tempting targets for theft and so are a major cause of serious social conflict. The Grand Valley itself is so densely populated that little significant wildlife is available for hunting. A few men who live on the edge of the Valley keep dogs and hunt for tree kangaroos and the like in the flanking high forests. In the Grand Valley, there were no fish until the Dutch began to introduce them in the 1960s.

The only water creatures which the Dani ate were crayfish from the larger streams.

Industrial Arts. Until the 1960s, when metal tools were introduced by outsiders, the Grand Valley Dani tools were of stone, bone, pig tusk, wood, and bamboo. Ground ax and adz stones were traded in from quarries in the Western Dani region, and the Jale, or Eastern Dani, got their stones from even further east. Other tools were made locally. They made no pottery or bark cloth. Gourds were used for water containers and also for penis covers. String rolled from the inner bark of local bushes was used extensively to make carrying nets, women's skirts, and ornaments. Rattan torso armor for protection against arrows was made by Western Dani but the Grand Valley Dani neither made it nor traded for it. Spears and bows and arrows were the weapons of war. The arrows were unfletched, with notched, barbed, and dirtied (but not poisoned) tips. By the 1980s, cloth, metal axes, knives, and shovels, as well as the detritus of modern life—cast-off tin cans and plastic bottles—had partially replaced traditional Dani crafts.

Trade. Even before contact, various seashell types had been traded up from the coasts of the island into the entire Dani area. Ax stones and flat slate ceremonial stones, bird of paradise feathers, cassowary-feather whisks, and spear woods were traded into the Grand Valley in exchange for pigs and salt produced from local brine pools.

Division of Labor. Gender and age are the major bases for division of labor. There are no full-time specialists; but there is some spare-time specialization. A few people are known as expert arrow makers or curers. Generally, men do the heavy work like tilling gardens or building houses, while women do the tedious work like planting, weeding, harvesting, and carrying thatch grass. Men weave the tight shell bands used in ceremonies, women make carrying nets, and both make string. Because of the very relaxed atmosphere between men and women, there is little activity totally hidden from either sex.

Land Tenure. Quite informal usage rights are the rule. Although there is little or no population pressure in the Grand Valley, the extensively ditched sweet potato gardens on the broad valley floor do represent quite a considerable labor investment, but even so, rights are casually and informally transferred. Large garden areas are usually farmed by men of a single sib or a single neighborhood. Fields are controlled by men, not women.

Kinship

Kin Groups and Descent. The Grand Valley Dani have exogamous patrilineal moieties and exogamous patrilineal sibs. Some sib names can be found also in groups outside the Grand Valley and there are hints, perhaps remnants, of a moiety system in Western Dani. In the Grand Valley, people are born into the sib of their father, but at birth all Grand Valley Dani are considered to be of the *wida* moiety. Before marriage, those whose fathers are of the *waiya* moiety "become waiya," the boys through an initiation ceremony, the girls without ceremony. The chief function of the moieties is to regulate marriage. Sibs are associated with one or the other moiety, never both. There are sib-specific bird totems and food taboos. Local segments of sibs keep their sacred objects in common, store them in the men's house of the most important man, and hold renewal ceremonies for these objects. Grand Valley Dani are not much concerned with tracing genealogy. Common sib membership is assumed to mean common ancestry, but people rarely know their ancestors more than a couple of generations back.

Kinship Terminology. The Dani have Omaha-type kinship terminology.

Marriage and Family

Marriage. Weddings take place only at the time of the great pig feast, which is held in an alliance area every four to six years. Moiety exogamy is invariably observed. Marriages tend to take place between neighbors, if not within a neighborhood at least within a confederation. Some marriages are arranged by the families, while others are love matches arranged by the individuals. Marriage begins a series of relatively equal exchanges between the two families, which continues for a generation, through the initiation and marriage of the resulting children. These exchanges consist of pigs, cowrie shell bands, and sacred slate stones. Immediate postmarital residence is patrilocal, although within a few years the couple is likely to be living neolocally within the neighborhood or confederation where both sets of parents live. Divorce is fairly easy, but long-term separation is more common. At early stages of tension, the wife, or the junior wife, moves out to another relative's compound for a time. Nearly half the men are involved in polygynous marriages. The Grand Valley Dani have remarkably little interest in sexuality. A postpartum sexual abstinence period of around five years is generally observed by both parents of a child. The minority of men who are involved in polygynous marriages may have sexual access to another wife, but for most men and all women there are no alternative outlets nor any apparent increased level of stress for those subject to the abstinence. Ritual homosexuality is absent. This extraordinarily long postpartum sexual abstinence has not been reported among the Western Dani.

Domestic Unit. It is easy to identify both nuclear families and extended families, but these units are usually less important than the compound group as a whole.

Inheritance. There is little real property to inherit. As boys grow up they join with their fathers in maintaining the sacred objects held by the local patrilineal sib segment. In a more general sense, sons—and to some extent daughters—of the wealthier and more powerful men benefit from their father's position.

Socialization. Child rearing is very permissive. Toilet training is casual. Children are rarely, if ever, physically disciplined and even verbal admonishment is rare. There is almost no overt instruction. Children learn by participating but not by asking questions. Since the late 1960s, government-sponsored schools, usually run by missionaries, have been teaching more and more Dani children to read and write in Indonesian.

Sociopolitical Organization

Social Organization. In the Grand Valley the largest territorial sociopolitical unit is the alliance, with several thousand people. Warfare and the great pig feast are organized at the alliance level. Each alliance is composed of several confederations, which are also territorial units containing from several hundred up to a thousand people. Confederations are usually named for the two sibs with the strongest representation. Many ceremonies, and the individual battles that constitute warfare, are organized on a confederation level, initiated by the confederation-level leaders. Within the confederation territory there are usually recognizable neighborhoods, but these are not true, functioning social units. Contiguous clusters of compounds, also making up physical units, are not social units. Each individual compound, although lacking formal organization, is the venue of the most intense social interaction. Moieties and sibs are nonterritorial, unilinear descent groups which crosscut the territorial units. The two moieties, being exogamous, are represented in every compound. A couple of dozen sibs may be represented in a confederation, even though it is dominated by members of only a few sibs. In Dani areas outside the Grand Valley, the confederation is the largest unit and alliances are absent.

Political Organization. Dani leadership is relatively informal, vested in nonhereditary "big-men" (that term is used in Dani). The leaders of the confederation and the alliance are well known, but they are not marked by special attire or other artifacts. They are men of influence, not power, and they emerge as leaders through consensus. Leaders take responsibility for major ceremonies and for initiating particular battles. The leader of the alliance announces the great pig feast and directs the final alliance-wide memorial ritual. Leaders are believed to have unusually strong supernatural powers.

Social Control. Grand Valley Dani have no formal judicial institutions, but leaders, using their influence, can resolve disputes up to the confederation level, assessing compensation for pig theft and the like. But beyond the confederation, even within a single alliance, disputes often go unresolved because rarely does anyone's influence extend across confederation boundaries. Norms were not expressed in explicit formal statements. Now the Indonesian police and army have taken over dispute settlement.

Conflict. Until the early 1960s, interalliance warfare was endemic in the Grand Valley. Each alliance was at war with one or more of its neighbors. Wars broke out when the accumulation of unresolved disputes became too great. A war could last for a decade. Then, as the original grievances began to be forgotten, fighting would slack off. At that point an alliance that had built up unresolved interconfederation grievances could split apart, resulting in re-formation of alliances and ties, whether of war or of peace, between alliances. The confederation itself remained relatively stable, but alliance groupings shifted. It was the ritual phase of war that lasted for years. Once begun, it was fueled by the belief that ghosts of the killed demanded revenge. Since both sides were Dani, with virtually the same culture, and the same ghost beliefs, the killing went on, back and forth. In the ritual phase of war, formal battles alternated with surprise raids and ambushes at the rate of about one incident every couple of weeks. Battles might bring 1,000 armed men together for a few hours on a battleground. A raid might be carried out by a handful of men slipping across no-man's-land hoping to kill an unsuspecting enemy. But a war would begin with a brief, secular outburst that had no connection with unplacated ghosts. Some confederations in an alliance would turn against their supposed allies and make a surprise attack on villages, killing men, women, and children indiscriminately. The alliance would be broken apart, and both sides would withdraw from a kilometer-wide area, which would become a fallow no-man's-land on which the periodic battles of the ritual phase of war would be fought. By the mid-1960s, the Dutch and then the Indonesians were able to abolish formal battles of the ritual phase of war, but sporadic raids and skirmishes continue in isolated parts of the Grand Valley.

Religion and Expressive Culture

Religious Beliefs. The Grand Valley Dani explain most of their ritual as placating the restless ghosts of their own recent dead. These ghosts are potentially dangerous and cause misfortune, illness, and death. Thus, attempts are made to keep them far off in the forest. Dani also believe in local land and water spirits. In the 1950s, the Western Dani region experienced nativistic cargo cult–like movements that swept ahead of the Christian missionary advance. But these movements had no effect on the more conservative Grand Valley Dani. Now, in the 1990s, many Dani—Grand Valley as well as others—are practicing Christians. Islam, the majority religion of the larger nation, was not able to cope with Dani pigs and has had little success there.

Religious Practitioners. Various people, mainly men, are known for their magical curing powers. Ritual as well as secular power is combined in the leaders at various levels. Leaders of alliances seem often to have exceptionally strong and even unique powers.

Ceremonies. During the time of war, ceremonies were frequent. Battles themselves could be seen as ceremonies directed at placating the ghosts. There were also ceremonies celebrating the death of an enemy or funerals for people killed by the enemy. At the cremation ceremony for someone killed in battle, one or two fingers of several girls would be chopped off as sacrifices to the ghost of the dead person. Men might occasionally chop off their own fingers or cut off the tips of their ears, but these actions were signs of personal sacrifice and mourning. Funeral ceremonies as well as wedding ceremonies continued at intervals after the main event. Both were concluded in the great pig feast held every four to six years, in which the entire alliance participated.

Arts. The Grand Valley Dani have practically no art beyond decorations on arrow points and personal ornaments of furs, feathers, and shells. Formal oratory was not important, but casual storytelling was a well-developed skill.

Medicine. The Grand Valley Dani have no internal medicine, but they do rub rough leaves on the forehead to relieve headaches. For serious battle wounds, they draw blood from chest and arms. Until the recent introduction of malaria and venereal diseases they were quite healthy.

Death and Afterlife. The Grand Valley Dani conceive of a soullike substance, *edai-egen* or "seeds of singing," which is seen throbbing below the sternum. It is considered to be fully developed by about two years of age. Serious sickness or wounds can cause it to retreat towards the backbone, whence it is recalled by heat and by curing ceremonies. At death, this feature becomes a *mogat*, or ghost, and it must be induced to go off into the forest where it cannot harm the living. Death itself is considered to be caused by magic or witchcraft but, although witches are known, there is no particular fear of them in the Grand Valley. Similar patterns of witchcraft belief occur among the Western Dani, but there witches are lynched.

Bibliography

Broekhuijse, J. Th. (1967). *De Wiligiman-Dani.* Tilburgh: H. Gianotten.

Gardner, Robert (1963). *Dead Birds.* Film. Produced by the Film Study Center, Harvard University. New York: Phoenix Films.

Heider, Karl G. (1990). *Grand Valley Dani: Peaceful Warriors.* 2nd ed. New York: Holt, Rinehart & Winston.

Larson, Gordon Frederick (1987). "The Structure and Demography of the Cycle of Warfare among the Ilaga Dani of Irian Jaya." Ph.D. dissertation, Department of Anthropology, University of Michigan Ann Arbor.

Matthiessen, Peter (1962). *Under the Mountain Wall: a Chronicle of Two Seasons in the Stone Age.* New York: Viking.

O'Brien, Denise, and Anton Ploeg (1964). "Acculturation Movements among the Western Dani." *American Anthropologist,* 66 no. 4, pt. 2:281–292.

Stap, P. A. M. van der (1966). *Outline of Dani Morphology.* Verhandelingen van het Koninklijk Instituut voor Taal-, Land- en Volkenkunde, vol. 48. The Hague: Martinus Nijhoff.

KARL G. HEIDER

Daribi

ETHNONYMS: Dadibi, Karimui, Mikaru

Orientation

Identification. "Daribi" is the name for a people of Papua New Guinea who speak a single language with little or no dialect differentiation. Among themselves they make a distinction between the Daribi of Mount Karimui (Migaru or Korobo) and those of Mount Suaru. The Karimui Daribi distinguish between the *kuai bidi,* inhabitants of the volcanic plateau, and the *buru aze bidi,* limestone-country people.

Location. Daribi occupy the volcanic plateaus of Mount Karimui and Mount Suaru and the area of limestone ridges to the west of Karimui in the south of the Simbu (Chimbu) Province, adjacent to the Gulf and Southern Highlands provinces at about 6° 30' S and 144° 30' to 144° 45' E. Human habitation averages between 900 and 1,050 meters above sea level, with some subsistence activity at higher and lower elevations. Except where broken by gardening and second growth, the area is covered by tall, midmontane rain forest and is drained by the Tua River, a main tributary of the Purari. Most rainfall occurs during the season of the South Asian monsoon (November–April); the rest of the year is drier, and overnight temperatures in June are often quite chilly.

Demography. Although the earliest census figures are unreliable, it would be realistic to estimate an increase from between 3,000 and 4,000 Daribi at the time of pacification (1961–1962) to more than 6,000 at present. This increase was largely the result of the suppression of malaria, which was endemic to the region before that time.

Linguistic Affiliation. The Daribi language is classified as a member of the Teberan stock-level Family of languages, which includes only one other language, Polopa, spoken by a neighboring people to the southwest. The Teberan is a family of the Teberan-Pawaian Super-Stock, which includes as well the Pawaian language, a large number of whose speakers also reside at Karimui. Most Pawaian speakers at Karimui are bilingual with Daribi; however, very few Daribi speak Pawaian.

History and Cultural Relations

According to their own ethnohistorical tradition, the Daribi lived originally near Mount Ialibu, in the southern highlands, and then moved eastward, inhabiting the deep valley of the Tua River to the west of Mount Karimui. During this time their staple food was sago, and they took advantage of the large limestone caverns there for shelter. They intermarried with the Pawaian people living at the base of Mount Karimui, eventually moving up onto the plateau. Many of the Daribi phratries trace their origins to Daribi-Pawaian marriages made at that time. Those Pawaian groups that were not assimilated by the Daribi were driven eastward ahead of the expanding population to the valleys of the Sena and Pio rivers, where they now reside. The Daribi seem to have been "pursued" by intermarrying Wiru peoples from the southern highlands in the same fashion as they drove the Pawaians, for several Wiru clans took up residence in the extreme west of the settled region at Karimui, and were driven back to the Wiru area late in the nineteenth century after a period of sorcery accusations and internecine warfare. These movements, and certainly the ability to settle inland, away from the rivers, seem to have been involved with the introduction of sweet potatoes as a staple crop. Daribi had their first non-Melanesian contacts with the explorers Leahy and Dwyer in 1930 and Champion in 1936, and they were pacified in 1961–1962, when an airstrip, patrol post, and Lutheran mission station were built at Karimui. Daribi were incorporated in the newly formed Chimbu District (Simbu Province) in 1966.

Settlements

Traditionally a small extended family, polygynous or based on a group of brothers, occupied a single-story longhouse in the center of a cleared swidden. The house was divided front-to-back into respective men's and women's quarters. Other, related families occupied similar quarters nearby. In times of warfare or uncertainty a number of such families or a lineage or small clan of up to sixty people would occupy a two-story longhouse (*sigibe'*), with the men's quarters in the upper story for defensive advantage and the women's quarters below. Since administrative control was established, residence in nucleated villages or hamlets has been the norm. Small extended or nuclear families occupy single-story longhouses facing the road in parallel rows, usually with a small yard or garden area surrounding each one.

Economy

Subsistence and Commercial Activities. In traditional as in present times, most significant production and consumption is centered on the family, with its sexual division of labor. Subsistence is based on bush fallowing, or swidden horticulture, with sweet potatoes as the staple crop. Sago is grown to supplement this in low-lying regions, and other important crops include bananas, pandanus, maize, yams, dry taro, *pitpit,* sugarcane, and sweet manioc. Tobacco is grown for home consumption as well as trade, but its earlier importance as a cash crop has been supplanted by cardamoms, grown extensively for commercial export. Pigs are raised for purposes of exchange, nurtured by women when small and then permitted to forage for themselves in the bush. Some chickens are also kept, as well as cattle to a limited extent. Hunting and foraging remain substantial contributors to general subsistence; the favored quarry is wild pigs and marsupials, and bush-fowl eggs, sago grubs, and a wide variety of mushrooms are major forage items. Limited amounts of fish and crayfish are obtained by damming streams.

Industrial Arts. Dugout canoes, wooden bowls, body shields, and bows were produced from hewn wood, whereas fences, rafts, houses, cane bridges, and arrows were constructed from raw forest materials. Traditional industry also included the crafting of bamboo pipes and musical instruments from bamboo and the production of bark cloth.

Trade. Tobacco is grown, cured over the domestic fires of the longhouse, and twisted into large, spindle-shaped packets to be used as the principal trade item. It is traded for decorative bird plumage with peoples living in more heavily forested areas. Before contact tobacco and plumage were traded, together with extracted pandanus oil, for salt, ax blades, and, later, pearl shells with South Chimbu peoples. Presently the feathers are exchanged for cash. Prior to extensive contact with Highland peoples, Daribi traded with the Polopa of the Erave River and the Wiru of Pangia.

Division of Labor. The basic division of labor is sexual and orientational: men work with vegetation above ground level, including the felling and cutting of trees, planting and tending tree crops, and construction of houses, fences, other external structures, and tools. Men also hunt, supervise animal husbandry, slaughter, butcher, and prepare meats. Women work with vegetation at or below ground level, clear brushwood, plant, weed, and harvest ground crops.

Land Tenure. Named tracts of land, bounded in most cases by watercourses or other natural features, are traditionally held in common by members of a clan or exogamous lineage group. Male members and their wives are permitted to use whatever land they wish within a tract for gardening, dwelling, or other productive purposes, provided only that it is not being used by someone else. Plants or tree crops, however, regardless of where they may be located, belong exclusively to the person who has planted them.

Kinship

Kin Groups and Descent. A Daribi child should, as a matter of moral principle, be recruited to its father's clan through payments (*pagehaie,* or, colloquially, "head" payments) made to a representative of its mother's line, usually the maternal uncle (*pagebidi*). Should the payments not be given, the maternal line has the right (not necessarily exercised) of claiming the child. The clan, which holds in common the wealth through which these payments are made, is thus ideally patrilineal. Clans are composed of *zibi,* minimally the sibling set that "becomes a group of brothers after the sisters marry out." Clans are grouped into phratries, tracing descent from a named male ancestor.

Kinship Terminology. A terminology of the Iroquois type is used with respect to consanguineals in one's own and ascending generations, whereas a Hawaiian-type terminology is used with respect to those in descending generations.

Marriage and Family

Marriage. Daribi traditionally betrothed girls from an early age, often infancy, and tried to betroth them to wealthy or prestigious men if possible. The people were traditionally highly polygynous; women were married at puberty, whereas men, who had to assemble a bride-price, normally married about ten years afterward. This imbalance in age permitted most men to be polygynous at middle age, and marriage to sisters or other close relatives of an earlier wife was encouraged. Daribi state summarily that they marry among those with whom they do not "eat meat" or share wealth. This makes the clan, which likewise shares in contributing meat and wealth to recruitment of its members, something of a "holding company" for wives. A woman's close relatives in her natal clan are called her *pagebidi,* and, as in the case of her offspring, her membership must be redeemed from them. In statistical terms, fully half of all marriages at any given time are the result of a transference of the betrothed or married woman to someone other than the originally intended spouse. Divorce often involves nothing more than a transference among men in a woman's clan of marriage; this transference is also the most common consequence of widowhood. Postmarital residence is virilocal by normative preference, though there are exceptions.

Domestic Unit. The domestic unit, or household, is determined more strongly by division of labor than by marriage, though a marital household is the norm. For example, a separate household was often formed (with its own building) of all the unmarried youths and widows past childbearing age in a community, so they might cooperate in gardening.

Inheritance. Since a person's pigs and wealth, including money, are most often dispersed in kin payments at death, inheritance frequently comes down to the right to share in clan lands and wealth. The garden of a deceased person goes to the surviving spouse or gardening partner; rights in bearing trees are inherited patrilineally.

Socialization. A child is not punished for its acts before it is felt to be rational, that is, before it "has a soul" and can speak. Male children are socialized by peers and by participation in male activities, female children through their involvement in women's gardening and child-rearing work.

Sociopolitical Organization

Social Organization. Collective activities, meetings and arbitration, work groups, and warfare and vengeance undertakings have in the past served as active foci for lineal, factional, and coresidential groupings. Often, but not necessarily, such task groupings coincide with the clan or even a coresidential clustering of clans. Before the institution of centralized administrative control, cooperative parties of men organized themselves in this way to clear large tracts of land for gardening or for military action. Influential men, often the eldest of a group of brothers, take the initiative in planning and supervising collective tasks, more through the exhorting of others than actual direction. Kin relationship is often the strongest or most consistent single factor in the galvanizing of these activities, though it is by no means the only one.

Political Organization. A coresidential grouping of the dimensions of a clan or village predictably divides, at any given time, into two opposed factions, roughly along the lines of kin affiliation or affinity. The men of a faction are the *hana,* followers and supporters of a big-man or significant leader (*genuaibidi*). Such leaders would often bid for the patronage of younger men by transferring betrothals to them or by feeding them with the surplus meals received each day from their pluralities of wives.

Social Control. Body-substance sorcery (*animani*) and secret murder through sorcery assassination (*keberebidi*) were often resorted to for vengeance; perhaps the threat of these actions helped to ensure social compliance. Certainly the most effective instrument of social control is "talk," that is, public approval and disapproval, an organ of consensual enforcement that has been amplified by the village-court system.

Conflict. Bouts of hysterical public anger, often escalating into factional confrontations, mark the stresses and strains of ordinary village life. If aggravated over a long period they may lead to residential splitting along factional lines. "Third parties," either leaders or adjacent groups, will often try to mediate these fights. Traditional warfare took the form of ambushes, skirmishes along boundaries, sieges, and occasional massacres by organized groupings of clans acting in concert.

Religion and Expressive Culture

Religious Beliefs. Whether or not they believe in them, and incidental to any profession of a religious faith, Daribi fear the displeasure, attack, or possession of ghosts (*izibidi*) and, perhaps less frequently, of "place spirits"—local beings dwelling beneath the ground, in ravines, or in trees. Ghosts, most likely those of friends or relatives, are thought to take action against those who betray them, and place spirits against those who violate their habitations.

Religious Practitioners. Traditional Daribi religious practitioners include spirit mediums, defined as "ill" because they have an insecure relation to possessing ghosts, and shamans (*sogoyezibidi*), who have "died" and attained a complete rapport with their spirits. Since most forms of mental and physical illness traditionally were considered to be effects of spirit possession, shamans functioned as effective curers and charged for their services even in precontact times. The large majority of both kinds of practitioners are women.

Ceremonies. The major traditional rite is the *habu,* performed to "bring back to the house" the ghost of someone who has died unmourned in the bush. In the habu, young men are "possessed" by the alienated ghost and spend weeks in the forest hunting animals and smoking the meat. When they return to the house they bring the ghost "on their skins," and it must be dislodged by wrestling with the "house people," after which the meat is blamed for the ghost's hostility and consumed as a mortuary feast. Other rites include those of marriage, initiation, and the pig feast, introduced from the highlands.

Arts. Depictive incision on arrow shafts and other implements is practiced. Daribi express themselves musically with the flute, the Jew's harp, and mourning laments. Storytelling (*namu pusabo*) is the best-developed artistic medium, along with lyric poetry.

Medicine. In addition to shamanic curers, traditional medicine included herbal remedies and a surgical practitioner (*bidi egabo bidi*) who removed arrows through a skilled knowledge of body movements.

Death and Afterlife. Traditional Daribi admitted human mortality but denied death through natural causes. The dead are believed to survive as ghosts who communicate with the living through spirit mediums and shamans and who travel, usually at night, along watercourses. They live together at an ill-defined place to the west, possibly in a lake.

See also Chimbu

Bibliography

Hide, Robin L., editor (1984). *South Simbu: Studies in Demography, Nutrition, and Subsistence.* Boroko, Papua New Guinea: Institute of Applied Social and Economic Research.

Hughes, Ian M. (1970). "Pigs, Sago, and Limestone." *Mankind* 7:272–278.

Wagner, Roy (1967). *The Curse of Souw.* Chicago: University of Chicago Press.

Wagner, Roy (1972). *Habu.* Chicago: University of Chicago Press.

Wagner, Roy (1978). *Lethal Speech.* Ithaca, N.Y.: Cornell University Press.

Weiner, James F., editor (1988). *Mountain Papuans.* Ann Arbor: University of Michigan Press.

ROY WAGNER

Dieri

ETHNONYMS: Dayerrie, Deerie, Diari, Dieyerie, Dieyrie, Diyeri, Dthee-eri, Koonarie, Kunari, Ti:ari, Urrominna, Wongkadieri, Wonkadieri

The Dieri are an Aboriginal hunting and gathering people of southern Australia's lakes region, who live on the Cooper River to the east of Lake Eyre. Their present territory is located at 139° E and 28°20' S. Their kinship system is similar in many respects to that of the Aranda, but it differs on two significant counts. First, the Dieri use a single term for both father's mother and father's mother's brother on the one hand and for mother's brother's (or father's sister's) children on the other. Second, the Dieri lack the Arandic characteristic of applying a single term to both mother's mother and mother's brother and to the mother's brother's children. Instead, the Dieri class mother's mother's brother's son's children with direct siblings (i.e., with brothers and sisters). Within the Dieri system, marriage is preferred with the mother's mother's brother's daughter's daughter (i.e., the children of two women related to one another as cross cousins are the preferred marrying pair). Direct cross-cousin marriage, however, is considered unacceptable (though special circumstances have been invoked to void this prohibition). A male child inherits from his father a totemic relationship with a particular natural species of the area to which the father himself is attached by descent and usage. Within this area is a totemic center with which a totemic being (*mura-mura*) is associated—one of several culture heroes thought to have traveled from southwestern Queensland to the current Dieri territory. A boy learns the lore and rituals of this totemic center from his father and other elder males of his father's line. This patrilineal totemistic heritage is similar to that reported for peoples of the Western Desert region of Australia. Crosscutting this patrilineal totemic system is one that is derived matrilineally, which appears to serve primarily to establish wife-giver and wife-taker categories but which also involves food taboos and permits a male to participate in some rituals of his mother's brother's clan. Initiation is an ongoing process for young Dieri men, culminating in a ritual known as *wilyaru*, which involves scarification of the initiates.

See also Aranda

Bibliography

Elkin, A. P. "The Social Organization of South Australian Tribes." *Oceania* 2:44–73.

Radcliffe-Brown, A. R. (1930). "The Social Organization of Australian Tribes, Part I." *Oceania* 1:34–63.

Radcliffe-Brown, A. R. (1930). "The Social Organization of Australian Tribes, Part II." *Oceania* 1:322–341.

Dobu

ETHNONYM: Edugaura

Orientation

Identification. Dobu (Goulvain Island on the earliest maps) is a small island (3.2 by 4.8 kilometers), an extinct volcano. It is also the name of the language of its inhabitants and, more generally, of those speakers of the same language in neighboring areas. The anthropologist Bronislaw Malinowski described Dobuans as a "tribe," implying a linguistic, cultural, and even political entity, but this wider sense of "Dobuan" was largely a construct of the first missionaries.

Location. Dobu Island is situated in Dawson Strait (9.45° S and 150.50° E), which separates the large mountainous islands of Fergusson and Normanby in the D'Entrecasteaux Archipelago of Milne Bay Province, Papua New Guinea. Dobu speakers occupy southeastern Fergusson, northern Normanby, and the offshore islands of Dobu, Sanaroa, and Tewara. The natural vegetation is lowland rain forest, though much of the settled area is covered with secondary forest or grassland. The region is tropical with two main seasons: the southeasterly winds dominate the year (May to November), while the northwest monsoon (December to April) brings heavy squalls. Average annual rainfall is about 254 centimeters, but droughts are not infrequent.

Demography. At the last census (1980) there were about 10,000 people in the Dobu-speaking area. They are centered on the island of Dobu with a population today of about 900 (though missionary William Bromilow estimated there were 2,000 in 1891). The tiny island of Tewara, to the north of Dobu, had a population of only 40 when anthropologist Reo Fortune worked there in 1928. At that time the Dobuan population (along with many others in the Massim) had been reduced by a half.

Linguistic Affiliation. The Dobu language, comprising numerous local dialects, is one of forty or more Austronesian languages belonging to the so-called Milne Bay Family of the Massim. Dobu's closest affiliations are with other languages of the D'Entrecasteaux. The Edugaura dialect of Dobu Island was adopted as a lingua franca by the Wesleyan Mission and is spoken throughout the central Massim and beyond.

History and Cultural Relations

In the late nineteenth century, Dobuans (Edugaurans in particular) were reputed to be fierce warriors and notorious cannibals who terrorized many of their neighbors. Their trading relations with the islands of Fergusson, Amphletts, and Trobriands to the north, and with the peoples of Duau (Normanby Island) and Tubetube to the south, were conducted in parallel with local raiding enterprises. Contact history began in the mid-nineteenth century with brief visits by whalers and pearlers, and later, in 1884, by "blackbirders" who forcibly recruited a number of men and killed others. Dobu was visited in 1888 by Administrator Sir William MacGregor on his first official tour of the newly proclaimed British New Guinea, and in 1890 by the Reverend George Brown, secretary general of the Australasian Methodist church, who was seeking a headquarters for his mission. By this date copra traders had already settled in the area, steel tools and trade tobacco were in circulation, and European-introduced epidemic diseases were beginning to deplete the population. The arrival on 13 June 1891 of William Bromilow and his missionary party of sixty-three (which included thirty Polynesian evangelists) was probably the most consequential event of local history. Within a few years Bromilow claimed to have pacified the district, though it was more than forty years before the whole Dobu-speaking area was Christianized.

Settlements

The "district" of Dobu Island contained about twelve "localities" or village clusters, each of which was constituted of a number of small, dispersed villages with an average population of about twenty-five persons. A typical village contains a circle of houses that face inward to a central, stone-covered grave mound, in which matriclan members of the village are buried. Paths skirt the village rather than passing through it, and the village is surrounded by coconut, betel nut, and other fruit trees. Houses are rectangular, traditionally with a steeply pitched roof; they are built on piles with a small front verandah. Walls and roof are made of sago-leaf thatch.

Economy

Subsistence and Commercial Activities. Swidden horticulture is "the supreme occupation." The main crop is the yam and its cultivation dominates the Dobu calendar. People without their own yam strains are "beggars" and find it hard to marry. Other indigenous crops are bananas, taro, sago, and sugarcane. Sweet potatoes, manioc, pumpkins, maize, and other crops were introduced more recently. Fishing is an important subsistence activity, and in forested areas men hunt wild pigs, birds, cuscus, and other small game. Pigs, dogs, and chickens are kept for domestic use as well as for exchange. Since the earliest mission days, Dobuans have earned cash by making copra, but migrant labor on plantations and in gold mines was the most important source of money during the colonial era, and it became an essential rite of passage for young men. Today Dobuans abroad are to be found as clerks, public servants, businesspeople, physicians, and lawyers. The rural population continues to engage in subsistence horticulture with some cash cropping (mainly copra and cocoa). The area is served by several wharfs and two small airstrips.

Industrial Arts. Traditional technology was neolithic and typical of Melanesia. Obsidian and stone ax blades were imported, but most other tools and weapons (bamboo knives, black-palm spears, wooden fishhooks, digging sticks, etc.) were made locally, as were the seagoing canoes used on trading and raiding expeditions. Clay pots were imported from the Amphletts (more recently from Tubetube in the southern Massim), but coconut-leaf baskets, pandanus-leaf mats, and skirts were made by each householder. Craft specialization was rare, unless in canoe carving, net making, and the manufacture of arm shells. The most crucial specializations were magical.

Trade. The traditional ceremonial *kula* exchange (*kune* in Dobu), for which the Massim is ethnographically famous, continues today with many modifications. Dobu remains an important node in this vast interisland network of exchange partners through whose hands arm shells (*mwali*) circulate to the south and shell necklaces (*bagi*) to the north. Today, most kune voyaging is done by chartered motor launch instead of by canoe. This streamlines activities and obviates much of the traditional ritual; it also enables women to participate. Subsidiary, "utilitarian" trade is now negligible, though traditionally kune involved (in addition to shell ornaments) stone blades, obsidian, pottery, wooden bowls, pigs, sago, yams, betel nuts, face paint, lime gourds and spatulas, canoe hulls, and even human beings. Live captives could be redeemed by the payment of shell valuables, or they could be adopted by their captors to replace dead kin. Kune was thus intimately connected to warfare, marriage exchanges, and mortuary observances.

Division of Labor. The most crucial specializations were magical, and these had significant economic implications as, for instance, in the control of rain and the growth of crops and pigs, in maintaining the abundance of fish, and in curing diseases. A husband and wife cooperate in gardening but their separate inheritances of seed yams require separate plots. Gardens are cleared and planted communally, but after the village magicians have performed their rituals, the gardens are the private domains of men and their wives. Bush clearing is done by men and women together, the men cutting the heavier timber. Men fire the debris and later wield the digging stick; women insert and cover the yam seeds. Women weed and mound the plants as they grow; men cut stakes and train the yam vines to climb them. Women dig the harvest; men plant and tend banana patches. Both sexes fish and make sago; men cook on ceremonial occasions. Traditionally, only men traveled on kune expeditions, yet only old women were thought to possess the magic to control the winds.

Land Tenure. The use of gardens and village lands is governed by matrilineage membership. A man inherits land from his mother or mother's brother. A father may give some garden land (never village land) to his son, though after his father's death the son is prohibited from eating the produce of this land. Nowadays there is a tendency for fathers to transmit land bearing cash crops (especially coconuts) to their sons.

Kinship

Kin Groups and Descent. The most important unit of Dobu social organization is the three-generation matrilineage (*susu,* "breast milk"). Each susu claims descent in the female line from one of several mythical bird ancestors of which the commonest are Green Parrot, White Pigeon, Sea Eagle, and Crow. The susu of a village putatively belong to a single matriclan, descendants of the same totemic bird. The matriclans of a locality are randomly associated and dispersed throughout the Dobu-speaking area.

Kinship Terminology. Iroquois-type cousin terminology is used while a father is alive, but after his death, Crow-type cousin terms are used (since a sister's son succeeds to his mother's brother's kinship status), and the dead man's son calls his father's sister's son "father."

Marriage and Family

Marriage. Marriage is forbidden between the owning susu of a village and between cross cousins; thus villages are exogamous, though localities tend to be endogamous. Premarital sex is permitted and adolescent promiscuity is the norm, though the anthropologist Reo Fortune characterized Dobuans as prudish in speech and public behavior. A betrothed couple work hard for a year for their respective inlaws. Marriage is marked by a series of exchanges of cooked and uncooked food, pork, fish, and game between the contracting villages and by a gift of arm shells from the groom's to the bride's group. Intervillage exchanges also occur annually in the name of each married couple. Ideally, marriage exchanges balance in the long run. Monogamy was the norm and polygyny was practiced by only a few wealthy men (*esa'esa*). Dobu is renowned for the practice of bilocal residence in which a couple live alternately, for a year at a time, in the village of each spouse in turn. Affines show great respect to village owners, but friction between the owning susu and incoming spouses gives rise to quarreling, village "incest," and attempted suicide. Fortune regarded the practice of bilocal residence as a compromise between the demands of the susu and those of the conjugal unit, though he judged it more destructive of the latter. Divorce is very frequent in Dobu. Bromilow listed twenty-two reasons for divorce (including "filthy language"), but Fortune accounted the commonest cause to be "cut-and-run adultery" with a village "sister" or "brother." Affines are feared as likely witches and sorcerers. In the revised edition of his book Fortune offered another interpretation of bilocal residence, stating that it is associated with an annual exchange of yams for arm shells between resident susu wives and their nonresident husbands' sisters.

Domestic Unit. The household normally comprises a married couple and their young children. Adolescent girls remain with their parents until marriage, but at puberty boys go to sleep elsewhere, usually with the girls of neighboring villages. After a man's death his children are prohibited from entering his village.

Inheritance. Village land, fruit trees, and most garden lands are inherited matrilineally. The corpse and skull of a person belong to the susu, as do personal names. Canoes, fishing nets, stone blades, ornamental valuables, and other personal property also descend within the susu. Magic, however, can pass from a father to one of his sons (as well as to his rightful heir), a practice that Fortune regarded as "subversive" of the susu.

Socialization. Both parents rear young children, and they are usually strict. Children avoid harsh treatment by taking refuge with their mother's sister and her husband, who are indulgent. Between ages 5 and 8, a boy has his earlobes and nasal septum pierced by his father or mother's brother, and about this time he is given a small garden plot of his own, and he may even be taught fragments of magic. At age 10 he is no longer struck for punishment, lest he (imitating his father) break his mother's cooking pots or (imitating his mother) behave cruelly to his father's dog. Boys of this age learn to throw and dodge spears, and by the time they are 14 they have begun to learn love magic and to sleep with girls. Fortune says little about the socialization of young girls.

Sociopolitical Organization

Social and Political Organization. The village (*asa*) comprises between four and a dozen susu and is the most important social unit for the organization of marriage and mortuary exchanges. Between four and twenty villages form a named locality, which traditionally appears to have had a headman, probably one who had inherited much magic and was prominent in kune. The localities of a district (such as Dobu Island) were normally hostile to one another, though they sometimes combined for war making (and kune expeditions) under the leadership of a strong "war chief and standard bearer." Such was Bromilow's "friend" Guganumore, who had tallied eighty-six captives and whose position was reified in 1892 by his appointment as a government chief. Dobu society is essentially egalitarian, and it lacks the ideology of hereditary rank found in Kiriwina to the north. In 1961 the Dobu Local Government Council was proclaimed, and today the Dobu area forms the constituency of an elected member of the provincial government. A number of Dobuans have also stood for national parliament, and their kune networks have proved effective in electioneering.

Social Control. In the absence of adjudicating authorities, dispute settlement and the redress of wrongs were matters for self-help. Sanctions were social (shame, ridicule, admonishment), supernatural (especially witchcraft and sorcery), or based on reciprocal response (revenge killing, sorcery feud, attempted suicide). The threat of sorcery was an effective means of enforcing economic obligations. Public harangues by the village headman were effective in shaming delinquents. Fruit trees were protected from theft by charms (*tabu*) believed to cause disease or disfigurement. Many of these sanctions still operate, somewhat modified by Christian ethics. Modern Dobu is served by a magistrate's court, though it is one of the local government councillor's tasks to settle disputes at the village level.

Conflict. Fortune represented Dobu as a society permeated by jealousy and suspicion. At its troubled heart was the syndrome of susu solidarity, marital antagonism, bilocal residence, and the ubiquitous fear of witchcraft and sorcery. Warfare was endemic in the nineteenth century, and the locality was the war-making unit. Furtive raids rather than pitched battles were the norm. Intermarriage between enemies was rare, though captives were sometimes adopted.

Religion and Expressive Culture

Religious Beliefs. As the site of intensive missionary activity since 1891, the Dobu area is now thoroughly Christianized and village churches (run by local lay preachers) are an important focus of community life. Sundays and holy days of the Christian calendar are observed, and commemorative dates of the Dobu mission are celebrated (notably the anniversary of Bromilow's arrival), when gifts of money are made to the church. Many Dobuans have become ministers and are found in communities throughout the Massim. Elements of the traditional religion survive, however, and beliefs in magic, witchcraft, and sorcery remain pervasive. Yam gardening is still accompanied by rituals, taboos, and magical incantations; the dogma persists that yams are "persons" and must be treated properly lest they abandon their owner's garden for another. Every woman is a potential witch (*werebana*) and every man a potential sorcerer (*barau*); as such their spirits are most active during sleep. Immortal spirit beings, commemorated in myth, validate magical systems and explain the Dobu world of "contending magical forces." The most important are Kasabwaibwaileta (the hero of kune or kula); Tauhau (creator of the White man, his goods, and his epidemic diseases); Yarata (the northwest wind); and Bunelala (the first woman to plant yams). Others are less anthropomorphic, such as Nuakiekepaki, the moving rock-man who sinks canoes. Many supernaturals are exemplars whose secret names are invoked in the incantations used to control them. Yabowaine was another supernatural who "watched over" war, cannibalism, and kune. He was believed to form the fingers and toes of unborn children, and on account of this creative function the first missionaries appropriated his name for "God," thereby immeasurably inflating his traditional role.

Religious Practitioners. Although there are ritual specialists as well as renowned diviners, most men and women use magic of their own inheritance. The uses of magic in gardening, in love, and in kune are highly competitive: "The ladder of social ambition is that of successful magic," Fortune wrote. The social distribution of magic thus coincides with the distribution of wealth and power.

Ceremonies. The most important ceremonies are periodic exchanges and feasts associated with marriage and death.

Arts. A rich mythology contains many legends that validate magical spells. Decorative art of the pleasing curvilinear style typical of the Massim was largely confined to houses and canoes. The bamboo flute and Jew's harp were used in courtship, and dancing to hand drums accompanied feasting. Many of the dance songs translated by Fortune are remarkable for their pathos and poetic beauty.

Medicine. Illness is almost invariably attributed to sorcery, witchcraft, or the breach of taboo; curing involves the settlement of grievances. Ginger is the most common magical prophylactic and curing agent. Many other plants and herbs are used, but their pharmacological efficacy is doubtful.

Death and Afterlife. Death and mourning continue the cycle of affinal exchanges and feasts. The surviving spouse's village gives yams, arm shells, and a pig (previously, a human captive) to the village of the dead spouse, who is buried by his or her own susu. After a year the latter release the widow or widower from mourning, and following this rite he or she may never again enter the village of the deceased. Large feasts (*sagali*) are held periodically in honor of the collective dead of a village, at which pigs and yams are distributed to other localities. The spirits of the dead went to Bwebweso, an extinct volcano on Normanby Island ("Bwebweso" means "extinguished"). Its portals were guarded by Sinebomatu (Woman of the Northeast Wind) who exacted a payment of betel nuts from each new arrival. The diseased and the deformed were consigned to a swamp at the foot of Bwebweso. The spirits of those slain in war also had a separate afterworld.

See also Goodenough Island, Trobriand Islands

Bibliography

Bromilow, W. E. (1910). *Some Manners and Customs of the Dobuans of S. E. Papua.* Brisbane: Australasian Association for the Advancement of Science.

Bromilow, W. E. (1929). *Twenty Years among Primitive Papuans.* London: Hodder & Stoughton.

Fortune, Reo F. (1932). *Sorcerers of Dobu.* London: George Routledge & Sons. Rev. ed. 1963. New York: E. P. Dutton.

Young, Michael W. (1980). "A Tropology of the Dobu Mission." *Canberra Anthropology* 3:86–104.

MICHAEL W. YOUNG

Easter Island

ETHNONYMS: Isla de Pascua, Pito-O-Te Henua, Rapa Nui

Orientation

Identification. Easter Island, the easternmost island in Polynesia, was so named by Jacob Roggeveen who came upon it on Easter Sunday in 1722. Easter Islanders evidently never had a name of their own for the island. "Rapa Nui" (also Rapa-nui, Rapanui) came into use in the 1800s and eventually became the preferred name for Easter Island throughout Polynesia. The origin of Rapa Nui is unclear but the name was evidently given by people from another island, perhaps Rapa. In 1862 and 1863 Easter Island experienced a severe depopulation that led to the destruction of much of its traditional culture. Subsequent contact with Chile, which took possession of Easter Island in 1888, has produced a culture containing many elements borrowed from South America. Easter Island is currently a dependency of Chile.

Location. Easter Island is located at 27°8' S and 190°25' W, about 4,200 kilometers off the coast of Chile and 1,760 kilometers east of Pitcairn Island, the nearest inhabited island. It is a triangular-shape volcanic high island with a total area of 180 square kilometers. The most prominent physical features are the three volcanic peaks, each located at one corner of the island. The land is either barren rock or covered by grass or shrubs, although parts were heavily forested in the past. Only flocks of sea birds and the Polynesian rat were indigenous to the island, with chickens, dogs, pigs, sheep, and cattle introduced by people from other islands or Europeans. The climate is tropical. Water was obtained from springs and by collecting rainwater.

Demography. Population estimates by European explorers in the eighteenth and early nineteenth centuries ranged from 600 to 3,000, although none can be considered reliable. There are indications that the precontact population could have been as much as 10,000 people. From 1862 to 1871 severe depopulation resulted from the kidnapping of about 1,000 men by Peruvian slavers, a smallpox epidemic, and relocation to Mangareva and Tahiti. In 1872 reliable missionary reports indicated only 175 people on Easter Island. The population continued to decline until the late 1880s and then slowly increased to 456 in 1934. In 1981, there were about 1,900 Easter Islanders on Easter Island and others living in Chile, Tahiti, and the United States. Easter Islanders make up about two-thirds of the island population, with the others being mainly Chilean military personnel or government employees.

Linguistic Affiliation. Easter Islanders speak Rapa Nui (Pascuense), a Polynesian language that has been described as closely related to the languages spoken on Tahiti, Mangareva, and by the Maori in New Zealand. Since contact, words from French, English, and Spanish have been added to the lexicon. Because of the Chilean presence, many Easter Islanders also speak Spanish. There is debate over whether symbols found carved in wood boards called *rongorongo* are a precontact written language, pictographs, symbolic ornamentation, or copies of Spanish documents left by early explorers.

History and Cultural Relations

The settlement of Easter Island has been a topic of considerable conjecture and debate. Thor Heyerdahl's *Kon-Tiki* expedition showed that the island could have been settled from South America, although linguistic and archaeological evidence suggests settlement from other Polynesian islands perhaps as early as A.D. 400. Wherever the first Easter Islanders migrated from, it is likely that, given the remote location of the island, they were relatively isolated from other Polynesians. First contact with Europeans was with the Dutch explorer Jacob Roggeveen in 1722. There is some evidence that because of deforestation and wars between subtribes, the population was already declining and the culture disintegrating at this time. The island was subsequently visited, usually infrequently and briefly, by a succession of Spanish, English, French, American, and Russian explorers, traders, and whalers. The first major and the most significant contact occurred in 1862 when Peruvian slavers raided the island and kidnapped about 1,000 men to the guano islands off the Peruvian coast. There the Easter Islanders were forced to mine guano for one year during which time 900 died. Facing an international scandal, the Peruvian government sent the remaining 100 men home, although only 15 survived the trip. Infected with smallpox, they spread the disease to those on the island, further reducing the population to perhaps 25 percent of what it had been in 1862. The depopulation, disease, fear of outsiders, and death of many leaders led to cultural disintegration and a loss of much of the traditional culture within a decade. Catholic missionaries arrived in 1863, beginning a small though continuous European presence to this day. Within ten years, all surviving Easter Islanders were converted to Roman Catholicism, with many of the economic and social practices taught by the priests replacing traditional culture practices. In 1888 Chile annexed the island and subsequently leased 160 square kilometers to the Williamson and Balfour Company, which established sheep ranching for wool. The remaining 20 square kilometers were set aside for use by the Easter Islanders. In 1954 governance of the island and the sheep-ranching business was turned over to the Chilean navy, and in 1965, in response to islander complaints, the island was put under civilian control. Easter Island is currently a dependency of Chile and Easter Islanders are Chilean citizens.

Settlements

Since 1862 the Easter Islanders have lived in or around the village of Hangoroa in the southwest corner of the island. European-style stone and wood houses have completely replaced the traditional forms. Before 1862, villages were located along the coast, leaving the interior mostly uninhabited. Dwellings included thatched huts, semisubterranean houses, and caves. Wealthier Easter Islanders evidently lived in larger houses, often with stone foundations. In addition to dwellings, villages often contained cooking shelters, underground ovens, stone chicken coops, turtle watchtowers, and stone-walled gardens.

Economy

Subsistence and Commercial Activities. Prior to 1862, Easter Islanders subsisted mainly on cultivated crops, with sweet potatoes being the most important. Taro, yams, sugarcane, bananas, gourds, turmeric, and arrowroot were also grown while berries and seabird eggs were gathered. Fish provided some protein, although fishing was never a major subsistence activity. Easter Islanders continue to farm small plots today, although maize is now the major crop and Chilean cuisine has replaced the native diet. Since the introduction of sheep ranching, sheep and cattle on the island have been the primary sources of meat. Most material goods are now obtained from the store on the island and from the Chilean government. In addition to farming and fishing, Easter Islanders now work for the government, in a few small businesses, and in the tourist industry.

Industrial Arts. Easter Islanders were highly skilled stonecutters and stone-carvers, masons, woodcutters, and canoe makers. Today, some carve wood images for the tourist trade. The stone-carving tradition had already been abandoned at the time of contact, though the large stone statues survived and drew the attention of visitors to the island. Easter Islanders also made various utensils, implements, and tools from stone and wood, baskets, nets, mats, cordage, tapa (a cloth made from bark), and body ornaments.

Trade. Because of their isolation, Easter Islanders evidently did not trade with other groups in Polynesia. There has been conjecture that some culture elements developed through contact with South America, most notably the facial images on the stone monuments. These ideas remain unproven.

Division of Labor. Men were responsible for planting the gardens, fishing, and building the stone structures. Women harvested crops and handled most domestic chores. There was also a well-defined occupational hierarchy, with expert reciters of genealogies and folklore, stone-carvers, woodcarvers, and fishermen paid for their services with produce. Stone-carvers were a privileged group with the role and status passed from father to son.

Land Tenure. In traditional times, land was owned by lineages with dwelling and farm plots alloted to families. Since 1888 Chile has maintained ownership of all of Easter Island and has restricted the Easter Islanders to land in and around Hangoroa. Newlyweds are given a few acres of land for their use by the Chilean government.

Kinship

Kin Groups and Descent. The population of Easter Island was divided into ten subtribes or clans (*mata*), each of which evidently occupied a distinct territory in precontact times. By historic times, subtribe members were more widely dispersed as a result of exogamous marriage, adoption, and capture during war. The ten clans formed two larger divisions, with one controlling the western half and the other the eastern half of the island.

Kinship Terminology. Traditional kin term usage followed the Hawaiian system, which has been modified over time to reflect changes in family organization.

Marriage and Family

Marriage. In traditional times, most marriages were monogamous, though some wealthy men had more than one wife. Marriages were generally arranged, with infant betrothal not uncommon. Today, marriage is by free choice, although the fathers of both the groom and bride are involved in approving and making arrangements for the marriage. Marriages are marked by three ceremonies—a civil ceremony, church ceremony, and a large feast hosted by the groom's father—reflecting the survival of a traditional practice. Upon marriage, the couple generally live with one family or the other until materials can be obtained to build their own home. In the past, many marriages ended in divorce, which could be initiated by either party for virtually any reason. The Roman Catholic church has made divorce more difficult and less frequent.

Domestic Unit. In the past, the basic family and residential unit was the laterally extended family composed of brothers, their wives, and their children. Today, the nuclear family is the norm, although other relatives such as grandparents and brothers might also be present. In the past and today, the father was the authority figure, although today the wife's father has more power than the husband's father and a son-in-law will often seek his father-in-law's approval for educational and career decisions. Under Chilean influence, the role of godparent (*compadre*) has developed, and godparents often play a role in child rearing.

Inheritance. In the past and today, both men and women could inherit and both men and women could leave property.

Socialization. Puberty in traditional times was marked for boys and girls by secluding them on an island for some months and then holding large separate feasts at the end of the seclusion period. These rites disappeared long ago, and puberty is no longer marked by ritual. The Chilean government provides a school for elementary education and some Easter Islanders attend high school in Chile.

Social and Political Organization

Social Organization. In addition to social distinctions based on kinship, Easter Island traditionally had four distinct social classes: noblemen (*ariki*); priests (*ivi-atua*); warriors (*matatoa*); and servants and farmers (*kio*). The ruler was the main high chief (*ariki-mau*) who traced his status to descent from Hotu-matua, the founder of the island. In reality, ariki were invested with considerable mana and were subject to numerous taboos, although they had little actual power. Little is known about the activities of priests, as the role had disappeared by the time missionaries arrived. Kio were war captives who worked for others or paid tribute in the form of percentage of their crops.

Political Organization. As noted above, the nominal rulers came from the ariki class, with succession to the position of high chief going to the oldest son at the time of his marriage. However, since this marriage was often delayed many years beyond that of most Easter Islanders, chiefs often held their position for some years. At the time of sustained contact, warriors were the actual political leaders, reflecting a long history of fighting among the subtribes and the almost continuous fighting that followed the kidnapping of men in 1862. Today, the Easter Islanders are governed by Chile, with a Chilean governor, civil service, and police force providing services. Easter Islander representation is through the mayor of Hangoroa.

Social Control. Most early observers described theft as a common occurrence, with items stolen both from Europeans and from other Easter Islanders. Revenge was the major form of social control (actually it often led to warfare rather than peace) in early historic times. Taboos on the king, nobles, various foods, places, crops, death, and so on were a major aspect of everyday life and were rigorously enforced. Taboo violators were subject to beatings and even death. Although traditional taboos have now disappeared, they were still a strong infuence in the 1860s. Today, the laws of Chile are enforced by the Chilean police and government officials on the island.

Conflict. Wars were evidently common between the subtribes and especially between the eastern and western factions. Wars were often for revenge and involved ambushes, burning and looting villages, and the taking of captives, some of whom were tortured. War with Europeans was short-lived, and after the kidnapping in 1862 many Easter Islanders fled to inland caves upon the arrival of European ships.

Religion and Expressive Culture

Religious Beliefs. The traditional pantheon included at least ninety different named gods and spirits divided into the two categories of high gods and lesser gods. High gods included the creator, the rain god, and the superior god (Makemake). Lesser gods included gods with more restricted powers, nature spirits, demons, and ancestor spirits. Religious ritual included offerings of food and tapa, communication through priests, and chanting. Traditional beliefs have now been completely replaced by Roman Catholicism.

Religious Practitioners. Priests, who could be men or women, were evidently drawn from the noble class. Little is known of the role and status of priests other than the fact that they acted as healers and communicated with the supernatural world through possession trance. Priests could also place curses that were considered especially harmful. There were also sorcerers whose skills were used to influence or cause harm to others.

Ceremonies. Ceremonies were held to bring rain, sanctify new houses, and to ensure a rich harvest as well as to mark all major life-cycle events. The annual feast of the bird cult (*tangata-manu*) and the feast of the Bird-Man were the most important ceremonies.

Arts. The best-known of the traditional arts centered on stoneworking and stone carving. The most dramatic expressions of this tradition are the 600 large (from 20 to 60 feet high) carved stone statues mounted on stone platforms called *ahu.* The statues are most likely portraits of ancestors and chiefs. Statue carving had ceased by the time of European contact, with some 150 statues sitting unfinished in the quarry and many toppled over. Petroglyphs have been found on the island, and some interior stone walls of houses are decorated with paintings. Traditionally, various body ornaments were carved and both men and women wore body tattoos. The carving of wooden images, which was a common activity in early times, has evolved into a tourist-based economic activity with human images much in demand.

Medicine. Healing was done by the priests who used steaming, massage, binding, a limited pharmacopoeia, and contact with spirits. Today, Easter Islanders use Western medical care provided by Chile.

Death and Afterlife. In the past, the body of the deceased was placed on the ahu platform and left to decompose. The bones were then buried in the ahu vault. Much behavior that would normally occur in the vicinity of the ahu was taboo during the time the body was displayed. The funeral ceremony involved a large feast with singing and dancing. Today, Roman Catholic practices have replaced the traditional ones, although the latter survived into the twentieth century, far longer than many other cultural traits. The body is now displayed in the home, followed by the church rite and burial in a coffin in the church cemetery. Interment is marked by hysterical grief. In the evening there is a feast with food taboos for the family of the deceased.

Bibliography

Barthel, Thomas (1978). *The Eighth Land: The Polynesian Discovery and Settlement of Easter Island.* Honolulu: University of Hawaii Press.

Cooke, Melinda W. (1984). "Easter Island." In *Oceania: A Regional Study,* edited by Frederica M. Burge and Melinda W. Cooke, 371–375. Washington, D.C.: U.S. Government Printing Office.

Ferndon, Edwin N., Jr. (1957). "Notes on the Present-Day Easter Islanders." *Southwestern Journal of Anthropology* 13:223–238.

Metraux, Alfred (1940). *Ethnology of Easter Island.* Bernice P. Bishop Museum Bulletin no. 160. Honolulu.

Eipo

ETHNONYMS: Eipodumanang, Goliath, Kimyal, Mek

Orientation

Identification. The Eipo and their neighbors live in the Daerah Jayawijaya of the Indonesian Province of Irian Jaya. The Eipo usually refer to themselves as "Eipodumanang," which means "the ones living on the banks of the Eipo River," but the term "Eipo" is sometimes extended to include the inhabitants of adjacent valleys. The term "Mek" (meaning water, or river) has been introduced by linguists and anthropologists to designate the fairly uniform languages and cultural traditions in this area.

Location. The Eipo inhabit approximately 150 square kilometers of land in the southernmost (upper) section of the Eipomek Valley, at approximately 4°25'–4°27' S, 140°00'–140°05' E. Settlements are found at elevations between 1,600 and 2,100 meters, but surrounding mountain ranges reach 4,600 meters. The terrain is for the most part steeply incised. Anthropogenic grassland is found in a wide circle around the villages. Rain forest exists between the garden areas and covers the mountains above about 2,400 meters up to the tree line at 3,500 meters. Annual rainfall in 1975–1976 was 590 centimeters, with rain mostly falling daily in the afternoons and evenings. Temperatures range from about 11–13° to 21–25° C. Little seasonal change is to be observed, but the time of flowering of a particular tree (*Eodia* sp.) is taken by the Eipo as a marker of certain feasts and other activities. In 1976 two severe earthquakes destroyed large areas of garden land and some villages; it is likely that similar catastrophes have occurred in the past.

Demography. The Eipo numbered close to 800 people in 1980; indications are that the population is growing.

Linguistic Affiliation. Eipo, of which there are three dialects, is a member of the Mek Family of Non-Austronesian languages, clearly separate from the Ok languages to the east, the Yali and Dani languages to the west, and languages spoken to the north and south. Local people traditionally understand—and, to a lesser extent, speak—one or two dialects or languages other than their own. Children usually learn their speech from their mothers (who, due to rules of exogamy, often come from different valleys) and often do not adopt the dialect spoken by the majority in a particular village. Bahasa Indonesia, unknown before the 1970s, is slowly gaining ground as a lingua franca.

History and Cultural Relations

No archaeological data are available for the Mek region, and ethnohistoric surveys are missing as well. It is probable, however, that parts of the Mek area have been inhabited for many thousands of years. Linguistic and historical research on the introduction and diffusion of tobacco shows that the Mek (and their Ok neighbors to the east) may have been central in this process, and comparative studies on religious beliefs prove that important concepts (e.g., that of a mythical ancestral creator) have traveled from east to west. While it is unknown as yet at what time the sweet potato (*Ipomoea batatas*) was introduced, one can conclude from the significance of taro (*Colocasia esculenta*) in all ceremonial religious contexts that this latter food plant was of vital importance in pre-Ipomoean times. The first known contact by outsiders with Mek peoples was made by a team of Dutch surveyors early in this century; they met a group of people near Mount Goliath in the south of the area and reported the first recorded words of a Mek language. Some other groups were contacted in 1959 in the course of a French expedition across West New Guinea. Its leader, Pierre Gaisseau, later returned with a film team and Indonesian military personnel in 1969, parachuting into the southern Eipo Valley where they conducted a small but sound survey on the area and the people. Members of an interdisciplinary German research team conducted research in the Eipo Valley and some adjacent areas between 1974 and 1980.

Settlements

The villages of the Eipo and their neighbors in the Mek area have 30–250 inhabitants and are usually built on spots that facilitate defense. One or more circular men's houses (which often have sacred functions) occupy conspicuous places, either in the center or at the end of the village. The much smaller and less well-built family houses, also of circular shape but sometimes with rectangular roofs, are the locations for family-centered activities. Women stay in seclusion houses, usually situated at the periphery of the village, during menstruation, childbirth, and puerperium, and sometimes during serious illnesses and for sanctuary. All men's houses and most family houses have elevated floors and a central fireplace. Protection against the cold of the night is not very adequate. Due to mission influence, which chiefly employs Dani evangelists and teachers, Dani house styles are becoming fashionable.

Economy

Subsistence and Commercial Activities. The Eipo and the Mek in general are skillful horticulturalists and make their gardens in various places: sometimes on steep self-draining mountain slopes, but also in flat, wet areas where ditching and building mounds are particularly important for the main staple crop, sweet potatoes. Mulching is widespread. Fallow periods are fifteen years or more; sufficient regeneration of the soil is judged by the size of a tree (*Trema tomentosa*) that soon starts to grow in old gardens. Numerous varieties of taro, some of which reach considerable size and weight, are also cultivated. They are reserved for ceremonies, especially feasts for guests. Other cultigens include leafy greens (which contribute most of the vegetable protein, especially for men), bananas, sugarcane, edible *pitpit,* native asparagus (*Setaria palmifolia*), various pandanus species, and other wild foods. Beans, cheyote (*Secchium edule*), cucumbers, maize, cassava, and peanuts have been introduced and successfully cultivated. The few domesticated pigs do not contribute much to the diet, only about one gram per day person; they are carefully raised and usually used only in ceremonial contexts. Small marsupials are snared or hunted, often with the help of dogs, but hunting is done more to satisfy emotional needs than to provide meat. Women and girls obtain valuable animal protein in the form of frogs, tadpoles, lizards, snakes, spiders, and other insects as well as the eggs and larvae of these animals. Tradition and religious taboos reserve these foods as well as most of the bird species for infants, girls, and women. In the past decade, the Eipo have become dependent on mission stations as sources of modern tools, clothing, tinned food, and other goods, which are purchased with money received from selling services or products to the mission.

Industrial Arts. The material culture is poor, even compared to other highlands groups, and when research was begun in 1974, the Eipo and many of their neighbors were still using stone, bone, and wooden tools. Their worldly belongings include string bags, bows, arrows, stone adzes, stone knives and scrapers, wooden digging sticks, boars' tusks and marsupial teeth used as carving tools, bone daggers and awls, lianas for starting fires by friction, bamboo or calabash containers for water, penis gourds for the men, and grass skirts for girls and women. The Mek cook in hot ashes, bamboo containers over the open fire, or in earth ovens for larger groups of people, especially guests.

Trade. The Eipo and other Mek groups may seem self-sufficient now, but traditionally they relied on various goods from the outside. Unpolished stone adze blades were produced by specialists in the Heime Valley and exchanged mainly for string bags and garden products. Other items that had to be imported included black-palm wood for bows, feathers of birds of paradise and cassowaries, and various highly valued shells.

Division of Labor. Traditionally, the only specialists were producers of stone adze blades; all other work activities were carried out, sometimes in sex-specific ways, by everyone. The clearing of virgin forest (rarely done traditionally), the felling of larger trees, and the building of houses or log and cane bridges are all male tasks. The physically demanding work of clearing secondary vegetation for new gardens is done jointly by men and women, as are various activities in the gardens, such as preparing the ground, planting, weeding, and harvesting. With regard to the latter, the women have a heavier workload than do men and are known to carry their own body weight (about 40 kilograms) for several kilometers at a time. Hunting and snaring, as well as killing domesticated pigs, is done by the men. Women make most of the handicrafts, especially string bags of various sizes.

Land Tenure. All land, with the possible exception of that in the very high mountains, belongs to individuals (mostly men) or clans. In the latter case the corresponding rights are usually exercised by the clans' most influential male members. Some clans, namely those who are said to have "always" lived in a certain area, may own much more land than others; in a few cases "latecomers" may not have any land property at all. Still, enough garden land is made available to everyone in a process of formal distribution. Among the Eipo it is possible to gain use rights to land that one has made into a garden if it has been unused or unclaimed for a certain period of time. Individually owned or clan-owned garden land is marked by specially planted *Cordyline* shrubs, the connecting lines of which designate the sacrosanct borders. Despite this, disputes over land are quite common and can lead to armed fights.

Kinship

Kin Groups and Descent. Descent is reckoned patrilineally. Clan origins are dated back to mythical times. Animals, the sun, and the moon are considered the respective forefathers of clans and are worshipped as totems. Patriclans and patrlineages are exogamous, a rule that is quite strictly adhered to, even when choosing premarital or extramarital lovers. Even children know surprisingly well the details of the intricate kinship network.

Kinship Terminology. Kinship terms follow the conventions of the Omaha type of system. Additional classification principles include the specification that mother's brother, mother's father's brother's son, and mother's brother's son are all called by the same term.

Marriage and Family

Marriage. The Eipo term *ka* signifies a marriageable clan, lineage, or partner; *kaib* means to secure a marriageable partner and is the term for arranging a marriage. This form is seen as ideal, but in reality it does not occur too often because both the bride and groom have the right to reject the arrangement and because love affairs are quite common. The latter may lead either directly to marriage or to the man's abducting the consenting woman from her husband, to whom she is often married as a second wife. Rather than a payment of bride-price there is a system of mutual exchange of gifts: the groom's side and that of the bride hand over substantial valuables, shell and feather decorations, tools, etc. With a few exceptions, particularly in young couples, virilocality is the rule. In the 1970s 12 percent of the men lived in polygynous marriages, all with two wives, except for one man who had three. Because of the facultative polygyny and the imbalanced sex ratio (133 for all age groups, a result of preferential female infanticide, which is one of the mechanisms controlling population size), approximately 5 percent of all men must live permanently without a spouse, whereas virtually all sexually active and/or physically healthy women are married. In one case, a woman was "officially" living with two brothers. Whether such polyandrous settings are institutionalized marriages or ad-hoc solutions is unknown. Premarital sexual intercourse is allowed. Fidelity is expected of married persons but not always observed. Separation, divorce, and remarriage occur frequently.

Domestic Unit. A family house is usually occupied by a woman, her husband (who may at times, however, eat and sleep in the men's house), her daughters, her sons younger than about 13 years old, and unmarried or elderly relatives. The confined space is often also shared with a dog or a smaller pig or two. Husband and wife may work together, and the gardens and adjacent areas are preferred places for sexual intercourse.

Inheritance. Inheritance is through the patriline. Tools, body decorations, and the like may also be given to other persons, especially if the deceased was unmarried.

Socialization. Infants grow up in an emotionally protective environment with much body contact, especially with their mothers, and are breast-fed on demand. Birth intervals are at least three years, but child spacing will probably decrease in the course of acculturation. Infants receive a variety of social, emotional, and intellectual stimuli as they frequently interact with various persons of different ages and sexes. The principle of granting all of a child's wishes is gradually replaced by educational and economic demands. More than actual corporeal punishment, the threat of it keeps children fairly well disciplined. Girls help with various domestic duties earlier than do boys. Beyond the age of about 3 years, socialization takes place more and more in peer groups. In the last one or two decades mission schools have introduced hitherto-unknown formal education, and they are taking over part of the socialization process.

Sociopolitical Organization

Social Organization. In order of increasing complexity and decreasing consanguineality, the following social levels exist: extended families, coresident groups, lineages and clans, men's house communities, villages, and political alliances of a number of villages. Among members of the same lineage or clan, loyalty is usually high. Men's-house communities, led by specific clans, play an important role as work groups and in political decision making.

Political Organization. On the basis of their intellectual, oratorical, social, and physical power, *sisinang* (big-men) lead village communities as persons who take initiative, pursue plans, and respect rules and traditions, though they also use them to their advantage. In this protomeritocracy, leadership is dependent on the actual power of the leader. Persons who show signs of losing their capacities lose their positions, too. Inheritance of big-man status from father to son is not institutionalized, but it sometimes occurs de facto.

Social Control. Big-men exercise a certain amount of social control, but more important is the process of enforcing social norms through public opinion. This process, in turn, is effected through gossip, discussion of disputed issues, and the use of extrahuman powers in black magic allegedly performed by female or male witches. The infliction of illness thus functions as punishment for social wrongdoing.

Conflict. Despite the fact that the Eipo are usually friendly and controlled, the potential for aggressive acts is quite high and does not need much triggering. Until recently, in both intraalliance fights and interalliance warfare, approximately 3–4 persons per 1,000 inhabitants died of violence per year. Verbal quarrels and physical attacks with sticks, stone adzes, and arrows was the usual sequence of escalation leading to fights in the village. Neighbors in adjacent valleys sometimes were hereditary enemies who fought wars that were less ritualized (and therefore less controlled) than the intraalliance fights; in the past these conflicts occasionally led to cannibalism. Formal peace ceremonies ended these wars for periods of months or years. Warfare against ideologically defined and dehumanized "others" increased one's own sense of identity and strengthened bonds within the group.

Religion and Expressive Culture

Religious Beliefs. The visible world is considered to be inhabited by numerous, usually monstrous, beings: souls of the deceased, zoomorphic spirits of the forests and rivers, and powerful shapers of nature and bringers of culture who, since mythical times, have influenced the life of people. Yaleenye (a name that means "the one coming from the east") is the most prominent such culture hero. Mythical powers, symbolized by holy relics, were traditionally housed and honored in sacred men's houses. Various ceremonies that pervaded everyday life were performed to ensure the well-being of humans, domestic animals, and food plants. Fundamentalist Christianity has replaced—sometimes radically—traditional practices and, to a lesser extent, beliefs. Syncretic ideas and ceremonies are quite common and cargo-cult concepts exist.

Religious Practitioners. Seers are the only ones who can communicate directly with the extrahuman sphere and its agents. They may also act as sorcerers, inflicting harm, disease, and death on others. Male cult leaders, who were sometimes also big-men, were responsible in the past for religious ceremonies. The small group of specialists in religious matters included healers.

Ceremonies. Until recently, the first and most important initiation of boys between about 4 and 15 years of age was a major event that involved participants from other valleys. It was held at intervals of about 10 years, depending on how many boys were available for this costly ceremony. Coinitiates kept a lifelong bond. Second and third stages involved, respectively, the bestowal of the cane waistband and penis gourd, and the presentation of the *mum*, a back decoration that hung down from the head. Large and costly ceremonial dance feasts for visitors strengthened ties with trade and marriage partners from other valleys. Warfare and alliance formation involved ceremonies, and the killing of any enemy was celebrated triumphantly. More rarely, great ceremonies, bringing together inhabitants from distant, sometimes inimical valleys, were held to ensure the fertility of the soil.

Arts. The Eipo make very few carved or painted objects. Some Mek groups have sacred boards and large sacred shields that were not used in war. Drums are known only in some areas, but the Jew's harp is found everywhere. The texts of profane songs and sacred chants convincingly use powerful metaphors and are highly sophisticated examples of artistic expression.

Medicine. Compared to other areas of New Guinea, surprisingly few plant medicines are used. Leaves of the stinging nettle are applied as counterirritants. Other traditional (psychosomatic) treatments, carried out by healers who were usually males, involved sacred pig's fat and chants to invoke the help of extrahuman powers. Healers usually were not paid for their services. In recent years modern medicines have been administered at some mission stations.

Death and Afterlife. The death of a person leads to emotional distress among others and is spontaneously and ceremonially lamented, sometimes for months. The corpse traditionally was placed in a tree and protected against rainfall with bark and leaves. After mummification the body was put under the roof of a garden house. Later, in a third ceremony, the bones were placed under rock shelters. The complete cycle of ceremonies was not performed in all cases, and today through mission influence the dead are buried. The souls of the deceased are thought to leave the body, as they do during fainting spells or severe illness, and it is hoped that they will quickly proceed to the mythical ancestral village of their respective clans high up in the mountains. The spirits of the dead are thought to be basically angry and jealous of the joys on earth, and people think they can come back to harm or, less frequently, to help the living.

Bibliography

Eibl-Eibesfeldt, I., W. Schiefenhövel, and V. Heeschen (1989). *Kommunikation bei den Eipo: Eine humanethologische Bestandsaufnahme im zentralen Bergland von Irian Jaya (West-Neuguinea), Indonesien.* Mensch, Kultur, und Umwelt im zentralen Bergland von West-Neuguinea, no. 19. Berlin: D. Reimer.

Heeschen, V., and W. Schiefenhövel (1983). *Wörterbuch der Eipo-Sprache: Eipo-Deutsch-English.* Mensch, Kultur, und Umwelt im zentralen Bergland von West-Neuguinea, no. 6. Berlin: D. Reimer.

Koch, G. (1984). *Malingdam: Ethnographische Notizen über einen Siedlungsbereich im oberen Eipomek-Tal, zentralen Bergland von Irian Jaya (West-Neuguinea), Indonesien.* Mensch, Kultur, und Umwelt im zentralen Bergland von West-Neuguinea, no. 15. Berlin: D. Reimer.

Schiefenhövel, W. (1988). *Geburtsverhalten und reproduktive Strategien der Eipo: Ergebnisse humanethologischer und ethnmedizinischer Untersuchungen im zentralen Bergland von Irian Jaya (West-Neuguinea), Indonesien.* Mensch, Kultur, und Umwelt im zentralen Bergland von West-Neuguinea, no. 16. Berlin: D. Reimer.

WULF SCHIEFENHÖVEL

Foi

ETHNONYMS: Fiwaga, Foe, Foi'i, Kutubuans, Mobi, Mubi

Orientation

Identification. The Foi inhabit the Mubi River Valley and the shores of Lake Kutubu on the fringe of the southern highlands in Papua New Guinea. They divide themselves into three subgroups: the *gurubumena,* or "Kutubu people"; the *awamena,* the middle-Mubi Valley dwellers; and the *foimena* proper, the so-called Lower Foi who reside near the junction of the Mubi and Kikori rivers. The term "Foi" formerly applied to the common language of all three subgroups. It was subsequently employed as an ethnonym by the first missionaries.

Location. Most members of the Foi population inhabit the banks of the middle reaches of the Mubi River, between approximately 143°25' and 143°35' E and between 6°27' and 6°30' S. The alluvial Mubi River Valley is approximately 670 meters in altitude and abuts the higher ranges of the central highlands in the Southern Highlands Province of Papua New Guinea. The region is in every sense intermediate between the highlands valleys to the north and the coastal regions of the Gulf Province to the south. The southeasterly monsoon brings considerable rainfall during the middle months of the year, while the months between October and March are relatively drier.

Demography. The 1979 Papua New Guinea National Census counted some 4,000 Foi and accounted for another 400 Foi living elsewhere in the country. Foi territory comprises 1,689 square kilometers, and the population density is 2.4 persons per square kilometer. However, the Foi settlement area is restricted to the banks of the Mubi River and the shores of Lake Kutubu; over 60 percent of their land is reserved for hunting and is not permanently inhabited. The Foi are consequently separated from their neighbors by buffer zones of uninhabited bush. To the north are the Angal-speaking groups of the Nembi Plateau; to the southwest are the Fasu or Namu Po people; to the east are Kewa speakers of the Erave River Valley. Directly south of the Foi are small groups of Kasere, Ikobi, and Namumi speakers of the interior Gulf Province.

Linguistic Affiliation. Foi and Fiwaga are the only languages within the East Kutubuan Family of the Kutubuan Language Stock. It is closely related only to the languages of the West Kutubuan Family, which includes the Fasu, Kasere, and Namumi languages, but it also exhibits some small amount of cognation with other interior Papuan languages such as Mikaruan (Daribi) and Kaluli.

History and Cultural Relations

It is likely that the Foi first entered the Mubi Valley from the southwest, bringing domesticated sago with them. Although the Foi were briefly contacted along the southern reaches of their territory at different times by explorers moving inland from the Papuan Gulf coast, it was not until Ivan Champion first sighted Lake Kutubu in 1935 and consequently visited the lake on foot during his Bamu-Purari patrol that regular contact was established between the Foi and Europeans in the form of the patrol post at Lake Kutubu. The Unevangelized Fields Mission began activities at both Lake Kutubu and the middle Mubi Valley in 1951, and by the late 1960s the traditional religious life of the Foi had been largely superseded by Christianity. From 1950 the Foi were administered from various highlands patrol posts until the early 1970s, when a new administrative center was built and government health stations were reestablished in the Mubi Valley. Australian administrators introduced various European and other foreign vegetables to the area, including Singapore taro, pumpkins, chokos, Cavendish bananas, and pineapples. In 1988, large oil reserves were discovered west of Lake Kutubu in Fasu territory. The Foi of the upper Mubi Valley traditionally traded and occasionally fought with their highlands neighbors to the north. They exported the reddish oil of the *kara'o* tree (*Campnosperma brevipetiolata*) and in return received pearl shells, pigs, and ax blades. The Foi of Lake Kutubu were rather more under the influence, because of their close ties with the intervening Fasu people, with the Bosavi complex to the west, and it appears as if the boys' homosexual initiation cult, the *gisaro-kosa* ceremonial complex, and other Bosavi cultural traits had moved eastward into Foi territory shortly before Champion's contact. In the last twenty years, the more populous and politically ascendant peoples of the highlands have exerted some amount of cultural hegemony over the Foi. The Foi have therefore experimented with the southern highlands pork-and-pearl-shell exchange in recent years. Relations with eastern and southern neighbors appear to have been more tenuous.

Settlements

Foi communal life centers around a men's longhouse, wherein reside the representatives of anywhere between three and thirteen patrilineally composed exogamous dispersed clans. Villages range in size from about 20 people to almost 300. In the village, women reside in smaller houses flanking the longhouse; the longhouse can reach lengths of 55 meters. The separate domiciles of men and women stem from Foi men's belief that contact with women's menstrual secretions is deleterious to their health. The Foi subsistence economy, however, revolves around nuclear family bush houses, scattered in the territory surrounding the longhouse village, where a man, his wives, and children reside on the man's property. Most Foi move back and forth between bush and longhouse regularly, but the longhouse is technically only a public, ceremonial venue. Mubi River villages are close to the river itself and much traffic is by dugout canoe.

Economy

Subsistence and Commercial Activities. The Foi depend upon the following subsistence methods roughly in this order of importance: sago processing, gardening, tree crop cultivation (including *marita* pandanus and breadfruit), foraging, fishing, and hunting. In addition, pigs are semidomesticated and are slaughtered both casually and, on ceremonial occasions, in large numbers. Traditionally, the Foi tended to divide their year into seasons, dominated by the onset of the rainy season in early mid-year, at which time they left the village and moved to the hunting preserves where they would trap, fish, and forage until the drier weather returned around October. They then returned to the village to cut new gardens (according to standard swidden methods), make sago, and care for pigs.

Trade. Foi men traditionally carried on and still maintain a vigorous trade with their highlands neighbors to the north. They export kara'o oil, black-palm bows, and cassowaries and in return receive pearl shells and shoats. In premission times, they also received cult objects and procedures in trade.

Division of Labor. Foi subsistence tasks are sexually dimorphic: women process sago, tend gardens, forage, check traps and weirs, care for pigs and children, and weave baskets and string bags. Men build houses and canoes, fashion weapons, do the initial tasks of garden land preparation and sago grove management, build traps and weirs, hunt with ax and dog, and engage in trade and ceremonial exchange. In premission times, the men also performed fertility and healing ceremonies.

Land Tenure. Land is owned by local clan segments as corporate units, though its individual members assert more or less permanent usufructuary rights in certain tracts. These rights are usually passed on from father to son. Women maintain their husbands' productive resources but maintain rights in their natal clans' lands, should the occasion arise. Land can be sold, and in precontact times it was often granted to immigrants as a means of extending patronage to refugees from other areas.

Kinship

Kin Groups and Descent. The local totemically named patrilineal clan is the exogamous unit among the Foi and varies considerably in size. Smaller unnamed "lineages" consisting of a man and his adult sons are the units of marriage negotiation, though the local clan is the unit of exogamy and bride-wealth distribution. Descent is patrilineal. Orphaned children are sometimes claimed by their mother's brother, the clan of "true origin" in the Foi view.

Kinship Terminology. To the extent that this is a useful characterization, the Foi have an Iroquois-type terminology. Adults often address each other by their teknonyms if not otherwise related. In the past, reciprocal food-sharing names (special personal names used by those who shared food without obligation to do so) were common as modes of address, and children of people who shared such a name often called each other by their parents' food-sharing name.

Marriage and Family

Marriage. Betrothal is arranged by the fathers of boys and girls at an early age. Upon the presentation of bride-wealth (consisting of pearl shells, cowrie shells, meat, and currency) by the groom's father and mother's brother to the same relatives of the bride, a girl takes up residence in her husband's house. Bride-wealth payments are often made in installments that stretch out for years after marriage. When a person dies, the spouse's clan makes funeral payments to the father's, mother's, and mother's mother's clans of the deceased. These payments effectively cancel any residual claims of outstanding bride-wealth. Divorce is infrequent. Polygyny is practiced by a small number of men.

Domestic Unit. A man has one or more bush houses in various parts of his territory where he and his wife or wives process sago, garden, and care for pigs. A man and his grown sons often live close enough to each other for their wives to cooperate in subsistence tasks.

Inheritance. A man passes on his wealth, land, and other property to his sons, real and adopted.

Socialization. Children stay with their mothers in the women's houses until about age 2, when boys move into the men's house with their fathers. Foi children learn by trial-and-error imitation rather than overt instruction and reward/punishment.

Sociopolitical Organization

Political Organization. Three or four villages occupying contiguous territories, whose longhouses are close to each other, constitute an extended community. Less than 10 percent of all marriages take place between villages from different extended communities. Within this unit, set battles did not occur, though sorcery and homicide did. The extended community was the traditional unit of warfare alliance and nowadays is the political unit of ceremonial exchange. In the 1970s the Foi borrowed the pork-and-shell-exchange cycle of their highlands neighbors. This involves periodic large-scale pig slaughters, fueled by the collection and disbursement of pledges of shell wealth. Debts in pork and shells accumulate with each pig kill and villages take turns in discharging their obligations to creditors. These activities are coordinated and controlled by big-men.

Social Control. Within each local clan, one or two men occupy positions of respect and authority, based on former prowess in warfare, success in negotiating marriages and exchange relationships, oratorical ability, magic, skill in healing, and reputed knowledge of sorcery. Each village has two to four such big-men who represent the village as a whole to outsiders. "Social control" among Foi depends on the degree to which the astuteness and judgment of big-men is acknowledged by other men.

Conflict. While major warfare between foreign and distant villages was not endemic, sorcery, ambush, and assassination were certainly regular occurrences in traditional times. Fear of sorcery and revenge killing and considerations of high death-compensation payments to the victim's kin constituted moderately effective sanctions against violence and homicide in the past; ethical commandments and fear of retribution in the Christian afterlife passed on by missionaries have been absorbed as models and incentives for correct behavior. Homicide and violence today are rare, suicide less so.

Religion and Expressive Culture

Religious Beliefs. In traditional times, Foi men engaged in a variety of cult activities all designed to ensure fertility and heal sickness by appeasing ghosts. All sickness except that caused by sorcery was believed to occur through the agency of ghosts. In addition, men sought to acquire ghosts' powers of magic, prescience, and sorcery for themselves. According to the Foi, all dead people become ghosts, and the power and the malevolence of certain kinds of ghosts are a result of the manner of death: violent homicide produces the most virulently malevolent and powerful ghosts, while the ghosts of dead people who die more peacefully are less efficacious and dangerous. Ghosts take the form of certain birds, chiefly fruit- and nectar-eating birds. The trees which attract such birds, including several *Ficus* varieties, are considered the favored abode of ghosts. Other places thought to attract ghosts are the spots where powerful magic spells were once performed, still pools of water, and whirlpools formed in sharp bends in the rivers. In the past, men fasted and slept near these places to establish contact with ghosts in dreams. Such cult activity ended in the late 1960s following effective missionization.

Religious Practitioners. Certain men became skilled in such healing techniques and renowned for their rapport with powerful ghosts. These men also took the initiative for inducting young boys into the cult secrets. Men attempt to purchase knowledge of sorcery and the associated substances, often from neigboring peoples. Knowledge of effective sorcery is associated with big-men.

Ceremonies. The "Bi'a'a Guabora" (arrowhead cult) was a secret male fertility cult designed to ensure success in hunting. Its rites were performed in conjunction with funeral ceremonies, widow remarriage, and the completion of a new longhouse. The *usane habora* was the major traditional healing ceremony. It was followed by a slaughter of pigs and the exchange for pork or shell wealth and nighttime men's dancing accompanied by drums. The *sorohabora* was a more secular pig kill and exchange to celebrate the completion of a new longhouse or an especially large canoe. The nighttime performances at these ceremonies included the singing of laments in the memory of deceased men. More recently, the Foi have borrowed the Mendi-Nipa *sa* pig kill and exchange, which has provided them with links to the regional exchange networks of the southern highlands.

Arts. The most highly developed art form among the Foi is ceremonial song-poetry, composed by women as sago work songs and performed by men. These songs are laments composed to commemorate deceased men. They make use of a wide range of imagery, the most important of which is the linking of the deceased's lifespan to the series of places he occupied and made use of during his life. The Foi also have a large corpus of myths that they recite in casual recreational contexts. Graphic art, by contrast, is nonexistent.

Medicine. The "Usi" and "Hisare" (ghost-appeasement cults) were the major cults of the middle Mubi area. They involved the preparation of certain potions, the learning of techniques of foreign-body removal from afflicted persons, and instruction in sorcery. Something over 60 percent of all boys were inducted into Usi in pre-1960 times. Adult men were also subject to a number of food taboos in traditional times, the rationale of which was to prevent premature aging and weakness by avoiding items associated with femaleness and old age. These taboos have relaxed somewhat since 1970.

Death and Afterlife. Ghosts were expected to leave the community of the living and take up residence in the afterworld located in the distant east. This belief now competes with vague ideas concerning Christian Heaven. A widow is thought likely to attract the attention of her dead husband's ghost and is considered particularly dangerous to other men for some time after her husband's death. For this reason, widows who are about to remarry have to undergo various purification rituals designed to forestall the anger of their former husbands' ghosts. Ghosts are also believed to be the agents by which men can induce illness in their sisters' children if they become frustrated over insufficiencies in the bride-wealth they have received for these women. On the other hand, men seek through dreams and in their healing cult rites to establish contact with ghosts whom they consider the source of magical techniques and knowledge of future events.

See also Kaluli, Kewa, Mendi

Bibliography

Weiner, James F. (1987). "Diseases of the Soul: Sickness, Agency, and the Men's Cult among the Foi of New Guinea." In *Dealing with Inequality,* edited by M. Strathern. Cambridge: Cambridge University Press.

Weiner, James F. (1988). The *Heart of the Pearl Shell: The Mythological Dimension of Foi Sociality*. Berkeley: University of California Press.

Weiner, James F., ed. (1988). *Mountain Papuans: Historical and Comparative Perspectives from New Guinea Fringe Highlands Societies.* Ann Arbor: University of Michigan Press.

Williams, F. E. (1940). *Natives of Lake Kutubu, Papua.* Oceania Monograph no. 6. Sydney: Oceania Publications.

JAMES F. WEINER

Fore

ETHNONYMS: none

Orientation

Identification. The Fore people are subsistence-oriented swidden horticulturalists who live in the Okapa District of the Eastern Highlands Province, Papua New Guinea. Although they shared a common language, they traditionally had no group name for themselves, no encompassing political organization, and no unifying collective ceremonies. The Fore are well known for being victims of an always-fatal, degenerative neurological disease, called *kuru,* which medical researchers now believe is caused by an unconventional, slow virus infection of the central nervous system that was transmitted in the past through cannibalistic consumption of those who died of the disease. With the discontinuation of this practice, Fore society is now recovering from the devastating effects of kuru.

Location. Fore territory, centered on 6°35' S and 145°35' E, is a wedge of approximately 950 square kilometers, bounded on the north by the Kratke Mountains and on the west and the southeast by the Yani and the Lamari Rivers, respectively. In this mountainous lower-montane zone, altitude varies from 400 to 2,500 meters, although most people live within the altitudinal range of 1,000–2,200 meters. Broad, grass-covered valleys occur in the north, a result of human clearing and cultivation activities. In the south, the tropical forest canopy is broken only by more recently cleared settlement sites as small groups of Fore continue to pioneer in uninhabited areas along their southern border.

Demography. There are approximately 20,000 Fore who are separated by the Wanevinti Mountains into the North Fore and South Fore regions, with the population of the latter being somewhat greater than that of the former. While the overall population density averages 21 persons per square kilometer, the North Fore people live at nearly twice the density as do the South Fore.

Linguistic Affiliation. The Fore language, with three distinct dialects, is the southernmost member of the East Central Family, East New Guinea Highlands Stock, Trans–New Guinea Phylum of Papuan languages. The Fore share territorial boundaries with speakers of seven other mutually unintelligible languages. Recently, linguist missionaries have developed an orthography for the language and Fore now exists in written form.

History and Cultural Relations

The ancestral home of the Fore people is unknown, but linguistic and genetic affinities and vegetative patterns strongly indicate migration routes from the north and east. Australian prospectors first penetrated the highlands in the early 1930s and Australian exploratory patrols entered the region in the late 1940s, bringing with them steel axes, sodium salt, and cloth. In the early 1950s, a Lutheran mission was founded at Tarabo, the colonial government opened a patrol post at Okapa, and various new garden crops, domesticated animals, items of clothing, and other manufactured goods were introduced. Also, subsistence activities began to be augmented by a nascent commercial economy. The first coffee seedlings were planted in 1955, and Fore men began to venture out of the region as migrant wage laborers. In 1957, the Kuru Research Center was opened at Awande to begin intensive study of this disease. Cannibalistic practices ceased about 1960, and since then the annual number of kuru deaths has fallen from about 200 per year to less than 10 per year at present. By the mid-1960s, Okapa had become the regional administrative center and boasted a hospital, school, and several small stores. Elections also had been held for the local government council. Today, most people have access to some formal education, medical care, and other government services, and many have converted to Christianity. The Fore have come to accept a common group identity, and the degree of social isolation and enmity has declined dramatically. They now live as active citizens of the Nation-state of Papua New Guinea.

Settlements

Fore settlements are relatively dispersed over the landscape with small groups of people living together at the edge of the forest in close proximity to their food gardens. The main residential unit is the hamlet which, in earlier times, typically consisted of one or two communal men's houses and a row of several smaller houses occupied by women and children. An open space with cooking pits separated the two types of dwellings. Behind the women's houses at the edge of the clearing would be one or two small structures where women stayed during menstruation and childbirth. The entire settlement was surrounded by a defensive stockade. Today, the men's houses and stockades are gone and most families live together in one house, often in larger aggregated villages.

Economy

Subsistence and Commercial Activities. Fore subsistence is based on a system of swidden horticulture and pig husbandry that is augmented to a small degree by hunting and foraging activities. New gardens are cleared in forested areas using slash-and-burn techniques. After fencing, the plots are planted using a digging-stick technology. The most important crop is the sweet potato, which is the staple food for both people and pigs. Pigs are a major form of wealth among the Fore and successful pig raisers are much admired. Treated like valued pets, pigs live in close physical proximity to their keepers and are fed garden produce daily. Gardens also contain smaller amounts of other tubers (taro, yams, manioc), *pitpit* (*Saccharum edule* and *Setaria palmifolia*), maize, winged beans, bananas, sugarcane, and a variety of leafy vegetables and herbs. In recent decades, many new crops have been incorporated into Fore gardens, including lima beans, peanuts, cabbages, pumpkins, onions, and papayas. Coffee growing is a major commercial venture in which nearly all Fore participate.

Industrial Arts. As with many of their neighbors, the Fore have largely abandoned local manufacture of clothing, tools, and utensils, relying on articles of Western manufacture that are purchased with the proceeds from cash crops. House building and fencing of gardens and interhamlet pathways are the principal male industrial arts; utilitarian net bags, made of hand-spun bark string, are still manufactured by women. Prior to the 1950s, Fore also extracted salt for local use and for trade from the ash of *Coix gigantea,* an indigenous tall grass. This last industry has been superseded by the introduction of commercial salt.

Trade. Regional trade was always an important means by which Fore acquired goods not available locally. Trade items passed through complex networks of hand-to-hand transactions between established trading partners who rarely lived more than one day's walk apart. In general, stone ax blades came from neighbors to the north and west in exchange for locally manufactured salt, fur pelts, bird plumes, and betel nuts; black-palm bows and arrowheads were traded from the southeast for salt and piglets; occasionally, a few shells were obtained from Papuan peoples two days to the south for tobacco and net bags. However, nowadays most Fore rely on small stores and the periodic market in Okapa to obtain nonlocal goods.

Division of Labor. The Fore define only a few tasks as the exclusive responsibility of men or women. In gardening, men fell the trees while women clear the underbrush and pile the debris for burning. Women then do most of the soil preparation and planting while men build the enclosing fences. The cultivation, tending, harvesting, and transporting of most crops falls to women, but men are free to assist with these tasks if they so choose. Pandanus and tobacco are cultivated only by men as are a few ritually important, red varieties of sugarcane, bananas, yams, and taro. Women undertake the primary burdens of pig tending under the close supervision of men. Childcare again ultimately falls to women although men and older siblings regularly assist. Most food is prepared and cooked by women with men taking major responsibility for obtaining firewood and preparing the earth-oven fires. Women traditionally made all items of clothing and net bags, and men fashioned weapons, stone axes, and some items of personal adornment.

Land Tenure. Land rights are held communally by the male and female members of local clan groups who currently occupy the land and control access to it. Garden plots are allocated for the use of member families, and occasionally nonmembers will be granted temporary usufructuary rights. No Fore land is individually owned.

Kinship

Kinship is a dominant organizing principle of Fore society. Although genealogies normally can only be recalled to the second ascending generation, all significant social groups are assumed to be based on shared kinship, with the predominant ideology stressing patrilineal connections. Fore kinship, however, is not a simple reflection of actual genetic relatedness of individuals. Previously unrelated newcomers are easily incorporated as kin through various mechanisms of adoption, affiliation, and mutual consent. By fulfilling the obligations of loyalty and cooperation expected of kin, people become "one blood."

Kin Groups and Descent. The Fore conceive of their kin groups as being hierarchically organized and based on recognized patrilineal descent. The smallest unit is called a *lounei,* or "line." Members of a given line usually reside together in a single hamlet and are an exogamous unit. Several lines together form the next group level, the subclan, members of which live in close proximity to each other and consider themselves closely related; they may or may not be exogamous. The largest kin-based group is the clan, composed of several subclans; the clan is not exogamous. Although members of a clan recognize a common territory, it is not uncommon for some members to reside outside these boundaries.

Kinship Terminology. Fore terminology distinguishes siblings according to sex and relative age and uses the Iroquois scheme for cousin terms. In the first ascending generation, bifurcate merging occurs.

Marriage and Family

Marriage. Marriage among the Fore involves the relatives of the bride and the groom in a lengthy and complex series of prestations. In the past, this could commence soon after the birth of the female when, following the custom of infant betrothal, she would be promised as the future wife of a young cross cousin. Among the North Fore, this preferred relationship between spouses includes both matrilateral and patrilateral cross cousins, but among the South Fore, patrilateral cross cousins are forbidden to marry. Today, it is more common for a couple to make known their intention to marry and thereby initiate the negotiations between their respective relatives concerning the bride-wealth payment that culminates all marriage ceremonies. The newly married couple resides with relatives of the husband. Many Fore men aspire to polygyny, but the lack of marriageable women caused by the high death rate from kuru means that relatively few men succeed. Although most younger widows do remarry, many men spend long periods without wives. Under these conditions, most marriages terminate with a death, and divorce accounts for only 5–10 percent of dissolutions.

Domestic Unit. In the past, the Fore observed strict residential segregation stemming from beliefs about the dangers posed to men by female menstrual pollution. All men above 8–10 years of age lived communally in large men's houses, and women and younger children resided in smaller separate houses. Today, residential segregation of the household is rarely maintained. Nuclear families, often augmented by elderly relatives or unmarried siblings of the husband or wife, occupy individual houses and are the primary production and consumption units in Fore society.

Inheritance. The Fore inherit land rights and valuables through their recognized patriline. Although women, after marriage, retain rights to land of their natal group, they cannot pass these on to their children.

Socialization. From birth, Fore infants enjoy nearly constant physical contact with parents, siblings, and other caretakers. As toddlers, they are free to investigate the world nearby and often are encouraged in spontaneous acts of aggression. From an early age, girls are expected to assist their mothers in gardening tasks. Young boys form small groups based on friendship and roam hamlet lands exploring, hunting, and playing together. Occasionally, such groups build their own houses and cook, eat, and sleep together. At 8–10 years of age, boys begin their formal initiation into the secret world of men where the values of cooperation, mutual support, and loyalty are reinforced.

Sociopolitical Organization

Social Organization. Fore society is characterized as relatively egalitarian, meaning that most significant distinctions in social status are based only on age and sex. There is no system of ranked statuses and no social classes. Nonetheless, inequalities do exist. Men dominate the public arena and consider themselves superior to women, who are called "the hands of men." Also, men compete with each other for political influence and prestige with the more successful individuals achieving regional prominence and increased access to wives, valuables, and resources.

Political Organization. The traditional political organization is based on the parish, or "district," which is composed of one or more adjacent hamlets whose members recognize and defend a common territory, share one sacred spirit place, and ideally settle internal disputes peaceably. Parishes are subdivided into "sections" which, in the past, were the effective military units. Parish sections responded jointly to threats and attack and negotiated the settlement of hostilities. Sections, in turn, are composed of "lines," which are exogamous descent groups as well as political units. Although parishes and sections are coresidential groups, rather than descent groups whose composition changes constantly, the tenuous group unity often is reinforced in the language of consanguinity with members referring to themselves as "one blood." All sections and parishes are led by leaders, called big-men, who command the respect and loyalty of their followers by demonstrating superior skill in activities necessary for survival of the group. They initiate and organize most group activities (including warfare), direct economic transactions with other groups, and recruit immigrants to bolster group numbers. A big-man must be a strong, dominating figure, an aggressive warrior, and a skilled orator and negotiator. He also must face constant competition from other would-be leaders who will usurp his authority if he falters. Today, the local political system is complemented by the national system of elective offices and Fore big-men often stand for provincial and national assembly seats.

Social Control. Big-men, as fight leaders and peace negotiators, play an important role in controlling the level of hostilities between parishes. The threat of sorcery also is a powerful means of social control for members of different parishes. Within parishes, unity depends on reciprocity and cooperation among members. Perceived violations of these group norms are publicly denounced by offended parties and often lead to demands for restitution. Actions especially prohibited within a parish are stealing, adultery, fighting with lethal weapons, and sorcery. The imposition of sanctions, however, rests largely on the authority of big-men and their ability to command the cooperation of others. Within households, the structured antagonism between men and their wives can be influenced by the intervention of close relatives and also is modulated by fear that wives secretly may contaminate abusive husbands with menstrual secretions.

Conflict. In the past, interparish warfare was a normal aspect of everyday Fore life. Driven by an ethic that demanded retaliation for actual or suspected wrongs, sporadic raids and counterraids were made into enemy territory to kill those thought culpable and to destroy their houses, pigs, and gardens. Fighting tended to occur between members of neighboring parishes, and at any given time a parish was likely to be at peace with some neighbors and actively prosecuting hostilities with others. By mutual consent, peace could be declared, but the tenor of interparish relations was subject to rapid turnabout.

Religion and Expressive Culture

Religious Beliefs. Fore religion consists of a complex body of beliefs concerning nature, human nature, and the spiritual realm. It is animated by a host of ancestor spirits, ghosts of the recently deceased, and nature spirits. Central figures in Fore cosmology include a sacred creator-spirit couple who emerged from a swamp in South Fore and traveled through the region, leaving humans and many useful species of plants and animals along the way. They also provided fundamental teachings for acceptable human existence emphasizing the themes of fertility, strength, cooperation, and loyalty that are expressed in myths and ritual activities. This couple exists in many manifestations among the Fore, and they make their presence known most frequently by giving their voices to the playing of sacred flutes on all important ceremonial occasions. Ghosts and nature spirits are capable of causing illness or misfortune when offended and of rewarding respectful behavior by ensuring abundant gardens and wild resources. In recent decades, many Fore have been evangelized by Christian missionaries.

Religious Practitioners. There are no specifically religious specialists among the Fore although some people, both men and women, are known for having superior knowledge of and access to the spirit world. Chief among these people are curers and sorcerers who are able to manipulate spiritual powers to their own ends.

Ceremonies. The most important ritual complex among the Fore revolves around the initiation of boys into manhood. Young boys are removed forcibly from the care of their mothers and taken to live with men. During the initiation stages, which last several years, they are taught the rationale and techniques of nose bleeding, cane swallowing, and vomiting designed to promote growth, strength, and fertility and to protect their health from the polluting powers of women. They also are instructed in the proper beliefs, behaviors, and responsibilities of adult Fore men. At puberty, young women also are secluded briefly, undergo nose bleeding, and are informed by older women of their new responsibilities. The Fore also hold periodic pig feasts once or twice each decade, often in conjunction with initiations. These are the largest social gatherings in the region and are highly competitive political events.

Arts. A major focus of Fore art is items of body adornment, including feather headdresses and shell headbands and necklaces. Traditionally, men also carved wooden bows and arrows and war shields while women fashioned clothing and knitted net bags with intricate geometric designs.

Medicine. Fore attribute most serious illness, including kuru, to sorcery, but lesser ailments may be caused by witches, ghosts, and nature spirits or may result from abrogation of social rules and expectations. Curers rely on preparations from the local pharmacopoeia of medicinal plants, incantation, bloodletting, and divination. Local curers, called "bark men" or "bark women," treat relatively minor illnesses, but sorcery-caused sickness requires the attention of powerful and widely known "dream men" who always live in a distant parish and may be non-Fore. These men perform acts of divination and curing using information gained in dream states induced by ingestion of hallucinogenic plant materials and heavy inhalation of tobacco smoke.

Death and Afterlife. Death is marked by extended mourning rituals, public display of the corpse, and the giving of gifts by paternal relatives to the maternal relatives of the deceased. In the past, the body commonly was eaten, especially by women, children, and the elderly and the remains were buried in an old garden site of the deceased. Human flesh was thought to promote fertility and regenerate both people and gardens. The Fore no longer practice mortuary cannibalism, and each line maintains a common burial ground for its dead. The spirit of the deceased is thought to remain for a time near the grave site and finally to move to one of the known spirit places to continue its afterlife indefinitely.

See also Sambia, Tairora

Bibliography

Berndt, Ronald M. (1962). *Excess and Restraint: Social Control among a New Guinea Mountain People.* Chicago: University of Chicago Press.

Gajdusek, D. Carleton (1977). "Unconventional Viruses and the Origin and Disappearance of Kuru." *Science* 197: 943–960.

Hornabrook, R. W. (ed.) (1976). *Essays on Kuru.* Faringdon, U.K.: E. W. Classey.

Lindenbaum, Shirley (1979). *Kuru Sorcery: Disease and Danger in the New Guinea Highlands.* Palo Alto, Calif.: Mayfield Publishing Company.

Sorenson, E. Richard (1976). *The Edge of the Forest: Land, Childhood, and Change in a New Guinea Protoagricultural Society.* Washington, D.C.: Smithsonian Institution Press.

DAVID J. BOYD

Futuna

ETHNONYMS: East Futuna, Hoorn Islands, Horn Islands

Orientation

Identification. Futuna and its neighboring island of Alofi (or Tua) are politically joined to Wallis Island under French administration as overseas territories. They were named the "Hoorn [or Horn] Islands" after the birthplace in Holland of one of the first European explorers to sight the islands. This Futuna must not be confused with West Futuna, east of Tanna in Vanuatu.

Location. Futuna is located 240 kilometers northeast of Vanua Levu (in Fiji), and 200 kilometers southwest of Wallis at 14° S, 178° W. Futuna and Alofi are both volcanic islands with steep mountainous interiors rising to the highest point of 850 meters. There are many streams and a plentiful supply of fresh water. Futuna is subject to cyclones.

Demography. In 1983 the population on the island of 44 square kilometers of land was 4,324, and it was growing at about 4 percent per year. In addition, approximately 4,000 Futunans were living in New Caledonia. About 50 French people are resident as administrators, teachers, and doctors.

Linguistic Affiliation. East Futuna is an Austronesian language, included in the Nuclear Polynesian Subgroup of the Polynesian Group. It is mutually understandable with Wallisian but distinct from West Futunan, and it has some close cognates with Samoan. French is now spoken by some of the younger Futunans, particularly those living in New Caledonia.

History and Cultural Relations

Occupation of Futuna has been documented for about 3,000 years, divided into three periods: Kele Uli, Kele Mea, and Kele Ula. Lapita-associated pottery has been found related to the first period, when first settlement apparently was on the coast. In the Kele Mea period, Futunans took up residence in the interior of the island in fortified sites; Alofi was also inhabited during this period. Kele Ula is the period covered by oral tradition, when Futuna was linked with Tonga and Samoa (and possibly Fiji) through visits by chiefs and their followers for both peaceable and warlike purposes. Oral tradition also records the arrival of a "Chinese" ship whose crew left numerous descendants. In 1837 Father Chanel, a French Marist priest, was one of the first Europeans to take up residence on Futuna; he was murdered in 1841, but the Catholic mission continued its strong presence. Chanel was beatified and his relics returned in 1976 to rest in a shrine on Futuna. In 1842, the *lavelua* (high chief) of Wallis sought protection from France, a move with which the two traditional leaders of Futuna agreed. Futuna, together with Wallis, became a protectorate of France in 1887 and a colony in 1913. In 1961, Futuna and Wallis became an overseas territory of France. Futuna was marginally involved in World War II with a few ships being wrecked there, particularly off its northern coast. When nickel mines opened in New Caledonia, Futunans took advantage of the opportunity to work for wages; the stream of migration has continued to the present day, with a few returning to their home island, especially in their old age.

Settlements

The island of Futuna is divided by the Vaigaifo River into two kingdoms, Sigave in the west and Alo (including the island of Alofi) in the east. Villages are located around the coastline of Futuna and linked by one road; there are no permanent inhabitants on Alofi. The main commercial and administrative center is in Leava in Sigave, but there are small shops and a church in each of the villages. Most of the houses are set on the inland side of the road, with their household garden plots behind the house. The oval-shaped thatched houses are surrounded by low concrete walls to keep the pigs from attacking the crops and have open sides, except for coconut-frond blinds that can be let down in bad weather. Most houses have very recently been wired for electricity and have outside piped water.

Economy

Subsistence and Commercial Activities. Futuna is a very fertile island with high rainfall, so everything grows well. The main dietary items are starchy vegetables with a little accompaniment, such as coconut, fish, or a *faikai* pudding. Taro and yams are the main root crops grown on a rotational system; breadfruit, bananas, and coconuts are also important. All of these crops are liable to cyclone damage such as that inflicted by Cyclone Raja in December 1986. At the eastern end of the island where the coastal belt is narrow, plantations are cut into the hillside; at the western end, extensive fields of irrigated taro are planted. Fishing is limited because of the lack of a protecting reef and high seas for most of the year. Men fish in the shelter of Alofi Island, using the few boats that are owned jointly; older women fish on the reef for smaller fish. Pigs predominate in the villages, roaming around their households and on the reef where they scavenge for food; each family has its own pigs as these are the main representation of wealth. Formerly copra was sold; now the people rely for cash on the few administrative and public-works jobs, the sale of handicrafts, pensions for those over age 60, and occasional gifts from relatives in New Caledonia.

Industrial Arts. Women spend a good part of their time weaving mats and beating tapa; both these items are shipped to New Caledonia as gifts for relatives and for sale. Some of the mats are also used locally as gifts on large communal occasions.

Trade. Goods are imported from New Caledonia for sale in Futuna, or sent as gifts by relatives. Futuna's imports far outweigh its exports, especially since copra has ceased to be a marketable crop.

Division of Labor. Men cultivate the land, including both household plots and the plantations farther afield. This task requires them to clear any vegetation, turn over the soil, plant, weed, and harvest the crops; the latter job may necessitate carrying loads of taro or *kape* (kava) several kilometers. Men also go fishing together, though this activity is considered more like sport than work. Women look after the household, take care of children, weave mats, and make tapa. Older women also fish on the reef. Children fetch water and act as runners between households, bearing goods and messages.

Land Tenure. The two halves of Futuna, Sigave and Alo, are distinct entities with separate land holdings; it is rare for a person to hold land in both kingdoms. Each *sau*, or leader, is custodian of all lands in his territory, and in former times waged war in response to any violation of his lands. In each village the headman was responsible for ensuring that lands were properly used, but individual families could cultivate their household land and also use the vacant land behind the village. Some village land was maintained in production by a group of men in order to provide a bountiful supply of yams and kape for any large communal feast. Families depended on their household strip for day-to-day supplies of taro, breadfruit, bananas, kape, and cassava. But in these days of large households, the men find it necessary to cultivate their own plantation land, and sometimes that of their wives, in order to grow enough to feed the family. Land rights are passed on to both sons and daughters, but a couple prefers to live on the man's land.

Kinship

Kin Groups and Descent. Kin ties linking a large number of Futunans into overlapping social entities center on brothers and sisters. The oldest sister has certain privileges within the family group. There is a strong protective relationship between brothers and their sisters as well as avoidance regarding certain issues with sexual implications. The privileged relationship to a father's sister (*vasu*) that allows the younger person to take food from her is restricted to royal lineages. Kin groups are the basis for working parties, such as for fishing, thatching, or making a canoe. Descent is reckoned through both mothers and fathers, mainly for inheritance of land rights or to trace a relationship to a chiefly family. "Family" to a Futunan means a bilaterally extended family, consisting of a wide-ranging group of people living both on Futuna and on Wallis, as well as in New Caledonia. Relatives are recognized even though contact may not have been sustained for several years.

Kinship Terminology. Kinship terminology is of the Hawaiian type where the terms for mother, father, brother, sister, and grandparents are extended to collaterals. Sibling terms are determined by the sex of the speaker.

Marriage and Family

Marriage. Marriage is preferred between two people of the same or neighboring villages, as long as they are not too closely related. The sau or one of his councillors must approve each marriage. The young couple is likely to live with either his or her parents, and the mother-in-law feeds her new daughter-in-law well lest the latter's family criticize her.

Domestic Unit. Two or more siblings and their spouses and children are likely to share a household together with additional kin or adoptive kin. Household size averages eight persons, representing three generations as well as some siblings of those in the older generation and their offspring. This is the main group that interacts within the village and beyond.

Inheritance. Land and property, such as kava-making equipment, canoes, and planting implements, are passed on from fathers to their children, while tapa beaters and special mats are passed on in the female line. Titles within the Tuiagaifo and Sau chiefly families are passed between two separate groups; e.g., the incumbent family passes the Tuiagaifo title to the person selected by the family group of the past incumbent.

Socialization. Children are raised within a very close family network that consists of many people. They are carefully guarded and watched over, and not allowed to roam far from home without good reason. This pattern dominates their lives even as adults. Every Futunan is bound into a system of "Faka Futuna" or "the Futuna Way," which he or she must honor and respect. It includes obligations to the traditional leaders and to the Catholic mission as well as to senior members of the extended family. This system has been extended to New Caledonia where the number of Futunans is large enough to continue the caring and sharing tradition.

Sociopolitical Organization

Social Organization. Traditionally, there were three social classes, with the sau, or chiefly group, at the head and the *aliki* as the assistant leader. The ordinary people were bound to their households. Kava was the classic means by which status was expressed in villages at both the district and island levels.

Political Organization. The two polities of Futunan society, Sigave and Alo, each have their own traditional leadership consisting of the sau, his family, aliki and village chiefs, and their families. The rest of the population is organized by village groups, each with its own *faipule* (village official) and advisers, all of whom are responsible to the sau. The sau has authority over internal affairs including settling disputes and signing passports; any Futunan wishing to go overseas must seek his permission. Villages are grouped according to traditional affiliations. Futuna also has eight elected members of the territorial assembly of Wallis and Futuna. The Catholic mission is also a notable political force in the lives of Futunans, as the Bishop of Wallis and Futuna, the two sau of Futuna, the lavelua of Wallis, and the high commissioner representing France share the power of decision making affecting the lives of Wallisians and Futunans.

Social Control and Conflict. The church is a very strong agent of social control, along with the families and the faipule of each village. Moral guidance is sought from the priests and nuns, and this source of authority has dominated the lives of Futunans for more than 100 years. The staves carried by the deacons in church, used to keep the congregation awake and seated attentively during services, are but one symbol of this control. Conflict between individuals and between families is resolved through mediation by a senior family member, the faipule, or, if serious enough, by a member of the sau's family.

Religion and Expressive Culture

Religious Beliefs. Traditionally, mana and *tapu* were concepts that were widely observed. The main gods included Tagaloa, the sky god; Mafuike, who brought fire to the islands; Sina and the demigod Maui; and ancestral gods and spirits of animals such as Feke (octopus), Fonu (tortoise), and Tafolaa (whale). The Catholic faith has dominated the lives of Futunans for 150 years, and it has diminished though not completely replaced faith in the supernatural powers of the sau. Futunans today attend Mass and belong to various groups within the Catholic organization, though a few have expressed their dissatisfaction with the dominance that the church has over their lives. There is a church in each village, as well as several shrines, all of which are carefully tended with flowers each week. A significant though unknown proportion of people's income is donated to the church for general upkeep as well as for ideological causes.

Religious Practitioners. The Catholic priests on Futuna are both European and Wallisian, as are the nuns. Futunans train at the Pacific Theological College in Fiji to enter the priesthood.

Ceremonies. The church calendar dominates, with First Communion as well as Christmas and Easter as major social festivities. Bastille Day (14 July) and Armistice Day (11 November), as well as a day commemorating Father Chanel's beatification, are all celebrated.

Arts. Tapa making and mat weaving incorporate uniquely Futunan designs. The Futunans' fine black-ink etching on tapa is particularly distinctive. Men carve wooden staves and other objects with particular designs, mainly for sale.

Medicine. A central hospital is located in Leava, Sigave, with a clinic in Ono village and another in Poi. The medical service is staffed with a French doctor and local nursing staff. Many Futunan people also use their traditional doctors, who may be women or men. They massage and rub affected areas using local oils and leaves; they may also give medicines made of local ingredients. Pregnant women in particular visit the Futunan doctor in order to ensure a successful birth. Some love potions are also administered when requested.

Death and Afterlife. Futunans are buried according to Catholic ritual in cemeteries in the dead person's village. Every funeral is followed by a special Mass each evening for six days following the death. A large feast also marks the passing of each Futunan. Catholic beliefs in the afterlife, such as Heaven and Hell, are very much part of Futunan thinking, resembling traditional beliefs in an immortal spirit and in an afterlife in a place known as "Lagi" (meaning "sky") or "Pulotu," while "Fale Mate" (literally, "house of suffering") was a kind of hell.

See also Rotuma, Samoa, Tonga, Uvea

Bibliography

Burrows, Edwin C. (1936). *The Ethnology of Futuna*. Bernice B. Bishop Museum Bulletin no. 138. Honolulu.

Kirch, Patrick (1976). "Ethno-Archeological Investigations." In "Futuna and Uvea (Western Polynesia): A Preliminary Report." *Journal of the Polynesian Society* 85:27–69.

NANCY J. POLLOCK

Gahuku-Gama

ETHNONYMS: Gahuku, Garfuku, Gorokans

Orientation

Identification. The name "Gahuku," like "Gama," is that of a tribe or district group, but the former has been extended by linguists to include a congeries of such units and the common language they speak.

Location. Gahuku occupy the open grassland and ridges immediately to the west of the town of Goroka, which is located at 6°5' S, 145°25' E and serves as the administrative center of the Goroka District of the Eastern Highlands Province of Papua New Guinea. Bounded to the north by the Bismarck Range, the Goroka Valley is drained by the Asaro and Bena Bena rivers and lies at an elevation of about 1,200 meters, with surrounding mountains reaching over 3,000 meters. Centuries of forest clearance have left little timber in the region, though the extensive grasslands are now being reforested through administration-sponsored schemes. A marked dry season sometimes led to periodic food shortages in the past, but about 190 centimeters of rain fall annually, mostly from November to March.

Demography. At first European contact in 1930, there were an estimated 50,000 people living in the Goroka area, but it is difficult to say how many of those were Gahuku. Currently, slightly more than 16,000 Gahuku speakers are officially recognized.

Linguistic Affiliation. Some linguists consider Gahuku to be a dialect, with Asaro (or Gururumba), of the Gahuku-Asaro language, which is grouped with Benabena, Fore, Gende, Gimi, Kamano, Siane, and Yabiyufa in the East-Central Family of the East New Guinea Highlands Stock of Non-Austronesian languages. Many Gahuku are bilingual in Asaro, Benabena, or Siane, and nowadays most younger adults and children speak Tok Pisin, with increasing numbers learning English in schools.

History and Cultural Relations

Archaeological evidence from the Kafiavana rock shelter indicates the presence of hunting and gathering populations in the Goroka Valley at about 9,000 B.C., with the transition to horticulture occurring probably thousands of years ago. While ancient trade linkages to distant coastal populations are suggested by cowrie shells dated at 7,000 B.C., the Gahuku did not experience direct contact with Westerners until 1930, in the form of an Australian gold prospecting party. This was soon followed by the creation of an aerodrome at nearby Bena Bena and the arrival of Lutheran missionaries in 1932. Goroka was established as an Australian administrative post in 1939, and World War II brought over 1,000 American and Australian servicemen to Bena Bena and Goroka. Postwar roads, airstrips, economic development, political changes, and proximity to the town of Goroka have all brought Gahuku fully into the modern world.

Settlements

Prior to intensive European influence, Gahuku villages, with populations ranging from 70 to 700 people, consisted of twenty to fifty houses, occupied by women and children, laid out in a straight line with one or two men's houses at the end. Villages were enclosed with double palisades and located on narrow tops of ridges for defensive purposes. Temporary houses were erected in the surrounding gardens, beyond which pigs were put out to graze in the grassy, unclaimed area separating villages. Groves of casuarinas and bamboo, as well as their ridge locations, clearly identified villages as distinct entities, and they were indeed centers of ritual and ceremonial life. Since pacification, villages have become more spread out, and traditional conically shaped grass houses have been replaced in many cases with rectangular houses with walls of woven cane and bamboo.

Economy

Subsistence and Commercial Activities. Gahuku subsistence is still based largely on garden crops, among which sweet potatoes are predominant, while bananas, yams, taro, greens, and legumes are also important. Mainly because of the lack of forest, hunting has been of little significance in recent times, but domestic pigs are a major source of protein as well as being of vital importance in exchange relationships. Since the 1950s, cash crops, especially coffee, have provided cash income, as have some employment opportunities in nearby Goroka.

Industrial Arts. Traditional implements, including wooden digging sticks and stone adzes, were manufactured from local materials but have now largely been replaced with steel tools. Men's bark "G-strings" and women's string aprons have also yielded to Western clothing. Locally made bows and arrows are still possessed and used by most men.

Trade. Until the 1930s the Gahuku lived in a fairly closed world, maintaining trade and exchange relationships with their nearest neighbors such as Asaro and Benabena and extending to the Ramu Valley, circulating salt, shells, pigs, plumes, and stone axes. Modern trade stores have now diminished the importance of these exchanges.

Division of Labor. Gahuku tasks were traditionally assigned almost exclusively by age and sex, with no occupational specialization. Young girls began early to learn their primary responsibilities of gardening, cooking, weaving string bags, and caring for children. Boys spent their childhood in play, but with initiation began to assume their male tasks of hunting, land clearing, construction, and warfare.

Land Tenure. While stands of bamboo and casuarinas were individually owned by the men who planted them, land was held collectively by patrilineal descent groups, membership in which conferred rights of use. In the vicinity of settlements such rights were clearly defined, but they became shadowy beyond those limits. With enemy groups often less than an hour's walk away, land outside of the garden areas was often contested. Individual claims to land, while not based in custom, have become increasingly important, and they have become grounds for disputes with the rise of entrepreneurship, especially regarding coffee plantations.

Kinship

Kin Groups and Descent. Gahuku reproduction beliefs allocate only a secondary role to women, who are viewed as mere receptacles for a man's semen, and a closer spiritual tie is held to obtain between a father and his child than that between a child and its mother. Descent is, accordingly, traced through males. The male members of patrilineages, tracing their descent through about four generations to a shared ancestor, usually reside together in the same village, where they exercise rights to specific areas of land and undertake communal labor tasks. Their identity is stressed further through ownership of pairs of sacred flutes and through the pooling and sharing of resources in bride-wealth transactions. Lineages are also joined into subclans and clans, which are named despite the lack of precise knowledge of all genealogical links that unite them. Clans are exogamous, are predominantly localized with their own plots of land, and act as corporate groups in a wide range of activities, including warfare.

Kinship Terminology. Gahuku distinguish between older and younger siblings, reflecting a general concern with seniority, but sibling terms are extended widely to all of the same generation within both the lineage and clan. The use of kin terms is modified by real age differences and for males by age-mate relationships, which usually come about through coinitiation and are marked by close bonds.

Marriage and Family

Marriage. While a central theme of Gahuku culture is that the "female principle" is antagonistic and dangerous to men, traditionally a man was considered as nothing, and could never become a full member of the community, without a wife who would bear him children. In the context of male initiation ceremonies, a group of males (at about 15 years of age) would be formally betrothed to girls (of about the same age) selected by lineage elders. Upon betrothal, a girl moved to her fiancé's village and into his mother's house. A newly betrothed male was secluded for a period of weeks while adult men gave him instruction, following which he was enjoined to avoid his betrothed completely for up to seven years before cohabitation could occur. During that period he would engage in institutionalized courtship in friendly villages, trying to persuade other girls to elope with him. Not uncommonly, betrothals were broken off when the girl was considered to be maturing too quickly or when she ran off with an older male. When the time for cohabitation arrived, the groom shot an arrow into his bride's thigh, they shared a meal in public, and she was ceremonially conducted to her new house in her husband's village. Like betrothals, few marriages were permanent, ending with the wife's desertion or litigation initiated by the husband or his lineage mates suing for the return of the bride-wealth (most commonly because of childlessness, which was invariably blamed on the woman). Polygyny, although allowed, was practiced by relatively few men. Under the influence of missions, schools, and other agents of change, long betrothals, if not arranged marriages, are now a thing of the past.

Domestic Unit. Given the belief that women were dangerous to men, male children were inducted into the men's house at about 10 years of age, where they lived with all initiated males of the village. The traditional household, then, consisted of a woman, her unmarried daughters, and young sons. A man's cowives, between whom relations were almost invariably hostile, were housed separately. While husbands and wives occasionally worked together in gardens, sexual segregation was extensive. Nowadays, however, married couples increasingly share residences, with the nuclear family forming the typical household.

Inheritance. Land claims of the deceased reverted to other members of the lineage or clan, and movable property typically was claimed by surviving male relatives.

Socialization. Children have always been at the center of adult attention in Gahuku culture, but men traditionally had little to do with male children until they moved into the men's house. Thus, early child rearing was left almost exclusively in the hands of women and older siblings. Beginning at about age 5, males underwent a series of initiation ceremonies, gradually being placed under the authority and supervision of the adult male community.

Sociopolitical Organization

Social Organization. Beyond the village, the tribe was the largest social grouping, encompassing 300–1,000 people. Comprised of two or more clans, it was named (e.g., "Gahuku" or "Gama"); it claimed a common territory; and its male members, supposing a common origin of some kind, were joined in friendship, allowing no warfare within the tribe and acting as a unit in carrying out initiation ceremonies and pig festivals. Sometimes pairs of tribes joined in alliance for warfare purposes; all tribes stood in permanent friend or enemy relationships with other like units.

Political Organization. Within the lineage, authority was linked to seniority and publicly held by males, who were regarded as the custodians of customary lore and knowledge. Beyond the boundaries of kin groups, an individual might become "a man with a name," renowned for his aggressive tendencies and skill in warfare, balanced with diplomacy. Such big-men often had outstanding oratorical abilities and served as leaders. Because "character" was believed to be inherited from one's father, a son was expected to succeed his father as "a man with a name," but succession was not automatic. With European contact, village officials were appointed by the Australian administration, and these officials have now been replaced with elected members of the provincial government.

Social Control. Showing disrespect for elders, lack of regard for agemates, failures to support fellow clan members or meet other obligations among kin, breaking rules of exogamy, incest, and adultery within the subclan or clan were grounds for public shaming or physical aggression, which was a predisposition of both sexes. Moots, with big-men taking major roles, aimed at peaceful resolution through consensus.

Conflict. While physical violence and feuding (*hina*) could erupt within groups as large as the tribe, this was considered as only a temporary solution to differences; eventually the dispute was to be resolved peacefully through compensation or ceremonial reconciliation. True warfare (*rova*), seen as a permanent state of existence between tribes and endemic until it was proscribed in 1950 by the Australian administration, could be considered a dominant orientation of Gahuku culture. Battles and raids, triggered by unresolved disputes over land or sorcery accusations, were conducted each dry season, with the objectives of destroying settlements and gardens, killing as many of the enemy group as possible, and forcing the survivors to seek refuge with allied clans or tribes.

Religion and Expressive Culture

Religious Beliefs. Traditionally, Gahuku possessed no systematic cosmology. They believed in no gods, and few demons or other malignant spirits inhabited their world. On the other hand, an impersonal supernatural force was tapped through ritual, especially through the deployment of sacred flutes that, when blown, united men with each other and their ancestors, endowing them with powers of growth and fertility. While Lutheran missionaries have settled in the area since the 1930s, their progress in converting the Gahuku to Christianity was slow until recent years.

Religious Practitioners. No formal priesthood existed, with major roles in rituals and ceremonies allocated simply to elders who were viewed as repositories of the requisite knowledge.

Ceremonies. Annually, during the dry season, male initiation ceremonies were held over a period of months, inducting groups of agemates into the *nama* cult of the men's house. These rites typically concluded with a pig festival also lasting several months, during which group obligations (e.g., to allies) were discharged through gifts of pigs and pork. Less regularly, perhaps every three to five years, a fertility rite was conducted to stimulate the growth of crops and both pig and human populations. Nowadays, Christian holidays, such as Christmas, are occasions for public festivals.

Arts. Like other New Guinea highlanders, Gahuku confine their artistic production almost totally to body decoration and ornamentation for ceremonies, festivals, and courtship.

Medicine. Bush medicines and purification techniques were traditionally employed on a self-help basis, but increasingly nowadays Western medical facilities are used.

Death and Afterlife. All deaths, whatever their apparent proximate causes, were attributed to sorcery, with women viewed as the principal accomplices, if not actual agents. A "breath-soul" animating principle was believed simply to depart at death, leaving behind only a shade, which usually showed no interest in the living. Until the introduction of Christianity, no belief in an afterworld existed for the Gahuku.

See also Gururumba, Siane, Tairora

Bibliography

Finney, Ben R. (1973). *Big-Men and Business: Entrepreneurship and Economic Growth in the New Guinea Highlands.* Honolulu: University Press of Hawaii.

Finney, Ben R. (1987). *Business Development in the Highlands of Papua New Guinea.* Pacific Islands Development Program Research Report no. 6. Honolulu: East-West Center.

Read, Kenneth E. (1952). "Nama Cult of the Central Highlands, New Guinea." *Oceania* 23:1–25.

Read, Kenneth E. (1954). "Cultures of the Central Highlands, New Guinea." *Southwestern Journal of Anthropology* 10:1–43.

Read, Kenneth E. (1965). *The High Valley*. New York: Charles Scribner's Sons. Rev. ed. 1980. New York: Columbia University Press.

Read, Kenneth E. (1986). *Return to the High Valley: Coming Full Circle*. Berkeley: University of California Press.

TERENCE E. HAYS

Gainj

ETHNONYMS: Aiome Pygmies, Gants, Ganz

Orientation

Identification. Gainj is the name for approximately 1,500 people who distinguish themselves from their culturally similar neighbors on the basis of language and territorial affiliation.

Location. The Gainj live in the Takwi Valley of the Western Schrader Range in Papua New Guinea's Madang Province. On the northernmost fringe of the central highlands, the valley covers approximately 55 square kilometers, centered at 144°40' E and 5°14' S. The area receives almost 500 centimeters of rain annually, with the heaviest rainfall occurring from December to April. The mean daily temperature, 22–24° C, varies little across seasons.

Demography. The 1,500 Gainj live in approximately twenty widely dispersed local groups, which vary in size from about 30 to 200 individuals. Local groups are ephemeral, with a half-life of about two generations; a continuous process of fission and fusion maintains the total number of groups at a fairly constant level. In recent years, the population growth rate has not been significantly different from zero, except for a brief period of growth following the first major influenza epidemic in 1969. Population size appears to be maintained by low fertility and density-dependent mortality. Life expectancy at birth is 29.0 years for females and 32.4 years for males; infant mortality is about 165 per 1,000 live births, with a slightly higher rate for females than for males.

Linguistic Affiliation. Gainj is classified with Kalam and Kobon in the Kalam Family of the East New Guinea Highlands Stock of Papuan languages. Many Gainj are multilingual, most commonly in Kalam, although men are also likely to speak Tok Pisin, and some schoolchildren speak Pisin and some basic English.

History and Cultural Relations

The first Australian colonial contact occurred in 1953, but the Gainj remained largely unaffected by the colonial government until the establishment of Simbai Patrol Post, 30 kilometers to the west, in 1959. The area was declared pacified in 1963, and male labor recruitment for coastal plantations began immediately and continues today. The Anglican church established a mission in 1969 and a school in 1974, now administered by the provincial government. A major event in Gainj history was the introduction of coffee as a cash crop in 1973, which has led in recent years to the development of a road and an airstrip in the area. Both pacification and these new routes out of the valley have led to more extensive relations with neighboring groups and the migration of some Gainj into the lowland areas near Aiome.

Settlements

Settlement is widely dispersed; there are no villages or nucleated settlements. House sites are distributed through the valley within bounded, nonoverlapping, named territories (*kunyung*) which operate as ritual and political entities. This term describes both the territory and the people who are said to belong to it. House sites are usually selected on the basis of available level ground, water supply, and proximity to current gardens. Each house is ideally occupied by a nuclear family and is primarily a place for sleeping and storing personal possessions. Houses are ovoid in shape and made of wooden frames covered with sheets of bark; roofs are thatched with sago palm leaves.

Economy

Subsistence and Commercial Activities. The Gainj are classic slash-and-burn horticulturalists. They clear land in secondary forest, cultivate plots for one to two years, and then permit them to lie fallow for eight to twelve years, to a maximum of about thirty years. Sweet potatoes are the staple crop; taro and yams also make up a lesser but significant part of the diet. Bananas, sugarcane, breadfruit, pandanus, *pitpit*, and a large number of domestic and wild greens supplement the basic root-crop diet. Introduced cultigens, such as corn, pumpkins, cassava, papayas, cucumbers, and pineapples, are grown in small amounts. Pigs and chickens are kept in small numbers but are rarely eaten, since they are valued as elements in bride-wealth and exchange. Men do some hunting, but this contributes little to household maintenance. Snakes, lizards, eels, insects, and rats are eaten but their total nutritive value is slight. In 1978, the Gainj marketed their first major coffee crop and are now the major coffee producers for Madang Province. Cash cropping has fostered local business cooperatives which buy and sell coffee beans and operate local stores in which coffee profits are used to buy manufactured items and imported foods such as rice, canned beef, and fish.

Industrial Arts. The most important locally produced items are all-purpose string carrying bags and skirts. Mats and some traditional weapons, spears and bows and arrows, are still manufactured.

Trade. The larger region within which the Gainj live was important in precontact times as a funnel for marine shells (especially cowrie and bailer shells) being traded up into the central highlands, and the Gainj participated in that trade to some degree. In addition, the Gainj area was an important source of bird of paradise plumes for the central highlands.

More recently, the Gainj have taken advantage of their fringe highland location by trading lowland cassowaries up to the central highlands, where they are used in bride-wealth payments.

Division of Labor. There is a sharp sexual division of labor. Women bear the major burden of everyday physical work. Women bear, nurse, and care for children; burn, plant, tend, and harvest gardens; provide wood and water; prepare and cook food; tend pigs; manufacture string and weave it into bags and skirts; collect wild foods and raw materials; maintain house sites; and care for the sick and dying. Women also maintain, harvest, process, and carry coffee. Men's labor is more sporadic and dramatic. No longer warriors, they clear and fence gardens, build houses, hunt, plant and sell coffee, and control ritual and politics.

Land Tenure. Gainj say "Yandena ofu" (I make gardens) in a particular kunyung. This applies to kunyung in which they have gardened, are currently gardening, and may garden in the future. Like the Kalam and Kopon, they are unusual in having no corporate groups controlling access to land or exercising rights over land as a group estate. Gainj garden in their own kunyung, in their birthplaces, and in the kunyung or birthplace of any grandparent, parent, sibling, cross cousin, spouse, or child. Access to land is also provided through corresponding spousal relationships. Men and women enjoy access to land and may garden in virtually all of the named territories. While there is no concept of individual ownership of land, for as long as an individual uses land it belongs to him or her, in the sense that he or she has exclusive rights to its produce. Trees can be individually owned and can be passed on at their owner's death. Once a garden has been abandoned, its owner retains no residual rights to it and the land is restored to the common fund. There is always a balance of land being withdrawn from and returned to the common fund. The semipermanent nature of coffee trees will undoubtedly affect further land use and availability.

Kinship

Kin Groups and Descent. Kinship is reckoned bilaterally. There are no descent groups. The important kinship groups are the nuclear family, the kindred, and the kunyung.

Kinship Terminology. On the first ascending generation, terminology is bifurcate merging. Terminology for one's own generation is more difficult to classify. Parallel cousins and opposite-sex cross cousins are called by the same terms as opposite-sex siblings; however, same-sex cross cousins are called by different terms than same-sex siblings. The terminology can be called modified Hawaiian, consistent with the generational terminology in the first descending and second ascending generations, or modified Iroquois, consistent with the bifurcate-merging terminology of the first ascending generation.

Marriage and Family

Marriage. Virtually all Gainj marry. The exogamous unit is the bilateral kindred, with membership delimited by the first degree of collaterality. Sister exchange is permitted but not preferred; it obviates bride-wealth if exchange is simultaneous. All other marriages require payment from the groom's kin to the bride's, although Gainj bride-wealths are small by highland standards. There is a preference for kunyung exogamy, but there are no negative sanctions for kunyung-endogamous marriages. Once a child has been born there is virtually no divorce. Men usually remarry after the death of a wife, while widow remarriage is correlated with the number of children a woman has borne. Postmarital residence is ideally patrivirilocal, but there is considerable variation in actual living arrangements. Polygyny is highly valued, but most marriages are monogamous.

Domestic Unit. The basic domestic unit is the household composed, ideally, of a nuclear family, although many households do in fact include nonnuclear members. The household is the basic unit of consumption and production.

Inheritance. Since land is not owned, the only heritable items are personal property, which is generally distributed along same-sex networks, although there are no rules as to disposition.

Socialization. Young children of both sexes are primarily socialized by mothers, although other concerned adults are often part of the process. Boys are initiated between ages 10 and 15; at that time they move into bachelors' houses, away from their mothers' influence. While it is not unknown for a child to be punished physically, it is unusual. Children are often permitted to learn the outcome of dangerous situations (e.g., playing near a fire) by painful experience.

Sociopolitical Organization

Social Organization. Traditionally, the kunyung acted as a group in ritual and warfare, although ties of cognatic kinship could excuse a man from fighting. Membership is not automatic, and descent is never invoked as a principle of recruitment. Group composition is phrased in terms of a shared, continuing, and primary nourishment from gardens within the territory. All those individuals who have received their principal nourishment from the gardens of the same territory share membership and kinship. While membership is fluid, changing membership requires considerable time, and people, particularly in-marrying women, may consider themselves members of two kunyung during the time their membership is in the process of change.

Political Organization. There are no hereditary political positions among the Gainj. Traditionally, local big-men were associated with each territory; the basis of their temporary ascendancy was their skill as fight leaders. The extensive competitive exchange systems that characterize many groups in the central highlands did not operate among the Gainj. Kunyung were the most important political units and their major function was warfare. However, even in warfare, individuals were permitted choice on the basis of conflicting cognatic kinship ties. Today, political unity is expressed in ritual dances and in business cooperatives, whose leaders are spoken of as big-men waging business wars. As is the case in much of highland New Guinea, a system of male dominance permits men to exploit the productive and reproductive abilities of women to their own political and economic advantage.

Social Control. Although the Gainj are citizens of Papua New Guinea and subject to its laws, the legal system operates as social control only in the most serious and public cases. On a more quotidian level, talk, including gossip and public discussion of improper behavior, are more important. By far the major form of social control is fear of sorcery and of sorcery accusations.

Conflict. Traditionally, warfare occurred between Gainj kunyung and between Gainj and Kalam. In the latter, participants were those kunyung directly involved and any allies they could muster, with no expectation that all Gainj would be involved. Warfare was small-scale, composed of forays rather than battles, and was usually precipitated by disputes between individuals or the need to avenge deaths. Gainj note that since pacification, sorcery and sorcery accusations have increased, and "fighting has gone secret."

Religion and Expressive Culture

Religious Beliefs. Malevolent spirits, associated with mythical cannibals and sorcerers, are believed to inhabit the permanently cloud-covered primary forest of higher altitudes. Each kunyung is said to have such a place associated with it that is safe for members but dangerous for nonmembers. Ancestral ghosts are believed to be at best neutral; at worst they are malevolent and cause illness and death among the living. There is a pervasive fear of human sorcerers. Some Gainj have become members of the Anglican church, but for most people membership appears to be nominal.

Religious Practitioners. Gainj recognize traditional healers and sorcerers.

Ceremonies. The major ceremony is a dance (*nyink*), which one kunyung sponsors while others attend as guests. Traditionally, nyinks ended a male initiation, but with fewer youth being initiated, dances may now be held to celebrate the opening of a trade store or the formation of a business cooperative. Men, decorated and wearing elaborate headdresses, sing, dance, and drum from dusk to dawn, before an audience of men, women, and children from the entire valley. Nyinks are still often the occasion for paying outstanding debts and beginning marriage payments.

Arts. As in much of the highlands, the principal art form is body decoration and the construction of elaborate headdresses.

Medicine. There are very few surviving traditional medical practitioners, mostly very old men. Like a number of highland peoples, the Gainj value Western medicine and would like to have greater access to it. There is a corresponding denigration of traditional medicine, and younger Gainj are not learning traditional methods. Moreover, local representatives of the provincial government and missionaries have discouraged traditional medicine, going so far as to imprison admitted practitioners. The traditional pharmacopoeia relied heavily on plants, especially ginger and stinging nettles. A local plant is also said to have been effective as both a contraceptive and an abortifacient. Occasionally, people still sacrifice pigs to ancestors in an attempt to cure illness.

Death and Afterlife. All deaths are believed to be caused by sorcery or by malevolent spirits. Ancestral ghosts are thought to inhabit the areas in which they died and may visit evil upon the living. They can be ritually appeased; sorcerers cannot.

Bibliography

Johnson, Patricia L. (1981). "When Dying Is Better Than Living: Female Suicide among the Gainj of Papua New Guinea." *Ethnology* 20:325–334.

Johnson, Patricia L. (1982). "Gainj Kinship and Social Organization." Ph.D dissertation, University of Michigan, Ann Arbor.

Johnson, Patricia L. (1988). "Women and Development: A Highland New Guinea Example." *Human Ecology* 16: 105–122.

Long, J. C., J. M. Naidu, H. W. Mohrenweiser, H. Gershowitz, P. L. Johnson, J. W. Wood, and P. E. Smouse (1986). "Genetic Characterization of Gainj- and Kalam-Speaking Peoples of Papua New Guinea." *American Journal of Physical Anthropology* 70:75–96.

Wood, James W., Patricia L. Johnson, and Kenneth L. Campbell (1985). "Demographic and Endocrinological Aspects of Low Natural Fertility in Highland New Guinea." *Journal of Biosocial Science* 17:57–79.

Wood, James W., Daina Lai, Patricia L. Johnson, Kenneth L. Campbell, and Ila A. Maslar (1985). "Lactation and Birth Spacing in Highland New Guinea." *Journal of Biosocial Science*, Supplement 9:159–173.

PATRICIA L. JOHNSON AND JAMES W. WOOD

Garia

ETHNONYM: Sumau

Orientation

Identification. The Garia live in southern Madang Province of Papua New Guinea. "Garia" is their own name for the language they speak, which is called "Sumau" by linguists after a prominent mountain peak in the area.

Location. Garia territory includes 80–110 square kilometers of land between the coastal plain of Madang and the Ramu River Valley, with central coordinates of 145°2' E, 5°28' S. The region consists of rugged, low mountain ranges, with the highest peaks reaching about 920 meters. The most important of these is Mount Somau, the mythological origin place of the Garia. Three principal rivers arise in these mountains and provide the routes of a major regional transportation and communication system. Most of the land is covered with dense jungle, broken up by occasional patches of savannah and secondary vegetation. The dry season (February–October) is one of high humidity and intense social and religious activity. During the rest of the year there is regular afternoon rain and people spend much of their time making and repairing implements and tools.

Demography. In 1950 the population consisted of about 2,500 people; by 1975 the resident population included slightly over this number, but another 700 or so Garia were away for employment elsewhere in Papua New Guinea.

Linguistic Affiliation. Sumau is classified with its nearest neighbor, Usino, in the Peka Family of Non-Austronesian languages. There is a high degree of multilingualism in the population, and since 1949 most Garia have been fluent in Tok Pisin and many also in English.

History and Cultural Relations

According to Garia oral traditions, they originated to the west of their current location as the first human beings, given birth to by a boulder assisted by a snake goddess. Following the political annexation of northeastern New Guinea by Germany in 1884, exploratory expeditions skirted Garia territory but had little direct contact with the people. These first foreigners were associated by the Garia with Nikolai Miklouho-Maclay, an earlier Russian explorer of the coast to the east, and they were considered deities called *magarai* (*masalai* in Tok Pisin) after Maclay. The most direct Garia contact with Europeans began with labor recruiters during World War I. Between the wars such recruiting intensified and a three-year term in European employment became routine for young Garia men. In 1922, Lutherans established a mission station and schools in the area, and by 1936 the Garia were considered fully "controlled" by the Australian administration, with government-appointed headmen, courts, head tax, consolidation of the population into villages, and abolition of tribal warfare. Although the Japanese occupied the Madang coast during World War II they had little direct impact on the Garia. However, during this period the missionaries were evacuated and several cargo cults swept through the region, one of which originated locally. At the close of the war plantations resumed operation and the missionaries returned to find much of the traditional religion reestablished amid the cargo-cult activity. The 1950s saw administrative attempts at economic development of the region, including the introduction of coffee as a cash crop, and in 1964 the Garia voted in the election for the first House of Assembly. Garia are now incorporated in the Usino Local Government Council and Lutheran and Seventh-Day Adventist missions are well established.

Settlements

Traditionally the Garia lived in small, scattered hamlets, each having fewer than fifty residents. There were three kinds of houses: men's dwellings; those for women and children; and clubhouses where adolescent males slept. All had earth floors and either leaf thatch on a beehive framework or slit-log walls with a palm or grass roof. In the 1920s Australian administrators introduced and enforced the coastal style of stilt houses, with bark walls, raised floors of black palm, and a palm or grass thatch roof. During the period of the 1920s–1950s people were required to concentrate their residence in fourteen large villages of up to 300 people each. Each village consisted of wards or sections named after the small areas of associated bush. Since the 1950s the Garia have largely gone back to their preference for intermittently shifting hamlets. In any case the population of a hamlet or village is unstable, consisting simply of those people who have, for the time being, common economic interests in the same area or who want to associate with a particular leader.

Economy

Subsistence and Commercial Activities. The Garia practice shifting cultivation; fencing assists in soil retention on the steep slopes of gardens. Each stage of garden work employs both secular and religious techniques, with garden leaders' magic necessarily preceding any other activity. Traditional staple crops include taro, yams, native spinach, *pitpit*, bananas, and sugarcane; in recent decades these have been supplemented with *Xanthosoma* taro, corn, coconuts, and European vegetables, all introduced by Europeans. The wet season is a time of food shortage, but the dry season is a time of plenty. Limited wild game in the region restricts hunting to a casual and individual pursuit. Fishing, using arrows and spears, is done mainly in the wet season. Chickens and dogs are kept, but domestic pigs are few and saved for ceremonial occasions and as items of bride-wealth and exchange at feasts.

Industrial Arts. Everyday items manufactured locally include net bags, conical clay pots, wooden plates, round wooden bowls, digging sticks, axes and adzes, bows, arrows, spears, cassowary-bone daggers, betel lime gourds, bamboo smoking tubes, and hand drums. Traditional stone tools have now been replaced by steel, and other Western implements are also popular.

Trade. Garia have long been linked with the Madang coast to the east and Usino and the Ramu Valley to the west through trade networks. Pots are the main item of export, being traded to the east for shell valuables and to the west for sorcery medicines, tobacco, wooden plates and bowls, stone axes and knives, and bows and arrows. Individual men make special trips for the purpose of trade or engage in barter in the course of pig exchanges. Nowadays there are trade stores in the area selling Western goods, but the networks of trade partnerships remain active.

Division of Labor. A sexual division of labor governs everyday activities, with males taking the responsibility for heavier garden work and construction. Net bags are made and used exclusively by women. In the work of producing pottery, the main trade item, women are charged with collecting the clay while men are the actual potters.

Land Tenure. All useful land is said to be owned and each demarcated area bears the name of the cognatic stock and human proprietors associated with it. All members of a cognatic stock have permanent rights of personal usufruct and the responsibility of collective guardianship over landholdings bearing its name. In the north, the holdings of a cognatic stock may be scattered within a general locality and rights are vested in individuals, while in the south land plots tend to be concentrated in huge tracts, rights to which are allocated to a group of agnates within the cognatic stock. Temporary usufructuary rights are usually granted to most members of a man's "security circle" (see the later section on social organization). Rights to land are inherited by male agnates, but they can also be purchased by male enates, especially sisters' sons.

Kinship

Kin Groups and Descent. Kinship is traced cognatically, but patrikin and matrikin are distinguished in everyday conversation and there is a marked bias toward patriliny. Patrilineages are the cores of cognatic stocks, maintaining exclusive corporate rights of guardianship of the land belonging to the cognatic stocks. The kindred is not a defined local group and all political allegiances are expressed in terms of interpersonal ties rather than group membership. In general, the kinship system may be said to be highly flexible and individualistic.

Kinship Terminology. The system is basically of the Iroquois type, but father's sister and mother's brother's wife are equated with mother, and both father's sister's husband and mother's sister's husband have a special term and are treated almost as affines.

Marriage and Family

Marriage. "Close kin," that is, cognates linked by marriages up to the second ascending generation, are forbidden to marry; more distant kin living within one's own political region are the preferred marriage partners. Usually a man, when he is in his early twenties, selects a wife (in her late teens) from potentially hostile people, and his subsequent behavior toward his affines is marked by extreme respect. All men aspire to polygyny, but marriage entails a major and prolonged economic burden for a man, with bride-price payments that must be tendered to his immediate and close affines for many years. During the first year of marriage the wife lives apart from her husband in his mother's house, after which time the couple may cohabit. The rules for second marriages, especially those involving widows, are more complex. Ideally, there should be no close consanguineal or affinal links between the parties, and bride-price must be paid by the new husband unless the couple elopes.

Domestic Unit. The basic domestic unit is an elementary or compound family, although families are not tightly knit and residential segregation of the sexes is maintained. Women are thought to be inherently dangerous to men; thus it is believed that men should not spend much time with women, and from adolescence until marriage a male is absolutely forbidden to associate with any female of child-bearing age. A husband and wife may work together at a garden site (with adolescent children usually planting on separate sites), but they will rest in separate groups formed on the basis of sex. Garden teams are socially irregular, formed around those men who wish to associate with certain middle-aged leaders, who supervise all gardening land.

Inheritance. Land rights are inherited by male agnates, ideally by sons but, when they are lacking, by true brothers and brothers' sons. Daughters rarely inherit land because they are considered to be the responsibility of their husbands.

Socialization. Parents and older relatives are the main socializing agents, frequently indulging and rarely disciplining children. When a child is able to walk and talk it is taught the basics of kinship terminology and associated duties. It learns that cooperation and support are earned by correct behavior and that one cannot survive as a socioeconomic isolate. Young children sleep with their mothers, which girls will continue to do until they marry. Young boys form play groups, while girls spend most of their time with their mothers. At about the age of 10, a boy begins a sequence of initiation ceremonies and moves into a clubhouse (sometimes leaving his parents' settlement), where he is segregated from all nubile women until he marries. Adolescent girls go through a first-menstruation ceremony but they remain living in their mothers' houses.

Sociopolitical Organization

Social Organization. The most important component of social organization is what anthropologist Peter Lawrence calls the "security circle," a (male) Ego-centered network based on kinship, descent, affinity, and special interpersonal relationships such as those arising from common economic interests, coresidence, trade partnerships, and coinitiation. Close kin constitute the core of the security circle, within which one may not marry; nor may one eat animals raised by other members of one's security-circle or engage in any violent behavior. While security-circle members are invariably dispersed across the landscape, they are obligated to cooperate with and provide support to one another.

Political Organization. While government-appointed headmen, and now elected officials, represent Garia in formal provincial and national assemblies, at the local level all social action, including pig exchanges, initiation ceremonies, gardening activities, and the establishment of settlements, is set in motion by the decisions of big-men. A man becomes such a leader by attaining a reputation based on his self-confidence, oratorical powers, and ability to assemble wealth for exchanges and to coordinate and supervise group activities. It is also essential that he demonstrate effectiveness in the superhuman realm, for he is depended upon to perform rituals as well as to be the catalyst for other events. A big-man's power rests on popular approval and he has no judicial authority.

Social Control. As a child learns at an early age, the withdrawal of cooperation and support are powerful Garia sanctions, and they are combined with shame and local criticism as ways to redress secular offenses. Garia emphasize self-regulation and when disputes do arise—over theft, invasions of gardens by pigs, homicide, adultery, or sorcery—they are expected to be settled in moots with the aid of neutral kin whose aim is compromise, which might involve compensation, retaliation, or, nowadays, a football match between the security circles of the respective parties. Most disputes are thus resolved or gradually fade into oblivion. The Garia say that in the past women were put to death for witnessing men's initiation secrets, but in general, and certainly in recent decades, breaches of taboos usually just result in moral condemnation and stigma. Punishment is left up to ghosts and the gods, who might visit the guilty party with crop destruction, bad luck, illness, or death.

Conflict. Garia never united in war against their neighbors, but on rare occasions intragroup warfare erupted over an unresolved sorcery feud.

Religion and Expressive Culture

Religious Beliefs. Traditional Garia religion was regarded as the cornerstone of the universe, an essential background to all social and technological activities. A pantheon of gods and goddesses was posited. These deities were believed to have shaped the physical environment, created human beings, and invented social and material culture. According to myths, after teaching people how to make things and engage in social affairs, the deities disclosed their secret names and the esoteric spells required to invoke their aid in making things happen. These creator deities were believed to live on, in corporeal form, in sanctuaries in the bush. Other entities in the traditional cosmology included hostile demons and personal doubles, who inhabited the bush but associated freely with people and could be either friendly or hostile. Finally, ghosts or spirits of the dead were the ultimate custodians of patrilineage estates, whose role primarily was to protect their living kin. The Garia perceived the relationship between human and superhuman beings as one of reciprocal moral obligations, and they saw religion as the primary operative force in life. Following early, partially successful attempts by Lutheran evangelists to convert the Garia to Christianity, much of this traditional religion was revived during World War II, when cargo cults swept through the area. In these cults, God (like traditional deities) was viewed as the ultimate source of material wealth (Western goods), and, if properly invoked through ritual, He would send these goods from Paradise using spirits of the dead as emissaries. While the cults as such lost favor and had disappeared by 1949, today Garia religion manifests the same kind of syncretic blend of old and new elements.

Religious Practitioners. Ultimately, Garia religion was and is individualistic, with each person required to win the moral commitment and support of the gods through performance of ritual, including invocations and food offerings. For joint undertakings, human and superhuman beings were mobilized through the conduct of ritual by big-men, whose knowledge of myths and spells is regarded as essential.

Ceremonies. During the dry season the most important ceremonies are held in the form of pig exchanges. These might be initiated by only a few people who use them to extend or buttress their security circles. Guests are invited from distant settlements and after an all-night dance to honor their hosts they receive pigs and food the next morning. The pig exchange is the most important occasion for paying ritual honor to the dead, who are also important allies in human affairs. A series of three separate initiation ceremonies marks a male's passage from puberty to marriage, during which he is taught the names and spells required to extend his security circle to include the deities and spirits of the dead. Also, those who are initiated together form special relationships based on this common experience and become members of each others' human security circles, however they may be otherwise related.

Arts. Ceremony provides the main context for Garia artistic expression, which focuses on: body ornamentation with floral decorations, shell and bone ornaments, and ornate bird-plume headdresses; music, employing hand drums, bamboo stamping tubes, and bamboo flutes; and dancing.

Medicine. The spirits of the dead are major allies in warding off disease and promoting good health, but grave illnesses may also be interpreted as retribution by ghosts or the gods for breaches of taboos. Otherwise illness is generally attributed to sorcery and treated by divination and extraction, skills learned by males during their initiation sequence.

Death and Afterlife. Three lands of the dead are postulated by Garia; while regionally based, they are believed to be supervised by Obomwe, the snake goddess who gave birth to mankind. The life of the dead is thought to replicate the life of the living, with ghosts living in settlements with their kin and visiting living relatives in dreams. If death has resulted from physical violence, the spirit of the deceased is believed to haunt the land of the living in search of revenge. Traditionally, the dead were exposed on tree platforms and the sons of the deceased would collect and preserve their bones as relics. Since the 1920s, under administrative and mission influence, Garia have buried their dead in village cemeteries or in the bush near the land a person was working when he or she died. At funerals, all of the security circle of the deceased assemble and comfort the bereaved as they express respect for the dead and help the soul on its road to the land of the dead. Garia believe that after two or three generations spent in the land of the dead, spirits are transformed into flying foxes (fruit bats) or bush pigeons.

See also Usino

Bibliography

Lawrence, Peter (1964). *Road Belong Cargo: A Study of the Cargo Movement in the Southern Madang District, New Guinea.* Manchester: Manchester University Press. Reprint. 1979. New York: Humanities Press.

Lawrence, Peter (1971). "Cargo Cult and Religious Belief among the Garia." In *Melanesia: Readings on a Culture Area,* edited by L. L. Langness and John C. Weschler, 295–314. Scranton, Pa.: Chandler.

Lawrence, Peter (1971). "The Garia of the Madang District." In *Politics in New Guinea,* edited by Ronald M. Berndt and Peter Lawrence, 74–93. Seattle: University of Washington Press.

Lawrence, Peter (1984). *The Garia: An Ethnography of a Traditional Cosmic System in Papua New Guinea.* Manchester: Manchester University Press.

TERENCE E. HAYS

Gebusi

ETHNONYMS: Bibo, Nomad River peoples

Orientation

Identification. Gebusi identify themselves as a distinctive Gebusi-speaking cultural group within the Nomad River area of the East Strickland River Plain, Western Province, Papua New Guinea. Gebusi perceive selective similarities between themselves and other Nomad River groups such as the Honibo, the Samo, and to a lesser extent the Bedamini to the east.

Location. Gebusi live near the northern edge of New Guinea's large south central lowland rain forest at approximately 6°17–22' S and 142°118–125' E. They are bordered on the north by the Hamam River, on the northwest by the Nomad River and the Nomad government station, and on the south by the Rentoul River. The dominant landform is relict alluvial plain, with erosion forming accordant ridges and valleys with relief up to 75 meters despite a flat rain-forest appearance from the air and a maximum elevation of 200 meters above sea level. Soils are clayey with no stone except in larger river beds. Primary rain-forest canopy is ubiquitous except over larger rivers and small settlement and garden clearings. Monthly median high temperature ranges between 32.5° C and 38° C, with an overall high of 42° C. Rainfall averages 416.5 centimeters a year, with a variable dry season from June to early November. Humidity is very high.

Demography. Gebusi numbered approximately 450 in 1980–1982, with a population density of 2.6 persons per square kilometer. Gebusi have suffered depopulation, partly from introduced epidemic influenza as well as from tuberculosis and other pulmonary and gastrointestinal diseases, resulting in an estimated 24 percent natural population decline from November 1967 to January 1982. This decline was counterbalanced by population inmigration, mostly from Bedamini to the east, leading to a net territorial population increase of 1.3 persons per year over this period.

Linguistic Affiliation. The linguist S. A. Wurm classifies Gebusi as part of the East Strickland Language Family within the South-Central New Guinea Stock of the Trans–New Guinea Phylum. Gebusi are part of a chain of related dialects extending from the Strickland River east to Mount Bosavi and Mount Sisa. A partial break in this chain exists between Gebusi and the Bedamini to their east, who share only 32 percent of their cognates. Bedamini expansion may have eradicated linguistic groups that were once intermediate.

History and Cultural Relations

Gebusi are one of some dozen cultural and linguistic groups inhabiting the Strickland-Bosavi area. Each ethnic group claims distinct customs and a named language. Features common to the entire area include: traditional residence in a communal longhouse, with men and women sleeping separately; social organization based on small dispersed patriclans, adult males coresiding through a combination of agnatic, affinal, and matrilateral ties; spirit mediumship in all-night spirit seances focusing on sickness and curing, sorcery or witchcraft, collective subsistence, and conflict; a single-stage initiation or celebratory transition into adult manhood; and all-night dance and songfest rituals between longhouses, during which a beautifully costumed dancer is accompanied by plaintive songs. Raiding between adjacent ethnic groups was common. Gebusi were the target of raids particularly by the much larger Bedamini population to their north and east, which has intruded strongly into border areas. Bedamini were pacified by government patrols in the late 1960s and early 1970s. Gebusi were first effectively contacted in 1962 and have had little subsequent contact with outsiders except for yearly government patrols, a recently established mission station (begun in the mid-1980s), and highly sporadic work with Western geological survey crews northeast of Nomad. In 1980–1982, spirit seances, sorcery inquests, male initiation, and ritual homosexuality were still practiced.

Settlements

From the air, Gebusi settlements appear as isolated footprints of clearing amid sprawling rain forest. In 1980–1982 there were seventeen principal residence sites with an average population of 26.5 persons and a range of 6 to 54 persons. Although widely spaced, smaller settlements tend to orient socially around larger ones, at which initiations and larger feasts and dances are held. Larger settlements have a communal longhouse 20 meters or more in length, roofed with sago palm leaves. The common cooking/socializing area of the longhouse is on ground level, with elevated rear portions sex-segregated into collective male and female sleeping and socializing areas. Longhouses are supplemented by numerous small garden houses and shelters occupied temporarily during extended gardening and foraging activities. Gebusi life-style is extremely mobile. On an average night 45 percent of the village's permanent residents have left the village for a garden house, a foraging shelter, or another longhouse settlement.

Economy

Subsistence and Commercial Activities. Gebusi subsistence combines rudimentary gardening, sago-palm processing, foraging, and fishing. Hunting is sporadically practiced and husbandry of semidomesticated pigs is rudimentary. Bananas are the primary starch staple, constituting perhaps 65–70 percent of the starch diet. Sago supplies roughly 25–30 percent and root crops about 5–10 percent of starch intake. Most gardens are unfenced, quickly cleared, and filled primarily with banana plots. Gebusi get their protein mostly from casual foraging activities that yield grubs, bird eggs, nuts, and riverine fauna. Despite this, many children appear malnourished, with large, symmetrically distended abdomens and underdeveloped musculature.

Industrial Arts. Gebusi industrial arts include the making by men of bows and arrows, drums, tobacco pipes, palm-spathe bowls, ritual decorations, and—since the introduction of steel axes and adzes—canoes; women weave fine net bags, sago pouches, ritual chest bands, and string skirts, and they also make bark tapa. In 1980–1982, cash cropping, wage labor, and outmigration were negligible, and there were no trade stores among Gebusi or at the Nomad station.

Trade. Indigenous trade was conducted opportunistically with no standard rates of exchange. Trade items produced by Gebusi included tobacco and dogs'-teeth necklaces. These were traded with adjacent groups for red ocher, cuscus-bone arrow tips, pearl-shell slivers, and, precolonially, ax heads made from stone found near the Strickland River.

Division of Labor. Men hunt, fish, cut down trees (including sago palms), build houses, and make weapons and most ritual decorations; women process sago, carry most garden produce and firewood, do most weeding and harvesting, and make string bags, skirts, sago baskets, and bark cloth.

Land Tenure. Land rights are patrilineal, but residence confers extensive usufructuary land rights and privileges. Most Gebusi do not live on or cultivate their fathers' land, though they may visit such land to exploit sago palms, nut trees, or special foraging resources. In principle, entire patriclans have rights to bounded areas of land, but clan members tend to be residentially dispersed outside of these areas. Conversely, intrusive or refugee clans, which may have no clan land in Gebusi territory, can be numerically and politically prominent within their communities. Land is not a significant matter of dispute and there is no discernible land shortage.

Kinship

Kin Groups and Descent. The only named and enduring Gebusi kinship group is the patriclan, with a population ranging from one to sixty-seven members, averaging eighteen. Clans recognize nominal "sibling" ties to a few other clans based on putative coresidence in the past. Genealogies are extremely shallow, with agnatic linkage traceable only to first or second cousins. Clans are residentially dispersed, with de facto subclans and patrilines virtually autonomous from one another despite having only one to three adult male members.

Kinship Terminology. Kinship terminology is bifurcate merging with Omaha cross-generational merging between mother/mother's brother's daughter, mother's brother/mother's brother's son, and child/sister's child. Affinal ties are extended from the entire wife-giving clan to the individual groom only.

Marriage and Family

Marriage. Marriage is ideally sister exchange; same-generation exchange of women between clans constitutes 52 percent of first marriages. A countervailing ideal of nonreciprocated romantic marriage is also strong. In either case, marriage is accompanied by neither bride-wealth nor bride-service. Divorce and polygyny are both infrequent; 14 percent of completed marriages are terminated by divorce, and 7 percent of married men are married polygynously. Polygyny usually results from the levirate; the small patriline or subclan has first claims over the widowed wives of its deceased men, just as it takes primary responsibility for supplying "sisters" in reciprocity for its male members' wives. Postmarital residence may be uxori/matrilocal, neolocal, or viri/patrilocal, with some statistical bias toward virilocality.

Domestic Unit. A married couple form the basic gardening unit, though many subsistence, foraging, and domestic tasks are conducted collectively by groups of men or women. The effective domestic unit is typically two or three nuclear families related by close agnatic, affinal, or matrilateral ties. Settlement coresidence among adult male wife's brother/sister's husband is 68 percent of that actually possible, 82 percent among mother's brother/sister's son, 85 percent among father's brother's son, 88 percent among wife's father/daughter's husband, and 92 percent among brothers. The settlement as a whole is comprised of several interrelated extended family clusters and is a domestic unit in sponsoring feasts.

Inheritance. Aside from long-term land resources such as sago palms or nut trees, there is little material property to inherit—perhaps only a pearl-shell sliver or a pig—and any such items are typically bequeathed to sons.

Socialization. This aspect of Gebusi life is generally affectionate and benign. Fathers as well as mothers are indulgent with young children; older children are seldom yelled at and virtually never struck. Boys' transition to the men's sleeping section of the longhouse is gradual and noncoercive, occurring between ages 4 and 7. Male initiation is a celebratory and nontraumatic transition to manhood at 17 to 23 years of age.

Sociopolitical Organization

Social and Political Organization. The Gebusi social and political order is extremely decentralized, with no secular leadership positions (i.e., no recognized big-men, headmen, senior elders, or war leaders). Adult men are surprisingly noncompetitive as well as egalitarian, and they are self-effacing rather than boastful; collective decisions emerge from general consensus. Settlements tend to act as de facto political units in feast giving and fighting, diverse clan affiliations among coresident men notwithstanding. Single-stage initiation and subsequent marriage confer full adult male status. There is little if any social inequality between wife givers and wife takers; affines exchange food equally in ongoing relationships regardless of the balance of women in marriage between them. Food gifts and subsequent exchanges affirm social ties in a noncompetitive fashion both within and between settlements. Gebusi do not use bride-wealth, bride-service, or homicide compensation. They employ person-for-person reciprocity in marriage and sorcery retribution where possible. Gender relations are a significant dimension of Gebusi sociopolitical organization; communal male prerogatives include legitimate control of rituals, feast giving, bow-and-arrow fighting, and large-scale collective activity. Women frequently participate as singers but dance only at initiations, are generally excluded from spirit seances, and may be sporadically beaten without reprisal by husbands. Women seclude themselves in their section of the longhouse during peak menstruation and males harbor nominal beliefs of female sexual and menstrual contamination. However, such belief appears to be more a topic of ribald male joking than a source of personal anxiety. Many women exercise significant influence in spousal choice—norms of sister exchange notwithstanding—and marital harmony is the norm on a quotidian basis. Male views of women are ambivalent, ranging from a positive image of women as attractive sexual partners and helpers—prominently encoded in the persona of the beneficent spirit woman—to derogatory attitudes concerning the sexual, productive, and reproductive status of older women.

Social Control and Conflict. Warfare between Gebusi settlement communities was infrequent in contrast to systematic raiding upon Gebusi by Bedamini. Gebusi ritual fights between settlements sometimes escalated to club-wielding brawls but rarely to bow-and-arrow fighting; they seldom resulted in casualties. The same is true of fights erupting occasionally over nonreciprocal marriage and adultery accusation. The most virulent incidents of Gebusi social control and conflict stem from sorcery attribution. Unlike many New Guinea societies, Gebusi sorcery suspects are often publicly accused, forced to undergo difficult divinatory trials, and executed. Between about 1940 and 1982, 29 percent of female deaths and 35 percent of male deaths were homicides, the vast majority resulting from sorcery attributions. The 33 percent of adult deaths due to physical violence extrapolates to a yearly homicide rate of at least 568 per 100,000 over the 42-year period. Yet there is no evidence that sorcery packets are actually made or used by Gebusi; Gebusi sorcery is the projective attribution of deviance. Most older individuals are eventually accused of sorcery. The perception of impartiality in elaborate spiritual inquests corresponds with both the consensus of diverse clan members to execute of one of their own community members as a sorcerer and the lack of violent resistance or revenge by the accused's kin. Statistically, however, sorcery attribution and attendant homicide are most common between affines related via nonreciprocal marriage, with both wife givers and wife receivers killed in equivalent numbers.

Religion and Expressive Culture

Religious Beliefs. The Gebusi cosmos is populated by numerous spirits, including those of fish, birds, and other animals. Of particular importance are the true spirit people (*to di os*), who aid the Gebusi in finding the causes of sickness, the identity of sorcerers, the location of lost pigs, and the success of anticipated hunting expeditions. Although spirits may cause transient illness, virtually all deaths among humans are believed to be caused by other living Gebusi through either sorcery or homicide. Sorcery is also seen as a predisposing cause of accidental death and suicide. Following spiritual indictment, sorcery suspects are enjoined to perform corpse or sago divinations in a largely futile attempt to establish their innocence.

Religious Practitioners. Spirit people are contacted by male spirit mediums in all-night spirit seances held on average once every eleven days. The spirit medium sits quietly in a darkened longhouse and self-induces a trance. His own spirit departs and is replaced by beautiful spirit women who chant in high falsetto voices. Their songs are echoed line by line by a chorus of men who sit around the spirit medium. During the seance, spirits perform spirit-world cures for sick Gebusi and have strong de facto authority in making sorcery pronouncements. Spirit mediums should be neutral parties in any sorcery attribution and have no special authority except via the spirit world in seances. They are not remunerated for their services, which are considered a civic duty.

Ceremonies. The harmony and beneficence of the Gebusi spirit world is celebrated in an all-night dance performed at feasts and other important occasions. The elaborate and standardized costume of the male dancer(s) brings together in iconographic form the diverse spirits of the upper and lower worlds, symbolizing their unity and harmony in dance. Sociologically parallel is the overcoming of real and/or ritual antagonism between visitors and hosts through feasting, drinking kava, dancing, and ribald male camaraderie during the night. On occasion, male homosexual liaisons take place in the privacy of the bush outside the longhouse. Gebusi believe boys must be orally inseminated to obtain male life force and attain adulthood. Insemination continues during adolescence and culminates in the male initiation (*wa kawala*, or "child becomes big") between ages 17 and 23. Initiation is largely benign. Initiates receive costume parts and other gifts from diverse initiation sponsors and reciprocate with major food gifts. Novices are ultimately dressed in beautiful red bird-of-paradise (spirit-woman) costumes and are the focus of several days of feasting and ceremony attended by most Gebusi.

Arts. Gebusi make fine initiation arrows, armbands, and string bags, and they design elaborate dance and initiation costumes.

Medicine. Curing is done primarily via the spirit world; there is little intervention of a physical nature.

Death and Afterlife. A divinatory outcome indicating guilt of a sorcery suspect validates the spirits' indictment and foreshadows execution and cannibalism of the suspect, whose spirit reincarnates thereafter as a dangerous wild pig. Until recently, bodies of persons killed as sorcerers were butchered and cooked with sago and greens in a feasting oven and cannibalized fully, except for the intestines, which were discarded. The cooked body was distributed and eaten widely throughout the community, excluding close relatives and classificatory agnates of the deceased. Other Gebusi are not cannibalized and upon death reincarnate in bird, animal, and fish forms appropriate to their age and sex. A funeral feast is held when death results from sickness or accident.

See also Kaluli

Bibliography

Knauft, Bruce M. (1985). *Good Company and Violence: Sorcery and Social Action in a Lowland New Guinea Society*. Berkeley: University of California Press.

Knauft, Bruce M. (1985). "Ritual Form and Permutation in New Guinea." *American Ethnologist* 12:321–340.

Knauft, Bruce M. (1986). "Text and Social Practice: Narrative 'Longing' and Bisexuality among the Gebusi of New Guinea." *Ethos* 4:252–281.

Knauft, Bruce M. (1987). "Reconsidering Violence in Simple Human Societies: Homicide among the Gebusi of New Guinea." *Current Anthropology* 28:457–500.

Knauft, Bruce M. (1989). "Imagery, Pronouncement, and the Aesthetics of Reception in Gebusi Spirit Mediumship." In *The Religious Imagination in New Guinea*, edited by Gilbert Herdt and Michele Stephen, 67–98. New Brunswick, N.J.: Rutgers University Press.

BRUCE KNAUFT

Gnau

ETHNONYMS: none

Orientation

Identification. Speakers of the Gnau language live in the West Sepik Province of Papua New Guinea. "Gnau" is the word for "no" in the local language. While they constitute a linguistic group, Gnau do not define themselves as members of a population extending beyond the village or villages known to them personally.

Location. Gnau villages are found on forested mountain ridges between the Nopan and Assini rivers in the Lumi Subdistrict of West Sepik Province, roughly between 142°9' and 142°21' E and 3°32' to 3°45' S. The environment is mostly lowland tropical rain forest and the climate is hot and humid, with a dry season lasting from November to March. Average annual rainfall is approximately 250 centimeters.

Demography. In 1981 the population of Gnau speakers was estimated at 980 people. Earlier population figures are unavailable or nonexistent, although there is evidence that as many as one-third of the Gnau died during a dysentery epidemic in the 1930s.

Linguistic Affiliation. Gnau, together with Olo (Wape) and others, is a member of the Wapei Family of Non-Austronesian languages. Today nearly all men and boys as well as some women and girls also speak Tok Pisin.

History and Cultural Relations

Prior to Western contact, Gnau villages were relatively isolated, apparently not participating at all in the extensive trade network that crisscrossed the region. Extravillage relations appear to have been limited to immediately neighboring groups and were often hostile in character. In the 1930s, Australian labor recruiters began to visit the area and Gnau men were hired for two-year terms on coastal copra plantations. World War II had little direct effect on Gnau life, but plantation workers, whose return to their home villages was delayed by the war, became important agents of social change in the postwar years. An Australian patrol post was established in the region in 1949, and by 1955 the administration had largely succeeded in ending Gnau intervillage warfare. The relative peace thus introduced resulted in an expansion of village hunting and gardening territory, and fostered more peaceful relations between individual Gnau villages. In 1951 a Franciscan mission was built in the area, followed in 1958 by an evangelical Protestant one. The missions established an airstrip, stores, schools, and a hospital. Gnau became taxpayers in 1957 and received the vote in 1964, when they began electing members of the National Assembly and, later, local government councillors. Taken all together, these contacts have transformed the Gnau from isolated villagers to a group defined by outsiders as a single people who are increasingly involved in the regional and national polity and economy.

Settlements

Gnau villages are built on hilltops, 300 meters or more above sea level—a settlement choice likely derived from the need for defense dating back to the precontact times of chronic intervillage hostilities. Villages are subdivided into named hamlets and subhamlets. Hamlets are surrounded by coconut palms, with village gardens located in the forest in the valleys below. Hamlets consist of men's houses, dwelling houses for women and their children, and "day houses" where men gather together and eat during the day. In the past each hamlet had one large men's house rather than the several smaller ones found today. Substantial houses and sometimes smaller huts are also built and maintained near the gardens.

Economy

Subsistence and Commercial Activities. The Gnau economy consists of slash-and-burn horticulture, hunting, gathering, fishing, and, most recently, participation in the regional cash economy. Although most men work for two years or more as laborers on copra plantations and on government projects, the Gnau are still somewhat isolated from the regional economy when compared to other, neighboring groups. Sago was the traditional staple, today supplemented with taro, yams, sweet potatoes, corn, bananas, pawpaws, *pitpit*, breadfruit, beans, coconuts, and sugarcane grown in the gardens. A family might maintain as many as six gardens simultaneously, integrating horticultural practices with hunting and gathering activities. Rice is grown as a cash crop only; the Gnau themselves purchase from stores what rice appears in their own diet. Pigs, wallabies, and cassowaries are the principal animals hunted. Fishing is done with nets or poison. Eggs, grubs, insects, and reptiles are gathered to round out the protein component of the Gnau diet.

Industrial Arts. The Gnau traditionally were self-sufficient in meeting their material needs, producing stone axes, bows and arrows, knives, baskets, string, fish nets, net bags, skirts, ornaments of shell and feather, containers, animal traps, wooden boxes, and armbands. Many of these items are still manufactured locally today. In the past they also made clay pots.

Trade. Because of this basic self-sufficiency, trade did not play a large role in the Gnau economy. Only a few items, notably shell ornaments and stone adze heads, were occasionally acquired from beyond the community. With the coming of the mission stations, the introduction of a government presence in the area, and the beginning of wage labor on the plantations, the Gnau have become more dependent on goods purchased at the local stores.

Division of Labor. Men hunt, build houses, maintain paths, make weapons and tools, and work at jobs outside the villages. Women gather water and firewood, make string, net bags, and other items, and have primary responsibilty for child care. Both men and women fish and gather wild foods. Cooking sago is done by women, but some other foods are cooked exclusively by men, and much day-to-day cooking is done equally often by men and women.

Land Tenure. All village land, garden plots, and stands of breadfruit, sago, and coconut palms are named and owned by the patrilineages of the men currently using them.

Kinship

Kin Groups and Descent. Gnau descent is reckoned patrilineally, and genealogies are traced to a much greater depth—between five and fifteen generations—than is commonly the case among New Guinea peoples. The descent groups are not localized in single villages, although in most cases a mythological charter connects the most distant known ancestors to specific locales. Within descent groups, individual lineages stand in "brother" relationships to one another. The largest descent groups, consisting of all people who trace patrilineal ties back to the founding ancestors and to associated ancient sites, are crosscut or even contradicted by local claims of direct ancestry, within which "brotherhood" may be ascribed by virtue of no criterion other than length of residence. Thus, although fairly accurate genealogies are maintained over a great many generations, agnation can and often is manipulated. For this to be done, however, any justification for claiming agnatic relationships is necessarily located in the remote past.

Kinship Terminology. Kinship terminology is based on the two concepts of "brotherhood" and "seniority," couched within the framework of a locationally defined descent group. All men who descended from the same founding ancestor and who are members of the same generation are classed as "brothers" and further distinguished as senior or junior with regard to one another.

Marriage and Family

Marriage. The agnatically constituted descent groups of the Gnau are exogamous, but villages, consisting as they most frequently do of members of a number of descent groups, are not necessarily so. Marriages are arranged between the families of the prospective spouses, and the new wife takes up residence with her husband. The rights associated with her that were previously held by her father and brothers pass to her husband upon payment of bride-wealth. The marriage remains provisional until the birth of the first child, however, so bride-wealth is not distributed until that time. Although this payment confers rights in and authority over the child on its father, the mother's brother retains some rights and obligations as well. A husband must be compensated for his wife's adultery by her lover or the latter is subject to attack by the offended husband. Neither widows nor widowers are socially required to remarry, but it is important for a widower to find himself a new wife to cook for him and care for his children. Widows may often seek to avoid remarriage in order not to obscure or confuse the rights of her children from her earlier marriage.

Domestic Unit. The conjugal unit of husband and wife plus their children does not correspond to a residential unit. The wife lives in her dwelling house with her small sons and her daughters until they marry, while the husband sleeps in a men's house that is shared with his brothers and older sons. Lacking coresidential markers of relationship, the smallest family unit can be defined in terms of those individuals for whom a woman cooks on a daily basis: these will be her husband and her unmarried offspring. The larger sense of family, constituting the range of individuals cooperatively involved in provisioning the household through pursuits other than gardening, will also include the husband's brothers. A widowed female with young children, if she chooses to remain unmarried, will attach herself to her brother's household, while a widowed man with no daughter old enough to cook for him may join the household of a married older brother.

Inheritance. Land and ritual lore are the most important heritable items in Gnau society, and they belong to the lineage. Access to both passes from fathers to sons. Although elder and younger brothers are distinguished terminologically and have different obligations, this distinction is not mirrored in inheritance patterns: older males do not inherit differently than their younger male siblings do. "Temporary" property, such as trees and produce, are inherited individually by a man's sons at the discretion of the owner. Women do not inherit.

Socialization. Very young children stay with their mothers, but as they become old enough to wander about they enjoy a great deal of freedom. As a boy grows up he moves from his mother's house to the men's house of his father's lineage and plays in groups with other boys of the village. Both boys and girls pick up necessary practical knowledge through observation and mimicking in play the behavior of their elders. The day-to-day care of young children falls largely to the mother, but certain points in the child's development call for ritual performances involving both paternal and maternal kin. During these times traditional knowledge and ritual lore are passed along. The mother's brother is expected to hold a ceremony that removes dietary taboos when a child reaches about 3 years of age, and he is also intimately involved in the puberty ceremonies of both boys and girls. The father and the father's lineage are obligated to compensate the mother's brother for this ritual involvement and to provide food for the accompanying feasts.

Sociopolitical Organization

Social Organization. Social units are organized according to two separate principles. The first is locational, based on claims of attachment to the place of one's birth and of one's ancestors' birth. Thus an individual's membership in a village is in part defined by the fact that he or she was born there, parents came from there, or a more distant ancestor can be shown to have been born there. Patrilineal descent provides the second principle of organization, establishing separate subdivisions (hamlets) within the confines of a single village and further subdivisions within the hamlet itself. Units of social cooperation and obligation are couched in terms of brotherhood relations or ties established by marriage.

Political Organization. Traditionally, Gnau communities had no recognized political unit or office and no overarching intervillage organization. Apart from skill in mobilizing people for defense in the days of intervillage warfare, kinship and affinal relations, deference of junior to elder, and personally achieved prestige were, and still are, the considerations that led to a man's being looked to as a leader. Since 1964, Gnau have begun participating in the election of representatives to the House of Assembly, and in 1967 they began selecting local government councillors. These developments have begun to bring the separate villages into more unified polities, and the newly instituted political offices serve as points of articulation between local communities and the national government.

Social Control. A system of taboos, many of them dietary, provides the framework for appropriate behavior. Infractions may be punished by the imposition of fines, as in the case of adultery. Some fear of retributive sorcery also contributes to social control, albeit in a negative sense: a woman's brother is thought to have the ritual and magical power necessary to influence the health—indeed, the life—of her children, and he might withhold that power should the husband's lineage fail to fulfill its obligations to the child or refuse to cooperate with the wife's kin.

Conflict. Serious conflicts often arose between villages prior to Western contact, and fighting was considered to be a highly prestigious activity. Except for the prestige conferred by success in war, there seems to have been little other real basis for intervillage hostilities: garden land and access to game were plentiful and there was little else by way of intervillage relations that might have given rise to friction. Gnau did not recruit allies throughout the region for warfare; rather, fighting was conducted on a strictly village-against-village basis.

Religion and Expressive Culture

Religious Beliefs. Specific locations within Gnau territory are each associated with a descent-group founder, who is thought to have left behind the ritual knowledge and practical lore necessary to proper living. The activities of these founding personages and the knowledge they left behind are recounted in myths and songs, which also refer to a wide variety of spirits. These spirits are often invoked in garden ritual and their influence is thought to be necessary to the success of a crop.

Religious Practitioners. All men learn ritual lore throughout the process of their socialization. The mother's brother is the ritual specialist called in for most of a boy's initiations, and every adult male has garden magic to perform. The ability to cause a death through magic appears to have been specifically limited; through this means a man is believed able to kill his sister's son.

Ceremonies. Villagewide ceremonies accompany important life-cycle events as well as major undertakings such as the erection of a new men's house. Such occasions will involve feasting, song, and dance. Of particular importance in traditional Gnau life was the Tambin, the major male initiation rite held by the boy's mother's brother and supported through payments of wealth and the provision of a feast by the father's lineage. A parallel rite is held for girls upon attaining puberty. In the Tambin, a number of boys who have reached puberty go into seclusion together, during which time they are bled and also receive blood taken from their mothers' brothers. This bleeding, caused by cutting the mouth and the penis, is central to Gnau male ritual and is considered to be absolutely essential for a man's development. It appears to have no direct parallel in the ritual for females.

Arts. Gnau material culture appears to be utilitarian for the most part, but ornamental items of shell and feathers are made. Gnau songs are elaborate expressions of local mythology. Singing to the accompaniment of slit drums and ritual dance form important elements of any Gnau ceremony.

Medicine. Illness is thought to be largely the result of violations of taboos. Cures are believed to be effected through the observance of dietary taboos, the use of herbs, and bloodletting.

Death and Afterlife. Traditionally, when an individual died the Gnau laid the corpse out on a platform where it was smoke-dried; today interment is practiced. The spirits of the dead are thought to watch over their descendants and may appear to speak to their survivors in dreams. Their assistance is sought through spells and ritual.

See also Wape

Bibliography

Lewis, Gilbert (1975). *Knowledge of Illness in a Sepik Society: A Study of the Gnau, New Guinea.* London: Athlone Press.

Lewis, Gilbert (1980). *Day of Shining Red: An Essay on Understanding Ritual.* Cambridge: Cambridge University Press.

NANCY GRATTON

Gogodala

ETHNONYMS: Girara, Gogodara, Kabiri

Orientation

Identification. The Gogodala live in the Western Province of Papua New Guinea. Earlier names for them were based on misunderstandings of a term for "language" or "speech" (*girara*) or the name of a small creek, "Kabiri." The basis for the name Gogodala is not known.

Location. A few Gogodala villages are found on the north bank of the Fly River, but most are located along the Aramia River, a major tributary of the Bamu. The region, at approximately 8° to 8°15' S and 142°30' to 143°15' E, is largely one of flat, swampy floodplain with numerous meandering watercourses; alternating mixed woodland and grassland are punctuated with low hillocks and ridges where settlements are placed. During the wet season (December–May) about 75 percent of the annual rainfall of 216 centimeters occurs and most of the area turns into a vast sea, with canoes as the only means of mobility among the hillocks that form islands in it. Bird life and wild game (including wallabies, cassowaries, and wild pigs, with some deer found nowadays) are abundant, as are mosquitoes.

Demography. Population estimates have changed somewhat since significant European contact began after the turn of the twentieth century, with a low of 5,000 proposed in 1916 and about 7,000 Gogodala speakers currently recognized.

Linguistic Affiliation. Gogodala is a Non-Austronesian language, the only other member of its family being Ari-Waruna, which is understood but not spoken by Gogodala. Linkages with peoples of the Fly River are indicated by the joining of Gogodala with Suki as a separate stock in the

Trans–New Guinea Phylum. Currently, most Gogodala also speak Tok Pisin, and many are fluent in English.

History and Cultural Relations

According to oral traditions, the ancestors of the Gogodala arrived in a large canoe from the direction of the Fly River, settling at the Aramia River after many years of wandering and being happy to find a region rich in sago, fish, and game. Physically, socially, and culturally they share many features with the peoples of the Trans-Fly region and southwest New Guinea. Almost all that is known of traditional Gogodala life is based on reports of government officers who visited them for brief periods in 1910–1916 and the work of the anthropologist Paul Wirz, who conducted fieldwork among them in 1930. Missionaries of the Unevangelised Fields Mission (now the Asia Pacific Christian Mission) established a station in Gogodala territory in 1934 and two years later local converts and native evangelists, in concert with the missionaries, were responsible for mass destruction of all traditional art and ceremonial paraphernalia. During World War II the people were left on their own, but intensified missionary efforts in the 1950s and 1960s resulted in drastic social change, including the total abandonment of traditional longhouses themselves. A cultural revival in 1972 culminated in the erection and dedication of a new longhouse as the Gogodala Cultural Centre, established as a museum, an educational center, and an assertion of cultural identity at Balimo, the site of the first mission station.

Settlements

Until the 1950s, a Gogodala village consisted of a single communal longhouse, elevated about 2 meters above the ground and surrounded by gardens made on the sloping sides of the chosen hillock, usually well inland from the river banks. These multistory fortresses were up to 200 meters long, each having a central chamber that extended the length of the building and served as a general social area. Men entered the house from either end and slept on an elevated platform above the chamber. Women entered the house from underneath, where pigs were kept and objects stored, and occupied cubicles along the sides, cooking on a lower floor and sleeping in an upper story. Since the 1960s all Gogodala villages have consisted of rectangular family dwellings made of split palm with sago-thatch roofs or, increasingly, galvanized iron sheeting.

Economy

Subsistence and Commercial Activities. Apart from sago extraction from trees in some of the swampy areas, gardens provide staple foods such as yams, taro, cassava, breadfruit, bananas, coconuts, and sugarcane. Recently introduced sweet potatoes, pumpkins, corn, and cucumbers are also planted. *Piper methysticum,* for the manufacture of kava, was traditionally cultivated in special manured garden beds, and it continues to be grown and used despite opposition from the missionaries. Fishing, with nets, traps, and poison, is an important subsistence activity, as is hunting, which yields game required for a variety of social exchanges. Carvings have recently become a major source of cash income.

Industrial Arts. Everyday implements such as bows and arrows, digging sticks, canoe paddles, fishing nets, and wicker fish traps were made from locally available materials, as were the wispy grass aprons traditionally worn by women and coarse fiber nets and bags. Despite abundant suitable clay in the area, no pottery was manufactured or used. In a region devoid of natural stone, the Gogodala were, and remain, remarkably skilled wood-carvers, intricately ornamenting house posts and dugout canoes, some of the latter being up to 12 meters long.

Trade. Prior to government control of the region, trading opportunities were restricted, as cannibal enemy groups resided to both the north and south of the Gogodala; with pacification, however, the Gododala traded European goods with the Kiwai of the Fly River for stone adz blades originating in the Torres Strait. Between Gogodala villages, there was frequent trade of tobacco, bird of paradise plumes, ornaments, and daggers, with the villages nearest the sea providing shell of various kinds.

Division of Labor. Traditionally, all men made their own implements for everyday use and were also responsible for construction, felling sago palms, gardening, and hunting. Women's tasks included making sago, fishing, cooking, weaving, and making twine; also, wild piglets captured by men on hunting trips were tended by women. While all men learned to shape wood at an early age, some boys were recognized as having special talents and were apprenticed to master craftsmen and artists who, although their everyday lives were the same as those of others, occupied a distinctive place in society.

Land Tenure. All lagoons, patches of forest, and sago swamps are owned by clans and subdivided according to subclan. A man may make gardens and hunt on the land associated with his own clan, and a woman fishes in the area belonging to her husband's clan, although she may be permitted also to use her father's clan's portion of lagoons and waterways.

Kinship

Kin Groups and Descent. Descent is reckoned patrilineally and Gogodala society is composed of eight exogamous, totemic clans, each of which has its own ceremonial canoe marked with its totemic insignia. A person traditionally was allowed to eat the primary totems of his or her mother's clan and those of unrelated individuals, but not that of his or her own clan. Clans are divided into subclans but also united into moieties, each of which includes four clans.

Kinship Terminology. Wirz's account of Gogodala kinship is incomplete, but it appears that there was a very strong tendency towards generational terms, with all women in the parental generation called by the same term and father's brother equated with mother's brother (but not father); sexes were distinguished, but otherwise one's own children were called by the same terms as one's brother's or sister's children; in one's own generation, elder and younger siblings were distinguished and it is likely that these terms were extended to cousins in a Hawaiian-type system.

Marriage and Family

Marriage. Marriages were contracted traditionally through sister exchange, with a man forbidden to marry a woman in his own, his mother's, or his father's mother's clans or any of his father's sister's children. Formerly polygyny was common but is now practiced by few; divorce was uncommon.

Domestic Unit. Traditionally, husbands and wives slept separately but all lived together with the entire community in the longhouse; nowadays, families form living units. While neither men's gardening activities nor women's fishing is shared with a spouse, whole families may spend days or weeks together in the bush seeking building materials and carrying out their various subsistence tasks.

Inheritance. Men bequeath their land and other property to their sons or, if they have none, to their brothers, with nothing left to daughters. A wife may be allowed to use her dead husband's land, but she claims no title to it.

Socialization. Babies are cared for by their mothers or older sisters; fathers are affectionate to infants but their active interest is said to wane with the growing independence of the child. In the early years, children are largely left to their own devices and spend much of their leisure time in the lagoons. From the age of 4, boys have their own canoes and race them, imitating their fathers. Young girls accompany their mothers to sago swamps and fish on their own; boys work with their fathers in the gardens and sometimes go along on hunting trips. It is a father's responsibility to teach his sons about daily life, while their mother's brothers transmit the secrets of manhood and cult life.

Sociopolitical Organization

Social and Political Organization. Moieties provided a dualistic organization to Gogodala society, with symmetrical subdivision into clans constituting the basic organizational framework, especially in matters of marriage, intercommunity relations, and ceremonial life. Although some sojourners indicated the existence of chiefs, Wirz's account based on fieldwork stresses an egalitarian ethic that colored daily life, with no recognized formal leadership positions.

Social Control and Conflict. Disputes arose traditionally over land or women, and at moots all were free to air their views. Subsequent truces or agreements were celebrated with races between clan-owned canoes. Prior to government control in about 1912, wars were waged arising from vendettas between Gogodala communities and disputes with the Kiwai and peoples to the north of the Aramia River. Head trophies were taken, but cannibalism was not practiced by the Gogodala.

Religion and Expressive Culture

Religious Beliefs. Ancestral totems (including the snake, crocodile, pig, bird of paradise, hornbill, eel, hawk, and cassowary) were at the core of traditional religion, and clan insignia were displayed on all implements, canoes, and ceremonial objects. A general spiritual force traditionally was believed to control most happenings in the world; it could be tapped through carved effigies (placed around longhouses and in gardens) and used to dispel sickness from the village and ensure growth and fertility. Virtually all of the traditional religion was supplanted by Christianity, beginning in the 1930s.

Ceremonies. The direct campaign waged by missionaries and evangelists beginning in the 1930s effectively destroyed what was evidently a very rich ceremonial life in Gogodala villages. Men made and drank kava to mark all feasts and celebrations, which included first-menstruation rites for girls and a cycle of initiation for males, the culmination of which was the spectacular ceremony inducting all adolescent males into the *aida* cult. Aida not only united the males of a village in a secret society but also bound together neighboring longhouses. Canoe races symbolized the competitive rivalry but also the complementarity of clans and communities at the conclusion of the aida ceremony and at truce making. Through the efforts of the Australian government and the Papua New Guinea National Cultural Council, the establishment of the Gogodala Cultural Centre in 1974 has revived local interest in and enactments of traditional ceremonial life in new, syncretic forms.

Arts. In the southern region around the Gulf of Papua, rich artistic traditions abound, and Gogodala styles have been regarded as perhaps the most abstract and individualistic of them all. Until the 1930s, Gogodala surrounded themselves with their art, elaborately carving and painting longhouse posts and joists, ladders, canoes, canoe paddles, drums, and nearly everything else. Light, balsalike wood and cane were the basic materials for flat, shieldlike masks and plaques, flat or round ancestral human figures, and three-dimensional totem effigies, all of which typically manifested the Gogodala hallmark of concentric designs incorporating asymmetric appendages. Destruction of these objects was related to the fact that nearly all artistic productions were based in Gogodala traditional religion, aimed at soliciting the intervention of ancestors in worldly affairs. Individuals distinguished locally as artists were believed to inherit their talents, and all had their individual styles. While all traditional art focused on the supernatural world, nowadays Gogodala artists produce most of their work for sale, and some of them have exhibited their work as far away as West Germany.

Medicine. Illness and death traditionally were attributed to attacks by spirits and sorcery; thus individuals wore personal charms, and effigies were placed outside longhouses and in gardens to ward off the spirits responsible. When these failed, numerous medicinal plants were used in treatment, which emphasized external applications rather than internal use. Since World War II, mission clinics have provided Western medical care.

Death and Afterlife. All early European visitors to the Gogodala remarked upon the coarse net veils completely covering the heads of relatives of the recently deceased. Such veils were worn in mourning for about a year, though high death rates through disease and warfare could result in at least some people wearing such veils almost perpetually. The dead were buried with their heads facing the east in shallow graves on ridges at some distance from the longhouse. If the deceased was male, an effigy was placed in his garden, warning all to take nothing from it until a feast was held at which all of the food from his garden and all of his pigs would be consumed by the community. The soul was believed to leave the corpse with the rising sun on the day following death, at which time it would travel to the west to its final resting place.

See also Kiwai

Bibliography

Beaver, Wilfred N. (1914). "A Description of the Girara District, Western Papua." *Geographical Journal* 43:407–413.

Beaver, Wilfred N. (1920). *Unexplored New Guinea.* London: Seeley, Service & Company.

Crawford, Anthony L. (1981). *Aida: Life and Ceremony of the Gogodala.* Bathurst, N.S.W.: Robert Brown & Associates.

Haddon, Alfred C. (1916). "The Kabiri and Girara District, Fly River, Papua." *Journal of the Royal Anthropological Institute* 46:334–352.

Lyons, A. P. (1926). "Notes on the Gogodara Tribe of Western Papua." *Journal of the Royal Anthropological Institute* 6:329–359.

Wirz, Paul (1934). "Die Gemeinde der Gogodara." *Nova Guinea* 16:371–499.

TERENCE E. HAYS

Goodenough Island

ETHNONYMS: Bwaidoka, Iduna, Kalauna, Morata, Nidula

Orientation

Identification. Goodenough Island (Morata on the earliest maps) was named by Captain John Moresby in 1874 in memory of a British naval colleague. The earliest ethnography, by Diamond Jenness and Rev. A. Ballantyne, focused on coastal Bwaidoka in the southeast; the most intensive studies, by Michael Young, concentrate on Kalauna, a mountain village in east-central Goodenough.

Location. Goodenough, at 9° S, 150° E, is the westernmost of three rugged islands of the D'Entrecasteaux Archipelago of Milne Bay Province, Papua New Guinea. With mountains rising to 2,440 meters it is the highest island in the group, though with an area of about 777 square kilometers it is second to Fergusson in size. Rain forest is extensive on these islands and the higher mountains are uninhabited. Secondary forest and grasslands prevail on the coastal plains and lower slopes. The region is tropical, with high temperatures and humidity throughout the year. There are two main seasons: the cooler southeasterly winds (May–October) dominate the year, while the hot northwest monsoon (December–March) brings sudden squalls. Rainfall is within the range of 152–254 centimeters per annum according to location. Serious droughts occur once or twice a decade, hurricanes even less frequently.

Demography. At the 1980 census there were about 12,500 islanders in residence and another 1,000 abroad. More than half of them live in the southeast of the island with a density of about 38 persons per square kilometer; elsewhere the population density averages 10 persons per square kilometer.

Linguistic Affiliation. The four languages of Goodenough (Bwaidoka, Iduna, Diodio, and Buduna or Wataluma) belong to the Milne Bay Family (or "Papuan Tip Cluster") of Austronesian languages. The dominant language on the island is Bwaidoka, adopted as a lingua franca by the Wesleyan (Methodist) Mission at the turn of the century.

History and Cultural Relations

The D'Entrecasteaux Islands have probably been inhabited for several thousand years, and some of the mountain-dwelling people of Goodenough yield blood-group markers that relate them distantly to mainland Papuans. Over the past two millennia Austronesian immigrants have decisively shaped the culture. Although the population is fairly homogeneous throughout the island, a subcultural distinction occurs between "people of the mountains" and "people of the coast." This distinction is blurred today because of the resettlement of many hill communities on or near the littoral, but all Goodenough communities claim their origin from Yauyaba, a "sacred hill" on the east coast, whence mankind emerged from underground. European contact began in 1874 with an exploratory visit by Captain John Moresby. Brief visits by whalers, pearlers, and gold seekers followed, and in 1888 Administrator William MacGregor visited the island on his inaugural tour of the newly proclaimed British New Guinea. Ten years later William Bromilow led the first Wesleyan Mission party from his headquarters in Dobu, and in 1900 a station was established at Wailagi in Bwaidoka. By that time traders had already created a regular demand for steel tools, cloth, and twist tobacco. A famine in 1900 forced many men into contract labor abroad, the beginning of a local tradition of migrant labor that earned for Goodenough Islanders the reputation of "the best workmen in Papua." Local warfare and cannibalism persisted in remote areas until the early 1920s, when the first census was conducted and a head tax introduced. World War II was traumatic: a small Japanese invasion force occupied the island in 1942, and after its extermination a massive Allied airbase was built on the northeast plain. After the war the Australian colonial administration resumed its benign neglect. Partly in response to an outbreak of cargo cults, a government patrol post was established in 1960, followed by a local government council in 1964. Since Papua New Guinea's independence in 1975, Goodenough Island (jointly with the Trobriand Islands) has elected a member to the national parliament. Nowadays two representatives are also elected to the provincial government of Milne Bay.

Settlements

The inhabited areas of Goodenough are found on the coast close to coral reefs, in the immediate hinterland, or in the foothills of the island's mountain spine. At contact Goodenough was divided into more than thirty geographical "districts," each containing one or more villages. Certain districts were loosely affiliated through common dialect and a degree of intermarriage. Throughout the 1920s, government officers encouraged mountain communities to resettle at more accessible locations near the coast. Many communities amalgamated. The present-day successors of the districts are twenty-three census groups or "wards" of the local government council. The population of these village communities averages 500. The houses of a hamlet cluster around one or more circular sitting platforms constructed of stone slabs, important symbols of descent-group continuity. Hamlets are surrounded by fruit trees: coconut, *areca* (betel nut), mango, breadfruit, and native chestnut. Houses are rectangular structures built on piles and with gabled roofs; they usually contain two or three small rooms, including a kitchen. There are two main house styles: a warm, boxlike structure with pandanus-leaf walls, which is favored by the hill communities; and a cooler coastal style with walls of sago-leaf midrib. Both types have black-palm floors and roofs of sago-leaf thatch.

Economy

Subsistence and Commercial Activities. Gardening is the main economic activity. Yams are the principal crop and their swidden cultivation dominates the calendar. Taro is a close second in importance, and bananas (plantains) third. Magic is used to ensure the growth of these crops and coconuts. Other crops (many of recent introduction) include sweet potatoes, manioc, sugarcane, sago, arrowroot, pumpkins, pawpaws, maize, and beans. Reef fishing and hunting for pigs and wallabies were more important traditionally than they are today since reefs and bush have been depleted. Mangrove crabs, freshwater eels, wild pigs, birds, cuscus, and other small game are still caught, but the main source of protein remains domesticated pigs and fowls (in some villages dogs are also eaten). Copra is the only significant cash crop, but transport and marketing facilities are poor. Since 1900 migrant workers have earned money abroad and remitted a share to kin. Wage labor became a mandatory rite of passage for young men, and to some extent it remains so, though many young islanders (including women) now work in towns as clerks and minor public servants.

Industrial Arts. Traditional technology included polished-stone ax heads, obsidian and bamboo knives, black-palm spears and clubs, single-outrigger canoes, wooden fish-hooks and digging sticks, twine nets for hunting and fishing, and fighting slings. Woven crafts included pandanus-leaf sleeping mats and coconut-leaf baskets. Except for canoes, hunting nets, and pottery, craft specialization was minimal.

Trade. Largely self-sufficient in resources and peripheral to the main Massim trade routes, the island's trade links were not extensive. Canoe technology was comparatively poor, and only a few communities made seagoing vessels. Most villages relied on visiting traders from western Fergusson, the Amphlett Islands, Kaileuna in the Trobriands, or Wedau and Cape Vogel on the mainland. Among the commodities exchanged were ax blades, clay pots, pigs, yams and taro, sago, betel nuts, arm shells and necklaces, nose shells, belts, lime gourds, baskets, and decorated combs. The wares from the pot-making villages in the north did not circulate as widely as did those of the Amphletts. There was also an institution of interdistrict ceremonial visiting, undertaken on foot or by newly completed canoes, to solicit gifts of pigs, yams, and shell valuables from hereditary trade partners. The gifts received had to be passed on to a third party, and ideally each expedition was reciprocated. This ceremonial exchange has obvious affinities with that of the *kula.*

Division of Labor. Husband and wife cooperate in gardening after the communal clearing of new plots. Clearing is done by men, though women help to plant and harvest crops and perform most of the regular weeding. Most domestic tasks are done by women, including cooking, washing, fetching water, child care, and pig rearing; women also gather shellfish. Men build houses, fish and hunt, butcher pigs, and cook in large pots on ceremonial occasions. Both sexes cut and carry firewood.

Land Tenure. The clearing and planting of virgin forest establishes a group's rights to that land in perpetuity. Garden and residential land is inherited patrilineally and is in theory inalienable. There is a hierarchy of corporate land rights within the clan, though the sibling set is operationally the most important land-owning unit, and sons inherit land and fruit trees directly from their fathers. Although a daughter inherits land and trees too, she is more likely to use her husband's. Her children may use her land only if their father pays a pig to her brothers. In some communities plots of land may be transferred following a death, as a form of payment to non-agnatic buriers. Such land may be reclaimed in the future after the true owners have performed a reciprocal burial service. These devices allowed an equitable distribution of garden land between groups, though in recent generations the planting of coconuts as a cash crop has made the tenure system more rigid.

Kinship

Kin Groups and Descent. Although the Massim is predominantly matrilineal, descent on Goodenough Island is patrilineal. The most important descent group is the *unuma,* a shallow patrilineage four to five generations in depth. On a sibling birth-order model, unuma are ranked according to genealogical seniority. The most encompassing descent group, comprising several unuma, is a localized, exogamous, named patriclan. The several clans of a community are distinguished from one another by different origin myths and unique "customs," such as secret magical formulas, designs, totem animals, taboos, and special artifacts. Every clan belongs to one of the ceremonial moieties.

Kinship Terminology. Hawaiian-type terminology is used, though sibling/cousin terminology is characterized by a double mode of classification, according to sex or relative age.

Marriage and Family

Marriage. Postmarital residence is patrivirilocal, which ensures a core of male agnates in each hamlet. Marriage is forbidden within father's and mother's clans. There are no preferential rules, though certain matches are favored: between exchange partners and between distant cognatic kin traced through outmarrying women. Infant betrothal used to occur, but free choice between partners of the same age is nowadays the norm. Most communities are large enough to sustain local endogamy, and about 85 percent of marriages are between partners belonging to the same village. Marriage is signaled by the bride and groom sharing their first meal in the boy's parental house. The bride lives there while her husband's kin work her hard to test her endurance; meanwhile the groom performs arduous bride-service for his affines. Exchanges of game, fish, and cooked food legitimate the marriage soon afterwards, but bride-price payments (of a pig, a few shell valuables, and a sum of money) are nowadays delayed for months or even years. They are eventually given to the bride's unuma for distribution—if the marriage survived the stressful early years. About one in three marriages ends in divorce: the usual complaints are of neglect, laziness, or infidelity. If weaned the children remain with their father, for they belong to his group. Remarriage is simple, though a new husband must repay the first husband his bride-price. Widow remarriage is a more delicate affair, and the new husband must make generous gifts to the dead husband's kin to allay any suspicion of complicity in his death. Monogamy is the norm, but a few instances of polygyny occur in most communities despite eighty years of missionary disapproval of the practice.

Domestic Unit. The household—the basic economic and commensal unit—is usually composed of a married couple and their children, including any they are fostering. Adolescents, widows, and widowers may occupy small houses of their own, though they usually join other households to work and eat.

Inheritance. All property (including magic and clan paraphernalia) is inherited patrilineally. Certain statuses such as exchange partnerships and traditional enemies are also inherited patrilineally, as are a father's exchange debts and credits. An eldest son normally inherits his father's land and trees and items of wealth not disbursed as death payments. This patrimony should be divided among his siblings according to need. Ritual property (magical knowledge in particular) is more jealously guarded and less likely to be shared equally among brothers. If a man is without close agnatic heirs he may choose to transmit his magic (as well as his land or other property) to his sister's sons, though this is apt to cause contention in the following generation. Women can own land, trees, pigs, and some ritual property, though their control or disposal of them is usually subject to the approval of their closest male agnates. As in most Melanesian societies, the dispersal of personal wealth at death prevents the accumulation of inherited wealth which could be converted into rank or class.

Socialization. Infants are breast-fed on demand and weaned fairly abruptly at about two years. Children are frequently handled by parents, grandparents, and older siblings. The mother's brother is also important in a child's upbringing, and makes regular gifts of food with the expectation of being repaid (in cash earnings or bride-wealth) when the child reaches maturity. The children of a hamlet form play groups of peers. From an early age they accompany their parents to the gardens where they are encouraged to make toy gardens. Although parents are indulgent they readily strike their disobedient children, with an open hand or whatever they happen to be holding. Children are taught early to control their appetites, though they are permitted, and even encouraged, to chew betel nuts as soon as this desire arises. Traditionally there was no formal initiation of boys or girls, though nowadays school itself serves to weaken a child's bonding to its parents.

Sociopolitical Organization

Social Organization. The typical village community comprises several local patriclans occupying one or more adjacent hamlets and consisting of a number of genealogically ranked patrilineages. Clans are linked by marriage and exchange partnerships; there may be further crosscutting ties based on traditional enemy relationships. The village is also divided into ceremonial, nonexogamous moieties, which form the basis of a reciprocal feasting cycle, though nowadays such festivals tend to be promoted purely as memorials for dead leaders.

Political Organization. Large-scale feasting is intrinsically competitive and in the postcontact era it has assumed political functions hitherto associated with local warfare and revenge cannibalism. A ramifying system of pig and vegetable food debts loosely integrates the neighboring communities that attend one another's feasts and exchanges. Leadership on Goodenough takes several forms. Warrior leaders were prominent traditionally and sometimes became tyrannical despots. At the clan and hamlet level, leaders are ideally the most senior men of their groups, but there are many opportunities for younger sons to achieve prominence if they are productive gardeners, capable organizers, and good orators. Competitive food exchanges, whether held between whole villages or between contending clans within a village, are an important political institution, one that has been elaborated greatly since pacification and the availability of steel tools. Despite the egalitarian ethos of Goodenough society, there are hints of hierarchy in many communities; e.g., the possession of ritual means of prosperity (and conversely, the coercive threat of famine) makes the leaders of certain clans unusually powerful. In heavily missionized communities, however, such ritual village "guardians" do not exist, and village leaders there tend also to be church leaders.

Social Control. Traditionally the redress of wrongs was a matter of self-help by kin groups. Islanders are still reluctant to appeal to external authorities, and it is the local government councillor's task to attempt the settlement of disputes at the village level. Traditional sanctions remain in use; most notable are public harangue, ridicule, ostracism, and revenge sorcery. Among the most important and effective sanctions is food-giving-to-shame, which in the postcontact era has served as a dramatic mode of conflict resolution. It displays many features of traditional warfare; hence the idiom, "fighting with food."

Conflict. In the nineteenth century small-scale warfare and cannibalism were endemic on Goodenough. Because the ultimate indignity to an enemy was to eat him or her, an escalating revenge cycle could ensue from a single act of cannibalism. Not all the clans of a community were enemies of all the clans of a neighboring community, and relations of alliance and hostility could crosscut district boundaries. The very size and compactness of modern communities exacerbate minor conflicts, making Goodenough people seem fractious and hypersensitive to slight. Food and women remain the sources of most conflict, though land disputes are becoming increasingly frequent.

Religion and Expressive Culture

Religious Beliefs. Goodenough has been missionized for almost a century, and village churches (United or Catholic) are ubiquitous. Most elements of the traditional religion survive, however, and the world view remains magical and animistic, including a great variety of anthropomorphic spirits. Ancestral spirits as well as immortal demigods are invoked in magical spells. Gardening is accompanied at all stages by rituals and taboos, and magic exists for every human activity, from love and war to birth and death. Each group has its own secret magic of appetite suppression and food conservation, the obverse of which is the sorcery that brings famine by inducing insatiable hunger. A dominant principle of the indigenous cosmology derives from a fatalistic and anthropomorphic application of the emotion of bitter resentment. A modern projection of this principle can be seen in the local cargo cults that blend Christian dogmas of sacrifice with traditional hero myths.

Religious Practitioners. The main ritual experts are those with inherited magical systems employed for the communal control of human appetite, the most important food crops, and the elements. All leaders make some use of garden magic on behalf of their groups, and most men and women possess a few inherited spells of their own.

Ceremonies. All life-crisis ceremonies involve the distribution of cooked and uncooked food. Other occasions of ceremonial feasting are harvests, housewarmings, canoe launchings, and other inaugurations. A feature of all such ceremonies is that the initiator or food-distributing sponsor may not eat. An important ceremony in the past was *manumanua*, a periodic ritual of prosperity, in which the magicians sat absolutely still for a day reciting myths and spells to banish famine.

Arts. Traditional wood carving (of bowls, drums, combs, lime gourds and lime sticks, war clubs, house boards, and canoes) was done in typical Massim curvilinear style. The arts of singing and dancing were highly developed, and mouth flutes were used in courtship. Rhetoric and storytelling are important skills, and there are oral traditions of myth and folktale.

Medicine. Most illnesses are attributed to sorcery, broken taboos, attack by ancestral or other spirits, misfiring magic, or malicious gossip. Curers, who almost invariably are also sorcerers, employ incantation, rubbing the body with doctored leaves, and spitting chewed ginger on the patient's head. Since the ultimate cause of many illnesses is believed to lie in disturbed social relations, curing may also require divination and the public confession of grievance.

Death and Afterlife. Burial customs vary across the island, with interment in side-chambered graves practiced in most communities but secondary burial of bones in caves occurring in the north. Elaborate washing ceremonies and food taboos are general but vary locally in detail, as do the sequences of mortuary feasts. For the majority of islanders nowadays the afterlife is a vague notion of the Christian Heaven. However, burial rites continue to acknowledge the traditional belief that spirits of the dead journey first to Wafolo, a point on northern Fergusson Island, and from there—guided by a spirit who dwells in hot springs—they travel north to the island of Tuma in the Trobriands.

See also Dobu, Maisin, Trobriand Islands

Bibliography

Jenness, Diamond, and Rev. A. Ballantyne (1920). *The Northern D'Entrecasteaux.* Oxford: Clarendon Press.

Young, Michael W. (1971). *Fighting with Food.* Cambridge: Cambridge University Press.

Young, Michael W. (1983). "Ceremonial Visiting in Goodenough Island." In *The Kula: New Perspectives on Massim Exchange,* edited by J. Leach and E. R. Leach, 395–410. Cambridge: Cambridge University Press.

Young, Michael W. (1983). *Magicians of Manumanua.* Berkeley: University of California Press.

MICHAEL W. YOUNG

Guadalcanal

ETHNONYMS: Guadalcanar, Kaoka

Orientation

Identification. Among the peoples inhabiting Guadalcanal Island, one of the Solomon Islands, there is found considerable variety of cultural practices and language dialects. This entry will focus upon the people of five autonomous villages (Mbambasu, Longgu, Nangali, Mboli, and Paupau) in the northeastern coastal region who share both a single set of cultural practices and a common dialect, called "Kaoka," after one of the larger rivers in the area.

Location. The Solomon Islands, formed from the peaks of a double chain of submerged mountains, lie to the southeast of New Guinea. At about 136 kilometers in length and 48 kilometers in breadth, Guadalcanal is one of the two largest islands of the Solomons and is located at 9°30' S and 160° E. Guadalcanal's immediate neighbors are Santa Isabel Island in the northwest; Florida Island directly to the north; Malaita in the northeast; and San Cristobal Island to the southeast. The islands are frequently shaken by volcanos and earthquakes. The southern coast of Guadalcanal is formed by a ridge, which attains a maximum elevation of 2,400 meters. From this ridge the terrain slopes northerly into an alluvial grass plain. There is little climatic variation, other than the semiannual shift in dominance from the southeast tradewinds of early June to September to that of the northwest monsoon of late November to April. Throughout the year it is hot and wet, with temperatures averaging 27° C and an average annual rainfall of 305 centimeters.

Demography. In the first half of the 1900s, the population of Guadalcanal was estimated at 15,000. In 1986 there were estimated to be 68,900 people on the island.

Linguistic Affiliation. The dialects spoken on Guadalcanal are classed within the Eastern Oceanic Subgroup of the Oceanic Branch of Austronesian languages. There is a marked similarity between the dialect of the Kaoka speakers and that spoken on Florida Island.

History and Cultural Relations

The Solomons were first discovered in 1567 by a Spanish trading ship, and they were named at that time in reference to the treasure of King Solomon which was thought to be hidden there. There was very little further contact with European trading and whaling ships until the second half of the 1700s, when English ships visited. By 1845, missionaries began to visit the Solomons, and at about this time "blackbirders" began kidnapping men of the islands for forced labor on European sugar plantations in Fiji and elsewhere. In 1893, Guadalcanal became a British territory in the nominal care of the government of the Solomon Islands Protectorate, but full administrative control was not established until 1927. An Anglican mission and school was built in Longgu in 1912, and missionizing activities increased in intensity. During this time, and again after World War II, a number of European-owned coconut plantations were established. From relative obscurity, Guadalcanal Island leapt to the world's notice during World War II when, in 1942–1943, it was the site of a definitive confrontation between U.S. Marines and Japanese forces. With the building of an American base on the island, adult males were conscripted for the labor corps and there was a sudden influx of Western manufactured goods. In postwar years, the remembrance of that time of relatively easy access to new and desired Western goods, as well as a reaction to the breakdown of the traditional sociopolitical and socioeconomic systems, contributed to the development of the "Masinga Rule" movement (often translated as "Marching Rule," but there is evidence that *masinga* means "brotherhood" in one of Guadalcanal's dialects). This originally was a millenarian cult premised on the idea that through appropriate belief and the correct ritual practice the goods and largess experienced during the war years could someday be made to return. It became, in fact, a vehicle by which to seek, and by 1978 to secure, the independence of the Solomon Islands from British colonial rule.

Settlements

Kaoka speakers occupy five autonomous villages, four of which are located on the coast; the fifth is a few miles inland. Each village is made up of a number of hamlets consisting of a cluster of four to ten households, each with its own dwelling and associated gardens, and in traditional times there would also be three shrines, each dedicated to spirit beings. There is only one building style, regardless of the purpose of the structure: a high-peaked, windowless, thatched-roof affair, with walls made of split saplings lashed together with strong vines and anchored to solid upright beams. Small stones and larger shingle from the beach are spread to make the flooring. Doorways are elevated from ground level, to keep village pigs from gaining entry. Each shrine is decorated with the skulls of ancestors and a carved palisade of representations of spirits is set before the entrance. Because of the local climate and the nature of building materials, a structure is unlikely to last more than five years before having to be rebuilt.

Economy

Subsistence and Commercial Activities. The people of Guadalcanal are slash-and-burn horticulturalists whose principal crops are yams, taro, sweet potatoes, and bananas. Although every head of household will raise a herd of pigs, for coastal peoples the bulk of the day-to-day protein intake is supplied by seafood: fish from the open sea, as well as crustaceans and shellfish gathered from the reefs. Bonito is a great delicacy, but it is unavailable during the season of the monsoons when the winds are too dangerously high for the canoes. The consumption of pork is reserved for important occasions such as weddings or funerals. Fishing is done from plank canoes or from the shore. While there are wild pigs on the island, hunting is not often indulged in and contributes very little to the household diet.

Industrial Arts. House construction is the most time-consuming of necessary tasks, and it is usually done by a party of kinsmen; it is not the work of specialists. Canoe building, however, is a specialized skill, and only a few men in the village are held to be fully capable of it. The canoe builder will lend his skills freely to fellow clansmen, but he expects compensation for his work in the form of strings of shell money from anyone not so related. Most other tools used in day-to-day living that are made locally are relatively simple: fishing lines, digging sticks, and the like. Other items once manufactured locally, such as knives, axes, articles of clothing, and household utensils, have been replaced by store-bought items of Western manufacture.

Division of Labor. Men clear and prepare gardens and build fences, houses, and canoes; they also fish both from the shore and at sea. Women gather shellfish and crustaceans from the reefs and do most of the day-to-day tending of the gardens (weeding, harvesting). Planting is a cooperative effort between men and women. What little hunting that occurs is done entirely by those few men considered particularly adept at it. Domestic chores are the province of women, though many tasks, including tending small children, is often passed along to older daughters. Interisland trading expeditions were traditionally carried out by groups of men of the village, but with the enforcement of colonial interdictions against raiding, such trade no longer requires the large defensive fleets of the past.

Trade. While each household is largely capable of securing an adequate subsistence, there was trade between coastal villages and people of the interior, as well as overseas trade with other islands in the vicinity—in particular with Langalanga Lagoon on the west coast of Malaita, and with people of San Cristobal Island to the southeast. Langalanga was the source of the shell money used as a currency in trade and for ceremonial purposes such as the payment of bride-price. In trade for these strings of shell disks, people of Guadalcanal provided surplus pigs and vegetables. San Cristobal was a principal source of porpoise teeth, also used as currency and in ceremonial exchange, and Guadalcanal provided tobacco in return. Trade with the interior parts of Guadalcanal Island involved the exchange of shell disks, porpoise teeth, salt, coconuts, and limes for tobacco, dogs' teeth, bowls, and shields. Trade was and still is carried out between individuals who have formed a partnership relationship, which is passed along from father to son or from maternal uncle to nephew. Most often, the traders from Langalanga voyage to Guadalcanal with their trade goods, and, though less frequently, the people of Guadalcanal sometimes make the opposite trip. The large canoes in which trading voyages are made are themselves a trade item made on Florida Island and by the people of Marau Sound on the extreme east coast of Guadalcanal.

Kinship

Kin Groups and Descent. Descent is reckoned matrilineally. Kaoka speakers recognize five dispersed matrilineal clans, said to have been created through the marriages of the five sons and five daughters of Koevasi, the culture heroine. Each daughter then became the founding ancestress of one of the clans. Localized subclans constitute the core population of each hamlet. Among the people of the interior, there are two matrimoieties, each consisting of a number of constituent matrilineal clans. A male does not usually take up residence in the territory of his clan until a few years after marriage, with the construction of his second house, so many of a hamlet's young adult males are, in fact, the sons of clan members but not clan members themselves.

Kinship Terminology. Among the interior people, a relatively straightforward Hawaiian system is found. Among the Kaoka speakers, the terms for parallel and cross cousins are the same, but they are terminologically differentiated from siblings.

Marriage and Family

Marriage. Marriage is said to be prohibited between members of the same matrilineage; therefore, hamlets are ideally exogamous but the village is not because it consists of hamlets of all five of the clans. The parental generation arranges marriages, holding that young people are unlikely to be appropriately pragmatic in choosing mates. Negotiations for marriage are initiated by the father of the young man, but the responsibility to solicit bride-price contributions is equally shared by the father's clan and that of the maternal uncle. Forced marriages are understood to be less than ideal, and strong objections by either of the couple are enough to break off the match. The bride-price goes, in roughly equal amounts, to the girl's patrilateral and matrilateral kin—much in the same way that it was collected by the boy's family. After the bride-price is paid, the groom's father arranges for a house to be built near his own, where the newly wed couple will live. Later the couple and their children will move to a hamlet associated with the husband's mother's subclan, where his rights—particularly to the use of land—are of greater significance. Divorce is rare, and the only recognized grounds are cruelty, incompatibility, or adultery. Because it is only in cases of serious bodily harm to the wife that her family can retain the bride-price that was paid, wives are under far more pressure to remain within a marriage than is the case for husbands, although ideally either spouse has an equal right to seek divorce. Polygyny occurred in the past, although it tended to be an option limited only to particularly wealthy and influential men, due to the burden of raising high bride-prices.

Domestic Unit. The household consists minimally of a married adult male, his wife, and children, but frequently it also includes an aging parent (either the husband's or the wife's) and unmarried siblings of the husband. In particular, an unmarried or divorced woman will turn to her brother's household as her proper home, should the need arise. A newly married son and his wife will live temporarily in the boy's father's house until their first independent dwelling is built nearby, but they will build future houses in the hamlet of the boy's uterine uncle.

Inheritance. Use rights to land for adult males follows clan membership, and clan lore is passed from uterine uncles to nephews. But a father will pass to his sons the practical knowledge and skills he has accumulated (e.g., garden magic, technical skills such as canoe building). Heritable personal property is minimal because at the death of an individual his or her closest kin ritually express their grief by the destruction of part of such property—clothing is burned, canoes are broken apart, and the like—but a man's principal heirs are always his uterine nephews.

Socialization. Children are reared primarily by their mothers for the first few years of life, but all members of the household and both maternal and paternal kin will intervene with corrections or scoldings when necessary. Children are expected to learn early on the value of sharing and respect for the belongings of others. Girls begin their practical training in adult skills and roles early on, but boys do not begin to go about with their fathers until they reach the age of 7 or so, at which time a man might make a small fishing rod for his son and take him down to the beach. At a fairly young age a father will give his son a small pig to raise, and both he and the boy's uterine uncle will begin to take his practical education in hand. Fathers teach their sons skills but not clan lore. If there once were boys' puberty rituals, all memory of them has been lost, but girls still undergo facial scarring when they are about age 12 or 13.

Sociopolitical Organization

Social Organization. The five dispersed matrilineal clans form the largest unit that establishes kin-based rights and obligations, specifically regarding hospitality, but at this level these rights and obligations are somewhat attenuated. The localized subclan of the hamlet serves far more significantly as a unit of organization—from this level community work parties for the clearing of gardens, women's gathering groups, and the like are drawn. For overseas trading expeditions, men from a number of hamlets in the village cooperate; these groups crosscut subclan ties.

Political Organization. The traditional system relied on the influence of senior men to whom others in the hamlet would turn for help in resolving conflicts or organizing work parties on a scale larger than the household. Leadership was traditionally based on the amassing of wealth (in the form of strings of shell money) and prestige. The largest unit of organization and cooperation—for overseas trading expeditions and for war—was the village, and the most influential of the hamlet headmen would lead his fellows in achieving consensus for such decisions. This system suffered early from the effects of colonization and missionization when the bases of village and headman influence were suppressed by church and administrative policies.

Social Control. Shaming was traditionally a principal means of securing appropriate social behavior, although recourse was often taken to the counsel of hamlet or village headmen when disputes or asocial behavior required outside intervention. Training from childhood is geared to inculcate qualities of cooperation, respect, and tolerance, but in the day-to-day life of the hamlet and village frictions do arise between individuals. At such times, other kin will try to intervene to bring the miscreant to his or her senses. When necessary a hamlet or village headman will step in to mediate and effect a reconciliation between mutually offended parties. Now recourse is taken to courts and government councils.

Conflict. Conflict might arise over theft or the killing of another man's pig, but the principal cause is said to be adultery. When this occurs between members of different villages, it may be redressed through "death sorcery." If an individual is thought to have been killed by sorcery, a diviner identifies the sorcerer and countersorcery is attempted. Open violence used to be resorted to if the victim was an important leader; this method involved hiring a party of warriors, not of the victim's subclan, who would undertake to kill the sorcerer and bring back his head, after which the kin of the slain sorcerer had to be paid compensation in shell money and teeth.

Religion and Expressive Culture

Religious Beliefs. Each of the five matrilineal clans derives its charter from stipulated descent from one of the five sons of the culture heroine, Koevasi, who is said to have created the first humans. Each clan has three classes of spirits—spirits of the dead, shark spirits, and snake spirits—all possessing *nanama,* which is a power that can be exerted by them on behalf of the living. Such intervention is sought through sacrifices to the shrine of one or another of these spirit types, and each has associated with it certain food taboos and restrictions as to who may be present at the sacrifice. One particular class of the spirits of the dead—warrior spirits—influenced success or failure in war, while all other ancestral spirits were primarily involved in maintaining the health of their living descendants. The assistance of shark spirits was sought in circumstances to do with fishing or overseas trading expeditions, and snake spirits were particularly helpful with regard to gardening. Ancestral spirits could be invoked by sorcerers to cause death or illness in others, as well as to remove the death or sickness spells cast by others. Christian beliefs and practices were introduced by Anglican missionaries in 1912, and the church has had no little success, although early efforts at missionizing went a bit astray—an attempt to translate the *Book of Common Prayer* into the Kaoka language in 1916 was received as gibberish. Today, however, both Christian converts and non-Christians tend to hold both the introduced religion and the indigenous one as valid, and there is a tendency to fit Christian teachings into traditional terms.

Religious Practitioners. Each shrine had a priest, knowledgeable in its specific taboos and procedures, to whom others of the clan or subclan would turn to conduct sacrifices or for divination. Magic and sorcery were practiced not by such priests but by men of the community to whom the ritual knowledge had been taught by paternal kin (for curative, agricultural, and fishing magic) or received from a clan relative (for death or sickness sorcery). Any effective headman was considered capable of casting spells, for it was held that his success was contingent upon access to the spirits' nanama.

Ceremonies. Ceremonial feasts were held on the occasion of weddings and funerals, as well as to celebrate a birth or the construction of a new house or canoe. Each householder in the subclan holding the feast contributes as much surplus garden produce and pigs as he can, for it is his largess on these occasions that gain him prestige and influence in the community. The planting of crops involves the use of garden magic, and invoking the assistance of spirits calls for a sacrifice, usually of a pig.

Arts. Animal ballets are often performed during the course of feasts. The composition of such ballets is determined by specialized choreographers and performed by skilled local dancers, always male. On the coast, only choral music accompanies the dances, but in the interior there are also orchestras of panpipes. Women have dances as well, although these are not associated with celebrations and consist simply of a shuffling circular movement to the accompaniment of a chorus.

Medicine. Disease and death were held to be caused by sorcery, for the most part, although they were believed also to result from the direct displeasure of spirits without the involvement of humans—in the case of taboo violations, for example. Treatment for illness required the assistance of a magical specialist, who through divination would attempt to determine the cause of the sickness and the appropriate curative procedures.

Death and Afterlife. The traditional religion held that one's deceased ancestors still could be petitioned by the living through the intervention of nanama, and mortuary practices reflect that belief. At the death of an individual, close kin gather to host a meal for the rest of the village. Burial practice varies according to subclan tradition and other factors and includes burial at sea, exposure of the corpse, and interment in the floor of the deceased's dwelling; this last is the most common. For two or three months the deceased's nearest kin observe a number of taboos, and villagers respectfully refrain from loud or boisterous behavior to avoid giving the appearance of taking pleasure in the death and thus giving rise to suspicions of sorcery. When enough time has passed and decomposition of the body is sufficiently advanced to permit the removal of the skull, the chief heir secures the services of a ritual expert to take and clean the head, which is then hung under the eaves of the house. A series of ritual payments have been exchanged between the kin of the surviving spouse and the kin of the deceased, and the deceased's clothing is burned by his or her brother or nephew. A feast is held to mark the end of the mourning period. The skull is then installed in the hamlet shrine and a small pig is sacrificed to the spirit of the dead person, which remains in the vicinity to influence the affairs of his or her survivors and descendants.

See also Malaita, San Cristobal

Bibliography

Belshaw, Cyril S. (1954). *Changing Melanesia.* New York: Oxford University Press.

Hogbin, Ian (1938). "Social Advancement in Guadalcanal." *Oceania* 8:289–305.

Hogbin, Ian (1964). *A Guadalcanal Society: The Kaoka Speakers*. New York: Holt, Rinehart & Winston.

NANCY E. GRATTON

Gururumba

ETHNONYMS: Asaro, Miruma

Orientation

Identification. The Gururumba are one of nine political sovereignties located in the upper valley of the Asaro River in the Eastern Highlands Province of Papua New Guinea.

Location. The Upper Asaro Valley is part of the Goroka Valley system, bounded on the east by a section of the Bismarck Mountains and on the west by the Asaro Range. The Gururumba control approximately 140 square kilometers on the west side of the valley at elevations ranging from 1,800 to 2,300 meters. Some 100 square kilometers of this is arable land and the rest is covered with semitropical rain forest. The climate is marked by an annual rainfall of 254 centimeters or more, with 75 percent of it falling in a November–April wet season.

Demography. In 1960 the Gururumba numbered about 1,300 of the 13,500 residents of the Upper Asaro Census Division, reflecting a population increase of about 10 percent during the previous decade. The cessation of indigenous warfare and the introduction of a rudimentary health-care system may largely account for this increase, as is also true of recent estimates of over 18,000 Asaro speakers.

Linguistic Affiliation. The people of the Upper Asaro Valley speak a dialect of the Gahuku-Asaro language in the East-Central Family of Papuan languages. Neo-Melanesian (Tok Pisin), a lingua franca introduced in the 1930s by Australians and others, is also commonly spoken.

History and Cultural Relations

The Gururumba and the other sovereignties in the Upper Asaro Valley all have traditional oral narratives that tell of their once being part of a smaller common population living farther downriver from where they are now. Warfare is said to have broken out, and the population split into various factions that moved to the different parts of the upper valley where their descendants are currently found. Archaeological evidence indicates that people have been living in this part of the highlands for some thousands of years. This long period of relative isolation was broken in the 1930s when Australian gold prospectors entered the region. There followed a period of exploration and the introduction of *Pax Australiana*. The Gururumba were first contacted by an Australian government patrol in 1948, and a one-track dirt road was extended into their territory in 1957. Prior to European contact the Gururumba had little exposure to peoples outside their valley boundaries. They knew and traded with other peoples with different languages, most important of whom were the Chimbu living across the 3,700-meter Asaro-Chimbu Divide. They were regarded by the Gururumba as powerful people and were actively recruited to establish permanent residences among them. The Gururumba were also familiar with the Gende-speaking peoples living in the Bismarck Mountains and the Gahuku and Siane speakers to the southwest and southeast.

Settlements

About one-third of Gururumba territory is in dense forest cover; the remaining portion is open grassland, studded with gardens and stands of planted casuarinas. Major villages, containing 150–300 people, are located between the Asaro River and the forest line, arranged in a linear pattern if located on ridges, or in a rectangular arrangement if not. The latter villages were also sites of important ceremonial events, which hundreds of people from other sovereignties and language groups would attend for several days at a time. Prior to European contact the villages were somewhat smaller, palisaded, and located in less-open positions on ridges closer to the forest for defensive reasons. Houses were round in floor plan with a center pole supporting radial rafters and a thatched roof. The walls were made of a double row of wooden stakes lined with grass and sealed with horizontal strips of tree bark. Each village consisted of one or two large houses, where all the adult men slept and ate together, and a series of smaller houses: one for each married woman, her unmarried daughters, and young sons. In either case, the houses were divided into a front half, where the door and hearth were located, and a back half used as a storage and sleeping area.

Economy

Subsistence and Commercial Activities. Subsistence was dependent on a system of swidden horticulture supplemented by hunting and gathering. The major domesticated food plants were sweet potatoes, yams, taro, sugarcane, and a variety of greens. Pandanus was a major wild food plant. The pig was the main domesticated food animal, but it was not raised primarily to yield a continuous meat supply. Pigs were important as prestations between individuals and groups, and they were slaughtered and eaten in such a manner as to facilitate the political economy rather than the larder. Many kinds of birds, marsupials, rodents, and reptiles were hunted and eaten, although primarily by women and children as these animals as food were taboo to adult men. Corn, peanuts, soybeans, and a variety of other European vegetables have been grown since the 1950s, as has coffee, which was the first commercial enterprise for the Gururumba.

Industrial Arts. There were no specialized artisans in traditional Gururumba society. Almost every adult knew how to produce the material necessities, although some people were recognized as being particularly adept at a certain process and thus their help was sometimes sought, as in making a particular kind of intricately decorated arrow.

Trade. Simple barter based on a system of equivalencies was the traditional mode of trade. Feathers of all kinds (but especially bird of paradise plumes), wood for bows, ornamental arrows, ceremonial stone axes, shells, salt, and pigs were important trade items, and the Gururumba made treks (at some risk) into other language areas, such as Gende and Siane, to obtain them.

Division of Labor. Division of labor was primarily by sex and age. The bulk of the gardening was done by the women, although certain garden tasks (cutting fence posts and building fences) were allotted to men, and certain plants (sugarcane and taro) were only grown by men. Men hunted, women collected; men built houses, women thatched; man made tools and weapons, women made a variety of bags, skirts, and bands of bast and other fibers; and men acted as guards against enemy attack while women worked in exposed gardens.

Land Tenure. The Gururumba comprise eight patriclans and it is through these that a person gains access to land. Each patriclan is named and identified with a territory clearly bounded by major ridge lines and watercourses, and encompassing all the major ecological zones, from the rich alluvial soils near the river through the hilly grassland and into the rain forest. The full extent of a clan territory is divided into named plots, each of which has a characteristic potential for certain kinds of crops and resources. These plots tend to be associated with particular lineages within clans, but one of the functions of clan leadership is to facilitate equitable distribution of productive and less productive plots.

Kinship

Kin Groups and Descent. The most important sodalities and networks were based on kinship, descent, and their extension through marriage. The patriclan was such a sodality, marked by a name and a territory. It also had two other important attributes and functions: it was exogamous, and thus controlled marriage; and it was the organizing unit for the *idzi namo* (pig festival), the climactic ceremonial event in an important cycle of prestations regulating the political economy. The genealogies of these units only extended back one or two generations beyond adult living members, however, and ended with two or three imputed "brothers" rather than a single named ancestor. This type of unit is signified by the bound morpheme-*juhu*, which was said to indicate "people who sit down together," thus emphasizing a commonality of place and purpose more than genealogy. Each patriclan is made up of three to five patrilineages and these are identified with particular founding males. Lineages were said to be to clans as staves are to a fence or internodal segments are to a stalk of bamboo. Again, the image emphasizes unity of segments rather than genealogical subordination. Other important descent relationships are those between mother's brother and sister's son and between men whose mothers are sisters or are from the same clan, thus giving a matrilineal bias to an otherwise patrilineal system.

Kinship Terminology. The kin term system is characterized by Omaha-type cousin terminology, an extension of parental and sibling terms to clan mates, and an elaboration of terms marking relative age for siblings and parental siblings of both sexes.

Marriage and Family

Marriage. Marriages are most importantly arrangements between clans rather than individuals, and residence is patrivirilocal. From the point of view of a male clan member it is important to send one's sisters and daughters as wives to as many other clans as possible to establish a network of reciprocities based on the obligations of kinship that develop through the joint responsibilities for children produced by these unions. Such networks were one of the main bases of political alliance among sovereignties. Divorce, then, most often involved negotiation between the two clans involved rather than between the individuals.

Domestic Unit. Because of residential segregation of the sexes, the domestic unit was not a residential unit. A woman, her unmarried daughters, and her sons who were too young to be taken into the men's house all lived together. The father/husband visited occasionally in their house but never slept there. He joined them on an almost daily basis to plan and carry out various tasks, but he spent most of his other time with the men's group.

Inheritance. Since males have ultimate control over land and its products, upon death claims to garden land would revert to the clan. Personal movable property might be claimed by the children of the deceased.

Socialization. Children have a variety of caretakers and socializing agents including older siblings, any adult of the same lineage, and peers. The latter are especially important as prepubescent males often form their own dwelling and eating groups.

Sociopolitical Organization

Social and Political Organization. The sovereignty to which the name "Gururumba" applies is a phratry: a group of patriclans occupying contiguous territory and having a sense of common origin. In addition they see themselves as a peace group and as allies against enemy clans outside the phratry. Disputes internal to the phratry should be settled by means other than killing, and members should aid one another if attacked by outsiders. The phratry was also an important ritual unit in the past. Within the territory of each Upper Asaro Valley phratry there was a ceremonial structure (*jabirisi*) where renewal rituals were performed at times when there was a consensus among the constituent clans that disastrous times had befallen them. Representatives of all of the clans participated. All phratries of the Upper Asaro Valley developed patterns of amity and enmity that shifted over time and could result in devastating warfare. Alliances among phratries were stabilized and maintained through a complex of marriages and large-scale food and wealth exchanges. These were organized by "men whose names are known" or big-men who occupied positions of consensual leadership in particular clans primarily because they were known to be adept at alliance-building through manipulating marriages and material resources such as pigs and shells.

Social Control and Conflict. Aside from personal quarrels, disputes might arise over land, especially plots with high potential for crops such as taro and others important in exchange activities. Disputes could be extended to involve whole lineages, villages, sibs, or phratries; fighting (*nande*) with hands, sticks, and stones might occur, but these conflicts were expected ultimately to be settled in moots presided over by big-men. Warfare (*rovo*), involving spears, axes, and arrows and intended to decimate the opposition, was restricted to enemy phratries and alliances, and it was endemic prior to European influence.

Religion and Expressive Culture

Religious Beliefs. Traditional Gururumba religious belief is focused on an inner cosmos of bodily fluids, energies, and spirit entities. All people are believed to have a vital substance that actualizes them both physically and emotionally. Illness and death are primarily the result of some diminution of the power of this substance through not taking proper precautions to protect it or through making some attack on it by sorcery or witchcraft. In addition, women have a particularly potent power in the form of their natural fecundity, which can be harmful to men if the men do not properly protect themselves. This is the rationale for residential segregation of the sexes along with other taboos that restrict male-female contact. There are also some persons (*gwumu*, or witches) who are thought to have a substance in them that causes them to do harmful and malevolent things to others.

Religious Practitioners. There are a few individuals who function as shamanic curers, but they are only called in for difficult cases, particularly those involving sorcery.

Ceremonies and Arts. The pig festival was the prime arena for expressive culture. The groups who were guests at such events came splendidly arrayed in elaborate body decorations of feathers, fur, shells, pigment, and colorful fiber ornaments. As many as 2,000–5,000 people might be assembled on a dance ground with many groups simultaneously performing dances and mobile dramas ranging from the farcical to the mythical. Dancers at such an event would also typically be wearing *ingerebe* on their heads. These decorations are small carved and painted boards fixed into the hair and surrounded with elaborate feather ornaments. They were also magical objects, believed to store up the energy of such events and later release it into gardens from trees where they were hung. Singing, drumming, and flute music were accompaniments to these events. Another such context was the initial installment of older boys into the men's house. The magical rituals transforming them from boys into men were kept secret from the women, but women made many of the special decorative items signaling adult male status first worn by these "new men" on their emergence from the men's house.

Medicine. Men's illnesses were generally attributed to semen loss or contamination by menstrual blood or to the causes to which all were vulnerable: sorcery, witchcraft, or attacks by ghosts. All adults knew some bush medicines and spells, but some older men were considered to know more and to be more adept. They would be brought in to divine the cause and prescribe a cure, especially in cases of suspected sorcery or witchcraft. Illness attributed to ghosts could be alleviated by propitiating or driving away the ghosts responsible.

Death and Afterlife. Death, especially for important men, was marked by a villagewide funeral ceremony, followed by burial, usually on land of the resident clan of the deceased. Each person was believed to have a spiritual essence, which was released at death; this essence might remain among the living for some time as a ghost. Ghosts occasionally helped the living by appearing in dreams and foretelling the future or revealing new magic, but more often they caused trouble including illness, accidents, rainstorms, trouble with pigs, madness, and even death. They staged these attacks in response to perceived affronts to their esteem or physical remains.

See also Chimbu, Gahuku-Gama, Siane, Tairora

Bibliography

Newman, Philip L. (1962). "Sorcery, Religion, and the Man." *Natural History* 71:21–28.

Newman, Philip L. (1962). "Supernaturalism and Ritual among the Gururumba." Ph.D. dissertation, University of Washington.

Newman, Philip L. (1964). "Religious Belief and Ritual in a New Guinea Society." *American Anthropologist* 66:257–272.

Newman, Philip L. (1965). *Knowing the Gururumba.* New York: Holt, Rinehart & Winston.

Newman, Philip L. (1981). "Sexual Politics and Witchcraft in Two New Guinea Societies." In *Social Inequality: Comparative and Developmental Approaches,* edited by Gerald D. Berreman, 103–121. New York: Academic Press.

PHILIP L. NEWMAN

Hawaiians

ETHNONYM: Hawaiian Islanders

Orientation

Identification. Hawaiians are the indigenous people of the Hawaiian Islands. Now a disadvantaged minority in their own homeland, they are the descendants of Eastern Polynesians who originated in the Marquesas Islands. The name "Hawai'i" is that of the largest island in the chain. It came to refer to the aboriginal people of the archipelago because the first Western visitors anchored at that island and interacted predominantly with Hawai'i Island chiefs.

Location. The populated Hawaiian Islands are located between 15° and 20° N and 160° and 155° W. The climate is temperate tropical, and weathered volcanic features dominate the terrain. Rainfall and soil fertility may vary significantly between the windward and leeward sides of the islands.

Demography. The aboriginal population is estimated at 250,000–300,000. Because of recurrent epidemics of introduced diseases, the native population had been reduced by at least 75 percent by 1854. In the late 1880s Hawaiians were outnumbered by immigrant sugar workers. According to the state's enumeration, Hawaiians today number about 175,000, or 19 percent of the state's population. Because of historically high rates of Hawaiian exogamy "pure" Hawaiians number only about 9,000.

Linguistic Affiliation. Hawaiian is closely related to Marquesan, Tahitian, and Maori. The use of Hawaiian was suppressed in island schools during the territorial period, and the language fell into disuse during the mid-twentieth century. Few Hawaiians can speak the language today. The colloquial language of most Hawaiians is Hawai'i Islands Creole, informally known as "Pidgin." Since the 1970s the University of Hawaii has been the center of attempts to revive the Hawaiian language through education. A few hundred children are enrolled in language-immersion preschools where only Hawaiian is spoken.

History and Cultural Relations

The date of first colonization is constantly being revised, but Polynesians are believed to have reached Hawai'i by about A.D. 300. There may have been multiple settlement voyages, but two-way travel between Hawai'i and other island groups was never extensive. By the time of Captain James Cook's arrival late in 1778, the Hawaiian chieftainship had evolved a high order of political complexity and stratification, with the Maui and Hawai'i Island dynasties vying to control the eastern portion of the archipelago. In their first encounters with the Hawaiians Cook's men introduced venereal disease. At Kealakekua, on the leeward side of Hawai'i Island, Cook was greeted as the returning god Lono, but he was later killed in a skirmish over a stolen longboat. Europeans nevertheless began to use the islands as a provisions stop, for Hawai'i was uniquely well situated to supply the fur trade and, later, North Pacific whalers. The Hawaiian chiefs became avidly involved in foreign trade, seeking to accumulate weapons, ammunition, and luxury goods. In 1795 Kamehameha, a junior chief of Hawai'i Island, defeated the Maui chiefs in a decisive battle on O'ahu Island, thereby unifying the windward isles. This date is taken to mark the beginning of the Hawaiian kingdom and Hawai'i's transition from chiefdom to state. An astute and strong-willed ruler, Kamehameha consolidated his rule and established a bureaucratic government. His successors were weaker and were continually pressured by foreign residents and bullied by colonial governments. High-ranking chiefly women and their supporters convinced Kamehameha II to abolish the indigenous religion shortly after his father's death in 1819. Congregationalist missionaries arrived a few months later and came to exert tremendous influence on the kingdom's laws and policies. In the 1840s resident foreigners persuaded Kamehameha III to replace the traditional system of land tenure with Western-style private landed property. The resulting land division, the "Great Mâhele," was a disaster for the Hawaiian people. The king, the government, and major chiefs received most of the land, with only 29,000 acres going to 80,000 commoners. At the same time foreigners were given the right to buy and own property. Within a few decades most Hawaiians were landless as foreign residents accumulated large tracts for plantations and ranches. The 1875 Reciprocity Treaty with the United States ensured the profitability of sugar. Planters imported waves of laborers from Asia and Europe, and Hawaiians became a numerical minority. A clique of white businessmen overthrew the last monarch, Queen Lili'uokalani, in 1893. Although President Grover Cleveland urged that the monarchy be restored, Congress took no action and annexation followed in 1898. While descendants of the Asian sugar workers have lived the American dream in Hawai'i, native Hawaiians suffered increasing poverty and alienation during the territorial period. Hawaiian radicalism and cultural awareness have been on the upsurge since the mid-1970s. Citing the precedent of American Indian tribal nations, activists now demand similar status for Hawaiians, and the movement for Hawaiian sovereignty has gained increasing credibility among the state's political leaders.

Settlements

In precontact times Hawaiians lived in dispersed settlements along the coasts and in windward valleys. Inland and mountain areas were sparsely populated. Hawaiian houses were thatched from ground to roof ridge with native grass or sugarcane leaves. Commoner houses were low and sparsely furnished with coarse floor mats. The dwellings of the chiefs were more spacious, with floors and walls covered thickly with fine mats and bark cloth. Because of taboos mandating the separation of men and women in certain contexts, a household compound consisted of several dwellings for sleeping and eating. The most important developments affecting Hawaiians since the mid-nineteenth century have been land alienation and urbanization. Small Hawaiian subsistence communities practicing fishing and farming persist in isolated rural areas of Maui, Moloka'i, and Hawai'i. On O'ahu, the leeward Waianae coast is a center of Hawaiian settlement. Significant numbers of Hawaiians also live on leased house lots in government-sponsored Hawaiian Home Lands communities within the city of Honolulu. Dwellings in the style of plantation housing predominate in working-class communities and neighborhoods throughout Hawai'i, and Hawaiian settlements are no exception to this pattern. In most Hawaiian villages and neighborhoods the houses are of single-walled wood construction, sometimes raised off the ground on pilings, with corrugated iron roofs. Rural Hawaiians may have small houses for cooking and bathing behind the main dwelling, a pattern that appears to be a holdover from Polynesian culture.

Economy

Subsistence and Commercial Activities. The first Polynesian settlers in Hawai'i subsisted largely on marine resources. In the ensuing centuries the Hawaiians developed extensive and highly productive agricultural systems. The staple food was taro, a starchy root that the Hawaiians pounded and mashed into a paste called *poi.* In wetland valleys taro was grown in irrigated pond fields resembling rice paddies. Intricate networks of ditches brought water into the taro patches, some of which doubled as fish ponds. In the late precontact period, concurrent with increasing political complexity, large walled fish ponds were constructed in offshore areas. These were reserved for chiefly use. The lee sides of the islands supported extensive field systems where Hawaiians grew dry-land taro, sweet potatoes, breadfruit, and bananas. The Polynesians brought pigs, dogs, and chickens to Hawai'i. Goats and cattle were introduced by Westerners before 1800. In the early 1800s, to avoid the chiefs' growing demands on the rural populace, some Hawaiians turned to seafaring, peddling, and various jobs in the ports. The shift from rural subsistence to wage labor intensified in the latter half of the century. Hawaiians—men and women—made up the bulk of the sugar plantation labor force until after 1875. According to 1980 state figures, about 23 percent of Hawaiians today are employed in agriculture. Some are independent small farmers who produce the traditional staple, taro, for sale to markets. But most Hawaiians are engaged in service jobs. Hawaiians are underrepresented in management and professional occupations and overrepresented as bus drivers, police officers, and fire fighters.

Industrial Arts. Indigenous Hawaiian crafts included mat and bark-cloth making, feather work, and woodworking.

Trade. Although the traditional Hawaiian local group was largely self-sufficient, there was specialization and internal trade in canoes, adzes, fish lines, salt, and fine mats. In the postcontact period Hawaiians have tended to leave store keeping and commerce to other ethnic groups.

Division of Labor. Most agricultural labor was performed by men in ancient Hawai'i, as was woodworking and adz manufacture. Women made bark cloth for clothing and mats for domestic furnishings, chiefly tribute, and exchange. Men did the deep-sea fishing while women gathered inshore marine foods. In most Hawaiian families today both spouses have salaried jobs outside the home.

Land Tenure. In the native Hawaiian conception land was not owned but "cared for." Use and access rights were allocated through the social hierarchy from the highest chiefs to their local land supervisors and thence to commoners. The most important administrative unit was a land section called the *ahupua'a,* which ideally ran from the mountain to the sea and contained a full range of productive zones. Typically a household had rights in a variety of microenvironments. The introduction of private land titles resulted in widespread dispossession in part because Hawaiians did not understand the implications of alienable property. The lands of the Kamehameha chiefly family descended to Princess Bernice Pauahi Bishop, whose estate supports the Kamehameha Schools in Honolulu for the education of Hawaiian children. The Hawaiian Home Lands, established by Congress in 1920, are leased to persons who can prove 50 percent Hawaiian ancestry. Originally conceived as a "back to the land" farming program, the Hawaiian Home Lands are now used primarily for house lots.

Kinship

Kin Groups and Descent. There were no corporate kin groups among Hawaiians at the time of contact. The chiefs could trace their genealogies back many generations through bilateral links, opportunistically linking themselves to particular ancestral lines as the political situation demanded. Commoners recognized shallow bilateral kindreds augmented by stipulated and fictive kin.

Kinship Terminology. In the Hawaiian language no distinction is made between parents and parents' collateral kin. Same-sex siblings are ranked by relative age, but brother and sister are terminologically unranked.

Marriage and Family

Marriage. In pre-Christian Hawai'i both sexes enjoyed near-complete freedom to initiate and terminate sexual attachments. Marriage was unmarked by ceremony and was hardly distinguished from cohabitation and liaisons, except in chiefly unions. The birth of children was the more important ceremonial occasion. Marrying someone of higher rank was the ideal for both men and women. Polygyny was the norm among the ruling chiefs, permissible but infrequent among the common people. Postmarital residence was determined by pragmatic considerations.

Domestic Unit. Both commoners and chiefs lived in large extended-family household groups with fluid composition. The indigenous religion mandated that men and women had to have separate dwelling houses and could not eat together.

Inheritance. Men were more likely to inherit land rights than women, while women were privileged in the inheritance of the family's spiritual property and knowledge. Since the legal changes of the nineteenth century land inheritance among Hawaiians has been mostly bilateral.

Socialization. In Hawaiian families today grandparents have an especially close relationship with their grandchildren, and they frequently take over parenting duties. As in other Polynesian societies, children may be adopted freely without emotional turmoil or secretiveness. Emphasis is placed on respect for age and mutual caring between family members.

Sociopolitical Organization

At the time of Western contact in 1778 the Hawaiian islands were politically divided into several competing chiefdoms. Hawai'i was an independent kingdom from 1795 to 1893 and a United States territory from 1898 until statehood in 1959.

Social Organization. Precontact Hawai'i was a highly stratified society where the chiefs were socially and ritually set apart from the common people. Rank was bilaterally determined and chiefly women wielded considerable authority. The commoner category was internally egalitarian.

Political Organization. Each island was divided into districts consisting of several ahupua'a land sections. Districts and ahupua'a were redistributed by successful chiefs to their followers after a conquest. The chief then appointed a local land agent to supervise production and maintenance of the irrigation system. The commoners materially supported the chiefs with tribute at ritually prescribed times. Rebellions and power struggles were common. In legendary histories cruel and stingy chiefs are deserted by their people and overthrown by their kinder younger brothers.

Social Control. The chiefs had absolute authority over commoners. They could confiscate their property or put them to death for violating ritual prohibitions. In practice, however, chiefs were constrained by their reliance on the underlying populace of producers. In Hawaiian communities today there is no sense of inborn rank and an egalitarian ethic prevails. Pretensions are leveled by the use of gossip and temporary ostracism.

Conflict. Warfare was endemic in the Hawaiian chieftainship in the century or two preceding Cook's arrival. After Kamehameha's conquest the Hawaiian warrior ethic declined to the extent that the monarchy could be overthrown in 1893 by a company of marines. Interpersonal conflicts among Hawaiians today typify the tensions present in any small-scale community, and they are for the most part resolved through the intervention of family and friends. Hawaiians are very reluctant to call in outside authorities to resolve local-level conflicts.

Religion and Expressive Culture

The religion described in ethnohistorical sources was largely the province of male chiefs. Sacrificial rites performed by priests at monumental temples served to legitimate chiefly authority.

Religious Beliefs. Chiefs were genealogically linked to gods and were believed to have sacred power (mana). Under what was called the *kapu* system women were denied many choice foods and could not eat with men. Pre-Christian beliefs persisted at the local level long after the chiefly sacrificial religion was overthrown. The indigenous religion recognized four major gods and at least one major goddess identified with the earth and procreation. Kū, the god of war, fishing, and other male pursuits, was Kamehameha's patron deity. Another god, Lono, represented the contrasting ethos of peace and reproduction. Women worshipped their own patron goddesses. Commoners made offerings to ancestral guardian spirits at their domestic shrines. Deities were also associated with particular crafts and activities. Although Congregationalists were the first to missionize in Hawai'i, the sect has few adherents among Hawaiians today. Roman Catholicism has attracted many Hawaiians, as have small Protestant churches emphasizing personal forms of worship.

Religious Practitioners. Before the *kapu* abolition younger brothers normatively served their seniors as priests. Major deities had their own priesthoods. The volcano goddess Pele is said to have had priestesses. Among the commoners there were experts in healing and sorcery, known as "Kāhuna," and such specialists are still utilized by Hawaiians today.

Ceremonies. The Hawaiian ritual calendar was based on lunar phases. Kū ruled the land for eight months of the year. Lono reigned for four winter months during the Makahiki festival when warfare was suspended and fertility was celebrated.

Arts. Chiefly men were sometimes tattooed, but this was not a general custom and most of the details have been lost. The carved wooden idols of the gods are artistically impressive, but few survived the dramatic end of the native religion. The hula, the indigenous dance form, had numerous styles ranging from sacred paeans to erotic celebrations of fertility. Various percussion instruments used included drums, sticks, bamboo pipes, pebbles (like castanets), gourds, rattles, and split bamboo pieces.

Medicine. Hawaiians today utilize Western medicine but may also consult healers and spiritual specialists, some linked to Hawaiian cultural precedent and others syncretic, drawing on other ethnic traditions. Hawaiians are particularly prone to spirit possession, and many believe that evil thoughts have material consequences on other people. Illness is linked to social grievances or imbalances.

Death and Afterlife. Ancient Hawaiians secreted remains of the dead in burial caves. The deceased's personal power or *mana* was believed to reside in the bones. Chiefs were particularly concerned that their enemies not find their remains and show disrespect to them after death. Those who broke the taboos, on the other hand, were killed and offered to the gods, and their remains were allowed to decompose on the temple.

See also Marquesas, Tahiti

Bibliography

Kirch, Patrick V. (1985). *Feathered Gods and Fishhooks: An Introduction to Hawaiian Archaeology and Prehistory.* Honolulu: University of Hawaii Press.

Kuykendall, Ralph S. (1938). *The Hawaiian Kingdom.* Vol. 1, 1778–1854. Honolulu: University of Hawaii Press.

Linnekin, Jocelyn (1985). *Children of the Land: Exchange and Status in a Hawaiian Community.* New Brunswick, N.J.: Rutgers University Press.

Valeri, Valerio (1985). *Kingship and Sacrifice: Ritual and Society in Ancient Hawaii.* Chicago: University of Chicago Press.

JOCELYN LINNEKIN

Iatmul

ETHNONYM: Yatmul

Orientation

Identification. The Iatmul live along the banks of the Middle Sepik River in the East Sepik Province of Papua New Guinea.

Location. The Middle Sepik area is dominated by the meandering river that regularly floods the whole valley and continuously changes its course as it flows from west to east into the Bismarck Sea. During the wet season, extremely heavy rains raise the water level 4–6 meters, turning the whole region into a lake that extends far into the northern grasslands (turning them into swamp) and to the Sepik Hills in the south. Floating grass islands, sometimes with whole trees and birds on them, are typical for that season as the rising floodwaters tear off parts of riverbanks and carry them downstream until they get stuck somewhere else. Iatmul territory begins about 230 kilometers up from the mouth of the Sepik and ends about 170 kilometers farther upstream. The Iatmul lead an almost amphibian way of life within the two main seasons, wet and dry, each lasting for five months with two intermediate months in between.

Demography. The Iatmul number about 10,000, and classify themselves into three territorial subgroups: eastern (Woliagui), central (Palimbei), and western (Nyaura). During the last few years many Iatmul have left the Middle Sepik, with nearly 50 percent of the population today living elsewhere in Papua New Guinea, temporarily or even permanently. There are Iatmul colonies, sometimes of considerable size, in the towns of Wewak, Madang, and Rabaul (on New Britain).

Linguistic Affiliation. Iatmul is joined with Abelam, Boiken, Sawos, and other Papuan languages in the Ndu Family of the Sepik-Ramu Phylum.

History and Cultural Relations

The Iatmul believe that they all originated from a hole in the ground in Sawos (Gaikundi) territory. Other oral traditions tell of drifting down the river on rafts, having started somewhere in the west. The Sepik Basin is, from the point of view of geology, relatively young, having achieved its present character around 1,000 years ago. The whole area was flooded by the sea until about 5,000 years ago; only gradually, when the coastline withdrew until it reached its present location, did the alluvial plains form and marine conditions change to those of fresh water. Linguistic and archaeological evidence suggests that the Ndu speakers came down into the Sepik Basin from a southern tributary. The Sepik River (called the Kaiserin-Augusta-Fluss during German colonial times) was a main passageway for colonial administrators traveling upriver by ship. During German rule the first official Sepik exploratory expedition took place in 1886, and it was followed by several others. After World War I, when Ambunti Patrol Post was established, the new Australian administration tried to suppress head-hunting. They finally succeeded in the mid-1930s by publicly executing convicted Iatmul warriors. The pacification of the Iatmul—a culture in which much emphasis was placed on male aggression and head-hunting raids—brought far-reaching cultural change from the outside world. Iatmul villages were in continuous contact with neighboring groups to the north and south, often in a symbiotic subsistence relationship with the Iatmul trading turtles and fish in exchange for sago. The Sawos were regarded as nurturing mothers in this regard. Women conducted the trade while men were involved in joint rituals with neighboring groups.

Settlements

Iatmul villages, containing 300–1,000 people, are built high on riverbanks. Villages often consist of three distinct sections, with a men's house in the center. Houses were often built in two rows, parallel to or at a right angle to the course of the river. The men's house was usually built in the center of an open space, the dancing ground. Older Iatmul men's houses, which were huge buildings up to 20 meters high and 40 meters long, are among the most impressive architectural achievements in New Guinea. They served as men's assembly houses in daily life and as religious centers during rituals. The dancing ground contained a ceremonial mound on which heads were displayed when brought back from a successful raid. Each section of the tripartite village owned a long war canoe that was a symbol of its cooperation during warfare, as was the ceremonial house for ritual life. The whole village usually constituted a defensive unit, whereas only a section of it may have made a raid on an enemy village. A village often was surrounded by fences and watchtowers. Traditionally, Iatmul houses were huge pile dwellings with the families of brothers living together in one house. Clans are classified into moieties, a fact that can be recognized in the layout of the village and the distribution of the houses there.

Economy

Subsistence and Commercial Activities. Traditionally the Iatmul were mainly hunters and gatherers, depending on fish and sago, with horticulture a secondary activity as the gardens on riverbanks are often inundated before the root crops (yams and taro) are ripe. Bananas and coconuts are regularly consumed. The hunting of game (wild pigs, crocodiles, and, rarely, cassowaries) is practiced only irregularly. Fishing is mainly women's work, using hooks, nets, and traps; when men fish they use spears. Among women there is an informal system of redistribution that provides fish to women who are unable to leave their houses because of illness, menstruation, childbirth, or old age. Although most Iatmul villages have sago stands, they have never been productive enough to guarantee a continuous supply. Therefore, Iatmul depend on sago produced by Sawos villages to the north and by some Sepik Hills villages to the south. Every few days Iatmul women transport fresh and smoked fish in their canoes to market places, most of which are located in Sawos territory. There, they barter fish for sago with women from bush villages. The women's trading expeditions take a full day and are carried out mostly by elderly women who are commissioned by younger women to do the bartering for them.

Industrial Arts and Trade. Most Iatmul villages specialize in the production of different kinds of goods that are used for trading. Aibom is well known for pottery, which traditionally was traded for sago throughout the Iatmul area; today it is sold for money as well. Chambri, a non-Iatmul border village to the south, specializes in firmly plaited mosquito bags manufactured by women. In all Sepik villages, where mosquitoes and malaria are endemic, these bags are used by entire families sleeping in them communally. Tambunum is renowned for its plaited bags, also produced by women, with various colored patterns. Iatmul carvings are among the most artistic in New Guinea. Men began producing them in large quantities when they found early travelers and art dealers interested in them. Anthropologists argue that Iatmul attained superiority and control over their neighbors by being a "cultural factory," producing sacred artifacts, spells, and knowledge and then exporting them. However, no reliable information confirming this can be found, except for an exchange of ritual items that must have taken place in both directions as indicated by Abelam paintings collected by early German explorers in Iatmul villages. As far as can be determined, irregular trading expeditions took place up southern tributaries and vice versa, with paint, edible earth, and bark used for medicinal purposes imported from these areas. Shell rings, turtleshell ornaments, and other valuables arrived in the Middle Sepik through the Abelam and Sawos regions and also from the upper regions of the Sepik River. Stone blades as well as pearlshells came from the highlands to the south.

Division of Labor. Subsistence activities, mainly the gathering of fish and sago, are carried out by women. Men make almost all implements used for subsistence (canoes, paddles, and tools for sago production) except fish traps, nets, and bags. Men build the houses and are also the ritual specialists.

Land Tenure. Lagoons and the open river are considered the property of the villages. Clans own rights to specific fishing and gathering locales. Garden land is also owned by clans or lineages and is allotted among the male members of the clan at the end of each flood season.

Kinship

Kin Groups and Descent. Iatmul patrilineal clans (*ngaiva*) are the organizational basis of the social order. Most clans are organized into pairs, with one considered the elder brother and the other the younger, both tracing their origin to a pair of brothers who are the founding ancestors. Genealogies are important evidence of landownership, the right to produce and possess ritual paraphernalia and ritual knowledge, and the right to perform specific ceremonies. Clan membership also determines a man's place within the men's house. Within clans there exists a further differentiation into pairs of lineages, with the senior lineage having some authority over the junior one.

Kinship Terminology. Different terms are used for matrilateral and patrilateral kin. In each generation siblings of the same sex are classified together as are parallel cousins, and in the parent's generation affinal relatives are addressed in terms used also for consanguineal kin.

Marriage and Family

Marriage. Three rules of marriage are reported: marriage with *iai* (father's mother's brother's son's daughter), marriage with *na* (father's sister's daughter), and sister exchange. But, marriages with other categories of women also took place. In marriage ceremonies the asymmetric relationship between wife givers and wife takers were acted out by an unequal exchange of goods (shell valuables, classified as male, and household goods, classified as female). Postmarital residence was patrilocal.

Domestic Unit. Several closely related nuclear families live together in a single dwelling. Each family has its own section and within it husbands and wives have their separate compartments. Cowives and wives of brothers are supposed to form a corporate unit for daily subsistence activities.

Inheritance. Inheritance of land and ritual knowledge follows rules of seniority insofar as the eldest son usually inherits knowledge, and thus power, that his siblings are denied. In rare cases a daughter may become the heir if a man has no son. In former times, the girl was then initiated with the men. Later, her sons inherited the knowledge from her father.

Socialization. Growing up in Iatmul culture is a gradual process of learning and experiencing tasks performed by adults. Children participate actively in the subsistence economy. The acquisition of a new skill and the first performance of a gender-specific task are celebrated for each girl and each boy individually. These ceremonies, *naven*, were carried out spontaneously by the mother's brother and/or his wife. Children spend much of their time in independent and autonomous groups. Girls grow gradually into women's roles. Boys, on the other hand, have to undergo an initiation which severs them from the women's world and forces them to adopt a male life-style.

Sociopolitical Organization

Social Organization. Local organization mirrors the social division into moieties, with named clans represented in many villages between whom relations are traced. The moieties are classified into "sky" (*nyaui*) and "earth" (or "mother," *hnyamei*). Each moiety is responsible for carrying out the initiation for the boys of the other; thus, boys get scarified by men from the other group. Iatmul men are classified also into an age-grade system, with four to six different degrees, depending on the village. Among the eastern Iatmul there exists a second nonlocalized moiety system that works as a competitive exchange system.

Political Organization. The men's houses are not only the religious center of Iatmul life but the political center as well. There discussions are held concerning all public matters on which a decision has to be made or action taken. Discussions are usually led by influential men who occupy the structural position of being endowed with ritual knowledge, a prerequisite for political leadership. Among men there is considerable competition and rivalry for political leadership. Speech making is an important factor in the decision-making process, and oratorical skill is a necessary condition for leadership. Speeches are delivered near the ceremonial "chair," a totemic representation of a founding ancestor whose judgment is solicited as a warrant for the truth. Another means to political leadership was to have a reputation as a powerful sorcerer or to be talented as a chanter.

Social Control. Traditionally, the men's house was also the center of jurisdiction in quarrels between members of different clans. Within a clan conflicts were settled by its own influential men. Women had informal power in social affairs; for example, a wife could refuse to provide her husband with food, and in serious matters she could call on her own family, mainly her brothers. At the community level, women were feared for their supposed polluting capacities, which were considered responsible at least in part for sorcery and witchcraft.

Conflict. Warfare was an important male activity and head-hunting was part of the initiation rite. Most attacks were against other Iatmul villages, particularly in the east.

Religion and Expressive Culture

Religious Beliefs. The men's house is a condensation of Iatmul religion, and it also reveals the connections between clans and their founding ancestors. In former days the house posts were beautifully carved, depicting parts of clan mythology and constituting thereby the foundation not only of the house but, symbolically, of the whole society. The building on the rectangular dancing ground represented the first grass island floating down the Sepik River as it is described in a myth of world creation. At the same time it represented the first crocodile, the primeval ancestor who emerged from the bottom of the flood. Today, the ground level of the men's house is used in everyday life by initiated men. It contains slit gongs, fireplaces, and sitting platforms as well as ritual objects of minor importance. The upper floor is used mainly for rituals, and the long flutes and other sacred paraphernalia are kept there. Iatmul culture is rich in myths that constitute the ideational background explaining how everything came into being. Myths in Iatmul culture are known by many people but only a few know the names of the actors and of the places. Names range among the highly valued secrets of clans. Myths can become reactivated through rituals, whereby the primeval time becomes the present and the dancing ground and the men's house become the original stage.

Religious Practitioners. The Iatmul acknowledged men and women who gained personal status through their knowledge and use of supernatural powers for healing and as intermediaries with the supernatural world.

Ceremonies. The men's house was the focus of different types of rituals: initiation, celebration of successful head-hunting raids, performances by masked figures, and celebrations of death ceremonies for important persons. In initiations boys were scarified, receiving the distinctive marks of a crocodile, the symbol of a ritually mature man.

Arts. Iatmul art is well known for its superb carvings, which were usually painted in a curvilinear style. Almost all art objects were used in ritual contexts and only through such use did they receive meaning. Also famous are the skulls overmodeled with clay and then painted. Apart from such preservable artifacts, Iatmul art consists of ephemeral art, such as body painting and decorations made of leaves, flowers, and feathers.

Medicine. Illness and difficult childbirths were treated with spells designed to invoke the powers of ancestors or supernatural forces such as the sun or moon. Healing often focused on symbolically casting off the illness.

Death and Afterlife. Legitimation of the present out of the past was accomplished through the preservation of relics (bones) of ancestors and through eating scrapings from them. Death meant crossing the border between the present and the past. The corpse was handled only by women. If the deceased had been an important man or woman, a representational figure was erected and his or her merits displayed. Occasionally after interment the skull was exhumed, modeled over with clay, and then installed during a special ceremony as an influential ancestor. Ghosts of recently dead relatives are relevant in shamanic seances as mediators between the living and the dead.

See also Abelam, Chambri

Bibliography

Bateson, Gregory (1936). *Naven.* Cambridge: Cambridge University Press. Rev. ed. 1954. Stanford: Stanford University Press.

Behrmann, Walter (1922). *Im Stromgebiet des Sepik.* Berlin: A. Scherl.

Lutkehaus, Nancy, et al., eds. (1990). *Sepik Heritage: Tradition and Change in Papua New Guinea.* Durham, N.C.: Carolina University Press.

Reche, Otto (1913). "Der Kaiserin-Augusta-Fluss." In *Ergebnisse der Südsee Expedition 1908–1910,* edited by Georg Thilenius. II. Ethnographie; A., Melanesien, vol. 1. Hamburg: L. Friederichsen.

Roesicke, Adolf (1914). "Mitteilungen Füber Ethnographische Ergebnisse der Kaiserin-Augusta-Fluss-Expedition." *Zeitschrift für Ethnologie* 46:507–522.

BRIGITTA HAUSER-SCHÄUBLIN

Kaluli

ETHNONYMS: Bosavi, Orogo, Waluli, Wisaesi

Orientation

Identification. "Bosavi kalu" (meaning "men of Bosavi") is the collective designation of four closely related horticulturalist groups who live in the rain forest of the Great Papuan Plateau. Of these four groups (Kaluli, Orogo, Waluli, and Wisaesi), the Kaluli are the most numerous and the most thoroughly studied.

Location. Kaluli longhouses are located along the northern slope of Mount Bosavi at roughly 142°38' to 142°55' W and 6°23' to 6°29' S, between the altitudes of 900 and 1,000 meters, in the drainage of the Isawa and Bifo rivers. This is a land of lush, largely virgin rain forest, where the vegetation is unbroken except for the small settlement clearings scattered throughout. Seasonality is not based on changes in temperature, because that averages between 29° and 32° C year-round. Rather, the year is divided into a relatively dry season (March to November) and a rainier one (December to February). During the rainy season there are frequent and violent rainstorms, with driving winds, torrential rains, and impressive thunder and lightning displays. The region is rich in birds and wild game, and it is cut through with myriad brooks and streams.

Demography. The Kaluli were estimated at 1,200 individuals in 1969 and 2,000 in 1987, which makes them the largest single language group on the plateau. Population levels for all plateau groups are thought to have been substantially higher in the precontact years, but the 1940s brought epidemics of measles and influenza, which devastated many of the groups. The Kaluli lost as much as 25 percent of their population to these epidemics, and their numbers have never fully recovered. Infant mortality rates today are quite high, and influenza epidemics still ravage the plateau periodically.

Linguistic Affiliation. Kaluli is a member of the Bosavi Family of Non-Austronesian languages, which also includes Beami (Gebusi).

History and Cultural Relations

Physiological and cultural evidence suggest that the Kaluli are more closely related to lowland Papuan cultural groups than to those of the nearby highlands, but there is no hard evidence to suggest that they originated anywhere outside of the general territory that they currently occupy. Early trade relations and cultural borrowings appear to have been predominantly with the peoples to their north and west. Throughout their existence, the Kaluli have been moving very gradually eastward, away from established settlement areas, moving ever more deeply into the virgin forests. Some of this movement may be attributed to a need to seek fresh garden lands, but it may also be explained in part as a defensive response to the expansionist pressures of the Beami and Etoro, traditional Kaluli enemies who live to the west and northwest of Kaluli territory. Warfare and raiding were common on the plateau, but there were longstanding trade relations between the Kaluli and certain of the other plateau groups, particularly with the Sonia to the west and the Huli of the Papuan highlands. First European contact on the plateau occurred in 1935, bringing with it the introduction of new goods to the regional trade network—most significantly, steel axes and knives. World War II brought a temporary halt to Australian government exploration of the plateau, which only recommenced in 1953. At this time, there began more frequent though still irregular contacts with Australian administrators and more direct interventions into the lives of the plateau peoples. Raiding and cannibalism were outlawed by 1960, and in 1964 missionaries built an airstrip near Kaluli territory to serve two mission stations established nearby.

Settlements

The Kaluli live in about twenty autonomous longhouse communities of approximately sixty individuals (or fifteen families) each. The longhouse is an elevated structure, about 18 meters by 9 meters, with a veranda at front and rear, and built roughly at the center of the community's garden lands. Inside, the longhouse is divided lengthwise down the center by a long hall, along either side of which are found the married men's sleeping platforms alternating with cooking hearths and, above the hearths, meat-smoking racks. Partitioned off from the men's platforms, and running the length of the structure along the outside walls, the married women's sleeping platforms follow the same pattern as the men's, and a wife will occupy the platform directly on the other side of her husband's partition. Very young children sleep with their mothers. Older male children and bachelors sleep together at the back of the longhouse, while marriageable women sleep communally at the front. The hallway, and the space just before the front and back doors of the longhouse are public areas. The area immediately surrounding the longhouse is cleared of forest growth, and here there are likely to be found a few small outbuildings to house visitors, and some of the land is planted in bananas, *pitpit,* and sugarcane. Other small shelters are built near the individual gardens that are scattered throughout the longhouse territory.

Economy

Subsistence and Commercial Activities. Sago is the staple of the Kaluli diet, processed from palms that self-propagate in the forest. This food is supplemented by garden produce—bananas, pandanus, breadfruit, *pitpit,* sugarcane, taro, and sweet potatoes. Protein is derived from wild game, lizards, fish, and crayfish. While the Kaluli keep domesticated pigs, these are only killed on ceremonial occasions, and the pig meat is distributed as gifts. Another ceremonially important food is grubs, which are incubated in sago-palm hearts and distributed like pork.

Industrial Arts. Items of Kaluli manufacture are few and, for the most part, simple: digging sticks, stone adzes, black-palm bows, and net bags. Longhouses and fences are built of forest materials, and dams are sometimes built in streams. Stone tools have largely been replaced by steel axes and knives. Kaluli also make necklaces of shell and fashion elaborate costumes and headdresses for their ceremonial dances.

Trade. Circulation of goods among Kaluli longhouses occurs in the context of ongoing, reciprocal gift exchange, as distinct from the more straightforward trade relations between Kaluli and non-Kaluli groups. Kaluli trade items such as net bags and black-palm bows in return for dogs' teeth, hornbill beaks, and tree oil from other plateau groups. These items are passed along with Kaluli goods to the Huli of the highlands in exchange for tobacco, vegetable salt, and netted aprons. Other items for which Kaluli trade include cowrie and small pearl shells from the coast, drums, and, more recently, glass beads, mirrors, and steel knives and axe heads.

Division of Labor. Some tasks are allocated according to a strict sexual division of labor. Men in groups do the heavy work of cutting down, dividing, and splitting the sago-palm trunk and pulverizing its core; they also clear the garden lands, build fences and dams, plant gardens and perform garden magic, hunt large game animals in the forest, fish, and butcher meat. Women process the sago pith, weed the gardens, tend the pigs, gather smaller forest prey and crayfish, and have the primary responsibilities of child rearing.

Land Tenure. Garden land and stands of sago palm are, to all intents and purposes, owned by individual men of the longhouse community, and each man is free to give, loan, or bequeath his property as he wishes. The general territory may be spoken of as belonging to the longhouse as a unit, but this group ownership does not imply any clan or lineage control over parcels of it. Ownership obtains as long as the land or sago is worked. Should it go unused for a generation, claims of ownership lapse. Rights in land and sago generally pass from father to son, secondarily to a man's brothers, his brother's children, or his sister's sons. Because the plateau is sparsely populated, there is little land pressure to give rise to property disputes.

Kinship

Kin Groups and Descent. Kaluli clans are patrilineal, exogamous, and dispersed throughout the longhouse settlements. Localized lineages of two or more such clans share residence in any single longhouse. While clan membership passes through the male line, an individual has claims of kinship both to the father's and mother's clans, with paternal kin providing ties within the longhouse and maternal kin providing linkages with his or her mother's kin in another longhouse of the territory. In practice, the sibling set—which includes one's actual siblings and all others of the same generation born of one's mother's sisters and father's brothers—takes priority over genealogical reckoning in establishing relationships. When a man marries, the importance of maternal kin for establishing extralonghouse relationships is superseded by ties to his wife's paternal clan.

Kinship Terminology. All kin two or more generations distant from an individual are called *maemu* ("grandfather" or "grandchild"), which is also the term used to designate people with whom one shares no discernible kin ties. Father and father's brother are called by the same term, as are mother and mother's sister. The offspring of all of these people are classified as siblings and share a common designation. The children of one's father's sister and mother's brother are termed cross cousins, though the mother's brother's daughter, upon bearing children, is reclassified with the term for "mother" and her children are classified as siblings. In practice, genealogical reckoning of relationships is preempted by classificatory assignment of a kin term, with no real effort made to pin down actual genealogical links.

Marriage and Family

Marriage. Kaluli marriages are arranged and usually set in motion by the elders of a prospective groom's longhouse, under the leadership of the groom's father. The young man and young woman to be wed are often quite unaware of marriage plans until bride-wealth negotiations are well advanced. Bride-wealth is collected from most if not all members of the groom's longhouse, regardless of actual kin ties, and it is shared out in the same manner by the bride's longhouse community. Sister exchange, or the provision of a groom's classificatory sister as marriage partner to a wife's classificatory brother, is the ideal, but it rarely occurs. Bride-wealth presentations are accompanied by great ceremonial, known as the "Gisaro," a ritual dance and song performance put on by the groom's kin and supporters. Upon payment of bride-wealth, the new wife is taken to the longhouse of her husband, but it may be weeks before conjugal relations begin. Marriage establishes a relationship of customary meat exchanges between the groom and his affines—particularly the father and brother(s) of the bride—which continue throughout the marriage. Polygyny is permissible, but it appears to be rare.

Domestic Unit. Within the longhouse, each nuclear family functions as a semiautonomous unit in gardening and in making its own meals. However, since so much of social and economic life is based on the cooperative efforts of the wider range of longhouse members, and since food tends to be shared throughout the community, the entire residential community can be viewed as the unit of consumption.

Inheritance. Other than land and sago, which usually pass from father to son, personal possessions are few. Net bags, bows, tools, or items of dress or adornment are given to the surviving spouse, the children of the deceased, or close age mates.

Socialization. Young children are raised by their mothers, with the help of other women and older female children of the longhouse. A girl learns her future role early on by watching her mother and, as she grows older, by helping in the mother's tasks. Young boys soon find themselves free of responsibility, and they are encouraged to play at games or roam the territory with their age mates to hunt or fish. As a boy becomes independent of his mother's care, he moves from her sleeping platform to the unmarried men's communal hearth at the rear of the longhouse, and here he is exposed to the talk and tales of men. During a boy's teens he traditionally enters into a homosexual relationship with an older man, for it is thought that he needs semen to promote his development into full manhood. Prior to contact, the unmarried youths of several clans would go into seclusion in the *bau a*, or ceremonial hunting lodge, for periods of as much as a year. During this time of seclusion from women, the men and boys would go on day-long hunting trips throughout the forest, and thus each boy would have the opportunity to learn in detail the features of his territory, the behavior of the forest animals, and other elements of men's lore. This practice did not constitute an initiation per se, but it did provide a period of intense immersion in the world of men.

Sociopolitical Organization

Social Organization. The longhouse is the most significant unit of social, economic, and ritual cooperation among the Kaluli, taking precedence over clan and lineage affiliation in most practical matters. Longhouses are tied to one another, however, through the gift-exchange relationships established between affines, sibling sets, and patrilaterally and matrilaterally reckoned kin, and these extracommunity relationships may be called upon by an individual to secure hospitality or support.

Political Organization. Kaluli society is essentially egalitarian, having no formally understood positions of leadership. Elders tend to wield more influence than younger men, but group action may be initiated by any adult male who can successfully enlist supporters for his cause.

Social Control. In the absence of formal leadership offices, social control is dependent upon informal sanctions such as gossip or ostracism, and an individual deemed guilty of a social or personal infraction may be met with demands for compensation by the aggrieved party or parties. Beliefs in spirits provide supernatural sanctions for violations of food taboos. The threat of retributive raids once served as an important means of discouraging serious transgressions, but the government no longer permits recourse to this sanction.

Conflict. The principal sources of conflict are theft of wealth or of women and (pre-1960) retribution for a death. Deaths are held to be the result of witchcraft, regardless of the apparent cause. In such cases, close friends and kinsmen of the deceased would determine the party responsible through divination and then organize a raiding party to attack the witch's longhouse. Members of the raiding party would converge on the longhouse at night, rushing the building at dawn with the express purpose of clubbing the witch to death. The body of the witch would be cut up and distributed to kin of the raiding party participants. Later, the members of the raiding party would pay compensation to the longhouse of the witch in order to prevent further retributive raids. Government intervention on the plateau brought retributive raiding and its attendant cannibalism to an end in the 1960s but provided no alternative means of redressing a death. Instead, an accused witch is now confronted and compensation is demanded, but there is no means to enforce payment.

Religion and Expressive Culture

Religious Beliefs. Kaluli believe that there is a spirit world that is coextensive with the everyday world of nature and subject to the same laws but that cannot be directly perceived. Every human is thought to have a spirit "shadow" (in the form of wild pigs for males, cassowaries for females) that wanders about in the forests of Mount Bosavi. A human and his or her shadow counterpart are linked in such a way that injury or death of one's shadow means that one will sicken or die. Along with the pig and cassowary shadows of living humans, the shadow world is peopled by three types of spirits: *ane kalu* (spirits of the dead), who are kindly disposed to the living and can be recruited to provide assistance when needed; *mamul,* who are generally aloof from humans but who during their hunts on Mount Bosavi may inadvertently kill a person's shadow animal, and whose ceremonial dances cause the thunderstorms during rainy seasons; and *kalu hungo* ("dangerous men") who inhabit specific creeks or other such locations in Kaluli territory and who will cause bad luck or bad weather when humans trespass on their property.

Religious Practitioners. Mediums are men who have married spirit women in a dream and who develop the ability to leave their physical bodies to walk about in the spirit world. At the same time, spirits may enter the medium's body and speak through him during seances to help people in curing an illness, locating lost pigs, or divining the identity of a witch. Witches (*sei*) can be male or female and generally do not themselves know of their evil aspect, which waits until its host sleeps and then prowls about in the night seeking its victims. Sei are thought not to attack their own kin, except on extremely rare occasions.

Ceremonies. The centerpiece of Kaluli ceremonial life is the Gisaro, which is performed at all major celebratory occasions such as weddings. "Gisaro" specifically refers to the songs and dancing performed for a host longhouse by visitors; the songs are composed to incorporate sorrowful references to important places and people who have died but who are remembered with fondness and grief. The ornately costumed Gisaro dancer performs his song in the central hall of the host longhouse, and his goal is to incite members of the host groups to tears with the beauty and sadness of his composition and the stateliness of his dance. When he has succeeded, longhouse men run up to the dancer and thrust burning torches against his back and shoulders, burning him. After all the singers of a Gisaro troupe have performed, the dancers leave small gifts for their hosts, as repayment for having evoked their tears and grief.

Arts. The ultimate artistic expression is the composition and performance of Gisaro songs and the proper execution of the accompanying dance. Visual arts are not highly developed, except in the elaborate costumes of the Gisaro dancers.

Medicine. Food taboos and the use of medicinal plants are commonly applied to treat illness, but most curing is done through the assistance of a medium, through actions he takes while traveling in the spirit world.

Death and Afterlife. Upon death, one's spirit immediately quits the now useless physical body and is chased into the forest by the longhouse dogs. The spirit is thus forced to walk on the Isawa River, which in this new noncorporeal state appears as a broad road leading west. Eventually, the spirit arrives at "Imol," a place of enormous fire, where he burns until rescued by a spirit woman who carries his charred soul back along the Isawa, stopping at spirit Gisaro ceremonies along the way. In this way, she gradually "heals" the soul, eventually bringing him to her spirit longhouse and taking him as her husband (in the case of the death of a woman, the spirit helper and eventual spouse is a male). Henceforth, the spirit will appear to humans as just another wild creature of the forest or will speak to his or her kin through a medium. Traditional mortuary ritual called for the body of the deceased to be slung in a hammock-link affair of cane loops, after the body had been stripped of ornaments and clothing, and hung at the front of the house near the unmarried women's communal area. Fires would be lit at the head and foot of the corpse, and during the next days friends and kin would view the body. Later, the body would be placed on a platform outside until decomposition was complete. The bones would be later recovered and hung up in the eaves of the longhouse. Since 1968, government edict has required that bodies be buried in a cemetery. Survivors of a deceased person assume food taboos during the period of mourning. These taboos are obligatory for the surviving spouse and children, but they are often voluntarily taken on by close friends and other kin as well.

See also Foi, Gebusi

Bibliography

Feld, Steven (1982). *Sound and Sentiment: Birds, Weeping, Poetics and Song in Kaluli Expression.* Philadelphia: University of Pennsylvania Press. Rev. ed. 1990.

Schieffelin, Bambi (1990). *The Give and Take of Everyday Life: Language Socialization of Kaluli Children.* Cambridge: Cambridge University Press.

Schieffelin, Edward L. (1976). *The Sorrow of the Lonely and the Burning of the Dancers.* New York: St. Martin's Press.

Schieffelin, Edward L. (1985). "The Retaliation of the Animals: On the Cultural Construction of the Past in Papua New Guinea." In *History and Ethnohistory in Papua New Guinea,* edited by Deborah Gewertz and Edward Schieffelin, 40–57. Oceania Monograph no. 28. Sydney: Oceania Publications.

NANCY E. GRATTON

Kamilaroi

ETHNONYMS: Camileroi, Euahlayi, Gunilroy

The Kamilaroi were an Aboriginal group located in New South Wales, Australia, along the Barwon, Bundarra, Balonne, and upper Hunter rivers and in the Liverpool plains. They are now nearly extinct and only a small number remain. The Kamilaroi language, which is no longer spoken, is classified in the Pama-Nyungan Family of Australian languages.

The Kamilaroi were nomadic hunters and gatherers with a band-level social organization. Important vegetable foods were yams and other roots, as well as a sterculia grain, which was made into a bread. Insect larvae, frogs, and eggs of several different animals were also gathered. Various birds, kangaroos, emus, iguanas, opossums, echidnas, and bandicoots were among the important animals hunted. Dingo pups were regarded as a delicacy. Fish were also consumed, as were crayfish, mussels, and shrimp. Men typically hunted, cleaned, and prepared the game for cooking. Women did the actual cooking, in addition to fishing and gathering. Individual Kamilaroi did not eat animals that were their totems, although the Euahlayi, a related group, did not observe this restriction.

Their complex kinship and marriage system has made the Kamilaroi a group of considerable anthropological interest. At the most general level of social organization, the Kamilaroi were organized into exogamous matrimoities. Both moities were divided into four marriage classes. Also present within the moities were various sibs and lineages, each represented by several totems and subtotems. Descent was matrilineal. The Kamilaroi had a four-class marriage system. Exogamy was the rule for each kin group, from the lineage through the moiety. Paternal half-sister marriage was reportedly the preferred form among the Euahlayi. The primary economic units were the bands, which were composed of several households. Matrilineages were represented by subtotems and organized into a matrisib, which had its own totem. The sibs were members of one or the other matrimoieties. Intersecting with these groups based on kinship and descent were the four marriage classes, all of which were common to both matrimoieties.

Rites were held to encourage the propagation of totems. There were initiation ceremonies for both sexes, with circumcision for boys. Shamans (*wireenun*) concerned themselves with curing illness and communicating with their dream spirits, who were often sent out on information-gathering missions. The Kamilaroi believed in an "All Father," the moral and kindly deity in the sky who received the souls of good Aborigines upon their death. Each individual was believed to have a soul, a dream spirit, and a shadow spirit. Sickness or death was believed to result if one's shadow spirit were molested or captured by a shaman. Some individuals also had the aid of a spirit helper.

Bibliography

Fison, Lorimer, and A. W. Howitt (1867). *Kamilaroi and Kurnai: Group Marriage and Relationship, and Marriage by Elopement.* Oosterhout, the Netherlands: Anthropological Publications.

Parker, K. Langloh (1905). *The Euahlayi Tribe: a Study of Aboriginal Life in Australia.* London: Archibald Constable.

Kapauku

ETHNONYMS: Ekagi, Ekari, Me, Tapiro

Orientation

Identification. The Kapauku live in the central highlands of western New Guinea, now Irian Jaya. Although they are generally treated as a single cultural group, there are variations in dialect and in social and cultural practice across Kapauku territory. The name "Kapauku" was given them by neighboring groups to the south, and the Moni Papuans, their neighbors to the north, call them "Ekari," but they call themselves "Me," which means "the people."

Location. The Kapauku occupy an ecologically diverse region of the west-central highlands, between 135°25' and

137° E and 3°25' and 4°10' S. Most of the region is above 1,500 meters, with three large lakes (Paniai, Tage, and Tigi), and five vegetation zones, including much tropical rain forest. Rainfall is plentiful and the average daily temperature ranges from 20° C to 60° C.

Demography. In the 1960s, the Kapauku population was estimated at about 45,000; today they number about 100,000.

Linguistic Affiliation. The Kapauku language (Ekagi) is classified within the Ekagi-Wodani-Moni Family of Papuan languages.

History and Cultural Relations

There is little information available regarding the history of the Kapauku prior to European contact, but they have long been horticulturalists (both intensive and extensive) and traders in the region. An important intertribal trade network linking the south coast of New Guinea to the interior ran directly through Kapauku territory, bringing the people of the region into contact with peoples and goods from far beyond their own territorial borders. European contact with the Kapauku did not occur until 1938, when a Dutch government post was established at Paniai Lake. It was quickly abandoned with the Japanese invasion of New Guinea. In 1946 the post was reestablished, and a few Catholic and Protestant missionaries returned to the area.

Settlements

The Kapauku village settlement is a loose cluster of about fifteen dwellings, typically housing about 120 people. Houses are not oriented to one another in any formal plan, as individuals are free to build wherever they please, as long as proper title or lease is held to the piece of land upon which the house is to be built. Dwellings consist, minimally, of a large house (*owa*), an elevated structure with a space beneath in which to shelter domesticated pigs. This building is divided into halves separated by a plank partition. The front half is the *emaage*, or men's dormitory. The back section is subdivided into *kugu*, or individual "apartments," one for each woman and her children. If the owa is insufficient to provide space for wives and children, outbuildings (called *tone*) are added.

Economy

Leopold Pospisil, the leading authority on the Kapauku, labels their economy as "primitive capitalism" characterized by the pursuit of wealth in the form of cowrie shell money, status distinctions based on such wealth, and an ethic of individualism.

Subsistence and Commercial Activities. Kapauku subsistence is based on the sweet potato, to which about 90 percent of cultivated land is devoted, and pig husbandry. Sweet potatoes are grown both for human consumption and to feed the pigs that, through sales, are a basic source of income and wealth. Commonly grown, but constituting a far smaller portion of the diet, are a spinach-like green (*idaja*), bananas, and taro. In the densely populated Kamu Valley, hunting is of small importance due to a paucity of large game animals, but it is indulged in by men as sport. Edible fish are absent from the lakes, but crayfish, dragonfly larvae, certain types of beetles, and frogs augment the diet, as do rats and bats. Farming is done both on the mountain slopes and in the valleys. Upland gardens are given over to the extensive cultivation of sweet potatoes, with long fallow periods between plantings. In the valleys a more intensive method is followed, using both mixed cropping and crop rotation. Households will generally cultivate at least one of each type of garden.

Industrial Arts. Kapauku manufacture is limited and, for the most part, not specialized. Net bags, for utilitarian and for decorative purposes, are made from woven tree bark, as are the armbands and necklaces worn by both men and women. Also made from this bark are women's aprons. Kapauku also manufacture stone axes and knives, flint chips, and grinding stones. From bamboo they make knives for the carving of pork and for surgical use. Other carving tools are fashioned from rat teeth and bird claws, and agricultural tools include weeding, planting, and harvesting sticks. Weaponry consists of bows and arrows, the latter of which may be tipped with long blades of bamboo.

Trade. Trade is carried out intra- and interregionally and intertribally, with trade links extending to the Mimika people of the coast. The two most important trade commodities are pigs and salt. Trade is generally conducted in shell currency, pigs, or extensions of credit, and the bulk of trading occurs during pig feasts and at the pig markets. Barter is a relatively unimportant means by which goods may be transferred. All distributions of food incur a debt on the part of each recipient to repay in kind to the giver. Pospisil notes that the Kapauku are lively participants in the selling of pigs and pork. Shell money (and sometimes an obligation to provide pork) is required in payment to a shaman for the performance of magic.

Division of Labor. There is a sexual division of labor. Tasks held to be the exclusive province of men include the planning of agricultural production, digging ditches, making garden beds, felling trees, building fences, planting and harvesting bananas, tobacco, chili peppers, and *apuu* (a particular variety of yam), while the burning of gardens, planting sugarcane, manioc, squash, and maize, as well as the harvesting of sugarcane, manioc, and ginger, are preferentially but not necessarily done by males. Exclusively female tasks include the planting of sweet potatoes and *jatu* (an edible grass, *Setaria palmifolia*) and weeding. Other tasks, such as planting and weeding taro and harvesting sweet potatoes, are usually done by women. All other tasks relating to agriculture are carried out by members of both sexes. The gathering of crayfish, water beetles, tadpoles, dragonfly larvae, and frogs is largely the task of women; the hunting of large game is an infrequent enterprise and is done only by men. Small game is hunted by young men and boys. Pigs and chickens, while usually owned by males, are tended by women or adolescent children, but only males are allowed to kill and butcher them. The weaving of utilitarian net bags is a woman's job, while the production of the more ornate and colorful decorative bags is the province of males.

Land Tenure. A particular piece of land is the property of the house owner, always male, with use rights accorded to members of his household. Sons inherit land from their fathers. Ownership implies rights of alienation of the land as well as usufruct rights.

Kinship

Kin Groups and Descent. Kapauku reckon descent along both maternal and paternal lines, but villages are patrilineal and exogamous, with postmarital residence generally patrilocal. The most important Kapauku kinship group is the sib, a named, ideally exogamous, totemic, patrilineal group whose members share a belief in a common apical ancestor. Two or more sibs group into loosely united phratries that have common totemic taboos but are not exogamous. Many of the sibs are further split into moieties. Kinship ties with other lineages (through affines) give rise to larger, political amalgamations known as "confederations."

Kinship Terminology. Kapauku kinship terminology is of the Iroquois type, but it diverges in the way in which parallel and cross cousins are differentiated: the sex of the nearest and the most distant link connecting the individual to his or her cousin determines cross- or parallel-cousin status. Kapauku kinship terms differentiate among paternal and maternal relatives, affinal and consanguineal relatives, and generationally.

Marriage and Family

Marriage. Marriage is ideally arranged between the families of the prospective groom and brothers and mother of the prospective bride. The preferences of the woman are considered secondary to the possibility of collecting a high bride-price but, in practice, her mother may set a forbiddingly high bride-price to discourage an unacceptable suitor. Elopements, while considered improper, occur with some frequency. In such cases the families of the eloping couple will likely accept the union by negotiating a bride-price after the fact. Courtship is often conducted in the context of the pig feast, when young men and women arrive at the host village from neighboring villages to dance and to be seen by members of the opposite sex. Premarital sex, while not approved of because of its possible negative effect on a woman's bride-price, is generally not punished. Premarital pregnancy, however, is severely disapproved. Divorce involves the return of bride-price, and the children generally remain with their mother until they reach the age of about 7, at which time they join their father's village. Polygyny, as an indicator of the husband's ability to pay multiple bride-prices, is the ideal. A widow is expected to remarry within a suitable period following the death of her husband, unless she is quite old or very sick, but the levirate is not assumed.

Domestic Unit. The household consists, minimally, of a nuclear family, but it more commonly also includes consanguineal or affinal kinsmen and their wives and children as well. In the case of wealthy and prestigious men, there may also be apprentices or political supporters and their wives and children. The household is the basic Kapauku unit of residence and, to a large extent, of production and consumption. Within the household, the house owner is titular head, responsible for organizing production activities and maintaining cooperation among the male household members. However, each married male has sole authority over the affairs of his wife or wives and his offspring, an authority which even the head of household cannot usurp.

Inheritance. Personal items, such as bows and arrows, penis sheaths, etc., are interred or otherwise left with the corpse of the deceased. Land and accrued wealth is inherited by males through the paternal line, ideally by the deceased's first-born son. If there is no son, a man's eldest brother inherits. Women do not inherit land.

Socialization. Children learn adult roles through observation and by specific training. Boys leave their mothers' apartments at the age of about 7 to live in the men's dormitory, at which time they are explicitly exposed to the expected adult male behaviors. There is no male initiation ceremony. Girls, upon achieving their menarche, undergo a brief period (two days, two nights) of semiseclusion in a menstrual hut during the time of their first two menstruations. During this time they are instructed in the responsibilities and skills of adulthood by close female relatives. After these periods of seclusion, girls put aside the skirtlike apparel of childhood and begin to wear the bark-thong wrap of adulthood.

Sociopolitical Organization

Social Organization. The Kapauku patrilineage is a nonlocalized grouping whose membership claims descent from a common apical ancestor. Its dispersed character makes it inutile for political purposes; rather, its functions pertain to the regulation of marriage, the establishment of interpersonal obligations of support (both personal and economic), and religion. The sib establishes shared totemic taboos that involve its members in relations of mutual ritual obligation, particularly in the matter of redressing taboo violations. Most day-to-day rights and obligations are incurred within the localized patrilineal group; it is to members of this group that an individual will turn for assistance in amassing the bride-wealth necessary for marriage, as well as for allies in conflicts arising with outsiders. Within the village, households are relatively autonomous, as each household head is able to call on fellow members for support in economic and ritual endeavors.

Political Organization. Kapauku leadership is based on personal influence, developed through the accumulation of wealth in shells and pigs, particularly through sponsoring pig feasts. A headman (*tonowi*) uses his prestige and wealth to induce the compliance of others, particularly through the extension or refusal of credit. Again, the principle of organization is based upon the tracing of at least putative kinship ties, and the larger the group of individuals united in a political unit, the more these ties are based on tradition rather than demonstrable links. The most inclusive politically organized group is the confederacy, which consists of two or more localized lineages that may or may not belong to the same sib. Such groups unite for defense as well as for offense against nonmember groups. The leader of the strongest lineage is also the leader of the confederacy, and as such this leader is responsible for adjudicating disputes to avoid the possibility of intraconfederacy feuding. He is equally responsible for representing the confederacy in dealings and dispute settlement with outsiders, deciding upon the necessity of war, and negotiating terms of peace with hostile groups. Leadership is ostensibly the province of men only, but in practice considerable influence may be wielded by women.

Social Control. Social control is effected in Kapauku local groups by inducement rather than by force. The primary form of inducement is the extension or withdrawal of credit. Since a headman's supporters are tied to him through his economic largess, the threat of a withdrawal of credit, or of a premature demand for repayment, provides strong inducement for others to accede to the headman's wishes. Sanctions such as public scolding or shooting an arrow into a miscreant's thigh are common, but in such cases the party being punished has the opportunity to fight back. Kin-based obligations to seek vengeance for the death of a lineage member are often invoked. Less frequently, to punish sorcerers, ostracism or death may be inflicted.

Conflict. Kapauku do not care for war, but members of a lineage are obligated to avenge the death of their kin. Warfare almost never occurs below the level of the confederacy, and it is most frequently occasioned by divorce. Wars are fought exclusively with bows and arrows. At the more localized level, disputes over economic interests or factional splits between two powerful headmen may lead to outbreaks of hostility to the point of violence. Such occasions may require the intervention of confederacy headmen.

Religion and Expressive Culture

Religious Beliefs. The Kapauku believe that the universe was created by Ugatame, who has predetermined all that occurs or has occurred within it. Ugatame is not, strictly speaking, anthropomorphized, although a creation myth—in which disease and mortality were first brought to the Kapauku—attributes to Ugatame the combined characters of a young woman and a tall young man. Ugatame dwells beyond the sky and is manifested in, but is not identical to, the sun and the moon. It is believed that, along with the physical universe, Ugatame created a number of spirits. These spirits, essentially incorporeal, frequently appear to Kapauku in the form of shadows among the trees, which can be heard to make scratching or whistling sounds. Less commonly, they will appear in dreams or visions, at times assuming human form. They can be enlisted by the dreamer or visionary as guardians and helpers, for good or for ill. The souls of the dead can similarly be persuaded to help their surviving kin.

Religious Practitioners. Magical-religious practitioners are of two classes: shamans (who practice magic for good purposes) and sorcerers (who practice "black magic"). Both men and women can become shamans or sorcerers through the acquisition of spirit helpers in dreams or visions and through the successful (as gauged by perceived results) use of magic. The shaman practices curative and preventive magic, while the sorcerer is concerned with causing harm to others (through illness, death, or economic failure). Ghouls are older women whose souls have been replaced during sleep by rapacious spirits hungry for the taste of human flesh. The ghoul, by all appearances a normal woman during the day, travels abroad in the night to dig up the corpses of her possessing spirit's victims and make a feast of their flesh. Women believed to be possessed in this way are not killed, for their death would simply release the possessing spirit to find a new hostess. Rather, ghouls are held to be the helpers of sorcerers, whose black magic is held responsible for the women's condition. It is the sorcerer's magic that must be countered, or the sorcerer must be killed, to stop the depredations of a ghoul.

Ceremonies. One of the most important Kapauku ceremonies is the *juwo,* or pig feast. This begins with a series of rituals associated with the construction of a dance house and feasting houses, after which follows a period of nightly dances, attended by people from villages throughout the area. After about three months a final feast is held wherein the sponsors slaughter many pigs and pork is distributed or sold. During this final feast day, trade in items of manufacture is also conducted.

Arts. Visual arts are not heavily represented in Kapauku culture, apart from the decorative net bags made by the men and the armbands and necklaces worn as bodily adornment. Dances, as part of the pig feast, are frequent. There are two principal dances, the *waita tai* and the *tuupe.* The *ugaa,* which is a song that begins with barking cheers, is followed by an individual's extemporaneous solo composition, the lyrics of which may contain gossip, local complaints, or a proposal of marriage.

Medicine. Illness is attributed to sorcerers or the spirits. Cures are accomplished by a shaman, who seeks a diagnosis and treatment from a spirit helper. Treatment includes the recitation of spells or prayers, the manipulation of magical plants, purification through the washing of body parts in water, and, at times, the extraction of bits of foreign matter from the body of the victim. Should an individual believe that he or she may be the target of sorcery, a preventive cure may be sought before the actual onset of illness.

Death and Afterlife. Death, regardless of the outward cause, is thought always to be caused by sorcerers or spirits. The soul goes to spend its days in the forest, but it returns to the village at night to assist its surviving kin or to seek vengeance in the case of wrongful death. There is no concept of an afterworld, in the sense of some "other" place in which the dead dwell. A principal concern of Kapauku funerary practices is the enlistment of the soul of the departed as guardian of its surviving kin. The more beloved or prestigious the deceased, the greater the care taken, through burial practices, to tempt them to such a role. The head is left exposed, sheltered under a cover of branches, but provided with a window. Cremation for fallen and unclaimed enemies and complete interment for those of little social status constitute the lower range of funerary attention.

See also Mimika

Bibliography

Pospisil, Leopold (1958). *Kapauku Papuans and Their Law.* Yale University Publications in Anthropology, no. 54. New Haven, Conn.

Pospisil, Leopold (1960). "The Kapauku Papuans and Their Kinship System." *Oceania,* 30: 188–205.

Pospisil, Leopold (1963). *Kapauku Papuan Economy.* Yale University Publications in Anthropology, no. 67. New Haven, Conn. Reprint. 1972. New Haven, Conn.: Human Relations Area Files.

Pospisil, Leopold (1978). *The Kapauku Papuans of West New Guinea.* 2nd ed. New York: Holt, Rinehart & Winston.

NANCY GRATTON

Kapingamarangi

ETHNONYMS: Kapinga, Kiriniti

Orientation

Identification. Kapingamarangi, one of the Polynesian outliers, is the southernmost atoll in the Eastern Caroline Islands of Micronesia. "Kiriniti" is a local rendering of the English "Greenwich."

Location. Located at 1°4' N, 154°46' E, the atoll consists of thirty-three flat islets forming a semicircle on an egg-shaped reef surrounding a central lagoon. Its total land area of 1.09 square kilometers supports a native vegetation of ninety-three different species of plants, but only five of these—breadfruit, coconuts, pandanus, *Alocasia* taro, and a nitrogen-fixing creeper—were useful as food. The average annual rainfall is 305 centimeters, but the atoll is subject to periodic drought, lasting from weeks to years.

Demography. The Kapingamarangi population fluctuated according to periods of adequate rainfall and extended drought, averaging about 450 people. Currently the population is much larger, with many Kapingamarangi living in Porakied village on Pohnpei.

Linguistic Affiliation. Kapingamarangi is a member of the Polynesian Family of Oceanic Austronesian languages. Most people speak at least one other language, including English, Japanese, and Pohnpeian.

History and Cultural Relations

According to local legend, the present Polynesian population is descended from Ellice Islands castaways of some 600–700 years ago (possibly supplemented by immigrants from Samoa). They arrived to find a small resident population (presumably Mortlockese) whom they appear to have culturally absorbed. Once settled, this population was extremely isolated, the only contacts being with castaways from the Gilbert Islands, the Mortlocks, the Marshall Islands, and Woleai. The latter two were culturally the most significant, with the Woleaians introducing plant medicines, sorcery, and a very important group fishing method, while the Marshallese slaughtered over half the Kapinga population in 1865. The first European ship entered the lagoon and established direct contact with the islanders in 1877. Thereafter, ships from Rabaul visited the atoll periodically, trading Western goods for copra. These contacts resulted in the introduction of both Western goods and plants and techniques from other islands. When the Japanese colonial administration assumed control of Micronesia from the Germans in 1914, shipping, trade, and travel became regular features of Kapinga life. With the constant need for labor on Pohnpei (a district center), men were taken there as work crews on road gangs and plantations. In 1919 the Japanese administration granted the Kapinga land in Kolonia to house emigrants to Pohnpei. This settlement, called Porakied village, has grown over the years to its present population of about 600, and it has been there that Kapingamarangi people have had their most intensive contacts with other islanders. Regular ship visits between Pohnpei and the atoll facilitate a flow of people, which increased in frequency after World War II and the advent of the United States Trust Territory of the Pacific Islands that succeeded the Japanese colonial administration. While the Japanese were interested mainly in commercial development, the United States has emphasized economic and political development, bringing people to Pohnpei for training to run development programs on the atoll. In 1979, Pohnpei District became a state of the Federated States of Micronesia, and Kapingamarangi is now a municipality of Pohnpei State, with its own constitution.

Settlements

On the atoll, residence compounds, all of which have names and well-defined boundaries, are located on the three central islets. In addition to the atoll community and Porakied, Kapinga people have maintained a small settlement on Oroluk Atoll since 1954 for copra production and pig and turtle husbandry.

Economy

Subsistence and Commercial Activities. Kapinga people continue to subsist on local products, especially coconuts, breadfruit, pandanus fruit, and taro. Of these, only taro requires constant care, which has intensified since the 1880s when *Cyrtosperma* largely replaced *Alocasia.* This variety of taro grew faster and larger than the native one and quickly became a staple. Coconut groves have largely replaced pandanus groves to accommodate the copra trade, the income from which has been augmented by government and municipal salaried jobs and the sale of handicrafts. Cash income is used to buy foods such as rice, coffee, sugar, tea, tinned fish, and candies; tools and utensils; and, recently, gasoline for the outboard engines that have largely replaced sails on the canoes. Imports are retailed by a cooperative, a branch of the Pohnpei Federation of Cooperatives, which buys copra from local producers.

Industrial Arts. Traditionally, Kapinga produced a variety of implements, using wood for houses, canoes, handles, paddles, breadfruit grating stands, poles, digging sticks, traps, and outrigger-canoe parts. Coconut husk was made into sennit cord and the cord into ropes and coir nets. Hibiscus and breadfruit bast was used for clothing and cordage. Shells were used for cutting, scraping, and abrading tools, and coconut and pandanus leaves made thatch and a variety of mats. Pandanus leaf was also used for canoe sails and, woven with a backstrap loom, clothing. Since World War II many of these items have been produced for the handicraft market, which yields a significant percentage of the income of Porakied villagers on Pohnpei. The copra trade allowed Kapinga to replace their shell tools with metal counterparts, and since the 1950s locally produced fishing lines and netting fiber have been replaced by mail-order nylon and other synthetics. Canvas sails have replaced those made from plaited pandanus leaf.

Trade. Other than copra production and commercial fishing and handicrafts on Pohnpei, the only other significant trade—again on Pohnpei—has been that of trade friendships between Kapinga and their Micronesian neighbors, usually involving the exchange of fish for vegetable foods.

Division of Labor. As in most Pacific societies, the division of labor is based mainly on gender and age. Women control the domestic sphere, centered in the residence compounds, where they cook, wash clothes, care for children, and do craft work (basketry and mat making). Women leave their compounds to help relatives in other compounds and to work in their taro patches, located on one of the central islets and three other outlying ones. The quintessence of manhood is fishing, but men also harvest fruit from trees and construct and repair houses and gear. Men also made both their own and women's wraparound skirts from hisbiscus and breadfruit bast before people adopted imported cloth. Because women are responsible for scheduling meals (and assessing food needs that require harvest trips to outer islet groves and taro gardens), they have a lien on men's time and canoes. Men have to schedule their work around the needs of their households.

Land Tenure. Kapingamarangi is typical of Oceanic atolls in its identification of relations regarding land with relations among kin. On a cultural level, land and kinship are defined in terms of each other. Every transaction in land, therefore, implies some sort of kin relation. Kapinga distinguish taro plots from "land," i.e., dry land used for groves. Taro plots are always owned by individual persons while "land" proper is owned either individually or, more often, by kin groups. Rights to dry land are either ownership rights or use rights. Ownership of land involves using it at will for any and all of its purposes, including residence; harvesting food, leaves, and wood; planting; and graves. Owners can also convey the land by will or gift. Use rights involve using land for some of its purposes (usually harvesting food, leaves, or wood) only with the permission of its owner. The application of these principles exemplifies the structure of kin relations and groups. Residence compounds are owned by descent groups called *madawaawa,* whose members are descendants of a former owner reckoned through both males and females. Garden land was and still is owned by individual persons or, more commonly, by cognatic descent groups called *madahaanau.* A person's or group's land usually consists of a bundle of rights in several plots scattered over different islets with part of the bundle coming from each parent.

Kinship

Kin Groups and Descent. Kinship groups are corporate with respect to two things: land and ceremonies. Group formation uses the cognatic descent principle of eligibility with one exception. The madawaawa, the group centered on house compounds, is really a descent category with a six- or seven-generation depth from whose membership groups can be recruited for specific purposes, such as feasts, funerals, house repair, and roof thatching; as groups form for these projects, people can opt in or out, with participation signaling group membership. For members of the secular class, such recruitment used cognatic descent. But since eligibility for the priesthood was inherited matrilineally, those madawaawa consisting exclusively of members of the sacred class were matrilineal (nonexogamous) lineages. These lineages functioned as a group during specific cult-house rituals and for weddings, funerals, and other celebrations of their members that specifically centered on the group's house compound. Similarly, the land-owning madahaanau functioned as ritual groups during life-crisis events of their members.

Kinship Terminology. Kapinga kin terms are of the Hawaiian type, distinguishing all ascending generation females as *dinana,* or "mother" from all ascending generation males as *damana,* or "father." All relatives in Ego's generation are called by the single sibling term, *duaahina,* and all descending generation relatives are referred to by the term for child, *dama.*

Marriage and Family

Marriage. Traditionally, there were no marriage rules other than those prohibiting sex between parents and their children and between full or half-siblings. Other than this narrowly defined incest rule, we find only marriage strategies, usually focused on protecting or augmenting a family's landholdings. Thus we find instances of polygyny, polyandry, cross-cousin marriage, parallel-cousin marriage, father's brother–brother's daughter marriage, wife sharing, and wife swapping between male parallel first cousins for purposes of conceiving a child. Marriages were usually arranged by parents. After an initial period of virilocal residence, the couple lived in the bride's mother's compound. A man practiced strict avoidance of all in-laws except small children of the compound. The considerable strains of uxorilocal residence make marriages brittle in their early years, and divorce has always been common (25–33 percent of all marriages).

Domestic Unit. The domestic unit is the household compound, which can contain as few as one or as many as five of what we would call nuclear families, each of which consists of one to twelve (or sometimes more) people. The core of a compound was a set of related women, their in-married spouses, and their children. Each household contains a woman, with or without spouse and children, but it may also contain a cousin or elderly relative. At puberty, boys move to the men's house to sleep, but they continue to eat and work at their natal compounds. Thus, a compound ranged in size from one to thirty or more people. Kapinga living on Pohnpei continue to organize their households by compounds wherever possible.

Socialization. Children typically grow up in a compound consisting of their (natural or adoptive) mother's female relatives, in-married men, and their children. Men of the compound spend little time there, appearing mainly for meals and to sleep. When a baby is old enough to be weaned, he or she is given to an older sibling for care. By age 4 or 5 children (especially boys) join peer groups and spend less time at their compounds and more time around the islets and the lagoon. Boys' groups are more stable than girls' groups, since girls are more useful to their mothers at a much earlier age. Boys begin to fish on the reef with pole and line at 7 or 8 years of age. Traditionally, there was no formal initiation of children, although a father gave a small feast when his adolescent son first began to sleep in the men's house, and a boy got his first loincloth when he caught one thousand flying fish. There was no comparable initiation for girls. Boys and young unmarried men constituted a work force for the men's house, which organized group fishing and provided labor for all cult house construction and repair projects. While a girl was socialized almost entirely by women of her own and related compounds, boys were socialized first by their mothers, then by their older siblings, then by their peers, and finally by men of their compounds and the men's house.

Sociopolitical Organization

Social Organization. The Kapinga social order was hierarchically organized: the household was nested in the compound, where males belonged to men's houses, which were controlled by their headmen and an elder male called the *tomoono.* These leaders were, in turn, accountable to the high priest, called *aligi,* who was responsible for organizing all cult house ritual and for communicating with the gods, who were the ultimate source of all authority.

Political Organization. The institution that integrated household compounds, descent groups, and the men's houses was the cult house, whose activities were organized by the priesthood. The high priest exercised a good deal of control over fishing and access to land resources through his ownership of breadfruit trees and drift logs (used to make canoes); by his ability to taboo the lagoon, deep sea, and trees; and by his decisions on timing of rituals. By restricting the number of canoes, he indirectly controlled the frequency of angling, lending a powerful saliency to men's houses, the other major alternative for fishing activity. Men's houses varied in number between two and five, and they exercised control over their members' time through the organization of group fishing expeditions, which could number as many as three during a day. Fishing was organized by a headman, while work groups were organized and provisioned by the tomoono. There was a good deal of competition between men's houses in fish catches and in song composition. The men's house located lagoonward of the cult house on the main islet provided the major work force for cult-house projects, and its tomoono had veto power over the granting of permission to construct canoes. He was also given the task of provisioning and caring for Europeans after contact. His liaison responsibility eventually evolved into a position of power that became a secular chieftainship (he was called "king") after the collapse of the cult house and conversion to Christianity in 1917.

Social Control. Disputes over land were ordinarily settled by the families involved, while those arising among men were normally settled in the men's house. Breaches of fishing or men's-house protocol were dealt with by the tomoono, while the high priest dealt with ritual violations, sometimes by execution, which ordinarily was done by putting the violator in a canoe and setting it adrift.

Religion and Expressive Culture

Religious Beliefs. There were three classes of spirits with whom people had to cope. The high gods were spirits who came to the atoll on the original canoe or were spirits of former high priests. The priesthood (with its sacred/secular class distinction) and the organization of people by age category were designed to deal with these powerful unpredictable beings. Another set of spirits, called the "line of ghosts," were spirits of recently and long-deceased people who inhabited the outer lagoon, coming ashore in a line at night to steal the souls of unwary people sleeping or wandering outside their houses. One simply avoided these spirits by trying not to attract their attention. Finally, there was a female spirit who inhabited the northern islets, enticing unsuspecting men at night to drive them crazy. A male spirit in the southern lagoon waited to molest women at night, making them ill. Being accompanied by someone of the opposite sex would forfend an attack by either.

Religious Practitioners. The priesthood was organized in a panel of twenty men, with ten on the side of the high priest and ten led by the "calling" priest. Each side consisted of five priests and five sergeants-at-arms, all ranked asymmetrically (i.e., the high priest outranked the "calling" priest, who outranked the next priest below the high priest, etc.) The high priest's job was to maintain a good relationship with the gods, to ascertain their desires and their moods, and to keep them well disposed to the community so that they would bring rain and fish and would not precipitate disasters such as droughts and gales.

Ceremonies. In addition to daily rituals of supplication, the high priest conducted major rituals called *boo,* of which there were five, conducted on an as-needed basis: renovation of the cult house, replacing of dark mats, replacing of bleached mats (used by the gods), canoe making, and freeing of parturient mothers from confinement. These rituals all used an identical format, differing only in the specific prayers and chants inserted. Lower-ranking priests had specific roles in these rituals. The ripening of breadfruit and the beaching of whales were also ritual occasions for which special prayers were given. Men fishing on the deep sea had to offer chants of supplication to the gods before commencing fishing. Special rituals also were performed during droughts and epidemics, at the sighting of ships, and to correct errors in performance of a prior ritual.

Arts. Arts native to the atoll were dance, song, and folktales. The Kapinga dance, called *koni,* was performed during and after major rituals. It involved a stereotyped stance with the body held rigid and the feet moving in place. The dance was accompanied by songs called *daahili* that were short sentences and phrases repeated in a monotone at increasing tempo. Their contents referred obliquely to events that were otherwise gossip—love affairs, being jilted, ridicule for some faux pas, and the like. The bulk of Kapinga song repertoire was the chant. The subjects of chants included prayers of supplication or celebration of the gods and other ritual formulas; eulogies; and accounts of fishing expeditions, the beachings of whales, and sexual encounters.

Medicine. Medicinal practices included bone setting, massage, special foods for specific illneses, and chanting by the priest in life-threatening situations. Plant medicines and sorcery were imported by a Woleaian in the 1780s.

Death and Afterlife. Kapinga believe that death is a natural part of the life cycle. They fear early, untimely death by accident, disease, or malicious spirits and socialize their children with lessons of reasonable caution at work, at play, and in those situations when spirits might be about. Because control over one's emotions is so important in forfending disaster, grief was and is considered particularly dangerous, attracting the attention of ghosts and leading to insanity. Funerals control personal emotion through the work of having to organize a major set of ceremonies and provision them with food for mourners and others. All of this activity takes place over a 24- to 36-hour period requiring intense concentration, work, and both the incurring and collection of debts. Chanting marks every stage of a funeral, providing its closure as entertainment. At death, the soul is said to leave the body forever. The souls of men and women go to the far lagoon to join the line of ghosts. Those of women who die in childbirth go to the goddess Roua in the deep sea, where they (and the souls of high priests) may return to the atoll as beached whales. Otherwise, the souls of high priests become new gods.

See also Marshall Islands, Nomoi, Pohnpei, Woleai

Bibliography

Buck, Peter (1950). *Material Culture of Kapingamarangi.* Bernice P. Bishop Museum Bulletin no. 200. Honolulu.

Emory, Kenneth (1965). *Kapingamarangi: Social and Religious Life of a Polynesian Atoll.* Bernice P. Bishop Museum Bulletin no. 228. Honolulu.

Lieber, Michael D. (1974). "Land Tenure on Kapingamarangi." In *Land Tenure in Oceania,* edited by Henry P. Lundsgaarde, 70–99. Honolulu: University Press of Hawaii.

Lieber, Michael D. (1977). "Change in Two Kapingamarangi Communities." In *Exiles and Migrants in Oceania,* edited by Michael D. Lieber. Honolulu: University Press of Hawaii.

Lieber, Michael D., and Kalio H. Dikepa (1974). *Kapingamarangi Lexicon.* Honolulu: University Press of Hawaii.

MICHAEL D. LIEBER

Karadjeri

The Karadjeri (Garadjui, Guaradjara, Karadjari) are an Aboriginal group located in the state of Western Australia, in the area of Roebuck Bay and inland to Broome. In 1984 there were thirty-five individuals. Karadjeri is classified in the Pama-Nyungan Family of Australian languages. The Karadjeri were hunters and gatherers with their subsistence territory defined with reference to various religious and sacred sites.

Bibliography

Capell, A. (1949). "Some Myths of the Garadjeri Tribe." *Mankind* 4:46–47, 108–125, 148–162.

Piddington, R., and M. Piddington (1932). "Report on Field Work in North-Western Australia." *Oceania* 2:342–358.

Kariera

The term "Kariera" refers both to a particular Western Australian people, with a distinct name and language, as well as to a specific form of social organization and kinship reckoning shared by several distinct groups (Nglera, Kariera, Ngaluma, Indjibandi, Pandjima, Bailgu, and Nyamal). The territory associated with the Kariera type of organization is defined by the drainage of the De Grey River, as well as portions of the region along both sides of the Fortescue River. In common with other Western Australian groups, the Kariera are traditional hunting and gathering people, locally organized into small bands and centered on nuclear families, which exploit a portion of the larger Kariera territory. The Kariera have a "four-section" system of descent-based social organization, in which two patrilineal, exogamous moieties are crosscut by two matrilineal moieties. This system establishes two sets of wife-giving and wife-taking sections, marked by kinship terms that denote the appropriate wife-giving group as one whose members include classificatory cross cousins: that is, a man is expected to marry either his mother's brother's daughter or his father's sister's daughter. Because these groups are reciprocally defined (i.e., if a man from section A is expected to marry a woman from section B, so too is a man from section B expected to marry a woman from section A) the system also entails sister exchange, at least classificatorily. Other aspects of the Kariera-type system, according to kinship usage, include the division of all relatives into three generations. Within a single generation further subdivisions occur along the male and female lines. For the males, one such division consists of the father's line, including among its number the husbands of the father's mother's sisters and the brothers of the mother's mother. The other division is along the mother's line and includes as well the husbands of the mother's mother's sisters and the brothers of the father's mother. Among the females, these two divisions are mirrored. Grandparents and grandchildren are terminologically merged as well, in two dimensions: between one another, a grandparent will use the same term for a grandchild as that grandchild uses for the grandparent; and a member of an intervening generation will refer to his or her grandparent with the same term appropriate for his or her grandchild of the same sex. Membership in either of the two patrilineal moieties is lifelong, and it is from this membership that a person derives his or her ritual and territorial claims—although with regard to territory, membership cannot be understood to construe rights to property in land, which are absent in traditional Western Australian Aboriginal societies. Rather, membership entials rights of access to ritually significant sites and the right and obligation to participate in a particular area's ritual ceremonies and to partake of its taboos. Such membership is also invoked to establish hunting rights within a particular band's territory, although nonmembers may be accorded temporary rights as well. The matrilineal moieties serve primarily to define appropriate marriage partners and, since postmarital residence is patrilocal, a wife exchanges her section affiliation (and therefore her patrilineage affiliation) for that of her husband. Among the Kariera, male initiation consists in the young man setting out on a long journey (of several months), which often will take him beyond the borders of his own section's traditional territory and may even bring him into contact with non-Kariera groups. Throughout the course of this journey he acquires knowledge of the surrounding lands and, more importantly, is gradually introduced into the ritual lore associated with the territory. On this journey, the young man seeks a wife, but he also establishes the rough outline of the "road," the specific portion of territory in which he will, as an adult, travel and hunt.

Bibliography

Radcliffe-Brown, A. R. (1930). "The Social Organization of Australian Tribes, Part I." *Oceania* 1:34–63.

Radcliffe-Brown, A. R. (1930). "The Social Organization of Australian Tribes, Part II." *Oceania* 1:206–256; 322–341.

Radcliffe-Brown, A. R. (1930). "The Social Organization of Australian Tribes, Part III." *Oceania* 1:426–456.

Keraki

ETHNONYMS: Morehead, Nambu, Trans-Fly

Orientation

Identification. The term "Keraki" generally refers to one of several small transhumant cultural groups living near the Morehead River in the Trans-Fly region of Papua New Guinea, applying principally to Nambu speakers but also including some of their immediate neighbors. The name also refers to one of the roughly nine small "tribes" into which the Keraki are divided.

Location. Keraki territory lies in the southwestern part of Papua New Guinea, just to the east of the Morehead River, at about 9° S by 142° E. The area is characterized by extremes of climate. During a considerable part of the rainy season, especially between January and March, much of the land is under water, and the Keraki are obliged to take up residence in semipermanent villages in one of a few locations along high ground. The rains abate in May or June, the country dries up, the land becomes parched, and the Keraki move to locations along one of the lagoons or larger streams, within reach of water. At the height of the dry season, the people often live in small clearings in the forest to escape the considerable heat.

Demography. In 1931, the ethnographic present for this report, F. E. Williams estimated the entire Keraki population at about 700–800. Recent estimates indicated 700 Nambu speakers and another 800 speakers of the Tonda and Lower Morehead languages.

Linguistic Affiliation. Nambu, Tonda, and Lower Morehead are three of the seven small Non-Austronesian languages that make up the Morehead and Upper Maro Rivers Family.

History and Cultural Relations

Owing to its sparse and scattered population, inhospitable climate, and apparent lack of potential for development, the Morehead area was little affected by European contact in the 1920s and 1930s when F. E. Williams conducted his basic ethnographic research. Even today, the region is somewhat isolated, with very little economic development. Cultural relations and communications among groups are hampered by flooding of the area in the wet season, lack of water in the dry season, and, in the precontact and early-contact era, by the constant raiding of powerful headhunters from across the border to the west.

Settlements

The semipermanent villages are usually located in or on the edge of a forest area, on high ground. The village itself is a clearing, planted with coconut palms, with houses irregularly scattered about. Gardens ring the village, and decorative plants and flowers grow within. Houses are of several types. The *mongo-vivi*, or "proper" house, is a long, oblong building with a ridged roof, stamped and hardened clay floor, and semicircular verandas on either end. A good-sized house is about 9 meters long, 3.6 meters wide, and 2.4 meters high, although dimensions vary considerably. These houses are used primarily for food storage, especially for yams. Typically, villages also contain a number of shelters, called *gua-mongo*, under which Keraki spread their mats. These shelters are simple open-sided structures consisting of four poles supporting a ridged roof. In contrast to the semipermanent villages, the temporary villages—which might be used as dry-season settlements, headquarters for large hunting parties, or other temporary encampments—usually contain only haphazard, roughly built houses, shelters, and lean-tos, with little attempt made to clear the brush.

Economy

Subsistence and Commercial Activities. The Keraki are subsistence farmers who practice swidden or slash-and-burn horticulture. Their staple crop is the lesser yam (*Dioscorea esculenta*). Gardens are prepared at the end of the dry season and completed by October or November, when the first sounds of thunder signal the beginning of the planting season. Several families usually cooperate in clearing a tract of land, which is subsequently divided into individually owned plots of about 45 meters square, separated from one another by timber markers laid along the ground. The entire area is customarily fenced against wild pigs, wallabies, etc. By June the yam vines, attached to 2-meter-long poles, have begun to turn yellow, and the harvest begins—desultorily at first, then more seriously as the vines wither. Yams are levered up or dug out with heavy spatulate digging sticks, then picked out by hand, and later sorted into piles for cooking, replanting, or for feasts. Other important root crops are taro, manioc, and sweet potatoes. Sugarcane, coconuts, and bananas are also grown, and various other fruits, especially papayas, complement the Keraki diet. Sago is rare and highly prized, thriving only in the few sago swamps that exist in Keraki territory.

Garden produce is supplemented by hunting, mainly for wallabies. These animals are taken either individually or collectively, by means of a drive, which is sometimes aided by grass burning. Cassowaries and wild pigs are hunted too, although pigs are also raised in small enclosures. Fishing is employed using a variety of techniques including stationary traps, hook and line, shooting with bow and arrow, and stupefying with poison root, but fish contribute relatively little to the Keraki diet.

Industrial Arts. Keraki have few manufactures beyond the simple utilitarian objects used in their daily lives. Personal ornaments are few. The only particularly well-finished pieces of woodwork are the drum, about 1 meter long, tapering to a longish waist in the middle, with a handle of one piece; the spatula, used for scooping out the pulpy interior of yams; and a boomerang-shaped hair ornament. Formerly, Keraki headhunters lavished considerable care on the making of carved, painted or barbed arrows for use in raids, and they also carved delicate wands or clubs called *parasi,* which were shattered over the heads of victims. Perhaps their most finely made objects are textiles, including mats, embroidered carrying bags, plaited belts and armlets, and finely worked women's mourning dresses.

Trade. Keraki engage in such considerable barter of all sorts of objects with neighboring peoples that it is difficult for the ethnographer to identify truly indigenous manufactures. However, since the Morehead area lacks appropriate natural stone, their most important trade was for stone axes and club heads, which, together with painted arrows, they obtained from the Wiram people in exchange for *melo* shells, used as a men's pubic covering. Other stone was obtained from Buji, on the coast near the mouth of the Mai Kussa River.

Division of Labor. As in most tribal societies, Keraki division of labor is based on age and sex. Women clean the houses and grounds, cook day-to-day meals, make textiles, and take primary responsibility for the children. Men hunt, build houses and shelters, conduct ritual matters, and do much of the cooking for feasts. Garden work is done by both sexes, although the sexes do perform slightly different tasks, with men doing most of the heavy felling, clearing, fencing, planting, and harvesting and women doing most of the daily weeding, cleaning, and harvesting.

Land Tenure. While the population density of the Morehead area is only about 0.2 person to the square kilometer, and the land is vast in proportion to the people, there are nevertheless rules of ownership, control, and inheritance of land. These rules are more closely observed for good land close to the semipermanent villages than for relatively useless land far from habitation sites. The whole territory is divided into large, named areas of about 13 to 15.5 square kilometers each, separated by natural boundaries and nominally owned by one of the nine Keraki tribes, but actually belonging to one of the villages of the tribe. Each of these major tracts is divided into a number of individually owned minor tracts. The *yure,* or owner of the land, gives formal permission to garden on the land, although this is commonly given to all who ask. Succession to yure-ownership is from father, through younger brother, and back to son; land may also be partitioned among sons and brothers.

Kinship

Kin Groups and Descent. Keraki society is divided into exogamous moieties of unequal size. One of these moieties is subdivided into three major sections. This moiety system overlays a system of local totemic groups. Descent is reckoned patrilineally.

Kinship Terminology. Kinship terminology is of the Iroquois type.

Marriage and Family

Marriage. Marriage is generally arranged by men, through "sister exchange," although "sisters" are frequently classificatory. Since two couples are created simultaneously, someone (typically a "bride") may still be adolescent when these exchanges are technically effected. In such cases, the girl becomes a member of the husband's household, even if the husband is still residing in the young men's house, and years may pass before the marriage is actually consummated. Polygyny is common: only about 55 percent of marriages are monogamous. Mates are chosen from outside the moiety and, generally, from outside the local totemic group. The levirate and sororate are both loosely practiced in a classificatory sense. Divorce is rare: since it directly affects another couple, considerable social pressure is brought to bear on women to uphold the marriage contract.

Domestic Unit. The basic domestic unit is the household, generally consisting of a man, his wife or wives, and their younger children. Occasionally a close relative may reside with them, but households are typically small and simply constituted.

Inheritance. Inheritance is normally patrilineal. A woman will leave her possessions to the "sons' wives" who live in her village.

Socialization. Keraki have no form of institutionalized instruction except during the seclusion and initiation of young boys, when they learn the secrets of the bullroarer and "sacred pipe," learn of hunting and other rituals, and hear secret mythological stories. At other times, children of both sexes are left to observe the day-to-day norms of behavior and to conduct themselves accordingly. By the norms of Western society, parents are quite indulgent and somewhat neglectful, although they do instruct and scold children when necessary.

Sociopolitical Organization

Social Organization. Keraki society is divided into tribes, with each tribe having three or four local section groups. Most villages belong predominantly to one section or another. Even when two sections are represented in the same village, section members live together. These local section groups, united by ties of kinship, common interest, and fellowship, are the most important units of Keraki social organization. They hunt together, make sago together, and often garden together. They cooperate in ritual matters: the group owns the major bullroarer and combines to initiate boys, it cooperates in fertility and death rituals, it acts as a group in the exchange of marriage partners, and it collectively organizes feasts. Formerly it raided together. These exogamous local groups become affinally linked to one another through exchange marriages. The two husbands become *tambera* or exchange partners, and they perform ritual services for each other's children. Other males of approximately the same age become *kamat* (sisters' husbands or wives' brothers), offering hospitality and friendship to their counterparts in the opposite local group.

Political Organization. The Keraki recognize hereditary headmen of the local groups described above. However, since these local groups are patrilineally organized and typically very small, consisting of only about thirty persons, the headman is usually the eldest active male. Leadership passes to a younger brother and then to the eldest son of the original headman. The headman exercises very little real authority. His "decisions" merely reflect the general consensus of opinion. There is no formal leadership above the local group level.

Social Control. Social control within the group is maintained largely through a sense of conformity, knowledge of the importance of reciprocity, feelings of in-group solidarity and support, and general conservatism. These are bolstered by fears of public reprobation or ridicule, retaliation through violence or sorcery, and the possibility of supernatural retribution.

Conflict. Conflict within the local group is rare, owing to the social control mechanisms described above. Occasional thefts and sexual jealousies are the most common exceptions. Fighting with Keraki people from outside the local group is called *guwari,* in which the men from one village descend in open invasion on the men from another village. Loud, wordy quarrels might develop into general brawls, sometimes with sticks and arrows used as weapons, but these fights usually end in reconciliation. In contrast to this was the *moku,* or head-hunting raid, directed against non-Keraki people, most commonly the Gunduman. These raids took the form of unexpected, often predawn raids. Heads were quickly severed with bamboo knives and attached to cane head carriers, whereupon the entire party fled. Once in their camp, the raiders cooked the heads, often eating a bit of flesh, usually from the cheek, and cleaned the skulls, which they erected on poles as trophies. Men who had taken heads achieved status and some measure of influence within the group. The Keraki were comparatively peaceful, however, more often being the victims of the aggressive Marind or Wiram people than the victors themselves, and their head-hunting raids were rather infrequent.

Religion and Expressive Culture

Religious Beliefs. Certain Keraki religious beliefs are embodied in myth and actually not known by a significant proportion of the population. There is an Originator and his family, who constitute the Sky Beings of *gainjan* times, when creatures were greater than they are today. These Sky Beings can grant or withhold favors to present-day human beings, and they may cause sickness by capturing a person's spirit. They may be appealed to through prayers or exhortations.

Religious Practitioners. The actions of Keraki religious practitioners are linked to the belief in magic, particularly sympathetic magic. All Keraki practice magic of various kinds, but specialist practitioners are of two main types: the rainmakers and the sorcerers.

Ceremonies. Keraki ritual life is quite varied. At the group level, exchange feasts are extremely important: they provide a stimulus for food production and bring together otherwise disparate groups. Hosts provide sociability, food, and sexual partners for male guests; these favors are then reciprocated at a return feast. At the individual level, by far the most important ceremony of male youth is the period of seclusion and initiation mentioned above, where young boys are taught ritual and mythological lore. In a practice not uncommon in the Trans-Fly, the initiates are sodomized by men from the opposite moiety in order to promote the boys' growth.

Arts. Keraki arts include wood carving, textile making, and aspects of music and performance associated primarily with ritual.

Medicine. Sickness and death are often ascribed to sorcery. Treatments for sorcery vary, but they often include bleeding or the extraction of some object introduced into the body.

Death and Afterlife. Deceased are buried in a house, often a yam house. The corpse is wrapped in bark and shallowly interred in a supine position with feet facing the south (toward the sea). Roughly a year of formal mourning and food avoidance follows, particularly for women, who cut their hair and then let it grow, refrain from washing, and wear *makamaka,* elaborate costumes constructed of multiple layers of plaited swamp grass. After interment, there is a small burial feast, followed by the erection of a small memorial and the burning of personal belongings. A larger feast signals the end of formal mourning. Women then remove the makamaka, and the memorial is uprooted. There is a belief in a soul that independently continues the existence of a person after death, but where it abides is unclear.

See also Marind-anim

Bibliography

Williams, Francis Edgar (1929). "Rainmaking on the River Morehead." *Journal of the Royal Anthropological Institute of Great Britain and Ireland* 59:379–397.

Williams, Francis Edgar (1936). *Papuans of the Trans-Fly.* Territory of Papua Anthropology Report no. 15. Oxford: Clarendon Press.

RICHARD SCAGLION

Kewa

ETHNONYMS: Kewapi, Pole, South Mendi

Orientation

Identification. The Kewa live in the Southern Highlands Province of Papua New Guinea and speak three major, mutually intelligible dialects. The name "Kewa" is not indigenous, in that areas are known only by the names of the clans that occupy them and not by more generic terms. It means, literally, "a stranger," and refers to people generally living south of Ialibu, the main center from which the first census was taken. The same name, with similar meanings, is found in other parts of the Southern Highlands Province. The people refer to themselves as those who speak the *adaa agaa(le)*, "the large/important language."

Location. The Kewa cultural area is located between 6°15' and 6°40' N and 143°7' and 144°1' E. One major river network, the Mendi-Erave and its tributaries, drains the whole Kewa area. Two prominent mountains, Giluwe (4,400 meters) and Ialibu (3,300 meters), lie to the north and northeast of the area. The area is part of the central cordillera, which is a complex system of ranges and broad upland valleys with forest, wild cane, and grasslands. There are many limestone escarpments as well as strike ridges composed of sedimentary rocks. The Kagua (1,500 meters) and Erave (1,300 meters) areas have extensive plateaus. The average yearly rainfall in the Kagua area (the central part of Kewa) is 310 centimeters and the temperature is 17–26° C during the day and 9–17° C at night. There is no marked wet-dry season, but June–August and December are usually the driest months.

Demography. As of 1989 the estimated population was 63,600 with a density from 15–40 persons per square kilometer, although in some areas it is much less. The population is growing at the rate of 2.7 percent per year, with a fluctuating resident population due to migration out to towns and plantations. In the 18–40 age bracket, 35–40 percent of the people are nonresident in their village or parish. The major towns in the Kewa area are Kagua and Erave, with Mendi and Ialibu on the northern border. Only Mendi has more than 1,000 permanent residents.

Linguistic Affiliation. Kewa is part of the Mendi-Kewa Subgroup of the Engan (West-Central) Family of languages. The Engan Family is, in turn, a part of a large group of Highlands languages (more than 60), which are in turn a segment of a much larger chain of languages that crosses Papua New Guinea and Irian Jaya. These languages are remotely related and are called Papuan to distinguish them from the Austronesian languages. Kewa also has some relationship, both culturally and linguistically, with groups to the south and west towards Lake Kutubu.

History and Cultural Relations

The ancestors of the Kewa most likely lived in the area now occupied by the Central Enga people, which is well to the north and northwest. There are very old trade links which extend southwest to Lake Kutubu and along the Kikori River, as well as northwest to the Upper Mendi. The first European visitors, patrol officers Jack Hides and James O'Malley, penetrated the Kewa area in 1935, followed by I. Champion and C. J. Adamson in 1936. There was little contact again until the early 1950s. Since that time both the missions and the government have built airstrips, schools, roads, and medical facilities.

Settlements

The parishes and villages that now exist have grown up around traditional dance grounds, as well as mission and government stations. People live in dispersed homesteads according to patrilineal lines. Several clan groups may reside in the same ceremonial dance ground territory with their respective men's and women's houses. More recently, nuclear family houses have become the rule. Homesteads are surrounded by fenced gardens, casuarina trees, cordyline leaves, and ditches to mark boundaries. There are often coffee groves as well. Every five to ten years a particular clan sponsors a pig kill and long (100–150 meters) low houses are built by the participants. The men's house is a low (2–3 meters at the peak, 1 meter at the sides), rectangular structure with grass roof, bark sides, and an open porchlike dwelling where food is communally cooked and eaten by the men. An entrance from the communal section of the house leads to individual sleeping platforms, slightly raised, each with a sunken fireplace.

Economy

Subsistence and Commercial Activities. The Kewa are subsistence horticulturalists and pigkeepers. Their dietary staple crop is the sweet potato, although native taro and introduced taro are planted as well. Sweet potatoes account for some 85 percent of the caloric intake. Harvesting of the sweet potatoes takes place 5–8 months after planting, depending on the soil and rainfall. The slashing, burning, and cutting of trees and the tilling of the soil are the duties of the men. Women assist in slashing and clearing of the grass, and they are responsible for the final clearing, planting, weeding, harvesting, and transport of the sweet potatoes. Sweet potatoes are baked in the ashes of the fire or in pots. The Kewa people have two main types of gardens: the *maapu* and the *ee*. The former is generally for sweet potatoes, cassava, sugarcane, and edible *pitpit,* although introduced vegetables may be cultivated as well. The sweet-potato vines are planted into mounds, circular or rectangular, which enhance drainage and use the natural compost from clearing and weeding. The *ee* is an overgrown *maapu,* or forest garden, and contains primarily greens and old sweet potatoes, which are also used as pig feed. Other common food crops are cucumbers, beans, corn, cabbages, onions, peanuts, and pumpkins. All of the foods mentioned as well as pineapple, bits of pork, and fried biscuits are commonly sold in the local markets. Two kinds of pandanus (the common screw pine), one with a large nut and the other with a long red fruit, are harvested. The main commercial crop is *Arabica* coffee, although tea, chili, and pyrethrum have been tried. The pig is the primary domestic animal and elaborate ceremonies and rituals are associated with it. Other animals include chickens, the occasional goat, a few cattle, and penned cassowaries.

Industrial Arts. Basket weaving is now common and various patterns are known. The materials are local reeds and vines, patterned with brown or black for contrast. Along the northeast border the people also weave walls from wild cane, which are in turn sold to other groups. Local artists incorporate designs into the weaving. Some stone axes and arrows are also prepared for tourists. Decorative weaving to secure the handles of ceremonial stone axes has long been practiced. In addition, umbrella mats, net bags and aprons, and wig coverings (for the men) are commonly made by the women. The men weave arm and leg bands, small purses, and previously carved wooden bowls. They still make arrows, bows, and spears, but they no longer carve or decorate shields. Industrial and commercial tasks are performed in the towns at vocational schools, or at mission centers.

Trade. Gold-lip pearl shells (*Pinctada maxima*) are still used, along with pigs, as the main items of exchange for wives. Also common as trade items are packets of salt and *tigaso* oil from the *Campnosperma* tree, which is purchased in the Lake Kutubu area and carried in long bamboo containers. Every village has small trade stores owned by the local clan or subclans. They sell axes, knives (which are also used in trade), fish and rice, matches, pots and pans, batteries, some clothing, kerosene, and other items. Kewa men trade plumes of the birds of paradise, parrots, cockatoos, and cassowaries, from which they make elaborate headdresses.

Division of Labor. In addition to their gardening duties, women are responsible for the husbanding of pigs, looking after the smaller children, and cooking food in the family residence or carrying it to the entrance of the men's house. The men collect and split firewood, plant sugarcane and edible *pitpit,* harvest pandanus nuts, hunt, and trade. Women are responsible for weaving net bags, net aprons, and thatching mats from pandanus leaves. The men weave the occasional arm- or legbands or fashion their own bark belts.

Land Tenure. Traditional claims on land are supported by the planting of pandanus trees and cordyline plants. Evidence of gardening and ditches are also a means of establishing clan and subclan ownership. Warfare has played an important part in present-day land claims and tenure. Upon arrival of the *Pax Australiana* all groups were given rights to the land where they were then residing. Tension exists in areas where land is less plentiful or where there are choice forests or potential garden plots. In some areas, such as the Sugu and Erave, endemic malaria has restricted the use of much land. There has been some attempt to introduce large-scale cattle production into the Sugu territory on available land. The most effective claim for land tenure is planting trees, digging ditches, and building fences.

Kinship

Kin Groups and Descent. The kin groups are loosely defined according to the *ruru* and *repaa.* The former is a collection of at least two generations of collateral male kin, their wives and children. The latter consists of a family (i.e., a husband and wife/wives) and their children, which has the potential of becoming a ruru. All land is allocated and claimed along these kinship lines, sometimes linked across widely separated areas due to the movements of the ancestors. Descent is reckoned through the male lineage with priority to the eldest male if there are brothers.

Kinship Terminology. The system is bifurcate collateral in the first ascending generation. In one's own generation, Iroquois-type cousin terms are used and all cross cousins are called by the same term but are terminologically different from siblings. Parallel cousins are classed as siblings. Siblings of the same sex have one term for the male and a different one for the female, whereas a single reciprocal term is used for siblings of the opposite sex. Males and females who are two generations removed use reciprocal terms.

Marriage and Family

Marriage. Marriage is clan-exogamous. Wealth is exchanged and negotiated by the father, uncles, or brothers of the bride with the woman's father or brother. The display of bride-wealth includes pearl shells, pigs, salt, indigenous oil, axes, knives, and cash. In some areas cassowaries are exchanged as well. Reciprocal gifts are exchanged on the part of the bride's group. The negotiation and acceptance of exchange items are pivotal in the marriage, just as their renegotiating is crucial in divorce settlements. Polygynous marriages are still common, although now most marriages are monogamous and take place within the tradition of exchange and the contemporary validation of the church. The new bride is expected to live and work with the mother-in-law while the groom prepares a house and clears land for gardens. Ideally, sexual relations take place after the negotiations are complete. Residence for the wife is primarily virilocal. Divorce is not uncommon, especially if there are as yet no children, and perhaps half of the "marriages" end in divorce, if trial marriages and casual liaisons preceding bride-wealth settlements are taken into account.

Domestic Unit. The nuclear family may live together in a house, once the household unit is established. Many adult male members of the households spend considerable time in the men's houses as well. If there are gardens some distance from the central parish locale, then temporary houses are built there. People from other areas who have some obligations to a family may be adopted into the family. The term for a family is *araalu,* meaning "duration of the father." Married households have menstrual huts nearby that also function as birth huts.

Inheritance. The adult senior male distributes the wealth. Most items pass on to the next brother(s) in line, but pigs that the wife or daughters have tended become their property. Land is awarded through the male lineage. In cases of land shortage, the husband may return to the wife's domain to receive some land. People near death are encouraged to voice their will where shells, household goods, and common items are concerned.

Socialization. Children are raised by their mother and aunts until they are 8–10 years old, when the males start to spend time in the men's house. Rarely are any children subject to physical discipline. They have no *kone* (responsible thoughts, behavior) until they are 6 or so and, since they may die at a young age, the parents would be remorseful if they had punished the youngsters. Young boys in the men's house are expected to be quiet and listen to the talk and tales of the elders. All young children learn how to interact in the culture by observing and listening. Traditionally, no formal initiation rites seem to occur for either sex. Participation in men's cult activities marks the point at which a young adult male is accepted into the male adult cult world, and it usually begins when the boy is about 14 or so.

Sociopolitical Organization

The Kewa area is divided into census divisions. Certain parish districts are identified for the census. The same groups elect village leaders, one of whom, as councillor, represents the people to the Local Government Council. The council attempts to set and collect taxes, to assume some responsibility for roads, aid posts, health centers, and schools, to give agricultural assistance, and the like. Provincial and national representatives are elected on the basis of population distribution to the local assembly and the national parliament.

Social Organization. A clan or ruru includes any patriarchal lineages of more than two generations. Subclans with sufficient population suffix the form *-repaa* to the name of the progenitor. Clans reside in a parish, which includes all of the persons associated with a particular tract of land. In time of war or large ceremonies, clan alliances are common.

Political Organization. Traditionally, the big-men were responsible for their clan groups. They become prominent through competition in exchange ceremonies, warfare, and the possession of goods, including wives. Each clan has at least one big-man who is expected to represent the clan. There is no broad-based concept of tribal or group leadership that extends beyond the parish, although influential men are known over a wide area by virtue of their trade relationships and fighting alliances. Both the government and the churches have their appointed big-men.

Social Control. Traditionally, large peace feasts were held, where gifts of pork were presented. Important men, who were rich by virtue of the pigs and pearl shells that they owned and the number of their wives, would distribute wealth to foster alliances and relationships throughout their areas. Local village magistrates serve the government and arbitrate lesser cases but anything that cannot be settled or that is considered major is referred to the government court. Courts are located at the provincial, district, or subdistrict headquarters: Mendi, Kagua, Ialibu, or Erave. Severe matters, such as murder, are dealt with by supreme court judges on their tours through the highlands.

Conflict. Most fighting was due to "payback," which could always be traced back to a couple of brothers who fought and then separated. It was always important to keep the number of deaths the same on the two sides, otherwise a further payback would be imminent. This is still the case. Other conflicts are domestic and settled within the clans and parishes. In the case of tribal warfare the district police are called in to maintain law and order. For local disputes the village magistrate is the first court of appeal. Most conflict is resolved only by prolonged negotiation and compensation. Suicide is not uncommon.

Religion and Expressive Culture

At least 80 percent of the Kewa population call themselves Christian, and most are baptized members of the Catholic or Lutheran churches. Other denominations in the Kewa area are: Evangelical Church of Papua, Wesleyan, Bible Church, United Church, Nazarene, Pentecostal, and Seventh-Day Adventist. The remaining Kewas are uncommitted or traditional animists. Syncretism is not uncommon.

Religious Beliefs. A belief in one supernatural being is widespread, often based on an interpretation of the sky being "Yaki(li)." Ancestral spirits can be particularly malevolent if not appeased properly. The most powerful spirits traditionally were those associated with various curing ceremonies. At a lower level, but still feared, are the nature spirits. Coexisting with Christianity is the widespread belief in and acceptance of sorcery. Traditionally, men's cults predominated, with associated secret languages and ceremonies. There is a widespread fear of both the power of sorcerers and the power of ancestral ghosts.

Religious Practitioners. Certain men are responsible for divining and effecting cures. Pigs and chickens are killed and presented in payment for their services. Sorcery includes incantations and exorcisms of potent items. The most vicious forms of sorcery are always considered to be from outside the region. Hair, nails, and feces can be used for potential harm.

Ceremonies. Exchange ceremonies provide social cohesion, especially large festivals that culminate in the killing of hundreds of pigs. Bride-exchange and compensation ceremonies are confined to the clans involved. With the advent of roads and accidental deaths, large compensation gifts are negotiated by the government. Churches have incorporated various special days and meetings into village life.

Arts. A few traditional musical instruments are made: the Jew's harp, drum, and flute. In some areas panpipes are also used. Combs and pipes are carved and designed from bamboo. The Kewa people excel in body decorations for special events, painting their faces with intricate, colorful designs. Wigs are decorated with beautiful plumes from birds of paradise, parrots, cockatoos, cassowaries, and other birds. Funeral decorations include clay for body painting and Job's tears (*Coix lachryma-jobi*) for necklaces.

Medicine. Illness is often attributed to the breaking of social taboos, such as incorrect preparation of food, not observing sexual abstinence at certain times, or not showing respect for the dead ancestors. Remedies are provided by healers and other experts, often using traditional herbs (such as ginger) and medicines. There are aid posts, health centers, and hospitals throughout the Kewa area.

Death and Afterlife. The bodies of important men are placed on elevated platforms; the bodies of lesser men and of women are suspended on poles. Grief is shown by painting the body with clay and tearing out the hair. The spirit of the departed person is assumed to reside nearby for some time. The more important the person was in life, the more important the spirit is in death. Healthy people do not simply die; their death is attributed to sorcery or foul play of some kind. Well-known diseases such as leprosy, hepatitis, worm infestation, pneumonia, malaria, and dysentery traditionally had curing functions associated with particular spirits. The spirits of the dead are called upon in remembrance ceremonies and some important graves now are marked with special small houses. The Kewa belief in the afterlife is evident in various myths and stories.

See also Foi, Mendi

Bibliography

Franklin, Karl J., and Joice Franklin (1978). *A Kewa Dictionary: With Supplementary Grammatical and Anthropological Materials.* Pacific Linguistics, Series C, no. 53. Canberra: Australian National University.

Josephides, Lisette (1985). *The Production of Inequality: Gender and Exchange among the Kewa.* London: Tavistock.

LeRoy, John (1985). *Fabricated World: An Interpretation of Kewa Tales.* Vancouver: University of British Columbia Press.

KARL J. FRANKLIN

Kilenge

ETHNONYMS: None

Orientation

Identification and Location. The Kilenge, subsistence swidden horticulturalists, live along a 4-kilometer coastal stretch on the northwest tip of the island of New Britain, 5°28' S, 148°22' E. They are part of the Kilenge-Lolo District of the province of West New Britain in Papua New Guinea. A reef about 1 kilometer offshore fringes the coastline, and the land rises from the beach to the peak of Mount Talave (an extinct volcano), some 1,834 meters high. The bulk of Talave shields the Kilenge villages from Langila, an active volcanic spur of the mountain. Rainfall averages some 300 centimeters per year, with much of the rain coming during the northwest monsoon (December to March). A marked dry period (July to September) causes occasional droughts. Daily temperature usually exceeds 25° C.

Demography. In 1982, approximately 1,000 Kilenge lived in northwest New Britain settlements. Another 400 to 600 Kilenge lived elsewhere as students, wage laborers, or their dependents. Family size averaged about five children per couple.

Linguistic Affiliation. The Kilenge speak a dialect of Male'u, a language they share with their inland Lolo neighbors. Male'u is an Austronesian language, part of the Siassi or Vitiaz Family of languages.

History and Cultural Relations

The Kilenge themselves are not sure of their origins: different legends variously ascribe their ancestors as coming from the north coast of New Guinea, the Siassi Islands, or the south coast of New Britain. Evidence suggests that their immediate forbears lived on the lower slopes of Mount Talave and slowly migrated down to the coast, arriving there about 150 years ago. The Germans began recruiting the Kilenge for labor around the turn of this century, establishing a pattern of wage-labor migration that persists today. Some depopulation resulted from a smallpox epidemic in the second decade of this century. World War II caused dislocation but few casualties. It also opened up new cultural and social horizons. Today, the Kilenge are marginally incorporated into the world economy. The Kilenge cultural repertoire, while related to those of other New Britain and Siassi Island groups, is unique in its particular configuration. The Kilenge are primarily endogamous, and they distinguish themselves from other people, particularly their bush-dwelling Lolo neighbors, in terms of their particular combination of locality, language, marriage, and culture. In the past, the Kilenge participated in the overseas trade network organized and maintained by the Siassi Islanders, exchanging their pigs, coconuts, taro, and Talasea obsidian for carved bowls and clay pots needed in their bride-price payments. They also mediated the exchange between the Lolo and the Siassi and maintained ties with the Bariai, Kaliai, and Kove to the east.

Settlements

Historically, the Kilenge lived in small hamlets centered around men's houses. Colonial rule saw the formalization of hamlet clusters into villages. Currently, the Kilenge live in three villages separated from one another by streams or stretches of bush. The villages are (from southwest to northeast) Portne, Ongaia, and Kilenge proper. The latter is further divided into three distinct sections: Ulumai'enge, Saumoi, and Varemo. Portne and Ongaia each have a population of about 250, while Kilenge proper has about 500 people. Other Kilenge settlements further east were destroyed by the eruption of Ritter Island in 1888 or in battles during World War II and were never resettled. Villages are built along the beach, and while most houses tend to be raised a meter or more above the ground, building materials and house styles vary widely, from bush materials (sago-palm roof thatching, woven coconut-palm-frond walls) to imported timbers and corrugated iron. Each village contains at least one large, distinctive building constructed directly on the ground: a men's house with a high-pitched roof.

Economy

Subsistence and Commercial Activities. Although they live on the coast, the Kilenge derive their primary subsistence from swidden horticulture rather than the sea. They slash-and-burn their gardens in the volcanic soils on the lower slopes of Mount Talave. Individual gardens are devoted to one of the three staple root starches (taro, yams, sweet potatoes), but they also contain up to twenty other types of plants, both native food (sugarcane, cassava, bananas) and various introduced fruits and vegetables. A single garden produces for no more than three years, then lies fallow for between ten and twenty years. Gardens are planned so that they will normally feed a family and the family's pigs and still provide a nonstorable surplus for ceremonial events. People commonly use coconuts for food and drink. Fish caught in the lagoon (with nets, hooks, explosives, or poisons), shellfish gathered from the reef, and marine animals occasionally supplement the diet, as does sago flour. Hunting wild pigs, cassowaries, and other birds and mammals contributes a little to the diet. Today, Kilenge also eat imported food (mainly rice and canned fish but also flour, canned meat, biscuits, etc.) purchased at local, group-owned trade stores. Villagers get money for their purchases through the production of copra (dried coconut meat), remittances from relatives in town, or the rare casual wage-labor opportunities offered by the Catholic mission or government station. The limited money available (1981 income estimate of less than $100 U.S. per capita) also pays school fees, purchases imported items (clothing, kerosene, soap, tobacco, etc.), and supports ceremonial activities.

Industrial Arts. The Kilenge are capable of producing most material items needed for daily life, although they rely increasingly on imported substitutes. All adult men should be able to build their own houses and canoes, but men with expertise in a given field are recognized as master artisans and are called on by others to supervise house building and canoe carving, to repair a fishnet, or to decorate ceremonial artifacts. Steel tools such as axes, adzes, and saws have completely replaced the traditional stone tools.

Trade. Local markets rise and fall sporadically. Regional trade has suffered with the decline of the Siassi trade system, but men grow tobacco for sale to other New Britain groups and women produce dancing skirts for the same market.

Division of Labor. Whenever possible, the Kilenge conduct work as a social, not a solitary, activity. Men clear the gardens, plant some crops, provide infrastructure (houses, canoes, fishnets), fish, butcher pigs and large sea animals, organize ceremonies and produce ceremonial paraphernalia, and control political activity. Women plant other crops, tend and harvest gardens, organize the household, prepare food for daily and ceremonial use, look after children, sweep the village, and gather shellfish from the reef. Both men and women make house walls and roof thatching, participate in required government and communal labor, and produce copra.

Land Tenure. Groups, rather than individuals, hold title to land. Most garden land (whether in use or fallow) and productive reef sections are controlled by localized men's house organizations (*naulum*). Recently cleared primary forest is controlled by the cognatic descendants of the clearer, but over time control reverts to the clearer's men's house group. Individuals own the gardens and trees they plant on group land. A government-backed attempt to introduce individual landholding met with little success in the early 1980s.

Kinship

Kin Groups and Descent. In Kilenge, a cognatic descent principle serves as a basis for recruitment of membership in various groups and organizations. Cognatic descent, wherein the sex of the linking kinsmen does not matter in the reckoning of the descent continuum, entitles people to group membership and various use rights, but actual membership in a unit depends on a host of possible reasons for activating or severing connections with a unit. People can therefore choose, rather than be assigned, group membership. The most socially significant kin-based group or organization is the naulum, or men's house. Each naulum, manifested in a named cluster of coresident, cognatically related individuals and their spouses, controls land, owns other tangible and intangible property, sponsors ceremonial events and cycles, and provides help and support to members. Naulum may or may not have physical men's house buildings. Individuals may be a primary, active member of one naulum while maintaining secondary membership in one or more other naulum. Other kin-based units include the *naulum kuria,* which is a subdivision of the naulum; unnamed resource-focused ramages composed of the descendants of the resource establisher; and unnamed sibling groups that provide members with mutual aid.

Kinship Terminology. Kilenge kinship terminology is a Hawaiian-type generational system modified by a form of sibling ranking, reflecting the importance of seniority in Kilenge culture.

Marriage and Family

Marriage. Some traditional marriage practices like bride-price persist, while others, such as polygyny and arranged marriages, are things of the past. Today, individuals choose their own partners, and they mark their marriages by bride-price payment, sanctification in the church, or both. Kilenge elders frown on simple cohabitation and forbid marriage within the naulum kuria. Bride-price payments consist of traditional valuables such as Siassi bowls and pigs, as well as cash. Payments are negotiated by the groom's father, gathered from the groom's parents' kindreds, and distributed by the bride's parents to their kindreds. Debts incurred by bride-price contributions enmesh young men in the local prestige exchange system. Upon either the bride-price payment or church wedding, the couple set up their own household. Virilocal residence is the statistical norm, but uxorilocal residence is common and accepted. Divorce rarely occurs: the Kilenge are Catholic, and they find it virtually impossible to reconstruct and return dispersed bride-price payments, even in the face of continued domestic violence.

Domestic Unit. The nuclear family household is the most common domestic unit, providing most labor needed for daily activities. Childless couples usually adopt one or more children for companionship and help with work. Elderly individuals, even those with limited physical capacity, take pride in maintaining their own households.

Inheritance. The eldest child inherits titles and statuses, contingent on his or her abilities. Children inherit traditional valuables and fixed resources (such as coconut trees) from their parents. People gain rights to land from their naulum membership. Adopted children may inherit material items and gain land rights through both their natal and adoptive families.

Socialization. The nuclear family is the main unit of socialization of children. Relatives and neighbors also participate in the process. Responsibility for proper initiation rests with parents or their elder siblings. Today, the government school acts as a major agent of socialization. In the past, the period of seclusion associated with initiation during puberty (circumcision for boys and ceremonial dressing for girls) provided time for intense indoctrination into Kilenge lore. Now, such seclusion would interfere with schooling, and ceremonial initiation occurs at a much younger age.

Sociopolitical Organization

Social Organization. Birth order, genealogical seniority, age, sex, and ability combine to provide one's relative status in Kilenge society. Solidarity decreases in intensity from the household level through sibling groups, men's house groups, villages, and Kilenge society as a whole. Kinship ties can crosscut organizational affiliations.

Political Organization. Traditionally, the men's house group, or naulum, served as the basic political unit. A *natavolo,* or hereditary leader, headed each naulum. Hereditary leadership candidates validated their claims to natavolo status by organizing ceremonies, trading expeditions, wars, and feuds and by arranging marriages. Today, under an imposed administrative structure, the village is the basic political unit. The senior natavolo in each village is ideally the village leader in traditional activities, but he must compete with appointed and elected government functionaries. The hereditary leader serves mainly as an organizer of ceremonies, but recently hereditary leaders have become prominent in commercial activities, using their status to organize their followers for business undertakings. Villagers elect representatives to the Gloucester Local Government Council, the West New Britain Provincial Government, the National Parliament in Port Moresby, and a variety of local bodies.

Social Control. Contemporary sanctions for serious offenses (murder, theft of imported goods) are the prerogative of the national government and its appointed agents (the police, village magistrates, the court system). Gossip and fear of sorcery act as powerful sanctions against violation of local norms and conventions. Traditionally, the hereditary leader of the men's house group acted as the final arbiter of social control. He could order the death, through physical or supernatural means, of a recalcitrant follower. He could also, through the use of sacred "*Nausang*" masks, have offenders beaten and their property confiscated. Followers could use sorcery on or assassinate a tyrannical leader, or they could join other men's house groups.

Conflict. In the past, naulum and naulum clusters went to war over violation of property rights, women, and sacred injunctions. A group's hereditary leader would assess his own strength and the potential enemy's strength, and then decide on a course of war or peace. Battles were fought as individual spear duels between lines of men. People related to members on both sides of the conflict would facilitate eventual peacemaking, but violations of sacred injunctions usually resulted in surprise attacks and extermination of the violator's group. Colonial rule saw the end of organized conflict. Open conflict is now settled either locally or, if violent, by the police. People pursue hidden conflict using sorcery.

Religion and Expressive Culture

Religious Beliefs and Practitioners. The Roman Catholics established a mission in 1929, and today most Kilenge are at least nominal Catholics. People maintain their beliefs in a variety of precontact phenomena: the power of sacred stones to change into humans or animals; forbidden places (*ngaselnga*) where malevolent spirits dwell; Nausang spirits manifested in masks; and sorcery. Most people know some magical formulas to help in work. Some people claim the power to find lost souls through dreaming; others claim to control weather. The Kilenge say that they know little sorcery, and they ascribe most acts of homicidal sorcery to their Lolo neighbors.

Ceremonies. A rich variety of ceremonial cycles, lasting up to five to seven years, provide the Kilenge with a context in which they initiate children, honor the dead, validate hereditary leadership, compete for group prestige, and exchange quantities of pigs and other traditional valuables.

Arts. The masks, headdresses, and dancing paraphernalia produced for the ceremonial cycles constitute the major items of Kilenge artistic production. Intricate songs and dances associated with the cycles demonstrate ability in the performing arts. Utilitarian items may be decorated, but most, with the exception of canoes, are left plain.

Medicine. The Kilenge rely on mission and government clinics for treatment of some major ailments, but they know spells and plants to relieve minor discomforts and go to curers when modern medicine fails.

Death and Afterlife. Funerals occur the day after a death. When people feel the death was caused by human malevolence, they will discreetly inquire about sorcery or consult diviners. Mortuary ceremonies for important people may last years, culminating in the destruction of the deceased's house. Attenuated ceremonies accompany the death of children or less important adults. The soul lingers by the grave for days or weeks and can present a threat to humans. Traditionalists say the soul then departs for Mount Andewa to the east, while committed Catholics believe the soul goes to Heaven or Hell.

Bibliography

Dark, P. J. C. (1974). *Kilenge Art and Life: A Look at a New Guinea People.* London: Academy Editions.

Grant, J., H. Saito, and M. Zelenietz (1986). "Where Development Never Comes: Business Activities in Kilenge, Papua New Guinea." *Journal of the Polynesian Society* 95:195–219.

Zelenietz, M., and J. Grant (1986). "The Problem with *Pisins*: An Alternative View of Social Organization in West New Britain." *Oceania* 56:199–214, 264–274.

MARTY ZELENIETZ

Kiribati

ETHNONYMS: Gilbertese (Gilbert Islands), I-Kiribati, Tungaru

Orientation

Identification. Almost all of the citizens of Kiribati have at least some I-Kiribati ancestors and have inherited land rights in the Gilbert Islands. The indigenous inhabitants of Banaba (Ocean Island) speak a Gilbertese dialect and practice a variant of Gilbertese culture but consider themselves a separate people politically. Most of the Banabans have lived on Rabi Island in Fiji since 1945. Another Gilbertese dialect is spoken on Nui in Tuvalu. The Gilbert Islands were named in honor of Thomas Gilbert, a British captain whose ship sighted some of the islands after transporting convicts to Australia in 1788. In default of a generally acceptable indigenous name, it was decided at the time of independence to adopt "Kiribati" (pronounced "kiribass"), the local respelling of "Gilberts," for the new nation. The poetic "Tungaru" usually connotes the ancestors and their savage or superhuman feats.

Location. The Gilberts comprise sixteen inhabited coral reef islands and atolls between 3° N and 3° S and between 173° and 177° E. The territory of the Republic of Kiribati also includes the raised coral island of Banaba, about 400 kilometers west of the Gilberts, and the Phoenix and Line Islands lying as much as 2,800 kilometers to the east. The average annual rainfall diminishes from north to south. The islands south of the equator and Banaba suffer from periodic droughts.

Demography. According to the 1985 census, Kiribati had a total population of 63,883. The average population density for the Gilbert Islands, which have a combined area of 279 square kilometers, was 219 persons per square kilometer. The growth rate averaged 2.0 percent per annum in the 6 ½ years between censuses. A third of the population was enumerated in the urbanized area of South Tarawa.

Linguistic Affiliation. I-Kiribati and Banabans speak a single language, usually known as Gilbertese. Linguists agree that Gilbertese belongs to the Oceanic Branch of the Austronesian languages, and its closest relatives are the other Nuclear Micronesian languages: Trukese, Ponapean, Kosraean (Kusaian), and Marshallese. The more distant connections of Nuclear Micronesian within Oceanic Austronesian are still being debated, but they seem to point toward the southern Solomon Islands and Vanuatu, with the languages of San Cristobal and Malaita as perhaps the strongest candidates. The pioneer American missionary, Hiram Bingham, Jr., devised a written form of Gilbertese based on the Latin alphabet that is still in general use, having undergone only minor modifications.

History and Cultural Relations

On linguistic and archaeological grounds, it is likely that voyagers from southern Melanesia arrived in the Gilberts long before A.D. 600, the earliest radiocarbon date obtained up to now. Kiribati language and culture show signs of borrowing from western Polynesia at some time after the islands were settled. The political and social structure of all the islands except for Butaritari-Makin and Banaba was forcibly unified, possibly in the seventeenth century, when armies led by Kaitu, Beru, and Uakeia of Nikunau introduced the meetinghouse organization. Regular contacts with Europeans and Americans began when merchant ships sailing new routes across the Pacific, New England whalers, and exploring expeditions discovered or rediscovered all the islands between 1765 and 1826. Resident traders bought coconut oil from 1846 to the 1870s and then switched to copra, which remains Kiribati's sole agricultural export. A British protectorate was proclaimed over the Gilberts and their Polynesian neighbors, the Ellice Islands, in 1892. The Japanese occupation of the Gilberts early in World War II ended with an American victory in the "particularly bloody battle at Tarawa" (as Richard Overy has aptly termed it) fought in November 1943. The phosphate mine on Banaba provided most of the colony's revenue and employment for its people from 1900 until the deposits were exhausted in the year of independence; I-Kiribati still mine phosphate on the neighboring independent island of Nauru. Since 1967, the Marine Training School has made it possible for many young men to get jobs as seamen on West German ships and to add greatly to their families' incomes through remittances. Four years after the Ellice Islands had separated from the colony to become the state of Tuvalu, the Gilberts also became independent as the Republic of Kiribati on 12 July 1979.

Settlements

Precolonial villages were social and political units centered on a meetinghouse (*te mwaneaba*). The settlement pattern was one of dispersed hamlets on descent-group lands, which usually ran across islets from west to east. Around 1900 the Resident Commissioner and government agents ordered villages consolidated along a road running parallel to the western (leeward) shore of each inhabited islet, even if that meant forcing people to move off their hereditary lands. They also compelled the islanders to build houses according to a uniform pattern. A house consists essentially of a roof covered with coconut- or pandanus-leaf thatch and supported by four or six wooden posts. Unlike most precolonial houses, the new-style ones have raised floors of split coconut-leaf midribs and can comfortably accommodate only one nuclear family. Following a colonial regulation, each family still builds separate houses for sleeping and eating. In the 1980s some relatively affluent people, such as the families of merchant seamen, and members of clubs organized for that purpose were erecting cement-block houses with galvanized-iron roofs and facilities for catching rainwater. Large meetinghouses are still constructed in more or less the traditional style, not only as sites for village councils and festivities but also by church congregations and neighborhoods.

Economy

Subsistence and Commercial Activities. The only crop that I-Kiribati cultivate regularly is the atoll taro *Cyrtosperma chamissonis*, which is grown in gardens dug down to the level of the freshwater lens or in natural swamps. The slower-growing varieties are often fertilized for years with mixtures of humus and leaf compost sprinkled into "pots" of plaited coconut fronds or braided pandanus leaves, until the leaves are as much as 3.5 meters high. The huge corms that develop as a result of this treatment are suitable for feasts and formal presentations. Smaller varieties, allowed to clone and not usually fertilized, are an everyday food on the northern islands. The only other important native vegetable foods are tree crops—coconuts, pandanus, and, mainly in the north, breadfruit. The coconut palm is also the source of toddy, the juice of the unopened flower spathe which is collected in a coconut shell as a fresh drink, boiled into molasses, or allowed to ferment. The numerous fishing methods include trolling behind a canoe furnished with a sail or an outboard motor, unrolling a line with baited hook into deep water from a smaller paddling canoe, catching flying fish with a coconut-leaf torch or kerosene lantern and a scoop net, searching the holes and pools of the nighttime reef with a scoop net and machete, netting on the reef at high tide, angling from the edge of the reef, and trapping fish behind a stone weir. Domestic animals, all of which are eaten, include dogs, chickens, and introduced pigs.

Industrial Arts. There are part-time builders of canoes, houses, and meetinghouses in every village. These men, like the few remaining navigators, enjoy respect and deference, but they receive no pay except their food while at work and perhaps a waist cloth when the job is finished.

Trade. Most adults hold shares in their village cooperative store, which is affiliated with a national federation. There are many even smaller general stores belonging to individuals, partnerships, and clubs. Women sell or give away all of their husbands' catches of tuna, flying fish, and shark that exceed household requirements.

Division of Labor. Men cultivate and harvest *Cyrtosperma* in the south, where the corms are a luxury food. In the north women do most of the routine fertilizing, and the custom that only a woman may dig up a corm is used as an argument for marriage. The I-Kiribati also believe that only men should climb trees. Men do the bulk of the fishing; women collect shellfish and catch land crabs, but occasionally they engage in other kinds of fishing as well. Work with leaves is restricted to women, who make mats, baskets, and thatch and produce cordage from fiber obtained from coconut husks. Men build houses and canoes and make smaller wooden objects. Women normally fetch water, cook meals, and wash clothes. The division of labor is not rigid, but persons who habitually perform tasks associated with the opposite sex are regarded as having changed their gender identity, like North American Indian *berdaches*.

Land Tenure. Both men and women inherit land rights from both parents, rights that are inseparable from one's status as a blood relative and a member of the community. The colonial administration abrogated the old rules, under which sons received larger shares than daughters and an eldest son (and sometimes an eldest daughter) more than younger children, in favor of an equal division. Parents customarily divide their lands in a way that assures each of their children of rights in as many of the parental descent groups as possible. If someone dies without leaving natural or adopted children, his land will be divided among his siblings or, lacking these, will revert to the estate of his father and mother. Most of the lands (though not the *Cyrtosperma* gardens) on Butaritari and Makin are the joint property of descent groups, necessitating a system of annual or weekly turns for collecting coconuts. A widespread Micronesian distinction between provisional titleholders or caretakers (who actually work the land and utilize its products) and residual titleholders (whose claims must be acknowledged by gifts and assistance) is the basis for several social relationships, such as those between brother and married sister and between guardian and ward.

Kinship

Kin Groups and Descent. Descent, like inheritance, is ambilineal. Everyone is affiliated with the descent groups (ramages) of several ancestors, although he or she is most active in a group associated with his or her own or the parents' place of residence. Before the introduction of lands registers, inactive memberships tended to lapse after a few generations, especially if the link to the group was a female ancestor. Members of a descent group who together with their spouses and children occupied a communal dwelling or hamlet on its estate constituted a residential group (*te kaainga*, a term used for a descent group conceived of as a landholding corporation and also for the land itself). Each descent group has traditionally been associated with a place in the meetinghouse (*te inaki*, literally "a vertical row of thatch," or *te boti*).

Kinship Terminology. Cousin terminology is Hawaiian-type: everyone with whom one shares an ancestor an equal number of generations removed can be referred to by the terms for "sibling of the same sex" or "sibling of the opposite sex." Other cognatic and affinal relatives are also classified by generation. Native kinship terms are not used in address.

Marriage and Family

Marriage. First marriages, in particular, ideally are arranged by the parents or at least require their consent, but elopements are becoming more common. In theory, persons who share an ancestor within three generations, or who trace descent from a more distant common ancestor but themselves belong to different generations, are forbidden to marry. In practice, reaction to a proposed marriage that would join together distant relatives depends on whether the immediate families of the young people have been treating one another as kinsfolk. Some families still follow the old custom of rejoicing publicly when a bride has demonstrated her virginity. Most young married people reside with the husbands' parents until they are considered ready for independent life. Until recently, they were also expected to reside permanently on land the husband had inherited either through his father or through his mother. A man who agreed to live with his wife's kin was thought to yield much of his authority over his household. A permanently separated couple is regarded as divorced by the community if not by the church. Once children have been born, kin on both sides will put pressure on the spouses to reconcile or will try to persuade an unmarried sibling to act as stepparent. Sororal polygyny is dying out.

Domestic Units. The people who cook and eat meals together are considered a family. The teenage boys and young unmarried men of the neighborhood often sleep in an unoccupied house but eat with their families. A nuclear family or a currently unmarried woman and her children are ordinarily the minimal family units. As their own children grow up and leave home, couples often begin rearing a second family of grandchildren or wards. Other helpful or dependent kinsfolk may be present as well. Families outside South Tarawa average 5.8 persons.

Inheritance. Parents leave their house to one of their children, often when they retire to stay with each of their children in turn. Portable artifacts are probably distributed informally, but large canoes tend to be treated like land. Items of esoteric knowledge, which are considered a kind of personal property, may be bestowed on a favorite child, on another young relative, or even on an outsider.

Socialization. A good deal of personal independence is conceded even to young children, who at least in theory have the right to own property and to decide with whom they will live. Small children are treated indulgently by everyone, even when they act aggressively. Older children are expected to help with household tasks, to show respect for senior kinsfolk, and to refrain from calling attention to themselves when adults are present. Physical punishment is acceptable once a child has reached the age of reason. Threats, ridicule, and scary stories about punitive agents from outside the family are commoner sanctions, however.

Sociopolitical Organization

Kiribati is a democracy with a popularly elected president and House of Assembly.

Social Organization. Chiefs were present in the central and northern Gilberts, but on several islands no single chief managed to hold undisputed power for very long. The most stratified societies in the late precolonial and early colonial periods were Butaritari-Makin and Abemama, which had conquered the neighboring islands of Aranuka and Kuria. The Butaritari-Makin hierarchy, which resembled those of other Micronesian societies to the north, was headed by a high chief who was a focus for redistributive activities. Below the high chief and his siblings and children were aristocrats, commoners, and descendants of strangers from other islands. Since the 1970s life-styles have reflected differences in family incomes, even in the villages.

Political Organization. The government of the republic provides a system of courts and health, educational, and agricultural services on the national and island levels. Elected island councils are responsible for repairing roads, maintaining schools, granting permission to build new houses, and filling some off-island jobs. Lands courts approve the inheritance and transfer of real property and resolve disputes over boundaries and the rights of coowners. Especially since independence, many of the powers of the island councils have been assumed by unofficial bodies of village elders that developed out of the traditional councils of heads of descent groups. The elders legislate on matters ranging from trips by the local soccer team to the prohibition of alcohol. They punish violators with fines, beatings, and occasionally exile. Wider consensus is reached by inviting delegates from other villages to a joint meeting or, as on Nonouti in the late 1960s, by organizing a single council for the whole island.

Social Control. The Kiribati ethos holds that an adult should be prepared to fight if challenged and be ready to avenge an injury or insult against himself or a member of his family. On the other hand, the wisdom and control over the passions that comes with age gives some older people the status of acknowledged peacemakers. Any assembly is thought to assert social norms over the selfish or shortsighted impulses of individuals. The fear of gossip and of secret or open mockery by neighbors are commonplace checks on deviant behavior.

Conflict. In the past, villages and intervillage factions fought to avenge offenses, to seize land, and to gain a chieftainship for their candidate. Wars became more destructive in the nineteenth century, when steel weapons and firearms were widely available and the activities of labor recruiters, traders, and missionaries weakened the social order and created new causes for conflict. In the presidential election preceding independence, the voters of Kiribati decided against having an army.

Religion and Expressive Culture

Religious Beliefs. The forerunners of the present-day Kiribati Protestant Church (K.P.C.), the American Board of Commissioners for Foreign Missions and the London Missionary Society, arrived in the northern and southern islands, respectively, in 1857 and 1870. The French Roman Catholic fathers of the Order of the Sacred Heart began work on Nonouti in 1888. Catholics (53 percent of the indigenous population) are in the majority from Tarawa northward. The K.P.C. (41 percent) holds a near-monopoly on Arorae and Tamana and retains majorities on a few of the other southern islands. About 2½ percent of the I-Kiribati adhere to the Baha'i faith. Mormons, Seventh-Day Adventists, and members of other Christian sects make up the remainder of the population. A good deal of social, recreational, and even economic activity centers on the churches.

Religious Practitioners. The expatriate (mostly French) Catholic clergy has been largely replaced by I-Kiribati priests and nuns. Local catechists conduct services on most islands between occasional visits by a priest. K.P.C. ministers are all I-Kiribati (except for a few from Tuvalu) but do not serve on their home islands. The priests of the old pagan religion interpreted omens and made offerings to deities that descended from time to time onto pillars of coral limestone and other shrines or took animal forms. Spirit mediums are probably still active, although they are possessed by recently introduced supernaturals and are regarded with great ambivalence. I-Kiribati deities (some with western Polynesian names) were believed to have been ancestors of descent groups that obeyed their taboos and relied on them for protection. Their associations with animals and natural phenomena gave them significance for the community as a whole.

Ceremonies. Early in the colonial period, indigenous dancing was permitted only on Christmas, New Year's, and the Queen's birthday. These holidays, with Independence Day replacing the Queen's birthday and Easter and Youth Day added, are still occasions for public feasting and dancing. Catholics celebrate the major feasts of the church in the same ways and sometimes by mass visits to their coreligionists in other villages.

Arts. The patterns of plaited sleeping mats, created by alternating light- and dark-colored strips of dried pandanus leaf, show off women's esthetic sense as well as their technical skills. Durable ornaments are made of spondylus, mother-of-pearl, and marine snail shells; in former times, dolphin, whale, and human teeth were also used. Kiribati sitting and standing dances, accompanied by singing and by clapping hands or beating on a box, are famous. Songs are still composed by traditional methods, although usually on a Western tonal scale.

Medicine. Illness is generally attributed to material causes, although attacks by ghosts, retribution for offending a parent or other superior, sorcery, soul loss, and divine punishment are advanced as explanations in particular cases. Indigenous curing methods include the use of proprietary herbal medicines and systems of massage and cautery.

Death and Afterlife. Nineteenth-century travelers reported that the body was kept in the house for three to nine days and even longer if the deceased had been prominent. Some months after burial the skull was removed and thereafter oiled and offered food and tobacco. Mission influence has been opposed to drawn-out funerals and of course to the custom of keeping a relative's skull on a shelf or carrying it around. The wake is still attended by a large number of kinsfolk, who contribute *Cyrtosperma* corms and money and eulogize the departed. Burial is in a village cemetery or in a grave next to the house. Despite strong Christian beliefs in an afterlife of rewards or punishments, people remember the old story that the god Nakaa welcomes souls at the north end of the Gilberts.

See also Nauru, Rotuma, Tuvalu

Bibliography

Geddes, William H. (1977). "Social Individualisation on Tabiteuea Atoll." *Journal of the Polynesian Society* 86:371–392.

Macdonald, Barrie (1982). *Cinderellas of the Empire: Towards a History of Kiribati and Tuvalu.* Canberra: Australian National University Press.

Silverman, Martin G. (1971). *Disconcerting Issue: Meaning and Struggle in a Resettled Pacific Community.* Chicago: University of Chicago Press.

Watters, Ray, and Nancy J. Pollock, project directors (1983). *Atoll Economy: Social Change in Kiribati and Tuvalu.* 6 vols. Canberra: Australian National University Press.

BERND LAMBERT

Kiwai

ETHNONYMS: none

Orientation

Identification. The Kiwai are a coastal people of southern New Guinea who live between the Pahoturi and Fly rivers and on the islands and river banks of the estuaries of the Fly and Bamu rivers. Almost all of what we know about these people comes from the work of Gunnar Landtman, who lived among the Kiwai of Kiwai Island in the Fly River Delta for two years from 1910 to 1912 and whose major descriptions were published in 1917 and 1927. This summary is based primarily on these descriptions.

Location. The Fly River Delta lies between 8° and 8°15' S and between 143° and 143°45' E. The Fly River is approximately 80 kilometers wide at its mouth, and Kiwai Island, which is 60 kilometers long and 5 to 10 kilometers wide, is the largest of the islands in the delta. The islands of the Fly and Bamu deltas are extremely low and swampy as are the river banks and coastlines near the mouths of these rivers. In tidal areas, vegetation consists almost exclusively of mangroves and nipa palms, but further inland there are large freshwater swamps and dry savannas. The average annual rainfall at the mouth of the Fly River is about 200 centimeters, most of which falls during the northwest monsoon from December to April. During this period it rains almost every day, and the rain is often accompanied by violent thunderstorms and high winds.

Demography. In 1980 there were approximately 13,400 Kiwai. This figure includes 7,800 speakers of Southern Kiwai, 2,000 speakers of Wabuda, and 3,600 speakers of Bamu Kiwai. The population density of the area is about 2.5 persons per square kilometer. There are no reliable early population estimates for the Kiwai, and there is no reliable information on population growth or decline.

Linguistic Affiliation. Stefan Wurm has identified seven languages in the Kiwai (or Kiwaian) Language Family. The people who call themselves Kiwai, and who are the subject of this summary, speak the Southern Kiwai, Wabuda, and Bamu Kiwai languages. The other four languages of the Kiwai Family are Morigi, Kerewo, Arigibi, and Northeastern Kiwai. The Kiwai Family is part of the Trans–Fly Stock which, in turn, is part of the Trans–New Guinea Language Phylum. According to Wurm, however, the languages of the Kiwai Family are "aberrant members" of the Trans–New Guinea Stock, and the apparent relationship between the languages of the Kiwai Family and the other languages of the Trans-Fly Stock may be the result of relatively recent contact rather than genetic relationship. The languages of the Kiwai Family also show strong connections with the languages of the Upper Fly River area, particularly those of the Ok and Awin-Pa Families.

History and Cultural Relations

The mouth of the Fly River was discovered by Europeans in 1842, and there was considerable contact between the Kiwai and European explorers, traders, and missionaries during the second half of the nineteenth century. By the time Landtman arrived in 1910, many Kiwai men spoke Pidgin English and had worked on pearl-shell boats in the Torres Strait and on plantations farther to the east on the southern coast of New Guinea. In 1884, the British established the protectorate of British New Guinea along the southern coast of New Guinea, and, in 1905, the southeastern quarter of New Guinea became the Australian Territory of Papua. Since 1975, the Kiwai have been citizens of the Independent State of Papua New Guinea.

The cultural similarities and differences both among the speakers of Kiwaian languages and among the Kiwai and their neighbors have not been well documented. Nonetheless, there appear to be broad cultural similarities between the Kiwai and the Marind-anim who live farther west along the southern coast of New Guinea and between the Kiwai and the Gogodala who live along the Aramia River to the west and northwest of the Kiwai.

Settlements

Villages, which range in population from about 50 to 500 persons, are built close to the water. Traditionally, the Kiwai built two types of houses: the móto, or communal dwelling where the women, children, and married men lived, and the dárimo, or men's house. Both types of houses had raised floors of split palm and thatched roofs that extended almost to the level of the floor. Some móto were very long—one measured by Landtman was 154 meters long—and were inhabited by the members of a single totemic clan, although two or three clans would sometimes occupy separate parts of the same house. The móto had an open passageway running lengthwise down the middle of the house and a row of fireplaces on each side. Each family had its own fireplace along the side of the house. The dárimo were constructed like the móto, but served as ceremonial houses and as residences for the unmarried men. On some occasions, married men would also sleep in the dárimo. Today, the móto and the dárimo are largely things of the past, and most villages consist of small single-family dwellings with raised floors of split palm, walls of sago palm frond stems, and thatched roofs.

Economy

Subsistence and Commercial Activities. The Kiwai are a horticultural people who get most of their food from their gardens. The alluvial soil of the Kiwai area is very rich, and they cultivate yams, taro, sweet potatoes, bananas, coconut and sago palms, sugarcane, and betel nuts. The Kiwai also hunt pigs, cassowaries, wallabies, snakes, lizards, crocodiles, and birds with bamboo bows and arrows. Larger game animals such as pigs, cassowaries, and wallabies are usually hunted with dogs. Dugongs and turtles are hunted with harpoons, and the Kiwai obtain fish with hooks and lines, spears, and traps. Fishing nets were not traditionally used by the Kiwai, but commercial nylon nets are now available. According to Landtman, a great many magical observances are associated with gardening and hunting, including the hunting of dugongs and turtles.

Industrial Arts. The Kiwai remain largely preindustrial. Prior to the arrival of Europeans, they used only stone tools, but by the time Landtman arrived in 1910 most Kiwai men had steel axes and knives. Any adult can produce the implements necessary for day-to-day living from materials found in the local environment.

Trade. Traditionally there was an extensive trade network among the Kiwai and their neighbors. From the people who lived further inland, the Kiwai obtained bird of paradise feathers, live cassowaries, bows and arrows, and garden produce, and from Torres Strait Islanders to the south they obtained harpoon shafts, shells, dugong and turtle meat, and stones for axes and clubs. In exchange, the Kiwai traded canoes, garden produce, sago, bows and arrows, mats, belts, grass skirts, and feathers. By far the most important Kiwai trade items, however, were the canoes that were traded primarily to the people of the Torres Strait in exchange for finished and unfinished stone tools. Landtman notes that it is not clear to what extent traditional trade took the form of barter since most things seem to have changed hands through mutual gift giving. Today, the Kiwai are able to buy steel tools, metal pots, Western clothes, radios, European-style foods, and other European articles from locally owned trade stores.

Division of Labor. The Kiwai have a loose sexual division of labor. Women's work includes taking care of children; carrying firewood and water; making sago; preparing food; making baskets, mats, and clothing; and fishing with hooks or traps in small creeks. Men's work includes building houses, making canoes, hunting, and open-water hunting and fishing with harpoons and spears. Both men and women garden. Men fell the trees and build fences, after which women prepare the garden. Planting may be done by either sex, although it is generally seen as men's work, and harvesting may be done by either men or women. The only exceptions are yams, which are planted and harvested only by men. In sago making, men chop down the palm and remove the bark, after which women chop and squeeze the pith. Beyond this rough sexual division of labor, there is rudimentary division of labor based on differences in skill in producing objects such as canoes, harpoons, and drums.

Land Tenure. Land is divided among the different villages, and, within the land owned by a village, land is divided among individual men, except for large swamps which belong to the entire community. While land is said to be owned by individuals, there is a strong notion that land actually belongs to a family or kin group. This prevents the alienation of land to outsiders and prevents women, who marry outside their kin group, from actually owning land. The Kiwai make a clear distinction between ownership and usufruct, however, and landowners are free to grant usufruct rights for the purpose of gardening to whomever they wish. Hunting and fishing are not restricted by landownership.

Kinship

Kin Groups and Descent. The Kiwai are divided into patrilineal totemic clans. According to Landtman, these clans are "strictly exogamous." In some areas the clans are grouped into moieties which have ritual functions and may or may not be exogamous. Married women remain members of their natal totemic clans. Descent is patrilineal.

Kinship Terminology. The Kiwai have Hawaiian-type cousin terms and generational kinship terms in the parental generation. According to Landtman, Kiwai kinship terms do not distinguish between parallel cousins and cross cousins. All cousins are addressed and referred to by the same terms as those used for siblings—terms that denote the sex of the sibling and his or her age relative to the speaker. There is, however, a special term that is used by cross cousins that is not sex-specific. Landtman also notes that matrilateral parallel cousins "are hardly considered to be related at all by blood, and no particular kinship terms are used between them; they are not, however, allowed to marry." There are five terms for members of the parental generation. Both the father's and the mother's older brothers are addressed and referred to with the term used for grandfather, and both the father's and the mother's older sisters are addressed and referred to with the term that is used for mother. Finally, both the father's and the mother's younger brothers are addressed and referred to with a compound term that includes the term for father, and both the father's and the mother's younger sisters are addressed and referred to with a compound term that includes the term for mother.

Marriage and Family

Marriage. Landtman suggests that often there was tension between individual desires and traditional marriage rules. Traditionally, a Kiwai man could marry only if he compensated his bride's father with a woman who was given as a wife to a man of the bride's family. Although some marriages began as love affairs, older people often ignored young people's wishes in arranging marriages because of this requirement of reciprocity. When Landtman was living with the Kiwai, marriages by exchange were still the rule, but marriage through the prestation of gifts to the bride's family (i.e., bride-wealth) was becoming increasingly common. Landtman argues that these gifts were primarily intended to indicate "the importance and prosperity of the donors," and he notes that reciprocal gifts were given by the bride's family to the groom's family. In some instances, a man could also obtain a wife by working for her father for a short period of time. Girls usually marry shortly after puberty. Men and women with the same totem cannot marry, nor can they marry if any of their four parents have the same totem. First cousins cannot marry, and boys and girls who are not related but have grown up together because of adoption cannot marry. There is no formal marriage ceremony, but a feast is usually held with the food provided by the groom's family. A groom should not have sexual intercourse with his bride until he has taken an enemy's head since sons who are born before their father has taken a head are subject to ridicule as they grow up. After marriage the woman moves into her husband's house. Polygyny is accepted but not generally practiced. According to Landtman, divorce was frequent and usually resulted from the wife's "incompetence" as a housekeeper and worker or from the wife's barrenness.

Domestic Unit. The nuclear family is the typical unit of production. Traditionally, the members of a totemic clan lived together in their clan's móto.

Inheritance. Land and personal belongings are divided among a man's sons. As his sons grow up a man will give them land with the final partition taking place at the time of the man's death. If a man leaves a widow and children, his sons are expected to support their mother and sisters. If a man does not have any sons, the land passes to his brothers who are supposed to look after the dead man's family. Some personal belongings are deposited in the grave, but the remainder is divided among the dead person's sons. Daughters are not entitled to inherit personal belongings, but they are often given some by their brothers.

Socialization. Children are usually nursed until they begin to talk. Women will sometimes rub ginger on their nipples to expedite weaning. A child's hair is not cut until the child begins to walk, and shortly thereafter his or her earlobes and septum are pierced. The hair is kept short until puberty when boys and girls begin to let their hair grow. Boys are not initiated at any one time but are introduced to different ceremonies as they take place. A boy, however, must have experienced the mogúru ceremony (see below) before he is ready to marry. After the mogúru ceremony, a boy will sleep in the dárimo or men's house. Landtman notes that, at least in some areas, boys "must practice sodomy in order to become tall and strong," but he states that he is not certain how widespread this belief and practice is among the Kiwai. Girls are initiated shortly after menarche. Their initiation consists of a procession and ritual bath, and the symbolism of the event emphasizes their transition from childhood to eligibility for marriage.

Sociopolitical Organization

Social Organization. There are no differences of rank among the Kiwai, and every man is the equal of every other. This is partly facilitated by there being little property which would constitute a difference in wealth. There are, however, some differences in status based on differences in skills. Successful gardeners, hunters, and harpooners, as well as renowned sorcerers, great warriors, and eloquent orators command respect and recognition from others. People with physical and mental disabilities are looked down upon, as are idlers, braggarts, and widowers who have not remarried. According to Landtman, women are almost equal to men. They possess property (except land), and they can do as they please with the things that they produce. They are, however, excluded from many public affairs and from men's religious secrets including myths and rituals. Landtman reports that a woman would be killed if she were to find out anything about the men's secrets but, outside the world of men's secrets, women publicly express their opinions and are listened to.

Political Organization. The Kiwai have no chiefs. Tribal authority is exercised collectively by several men, each of whom is the head of a totemic clan. Leaders are middle-aged men of some exceptional ability, and their influence decreases as soon as they begin to lose their physical and mental powers.

Social Control. In the case of violent death, revenge (either by sorcery or physical attack) was taken on the murderer as soon as possible. Revenge was the responsibility of the entire clan. Prior to pacification, almost every homicide led to fighting, but nowadays compensation is the usual way of settling a homicide.

Conflict. The Kiwai distinguish between hostility between clans of the same village or between related village communities and conflict between tribes that are hereditary enemies or that regularly raid one another. The first type of conflict involves few fatalities. The second type has the purpose of killing as many enemies as possible, destroying their property, and taking the heads of the people who are killed. Most conflicts are over women.

Religion and Expressive Culture

Religious Beliefs. Landtman gives little information about Kiwai religious beliefs, but he notes that their religious beliefs are not systematic. The Kiwai believe in a vast number of supernatural beings including various types of water beings, wicked female beings, and beings associated with certain localities. Virtually every conspicuous place in the landscape is thought to be the abode of a mythical being, some of which are humanlike and others of which are like animals or trees. Like many other groups in southern New Guinea, the Kiwai have a large number of myths about the life of Sido who the Kiwai believe was the first man to die and open the way to Adiri, the land of the dead.

Religious Practitioners. There are no priests and no specific training is necessary for those who perform religious ceremonies. Sorcery is learned on an individual basis from other sorcerers, and a sorcerer can demand, and will receive, almost any payment for his services. A common payment is sexual access to the client's wife. Sorcerers work by getting some part of their intended victim's body (e.g., nail or hair clippings) or personal possessions. According to Landtman, "every Kiwai man practices sorcery, without which he would have no success in any of his occupations or undertakings."

Ceremonies. The Kiwai have a large number of ceremonies including ceremonies undertaken prior to a fight expedition and ceremonies designed to make young men fearless and invulnerable in battle. They also have several important secret ceremonies including the hóriómu, the mogúru, and the mimía. The hóriómu is connected with the cult of the dead and is held each year at the beginning of the dry season (in April or May). The ceremony lasts several weeks, occupying a few hours each day before sunset. The mogúru is the most secret and most important ceremony of the Kiwai people. Traditionally, it was held once or twice a year in the dárimo. The two main purposes of the mogúru are the sexual instruction of boys and girls who have reached puberty and the preparation of a magical concoction made of herbs and semen collected from the vaginas of women following promiscuous sexual intercourse. The mimía or fire ceremony is connected with the initiation of young men. During the ceremony, the young men are burned and beaten and given magical substances that are believed to make them strong.

Arts. The Kiwai produce a great deal of representational art, and even their utilitarian wooden implements (e.g., digging or walking sticks) are often carved to represent a human face or body. Musical instruments include hourglass and cylindrical drums, rattles made from seed pods, reed whistles, panpipes, bamboo and reed flutes, shell trumpets, Jew's harps, and bullroarers. The Kiwai also make elaborate ceremonial masks from wood and turtle shells.

Medicine. Illness is believed to be caused by comets, earthquakes, sorcery, or the abduction of a person's soul by a spirit. Menstrual blood is believed to be particularly deleterious to men's health. In the case of fever, the patient is bled from the part of the body where the illness is thought to be located. Sick people are given food that is considered "strong" such as pig meat, shark meat, taro, or sago. Bananas are not eaten because they are soft, and dugong and turtle meat may not be eaten because they are associated with the spirit world. It is also bad if a sick person comes into contact with someone (man or woman) who has recently had sexual intercourse.

Death and Afterlife. Wailing begins immediately after a person dies and continues through the night. The next morning, the dead person's face is painted black, white, and red and the body is dressed in a headdress and shell ornaments. The body is then placed in a sitting position near the door of the house. After being displayed, the body is placed on a board and carried a short distance from the village where it is placed on a platform. If the person was murdered and revenge has already been taken, the murderer's head may be cut off and placed as a pillow under the head of the deceased. Water is poured over the body daily to speed decomposition. When only bones remain, they are washed and then buried in a garden belonging to the dead person. Sometimes the skull of the deceased is kept and decorated by his widow. The widow spends a period of time secluded in an enclosure of mats in the móto. A widower will not go into seclusion, but he will spend several days crying for his wife and will refrain from hunting and fishing for a long time. Both widows and widowers wear a mourning garb made of grass and consisting of a cap with long fringe and a fringed covering for his or her shoulders, chest, arms, and legs. No drums may be beaten until a feast is held a few weeks later to end the period of mourning. Ordinarily the spirits of the dead are invisible, but sometimes they can be seen and touched. A ghost may not always start its journey to the land of the dead immediately but may instead linger for a time near its former home. The Kiwai are particularly afraid of the ghosts of sorcerers and persons who have met a violent death or have died in an unusual way. Even after spirits have gone to the land of the dead, they may return to give messages to the living either through dreams or appearing to them directly. Ghosts may also possess living people.

See also Marind-anim, Torres Strait

Bibliography

Landtman, Gunnar (1917). *The Folk-Tales of the Kiwai Papuans.* Acta Societatis Scientiarum Fennicae, vol. 47. Helsinki: Finnish Society of Literature.

Landtman, Gunnar (1927). *The Kiwai Papuans of British New Guinea.* London: Macmillan.

Wurm, Stefan (1951). *Studies in the Kiwai Languages, Fly Delta, Papua, New Guinea.* Acta Ethnologica et Linguistica, no. 2. Vienna: Institut für Völkerkunde der Universität Wien.

Wurm, Stefan (1973). "The Kiwaian Language Family." In *The Linguistic Situation in the Gulf District and Adjacent Areas, Papua New Guinea,* edited by Karl Franklin, 219–260. Pacific Linguistics, Series C, no. 26. Canberra: Australian National University.

MARK BUSSE

Koiari

The Koiari (Grass Koiari) numbered about 1,800 in 1973. They live at about 9°S and 148° E in Port Moresby Subprovince, Central Province of Papua New Guinea. They are closely related to the Mountain Koiali (Mountain Koiari) who are found farther inland and at higher elevations.

See also Motu

Bibliography

Groves, Murray, et al. (1957). "Blood Groups of the Motu and Koita Peoples." *Oceania* 28:222–238.

Lawes, W. G. (1879). "Ethnological Notes on the Motu, Koitapu, and Koiari Tribes." *Journal of the Royal Anthropological Institute* 8:369–377.

Kosrae

ETHNONYMS: Kusaie, Strong's Island, Ualan (Ualang)

Orientation

Identification. Kosrae is the easternmost of the Caroline Islands. Until 1977, most maps identified it as "Kusaie," but the inhabitants have always known it as "Kosrae." The island is now one state of the Federated States of Micronesia.

Location. Kosrae is located at about 5° N and 163° E. Like other Micronesian high (volcanic) islands, its interior consists of rugged mountains. Today large parts of its 110 square kilometers have been cleared of rain forest for cultivation and settlement. Abundant rainfall, averaging about 500 centimeters annually, supports lush vegetation and feeds the many rivers. The island is surrounded by a small fringing reef, which provides both fish and canoe transportation.

Demography. Before the first contact with technologically advanced Western powers in 1824, the population was about 5,000. During the whaling era between the 1840s and the 1860s, new diseases were introduced that decimated the population. Only 200–300 Kosraens were alive in the 1870s, and many outsiders predicted total extinction. Population numbers began to recover in the 1880s and a steady growth began that continues into the present. Today the resident population is around 6,000.

Linguistic Affiliation. The Kosraen language is unique to the island and is not mutually intelligible with any other modern tongue. It is one of the Nuclear Micronesian languages, its closest historical relations being with Pohnpeian and Marshallese.

History and Cultural Relations

Archaeological work done mainly in the 1980s shows that Kosrae was definitely settled by the early first millennium A.D., although future research is expected to push this date back to the first millennium B.C. The society was highly stratified at the time of initial contact with the West. In aboriginal times, Kosrae shared many common cultural features with surrounding islands, including: matrilineal lineages and clans; social rank defined by affiliation with kin groups defined as "noble" or "commoner"; noble control over land worked mainly by commoners; elaborate redistributive exchanges; and settlements oriented around a group of close relatives sharing access to a single cook house. For several decades after their 1824 discovery by Europeans, Kosraens were victimized by whaling crews, who made deals with chiefs for the island's abundant foods, water, and female companionship. The first missionary established a station in 1852 and virtually the entire population was Christianized in the 1870s. During the Japanese mandate of 1914–1945, extensive economic development occurred, run by and for the benefit of the Japanese companies and government. The United States was granted control over Micronesia at the end of World War II. After two decades of relative neglect, in the 1960s the U.S. administration poured in money for education, health care, public works, and development projects. Employment with the government became and remains the major source of jobs and cash income, spent on food, building materials, vehicles, and other imports. Most Kosraens continue to acquire the bulk of their subsistence from traditional crops and fishing, but imports have replaced almost all other native manufactures.

Settlements

In aboriginal times, commoners lived in scattered clusters of houses averaging only about thirty to fifty people. The strong distinction between nobility and commoner was apparent in the residential segregation: noble families lived on the tiny island of Lelu located in a small bay off the east coast. Their fine residences were surrounded by enormous stone walls built of layers of basalt crystals laid horizontally, reaching heights of 7.5 meters. Nobles, served by numerous retainers, lived within these magnificent courtyards, into which no commoner could set foot without permission. In the twentieth century, the pull of access to church, stores, and other services led to increased nucleation of settlement. Today most of the population lives in one of four concentrated villages. The ancient political center of Lelu remains the capital and commercial center.

Economy

Subsistence and Commercial Activities. Aboriginally, subsistence was based on breadfruit, coconuts, bananas, taro, yams, and sugarcane. Breadfruit was the staple when in season. It was preserved in leaf-lined pits for times of scarcity. Each settlement included at least one earth oven, used for cooking. Soft taro was made into a feast food called *fahfah* by men trained in the elaborate skills needed to prepare it properly. Coconuts were reserved for the noble class. Another important crop was kava, a drink made from the roots of a plant that grew in the mountains. It was prepared for and served to members of the nobility by specialists. Fish were harvested mainly from the lagoon using nets. A medium of exchange made of shells existed, but little is known of its specific uses. In modern times, daily food for most families is a mixture of imported rice, tinned meats and fish, and locally produced fish and tree and root crops. Fahfah and pork are mainly feast foods.

Industrial Arts. Like other Micronesians, Kosraens in precontact times were especially skilled in the construction of canoes. In prehistoric times, at least, they also possessed the knowledge needed to mine and transport the basalt used to build the impressive stone walls enclosing chiefly compounds on Lelu Island. Skills needed to work with modern tools developed during the Japanese mandate, and today many islanders are electricians, carpenters, and heavy-equipment operators.

Trade. Old Kosrae was visited by neighboring atoll dwellers for purposes of trade, although evidence suggests that Kosraens themselves rarely ventured far beyond the shores of their lush homeland. German traders had firmly established the exchange of copra for imported Western articles by 1890. The sale of copra remained the major source of cash income into the 1960s. During World War II, Kosraen fields provided food crops taken to the Japanese garrison stationed in the Marshalls. Today about one in four Kosraens of appropriate age has a job, trading labor for cash used almost entirely to purchase goods imported from Japan, Australia, and the United States. Privately owned stores have sprung up to supply the new demand.

Division of Labor. Even in aboriginal times, there were crafts specialists, including cooks, fahfah makers, kava makers and servers, nannies, canoe builders, and fishers. Most or all of these specialists were attached to and provided their services for chiefs. Gender also determined the allocation of tasks: women were weavers of mats, nets, baskets, belts, and clothing, while men were cultivators, builders, cooks, and makers of earth ovens. Both sexes fished. The titled nobility did little or no farming, construction, or other forms of manual labor.

Land Tenure. Before the middle decades of the nineteenth century, the principal chief controlled the allocation of all the land on the island. He allocated control over particular districts, with their natural resources and commoner residents, to other members of the noble class. Commoners, and in theory other members of the nobility, used the land only by his leave. In return, commoners were obliged to supply regular tribute and labor services to the chief to whom their district was assigned. Today ownership is in the hands of individuals, although a group of siblings will occasionally maintain control over plots.

Kinship

Kinship Groups and Descent. Few details are known of kinship and family relations in aboriginal times. There were matrilineal clans, segmented into lineages. Clans were ranked, as were lineages within them. Certain lines of descent within at least two or three clans were considered noble, the others commoner. Whether kin groups were assigned common rights to resources or owned common property is unclear, although such rights were commonplace in neighboring islands. Clans, lineages, and matrilineal descent itself are now only memories on the island. Modern Kosraens trace their relationships bilaterally, and the kin group is the operative unit. Members of an individual's kindred are called upon for occasional communal labor and to make contributions at weddings and funerals.

Kinship Terminology. A modified Hawaiian terminology was used in precontact times. Modern Kosraens continue to use generational terminology in many contexts, but the English word *cousin* has been added to use when one wishes to distinguish degrees of relatedness within one's own generation.

Marriage and Family

Marriage. The old clans were presumably exogamous, and today exogamic restrictions apply to second cousins. Traditionally, chiefly polygyny occurred, but this ended with Christianization and modern Kosraens are so rigorously monogamous that divorce is extremely uncommon. In modern times people choose their own spouses, although parental approval is always sought and remains almost essential. Newly married couples frequently live alternately with both sets of parents for a year or more until they build a house of their own, ideally on the land of the husband if he has sufficient land and if relations with his kin are amiable. The bond between husband and wife creates new affinal relationships and binds the two sets of kin with mutual obligations of economic and social support.

Domestic Unit. Nuclear families are statistically the most common living group, but a variety of domestic arrangements occur. Children normally live with their biological parents, but this is complicated by high rates of adoption, which in the 1970s reached 25 percent in one village. A middle-aged couple with married offspring may have one or more of their children's family living with them temporarily or for long periods. Occasionally, brothers will live together with their families for short periods or even semipermanently. Elderly couples may live alone or with one of their children, according to familial circumstances.

Inheritance. In modern times, inheritance of real property is determined by a will—ideally, a written one—left by the owner, who usually attempts to provide all his male children with land suitable for the cultivation of various crops. With population growth, fragmentation of parcels often makes this impossible. Disputes among potential heirs are common, caused often by the fact that a man favors some of his children over others.

Socialization. Due to the large average family size and the fact that relatives usually live close by, young children grow up in a nurturing atmosphere. Infants are coddled by young and old alike. Although there is variation, physical punishment occurs from the age of 2, and verbal scolding is common. Children begin to perform simple household tasks such as sweeping and fetching as early as age 3 or 4. Girls help their mothers extensively with washing and other chores once they reach the age of 9 or 10. Boys accompany their fathers and older brothers to gardens at similarly young ages, and in fact today much of the harvesting of gardens is done by teen-aged boys, partly because their fathers are so often employed for wages.

Sociopolitical Organization

Social Organization. In traditional times, gender, kinship, and rank served as the main organizing principles of society. One was born into a noble or commoner kin group, and there seems to have been little possibility of social movement between these classes. Interaction between classes was governed by a rigid etiquette, including special forms of speech used by commoners towards nobles. Commoner labor and tribute provided the nobility with most of their necessities as well as luxury items. Only those of noble rank were allowed to hold titles and to control the resources and labor that titles carried with them. Hereditary rank distinctions now belong to the past, victims of nineteenth-century Christianization. Modern Kosraens with nobility in their ancestry, however, seem proud of their heritage.

Political Organization. In aboriginal days, political authority rested largely in the hands of the chiefs. One privilege enjoyed by the nobility was that of competing for one of eighteen ranked titles, whose holders were appointed by the principal chief, "Tokosra." The Tokosra was so powerful that early Western visitors referred to him as a king, noting that the people treated him like a god. The office of Tokosra was hereditary within a certain lineage of the freshwater-eel clan. Once he succeeded, the Tokosra appointed other male members of the nobility to the titles; their wives acquired the associated female titles. Because the titles were ranked and carried control over the resources and commoner labor of particular districts on the island, considerable competition and conflict arose among the nobility for appointment and promotion. Ordinarily, this took the form of feasting and rendering extra service and gifts to the Tokosra, in order to win a title or to be promoted to a higher title carrying control over more resources and people. Armed conflicts also are known to have occurred over succession. The fifty to sixty named districts were the lowest level of the political structure, where the commoner population lived and worked. Each district was headed by a commoner overseer, who acted as a mediator between the residents and the chief assigned to administer the district. With the loss of population and Christianization in the last decades of the nineteenth century, this political system declined. Today the island has its own state legislature and sends elected representatives to the Congress of Micronesia.

Social Control. As in other complex chiefdoms, the titled nobility of old Kosrae had many rights over the persons and properties of commoners, which they used to reward diligence and support as well as to punish laziness and recalcitrance. Since the island became Christian 100 years ago, the main source of social control has been the church membership and church-sponsored activities. Those who smoke tobacco, drink alcohol, have illicit sexual relations, or are in a state of anger or conflict with their relatives or neighbors face excommunication and the possibility of eternal damnation. The threat of excommunication remains a deterrent against antisocial or culturally prohibited behaviors. Reinstatement occurs by means of public confession and repentance at a monthly service.

Conflict. Little is known of interpersonal conflicts in precontact days. Recurrent, patterned, large-scale conflicts were associated with political and prestige rivalries, primarily among the titled nobility. Although usually rivalries took the form of competitive feasting and gift giving, in 1837 one chief, together with his six brothers and commoner supporters, deposed an unpopular Tokosra by force. Also, prior to contact, quarrels over just which lines in one clan were truly noble led commoners in several districts to rebel (unsuccessfully). Unfortunately, little is known of the frequency and intensity of such rebellions. In modern times, the church's influence has spared the island from some of the fighting associated with young male drunkenness in much of Micronesia—although such violent encounters are far from uncommon on weekends. Intrafamily conflicts occur, as everywhere, but are usually settled quickly. Perhaps the main source of serious, enduring disputes today is land. Close relatives (e.g., siblings) quarrel over inheritance and use rights. The failure of previous generations in settling land issues means that distant relatives often find themselves at odds over ownership of particular parcels. Nevertheless, Kosrae is a remarkably peaceful island overall. Almost all fighting is alcohol-related, and as late as the 1970s no one could recall a violent death except for those associated with World War II battles.

Religion and Expressive Culture

Religious Beliefs. Little is known of the aboriginal religion, other than that it was polytheistic and involved ritual processions to Lelu led by priests. A goddess of breadfruit seems to have been most important. Modern Kosraens are known throughout Micronesia for their staunch religiosity and the church is very much the center of their public life. They believe that membership in the Kosraen church is necessary for their salvation. The sincerity of one's commitment to the church and to God is shown by one's "work," such as regular attendance at church services and social functions, living a clean moral life, and monetary support of church activities and building programs.

Religious Practitioners. Today each village has its own church, its own pastor and deacons, and a plethora of offices and committees. There is in addition an overarching committee that meets periodically to deliberate issues that face the Kosraen church community as a whole. Competition for annually elected high offices in the village churches is largely covert but nonetheless serious, for incumbents enjoy considerable respect.

Ceremonies. Aside from Sunday services (morning, afternoon, and evening), the church organizes a variety of social as well as religious activities. Most of these involve feasts, for which people spend weeks preparing. Major annual events include Liberation Day (which commemorates the day U.S. forces captured the island from the Japanese), Christmas, and installation days for winners of high church offices. Dedications of new church buildings also are islandwide events.

Arts. In aboriginal times, bodies were decorated with tattoos. Pandanus leaves used to make sleeping mats and clothing were dyed and woven into geometric patterns. Very finely woven belts were made of banana fibers dyed and woven into pleasing designs. Today, only the weaving of mats survives. Other than a few crafts produced for the very limited tourist trade and the sewing of dresses for use on ceremonial occasions, Kosraens are uninterested in expression through graphic arts. Great creativity is shown, however, in composing new hymns to be sung in church at several year-end events.

Medicine. Little is known of precontact treatments. Today people seek care at a new hospital completed in the late 1970s. A few women continue to practice folk medicine, especially massages, which are often given to pregnant women.

Death and Afterlife. Funerals receive extensive ceremonial treatment. The body lies in state for three days, usually at the house of the deceased's closest male relative. Relatives and friends visit the family, to pay their respects and to "cheer them up." To supply the hundreds of guests, close kin of the family contribute enormous quantities of food, today mainly imports. Aside from year-end church events, funerals and weddings are consistently the largest social gatherings on the island.

See also Yap

Bibliography

Fischer, John L., and Ann M. Fischer (1966). *The Eastern Carolines.* New Haven, Conn.: Human Relations Area Files Press.

Peoples, James G. (1985). *Island in Trust.* Boulder, Colo.: Westview Press.

Ritter, Philip L. (1978). "*The Repopulation of Kosrae.*" Ph.D. dissertation, Stanford University.

Ritter, Philip L., and Lynn T. Ritter (1982). *The European Discovery of Kosrae Island.* Micronesian Archaeological Survey Report no. 13. Saipan, Commonwealth of the Northern Marianas.

JAMES G. PEOPLES

Kurtatchi

ETHNONYMS: Buka, Timputs, Tinputz, Wasio

Orientation

Identification. Strictly speaking, the name "Kurtatchi" refers to a single village, the subject in 1930 of a classic ethnographic study by Beatrice Blackwood. Modern usage would suggest designating the people by the language they speak, Tinputz.

Location. Tinputz speakers occupy part of the northernmost portion of the island of Bougainville, near the passage separating Bougainville from Buka Island, approximately 5° S and 154° E. The area ranges from sea level to about 100 meters above, in moderately high relief; the characteristic slope is one of high gradient. Temperatures range from 22° to 32° C, and 250 to 300 centimeters of rain are more or less evenly distributed throughout the year.

Demography. In 1930, Kurtatchi village contained 136 people. The entire population of Bougainville before European contact has been estimated at 45,000. In 1963, there were an estimated 1,390 Tinputz speakers. There has been a sharp increase in Bougainville's population since that time.

Linguistic Affiliation. Tinputz forms a family with Teop and Hahon; together with the Petats, Banoni, and Torau families and the Nissan and Nahoa languages, they are part of the Bougainville Austronesian Stock. Today, most younger people also speak Tok Pisin, the lingua franca of Papua New Guinea, or English.

History and Cultural Relations

There is evidence of human occupation on Buka Island more than 28,000 years ago. Speakers of Austronesian languages like Tinputz have been regarded as late arrivals in Bougainville, relative to people in the southern part of the island, who speak entirely different languages. Almost certainly Austronesian languages were spoken there more than 3,000 years ago. Austronesian communities in north Bougainville and Buka Island formed a cultural group, distinguished from southerners by such characteristics as use of large plank canoes, greater importance of fishing and trading, formal initiation for boys, inherited political rank, prohibited cross-cousin marriage and, probably, cannibalism. Bougainville Island was sighted in 1768 by the French navigator for whom it was named. During the latter part of the nineteenth century, traders and labor recruiters operated on the island, to which Imperial Germany laid claim in 1886. Australia administered what had been German New Guinea from 1914 to 1975. Since then, Bougainville has been part of the North Solomons Province of the independent nation of Papua New Guinea. Europeans took up land in Bougainville, including the Tinputz area, for coconut plantations beginning in the early 1900s and continuing until World War II. Tinputz speakers, who had been recruited for plantations elsewhere in the Pacific, also were employed locally. Bougainville was occupied by the Japanese in World War II, and subsequent military action did considerable damage to the island and its people. Since that time, rapidly changing political and economic conditions have sometimes proved socially disruptive throughout Bougainville.

Settlements

Tinputz speakers lived in scattered hamlets along the coast, atop cliffs which rose up from the shore, and, less often, slightly inland. People were under continual pressure from the government and missions to consolidate settlements, which were probably smaller in precontact times. Houses were aligned, and the hamlet was fenced except toward the shoreline. An important feature of each hamlet was a men's house, especially used for boys' initiation. Houses were built directly on the ground of sago-palm thatch, in the shape of a broad Gothic arch, a form distinctive of the Austronesian-language speakers of the north. Australian administrators urged people to build houses raised on piles for hygienic reasons, and today some Tinputz live in houses made of European materials with floor plans like those found in more urban settings.

Economy

Subsistence and Commercial Activities. Tinputz were typical Melanesian swidden horticulturalists, growing taro as a staple crop. Coconuts were grown for food and, after contact and with administration encouragement, as a cash crop. When a taro disease swept through Bougainville during World War II, sweet potatoes became more important in the diet. Bonito fishing was an important male activity. Some Tinputz men worked as plantation laborers in Bougainville and elsewhere before World War II, but they devoted more time to their own cash crops thereafter. A major cash crop today is cocoa. Those Tinputz with higher education, like their peers elsewhere in Papua New Guinea, are now employed in the modern, urban economic sector.

Industrial Arts. Traditional crafts included canoe building, wood carving, and making mats, baskets, and rain hoods from pandanus leaves. Most of these arts are still practiced.

Trade. The most important form of traditional exchange was between coastal and inland villages, trading fish for taro. Tinputz also exchanged various items for pottery produced on Buka. Two forms of currency were used traditionally: strings of teeth, either of flying fox or porpoise, and strings of shell discs. However, these were special-purpose currencies only, used for marriages and other socially important occasions. Tinputz and other Bougainvilleans began sporadic trading with European ships in the nineteenth century, exchanging coconuts and other food items for metal tools, among other things. European administrations imposed a head tax early in the colonial period, which forced the development of a cash economy: the islanders began to produce copra and to work for wages. Today all are involved to some degree in a modern cash economy.

Division of Labor. Like other Melanesians, Tinputz traditionally divided subsistence tasks according to gender: men did the heavy work of clearing land for gardens, built fences, houses, and canoes, hunted, and fished beyond the reef while women gardened, cooked, gathered marine life from the reef, and bore most responsibility for child rearing. Men were much more active than women in the economy established during the colonial period, working as casual or indentured laborers, and are still overrepresented in higher education and the cash economy. However, women today may grow and market cash crops.

Land Tenure. Blackwood describes land as belonging to a village, but with managerial rights vested in the highest-ranking clan. It is most likely that rights to land could be obtained through more than one kind of social connection: clan membership, locality, marriage, or individual kin networks. Trees might be individually claimed and today, when much land is planted in cash-crop trees, there are more disputes over land as people seek individual ownership in a European pattern.

Kinship

Kin Groups and Descent. The basic kin group is the matrilineage, traditionally occupying a single hamlet, to which the lineage claimed ultimate rights in land. Matrilineages were grouped into exogamous clans which, being dispersed, did not normally act as corporate units. Like other Bougainvilleans, Tinputz were uninterested in genealogy in a Western sense.

Kinship Terminology. Tinputz terminology was a variant of the Iroquois system, in which siblings are equated with parallel cousins and terminologically distinguished from cross cousins.

Marriage and Family

Marriage. Blackwood maintains that there was no preferred marriage pattern, only restrictions. Cross cousins as well as parallel cousins were forbidden to marry. Child betrothal was common, typically negotiated between the boy's father and the girl's mother. Marriage involved a series of exchanges of food and other items between the two sets of relatives; a bride-price was paid in porpoise or flying-fox teeth currency. Polygyny was confined to men of higher rank. A man might inherit his brother's widow and a widower lay claim to his deceased wife's sister. Residence after marriage was uxorilocal; divorce was frequent and easy. Today, polygyny and child betrothal have ceased, but bride-wealth is still paid in traditional valuables. Furthermore, marriages are contracted beyond the language, or even the ethnic group, since educated young people are more likely to seek out their peers in adopting European life-styles.

Domestic Unit. Traditionally, households consisted of a married couple and immature children. In polygynous marriages, each wife had her own dwelling. Occasionally an aged parent of either sex might join an adult child's household. During their initiation period, adolescent boys lived in the men's house. The nuclear family household continues to be the norm today, while adolescent children may go away for secondary education.

Inheritance. Since much of a deceased person's property, such as pigs or productive trees, was traditionally consumed or destroyed during funeral observances, inheritance was not of great significance. Traditional valuables and rank were inherited matrilineally. Today, cash-crop trees or money normally pass from parents of either sex to their children.

Socialization. An individual's kindred was the group of greatest influence in daily life, and fathers took an active part in caring for small children. Many events in a child's life, such as first appearance in public after birth or a first trip to the garden, were marked with ceremonies, especially if the child was of high rank. However, the most distinctive aspect of socialization among the Tinputz and several other Austronesian groups in Bougainville was the initiation of boys, involving the wearing of the *upe* hat. This distinctive headgear was made from leaves of a fan palm, stretched over a bamboo frame to form a cylindrical, or melon, shape. Although the upe was light, it was clumsy and the wearer had to learn to keep it in position during daily activities. For several years, beginning at age 8 or 9 until the upe was formally removed, the boy was never supposed to be seen by a woman without the hat. The removal ceremony involved cutting the boy's hair, which was quite long by that time. A girl, especially an eldest daughter or one of high rank, might be the subject of seclusion and celebration at menarche, but such observances were not carried out for all. Today, socialization for both sexes involves formal education, at least to the primary level and extending for a few to tertiary schooling.

Sociopolitical Organization

Social Organization. Traditional Tinputz society was relatively egalitarian, especially in comparison with some other Melanesian groups. Relations between the sexes tended toward complementarity, rather than hierarchy; women as well as men could inherit high rank. Today, distinctions of wealth and education are more notable.

Political Organization. Traditional Tinputz hamlets appear to have operated as autonomous units. Within each hamlet, the senior male and female of the most important lineage were recognized as *tsunaun,* a "person of importance." It is not clear how much real power the tsunaun exercised before European contact, but the position seems to have been one of influence and status, rather than necessarily of political authority. Tsunaun were certainly treated deferentially and stages in their life cycle were occasions for elaborate ceremonies. Male tsunaun normally had several wives. Rank was not based on property; succession passed matrilineally. German and Australian administrations appointed village headmen, and today Tinputz elect representatives to the Provincial Assembly and to the Papua New Guinea House of Assembly.

Social Control. The tsunaun was supposed to settle disputes within his own village, and may have had the power to pass the death sentence on someone guilty of persistent antisocial behavior. However, a much more pervasive method of social control lay in the fear of harmful magic that could be performed by a victim against an offender. The usual way of expressing anger was to break up one's own personal possessions. Today Tinputz are subject to the laws of Papua New Guinea, which include a system of village courts for settling local disputes.

Conflict. A state of sporadic warfare existed before colonization, especially between coastal and interior dwellers, but also among coastal people themselves. A tsunaun was expected to lead his village or even a group of villages in such conflict. It seems that warfare took the form of raids and ambushes, rather than pitched battles. One motive for raids was the capture of prisoners to be eaten. Colonial administrations regarded eliminating warfare as a first task, but groups living inland from the Tinputz continued cannibal raids on coastal villages until after World War II.

Religion and Expressive Culture

Religious Beliefs. To a Western observer, traditional Tinputz life seemed filled with supernaturalism. Most daily activities involved consideration of spells, magic, and attention to spirit beings. Tinputz do not seem to have recognized a category of supernaturals that might be called "divinities." By far the most important spirits were those of deceased humans. Although they were generally regarded with dread, they might also be propitiated and called upon to aid in gardening and other activities. The same term, *ura,* was applied to spirits thought to inhabit particular locales. Roman Catholic missionaries began work in Bougainville in 1902, and Methodist and Seventh-Day Adventist missionaries arrived after World War I. Methodist (now United Church) presence is today very strong in the Tinputz area.

Religious Practitioners. There were no full-time religious specialists, but many individuals were believed to have special knowledge to influence events (e.g., every village had its rainmaker). Mission teachers and United Church pastors play a role in today's religious life.

Ceremonies. As noted, life-cycle ceremonies were the most significant for Tinputz, but almost any activity might have associated with it spells or magical substances. Missionization brought Sunday and other Christian observances.

Arts. Music, dance, and other aesthetic activities were intimately connected to ceremonial life. Slit gongs, wooden trumpets, panpipes, bullroarers, musical bows, and Jew's harps were used for different occasions. Utilitarian objects like lime pots and canoe paddles were decorated, but carved wooden figures, especially of ura spirits, were traditionally associated with religious observance.

Medicine. Tinputz did not make the Western distinction between medicine and religion. Illness was thought to be brought by malevolent spirits or magic performed by an enemy. Although plant and other materials were used for curing, their efficacy was as much supernatural as pharmacological. Western medicine has stamped out yaws and Hansen's disease, but malaria continues to be a serious health problem.

Death and Afterlife. Except in the case of the very young or very old, Tinputz regarded all deaths as caused by malicious human or spirit beings. The dead were believed to go to the active volcano at Mount Balbi, but some remained near the living in the form of ura. Tinputz living on the shore originally threw the dead into the sea; however, burial had been adopted even before Christianity became dominant. Mourning was enjoined for widows and, in the case of a tsunaun's death, for a whole village.

See also Nissan

Bibliography

Allen, Jerry, and Conrad Hurd (1963). *Languages of the Bougainville District.* Ukarumpa, Papua New Guinea: Summer Institute of Linguistics.

Blackwood, Beatrice (1935). *Both Sides of Buka Passage.* Oxford: Clarendon Press.

Oliver, Douglas L. (1949). *Studies in the Anthropology of Bougainville, Solomon Islands.* Cambridge, Mass.: Peabody Museum, Harvard University.

Spriggs, Matthew (1984). "The Lapita Cultural Complex: Origins, Distribution, Contemporaries, and Successors." *The Journal of Pacific History* 19:202–223.

EUGENE OGAN

Kwoma

ETHNONYMS: Nukuma, Washkuk, Waskuk

Orientation

Identification. The Kwoma are located in the Ambunti Sub-Province of the Sepik River region of Papua New Guinea. The people are divided into two dialect groups. One is located in the Washkuk Hills, a range of low mountains on the north side of the Sepik adjacent to the Ambunti Patrol Post; the other is situated to the north and west of the Washkuk range along tributaries of the Sepik. Members of the former identify themselves as "Kwoma," or "hill people," and refer to the latter as "Nukuma," or "headwater people." Linguists give the name Kwoma to the language as a whole and Nukuma to its northern dialect. "Washkuk" or Waskuk is a government name of uncertain derivation for the language and the people.

Location. The total area the people occupy coincides roughly with that of the Washkuk Hills Census District, an area of 485 kilometers located between 4° and 5° S and 142° and 143° E. Climate is of the tropical-forest type.

Demography. Kwoma speakers in the Washkuk Hills number approximately 2,000, Nukuma speakers 1,200. Population density is 5.8 persons per square kilometer.

Linguistic Affiliation. Kwoma is one of ninety or so distinct Papuan or Non-Austronesian languages that make up the Sepik-Ramu Phylum. Kwoma is classified in the Nukuma Language Family.

History and Cultural Relations

Kwoma trace their origin to various "holes" in the ground in Nukuma territory. Linguistically, Kwoma is closely related to Kwanga, spoken by a substantially larger population in the southern foothills of the Torricelli Mountains 48 kilometers to the north, and almost certainly the Kwoma people have migrated during recent centuries from this region to their present sites. First European contact took place shortly before World War I, when the region was under German control, but European society had minimal impact until after World War II. Christian missions have been active since the 1950s, and most people are nominal adherents to one denomination or another. Most men have worked for several years elsewhere in Papua New Guinea as wage laborers or in the employ of churches, the army, or the police force. In everyday life people speak Kwoma among themselves, and New Guinea pidgin with outsiders. Few speak English.

Settlements

Traditionally, the population was divided among a number of large but discrete settlement groups composed of numerous hamlets separated by gardens and stretches of forest. In the Washkuk Hills all settlements were located on hilltops. At the center of each hamlet was one or more huge ceremonial buildings (in pidgin, *haus tambaran*), which were used as men's clubhouses and as the venues for rituals. Dwellings were scattered in a rough circle around the periphery of the hamlet. Following pacification around 1945, settlements in the Washkuk Hills were relocated to sites next to or near waterways. Several of these settlements simultaneously divided into two or more distinct villages. Contemporary villages are more consolidated than formerly and are composed of wards occupied by members of individual clans; most of them have one or more centrally situated ceremonial buildings. In common with those of other "hill" cultures in the same region, houses formerly were built directly on the ground. Today houses (but not kitchens) tend to be raised on piles. During the day, when they are not working out of the village, people sit outside (or underneath) their houses; this facilitates friendly interaction with neighbors and passersby, the importance of which Kwoma emphasize.

Economy

Subsistence and Commercial Activities. Kwoma subsist principally on wild sago, which is locally abundant, and the produce of swiddens, including yams, taro, and bananas. Animal protein is provided predominantly by fish. Kwoma do not keep domestic pigs, though pigs and cassowaries are occasionally hunted for food, mainly on ceremonial occasions. The Sepik River region has little economic potential in Western terms. Very few Kwoma earn income from cash crops or other commercial activities. The main cash crop is coffee. In villages, individual families often run small trade stores, selling such goods as batteries, kerosene, and soap.

Division of Labor. In economic activities there is a division of labor between the sexes: men undertake the heaviest tasks such as house building and clearing forest for gardens, while women perform the majority of household duties. But the division is not rigid and men regularly assist with such activities as cooking and the care of children and women with garden clearing and maintenance. Sago processing, the major economic activity, is undertaken by the male and female members of individual households working independently.

Trade. Kwoma villages closest to the Sepik trade with adjacent river villages. Trade is conducted both privately through ties of "friendship" and at regular markets. Kwoma exchange sago and other "bush" products such as betel nuts for fish and currency shells. Trading at markets is conducted by women.

Land Tenure. Land is used mainly for subsistence purposes; the low population density up to now has helped to ensure against pressure on this resource.

Kinship

Kin Groups and Descent. The basic kin groups are named, exogamous, patrilineal, patrilocal clans. In theory, members of a single clan trace descent by known agnatic links from a common, named, human male forbear. Some clans are agnatically linked through their founders to other exogamous groups, but such larger patrilineal units are not named and do not unite for action in any context. Each clan "owns" a large number of totems, principally plants and animal species. Totemic species are classified as either "male" or "female": "male" species (e.g., different types of fish) provide the majority of men's names, "female" species (e.g., most birds, including the cassowary and birds of paradise) the majority of women's names. Clans that share the same or similar sets of totems form named divisions of classes; such divisions cross village, tribal, and even linguistic boundaries. Members of clans in the same totemic division regard each other as kin. A person's other major class of relatives are those by marriage. People who are neither kin nor affines are "unrelated" or "strangers." Clans in the same totemic division may intermarry.

Kinship Terminology. Kwoma terminology follows the Omaha system. Relationship terms also conflate laterally members of individual clans of the same sex and relative age, regardless of the degree of genealogical connection. Thus, a person refers to all clanswomen of his or her own generation as "true sisters" and kinsmen of his or her first ascending generation as "true fathers." "Classificatory" sisters and fathers are persons of equivalent sex and generation in other clans in the same totemic division.

Marriage and Family

Marriage. As with many Papua New Guinea societies, individual marriages give rise to alliances between groups that endure for up to four generations. Such alliances are made manifest, and defined, by continuing asymmetrical exchanges of food and wealth objects between members of wife-giving and wife-taking lines; food goes to wife-taking lines, wealth (in "payment" for the food) to wife-giving. Members of such lines also exchange a variety of reciprocal economic and political services, such as assistance in gardening, house building, and, formerly, warfare. The major occasions on which members of a wife-taking line give wealth to members of a wife-giving line are: at marriage (from the husband to the wife's brother); when the oldest child of the marriage reaches puberty (from the children's father to their mother's brother); and on the deaths of the wife and each child. The death payment for an unmarried girl, like that of a son, goes to the deceased's mother's clan; the death payment for a married woman, like her bride-wealth payment, goes to her natal clan. For the duration of an affinal alliance no further marriages may take place between the same two lines (though they may between other members of the same two clans). This restriction means that marriage is prohibited with a wide range of relatives, thus ensuring that marriages, and hence political alliances, are widely dispersed between clans and villages. Kwoma do not "prescribe" marriage with particular categories of relatives. A person's choice of a spouse should be acceptable to their clan as a whole, and traditionally an individual's first marriage was arranged. Clans corporately participate in the bride-wealth, puberty, and death payments in which their members are involved, either as donors or receivers of wealth. Clans that become too small to make such inter-group prestations independently fuse with other groups and pool their resources. Clans that grow too large for all members to receive a significant share of a bride-wealth or death payment divide into two or more separate clans. Divorce is strongly discouraged, especially during the early years of a marriage when part of the bride-wealth payment would have to be returned, but marriages may legitimately be terminated because of factors such as serious personal incompatibility, abandonment by a spouse, or a man taking an additional wife polygynously without the first wife's approval as convention requires. If a woman dies shortly after she marries, her clansmen may provide a clan sister in her place; when a man dies his widow is strongly encouraged, but cannot be compelled, to marry leviratically.

Domestic Unit. Each family, monogamous or polygynous, owns at least one "sleeping house" (in which men sleep with their wives and their children) and an adjacent kitchen. All sexually mature females in a household have separate hearths in which they do their own cooking. In polygynous households each wife usually has a separate house, or a walled-off section of a common house. Polygyny is practiced by only a minority of men, usually village seniors, many of whom acquire additional wives as part of the levirate. A woman may agree to her husband taking a second or subsequent wife (e.g., an older brother's widow) only if the marriage remains nonsexual. Younger women prefer to marry monogamously, since sexual jealousy between cowives of childbearing age is common. When sons in a household reach adulthood they normally build houses next to their father's, to which they bring their wives at marriage.

Inheritance. Clans are independent land-holding and ritual units, and a clan's estate in land and ritual paraphernalia, as well as such intangible property as totemic names and exchange rights in clan-exogamous females, are inherited by their male members. Out-married clan females are often allocated usufructuary rights in parcels of their clan's land, but they cannot pass these rights to their children. A man's and woman's movable personal property, such as spears, cooking vessels, pets, and transistor radios, is not inherited by a clan member but passes to other groups as part of their death payments.

Socialization. Child rearing is the responsibility of the parents and older siblings. Emphasis is placed on self-reliance and strength in interpersonal relations but also on awareness of the rights of others. Children learn principally by observing and imitating. By about the age of 10 girls have acquired all of the economic skills a married woman requires to maintain a household, and by the same age boys can perform most routine masculine activities. Traditionally, boys at or near puberty were incarcerated for several weeks in enclosures in which magic was performed on them to encourage their growth and make them skilled hunters, and in which they received intensive instruction in the society's complex dual literature. Each boy was assigned a "ceremonial father" from his clan who looked after him during initiation and became a lifelong ally. Older men commonly underwent a simultaneous period of seclusion during which outstanding big-men instructed them in advanced magical and ritual techniques. Both initiation rites, named "Handapiya" and "Nal" respectively, have effectively now been abandoned. Today, men's initiation takes the form of first participation in one or another of the first two yam harvest ceremonies, "Yena" and "Minja." The sculptures displayed during these rites, though differing in form, both constitute highly condensed symbolic expressions of traditional ideals that men still hold in relation to themselves, principally those of men as hunters of animals and killers of others in warfare, and as creators: horticulturally as growers of yams and in human terms as procreators of children. When novices participate in these ceremonies and gradually acquire familiarity with the hitherto secret sculptures, including the way they are painted and decorated, they begin in earnest to master their community's esoteric knowledge and to inculcate these masculine ideals.

Sociopolitical Organization

Political Organization. Kwoma are divided into a number of named, politically autonomous tribes. Traditionally, the clans composing a tribe formed a discrete settlement group (see above); today several tribes can be divided into two or more villages. Leadership at the tribal level is exercised by men who have risen to positions of prominence through their debating skills, their greater knowledge of social and ritual matters, and, formerly, their prowess in warfare. "Big-men" usually are also outstanding artists. There are no inherited political offices. Political leaders reach the height of their power in their sixth and seventh decades. Men under the age of about 50 carry little weight in tribal politics. Today, individual villages elect councillors to represent them in the Ambunti Local Government Council.

Conflict and Social Control. Formerly, warfare between tribes was common. Warfare between clans in the same tribe was strongly reprobated, but such clans were and still are believed to fight with sorcery, suspicion of which is the major cause of lasting ill-feeling between individuals and clans in the same tribe. Intratribal conflict ideally is resolved nonlethally, through discussion, mediation by clan leaders, (traditionally) fighting with sticks, and payments of compensation in shell wealth. Village leaders regularly convene meetings in the ceremonial houses, attended by all members of the local community, to resolve disputes and discuss other matters of village concern. Long-standing unresolved conflict is believed to precipitate retaliatory sorcery.

Religion and Expressive Culture

Religious Beliefs. Although nominally Christian, Kwoma have a traditionally oriented ritual and aesthetic life. They believe in a complex pantheon of spirits. These fall into two categories: "bush" or "water" spirits occupying streams, boulders, or other natural features, collectively termed (in pidgin) *masalai*; and clan spirits depicted by ceremonial carvings.

Ceremonies. The three major contemporary Kwoma rituals focus on the harvesting of yams; in each, men display different styles of painted and decorated wooden sculptures depicting powerful clan spirits (the agents thought responsible for the continuing fertility of yam gardens) and dance around these sculptures singing complex song cycles that celebrate incidents of note in the histories of individual clans. Previously, Kwoma performed a separate yam-planting ceremony that focused on the display of a distinctive style of carved female figure, but this ritual has now been abandoned. Women's participation in rituals is limited to dancing and singing outside men's houses on specific ceremonial occasions; women know the songs men perform and enthusiastically join in the choruses.

Arts. Like other Sepik peoples they are famous for their plastic art, principally wood carvings and paintings on bark. The bulk of plastic art decorates ceremonial buildings. The ceilings of these structures are lined with hundreds of paintings of totemic species, and the posts and beams are lavishly carved with sculptures depicting mythological personages and spirits. Kwoma men's houses are among the greatest of all artwork in the Pacific region.

Medicine. All serious illnesses, and deaths other than those from direct physical violence, are attributed to sorcery. Kwoma believe that serious illnesses (e.g., tuberculosis) can only be cured effectively if the initial conflicts that gave rise to the sorcery that caused them are resolved.

Death and Afterlife. Kwoma do not dwell on the afterlife and have no notion of a person's actions being punished or rewarded in the hereafter. The souls of the dead are thought to live in ghostly villages deep in the forest or, in the case of the most prominent men, in a subterranean world entered through lagoons. Kwoma practice double burial. The second burial, which takes place a year or more after the first, coincides with the complete decomposition of the body and marks the formal end of the period of mourning and the permanent departure of the deceased's soul for the land of the dead. Corpses were formerly exposed on platforms; today they are buried in cemeteries. Although now illegal, a traditional practice persists in which various bones are recovered during the second burial and fashioned into daggers and other items of traditional adornment. Skulls of outstanding warriors and debaters are buried beside the main posts of men's houses to give added "strength" to the buildings.

Bibliography

Bowden, Ross (1983). *Yena: Art and Ceremony in a Sepik Society.* Oxford: Pitt Rivers Museum.

Bowden, Ross (1983). "Kwoma Terminology and Marriage Alliance: The "Omaha" Problem Revisited." *Man* 18:745–765.

Whiting, John W. F. (1941). *Becoming a Kwoma: Teaching and Learning in a New Guinea Tribe.* New Haven: Yale University Press.

ROSS BOWDEN

Lak

ETHNONYMS: Butam, Guramalum, Laget, Lambel, Pugusch, Siar, Siarra

Orientation

Identification. Lak is the name of a coastal Papua New Guinea population and encompasses two groups that are no longer distinct: inland dwellers who relocated to the coast at the time of Western contact (c. 1900) and an original coastal-dwelling group. The name has been adopted by the New Ireland provincial government and designates an electorate composed almost exclusively of Lak speakers. The word "Lak" corresponds to the English word "hey" and is commonly used as a greeting.

Location. The Lak reside on the southernmost eastern coast of New Ireland, inhabiting a strip of land that rarely extends more than a quarter of a mile inland before steep foothills make settlements and gardening untenable. Siar village, at the center of the Lak electorate, lies roughly at 153° E, 4°30' S. The northern border of the Lak area is marked roughly by the Mimias River and the beginning of the Susurunga region. Included in this region are two outlying islands with significant settlements, Lambom and Lamassa. The region is largely tropical rain forest and lies just below the equator. The rainy season is generally between June and September, the period of *taubar,* or the southeast monsoon. This period stands in contrast to *labur,* the months in which the northwest wind is strongest and rain may be as infrequent as once every twenty days. This alternation reverses the pattern typical of northern New Ireland and the neighboring Gazelle Peninsula of New Britain.

Demography. There are no reliable estimates of the precontact population. Today, there are roughly 1,700 Lak speakers. While the population is currently expanding, this figure represents the effects of depopulation brought on by world war and disease in the 1940s and 1950s.

Linguistic Affiliation. Lak is a member of the Patpatar-Tolai Subgroup of Austronesian languages. There is no great dialectal variation across the region. Use of the vernacular is strong, even though all but the most elderly women speak Melanesian pidgin (Tok Pisin) fluently. Formal linguistic study of Lak has yet to be undertaken.

History and Cultural Relations

While a number of European explorers laid anchor at Cape Saint George (including Dampier, Carteret, Bougainville, and Duperry), only Duperry's crew, in 1824, made contact with the population. Two members of this crew, Blosseville and Lesson, were the first to report of the *duk-duk,* or masked men's society, in New Ireland. The last half of the nineteenth century saw a great deal of "blackbirding," or impressment of New Irelanders into plantation service in Australia and Samoa; however, few Lak speakers fell victim to such servitude because of their continued movement from coast to interior and their generally hostile attitude toward Europeans. In 1880, Charles Bonaventure du Breuil, the self-styled "Marquis de Rays," chose the Lak region as the site for "Port Breton," a large-scale attempt at colonization that led to famine for the colonists and a jail term for their leader. Major European penetration of the area did not occur until 1904, when Germany enforced its colonial claim by sending a punitive expedition against an interior Lak group. By about 1915, most of the interior groups had relocated to the coast, where copra planting and trade with Europeans were well under way. By this time, pacification was complete. Following World War I, the area reverted to English and then Australian control, but the region appears to have seen even less Western contact with time.

Settlements

Lak settlements are small and dispersed. A large village consists of ten to fifteen houses, containing at most seventy to eighty people. Villages are usually affiliated with nearby satellite hamlets, each consisting of one to three houses. Only in densely populated Lambom Island, where land and water are scarce, is this pattern altered. Men gather to build houses collectively, but each house is occupied by a single nuclear family. At the margin of each community is a *triun,* or place forbidden to women and children. This area is used for men's society activities. Near the triun, or sometimes within the village proper, is a men's house (*pal*). Bachelors, but also all men whose daughters have reached puberty, sleep in the pal. Lak villages are located along the coast in areas cleared of coconut palms. Copra stands and betel palms ring the villages, while gardens lie farther off.

Economy

Subsistence and Commercial Activities. The household is the basic unit of production and consumption, though villages are also knit together in extensive food-sharing relations. The staple is taro in the northern half of the district, and a combination of manioc and sweet potatoes in the south. Every household plants two concurrent swidden gardens, one along the beach, which is devoted exclusively to manioc and pineapples, and a more diverse garden inland, which may contain taro, yams, sweet potatoes, melons, sugarcane, bananas, spinach-type greens, and a variety of newly introduced vegetables. Tubers are planted with a digging stick. Gardens are fenced and set with traps to prevent domestic and wild pigs from ravaging crops. Manioc is grated, mixed with coconut oil, and baked in earth ovens to form a kind of bread (*gem, komkom*). Individual-size portions of this bread are exchanged between households two or three times a week, along with plates of cooked food. The people also gather a great range of wild fruits and nuts. The major source of protein is pigs, especially those raised within villages, which are mainly killed as part of mortuary commemorations. These pigs roam freely through villages, despite efforts to fence them as a way to improve village hygiene. Wild pigs and cuscus are hunted with spears. Reefs provide a great variety of shellfish. Lak also fish and are adept at catching large ocean-dwelling turtles. Turtle eggs are collected from the beach and are highly prized. Each household also harvests coconuts and cocoa as a source of hard currency. As of 1986, this arduous work netted an enterprising household no more than $400 yearly. The major cash expense for households involves fees for schooling, and few are able to send children to high school.

Industrial Arts. Items produced include canoes, plaited mats and baskets, wooden bowls, and traps to snare feral pigs.

Trade. Intervillage trade currently centers on pigs, which are transported live between lineage leaders planning to host mortuary commemorations. In the precontact period, Lak traded foodstuffs and ritual paraphernalia in an interisland network that stretched between southern New Ireland and the outlying islands of Nissan and Anir.

Division of Labor. The sexual division of labor among the Lak is less pronounced now than in the precontact period. Men and women both clear garden land, plant, and harvest; and both string the *nassa* shells that are used as traditional currency (*sar*). However, maintaining gardens is largely women's work, while men appear to have exclusive control over magic designed to improve garden yields and foster growth of pigs. Hunting is a collective male affair, as is all major ritual. Men alone fish. Women perform all domestic chores.

Land Tenure. Garden land among the Lak is inalienable. It is a possession of matrilineal segments, which is under the exclusive stewardship of the segment big-man, or *kamgoi*. All garden land currently under cultivation by a village is owned by the dominant segment in the area. The segment kamgoi allows all residents to plant on the land. This stewardship, however, does not allow him direct control over village garden production. Because garden land is abundant, disaffected village dwellers can always resettle in areas in which their own segment controls land. While ownership of garden land is theoretically inviolate, tenure over land does in fact change. This occurs in two ways. First, segments (such as lineages, or *kampapal*) do move between larger matrilineal units (*kamtikan oon*). Second, if a big-man can convince his supporters to follow him, landowning segments can sell land to individuals, provided that this land is used only for cultivation of coconuts or cocoa (i.e., cash crops). Evidently, rent or lease arrangements are also possible.

Kinship

Kin Groups and Descent. Lak society is characterized by dual organization: every Lak belongs to either "Bongian" (sea eagle, *Haliaetus leucogaster*) or "Koroe" (fish hawk, *Pandion leucocephalus*) moiety; and members of one moiety must marry into the other. Each village is considered Bongian or Koroe, depending on the dominant landowning segment in the area. This designation is important for rituals that regulate relations between moieties. Thus, the first time a member of the opposite moiety sleeps or dances in the village, he will be showered with gifts, which must, however, be repaid shortly after. Recruitment to moiety and clan membership is matrilineal. Lak clans are thus partitioned into two sets. Interestingly, two of the largest Lak clans bear the same names as the moieties, suggesting that the other clans are perhaps newer to the region. Lineages are demarcated by their right to erect men's houses; they also have ancestors who are invoked in men's ritual.

Kinship Terminology. Kinship terminology is of the Iroquois type. Affinal terms are extended to all members of the opposite moiety.

Marriage and Family

Marriage. The only marriage rule among the Lak is that of moiety exogamy. While marriages between certain Lak segments are more common than one would expect by chance alone, these unions do not reflect prescriptive rules. Polygyny, once common among big-men, is no longer practiced. A large bride-price is required for all marriages, though marriages are no longer arranged in any strong sense. Postmarital residence is variable and usually depends on the relative strength of each spouse's segment leader. Thus, a man marrying a big-man's daughter is likely to reside in the big-man's village at least for the early years of the marriage. Affinal lineages have a great stake in marriages and are involved in a series of ritual exchanges that commemorate births and deaths. Exchanges of pigs are also common to shame a husband who has struck his wife, for example. Divorce is an option for men and women; in such cases, children usually remain with the mother and her lineage.

Domestic Unit. The basic domestic unit is the household, composed of either a nuclear or extended family. Each household cooks and gardens separately.

Inheritance. Inheritance is matrilineal in the case of the two goods that matter most, land and ritual objects. However, fathers give money to their sons, so that the sons are able to purchase land and access to ritual. In this way, fathers manage a hidden form of patrilineal transmission.

Socialization. Children are indulged until about age 5 or 6. At that point a major crisis is typical. The child is denied something and may throw a tantrum for hours, in which he rends his clothes and flings sand at himself and at those around him. When the tantrum is finished, he understands that he must begin to assume new duties. Girls as young as 5 years old are a valuable resource for households, and they are put to work carrying heavy garden produce. Boys are brought into the realm of productive labor later, when they are first given a plot to cultivate at about age 15 or 16. The real assumption of adult responsibilities for young men comes with marriage, when all at once they must build a house, plant a garden, perform bride-service for their father-in-law, and begin to amass the wealth that will allow them to move up in the men's secret society and hold their own as a participant in an extensive system of competitive feasting.

Sociopolitical Organization

Social Organization. The Lak village is above all a food-sharing unit. Households eat separately, but strong sanctions enjoin them to circulate food products whenever there are surpluses. In fact, the people create an artificial surplus in their exchange of komkom, the manioc product that circulates between households on a regular basis. A household will prepare thirty or so packets of manioc bread, send half to other households (which are conveyed by small children), and receive about that much in return. Every household in the village is supposed to participate in the exchange. This exchange relation represents the ideal solidarity of the village. Such solidarity must be contrasted with *tondon*, "the work of marriage and of death," that is, the exchange relations that define lineages as competitors and partners in complex pig-providing exchange relations. This opposition between lineages is mainly evident in the context of mortuary ritual. Lineage membership overrides the claim of village solidarity only in ritual. Thus, all village men congregate in the men's house of the big-man of the village, despite varied clan membership. Lineages are not localized in villages, and villages include members of many segments.

Political Organization. Political leadership among the Lak is typical of coastal Melanesian big-man systems: a big-man (kamgoi) emerges by working harder than others to amass wealth in the form of pigs; this achievement makes him central in the competitive feasts that define interclan relations and also allows him to purchase control over segment ritual objects, such as the *tubuan* and duk-duk masks critical for segment leadership. The consummate big-man convinces others to put their labor in his service and in this way rises quite quickly as a leader. He may even use the feasting system to incorporate lineages within his own segment. The Lak big-man hosts mortuary feasts for all deceased of his segment, and he may also manage its collective stock of shell money.

Social Control. Enforcement of ritual sanctions is carried out by the tubuan: masked figures appear at night and fine an offender; earlier, they might have killed the offender using a special axe (*firam*). Enforcement of civil disputes is turned over to village courts, in which an elected village member uses public opinion to resolve bride-price disputes, sorcery accusations, and minor infractions of daily etiquette. Disputes may be taken to a provincial officer if they involve bloodshed.

Conflict. Before pacification, feuding was endemic. Roaming bands undertook cannibalistic raids.

Religion and Expressive Culture

Religious Beliefs. The traditional religious beliefs of the Lak focused on a set of creators: two brothers, Swilik and Kampatarai, and their grandmother. Swilik created the Lak landscape and gave them moieties to regulate marriage. He has been assimilated into the Christian god, as the Lak have been progressively missionized. Other religious beliefs center on lineage ancestors and *marsalai,* spirits associated with particular features of the landscape.

Religious Practitioners. Lak shamans (*iniet*) serve as healers and sorcerers, but few of them remain. More common is the *tenabuai,* an expert in magic associated with betel nuts.

Ceremonies. Dances, accompanied by music and drums, mark the major mortuary feast. These are twenty-four hour events and may bring hundreds of people together. Big-men host "teams" of young men, who try to outdo one another as dancers. Men also practice secret ceremonies associated with tubuan and duk-duk masks, as well as other ceremonies revolving around bullroarers (*talun*).

Arts. Ritual objects are the focus of artistic effort, but designs are relatively spare when compared to those of other Melanesian peoples. Most Lak villages have large, unadorned slit gongs used in ritual, but these instruments are no longer being made. Houses are not decorated, and canoes show little elaboration.

Medicine. Traditional healing is performed by the iniet, or shaman, who is schooled in an extensive indigenous pharmacopoeia. Treatments are costly and typically take the form of long-term sessions, in which the iniet casts spells on plant materials and blows them onto the afflicted person. Currently, Lak make use of both traditional remedies and Western medicine.

Death and Afterlife. Lak fear the recently deceased, who are said to roam the village and lure others to the netherworld. The prominent dead man is apparently incorporated into ritual paraphernalia, as in current betel-nut magic. In the past, this practice was more common, as dead lineage leaders slowly took on the status of lineage ancestors. Lineage dead are seen to be somewhat capricious, visiting sickness or misfortune on the living with no apparent motive.

See also Nissan, Tolai

Bibliography

Albert, Steven M. (1987). "Tubuan: Masks and Men in Southern New Ireland." *Expedition* 29:17–26.

Albert, Steven M. (1988). "How Big Are Melanesian Big Men: a Case from Southern New Ireland." *Research in Economic Anthropology* 10:159–200.

Albert, Steven M. (1989). "Cultural Implication: Representing the Domain of Devils among the Lak." *Man* 24:273–289.

Schlaginhaufen, O. (1908). "Orientierungsmarsche an der Östkuste von Süd-Neu-Mecklenburg." *Mitteilungen aus den deutsche Schutzgebieten* 21:213–220.

Stephan, E., and F. Graebner (1907). *Neumecklenburg: Die Kuste von Umuddu bis Kap St. Georg.* Berlin: D. Riemer.

STEVEN M. ALBERT

Lakalai

ETHNONYMS: Bileki, Muku, Nakanai, West Nakanai

Orientation

Identification. The Lakalai are distinguished from speakers of related dialects and languages, all labeled Nakanai, by the absence of the phoneme *n* in their language. Most have learned to pronounce this phoneme through exposure to Pidgin English, and they often identify themselves to outsiders simply as West Nakanai.

Location. Located approximately 150°30' to 150°6' E and 5°25' to 5°40' S, Lakalai villages are on the central and eastern part of the Hoskins Peninsula on the island of New Britain. The climate is warm and humid by day, cool at night, with an annual rainfall of about 355.6 centimeters and a well-marked rainy season when the northwest monsoon blows from December through March. An active volcano, Pago, erupted frequently early in the century, leading to abandonment of many villages as ash falls destroyed crops. The volcanic soil is fertile, but freshwater sources are few and generally close to the beach, as, perforce, are most of the villages.

Demography. The population increased from under 2,700 in 1954 to almost 6,500 in 1980. The expansion reflects recovery from depopulation occasioned by Japanese occupation during World War II, coupled with the abolition of warfare and access to Western medicine. Many Lakalai now want to limit family size to about five children.

Linguistic Affiliation. Lakalai is an Oceanic (Austronesian) language, the westernmost of a chain of dialects also spoken in Ubae, in the West Nakanai Census Division, and in coastal villages of Central Nakanai Census Division, to the east. Their closest relatives are East Nakanai (Meramera, Ubili), still farther east, and, to the west, Xarua and the languages of the Willaumez Peninsula (Bola or Bakovi, and Bulu). An early theory that this whole group of languages, classed together as Kimbe or Willaumez, represented a back-migration from islands located much farther east is probably incorrect.

History and Cultural Relations

Culturally, Lakalai differ very little from speakers of related branches of Nakanai to the east and from other residents of the West Nakanai Census Division, some of whom (the Bebeli or Banaule) speak a very different language. Prior to World War I, when New Britain was still part of German New Guinea, labor recruiters began to visit the Lakalai region, occasionally "blackbirding," kidnapping men to work on plantations as far away as Samoa. Many young men voluntarily went to work on plantations on the Gazelle Peninsula of East New Britain, where European settlements date to the nineteenth century, and returned home with steel tools and other European goods. As the region east of Lakalai became pacified, Tolai traders from the Gazelle Peninsula began visiting Lakalai. Ties with the Tolai, whose language was used by the Methodist mission, are still strong, and initially they helped lay the groundwork for the acceptance of foreign missionaries.

Nevertheless, major social change did not occur until the imposition of Australian rule and the arrival of Christian missionaries (Methodist and Roman Catholic) in the 1920s. Warfare was suppressed and traditional political organization partially replaced by a system of government-appointed officials. In 1968, local government councils were instituted. The desire for foreign goods such as steel tools, and later the need to pay taxes, led almost all unmarried men to engage in wage labor outside Lakalai. With the establishment of government schools to replace or supplement mission schools, education improved greatly after 1968. By the 1970s, several men had gained degrees at the national universities, but today school fees are an increasing burden for parents. Lakalai is now linked by road to the provincial capital at Kimbe, and the greatly increased contact with outsiders has considerably altered village life. All Lakalai are Christians, the majority Roman Catholic, though many traditional beliefs remain. An antigovernment cargo cult that began in 1941 flourished for decades but was quiescent by the 1980s. Cash earned from markets and cash crops is supplemented by money sent by children working elsewhere, repaying sums spent educating them.

Settlements

Traditionally, villages were small, probably containing no more than 150 inhabitants, but most were divided into two or more named hamlets, each with its own men's house, feasting area, and dance plaza. The hamlet contained shade and fruit trees but was kept free of weeds and grass. Many family houses contained an extended family, but each adult woman had her own cooking hearth. Each village shared a garden site and freshwater supply. Two or more adjacent villages constituted a territory within which relations were usually friendly. Villages of the same territory were connected by paths, intermarried, attended each other's ceremonies, and collaborated in warfare. The colonial authorities objected to the fissioning of established villages, and present-day ones are much larger and often lack men's houses, but hamlet affiliation is still important. Also as the result of government pressure, most dwellings are now built on piles, with separate cooking houses based on the ground and often slept in by the elderly.

Economy

Subsistence and Commercial Activities. The traditional starch staple was taro, harvested and replanted daily. Because of a taro blight, beginning about 1960, this crop has been largely replaced by introduced crops, particularly manioc and sweet potatoes, and increasingly by purchased rice. Many other crops, both traditional and introduced, are grown; breadfruit, coconuts, bananas, papayas, *Canarium* almonds, and a variety of greens are the most important. In the past, various wild foods supplemented the cultigens, but now the only important one is sago. The hunting of small wild game such as marsupials and birds has also been abandoned, but wild pigs are still an important contribution to the diet, being netted, trapped, or nowadays killed with shotguns. The everyday protein supply comes from fish, shellfish and, during most of the year, megapode eggs laid in holes in a thermal region that the nearby eastern villages try to keep for their exclusive use. Those who have the cash often buy canned fish or meat, but no one is dependent on food from trade stores. Some tobacco is grown, and many betel (areca) nuts. Markets just beyond Lakalai are now accessible by road, and women sell surplus coconuts, betel nuts, megapode eggs, and fruit to foreigners living near government posts. Some of these foreigners also buy fish from Lakalai men. Cash crops are now a major source of income. The principal ones are coconuts (from which copra is made), cacao, and, most recently, oil palm.

Industrial Arts. Traditionally, these included highly decorated canoes, spears (some covered with shells for use in marriage payments), carved shields, slings, a variety of nets, coiled and plaited baskets, bags, pandanus sleeping mats, and bark-cloth slings for carrying babies. Elaborate painted bark-cloth masks and carved objects were made for ceremonies, and dances were accompanied by wooden slit gongs and hourglass drums. Specialists made ornaments of tortoiseshell, shell, and plaited fiber. The manufacture of ornaments, bark-cloth slings, traditional weapons, and special canoes used for racing has been abandoned.

Trade. This was regarded as highly dangerous, necessitating contact with clan mates who lived in enemy territory. The Lakalai received obsidian, red paint, and tortoiseshell from the Willaumez Peninsula, and they passed on shell beads traded from the east by the Tolai, who bought the shells from which they manufactured their own shell money (*tambu*) in Nakanai-speaking regions. Tambu shells are still sold to the Tolai, nowadays for cash.

Division of Labor. Cooperation in such enterprises as house building and canoe manufacture typically involves hamlet mates together with affines and consanguineal kin from other hamlets of the village. For small-scale enterprises, men are likely to cooperate with partners specially selected to share a particular activity. They often exchange food with each other. Men clear bush, fence gardens, build houses, fish in the sea, and hunt. Until warfare over control of the egg fields ended, they also collected megapode eggs; now women do. Men manufacture fish nets and pig nets, canoes, and the coiled baskets used by women. Men and women cooperate to make sago. Women plant and harvest all garden crops, cook everything except food for special men's feasts, fish with hand nets in streams, collect shellfish in swamps, and care for domestic pigs. They manufacture bags, pandanus sleeping mats, and skirts, some of which are used as dowry and marriage payments. Child care is increasingly shared by both parents. Of the cash crops, men plant and harvest coconuts and oil palms, though women may help in the preparation of copra. Both sexes plant and harvest cacao.

Land Tenure. Land is vested in the clan, and use rights to garden on it are granted by the senior resident male to non-clan members such as children and grandchildren of men of the clan and phratry mates. With the expanding population and much land permanently under cash crops, clan segments have begun to be less generous to other outsiders. Trees are inherited separately but revert to the landowners if no direct descendants of the planter remain in the area. Some productive reefs are also claimed by clans.

Kinship

Kin Groups and Descent. Every Lakalai is born into a named, nonlocalized, agamous matrilineal descent group, called a "sib" or "clan" in the literature. Each has several food taboos, which differ for subclans, and a sacred place (*olu*) in which the dead of the clan reside. Clans that share an olu or a food taboo consider each other "brothers" and so constitute phratries. The clan owns garden land, incorporeal property such as mask designs and magical spells, and portable wealth used to finance marriages of clan members and to settle feuds. Because clans are dispersed throughout Lakalai, only the local segment constitutes a social group, headed by the senior male. The father's clan also feels responsibility for the "children of the clan." Finally, all coresidents of a hamlet regard each other as members of a bilateral kindred.

Kinship Terminology. Kinship terminology is Iroquois-type, with relative age being indicated for siblings of the same sex. Because of consanguineal, clan, phratry, and hamlet ties, kinship terms are extended to all members of the village, many being related in more than one way. Classificatory siblings are preferred to those labeled as cross cousins, with whom there is an avoidance relationship. Cross cousins may be married by arrangement, but marriages resulting from love affairs typically involve classificatory siblings.

Marriage and Family

Marriage. Marriages may be either arranged by the father and mother's brother of each partner, acting together, or result from elopement, if the kin of the couple give their approval. Sister exchange is liked, but it still involves bride-wealth, which is contributed by the groom's clan and that of his father and is highest for arranged marriages. Divorce is rare after the birth of the children, most of whom stay with the mother, especially if she did not instigate the divorce. Many men try polygyny as an alternative to divorce, but women strongly dislike the practice, and stable polygynous marriages are rare. Both the sororate and the levirate are practiced. Postmarital residence is normally patrivirilocal until the groom's father dies, at which point the man may join other kin, including clan mates. Christianity and other Western influences have greatly reduced the incidence of arranged marriages. An increasing number of younger Lakalai, especially men, marry non-Lakalai.

Domestic Unit. A woman usually lives with her husband's kin until several children are born, at which time the couple build a house of their own but may still share it with the husband's married brother or other kin. Increasingly, partly because of mission pressure, a young couple may have their own house much earlier.

Inheritance. Most wealth is held by men, who can dispose of it before death, with the bulk being kept for the bride-wealth of sons. Productive trees may be planted for children of both sexes. Some magic, being clan-owned, should only be taught to a sister's child.

Socialization. This is primarily in the hands of the parents, aided by the father's elder brother. The mother's brother may give instruction, but unlike the parents and the father's brother, he should not scold or strike a child. Children are warned against involvement in clan feuds, and taught to behave in ways that will make them desirable spouses. Sexual behavior is relatively free, but a girl is expected to be secretive about her affairs. Extramarital pregnancy is strongly disapproved.

Sociopolitical Organization

Social Organization. Under the leadership of one or more senior men, the hamlet acts as a unit in economic activities, including putting on feasts and sharing food received at feasts given by other hamlets. All protein food should be shared within the hamlet. Rivalry between hamlet heads, and covert clan feuds, weaken village cooperation, but crosscutting kin ties bind residents together, as does common reliance on a few ritual specialists such as a garden magician. Clan mates need not live in the same hamlet, and they act as a unit only at weddings and when producing masks and performing dances for ceremonies. A woman, as the continuation of the descent group, should be respected by her brother, but in general women are denigrated, and male solidarity, including that between brothers-in-law, disadvantages women. An abused wife may, however, shame her husband by cursing him in public, or she may leave him if her kin agree that she has been badly mistreated. Too much contact with women, and especially with menstrual blood and blood shed in childbirth, is thought to weaken men. In the past, men usually slept in a separate men's house and avoided contact with young babies, considered contaminated by the aura of childbirth. These attitudes have weakened greatly in recent years, but some menstrual taboos are still observed. The overall position of women has improved somewhat because of missionary influence.

Political Organization. Each hamlet is led by one or more senior men, literally called "big-men." They must have demonstrated ability to finance marriages and otherwise care for dependents and to sponsor ceremonies. In addition, each clan segment is headed by the senior male. In the past, leading warriors who also belonged to a clan holding land near the village were invested with a wristband containing a powerful spirit, which enabled them to settle quarrels as well as to continue success in battle. Because these men, called *suara,* tended to promote the interests of their own clans and hamlets, the ideal solution was agreement by all the big-men to elect one as village chief. He carried no arms and was supported in his decisions by the remaining suara. Without such a chief, hamlets and villages often broke up. At present, elected officials handle village affairs, but hamlet and clan heads continue as in the past.

Social Control. Fear of being shamed by their elders and inability to finance their own marriages help to keep younger men well-behaved. In the past, threats of sorcery and beatings and the intervention of suara impeded open wrongdoing. Today, village courts and the external police and judicial system are resorted to when the scolding of elders is ineffective. Fear of Hell is also said to influence some of the more devout Christians.

Conflict. In the past, conflict between territories was often triggered by offenses such as the abduction of a woman or theft of a pig across the boundaries. When tired of fighting, the war leaders, united by their possession of the same kind of wristband, oversaw formal peace ceremonies at which compensation was paid for deaths.

Religion and Expressive Culture

Religious Beliefs. A single god, Sumua, resides in the volcano and controls the taro crop. Although beliefs about him were incorporated in the cargo-cult myth, he is thought to have become inactive with the spread of Christianity. Uncleared bush and the high seas are the domain of a variety of spirits, which can also enter villages after dark. Ghosts of near kin may be helpful, but in general spirits are at best unpredictable and are likely to be dangerous to the living.

Religious Practitioners. Specialist magicians perform garden magic for the benefit of coresidents; specialist war magicians were equally useful in the past. Weather magicians are often hired to bring or prevent rain. Most men know spells for love magic, hunting, and fishing. Most older men are thought to know death-dealing sorcery, but deaths tend to be blamed on a few whose ancestors were renowned sorcerers. Both sexes rescue souls captured by ghosts and act as curers. Women are most likely to know magic relating to female fertility and child growth.

Ceremonies. The most important but most infrequent is the *mage,* which honors the dead kin of the sponsor. The climax involves dances and other performances and the distribution of feast foods, including domestic pork. Sponsoring mage is a major avenue to renown. Every dry season, men wearing masks (*valuku*) peculiar to their clan parade through the villages, sometimes chasing and beating women and children. In the past, when boys reached maturity, groups of them assumed a special headdress and also paraded, indicating their readiness for marriage. A joint ceremony honoring young girls occurs when they first put on leaf skirts. Other small ceremonies celebrate a girl's menarche and the first time a first-born child of either sex does something new. All ceremonies are generally enjoyable occasions, and religious aspects are minimal, even for the mage and the valuku. A father is obliged to sponsor ceremonies honoring his children; men competing for status put on more spectacular ceremonies than the occasion demands. The form and content of ceremonies has altered in recent years, but all persist apart from the one indicating maturity for boys.

Arts. Designs for masks, face paint worn by dancers and other participants in ceremonies, carved and painted canoes, and shields are all of the same sort, and all of them belong to the clan of the person who first discovers the design (often in a dream) or invents it. The Lakalai greatly value innovation in art, even though new designs must conform to a fairly rigid pattern, and they also praise new songs and dances. Major artists are men, but women compose songs, especially dirges, and sometimes learn new mask designs and songs in dreams. Men are the principal performers in dances and mage, in which they hope to attract the sexual interest of female spectators.

Medicine. Most remedies involve spells, but minor ailments may be treated by herbs alone. Today, Western medicine supplements traditional cures.

Death and Afterlife. Traditionally, the dead were buried in the house floor. If a mage was planned, the left humerus was exhumed so it could be used as the focus of the ceremony, and afterward it was attached to a spear with which a man was killed. With the prohibition of all these activities by the Australian government, the dead are now buried in village cemeteries, and other relics take the place of the humerus. Mourning involves the seclusion of the widow and long-term abstention from favorite foods by all close kin, and it is still observed in attenuated form. Souls of the dead are simultaneously thought to live in the olu, in a ghostly village in the bush, in the cemetery, and in the Christian Heaven.

See also Tolai

Bibliography

Chowning, Ann (1965–1966). "Lakalai Kinship." *Anthropological Forum* 1:476–501.

Chowning, Ann (1973). "Inspiration and Convention in Lakalai Paintings." In *Art and Artists of Oceania,* edited by S. M. Mead and B. Kernot, 91–104. Mill Valley, Calif.: Ethnographic Arts Publications.

Chowning, Ann, and Ward H. Goodenough (1965–1966). "Lakalai Political Organization." *Anthropological Forum* 1:412–473.

Goodenough, Ward H. (1971). "The Pageant of Death in Nakanai." In *Melanesia: Readings on an Area,* edited by Lewis

L. Langness and John C. Wechsler, 270–290. Scranton, Pa.: Chandler.

Valentine, Charles A. (1961). *Masks and Men in a Melanesian Society: The Valuku or Tubuan of the Lakalai of New Britain.* Lawrence: University of Kansas, Social Science Studies.

Valentine, Charles A. (1965). "The Lakalai of New Britain." In *Gods, Ghosts, and Men: Some Religions of Australian New Guinea and the New Hebrides,* edited by P. Lawrence and M. J. Meggitt, 162–197. Melbourne: Oxford University Press.

ANN CHOWNING

Lau

ETHNONYMS: None

Orientation

Identification. Lau is a chain of about 100 small islands and reefs spread over an area of about 1,400 square kilometers in the South Pacific. Geographically and culturally, Lau is intermediate between Melanesian Fiji and Polynesian Tonga. Lau is made up of three major divisions: the islands of southern and central Lau including Lakemba, Oneata, Mothe, the Kambara group, the Fulanga group, and the Ono group; the Exploring Islands; and the Moala group. While the British colonial government considered all three divisions to be part of the Lau group, native Lauans considered only the central and southern islands that formed the chiefdom of Lakemba to be Lau.

Location. The Lau islands are located between 16° 43' and 21° 2' S and 178° 15' and 180° 17' W. Three types of islands are found in the chain. Volcanic high islands are well watered with rich soil and support intensive horticulture. Limestone islands have little water and poor soil, though they do have heavily forested basins and lagoons rich with fish and shellfish. Islands composed of both volcanic rock and limestone display a combination of the above features. Lau has a tropical climate with a dry season from April to October and rainy, warm weather the rest of the year.

Demography. Reliable population figures for early contact times are unavailable. In 1920, the population was estimated at 7,402. An estimate in 1981 reported 16,000 Lau speakers.

Linguistic Affiliation. The indigenous language of Lau is a member of the Eastern Fijian Subgroup of Central Pacific Austronesian languages. The modern Lau dialect is evidently a mixture of the now-extinct traditional dialect, the dialect of Bau Fiji, and the Tongan language.

History and Cultural Relations

Abel Tasman, the Dutch explorer, came upon the Fiji Islands in 1643. Little is known about Lau prior to the early nineteenth century, although the islands were visited by Cook, Bligh, Wilson, and other European explorers and traders. The culture of Lau reflects the influence of the western Fiji Islands, Tonga, and British colonialism. In the first half of the nineteenth century, Lau was under the control of the Mbau chiefdom located on east Viti Levu. At the same time, however, contact with Tonga was increasing and Tongan villages developed on some Lau islands. The Tongan chief, Maafu, was sent to Lau to rule the Tongans and by 1864 had successfully taken control of some Lau islands and threatened Mbau supremacy. In 1874, Fiji became a British colony, thus effectively ending both Mbau rule and preventing Tongan rule. Under British influence before and following annexation, Lauans were subject to intensive missionization and involvement as plantation workers in the copra industry. With the post–World War I decline in the copra market, Lau became something of an economic and cultural backwater in comparison to western Fiji. In 1970, Fiji achieved political independence and Lauans have been active participants in national economic and political matters.

Settlements

About 30 of the 100 Lau islands are inhabited. Villages are located along the coast and are often surrounded by coconut palm and breadfruit tree groves. Village land is owned by clans, with each clan controlling a strip of land running from the shore inland to the mountain slopes. Villages often contain dwellings of various sizes, men's houses for each clan, kitchen huts, oven shelters, a garden shed, canoe shelters, ceremonial ground, and a burial ground. Houses are often similar to those on Tonga, raised on an earth mound with substantial wooden posts, walled, and constructed with thatched roofs. Some villages also have a store, reservoir, a mission church, and a temple. On the hills of some islands there are the remains of stone fortresses that have fallen into disuse with the cessation of interisland warfare.

Economy

Subsistence and Commercial Activities. Little, if any, horticulture was practiced before the introduction of manioc and sweet potatoes. It is believed that the gathering of plant foods supplemented by fishing, pig and chicken raising, and hunting sea turtles and crabs provided subsistence prior to the introduction of horticulture. Horticulture led to the development of a diversified subsistence economy based on yams, breadfruit, sweet potatoes, bananas, fish, and fowl. Pigs and sea turtles are now feast foods. Copra is the main commercial crop. Lauans, because of their relatively small population and isolated location, have not been drawn into the national economy to the same extent as Fijians in the western islands.

Industrial Arts. Woodworking is highly developed. Much of the raw material comes from the heavy forests on the limestone islands. Buildings of various types and sizes are constructed, both sailing and paddling canoes are made, and men carve wooden bowls, headrests, slit gongs, cups, and weapons. Women make bark cloth and mats from pandanus leaves.

Trade. Interisland trade was active in traditional times and involved raw materials (timber, bark, vegetable oils), food (breadfruit, yams, taro, kava, shellfish, turtles), and manufactured items (canoes, bowls, mats, bark cloth). External trade with Europeans centered on the exporting of copra in exchange for manufactured items such as metal tools, matches, tobacco, cloth, and fuel. Trade with Tonga involved the exporting of timber and providing military training for Tongan nobles.

Division of Labor. The division of labor by sex relegates to men the tasks of house building, canoe making and sailing, woodworking, and sennit manufacture. Women make and decorate bark cloth, make mats, refine coconut oil, roll fish lines, and make nets. Both men and women make baskets from pandanus leaves. Carpenters often build or assist in the building of houses and are compensated for their services. In traditional times, priests and two types of curers (diagnosticians and healers) were prominent members of the community.

Land Tenure. In the past, clans owned the hamlets located in the interior. With the establishment of villages along the coast, clans became the owners of plots of land running inland from the coast as well as the gardens. Rights to bush lands and lagoons are controlled by the villages. Through a system called *kerekere* unused land is rented to others.

Kinship

Kin Groups and Descent. At the highest level of kinship organization are five ranked phratries. The lowest-ranking phratry is that of the "land people." The land people are commoners and comprise 80 percent of the Lau population. The upper class is made up of the 20 percent of the population in the other four phratries. The chief's phratry (the Nakauvandra people) ranks the highest and forms the nobility. The three other phratries consist of two carpenter phratries and the phratry composed of the Tongans or "sea people." Phratries are composed of exogamous, patrilocal, patrilineal clans. Clans are localized economic and ceremonial units. Each clan is made up of subclans or of nuclear family households.

Kinship Terminology. Kin terms are classificatory, with a clear distinction made between cross and parallel cousins.

Marriage and Family

Marriage. Modern Lauan society is completely monogamous, although before the advent of Christianity polygny was practiced by high-ranking men, especially by chiefs. Cross-cousin marriage was preferred, though not all marriages were of this ideal type. Marriages were clan- and sometimes subclan-exogamous, with a pattern of preference for some pairs of clans and subclans. Postmarital residence was patrilocal, although matrilocal residence and matrilineal descent did occur in special circumstances, such as when there was a need to keep a clan from dying out. Separation and divorce are not common.

Domestic Unit. The typical household unit (*vuvale*) consists of a man, his wife, their children, and often additional relatives. Each household owns a dwelling house, a kitchen hut, an oven shelter, and sometimes a men's house. The household is the basic unit of food production and consumption.

Inheritance. Property, status, and specialized knowledge such as that of medicines and spells is passed from parents to children. Most valuable property is passed from fathers to sons. Mothers pass bark-cloth designs to their daughters.

Socialization. Relations between parents and children are governed by the same principles of status and respect that govern the relations between adults and between social groups. Children respect and obey their fathers and various material possessions of the latter are taboo. Relations with one's mother, who is not a member of one's clan, are freer and easier. Grandparents play a major role in child care and have especially close ties to their grandchildren. In traditional times, boys between the ages of 7 and 13 underwent a group superincision operation followed by four days of seclusion and a feast. There was no comparable ceremony for girls. Since British colonial times, formal education has been available on most inhabited islands.

Sociopolitical Organization

Social Organization. Lauan society is characterized by an autocratic, stratified type of social organization with a close integration of the political, stratification, and kinship systems. Notions of status and rank pervade all aspects of Lauan society and govern relations between individuals and social groups. In understanding Lauan society, it is important to bear in mind that Lauan culture reflects a fusion of three cultural traditions: early Polynesian, Melanesian, and Western Polynesian. Today, these traditions are reflected in the tripartite division among the land people, Nakauvandra people, and the Tongans or sea people. The land people were the earliest inhabitants of Lau. About ten generations ago, the ancestors of the Nakauvandra people immigrated to Lau and brought with them a highly organized and complicated system of social ranking that was reflected in their hierarchy of gods. The height of Tongan influence was in the mid-nineteenth century.

Political Organization. The chiefdom is the largest political unit in Lau. It is made up of groups of islands or minor chiefdoms that are united in tributary relationships to the high chief at Lakemba. The minor chiefdoms are composed of villages, which were made up of hamlets in traditional times. The minor chiefdoms are ranked according to their relationship to each other and to the high chief, and the villages that make up the minor chiefdoms are ranked according to the status of the clans of which they are composed. Under British administration, village headmen were appointed by the colonial government. Today, Lauans participate in national politics, which are marked by ethnic-based rivalry between native Fijians and Asian Indians and rivalries between different chiefdoms.

Social Control. The concepts of status and rank and associated behaviors, especially taboos on the objects and behaviors of the chiefs, were important ordering mechanisms in traditional times. At various times, the missionaries, Tongan chiefs, British officials, and clan alliances based on marriage have served as social-order mechanisms.

Conflict. Internal warfare evidently increased in frequency after the arrival of the Nakauvandra people and often concerned intervillage and interclan competition for status and competition between nobles for power. Warfare generally took the form of surprise raids and ambushes with an emphasis on keeping one's own casualties to a minimum.

Religion and Expressive Culture

Religious Beliefs. The settlers from Melanesia who founded the chief's phratry (the Nakauvandra people) introduced an ancestor cult to Lau. In this cult, the hierarchy of the clans is reflected in the hierarchy of the ancestor gods. Offerings are presented to the gods by hereditary priests for the purpose of obtaining *mana.* According to Laura Thompson, the Lau are totemic in two senses. First, there is a form of totemism associated with the land people who believe that they descended from some local natural phenomena. These groups practice island endogamy. The second form of totemism is associated with the clans, many of whom possess as many as three totems, although there was no belief in descent from the totems. Most Lauans had converted to Christianity by the close of the nineteenth century, with Methodism being the most popular denomination.

Religious Practitioners. Each island chief had a hereditary priest who acted as a seer and sanctified the chief's status and authority. The priest was responsible for worshipping the ancestor god, an activity carried out through possession trance. There is some evidence that in the past the priest was as powerful as the chief. Today, the position of priest is essentially an honorary one.

Ceremonies. Ceremonialism involves the presentation and reception of gifts (formerly to the ancestor god by the priest, but since the advent of Christianity, to the chief), kava drinking, a feast, and dancing accompanied by a form of rhythmic chanting called *meke.* The most important traditional ceremony was the first fruit of the land ceremony (*sevu ni vanua*). Life-cycle events were also marked by ceremonies, as were activities of the chief such as his installation and payment of tribute to him. The elaborateness of a ceremony reflected the status of the host or of the object of the ceremony.

Arts. Artistic expression was manifested mainly through the preparation, stenciling, and painting of bark cloth by women, the weaving and decoration of mats, and dancing. Dancing was a major component of all ceremonies and often involved much preparation and practice beforehand. The rhythmic chanting (meke) was accompanied by dancing, gesturing, and drumming.

Medicine. Illness and death were attributed to supernatural forces including sorcery and possession by an evil spirit. Illness was often viewed as supernatural punishment for a taboo violation. The cause of an illness was first identified by a diagnostician who then referred the person to the appropriate curer who specialized on the basis of the cause. Curers used talking, massage, vegetable medicines, surgery, and purification ceremonies.

Death and Afterlife. Persons near death are prepared for death by close relatives. Death is marked by wailing, a ceremony, the giving of gifts, numerous taboos, burial, and a mourning period. The elaborateness of all of these is directly related to the status of the deceased. Lauans believe that all people have a good soul and a bad soul. Ideas about the destiny of the soul after death are unclear.

See also Bau, Tonga

Bibliography

Bunge, Frederica M., and Melinda W. Cooke, eds. (1984). *Oceania: A Regional Study.* Washington, D.C.: U.S. Government Printing Office.

Hocart, Arthur M. (1929). *Lau Islands, Fiji.* Honolulu: Bernice P. Bishop Museum.

Thompson, Laura (1940). *Southern Lau, Fij: An Ethnography.* Honolulu: Bernice P. Bishop Museum.

Lesu

ETHNONYM: Notsi

Orientation

Identification. Lesu is a village on the east coast of the island of New Ireland, Papua New Guinea. Lesu also refers to the people who live in the village. The Lesu are one of the nine main indigenous ethnolinguistic groups of New Ireland. Other groups include the Nokon, Mandak, Usen Barok, Nusu, and Lavongai. There is no social cohesion among these groups and, prior to European dominance, various groups as well as villages within groups were often at war with one another. Contact between villages is confined mainly to joint attendance at ceremonies. This summary describes Lesu as it existed in the late 1920s. More recent information is generally unavailable, although it can be assumed that Lesu has been largely Westernized and there is reason to believe that the Lesu language is no longer spoken.

Location. Lesu village runs for about 5 kilometers along the northeast coast of New Ireland at 2° 30' S and 151° E. The environment is tropical with life oriented both to the sea and to the interior with palm trees, bamboo groves, taro gardens, and heavy undergrowth.

Demography. The precontact population of Lesu is unknown. The Lesu experienced severe depopulation while under German control from 1884 to 1915 due to recruitment of men and women as laborers on copra plantations on and off the island and because of the spread of diseases, especially tuberculosis. In 1930 there were 232 people in Lesu. Current estimates of 1,100 speakers of the Notsi language include Lesu and some of their neighbors.

Linguistic Affiliation. Lesu villagers speak Notsi, a member of the Northern New Ireland Subgroup and New Ireland–Tolai Group of Austronesian languages.

History and Cultural Relations

The precontact history of Lesu is unknown. The Lesu were localized on the east coast at the time of European contact. New Ireland was visited by Dutch, English, and French explorers and traders in the seventeenth and eighteenth centuries. Germany controlled New Ireland as a colony from 1884 to 1914. During this period many Lesu were recruited to work on German and English plantations elsewhere on the island and on other islands, and a road was built with native labor along the east coast. These two developments brought the Lesu into more frequent contact both with Europeans and other New Ireland groups. Beginning in the late nineteenth century, missionaries entered New Ireland; the Lesu eventually were influenced most by Roman Catholic and Methodist missionaries. In 1914, New Ireland came under Australian control and remained so until 1942 when the island was occupied by Japan. Australia resumed control in 1945. In 1949 New Ireland became part of the Trust Territory of New Guinea and has been a province of the nation of Papua New Guinea since 1975.

Settlements

Lesu consists of fifteen named hamlets, all located along the sea. The hamlets contain from two to eight thatched, bamboo-walled houses and a communal cooking area. Larger hamlets also have men's houses on the shore, a cemetary, and cook houses. There is also a mission station. An individual's identity is based on residence both in Lesu and in a specific hamlet. Taro gardens are located inland, with Lesu land extending 8 or 9 kilometers in from the sea.

Economy

Subsistence and Commercial Activities. The Lesu are slash-and-burn horticulturalists, with taro being the staple crop grown in fenced gardens a kilometer or more inland from the village. Yams are also grown, though they are less important than for other New Ireland groups. Fish are taken with nets, traps, or spears; crabs, mussels, and coconuts are gathered; and wild pigs are hunted. At various times, subsistence activities have been supplemented by income derived from the sale of land, wage labor on coconut plantations, and work for colonial governments. Specialists are paid for their services with shell money (*tsera*) or European currency. Magicians and healers command high fees for their services, although all service providers—such as dancers at ceremonies and house builders—are paid.

Industrial Arts. Baskets are plaited from coconut-palm leaves, fishing nets are woven from plant fibers, and carving is done in wood and tortoiseshell. Canoe building had disappeared by the 1930s. *Malanggan*, ritual carvings used in death rituals, are the most important crafted objects. They are made by specialists working under carefully controlled conditions; in the past only men were allowed to see them.

Trade. Exchange between individuals and groups was based on reciprocity and the purchase of goods and services through the payment of tsera. A unit of tsera is one arm's length of strung flat shells. Tsera were made by specialists on the island of Lavongai, north of New Ireland. Items were never sold at a profit (i.e., for more than they were first purchased for). With the establishment of Australian control, the shilling replaced the tsera as the medium of exchange.

Division of Labor. Most tasks are assigned on the basis of sex. Men clear gardens, plant trees, gather sago, fish, hunt, prepare meat for cooking, build and repair houses, and make masks, canoes, nets, spears, and ornaments. Women plant taro and yams, gather crabs, feed pigs, haul water, keep house, and carry most burdens. Both men and women make mats and baskets, care for children, and serve as healers and magicians. Women are restricted from certain categories of knowledge such as some myths, some types of magic, and some supernatural beliefs. Magicians, healers, carvers, and net weavers traditionally were paid part-time specialists.

Land Tenure. The Lesu distinguish between two types of land. Clan land, which is in small parcels, is where the clan totemic animals live and is owned by the clan. All other land and rights to use of the sea are owned communally by the entire village. The custom is for people to plant gardens on land previously used by their parents, preferably the wife's parents. Ownership of trees and plants on the land rests with the individual gardener, who is usually the woman who works the plot. Purchase of land by colonial governments has complicated the question of ownership.

Kinship

Kin Groups and Descent. Lesu society is divided into two exogamous moieties, the Hawk (Telenga) and the Eagle (Kongkong) moieties. Each moiety is composed of a number of matrilineal clans, with each clan associated with totemic animals and parcels of land or sections of sea. Moieties maintain reciprocal ritual obligations regarding pregnancy, birth, first menstruation, circumcision, marriage, and death. Clans are the basic economic unit and clan members are expected to cooperate in all major projects. However, individuals are often conflicted over loyalties to the clan versus those to their residential family. While the inheritance of status strictly follows the matrilineal line, the rules governing the inheritance of property are less rigid, though items generally go from a man to his sister's son.

Kinship Terminology. Kin terms follow the Iroquois system.

Marriage and Family

Marriage. In the past, polygynous marriage was preferred, and many men had two wives, with a few very wealthy men having three or four. Polyandry also occurred, though with considerably less frequency. Under European influence, all marriages are now monogamous. Cross-cousin marriage was preferred, with a mother's brother's daughter's daughter or father's sister's daughter's daughter the most desirable mate for a man. This preference meant that men often married a woman one generation removed from themselves. Divorce was easy and frequent, with the wife always retaining custody of the children. Postmarital residence is matrilocal, though marriages within a hamlet were common, and therefore men often did not have to relocate to a new one. For the Lesu, incest was the most serious norm violation, so various restrictions and taboos operated to control contact between men and women whose relations would be considered incestuous.

Domestic Unit. The nuclear family household is the basic domestic unit. It consists of the husband, wife, unmarried daughters, and sons under the age of 9 or 10. Boys older than 9 or 10, unmarried men, and men whose wives are pregnant or nursing live in the men's house, though much of their daily activity centers on the household. In polygynous families, each wife and her children usually occupied a separate dwelling.

Inheritance. Although inheritance of knowledge and material objects is preferentially matrilineal, in practice the desires of the owner of the property or the family are more influential than the clan rules.

Socialization. Infants are indulged by their mothers and fathers and developmental events such as the first tooth are marked by feasts. Children are observers of and participants in the daily lives of the adults in their household and in the community. Very early on, a clear distinction is made between boys and girls, with the two kept separate. Age groups for boys are encouraged but not for girls. In the past, boys age 8 to 11 underwent an elaborate initiation rite, lasting eight months with an additional two months for preparations. The rite included seclusion in a specially built dwellng, circumcision, feasting, dancing, speech making, and an exchange of wealth. The initiation rite was always accompanied by the malanggan rite during which the malanggans were displayed and then destroyed. Under Roman Catholic influence, the duration of the initiation rite was shortened and it was followed by instruction at the mission. First menstruation was marked by feasting and ritual bathing which signified that the girl was now an adult and ready to marry.

Sociopolitical Organization

Social Organization. An individual's place in the Lesu social order was based on kinship, locality, and gender. The exogamous nature of the moieties and the reciprocity involved in relations between individuals, families, clans, and the moieties were the major forces welding the fifteen hamlets into a cohesive group. Status distinctions between individuals and families were based on wealth and degree of magical knowledge, which itself provided wealth through payments for magical services.

Political Organization. Community leaders (*orang*) were important old men in each clan who formed an informal council that decided issues for the village. Orang status was not inherited but was based on age, wealth, strength of personality, magical knowledge, and oratorical ability. In the past, there was also a warrior chief—a role that disappeared with the cessation of intervillage warfare. Under European administration an intermediary (*luluai*) was appointed to act as the village's representative. This person was sometimes also an orang, but whether he was or not, he always consulted with the orang council. Today, village representatives are elected.

Social Control. Incestuous relations were the most serious violations of norms and various mechanisms such as taboos and avoidance served to prevent incest from ever occurring.

Conflict. Prior to German colonization, warfare between the Lesu and other island groups was evidently quite common. Wars were often begun for revenge and ended through negotiation and the payment of compensation. Conflict between the Lesu hamlets was rare.

Religion and Expressive Culture

Religious Beliefs. Lesu religion centered on the use of magic to control virtually all aspects of life. Various types of magic were distinguished, including taro, rain, fishing, shark, war, love, black (to kill), and magic to counteract black magic. Magic was created through the recitation of spells. Under the influence of Christian missionaries, Christian beliefs came to coexist with traditional ones.

Religious Practitioners. Magicians were the ritual specialists. Both men and women could be magicians, though most were men. Magicians were paid for their services and were often the wealthiest and highest-status individuals in the village. Each magician had extensive knowledge of only one type of magic, plus some basic knowledge of medical magic. Magicians thought to practice black magic might be put to death by the relatives of the victim.

Ceremonies. Ceremonies were held for all the major life-cycle events—birth, initiation of boys, first menstruation of girls, marriage, and death. Ceremonies involved dancing, drumming, and feasting. Malanggan rites, which might be conducted separately or, more commonly, as part of the male-initation ceremony, were the most significant ceremonial events.

Arts. As noted above, wood carving, especially of the malanggans, is the most elaborated art form. All rituals are accompanied by dancing, both by men and women, with the former often costumed and masked. More elaborate dances are accompanied by drumming and singing. Body decoration is considered important and takes the form of hair decorations and facial makeup. The Lesu have a rich mythology and repertoire of folktales, many of which are recited or acted out as part of ritual activities.

Medicine. Illness is attributed to either natural causes or magic. The former are treated by healers (men or women) who use plant treatments such as passing leaves over the wound or having the patient chew certain leaves. Illnesses attributed to magic are treated by magicians who seek to counteract the magic.

Death and Afterlife. The Lesu believe in ghosts of the dead who can be called on to assist the living. However, the services of such ghosts do not play a major role in daily life or in religious belief and practice. Death is marked by a ceremony with wailing, dancing, feasting, and gift exchange. The deceased is buried in a coffin in the cemetery. After the burial, various taboos and restrictions disrupt normal activities in the hamlet for some weeks. The higher the social status of the deceased, the more elaborate the rites.

See also Mandak

Bibliography

Powdermaker, Hortense (1933). *Life in Lesu: The Study of a Melanesian Society in New Ireland.* New York: Norton.

Loyalty Islands

ETHNONYMS: Dehu, Iaai, Nengone, West Ouvean

There are four major resident groups in the Loyalty Islands of Melanesia: Dehu, also known as De'u, Drehu, Lifou, Lifu, and Min; Iaai, also known as Iai and Yai; Nengone, also known as Mare and Iwatenu; and West Ouvean, which is also known as Faga-Uvéa and Ouvean. In 1982 the population of the islands was approximately 22,100. The Loyalty Islands are located in the southwestern Pacific, just northeast of New Caledonia, which they were affiliated with in an areawide trading network. Dehu, Iaai, Nengone, and their various dialects are classified in the New Caledonian Group of the Austronesian Language Family. West Ouvean and its variants are classified in the Polynesian Group of Austronesian languages.

See also Ajie

Bibliography

Faivre, Jean Paul (1955). *La nouvelle Calédonie: géographie et histoire, economie, démographie, ethnologie.* Paris: Nouvelles Éditions Latines.

Guiart, Jean (1963). *Structure de la chefferie en Mélanésie du sud.* Paris: L'Institut d'Ethnologie, Université de Paris.

Mae Enga

ETHNONYMS: Western Central Enga

Orientation

Identification. The Mae form a cultural and geographical subdivision of the Enga, who comprise most of the inhabitants of Enga Province in the central highlands of Papua New Guinea. The Melpa to the east first called them Enga, a name that European explorers and later the people themselves have adopted.

Location. Wabag, the administrative center of Enga Province, is situated at about 5°30' S and 143°45' E. Mae exploit river valleys and mountain slopes between about 1,820 and 2,700 meters above sea level. Forested high ridges are uninhabited. Mean annual rainfall is about 300 centimeters, varying between 228 and 320 centimeters. Rain falls about 265 days a year, but there is a summer wet season (November to April) and a winter dry season (May to October). Winter droughts may occur, and at altitudes above 2,500 meters, winter frosts are common; both may cause food shortages.

Demography. In 1960 the then Wabag Subdistrict of about 8,710 square kilometers supported an indigenous population estimated at 115,000, of whom about 30,000 were Mae. Central Enga population densities ranged from about 19 to 115 persons per square kilometer. By the mid-1980s the population of Enga Province exceeded 175,000, including at least 45,000 Mae, and population densities were generally higher.

Linguistic Affiliation. Mae speak a dialect of Enga, one of the West-Central Family of the Central Highlands Stock of Papuan languages of Papua New Guinea.

History and Cultural Relations

Archaeological research in the central highlands indicates that horticulturalists were active in the Enga area at least 2,000 years ago, and probably earlier. These pre-Ipomean cultivators were presumably ancestral to present-day Enga, but their place of origin is unknown. Enga, including Mae, have for centuries maintained with non-Enga neighbors social contacts such as marriage, sharing of rituals, economic exchanges, and raiding. In 1930 Enga first encountered European gold prospectors and in 1938 field officers of the Australian colonial administration. By 1948 Wabag Subdistrict headquarters was established and the government permitted miners and Christian missionaries to enter the area. Between 1963 and 1973 the administration set up six elected local government councils, representatives of which in 1973 comprised a district-wide Area Authority. In 1964 Enga, like other residents of the then Territory of Papua New Guinea, elected representatives to the new House of Assembly, which in 1975 became the National Parliament after the country secured political independence from Australia. In 1974 Enga Province was proclaimed and in 1978 Enga elected a provincial assembly and government.

Settlements

Mae do not live in compact villages. Men and women occupy separate houses dispersed among the gardens and groves in the territory held by each clan parish, whose population of clansmen, their in-married wives, and their children averages about 400 persons and exploits about 5.2 square kilometers of irregular terrain. One-story dwellings hug the ground and are built with double-planked walls and thickly thatched roofs to keep out cold and rain. Houses are all much the same size and are externally similar but, whereas a woman's house usually shelters one wife, her unwed daughters, her infant sons, several pigs, and family valuables, the average men's house contains about six or seven closely related agnates, including boys, and their equipment. Wabag township is now a public service and commercial center of between 2,000 and 3,000 residents (including 100 or more non-Enga and Europeans) and has paved streets, Australian-style wooden houses, electricity, and piped water. All-weather roads link Wabag with administrative posts and mission stations within Enga and with neighboring provincial centers.

Economy

Subsistence and Commercial Activities. Mae were and most remain subsistence gardeners. They employ an intensive and productive system of long-fallow swidden cultivation, which utilizes family labor, simple tools, and effective techniques of composting and draining to grow the staple sweet potatoes, supplemented by taro, bananas, sugarcane, pandanus nuts, beans, and various leaf greens, as well as introduced potatoes, maize, and peanuts. Since the 1960s coffee, pyrethrum, potatoes, and, most recently, orchids have become the main commercial products of the cultivators. Domestic pig raising, important in the horticultural cycle, not only provides most of the meat in the daily diet but also the pork and live pigs that figure in public distributions of valuables to mark marriages, illnesses, deaths, and homicides. Small herds of introduced cattle, water buffalo, sheep, and goats are kept but have little commercial significance.

Industrial Arts and Trade. Traditionally Mae traded ash salt and occasionally pigs and pandanus nuts with neighboring societies in return for regional specialties, including cosmetic tree oil, stone axe blades, palm and forest woods to make weapons and drums, plumes, and marine shells. At home these and other valuables such as pigs and cassowaries circulated freely through the *Te* ceremonial exchange cycle and the prestations associated with births, deaths, and marriages. Local crafts were (and still are) limited mainly to men's construction of houses and bridges and production of weapons, implements, and personal ornaments, while women made net carrying bags and men's aprons. Artisans competent in Western trades are scarce in Enga and most of these, especially mechanics, carpenters, and builders, work for the National Works Authority based in Wabag. Also located there are the few bank branches and general stores that serve the Mae. Scattered through the clan territories are scores of tiny and unprofitable trade stores that sell canned foods, kerosene, soap, cigarettes, etc., as well as a number of all-night dance halls where beer is sold and a few bush garages and carpentry workshops. Many women sell small quantities of vegetables at local markets that have sprung up in Wabag and near missions and schools. Some women with sewing machines make simple clothes for the market.

Division of Labor. Division of labor by sex is marked among Mae. Men undertake the initial concentrated and heavy work of clearing, fencing, ditching, and deep tilling of gardens and coffee plots, after which their wives and daughters sustain the constant round of planting, weeding, repairing fences, and daily harvesting of food plants, plus picking and processing coffee in season. Women also tend family pigs, care for infants, prepare and cook food, and carry firewood and water. Men build all houses, while women gather grass for thatch and provide food for the workers. In short, women's work provisions Mae domestic economy and supports male and political and ceremonial activities.

Land Tenure. Within the 520 or so square kilometers comprising the Mae district, sharply localized patriclans traditionally claimed rights to all the arable lands and other high forests and marshlands whose resources they could exploit; and neighboring clans frequently engaged in bitter warfare to defend or to extend their territories. Since the 1960s the combination of a rapidly increasing population and the diversion of arable areas from food growing to coffee and cattle production has exacerbated interclan conflicts over access to land and other economic assets, as well as to political office. The numbers of Mae emigrating to other provinces to seek urban or rural employment have not been so great as to ameliorate the situation.

Kinship

Kin Groups and Descent. All Mae are members of segmentary agnatic descent structures, within which residential and cultivation rights to land are successively divided. The largest agnatic descent group, with as many as 6,000 members, is the eponymously named and nonexogamous phratry, each of which comprises a cluster of contiguous clans (average about eight, range four to twenty) whose eponymous founders are thought to be sons of the phratry founder. The mean size of the exogamous and localized patriclans is about 400 members, with a range from about 100 to 1,500. A clan contains from two to eight named subclans generated by the putative sons of the clan founder. The subclan in turn is divided into from two to four named patrilineages established by sons of the subclan founder. Patrilineages contain twenty or more elementary (monogamous) and composite (polygynous) families whose heads are usually held to be great-grandsons of the lineage founder.

Kinship Terminology. The Iroquois bifurcate-merging system of kin terms, which the Mae system resembles, distinguishes generation levels but not seniority within generations. Mae also recognize terminologically four wider categories of kin: agnates, other patrilateral cognates, matrilateral cognates, and affines.

Marriage and Family

Marriage. Until the 1960s polygyny was an indicator of social and economic worth, and about 15 percent of married men had two or more wives; nowadays monogamy is becoming more common. The levirate is the only marriage prescription, and most of the numerous prohibitions are phrased in terms of agnatic descent-group affiliation. The most important are that a man should not wed within his own patrician or within the subclans of his mother or his current wives. Parents, especially fathers, generally choose the spouses when their children first marry. Postmarital residence ideally is patrivirilocal. Because marriage unites the clans of both bride and groom in valued long-term exchange relations, divorce is difficult to achieve, even by husbands. Adultery is deplored, and the few erring wives are brutally punished. All of these norms and constraints have eroded noticeably of late due to the influence of secular education and Christian missions, wage earning and mobility of young adults, and the growing consumption of alcohol.

Domestic Unit. Because men regard female sexual characteristics, especially menstruation, as potentially dangerous, women may never enter men's houses and men, although they visit their wives' houses to discuss family matters, do not sleep there. Nevertheless, the elementary family of husband, wife, and unwed children constitutes the basic unit of domestic production and reproduction. A polygynous man directs the pig tending and cultivation done separately by his wives in their individual households, and he coordinates their activities to meet the public demands of his clan or its component segments.

Inheritance. Men bequeath rights to socially significant property such as land, trees, crops, houses, pigs, and cassowaries more or less equally to their sons as these sons marry. Daughters at marriage receive domestic equipment from their mothers.

Socialization. Women train their daughters in domestic and gardening skills from infancy until adolescence, when they marry and join their husbands' clan parishes. At about age 6 or 7, boys enter the men's house of their father and his close agnates, all of whom share in the boys' economic, political, and ritual education.

Sociopolitical Organization

Since 1975, Mae have been citizens of the Nation-state of Papua New Guinea, a member of the British Commonwealth of Nations with a Westminster system of government.

Social Organization. Traditional Mae society was relatively egalitarian and economically homogeneous and remains largely so in the 1980s despite the effects of international commerce. The 120 or so patriclans are still significant landholding units, and they and their component segments are corporately involved in a wide variety of events. A clan engages in warfare and peacemaking; initiates payments of pigs and, today, money as homicide compensation for slain enemies and allies; organizes large-scale distributions of pigs and valuables in the elaborate interclan ceremonial exchange cycle; and participates in irregularly held rituals to propitiate clan ancestors. No hereditary or formally elected clan chiefs direct these activities; they are coordinated by able and influential men who, through their past managerial successes, have acquired "big names." The arable land of a clan is divided among its subclans, which hold funeral feasts for their dead, exchange pork and other valuables with matrilateral kin of the deceased, and also compensate the matrikin of members who have been insulted, injured, or ill. Bachelors usually organize their purificatory rituals on a subclan basis. Subclan land is in turn divided among component patrilineages, whose members contribute valuables to bride-price or to return gifts as their juniors wed those of lineages in other clans. Lineage members also help each other in house building and in clearing garden land. Today clan solidarity, as well as interclan hostility, importantly determines who individual voters support in national, provincial, and local council elections. All of these Australian-inspired governmental entities provide the extraclan public services, such as schools, clinics, courts, constabulary, post offices, and roads, on which Mae now depend heavily.

Social Control and Conflict. Within the clan social control is still largely exercised through public opinion, including ridicule, implicit threats by agnates to withdraw the economic support and labor on which all families rely, and the pervasive influence of prominent big-men in informal moots. The ultimate sanction, even within the household, is physical violence. Formerly clans within a phratry or neighborhood could resort to similar courts jointly steered by their big-men to reach reluctant compromises; but such negotiations, especially over land or pigs, frequently erupted in bloodshed. The Australian colonial administration supplemented courts with more formal and fairly effective Courts for Native Affairs, which after independence were replaced by Village Courts with elected local magistrates. Nevertheless, clans in conflict, whether over land encroachment or homicides, still turn quickly to warfare to settle matters despite attempts by armed mobile squads of national police to deter them.

Religion and Expressive Culture

Religious Beliefs. The traditional system of Mae magical-religious beliefs and practices, like those of other Central Enga, are strongly clan-based, and many animist assumptions still orient popular ideology and social behavior, despite the apparent impact of Christian mission proselytizing since 1948. Mae believe the sun and the moon, "the father and mother of us all," have procreated many generations of immortal sky people who resemble Enga in being organized in an agnatic segmentary society of warlike cultivators. Each celestial phratry sent a representative to earth to colonize the hitherto empty land. The now mortal founder of each terrestrial phratry married, had children, and allocated lands and property to his sons as they wed daughters of other phratry founders. Thus were originated the named fraternal clans, each of which today rightfully occupies the defined territory inherited patrilineally from the founder. Each clan still possesses some of the fertility stones carried to earth by the phratry founder. Buried in the clan's sacred grove, they are the locus of the spirits of all the clan ancestors, including ghosts of deceased grandfathers. A man therefore has the right to exploit a tract of land because, through his father, he is a legitimate member of that clan, shares in the totality of clan patrilineal spirit, and is intimately linked with the localized clan ancestors. In addition to the continuing, often injurious interventions into human affairs of recent ghosts and of ancestral spirits, Mae also assert the existence of aggressive anthropophagous demons and of huge pythons, both of which defend their mountain and forest domains from human intrusions.

Ceremonies. Although lethal sorcery is uncommon, many men privately use magic to enhance their personal well-being, to acquire valuables and pigs, and to ensure military success. Clan bachelors regularly seclude themselves in groups to remove by magic and by washing the dangerous effects of even inadvertent contacts with women, after which the whole clan feasts its neighbors to celebrate the young men's return to secular life. Women employ magic to cleanse themselves after menstruation and parturition and occasionally to protect their garden crops. Following a family illness or death, a female medium conducts a seance or a male diviner bespells and cooks pork to identify the aggrieved ghost. The family head then kills pigs and ritually offers cooked pork to placate that ghost. Occurrences of clanwide disasters such as military defeats, crop failures, epidemic illnesses, or deaths of people or pigs stimulate clan leaders to arrange large-scale offerings of pork and game while hired ritual experts decorate the fertility stones to mollify the punitive clan ancestors.

Arts. The main expression of visual art is at clan festivals and rituals when dancing and singing men lavishly adorn themselves, and often their daughters, with plumes, shells, paints, and unguents. Musical forms and instruments are simple, but poetic and oratorical expression is elaborate. Formerly, painting and sculpture were uncommon, but since the 1970s a small school of Enga painters has flourished in Wabag.

Medicine. Local experts traditionally resorted to simples for minor complaints, bespelled foods for "magically induced" illnesses, and performed crude and often fatal surgery for serious arrow wounds. Nowadays, people usually visit government and mission clinics for treatment.

Death and Afterlife. Death, whether violent or from illness, is usually attributed to ghostly malevolence, less often to human sorcery or to demons' attacks. It is always a significant political event, entailing simple burial ceremonies, lengthy domestic mourning, and elaborate funerary feasting and exchanges of pigs and valuables. The angry ghost of the deceased is expected to kill a family member in retaliation before joining the corpus of clan ancestral spirits in the clan stones.

See also Melpa

Bibliography

Carrad, B., D. Lea, and K. Talyaga (1982). *Enga: Foundations for Development.* Armidale, N.S.W.: University of New England Press.

Gordon, R. J., and A. J. Meggitt (1985). *Law and Order in the New Guinea Highlands.* Hanover, N.H.: University Press of New England.

Meggitt, M. J. (1965). *The Lineage System of the Mae Enga of New Guinea.* Edinburgh: Oliver & Boyd.

Meggitt, M. J. (1974). *Studies in Enga History.* Oceania Monograph no. 20. Sydney: Oceania Publications.

Meggitt, M. J. (1977). *Blood Is Their Argument: Warfare among the Mae Enga.* Palo Alto, Calif.: Mayfield.

Waddell, E. J. (1972). *The Mound Builders.* Seattle: University of Washington Press.

MERVYN MEGGITT

Mafulu

ETHNONYMS: Fuyuge, Fuyughé, Goilala, Mambule

Orientation

Identification. Mafulu is the name, based on the pronunciation used by the neighboring Kunimaipa speakers, for the people of Mambule, their nearest community of Fuyuge speakers. The Sacred Heart missionaries generalized Mafulu to include all of the Fuyuge-speaking inhabitants of the Auga, Vanapa, and Dilava river valleys. It is now also applied to people living in the Chirima Valley. Mafulu who have moved to Port Moresby since World War II are often identified, together with the Tauade from the neighboring valleys, as Goilala.

Location. The Mafulu inhabit the Goilala Subdistrict in the Central Province of Papua New Guinea, at about 8°30' S and 147° E. Communities are located in the sparsely populated Auga, Vanapa, Dilava, and Chirima river valleys, inland from Yule Island, north of Port Moresby, and south of Mount Albert Edward in the Wharton Range of the central cordillera. Although they are separated from the coast by steep gorges, the high (1,000-meter) mountainous foothills in which they live have more gentle ridges, broad forested valleys, and occasional expanses of *kunai* grass. Temperatures in the Goilala Subdistrict range between 7° C and 24° C. The average rainfall for the Subdistrict is 262 centimeters per year. The dry season runs from June through October and early November. The rainy season begins in late November or December and lasts until May, with the heaviest rains in January, February, and March.

Demography. There are no reliable early population estimates. According to the 1966 census, there are approximately 14,000 Mafulu in the Goilala Subdistrict.

Linguistic Affiliation. Fuyuge, the language spoken by the Mafulu, is the largest member of the Goilalan Family of the Trans-New Guinea Phylum of Papuan (Non-Austronesian) languages. Fuyuge has appeared in the linguistic literature as Fuyughé and Fujuge, Asiba, Chirima, Gomali, Kambisa, Karukaru, Korona, Mafulu, Mambule, Neneba, Ononge (Onunge), Sikube, Sirima, Tauada, and Vovoi. Fuyuge is quite divergent from the other two members of the language family, sharing only 27 percent of its vocabulary with Tauade and 28 percent with Kunimaipa. The dialects of Fuyuge differ considerably from valley to valley. Some vernacular-language religious materials were produced by the Sacred Heart Mission.

History and Cultural Relations

Before European contact, the Mafulu maintained trade and exchange relations with the neighboring Tauade and Kunimaipa and with the more distant Mekeo. Early contact between the Mafulu and the Sacred Heart Mission and the government in the late 1880s was characterized by open conflict. In 1905, the Sacred Heart Mission was established at Popolé. Ethnographic research has been limited to R. W. Williamson's research in 1910, which remains the basis for most ethnographic data on the Mafulu and is the time of reference for this summary. Additional material was written (and some published) by members of the Sacred Heart Mission and reflects pre–World War II Mafulu society. Mafulu communities were not directly affected by combat during World War II. Following the war, many young men left the area to work as laborers on plantations along the coast and at Kokoda. More recently, others have moved to the Port Moresby area for employment. The region itself has remained relatively isolated because the mountainous terrain has hindered the development of roads. The region is serviced by a small, local airstrip.

Settlements

Communities are composed of several villages (from two to eight). Villages are usually identified with particular clans and maintain closer ties to villages of the same clan within the community. The number of houses in each village varies considerably from six or eight to thirty. Traditionally villages, situated along the crests of ridges, were surrounded by stockades for defense. Houses were built in two parallel rows with an open mall between the rows. The *emone* or "men's house" sat between the two rows of houses at one end. Special dancing villages, which brought together people from other villages in the community, were built for large feasts held about every ten to twelve years.

Economy

Subsistence and Commercial Activities. The Mafulu are swidden horticulturalists, whose main crops are sweet potatoes, taro, yams, and bananas. Sugarcane, beans, pumpkins, cucumbers, and pandanus are also cultivated. They breed pigs, and they hunt wild pigs, cassowaries, wallabies, and bandicoots with the assistance of domesticated dogs. The household is the basic unit of production and consumption. Most food is either roasted or steamed in sections of bamboo, while pig and other meat may be cooked in earth ovens.

Industrial Arts. Items produced include bark cloth (tapa), used for bark-cloth capes, widows' vests, dancing aprons, and loin cloths. Netting is used for string bags, hunting nets, and hammocks. Smoking pipes are made from bamboo. Stone adzes, used in the past to cut down trees and clear gardens, have given way to steel bush knives and axes. Spears, stone clubs, bows, and bamboo-tipped arrows are used in warfare and hunting. The Mafulu also make various musical instruments.

Trade. Trade consists primarily of pigs, feathers, dogs'-teeth necklaces, and stone tools. The Mafulu trade stone tools and pigs to the Tauade and others in neighboring valleys, who lack the appropriate stone or skills, in exchange for feathers, dogs'-teeth necklaces, and other valuables. They also trade valuables to peoples on the coast for clay pots and magic.

Division of Labor. Women are responsible for planting sweet potatoes and taro, clearing the gardens of weeds, collecting food from the gardens and cooking it, and gathering firewood. They also care for the pigs. Men's work consists primarily of planting yams, bananas, and sugarcane, cutting down large trees, building, and hunting. They also help women with their work.

Land Tenure. Members of a clan hold the rights to land which are exercised by resident clan members. Village land is owned by a particular clan, though individuals have private usufructuary rights to the land and ownership of the houses they build there for the period their houses stand. The neighboring bush is also owned jointly by the clan. Individual gardeners control access to cleared land until it returns to uncultivated bush, at which point jurisdiction reverts to the clan. Hunting land is property of the clan land, with access controlled by, though not restricted to, clan members. No individual has the right of disposal over clan land.

Kinship

Kin Group and Descent. Kinship ideology is patrilineal. In practice, however, an individual may move to the village of collateral relatives and assume membership in the clan of that village without losing affiliation with the clan of his or her previous residence. Clan membership is based on common descent and coresidence. Clans are unnamed nontotemic groups that are identified by the names of their chiefs. The chief is the embodiment of the "prototype" (*omate*) given by a mythological ancestor.

Kinship Terminology. There is insufficient data on kin terms to determine the terminological system. It is probably similar to that of the linguistically related Tauade (Goilala).

Marriage and Family

Marriage. Polygamous marriages are common, particularly among men with prestige. Clans and villages are exogamous. There does not appear to be any pattern of intermarriage among communities. Normally, a marriage proposal is made by a boy through one of the girl's close female relatives. However, marriages by elopement and childhood betrothal are also practiced. A gift of a pig and other bride-wealth legitimize a marriage. Postmarital residence is patrilocal. Divorce is not uncommon. A wife usually initiates divorce by leaving her husband's house and moving into the home of her parents, her brothers, or a new husband. Although there may be claims for a return of bride-wealth following divorce, they are usually ineffective.

Domestic Unit. The household is composed of a husband, his wife (or wives), and their children. Other members of the extended family may also join the household. The cowives and their female and young male children sleep together in a single house, while the husband and his adolescent sons usually sleep in the village men's house.

Inheritance. Inheritance is patrilineal. Personal, movable property is divided among sons or other male kin at the death of an owner. Women only inherit personal, movable property and have no effective claims to land.

Socialization. Children participate in many day-to-day activities with adults, such as gardening and aspects of hunting. Games often involve taking the roles of adults. Children attend primary schools administered and staffed by the district department of education.

Sociopolitical Organization

Social Organization. The largest effective social group is the community, composed of several villages. Villages of the community (particularly those of the same clan) cooperate in feasting, ceremonies, protection, and occasionally hunting and fishing. The number of villages of the same clan within a community varies as they divide and recombine over the course of several years. Villages of the same clan within a community have a common chief (*amidi*) who normally succeeds to his position by primogeniture. The chief's ceremonial emone, the men's house in the village where he lives, is the site of feasts. Clans are not named, nor do they share a common totemic emblem. Instead, people identify their social affiliation by using the name of their amidi.

Political Organization. The community is the largest political unit. Each clan within the community has a chief who has a house in each village of his clan. His basic residence, however, is in the same village as his ceremonial men's house. The amidi's only authority is as the hereditary leader of his clan within a community. There are also clan leaders for warfare, division of pigs, and other political activities. Decision making within communities is done cooperatively by the amidi of the clans in the community and other leaders.

Social Control. The amidi only exerts control within a village in his role as the senior member of a clan. In most instances of homicide, seduction etc., members of the aggrieved clan or village take retribution themselves on the offenders if they are from outside the community. Gossip and the threats of shame and retribution induced by self-mutilation or suicide also control open disagreement and violence in the community.

Conflict. Even after European contact, raids between communities continued. The most frequent causes of disputes were the seduction of wives and theft of pigs. The warfare and sorcery that often followed was waged between communities. Retribution could be taken on any member of the opposing clan or community. Early missionary sources state that cannibalism was not practiced, but this report is disputed by ethnographic and later missionary accounts.

Religion and Expressive Culture

Religious Beliefs. According to Mafulu legend, Tsidibe, the hero of Mafulu mythology, crossed the mountains from the north and introduced the prototype or omate of humans, crops, animals, and social activities to the region. Tsidibe's passage is marked by stones and odd-shaped rocks. The current amidi is the embodiment of the omate, without which women, animals, and the crops of the clan could not reproduce. The Mafulu fear spirits of the dead, particularly those of the amidi, which are often held responsible for illness and accident. After 1905 the Sacred Heart Mission Christianized most of the Mafulu, established a training center for local catechists at Popolé, and produced vernacular-language religious materials.

Religious Practitioners. Magicians or sorcerers had powers to cause and cure illness and death. They were also able to divine the progress of an illness. The power to cause illness was only to be exercised as retribution against people from other villages. Following the introduction of Christianity and the establishment of a religious training school, the region has produced Roman Catholic catechists.

Ceremonies. The principle ceremony is the *gabé*, a large intertribal feast, which draws many guests from numerous distant communities. Gabé are spaced about ten to twelve years apart to enable the hosts to develop large gardens and litters of pigs needed for the feast. In addition to the social dimension, this feast involves the washing and final disposal of the bones of a dead amidi. During the feast, the bones that had been hung in the emone are brought out, splashed with blood from the pigs killed for the feast, and then redistributed to the amidi's close relatives. Rites of passage for boys and girls can be performed concurrently with the gabé, though separate pigs are required for each ceremony. Traditionally, there were particular ceremonies for the birth of the chief's first child. Other ceremonies performed for all children included admitting both boys and girls to the emone (though only boys could sleep there). The assumption of a perineal band, which was preceded by a lengthy seclusion, was performed prior to adolescence. Ceremonies were also held when boys' and girls' noses and ears were pierced, when boys were given drums and songs, and when people were married. Death and mourning ceremonies for chiefs differed from those of others.

Arts. Plastic arts consist primarily of painting tapa dancing aprons, burning or cutting abstract designs on smoking pipes, and constructing feather headdresses for dances. Musical instruments consist of kundu-style drums that are used to accompany dancing at feasts, Jew's harps, and flutes.

Medicine. Some traditional herbal medicines (unidentified) were ingested for stomach ailments and applied topically to wounds.

Death and Afterlife. People are believed to have a ghostly spirit that inhabits the body during life and leaves at death. Ghostly spirits become malevolent and are held responsible for illness and misfortune. After death and mourning rituals are complete, ghosts retreat to live in the mountains where they may take the forms of various plants and animals.

See also Mekeo, Tauade

Bibliography

Dupeyrat, A. (1954). *Savage Papua: A Missionary among Cannibals.* Translated by E. and D. de Mauny. New York: E. P. Dutton.

Dupeyrat, A. (1956). *Festive Papua.* Translated by E. de Mauny. London: Staples Press.

Dutton, T. (1973). *A Checklist of Languages and Present-Day Villages of Central and South-East Mainland Papua.* Pacific Linguistics, Series B, no. 24, Canberra: Australian National University.

Haddon, A. C. (1946). "Smoking and Tobacco Pipes in New

Guinea." *Royal Society of London Philosophical Transactions*, Series B, no. 232, pp. 1–278. London.

Hallpike, C. (1977). *Bloodshed and Vengeance in the Papuan Mountains: The Generation of Conflict in Tauade Society*. Oxford: Oxford University Press.

Williamson, R. W. (1912). *The Mafulu: Mountain People of British New Guinea*. London: Macmillan.

WILLIAM H. MCKELLIN

Mailu

ETHNONYM: Magi

Orientation

Identification. The Mailu are a Papuo-Melanesian people of the southern coast of eastern Papua New Guinea and its adjacent islands. In addition to serving as a generic term for the people as a whole, who also at times refer to themselves as Magi, the name "Mailu" also refers to the most important village of the area, on Mailu Island.

Location. Mailu territory extends along the southern Papuan coast from Cape Rodney in the east to Orangerie Bay in the west, and there are several villages on the larger of the offshore islands along this portion of the coast. Rainfall is quite heavy here, during both the "dry" season of the southeast trade winds (May to November) and the even wetter season of the northwest monsoons (January to March). The climate is tropical, supporting a rain-forest vegetation throughout much of the territory; the topography changes to flatter swamplands in the western reaches of the region. Mailu Island, alone in the region, has ample clay suitable for pottery; it has no swampland, however, and therefore its inhabitants are dependent upon the mainland for access to sago.

Linguistic Affiliation. Magi is one of the languages in the Mailuan Family.

Demography. In 1980, the population of Mailu speakers was estimated at 6,000.

History and Cultural Relations

Archaeological evidence attests to the presence of a pottery-using people in the Mailu area—both along the coast and on some of the islands—as far back as 2,000 years ago. The people of what is now known variously as Mailu Island or Toulon Island appear to have established dominance in the region very early on; because of their monopoly of both pottery making and oceangoing canoes they were able to assume ascendancy in direct trade as well as serving as distributors who enabled trade between other communities. This ascendancy was reinforced by raids carried out against coastal villages, which had the effect of driving the population back from the coast to more easily defensible hilltop villages. First European contact occurred in 1606, when Torres anchored off Mailu Island; this brief encounter was not a pleasant one, for the men of the ship killed many of the villagers and kidnapped fourteen children. Nearly 300 years later, in the late 1800s, this region was made part of the Protectorate of British New Guinea, bringing the influence of missionaries and administrators and introducing European goods to the local economy. Mailu men began working for Europeans, particularly in maritime industries, very early on in this period, with the effect of introducing new forms of wealth and new ways to acquire it. The London Missionary Society established a mission on Mailu Island in 1894. Government and missionary intervention brought an end to traditional raiding and its consequent head-hunting, thereby contributing to the end of male initiatory practices that centered on the acquisition of heads in war. In 1914, Bronislaw Malinowski arrived in the Mailu territory to do his first fieldwork.

Settlements

Mailu villages are laid out in two facing rows of family houses, built on stilts, separated by a broad road. Prior to European contact, men's houses (*dubu*) were built in the center of this road, running perpendicular to the dwelling houses. Houses were two-storied affairs, the upper floor consisting of a single, windowless room enclosed on all sides by the heavy thatch of the roof and entered by means of a ladder and trapdoor arrangement from below. The lower floor is open on all sides, but pandanus or woven reed mats are used as temporary, movable screens when needed. The ridgepoles of the buildings are elaborately carved, and pig jaws and fish tails are hung on the supports at the front of the buildings as decoration. There is no specialization of functions for the living areas of the houses, and no specifically men's or women's areas, although men tend to congregate at the roadside end and women toward the back of the buildings. Fenced gardens are built behind the houses.

Economy

Subsistence and Commercial Activities. On Mailu Island, while some cultivation is done, the gardens are of far lesser significance than in mainland communities. Rather, the island economy centers around pottery making, fishing, and seagoing trade. Fishing is done with spears and nets, by individuals as well as in groups of two or three. Pottery is made of coiled ropes of clay. Gardens are of the swidden type, with long fallow periods between crop cultivation. Among the produce grown are bananas, taro, yams, and sugarcane. Coconut and betel palms are planted near the village but not in the fenced gardens. Sago palms are cut down and processed for their starch. Europeans have introduced papaws and pumpkins to the gardening repertoire. Pigs are raised in the village, but only sows are kept—these are permitted to range into the forest and mate with wild boars. Hunting is an important component of the mainland subsistence economy—game customarily sought includes wallabies and wild pigs, which are driven into nets and speared, and a variety of birds that are caught in traps. Along the coastal reefs, shellfish are gathered.

Industrial Arts. Mailu manufacture, beyond the construction of their houses, includes the building of fences for the gardens, the weaving of mats from pandanus leaves and reeds, basket weaving, the making of arm shells, and the forging of stone implements. On Mailu Island, the two most significant items of manufacture are the coiled clay pots and, of course, the canoes upon which the island economy is based.

Trade. The Mailu Islanders, with their big, oceangoing canoes, participate in a wide-ranging trade network that extends beyond their own territory. Trade is a seasonal occupation: from July through August, Mailu travel westward with locally manufactured pottery in order to trade for betel nuts with the Aroma. On the return voyage they will stop to fish for shells with which to make the shell armbands that are used throughout the region as trade items. From September through October they sail west again, carrying a cargo of surplus sago to trade for pigs and dogs. During November and December, they voyage eastward with the pigs and dogs to trade for arm shells, ebony carvings, baskets, and (prior to the introduction of steel axes) polished-stone axe blades. Traditionally, Mailu also traded boar tusks, shell disks, and imported netted string bags. This trade was not only the centerpiece of the islander's subsistence economy; it also provided the necessary wealth to support the big feasts (*maduna*) held by the village clans every year.

Division of Labor. Pottery making is done only by women; arm shell manufacture, seagoing trade, canoebuilding, house construction, and hunting are all done only by men. Garden clearing and the construction of garden fences are men's tasks, while all weeding is done by women. Women do all the day-to-day cooking. Except for limited night fishing with torches, women do not fish. Pig tending is primarily a woman's task. Men make their own tools or trade for them. Child care is the province of women.

Land Tenure. Ownership of garden lands and canoes is vested in the local clan section, under the direction of the headman. Dwelling houses belong to the household head, and ownership passes from him to his eldest son, while in the past the men's houses were held corporately by the clan. Rights to individual coconut and betel palms are held individually.

Kinship

Kin Groups and Descent. Mailu clans are patrilineal, dispersed over several villages. Local (village-level) clan "sections" are named, exogamous, and agnatically recruited. An in-marrying woman exchanges her clan membership for that of her husband, and her children, though initially held to belong to her brother (thus to her father's lineage), are normally claimed at some point by her husband through the gift of a pig. It is not unusual, however, for a childless man to adopt one of his sister's sons.

Kinship Terminology. Mailu employ a system of classificatory terms for all relatives of previous generations (i.e., grandparents, parents, uncles, and aunts) in order to get around the taboo of using personal names when speaking of or directly addressing these relatives. These terms mark not only one's genealogical position but also differentiate between elder and younger members of a single generation. However, while several different relations may be designated by a single term (e.g., a man's elder brother, his father's elder brother's son, and his mother's sister's elder son may all be referred to by the term *uiniegi*), other terms or qualifiers are used to mark more specifically the actual relationship of the relative when necessary.

Marriage and Family

Marriage. Mailu marriages are arranged through betrothal, often when the girl is still quite young but usually when she has reached her mid-teens. The boy's family provides a series of gifts of increasing value over time, and both families participate in roughly equivalent food exchanges. Upon betrothal, both the boy and girl are expected to remain celibate—an affair by either one is sufficient to nullify the betrothal. Bride-wealth is paid in pigs, tobacco, and other items of locally recognized wealth. Since pigs can only be given away at feasts, at some point prior to the actual marriage the contracting parents of the betrothed pair will use the occasion of a maduna to make this gift. Marriage itself is not marked by elaborate ceremony: the bride prepares a meal for her betrothed in his father's house, then returns to her own for an interval of about a week. After that time, the marriage may be consummated, and the bride leaves her family home to live in her father-in-law's house, assuming membership in his clan. With marriage, a man enters into avoidance relations with certain of his wife's kin, most particularly with her older sister. Polygyny is permitted but rarely practiced, due to the great expense of pig-based bride-wealth entailed by marriage. Adultery is considered a grievous offense for both men and women, but the punishment of an adulterous wife—a severe beating, even death—is far more onerous than the public censure and gossip that serves as punishment for a man's adultery. Divorce appears to be possible but rare.

Inheritance. Personal ornaments and wealth are inherited by a man's "real," as opposed to his classificatory, brothers. His coconut palms are passed to his brothers and his sons. The ownership of a house passes to the eldest surviving son. Women do not hold or inherit property, except in cases where a woman's father dies without sons.

Socialization. During their early years, Mailu children are cared for by their mothers and other female members of the household. Children enjoy a great degree of independence, rarely being corrected or chastised and generally being left free to indulge in games and sport. Boys are given miniature boats, similar in design to those used by their elders on the seas, and they are also provided with small versions of hunting and fishing nets and spears. For both boys and girls, early training in their adult roles is acquired by observing their elders at their daily tasks and by helping out when they possess sufficient skill and interest; this participation is allowed to develop at its own pace. Both boys and girls have their ears (and, formerly, the nasal septum) pierced shortly after birth. At about the age of 4, girls begin to undergo the long process of body tattooing, which culminates when they have attained marriageable age with the tattooing of their faces—done in conjunction with women-only feasts. Male initiation, which once was an important ritual event and required the acquisition of human heads during a raid, is no longer practiced. Infanticide is practiced when twins are born—the younger twin is killed—or when the mother dies in childbirth, as well as in the case of an illegitimate birth.

Sociopolitical Organization

Social Organization. Traditionally, Mailu households were under the ostensible direction of the eldest male, though since each adult male had his own gardens his self-sufficiency ensured a certain degree of independence. Enterprises requiring the cooperation of large numbers of people (trading voyages, garden clearing, the giving of major feasts) drew their personnel from beyond a single household's membership, and leadership in such cases was sought from influential individuals (headmen) in whom the participants had confidence. Clan affiliation determined the men's house to which one belonged, when men's houses were still being built, and it also served as the organizing principle for contributions of wealth in the pig feasts.

Political Organization. There is no traditionally recognized central authority among the Mailu, although elders generally provided leadership by dint of their prestige and reputation for sound judgment. Once Mailu territory came under colonial rule, individuals were picked by the administration to act as go-betweens, but this imposed leadership has no validation in traditional practice.

Social Control. Within the village, elders—and particularly headmen—might be called upon to mediate disputes and settle grievances. Major offenses such as the adultery of a woman or the killing of kin are sanctioned by death, but for lesser offenses the force of public opinion serves to punish offenders. Sorcerers within the village were usually appeased rather than punished.

Conflict. Warfare between villages was common prior to the arrival of missionaries and Western administrators, and it was conducted primarily for the purpose of collecting heads, which were of ritual importance in male initiation rites. Wars were fought with spears and clubs. Intervillage hostilities might arise over the suspicion of sorcery or in retribution for earlier raids.

Religion and Expressive Culture

Religious Beliefs. Mailu indigenous beliefs hold that a culture hero, called Tau or Samadulele, sailed with his mother from out of the West, bringing with him the pigs, sago, coconut, and betel nuts that form the core of Mailu economy and ceremonial life. However, outside of the chants performed during the "Govi Maduna," the largest ceremony performed by Mailu, the importance of this mythological personage is unclear. Of more direct, day-to-day importance in Mailu ritual life are two classes of spiritual beings. The first, spirits of the ancestors, are benevolent, and they are often consulted for protection and advice. They are held to reside in the skulls of the deceased, which are kept in the houses of their descendants. The second class of spirits are malevolent female beings who take possession of living persons, causing their unwitting hosts to commit murder or destroy property.

Religious Practitioners. All adult males possess some magical knowledge involving the use of herbs, incantations, and special taboos. This magic is used to protect one's garden, bring good luck in the building of a canoe or the making of tools, ensure a good crop, or other such individual concerns. Such knowledge is privately held, taught by a father to his sons, and a man will as a rule initiate his wife into this knowledge as well. Magic intended to secure protection for communally important enterprises such as a trading expedition or a big feast is performed by the more important members of the community. Sorcerers have private magical knowledge of a more destructive nature, but they are not thought to be anything other than mortal. Their magic permits them to travel unseen at night, during which they try to cause injury and even death to their rivals. Sorcery is believed to be widespread within Mailu society.

Ceremonies. The central ceremonial occasion of Mailu life is the Govi Maduna, a great annual pig feast held after the last of the year's trading voyages. The maduna is hosted by the entire village, although its initial sponsors may be drawn from only some of the clans represented therein. Because pigs can be exchanged only during the maduna, a number of other ritually important events are encompassed by it, such as the payment of pigs by the family of a prospective groom to the bride's kin and the assumption of paternal rights to a child. Each of the village's clans is represented by its local headman, who supervises his portion of the feast preparations, solicits contributions of food from his kin, and makes speeches during the festivities. Prior to the big feast, there is a series of lesser feasts of shorter duration and narrower scope—the big feast brings together people from a great many villages, while the lesser ones involve people from a smaller radius. During the course of the smaller feasts, promises of contributions to the upcoming maduna are solicited, and throughout this period wealth is collected to be used in a trading voyage to Aroma territory to get the pigs that will be slaughtered by each clan during the feast.

Arts. Mailu visual arts consist of decorative carvings on house posts, canoes, and a variety of utensils. The designs employed in the decorative arts are similar to those used by the Southern Massim and appear to have originated with them. Songs and dances performed in the Mailu feasts also appear to have originated elsewhere—with the Southern Massim as well as with other neighboring groups. Many of the dances involve mimicking the movements of birds or animals, while others involve the pantomiming of important day-to-day activities, such as preparing a garden or building a canoe.

Medicine. Illness, always attributed to sorcery, is treated by incantations, massage, and the sucking out of foreign matter (inserted magically by sorcerers) from the body of the patient. Medical practitioners are almost always male, and they charge high fees—payable in armbands and other local forms of wealth—for their services.

Death and Afterlife. Death is assumed to be caused ultimately by the action of a sorcerer. Upon death, two spirits are said to survive the corpse. One spirit departs the body and travels to the southwest where a ladder permits his or her descent into Biula, a subterranean underworld. The second spirit is thought to reside in the skull of the deceased, and it is this spirit with which a person's survivors communicate when seeking advice or assistance. Initially, the spouse and classificatory siblings of the deceased shave their heads, blacken their skin with burned coconut fiber, put on special armbands and other adornments, and assume mourning dress that conceals the entire body and face. Immediately upon discovery of a death, these close kin set up a wailing lamentation, while less close relatives of the deceased bring coconuts for distribution throughout the village. As soon as possible after a death, the body is washed and decorated and a chant is performed over the corpse in an effort to determine the sorcerer responsible (the corpse is thought to react violently at the naming of the sorcerer's village). As soon as may be after these preparations, the body is buried either under the house of the deceased or in his gardens. If the latter burial is performed, a small mortuary hut is built over the grave. A series of small feasts are held during the ensuing period of mourning, and after about two to three months the body is dug up to retrieve the head, which thereafter is kept in a small basket in the house of the surviving members of the deceased's household. A final, large-scale mortuary feast is held between six months to a year after the death, often as part of the maduna, where one of the nearest kin (though never the father or the widow of the deceased) performs a dance with the deceased's head. At this time the mortuary hut is destroyed, and the period of public mourning comes to an end.

Bibliography

Abbi, B. L. (1975). *Traditional Groupings and Modern Associations: A Study of Changing Local Groups in Papua and New Guinea.* Simla: Indian Institute of Advanced Study.

Malinowski, Bronislaw (1967). *A Diary in the Strict Sense of the Term.* London: Routledge & Kegan Paul.

Malinowski, Bronislaw (1988). *Malinowski among the Magi: "The Natives of Mailu."* Edited with an introduction by Michael W. Young. London: Routledge & Kegan Paul.

NANCY GRATTON

Maisin

ETHNONYMS: Kosirau, Kosirava, Maisina

Orientation

Identification. Maisin-speaking people live in Papua New Guinea. All but the remote Kosirau people refer to themselves as Maisin. Westerners called these groups Kosirava and Maisina in early reports.

Location. Maisin speakers occupy three areas in Tufi Subdistrict of Oro Province in Papua New Guinea. The Kosirau live in small isolated settlements within the vast swamps of the Musa River basin. A second group of Maisin speakers shares the village of Uwe with Korafe speakers on the northeast coast of Cape Nelson. The largest portion of the population lives in eight villages along the southern shores of Collingwood Bay. Behind the coastal villages stretches a vast area of unpopulated forest, swamp, and mountains. The region is very isolated from the rest of Papua New Guinea. There are no roads. The only access is by boat or small plane into grass airstrips. There are two distinct seasons. The northwest monsoons are accompanied by heavy rainfall between November and April. Around May, the winds switch to the southwest and the weather becomes dry, cooler, and breezy.

Demography. The 1980 National Census suggested a total Maisin population around 2,000. Of that number, approximately 1,400 lived in the rural villages while the rest had migrated to the cities. The population density along the coast was about 10 persons per square kilometer.

Linguistic Affiliation. There are two dialects: Maisin and Kosirava. Maisin attracted scholarly attention from an early date as a rare example of a language that combines grammatical features from both Austronesian and Non-Austronesian sources; thus Maisin has been variously classed as "mixed" or as "Non-Austronesian."

History and Cultural Relations

There is archaeological evidence of human occupation of southwestern Collingwood Bay going back 1,000 years, with trading links to Goodenough Island and the much more distant Trobriand Islands to the east. The Maisin relate that they are relative newcomers to the coast who have displaced the original inhabitants. Elders say that their ancestors emerged from underground about seven generations before the 1980s at a site on the western edge of the Musa Basin. Those who remained behind became the Kosirau; others made their way along coastal and interior routes to their present locations. At the time of European contact in 1890, the Maisin had a widespread reputation as ferocious warriors, employing huge canoes to sweep down upon their neighbors. In 1900, the administration of British New Guinea established a station at Tufi on Cape Nelson and, within a year, forcibly brought intertribal raiding in the area to a halt. The following year, the Anglican New Guinea Mission opened a church and school in the largest Maisin village of Uiaku. Over the next thirty years, the Maisin gradually became integrated into the emerging colonial society: most young people converted to Christianity and young men routinely signed up to work on distant plantations and in mines. Although Collingwood Bay lay outside the sphere of the Japanese invasion in 1942, all able-bodied Maisin men served as laborers with the Australian forces. Following the war, the pace of national integration quickened. Many Maisin young people attended new secondary and tertiary schools and entered the professional labor force. Those who remained behind experimented with a number of cash crops, most of which failed.

Settlements

The nine coastal villages range in size from less than 100 to more than 300 people. All but two of the villages are situated in clusters of two or three other communities. Local populations rise and fall considerably as people move between villages and town. A few villages are composed of a single kin group, but most are multinucleated settlements of patriclan hamlets, strung out along the coast. Most hamlets are arranged in two roughly parallel lines following the edge of the shore. A few hamlets, homes of the higher-ranking clans, have houses arranged in a rough circle around a bare earth plaza, traditionally used for feasting and dancing. Where hamlets are not contiguous, paths connect them to other parts of the settlement and to the gardens and other settlements. The three largest villages possess simple churches, school buildings (including houses for teachers), medical aid posts, and community trade stores. Prior to contact, Maisin constructed their dwellings on mangrove posts, 3 to 4 meters above ground. A platform on the bottom level served as a cooking area and shelter during the day, while an upper level room, entered by means of a ladder, served as sleeping quarters. Since the 1920s, the Maisin have built rectangular houses with windows and verandahs, along the lines of house styles introduced by the colonial administration in the 1920s. The houses are still on posts and constructed mostly of bush materials. In the mid-1980s, some villagers, with funds provided by working relatives, began to construct houses with metal roofs.

Economy

Subsistence and Commercial Activities. The Maisin practice slash-and-burn horticulture, shifting their gardens every two to three years. Staples include taro, sweet potatoes, plantains, and sago supplemented by coconuts, papayas, sugarcane, watermelons, squash, and sweet bananas. The usual gardening tools are digging sticks and machetes. Villagers enjoy fish and shellfish, which they gather by hand, line, net, and spear. They also hunt wild pigs, cassowaries, wallabies, and birds in the dense forests that surround the villages using spears and shotguns. They supplement this local diet with white rice and tinned meats and fish purchased in local trade stores. Domestic animals include chickens, dogs, and cats. The Local Government Council banned village pigs in the mid-1960s. There is a tiny commercial market for copra and a somewhat larger one for tapa. Villagers receive most of their cash and commodities as gifts from relatives working in the towns.

Industrial Arts. Maisin villagers continue to produce much of their material culture: string bags, tapa, houses, and outrigger canoes. They purchase some items, like clay cooking pots, from neighboring peoples. Many items, such as clothing, fishing nets, and cooking utensils, are quickly being replaced by factory products.

Trade. Into early colonial times, Maisin traded tapa, stone axe blades, and food for shell and obsidian with peoples to the east on Cape Vogel and Goodenough Island. They continue to trade occasionally with interior tribes for net bags, dogs, and feathers and with Wanigela people for cooking pots. Sometimes they exchange tapa for these things, but more often they pay money. Small trade stores, often operating out of village houses, sell tobacco and a few tinned items. Some villages hold weekly markets where women sell or exchange garden produce and tapa.

Division of Labor. There is a marked division of labor in most areas of life. Men clear and burn off garden land, erect fences against bush pigs, and help women plant crops. Men also hunt, fish, and build houses and canoes. Women plant, weed, and harvest gardens and gather wild foods from the bush, rivers, and mangrove swamps. They carry produce and firewood from the gardens to the villages and cook the meals. Women also weave string bags and beat tapa. Men and women both prepare sago, often together.

Land Tenure. Low population density and a relatively moderate climate provide the Maisin of southern Collingwood Bay with a rich food base. Land passes down through the male line, although villagers frequently make gardens on the lands of their affines and matrilineal relations. Patriclans also claim large areas of forest and grassland and occasionally stretches of coast.

Kinship

Kin Groups and Descent. Patriclans occupying hamlets within the village form the most stable kin groups. They vary greatly in composition. The smallest comprise single lineages, while the largest are composed of smaller named subclans, each occupying different areas of the hamlet or separate hamlets. Patriclans occupying land in different hamlets or villages often have close historical associations with each other. Patriclan identities are indicated by land claims and by emblems, including tapa designs, ritual customs, types of magic, lime-spatula designs, body decorations, and plant tokens. They are also affirmed—and disputed—in migration stories. Maisin distinguish two ranks of patriclan: the *kawo* and the *sabu*. The higher-ranked kawo clans enjoy certain ritual prerogatives, including the right to host feasts and dances in their hamlet plazas and to wear certain ornaments such as chicken feathers. Whatever importance these ranks had in the past when warfare and intertribal feasting were common, they have little practical or political influence today. The patriclans are rarely significant in the day-to-day affairs of the villages. Villagers generally call upon close cognatic kin and affines to form work groups and to host or participate in ceremonials and formal exchanges. Active kin groups, then, vary greatly from occasion to occasion. Descent is formally patrilineal, but as in much of Melanesia, there are many exceptions to the rule.

Kinship Terminology. Iroquois-type terms are used and relative age is distinguished.

Marriage and Family

Marriage. Until the recent exodus to the towns, the vast majority of Maisin married close to home, although almost always outside of their own patriclan. Sister exchange was the preferred form of marriage since it required no bride-wealth payments. Many such arrangements, however, broke down and in the past, as today, young people exercised considerable choice in their marriage partners. Premarital intercourse is common. Many individuals will temporarily live with a series of partners before settling with their permanent spouse, often after children are born. Husbands are expected to raise bride-wealth and the couple should also arrange formal prestations to the wife's kin to mark the birth and maturation of their firstborn. Many villagers complain, however, that couples today delay and often never meet their exchange obligations. Some couples are initially married in the church, but most wait, often until they have children, before seeking a priest's blessing of their union. Upon marriage, most couples settle initially with one of the husband's clansmen before building their own house in the patriclan's hamlet. The church frowns on divorce, but it is common and informal. Monogamy is the norm, but a few polygamous marriages occur in most villages.

Domestic Unit. A household, usually with a nuclear family at its core, makes up the basic working unit: gardening and consuming together. Parents, grandparents, adult siblings, aunts and uncles and other kin often enlarge the household. As older relations lose their ability for physical labor, their children build small satellite houses where they live in semiseclusion.

Inheritance. Most ritual property is bestowed upon the eldest, particularly if it is a boy. Sons inherit land equally and daughters are allowed to garden their fathers' land after they marry. They may not, however, pass this right to their own children.

Socialization. Infants and children are raised by their parents, close kin, and siblings. Older children provide much child care for younger siblings and cousins. Adults teach children to be respectful and cooperative by example and by chiding, rarely by punishment. From age 6 or 7, children spend a considerable amount of their time in school. Formerly, all males underwent short initiations into their patriclans. Much larger ceremonies were staged for firstborn children, male and female, and these occasionally still take place. Most Maisin girls still have their faces tattooed during puberty. As more children have entered distant high schools and as more villagers have left for jobs in the towns, traditional puberty practices have declined.

Sociopolitical Organization

Social Organization. The Maisin live in a relatively egalitarian society. Kinship obligations, marked by steady informal and formal exchanges, tend to level out differences in wealth and power and to provide support for the weak and elderly in the communities. Maisin frown upon those who show too much independence or who put themselves above others. However, some categories of people exercise more influence and expect to be treated with deference: parents over children, elders over younger persons, kawo clans over sabu clans, wife givers over wife takers, and men over women.

Political Organization. Maisin divide political activities into three domains: the "village side," the "mission side," and the "government side." "Village side" affairs include life-cycle ceremonies, exchanges, and land and sorcery disputes. These are matters handled between kin or kin groups, in which patriclan elders play a dominant role. "Mission side" affairs include the efforts of the church councils and Mothers' Unions to provide moral and monetary support for clergy and teachers. "Government side" affairs embrace the work of the Local Government Council and village business groups to promote development projects and locally organize for provincial and national elections. Frequently the same men become leaders in all three domains, largely through strength of personality, education and experience outside of the rural areas. Senior women have an indirect but important influence, especially in "mission side" and "village side" affairs. However, men dominate public politics.

Social Control. Informal sanctions, such as gossiping and strongly internalized values of respect and equivalence, provide the chief sources of social control. Fear of sorcery is another important sanction. Miscreants who are not brought into line informally may face a full village meeting or, in serious cases, be taken to court at the subdistrict government station.

Conflict. Warfare and raiding were common until around 1910. Maisin elders speak with some nostalgia of the great warriors in the past, but the only major conflict living Maisin have witnessed was that between the Japanese and Allies during World War II. Most conflicts today occur over land or sorcery accusation and rarely involve violence.

Religion and Expressive Culture

Religious Beliefs. Most Maisin believe that the spirits of the recent dead exercise a considerable influence, both for good and bad, over the living. Encounters with bush spirits can cause serious illness, particularly to women and children. Despite many attempts to get rid of sorcery, Maisin believe that various kinds continue to be practiced by villagers and by outsiders and they attribute most deaths to this cause. God and Jesus are very distant deities, sometimes encountered in dreams. Faith in them, it is said, can overcome the evil caused by sorcerers and spirits. With a handful of exceptions, Maisin are Christians. Most of the coastal people are second- or third-generation Anglicans while the Kosirau converted to the Seventh-Day Adventist church in the 1950s. Villagers accept this version of Christian teaching and liturgy, but they also encounter local bush spirits, ghosts, and sorcerers and most practice garden magic and make use of indigenous healing techniques and practitioners. There is considerable diversity in religious belief, depending in large part upon an individual's education and experience outside of the villages.

Religious Practitioners. Six Maisin men have been ordained as priests, and many more have served as deacons, members of religious orders, teacher-evangelists, lay readers, and mission medical workers. The Anglican Church has been almost entirely localized and, since 1962, an indigenous priest has served the Maisin. Healers can also be found in most villages—men and women who possess superior knowledge of indigenous medicines, bush spirits, and the interactions between human souls and the spirit world (including God).

Ceremonies. At the time of European contact, funerals, mourning rites, initiations of firstborn children, and intertribal feasts were the main ceremonial occasions. All were marked by large exchanges of food, shell valuables, and tapa cloth. Initiations and intertribal feasts were also occasions for days, sometimes weeks, of dancing. The chief ceremonies today are Christmas, Easter, and patronal feast days. Huge feasts are often held on such days, along with traditional dances by troops in indigenous costume. Life-cycle ceremonies—particularly firstborn puberty celebrations and mortuary rituals—are the other chief occasions for ceremonies.

Arts. Maisin women are famed throughout Papua New Guinea for their exquisitely designed tapa (bark cloth). Primarily serving as the traditional clothing for men and women, tapa today is a major item of local exchange and a source of cash. It is sold via church and government intermediaries to artifact shops in the cities. Most women receive elaborate facial tattoos in late adolescence, with the curvilinear designs covering the entire face that are unique to the region.

Medicine. Maisin attribute illnesses to "germs" or to spirit attacks and sorcerers, depending upon whether they respond to Western medicine. Villagers make use of local medical aid posts and a regional hospital, as well as home remedies and the services of village healers.

Death and Afterlife. Traditionally, Maisin believed that spirits of the dead inhabited the mountains behind their villages, frequently returning to aid or to punish kin. Villagers still encounter the recent dead in dreams and visions—attributing both good luck and misfortune to them—but they now say that the deceased reside in Heaven. Although they have been greatly modified by Christianity, mortuary ceremonies continue to present the most "traditional" face of Maisin society. Villagers mourn a death collectively for three days following the burial, during which time they avoid loud noises and work in the garden, lest they offend the soul of the dead person or its living relatives. Bereaved spouses and parents go into semiseclusion for periods lasting from a few days to several years. They are brought out of mourning by their affines, who wash them, trim their hair, and dress them in clean tapa and ornaments in a ceremony that is almost identical to the puberty rites for firstborn children.

See also Goodenough Island

Bibliography

Barker, John (1985). "Maisin Christianity: An Ethnography of the Contemporary Religion of a Seaboard Melanesian People." Ph.D. dissertation, University of British Columbia.

Barker, John (1989). "Western Medicine and the Continuity of Belief: The Maisin of Collingwood Bay, Oro Province." In *A Continuing Trial of Treatment: Medical Pluralism in Papua New Guinea,* edited by Stephen Frankel and Gilbert Lewis, 69–93. Dordrecht: Kluwer.

Ross, Malcolm (1984). "Maisin: A Preliminary Sketch." *Papers in New Guinea Linguistics* 23:1–82. Pacific Linguistics, Series A, no. 69. Canberra: Australian National University.

Tietjen, Anne Marie, and Lawrence J. Walker (1985). "Moral Reasoning and Leadership among Men in a Papua New Guinea Society." *Developmental Psychology* 21:982–992.

JOHN BARKER

Malaita

ETHNONYMS: 'Are'are, Fataleka, Kwaio, Kwara'ae, Langalanga, Lau, Sa'a, To'aba'ita

Orientation

Identification. Malaita is one of six large islands in the double chain that forms the Solomon Islands, formerly the British Solomon Islands Protectorate. As the most populous island in the Solomons, Malaita has long been a source of plantation labor, and in earlier decades its people were famed and feared for their violent resistance to European invasion. The island remains noteworthy for its strong cultural conservatism.

Location. Running northwest to southeast and being about 160 kilometers long and up to 40 kilometers wide, Malaita lies at 9° S and 161° E. The island is mountainous (rising to 1,540 meters) and comprised of rain forest, with lagoons along parts of both coastlines. The island of Maramasike is separated from Malaita proper by a narrow channel.

Demography. Malaita had a population in 1986 of about 80,000, with some 20,000 more Malaitans living elsewhere in the Solomons.

Linguistic Affiliation. Malaita languages fall into the Malaita-San Cristobal Group of the Southeast Solomonic (Oceanic Austronesian) languages. Southeast Solomonic may turn out to fall within a subgroup of Eastern Oceanic languages, along with North-central New Hebridean, Fijian, Polynesian, and Nuclear Micronesian languages; but so far the evidence is inconclusive, clouded by the shared retention in all these languages of many Proto-Oceanic features. Malaita is divided into a series of languages or dialects (mainly running in stripes across the island) although their precise relationship is not yet established. The most recent subgrouping establishes a subgroup of Northern Malaita languages, consisting of a northern dialect cluster (To'aba'ita, Baelelea, Baegu, Lau, Fataleka), Kwara'ae (with 18,000 speakers, the largest language group), Langalanga, and Kwaio. (There is some evidence that the latter two, along with two smaller language groups, form a separate Central Malaita Group.) 'Are'are and Sa'a (spoken on Maramasike) seem to form a subgroup with the Makira (San Cristobal) languages, although on cultural and other grounds a closer affinity of 'Are'are with the Malaita peoples to the northwest (Kwaio, etc.) seems likely.

History and Cultural Relations

Malaita was largely avoided in the early whaling and trading period (pre-1860) because of its inhospitable coastline and inhabitants. About 1870, Malaitans began to be kidnapped (and were later indentured) in the labor trade to Queensland, Fiji, Samoa, and New Caledonia plantations, a process notable for violent confrontations and heavy loss of life. Mission enclaves were established at the turn of the century. Pacification of Malaita began in 1909 but was not completed until 1927, after the assassination of a district officer by Kwaio warriors. Malaita was mostly spared the direct ravages of World War II, but laborers working with American troops were central in a postwar anticolonial resistance movement, Maasina ("Marching") Rule, focused on recognition of customary law and the codification of custom, indigenous representation in the process of administration, improved pay, dignity, and working conditions, and communal reorganization along military lines. The Solomon Islands gained independence in 1978, and today Malaitans play many important roles in national life.

Settlements

Very sharp contrasts in ecological adaptation distinguish the "bush" peoples of the Malaita interior from those of the lagoons of the northeast coast (Lau speakers, who also have a colony on Maramasike) and the lagoons of the central west coast (Langalanga speakers). The former, living on islets and on coral platforms dredged from the lagoon floor, specialize in fishing (in the lagoon and the open sea) and in bartering fish and other marine products for root vegetables and forest products offered by peoples of the adjacent mountains. The Langalanga speakers may earlier have had a similar adaptation, but in recent centuries their fishing has been complemented and overshadowed by the specialized production and export or barter of shell valuables. What follows deals primarily with the numerically preponderant "bush" peoples, but it also briefly examines the "saltwater" variants on common cultural themes (the contrast between *tolo* or "bush" and *asi* or "sea" is widely drawn in Malaita languages). In bush areas, settlements were scattered homesteads or tiny hamlets, clustered close enough for collective defense and frequently moved because of pollution violations or gardening cycles. Each settlement mapped out a cosmological pattern in which the men's house above and the menstrual hut below became symbolic mirror images, with domestic houses in between. During the colonial period, missions, labor recruiters, and the government encouraged movements to the coast; and these movements were accelerated by the postwar Maasina Rule anticolonial movement. Nowadays, the Malaita population is mainly concentrated along the coast in substantial villages, except in remaining pagan areas (notably the east Kwaio interior) where old patterns still prevail; large Malaita populations have also resettled around Honiara, with pockets elsewhere in the Solomons.

Economy

Subsistence and Commercial Activities. In bush areas of Malaita, taro was the primary subsistence crop, grown in a continuous cycle in forest swiddens. Yams were a secondary subsistence crop, but because they were grown in an annual cycle, they were accorded ritual importance. Plantains and a range of other cultigens and forest products augmented these starchy staples. (The taro plants were devastated by viral and fungal blights after World War II, and sweet potatoes—culturally disvalued but convenient—have become the dominant staple.) Animal protein came from fish, grubs, birds, cuscus, opossums, and other game, as well as domestic pigs. The latter (and their theft and defense) were a focus of cultural attention; the pigs were used mainly in sacrifices, mortuary feasts, bride-wealth, and compensation payments. Strung shell beads and dolphin teeth served as mediums of exchange, used in bride-wealth, homicide payments, compensation, and mortuary feasts. Red-shell discs produced in Langalanga (especially the ten-stringed *tafuli'ae* of northern Malaita) were widely used, but Kwaio produce their own white-shell beads, which in standard lengths and combinations (denominations) serve as an all-purpose medium of exchange. For 120 years, Malaitans have been locked into a system of circulating male plantation labor (originally to Queensland, Fiji, Samoa, and New Caledonia, and, in this century, to internal plantations). In the last 20 years, this adaptation has increasingly given way (except for the diehard pagans) to peasant production of copra, cocoa, and livestock, to petty entrepreneurship, and to wage labor in urban settings. Today, Malaitans occupy every rung of a developing class system, ranging from prosperous businesspeople and parliamentarians to a marginalized and violently predatory urban underclass.

Industrial Arts. Traditionally, chipped chert adzes were the primary felling and cutting tools. Other elements of early Malaita technology included pouches and bags woven from bush fibers, river fish and bird nets, intricate fishhooks, and large composite seagoing canoes with caulked planks and high prow and stern. In contrast to the relative elaborateness of their weaponry and some aspects of their maritime technology, Malaita bush peoples specialized in a kind of throwaway tool technology: crudely chipped chert adze blades were used in place of older ground basalt blades; giant bamboo was used for water, cooking, and construction; today, digging sticks are not even fire-hardened (at least among the Kwaio). With highly uneven access to education and Westernization on Malaita during the last forty years, Malaitans now span a technological range from engineers, doctors, and pilots to subsistence cultivators using magic and digging sticks.

Trade. Precolonial trade systems included the far-flung Langalanga networks, through which shell valuables were traded for pigs, produce, and other items, and the well-organized markets (especially on the northeastern coast) where Lau bartered fish and marine products for taro, yams, *Canarium* almonds, and forest products with interior populations (Baegu, Baelelea, Fataleka, To'aba'ita). Chert for adze blades and other scarce materials seem also to have been traded.

Division of Labor. Men and women had complementary roles in the division of labor, with women doing the bulk of everyday garden work, foraging, domestic labor, and child care and men felling trees, fencing land, fishing, and fighting.

Land Tenure. Primary rights to land are obtained through tracing patrifiliation, but secondary rights are also granted to those with maternal links to ancestors.

Kinship

Kin Groups and Descent. Throughout the Malaita interior, descent-based local groups having primary interests in estates in land and primary connections to ancestors are the most important sociopolitical units. Everywhere, the ideal pattern is for virilocal residence and patrifiliation, with children growing up in their father's place and developing a primary attachment there to lands and ancestors. Ideally, then, members of the group should all be connected to the founding ancestors through patrifilial chains (and those who are, are distinguished as "agnates"). However, throughout Malaita, connections with maternal relatives (and, through them, to lands and ancestors) are regarded as very important and complementary to connections to and through paternal relatives. "Nonagnates" are recognized as having secondary rights of residence and land use. Such ties are extended through father's mother, mother's mother, and more distant kin; and ancestors related through such links were commonly propitiated. Life circumstances—uxorilocal residence, parental divorce, or widowhood—can lead children to grow up with maternal kin. When they do, they are accorded de facto rights of residence and land rights as though they were agnates: what matters is commitment to lands, ancestors, and kin and intimate knowledge of a place and its rituals and taboos. Given the ideological emphasis on agnation (at least in some contexts) and countervailing ideologies of symmetric bilaterality, and given the varying statistical composition of groups, it is no wonder that ethnographers have differed in characterizing Malaita social structure. Among the Lau speakers of the lagoons, densely concentrated in large villages, descent groups are quite squarely agnatic. In some parts of Malaita, segmentary ritual and political relationships above the level of local descent-based groups were accorded importance. In the north, eight clusters of descent groups were recognized, with the politically dominant and ritually senior "stem" groups of each cluster connected to one another by putative agnatic links (but with some other groups within each cluster connected to the "stem" group by nonagnatic links). In Kwaio, such higher-level linkages operate only through ritual links between shrines and their priests.

Kinship Terminology. Kinship terminology ranges from a symmetric Iroquois-type pattern in Kwara'ae (systematically distinguishing cross from parallel kin in the middle three generations according to relative sex of the last connecting links) to a basically Hawaiian-type pattern in Kwaio (broken only by a self-reciprocal mother's brother/sister's child category). Intermediate are systems (such as To'aba'ita) with a partial Omaha-like skewing in which the mother's brother/sister's child category is incorporated into the grandparent/grandchild category (which occurs in all the Malaita terminologies).

Marriage and Family

Marriage. Marriage is generally serially monogamous, although polygyny is possible in some places. Bride-wealth is universal. Prohibitions on marriage generally are bilaterally based, with marriage between close cousins normatively prohibited. As noted previously, postmarital residence was initially virilocal, although in some areas later flexibility in residential attachment was possible. Divorce was possible but difficult because of bride-wealth.

Domestic Unit. Domestic family groups (prototypically nuclear families but often augmented by widows, bachelors, spinsters, and foster children) are the primary units of production and consumption.

Inheritance. Inheritance assigns rights to those who create property and transmits these rights to and through children. Normatively, although sons and daughters inherit rights, sons transmit primary rights to their children and daughters transmit secondary rights. A steward, ideally a senior agnate, acts as a spokesperson for collectively held land and other property.

Socialization. Children are highly valued and caringly nurtured, with women having the primary responsibilities for early child care and training. Sexual polarization early separates boys' and girls' life experiences (though there are no formal initiations), with boys being much more free to hunt and play and girls beginning early a regimen of hard labor and child care. Boys spend progressively more time with men, stay in men's houses, and participate in ritual.

Sociopolitical Organization

Social Organization. In bush areas, a fierce egalitarianism based on achievement rather than rank traditionally prevailed. However, in some coastal areas (e.g., Lau and Maramasike) ideas of hereditary rank had some currency.

Political Organization. A pervasive ideology on Malaita distinguishes three leadership roles: that of "priest," who acts as the religious officiant of the descent group (see below); that of "warrior-leader" (*ngwane ramo*), a bounty hunter and fighting leader; and that of a secular leader (in the Northern Malaita dialect, *ngwane inoto/inito'o*). Characterizations of the latter range from a hereditary chief (*araha* in Maramasike) to a smallish big-man in the most politically fragmented bush areas, such as Kwaio and northwestern 'Are'are. Other areas combined an ideology that the senior agnate of a descent group acted as its secular leader with a recognition of de facto leadership achieved through entrepreneurial success. In Lau and southeastern 'Are'are, hereditary leaders commanded prestige and had considerable authority in peacemaking and other intergroup relations. The colonial government appointed headmen as agents of administrative control. Partly in counter to this, in the Maasina Rule movement Malaitans put up a hierarchy of chiefs to lead them in an anticolonial struggle. The leaders were imprisoned in 1947, then released and incorporated into the process of gradual, indigenous-led participation in government, culminating in national independence in 1978. Today, Malaita (including Polynesian outliers) forms the Province of Solomon Islands, with a premier and a Provincial Assembly. Interest in "custom" remains strong, even in relatively Westernized areas, and "paramount chiefs" are being given legitimate status, even in bush areas where variant big-man systems prevailed.

Social Control and Conflict. Blood feuding was endemic on Malaita, with larger-scale warfare infrequent but dramatic and culturally celebrated in epic chants of ancestral deeds. Using bows and arrows, clubs, and spears, warriors challenged one another in direct combat or sometimes launched attacks in force against an enemy group in a fortified refuge, led by a shield-bearing fight leader. More often, killings were stealthy executions to gain vengeance, often on behalf of another group, to collect a bounty of valuables and pigs. Cannibalism was apparently practiced at least sporadically everywhere on Malaita; it seems not to have been primarily motivated by a quest for spiritual power, or even for protein, but rather represented a relegation to animal status of enemies or of social offenders (such as adulterers) whose conduct took them out of the bounds of human society. In northern Malaita, sorcery accusations were a common cause of killings; in central Malaita, sorcery was a less-central theme, and seductions were the most common cause of killings (a puritanical sexual code enjoined the execution of adulterers and often led to the killing by their own kin of young women whose sexuality had been invaded, even by a proposition). Curses and other insults also triggered brawls and killings. Principles of collective accountability in blood feuding often led to the killing of a substitute victim, a close or sometimes distant relative, if the seducer or sorcerer could not be killed himself. A cultural distinction was made (at least among the Kwaio and 'Are'are) between powers of productivity (and associated magic and ritual) and powers of destruction (warfare, theft, vandalism): a kind of uneasy tension existed between groups whose primary commitments were to stability and prosperity (and whose safety lay in their capacity to put up blood money against transgressors) and groups whose ancestors incited and supported killing, theft, and destruction (and whose living was consequently too unstable to allow sustained productivity).

Religion and Expressive Culture

Religious Beliefs. The precolonial religious system on Malaita centered on the propitiation of ancestral spirits (*akalo, agalo, adalo*) through the consecration and sacrifice of pigs. Each descent group had one or more focal shrines where religious officiants sacrificed; hierarchies of shrines and priesthoods marked higher levels of segmentary connection between groups and bonds to common ancient ancestors. In communities with maritime orientations (Lau, Langalanga, Maramasike), sharks were seen as spirits and were accordingly propitiated. Some Malaita peoples, particularly those in the north and south with maritime orientations, had extensively elaborated cosmologies positing multiple levels of creation and elaborated bodies of myth. Cosmologies and myth were less developed in bush areas, especially in central Malaita. Divination, dreams, and omens provided daily communication with the spirits. When displeased with their descendants, the ancestral shades visited sickness and death on the living; when pleased, they supported and protected them from malevolent "wild" spirits and empowered their efforts (in production and violent deeds) by "*mana*-izing" them. [In Malaita languages, cognates of *mana* were used mainly verbally: "be effective, be potent, be true, be realized" and (speaking of or to ancestors) "support, empower." They were also used as verbal nouns, such as "*mana*-ness," "*mana*-ization," or "truth."] The sacred (*abu*) men's houses and shrines where men symbolically gave birth to spirits through mortuary rites were a mirror image of the dangerous (abu) menstrual huts and childbirth areas where women gave birth to infants, a cosmological scheme that was mapped in the spatial layout of settlements. The traditional religious system functions still in pockets of pagan settlement, particularly the mountainous Kwaio and 'Are'are interiors. Elsewhere on Malaita, Christianity (principally the South Sea Evangelical, Catholic, Anglican, and Adventist churches) holds sway. Fundamentalist Christians, in particular, see themselves as being in continuous struggle with the ancestors that are viewed as manifestations of Satan.

Religious Practitioners. Traditionally kin groups had "priests" (in North Malaita, *fataabu*) who took primary responsibility for conducting sacrifices and other rites and maintaining relations with the spirits. Divinitory powers were believed to be quite commonly distributed, but certain persons were thought to have extraordinary powers and were widely sought.

Ceremonies. The death of an important or sacred person plunged a descent group into an intense and dangerous communication with the dead. This liminal separation from other living people was gradually ended by rites of desacralization and an eventual mortuary feast (north Malaita *maoma*, Kwaio *omea*), which was also an occasion for largess and competition involving large-scale exchanges of prestations (particularly shell valuables and pigs) in the fulfillment of kinship obligation.

Arts. The most notable artistic achievement on Malaita consisted of panpipe music, with orchestras of eight or more musicians playing matched sets of scaled pipes. The contrapuntal structures of this music are beautiful and complex, using as many as seven or eight melodic voices. In some genres, the panpipers accompanied formations of dancers, and they themselves performed intricate movements while piping. Another noteworthy musical genre is epic chanting, in which deeds of ancestors are recounted with harmonized accompaniments. Other musical forms include stamping tubes, Jew's harps, and other flute varieties. The most striking graphic arts took the form of bodily ornaments—women's heirloom jewelry (chest pendants, nose sticks, earrings, necklaces), intricately plated ornamental combs worn by men, arm shells, chest pendants, belts, and bandoliers. Weapons, batons, betel mortars, bowls, and other items were carved and/or decorated with nautilus inlay.

Medicine. Magic was highly elaborated, and it followed the sharp cultural separation between productive and destructive powers. Gardening, feast giving, fishing, fighting, and stealing all called for elaborate magic.

Death and Afterlife. Throughout Malaita, the souls of the dead were believed to travel to the land of the dead (associated with a small island off the northwestern tip of Malaita), while their shades hovered about the community, propitiated by the consecration of pigs and placated by purificatory sacrifice. The shades of the dead monitored the strict pollution taboos that compartmentalized menstruation and childbirth and sharply separated men's and women's realms, and they also supervised the strict observance of ritual procedures.

See also Guadalcanal, Ontong Java, San Cristobal

Bibliography

Hogbin, H. Ian (1936). *Experiments in Civilization.* London: Routledge & Kegan Paul.

Ivens, Walter J. (1927). *Melanesians of the South-East Solomons.* London: Kegan Paul.

Ivens, Walter J. (1930). *The Island Builders of the Pacific.* London: Seeley & Service.

Keesing, Roger M. (1982). *Kwaio Religion.* New York: Columbia University Press.

Keesing, Roger M. (1983). *'Elota's Story: The Life and Times of a Solomon Islands Big Man.* New York: Holt, Rinehart & Winston.

Ross, Harold (1972). *Baegu: Social and Ecological Organization on Malaita.* Urbana, Ill.: University of Illinois Press.

ROGER M. KEESING

Malekula

ETHNONYMS: Laus, Mewun, Seniang, Small Nambas

Orientation

Identification. This summary focuses on South West Bay, the home of several culturally similar ethnic groups, including the Laus (or Small Nambas), Mewun, and Seniang.

Location. The island of Malekula, at 167° E and 165° S, is the second-largest in Vanuatu. About 88 kilometers long and 48 kilometers at its widest, Malekula has few mineral resources aside from its fertile volcanic soil. Although there are no active volcanoes on the island, earthquakes are common. The southwestern part of Malekula is quite mountainous and covered with rain-forest vegetation. The climate provides a year-round growing season, divided into wet and dry periods, with most rainfall occurring between November and March, while drier, cooler weather dominates the region from April through October. Hurricanes are likely in January and February.

Demography. A detailed census of Mewun in 1974 recorded 482 people; the population of Seniang was about the same, while that of Laus was estimated at 125. In all three groups there is a surplus of bachelors, which seems to occur spontaneously but which has had an impact on social organization.

Linguistic Affiliation. All three groups speak Austronesian languages of the Malekula Coastal Subgroup. The languages (referred to locally as Ninde [Mewun], Nahava [Seniang], and Mbotegate [Laus]) are not mutually intelligible, but some residents are bi- or even trilingual.

History and Cultural Relations

The first sustained contact between South West Bay inhabitants and Europeans began in 1896 when a Presbyterian missionary settled there. As the missionary's power and following grew, the incidence of interethnic and intervillage warfare—previously an integral part of local life—declined, and by 1960, all people from Mewun and Seniang had moved into mission villages. Laus has remained, for the most part, unconverted, although a few people from this region have moved into Mewun and Seniang villages on the bay in the last decade or so. Colonization followed missionization as religious representatives inspired political interest in the region and the islands became the Anglo-French Condominium of the New Hebrides in 1906. For seventy-four years the country had two colonial governments and three official languages (English, French, and Melanesian Pidgin). There also were dual or parallel systems in nearly every domain—judicial, educational, monetary, and medical. This political arrangement, sometimes called the "Pandemonium," often operated roughly or ineptly, thereby leaving local people much autonomy. In 1980, after electing a government, the condominium became the nation of Vanuatu.

Settlements

Prior to the twentieth century most people lived in the foothills surrounding South West Bay, but missionization was the main catalyst for resettlement along the shores of the 9.6-kilometer-long harbor. Today the Mewun live on the northern half of the bay, the Seniang live to the south, and the unmissionized people of Laus remain farther inland in a number of small settlements. Traditionally all three groups lived in small settlements of fewer than fifty people, with separate residences for men and women arranged around a central clearing where dances and other ceremonies could take place. Children initially lived with their mothers, with boys moving into the men's house when they reached the age of 5 or 6. Since missionization, the Mewun and Seniang have settled in larger villages of 100–300 residents. Missionized villagers were required to have two houses, one for sleeping and the other for cooking, because it was considered unhealthy for residents to sleep in smoky areas. Although men and women were expected to live and sleep together, many Mewun used their two houses to preserve their traditional custom of sleeping apart; while women and children slept in the official sleeping houses, their husbands often slept in the family kitchens. This separation of the sexes has remained common up to the present. Traditional house styles with walls of black palm and thatched roofs made of *tangura* palm have given way in mission villages to walls and elevated floors of woven bamboo; nowadays, some families prefer corrugated tin roofs because they last longer and can be used to catch supplies of rain water.

Economy

Subsistence and Commercial Activities. Swidden horticulture provides the subsistence base, and either yams, taro, cassava, bananas, or sweet potatoes are usually eaten daily. Yams are probably the preferred form of carbohydrates, but they can be harvested only in the dry season. Yams store well for several months but the local supply is usually exhausted halfway through the rainy season. The traditional food remains the *laplap* or "pudding." This is made of one of the staple foods flavored with coconut cream and either protein or local greens. The protein supply is varied, including pork, fish, shellfish, turtle, chicken, or tinned meat or fish, but it is of limited quantity. Boiled rice is an increasingly common component of the diet. Cash crops include copra, cocoa, and a small coffee crop. There is little else in terms of commercial activity, but a local bakery operation and the sale of handicrafts to a cooperative in the capital city are two small enterprises that have endured.

Industrial Arts. Women weave mats and baskets of coconut and pandanus leaves. Nowadays men make canoes, but this is a new art. When the first missionary arrived, local people were still using rafts for ocean travel, but through mission influence they soon learned to carve outrigger canoes.

Trade. Trade among the three ethnic groups has rarely focused on essential items. In early colonial days, Mewun and Seniang people would hold "markets" to exchange yams with one another. Cultural artifacts, including special dances and unintelligible songs in foreign languages, are still traded within and between the groups.

Division of Labor. Traditionally—and still among the Laus—house building was a male task; however, in mission villages it is a cooperative task involving both sexes. So, too, yam gardens are now the exclusive province of men only in Laus; in Mewun and Seniang today, women work in yam gardens unless they are menstruating. Men and women share other agricultural tasks, and, while only men hunt, both men and women fish and gather shellfish. Although both sexes can be involved in cooking, ceremonial cooking for feasts, funerals, etc., is usually supervised by men.

Land Tenure. Land is inherited patrilineally. Married women retain usufruct rights to their brothers' coconut land and may gather the nuts without asking permission. In the past few decades, some men have found themselves with few heirs but much land. To prevent encroachment by Europeans, some men in this situation have given parcels of land to their sisters' sons. However, this new practice has led to a plethora of court cases, so men reportedly are moving away from this innovation in land inheritance. Although women do not usually hold or inherit land, there are instances where women are the sole heirs of a patrimony, and these women sometimes hold and control family land until their sons mature.

Kinship

Kin Groups and Descent. In all three groups the community is divided into a number of localized, patrilineal, exogamous descent groups called "clans" by their first ethnographer, A. B. Deacon. Each clan member can trace descent from a village or locality. Place membership appears to be a stronger factor in unity than clan membership per se. Children belong to the place of their father, but they can be adopted into other places on occasion. Members of a clan or place share a specific totem and a sacred place where group rituals were performed in precontact times. The descent group is the landholding unit, and food and other valued items are frequently shared by members.

Kinship Terminology. All three ethnic groups use Crow-type kinship terms in a patrilineal descent system. This combination is unusual, found in only two other Oceanic ethnic groups.

Marriage and Family

Marriage. Polygyny is still found in Laus and was common in Mewun and Seniang before they were completely missionized. Polyandry also occurred in traditional times among the Mewun. Members of the three groups occasionally intermarry. Substantial bride-wealth is required; in all three groups this can consist of a combination of pigs and cash, though a Laus bride-price is likely to include more pigs than bride-prices in Mewun and Seniang. With the current surplus of bachelors, older married men seek to control younger bachelors through their control of marriage choices for young women. In order to marry, most young men must obtain the approval of older men and use either bride-wealth or sister exchange to contract engagements. Postmarital residence is patrilocal. Although women move to their husbands' land when they marry, a widowed woman is almost always required to return to her patrilocality, leaving her children behind with her deceased spouse's relatives. This move, however, may not always involve a change in villages for her. Since mission villages in Mewun and Seniang are composed of several different patrilines, she may simply relocate to a different quadrant of the village and begin to farm the land of her patrilineal relatives. Divorce is illegal and almost absent in South West Bay. The few people who have separated from their spouses have left the bay for either Port Vila or Luganville (Vanuatu's only two cities) where they can form liaisons with new spouses.

Domestic Unit. The basic domestic unit is composed of relatives who share food and eat from a common fire. This may or may not coincide with a dwelling unit or household.

Inheritance. Inheritance is patrilineal. Daughters are given pieces of their fathers' territory to use before marriage and after they become widows. However, this is usually not inherited by their sons.

Socialization. Children are raised to interact with one another peaceably, so it is extremely rare to see children fighting or a parent striking a child. The threat of shame is often employed to ensure correct behavior. Most Mewun and Seniang children go to school until the third grade. While a large percentage finish primary school, only a few progress to secondary school. The district schools were established in the early 1900s by the resident Presbyterian missionary. Before independence, a few children from Mewun and a larger group from Seniang went to a French boarding school in southeastern Malekula. Laus children, for the most part, are not formally educated, although a few attend the mission schools in Mewun.

Sociopolitical Organization

Social Organization. The basic organizing principle is that of a common "place." Ancestral "place" commonly coincides with patrilineality, but there is plenty of room for ascription when suitable. Rights to "place" can be gained by adoption and long-term contiguity and commensality. Mission villages in Mewun and Seniang usually include residents from several "places." Members of a "place" are exogamous and cooperate on work teams; they also pool their resources for bride-wealth and funerary contributions. Members of a "place" will also share rights to unique artistic creations (dances, artifacts, songs, etc.), said to be given to members as gifts from the spirit world. These cultural artifacts can be bought and sold between "places." The emphasis on "place" seen in South West Bay apparently is significant throughout Vanuatu; not only is it noted by anthropologists in other parts of the archipelago, but the newly invented (postindependence) pidgin word for "citizen" is *man ples* (or *woman ples*)."

Political Organization. The traditional political system operated through a combination of personal and positional power. A men's graded society developed in all three South West Bay ethnic groups. By earning his way up the ladder of ritual position (each position involving payments and bestowing ritual privileges on the aspirant), a man could reach the top grade, at which point he became a spiritually powerful and feared person. High-ranking men were likely to have several wives, often obtained from different ethnic groups, and great wealth in pigs. Laus men still have a graded society, or *nimangi*. A shadow graded society also exists for Laus women and was described for Mewun and Seniang in traditional times. Since missionization of Seniang and Mewun, official political power in the form of chiefdoms has been rotated every year or two among various members of each "place." Prior to independence, Mewun and Seniang were each represented by an assessor, who officiated at the trials of small offenses but called in the British or French district agents in cases of major disputes or crimes. Outside the official realm, power is held by big-men who are empowered by their ability to control large networks of kin and affines and by their speaking talents. In general, postcontact power is much more diffused among socially prominent citizens, political representatives, and church officials than it reportedly was in earlier times.

Social Control. The most frequent causes of intragroup conflict are land disputes and adultery. In Mewun and Seniang, such disagreements are settled by long discussions monitored and guided by elected chiefs. Adultery is frequently punished by fines, levied on both parties, or by public service, such as caring for communal grounds or repairing public property. In Laus, disputes are still settled by big-men, just as they were in Mewun and Seniang prior to missionization.

Conflict. Until the arrival of Europeans, warfare was an integral part of life in South West Bay. Members of a descent group usually remained at peace with one another, but war could break out between different kin groups within Mewun, Seniang, or Laus. Aggression between members of these cultural groups was also common before missionization. Disputes between groups nowadays are most commonly over adultery or land. When these disagreements do occur, the cases are tried by chiefs from the involved communities. Very severe crimes, such as assault and battery, are tried by the national court system and guilty parties may serve prison terms. Whenever possible, disputes are settled by reciprocal exchanges of goods or services. The object of all locally tried court cases is the reduction of ill will between the parties, so all court proceedings tend to involve a great deal of negotiation rather than arbitrary legal sanctions.

Religion and Expressive Culture

Religious Beliefs. Although people of Seniang and Mewun consider themselves good Presbyterians, they nevertheless share certain beliefs with the unmissionized people of Laus. Essentially, all three groups believe the world is inhabited by spirits, some of whom take on human form temporarily until the death of a person sets the spirit loose again.

Religious Practitioners. Certain men are reputed to be especially clever in magic. Their services are sought to resolve human problems or punish grievances. Traditionally, there was said to be one shaman for each patrilocality. Some women also are said to have great powers to dream and thereby enter the spirit world where they can find ways to cure human illnesses and other problems.

Ceremonies. Ceremonial dances, usually accompanied by giant slit gongs or drums located in village dance areas, are frequently held in Laus. For example, funerary dances, performed with puppets made from cobwebs and clay, are part of the rituals for the dead. Prior to missionization, all three groups had nimangi grading systems. Advancement along the ladder of grades always involved ceremonies, including special dances and pig slaughters, for each level attained. One of the most famous Mewun ceremonies, apparently defunct since missionization, was known as the "Making of Men" ceremony, or "Nogho Tilabwe." Performed periodically, it was believed to increase fertility and preserve the health and strength of the Mewun population. A South West Bay precontact ceremony that has been reworked into local Presbyterian ritual is a yam harvest festival, followed by exchange of yams in memory of the dead. When the first yams are harvested, families decorate them with colorful flowers and leaves before taking them to the local church where they are blessed. After the ceremony, each yam is given to someone who is unrelated to the dead person commemorated by that yam. Since independence, when most missionaries left, Mewun and Seniang people have revived a number of old dances and ceremonies, which they researched among local elders with anthropological zeal and precision.

Arts. Southern Malekula has been praised as a center for exceptionally fine art. Most famous are the *rhamberamb*, or life-sized funerary statues of the dead, which are prized by museum collectors. While the people of Laus have continually created these and other art objects for ceremonial use, there has also been a renaissance of traditional art objects in Seniang and Mewun since Independence.

Death and Afterlife. All three ethnic groups believe that the spirits of the dead are dangerous influences on the living for a year after the deceased's funeral. Mewun mourn for twelve hours following a death and then take pains not to anger the deceased's troublesome spirit presence. After a year has passed, spirits pass to the land of the dead, which is under the surface of the earth and referred to as "dark Paradise."

See also Pentecost

Bibliography

Deacon, A. Bernard (1934). *Malekula: A Vanishing People in the New Hebrides.* London: Routledge & Kegan Paul.

Larcom, Joan C. (1980). "Place and the Politics of Marriage: The Mewun of Malekula, New Hebrides." Ph.D. dissertation, Stanford University.

MacClancy, Jeremy (1981). *To Kill a Bird with Two Stones: A Short History of Vanuatu.* Port Vila, Vanuatu: Vanuatu Cultural Centre Publications.

Sope, Barak (1976). *Land and Politics in the New Hebrides.* Suva, Fiji: South Pacific Social Sciences Association.

Weightman, Barry, et al. (1981). *Vanuatu: Twenti Wan Tingting Long Taem blong Independens.* Port Vila, Vanuatu: Institute of Pacific Studies.

JOAN C. LARCOM

Manam

ETHNONYM: Vulkan Islanders

Orientation

Identification. Manam Island, formerly called Vulkan-Insel or Hansa-Vulkaninsel by the Germans, and its outlier, the small island of Boesa (Aris-Insel) 6.5 kilometers to the northwest, are part of the Schouten Island archipelago, a chain of small volcanic islands that stretches along the northeast coast of Papua New Guinea. Near the mouths of the Ramu and Sepik rivers, Manam is part of the north coast and Sepik River culture areas.

Location. Situated just south of the equator at 4°5' S and 145°3' E and within the Pacific Ring of Fire, Manam is a small cone-shaped island about 13 kilometers across and 40 kilometers in circumference. A still-active volcano with craters that reach a height of 1,350 meters, it continuously spews forth ash and occasionally erupts molten lava. In 1957 the entire population was evacuated to the mainland for a year, at the end of that time returning to the remains of ash-covered villages on the island. Manam is 16 kilometers from the mainland district station of Bogia, near Hansa Bay in Madang Province. There are no rivers or permanent streams on the island. Northwest monsoon winds bring a rainy season that lasts from November to April, traditionally a time for canoe building and the staging of feasts and ceremonies. From May to October, southeast trade winds bring a dry season that was always a time of scarcity before the advent of trade stores.

Demography. In 1982 the population of Manam was estimated to be 6,400, with another 420 people on Boesa Island. Despite the fact that many younger Manam have chosen to live permanently on the mainland because of the limitation on available land on the island, the Manam are concerned about a rapidly increasing population. The village population is predominantly indigenous Manam Islanders, with only a small number of in-marrying spouses from mainland Papua New Guinea.

Linguistic Affiliation. Manam, with Wogeo, is classified in the Siassi Family of Austronesian languages. The Manam refer to their language as "Manam pile" (Manam speech or language). Although the same language is spoken throughout the island, it is undergoing a sound shift and two forms are currently spoken on different halves of the island. Most Manam also speak Tok Pisin (Melanesian Pidgin) and some—mostly younger educated people—also speak English.

History and Cultural Relations

Austronesian speakers arrived in New Guinea later than Papuan speakers, bringing with them items such as the domesticated pig, outrigger canoes, and navigational skills. The Proto-Austronesian Lapita culture, centered in the Bismarck Archipelago since at least 1,600 B.C., is believed to be ancestral to the Manam. The Manam themselves say that they came from the west prior to settling on Manam. Early written references to Manam are found from the sixteenth century on in the ships' logs of Europeans who noted the island's volcano. Regular contact with Europeans began when the Germans claimed sovereignty over northeast New Guinea in 1884. There have never been nonindigenous coconut plantations on Manam; however, over the years many Manam have worked as contract laborers on coastal plantations and in the goldfields of Wau and Bulolo. Since its establishment on the island in 1925, the Society of Divine Word Catholic mission has been the most significant Western influence. During World War II the Japanese occupation of the mainland caused the Manam to abandon their villages to live in the jungle for the duration of the war. The end of the war opened the way to considerable change, including much interest in the cargo cult and protonationalist activities of the Rai Coast leader Yali, native production of copra for sale, and the development of other commercial activities. These enterprises, combined with increasing educational and job opportunities on the mainland, have led to a continuing dependence on cash and a consumer economy. The Manam have traditionally maintained exchange relations with hereditary trade partners (*taoa*) on the mainland. There is little or no contact with other Schouten Islanders. Trade most frequently occurs with the Momboan villages on the coast directly across from Manam and with Kaian, Boroi, Watam, and Marangis villages near the Ramu River.

Settlements

There are fourteen villages on Manam and two on Boesa ranging in size from around 115 to 1,000 people, with the average being about 500. Villages are scattered settlements ranging from the beach up the mountainside into the jungle. Gardens are usually located on the mountainside beyond the settled area. Houses are built of wood with roofs of coconut-frond thatch and walls of woven bamboo or coconut-frond siding. Each village has a central cleared ceremonial ground and a large men's ceremonial house (in Tok Pisin, *haus tambaran*) prohibited to women. Other settlements include a small volcanology observatory, a government subdistrict headquarters, and two Catholic missions, each with a church and government-run school. A dirt road partially circles the island, but vehicles are few and travel between villages is primarily by foot, boat, or canoe.

Economy

Subsistence and Commercial Activities. The Manam are fishers and subsistence gardeners who practice slash-and-burn horticulture. Because of the relatively poor soil and lack of groundwater, a limited variety of crops is grown. Most important among them are taro, sweet potatoes, cassava, and bananas. Yams, prevalent on the mainland, do not grow well on Manam. Tree crops, such as breadfruit, coconuts, and *Canarium* almonds, supplement the vegetable diet. Fishing is seasonal, the monsoons hindering fishing on the south side of the island. Pigs are an occasional source of protein but are most important as wealth items used in both local and external trade. Other domesticated animals include chickens and dogs. The latter, primarily raised for hunting and protection, are sometimes eaten. Copra, sold either locally to distributors or directly to the Copra Marketing Board in Madang, is the only cash crop. Coffee and cacao, important mainland cash crops, are not viable on Manam. At present, cash from copra is used to buy rice, tinned meat, fish, and other imported foods purchased at trade stores on the island.

Industrial Arts. In comparison with many mainland people, the Manam practice relatively few industrial arts. They produce no pottery, carved slit drums, dyed grass skirts, woven baskets, or net bags; instead, they obtain these items from mainland trade partners. Their most important craft, in the past and to a lesser extent at present, is the construction of outrigger canoes. While men used to sail large canoes on trading expeditions to the mainland, canoes are now used only for travel between villages and to carry passengers and cargo on and off boats going to and from the mainland. Carving is men's work. In addition to canoes, other items carved include masks, combs, betel-nut mortars, coconut-shell containers, headrests, and canoe paddles. Women used to make their own pandanus-fiber skirts, while men made their own bark belts. Commercial clothing has replaced these items although they are still worn for special dances and ritual performances.

Trade. In the past men visited their mainland trade partners (taoa) to exchange pigs, *Canarium* almonds, betel nuts, and tobacco for sago, ritual paraphernalia, and dogs'-teeth and boars'-tusk valuables. The institution of hereditary trade partners still functions, although trips to the mainland are now made by motorized canoes and boats. There are also small markets, a Western innovation, at the mainland and at the mission stations on Manam where women sell produce and betel nuts, tobacco, *Canarium* almonds, etc.

Division of Labor. The primary division of labor is between men and women. Men are the main participants in all activities associated with the sea: the construction and use of canoes, fishing, and overseas trading expeditions. While both men and women work in the gardens, the bulk of the routine labor of planting, weeding, and harvesting is performed by women. Men help with the heavy labor associated with the initial clearing of new gardens and construction of fences, and some husbands also help their wives with planting and weeding. Only men, however, climb large trees to harvest breadfruit, *Canarium* almonds, coconuts, etc. Both men and women tend pigs, but only men slaughter them and distribute the meat. Only women cook food, chop and gather firewood, and fetch water. Both sexes are involved with the production and sale of copra.

Land Tenure. Land is communally controlled by kinship groups, while other productive resources such as trees are individually controlled. Both men and women can inherit land and other productive resources from both paternal and maternal relatives. However, men inherit more resources than do women and as land becomes a scarce resource fewer claims of access to land through maternal relatives are permitted by matrilateral kin.

Kinship

Kin Groups and Descent. Individuals belong to named localized exogamous clan groups called *bagi* or *ungguma* whose membership is based on patrilineal descent. Villages are composed of between two and ten bagi. Matrilineal kin, especially the mother's brother, are also important. Homesteads are extended family compounds situated on clan-owned land.

Kinship Terminology. Hawaiian-type cousin terms are used, and siblings are distinguished by relative age and sex.

Marriage and Family

Marriage. Although most marriages are monogamous, polygamy is still practiced. Village chiefs in particular have more than one wife. All marriages used to be arranged, but now young people usually decide who they will marry. The groom's family gives bride-wealth to the bride's relatives. With the exception of village chiefs, marriage tends to be endogamous within a village and residence patrilocal. A marriage is not considered final until the birth of a couple's first child. Prior to that divorce is relatively easy and frequent among young couples.

Domestic Unit. The nuclear family is the basic family unit although extended family households are common. In polygamous households each wife has her own hearth and gardens and cooks for her husband and children. Parents desire at least one child of each sex and adoption of children is a common practice between siblings. Firstborn children, especially male, receive special attention and have special rights and duties.

Inheritance. Both men and women inherit property from their parents, although firstborn males inherit more than other siblings. Claims to a man's property are made by his adult children through the performance of a ritual feast called *boro da paso* held in his honor while he is still alive.

Socialization. Although women are the primary caretakers, men often help with child care. Older siblings also share in the responsibility of raising younger children. Sex segregation and socialization into gender roles begins at a young age. Shame is a dominant concept used to shape conformity to culturally appropriate behavior.

Sociopolitical Organization

Social Organization. Unlike most New Guinea societies which are egalitarian, Manam is hierarchically organized into two hereditary social groups: an elite (*tanepoa*) and commoners (*gadagada*). Membership is based on patrilineal descent.

Political Organization. In precontact times Manam villages were politically autonomous. Each village was ruled by a hereditary chief called *tanepoa labalaba,* a position based on primogeniture. Each clan had a leader (*bagi sema*) whose position was also based on primogeniture. Although the Manam now elect a village councillor to represent them on the island's Local Government Council, in effect tanepoa labalaba are still the village leaders. The Manam also elect national and provincial representatives.

Social Control. In the past the tanepoa used the threat of sorcery and physical violence to exert social control. At present tanepoa and village councillors adjudicate local civil cases of adultery, divorce, theft, etc., or they refer offenders to the district officer and court.

Conflict. In the past incidental fighting and formal warfare, both between villages and between the Manam and mainland groups, were endemic. Conflicts were settled by negotiation of the payment of pigs and valuables. At present, although physical violence still erupts, payment of monetary compensation or jail are the main sanctions against conflict.

Religion and Expressive Culture

Religious Beliefs. The majority of the Manam are nominally Catholic, but various indigenous beliefs and practices based on supernatural spirits and powers are still meaningful. *Masalai* (Tok Pisin), which are culture heros and ancestors, are important supernatural beings. Masalai easily change from human to animal or inanimate form. Masalai snakes are particularly important as they are associated with the origin of the Manam people. The most important culture hero is Zaria, a female believed to inhabit the volcano and to be the source of its fire. Since the end of World War II interest in various millenarian movements has periodically surfaced. At present, in addition to Catholicism, Seventh-Day Adventists and several evangelical sects also have a small number of followers.

Religious Practitioners. There are no formal religious positions, but some individuals inherit supernatural power (*marou*) from their ancestors that enables them to perform canoe magic, influence the winds, ensure an abundance of tobacco, etc. A tanepoa labalaba in particular is thought to have the power to ensure the fertility of crops and the well-being of his villagers. Through trances, *aeno aine* or "sleep women" are believed to be able to mediate between the living and the dead to determine the cause of illness.

Ceremonies. Individual life-cycle events such as birth, puberty, marriage, and death are marked with special rituals. Each village holds an annual New Year's celebration known as "Barasi" in May or June. The most frequent intervillage ceremony is a type of dance and pig exchange called a *buleka*. Christian holidays such as Christmas and Easter are also observed.

Arts. Music and singing are the dominant arts. In addition to their aesthetic role, they have important political and economic functions. Dance, with men as the primary performers, is also a major art and new dance complexes are important trade items. Carving, an artform with a traditional iconography, is of minor importance.

Medicine. The Manam follow both indigenous and Western medical practices. Belief that pollution from blood, semen, and certain foods can be the cause of illness is gradually disappearing, but illness and death are still not believed to occur naturally. To the Manam they indicate a moral imbalance in the social world of the individual. Indigenous medical practices include the performance of curing ceremonies to reveal the social conflict causing an individual's illness. Most Manam also use the services of the government-sponsored clinic run by the Catholic sisters.

Death and Afterlife. Immediately upon death individuals gather to wail, sing mourning songs, and "give face" at the home of the deceased. People sleep outside the deceased's home until after the funeral feast has been held, approximately five days later. A second funeral rite should occur several years later when the deceased's relatives hold a special feast to commemorate the dead. The dead are believed to continue to exist as spirits who communicate through dreams and influence events in the world of the living.

See also Wogeo

Bibliography

Boehm, Karl (1983). *The Life of Some Island People of New Guinea.* Berlin: Reimer Verlag.

Lawrence, Peter (1964). *Road Belong Cargo.* Melbourne: Melbourne University Press.

Lutkehaus, Nancy (1985). "The Flutes of the Tanepoa: Hierarchy and Equivalence in Manam Society." Unpublished Ph.D. dissertation, Columbia University.

Maburau, Anthony (1985). "Irakau of Manam." In *New Religious Movements in Melanesia,* edited by C. Loeliger and G. Trompf, 2–17. Suva, Fiji, and Port Moresby: University of the South Pacific and University of Papua New Guinea.

Wedgwood, Camilla (1934). "Report on Research in Manam Island, Mandated Territory of New Guinea." *Oceania* 4:373–403.

NANCY CHRISTINE LUTKEHAUS

Mandak

ETHNONYM: Madak

Orientation

Identification. Mandak is a linguistic-cultural designation for people living in central New Ireland, Papua New Guinea. "Mandak" means "boy" or "male" and is used by New Irelanders to refer to those speaking the various dialects of Mandak. Further sociocultural distinctions are made by reference to particular Mandak villages.

Location. The Mandak live in central New Ireland on the east and west coasts and in the interior on Lelet Plateau, between 3°6' and 3°20' S and 151°47' and 152°8' E. This tropical area has a wet season dominated by the northwest monsoon winds from December to May and a dry season with prevailing southeast trade winds from May to October, divided by transitional calmer, more humid weather. Rainfall varies considerably according to local topographic conditions, with periodic drought a potential problem in some coastal areas. Mean monthly temperatures range from the high 20s to about 32° C.

Demography. The Mandak numbered about 3,324 in the 1960s, of which some 500 resided in the interior Lelet region. From about 1920 to 1950, New Ireland experienced depopulation due to Western contact. By the late 1950s, the population had stabilized and began to increase in some areas. Because of the loss of all census data for New Ireland during World War II, government records are available only from 1949 to present. A census of east coast villages made by E. W.

P. Chinnery in 1929 shows larger village populations than the 1949 government census.

Linguistic Affiliation. Mandak, with five dialects, is an Austronesian language, classified with Lavatbura-Lamusong in the Madak Family. Linguistic variation is also found at the subdialect level from village to village.

History and Cultural Relations

Little is known about the Mandak before Western contact. Present coastal populations include, either by village or intermingled within a village, people who claim to have originated in their present locations and those who relocated from inland settlements at the urging of German and Australian colonial governments in the early twentieth century. During the seventeenth and eighteenth centuries, New Ireland was visited by Dutch, English, and French explorers and blackbirders. Germany claimed New Ireland as a colony, renamed Neu Mecklenburg, between 1884 and 1914. In the early 1900s, German and English colonists planted coconut plantations on land taken from the local people for minimal recompense. During this period, the German administration used local labor to build a road along the east coast for almost 200 miles from Kavieng in the north to Namatanai in south central New Ireland. At the outbreak of World War I, Australia took over New Ireland, administering it as part of a mandate from the League of Nations from 1921 to 1942, when the Japanese invaded and occupied New Ireland. Australia again resumed control in 1945, with New Ireland becoming apart of the Territory of Papua New Guinea in 1949, administered by Australia under the United Nations. In the 1950s, the Mandak began planting their own coconut plantations for the copra market, adding cacao trees a decade or so later as a second cash crop. The Mandak have been part of independent Papua New Guinea since 1975. Christian missions have exerted a strong influence among the Mandak. Methodist missionary work in New Ireland began in the late nineteenth century, followed by Roman Catholics in the second decade of the twentieth century.

Settlements

At first contact, the Mandak were living in interrelated hamlets grouped together into villages. Today, villages range in size from about 50 to 230 people. Some retain the older settlement pattern of discrete, dispersed hamlets, while others, particularly the smaller resettled inland settlements, display a more centralized appearance. Hamlets range in size from 1 to 40 people living in one to ten nuclear family houses. A men's house, surrounded by a low stone wall, is found in most hamlets.

Economy

Subsistence and Commercial Activities. The Mandak combine subsistence agriculture with raising and selling coconuts and cacao beans. Main subsistence crops include taro, sweet potatoes, and yams, varying in significance regionally. Gardens are located from 1 to 3 miles inland from coastal settlements. Also grown are bananas, papayas, beans, leafy green vegetables, melons, breadfruit, pineapples, and a variety of nut and fruit trees. In earlier times, sago served as a famine food and is still occasionally processed today. In coastal areas, fishing provides varying amounts of fish seasonally, along with shellfish and occasional sea turtles. The Mandak raise pigs and chickens, the former for ceremonial exchanges, the latter for small-scale special occasions. Men occasionally hunt feral pigs for less-important social events. Marketing coconuts and cacao beans provides the Mandak with a reliable, though fluctuating, income. A few individuals in each village operate small trade stores, selling canned meat, coffee, tea, sugar, kerosene, and other items.

Industrial Arts. Items produced locally from coconut and pandanus leaves and other plant fibers include: large food-carrying baskets for women, smaller baskets for men and women, lime pouches, sitting mats, and rain covers. Also crafted are small bamboo and large hollow-log slit gongs, fishing nets, single-outrigger canoes, and log rafts. Canoes and fishing nets are no longer made in some areas. Polished-shell bead strands used in ceremonial exchanges, shell pendants, and arm bracelets are produced in some areas. Production of white-shell bead strands ceased after World War II, after a local leader forbade their use in exchanges in preference to red-shell strands produced elsewhere.

Trade. Before island settlements moved to the coast in the first decades of the twentieth century, coastal women traded fish for vegetable foods with inland women. Items traded between individuals in different villages, within or beyond language areas, include: shell valuables (red-shell bead strands), shell bracelets, pigs, rituals and ritual paraphernalia, song-dances, and magic spells.

Division of Labor. Labor cooperation varies contextually from small networks of individuals sharing an enclosed garden, to larger groups cultivating gardens for a special mortuary feast, to an entire village cooperating in fishing and ceremonial feast preparations. Gender demarcates the division of labor: men clear secondary-growth areas for gardens and fence them against pigs, while women plant, tend, and harvest the root crops; men fish, while women gather shellfish. In building houses, men perform the heavier work while women prepare the palm-frond roofs. Women do the daily cooking, generally in individual household earth ovens, while for feasts they cut and peel root crops to be cooked in large earth ovens constructed by men. Both sexes cooperate in harvesting coconuts and preparing them for market and in collecting cacao beans. Men take the copra to market in trucks, usually rented, with male drivers.

Land Tenure. Land is generally owned by lineages, but it is used for subsistence gardens in flexible arrangements with affines and offspring of male lineage or clan members. Offspring may gain permanent rights to portions of their father's land at his death by making certain exchanges to members of his lineage or clan at his mortuary feast. In situations where a lineage or clan has few members and no heirs (clan or paternal offspring), someone with other ties to the clan may establish claims to clan land by making contributions to mortuary feasts of the last remaining clan members. In some areas, a man or woman may claim land rights from his or her mother's or father's paternal kin at the latter's death, by making an exchange at a mortuary feast to the deceased's lineage. Land transfers were complicated by colonial laws that required cash payments for land leaving the clan.

Kinship

Kin Groups and Descent. Mandak individuals belong at birth to the lineage, clan, and moiety of their mother. There are no known relationships between clans of the same moiety, nor generally between lineages of a clan. Moieties are exogamous. Kinship relations are expressed in varying references to shared or exchanged nurturance, between individuals and between groups. The relationship of a man and his lineage, clan, or moiety to his offspring is expressed as one of nurturance. At an individual's death—if a man, his offspring and spouse; if a woman, her spouse—give wealth to the deceased's clan for nurturance received from the deceased and his or her clan.

Kinship Terminology. Kinship terminology is a variant of the Iroquois type.

Marriage and Family

Marriage. Before extensive mission influence, both polygyny and polyandry were accepted forms of marriage among the Mandak, although it is said that only a few men had more than one wife and that polyandry also was not common. Moiety and clan exogamy are stressed. Villages are not exogamous and there is some preference for marrying within the village. A bride-price is given by the husband's lineage to the wife's lineage. No single option is stated as a preferred form of postmarital residence. Usually, a couple moves several times during their married life. For the oldest male of a sibling group, preferred residence is in his lineage hamlet. Divorce is allowed, with young children usually staying with their mother.

Domestic Unit. Basic domestic units include separate households for single adult women (divorced, widowed, unmarried), for nuclear families, and sometimes for single men, who usually, however, live in a men's house.

Inheritance. Inheritance is ideally matrilineal for land and certain forms of magic, although an individual, male or female, may inherit some land and receive magic spells from his or her father.

Socialization. Both parents discipline their children, generally verbally, with an occasional switching. Older siblings also exert some control over their younger siblings. Adoption of children is common, usually between closely related kin. Male youths, from about age 12 into their early 20s, have considerable freedom of movement, with little social responsibility. Most children go to local schools up to about age 12, with some going on to secondary (usually boarding) schools and then college or technical school.

Sociopolitical Organization

Social Organization. The dynamics of the social system are characterized by oppositions elicited in different contexts. At the broadest level, the matrilineal, exogamous moieties are contrasted as complementary units, giving or receiving nurturance from one another through men's work in the procreation and nurturance of their offspring. The same contrast may be evoked in relating clans, lineages, or individuals. Same-unit membership (of moiety, clan, lineage) entails a focus on shared nurturance. The hamlet is owned and identified with a lineage, ideally with the social unit's oldest male in control of its men's house. Hamlets may include members of different clans, through affinal, paternal, and other ties to the owning lineage. Social units are not localized, and thus they may be spread over a number of villages, while the social unit's identity is localized in one hamlet and its men's house in whose adjacent yard lineage members are buried.

Political Organization. Political power adheres in the activities of big-men. All middle-aged and older men are recognized as having the capacity for political influence. The oldest man of the lineage is regarded as the representative of that social unit, for purposes of land arbitrations, feast sponsorship, and in certain formal feast exchanges. One or more men of each village may be recognized as having particular "strength" and "power." Such men are more active than others in sponsoring social events and in gaining village consensus in large-scale village cooperative action. Such men's reputations extend beyond their own community to other villages. A variety of appointed (during early colonial decades) and then elected (since the 1960s) officials at the village, regional, and (since 1975) national level are involved in Mandak political activities. At times the big-man system works partly within these institutionalized authority positions, while at other times it coexists separately.

Social Control. In precontact times, there was no formalized social control at the village level. Usually, conflicts were handled either by fighting or clandestine sorcery. Fear of sorcery attack or retaliation continues to serve as a powerful means of social control. Today, minor social disputes are handled at the village level in weekly meetings, established by German and Australian colonial governments, with various fines allotted by discussions led by big-men. Major problems are handled by formal courts at the regional level.

Conflict. Up to the 1920s, before pacification by colonial forces, sporadic warfare occurred both within and between villages.

Religion and Expressive Culture

Religious Beliefs. Christian missions were established in the Mandak area in the late nineteenth and early twentieth centuries. Today, most of the Mandak are nominally members of a Christian sect, Methodists and Roman Catholics predominating. In addition, many people adhere in varying degrees to views of a world inhabited by a variety of nonhuman spirits, most of which are dangerous to humans who come into contact with them. Each clan has one or more powerful spirits or power embodied in an animal form, in sea life, or in a landscape feature on clan land. Spirits of the dead, particularly those of individuals who died a violent death, can be a source of danger to humans who encounter them. Unseen power or energy is thought to be a source of varied forms of control by humans who know how to direct it through magic spells. The use of magic, for both positive and negative purposes, is a common subject of concern in Mandak lives.

Religious Practitioners. Most adult men and women are thought to possess some magic spells, although only some men are capable of performing stronger forms of sorcery, ritual empowerment, and such specialized forms of magic as used in shark catching, sea becalming, and weather control. Village church leaders are usually from among the local male population.

Ceremonies. Ceremonial life focuses on mortuary feasts, of which there are various forms, including: the burial of a deceased individual; later mortuary feasts relevant to a single deceased individual; and large-scale clan-sponsored mortuary ceremonies involving dances and distribution of pigs, taro, and sweet potatoes. *Malagan* ceremonies occur in this area, although unevenly since the 1950s. Malagan refers to both a material object—carved wood or woven; mask, figure, or frieze—and its attendant rituals, usually as part of a large-scale mortuary ceremony.

Arts. The major artistic focus here involves malagan productions. Men's or women's songs and accompanying dances are important features of final mortuary ceremonies.

Death and Afterlife. The Mandak subscribe to a variety of beliefs concerning death and afterlife, from Christian doctrines to pre-Christian beliefs. In regard to the latter, an individual's spirit becomes either a restless, roaming spirit if the individual died a violent death (as from sorcery, accident, murder) or a more peaceful spirit, believed formerly to go to small nearby islands. Either type of spirit can serve as an aid to the living in various forms of magic and ritual or as a source of new ritual or song-dance.

See also Lesu

Bibliography

Brouwer, Elizabeth (1980). "A Malagan to Cover the Grave: Funerary Ceremonies in Mandak." Ph.D. dissertation, University of Queensland.

Chinnery, E. W. Pearson (1929). *Studies of the Native Population of the East Coast of New Ireland.* Territory of New Guinea Anthropological Report no. 6. Canberra: H. J. Green, Government Printer.

Clay, Brenda J. (1977). *Pinikindu: Maternal Nurture, Paternal Substance.* Chicago, Ill.: University of Chicago Press.

Clay, Brenda J. (1986). *Mandak Realities: Person and Power in Central New Ireland.* New Brunswick: Rutgers University Press.

Kramer, Augustin (1925). *Die Malanggane von Tombara.* Munich: Georg Muller.

BRENDA JOHNSON CLAY

Mangareva

Mangareva, also known as the Gambier Islands, consists of four small volcanic islands located southeast of the Tuamotu Archipelago in French Polynesia at 22° S and 128° W. The islands have a land area of about 29 square kilometers. In 1987, 1,600 speakers of Mangarevan were reported living on the islands. Estimates of the population in the past range from a high of 8,000 at the time of first contact to a low of 1,275 in 1824. In recent years, as on many smaller Polynesian islands, there has been a notable out-migration to larger islands such as Tahiti and urban centers. Mangarevan is an Austronesian language closely related to the languages spoken on the Marquesas Islands. In the past and today, Mangarevans subsist on a combination of fishing and horticulture, with breadfruit, coconuts, taro, bananas, and sugarcane the most important crops.

See also Raroia

Bibliography

Buck, Peter H. (1938). *Ethnology of Mangareva.* Bernice P. Bishop Museum Bulletin no. 157. Honolulu.

Sahlins, Marshall D. (1958). *Social Stratification in Polynesia.* Seattle: University of Washington Press.

Manihiki

ETHNONYMS: none

Manihiki is separated by 40 kilometers of open sea from its twin atoll of Rakahanga. It consists of two large islets and many smaller ones in the northern Cook Archipelago. There were 905 residents of the atolls in 1966. The languages are classified in the Eastern Polynesian Group of Austronesian languages. Prior to 1852 the people of Manihiki and Rakahanga would regularly migrate en masse from one atoll to the other, to allow natural regeneration of the abandoned atoll. Missionaries ended these cyclical movements and there are now permanent populations on both atolls. The senior line or moiety is supposed to reside on the lagoon side of the islets, while the junior line resides on the ocean side.

The primary staples are coconuts and swamp taro, in addition to sea foods. There were no pigs, dogs, or chickens on the atolls when Europeans arrived. Important kin groups are moieties, bilateral descent groups, and lineages. Descent is bilateral, with a patrilineal emphasis. All land is divided between the moieties and then allocated to descent groups. Arranged marriages are common and residence tends to be patrilocal. Polygyny was permitted for the chiefs, although all marriages are now monogamous. The core of a household is a single nuclear family (*puna*). Membership in a household is flexible, however, and many combinations of relatives can be found. The people of Manihiki and Rakahanga are organized into moieties (one senior and one junior), both of which fissioned sometime in the past to create four submoieties or descent groups. Out of these lineages twenty-five households have been established. The entire population is evidently descended from a single family, and so it constitutes one great bilateral kin group. Before the moieties were established the people were led by one chief or *ariki*. When the community split so did the office of ariki, with his ritual powers and responsibilities going to the senior line and his economic powers going to the junior line. Each of the four lineages also have leaders, who collectively make up the chiefly council.

All of the people are now Christian, although the concept of *tapu*, "sacredness," was important in the past. There are two ceremonial stone platforms (*marae*), one for each moiety. The native priests were the guardians of the gods, to whom they offered sacrifices at the marae.

See also Cook Islands, Pukapuka

Bibliography

Buck, Peter (1932). *Ethnology of Manihiki and Rakahanga.* Bernice P. Bishop Museum Bulletin no. 99. Honolulu.

Wiens, Harold (1962). *Atoll Environment and Ecology.* New Haven: Yale University Press.

Manus

ETHNONYM: Manusian

Orientation

Identification. The terms "Manus" and "Manusian" denote people native to Manus Province, Papua New Guinea. Manus also denotes the Titan-speaking people of the coast and offshore islands of the southeastern part of the province, who had the most intense early contact with White colonists. People can refer to each other by their language, village, or local area names, often the same. Also, they can use terms that denote other significant differences. Examples include electoral district names, terms denoting "islanders" (historically fishing and trading people) or "mainlanders" (historically agriculturalists) and terms denoting residents or those who have migrated elsewhere.

Location. Manus Province consists of a mainland (the main island of Manus and the barely separated island of Los Negros) and offshore islands, mostly to the southeast and north. It also includes several islands to the far west, inhabited by a set of ethnically distinct people not discussed here. Manus is in the Admiralty Islands at about 2° S and 147° E. The mainland is about 96 kilometers long and 24 kilometers wide, about 272 kilometers north-northeast of the Madang coast on the main island of New Guinea. It and some larger, volcanic islands are relatively fertile, but many smaller islands are infertile sand cays. The seasons are those of the southeast trade winds (April to October) and the northwestern monsoon (October to April). The monsoon has higher tide levels, greater cloudiness, and frequent storms, but the whole year is hot and wet.

Demography. In 1980, there were about 26,000 Manus people, of whom about 6,000 lived elsewhere in Papua New Guinea. This is more than twice the population reported in the first reliable estimates, early in the twentieth century.

Linguistic Affiliation. Manus languages are a distinct family of Austronesian languages, with four subfamilies: Eastern Mainland Manus (the largest), Western Mainland Manus, Northern Islands, and Southeastern Islands. There is little agreement on the origin of the languages. Estimates of their number range from eighteen to forty, and they share some grammatical and vocabulary elements. Many people from small, linguistically unique villages may understand three or four different languages; almost all speak Melanesian Pidgin; most speak some English.

History and Cultural Relations

Earliest European contact with the Manus mainland was in the sixteenth century, but first substantial contact was in the nineteenth century, with pearlers, whalers, and bêche-de-mer fishermen. Germany annexed Manus with the rest of German New Guinea in 1884 and was replaced by Australia in 1915. Colonial administration was based on appointed village headmen. Resistance to colonization was fierce in some areas: control was not complete until about 1920. A few copra plantations were established by 1910 and mission activity began shortly after. However, relatively little land was alienated for plantations. By World War II, most Manus were Christian—primarily Catholic, Seventh-Day Adventist, or Lutheran—but Christianity supplemented rather than displaced indigenous beliefs. After World War II, there was agitation for social, economic, and political improvement. Partly as a result, education provision increased, village officials were elected rather than appointed, and there was encouragement of village cooperatives. Public services expanded through the early 1980s, when government financial difficulties led to slight contraction. Shortly after the independence of Papua New Guinea in 1975, the province acquired an elected assembly.

Settlements

Villages rarely have more than 400 residents. They frequently are made of hamlets, sets of houses built around a central clearing, often with an associated patriclan's men's house. Hamlets and village sections are connected by paths. These hamlet clearings and the areas around houses are cleaned carefully. Households often maintain a dwelling house with a separate house for cooking. Houses may be built on the ground or on posts (up to about 6 feet) and may be of one or two stories. The household usually is a nuclear family, though a married child may build a house adjacent to the parents' dwelling. Manus has two urban areas. Lorengau, the provincial capital and market center, is a harbor town with about 4,000 people. Lombrum, a Defense Force naval base, has about 1,500 people. both were built during Australian control with commercial housing materials.

Economy

Subsistence and Commercial Activities. The household is the basic economic unit. The subsistence base for rural villagers is arboriculture and swidden agriculture (traditional for mainland villagers) or fishing (traditional for islanders). Agriculturalists harvest sago palms and various tree fruits and nuts, and they grow taro, sweet potatoes, leafy greens, and bananas. Fishing people catch many varieties of reef fish and some pelagic species, as well as the occasional shark or sea turtle. Almost all villages maintain coconut palms: coconut is an important food and source of cooking oil; many households use it to produce copra for occasional sale and in some areas it is an important commercial crop. Cocoa is also an important commercial crop in a few areas. Many households grow small quantities of leafy greens, squash, sugarcane, and bananas, and areca (betel) nuts, and betel peppers. Pork is important for feasts, and so in most villages a few pigs are reared. Indigenous food sources are supplemented by imported items, especially rice, tinned fish and meat, biscuits, tea, coffee, sugar, beer, cigarettes, and twist tobacco. These are available in small village shops and in greater variety more cheaply in Lorengau and Lombrum.

Industrial Arts. Before colonization, people produced a range of manufactured items. By the mid-1900s, imported substitutes displaced most indigenous manufacture, though most houses and canoes are still made of local materials. Handicraft production is reviving in some areas, for sale to tourists.

Trade. Manus originally had a complex system of trade that reflected village ecological differences, primarily between mainland agricultural villages and island fishing villages. This fish-for-starch trade weakened after World War II as mainland villagers, and in some instances islanders, moved to the coast and took up both agriculture and fishing. However, there remain many markets between pairs of island and mainland villages, but by about 1970 these generally had become cash-only rather than barter markets. In addition, many villages had access to special natural resources: clay for pots, obsidian for knives and spear points, beds of shell for shell money, etc. By about 1970, imported manufactures replaced these items and trade for them largely disappeared. Some villages carry fish and agricultural produce to Lorengau and Lombrum for sale in the marketplaces, and they buy and sell there from each other as well.

Division of Labor. The sexual division of labor is pronounced, though weaker than it had been. Men make housing (including village buildings like aid posts, schools, and churches), canoes, and sails, tend coconut and sago palms, and do some preparation of gardening land. Women do much other agricultural work, including pounding and washing sago, splitting and scraping coconuts, and preparing oil. Women also clean the house and its nearby area and village paths. In fishing villages, both men and women fish in nearby waters, but usually only men fish outside the surrounding reef. In some villages, different fishing techniques are clearly restricted to men or women. Although men claim formal control, in many villages women exert strong informal influence on much ceremonial activity. Villagewide cooperation for communal projects is difficult, as the villagewide structures that could be activated to induce cooperation are relatively recent and weak. An important division of labor for many villagers is between migrants and residents. Migrants remit money, important for the economic well-being of residents. In return, residents perform ritual and social activities necessary for the social and spiritual well-being of migrants (e.g., life-crisis and healing rituals).

Land Tenure. Land rights are inherited and there is almost no land sale. Parcels of land belong to agnatic groups, with sections of such parcels controlled by the group members who garden or build on them. In fishing communities, agnatic groups commonly hold marine rights, but the complexity of the system of tenure varies. Usually, areas of the surrounding reef and sea are claimed by agnatic groups, but specific parcels are not controlled by individuals in the way land is. In some villages there is ownership of fishing techniques of different sorts and of the right to catch certain species of fish. In the past these rights may have been of economic significance, but presently they are of little significance among subsistence fishing people. In principle, land in urban areas can be bought and sold by individuals as private property. However, some village groups claim to be ancestral owners of urban land and they have tried to assert that ownership.

Kinship

Kin Groups and Descent. The politically dominant kin groups are village-based, patrilineal descent groups that can loosely be called patriclans, internally differentiated into lineages. These groups are concerned primarily with land and sea tenure, but they also participate in exchange. People inherit group membership from their fathers; in some areas women adopt their husband's on marriage. There are also province-wide matriclans that do not have complex internal differentiation, though their importance varies around Manus. These matriclans are concerned mainly with health: treating pollution caused by contact with forbidden items, purification at stages of the life cycle. In addition there are local cognatic stocks (with patrilateral biases), one descending from each married couple in the past and present. These relationships are activated primarily during ceremonial exchanges, and as exchanges are frequent and important economically, these stocks are important. Villagers inherit all the stock memberships of both parents.

Kinship Terminology. Terminology varies, but it commonly stresses the relationship between the descendants of brothers and of sisters. Generational skewing of the Crow type occurs.

Marriage and Family

Marriage. Village endogamy and patriclan exogamy seem to have been enduring marriage preferences (matriclans are not significant here). In addition, other patterns have appeared at different times and places, shaped by political and economic interests. Notable among these is cross-cousin marriage and intervillage marriage (especially among elite families). Since conversion to Christianity, patterns have been shaped by church rules as well. Marriage entails payment of bride-price, which in the past made it susceptible to the manipulation of entrepreneurial big-men and in the present makes it an important conduit through which money passes from migrants to residents. Patrivirilocal residence is commonly preferred. Acceptability of divorce and illegitimacy vary widely, shaped in part by religious affiliation.

Domestic Unit. The domestic unit is the married couple and their unmarried children. Husband and older sons are no longer expected to sleep routinely in the patriclan's men's house, but they may do so occasionally.

Inheritance. The right to make decisions about real property is inherited patrilineally. Personal property can pass from parents to children or from sibling to sibling.

Socialization. The main institutions that socialize children are parents, schools, and churches (the last two at times being the same). As well, certain classes of relatives often have special responsibility for the child's welfare. Parents and other relatives, schools, and churches frequently are seen to have distinct spheres of competence: traditional and village skills, urban and Western skills, and Christian morality, respectively. Physical punishment of children is expected only in restricted circumstances. While some socialization may have occurred during initiation procedures in the past, these rites no longer exist.

Sociopolitical Organization

Social Organization. Villages are organized around the structure of patriclans, which shape rights in real property, and the structure of cognatic stocks, which shape participation in exchange. (Matriclans are relatively unimportant here.) Patriclans and stocks are localized and do not facilitate intervillage relationships. Patriclans are small (at times no more than five or six resident adults), and lineages are even smaller. Thus, they commonly recruit nonmembers for productive and ceremonial activities, typically from cognatic stocks descended from out-marrying patriclan (or lineage) women of earlier generations. This is often described as a distinction between the line (descendants) of the man (the brother) and the line of the woman (the out-marrying sister). A distinction between a line of the man and a line of the woman first appears at marriage, between the line of the groom and of the bride. For the children of the marriage, the distinction is between the line of the father and of the mother. In subsequent generations, it is the line of the man and of the woman. Villagers also distinguish residents and migrants, though this is reflected in practices rather than structures. Many ceremonial exchanges are organized to accommodate the schedules and wishes of important migrants, and the rules and practices of contribution and distribution help assure that migrants' contributions remain in the hands of residents.

Political Organization. Village political organization revolves around patriclans and village factions. Hereditary patriclan leaders are supposed to lead patriclan activities and influence patriclan political decisions, though within a general framework of consensus. Often, different village patriclans were responsible for villagewide activities, such as making war, making peace, and village governance. Patriclans and their leaders are more powerful in those villages where clan land is of prime economic significance, not overshadowed by introduced economic resources that are beyond the control of villages (especially wage labor). Village factions often reflect patriclan differences, but also reflect different orientations to contemporary conditions and issues. Most common are different orientations to modernization, tradition, and Christianity. Villages have formal governments, including an elected village leader and assistant, elected magistrates and constable, and usually an elected representative to the local subprovincial governing body. Electoral districts for provincial and national parliaments include more than one village, and elections for these bodies often unite villagers in support for the candidate from their village. Provincial party allegiance is weak and people often say that representatives are swayed by gifts and favors.

Social Control. Ideally, relations within the patriclan are amicable. This is less true of relations between patriclans and villages, which may be tense and even violent. Behavior is controlled in three ways. One is the sanction of agnatic ancestors, who monitor the acts of their living descendants and in cases of unresolved grievance may inflict illness, which can be fatal. Someone suspecting an ancestral illness will call a meeting of relatives, where all are to confess their hidden grievances and resolve them. As ancestors monitor migrants as well as residents, this helps tie migrants to their natal village. Second is the power of specific classes of ego's kin (especially classificatory father's sister, father's sister's daughter, and father's sister's son). These have the power to bless or curse, and can use their power to ensure ego's proper behavior. Third is the village court system. Cases of slander and petty theft, as well as more serious matters, are routinely heard by village magistrates. Higher-level courts are seldom used.

Conflict. Prior to colonial control, raiding and open warfare between villages were common. Conflict was common when mainland or island groups moved to coastal land, and so it helped maintain the ecological division of villages and the related trade system. Intravillage, interclan fighting occurred, but such conflicts seem to have been unusual and informal, though sorcery attacks among villagers did occur. Such fighting could lead to village fission. Modern intervillage conflict is not common, occurring mainly when residents of one village use the land or seas of other villages. There is conflict between villages and government over the imposition of taxes and, more recently, over provincial government policies. Such conflicts reflect a recurring regional division between southern and northern Manus.

Religion and Expressive Culture

Religious Beliefs. Indigenous religion revolves around the dead rather than gods. Ancestors monitor the acts of their agnatic descendants and punish wrongdoing by taking the substance of an individual's soul. A recently dead ancestor could be adopted as household patron and protector. There are also malevolent spirits, which can be controlled by sorcerers. Most Manus are Christian, and denominational beliefs have been modified in different ways by their mixture with indigenous cosmology.

Religious Practitioners. Divining in various ways is common, and many villages have two or three practitioners, who are not distinguished by special title or ritual. Some people are thought to control malevolent spirits, but few admit to this activity. Many people have entered the service of the church as catechists and lay officials, and some have been ordained.

Ceremonies. Dancing and feasting are performed only as part of other activities, especially men's-house raising, marriage and bride-price exchange, visits by important government and church officials, major provincial occasions, and important sporting events. Exchanges are frequent and are always accompanied by a degree of ceremonial activity, especially speech making and feasting. Church services are well attended.

Arts. Everyday objects, houses, and canoes could be carved and painted in the past, though this is less common in the present. Woven mats and baskets, lime gourds, and lime sticks frequently are decorated. Indigenous valuables (shell money and dogs' teeth) were and are treated as decorative as well as valuable. They are mounted on beadwork belts made with bright designs. People also make decorative beadwork-and-shell bracelets and necklaces.

Medicine. Before colonization there was extensive use of plant matter as medicine, and some is still used. Much illness is thought to be caused by ancestors and much medical practice involves locating and resolving the source of such illness. Illness caused by contact with matriclan totems, potentially fatal, is usually not worrisome as it is treated easily by the invocation of matriclan ancestors by matriclan women. With colonization, church and government health services spread; now they are often the treatment of first resort, though failure of nurses or physicians to diagnose and treat a complaint quickly can be taken to mean that an ancestral illness exists.

Death and Afterlife. Almost all deaths, even of the very old, are laid to ancestral illness or sorcery. The human spirit reluctantly leaves the body after death, usually before burial. Spirits exist in a parallel, invisible world, where they continue to act as normal people. As already described, they monitor the behavior of their agnatic descents, punishing where necessary. In addition, they may take revenge on some of the living to redress old complaints or their own death. The most recent dead are the most active, and after three or four generations the spirit no longer affects the living. This set of beliefs overlays Christian beliefs in Heaven and Hell, angels being the spirits of the dead.

Bibliography

Carrier, James, and Achsah Carrier (1989). *Wage, Trade, and Exchange in Melanesia: A Manus Society in the Modern State.* Berkeley: University of California Press.

Fortune, Reo (1935). *Manus Religion.* Philadelphia, Pa.: American Philosophical Society.

Mead, Margaret (1934). "Kinship in the Admiralty Islands." *American Museum of Natural History Anthropological Papers* 34:189–358.

Mead, Margaret (1930). *Growing Up in New Guinea.* New York: William Morrow. Reprint. 1963. Harmondsworth, England: Penguin.

Schwartz, Theodore (1963). "Systems of Areal Integration: Some Considerations Based on the Admiralty Islands of Northern Melanesia." *Anthropological Forum* 1:56–97.

Schwartz, Theodore (1962). "The Paliau Movement in the Admiralty Islands." *American Museum of Natural History Anthropological Papers* 49:211–421.

JAMES G. CARRIER

Maori

ETHNONYM: Te Maori

Orientation

Identification. The Maori are the indigenous inhabitants of New Zealand. Culturally, they are Polynesians, most closely related to eastern Polynesians. After contact with Europeans, the people now known as the Maori began using the term *tangata maori,* meaning "usual or ordinary people," to refer to themselves.

Location. The Maori were originally settled primarily in the northern parts of North Island, New Zealand. South Island was much more sparsely settled.

Demography. When Captain Cook visited New Zealand in 1769 the indigenous population was probably between 200,000 and 250,000. The population declined after contact with Europeans, but it began to recover at the beginning of this century and now approaches 300,000.

Linguistic Affiliation. Maori is classified as part of the Polynesian Group of the Eastern Oceanic Branch of the Austronesian languages. Approximately one-third of the Maori still speak their ancestral language, with the vast majority fluent in English as well.

History and Cultural Relations

New Zealand was evidently settled in three waves by travelers from Polynesian islands in A.D. 950, 1150, and 1350. The early arrivals, the Moriori, subsisted mainly by fishing and hunting the moa and other birds that are now extinct. The final (pre-European) immigration was that of the "seven canoes of the great fleet." The people of the great fleet assimilated the original inhabitants by marriage and conquest. The immigrants of 1350 arrived with their own domesticated plants and animals (several of which did not survive the transition from a tropical to a temperate climate), and they subsequently developed into the Maori of the present historical period. Whalers and sealers were common visitors to New Zealand in the 1790s and their relations with the Maori were generally unfriendly and often violent. The first missionaries arrived in 1814 and by the 1830s large numbers of Europeans and Australians were settling in New Zealand. With the Treaty of Waitangi, signed in February 1840 by many (but not all) of the indigenous chiefs, the Maori relinquished sovereignty over New Zealand land and in turn received British recognition and protection, as well as guaranteed rights to their native lands. A period of rapid acculturation ensued, lasting until 1860. The years 1860–1865 saw many battles between the Maori and the government of New Zealand, mainly over questions of land rights and sovereignty. By 1900 their population slide had reversed and the Maori began to play a more active role in New Zealand society. They received permanent Maori seats in the national legislature, and most discriminatory laws were repealed. At present the Maori are a legally recognized minority group (about 10 percent of the population), and they receive special legal and economic considerations on these grounds. Since the 1960s there has been a move to revitalize the Maori language and the Maori are attempting to preserve their cultural heritage while living side-by-side with the "Pakeha" (New Zealanders of European descent). This summary focuses on traditional Maori culture.

Settlements

Today the Maori are overwhelmingly an urban population, located primarily in towns and cities of the northern sections of North Island. In the past there were two types of Maori settlements: fortified (*pa*) and unfortified (*kainga*). Pa, in which people took refuge in wartime, were usually located on a hill and were protected by ditches, palisades, fighting platforms, and earthworks. Houses in the pa were closely crowded, often on artificial terraces. Kainga were unfortified hamlets consisting of five or six scattered houses (*whare*), a cooking shelter (*kauta*) with an earth oven (*hangi*), and one or two roofed storage pits (*rua*). Most farmsteads were enclosed in a courtyard with a pole fence. Most buildings were made of pole and thatch, but some better-made ones were constructed of posts and worked timber.

Economy

Subsistence and Commercial Activities. Maori subsistence depended on fishing, gathering, and the cultivation of sweet potatoes, or *kumara* (*Ipomoea batatas*), some taro, yams, and gourds. Fishing was done with lines, nets, and traps, while fowling was done with spears and snares. Items gathered include shellfish, berries, roots, shoots, and piths. Rats were also trapped and eaten. In infertile areas or in harsh seasons uncultivated fern roots provided an important starchy supplement. Kumara was planted in October and harvested in February and March; winter was the most important hunting season. Getting food was a time-consuming and arduous business.

Industrial Arts. The Maori made tools from stone and wood. Important mechanical aids were wedges, skids, lifting tackles, fire ploughs, and cord drills. Most material items were highly decorated. Major manufactures included flax mats, canoes, fishing equipment, weapons, elaborate digging sticks, cloaks, and ornaments, among others.

Trade. Goods and services were conveyed or compensated through gift giving between individuals. Items and services did not have set values, and the Maori lacked any form of true money. Items most often exchanged were food, ornaments, flax coats, stone, obsidian, and greenstone. Generosity was valued as it enhanced a person's mana, or psychic power. There was a coastal-interior exchange of sea and agricultural products for forest products and greenstone from the west coast of South Island was exchanged for finished goods from the north.

Division of Labor. Men were responsible for felling trees, clearing ground for cultivation, planting, trapping birds and rats, digging fern roots, deep-sea fishing, canoe making, carving, stoneworking, tattooing, and performing esoteric rites. Women were responsible for gathering, weeding, collecting firewood, carrying water, cooking, plaiting, and weaving. Especially skilled individuals could become specialists (*tohunga*) as carvers, builders, and raft makers. The Maori preferred to work cooperatively, with particularly odious jobs left to the slaves.

Land Tenure. Nearly all land was owned by the various descent groups or tribes. Each group controlled a parcel of tribal territory and granted rights of usufruct and occupation to its members. Only the group could alienate the descent group's land, and then only with the permission of the entire tribe. Border disputes were a common source of fighting. The nuclear family (*whanau*) of a descent group held rights to specific resources and parcels of land, which could be conveyed to the members' children. Rights of use could be extended to nonmembers only with the permission of the entire descent group.

Kinship

Kin Groups. The largest kin groups in Maori society were the so-called tribes (*iwi*). The iwi were independent political units that occupied discrete territories. An iwi was a large, bilateral descent group encompassing as its members all descendants, traced through both male and female links, of the tribe's founder (by whose name most tribes were known). The Maori were organized into some fifty iwi, of varying size and prestige. The iwi, in turn, were made up of a number of sections known as *hapu*. The hapu also owned a discrete territory and consisted of all individuals bilaterally descended from a founding ancestor. The hapu were much more important than the iwi with regard to land use and communal projects among their members. Most of the members of a hapu lived, along with in-marrying spouses and slaves, in one or two communities. Since they were defined bilaterally, an individual was often a member of and could affiliate with more then one hapu. A household became officially affiliated with a particular hapu by demonstrating a genealogical link conferring membership and by participating fully in the group's daily life. Descent was reckoned bilaterally, with a patrilateral emphasis, especially in chiefly families.

Kinship Terminology. Maori kin terminology was of the Hawaiian type.

Marriage and Family

Marriage. Maori youth enjoyed premarital sexual freedom and were expected to have a series of discreet love affairs before marrying. The choice of a marriage partner was made by the senior members of the whanau (household). Marriage served to establish new relations with other kin groups and brought new members into the hapu. Aristocrats often betrothed their children as infants. Marriages were nearly always between members of the same tribe and often between members of the same hapu. First and second cousins were ineligible as marriage partners. Most marriages were monogamous, though chiefs often took several wives. Gifts were exchanged by both partners at the weddings of commoners while aristocratic women brought a dowry often in the form of land and slaves. Divorce was common and easy, based simply on an agreement of husband and wife to separate. Residence was flexible, but often patrilocal. Children were greatly desired and commonly adopted from relatives. Abortion, infanticide, and postpartum sexual abstinence were the primary methods of population control.

Domestic Unit. The basic social unit was the household (whanau), often comprised of an extended family, including a male head (*kaumatua*), his spouse(s), their unmarried children, and their married sons, along with the latter's spouses and children. Many households also had resident slaves.

Inheritance. A dying person would make a final testament disposing of his or her property. Most of the estate was divided fairly equally among the surviving children, except that certain types of hunting, fishing, and craft equipment went only to the offspring of the same sex.

Socialization. Children were generally educated by their relatives, especially grandparents, through songs and stories. Games often imitated adult activities and were competitive. Aggressiveness and competitiveness were encouraged.

Sociopolitical Organization

Social Organization. The interrelationships among households, hapu, and iwi has been described above. While iwi were fixed in composition and number, new hapu were created through fission. When a hapu grew too large to function effectively some of its members would break off and establish a new hapu under the leadership of one of the chief's sons or younger brothers. The tribes whose ancestors arrived in New Zealand in the same canoe were considered to constitute a *waka,* literally "canoe." A waka was effectively a confederation whose members felt some obligation to help one another. This special relationship did not, however, rule out warfare between two tribes of the same waka. The Maori were ranked into three social classes, determined by the source of one's line. Members of the two highest classes were both free people, while those descended from the oldest males of each generation formed the aristocracy (*rangatira*). Those from more junior lines, or whose ancestors had lost status, were considered commoners (*tutua* or *ware*). The question of precisely where a particular line stood in these two classes was often a source of controversy. Difference in rank was directly correlated with degree of sacredness (*tapu*) and mana of each individual and group. Finally, there were the slaves (*taurekareka*), mainly war captives, who stood outside the descent system.

Political Organization. Each hapu had a chief (from the rangatira). The rangatira of the most senior hapu was the paramount chief (*ariki*) of that tribe. The tribe was therefore the highest politically integrated unit in Maori society. Both chieftainships were passed on patrilineally to the first son in each generation. In some tribes a senior daughter was also given special recognition. Chiefs were of high rank and generally quite wealthy. They exercised great influence but lacked coercive power. The chiefs organized and directed economic projects, led *marae* ceremonials, administered their group's property, and conducted relations with other groups. The chiefs were often fully trained priests with ritual responsibilities and powers, most importantly the right to impose tapu. The rangatira and ariki were, in their persons, very tapu and had much mana. The household heads or kaumatua as a group constituted the community council (*runanga*) which advised and could influence the chief.

Social Control. Penalties for crimes ran from gossip, reprimand, and sorcery to seizure of property, beating, and execution.

Conflict. Conflict between different hapu and different tribes was common and often led to warfare. The defeated were most often enslaved, killed, or eaten. Women and children were the most likely persons to be spared.

Religion and Expressive Culture

Religious Beliefs. The Maori held an essentially spiritual view of the universe. Anything associated with the supernatural was invested with tapu, a mysterious quality which made those things or persons imbued with it either sacred or unclean according to context. Objects and persons could also possess mana, psychic power. Both qualities, which were inherited or acquired through contact, could be augmented or diminished during one's lifetime. All free men were tapu to a degree directly proportional to their rank. Furthermore, an object or resource could be made tapu and therefore off-limits. The punishment for violating a tapu restriction was automatic, usually coming as sickness or death. The Maori had a pantheon of supernatural beings (*atua*). The supreme god was known as Io. The two primeval parents, Papa and Rangi, had eight divine offspring: Haumia, the god of uncultivated food; Rongo, the god of peace and agriculture; Ruaumoko, the god of earthquakes; Tawhirimatea, the god of weather; Tane, the father of humans and god of forests; Tangaroa, the god of the sea; Tu-matauenga, the war god; and Whiro, the god of darkness and evil. There were also exclusive tribal gods, mainly associated with war. In addition, there were various family gods and familiar spirits.

Religious Practitioners. The senior deities had a priesthood (*tohunga ahurewa*), members of which received special professional training. They were responsible for all esoteric ritual, were knowledgeable about genealogies and tribal history, and were believed to be able to control the weather. Shamans rather than priests served the family gods whom they communicated with through spirit possession and sorcery.

Ceremonies. Most public rites were performed in the open, at the marae. The gods were offered the first fruits of all undertakings, and slaves were occasionally sacrificed to propitiate them. Incantations (*karakia*) were chanted in flawless repetition to influence the gods.

Arts. Most of the material objects of the Maori were highly decorated. Their statues and carvings, especially with filigree motifs, are admired worldwide and are the frequent subject of art museum exhibitions.

Medicine. Sickness was believed to be caused by sorcery or the violation of a tapu. The proximate cause of illness was the presence of foreign spirits in the sick body. The medical tohunga accordingly exorcised the spirits and purified the patient. The therapeutic value of some plants was also recognized.

Death and Afterlife. The dying and dead were taken to a shelter on the marae. The body was laid out on mats to receive mourners, who came in hapu or tribal groups. After a week or two of mourning the body was wrapped in mats and buried in a cave, in a tree, or in the ground. Often after a year or two the ariki would have the body exhumed, and the bones scraped clean and painted with red ochre, to be taken from settlement to settlement for a second mourning. Afterward, the bones were given a second burial in a sacred place. The spirits of the dead were believed to make a voyage to their final abode, a vague and mysterious underworld.

Bibliography

Best, Elsdon (1924). *The Maori.* 2 vols. Memoirs of the Polynesian Society, no. 5. Wellington.

Buck, Peter (1949). *The Coming of the Maori.* Wellington: Maori Purposes Fund Board and Whitcombe & Tombs.

Firth, Raymond (1929). *Economics of the New Zealand Maori.* Wellington: Government Printer.

Hanson, F. Allan, and Louise Hanson (1983). *Counterpoint in Maori Culture.* London: Routledge & Kegan Paul.

Metge, Joan (1967). *The Maoris of New Zealand, Rautahi.* London: Routledge & Kegan Paul. Rev. ed. 1976.

CHRISTOPHER LATHAM

Mardudjara

ETHNONYMS: Jigalong, Mardujarra

Orientation

Identification. The Mardu Aborigines are part of the Western Desert cultural bloc, which encompasses one-sixth of the continent of Australia, and is notable for its social, cultural and linguistic homogeneity. "Mardu," meaning "man" or "person," was coined as a collective label because there was no such traditional term. Constituent dialect-name groupings include the Gardujarra, Manyjilyjarra, Gurajarra, Giyajarra, and Budijarra.

Location. The territories of the Mardu straddle the Tropic of Capricorn between 122° and 125° E in one of the world's harshest environments. Rainfall, the crucial ecological variable, is very low and highly unpredictable. Permanent waters are rare, and both daily and seasonal temperature ranges are high (-4° C to over 54° C). Major landforms include: parallel, red-colored sand ridges with flat interdunal corridors; stony and sandy plains (covered in spinifex); rugged hilly areas with narrow gorges; and acacia scrub thickets and creek beds lined with large eucalyptus trees. Animal life includes kangaroos, emus, lizards, birds, insects, and grubs, which together with grass seeds, tubers, berries, fruits, and nectars formed the basis of the traditional Aboriginal diet.

Demography. It is impossible accurately to estimate the precontact populations here termed Mardu. They were scattered in small bands (fifteen to twenty-five people) most of the time, and population densities were very low: about 1 person per 91 square kilometers. Today there are about 1,000 Mardu, most of whom live either in the settlement of Jigalong or in a number of small outstation communities that have been established in the desert homelands within the past decade. Both the general population size and the ratio of children to adults have grown greatly since migration from the desert.

Linguistic Affiliation. All Mardu groups speak mutually intelligible dialects of the Western Desert language, the single-biggest language in Australia. There are currently several thousand speakers of this language.

History and Cultural Relations

Shielded by their forbidding environment, the Mardu were left largely undisturbed until relatively recently. They were attracted from the desert to fringe settlements: mining camps, pastoral properties, small towns, and missions, initially for brief periods. However, inducements offered by Whites who desired their labor (and, in the case of women, sexual services), plus a growing taste for European foodstuffs and other commodities, drew them increasingly into the ambit of the newcomers. Inevitably, they eventually abandoned their nomadic, hunter-gatherer adaptation for a sedentary life close to Whites. Migration began around the turn of the century and ended as recently as the 1960s. The Mardu remain today among the more tradition-oriented Aborigines in Australia. Jigalong was founded as a maintenance camp on a rabbit-control fence, and it later became a ration depot for the indigent Aborigines who had begun congregating there in the 1930s. It was a Christian mission for twenty-four years from 1946, but race relations were often tense and the Aborigines resisted all efforts to undermine their traditions. Many Aboriginal men and women worked on pastoral leases as laborers and domestics, but there was a dramatic downturn in this form of employment following the advent, in the 1960s, of laws requiring parity of wage levels between Aboriginal and White workers in the pastoral industry. Jigalong became a legally incorporated Aboriginal community in 1974, assisted by White advisers and funded almost entirely from governmental sources. Government policy since the early 1970s has promoted self-reliance and the retention of a distinctive identity and traditions. For the Mardu, access to alcohol and increasing Westernization pressures have led to considerable social problems, which remain unresolved. A recent movement to establish permanent outstations on or near traditional Mardu lands is partly in response to these pressures, particularly the damaging effects of alcohol, but it also relates to the advent of large-scale mining exploration in the desert. The Mardu strongly oppose these activities, and since the formation of a regional land council in the mid-1980s, a major concern has been to protect their lands from desecration and alienation.

Settlements

Most Mardu live today at Jigalong or in smaller outstations on the western side of the Gibson Desert, but a few (mostly the steady drinkers) live in or on the fringes of towns in the region. Mobility remains high, especially between Jigalong, whose population is around 300, and the outstations, which range in population from about 20 to 100 people. Jigalong has an airfield, graded dirt roads connecting it to the main highway to the west, telephone and radio contact, television, and many motor vehicles. It has a large school, a medical clinic, a sewage system, electricity, water supply, a well-stocked community-owned store, and many European-style houses for White staff and Aborigines. However, many people still live in squalid and unhygienic conditions. The outstations are still being developed, but most have basic necessities such as water supply and radio transceivers, and the large ones each have an airfield, a school, electricity generators, and refrigeration.

Economy

Subsistence and Commercial Activities. The total autonomy of the traditional hunting and gathering economy and the partial self-sufficiency of pastoral employment have been replaced by massive unemployment and a highly dependent, welfare-based existence. The Mardu region is ecologically extremely marginal, so the prospects of developing profitable local land-based industries are slim. Jigalong runs a cattle enterprise, and various other economic schemes have been tried, without success. All the settlements are heavily reliant on the importation of foodstuffs, despite the continuance of hunting and gathering activities. At Jigalong, the large settlement economy provides salaried work for Aboriginal office and store workers, teacher and health aides, maintenance workers, and pastoral employees. Besides kinship, gambling with cards is an important medium for the redistribution of cash. The Aborigines have adopted a wide range of material items from the Whites, but they have strongly resisted changes in basic values relating to kinship and religion.

Trade. Formalized trading networks were absent in the Western Desert, but scarce and highly valued items, such as pearl shells and red ocher, diffused widely throughout the region as a result of exchanges between individuals and groups, mostly within the context of ceremonial activities. Group exchanges centered on religious lore, both material and nonmaterial, and the exchange of mundane material items, such as weapons or tools, was clearly subsidiary to religious concerns. Most individual transactions were gift exchanges conducted within the framework of kinship and affinal obligations.

Division of Labor. The gender-based division between women as gatherers (and hunters of small game) and men as hunters is still seen, but these activities are no longer fundamental to subsistence. Women are the main cooks, housekeepers, and office workers, whereas men prefer to work outdoors. Children stay at school into their mid-teens, so their economic impact is slight, but girls tend still to marry at a younger age than boys and to assume full parental responsibilities earlier.

Land Tenure. Traditionally, bands were the basic land-occupying, economic unit, while large territorially anchored entities, known as estate groups, were associated with land "ownership." Although they contained a core of patrilineally related males, these groups had multiple criteria for membership, and it was possible for active adults to be involved significantly in more than one such group. Since land was inalienable, property rights were more often conceptualized in terms of responsibility for, rather than control over, sites and resources. In both ethos and practice, Mardu society strongly favored inclusivity and the maximizing of rights and obligations. Today, the Jigalong area is an officially recognized Aboriginal Reserve, but the Mardu have yet to obtain firm tenure to the traditional homelands. An Aboriginal Land bill, introduced in the State Parliament in 1985, failed to become law. A long-term lease scheme has since been established but the Mardu are pessimistic that governments will recognize their claims to traditional land, as mining interests continue to take precedence over Aboriginal concerns.

Kinship

Kin Groups and Descent. Although dispersal and traditional local organization have given way to aggregation in sedentary communities, kinship remains a fundamental building block of Mardu society, and everyone relates to everyone else primarily in terms of classificatory kinship norms. Kinship and religious ties link Aborigines right across the vast Western Desert. The Mardu are drawn from dialect-named territorial divisions that unite territory, language, and kin groups. These larger units, sometimes wrongly called "tribes," never existed as corporate entities, and though boundaries existed, they were highly permeable. The most visible group was the band, whose camping arrangements reflected the several family groups that made up this flexible aggregation. Within every dialect-named area were a number of bands and at least one "estate," the highly valued heartland that contained major sacred sites and important waterholes and constituted the locus of the estate group. The Mardu kinship system is bilateral, but traditionally there was a clear patrivirilocal tendency in "residence" rules and practices, as well as a strong preference for children to be born somewhere in or near the estate of their father. Both the estate group and the band tended to have a core of people related patrilineally. There were no lineages or clans, and genealogical depth was limited (aided by taboos on naming the dead).

Kinship Terminology. Terminology is bifurcate-merging and occurs in association with a section system, with the division of society into four named categories. Many of the seventeen different terms of address used by each sex are shared by male and female speakers. Mardu also employ a large and complex set of dual-reference terms. There is a generational emphasis; thus, for example, all people in one's grandparent and grandchild generations are merged under two nearly identical terms, differing only for the sex of the person addressed. Patterned sets of behaviors associated with each kin term can be seen as ranging along a continuum from joking to avoidance relationships.

Marriage and Family

Marriage. Classificatory bilateral cross-cousin marriage is the prescribed form. Polygyny was a social ideal not always realized in the past, and today it is still practiced but is not common. Infant betrothal was once the norm, all adults married, all widows remarried, and divorce was rare. Today, many widows remain single, and young, unmarried mothers are common. Marriage rules are less often obeyed, but they still have considerable force and transgressors are physically punished. Traditionally, men could not marry for at least a decade after their first initiatory rites, which occurred around age 16–17, but today men in their early twenties are marrying, and far fewer betrothals result in marriage.

Domestic Unit. Traditionally, the commensal unit was the nuclear or polygynous family and this remains largely the case. Most people camp near close relatives and there is a great deal of visiting and casual eating at the camps or houses of others. Generosity and sharing remain prime values and most households provide food and shelter for a shifting number and range of relatives.

Inheritance. Material possessions were minimal, and were generally buried with a person upon death; today, they are burned or given away to distant relatives, and houses, or areas surrounding the deceased's camp, are vacated for months or years at a time following a death.

Socialization. Infants and children are raised by parents, siblings and other close coresident relatives; grandparents typically play an important role as socializers. Children tend to be greatly indulged by adults and can always get money and food from a wide range of relatives. Freed from the necessity of observing kinship rules, they spend much time at play in large groups. Traditionally, they spent more time with women, whom they accompanied on food-gathering expeditions. Today, most attend school from the age of 5 or 6, but this requirement is frequently breached. At the onset of the teenage years, the fortunes of boys and girls begin to diverge dramatically. The transition of girls into wives and mothers is unmarked by ritual, whereas boys enter upon a protracted and ritually highly elaborated process that transforms them into adults. This culturally very important transition takes about 15 years from the first physical operations, such as nose piercing, to the final stages preceding first marriage, which occurs in the late twenties and marks the young man as socially adult.

Sociopolitical Organization

Social Organization. Families, bands, estate groups, and "big meetings" (periodic aggregations of people from a number of neighboring dialect-named territories, who met to conduct ritual and other business) were the major elements of social organization traditionally. These were crosscut by a multiplicity of memberships (totemic, kin-based, ritual-grade, etc.), including moieties and sections, which welded desert society together. Today, the families and the "big meetings" remain important institutions, but they exist parallel to introduced forms such as committees and councils.

Political Organization. In former times, political action was the domain of small groups, and sex and age were the main criteria for differentiation. Although the status of women was lower than that of men, an egalitarian ethos prevailed, and leadership was very much context-dependent and changeable. Most of the time, the norms of kinship provided an adequate framework for social action and the allocation of roles. The social and political autonomy of the traditional band and estate group has been replaced by encapsulation and minority status within the nation-state and the introduction of Western-style institutions such as elections and councils. High mobility and involvement in regional land councils reflect a continuing interest in the wider Western Desert society as "all one people," and the Mardu spend much time and effort maintaining these contacts. Politically, they remain dependent on governments for survival and on White advisers for assistance in dealing with the bureaucracies of Australian society. In the past few years, however, there has been a marked increase in Mardu political awareness and confidence in dealing with outsiders.

Social Control. Traditional social controls relied heavily on a high level of self-regulation, but physical sanctions were invoked on occasion. Western influences have seriously undermined these controls in the contact situation. For example, spearing and other forms of physical punishment have occasioned police interventions and arrests of "lawful" punishers; unprecedented numbers of children have led to problems of vandalism; there is an increasing incidence of marriage between improperly related partners; and young women have successfully resisted attempts to marry them off to their betrothed partners. Alcohol has contributed greatly to a loosening of traditional social controls, and uncontrolled violence (as well as drunken driving) has led to many deaths.

Conflict. Conflict was closely controlled traditionally, and the ritualized settlement of disputes was a vital preliminary to every "big meeting." Today, adding to less easily controlled intracommunity conflicts are political struggles, mostly with mining companies but also with a neighboring Aboriginal group that has long sought, unsuccessfully, to bring the Mardu under its control.

Religion and Expressive Culture

Religious Beliefs. Religion, like kinship, is pervasive in Aboriginal society. Founded on the notion of a creative era, now commonly known as "the Dreaming," when everything came into being and the rules for life were instituted by ancestral beings, religion is embodied in the landscape, myths, rituals, song lines, and sacred paraphernalia. Life was profoundly under spiritual authority, but prayers and worship had no place. Men controlled the most powerful, inner secrets, and ritual performance was believed to ensure the continuance of society, under the watchful eyes of all-powerful, but withdrawn, spiritual beings. Their continued release of life force into the physical world was held to be dependent on the proper observance of "the Law" (their legacy to the living, in the form of a blueprint for the proper conduct of social life) and the correct performance of ritual. Totemism provided each individual with direct and unique links into the realm of the Dreaming and were important in the formation and maintenance of identity. Despite intensive contact with Whites and a diminution in the frequency of ritual activities, beliefs in the reality of the traditional religion remain strong among Mardu, and all young men continue to be initiated into its secrets. Beliefs in a range of benevolent and malevolent spirits remain strong, and Mardu retain strong fears of travel to distant areas whose spirits do not know them and therefore are likely to be dangerous. A small minority of Mardu profess Christian beliefs, but none to the exclusion of the traditional religion.

Religious Practitioners. Virtually all Mardu participate in aspects of the religious life, and while different ritual complexes involve different roles or grades, there are no specialist practitioners.

Ceremonies. The traditionally rich ceremonial life, much of which included all community members, now has to compete with many other distractions. It is now more seasonal, and most "big meetings" are held in the very hot summer period. Some kinds of ceremony are no longer performed, but those surrounding male initiation remain as significant as ever, and generally involve several hundred Aborigines from widely separated communities. Ceremonial activities are still generally accorded priority over sociopolitical dealings with the wider society.

Arts. Most artistic endeavor was confined to religious contexts and entailed the manufacture of sacred objects, body decorations, and ground paintings. The making of weapons and other artifacts for sale to Whites has been an informal and minor part of the local economy for several decades.

Medicine. About 10 percent of Mardu males are magician-curers (*mabarn*), part-time specialists who employ magical means to cure (and, allegedly, to harm) people. A range of "bush medicines" is also known and employed by the Mardu, who also have frequent resort to Western medicines and treatment. Belief in the powers and efficacy of mabarn and magic remains unshaken.

Death and Afterlife. The ceremonies surrounding death were not highly elaborated among the Mardu. Their objective was to ensure the passage of the newly released spirit of the deceased back to the place from whence it had emerged, as a spirit child, to enter the body of its mother. Loud mourning, self-injury, and ceremonial exchanges continue to mark death, but there is now only a single burial, since inquests using dug-up bones, prior to reburial, are no longer held. Mabarn attend the burial to speak to the spirit and urge it to leave peacefully and to not harass the living; Christian prayers are also offered in some cases. The Mardu have no beliefs in reincarnation.

See also Aranda, Ngatatjara, Pintupi, Warlpiri

Bibliography

Tonkinson, R. (1974). *The Jigalong Mob: Aboriginal Victors of the Desert Crusade.* Menlo Park, Calif.: Benjamin Cummings.

Tonkinson, R. (1978). *The Mardudjara Aborigines: Living the Dream in Australia's Desert.* New York: Holt, Rinehart & Winston.

Tonkinson, R. (1987). "Mardujarra Religion: A Profile of the Religious System of the Mardujarra Aborigines." In *The Encyclopedia of Religion,* edited by M. Eliade, 196–201. New York: Macmillan, Free Press.

Tonkinson, R. (1988). "Mardujarra Kinship." In *Australians to 1788.* Vol. 1, *Australians: a Historical Library,* edited by D. J. Mulvaney and J. P. White, 196–219. Sydney: Fairfax, Weldon & Syme.

Tonkinson, R. (1988) "One Community, Two Laws: Aspects of Conflict and Convergence in a Western Australian Aboriginal Community." In *Indigenous Law and the State,* edited by B. Morse and G. Woodman, 395–411. Dordrecht: Foris.

ROBERT TONKINSON

Marind-anim

ETHNONYMS: Kaja-kaja, Tugeri

Orientation

Identification. Marind (*anim* means "people") is the name by which some forty territorial groups (subtribes) in New Guinea identify themselves vis-à-vis foreigners. The traditional culture, especially the religious system, has been dramatically changed through Western contact, although many Western material goods are avoided and the Marind prefer to associate with one another. The description which follows focuses on the traditional culture.

Location. Marind occupy the southeastern coastal area of Irian Jaya (the western half of New Guinea) from the southern entrance of the Muli Strait southeastward to about 30 kilometers beyond Merauke, with, at some distance from the international border, the enclave of Kondo. Farther inland, they occupy the upper Bulaka River region and all the land east of it to the Eli and Bian rivers, an area usually called the Okaba Hinterland. Marind territory also includes the Bian and Kumbe river valleys and part of the lower Maro with all the land between. The land is lowland, mainly savanna alternating with swamps; in the upper river areas, it is mostly low hills and swamps. Resources include coconuts on sandy ground, sago in the swamps, eucalyptus trees on the savanna, wallabies in the grasslands, and fish in the rivers and sea. The monsoon climate provides heavy rains during the northwest monsoon (end of December until April) and relative cool when the trade winds pass through from June to early October. The transition periods are hot and sticky.

Demography. In 1902 when the area was brought under control, the Marind numbered some 8,000 on the coast and up to 6,000 inland. By 1950 the population had decreased by more than 50 percent due largely to imported diseases. An additional factor was the pacification itself, which ended the kidnapping of children from other groups who were the targets of Marind head-hunting raids. As the Marind were decreasing in numbers long before pacification, the adoption of these stolen children was an important source of new tribal members.

Linguistic Affiliation. Marind is one of the three languages that together constitute the Marind Family of the Trans–New Guinea Phylum of Papuan languages. Marind has eastern and western dialects along the coast and at least three inland. The upper Bian people speak a special dialect that is classified as a separate language, closely related to Marind.

History and Cultural Relations

The Marind presumably entered their present habitat from the north. In the Middle Fly region live the Boazi, their closest linguistic and cultural relatives. The Boazi are also organized into subtribes, with one key difference: the Boazi subtribes fought one another, while the Marind head-hunting raids were directed at far-off groups, usually sparing non-

Marind neighbors. Consequently, the Marind lived in peace practically everywhere, although non-head-hunting conflicts did occur among Marind groups.

Settlements

In the interior, the scattered location of sago groves leads to dispersed subtribe settlements, rarely numbering more than 50 or 60 inhabitants. The coast offers more favorable conditions, with coconut palms on sandy ridges and swampy areas at the back of the ridge suitable for sago cultivation. Here, settlements take the form of villages with up to 200 inhabitants, with subclans from each of the four phratries present in each. In the settlements, members of different subclans occupy different wards, each ward having a number of men's houses with one or two women's houses nearby. A men's house usually holds six or seven men of the same lineage and an occasional relative. At the back of the settlement are daytime shelters for boys and adolescent males. All houses are huts, set up in one or two irregular rows. When there are two rows, they are set in parallel lines with an open space down the center.

Economy

Subsistence and Commercial Activities. Sago is the staple food, supplemented by coconuts, bananas, and the products of hunting and fishing. On festive occasions, there is pork from domesticated pigs, and taro and yams grown in elevated garden beds erected for that purpose (coastally), or grown in forest clearings (inland). Such gardens are also used for bananas and kava, the latter being (along with betel and, recently, tobacco) a favored stimulant.

Industrial Arts. The traditional Marind were a Stone Age culture, with a self-subsistent economy except for stone implements such as axe blades and club heads, which were imported from the mountains.

Trade. Information about traditional trade is lacking. As shells are used for jewelry in mountain societies, it seems reasonable to infer that shells were traded north and stone implements south.

Division of Labor. Most of the daily work is allotted to women: household chores, planting, weeding, harvesting, making sago, and collecting small fish and shellfish. The men hunt, do some fishing, build garden beds, and make forest clearings. They also build canoes, construct fences, and frame the huts, although their main tasks are ritual and warfare.

Land Tenure. The subtribe's territory and fishing grounds are divided between the main clans. Gardens and planted trees belong to individuals and are inherited patrilineally.

Kinship

Kin Groups and Descent. Descent is strictly patrilineal. Subtribe endogamy prevails, though intergroup marriages do occur, sometimes even between locally distant groups. As an expanding culture with much intercommunity traffic, the local clans and subclans—each with its own totems and totemic relations—have been arranged as parts of nine, or sometimes ten, superclans, whose names are used for identification and allegiance during intercommunity travel. Analysis of the marriage relations among these clans suggests that they are further arranged into four exogamous phratries, with only one having a name. The four phratries are represented in every subtribe and everywhere they are aligned in pairs into two moieties, "Geb-zé" and "Sami-rek." These moieties play an important role in Marind rituals. In one or two places along the coast and in a number of inland subtribes (on the upper Bian without exception) the moieties are exogamous.

Kinship Terminology. Kin terms are of the Dakota type with ample opportunity to emphasize age differences between members of one generation.

Marriage and Family

Marriage. Sister exchange is the preferred form of marriage, with first-cousin marriage prohibited. In many inland communities, the partners must be brother and sister, a rule which often requires the parents to adopt an exchange partner. Elsewhere, classificatory "siblingship" suffices and even that is not a firm rule, as the preferences of the future spouses are given a certain degree of consideration. First-marriage partners are usually age mates. Polygyny is rare. Traditionally, most marriages were long-lasting, which is surprising, given a number of Marind customs that might have undermined the stability of marriage. These customs include wives' involvement in ritualized group sex and husbands' involvement in homosexual relations with their sisters' adolescent sons.

Domestic Unit. Segregation of the sexes is strict and men may not stay for long in their wives' houses. However, the women's houses stand so close to the men's house that every word can be overheard on both sides.

Inheritance. Land, gardens, trees, and male ornaments and utensils are inherited patrilineally; female ornaments and goods are inherited matrilineally.

Socialization. Girls grow up by themselves, while boys are thought to need extra care. At a young age, boys go to sleep with their fathers in the men's house. As puberty approaches, they are no longer allowed to be in the village or on the beach during the day. They are entrusted to a mentor (the mother's brother) and sleep with him in his men's house. For three to four years, seclusion is severe until the boy passes to a higher age grade that allows for more fun. The passage is a family affair, marked by gift giving between the boy's parents and his mentor. Gift exchange also occurs when at age 18 or more the boy returns to his father's men's house to be married soon afterward. Women, who do most of the daily work and provide more of the daily food, have no say in matters of ritual, though they cooperate in minor rites. Girls are initiated into the *Mayo* fertility cult at the same age as the boys. Women are sometimes allowed to have ceremonial dances of their own, modeled on the magnificent ones performed by the men, and girls go through age grades like the boys, although the girls' age grades lack social significance.

Sociopolitical Organization

Social Organization. As mentioned above under kinship, Marind social organization is based on the ties formed through the structure of subclans, clans, phratries, and moieties spread across the various inland and coastal communities. These ties are reinforced through the religious beliefs and cult activities discussed below.

Political Organization. Despite the absence of any form of all-encompassing political organization, there was a sense of "belonging together." This sense found expression in the placement of local clan names under the labels of the nine or ten superclans, which were found all across Marind-anim territory. A more important source of solidarity was found in the great cults. The "Imo," followed by a number of inland subtribes and a few communities on the coast, acknowledged a central leadership that was settled on the coast. The "Mayo," the biggest and most impressive of all, lacked such leadership. It originated in the far-eastern coastal region and spread all along the coast where the initiation rites were performed by every subtribe for itself once every four years during a period lasting from six to nine months. In the first year of the four-year cycle the Mayo was celebrated by the subtribes in the far-western communities, the second year in the midwestern, the third year in the mideastern, and the fourth year in the far-eastern.

Social Control. Social control is largely informal. Apart from the leader of the Imo cult, the Marind have no other official authorities, save for the leading men of the men's houses whose influence is restricted and in practice is dependent on their age and personality. A more effective means of guaranteeing modest behavior is the fear of sorcery, which can be committed by or on behalf of anyone who bears a grudge.

Conflict. Disagreements over issues such as women or the use of garden land will usually be resolved if the disputants are members of the same community. If left unresolved, a grudge may be held until an accidental death leads to a suspicion of sorcery, a belief that is alternately the cause and the consequence of the prevailing mistrust between members of different subtribes. Accusations of sorcery often lead to serious brawls involving bloodshed, although heads are not taken and peace will eventually be restored through pressure exerted by other community members.

Religion and Expressive Culture

Religious Beliefs and Practitioners. Today, the Marind are largely Christians: some are Protestants, but the majority are Catholics. While the beliefs and practices have changed accordingly, the past is still remembered and scenes borrowed from traditional rites are sometimes reenacted at festive occasions. In traditional Marind-anim culture, every clan and subclan stood in a specific relation to several of the innumerable phenomena in nature and social life that are relevant to human existence. The clans being organized into the Geb-zé and Sami-rek moieties, these totemic relations were ordered in a system of dual oppositions, with each moiety leading in some areas and following in others. The Geb-zé moiety was associated with male sex, homosexuality, the sun and moon, going east with the southeast monsoon, the daytime, life, dry land and the beach, the coconut, the stork, and the cassowary; its members led the great cults. The Sami-rek was associated with the female sex, heterosexuality, the underworld, going west with the northwest monsoon, night, death, the sea, the swamp and inland region, the sago palm, the dog, crocodile, and pig; its members led the head-hunting expeditions and the great feasts that followed them. All phratries sustain dialectical connections with the opposite moiety, connections which are founded in myth. Thus the dualism of the whole repeats itself in parts, creating a dialectical system of opposites that has a logic of its own. The dramatis personae in myth are the *dema,* the ancestors of the clans. They play a dominant role in the ceremonies of the great cults and their names are invoked in magic, the minor rites accompanying everyday activities and needs. Such invocation is particularly effective if pronounced by a member of the clan originating from that dema. The belief involves the close cooperation between the subtribes constituting a settlement.

Ceremonies. The major ceremonies associated with the big cults are also initiation ceremonies associated with rebirth and the promotion of life. To that end the mythical history is staged and its main features symbolically represented. Of particular importance is the origin myth with the two central themes of antagonism between the sexes and life originating from death. The myth overtly recognizes the male as superior, while symbolically confirming the real superiority of the female, who produces life by giving birth to the (sun) bird. The life from death theme is symbolized by the coconut (symbolizing the human head) that sprouts when buried and is confirmed by the head-hunting that followed the initiation rites. The Mayo Marind rites also emphasize the female, while the Imo rites emphasize a slightly different theme, particularly the association of the female gender with death and decay, and celebrate male triumphs in warfare. Information on the cults of the Kondo and Upper Bian groups is incomplete.

Arts. The Marind are masters at body decoration. Their dances and ceremonies are a feast for the eye. The decoration of objects is of minor importance, with the exception of carved ceremonial spears and some images used in Mayo initiation rites. Singing, accompanied by drumming, for both ceremonial purposes and pleasure is important.

Medicine. Illness is cured by shamans whose cures are restricted to the extraction of foreign objects supposedly placed in the victim's body by hostile sorcerers. The shamans are often well-versed in mythology and some play a major role in rites.

Death and Afterlife. Death and the dead are of little importance, except among the Upper Bian where they are identified with the dema. The dead are believed to travel underground to the far east, where, like the sun, they will emerge to go to the far west, where, passing the spot where the sun sets, they will go on to the land of the dead which is just beyond. They will return to sit aside at big feasts, but they have no role to play.

See also Boazi, Keraki, Kiwai, Muyu

Bibliography

Baal, J. van (1966). *Dema: Description and Analysis of Marind-anim Culture.* The Hague: Martinus Nijhoff.

Baal, J. van (1984). "The Dialectics of Sex in Marind-anim Culture." In *Ritualized Homosexuality in Melanesia,* edited by G. H. Herdt. Berkeley: University of California Press.

Drabbe, P. (1955). *Spraakkunst van het Marind.* Studia Instituti Anthropos II. Vienna and Mödling: Anthropos Institut.

Geurtjens, H. (1933). *Marindineesch-Nederlansch Woordenboek: Verhandelingen Bataviaasch Genootschap* 71. Bandoeng, Java: A. C. Nix.

Wirz, Paul (1922–1925). *Die Marind-anim von Holländisch-Süd-Neu-Guinea.* Hamburgische Universität, Abhandlungen aus dem Gebiet der Auslandskunde, Band 10 and 16. Hamburg: Friederichsen.

J. VAN BAAL

Maring

ETHNONYMS: none

Orientation

Identification. The Maring are a linguistically and culturally distinct people of the interior highlands of New Guinea, made up of twenty-one named clan clusters divided, geographically, into two groups: one occupying the mountains of the Simbai Valley of Madang Province; the other located in the Jimi Valley of the Western Highlands Province. Despite this geographic separation, the linguistic, social, and cultural evidence links both Maring populations most closely to the peoples of the western highlands.

Location. Maring territory, extending about 350 kilometers, is located at approximately 5° S and 145° E, in the Bismarck mountain range. The land is heavily forested and of high relief. The year is split into relatively wetter and drier seasons, but the difference in rainfall between these two periods is not particularly great. Rainfall is usually at night. Temperature variations are slight throughout the year, with average daily temperatures fluctuating between lows in the 60s and highs in the 70s.

Demography. Population estimates for the Maring were in excess of 7,000 in 1988. Individual clan-cluster territories support populations ranging from 150 to 900 people.

Linguistic Affiliation. The language of the Maring belongs to the Jimi Subfamily of the Central Family of the East New Guinea Highland Stock.

History and Cultural Relations

Linguistic and other evidence suggests that the Maring came into their present territory from some undetermined region to the south. Traditional trade relations have long existed between the Maring and other peoples of the region. Contact with Europeans came late to Maring territory; the first Australian patrol did not arrive in the region until 1954, and governmental control of the area was not fully effected until 1962. However, the indirect effects of an Australian presence were felt as early as the 1940s, as steel tools entered the regional trade network and European diseases (dysentery and measles) struck the region. Also predating the actual entry of Australians in the region was the arrival of cargo cults, which were introduced by peoples from the north of Maring territory and had a brief popularity in the 1940s. However, after the Marings' early participation in cargo-cult activities, such practices quickly fell into disuse. As part of the Australian government's efforts to bring the Maring into its orbit, a headman (*luluai*) and assistant headman (*tultul*) were appointed, but these positions had little to do with local affairs, serving only as points of contact for dealings with the government.

Settlements

The Maring settlement pattern has been described as "pulsating," with house clusters and homesteads scattered throughout a clan cluster's territory most of the time but undergoing a sort of nucleation at certain times in the ritual cycle, when nearly everyone in a clan cluster is housed near the clan cluster's central dance ground. Populations tend to disperse as pig herds increase, then temporarily come together around a dance ground when ritual cooperation throughout the clan cluster is necessary. This gathering together rarely lasts for more than a year before the process of territorial dispersal begins again. During the "nucleated" settlement period, one finds residential compounds, consisting of matrilaterally related kin, clustered around the traditional dance ground of the clan cluster, with individual gardens on the adjacent land. A single compound will consist of a men's house, in which two to eleven men and postinitiation boys sleep and eat; and individual women's houses, located downhill from the men's house, in which live women, their young children and unmarried daughters, and, at times, other female kin in temporary need. Pigs are kept in individual stalls in the women's houses, each stall having its own entrance from the outside. All buildings are made of wood frames, thatched with pandanus leaves, and sometimes built on stilts. "Modern" homesteads no longer construct a separate men's house, but within the single dwelling shared by men and women the separation of male and female is still maintained. Near the dance ground a "magic house," where men of the clan cluster congregate, serves as an important public forum.

Economy

Subsistence and Commercial Activities. Maring subsistence is based upon slash-and-burn gardening, pig husbandry, and some hunting and gathering in the rain forest, as well as fishing—primarily for eels—in the rivers of the territory. Gardens are planted with taro, sweet potatoes, manioc, and bananas. Also grown are sugarcane, pandanus, and a variety of greens. Maize has been introduced to the region. Pig husbandry is of great importance, but Maring do not breed pigs domestically. Rather, all male pigs are castrated young in order to ensure that they will attain large size. Female pigs may breed with feral boars, but this is prevented whenever possible, again with an eye to assuring greater growth. Instead, pig herds are increased primarily through trade. Hunting and gathering also contribute to the subsistence economy, but to a markedly lesser extent. Nonetheless, hunting is considered to be a highly prestigious male activity. Eeling is important, as eels are a significant ritual food. In the past, Maring manufactured salt for trade.

Industrial Arts. Maring use simple technology: digging sticks, axes, and bush knives are the only gardening tools; bows and arrows and snares, as well as pits and deadfalls, are used in hunting; and spears, axes, and wooden shields complement the bows and arrows as weapons of war. Other items of local manufacture include net bags, aprons, loincloths, caps, waistbands, and armbands. Maring trade for steel tools, as they did for their earlier stone versions. Containers are made of hollowed gourds and bamboo tubes.

Trade. Much, if not most, circulation of goods is carried out through participation in relationships of exchange within the clan cluster, or between two clan clusters. However, Maring traditionally traded salt outside of Maring territory with peoples to their south in order to acquire stone tools, pigs, feathers, shells, and some furs. Most exchange relations, however, are between a man and his wife's agnates, his sisters' husbands' kin, his mother's agnatic kin, and the agnatic kin of his daughters' husbands. In recent years, interclan markets have been introduced. The items sold at these markets are principally foodstuffs, both raw and cooked, and while these markets are patterned after "modern" ones, they in fact simply provide a new forum for essentially balanced exchanges between individuals.

Division of Labor. Maring men fell trees, build houses and fences, hunt, and fish for eels. Women do the bulk of the gardening work, weeding, harvesting, and the burning off of used plots to clear them of refuse. Women and young children also handle the responsibilities of pig rearing, but men butcher the meat. Gardening is done in male-female pairs consisting of husband and wife, brother and sister, or daughter and widowed father. An individual will participate in several such pairs simultaneously. Child care is a woman's task.

Land Tenure. All gardening lands are held in the name of the clan cluster and subclan, and individuals ostensibly have access to that land only through membership therein. However, a nonmember of a clan cluster may be granted access to land on the basis of recent or historic marriage relations between the two clan clusters.

Kinship

Kin Groups and Descent. Each Maring clan is held to be derived from the descendants of a group of fatherless brothers. Each of these founding brothers stands as the founder of a subclan, and an individual's membership in the subclan is based on claiming patrilineal descent to one or another of these brothers.

Kinship Terminology. Maring kin terms are Iroquois-type for one's own generation and bifurcate-merging on the level of the first ascending generation. On all other generational levels, both ascending and descending, the terminology is generational.

Marriage and Family

Marriage. Marriageability is determined according to both matrilateral and patrilateral relationships: one cannot marry a woman from one's mother's clan nor one from one's own subclan unit, but marriage between subclans of a single clan is permissible. Marriage with a local woman is preferred, for the husband acquires land rights from his wife's kin. Rights in women are held by the clan, through the person of the woman's eldest brother. This brother, who receives the greatest share of the bride-wealth, chooses an appropriate husband, and it is not unusual for a certain high degree of tension to exist between a man and his sister should his choice not meet with her approval. Sister exchange is the ideal, and it requires the lowest bride-wealth. A woman may, and often does, pick her own husband, but such alliances must be regularized by the payment of bride-wealth to her kin. Should this payment not be quickly forthcoming, Maring traditionally resolved the situation by going to war against the husband and his kin. Today such problems are brought to court, but this solution is rarely satisfactory as the courts, reflecting a Western tendency to prefer the rights of the individual over those of the group, tend to find against the errant sister's kin. Maring marriage itself is not ritually marked, beyond an initial token payment of bride-wealth and the fact that the woman takes up residence in her new husband's mother's house. Eventually her husband will build her a house of her own, usually around the time of the birth of their first child, and it is also at this time that the husband generally fulfills the remainder of his bride-wealth commitment. Until the birth of children and this payment of major bride-wealth, divorce is simple and rather common. Marriage is usually monogamous, though polygyny is considered ideal. However, bride-price considerations make it difficult for men to afford acquiring more than one wife.

Domestic Unit. The basic domestic unit consists of a man, his wife, and their children. This arrangement is not, however, a residential group, as men live in their separate houses (or separate parts of the "modern" dwelling structures), and a woman's house may shelter some of her female kin at times. The core unit within the family is the gardening pair, but a gardening pair may also be composed of a man and one of his own female kin, as noted earlier.

Inheritance. Men inherit rights in land patrilineally, while individual, movable property is passed on at the discretion of the owner or the owner's survivors.

Socialization. Young children are kept with their mothers, and as they become old enough to help out they participate in gathering activities with her. A daughter remains with her mother until marriage; she learns the necessary skills and appropriate behaviors of a woman through instruction and observation. Boys around the age of 8 undergo initiation and then move into the men's house of their fathers. It is largely through observation of and association with the adult males of his patriline that a boy acquires adult knowledge.

Sociopolitical Organization

Social Organization. Each Maring clan cluster maintains a single territory, and its members cooperate economically, ritually, and in war. Within that territory, however, the day-to-day gardening activities and responsibilities of providing for the subsistence of individuals are carried out by smaller groups: the gardening pairs (husband and wife; brother and sister; daughter and father); brothers; and men related through marriage.

Political Organization. The largest Maring political unit is the clan cluster. There is no chiefly office, either hereditary or elected, nor are there any other formally recognized offices. Even the concept of big-men is somewhat inappropriate. An individual may gain the support or assistance of others for a particular enterprise through his own powers of persuasion, but any and all Maring men may, if they choose, participate equally in decision making. Attributes which contribute to a man's leadership potential are the ability and willingness to express an opinion on issues; a strong, outgoing personality; physical strength; and a reputation for intelligent or successful leadership in previous situations. All this being said, the arena within which leadership may be exercised is quite limited. It rarely extends beyond the level of the subclan and is most strongly felt among the individual's coresidents in the men's house. Generally, the leader is merely the first to act upon whatever group activity the consensus of the group appears to support. The government-appointed luluai and tultul are offices of no local relevance, and the appointees enjoy no special influence in the community.

Social Control. Social control is largely effected through beliefs in and observances of taboos, as well as through the operation of community pressures brought to bear upon the nonconforming individual. Government courts exist, and cases are sometimes brought to them, but this practice is not common given the personal and economic costs of bringing a suit and the lack of fit between court conceptions of justice and those of the Maring. Serious offenses— such as wife stealing, rape, pig killing, crop stealing, and sorcery— traditionally called for blood vengeance to be sought by the principal offended party, which in the case of wife stealing or rape would be the brother or husband of the woman involved.

Conflict. Fighting among the Maring rarely escalates to warfare within a local population—there are simply too many ties of interdependency for the community to allow hostilities to continue, even if the principals are of different clans. If such disputes cannot be resolved peacefully, the local group may split and take up relations of enmity, but this occurrence is relatively rare. Warfare, properly called, occurs between two separate local populations and was traditionally precipitated by serious offenses such as wife stealing. With their inception in an interpersonal dispute, hostilities call into play sets of allies recruited from the cognatic and affinal relations of the principal combatants. Fighting is highly ritualized and carried out in stages; the first stage requires that the offended party summon the offenders to a designated place in the forest, which will be cleared expressly for the purpose of battle. Shamans (*kun kaze yu*) perform rituals and summon spirits before the battle, and "fight-magic men" perform spells over the weapons and the warriors. The fighting itself is strictly regulated, with the adversarial groups lined up opposite one another on the fight grounds and shooting arrows at one another. Wounds are minimal and deaths are rare. After this "small" fight, if the dispute has not been resolved, ritual preparations for the second stage of hostilities (*ura kunuai,* "true fight") are begun. This second stage of fighting is done with axes, jabbing spears, and bows and arrows. At this level of fighting, fatalities are less rare than in the "nothing fight," and the combat may go on sporadically over a period of weeks, ending only when one side or another can no longer hold the support of its allies. During the course of the war, fighting would be interrupted because of rain or to permit the kin of a slain warrior to mourn the deceased. Wars ended in one of two ways. In the first case, one side might successfully rout the opposing force, after which they would burn their victims' gardens and houses and kill all the people they could find in the enemy's territory. The territory itself, however, was not occupied by the victors, for it was believed still to harbor the ancestral spirits of the previous owners. In the second case, one side might call a truce, which would be ritually marked by a pig feast and the planting of a ritually important bush called the *rumbim.*

Religion and Expressive Culture

Religious Beliefs. Central to Maring beliefs is the worship of ancestors. Maring origin myths refer to a group of brothers traveling from the southwest to what is now Maring territory and finding a group of sisters, whom they married. These marriages gave rise to the current Maring clans. These founding brothers and the spirits of all other ancestors constitute the principal supernatural forces recognized by the Maring. Without the assistance of ancestral spirits there can be no success in gardening, hunting, pig rearing, or warfare. A separate class of ancestral spirits, the *rawa mugi,* live in a special part of the territory and are the spirits of warriors killed in battle. Other spirits, not ancestral or even of human origin, inhabit the Maring lands, and, along with the rawa mugi, are associated with natural resources or physical attributes of the region. One special spirit (or group of spirits) is the "smoke woman," through whom shamans communicate with the spirit world.

Religious Practitioners. Shamans and fight-magic men are always male, and it is their ritual knowledge, along with the shamans' access to the spirit world through the smoke-woman spirits, that makes them indispensable in preparations for war. The Maring also believe in the existence of sorcerers, who are capable of causing death or illness through magical means and who are identified as men who possess great wealth but are not appropriately generous to others.

Ceremonies. The most well-known of Maring ceremonies is the *kaiko,* which is in fact a series of ritual events, extended over the course of a year or more, that traditionally terminated with the start of a war. The kaiko has two periods. The first is marked by the planting of stakes around the border of a settlement's land, a procedure that often involves the annexation of abandoned land not previously claimed by the local group. This first period is a time when garden produce is accumulated and work is done to prepare the dance ground. At the start of the second stage, a shaman contacts the smoke woman to gain the approval of the spirit world for the upcoming celebrations. A ritually planted rumbim shrub is uprooted and deposited on the border of the local group's territory along with other ritual objects, and the residential area and dance ground are ritually cleansed. Throughout the kaiko year, the host group sponsors dances to which other groups, linked by kin or trade relations to the host group, are invited. Men and some unmarried women who attend the dances don elaborately ornamented dress, which includes feathered headdresses, fur-trimmed waistbands and loincloths, and face pigments. Performances of stomping dances and of songs go on all night—interrupted at some point in the evening with a feast prepared by the host village—and end at dawn. This celebration is followed by a period of trading between the host group and their invited guests. The songs sung and the foods presented at the feast differ according to the portion of the kaiko year in which the dance is held. The final kaiko feast (*konj kaiko,* or pig kaiko) involves the relaxation of food taboos, a series of ritual addresses to the ancestors, and the initiation of such youths of the settlement as are ready to undergo ritual dedication to the rawa mugi. The culmination of the pig kaiko is a huge pig feast, with as many as 100 pigs slaughtered and thousands of pounds of pork distributed among the guests of the host group. During this last stage of the kaiko, individual obligations (such as death payments and compensation for favors or for grants of land) may be fulfilled, and bride-wealth negotiations may be initiated. At the end of the kaiko, any truces that were in effect between hostile groups are terminated, and traditionally this was a time when warfare was quite likely to erupt.

Arts. Maring decorative arts are limited, finding fullest expression in bodily adornment. Dance and song, accompanied by drums, are important in Maring ritual.

Medicine. All illnesses and deaths are held to be the result of purposeful action by another being, whether spirit or human, or the result of the violation of taboos. Certain plants are held to be medically efficacious.

Death and Afterlife. The dead join the ancestral spirits, who are tied to the clan and subclan territories, except in the case of warriors killed in battle, who become rawa mugi and go to dwell in the northern part of Maring territory. When someone dies, the body is left to lie in state for several days, then is exposed on a wooden outdoor platform until the flesh has rotted away and only bones are left. During this time, women maintain a constant vigil to keep away spirits, sorcerers, and animals who might interfere with the body. Some small bones are ultimately claimed by matrilateral female kin, while the remainder of the body is buried in a sacred "grove of the ancestors" and the grave is fenced and planted with rumbim. As a sign of intense mourning, a woman may chop off the joint of a small finger. Australian regulations regarding hygiene have banned the exposure of the corpse in the traditional manner, and the Maring now wrap the body in cloth and place it on a shelf dug out of the wall of the grave, in order to comply with government rules.

See also Melpa

Bibliography

Clarke, William C. (1972). *Place and People: An Ecology of a New Guinean Community.* Berkeley: University of California Press.

Healey, Christopher J. (1986). *Pioneers of the Mountain Forest.* Oceania Monograph no. 29. Sydney: Oceania Publications.

LiPuma, Edward (1988). *The Gift of Kinship: Structure and Practice in Maring Social Organization.* Cambridge: Cambridge University Press.

Rappaport, Roy (1968). *Pigs for the Ancestors: Ritual in the Ecology of a New Guinea People.* Rev. ed. 1984. New Haven: Yale University Press.

NANCY E. GRATTON

Marquesas Islands

ETHNONYMS: 'Enata, Marquesans, Te'enana

Orientation

Identification. *'Enana* and the cognate *'enata* simply mean "people," and this word was contrasted with *hao'e,* which came to mean "white foreigners." "Marquesans" derives from the Portuguese name of the island group, "Las Marquesas de Mendoca."

Location. The Marquesans inhabited the six larger islands of the Marquesan Group: Nukuhiva, 'Ua Pou, 'Ua Huka, Fatuiva, Tahuata, and Hova Oa; smaller islands such as Eiao were perhaps intermittently occupied. The rugged islands are divided by deep valleys, which are often well watered and which sustain rich vegetation, in contrast to the arid, eroded, and frequently excessively steep slopes. The group is situated around 8–11° S and 140° W. The closest inhabited islands were atolls in the Tuamotu Archipelago, about 450 kilometers to the south and southeast; larger Polynesian populations were more remote. Many Marquesans now live in Tahiti, the central island in the Overseas Territory of French Polynesia.

Demography. Estimates of precontact and early populations are highly variable and insecurely founded. A figure of 35,000 is much lower than many figures cited, but it seems justified by comparative evidence from better-documented islands. While some depopulation took place between 1800 and 1840, there was a more tragic decline associated with smallpox and other epidemics in the subsequent half-century. A reliable estimate in 1842 was just over 20,000; this fell to 5,000 in the 1880s and reached a low point of less than 2,000 during the 1920s. The population has gradually increased since then, and in the mid-1980s there were about 5,500 Marquesans resident in the islands, and several thousand people of Marquesan origin or descent were living in Tahiti at that time.

Linguistic Affiliation. Marquesan is a language in the Eastern Polynesian Group of Austronesian languages, closely related to Hawaiian and Tahitian. A complex pattern of dialect variation has diminished in recent decades, but there are still distinct differences between southern and northern parts of the group and a variety of local peculiarities.

History and Cultural Relations

The Marquesas Islands, like the Society Islands, appear to have been settled from western Polynesia by about 200 B.C.; populations spread gradually from the larger and more hospitable valleys on the southeastern coasts of the large islands to occupy more arid and rugged areas throughout the group. There is little evidence for exchange or sustained contact with other eastern Polynesian populations, and it appears that Marquesan societies developed essentially in isolation during the periods preceding European contacts in 1595 and 1774. Marquesan culture emerged as a singular form, but it was still recognizably related to other Polynesian groups; there were numerous correspondences between the traditional institutions of the islands and those in Tahiti, Hawaii, and other eastern Polynesian archipelagoes. Early contacts with European explorers entailed barter and sexual relations, but since most vessels' visits were of short duration, they had little impact. The first substantial European intrusion into Marquesan affairs was that of David Porter of the U.S. Navy in 1813; Porter fortified a settlement for his operations against British whaling vessels and became embroiled in local warfare against the occupants of Taipi Valley (later made famous in Herman Melville's novel, *Typee*). For the first time, Marquesans were profoundly impressed by the efficacy of firearms and the power of Whites, and chiefs and warriors throughout the group subsequently made great efforts to obtain the former and make friends with the latter. Trade thus developed a more systemic presence in the Marquesan economy. Both Protestant and Catholic missionaries attempted to gain footholds in the group, but they had very little influence in the period up to 1840, a time of severe depopulation. The French annexed the islands in 1842 but subsequently maintained a minimal presence. In the middle decades of the nineteenth century, the Catholic mission's influence grew, and by the 1880s most Marquesans were nominally Catholic. The French gave indigenous chiefs no recognition, and the combination of a fluid indigenous hierarchy, disease, and intrusions led to a decline of tribal political forms. By the 1870s, chiefs appear to have been unimportant, and in the twentieth century rights to such titles rarely have been claimed or deployed. While in the late eighteenth and early nineteenth centuries social life was marked by collective endeavors in warfare, ceremonial feasting, and nondomestic production for segregated rank groups, Marquesas society of the late nineteenth and twentieth centuries has had a more nucleated character, consisting of immediate families engaged in production for consumption and some cash cropping. Tribal divisions have ceased to be significant, and public ceremonies are now almost exclusively church or state events (such as Bastille Day). State services were limited until the 1920s, and institutionally the Catholic mission is still very prominent. Major changes followed the establishment of the French nuclear testing program at Muroroa Atoll; salaried employment associated with the construction of the test site itself and substantial military and administrative facilities on Tahiti was only part of a much bigger wave of economic expansion that brought more consumer goods and a marked increase in dependence on imported products. Recent political developments in the territory of French Polynesia have led to greater local representation and consultation on development and political matters, but the history of contact between Marquesans and Whites has generally been marked by the denial of self-determination for Marquesans and this policy has rarely been actively resisted.

Settlements

The form of island geography had a strong influence on the dispersal of aboriginal settlements. Before contact, the population density was high, and most valleys were densely occupied, even in their upper reaches, by "tribal" groups (*mata'eina'a*) usually consisting of 200–800 people. In some cases these groups occupied more than one valley, or valleys were occupied by more than one mata'eina'a. Frequent warfare meant that territories changed, and dispossessed groups were often forced into marginal areas such as small arid valleys and smaller islands. French administration has concentrated health services, schools, and employment in the towns of Taiohae, Nukuhiva, and Atuona, Hiva Oa, as well as in smaller centers on each of the other islands. Consequently, these valleys now have substantial populations, while other sites of formerly dense occupation are abandoned or sparsely inhabited. Contemporary settlements are usually clustered by the shore; churches and sports fields are prominent.

Economy

Subsistence and Commercial Activities. The Marquesans were and are horticulturalists, and they were distinctive in Polynesia for particular emphasis on the cultivation of breadfruit, which was preserved and fermented in large pits. Bananas, plantains, and various tubers were cultivated, and there was a limited amount of taro irrigation. Fishing was always of considerable importance, but pigs were kept mainly for ceremonial consumption. Since European contact, citrus, cassava, cattle, goats, and various other plants and animals have been introduced that broaden the subsistence base considerably. Now, however, imported foods such as rice and tinned fish have displaced locally produced vegetables. There are many coconut trees, from which the cash crop copra has been produced since the last century; this is generally of low value, and attempts have been made to broaden the islands' commercial base with coffee, timber, and various other crops, but these have not yet been extensively developed.

Industrial Arts. Before contact and during the nineteenth century, there was a broad range of specialist craft producers, who made wooden articles, ornaments, stone utensils, and weapons; women produced tapa (bark cloth) and mats. At various stages these crafts were abandoned, but wooden and stone articles are still produced for handicraft shops in Tahiti and the tourist resorts on the larger islands, rather than for the Marquesans themselves. Women on the island of Fatuiva now seem to be the only eastern Polynesians who still produce tapa, which is sold to visitors on yachts or to agents for Tahitian shops.

Trade. Although there appears to have been little precontact voyaging or trade between the Marquesas and other eastern Polynesian archipelagoes, exchange in birds' feathers (for ornaments), adz stone, and turmeric took place within the group. Small stores, often run by Chinese, are found in most settlements and a great deal of food and manufactured articles are imported via Tahiti.

Division of Labor. In the early contact period food production and consumption were segregated in various ways; fishing and house building were male activities, while women produced mats and bark cloth. Some male servants engaged in "female tasks," while high-ranking women were relatively unconstrained by sex roles and could, for example, go to war with men. Although the sex-typing of occupations is not sharp and women as well as men engage in a variety of forms of wage labor, Christian mission influences and the policies of the colonial administration have meant that women are primarily associated with the home and men with various external revenue-generating or food-collecting activities.

Land Tenure. In the early nineteenth century there was great emphasis on the rights of firstborn children (whether male or female) to inherit property, and those who followed often fell into some dependent status. However, the complexities of a cognatic system, and the fact that marriage often took place within valleys (such that individuals would not move far from their natal lands) meant that land rights were highly contested; even if the firstborn was the theoretical owner, others might have use rights that were, in effect, unconditional. Prominent warriors and others of high status often owned substantial tracts of land that were farmed by dependents who effectively exchanged their labor for security and access to the means of production.

Kinship

Kin Groups and Descent. The main units in Marquesan society were territorial rather than descent-based; although residence was normally patrivirilocal, cognatic reckoning permitted strategic affiliation and mobility. With mata'eina'a ("tribes") the main corporate action groups were factions associated with a particularly powerful figure, which developed through political manipulation and economic dependence, and *tapu* grades associated with particular occupations, such as fishing, wood carving, etc.; these groups were sometimes also feasting and ritual groups.

Kinship Terminology. Marquesan kin terms are of the Hawaiian type.

Marriage and Family

Marriage. The Marquesas are well-known in comparative marriage studies for the institution of nonfraternal polyandry, but this feature of their society often has not been adequately contextualized within indigenous rank structures and economic relations. Only women of high rank had secondary husbands, who were virtually always also servants or otherwise of much lower status than their primary, often chiefly, husbands. Conjugal relations varied with social status: in the upper levels, marriages were often contracted between elite families from different valleys or islands, for the purpose of initiating or consolidating political alliances; at middle levels, there was greater local endogamy; and relations among commoners were said to be more fluid and promiscuous.

Domestic Unit. Marquesan men and women of rank often ate in segregated clubhouses, while dependents had no autonomous households of their own. Hence domesticity was structured by wider economic and ritual relations, especially by tapu principles that required those of rank, and most men generally, to eat separately. Polyandry, and the associated relations of rank and dependence, broke down in the second half of the nineteenth century, and families approximating the Western nuclear model developed.

Inheritance. In the nineteenth century inheritance was structured by the principles of primogeniture and birth-order-based rank; in the northern part of the group especially, it appeared that children other than the firstborn would inherit little. Inequality was, however, qualified by the extension of use rights and altered by periodic seizures and redistributions of land.

Socialization. Infants and children were raised by both parents and older siblings; adolescents and young adults were expected to behave in a relatively uncontrolled and antisocial manner.

Sociopolitical Organization

Social Organization. Marquesan society was hierarchically structured on the basis of tapu principles, ritual occupations, sex, age, chiefly rank, and property. Power acquired through warfare or shamanistic accomplishment was as important as legitimate claims to rank. As indigenous rank structures broke down, other forms of privilege associated with particular forms of paid employment developed. The class distinctions now apparent in the Marquesas are the same as those that exist elsewhere in French Polynesia, and they derive from education, government or professional employment, and in some cases investment.

Political Organization. As in other eastern Polynesian groups, there were "chiefdoms," but these did not usually constitute clearly defined territorial domains. Within valleys, there were often several competing chiefs, sometimes with crosscutting loyalties. Most islands were split into dual divisions, the constituent tribes of each notionally sharing descent from one of a pair of brothers. In the northern part of the group this division did seem to structure warfare, but even there conflict within as well as between the groups occurred. There was no chiefly leadership at the division level.

Social Control. In the early nineteenth century disputes were resolved through arbitration or fighting; the losers in any major conflict sometimes left the islands in canoes to search for a new home. Sorcery was widely practiced, but it was done in the interests of individuals rather than as an expression of collective authority. Marquesan law was never recognized by the French colonial regime.

Conflict. Warfare was endemic in early contact society, and it was systematically linked with rivalrous feasting and competitive food production in the struggle for prestige and land. Factional disputes within particular valley populations were also common, and they often resulted in the displacement of chiefs and other prominent families.

Religion and Expressive Culture

Religious Beliefs. Indigenous religion was strongly dualistic, postulating a living world of light (*ao*) and a world of ghosts, deities, darkness, and night (*po*). The presence of deities (*etua*) in this world was believed to be vital for making work efficacious and for securing life and prosperity. There was an extensive hierarchy of deities, ranging from the founding originators of the cosmos to their particular expressions in the gods of occupations and places, and there also were apotheosized shamans and chiefs, often linked with local temples (*me'ae*). The aggrieved ghosts of major shamans were often propitiated to relieve famine, and many lesser figures were associated with illness and other misfortunes. Since the late nineteenth century, more than 90 percent of Marquesans have become Catholics, most of the remainder being Protestants descended from Hawaiian mission teachers. Modern Marquesan religion has not been adequately investigated, but syncretic elements appear to persist, including belief in a range of evil spirits, such as ghosts of women who have died in childbirth.

Religious Practitioners. There were two major classes of indigenous priests: shamans (*tau'a*), who were directly inspired by deities and in some cases were thought responsible for agricultural fertility; and *tuhuna o'ono,* who recited chants at chiefly ritual and performed sacrifices. Of these, there were many particular specialist healers and priests associated with occupations such as fishing. Sorcerers were renowned and widely feared.

Ceremonies. Traditionally, the largest events appear to have been commemorative mortuary feasts for chiefs and shamans; these ceremonies often took place some years after death and required considerable quantities of food and many human sacrifice victims. Major ceremonies were also associated with the life crises of chiefs and chiefly children, especially the firstborn. The main public events now are mostly church events, along with some French national days.

Arts. Both men and women, especially those of high status, were extensively tattooed using anthropomorphs and abstract designs that also recurred in wood carving and on ornaments. Massive stone *tiki* (anthropomorphic ancestral figures) and petroglyphs were also carved.

Medicine. Illness was attributed to soul loss, possession, or sorcery. Healers generally treated illness in one of three ways: they identified the cause in tapu violation, resulting in an offense to a deity; they removed harmful objects or spirits from the body; or they diagnosed sorcery, which might be lifted if fines were paid. The range of herbal medicines was extensive.

Death and Afterlife. Death was usually attributed to sorcery. Spirits were thought to roam the islands for a period and then congregate at certain rocky headlands where they would plunge beneath the sea and into the afterworld, known as Havai'i, which was supposed to be internally differentiated. Those of higher status, who had more pigs or human victims sacrificed for them, were sent to more pleasant parts; those whose tattooing was not rubbed off their skin after death were not admitted at all but instead had their spirits torn to pieces.

See also Hawaiians, Tahiti

Bibliography

Dening, Greg, ed. (1974). *The Marquesan Journal of Edward Roberts.* Canberra: Australian National University Press.

Dening, Greg (1980). *Islands and Beaches: Discourse on a Silent Land.* Honolulu: University of Hawaii Press.

Kirkpatrick, John (1983). *The Marquesan Notion of the Person.* Ann Arbor: University of Michigan Research Press.

Thomas, Nicholas. (1990). *Marquesan Societies: Inequality and Political Transformation in Eastern Polynesia.* Oxford: Oxford University Press.

NICHOLAS THOMAS

Marshall Islands

ETHNONYMS: Bikini, Enewetak, Kwajalein, Majuro, Rālik, Ratak

Orientation

Identification. The Republic of the Marshall Islands, formerly part of the Trust Territory of the Pacific Islands, gained independence as part of a Compact of Free Association with the United States in 1986. Marshall Islanders now speak mutually intelligible dialects of the same language, and each atoll group recognizes cultural affinities with at least some other atolls in its area. In precolonial times sporadic contact was maintained among all atolls—even the most distant—and occasionally the strongest chiefs were able to extend their reign over several atolls of the central Ratak or Rālik cultures for short periods of time. A common Marshall Islands identity, however, is a volatile notion developed in response to Western geopolitical agendas.

Location. The Marshall Islands cover an area of 1.95 million square kilometers in the west central Pacific Ocean, with a combined land mass of just under 180 square kilometers. The group is located between 160° and 173° E and 4° and 20° N. Its twenty-nine atolls (nineteen currently inhabited) and five coral pinnacles (four with human occupants) are simultaneously linked together and separated by the sea. The vast stretches of ocean help maintain an average temperature of 27° C with very little diurnal or yearly variation. Rainfall increases as one nears the equator, with around 152 centimeters per year in the north and 460 centimeters per year in the south. The dry part of the year, December through April, is typified by brisk breezes, and the central month of the wet season, August, may have periods of total calm. For much of the year, a light trade wind, most often northeasterly, provides mellow air conditioning. Typhoons, however, are not uncommon in the winter months.

Demography. The population of the islands in 1988 was 43,335, with the vast majority of people concentrated on the capital, Majuro Atoll (19,664), and on Ebeye, Kwajalein Atoll (8,277), across from the missile testing and tracking center on the Kwajalein islet. In the 1850s and 1860s missionaries very roughly estimated individual atoll populations to be between 100 and 2,000–3,000. The port towns and government centers supported by three waves of colonizers (Germany, Japan, and the United States) have provided the impetus and ability to alter the delicate balance between human populations and local atoll environments.

Linguistic Affiliation. Marshallese is a member of the Micronesian Family of the Oceanic Austronesian languages, and it shares the largest number of roots with the languages of Fiji, Nauru, and nearby locales like Pohnpei. Currently there are three dialects of Marshallese, though greater diversity undoubtedly existed in the nineteenth century. Translations of the Bible in the 1860s and 1870s made a missionary-inspired variant of Rālik dialect the standard for over a century. This text, read by nearly every Marshallese, was retranslated in a less awkward style in the 1970s and 1980s. Ratak dialect, spoken in the windward atolls of the Marshall Islands, is grammatically similar but lexically distinct from Rālik dialect, and Enewetak and Ujelang modes of speaking once differed so radically in both lexicon and grammar as to be considered a totally different language by local residents. The construction of a common dictionary and standard grammar has become one unifying focus since Marshallese independence.

History and Cultural Relations

Europeans first became aware of the atolls of the Marshalls' area in 1529 when Alvaro de Saavedra Ceron stopped briefly at two atolls, most likely Ujelang and another atoll in the northwest part of the region (Enewetak or Bikini), though Magellan had sailed through the Marshalls' latitudes without sighting land in the previous century. On behalf of Spain, voyagers on the *San Lucas* laid claim to some Rālik and Ratak atolls in 1565 and, while European visitors were infrequent for the next two centuries, explorers again sought landings in search of water and supplies in the late eighteenth and early nineteenth centuries. The Marshalls, like the neighboring Gilberts, were named for British explorers traveling from New South Wales to Canton in 1788. The nineteenth-century Russian explorer Otto von Kotzebue was the first to develop a serious interest in the people of Ratak and, not long after his visit, whalers began to frequent the area. The American Board of Commissioners for Foreign Missions (ABCFM), which had sent missionaries to Hawai'i in 1819, expanded their attempt to save islanders' souls to Micronesia in 1852, and by 1857 a mission station was founded on Ebon in the southern Rālik chain. Subsequent mission stations were established on even the most distant atolls like Enewetak by the mid-1920s. Likiep, which was purchased in 1877 as a copra plantation by A. DeBrum (a partner in Adolph Capelle & Co., an early trading firm), is the only atoll not heavily influenced by ABCFM descendants. For most Marshallese, the Catholic beliefs of Likiep residents were used to construct the religious "other," until a plethora of religious forms appeared on Majuro in the 1970s and 1980s. When the market for whale oil was replaced by coconut oil in the latter half of the nineteenth century, Marshall Islanders were drawn into a European- and American-dominated marketplace. Copra demanded land, laborers, and overseers, and Marshall Islands land tenure, family form, and chieftainship reshaped themselves to accommodate these demands. German copra firms sparked the expanding colonial interests, and in 1885 Germany claimed much of the west central Pacific, including the Marshalls, as its own. For thirty years mission forces and German administrators battled with one another, but as imperial Germany focused its efforts on war, Japan rapidly laid claim to Micronesia. Ironically, their own thirty-year reign would be terminated by another world war but, in the interim, the Japanese became the only committed colonizers of the Marshalls. Japan expanded copra production, opened Japanese-operated copra stations on most atolls, and convinced Marshall Islanders that, through diligence and obedient training, they could become Japanese citizens. In the late 1930s Japan's intentions shifted, and Marshallese were drafted as supporters while Japan prepared for war. Early in 1944 the Marshalls were involved in a holocaust involving battles between American and Japanese forces. Lives were lost and the physical forms of islets were transformed. They were denuded of vegetation and literally blown away by bombing and shelling. Within two months American military forces were in firm control of the critical atolls, and the strategic value of Marshallese soil was established in their minds. While America's hands-off colonial policies slowed the developmental programs begun by the Japanese, the strategic importance of the islands eventually resulted in more radical changes in the Marshallese life-style. Monetary compensations for nuclear damages on out-of-the-way Enewetak and Bikini atolls, for concomitant radiation-related suffering on Ronglab and Uterik, and for missile-tracking experiments and facilities on Kwajalein and Enewetak have created radical disparities of wealth among atoll dwellers. These changes, along with the bureaucratic expansion accompanying the creation of the Republic of the Marshall Islands, account for the significant demographic shifts witnessed today.

Settlements

With the exception of the urban settlements on Majuro and Kwajalein, most atoll dwellers live in small villages near the centers of the largest islets, on smaller atolls, or in dwellings dispersed along the lagoon side of these islets. Second dwellings may be maintained on smaller outer islets where families may go in search of fish or birds or during times of starvation. These islets are not permanently inhabited since they lack the underlying lens of brackish water that permits year-round settlement. Homes are built on pebbled grounds kept scrupulously clean and free of grass and weeds, and dedicated property owners maintain the lines of coconut palms that run from ocean side to lagoon and that delineate individual land parcels, which are kept cleared of underbrush, trash, and fallen fronds.

Economy

Subsistence and Commercial Activities. In the urban centers wage labor provides one major source of income, though others live on the strategic-testing compensations mentioned above. On the outer atolls, the household is the fundamental unit of production, though larger extended family units or sections of a village or islet commonly work together to prepare for feasts. Collecting and fishing provide the staples and the complements. On northern atolls, fish and birds accompany arrowroot, pandanus, coconuts, and some breadfruit, whereas the southern atolls provide larger quantities of breadfruit and, in ideal circumstances, taro. In many instances, rice, flour, and sugar have replaced traditional staples and added significantly to the nutritional impoverishment of the diet. Copra production allows access to these staples and to cloth from which to fashion Western-style clothing for even the poorest of atoll dwellers. Pigs and chickens, foods often seen at feasts, provide an added source of protein to the local diet.

Industrial Arts. Sailing canoes, pandanus mats, bark-cloth and woven coconut-frond clothing, pandanus or coconut-leaf baskets, coir (coconut sennit), and post-and-beam dwellings thatched with pandanus fronds were among the most critical of traditionally manufactured items. Nowadays, tin and plywood dwellings are replacing thatch, outboard motor boats are fashioned from plywood, canoes have been reduced to handicraft size, and a plethora of other handicraft items made from coconut or pandanus fibers supply the tourist market.

Trade. Interatoll trade was mainly in spouses, magic, and quests for chiefly control, but during the copra-trading era the center and periphery pattern in use today was introduced and institutionalized. Copra moves toward the center (Jaluij at first; more recently, Majuro), and the flow of Western foods, cloth, and small trade items is disseminated out in concentric rings of increasingly insignificant supply and consequence. Central Marshall Islands chiefs increased their power and stability by becoming the brokers who controlled incoming copra and outgoing goods.

Division of Labor. The division of labor is based on gender and age, with males controlling activities in the sea and sky (fishing, canoe building, gathering drinking coconuts or coconut fronds) and females dominating activities on the land (digging arrowroot or gathering pandanus fronds). Females also control the domestic space and are associated with activities in the village, while men work in the outlying bush and travel freely to foreign lands. Children often watch over their younger siblings, though young girls begin training in domestic life quite early while young boys are given considerable freedom to develop their careers as fishers and roaming foragers. The old busy themselves with repairs, child rearing, and activities close to home as long as they are able. Larger cooperative groups—sailing groups, religious groups, or groups representing sections of an islet or atoll—often cooperate for more specialized purposes.

Land tenure. Like kinship organization, land tenure varies significantly from one part of the Marshalls to another. Enewetak, Ujelang, and Bikini customs, affected differently by the copra complex and also altered by relocation, are the least like other Marshall Islands groups. Land rights are held in perpetuity by all members of a clan, living and nonliving, and are inalienable. Living people have use rights to that land as long as they maintain and improve it. In the central Marshalls' chains, chiefs have a right to the first fruits of the land, are given a share of the profits on copra produced on that land, and are allowed to dispossess those who fail to care for the land. Local overseers (*alab*), elders in a matriclan, manage the land in behalf of the chiefs. On Enewetak, chiefs are assisted with copra production on their own land but cannot dispossess landowners. Alab, extended family or household heads, may advise a chief but do not manage land on his or her behalf. In the Central Marshall Islands primary land rights are vested in matrilineages, whereas on Enewetak land rights may be claimed through either one's mother or father, though care of the land is critical to maintain a claim.

Kinship

Kin Groups and Descent. Each Marshall Islander is born into the clan of his or her mother and, minimally, clan members can expect to be welcomed by fellow clanmates even on distant atolls. Each clan is divided into lineages and lineage segments in the Central Marshall Islands, whereas on Enewetak and Ujelang people are members of bilateral extended families in which each member can trace a relationship to a common ancestor, usually a woman.

Kinship Terminology. Kinship terminology varies slightly throughout the group of atolls, but overall it is of the Hawaiian type.

Marriage and Family.

Marriage. Polyandry and particularly polygyny have legendary and ethnohistoric precedent, but such practices are rare in mission times. Clan exogamy is preferred, though marriage between members of the same clan is permitted if the partners to the marriage are not closely related. Atoll endogamy is a direct reflection of the physical and social isolation of any particular group, and atolls within close sailing distance of one another often maintained long-term marriage exchanges. The flexibility in postmarital residence provides, along with adoption, a way to balance the rapidly shifting relationships between clan affiliation and landholding commonly encountered in atoll environments. Residence decisions also reflect the respective position of each partner vis-à-vis larger domestic units. Divorce is allowed, though uncommon. Many early experimental marriages do not last, the children of those unions commonly being adopted by the mother's family of orientation or remaining with the mother and being adopted by her subsequent spouse.

Domestic Unit. The basic domestic unit is the household, those living under the same roof beam (*barowōj*), most commonly a small three- or four-generation extended family.

Inheritance. Inheritance is multilineal, with inheritance of land, political power, names, magical force, and other items each reflecting a person's rights in different groups.

Socialization. Infants remain close to one of their mothers ("real" or classificatory), though toddlers and young children are largely cared for by siblings slightly older than themselves. Females are trained from an early age in domestic skills, while male children roam into the bush lands and emulate the fishing, sailing, and tree-climbing skills of their male superiors. Formal schooling was introduced by the missionaries and still follows the American style. Outer-island schools go through eighth grade, with the most skilled students pursuing high school in one of the population centers.

Sociopolitical Organization

Social Organization. The social order is characterized by flexible arrangements for group membership and for claiming rights to land. In the Rālik and Ratak chains, several atolls may be governed by a single chief, but throughout the Marshall Islands each atoll member maintains a critical identity as "a person of Mili, of Ujae," or of some other atoll. Atolls are further divided into islets or districts, each associated with possible affiliations of residence or land-tenure claims established by tracing through a matriclan or conical clan. Sailing groups, fishing groups, and religious groups also exist, and claims to an identity in those groups, as with islet, district, or atoll residence, must be reinforced by active participation and cooperation. The solidarity developed through such commitments of time and energy provide one measure of cohesiveness and of conceptual value. Intra-atoll marriages and intra-atoll exchanges maintained for many generations promote an overlapping of identities and shared interests that results in increased solidarity. Several clans are typically represented on each atoll, and while some clans are found throughout the

Marshall Islands, others are restricted in their membership to one or two atolls. Other than chiefly lineages, the power of a clan and of its constituent lineages or bilateral extended families depends on the number of living representatives and upon their access to land.

Political Organization. Leadership identities are claimed through sacred lines of paramount chiefs who ultimately trace descent directly from ancient deities. These identities pass matrilineally except on Enewetak and Ujelang atolls where such identities are transmitted patrilineally. Ratak and Rālik chiefly lines have intermarried with some frequency, whereas the chiefs of Enewetak, Ujelang, and Bikini were so isolated prior to German times that few intermarriages occurred with Ratak and Rālik chiefs. Chiefs who represent an atoll or district are more localized, as are clan elders who head extended families, speak in their behalf, and, in many areas, serve as intermediaries between chiefs and commoners in matters concerning land. Traditionally, religious and magical specialists balanced the chiefs' earthly powers with knowledge of curing, sailing, and fishing, predicting the weather, and mediating between humans and deities. Warriors and specialists in the arts of love, song, and dance also held respected positions in the ancient social order. The Republic of the Marshall Islands government, designed on the parliamentary pattern, balances elected officials in one house with the house of chiefs, in which membership may be gained only by virtue of hereditary claims through a recognized chiefly line.

Social Control. While a formal legal apparatus exists to deal with criminal activities in the Marshall Islands, fear of God's wrath, of ancestor spirits, and of the negative judgments of others in one's community or group provide the major sources of social control.

Conflict. Conflict is always a threat to the solidarity of the group and, unless one is inebriated (and not really one's self), occurs only with "others"—with members of other clans, other island or national identities, or other competitive song fest groups.

Religion and Expressive Culture

Religious Beliefs. Nearly all Marshall Islanders now anchor part of their identity in one of several forms of Christian belief, but indigenous interpretations of these beliefs differ substantially from common European and American significances. The traditional polytheistic pantheon included numerous deities, local and regional, female and male, with specialized domains of control. Many major deities are represented by constellations that figure significantly in the cycle of renewal and regeneration that secures the future of earthly life. Other deities were local in character and were associated with local shrines—coral heads, pools of brackish water in the open sea, pandanus, or coconut trees. Ancestor spirits, now as in the past, continue to interact with living humans and mediate between the daily actions of living humans and the sets of taboos and moral guidelines set by high-ranked deities.

Religious Practitioners. Traditional religious specialists have been replaced with indigenous Christian mission pastors, but seers, curers, purveyors of evil magic, and weather magicians are still common.

Ceremonies. *Kūrijmōj,* the local celebration of "Christmas", with many weeks of singing and dancing competitions, feasting, and accompanying exchanges and games, is the largest ritual event. Each extended family or lineage segment also sponsors large first-birthday celebrations after the birth of a child.

Arts. Traditionally, Marshall Islanders fashioned the body into an ornate object of artistic and social expression with tattoos. Outlawed by mission and government restrictions, forms of artistic expression are now largely musical, though dance (once frowned on by missionaries) is making a resurgence, and Marshallese handicraft items, mats, and finely crafted sailing canoes are respected throughout the Pacific.

Medicine. Indigenous herbal medicines ingested or rubbed on the body, massage, and incanted cures are freely mixed with the suggestions of local health aides.

Death and Afterlife. Death, the appropriation of the breath and life's force from living humans, results from the actions of other beings, either living or dead. People carry many of their personality characteristics with them after death. They continue to interact with the living, though their physical features become desiccated, and their vaporous beings are not easily controlled by the living. Recently dead community members remain nearby, often sanctioning those who misbehave. Certain people are protected by recently dead namesakes or close relatives, but other cantankerous ancestral spirits may frighten people, not to sanction them, but to maintain their ambivalent reputations amongst the living. The most dangerous spirits are believed to come to an atoll from outside, often bringing misfortune, illness, or death.

See also Bikini, Kapingamarangi

Bibliography

Carucci, Laurence M. (1980). "The Renewal of Life: A Ritual Encounter in the Marshall Islands." Ph.D. dissertation, Department of Anthropology, University of Chicago.

Hezel, Francis X., S.J. (1983). *The First Taint of Civilization.* Honolulu: University of Hawaii Press.

Kiste, Robert, and Michael Rynkiewich (1976). "Incest and Exogamy: A Comparative Study of Two Marshall Island Populations." *The Journal of the Polynesian Society* 85:209–226.

Mason, Leonard (1954). "Relocation of the Bikini Marshallese: A Study in Group Migrations." Ph.D. dissertation, Department of Anthropology, Yale University.

Spoehr, Alexander (1949). *Majuro, a Village in the Marshall Islands.* Chicago: Field Museum of Natural History.

Tobin, Jack A. (1958). "Land Tenure in the Marshall Islands." In *Land Tenure Patterns: Trust Territory of the Pacific Islands.* Vol. 1. Guam: Office of the High Commissioner.

LAURENCE MARSHALL CARUCCI

Mejbrat

ETHNONYMS: Brat, Mejprat, Meybrat

Orientation

Identification. The Mejbrat are swidden cultivators of the Bird's Head Peninsula of Irian Jaya.

Location. Mejbrat territory is located in the inland of the Bird's Head Peninsula, in a mixed riverine and lacustrine region some distance from the coast. There are four minor lakes in the region, each surrounded by a marshy grassland zone which is itself encircled by a hilly, secondary-forest zone. Beyond this forest belt there is mountainous high country, densely covered with primary-growth, tropical rain forest vegetation. The inhabited portions of Mejbrat territory are crisscrossed with paths that link settlements and dotted with swidden gardens.

Demography. Recent population figures for the Mejbrat are difficult to come by, but there were 16,000 Mejbrat speakers estimated in 1956.

Linguistic Affiliation. Brat, with seven dialects, is a member of the Central Bird's Head Family of Non-Austronesian languages. The language appears to have been much influenced by Malay, introduced through Moluccan traders in the region as early as the 1600s.

History and Cultural Relations

Indirect contact with peoples not indigenous to the region occurred as early as the sixteenth century, when the first Moluccan traders arrived to seek slaves and locally available spices (principally nutmeg). The Dutch arrived on the peninsula at the start of the seventeenth century. It was not until the 1920s, however, that any sort of government presence was directly felt in the Mejbrat territory, and sustained programs of government intervention—organizing the inhabitants into registered *kampongs* or villages—did not occur until 1934. This process of village formation continued until well into the 1950s before it was completed. The largest of these kampongs had a school that doubled as the local mission church, and the schoolteachers—Indonesian or Papuan—did double duty as missionaries. Most of Mejbrat territory was missionized by the Protestant church, but the eastern portion of the area became Catholic. There is little information available regarding the history and cultural relations of precontact times, but it seems safe to say that there was trade both within the Mejbrat territory and between Mejbrat and non-Mejbrat.

Settlements

Kampong formation was intended to introduce nucleated settlements of several Mejbrat households each, with dwellings facing one another across a central road or path and, in some cases, associated with a local church-school, but today these artificial villages are generally uninhabited or sparsely populated. Mejbrat traditional settlements consist of scattered homesteads, each located close to its associated swidden gardens and all loosely centered on a regional "spirit house," the location where the founding spirit was thought to have emerged from beneath the ground. Mejbrat dwellings are wood-framed, pandanus-thatched, and built on stilts. Mejbrat do not build separate men's houses.

Economy

Subsistence and Commercial Activities. Mejbrat subsistence depends heavily upon the cultivation of taro, the principal crop, which is grown along with yams and sweet potatoes in the swidden gardens. Most of the people's protein needs are met by gathering grubs and larvae, locusts, lizards, snails, frogs, eggs, birds, and mice. The Mejbrat hunt with blowguns and spears, killing flying foxes, wild boars, opossums, and kangaroos, but the meat gained from hunting is used primarily in ceremonial exchange, rather than constituting a major part of the day-to-day diet. Fishing in the lakes and rivers is more important in some regions than in others, depending upon the availability of fish. It is most important for the people living near the three central lakes of the territory, for these lakes have been stocked by the territorial government. Fishing is done with poison, with traps in dammed rivers, and with baited lines, as well as with spears. Nonsubsistence cultivation features the introduced cash crops of ground nuts, green peas, and beans. Maize has long been grown as a trade crop in the northern parts of the region.

Trade. Throughout their known history, Mejbrat peoples have participated in extraregional trade. Moluccan traders brought bush knives, black sugar, rice, and—most importantly—cloth to the region from which they sought local bark, nutmeg, and slaves. This trade was by means of "advance payment"—the trade goods were left for local consideration, to be compensated for by later delivery of the desired local goods. By the time that the Dutch arrived in the seventeenth century this trading system was already in place, and they introduced finer cloth—of cotton—as well as chinaware and iron to the inventory of items imported into the region. By the nineteenth century gongs and glass beads, as well as guns and opium, had also been introduced into the local trade system. Trade within the region centered on ceremonial exchange, conducted under the auspices of feast cycles. The principal form of wealth circulated interiorly is woven, patterned cloth.

Industrial Arts. Items of local manufacture include bark cloth, generally embroidered according to patterns found on imported cloth, string bags, and the basic tools and utensils used in gardening, hunting, and fishing: digging sticks, blowguns, fish traps, fishing lines, and the like. Men weave decorative armbands. Houses are made of wood frames with pandanus-leaf thatching. Dams are built of brush.

Division of Labor. Men do the heavier tasks in house building: preparing the wood frames and attaching the thatch. Women, however, prepare the pandanus-leaf bundles used in thatching. While both men and women work at preparing garden lands by burning off the ground cover, only men build the swidden fences, and the bulk of actual gardening chores fall to women. Men dam rivers and prepare the poison used in fishing, but aside from spear fishing, which is done by both men and women, it is the women alone who fish with lines, spread the fish poison, collect the stunned fish, and use the fish traps. Hunting—with snares, spears, or blowguns—is done only by men. Gathering activities are considered women's work. Women, as wives, hold the wealth of a household, in the form of special cloths.

Land Tenure. Access to land follows the female line: a married man establishes gardens in the territory of his wife's father's maternal kin; unmarried men work the gardens of their mother's brother's wife. But since the bulk of gardening is done by women, and since the produce of the garden is considered to be women's property, it is perhaps improper to speak of "men's gardens" in any case.

Kinship

Kin Groups and Descent. Mejbrat stress horizontal relationships over lineal ones in reckoning relatedness. The primary kin ties are those established through one's mother's brother, sister's son, and through siblingship. However, these relationships are subject to a certain amount of manipulation. The consanguineal family, consisting of a male, his mother, mother's brother, and mother's brother's daughter (or, conversely, a female, her father, father's sister, and father's sister's son), appears to be the most significant unit of relationship and organization. There appears to be a crosscutting pair of moietal divisions, the first based on geographical separation ("shore" people versus "hill" people) and the second determined according to ancestral association with one or another of the regional spirits (*dema*). These crosscutting divisions establish wife-giving and wife-taking groups.

Kinship Terminology. "Proper" kinship terminology is largely Iroquoian, although informal usage tends toward the Hawaiian. Generational terms can be characterized as bifurcate-merging.

Marriage and Family

Marriage. The single most important unit for the Mejbrat subsistence economy is the husband and wife gardening pair, so there is strong societal pressure for all adult males to be married. Polygyny is thought of as the ideal, but it occurs infrequently. The preferred husband will be someone who is both geographically and genealogically distant from the wife-giving group. The wife-giving group, usually represented by the prospective bride's elder brother, selects an appropriate spouse; and the bride-wealth—paid in cloths, meat, fish, palm wine, and physical labor in clearing swiddens, etc.—is negotiated, with most of it to be paid during the course of the Mejbrat feast cycle. Wife givers reciprocate with prestations of lesser value: taro and other garden produce, net bags, and string. Most of the cloths that make up the wife taker's prestation go to the new wife and form the nucleus of the new household's wealth.

Domestic Unit. Mejbrat wives are considered important decision makers and enjoy a high degree of respect within the marital unit for three major reasons: because a wife's gardening labor is very important; because Mejbrat hold that a woman's garden produce belongs to her; and because, with uxorilocal residence, married women live near to close, supportive kin. In the early days of marriage, a young wife will temporarily live with her husband's mother, but the couple quite soon establishes its own household in the area of the wife's father's maternal kin. When children are quite small they live with their parents, but upon attaining the age of initiation a boy will go to live for extended periods of time with his mother's brother and a girl will spend much time in the household of her father's sister. A household proper will consist, therefore, of a husband and wife, their uninitiated children, and, often, an initiation-age niece or nephew as well.

Inheritance. Access to garden lands follows the maternal line through wives. Other property tends to pass from mother's brother to sister's son and from father's sister to brother's daughter. Esoteric lore is passed along the same lines as movable property, but it is taught rather than inherited.

Socialization. Young children, still living within the natal family, are cared for and disciplined by their mothers. Education in the appropriate skills and lore is the job of the mother's brother (for boys) or the father's sister (for girls). Both sexes undergo initiation under the guidance of the appropriate uncle or aunt.

Sociopolitical Organization

Social Organization. Mejbrat social organization centers on the consanguineal family, defined in terms of the mother, mother's brother, and mother's brother's daughter. The sibling relationship, with a differentiation between elders and juniors, also strongly influences the organization of people into cooperative groups.

Political Organization. Mejbrat society is essentially egalitarian, but a "first among equals" big-man system based on prestige and wealth is notable. Leadership status can be achieved by women as well as by men, but the range over which this leadership may be exercised is quite small—essentially limited to the household settlement. Government efforts to organize the Mejbrat into kampongs has had little apparent impact on Mejbrat political and social life: the kampongs tend to exist solely on paper, and the Mejbrat continue to follow traditional settlement and organizational patterns. This situation can be attributed largely to the fact that governmental organizational expectations, being of a Western, male-centered model, are contradicted on all levels by traditional Mejbrat practice.

Social Control. Most of Mejbrat social control is effected through the belief in and observance of taboos regarding interpersonal behaviors. A rich system of totemic beliefs and supernatural sanctions serve to keep most problems in check. However, fines of cloth wealth may also be levied against an offending party—if a young man is caught engaging in premarital sex, for example, the family of the young woman involved is entitled to demand that he "show respect" through payment of a great many cloths.

Warfare. There is no information available regarding Mejbrat warfare prior to the arrival of the Moluccan traders in the region, but it is known that once slaving was introduced the Mejbrat engaged in warfare. Dutch control eventually brought slaving to an end, and the Mejbrat are not known to be particularly interested in large-scale conflict.

Religion and Expressive Culture

Religious Beliefs. The Mejbrat conceive of the earth as a flat disk, at the center of which is a large island. People live on the top of this island, while spirits live on its other side. Communication between these two worlds takes place at "places of emergence" through which spirits can pass. Each of the

Mejbrat settlement territories has a mythological charter, or myth of origin, associated with one of these places of emergence: through this site the founding dema or spirit woman arose with her consort to create the physical world known to humans. This concept of the dema is not, however, a simple one: the dema is variously understood to be a local founding spirit, a sort of unifying principle (called, in this instance, "Ratu"), or a guiding spirit for human *mechar* (magical and ritual) experts. Many Mejbrat beliefs are couched in terms of complementary principles: hot and cold, female and male, slowly growing and active. Magical items (particularly small round stones) are selected for the way in which, through their color or shape, they suggest one or another of these principles.

Religious Practitioners. All adults, both men and women, are ritual practitioners to some degree in their obligations during the initiations of Mejbrat youths and girls. Only women appear eligible to act as mechar experts, however—perhaps because much of their skill involves the invoking of and conversing with the female dema spirits. Mechar experts appear in rituals as female transvestites and practice divination.

Arts. There is little information on Mejbrat arts. Women embroider bark cloth with designs taken from the patterns found on the imported cloths that constitute the bulk of Mejbrat wealth. Songs and dances are important elements of the feast cycle.

Medicine. All illnesses and deaths are thought to derive from an imbalance occurring between the principles of "hot" and "cold" that may be the result of active intervention by witches or of violations of taboos. A cure requires divination to discover the cause of the problem, and if the problem is deemed attributable to witchcraft, a course of countermagic may be followed. Otherwise, the application of ritual objects or of "hot" or "cold" herbs or foods will be attempted in order to reinstate the proper balance and thus to bring about a cure.

Death and Afterlife. When a person dies, Mejbrat believe that his or her spirit travels below the ground to reunite with the dema of the region. Details of funerary practice are sketchy, but it is clear that the responsibility for proper burial ritual, including the giving of a burial feast, falls to the son of the deceased and that this son is given the skull to retain after the rituals are completed. Failure to properly carry out the appropriate funerary rituals results in the spirit of the dead leaving the territory and joining his or her dema, unleashing the possibility of misfortune upon the living.

Bibliography

Elmberg, John-Erik (1955). "Fieldnotes on the Mejbrat People in the Ajamaru District of the Bird's Head, Western New Guinea." *Ethnos* 20:2–102.

Elmberg, John-Erik (1965). "The Popot Feast Cycle." *Ethnos* (Stockholm) Supplement to vol. 30.

Elmberg, John-Erik (1968). *Balance and Circulation: Aspects of Tradition and Change among the Mejprat of Irian Barat.* Monograph Series, Publication no. 12. Stockholm: Ethnographical Museum.

NANCY E. GRATTON

Mekeo

ETHNONYM: Bush Mekeo

Orientation

Identification. The Mekeo peoples live in village communities on the coastal plain of southeast Papua New Guinea. Although they divided themselves traditionally into four distinct tribes, the people share a language, a culture, and a pattern of social organization that vary only slightly from tribe to tribe.

Location. The Mekeo region lies between 7°15' and 8°45' S and 146°20' and 146°45' E, 100 kilometers to the northwest of the capital city, Port Moresby. It consists of nearly 400 square kilometers of low-lying fluvial plain with varied grassland, forest, riverine, and swamp habitats. Villages are situated along the meandering tributaries of the Angabanga and Biaru rivers. There are two seasons: a "wet," during the northwest monsoon from December until April; and a "dry," from May through November. Annual rainfall averages between 100 and 180 centimeters, and temperatures fluctuate between 20° and 30° C.

Demography. Very rough estimates of the precontact population range from 10,000 to 20,000. Probably 80 to 90 percent of the population died from epidemic diseases during the first fifty years of contact. In 1980, the population was 8,603. Densest concentrations exist in the central villages of Veifa'a, Aipiana, and Inawi, with over 1,000 persons each. Other villages range between 150 and 900 persons. All communities today are administered as part of the Kairuku Subprovince headquartered at Bereina township (population 577). Roughly one-fifth of ethnic Mekeo now live in Port Moresby or the other towns and cities of Papua New Guinea, supported by wage or other cash income.

Linguistic Affiliation. There are three dialects of Mekeo, which belongs to the Central Family of the Western Subgroup of Austronesian languages.

History and Cultural Relations

Archaeological evidence indicates the Mekeo region has been inhabited by presumably Austronesian-speaking agriculturalists for at least the last 2,000 years. Oral traditions cite a dispersal from the ancient villages of Isoisovapu and Isoisovino—supposedly, a joke over whether a bird's screams came from its mouth or its anus led to a quarrel among the ancestors, and in anger they separated to found distinct villages and tribes. Contacts with Europeans began in 1846 and intensified from 1875 onward with the arrival of French Catholic missionaries (Sacred Heart order). British colonial agents "pacified" the Mekeo and brought them under administrative control in 1890. In the early decades, the people suffered numerous epidemics of foreign disease and massive depopulation. The waves of death led to an escalation of traditional sorcery for which the Mekeo are still renowned. Under Australian domination after 1906, villagers were often forced to carry supplies for government patrols into the mountainous interior. At home, they were required to plant cash crops, dig latrines, pay an annual tax, and clear footpaths and cemeteries. In 1929 and 1941, there were brief outbreaks of anti-European millenarian (cargo cult) activity. During World War II, many men were conscripted as carriers for the Allied forces. Since then, increased educational opportunities, the nearby growth of Port Moresby as an urban center, new local, provincial, and national policies, and various development projects have combined to expand Mekeo perspectives well beyond the village horizon. Nevertheless, the people retain a culturally conservative outlook. Precontact relations among Mekeo and neighboring Roro, Kuni, Kabadi, Goilala, and Toaripi tribal groups concentrated on warfare and trade in traditional wealth. Since contact, intergroup hostility has been expressed mostly in terms of sorcery suspicion and accusations. Marriage across tribal lines remains infrequent, but it is increasing. Many trade relations among the inland and coastal networks have persisted into modern times, but their importance is gradually diminishing.

Settlements

Villages are typically rectangular in layout and cleared of all vegetation except coconut palms, betel palms, and breadfruit trees. Domestic dwellings are raised on stilts and roofed with palm thatch or corrugated iron. Interior rooms include a kitchen and sleeping room(s). Most casual socializing occurs outside, on an attached platform or veranda. Houses are aligned in rows along both sides of the open central thoroughfare that runs the length of the village. Architecturally impressive clan clubhouses face one another from opposite ends. The houses of clan chiefs and sorcerers are specially decorated and constructed of more durable materials than those of ordinary villagers. Bachelors' dormitories are erected to the rear of the other buildings. Each village also has a church and cemetery erected nearby. Nowadays, it is not uncommon for some enterprising Mekeos to operate small commercial village trade stores.

Economy

Subsistence and Commercial Activities. The Mekeo are primarily slash-and-burn agriculturalists. They subsist chiefly on sweet potatoes, taro, coconuts, plantains, yams, breadfruit, sugarcane, and a variety of other indigenous and introduced crops. Pigs and fowl are also domesticated, but they are usually reserved for ceremonial occasions. Nonetheless, villagers are able to supplement their vegetable diets substantially by hunting wild game (bush pigs, wallabies, cassowaries, and other birds) and fishing. Since contact, many commercial ventures have been launched by the government and missions or at the people's own initiative, involving rice, copra, coffee, cattle, and cocoa production, as well as trucking, fishing, canoeing, and trade-store retailing; most have proven unsuccessful in the long run. In recent years, a few families have benefited from mechanized dry-rice production. The most significant sources of cash for many villagers remain the lucrative betel-nut trade in Port Moresby and the wages sent home by salaried relatives living in urban centers.

Industrial Arts. Most adult men and women are competent in all gender-appropriate activities as defined by the culture, although differing degrees of individual skill are acknowledged. Men and women both possess carpentry skills, but different and complementary ones. Men perform the tasks of canoe construction, wood carving, and tool and weapon manufacture. Women spend much of their leisure time weaving string bags.

Trade. The Mekeo region is crisscrossed by a network of hereditary trade partnerships between individuals and groups. Fellow tribesmen and women exchange food, pigs, pots, string bags, valuables of shell, feathers, and dogs' teeth, and nowadays money at marriage, death, and various other occasions. Along intertribal trade routes in the past, pottery, salt, pigs, dogs, dried meat, lime, betel nuts, shells, tooth and feather valuables, bark and bark cloth, canoes, black palm for weapons, stone axe heads, carved cassowary-bone implements, and pandanus nuts were commonly traded. Weekly markets are still held where Mekeo women exchange their garden produce for fish and shellfish caught by the coastal Roro peoples.

Division of Labor. Tasks are assigned chiefly according to age and gender. Men do the heavier cutting and clearing of food gardens, women the lighter clearing, planting, and harvesting. Only men hunt, but both women and men fish according to distinct methods. Women are responsible for the cooking and serving of food, whereas men specialize in preparing and secretly wielding their various types of magic and sorcery ritual. Young and old help in child rearing, but it is grandparents and elder sisters who tend to young children when the parents are occupied. From the age of 10 or so (nowadays, upon completion of school) until they marry, adolescent males are freed from the demands of work and concentrate on courting and love magic. In the past, the young men also served as the community's warriors.

Land Tenure. All land is owned by patrilineal clan groupings. The "peace chief" of each clan has nominal control of its lands, but for important decisions he must consult the entire clan as a unit. All members of the clan, male and female, possess rights to particular tracts for gardening, hunting, fishing, and house sites, primarily according to where their fathers had worked and lived. Usually, though, it is only the male members who actually exert these rights and pass them on to their children. Persons of other clans are often allowed access to garden land, but they are forbidden to plant permanent tree crops (e.g., coconut or betel palms) as these are owned separately from land and serve as boundary markers. The recent adoption of commercial rice farming in some areas has economically favored those families and clans with claims to large tracts of land.

Kinship

Kin Groups and Descent. Kin groups (*ikupu*) are based on patrilineal descent, and ideally they include lineage, subclan, clan, and moiety units. Male members of a lineage are closely related through male links, usually reside and garden cooperatively, and have hereditary claim to the same kinds of specialized ritual knowledge (e.g., peace, sorcery, curing, war, weather, hunting). Male members of lineages who collaborate on a day-to-day basis, who gather at the same clubhouse, and who come under the authority of the same "peace chief," constitute a subclan's core. Subclans usually form the residential blocks of village organization. Distantly related subclans, each with their own chiefs and other officials, are ranked as senior and junior branches of the same clan and, whether they live together in the same village or not, are expected to participate in feasts and ceremonies as a unit. In some instances traditionally, a patrilineal connection was presumed to unite distinct clans of a tribe into moieties.

Kinship Terminology. Villagers use a Hawaiian-type system of classifying relatives, with terms differentiating kin according to generation, gender, and, in one's own generation, relative age, birth order, and marriageability.

Marriage and Family

Marriage. Most villagers marry within their tribe, but by rule they must marry someone outside their own clan and their mother's clan. In the past, parents arranged the matches of their children prior to cohabitation. Most couples today elope, so the marital exchanges of pigs and other wealth between in-laws take place after the birth of the first child. Under Catholic influence, relatively few marriages are polygynous, and divorce is fairly uncommon. In precontact times, divorce was also probably rare, because of the bride-wealth payments accompanying arranged marriages. Postmarital residence is patrivirilocal by rule.

Domestic Unit. Mekeo households usually consist of a man, his wife, their unmarried children (excepting bachelor sons), and, once he marries, the eldest son, his wife, and their children. Kin of various other types are frequently included, however. In most daily activities, members of a household cooperate closely. In households with more than one married woman, couples garden on discrete plots, and each wife prepares food separately at her own hearth. Unmarried sons living in bachelors' dormitories or in the clan clubhouse contribute only minimal effort to household labors and receive little of its fruits.

Inheritance. Rights held by men with respect to house sites, garden land, shells and other valuables, magical spells and paraphernalia, and hereditary titles are ideally passed patrilineally. Eldest sons hold a distinct advantage over their younger brothers. Women's durable wealth in clay pots and cooking utensils is inherited by their sisters and daughters. Intimate personal property of both men and women is ritually destroyed in funeral ceremonies.

Socialization. Grandparents, siblings, and other kin help raise young children. Weaning and the arrival of a younger sibling coincide with the fairly abrupt withdrawal of maternal indulgences. A child is encouraged thereafter to find its primary gratification in the play and company of its peers. Elder siblings are held responsible for their juniors, and, above all, sharing is emphasized. Boys and girls are reinforced differentially from early ages. At marriage, many young women suffer sudden trauma in being separated from their lifelong playmates.

Sociopolitical Organization

Through parliamentary elections and representation, contemporary Mekeo villages are integrated as units into the local, subprovincial, provincial, and national governments of the independent country of Papua New Guinea.

Social Organization. Prior to European contact, Mekeo tribes were autonomous sociopolitical units organized by principles of patrilineal descent, cognatic kinship, hereditary chieftainship and sorcery, mutual support in war, and formalized "friend" relations between clans. "Friends" still intermarry preferentially and reciprocate hospitality and feasts. They ritually release each other from mourning, install one another's heirs to chiefly and sorcery office, and inaugurate each other's clan clubhouses. Relations among clanspeople and "friends" dominate daily village life.

Political Organization. Leadership and decision making are largely in the hands of hereditary clan and subclan officials and ritual specialists. These offices are passed from father to eldest son. The most important of these positions are the "peace chief" (*lopia*) and his "peace sorcerer" (*unguanga*). Their legitimate sphere of authority concerns all aspects of interclan "friend" relations. The powers of "war chiefs" (*iso*) and "war sorcerers" (*fai'a*) are now obsolete, but titleholders are still accorded considerable respect. In the past, other specialists wielded ritual control over gardening, hunting, fishing, weather, courting, curing, and food distribution. Villagers are subject to the authority of their mothers' and spouses' clan officials as well as their own.

Social Control. Informal sanctions such as gossip and fear of public shame effect substantial control in most situations of daily village life. Serious infractions against the legitimate authority of the lopia are punished, or are believed to be punished, by the unguanga. Unguanga are said to use snakes and poisons as well as spiritual agents to make their victims fall sick or die. The Mekeo belief that all deaths are caused by sorcery has greatly supported the power of sorcerers and chiefs. The introduction of money and European manufactured goods has reportedly allowed wealthy individuals to pay sorcerers illicitly to do their bidding, rather than that of the legitimate chiefs'. Government regulations are enforced by village courts, elected village councillors, police, government courts, and other state apparatuses. Catholic missionaries and Christian morality also foster conformity in many spheres of modern village life.

Conflict. In the past, intertribal warfare was waged over land and in revenge for previous killings. With "pacification," conflict is expressed in competitive courting and feasting and in accusations of adultery and sorcery.

Religion and Expressive Culture

The religious experience of most villagers consists of elements drawn from traditional mythological and ritual sources and from Catholicism.

Religious Beliefs. The indigenous myths and rituals are focused upon the spirits of the ancestors and the immortal culture hero, Akaisa. Akaisa gave the people's ancestors all their customs and social institutions. Villagers now also revere the Christian figures of God, the Old Testament prophets, Jesus, Mary, Joseph, and the saints. Many villagers liken Akaisa to a "Mekeo Jesus Christ." In addition to Akaisa, his younger brother, Tsabini, ancestral spirits, and the Christian figures, the Mekeo recognize a separate category of nonhuman, shape-changing bush spirits (*faifai*) associated with particular animal species that live underground or underwater. When disturbed, these spirits can cause villagers to fall ill or human females to give birth to monsters.

Religious Practitioners. Clan chiefs and sorcerers are regarded as the ritual descendants of Akaisa and continue to wield his sacred powers in the performance of their offices. Other practitioners specialize in rituals of hunting, gardening, curing, courting, and so on, on behalf of their communities. All adult men are competent to perform a variety of secret, inherited rituals vis-à-vis the spirits of their own ancestors. European and indigenous Catholic priests and catechists perform Christian sacraments and ceremonies.

Ceremonies. The most important religious ceremonies involve the public installation of clan chiefs and sorcerers, burial rites, and the lifting of mourning restrictions for relatives of the deceased. Other rituals attend birth, the first wearing of clothes, male indoctrination, marriage, pregnancy, and homicide. Catholic ceremonies include Mass and the other sacraments and festivals for the village patron saints.

Arts. All Mekeo graphic arts have a distinctive geometric motif. Named designs are represented in the carved insignia of chiefs' houses and clan clubhouses, female body tattoos, ceremonial dress and ornaments, face paint, woven string bags, men's dance drums, wooden weapons, lime gourds, and carved cassowary-bone utensils. Drums and flutes are played by men in traditional courting, but guitars have become popular with contemporary youths. For war chants and dances, spears and bows are banged as rhythm sticks. Magic spells, although secret, and songs of various styles all possess a poetic form.

Medicine. Numerous plant, animal, mineral, and human bodily substances are used by sorcerers and other specialists in effecting ritual changes in their intended victims, whether to make them ill, weak, lazy, fall in love, or die, or to alleviate these conditions. Most medicines are secret, and knowledge of them is passed from fathers to sons and mothers to daughters.

Death and Afterlife. Death is believed to be the combined result of human and spiritual agency. It is always a social, not just a biological, fact, and it calls for secret revenge by the surviving relatives. Public treatment of the dead is initially directed toward burial and the expression of grief and loss. Months afterward, the mourning clan's lopia organizes a large feast at which "friends" in other clans are given special gifts of food. In return, the "friends" remove the mourners' pollution and restrictions so they can return safely to the world of the living. The deceased's bodily relics are publicly destroyed at the death feast, but close relatives will secretly keep hair, bones, or teeth for use in ritual and sorcery charms and as a means of communicating with the dead. Death feasts are also important in rearranging the relationships and obligations among the living in the absence of the deceased.

See also Mafulu, Tauade

Bibliography

Guis, J. (1936). *La vie des Papous.* Paris: Dillen.

Hau'ofa, Epeli (1981). *Mekeo: Inequality and Ambivalence in a Village Society.* Canberra: Australian National University Press.

Mosko, Mark S. (1985). *Quadripartite Structures: Categories, Relations, and Homologies in Bush Mekeo Culture.* Cambridge: Cambridge University Press.

Seligmann, C. G. (1910). *The Melanesians of British New Guinea.* Cambridge: Cambridge University Press.

MARK S. MOSKO

Melpa

ETHNONYMS: Hageners, Mbowamb, Medlpa

Orientation

Identification. The Melpa people live in the Western Highlands Province of the independent state of Papua New Guinea. They are a homogeneous ethnolinguistic group, bounded on the west by the Enga and on the east by the Wahgi peoples.

Location. The Melpa live in a location which is approximately between 144° to 145° E and 5° to 6° S. Geographically, their area consists of montane valleys and mountain slopes, varying between 400 and 2,100 meters above sea level. The bulk of the population lives at altitudes between 1,500 and 1,800 meters above sea level. The climate is marked by a relatively wet period from October to March and dry from April to September. Temperatures vary from seasonal lows of 4° C or less to highs of 27° C or more. Annual rainfall is in excess of 250 centimeters. In the dry season there may be periods of drought and nocturnal frost. Otherwise, the climate is benign and the planting of crops continues year-round.

Demography. The 60,000 or more Melpa speakers occupy the areas south and north of the modern township of Mount Hagen. Population density varies with ecology, but exceeds 134 persons per square kilometer in parts of the Wahgi Valley and Ogelbeng Plain just outside of the town, tapering to fewer than 19 persons per square kilometer in the northern parts known indigenously as "Kopon" (Dei Council). Annual growth of the population since colonial times is calculated at slightly over 2 percent per annum.

Linguistic Affiliation. The Melpa language is spoken by more than 60,000 persons. It belongs to the East New Guinea Highlands Stock of Non-Austronesian languages and to the Central Family within that stock. The nearest related languages are spoken in the Nebilyer Valley, Tambul, and Ialibu south of the Melpa area. To the east the Wahgi and

Chimbu languages and to the north the Maring, Narak, and Kandawo languages also belong to the same family.

History and Cultural Relations

Intensive horticulture has been practiced in the area for some 9,000 years, starting in fertile drained swamps and moving later to hillsides when sweet potatoes became available to replace taro as the staple crop, an event estimated to have occurred within the last few hundred years. Trading networks brought shell valuables, plumes for decoration, salt, and stone axe blades from distant parts. Europeans discovered the area in 1933 as part of an exploratory drive in search of gold in the highlands creeks. The brothers Michael, James, and Danny Leahy and the Australian Patrol Officer James L. Taylor were prominent in the process of discovery and initial pacification. Mount Hagen was established as a center for mission activities, trade, and administration. Until the 1950s, major contact with the outside world was by air. Nowadays the Highlands Highway to the coastal port of Lae on the north coast of Papua New Guinea is the chief channel for goods to enter and leave. Until 1975, Papua New Guinea was under Australian colonial control, and Western Highlands was a district. At independence, the districts became provinces and from the late 1970s these gained their own provincial assemblies and governments in addition to the National Parliament.

Settlements

The indigenous form of settlement is the hamlet or extended family homestead situated close to gardening areas within a clan territory. Pathways lead from one settlement to another. Some settlements have a ceremonial ground associated with them. This is particularly likely to be so if one of the residents is a political leader (a big-man). There are two kinds of houses: men's houses, usually round and occupied by men and boys from the time they are 8 or 9 years old; and women's houses, long and sometimes with a special compartment for pig stalls, in which the women and their unmarried daughters live. Houses are made from posts, bark, woven cane, and thatching grass. Missions introduced "line villages" with family houses instead of separate men's and women's houses. These innovations have had variable success. Houses nowadays tend to be built near roads, introduced since colonial times.

Economy

Subsistence and Commercial Activities. Traditional subsistence rests on the cultivation of sweet potatoes, in mounds or squares surrounded by drainage trenches. In fallow areas among trees the people also make vegetable gardens for cucumbers, beans, maize (introduced), sugarcane, and bananas (both for cooking and for eating ripe). These gardens are nowadays supplemented or even replaced by areas planted with coffee from which cash is earned. Vegetables are also taken for sale in Mount Hagen market. Trade stores dot the countryside, in which introduced clothing, foodstuffs, and household utensils can be bought.

Industrial Arts. In precolonial times, a number of stone-axe quarries were operated, and the rough-cut or polished stones were exported as well as being used locally. Europeans brought steel tools that replaced those of stone. Prehistoric mortars and pestles are found archaeologically, but these items were used by the Melpa as cult objects rather than tools.

Trade. Over time, exchange networks extended beyond the Melpa area in all directions, but particularly westward with Enga speakers, with whom stone axe blades were exchanged for salt packs. Major religious cults also diffused into the area from the south and southwest via Tambul. The low-lying northern areas were sources of fruit, pandanus, and bird plumes. The Melpa *moka* ceremonial exchange chains linked together many groups in the area itself in a complex set of obligations to make prestations of pigs and shells between exchange partners from different groups. Trade nowadays is in coffee, exported to the world market.

Division of Labor. The indigenous division of labor is by sex. Men create garden areas, fence them, and plant luxury crops. Women plant greens, the staple sweet potatoes, and taro. They harvest gardens and keep them free of weeds, and they are also largely responsible for feeding the pig herds that are essential to the prestige economy.

Land Tenure. Land is generally inherited by sons from their fathers as they grow up and marry. Daughters can be allocated portions to use even after marriage, but marriage is usually virilocal and a wife expects to garden mostly on her husband's land within his clan area.

Kinship

Kin Groups and Descent. Descent groups are normatively patrilineal, but there is a counterbalancing stress on matrilateral relationships and on affinal alliances expressed through exchange and in shifts of residence to the maternal group in case of in-group conflict or economic advantage. Exogamous clans are clustered into tribes and divided into subclans and smaller units that act as groups in exchange activities.

Kinship Terminology. Kinship terminology follows the Iroquois system with bifurcate-merging terms for collaterals. Most kin terms are self-reciprocals in address but not in reference.

Marriage and Family

Marriage. Marriage takes place through an exchange of payments of a bride-wealth type. Payments are high and require the cooperation of kin groups. The items are pigs, shells (traditionally), and cash (nowadays). Reverse prestations are made from the bride's side, including an endowment of breeding pigs over which she has significant control. Residence is normatively patrivirilocal. Divorce does occur and is marked by the return of a part of the bride-wealth, especially if the woman is judged at fault or has produced no children for the husband's clan.

Domestic Unit. A newly married couple may either build a fresh women's house for the bride or may use space in an existing women's house. Over time they will build houses for themselves, close to the man's settlement.

Inheritance. Land rights are the most important for inheritance, and land is parceled out according to the needs of children at their marriages. Most land goes to sons. Married daughters may be given cultivation rights at their natal place also.

Socialization. A postpartum taboo is observed for two to three years, after which children are weaned. Training is not severe, and children are treated with tolerance. There is no formal group-based initiation ritual for either boys or girls, but boys shift to the men's house well before puberty. Puberty for boys is marked by the donning of a wig made from human hair. Traditionally, both sexes learn by the "look and learn" method. Nowadays, most children go at least to primary school.

Sociopolitical Organization

Social Organization. Clans are primarily linked by marriages and the exchange ties that flow from them. Clans of a tribe generally had obligations to give support in serious warfare, but internally they might also fight each other. Tribal warfare has returned in the 1970s and 1980s with the partial breakdown of government control.

Political Organization. The indigenous leader is the big-man (*wö nuim*) who does not formally succeed to an office but with the aid of his kin establishes a dominant place in the networks of moka exchange. In precolonial times, big-men held a greater monopoly over shell wealth, which disappeared after Europeans brought in thousands of these previously scarce items. Big-men must also be good speakers and negotiators. Nowadays, the big-man system operates along with the introduced roles of councillors, provincial members, and members of the National Parliament, all of whom are elected every four or five years.

Social Control. Force played a major role in relations between groups in the past, modified by the negotiating skills of big-men. Internally, conflicts were settled by moots. Nowadays, these are replaced by official Village Courts and by a range of other introduced courts.

Conflict. Conflict is endemic in Melpa society, counterbalanced by strong norms of friendship between kin and exchange partners. The resurgence of political conflict between groups is a serious contemporary problem. It is fueled both by economic change and by continuity of a revenge mentality.

Religion and Expressive Culture

Religious Beliefs. Everyday religion in the past was centered on the family, lineage, and clan ghosts, to whom pork sacrifices were made in cases of sickness and at times of political danger (e.g., prior to warfare). In addition, circulating cults moved through the area, exported from group to group. Nowadays, many Melpa are members of various Christian churches in the area.

Religious Practitioners. Religious experts (*mön wö*) were significant in both local and circulating cults. They were both curers and intercessors between people and spirits. Some learned from their fathers, others by apprenticeship to existing experts. Women could become mediums possessed by spirits and able to reveal secrets.

Ceremonies. The climactic ceremonies of the circulating cults were impressive public affairs, in which the male participants danced out from the cult enclosure and distributed pork to hundreds of guests.

Arts. Self-decoration was, and is, an art and a major preoccupation of the people at festival times, both for cults and for moka exchanges. Other arts include the composition and performance of courting songs, laments, and songs for ceremonies, the playing of flutes and Jew's harps, and the chanting of epics.

Medicine. The mön wö knew ranges of spells to cure sickness. Adults in general were acquainted with a small number of herbal remedies. Often sickness was attributed to moral causes. Wrongdoing within the group was thought to bring an unfavorable reaction both from ghosts and from the group "*mi*," a sacred object or creature associated with the group's origins. For these spirits indigenous sacrifices had to be made. Nowadays, people make prayers in the Christian churches (Catholic, Lutheran, Pentecostal, Seventh-Day Adventist) for sickness, and they visit hospitals and aid posts for pragmatic treatment. Mön wö still practice their art, however.

Death and Afterlife. Death is marked by elaborate mourning and later by a funeral feast with special emphasis on gifts to maternal kin. Formerly, the corpse was exposed and after a while its bones were removed for use in shrines; nowadays, bodies are buried. Traditionally the dead are thought to travel down watercourses to a place in the low-lying northern Jimi Valley called "Mötamb Lip Pana." Spirits of the dead are believed to come back in dreams, however, and to continually influence the living with their benevolent or malevolent presence. Small skull houses were constructed in the past for personal sacrifices. Nowadays, many people are baptized and few maintain skull houses, but belief in the activities of spirits continues to influence people's interpretations of events, and indigenous notions underlie many Christian practices.

See also Chimbu, Mae Enga, Maring

Bibliography

Brandewie, Ernest (1891). *Contrast and Context in New Guinea Culture.* St. Augustin, Germany: Anthropos Institute.

Strathern, A. J. (1971). *The Rope of Moka: Big-Men and Ceremonial Exchange in Mount Hagen, New Guinea.* Cambridge: Cambridge University Press.

Strathern, A. J. (1972). *One Father, One Blood: Descent and Group Structure among the Melpa People.* Canberra: Australian National University Press.

Strathern, A. M. (1972). *Women in Between: Female Roles in a Male World.* London: Seminar Press.

Strauss, H., and H. Tischner (1962). *Die Mi-Kultur der Hagenberg-Stämme.* Hamburg: Cram, de Gruyter & Co.

Vicedom, G. F., and H. Tischner (1943–1948). *Die Mbowamb.* 3 vols. Hamburg: Friederichsen, de Gruyter & Co.

ANDREW STRATHERN

Mendi

ETHNONYMS: Angal, Anganen, Nembi, Wola

Orientation

Identification. "Mendi" refers to the people of the Mendi valley. In precolonial times, Mendi had no collective name for themselves; nowadays, they still speak a variety of languages and dialects, and Mendi Valley clans have active sociopolitical relationships of long standing with peoples living elsewhere (e.g., in Ialibu, Tambul, Kandep, the Lai Valley, and Kagua).

Location. The Mendi Valley is located at 6° to 6°10' S and 143°35' to 143°45' E, in the Mendi Subprovince of the Southern Highlands Province, Papua New Guinea. Flanked to the east by Mount Giluwe and to the west by limestone ridges separating it from the Lai Valley, the Mendi is about 40 kilometers long and V-shaped. Most Mendi live north of Mendi town (the provincial government center, altitude about 1,620 meters above sea level). The topography of the valley is fairly rugged: gardens are planted up to about 2,400 meters above sea level. There is a large boggy area in the far northeast around Lake Egari. The valley receives about 280 centimeters of rain per year with only a slight wet/dry seasonal contrast. Approximate average daily temperature range from 7° to 24° C, with high-altitude areas regularly experiencing mild to severe crop-damaging frosts.

Demography. The first government census was conducted in 1956, but no figures are available before patrol reports dated 1959–1960 and 1961. Based on these reports, anthropologists estimate the Mendi population of the late 1950s to be about 24,000. At the time of the 1976 government census, some 28,500 people lived in the Mendi Valley. Population density is moderate by highlands standards, and Mendi are not land-short.

Linguistic Affiliation. Mendi call their language "Angal Heneng" (meaning "true words/talk," or normal speech). Dialects or closely related variants are spoken in the Lai Valley and by Wola people living in the Was (Wage) to the west, as well as by people living in the Nembi to the southwest and south, where Angal Heneng and Kewa intersect in the speech of the Anganen, called "Magi"—about 55,000 speakers in all. These languages have been classified as the Mendi-Pole Subfamily which, together with Wiru, Kewa, Huli, Enga, and some others, belong to the West-Central Family (totaling 330,000 speakers). However, in the northeastern Mendi Valley, people speak primarily Imbonggu (or Aua)—a language that is mostly heard in Ialibu Subprovince to Mendi's east (and which, as a dialect of Hagen, belongs to the Central Family of languages spoken in the Western Highlands and Chimbu Provinces). These Imbonggu speakers are technically "Mendi": they belong to Mendi Valley tribes and intermarry with other Mendi. Generally, in the Mendi area as elsewhere in Papua New Guinea, there is no necessary relationship between language and cultural identity. That is, those who consider themselves to have a common culture may speak quite different languages; conversely, people speaking the same language may have distinct cultures.

History and Cultural Relations

Under Australian rule, Mendi became administrative headquarters for the Southern Highlands (then "District") in 1950–1951. Like most of the rest of the province, Mendi remains one of the least economically developed parts of Papua New Guinea, having been a significant site neither of expatriate nor of locally run market-oriented enterprises until recently. The colonial history of the province, from the 1950s through independence in 1975, was dominated instead by government administrators and missionaries. However, soon after independence the province initiated a large World Bank–funded integrated rural development project. That project, together with the recent discovery of mineral resources, will undoubtedly have important repercussions. Of course, Mendi "history" predates the colonial period. While some Mendi groups view themselves as autochthonous, others claim to have immigrated into the valley from the north and northeast five or more generations ago. Mendi oral traditions record shifting group alliances and expanding populations.

Settlements

Despite a partial congruence of names, government "census units" (with populations mostly between 200 and 800) do not correspond with indigenous localities (with perhaps 20–100 residents). Each locality (*su*, meaning "ground") is associated with an individual clan (or subclan) section, and is socially centered around a clearing (*koma*) where meetings and collective events are held. Strictly speaking, there are no villages. Residences are dispersed within clan territories, their fences separating community footpaths and clearings from garden areas. Farmsteads usually include an oval men's house, a long women's house (in which the family's pigs are also stalled at night), and other buildings (e.g., a menstrual seclusion hut). New-style houses have sleeping compartments for both men and women.

Economy

Subsistence and Commercial Activities. About 50 percent of garden produce is fed to herds of domesticated pigs, which are treated as "wealth" and are central to everyday and ceremonial gift exchanges. Sweet potatoes, which are both the human staple and pig fodder, are planted in mulched 3-meter diameter mounds, located in fenced garden plots, and harvested daily, year-round. Gardens are commonly kept in production continuously for thirty years or more; individual mounds may be fallowed for a few months between harvesting and replanting. Greens and sugarcane are planted in and around the sweet potato gardens, as are a wide variety of European vegetables (which may be consumed locally or, more often, offered for market sale). Especially since the mid-1970s, Mendi have experimented with coffee production, small-scale cattle projects, and other marketing endeavors. Mendi also run small retail stores and transportation companies, as well as seeking employment in town and farther afield.

Industrial Arts. People produce many of their own tools, and also rework items of Western manufacture into their tool kit. The two most important rural tools are wooden digging sticks or spades (used for clearing and planting gardens) and steel axes (for clearing forest and preparing house-building and fencing materials). Women turn fiber into twine for making apparel and net bags. People also make other containers, culinary implements, and hunting equipment.

Trade. While their social field has expanded enormously in the last generation, even in precolonial times Mendi traded regularly with peoples living outside the valley. Women and men walked four or five days northwards to Kandep to obtain salt (used for trade and consumption) from their distant matrilateral kin. Kandep high country was also a source of pig-breeding stock. For these things, Mendi exchanged southern products like pearl shells and *tigaso* tree oil (used for gifts and adornment), which they obtained from trade partners in Erave, Kagua, and Lake Kutubu. Mendi used to be key conduits for the movement of pearl shells from the south coast northwards into the highlands.

Division of Labor. Gender and age are the key dimensions. Men do ax work (like forest clearing and fence making); women do most of the everyday gardening (planting, weeding, harvesting) and pig care. Individuals control the disposition of the food they plant, so women are responsible for most everyday cooking and hospitality. While there are no strong taboos on crossing these conventional lines, men appear to do women's work more frequently than vice versa. Clan events are strongly gendered: men alone are responsible for collective feast making (butchering pigs, cooking port and vegetables, and providing sugarcane and exotic refreshments like beer and store-bought meat) as well as parade performances, wealth exchanges, and oratory.

Land Tenure. Men usually reside and garden in their father's locality; however, they may maintain active use rights to gardens in their mother's place as well whether or not they relocate there. Most women continue to garden in their natal-clan territory after they marry. Insofar as "place" partially defines clanship, clans retain inalienable control over both garden and forest lands; nonclanmembers may gain temporary use rights but may not make long-term claims on the land (for example, by planting trees). Fallow land (or the unused land of declining groups) may be claimed by any member of the local clan.

Kinship

Kin Groups and Descent. There are no descent groups and genealogies are shallow. Common social identity is constituted in terms as much of locality and food sharing as of ancestry. As elsewhere in the highlands, Mendi favor affiliation with their father's clan, but strong substantive connections are recognized on the mother's side as well. Both relations are actively acknowledged and negotiated in gift exchanges. The term "clan" is used here in the interest of consistency with the published ethnography of Mendi and its neighbors. In this somewhat unconventional usage, a "clan" is not a "descent group" (i.e., a kin group whose membership is based on a descent rule); however, it corresponds with such descent-based groups functionally (see below, "Social Organization"). Mendi employ idioms of brotherhood and patrilineal ancestry rhetorically in calls for group unity, but they do not use them to talk about membership criteria. Even the rationale for affiliation with one's father's group is not explained as a genealogical principle. In Mendi clans nowadays, the rights and status of nonagnatic "sister's sons" are indistinguishable from those of agnatic members.

Kinship Terminology. Mendi kinship terminology is a version of the Omaha type, insofar as father's brother's son and father's brother's daughter are equated with brother and sister and distinguished from father's sister's son or daughter, mother's brother's son or daughter, and mother's sister's son or daughter (who are all referred to by a single term).

Marriage and Family

Marriage. Young people have considerable control over whom they will marry. They generally practice clan exogamy and tend to intermarry with members of neighboring, allied clans. Marriage conventions also discourage lineage "brothers" from marrying lineage "sisters," which diversifies lineage members' exchange partnerships. Weddings involve an extended exchange of wealth between the bride's and groom's kin networks, with more moving from the groom's to the bride's. These prestations are important pretexts for initiating exchange (*twem*) partnerships, a key Mendi social relationship. Postmarital residence is usually virilocal, and polygamy is not uncommon. Divorce can be initiated by the husband or wife, but it may require the return of wedding wealth. Divorced women often take their young children with them, and they are welcomed back into their natal clans.

Domestic Unit. Household size and composition vary. Most include a husband and at least one wife, their children, and often also an elderly widowed parent or an unmarried or divorced sibling of the husband or wife. Persons occasionally live alone.

Inheritance. Fathers are expected to redistribute gardens to their children, and both parents pass on specialized (ritual or gendered) knowledge to them. Parents help sons with bride-wealth.

Socialization. While women and older girls do most of the child care, Mendi men also look after small children. Men not infrequently encourage their 3- and 4-year-old sons to accompany them in the hope that the latter will develop a sense of loyalty. Children may nurse at will, and they often do so past the age of 3. While both mothers and fathers are affectionate and indulgent with their children, they readily use force to discipline them. For their part, children frequently "talk back" to and strike their parents (a trait adults sometimes even encourage). If they feel unfairly treated at home, they may move in temporarily with other relatives (who readily accept them). Young people are encouraged to participate in gift exchange. Mendi are unusual among highlanders for not practicing initiation. Many children attend local community schools; some go on past the sixth year to residential mission or government high schools in Mendi town or elsewhere in the Southern Highlands; and a few have postsecondary educations.

Sociopolitical Organization

Social Organization. Individuals usually identify themselves with the named clan and subclan (*sem onda* and *sem kank,* meaning "large family" and "small family," respectively) of their father; while this social identity is defined by birth, it can be renegotiated by continued residence in a place and "brotherly" cooperation in clan events. Clanship is a relationship of shared responsibility: for example, for collective defense, for making contributions to clan-sponsored prestations, and for giving unsolicited aid in small-scale wealth distributions at times of marriage and death. In counterpoint to their clan obligations, over the course of their lives individuals also create networks of exchange (twem) partnerships with affines, maternal kin, and other nonclanmembers, on whom they depend whenever they need valuables (e.g., pigs, pearl shells, money). A person's external exchange partnerships constitute the source of his or her personal "autonomy" and power within the clan. The structures of interclan alliances and individual exchange partnerships only partially correspond with one another. While clanship is predominantly a relation among men, twem partnerships can also be constructed between women and men and among women. Local groups are generally known by both a place and a clan name (e.g., Senkere Molsem). Such local clan sections have close sociopolitical relations both with other sections of the same clan living in different localities (e.g., Molmanda Molsem)—whether or not they are contiguous—and with neighboring sections of different clans belonging to the same tribal alliance. Among members of one tribal alliance of clans, contiguity creates stronger relations of cooperation than does common clanship.

Political Organization. There are no formal councils or inherited positions. Leadership is achieved by consistently exemplary contributions to clan wealth distributions and by an outspoken, active interest in shaping clan policy through private persuasion and public oratory. Political participation in interclan wealth distributions—whether by big-men (*ol koma*) or ordinary men—depends at least as much upon having created a personal exchange partnership network as it does on having a large, productive household and direct access to female labor. Women are excluded from clan policy making. Whereas nonagnatic status may have disadvantaged men (e.g., preventing them from becoming big-men) in the past, it no longer does. While there is no political organization encompassing the Mendi Valley as a whole, territorially contiguous clans often ally themselves as pairs into named tribes of up to about 1,500 members. Neighboring tribes—comprising perhaps 3,000 people—who support one another in warfare and exchange, may refer to one another as "brothers" and link names (e.g., Surup and Suolol becoming Surup-Suol).

Social Control. There are moral restrictions on bloodletting within the clan and, to a lesser extent, between clans. It is thought that ancestral spirits (*temo*) will mete out justice in cases of intraclan violence. A strong moral emphasis on reciprocity—reinforced by fears concerning jealousy-induced sorcery and witchcraft—encourages people to participate in the exchange of wealth.

Conflict. Prior to colonial rule, Mendi tribes and clans were the main war- and peace-making units. After 1950, local warfare was suppressed as a main means by which the Australian administration established its authority. However while bow-and-arrow warfare did decline, conflict continues to this day under the rubric of sorcery (*tom*). That is, Mendi consider most deaths (except those among infants and the aged) to be politically motivated; they insist that collectivities accept responsibility for death by making public wealth compensation (*maike*) to the group of the deceased.

Religion and Expressive Culture

Religious Beliefs. Mendi revere their ancestors, who are thought to have an influence on the affairs of the living. Additionally, prior to the 1970s, Mendi participated in fertility cults meant to ensure human welfare. The rationale for several of the most important cults is contained in legends that make reference to male and female agents whose actions are believed to have shaped the landscape and given humans their present-day form. Several Christian missions—notably Catholic and United Church—were influential in Mendi as of the 1970s and 1980s; however, their influence was at least as much socioeconomic and political as it was spiritual.

Religious Practitioners. In former times, men with special knowledge (sometimes acquired from their fathers) acted as fertility-cult leaders. Nowadays some men have reputations as sorcery exorcists (*nemonk ol*), and a few women and men own spells and procedures for curing ills or for attracting wealth and/or spouses. Exorcists and curers receive small payments.

Ceremonies. Public ceremonialism now centers around occasions for wealth exchange: marriage, death, and the strengthening of political alliances.

Arts. Body decoration and feather-headdress-bedecked wigs—both worn mostly by men during public clan events—are the most notable visual arts nowadays. Clan parade formations and chants are striking performances. Public oratory depends on metaphor and theatrical gesture; it is subjected to formal (not just substantive) evaluation. While their tunes are repetitive, the courting and mourning songs men and women sing involve poetic improvisation. Women crochet decorative net bags using local and imported designs; even the patterns followed in planting gardens may have an aesthetic dimension.

Medicine. Sorcery exorcism and other curing procedures employ forest resources (leaves, bark) as well as a range of imported substances. In precolonial times, autopsies were performed to determine cause of death, and surgery was undertaken to extract arrows. Nowadays, rural aid posts, staffed by local medical orderlies, link communities with the provincial hospital in Mendi town. However, there are a host of conditions (including pregnancy and childbirth) for which Mendi are reluctant to use these services.

Death and Afterlife. Deaths are heralded by yodeling cries relayed from locality to locality. During the mourning period a feast (*komanda*) is organized, gifts are given to solicit mortuary prestations (*kowar*), which are often made to the deceased's maternal relatives, and community discussion centers around determining the cause. The body is usually interred in the local group's cemetery to keep the deceased's spirit (temo) around to watch over the living. In precolonial times, the skulls of ancestors were kept in special houses where pigs were killed when family members were ill.

See also Foi, Kewa

Bibliography

Lederman, Rena (1986). "Changing Times in Mendi: Notes on Writing Highland New Guinea History." *Ethnohistory* 33: 1–30.

Lederman, Rena (1986). *What Gifts Engender: Social Relations and Politics in Mendi, Highland Papua New Guinea.* Cambridge: Cambridge University Press.

Lederman, Rena (1987). "The Meaning of Residence in Mendi." In *The Survey under Difficult Conditions,* edited by T. McDevitt. HRAFlex Ethnography Series, no. OJ1-006. New Haven, Conn.

Lederman, Rena (1990). "Big-Men Large and Small? Towards a Comparative Perspective." *Ethnology* 33:3–15.

Mawe, Theodore (1985). *Mende Culture and Tradition: a Recent Survey.* P.N.G. National Museum Record no. 10. Boroko, Papua New Guinea: Institute of Papua New Guinea Studies.

Ryan, D'Arcy (1961). "Gift Exchange in the Mendi Valley." Ph.D. dissertation, Sydney University.

RENA LEDERMAN

Mimika

ETHNONYM: Kamoro

Orientation

Identification. The Mimika people are named after the Mimika River in the central district of Irian Jaya Province of Indonesia (formerly Netherlands, or Dutch, New Guinea). "Kamoro" means "living person" as opposed to "ghosts." There is no native name for the area, but as *wènata,* "real human beings," they contrast themselves with "not-real persons" such as the adjacent Asmat and Kapauku.

Location. The area is located between 4° and 6° S and 134°59' to 136°19' E, bounded by the Utakwa River in the east and the shores of Etna Bay in the west. The people inhabit the lowlands traversed by some sixty swamp and mountain rivers and creeks. The southeast monsoons bring rains that last from June to mid-September, but wet and dry seasons are not clearly demarcated.

Demography. A population of approximately 8,600 (1955) lives in about thirty villages. Since 1962, Indonesian migrants have also settled in the area.

Linguistic Affiliation. The Kamoro language, of which six to eight dialects have been identified, is a member of the Asmat-Kamoro Family of Non-Austronesian languages.

History and Cultural Relations

Oral traditions trace the origins of the Mimika people to conflict over sago groves among four local groups living in the lowlands east of the Utakwa River. An exodus to the southwest triggered a chain reaction among other groups in the east moving to the west. Linguistic evidence does point to a genetic relationship between Asmat (east of Mimika), and Sentani, far to the northeast on the north coast of Irian Jaya, thus suggesting a possible prehistoric northeast-southwest migration. Historic contacts with foreigners began perhaps as early as A.D. 1600, with Chinese, Indonesian, and Dutch traders entering the area from the west via Etna Bay. In the early twentieth century, while the area was under Dutch administration, Ceramese Islamic traders appointed nominal local representatives (*radjas*) in western Mimika, leading to a rush for ironware, textiles, earrings, and beads in exchange for resin, local foods, and slaves. In general, attitudes towards foreigners passed through several stages: enmity and cautious rapprochement; goodwill inspired by a strong desire for Western commodities; disappointment and passive resistance to interference with a seminomadic way of life; and, finally, following Japanese occupation during World War II, coexistence and resignation to the strangers' permanent presence. The entire Mimika population has now been baptized, but due to a paucity of marketable resources, economic development has been slow.

Settlements

The largest population concentration is found in the central and eastern regions, where villages range from about 60 to 400 inhabitants. In the past people lived in tiny dispersed temporary dwellings scattered around semipermanent longhouse settlements, and everyday life still consists of moving up and down between sago groves upstream and fishing grounds downstream. The traditional longhouse pattern is still followed in the temporary settlements for sago production, fishing, and foraging, but in the villages people have adopted separate family dwellings introduced by missionaries and the Dutch administration.

Economy

Subsistence and Commercial Activities. In order of importance, major subsistence activities are: sago making; foraging; fishing; some slash-and-burn gardening of tobacco, bananas, and tubers (especially in upstream settlements); and hunting. Coconut palms are grown in all villages, but cash cropping is of minor importance. Industrial art is limited and controlled by Indonesian merchants. It concerns the supply of timber for the local mill and some ironwood for export purposes. Cash earnings are mainly dependent on migrant labor outside the district in urban centers. Up-to-date and reliable information is not available. Food production was part of a cycle of extensive and shorter ceremonies, but this rhythm has been interfered with by duties connected with government administration. Many villagers leave for the sago and fishing grounds on Mondays and return to the villages on Saturdays in order to attend church services. A substantial amount of work has to be done for the village, the school, and for payment of taxes. Timber provides some cash earnings, but migrant labor in urban centers is economically more important. Trade stores are owned by Chinese or Indonesian tradespeople.

Industrial Arts. Mimika material equipment is simple and adapted to a seminomadic way of life. Apart from implements, two types of canoes were manufactured—dugouts, used in river travel, and seagoing canoes with high, sharp bows.

Trade. Traditional trade was of secondary importance. It still concerns the exchange of canoes for the right of sago production in West Mimika, where sago groves are scarce in the furthermost coastal areas. Inland people of Eastern Mimika trade tobacco to coastal communities. Tobacco was also obtained from Highland Papuans in exchange for inferior iron tools.

Division of Labor. The sexual division of labor functions as a device to institute a reciprocal state of interdependence between the sexes. Women play a major role in the production of sago, catching fish, foraging, collecting shellfish, cutting and transporting firewood, and preparing food. They also control the use of canoes, mats, bags, and the food supply. Men are the producers of canoes, tools, weapons, and implements for fishing and hunting; the construction of semipermanent longhouses and village dwellings is also their responsibility. Men also do most of the gardening (though this is of minor importance) and are nowadays the wage earners. The greater part of ritual activities are performed and controlled by men, but elderly women wield remarkable power and also have much ritual knowledge. There is a "guild" of drummers/singers, and there are specialist wood-carvers of high repute.

Land Tenure. Since land tenure is an aspect of a flexible social organization in which power and authority are diffused, the rules allow for much variety. Also, territory boundaries are much more sharply defined with regard to waterways than to the land itself, owing to the vital role of canoes as a means of transport. Land rights are inalienable to strangers or foreigners, though such people may be permitted to use the land. Sago groves belong to groups of siblings, cousins, and their children, but the use of sago groves (like fishing grounds) is extended to kin and affines of the persons who claim possession. Men usually act as spokesmen, but women are extremely influential. Tidal creeks, which can be closed off with a weir for fishing purposes, are owned and controlled by sisters, female cousins, or a mother and her daughters. Gardens are usually owned by older married couples. Trees are subject to individual possession, either by men or women. Since kinship is strongly classificatory and includes relationships based on adoption, friendship, and other considerations, the actual use of land and creeks is fairly nonrestrictive and collective. Land disputes mainly occur between villages with adjoining territories.

Kinship

Kin Groups and Descent. Kinship is closely associated with gender. The relation between siblings is a key metaphor for kinship, descent, marriage, and sociopolitical ties in myth and cosmology. But there is a clear male bias in that a male is said to have offspring originating from his penis (*kamare*)—his *kamarima* are his children and his brothers' children—and offspring from his anus (*wa*)—his *watako* are his sisters' children. By contrast, a woman does not have metaphorical offspring from the front and behind. Yet, while males are considered to model the fetus by means of frequent coitus—explicitly likened to carving a "spirit pole" (see below)—it is women who ensure the succession and reproduction of human beings in matrilineal descent groups. Thus in kinship, as otherwise, women and men have a complementary relationship, each sex contributing in its distinctive way.

Kinship Terminology. Consistent with the structural importance of "siblingship," kinship terminology stresses "horizontal" (generational) rather than "vertical" (lineal) ties and categories. It has a bilateral Hawaiian-type slant stressing generation and relative age. However, again gender comes in: "inferior" and "male" wife takers are terminologically distinguished from "superior" and "female" wife givers. The former, referred to as *kaokapajti* (sister's husband and daughter's husband) are required to render a wide variety of services. A man without kaokapajti is a social nobody. There are two modalities of matrilineal descent groups, each being associated with ideal preference for uxorilocal or matrilocal residence. The first modality, a vertical one, includes all matrilineal descendants of a named woman over three generations. In the fourth generation the focal point shifts to a woman of the second generation. The second modality, a horizontal one, includes siblings and cousins who claim to have one maternal grandmother in common. The two modalities represented by various groupings constitute the core of people who share a tract of land (*taparè*). The relationship between these groupings is usually putatively matrilineal.

Marriage and Family

Marriage. Marriage is ideally a matter of direct sister exchange between two groups, but indirect exchange by means of bride-wealth has been widely accepted as a substitute. The relationship between bride takers and bride givers is subject to rules of avoidance and joking, with bride givers' joking being more aggressive. The ideal preference is for uxorilocal or matrilocal residence.

Domestic Unit. The domestic unit consists of a married couple, their unmarried children, and a varying number of dependent relatives, all of whom usually eat and sleep together. Its composition and relation to its neighbors reflect the traditional longhouse community, replaced by separate family dwellings in the villages but still operating in the temporary settlements near sago and fishing grounds. Married couples had their own living quarters but were also part of matrifocal longhouse communities. Frequent intermarriage within coresident extended longhouse communities and strong ties between siblings blurred the residence parterns. The concentration of traditional communities in villages and the combination of villages in compounds have added to this blurred picture. Each domestic unit operates and cooperates with other units in an autonomous fashion. Working parties are of varying constitution, with a preference for small parties of six to ten persons, subdivided in pairs.

Inheritance. The mobility involved in the food quest and the flexible nature of kinship and descent, as well as the fact that tenure and use of land and fishing grounds operate along a sliding scale between individual and collective claims, all militate against clear-cut rules of inheritance. However, the multifarious ritual functions and the command of natural phenomena such as weather, mosquitoes, and various types of disease are subject to strict rules of predominantly patrilineal inheritance.

Socialization. Babies are well looked after not only by their mothers but also by their fathers, who share the normal duties with their wives. The demands of mobility for the food quest involve the two parents equally; as a result, weaned babies are often left in the care of slightly older siblings, supervised by one or two elder persons. Groups of children roam the village and learn to look after themselves at an early age. Games children play are predominantly in imitation of adult duties. Sexual segregation sets in after the separate rites of passage for male and female adolescents.

Sociopolitical Organization

Social Organization. The largest group with corporate functions was the longhouse community of the semipermanent settlements, the core of which is constituted today by the two modalities of matrilineal descent. Each longhouse community was associated with two to four others, constituting extended longhouse communities, which were a unit in warfare, feasting, and the exchange of women. At present these communities usually live "together-apart" in villages, sometimes working cooperatively but remaining autonomous in many ways. A striking feature of Mimika social organization is its dual structure, which is expressed in the settlement pattern, land tenure, ceremonies, and ritual. However, moieties in the technical sense of the word do not occur; duality is, rather, a general structuring principle.

Political Organization. Longhouse communities in their present configuration in villages recognize one or more elderly men as their "great men." Their position is not a hereditary one; their authority and power depend on personal intellectual and oratorical skill and the number and strength of their kinship and affinal relations.

Social Control and Conflict. Personal courage and a certain amount of mental imbalance were required for the position of warlord, who often was not identical with the leader of everyday life. In warfare, extended communities were joined in ever-changing federations, which carried out raids against each other.

Religion and Expressive Culture

Religious Beliefs. Mimika cosmology is characterized by a dual complementary division, following the male-female distinction, with west, inland, and upstream associated with women and east, coast, and downstream associated with men. The chief mechanism of the cosmos, as of history and social relations, is reciprocity. The adoption of Christianity has greatly altered the rituals that incorporate these themes, though a revival of traditional ceremonies swept through the area in the 1950s.

Religious Practitioners. Male and female elders possess detailed knowledge and conduct the rituals performed by members of their respective sexes.

Ceremonies. Two chief rituals, "Kaware" and "Emakame," are complementary and are considered to relate to each other as male to female. They are said to be the "mothers" of all other ceremonies, which mainly concern rites of passage, marking birth, adolescence (by piercing the nostrils of males), and death. Kaware epitomizes male control of ritual functions and secrets and of communication with the invisible underworld; Emakame is the paradigm of the female powers of production, reproduction, and erotic life.

Arts. Mimika art mainly functions in ceremonial contexts, as in the shieldlike carvings (produced by men) that represent ancestral mothers and the recent dead. The most spectacular objects are the monumental spirit poles (*mbitoro*), which have a clear affinity with the well-known Asmat *bis* poles. Mbitoro depict two highly stylized male and female human figures, representing individuals of some repute who have died recently, and are placed in front of the ceremonial houses erected for nose-piercing rites. The mbitoro figure recurs in drum handles, and many utilitarian objects are ornamented with carved figures of hornbills and cassowaries.

Medicine. Each type of disease has its own male or female specialist who commands its special formula and method of physical treatment; no general practitioners exist.

Death and Afterlife. It is believed that ghosts and men once lived together in peace, even intermarrying. However, death originated owing to infractions by humans of the rule of reciprocity. The spirits of the dead live in parallel villages in the underworld, where the environmental setting is perfect: no more mud, but beautiful sand and gardens. The male culture hero who carries the sun as a torch through the sky daily descends to the underworld, following a trail that connects the villages, and rises to the eastern sky in the early morning. Nowadays, God, Jesus, and Mary are also said to have their abode in the underworld. When a person dies, parting from the living takes several years, at the conclusion of which men and women of some repute impersonate the deceased in a masquerade, during which relatives and friends mourn and praise the deceased and finally invite the dead person to depart and to leave the living in peace. The "spirit," localized and fragmented in the moving parts of the body, leaves the body, goes upstream, and then descends to the underworld through a hole under a tree.

See also Asmat, Kapauku

Bibliography

Kooijman, Simon (1984). *Art, Art Objects and Ritual in the Mimika Culture.* Mededelingen van het Rijksmuseum voor Volkerkunde, no. 24. Leiden: Brill.

Pouwer, Jan (1955). *Enkele aspecten van de Mimika-cultuur (Nederlands zuidwest Nieuw Guinea).* The Hague: Staatsdrukkerij- en Uitgeversbedrijf.

Pouwer, Jan (1956). "A Masquerade in Mimika." *Antiquity and Survival* 1:373–387.

Pouwer, Jan (1975). "Structural History: A New Guinea Case Study." In *Explorations in the Anthropology of Religion: Essays in Honour of Jan Van Baal,* edited by W. E. A. van Beek and J. H. Scherer, 80–112. The Hague: Martinus Nijhoff.

JAN POUWER

Miyanmin

ETHNONYMS: Blimo, Mianmin, Wagarabai

Orientation

Identification. The Miyanmin live in Telefomin District of Sandaun (West Sepik) Province and Ambunti District of East Sepik Province, Papua New Guinea. There are two divisions: the mountain-dwelling southeastern Miyanmin refer to themselves as *am-nakai* or (cultured) "house people" and to the northwestern, low-altitude Miyanmin as *sa-nakai* or (wild) "forest people." Although it is now accepted, the name "Miyanmin" was originally the usage of the neighboring Telefolmin people for a now-extinct Miyanmin local group.

Location. The majority of Miyanmin live at around 1,000 meters in the Donner, Thurnwald, and Stolle mountains in the central cordillera of New Guinea, an area drained by the Upper Sepik, August, and May rivers. A smaller number live in the lowlands on the Upper August River, in the West and Landslip ranges and at the head of the Right May (Mai) River. The total area exceeds 3,800 square kilometers. It is an area of high rainfall and low seasonality and embraces a variety of forest types including midmontane beech and conifer forest, lower-montane oak and mixed rain forest, and lowland rain forest.

Demography. Mianmin speakers number approximately 1,800. Overall population density is 0.5 person per square kilometer. Of this total, the population of the higher-altitude Miyanmin groups of the southeast is approximately 1,150, with a crude population density of 8 persons per square kilometer.

Linguistic Affiliation. They speak a Papuan language called Mianmin, which is a member of the Mountain Ok Subfamily of the Ok Family of languages. Wagarabai is the name given to the dialect of Mianmin spoken by people living at low altitudes on the northern frontier.

History and Cultural Relations

Regional scholars have adopted the linguistic designation Mountain Ok to refer to the culturally related peoples living in and around the Sepik River source basin of Ifitaman. These related peoples include the Telefolmin and Atbalmin, southern neighbors of the Miyanmin and their traditional enemies. The northern frontier contacts groups such as the Iwam and Abau who are speakers of Upper Sepik languages. The indirect evidence of forest burning in Ifitaman suggests the presence of people in the Mountain Ok area at least 17,000–15,000 years ago with agriculture appearing in the region about 3,500 years ago. The linguistic separation of the major Mountain Ok groups may have occurred between 2,000 and 3,000 years ago. Mountain Ok groups share the belief that they were founded by an ancestress named Afek and that their separate existence is due to the travels of Afek or her sisters. The Miyanmin attribute their origin to one of these sisters. The most recent expansion and large-scale movement in the region began some 300 years ago. The Mountain Ok peoples were discovered by Richard Thurnwald and the German Sepik River expedition of 1912–1914. The expedition may have made visual contact with Miyanmin in the May Valley and the western Thurnwalds in 1913. This pattern of fleeting contact was sustained through subsequent visits by Westerners between 1927 and the 1950s when systematic pacification was initiated by Australian colonial authorities. This coincided with the heavy impact of introduced diseases that continued through the late 1960s. Heavy fighting between the Miyanmin and neighboring groups in the 1950s and 1960s resulted in court trials and mass jailings. In response, several Miyanmin groups in the eastern Thurnwalds began to develop a local modernization plan and mass conversion to Christianity even before missionaries entered the area directly. The plan, which continues to evolve, includes the construction of bush airstrips as centers for education, health care, and commerce. The movement has now extended to many other groups. Today, most men have worked as laborers elsewhere in Papua New Guinea. A number of young people have attended high school or mission institutions, some have received vocational training in health care and education, and one is in university.

Settlements

The Miyanmin are organized in local parish groups ranging in size from 40 to 200 members that claim large territories. At any given time, a parish or a cooperating group consisting of members of two parishes might occupy only a small portion of a group territory. Except when pioneering a new area, people live in dispersed hamlets that range in size from two women's houses and a men's house to as many as fifteen women's houses and several men's houses. Nuclear and polygynous families maintain houses in hamlets identified with each spouse's kin group and move between them seasonally. These houses are built on posts with bark floors and walls and tree-leaf or palm thatch roofs. Polygynous cowives share the same roof but have separate doors and hearths in an unpartitioned house. Women's houses are of similar size and design, but they vary in small details reflecting their builders' personal styles. Men's houses are raised above women's houses and command approaches to hamlets, which are typically located on scalped ridges, mountain spurs, or riverbanks. In addition to residential structures, every parish has three kinds of specialized buildings: a large dance house that also serves as a longhouse during the initial phase of settlement; a men's cult house in which ancestral bones and other ritual objects are kept from the sight of women and children; and a dormitory and ritual site for boys undergoing initiation. The overall settlement pattern is dynamic with hamlets built and abandoned constantly in response to game abundance and the availability of garden land. Modernization has changed settlement patterns and house styles. Settlements around airstrips, such as Mianmin in the Hak Valley, Yapsiei on the Upper August River, and Hotmin at the junction of the May and Right May rivers, have grown to unusual size due to the services and amenities they provide, which include schools and health care. Modern houses are highly idiosyncratic in style, floor plan, and materials. Family houses have replaced women's houses, and men's houses now shelter bachelors alone. The Hak Valley settlement now has as many as 400 persons with more than sixty family houses, leading to many social and environmental problems.

Economy

Subsistence and Commercial Activities. The Miyanmin are shifting cultivators and hunters and also keep small numbers of domestic pigs. People of the lowlands depend more on sago (*Metroxylon sago*) and aquatic resources. People say that "taro is our bones." Taro (*Colocasia esculenta*), produced using the slash-mulch technique, are the staple, with a variety of other traditional vegetables, such as squash, bananas, beans, and greens, also grown. Sweet potatoes (*Ipomoea batatas*) and introduced Western vegetables, such as commercial banana varieties, tomatoes, papayas, pineapples, and cabbages, have increasingly been grown around airstrip settlements both for subsistence and for their perceived commercial potential. Wild pigs, possums, wallabies, rats, cassowaries and other birds, snakes, lizards, frogs, insects, and other small terrestrial fauna continue to provide most of the high-quality protein in the diet. Hunting has declined around airstrip settlements, leading people to intensify pig husbandry. Cash sales of fruit and vegetables were part of the community modernization plan that developed in the 1960s. Today, people of several communities with access to an airstrip realize modest incomes from such sales in markets at Telefomin and Tabubil, the town serving the Ok Tedi gold and copper mine. In villages, cooperative trade stores organized along kinship lines sell tobacco, salt, soap, rice, canned fish, cloth, kerosene, and similar commodities.

Industrial Arts. Traditional male crafts included the carving of war shields and clubs, arrow foreshafts and points, bows, and bamboo blades and spatulas, using implements of stone, cassowary bone, pig tusk, and rat's tooth, and cane work for hafting and personal adornment. Women made string bags and personal ornaments for everyone, pandanus-leaf mats, raffia skirts, and bark cloth. Few are trained in Western trades, though some men have picked up particular skills while pursuing contract labor. The fashioning of scrap metal into useful objects, such as arrow points and prongs, graters, and sickles, is common.

Trade. Traditionally, there was modest trade among parishes in capital and prestige goods such as palm-wood bows, arrow points and foreshafts, stone tools, shell ornaments, plumes, and cuscus fur. Individuals might visit kin and friends in other parishes to collect raw materials at their source. Participation in regional trade networks was disrupted by endemic warfare, although the eastern Miyanmin did maintain a trade relationship with a riverine group on the Lower May.

Land Tenure. Cognatic parishes and patrilineages claim land and may assert this control in relation to other parishes and, in modern times, within parishes with an airstrip settlement where there is pressure on agricultural and forest resources.

Division of Labor. There is a marked but flexible sexual division of labor in all spheres. In agriculture, men engage in tree clearing and women remove branches and undergrowth and do the planting. All sexes weed and, while women do most of the routine harvesting, men harvest some of the taro for feasts and ceremonies. In construction, men gather timber, do structural work, and lay the roof, while women gather leaves for roofs and clay with which they make the hearths in all houses. Men hunt the larger and more distant game, although women and children may serve as beaters in pig hunts. Women hunt possums, bandicoots, and rats as well as smaller animals.

Kinship

Kin Groups and Descent. The parish is the basic group with corporate functions to which all Miyanmin belong. Although the genealogical composition of the predominantly endogamous parish is cognatic, the ideology of membership refers to coresidence rather than descent. Parishes are often paired in cooperative alliances forged by intermarriage. Descent is strongly emphasized in small patrilineages, typically four in number, of which am-nakai parishes are composed. These lineages are named after past big-men, are exogamous jurally, and are units of fission in the context of intragroup conflict. They are identified with particular hamlets whose resident population is comprised of a core of one or two nuclear families headed by male elders of a lineage and a transient population of affines and matrikin. Some sa-nakai local groups are breakaway patrilineages of am-nakai parishes. Because postmarital residence is bilocal, matrikin, agnates, and affines are equally important.

Kinship Terminology. There are two discrete systems. The first is a metaclassification with six terms that distinguish consanguineals from affinals. For the former, generation and gender are distinguished. For the latter, spouses are distinguished from other affines. The second classification consists of forty elementary, derivative, and descriptive terms in common use. Cousin terms are of the Hawaiian-generational type with bifurcate-merging terms for members of the first ascending generation of ego's gender and lineal terms for the opposite sex. Birth order and relative age are also distinguished. Thus, from the standpoint of a male ego, father's (elder) brother has a term derived from father with father's younger brother having his own term. Father's brothers are distinguished from mother's brothers while mother's sisters are equated with father's sisters.

Marriage and Family

Marriage. Most first marriages, involving young people whose parents are alive, are by consent. Fathers dote on their daughters and desire sons-in-law who will hunt for them. Women may be compelled to marry against their wishes when they are the wards of their brothers or other male kin. The most common form of marriage among members of largely endogamous parishes is sister exchange, with free marriages the next most common form. The remaining marriages involve capture and widow remarriage. For intraparish marriages, bilocal residence amounts to bride-service. Interparish marriages are equally divided between sister exchange and uxorilocality, with elopement and delayed reciprocity accounting for most of the remainder. Marriage with members of one's own or mother's patrilineage (i.e., classificatory siblings) is jurally prohibited, with the few exceptions involving spouses who never shared residence while growing up. The high proportion of parish-endogamous marriages reinforces solidarity and generates the cognatic appearance of the group, while the somewhat less frequent interparish marriages create and maintain durable patterns of cooperation. Death payments are demanded when a parish member who is residing uxorilocally in another parish dies. Traditionally, divorce was rare among the am-nakai groups while reportedly common among the sa-nakai groups. It is increasingly common in modern times, however. Polygyny is not associated with high social status but instead involves a man's need to augment the labor of a disabled first wife or his desire to acquire a young sex partner. Polygynous marriages are tense and are the most likely to end in divorce. Cowives do not attend each other in childbirth. Widows are encouraged to marry leviratically.

Domestic Unit. The elementary family of husband, wife (or wives), and children is the basic unit of consumption and production. Traditionally, while childless married couples might sleep together in the wives' houses, men typically spent the night in a men's house, which women never visited. Today, it is increasingly common for the entire family to sleep under one roof, although modern houses are likely to be partitioned.

Inheritance. Traditionally, a man or woman's sparse movable property, along with certain cultivated trees and the portion of their taro planting stock that survived mortuary destruction, was inherited by their children. People inherit their right to use land from both the maternal and the paternal lines and claims may extend many generations into the past.

Socialization. Men and women share equally in the care of children. Father-son relations are frequently tense. In mitigation, boys have very close relationships with their cross uncles who, for example, tutor them in crafts and related fields of knowledge. Girls' relationships with their mothers and other women are relaxed and highly supportive; they join in daily tasks at a young age. For boys, most learning occurs in same-sex, near-peer play groups. Traditionally, boys were removed from their mothers' houses after puberty to commence their advance through the male initiation cycle. There are no puberty or initiation rites for women. Today, some children have access to a community primary school.

Sociopolitical Organization

Social Organization. Traditional society was highly egalitarian with generalized sharing of resources within parishes and with visiting members of paired or allied parishes being an absolute value. Patrilineages were and remain significant landholding units with parishes then and now involved in external challenges to sovereignty. Modernization, however, has increased the frequency of disputes over resources, and assertions of lineage-based rights are today much more visible than they were in the 1960s, particularly around the airstrip villages.

Leadership. Miyanmin conform to the big-man pattern that has been identified for other fringe highland groups in which unstratified leadership roles are diffused widely and competence is defined narrowly in relation to such activities as agriculture, hunting, ritual, curing, and intergroup politics or war. Nevertheless, traditional war leaders were esteemed highly and parish oral history is organized in a framework comprised of the names of a succession of such men over ten or more generations.

Political Organization. Traditionally, the Miyanmin parishes were autonomous units with many concerns upon which they could act, including interparish affairs. A parish was also a ceremonial group, maintaining a cult house, organizing religious ceremonies, and building a dance house in connection with festivals attracting regional participation. Among the higher-altitude am-nakai groups, parishes were often paired in close cooperative relationships functioning jointly to exploit land. The ten am-nakai parishes of the Thurnwald Range and May Valley also formed a military alliance to campaign against the Telefolmin and Atbalmin to the south or to prey on excluded Miyanmin groups, including some of the sa-nakai, and riverine peoples of the Lower May. Since the national independence of Papua New Guinea in 1975, Miyanmin are conscious of their citizenship, identify with the "Pan-Min" movement of the Mountain Ok peoples at large that was sparked by the development of gold and copper mines in the region, and attempt to participate in political affairs. This participation has been stymied because of their small population.

Conflict and Social Control. Miyanmin warfare included cannibalism, the abduction of nubile women and children of either sex, plunder, and the destruction of enemy assets. Among the am-nakai social control was exercised through public opinion, through consensus building in men's-house or cult-house discussions in which elders and big-men may have greater voices, and, in extreme cases as in the context of an adult death, through the mediumship of a shaman in a mortuary ritual. Threats to social order range from domestic pigs damaging gardens, to disputes over property, to adultery and other offenses involving women, to homicide. At all levels, including within households, individual violence or its threat is the typical sanction, sometimes augmented by public opinion. The highest levels of intraparish conflict in which public opinion is divided can lead to parish fission and long-term enmity. Interparish disputes frequently culminated in brief, violent clashes with a few deaths, burned houses, and territorial losses. Losers were allowed to return to salvage planting material from their gardens. Contrastingly, the sa-nakai groups are stereotypically anarchistic with high levels of interpersonal and intergroup violence and low group solidarity.

Religion and Expressive Culture

Religious Beliefs. Today, most Miyanmin are Christian and, possibly excepting sorcery, traditional religious behavior and belief is retained only by the old. Churches have replaced cult houses, schools the initiation cycle. Traditionally, the Miyanmin believed that their world, including the physical world, neighboring peoples, and the land of the dead, was created by Afek or her younger sister. In addition to spirits, the sun and moon were recognized as remote supernatural beings. The Miyanmin also believed in bush demons associated with certain watercourses, trees, habitats, and objects that sanctioned taboo violations, caused sickness, and interfered with routine processes such as arrow flights. They also believed in a mythical rainbow-hued serpent that was responsible for human aggression.

Religious Practitioners. Traditional ritual leaders included shamans or "death seers" and elders. The latter served as arbiters of cult-house rituals, with one of their number serving as its principal keeper. Today, many local groups have indigenous Baptist pastors, one of whom is appointed by the Sepik Baptist Union to serve as circuit pastor.

Ceremonies. Traditional rituals were of three types: initiation; spirit intervention (including mortuary); and demon control (including curing). The initiation cycle consisted of twelve named rituals to advance boys and men through four statuses. Mortuary rites consisted of three phases: the burial wake; the seance; and garden destruction. The wake occurs on the day following the death and is marked by the violent arrival of visitors who either themselves bring the house of the deceased under mock attack or are themselves consumed in a brawl. The tree interment occurs in late afternoon. That night, a shaman conducts a seance in order to contact spirits, establish a cause of death, and set an appropriate course of action. The following day, male kin descend on the deceased's gardens and uproot and destroy a portion of the taro. Shamans also conduct rituals to cure illness, to foresee the course of battle, and to warn individuals of possible danger. Today, church services are held every Sunday morning and baptism by immersion is carried out when required. Since the "Rabaibal" movement swept the Ok area in the 1970s, small, informal groups have gathered from time to time to receive the Holy Spirit that is manifested in individual trances and the appearance of bright lights.

Arts. Miyanmin art is expressed in personal adornment with paint, fur, feathers, palm fronds, beads, twine, flowers, and cane and in the production and decoration of utilitarian objects in media such as bark twine, wood, and bamboo.

Medicine. In addition to curing rituals, people make use of plant materials to cure sores, staunch bleeding, promote healing, relieve respiratory symptoms, control pain, and act as general tonics.

Death and Afterlife. Traditional practice was to place the dead on tree platforms and recover the bones later for placement in a cult house along with the mandibles of wild pigs believed to have been taken due to the intervention of the deceased's spirit. When people die, they become spirits and move to the land of the dead, which is already inhabited by indigenous spirits and other ancestral spirits who tend to reside with their own kind. The spirit of the newly dead will marry into the indigenous group, have children, and engage in normal activities such as hunting, and in most cases they will have a benign influence on the affairs of the living, assisting in agriculture, hunting, warfare, and the like. Rarely, a person who died angry might reside with another group's ancestral spirits and seek vengeance. Today, most groups bury the dead and hold a simple graveside prayer service.

See also Telefolmin

Bibliography

Gardner, Donald S. (1983). "Performativity in Ritual: The Mianmin Case." *Man* 18:344–360.

Gardner, Donald S. (1987). "Spirits and Conceptions of Agency among the Mianmin of Papua New Guinea." *Oceania* 57:161–177.

Morren, George E. B., Jr. (1981). "A Small Footnote to the 'Big Walk': Development and Change among the Miyanmin of Papua New Guinea." *Oceania* 52:39–63.

Morren, George E. B., Jr. (1984). "Warfare on the Highland Fringe of New Guinea: The Case of the Mountain Ok." In *Warfare, Culture, and Environment,* edited by B. Ferguson, 169–207. Orlando, Fla.: Academic Press.

Morren, George E. B., Jr. (1986). *The Miyanmin: Human Ecology of a Papua New Guinea Society.* Ames: Iowa State University Press.

Morren, George E. B., Jr., and David Hyndman (1988). "The Taro Monoculture of Central New Guinea." *Human Ecology* 15:301–315.

GEORGE E. B. MORREN, JR.

Motu

ETHNONYMS: none

Orientation

Identification. At the time of their first recorded contact with Westerners, in 1872, the Austronesian-speaking people known as Motu lived in thirteen nucleated seaside villages on the south coast of the New Guinea mainland, immediately east and west of Port Moresby (9°29' S, 147°8' E), the first center of European settlement and the present capital of Papua New Guinea. One further Motu village was established subsequently. Three Motu villages, Elevala, Tanobada, and Hanuabada, were located close together on the shore of Port Moresby harbor, only a mile or so to the west of the present city's docks and commercial center. The Motu shared this coastline and its hinterland with a non-Austronesian-speaking people, the Koita, who occupied small residential enclaves in a number of Motu villages in addition to their own independent villages in the immediate hinterland. Today, Motu still inhabit the same fourteen seaside villages, though many of them have migrated from villages outside Port Moresby into its suburban residential areas. Most Motu villages were traditionally built over the water in tidal shallows, facing a barrier reef some distance offshore.

Location. From about April to November, when the southeast trade winds blow in from the sea, the Motu coast is hot and dry. Between November and March, the northwest monsoon brings some rain and increased humidity. The slopes, low hills, swamps, and valleys of the immediate hinterland behind and between Motu villages, where traditionally the Motu maintained gardens and occasionally hunted game, were sparsely covered with humid tropical savanna, mainly dry grass and stunted eucalypti. At the edges of the barrier reef, along the inshore beaches, and in the waters between, Motu fished.

Demography. Although no precise figures are available, from the random observations of early missionaries and other visitors the total population of all Motu villages at the time of first contact, including the small Koita minorities in some villages, has been estimated at between 4,000 and 5,000. Subsequently, in the early decades of colonization, there were increases and decreases in particular villages and a slight but not spectacular increase overall. After World War II, however, with rapid urbanization, a shift from a subsistence economy to wage labor, and improved medical services, the Motu population began to increase rapidly. For example, village population records show that the total population resident in the fourteen Motu villages increased between 1954 and 1968 from approximately 7,500 to 13,500. Precise figures on a village basis are no longer available, but the Motu population has continued to increase rapidly and may now number more than 25,000. Doubtless because of their proximity to Port Moresby, the Motu have played a role in the history and development of Papua New Guinea disproportionate to their numbers.

Linguistic Affiliation. In common with some other peoples scattered over Papua New Guinea's coastal periphery and offshore islands, the Motu speak an Austronesian language, classified in the Central Family, Eastern Subgroup.

History and Cultural Relations

Available archaeological evidence suggests that the Motu, seafarers with their own distinctive maritime culture and ceramic tradition, first occupied their present habitat comparatively recently in the history of settlement on New Guinea's southern shores. From 1872, when the first Christian missionaries arrived, through the entire colonial period inaugurated in 1884 with the establishment of a British protectorate, Motu—particularly in the Port Moresby villages—participated actively and significantly in the social, economic, and political developments that culminated in the establishment of Papua New Guinea as an independent nation-state in 1975. The early colonial government employed Motu speakers—including policemen recruited from the Solomon Islands who acquired a knowledge of simplified Motu when stationed in Port Moresby and, subsequently, Motu themselves—in remoter administrative districts. As a result, a simplified version of the Motu language, at first called "Police Motu," but now known officially as "Hiri Motu," became established as a lingua franca in Papua. Motu from Port Moresby villages, educated in English at their mission school, were also recruited to clerical or commercial jobs in Port Moresby. Nevertheless, before World War II, only a small proportion of Motu in the Port Moresby villages and almost none from other villages worked for wages, and most villagers made their living from traditional subsistence activities. Since World War II, Motu—first from the Port Moresby villages and then from the remoter villages as they were connected to the town by road—have increasingly entered the work force of Port Moresby's expanding commercial, industrial, and service economy, until today almost all Motu men and many women work full-time for wages in the town; those from nearer villages commute daily, and those from remoter villages live in town during the working week and return home at the weekends. As the Motu work force was absorbed into the urban economy, traditional economic enterprises declined and eventually disappeared. Apart from a few commercial fishermen, most able-bodied Motu men and many women are today urban workers: entrepreneurial, professional, white-collar, and blue-collar. Traditionally, Motu maintained trading relationships and lived in peace with some of their immediate inland neighbors, with whom they traded mainly fish for vegetables and fruit, and with the Erema and Toaripi peoples some distance west across the Gulf of Papua, to whose villages they made annual overseas trading expeditions (known as *hiri*), exchanging pottery and ceremonial ornaments for sago, canoe hulls, and areca nuts. Outside of these exchange relationships, contacts with other neighboring peoples prior to colonization were fortuitous and hostile.

Settlements

Motu villages were traditionally closely nucleated, the houses typically built out in lines over the water. Wooden walkways linked the houses in each line. Each of the independent, localized descent groups (*iduhu*), which together constituted the village polity, occupied its own line of houses. Although large numbers of Motu still live over the water in this way, many others have now built houses ashore. Traditionally, Motu traveled between villages by canoe or on foot, but now all Motu villages are linked to Port Moresby, and they can thus be reached from each other, by road.

Economy

Subsistence and Commercial Activities. Traditionally, Motu grew yams and bananas, with other minor crops, in garden plots scattered along the shore and over the coastal hillsides, maintained clusters of coconut palms near their villages, reared pigs (primarily for ceremonial purposes), fished, and gathered shellfish and crabs. They did not, however, produce enough staple food to meet their needs, so they augmented their food stores by trading fish, pottery, and ceremonial ornaments with their neighbors and overseas trading partners.

Industrial Arts and Division of Labor. Traditionally, there were no specialist craft workers among the Motu. The only division of labor was sexual. All men fished, sailed on the hiri, and constructed canoes, houses, and fishing nets. All women gathered crabs and shellfish, manufactured pottery, cooked, and fetched water. In the gardens, the soil was first broken by men and then weeded and cleared by women, but crops were planted, tended, and harvested by both sexes together.

Trade. Trade transactions usually took the form of reciprocal gift exchanges, but on the hiri direct barter supplemented gift exchange. Gift exchanges involving ceremonial valuables (mainly arm shells and other ornaments, pigs, and yams) occurred between individuals and groups in different villages or iduhu at feasts with dancing, often associated with mortuary rites, and between kin and affines during marriage ceremonies. Except for a few commercial fishermen, Motu have not tried to find commercial markets for their traditional produce or to introduce new cash crops.

Land Tenure. In theory, Motu hold that rights to use or alienate any piece of land are shared by all descendants, through males or females or both, of the person who is known to have first cultivated or occupied it. In practice traditional rights to residential or garden land were mainly exercised by agnatic descendants, since males and their immediate families tended to live in the residential section (iduhu) and cultivate the land of their fathers, whereas females married out. In colonial and postcolonial times, however, when Motu sold land for cash sums that were easily divisible, all descendants of the original occupant shared in the proceeds.

Kinship

Kin Groups and Descent. There are two significant corporate groups in a Motu village: the household, comprising one or more nuclear families; and the iduhu, comprising a number of households located together in their own residential section of the village. Nuclear families within a household, and households within an iduhu, are usually linked by agnatic ties: between fathers, sons, and brothers in a household, and between agnatic descendants of its founder in an iduhu. Some rights (e.g., to share in an iduhu's fishing catch) extend also to sisters and their children, and some (e.g., to land) extend to further descendants bilaterally, but the core members of the iduhu with the strongest claims to its scarce material and ritual resources are agnates. Females marry out, but subsequently retain close bonds with their fathers and brothers.

Kinship Terminology. With one complication, Motu kinship terminology is of the so-called "Hawaiian" type, distinguishing cognates of one's own generation only by age (*kaka,* older; *tadi,* younger) or sex (*taihu,* opposite sex) and applying only one term (*tubu*) to all cognates of one's grandparents' or grandchildren's generation. The complication occurs in the terms used by proximate generations: In the generation of one's parents, mother's male cognates and husbands of father's female cognates (both called *vava*) and father's female cognates and the wives of mother's male cognates (*lala*) are distinguished from father and his male cognates (*tama*) and mother and her female cognates (*sina*), and these distinctions operate reciprocally for cognates of one's children's generation. This type of terminology, sometimes called bifurcate-merging, is associated with classificatory brother-sister exchange marriage, which was traditionally not uncommon among the Motu.

Marriage and Family

Marriage. Although, traditionally, important men sometimes married several wives, Motu marriages today are monogamous. There is a rule against marrying any cognate but traditionally marriage within the village was preferred, which sometimes severely limited the range of choices and encouraged relaxation of the rule in the case of distant cognates. Traditionally, too, marriages were arranged, and childhood betrothals were common, but nowadays young people are mainly free to choose their own spouses. Gift exchanges traditionally accompanied various stages in the process of betrothal and marriage, culminating in the main presentation of bride-wealth (in the past consisting mainly of arm shells but now including substantial sums of money). In recent times, bride-wealth inflation, led by wealthier Motu, has delayed or impeded this final legitimation of marriages according to Motu custom among the less wealthy. Residence after marriage was traditionally viripatrilocal. Divorce, involving a return of bride-wealth, was possible but infrequent.

Domestic Unit. Traditionally, household members pooled foodstuffs and cooked together, but component nuclear families ate separately. Households, or sometimes component nuclear families within households, maintained their own garden plots. Each household had its own small fishing nets, though larger nets were owned and operated by the whole iduhu.

Inheritance. Houses and major household effects were (and are) usually inherited by the householder's oldest son. Other sons and their families might continue to live there, but they would seek eventually to establish their own separate households.

Socialization. All members of the household help in caring for and raising children, but mothers undertake the major chores. Traditional skills were learned by boys from their fathers and other senior men of the household, and by girls from their mothers and other senior women.

Sociopolitical Organization

Although there are perceived to be specific historical links between certain Motu villages, traditionally all villages were politically independent and there was no formal sociopolitical organization above the village level.

Social Organization. Normally, the senior married male agnate is recognized within an iduhu as its leader, and within a household as its head, and the status of other male members is determined by genealogical seniority both between and within generations. At the village level, there was traditionally no formal status hierarchy, but prominent men, for the most part iduhu leaders, competed for status and influence through the sponsorship and management of enterprises that conferred prestige, such as hiri expeditions, feasts with dancing, bride-wealth payments, and (in precolonial times) feats of military leadership. Nowadays, in the cash economy, Motu men of outstanding achievement seek—through bride-wealth payments, hospitality, and other forms of conspicuous consumption—to convert wealth into status, influence, and, ultimately, public office.

Political Organization. Political decisions at the village level were traditionally achieved and maintained through public debate, in which political leaders (big-men) used a rhetoric invoking their superior achievements and prestige, which in turn reflected the range and size of their support networks, to "shame" other participants out of contention until a clear victor or a winning consensus emerged. In the modern postindependence polity, important decisions affecting the Motu are made by politicians who build on local support to pursue power through formal organizations (including political parties) and informal alliances, all operating within a wider structure of democratically elected local, regional, and national legislatures and their supporting bureaucracies.

Conflict. At the village level, competition and conflict were endemic and essential features of the traditional Motu way of life: ultimately, victory over their rivals in the rhetoric of the political arena motivated individuals and groups to work, compete, and achieve to their maximum capacity. Victory was never complete, defeat rarely absolute; the pursuit of advantage was never-ending. Consensus—or, in its absence and as a last resort, physical confrontation—might temporarily give victory in a dispute to one party over the other, and the loser might offer a gift to placate the winner for the time being, but most losers withdrew only to fight again another day. Beyond the village, oral traditions and early historical records suggest that Motu engaged in warfare or conducted raids intermittently against other neighboring peoples and even sometimes against other Motu villages. Such warfare, endemic in this area, was eventually suppressed by the British administration after its establishment in 1884.

Social Control. Within the iduhu, traditionally, social control was usually maintained and conflict avoided or resolved through the exercise of agnatic authority, supported by ancestral ritual sanctions.

Religion and Expressive Culture

The Motu were the first people in mainland Papua New Guinea to receive Christian missionaries, and most Motu are now church members. For some generations, however, Christianity and traditional religious beliefs coexisted.

Religious Beliefs. Motu traditionally believed that their well-being depended on the continued support of their ancestral spirits, who were believed to go after death to a place of plenty over the sea, to the west, but who were thought also to maintain a concern for, and spiritual contact with, their living descendants in the village. Households and iduhu regularly performed mystical rites instituted by their ancestors to promote success in such enterprises as gardening, fishing, and the hiri. The ancestors of a household or iduhu were thought to monitor the behavior of members and to punish misbehavior by inflicting illness or misfortune.

Religious Practitioners. There were no specialist religious practitioners in traditional Motu society, except for diviners who could identify certain illnesses and calamities as punishments for particular infringements of the ancestral code or as the effects of sorcery (*mea*) or witchcraft (*vada*). The Motu believed that, in general, only Koita and other neighboring peoples practiced sorcery and witchcraft, but individual Motu could buy or otherwise enlist their services or skills.

Ceremonies. To gain the ancestors' support or to placate them, Motu traditionally held private ceremonies at the sacred place (*irutahuna*) of a house or canoe. Following the death of an important household member, to ensure a successful transition to the world of ancestral spirits, a series of public ceremonies took place over several years or more, culminating in a major feast with dancing (*turia*) during which the deceased's bones were disinterred.

Arts. Traditionally, Motu women were elaborately tattooed, but the practice has now ceased. Their ceramics (cooking pots, water jars, and food platters) were elegant but plain, with little decoration. Motu achieved their most spectacular artistic expression in their dances in which, with elaborate feather headdresses, brightly painted faces, arm shells and plaited amulets, colorful grass skirts on the women, and elegant perineal bands on the men, they danced in various formations to the percussion rhythms of wooden hourglass drums. Early missionaries viewed Motu dancing as a prelude to sexual abandon, and they forbade it. For some generations, Motu were divided between Christians, who did not dance, and pagans, who did. Although the Christians eventually won, some of the dance forms still survive, but only as cultural relics performed occasionally for tourists or in historical pageants.

See also Koiari, Namau, Orokolo

Bibliography

Belshaw, Cyril S. (1957). *The Great Village.* London: Routledge & Kegan Paul.

Dutton, Tom, ed. (1982). *The Hiri in History.* Pacific Research Monograph no. 8. Canberra: Australian National University.

Groves, Murray (1960). "Western Motu Descent Groups." *Ethnology* 1:15–30.

Seligmann, C. G. (1910). *The Melanesians of British New Guinea.* Cambridge: Cambridge University Press.

MURRAY GROVES

Mountain Arapesh

ETHNONYMS: Arapesh, Bukiyip

Orientation

Identification. The name "Mountain Arapesh" is used today to designate speakers of the three eastern dialects of the Arapesh language in the East Sepik Province of Papua New Guinea. The people described here, however, are the group Margaret Mead and Reo Fortune intended by the name, the people who occupied the southern two-thirds of the northeast dialect region. Although the Mountain Arapesh are called "Pukia" and "Bukiyip" by their neighbors, they have no name for themselves: "Arapesh" is simply their word for "friends" or "humans."

Location. Mountain Arapesh territory is located in the central mountains of the coastal Prince Alexander and Torricelli ranges, between 3°27' and 3°34' S and 143°09' and 143°19' E. Annual rainfall exceeds 250 centimeters over most of the area.

Demography. In 1932, there were at least thirteen and possibly more than twenty Mountain Arapesh "localities" with 200–300 people each, giving a total population between about 2,600 and 6,000 and a population density somewhere in the range of 9–20 persons per square kilometer.

Linguistic Affiliation. Mountain Arapesh is the northernmost of the Bukiyip dialects, which are linguistically chained with the Muhiang dialects to the west. This dialect chain is part of the Arapesh Language Family, commonly assigned to the Kombio Stock of the Torricelli Phylum.

History and Cultural Relations

The Mountain Arapesh are bordered by the Ndu-speaking Boiken in the east, the Kaboibus Arapesh (Mead's "Plains Arapesh") in the south, the Muhiang Arapesh in the west, and the Beach Arapesh in the north. Beyond the fact that their occupation of the coastal ranges predates the arrival of the Ndu-speaking people to their south, little is known of the Mountain Arapesh prior to European contact around the turn of the century. Contact itself had an enormous impact on their life: by the time Mead and Fortune studied them in 1932, stone tools had disappeared, warfare had been suppressed for over a decade, missionaries had become regular visitors, more than 20 percent of adult males were away working on European stations or plantations, and there had been at least one cargo cult. During World War II, fierce fighting between the Japanese and Australians prompted many Mountain Arapesh to desert their villages for the bush, and the following decade saw large-scale migration out of the mountains to the coast and inland foothills. Consequently, it is doubtful if life in the few Mountain Arapesh settlements remaining today bears much resemblance to that described by Mead and Fortune.

Settlements

The Mountain Arapesh lived in small hamlets of about six houses located on the leveled crests of densely forested, razorbacked ridges. Each hamlet was owned by a patrilineage, though under the fluid nature of Mountain Arapesh social organization, residents often included households belonging to other patrilineages. In each locality, there was also a central *wabul,* or "feasting village," where the locality's ceremonial feasts and *tambaran* cult houses were sited. There were two basic house structures: the pile house, raised 3 feet off the ground on stilts and occasionally gabled; and the ground house, built directly on the earth. They were thatched with sago palm fronds or tiles of sago leaflets and walled with sago bark shingles, sago fronds, or coconut fronds.

Economy

Subsistence and Commercial Activities. The mainstays of Mountain Arapesh subsistence were yams and taro, cultivated separately by slash-and-burn horticulture, and a feasting dependence on sago. Supplements included bananas, greens, sugarcane, bamboo sprouts, breadfruit, coconuts, and a wide variety of game, including pigs, cassowaries, a range of smaller ground and arboreal mammals, birds, grubs, and fish. Pigs and dogs were the main domestic animals.

Industrial Arts. Mountain Arapesh manufactures included tools, weapons, cooking and eating utensils, net bags, basketry, clothing, and body ornaments.

Trade. Self-sufficient in subsistence items, the Mountain Arapesh nonetheless were active participants in the Sepik Basin's extensive ritual, artistic, and ceremonial trade. Their principal traffic was in stone tools, bows, net bags, pottery, carved plates, masks, shell valuables, dogs' teeth, musical instruments, magic, songs, and dance complexes. Their own productions for this trade were rather meager, prompting Mead to label them an "importing culture," but they occasionally exported pigs, puppies, net bags, carved plates, sago, bird feathers, tobacco, and hospitality.

Division of Labor. There was a distinct division of labor. Men were responsible for fighting, hunting, clearing and fencing gardens, planting and harvesting the yams and sago, cooking ceremonial food, carving, and building houses. Women reared pigs, did the daily cooking and most of the portering, planted and harvested taro, bananas, and greens, fetched water, and foraged for firewood, bush foods, caterpillars, and grubs. Both sexes participated in child care, fishing, and the manufacture of ornaments, clothing, and twine.

Land Tenure. The living conceived of themselves not as owning the land but rather as belonging to it. The land, the trees growing on it, and the game supported by it belonged to the shades and *walin* (spirit of the lineage), and in this sense land was associated with the lineage. In theory, a man could dispose of the lands he inherited as he wished; in practice, he favored his sons, though sometimes he conferred land on his brothers' or on his sisters' husbands and sons. Fishing and transit rights were vested in the settlement as a whole.

Kinship

Kin Groups and Descent. The principal kin groups had a patrilineal ideology, often spanning many generations, but individuals frequently affiliated with, or were adopted into, groups to which they had no patrilineal link. Some of these "patrilineages" recognized themselves as collateral descendants of an eponymous ancestor and therefore could be called "clans." Patrilineages were named and totemically identified with a walin (plural: *walinab*) spirit. Alitoa locality contained eleven such patrilineages, each with an average of 3.8 households and twenty members.

Kinship Terminology. Kinship terminology was of the Omaha type.

Marriage and Family

Marriage. The Arapesh girl was betrothed between the ages of about 6 and 10 to a husband a few years her senior. According to Mead, sometime before the appearance of her secondary sexual characteristics she moved to his hamlet to be "fed and grown . . . until she becomes one of them." Marriage was proscribed within one's own lineage and with those from which one's lineage had either given or received women in the preceding three generations. Marriage involved bridewealth payments and initiated a relationship in which shell valuables and raw meat moved from the groom's to the bride's descent group at the births, woundings, and deaths of their children. According to Mead, "for one marriage that fails . . . the great majority succeed"; divorces, when they occurred, were engineered as "abductions" of the wife. A preference was expressed for "true" or "near" sister exchange, but only about 4 percent of Alitoa-locality marriages were real sister exchanges. Marriage was virilocal, with many women marrying beyond the locality (55 percent in Alitoa), usually towards the sea. Polygyny was pervasive: sixteen of the forty-two households in Alitoa locality were polygynous. Men with more than one wife benefited in a multitude of political, economic, and social ways, but polygyny resulted most commonly from the levirate.

Domestic Unit. The nuclear, frequently polygynous, family formed the basic household, with the father's parents, unmarried siblings, and sons' betrotheds the most common additions. This group averaged five individuals, with a range of about two to nine, and occupied either an entire hamlet or several adjacent houses in a hamlet.

Inheritance. Individuals owned whatever they had made, purchased, or been given, and they could dispose of it as they wished. Some clans owned *ginyau,* or traditional heirlooms, but it is unclear how these items were inherited.

Socialization. Although mothers devoted more time to child rearing than fathers, both parents delighted in the task. As the child grew older, he or she often left the parental home to stay awhile with other relatives, and around the age of 7 or 8, girls went to live with and be raised by their betrothed's kin. Gentleness, docility, responsiveness, and cooperativeness were the cardinal virtues that the socialization process sought to instill.

Sociopolitical Organization

Political Organization. The patrilineages of several hamlets formed a named "hamlet center" or "village." Several hamlet centers in turn formed a "locality" or "sovereign group" of 200 to 300 people: Alitoa locality had four hamlet centers and a total population of 217. Localities were territorially defined and, in essence, were military confederacies. Their patrilineages were divided on a territorial basis between the *Ginyau* and *Iwhul* moieties, totemically represented in most cases by the hawk and parrot, respectively. Adult males inherited, usually patrilineally, a competitive exchange partner (*buanyin*) from the opposite moiety, and the exchange of yams, pigs, and game between these partners played a prominent role in political practice. There being no concept of rank, hereditary authority, or organized leadership, politics revolved around big-men, who climbed to influence on the basis of ability, ambition, and performance in feast giving and exchanges with buanyin, gift friends, and *gabunyan* partners. Gift friendships and gabunyan partnerships were the principal links besides marriage among localities. Each patrilineage had gift friends in neighboring localities, and these partnerships linked localities into one of three major trading "roads" that crossed the mountains from the inland foothills to the sea, providing safe routes to move abroad and trade in "secular" items of ceremonial and artistic culture. The gabunyan partnerships existed between the most important men of the localities and were vehicles by which a locality purchased the "esoteric" dance complexes, masks, and services related to the *wareh* (tambaran) initiation cult.

Conflict. "Warfare was good Arapesh custom," and approximately half of the older men claimed at least one battle kill to their credit. Sometimes war broke out among the patrilineages of a locality, but more usually it occurred among localities, especially those lying on different trade routes. Interlocality fighting was precipitated primarily by the abduction of women (with their consent), and it took the form of ambushes on hamlets or confrontations across traditional battlefields situated on locality frontiers. On very rare occasions, conflict within a patrilineage also precipitated homicide.

Social Control. Mead may have overemphasized the gentle and unaggressive nature of Mountain Arapesh life, but it is clear that docility and altruism were highly valued. There were few mechanisms for controlling deviance but, informally, gossip and ostracism evidently were used to advantage. At a more formal level, sorcery and invocations to the ancestors were available to the disgruntled, and a man could revenge himself on a delinquent sister's husband by cursing the sister and her children to death. Men who had been publically abused by a wife or young relative might be subject to the discipline of the tambaran, also called the wareh, carried out by a group of men who came at night to destroy some man's property.

Religion and Expressive Culture

Religious Beliefs. Mountain Arapesh cosmology was not tightly integrated. The elements of the universe were viewed as either "given" or as the vaguely defined creations of walinab spirits, and they were believed principally to be influenced by ancestral spirits, walinab, and magical forces. The principal supernaturals were the walinab spirits and the ancestral shades. The giant walinab were responsible for rainbows. Lesser walinab occupied waterholes, bogs, and declivities and occasionally appeared as monstrous, two-headed snakes or lizards or as deformed animals. Each patrilineage was identified with a walin spirit that was believed to associate mystically with the group's ancestral shades and guard its lands against trespass and transgression.

Religious Practitioners. Since knowledge of many magical and ritual practices was widely diffused through the community, there was limited opportunity for the emergence of formal religious or magical specialists. The main exception was the patrilineage with the traditional right to act as incisor in male initiation, though an individual or patrilineage occasionally gained a temporary specialism in some novel, imported ritual practice.

Ceremonies. The main ceremonies were associated with the life cycle, the wareh (tambaran), and feasts for exchange partners. Birth, preadolescent growth, initiation, marriage, menstruation, and death were observed for both sexes in rites varying in complexity from the simple taboos associated with preadolescent growth to the elaborate, interlocality male initiation rituals. Tambaran rituals, involving a noise-making device represented as a being, were staged during male initiations or when an important man had been insulted by a wife or young relative. Large ceremonies were also held to feast buanyin or gabunyan as a return for previous feasts, to "pay" for initiation services, to celebrate house construction, or to purchase elements of the tambaran complex.

Arts. Although most graphic, plastic, and ephemeral art was imported, the Mountain Arapesh produced plaited armlets and belts, dogs'-teeth decorations, ornamented spinning tops, masks, painted sago-bark panels, and slit gongs. Songs appear to have been the major ephemeral productions.

Medicine. The principal cause of sickness was sorcery performed on a victim's exuviae, though ancestral spirits, walinab, pollution by females or the young, protective magic placed on property, and infractions of ritual and taboo were also frequently blamed.

Death and Afterlife. The soul (*mishin*) was believed to survive death as a white spirit that departed variously to the ocean, its patrilineage's walin or borderlands, or to old breadfruit trees. After relatives had been summoned on the slit gongs, the corpse was mourned formally for up to a day and then buried in a grave at the center of the hamlet plaza, under a little house containing some food and the deceased's personal property. The bones of particularly esteemed individuals were later exhumed and, in the case of males, used magically to acquire the deceased's special abilities.

See also Yangoru Boiken

Bibliography

Fortune, Reo F. (1939). "Arapesh Warfare." *American Anthropologist* 41:22–41.

Mead, Margaret (1939–1949). *The Mountain Arapesh*. 5 vols. New York: American Museum of Natural History Anthropological Papers.

Rubel, Paula G., and Abraham Rosman (1978). *Your Own Pigs You May Not Eat*. Chicago: University of Chicago Press.

PAUL ROSCOE

Mundugumor

ETHNONYMS: Biwat, Mundokuma, Mundugamor

Orientation

Identification. The Mundugumor live in the area of the central Yuat River in the East Sepik Province of Papua New Guinea. "Mundugumor" is an old name relating to their art styles; contemporary residents typically refer to themselves as "Biwats," the name of one of their villages as well as the name sometimes given to the Yuat River.

Location. The dominant geographical feature of the Sepik region is the Sepik River itself, which meanders down from mountains through the hills, swamps, and grassland plains of the province. One of its major tributaries is the Yuat, a swift-moving and strongly currented river that floods periodically. Although swamps and grasslands predominate to the north and south, the Mundugumor environment includes rain forest as well. The climate is tropical; the rainy season extends from approximately November through March.

Linguistic Affiliation. Biwat is a member of the Yuat Language Family.

Demography. The total population of the Mundugumor at the beginning of this century was probably about 1,000 people. Land and environmental resources were ample to support such a population. However, the population has increased steadily, and now land and resource pressures are being felt. Many people today leave the area and obtain jobs in towns and cities; some participate in resettlement schemes in nearby areas such as Angoram.

History and Cultural Relations

Little is known about the history of the Mundugumor before Western contact. Tradition says that the villages were founded by people coming from the west. A significant event was a change in the course of the Yuat River, a change that left two of the villages in the bush and made river villages of the other four. Western contact came early in this century in the form of German and Australian traders, administrators, and missionaries. Warfare and raiding as well as many ceremonial activities ceased. Men began to leave their villages to work on coastal plantations for extended periods. Although a complete mission station with airstrip and resident priest was not established until 1956, mission effects were present much earlier. There is now a school in the village of Biwat, and many children continue additional education outside of the area and go on to skilled and professional jobs in urban settings.

Settlements

The Mundugumor were composed of six villages: four along the banks of the Yuat River and two in the bush. Village size probably ranged from 108 to 200 people. Villages were not compact, nucleated settlements but rather a series of hamlets associated with one another. There were no central plazas or permanent ritual or men's houses. Today, the four river villages have almost grown together, but traditional house style has changed little. Houses were made from natural materials of sago ribs and leaves, oil-palm bark, and substantial posts and were built approximately 5 feet above the ground. Some families constructed additional temporary shelters near their distant gardens.

Economy

Subsistence and Commercial Activities. The traditional subsistence base was sago supplemented mainly by fish but also by game and garden produce. Gardens yielded bananas, coconuts, taro, sweet potatoes, and yams. A few pigs were kept as well. Pigs, cassowaries, marsupials, and birds were hunted. Betel nuts and tobacco were important crops that gave the Mundugumor hegemony in the regional trading system. Tobacco and betel nuts are still important as commercial crops, but introduced cash crops such as coffee, rubber, copra, and rice are also important. A few cattle are kept today as well as pigs and chickens.

Industrial Arts and Trade. There were no craft specialists; most adults made items of material culture that they needed. However, the Mundugumor did not make pottery or large baskets but traded tobacco, betel nuts, and garden products for them with their inland neighbors. Their environment lacked stone, so they traded shell and shell rings (obtained from downriver groups) with upriver peoples for stone and stone tools and other mountain products.

Division of Labor. There was an informal division of labor by age but by far the most important division of labor was by sex. Men conducted most of the ritual events, cleared the land for gardening, hunted, and did the major work in house and canoe construction. Men also conducted warfare and intergroup raiding. Women were in charge of day-to-day living and did most of the subsistence labor: they gardened, fished, cooked, and cared for the children. Sago processing required the participation of both men and women, men to cut and women to scrape.

Land Tenure. Land was loosely associated with patrilineal groups but people had the right to ask to use land that belonged to any relative with whom they were friendly and who had adequate land; rarely were such requests denied.

Kinship

Kin Groups and Descent. There were, and are today, patrilineal clans, but apart from being loosely associated with particular tracts of land, these groups were relatively unimportant. An individual's kin network, including affinal and matrilateral relatives, was more important. Exchange transactions among these kin down through the generations were very significant. Although Margaret Mead labeled these "ropes" descent groups, the term "rope" more likely served as a metaphor for the complex series of exchanges that commenced with a brother-sister exchange marriage and ended with another exchange marriage five generations later (rarely accomplished). These transactions highlighted the important roles of mother's brother and father's sister as well as brother and sister.

Kinship Terminology. Hawaiian-type terminology was used in one's own first descending generation, but Iroquois-type terms were used in the first ascending generation; that is, mother's brother was distinguished from father and father's sister distinguished from mother. It was possible to modify the kin terms for brother and sister to describe a "distant" sibling. A distinction was also made between older and younger same-sex siblings.

Marriage and Family

Marriage. Marriage formed the basis for Mundugumor social organization not only because a married couple was the core of a household but also because the affinal bond it created was a central cooperative bond and because it provided the structure for all significant exchange transactions for several generations. Brother-sister exchange was the preferred way to marry. A man carefully guarded rights to his sister against both his brothers and his father, who might try to use her in an exchange for a wife for themselves. Ideally these marriages were between distant siblings (classificatory cross cousins). On occasion marriage occurred by payment rather than sister exchange, but these unions usually involved undesirable women or very influential men. Some powerful men enticed women to marry them and offered no compensation, and women stolen from enemy groups were rarely reciprocated. Residence was predominantly patrivirilocal, but a man was under some pressure to live and work with his affines if he had not reciprocated a sister to his wife's brother. Marriages were especially unstable in the early stages, and women not infrequently packed up and went home to their own families or men refused to acknowledge new wives. But after the birth of children, marriages tended to become more stable. Polygyny was an ideal men tried to accomplish, but only a few of the more powerful leaders had more than two or three wives.

Domestic unit. Household organization depended on the number of wives present. In a simple man's household, one or two wives and their children might occupy a single structure. In a leader's hamlet, there might be a house for each of several wives, a house for adolescent sons, and a separate house for the household head. Each wife had her own hearth and cooked separately for her husband. The senior wife often cooked for all of her husband's children.

Inheritance. Inheritance rules varied. Access to land of course descended patrilineally, but a variety of other goods and rights went to sisters' children and from them to classificatory sisters' children.

Socialization. Children were not especially loved or prized, and newly married couples did not always look upon pregnancy with happiness. Women and men both disliked the taboos that were incumbent upon them during pregnancy and with newborns, and mothers resented the restrictions on their freedom that children required. Children were cared for but not especially nurtured. Both boys and girls grew up assertive, tough, and independent.

Sociopolitical Organization

Social and Political Organization. The basic social organization was provided by networks of related kin more than the patrilineal clans; interpersonal alliances shifted frequently. Leadership was achieved by individuals who were fierce in warfare and raiding, aggressive, and capable of attracting adherents through the manipulation of exchanges. These strong leaders earned many wives (who produced tobacco and other produce for them) and had the support of their affines as well as less-dominant kin of their own and meeker men seeking shelter. Contemporary Mundugumor participate in the parliamentary democracy that is the independent nation of Papua New Guinea. They elect representatives to a variety of local and national legislative bodies. Although war leaders have vanished, individuals who excel in various new endeavors, such as education or business, have significant influence.

Social Control. A variety of sanctions operated. Physical coercion was not uncommon, but at least as important were crosscutting kinship ties and obligations that generated conflicting loyalties. A strong egalitarian ideology also tended to prevent the construction of permanent alliances, and strong men could not violate rules and norms excessively or their followers would defect to their rivals.

Conflict. Conflict was common. Intracommunity disputes arose over a variety of concerns, most frequently the arrangement of brother-sister exchange marriages or adultery. Mundugumor villages fought one another over a variety of issues including the maintenance of reputation and honor. Warfare and raiding were also prevalent before colonialism; raids were staged on enemy villages in order to kill as many of the enemy as possible. Alliances with other groups were precarious and shifted frequently.

Religion and Expressive Culture

Religious Beliefs. The Mundugumor acknowledged the existence of a variety of unseen but controllable forces in the universe. Much of their religious activity centered around trying to affect or control these forces. As a result of missionary activity, today the majority of people adhere to the Catholic faith but acknowledge that some of their old beliefs still remain. The Mundugumor pantheon was not a complex one. Most prominent were a variety of water and bush spirits that were associated with particular tracts of land. Spirits of the dead also were recognized. Mythical persons were able to tap into different kinds of unnamed power contained in the universe at will.

Religious Practitioners. There were some people who were more adept at dealing with these forces than others: curers, diviners, some ritual specialists, but none of these positions was recognized and permanent. Individuals also owned (inherited or bought) their own means of control—spells, charms, and so on—and by a variety of magical acts attempted to harness the forces postulated by them.

Ceremonies. There were many ceremonial and ritual activities, including acts to ensure good gardening (especially of the long yam) and to ensure safe life-crisis passages. Initiations focused on admitting young men (and sometimes women) to view sacred objects; each such object had its own separate ritual initiation.

Arts. Mundugumor art was predominantly concerned with the sacred and efforts to control it. Sculpture and painting were the main media, and the style was affected by the mainstream art of the Middle Sepik region.

Medicine. Curing rituals focused on ascertaining the cause of the illness—sorcery, soul loss, taboo violation, etc.—and attempting to correct the situation.

Death and Afterlife. Death that was not the result of obvious natural causes such as warfare was usually attributed to sorcery. After death, a part of an individual's nonphysical essence left the body and became a ghost who inhabited areas associated with the patrilineal clan. Mortuary rituals were designed to care for the body and release the ghost from the village.

Bibliography

McDowell, Nancy (forthcoming). *The Mundugumor: From the Field Notes of Margaret Mead and Reo Fortune.* Washington, D.C.: Smithsonian Institution Press.

Mead, Margaret (1934). "Tambarans and Tumbuans 1935 in New Guinea." *Natural History* 34:234–246.

Mead, Margaret (1935). *Sex and Temperament in Three Primitive Societies.* New York: William Morrow.

NANCY MCDOWELL

Murik

ETHNONYMS: Karau, Kaup, Mayet

Orientation

Identification. The term "Murik" is generally used to refer to people living in five villages (Kaup, Big Murik, Darapap, Karau, Mendam) along the north coast of Papua New Guinea, west of the mouth of the Sepik River. Local differentiations designate three clusters of related villages from west to east: Kaup, Mayet (Big Murik), and Karau (Darapap, Karau, and Mendam). Originally "Murik" was used by coastal peoples to the west to refer to the Mayet. The Murik are culturally similar to other peoples of the region, but language and subsistence bases differ widely. The Murik, with the exception of Kaup, are generally "landless," and they trade throughout the region.

Location. The Murik reside along the north coast of Papua New Guinea in the East Sepik Province in the Sepik estuary, an area of mangrove lakes, swamps, and sandy beaches. The Murik Lakes region is humid and flat. The villages are located on narrow sandbanks that separate the lakes from the open ocean. During the wet season, November to May, a northwesterly wind prevails, bringing blustery late-afternoon winds, thunderstorms, heavy rainfall, and somewhat cooler temperatures. The transition from wet to dry season is marked by extreme high "spring" tides and by periods of complete stillness. Despite high humidity during the dry season, approximately June to October, there are droughts of several weeks' duration that cause severe shortages of fresh water. The northeasterly onshore breezes of this season, combined with longer periods of clear weather and calm seas, lead the Murik to refer to this as the good season for travel to town markets and visits to trade partners throughout the region.

Demography. The indigenous population of the villages is approximately 1,500 people. Village size varies from 80 to 450 people. Several hundred Murik live in the provincial capital, Wewak, and other towns. The postcontact population of the villages remains fairly constant due to out-migration.

Linguistic Affiliation. Murik is a Non-Austronesian or Papuan language of the Nor Family, which includes Chambri, Karawari, Yimas, Angoram, and Kopar. These groups are scattered throughout the Sepik Basin, suggesting a history of extensive migration. Many Murik know several languages of the region. Formerly communication with trade partners was ensured by sending children to live in a trade partner's village for a year. Most Murik now speak the vernacular and Melanesian Pidgin.

History and Cultural Relations

Recent archaeological evidence suggests that the mangrove lakes are the result of the river filling in an extensive inland sea 1,000 years ago. The Murik origin myth describes an extensive migration from Moim, on the Sepik River near Angoram, to the coast and offshore islands, eventually settling in the Murik Lakes at least 400 years ago. During the migration period, the Non-Austronesian or Papuan people from the Sepik Basin had extensive contact with Austronesian-speaking peoples who inhabited the offshore islands and some regions of the coast. Murik culture thus became an integration of Austronesian and Non-Austronesian cultural features. The first recorded mention of Murik is in 1616, when they visited a Dutch sailing vessel piloted by Jacob le Maire. Subsequently, German survey expeditions of the Sepik River collected artifacts from the region. Because the land was unsuitable for establishing copra plantations, this area was little influenced by traders and planters during the years of German colonial administration (1884 to World War I). By about 1913, a German Catholic missionary, Father Joseph Schmidt, S.V.D., had established a mission station at Big Murik. He remained there until 1942. German New Guinea was placed under military occupation by an Australian military force from 1914 to 1918. During this period German troops landed at Kaup and proceeded through the Murik villages, burning the men's houses and destroying many sacred objects in punishment for a Murik head-hunting raid. This event was followed by a long period of relative quiet during which the Murik extended their trade network and some took up work in towns, on plantations, and in various branches of colonial government. In 1942 the Japanese occupied the Murik Lakes for approximately nine months, followed by a bombing raid by Australian and American forces in 1943. Many people were killed and injured and the rest fled to the mangroves. Under Australian administration, the Murik took advantage of opportunities for education and employment. During the transition from colonial to independent government, Michael Somare of Karau village became a national political leader and was elected first Prime Minister of Papua New Guinea (1975). Mission influence since 1942 has been mainly through the Catholic mission at Marienberg. In 1952 a Seventh-Day Adventist church and school were established in Darapap village.

Settlements

The villages located on the ocean beach have been subjected to extensive damage from onshore storms and high seas. Where sufficient land is available, houses are arranged in sections by descent group. In Big Murik, Darapap, and Karau this orderly arrangement has been disrupted by shifts in the coastline and land shortages. The present village sites face the mangrove lakes. Houses are built on stilts from 4 to 8 feet above the ground. Shells and coconut refuse accumulate below houses to increase the dry land area. Canoes are built and maintained in proximity to the owners' houses. Large ceremonial houses (*taab*) are constructed by descent groups to house sacred objects and to perform secret rituals. Smaller men's houses (*kamasaan*) are used for daily gatherings to discuss village affairs and to work on carvings. Very large domestic dwellings, inhabited by a senior woman and her family, are designated as ceremonial houses for women's ritual (*sambaan iran*). Household composition varies with the domestic life cycle but usually includes an extended family of three or four generations. New houses are built by young couples as their family outgrows the extended family household. Villages have small garden plots and coconut groves nearby, and coconut, betel, and fruit trees grow in and around the village. The mangroves are laced with hand-cut channels for fishing and harvesting shellfish. Many families also maintain fishing houses deep in the mangroves.

Economy

Subsistence and Commercial Activities. Subsistence is based on fishing and trade. Both men and women fish in the lakes and ocean, but women gather most of the shellfish from the mangroves. The staple starch is sago, obtained by trade with villages on the inland side of the lakes. Garden produce and pigs, used primarily for ritual feasts, are obtained from trade partners in coastal and lower river villages. Gardens are maintained by those who feel so inclined and are often pillaged by foraging children before the fruit is ripe. Murik engage in extensive commercial activities. They trade smoked fish, fresh shellfish, baskets, and shells for garden produce, betel nuts, tobacco, and pigs. Manufactured items such as pots, plates, and canoe logs are sought in exchange for baskets. The most prestigious trade involves nonmaterial goods such as carving motifs, basket designs, magic, songs, and dance complexes. Cash income is obtained through remittances from relatives working in towns and through the sale of fish, shellfish, baskets, and tourist carvings in town markets. The money is used for transportation (outboard motors and fuel), school fees, clothing, and small household items.

Industrial Arts. Murik men have a distinctive carving style. Many ritual and household objects are made of carved wood, including canoes, paddles, house posts, male and female figures, masks, food pounders, plates, and betel mortars. Women weave twill-plaited baskets or bags of various sizes decorated with colored and raised designs. Designs are owned by descent groups or by individuals and transmission of designs is carefully monitored. The baskets that are traded or sold to non-Murik and tourists usually carry designs designated for public use.

Trade. A history of extensive trade along the coast, river, and offshore islands has been documented from bibliographic sources. Men and women have inherited trade partners in other villages with whom they maintain obligations over multiple generations. Trade for sago is tinged with hostility, but it goes on of necessity throughout the year. Trade with coastal and island villages is conducted as hospitality and confined to the dry season. Coastal and island trade activities occur in preparation for ritual performance.

Division of Labor. There is a high degree of cooperation among men and women on behalf of the household and the descent group. Few tasks are exclusively male or female. In general, men's work includes fishing, carving, house building, maintaining coconut groves, organizing village affairs, and conducting overseas trade. Women's work includes cooking, fishing, processing the catch, basket weaving, primary responsibility for raising children, and selling in the market. Men and women collect firewood, maintain canoes, care for children, and trade for sago.

Land Tenure. Several types of land are distinguished—villages, coconut plantations, gardens, and mangroves. Open lakes are fished by all Murik. Land and mangrove waters are owned by the eldest sibling of the senior generation. He or she inherits from one or both parents the right to regulate use of land on behalf of the sibling group. Access to various types of land is allocated according to a rule of primogeniture.

Kinship

Kin Groups and Descent. Descent groups trace their origin to an eponymous named couple, brother-sister pair, or man with several wives. Each group has a history describing their arrival in the Murik Lakes from elsewhere in the region. These are named, corporate groups in which descent is traced ambilineally. Giving names to individuals is an important way of indicating group membership(s). Individual claims to membership are activated by participating in cooperative enterprises and ritual work. Groups compete for members by sponsoring life-cycle rituals on behalf of individuals, especially firstborns. Leadership within the descent group is validated by organizing trade activities, rituals, feasts, and dance performance.

Kinship Terminology. Terminology is of the Hawaiian type with special terms for mother's brother and father's sister.

Marriage and Family

Marriage. Marriage among the Murik is best characterized as brittle monogamy that eventually stabilizes around parenting responsibilities. There is no ritual to mark a marriage, but assent of parents and assurance of appropriate genealogical distance are important. The rule of exogamy is that spouses should be at least third cousins, though occasional exceptions occur, usually due to confusion over adoptive ties. The Murik say they formerly practiced sister-exchange marriage and never paid bride-wealth. Marriage to outsiders is considered acceptable, even advantageous, as it establishes kin obligations that may be exploited for trade purposes. There is customarily bride-service of several years, during which ideally the son-in-law builds a new house for his wife's parents. Then the couple may reside where they choose. Women say they prefer to live near their mother and sisters, while men say that they have better access to resources when living near their father and brothers. Married children may always move back to the parental household in case of conflict or divorce. The terms of divorce are settled among the descent groups of the marriage partners.

Domestic Unit. Married couples are responsible for the maintenance of their own nuclear families, but the unit of production is the sibling group. Adult siblings and their spouses cooperate in child care, food processing, trade, and daily exchange of foodstuffs, canoes, and fishing equipment.

Inheritance. Inheritance may be claimed through the father and/or mother and follows a rule of primogeniture within sibling groups. A firstborn sibling legitimates his or her position of ownership, responsibility, and leadership through work. He or she may be displaced by an ambitious younger sibling who must ritually retire older siblings in sequence. There is a strong preference for inheritance from father to son, but mother-son and father-daughter inheritance are not unusual.

Socialization. Children are encouraged to be independent and to take initiative. There is a low demand for obedience but a high expectation that older children, especially firstborns, assume responsibility for and indulge younger siblings. Classificatory mother's brothers and father's sisters spontaneously celebrate first achievements. These same ritual actors encourage social competence in children by publicly mocking their faux pas.

Sociopolitical Organization

Social Organization. Social organization is oriented toward the proliferation of ties to other individuals and groups through exchange relations. Adoption, fictive kinship, exogamy, and assimilation of others into Murik villages are means to this end. Descent groups are residentially dispersed and convene to legitimate the transfer of status and to coordinate trade and ritual work. Village loyalty is extremely high. Villages are affiliated through intermarriage, but those who marry in lack a local support group of cognatic kin.

Political Organization. Senior members of the descent groups in each village provide political leadership. These individuals control the descent-group insignia (*suman*), named ornaments of shells, feathers, and other valuables assembled and displayed on ritual occasions. The firstborn of a descent group in each village controls the suman, in whose presence there may be no conflict or violence. He or she thus manages resources, evaluates membership claims, and settles disputes. Transfer of suman from one individual to another must be legitimated by the combined leaders from all of the villages who give prior approval and attend in person the ritual bestowal of suman.

Social Control. Wrongdoing and guilt are indicated by untoward events, illness, or unexpected death. The causes are established by consulting oracles and developing a consensus interpretation. Public exposure of the offense is sufficient to curtail its consequences. Gossip and aggressive joking are important mechanisms of social control, as are mocking and mimicry by formal joking partners who must be compensated for their performances.

Conflict. Intratribal conflict occurs most frequently over sexual jealousy and group membership claims. These are settled either by a public hearing or negotiations among descent-group leaders, who may award compensation in the form of pigs. Prior to European intervention, armed conflict with non-Murik peoples, particularly the sago-producing villages, was the norm. Neighboring peoples sometimes arranged for the Murik to rid them of suspected sorcerers and other enemies.

Religion and Expressive Culture

Religious Beliefs. The indigenous religion is based on a multiplicity of local spirits who are instrumental in causing illness and death, in inspiring homicidal rage during headhunting and warfare, and in acting as individual guardians. Ancestor spirits maintain a continuous relationship with the world of the living and point out flaws in social life by making ill some member of the transgressor's family. Ceremonies to propitiate spirits and to ensure the vitality of the community are performed by the men's and women's secret societies. Present-day Christianity is practiced in a syncretic form and was originally accepted as a potential means to domination of others by providing access to a superior source of sacred power.

Religious Practitioners. Individuals learn, usually from a parent, special magic spells for effecting dream travel, weather control, healing, etc. Sexual prowess and strength in fighting are acquired from spirits who inhabit carved figures and masks on ritual occasions. Access is regulated through initiation into the secret societies of men and women. Some individuals are susceptible to possession by various kinds of spirits.

Ceremonies. There is an extensive series of life-cycle rituals, only some of which are observed for any one individual. Rituals celebrating specific first accomplishments are opportunities for establishing descent-group claims and are most often performed for firstborns. The four stages of initiation into the secret society of men or of women, retirement from the position of descent-group leader, mourning, and the end of mourning are other opportunities to reinforce or change descent-group affiliations. Other ceremonial occasions include consecration of domestic and cult houses and canoe launching.

Arts. Murik men make many kinds of carved wooden objects and body decorations of woven fiber, shell, and animal teeth. An elaborate series of fantastic spirit figure costumes is owned, made, and displayed by the age grades of the men's secret society. Murik women achieve regional reputations for their skill in weaving twill-plaited bags. Formerly they also wove large sleeping bags that had room for several people in them.

Medicine. The Murik attribute most illnesses to social causes, which means therefore that they have social remedies. Following diagnosis, symptoms are treated through herbal remedies or bloodletting; however, illness recurs if the social cause is not addressed. Malaria, colds, and headache are so common that they are not diagnosed as social ailments but are presumed to be caused by overwork and exposure. Aspirin is valued as a general remedy. Other forms of Western treatment are sought only after traditional remedies have failed.

Death and Afterlife. Death is believed to result from social causes. It is considered appropriate for old people, who have indicated their willingness to leave the realm of the living by asking that their particular basket be woven. Death is always an occasion for sorrow and loneliness, but when a child or an adult in the prime of life dies, the reaction is one of rage and sorcery is suspected. Death, fainting, and dreaming are evidence that the soul (*nabran*) has left the body. Upon death the soul hovers near close kin and may try to lure them away to the realm of the dead by offering food in a dream. Therefore, mourners are in a polluted state and do not cook or obtain foodstuffs. At the end-of-mourning ceremony the soul becomes an ancestor, sent away to a permanent dwelling place among the mangroves where other deceased members of the descent group reside. As an ancestor, it is propitiated for assistance, and it oversees the conduct of social affairs.

See also Wogeo

Bibliography

Barlow, Kathleen (1985). "The Role of Women in Intertribal Trade among the Murik of Papua New Guinea." *Research in Economic Anthropology* 7:95–122.

Lipset, David M. (1984). "Authority and the Maternal Presence: An Interpretive Ethnography of Murik Lakes Society, East Sepik Province, Papua New Guinea." Unpublished Ph.D. dissertation, University of California, San Diego.

Meeker, Michael, Kathleen Barlow, and David Lipset (1986). "Culture, Exchange, and Gender: Lessons from the Murik." *Cultural Anthropology* 1:6–73.

Schmidt, Joseph (1923–1924). "Die Ethnographie der Nor-Papua (Murik-Kaup-Karau) bei Dallmannhafen, Neu-Guinea." *Anthropos* 18–19:700–732.

Schmidt, Joseph (1926). "Die Ethnographie der Nor-Papua (Murik-Kaup-Karau) bei Dallmannhafen, Neu-Guinea." *Anthropos* 21:38–71.

Schmidt, Joseph (1933). "Neue Beiträge zur Ethnographie der Nor-Papua (Neuguinea)." *Anthropos* 28:663–682.

Somare, Michael (1975). *Sana: An Autobiography of Michael Somare.* Port Moresby: Niugini Press.

Swadling, Pamela, et al. (1985). *The Sepik-Ramu.* Boroko: Papua New Guinea National Museum and Art Gallery.

Tiesler, Frank (1969). *Die intertribalen Beziehungen an der Nordküste Neuguineas im Gebiet der Kleinen Schouten-Inseln.* Berlin: Akademie Verlag.

KATHLEEN BARLOW

Murngin

ETHNONYMS: Miwuyt, Wulamba (Cultural Bloc), Yolngu, Yuulngu

Orientation

Identification. Yolngu has generally replaced the term Murngin to refer to the indigenous people of the northeastern part of Arnhem Land in Australia. "Murngin" was the term that the anthropologist Lloyd Warner adopted in the 1930s to identify the region and its culturally similar peoples. Linguists working in the area in the 1960s and 1970s introduced the term "Yolngu language," since *yolngu* is the word for "Aboriginal human being" in all the dialects. Aboriginal people in the Yolngu-speaking area refer to themselves as yolngu (as well as identifying all Aboriginal Australians as yolngu). Within the Yolngu area are some twenty such language-named, land-owning groups. In addition to the names of language groups, Yolngu people describe and name themselves in a number of other ways, including the location and features of the land they own or where they live (for example, "beach people" or "river people").

Location. The Yolngu area is roughly triangular and is located between 11° and 15° S and 134° and 137° E. The northern and eastern "sides" are coastal and the third "side" runs inland southeast from Cape Stewart on the north to south of Rose River on the east. Northeastern Arnhem Land is monsoonal, with northwest winds bringing rain from about December until April or May.

Demography. The Aboriginal population within the Yolngu area is estimated at 3,500; the population is largely in developing towns and settlements that were formerly Protestant missions.

Linguistic Affiliation. Yolngu languages are classified as Pama-Nyungan along with others covering seven-eighths of Australia, but they are isolated geographically from other Pama-Nyungan languages. Yolngu speakers classify their languages according to their pronominal systems into some nine groups, and each group is labeled by their shared demonstrative "this/here." Two of the largest groups, in terms of number of named languages, also classify their speakers by moiety: *dhuwal* languages are all Dhuwa moiety, and *dhuwala* languages are all Yirratja moiety. Since the 1970s and the development of adult education and bilingual education programs, a substantial amount of written material is being produced in the Yolngu languages.

History and Cultural Relations

In Western Arnhem Land, an area to the west of the Yolngu, archaeologists have excavated several living sites more than 30,000 years old and one that may be more than 50,000 years old. It is likely that the Yolngu have been in northeastern Arnhem Land for a comparable period of time. Yolngu had only sporadic contacts with non-Aboriginal people until European occupation of the Northern Territory was under way in the last quarter of the nineteenth century, except for regular visits by Macassans, traders from the Celebes, who gathered bêche-de-mer annually from the late seventeenth century until 1907. Yolngu assisted the Macassans in gathering and processing the bêche-de-mer, and they obtained from them iron tools, cloth, tobacco, and the techniques of dugout-canoe construction. In the nineteenth century, explorers and prospectors began to make their way overland; around the coast government customs boats patrolled. The Arnhem Land Aboriginal Reserve, created in 1931, includes the Yolngu area. Hostilities involving Japanese bêche-de-mer collectors and a police expedition in 1932 led to the establishment of a mission station on the Gove Peninsula to serve as a buffer between the Yolngu and the increasingly frequent incursions of non-Aborigines into the area. Other missions had been established earlier, two on the north coast and one on the south coast. Each of these missions became centers of gradually increasing Yolngu population. During World War II some Yolngu were killed in Japanese air attacks, some served in an Australian unit in Dutch New Guinea, and many become acquainted with Europeans. After the war, increasing numbers of missionaries and government personnel were based in the Yolngu settlements, and efforts to implement the federal policy of assimilation were intensified. Although gradually accepting Christianity, Yolngu generally resisted complete assimilation into the dominant British-derived society. Federal governments espousing multiculturalism and favorably disposed to some degree of Aboriginal self-determination enacted land-rights legislation in 1976 (which made the Arnhem Land Reserve an inalienable freehold, also called "Aboriginal Land") and began to support a widespread decentralization movement as Yolngu started to move back to their traditional lands. Settlements established there, although increasing in number and intended to be permanent, remain attached to the larger towns (formerly missions) and are serviced by them. Yolngu people are committed to the development of economic independence, although it must be based to some extent on mining on their land, to which in principle they object. They are also committed to the development of a bicultural society at a rate of change under their control.

Settlements

Population of the four major Yolngu towns (called "townships") ranges from approximately 1,000 to 2,000, including the permanent or semipermanent residents of the outstations or homeland centers serviced from the towns. The towns reflect their origins as missions, with a central area containing administration buildings and usually a church, as well as substantial well-constructed houses. Nearby, sometimes in the center and radiating away from the center, are the houses of the Yolngu people. This housing was at first of traditional shelter design, seasonally appropriate; subsequently, it was made of bush timber and corrugated iron; later, framed corrugated iron on cement slab was used. Increasingly houses have been built closer to standard Australian outback design, and still more recently they are of cement-block construction. At homeland centers, construction remains predominantly of bush timber or corrugated iron, with earth or sand floors, although some "kit houses" are now being erected. The largest center in the Yolngu area is the mining town at Nhulunbuy, with an estimated population of 3,500; fewer than 50 are Yolngu. In the other centers, non-Aboriginal residents are about 8 percent of the population and are mostly employees of the Yolngu towns and organizations.

Economy

Subsistence and Commercial Activities. The Yolngu economy was based exclusively on hunting and gathering until the establishment of the missions and the gradual introduction of market goods. Hunting and gathering remain important for Yolngu both in terms of subsistence (especially at the homeland centers) and of identity, even though motor vehicles, aluminum boats with outboard engines, guns, and other introduced objects have replaced indigenous tools. Small amounts of cash were introduced in the 1940s and 1950s; in 1969 federal training grants began to provide limited wages, and social service benefits were generally being paid. Standard wages were in place by the mid-1970s, but social services remain the major source of cash income for Yolngu and unemployment (in European-Australian terms) remains at over 50 percent. Most employment is provided by government agencies in administrative and service jobs. Yolngu on the Gove Peninsula have established business enterprises mainly related to contract work for the mining company.

Industrial Arts. For a few men and women in each Yolngu town or outstation the production of arts and crafts—bark paintings, carvings (chiefly but not exclusively made by men), woven net bags and baskets (exclusively produced by women)—is a significant source of income, but it is not nearly sufficient to preclude the need for social-security support.

Trade. Yolngu traditionally had trading partners who exchanged scarce commodities such as highly prized stone, ochres, and other objects of ritual value; trading relationships were important both socially and economically, and the network of trade, although attenuated, remains.

Division of Labor. In the past, women regularly gathered and processed vegetable foods as well as provided substantial amounts of protein (shellfish at coastal sites, small animals such as goannas and snakes at inland sites), while men provided less regularly taken but highly prized large animals (turtles, dugongs, and fish at coastal sites, and kangaroos, wallabies, emus, opossums, bandicoots, and echidnas at inland sites). This division of labor still exists, although women as well as men now line fish and men continue to use the spear and spear thrower for fishing. The division of labor in wage and salary jobs tends to follow the Euro-Australian pattern.

Land Tenure. Land is owned by language-named clans; the parcels comprising a clan's estate may not all be contiguous, and ideally they include both coastal and inland areas. Individuals inherit ownership rights in the clan estate from their father and responsibilities for and use rights in their mother's estate. They may also have subsidiary rights in an area where they were conceived (where their father found their spirit before it entered their mother) and also where they were born. In addition, individuals have interests in and responsibilities for their mother's mother's estate, including the potential right of inheritance should there be no males in their mother's mother's clan. Federal legislation in 1976 formally recognized Yolngu title along with the Aboriginal title of all Aboriginal reserve lands.

Kinship

Kin Groups and Descent. The main corporate kin groups are patrilineal clans that own land and the ritual objects and ceremonies that validate their title. In the case of large clans, this function may be assumed by subclan or lineage groups. Kinship provides the primary medium of social identity in the Yolngu social domain; each person is reckoned as kin to every other person, and kin links may thus be traced through several different relatives. Matrilineally defined relationships establish rights and duties complementary to those of patrilineal descent but not corporate landowning groups.

Kinship Terminology. Yolngu use some twenty-four kin terms (as well as some optional extras) to distinguish lineal and collateral, marriageable and nonmarriageable relatives; the analysis of their system of kin classification continues to provide fertile ground for anthropological debate.

Marriage and Family

Marriage. Polygynous marriages, formerly regarded as most desirable, are increasingly rare. Moiety and clan exogamy are observed, and within these parameters, families arrange marriages: ideally a young man is assigned a mother-in-law who is his mother's mother's brother's daughter (most likely and most desirably a classificatory relative in this category). Marriages in the past and to a large extent today maintain or extend alliances between lineages. A young man performs bride-service. Divorce was not formerly institutionalized, but permanent separation of spouses was not uncommon.

Domestic Unit. A man and his wife or wives, who are often sisters, and their children eat and sleep together, whether living in houses in towns, or in houses or shelters at homeland centers. Brothers with their wives and children frequently live in close proximity. Women in such a hearth group or household forage together, and brothers often hunt together.

Inheritance. Joint rights in land inhere in the patrilineal group into which each person is born; in the same way, ownership of a language is inherited. A lineage is a potential inheritor of land belonging to the patrilineal group of a real or classificatory mother's mother, should there be no males remaining in that group. Movable property is disposed of through exchange. Formerly a deceased person's personal property was destroyed, but now if such property is valuable it is ritually purified and distributed to relatives on the basis of their attachment to the deceased.

Socialization. Infants are almost always in physical contact with caretakers, children are not physically punished or threatened by adults, and infants and very young children are never overtly denied whatever they wish. Yolngu are proponents of bicultural education ("two-way education") and some are gaining university degrees and designing their own school curricula as well as administering and teaching in their schools.

Sociopolitical Organization

From the point of view of the Australian government, the Yolngu are citizens of Australia, although the entitlements of citizenship have been acquired piecemeal. As citizens they are subject to the administration of both Australian commonwealth and Northern Territory law. Special status exists in terms of the legislative provisions defining "Aboriginal land" and in limited recognition of some aspects of customary law. Yolngu towns receive financial support for their infrastructure maintenance and development from federal funding authorities and/or from the Northern Territory, depending on the legislation under which they are incorporated.

Social Organization. Yolngu society is based on principles of descent and the categories and groups within it are related through the idiom of kinship. In addition, the factors of age (both absolute and relative), birth order, and gender all influence the organization of social groups. Thus, through the operation of pervasive dualism, the universe is divided into two mutually exclusive but complementary name moieties, Dhuwa and Yirritja, and each individual is by birth a member of the moiety of his or her father. Each language-named clan is either of the Dhuwa or the Yirritja moiety; clans of the same moiety are linked through a shared myth while clans of the opposite moiety, through lineages within them, are linked by marriage alliances. Clans or particular lineages of alternate generation defined by matrifiliation are closely linked—or merged—through shared interests in land and ritual performance. Yolngu place a high value on personal autonomy and individual achievement.

Political Organization. Leadership roles in Yolngu society are defined by seniority, which is determined by birth order.

The oldest man in a sibling set exercises (or should exercise) primary authority over his brothers and sisters and their families. The oldest man in a clan should be its head, with his next-younger brother "second" to him. The expectation that the oldest man in a clan will be its head mitigates the strict ranking of lineages, and in practice if the first son of the first son is still regarded as too young to assume the headship, a younger brother of a deceased head will usually assume the headship. Here exist the grounds of competition for the headship. The rule of seniority operates with respect to both men and women; except that in public men usually exercise authority, birth order is more salient than gender in Yolngu political process. Leaders should be skilled orators, and have the obligation to "look after" all the people who acknowledge their position as leader. To be implemented, a decision must represent a consensus; until a consensus is reached, no decision has been made. These principles of authority and decision making still govern Yolngu political life, even though elected councils are responsible for administering the towns. Yolngu are increasingly active in Northern Territory politics, both through the activities of the Northern Land Council and interaction with elected officials of the territory government. A Yolngu man is currently serving as an elected member of the Northern Territory Assembly.

Social Control. One of the chief responsibilities of a Yolngu leader is to manage the procedures of dispute settlement. When a member of his clan requests his help to gain satisfaction for some grievance, he may intervene personally to attempt to bring about a resolution; he may convene family meetings or clan moots to ensure the involvement of all those whose concurrence in the matter in dispute and the appropriate outcome is necessary for settlement. People may call attention to a grievance by a public and very loud announcement; if they also threaten physical assault, certain kin should immediately respond: a sister and/or brother-in-law to provide physical restraint, and a lineage leader or clan head to urge calmness and to undertake to arrange satisfaction for the grievance.

Conflict. In the past, blood revenge (payback) prevailed; it was incumbent on certain kinsmen of a deceased person to avenge his or her death. Since deaths were rarely attributed to a "natural" cause, at almost any time people were planning a revenge expedition or were fearful of being subjected to one. It has frequently been said that the only sources of conflict among Yolngu (or Aborigines in general) were women and corpses. Yolngu deny this; rather, they say that serious disputes concern interests in land. The *makarrata,* which has been described as a "peace-making" ceremony, or as a "trial by ordeal," is ritualized revenge. A successful outcome is signaled by blood flowing from a wound inflicted in the thigh of a principal offender and is accepted as balancing accounts, at least during the time required for the performance of the ceremony. A custom referred to as *mirrirri* relates to special kinds of avoidance behavior expected between brothers and sisters regarding a reference to a woman's sexuality—a reference which, if made in the hearing of her brother, causes him to attack that sister or any other woman he calls sister. Nowadays, while a man might not attack his sister or "sisters" with a spear, people are still very circumspect about any reference to a woman's sexuality in the presence of her brother.

Religion and Expressive Culture

Religious Beliefs. Religious beliefs center on the myths that tell the travels and activities of spirit beings "in the beginning." The earth was much as it is now, but the acts of the spirit beings at that distant time in the past set the patterns of proper behavior for the Yolngu who would follow, and left signs of their presence in the land. "Wangarr" refers both to spirit being and distant time past; it is comparable to what has been called "the Dreaming" or "the Dreamtime" in other accounts of Aboriginal religion. The spirit beings named plants and animals in the language of the people on whom they bestowed the land and performed ceremonies that present-day owners of the land should perform. They transformed parts of the landscape during their journey. At what would be a clan's most important sacred site, they left a part of themselves; in some cases they stayed and "are always there." For the Yolngu, Wangarr continue to exist and to manifest themselves in both the seen and the unseen world. For individuals, the most important ones are those of their father's and their mother's clans. Healers (*marrnggitj*) have spirit familiars, often referred to as their "spirit children," who assist them in their curing practices. Since the arrival of the missions, all Yolngu have some knowledge of Christianity and to a varying extent have become active church members.

Religious Practitioners. Since all Yolngu are expected to participate in religious ritual—and most do—all are practitioners. All men sing the ritual songs and at some time do the appropriate dances; all women perform the women's dances that are required for the enactment of some phases of ceremony. Traditional ritual specialists are men who commit to memory a large corpus of sacred names (sometimes called "power names")—names of clan lands, sites, spirit beings, and their appurtenances—and who intone them in the manner of invocations at certain junctures in ritual performance. Some Yolngu men have been ordained as ministers in the Uniting Church (the successor of the original mission Methodist church); for most Yolngu it is important that their Christianity has been Aboriginalized. Some of the ritual of Yolngu ceremony and its sacred objects have been incorporated in the iconography of the Yolngu Christian churches.

Ceremonies. The major ceremonies of the Yolngu focus on death; their mortuary rituals are an elaborate and important part of their culture, although they have undergone certain changes since the advent of the missions. The initial phases of induction into ritual adult manhood were often conducted at this time too, when ritual paraphernalia had been renewed and all the appropriate relatives were gathered. Marriage arrangements, trade, and other negotiations were also conducted during the time of ceremonies, which tended to be at the end of the dry season. Rituals at which the clans' most sacred ritual objects are freshly decorated, displayed, and their meanings explained are the most restricted of all: these ceremonies are directed by the oldest men; only mature men who have demonstrated their worthiness are admitted; and the meanings are imparted incrementally. These objects are of the greatest importance to Yolngu, their significance indicated by their having been called "title deeds" to land.

Arts. Performance of ritual is judged by canons of aesthetics which make it a form of art as well as religious practice; individual dancers, singers, and drone pipe players are noted and praised for their performance style. Men learn to paint the figures and designs that represent or symbolize their clan's and their mother's clan's heritage, both ritually on bodies on religious occasions and at present on sheets of prepared bark as commercial fine art. Women have also produced commercial fine art since the 1970s. In the houses of Yolngu living in towns, bark paintings and carvings are displayed for the aesthetic pleasure they give as well as for their religious meaning.

Medicine. Yolngu may now avail themselves of Western medicine and also call on the services of a marrnggitj for diagnosis and/or treatment, especially if the cause of illness is suspected to be sorcery or inadvertent entry into a spiritually dangerous place. Yolngu have in addition a large pharmacopoeia based mainly on indigenous plants, the knowledge and use of which most people have some familiarity with.

Death and Afterlife. At the time of death, the soul, or its malign aspect, remains about the place of death and is a threat to close family members. One objective of the purificatory rites performed to "free" both survivors and material objects associated with the deceased, including houses, is protection from the malignity of the soul. During the extended course of the mortuary ritual, the soul is guided to some particular area or site on its own clan land, usually a place where, along with other souls of its clan, it awaits reincarnation.

Bibliography

Berndt, R. M. (1952). *Djanggawul; an Aboriginal Cult of North-Eastern Arnhem Land.* London: Routledge & Kegan Paul.

Berndt, R. M., and C. H. Berndt (1954). *Arnhem Land: Its History and Its People.* Melbourne: F. W. Cheshire.

Morphy, H. (1984). *Journey to the Crocodile's Nest: An Accompanying Monograph to the Film "Madarrpa Funeral at Gurka'wuy."* Canberra: Australian Institute of Aboriginal Studies.

Warner, W. L. (1937). *A Black Civilization: A Social Study of an Australian Tribe.* New York: Harper & Bros. Rev. ed. 1958. New York: Harper & Brothers.

Wells, A. E. (1963). *Milingimbi.* Sydney: Angus & Robertson. Reprint. 1976. *Life in the Crocodile Islands.* Adelaide: Rigby Seal Books.

Williams, N. M. (1986). *The Yolngu and Their Land: A System of Land Tenure and the Fight for Its Recognition.* Stanford, Calif.: Stanford University Press.

Williams, N. M. (1987). *Two Laws: Managing Disputes in a Contemporary Aboriginal Community.* Canberra: Australian Institute of Aboriginal Studies.

NANCY M. WILLIAMS

Muyu

ETHNONYMS: none

Orientation

Identification. The Muyu live just south of the central mountains of Irian Jaya, just along the border with Papua New Guinea. The name Muyu is taken from the Muyu River, a tributary of the Kao River, itself a tributary of the Digul River.

Location. The Muyu area is between 5° and 7° S and 140°5' and 141° E. The Muyu people originally inhabited the hilly country between the central highlands and the plains of the south coast. There is no clear wet or dry season in the Muyu area. The average (heavy) rainfall is between 400 and 650 centimeters per year, depending on the location in the area.

Demography. In 1956 the Muyu people numbered 12,223. At that time the total number of inhabitants of the administrative subdivision of Muyu was 17,269, although not all Muyu then lived in the subdivision. Muyu settlements were mostly found near Merauke (410 inhabitants in 1954). In 1984 about 7,000 Muyu fled over the border into Papua New Guinea, because of dissatisfaction with the situation in their own area. In 1989 a few thousand returned to Irian Jaya, partly to the Merauke area on the south coast. The population density averaged about 3 persons per square kilometer in 1956. The population growth rate is not high, but at the moment no exact figures are known. Traditionally, the Muyu are very mobile and easily migrate to other areas with more economic opportunities.

Linguistic Affiliation. The Muyu speak dialects of Kati in the Ok Family of Papuan languages. A thorough analysis of the Muyu language and its relations with the languages of the surrounding people has yet to be done.

History and Cultural Relations

The Muyu probably migrated from the area of the central mountains to the present Muyu area. Because of their trade system they maintained many relations with the neighboring groups. The first contact with non-Papuan people was probably in the period between 1907 and 1915, during a general military exploration of Dutch New Guinea. In 1902 a Dutch Indies administration post was opened on the southeast coast of Dutch New Guinea as the capital of the South New Guinea Division, which included the Muyu area. Foreign relations further developed between 1914 and 1926 when birds of paradise were hunted in South New Guinea by Chinese, Japanese, Australians, and Indonesians, according to Muyu stories. Some young Muyu followed the bird hunters to other parts of the Dutch Indies and Merauke. In 1927 the Upper Digul Subdivision was delineated with Tanah Merah as the capital and the Muyu area as a part of it. From Tanah Merah the first administrative interventions began, especially to control the frequent revenge killings. In 1933 the missionaries of the congregation of the Sacred Heart established a mission post at Ninati, in the Muyu area, followed by the government in 1935, when the Muyu area became a "district" (a sub-subdivision). The contacts between the Muyu and the foreigners, missionaries, and officials then became more intensive. The Muyu became a subdivision in 1955, with a "controleur BB" (officer of the civil service) as its head, who was responsible to the "resident" of the South New Guinea Division at Merauke. In 1963, when Dutch New Guinea became a province of Indonesia, the Muyu area became a *kecamatan,* with a *camat* as its chief, as a part of the *kabupaten* Merauke, with a *bupati* as its head. Because of dissatisfaction with lack of development, unfair treatment by the military, and pressure by the OPM ("Organisasi Papua Merdeka," the organization of freedom fighters), about 7,000 Muyu people fled to Papua New Guinea.

Settlements

Before the interventions of the government and the mission a striking feature of the Muyu culture was the dispersed form of settlement. The patrilineal lineages constituted territorial units, ranging from about four to sixty inhabitants. But even within these settlements, houses were dispersed because of the strong urge to build one's house on one's own land. Thus every adult man with a nuclear family had his own individual land, as the whole Muyu area was divided into individually owned plots. If possible, the Muyu lived in their gardens, which were clearings in the forest. The houses were well built at a height of about 10 meters, either on the trunks of trees that had been cut to that height or on poles of that length, for safety reasons. The floors and walls were made of strips of palm tree wood, bound with rattan cane and roofs thatched with sago palm leaves. After 1933, first the mission and then the government urged the Muyu to live together in villages of about 150 to 400 inhabitants each in order to be more easily reached by the mission and the government. Only in villages of such a size could schools, houses for school teachers or catechists, and guest houses (*pasanggrahan*) for visiting officials be built and maintained. Village houses were built close together neatly in a row along both sides of the road. Today the houses are usually built in the same styles as before and also on poles, but now the poles are at a height of only 1 to 3 meters.

Economy

Subsistence and Commercial Activities. The Muyu are slash-and-burn horticulturalists. The stone ax was used for clearing wood; it has been replaced by imported iron axes and machetes. The main crops are many varieties of bananas and root crops. Most important among the latter are yams, sweet potatoes, tobacco, and breadfruit. Sago palms are found and planted along the small rivers and in swamps, and they are a staple food crop for the southern Muyu. Commercial crops are difficult to grow in the Muyu area because of the heavy rainfall and poor soils. In 1960–1962 rubber and cacao were planted as commercial crops, with rubber providing hope for the development of the Muyu area. But the Indonesian government apparently has not been able to continue these efforts and the promising developments have stagnated. Pigs are the most important domestic animals.

Industrial Arts. No important traditional industrial arts were known, with even stone axes imported from neighboring tribes. The Muyu did make their own bows and arrows, their drums, and in the southern part dugouts for crossing the rivers. The northern Muyu made rattan-cane suspension bridges. As far as is known, no new industrial arts have been introduced.

Trade. The Muyu had their own money system (cowrie shells) with which a trade system was developed. Pigs, pork, bows, tobacco, magic stones, formulas, ornaments, and services (namely the murder of an enemy) were traded. Shell money (*ot*) also played an important role in bride-price payments. For most Muyu traditional money has been replaced by "modern" money. In 1954 a Chinese *toko* (trade store) was opened and the Muyu eagerly shopped for imported goods. After 1963 the supply of these goods decreased, and local inflation occurred with high prices (in Indonesian money) for local products such as pork and for bride-prices.

Division of Labor. Every wife has her own garden. The husband does the heavy work in the garden such as cutting trees, but the women clear most of the garden, grow the crops, and tend the pigs.

Land Tenure. All rights rest with the individual. The entire Muyu region is divided into bits and pieces of land, each with its separate owner who is known to all neighbors. Upon a man's death his land and fishing ground are divided among his sons. Of course no registration of these rights is available in a culture without script. The danger in the "modern" situation is that these rights will not be fully recognized by the government and land will be taken without proper procedures and compensation, leading to conflicts.

Kinship

Kin Groups and Descent. As noted above, the Muyu were organized in patrilineages, which were also territorial units. The nuclear family was a very important unit, which formed a household. In the present situation several lineages (about ten to twenty) live together in a village. The Muyu kinship system is probably based on the ideal marriage with a mother's brother's daughter, the so-called exclusive cross-cousin marriage.

Kinship Terminology. Kin terms followed the Iroquois system.

Marriage and Family

Marriage. Polygynous marriage is, and was, present, especially for men who could afford to marry more than one wife, who enhanced the man's wealth by caring for gardens and pigs. The Roman Catholic church attempts to introduce and maintain the value of the monogamous marriage. The basis of the marriage system is the institution of bride-price that provides the bride giver with the wealth he needs to obtain another wife for himself or his son. Bride-price thus makes the exclusive cross-cousin marriage and the open asymmetrical system possible. Especially in the southern part of the Muyu area, marriage to mother's brother's daughter was the ideal, while marriage with father's sister's daughter was forbidden. The bride-price also gave people much freedom of choice in selecting marriage partners. To a certain extent, freedom of choice exists also for the potential bride and groom, though in former times great pressure and even force could be applied to a woman if a high bride-price was available and could be paid in cash. The marriage system also supported the trade system by maintaining or creating trade contacts along trade routes even in remote areas. Postmarital residence was patrilocal and an independent family household was established. In the present village system, with several lineages living in one village, the bride can come from the same village as the groom. Today, the different lineages no longer necessarily live separately in different quarters of a village. Divorce is not common among the Muyu, because of the bride-price. The Roman Catholic church also discourages divorce.

Domestic Unit. The nuclear or polygynous family is the most common domestic unit living as a household in their own house.

Inheritance. Land and fishing waters are divided among surviving sons, the eldest son receiving somewhat more than the others. The rules of inheritance regarding articles of value are much the same as those regarding land. Here too it is the sons who inherit. However, the wife and daughters also receive a small part of this property.

Socialization. Children are raised by both parents, but after age 5 or 6 the boys spend more time with their fathers and the girls with their mothers. Emphasis is placed on independence and individualism, which means that from an early age the children have to take care of themselves as much as possible, such as fetching water for themselves or keeping their own gardens.

Sociopolitical Organization

The Muyu area is now a part of the Indonesian state, practically since 1963 and formally since 1969. Indonesia is a republic with a president as head of state.

Social Organization. In Muyu society there was a strong tendency toward equality in position, though the rich (*kayepak*) might have more influence. Through the process of modernization or development new classes of educated people have arisen, who have more status and modern wealth. But most of these people live outside of the Muyu area because of the few economic opportunities in the area.

Political Organization. The Muyu society had no broader sociopolitical organization than the lineage. The lineages themselves were small and loosely structured, without formally recognized chiefs. The kayepak could exert much influence inside and outside their own lineage because of their ability to help other people with their wealth or to threaten them by hiring murderers. The Muyu had no courts or councils for solving conflicts, and social order was maintained by taking justice into one's own hands, by taking revenge by murder, or by asking compensation for suffered damage. In traditional times, conflicts were common, resulting in an atmosphere of fear, distrust, and caution. Becoming a part of a state, first the Dutch colonial state in 1935 and then the Indonesian state in 1963, the Muyu became part of a foreign-dominated system. Modern villages have a village head (*kepala kampong*), who formerly was appointed by the colonial administration but who now can be elected. The village head is responsible to the camat, the head of the district (subsubdivision). The position of the village head is weak and tenuous, because of the lack of traditional chiefs in Muyu society. Ideally, the Indonesian government provides a range of services including schools (via the Roman Catholic church), police, courts, health services, and development projects. In reality, there is still too little development, which was one reason so many Muyu fled to Papua New Guinea in 1984.

Social Control. Traditionally, informal social control was maintained by the threat of man and by supernatural beings (ancestor spirits). Today, social control is exercised by the administration, with headmen, police, and military people, and by the church, with teachers, catechists, and priests.

Conflict. In the past recourse to violence, murder, or warfare generally arose from suspicion about causes of illness or death, disputes over debts, and unauthorized relations with women. Today, the ideal is that courts will resolve these conflicts in society, though the village head will often try to solve them informally.

Religion and Expressive Culture

Today, most Muyu are Roman Catholics. In the past, their traditional religion included beliefs in divine and other supernatural beings, myths about the origin of the Muyu and their way of life, religious ceremonies, religious-medical practices, etc. There was no uniformity throughout the entire region, which is not surprising, considering the dispersed settlement patterns, the open structure of the lineage, the many trade contacts, the marriage system, and the individualistic way in which knowledge of the supernatural was transferred. Some traditional religious beliefs and practices are maintained beside the Christian beliefs and practices.

Religious Beliefs. The Roman Catholic version of the Christian religion was brought by West European (Dutch) missionaries with the help of Indonesian (Kaiese) catechists and schoolteachers. This gave a special character to the contents of the Christian message and practice, which did not replace the existing religion but added new ideas and practices to it. For the central Muyu, Komot is the most important supernatural being. The myths tell how he arranged the life of the Muyu as it was. Komot has also great signifance for the hunt. An important myth for most of the Muyu is that about Kamberap, a primeval man from whom both the sacral pig and the regular domesticated pig originated. This myth explains that all the foreigners and their wealth originated from the Muyu area. In connection with these ideas the Muyu believe that the foreigners keep secret the way in which they get their knowledge and wealth. In several salvation movements (cargo cults) the Muyu tried with supernatural means to discover the secret and obtain the same wealth, knowledge, and position as the foreigners. These ideas are still present even if they do not find expression in salvation movements, though they probably did play a role in the decision to flee to Papua New Guinea in 1984. In addition to the Christian God, supernatural beings of the traditional religion play a role in daily village life, including Komot and the spirits of deceased ancestors, especially those of rich ones. They help if the Muyu live according to the rules and cause illness and death if the Muyu break the rules.

Religious Practitioners. There were no traditional religious specialists. The ceremonies, such as the slaughtering of the sacral pig (*yawarawon*) and the initiation of boys with the swinging of the bullroarer (*mulin*) and the playing of the sacral flutes (*konkomok*) can be arranged by any adult. Knowledge about the supernatural is transferred in an individualistic way from father to son and mother to daughter. Magic stones or formulas can also be bought from other people. Roman Catholic religion is taught by the catechists, schoolteachers, and priests, who also organize and lead the ceremonies. Most of the catechists and some of the schoolteachers are Muyu. Priests are either Dutch settlers or Indonesians from other islands.

Ceremonies. The Roman Catholic church follows the church calendar, though in remote villages not all the ceremonies are always held, as the priests can only visit the villages once every several months. Traditional ceremonies are still held, such as those for the pig feasts, the boys' initiations, and certain illnesses.

Arts. The Muyu culture is not artistically rich. Material objects include the short hand drums with some decoration and the big shields from behind which the warriors could shoot their arrows. They also have songs and dances, which are not yet described.

Medicine. Several cures are based on the idea that the spirits of deceased ancestors (*tawat*) have caused the diseases. No cures are known for diseases inflicted by sorcery. These afflictions will cease only if the person who applied the means (*mitim*) retrieves it from the position in which he placed it to cause the disease. Through the missionaries and the government, modern medicines were introduced, especially in the modest hospital at Mindiptana.

Death and Afterlife. As soon as someone dies, his next of kin are informed, even if they live in other settlements. If they don't live too far away, they will come to view the deceased, and the women will take part in the lamentations. To express sorrow one may try also to avoid being suspected of causing death. In former times the body could be buried, dried over a fire, or wrapped and left to dry by itself. In the latter case the body was usually laid on a rack near the dwelling. After some time, when there was an occasion during a pig feast, the bones were rubbed with pig's fat and buried. Today, the bodies are only buried under pressure from the government. The reason behind the more extensive treatment of the body was not just love for the deceased but also fear of his tawat. If the spirit is not satisfied, there will be harmful consequences for pig raising and horticulture. In traditional religious beliefs the spirits of the deceased went to a special dwelling place for tawat, a settlement like those of the living but with a carefree existence. In general the idea of the dwelling place of the dead was not important to the Muyu. Far more significant was, and is, the idea that the spirits continue to play an important part in the daily lives of the living. The Christian ideas of Heaven and Hell are now also playing a role, though it is not yet clear which ideas are predominant. Today, the Roman Catholic burial ceremonies are used if a catechist, school teacher, or priest is available.

See also Marind-anim, Ningerum

Bibliography

Schoorl, J. W. (1957). *Kultuur en Kultuurveranderingen in het Moejoe-gebied* (Culture and culture change in the Muyu area). The Hague: Voorhoeve. Reprint. 1990. Translation Series. Leiden: Royal Institute of Linguistics and Anthropology.

Schoorl, J. W. (1988). "Mobility and Migration in Muyu Culture." *Bijdragen tot de Taal-, Land- en Volkenkunde* 145:540–556.

PIM (J. W.) SCHOORL

Namau

ETHNONYMS: Koriki, Purari

Orientation

Identification. "Namau" is a term used to designate both the region and its inhabitants by the people who live in the Purari River delta region of the south coast of Papua New Guinea. Some local people, however, prefer the name Purari. The Koriki are one of the several named tribes in the area, which also include the I'ai, Kaimari, and Maipua.

Location. Namau territory, centering on about 7°30' to 7°45' S and 145° E, consists of the swampy marshlands formed by the five major mouths of the Purari River. The climate is very wet with high daytime temperatures. The region is essentially mud and water with islands of drier land scattered about and freshwater marshes that support sago and nipa palms. Nearer the coast one finds extensive mangrove stands. The waterways provide an avenue of communication and travel between island settlements as well as a rich variety of fish for the local diet.

Demography. Recent estimates suggest a total of about 6,500 speakers of the Purari language. It appears that the region suffered a population decline in the first half of the twentieth century, but it has been showing a slow, steady increase since 1956, perhaps due in part to the introduction of Western health care.

Linguistic Affiliation. Purari is considered by linguists to be an "isolate," unrelated to its nearest neighbors, such as Northeast Kiwai to the west and Orokolo to the east.

History and Cultural Relations

Information about the Namau prior to European contact is sketchy. Two of the groups (Kaimari and Maipua) have oral traditions suggesting that they may have migrated into the region, perhaps from the southwest, but no such tradition appears to exist for the other groups. The Namau were known to have been very warlike, and both head-hunting and ceremonial cannibalism formed important parts of traditional ritual culture. The first European contact took place in 1894 and government involvement, labor recruitment, missionary activities, and efforts at modernization followed shortly thereafter. Many men of the region served in the Papuan Infantry Battalion during World War II. As happened elsewhere in New Guinea, this experience and exposure to Western goods and values resulted in a high degree of local dissatisfaction in the postwar years. For the Namau, this unrest found expression in the Tommy Kabu movement, which was an effort to introduce a cooperative economy, break up the old ceremonial system, and achieve local political sovereignty. The movement did not receive adequate government support and by 1955 had achieved little by way of positive gains, in part because it lacked the people and the skills to carry out its economic program.

Settlements Namau settlements, containing up to 2,500 people, traditionally were built on islands of drier land scattered throughout the swamps. Dwellings had a high front elevation, rising up to as much as 20 meters with a roof line that sloped rearward to a back elevation of 4–5 meters. These dwellings were built on stilts to protect the structures from flooding during high-water periods. Men and women had separate houses, both built according to this structural style and partitioned on the inside. The partition-formed alcoves in the women's house provided separate quarters for each woman and her young children. The men's house, or *ravi,* served also as an important ceremonial center. Its alcoves, which ran in two parallel rows along the sides of the building, each had its own hearth and belonged to a small patrilineally related group of men and initiated youths. Modernization efforts, including the Tommy Kabu movement, have resulted in the adoption of European house design and the relocation of settlements to drier land areas, and the ceremonial centers/men's houses are no longer built.

Economy

Subsistence and Commercial Activities. Namau subsistence depends on taro, sweet potatoes, sago, coconuts, and bananas, as well as fish and great quantities of crabs from the rivers and streams. Game hunted for food includes wild pigs and wallabies. Gathered foods, such as grubs, also contribute to the diet, as do birds, though to a rather limited extent. Rattan, important in the construction of ritual masks and effigies as well as for house building, is obtained during large expeditions upriver. After Western contact the men of Namau were recruited to work for wages on European-owned plantations.

Industrial Arts. Namau build houses and canoes, make weapons and utilitarian items such as fishing nets and bows, and fashion ritual and ornamental objects from feathers, pearl shells, and rattan. Much of Namau manufacture is ornately carved with totemic motifs. Canoes are made primarily for local use, although sometimes they are sold. These vessels are not equipped with outrigging and the bows are carved with totemic designs.

Trade. Apart from exchanges occurring in ceremonial contexts, the only significant trade occurred with visits of Motu canoes taking part in the vast *hiri* trading system.

Division of Labor. Men build houses in cooperative groups recruited from patrilineally related kin. Canoe building is done only by men, as is the making of masks and effigies. Hunting is men's work as is most gardening and the tending of coconuts. Men also fish with bows and arrows or spears, but primarily for sport rather than as a subsistence activity. Women, on the other hand, engage in more serious fishing, using hand traps, hand nets, or long nets spread across streams. Women also process sago once the trees have been felled and floated downriver by the men. Gathering crabs and other food items may be done by either sex, but it tends to be done primarily by women. While all adult men are expected to be capable of building or making whatever they might need to secure a livelihood, an individual may develop a reputation as a particularly fine carver or boat builder and achieve a sort of specialist status among his fellows.

Land Tenure. Land for settlements and gardening, as well as associated waterways, is associated with local patrilineal groups rather than being vested in individuals. Rights to land are inherited patrilineally, with all sons having rights to the land of their fathers' groups.

Kinship

Kin Groups and Descent. Namau reckon descent patrilineally, allocating membership in one or another of several "river clans" (i.e., clans that derive their names and totemic associations from the rivers of the district). These river clans, dispersed among local, exogamous, patrilineal groups, are themselves assigned to exogamous moieties. By 1955, however, the traditional clan and moiety system no longer had any important functions, and Namau society has moved instead toward a kindred system.

Kinship Terminology. Namau kinship terms are of the Hawaiian type.

Marriage and Family

Marriage. Traditionally, Namau marriages were polygynous and marriages were often arranged while the potential spouses were still quite young. Wife stealing was also not uncommon and was a source of conflict that led easily to open hostilities between groups. Bride-wealth was required, and postmarital residence was patrilocal. Wife exchange appears to have been common in traditional Namau society. Divorce does not appear to have been an option for women, and husbands were held to be fully within their rights in beating their wives. Relationships among cowives were frequently not peaceful. Among the other social and cultural changes occurring by the 1950s was a dissolution of the old marriage system and its connections with the descent system. Nowadays individuals have much freedom in contracting marriages and the nuclear family is of central importance.

Domestic Unit. In the past cowives shared a single dwelling, but each had her own partitioned section in which she and her young children ate and slept. Women worked in their own gardens and cooked for their own children. In recent decades, the nuclear family has become a residential and work unit.

Inheritance. Heritable property passes from parents to children, with sons inheriting their fathers' shell ornaments, canoes, pigs, and dogs, and daughters their mothers' tools and personal effects.

Socialization. During their early years, children are largely cared for and disciplined by their mothers. In the past, a series of initiation rites served as the vehicle by which older children, especially boys, were taught the skills, practices, and lore of adulthood. At about 8 years of age boys were taken on a journey upriver to be initiated into the totemic groups of their patrilineal clans. At about 13, boys of the same patriclan underwent a period of seclusion and ceremony in a specially built ravi, after which they took on the status of warriors.

Sociopolitical Organization

Social Organization. Traditional social organization centered on the exogamous moieties, the river clans, and localized patrilineages, all of which established appropriate marriage partners and gave structure to affinal relations. At the hamlet or settlement level, the ravi brought together men of several different patrilineal groups, but each group maintained its own wickerwork mask and ritual obligations. Cooperation within the settlement often necessarily crosscut lineage membership (e.g., in matters of warfare or large-scale projects such as house building). Other cooperative efforts, such as the collection of bride-wealth, were carried out within the confines of the specific local patrilineage.

Political Organization. Traditionally, each Namau village had its own chief, as did each moiety, but a man was expected to lead with consent. In general, personal attributes of physical strength and success in warfare and raiding contributed to the prestige needed for effective leadership. For the most part, a leader's influence did not extend beyond the hamlet level and it was primarily concerned with mobilizing men for war, for ceremonial occasions, and for communitywide projects. The Tommy Kabu movement was an effort to unite the Namau economically and politically into a cooperative, sovereign unit, and for a time the newly introduced Purari villages tried to establish their own police, jails, and courts. These forms have all been superseded by participation in the modern provincial and national governments.

Social Control. Traditional Namau methods of social control centered on a system of totemic beliefs and associated taboos. Fears of sorcery served as checks on individuals with regard to gross antisocial behavior. If a wife did not perform her duties adequately, her husband was considered to be within his rights if he beat her; in the case of a wife's adultery she might be beaten to death.

Conflict. War was an important aspect of traditional Namau culture, which called for the taking of heads and ritual cannibalism in certain of its ceremonies, particularly in the initiation of youths. Hostilities might arise over allegations of sorcery, theft, or wife stealing, and raids were made on neighboring Purari groups. Battles were fought between two roughly equivalent ranks of warriors who faced one another and shot off a rain of arrows until one or more of the enemy had been seriously wounded or killed. Efforts appear to have been taken to keep the casualty levels equal on the two sides.

Religion and Expressive Culture

Religious Beliefs. The central concept in Namau religion was *imunu,* an all-pervading force (like mana elsewhere in Oceania) that took a different form in each kind of being or object. Thus river spirits were regarded as the mythological sources of the river clans, and other natural phenomena and local fauna were believed to have their own spiritual forces. Vengeful ghosts or spirits of slain warriors as well as the spirits of ancestors were thought to be able to trouble the living.

Religious Practitioners. Traditional Namau ritual life was a male province; women were not initiated into the esoterica of a patrilineage's river spirit or totem. Each ravi had two or more hereditary priests, who presided over ceremonies. Sorcerers, too, were thought to be men, characterized by an excess of ambition, willful failure to fulfill kin-based ritual obligations, and a lack of generosity.

Ceremonies. Large wickerwork masks and effigies featured importantly in traditional ceremonies, which were held for boys' initiations and other life-cycle events as well as to secure success in or celebrate victory after wars. Marriages, however, do not seem to have been marked by a particular ceremony.

Arts. The most dramatic of all Namau artistic productions were the woven masks, of which there were two types: the large *kanipu,* which were maintained in the men's house; and the *aiai* masks, constructed for specific ceremonies and later burned. The dominant motif on masks as well as in most Namau carving (of bowls and spoons, canoe prows, etc.) is the stylized representation of a face. Other Namau decorative arts include carved bark ceremonial belts, carved combs and drums, and pearl-shell breastplates. Noseplugs, earplugs, scarification, shaving heads, and hairdressing were elements of bodily adornment.

Medicine. Namau traditionally believed that all illness and misfortune ultimately resulted from the activity of spirits, with or without the involvement of a human agent through sorcery. Cures thus centered on entreating or cajoling the responsible spirit to stop the attack. For this a ritual specialist, versed in the skills of communicating with the spirits, was called in. In 1949 the London Missionary Society built a hospital in the region, and each of the larger village-style Namau settlements now has a local clinic dispensing Western-style health care.

Death and Afterlife. In the past, kin expressed mourning by observing food taboos and covering themselves with mud and dirt. Usually the deceased was wrapped in a mat and left to decompose in its house (now abandoned) with the bones later kept as relics or charms; sometimes, especially under mission influence, the corpse was buried in the village. A ritual feast for the dead brought together all members of the tribe; food was accumulated by the relatives of the deceased and the spirit of the latter was thought to extract the essence of the food, leaving behind its physical form to be shared by mourners and guests. The feast officially released mourners from their external forms of mourning and the associated food taboos. It was thought that the spirit of the deceased stayed in the vicinity and might return as a ghost to annoy or harm its kin.

See also Motu, Orokolo

Bibliography

Holmes, J. H. (1924). *In Primitive New Guinea.* London: Seeley Service.

Maher, Robert F. (1961). *New Men of Papua: A Study of Culture Change.* Madison: University of Wisconsin Press.

Williams, F. E. (1924). *Natives of the Purari Delta.* Territory of Papua Anthropology Report no. 5. Port Moresby: Government Printer.

NANCY E. GRATTON

Nasioi

ETHNONYM: Kietas

Orientation

Identification. The name "Nasioi" has been employed by Europeans since the beginning of the twentieth century, and it is best thought of as a linguistic term. Speakers of the Nasioi language and its dialects have referred to themselves by many names, usually reflecting locality. "Kietas" is now commonly heard from other Bougainvilleans and missionaries.

Location. Nasioi occupy a large part of the southeastern portion of the island of Bougainville, from the coast around the port of Kieta inland for approximately 29 kilometers, between 6° and 6°12' S. Their villages extended from the coast through the valleys up to altitudes 900 meters above sea level. Thus they occupied several different ecological niches; this settlement pattern conditioned exchanges of produce before European contact and created differential impacts of colonialism and social change. Mean annual temperature at sea level is 27° C, and the temperature varies over a wider range during a 24-hour period than in terms of monthly mean variation. Temperature is estimated to decrease with altitude at a rate of about 3.5° per 300 meters. Rainfall of approximately 300 centimeters annually is distributed more or less evenly throughout the year.

Linguistic Affiliation. Nasioi and Nagovisi form the Nasioi Family in the Southern Bougainville Stock of Non-Austronesian languages. The language includes several distinct dialects and a number of villages contain speakers of other languages as well. Today, most younger people speak Tok Pisin (the lingua franca of Papua New Guinea) and/or English.

Demography. In 1963, Nasioi speakers were estimated at 10,654. There has been a sharp growth in Bougainville's population since that time, and annual natural increase is estimated at close to 4 percent. Although the 1980 census for the island does not distinguish among language groups, a figure of 14,000 may be extrapolated for Nasioi.

History and Cultural Relations

It is assumed that speakers of Non-Austronesian languages like Nasioi were the first arrivals on Bougainville and that Austronesian speakers followed later. There is evidence of human occupation on nearby Buka Island more than 28,000 years ago, and a date in excess of 30,000 B.P. for the ancestors of Nasioi seems reasonable. The Non-Austronesian speakers of south Bougainville were distinguished from their Austronesian neighbors by such characteristics as preferred cross-cousin marriage, achieved leadership and, probably, head-hunting. Bougainville Island was sighted in 1768 by the French navigator for whom it was named. Beginning in the latter nineteenth century, Nasioi living on the coast were among those Bougainvilleans most frequently contacted by traders and other Europeans because of the natural harbor at Kieta. Roman Catholic missionaries settling near Kieta in 1902 were the first Europeans known to reside on the island, and Imperial Germany (which had claimed the island in 1899 as part of its New Guinea colony) established an administrative headquarters there in 1905. By 1908 colonizers had begun to alienate Nasioi land, establishing coconut plantations and employing Nasioi as laborers. Australia administered what had been German New Guinea from 1914 to 1975, first as a League of Nations Mandate and later as a United Nations Trust Territory. Bougainville suffered severely during World War II under Japanese occupation and the subsequent Allied effort to retake the island. By the beginning of the postwar era, the Nasioi had become increasingly dissatisfied with the colonial situation in which they found themselves. These social disruptions were sharply increased by the construction, beginning in 1968, of a gigantic copper mine on Nasioi land heretofore untouched by European economic interests. Since then, Nasioi life has been characterized by continued rapid social change; by increasing discontent with the mine, with other European interests, and, after 1975, with the central government of Papua New Guinea; and by more and more militant expressions of that discontent. In 1988, what might be called the injuries of colonialism culminated in violence led by a self-styled "Bougainville Revolutionary Army" composed mostly of Nasioi that closed down the mine, resisted forces sent by the Papua New Guinea government, and declared Bougainville an independent state. As of August 1990, a new peace treaty had been signed with the central government, but the future of the Nasioi remains problematic. Thus the people in Bougainville most directly affected by colonialism in various forms have had the most tempestuous modern history of social change in the island.

Settlements

Whether they lived along the coast, in the valleys, or on mountain slopes, Nasioi dwelt in small, scattered settlements, often consisting of no more than one or two households. Because of continuous pressure from the administration, by the 1960s villages were larger and oriented around a central "main street." Most houses were built on piles, though some households had separate cooking huts set directly on the ground. Houses had rectangular floor plans, walls of split bamboo, and roofs thatched with sago-palm leaves. By the 1970s, Nasioi active in a modern cash economy were building houses of European materials.

Economy

Subsistence and Commercial Activities. Traditional Nasioi subsistence was conditioned by the differing ecological niches (coastal, valley, and hillside) in which the population settled, but the general pattern was that of typical Melanesian swidden horticulturalists. Taro was a staple crop until a plant blight swept through the island in World War II; thereafter, sweet potatoes became more important. Coconuts and sago were raised at lower altitudes. Nasioi men were employed on local plantations before World War II, but subsequently they began to take more interest in cash crops: first copra, then cacao. Although resentment of the copper mine kept many Nasioi from working there, a larger number were employed by the various contracting firms during construction of the mine, roads, and towns during the 1970s. Educated Nasioi are now employed in the modern, urban sector in Bougainville and elsewhere in Papua New Guinea.

Industrial Arts. Traditional crafts included carving, basketry, and, on the coast, pottery making. By the 1960s, few Nasioi practiced these arts; instead, they purchased comparable items in trade stores.

Trade. Items of produce were exchanged among people settled in different environments: coastal people produced pottery, sago, fish, and salt; valley dwellers grew coconuts and raised pigs; and hill dwellers traded baskets, bows and arrows, and game. Nasioi obtained shell currency from the Solomon Islands, via their neighbors in south Bougainville, but this currency was for special purposes (e.g., marriage) only. Nasioi on the coast began trading with European ships in the nineteenth century, in particular exchanging coconuts for metal tools. Early on, German administrators encouraged copra production as well as wage labor. Today all Nasioi participate to some degree in a modern cash economy.

Division of Labor. Subsistence work was divided according to gender: men did the heavy but intermittent work of clearing forests and fencing gardens, while women engaged in the steady production of garden foods. Men hunted possums, birds, and feral pigs; they also harvested betel nuts. Women collected freshwater crayfish, made baskets and mats, and bore the major responsibility for child rearing. Men were much more active than women as the economy became modernized, especially as wage laborers, and they are still more prominent in the cash sector. However, women today grow and market cash crops, and increasingly they go on to higher education.

Land Tenure. Land seems to have been plentiful in the traditional setting. Rights to land were in the first instance achieved by clearing virgin forest and were most often inherited through matrilineal kinship ties. However, rights could also be established through marriage, residence, individual kin networks, or ceremonial exchanges. Land could never be alienated beyond the local group. As elsewhere in Papua New Guinea, it was easier to establish than to extinguish claims to land. Nasioi entry into cash cropping, a rapidly increasing population, and, above all, the presence of the copper mine have created massive problems because of the incongruity of traditional land tenure with modern economic structures.

Kinship

Kin Groups and Descent. Basic to Nasioi social organization was the dispersed matrilineal clan (*muu'*). Such clans were ideally exogamous. Since Nasioi paid little attention to genealogy in Western terms, clan membership provided people with a fixed place in the social system as well as a basis for making land claims. Entire clans did not operate as corporate units, but localized segments did carry out important social activities as ad hoc groups.

Kinship Terminology. Traditional Nasioi terminology was a variant of the Iroquois system, in which siblings were equated with parallel cousins and terminologically distinguished from cross cousins. Other equations were father with father's brother and mother's sister's husband, and mother with mother's sister and father's brother's wife. Distinctive "aunt" and "uncle" terms were applied to father's sister and mother's brother's wife and to mother's brother and father's sister's husband, respectively.

Marriage and Family

Marriage. Traditional marriage among the Nasioi was ideally between bilateral cross cousins; thus a boy would marry a girl who was at once his mother's brother's and father's sister's daughter. Even if such a genealogical relationship did not obtain, the pattern was of continuing exchange between two clans, on a model of balanced reciprocity that operated in other realms of social life. Child betrothal was common, often negotiated between the mothers of the children. Exchange of food and other valuables was supposed to balance; there was no bride-price or dowry as ordinarily defined. If a widow remarried, either she or her intended new husband might be expected to make a prestation to the clan of her deceased husband. Polygyny was rare, practiced only by unusually industrious men. Residence after marriage was uxorilocal, and divorce was easy. Cross-cousin marriage, polygyny, and child betrothal came under early attack from missionaries and are not normative today. Because educated young people are more likely to seek out others of comparable accomplishments, modern marriages may be contracted between Nasioi and other groups, including other Papua New Guineans and Europeans.

Domestic Unit. Households traditionally consisted of a married couple and immature children. Sometimes an aged parent or other relative might join a kinsman's household. The nuclear family household continues to be a norm; in the 1960s and thereafter adolescent boys (either relatives or friends) might establish their own group household, since it was considered inappropriate for such youth to dwell under the same roof with parents who were still sexually active.

Inheritance. Much of a deceased person's property was consumed or destroyed during funeral rituals, so that there was little to inherit. Land rights were inherited matrilineally in the first instance, but other factors such as a major prestation of food from the deceased's children to his clansmen might prevail. Today, cash-crop trees or money normally pass from parents of either sex to their children, but the conflict between tradition and demands of the new economy increases the likelihood of disputes.

Socialization. While mothers had primary responsibility for child care, fathers, older siblings, and the entire settlement took an active interest. Life-cycle events, such as a first trip to the garden, were often the occasion for ceremonial exchanges, which varied considerably as to scale and elaboration. Often the child's "aunts," who were members of a different clan, performed sometimes ribald songs or dances to mark the event; they were then given food, betel nuts, or other valued items as compensation. A girl's menarche might be marked by a short period of seclusion, followed by a feast with singing and dancing. This practice was discouraged by missionaries and, in the 1960s, was usually confined to the daughters of ambitious men. There were no ceremonies to mark a boy's adolescence. Today, formal education has replaced most, if not all, traditional observances.

Sociopolitical Organization

Social Organization. Even by the standards of south Bougainville, traditional Nasioi life seems to have been relatively egalitarian. Women, on whom society depended for subsistence and the continuity of the clan, exercised considerable influence, especially in such matters as marriage arrangements. One of the problems in modern Nasioi life is the conflict between the ideal of balance and equivalence in society with the formation of strata based on differences of wealth and education.

Political Organization. A pattern of small, scattered settlements characterized Nasioi life before colonization and is correlated with political atomism. The typical Melanesian role of big-man thus took a very modest form among Nasioi. A Nasioi *oboring* (big-man) established his position by industry, generosity, and wisdom, but he remained a person of influence, not authority. The status of oboring was achieved by giving feasts, and it was not normally inherited. Today, when many Pacific Islanders are eager to "reinvent tradition," Nasioi claim that "paramount chiefs" were customary, although early published accounts and informants' reports dating from 1962 contradict this. Because of their post–World War II discontent with the social changes brought about by colonialism and subsequent political and economic developments, Nasioi have for the past forty years been especially vocal in demanding Bougainville's succession, first from the Trust Territory of New Guinea and now from the independent nation of Papua New Guinea. As of August 1990, the Nasioi-led "Bougainville Revolutionary Army" claims authority over the entire island.

Social Control. The oboring might use his influence to settle disputes in his locality, but he had no real authority to do so. Public opinion and shaming also encouraged conformity, and a victim might destroy his or her own property to show chagrin and to rally the support of others. However, the most effective form of social control before colonialism seems to have been the fear of sorcery that could be performed against anyone who committed an offense. Nasioi opposition to Australian colonial authority in the 1960s and 1970s left a vacuum in social control, and intergenerational conflict today seems to be increasing.

Conflict. Perhaps because of abundant land, genuine warfare does not seem to have been characteristic of traditional Nasioi life. Violent conflict more often took the form of individual homicide and revenge. Once a single act had been "balanced" by another or by material compensation, the affair was considered over; that is, Nasioi did not feud. Today the peaceable practices of the Nasioi are being altered by contact with the more violent customs of other Papua New Guineans; the recent level of organized violence in Nasioi is unprecedented.

Religion and Expressive Culture

Religious Beliefs. Although the Nasioi also believed in supernatural beings who inhabited the forests and rivers, the outstanding characteristic of traditional Nasioi religion was the belief that humans are dependent on the spirits of the dead (*ma'naari*) for material well-being. Offerings of special food (e.g., pork) and invocations were made to ensure the favorable attention of these spirits. When Roman Catholic missionaries began to work among the Nasioi, many converts seemed to regard the Christian pantheon as a set of especially powerful ma'naari. Seventh-Day Adventist missionaries arrived in Nasioi territory in the 1920s and Methodists in the 1930s. After the disruption of World War II and with growing discontent over their colonial situation, the Nasioi began to display cargo-cult beliefs. These often syncretized traditional beliefs and introduced Christian notions, with the goal of changing Nasioi life to be more like that of the European colonizers. The Tok Pisin term *longlong lotu* or "crazy church" was sometimes applied to these beliefs and practices, which were attacked by the colonial administration. At present, adherence to Christianity seems to have suffered while various cargo cults thrive.

Religious Practitioners. Nasioi did not have full-time religious practitioners. Individuals were thought to have special knowledge (e.g., of sorcery), usually derived from a familiar spirit. After missionization, a number of Nasioi became teachers and catechists, and the present Roman Catholic bishop of Bougainville is a Nasioi. At least one Nasioi has sustained his position as a cargo-cult leader for more than two decades.

Ceremonies. Propitiation of ma'naari and life-cycle events occasioned the most common ceremonies; the former kind were usually individual activities. Missionization meant Christian observances, which may have fallen off during recent unrest. Cargo-cult ceremonials often relate to the remains of the dead, showing continuity with the past.

Arts. Although utilitarian objects like combs were occasionally decorated, the Nasioi seem to have emphasized music and dance over graphic and plastic arts. Slit gongs, wooden trumpets, panpipes, and the Jew's harp were employed, and dances sometimes involved cross-gender performances. Modern Nasioi enjoy "string bands" and other Pacific adaptations of Western music.

Medicine. Illness was thought to be most often the result of sorcery. Various plant materials were employed in curing, but the ultimate efficacy of cures depended upon the assistance of spirit helpers. Some individuals were thought to be especially skillful at dealing with bone and muscle injury. Western medicine is today valued for certain ailments; despite the initial success of a malaria eradication campaign, the disease has once again become a serious health problem.

Death and Afterlife. Nasioi believed most deaths, except those of the very young and very old, were ultimately caused by sorcery or malevolent spirits. A human was thought to have two souls; the one that stayed near the living was important, as noted. Informants were vague about the fate of the other soul or shadow. Nasioi cremated the dead, though they sometimes preserved the lower mandible in a clanmember's house. These rites were traditionally important, but following contact missionaries introduced burials and cemeteries. Since the 1970s, however, cremation has revived, as Christian practice has weakened and cargo cults have maintained vitality.

See also Siwai

Bibliography

Frizzi, Ernst (1914). *Ein Beitrag zur Ethnologie von Bougainville und Buka mit speziellen Berücksichtung der Nasioi.* Baessler-Archiv no. 6. Leipzig and Berlin: B. G. Teubner.

Ogan, Eugene (1971). *Business and Cargo: Socio-economic Change among the Nasioi of Bougainville.* New Guinea Research Bulletin no. 44. Canberra: Australian National University Press.

Ogan, Eugene (1971). "Nasioi Land Tenure: An Extended Case Study." *Oceania* 42:81–93.

Oliver, Douglas L. (1949). *Studies in the Anthropology of Bougainville, Solomon Islands.* Papers of the Peabody Museum, Harvard University, vol. 29, nos. 1–4. Cambridge, Mass.

EUGENE OGAN

Nauru

ETHNONYMS: Navodo, Nawodo, Pleasant Island

Orientation

Identification. Nauru is an independent republic, an associate member of the British Commonwealth, and a member of the South Pacific Commission and the South Pacific Forum. The indigenous term for the island is Nauru, but early European visitors gave it the name of "Pleasant Island," which was used briefly.

Location. The single raised coral island of Nauru is located in the center of the Pacific basin, at 0°25' S, 166°56' E. It has a narrow fringing reef that drops off very steeply to the ocean floor. A fertile belt some 150–300 meters wide above the shoreline encircles the island. On the inland side a coral cliff rises to a height up to 300 meters above sea level; this central plateau once bore the richest deposit of phosphate rock in the Pacific, but this deposit is almost mined out, leaving stark coral pinnacles.

Demography. At the last census in 1983 the Nauruan population was 4,964, with another 2,134 residents from Kiribati and Tuvalu and 263 Europeans, almost all employed by the Nauru Phosphate Commission. Since the previous census in 1977 the proportion of Nauruans has increased from 57 percent to 62 percent. Nauruans have a positive-growth population policy partly because of a series of declines in the past, including reduction to 589 persons during World War II.

Linguistic Affiliation. Nauruan is classified as an isolate within the Micronesian Family of Austronesian languages. It contains many Kiribati words, but it has deviant features that do not fit easily with neighboring Micronesian or Polynesian languages. Most Nauruans also speak English.

History and Cultural Relations

Little is known of Nauruan prehistory except what is suggested by myth and legend. Tradition holds that Nauru was settled by Tabuarik, who came from Kiribati—as did subsequent boatloads of Kiribati people—and took over the island from a small group living there. In more recent times the island was visited by whalers and escaped convicts from Norfolk Island and Australia. In 1886, an Anglo-German declaration assigned Nauru to Germany, who administered the island until 1914; after World War I the island became a League of Nations mandate under Australian administration. Following World War II, when the Japanese occupied the island, Nauru was a United Nations trusteeship administered by Australia until 1968 when it became an independent republic. Its economic history is based on the discovery of phosphate in 1899, the mining of which commenced in 1906. Beginning in 1919 the British Phosphate Commissioners (BPC) administered the mining operation and took proportionate shares in the phosphate mined. The BPC initially paid those Nauruans whose land was mined a royalty of one half-penny per ton of phosphate shipped. Inadequate returns to Nauruans for their phosphate has been a contentious issue for which Nauruan leaders have sought redress. Since independence the Nauru Phosphate Corporation has sold the phosphate on the open market for high returns, and Nauru has taken a positive lead in Pacific island affairs, choosing to share some of its wealth through airline and shipping links with countries that have limited communication networks.

Settlements

All residences are in one of twelve districts located in the narrow coastal belt, except for one village beside Buada Lagoon in the interior. The administrative center and contract worker housing, together with some Nauruan housing, are concentrated in the southwest corner of the island. Formerly housing was provided free by the government from phosphate royalties, but some individuals used their own phosphate income to build larger, more elaborate houses. Housing styles are thus varied but reminiscent of those found in any Western metropolitan country. In each district there is a primary school and at least one small store and a gas station. There are two main churches as well as three smaller chapels. The districts are linked by a road that encircles the island, with side roads serving the special housing areas. The interior village around Buada Lagoon is linked by road to the coastal area, with a branch road serving the current location of mining. This interior road network is decreasing as the phosphate is taken out and only the coral pinnacles remain.

Economy

Subsistence and Commercial Activities. Phosphate mining is now the base of the economy, though copra was the first source of cash before 1906 when mining commenced. Phosphate royalties have been invested both by individuals and by the government against the time when mining ends. Nauruans' income is derived mainly from these royalties, but also from employment and pensions. About half of the Nauruan population is privately employed or works in the administrative arm of government, teaching, or NPC administration. All consumer goods are imported to Nauru, mainly from Australia.

Industrial Arts. Several Nauruans have opened repair shops for cars and electrical appliances, based on some training gained in Australia and local apprenticeship. The expertise for mining operations is still largely in the hands of non-Nauruans.

Trade. Phosphate took over from copra in 1906 as the main source of trade income, and since independence this has increased tenfold. The Nauru Cooperative Society, formed in 1923 as the major controller of imports of foods and general merchandise, has been superseded by the Nauru Corporation, which is controlled by the Nauru Local Government Council. In addition there are a number of small stores in town run by Chinese who employ young Kiribati and Tuvalu girls as shop assistants. Nauruans take trips to Australia or Fiji to make major purchases.

Division of Labor. Formerly men were in charge of fishing while women cared for the household and children and made handicrafts. Today women's and men's tasks are much less differentiated, with both sexes holding paid jobs or assisting with household maintenance. Some men still go fishing, but mainly as sport. Kiribati men fish from canoes and sell their produce on the island.

Land Tenure. Nauruans hold land by virtue of being born of Nauruan parents; non-Nauruans cannot hold land. Land is passed on in named parcels from a parent to all children, such inheritance being recorded with the Nauru Lands Board. Thus individual Nauruans hold rights in several parcels but some of these shares may be very small. Those rights are the basis on which compensation for mining is paid. In addition to land, Nauruans also own rights to fishing places, lagoons, useful trees, goods, songs, and dances.

Kinship

Kin Groups and Descent. Every Nauruan belongs to an extended kin group consisting of both mother's and father's relatives as the largest affiliation. In addition a Nauruan is born into the mother's clan group. Formerly there were twelve named clans but today only ten exist, the main function of which is to regulate marriage.

Kinship Terminology. The system used is basically of the Hawaiian type, with classificatory terminology distinguishing generations and mother's relatives from father's.

Marriage and Family

Marriage. A couple intending to marry must be from different clan groups, and they must seek approval of their respective district councillors. Most marriages take place in church though today there are a few common-law marriages. Divorce is uncommon, but separation is more frequent, especially for Catholic couples. The birth of a child must be registered if the child is to receive the rights of being Nauruan, even if the birth takes place outside of Nauru.

Domestic Unit. The family unit consists of a wide group of relatives on both the father's and mother's side. Adoption is relatively common, especially by a Nauruan who has no children of his or her own. If accepted by the community, an adopted relative receives the same rights to land and residence as does a blood relative. A Nauruan household is likely to comprise an older couple with one or more married children and grandchildren, for an average size of eight persons per household.

Inheritance. Rights to land, useful trees, goods, songs, dances, and all other possessions are passed on from parents to all children, both natural and adopted.

Socialization. Children are much loved and treated with care and affection by both parents and all members of the domestic unit. Schooling is highly valued by parents, who may make financial sacrifices to send daughters and sons to secondary schools in Australia and New Zealand. Children are raised to think of themselves as Nauruans and to speak the Nauruan language.

Sociopolitical Organization

Social Organization. Nauruan society used to have three status groups: the Temonibe, the Amengename, and the Itsio. The first two were landholding groups, while the Itsio consisted of those who sought the protection of a Temonibe. Membership in the first two groups was by birth. The Temonibe were very highly respected and usually owned more land. They took on leadership in war or in large economic undertakings, but they were not chiefs. Today these three status groups are no longer significant.

Political Organization. The modern Republic of Nauru has an elected parliament of eighteen members, headed by a president. The councillors are elected from each district, as are members of the parliament. District chiefs were an innovation of European administration in 1927, and they gained significance when the Nauru Local Government Council (NLGC) was formed in 1951. Nowadays the NLGC controls most internal affairs.

Social Control and Conflict. Informal control is still maintained within Nauruan families, but formal control is in the hands of the Nauru police force and the judiciary, which consists of a supreme court, a chief justice (based in Melbourne, Australia), and district and family courts.

Religion and Expressive Culture

Religious Beliefs. Nauruans had their own traditional cosmology with beliefs in spirits and gods such as Tabuarik, who was represented in a stone now removed by mining activities. Family ancestors were honored with food offerings on an altar outside each family homestead. The centenary of the landing of the first London Missionary Society representatives was celebrated in 1987, and today most Nauruans are members of either the Nauruan Congregational church (60 percent) or the Roman Catholic church (33 percent). A breakaway Protestant church was formed in 1977 under the American Pentecostal church, but it has not drawn many adherents from the two established churches.

Religious Practitioners. Five Nauruans are ordained as pastors of the Congregational church, the younger ones having trained at Pacific Theological College in Fiji. The Catholic priest is appointed from Rome.

Ceremonies. Independence Day is celebrated on January 31; and "Amram Day" is observed in October to recognize the important day in 1933 when a Mrs. Amram gave birth to the 1,500th Nauruan. In addition, church feasts, marriages, and deaths are celebrated. Most festivities are marked with elaborate food sharing.

Arts. Weaving and other traditional arts are no longer practiced due to the lack of materials.

Medicine. Two hospitals serve the needs of Nauruans and other residents, but if other services are required patients are transported to Australia. Filariasis, leprosy, and tuberculosis are under control, but Nauruans have been noted as having a high incidence of diabetes and glucose intolerance.

Death and Afterlife. Funerals are conducted according to the faith of the deceased. A Nauruan is buried in the cemetery of the district to which he or she belonged. Such funerals are marked by feasts.

See also Kiribati, Tuvalu

Bibliography

Macdonald, Barrie (1988). *In Pursuit of the Sacred Trust.* New Zealand Institute of International Affairs Occasional Paper no. 3. Auckland.

Pollock, Nancy J. (1987). *Nauru Report to Commission for Rehabilitation of Nauru.* Melbourne: Government Printer.

Viviani, Nancy (1970). *Nauru: Phosphate and Political Progress.* Canberra: Australian National University Press.

Wedgwood, Camilla (1936). "Report on Research Work in Nauru Island, Central Pacific." *Oceania* 6:359–391; 7:1–33.

NANCY J. POLLOCK

New Georgia

The New Georgia group of islands is located in the south-central Solomon Islands between 8–9° S and 156–158° E. The group consists of the main island of New Georgia, nine other large islands, and numerous atolls. Among the major ethnolinguistic groups on New Georgia are the Kuaghe (also known as Kusaghe), Marovo, and Roviana. The Kuaghe, who numbered 1,059 in 1976, live on north New Georgia; the Marova (4,576 in 1976) on south New Georgia, Marova Lagoon, Vangunu Island, and Nggatokae Island; and the Roviana (5,365 in 1976) on north-central New Georgia, Roviana Lagoon, and Vonavona Lagoon. All speak languages classified in the New Georgia Group of Austronesian languages. Roviana, which was the primary language of many New Georgians, is being replaced by Solomons Pidgin, a combination of English words and Melanesian grammar with local dialect variation.

See also Choiseul

Bibliography

Capell, Alfred (1943). "Notes on the Islands of Choiseul and New Georgia, Solomon Islands." *Oceania* 14:20–29.

Goldie, J. (1909). "The People of New Georgia: Manners and Customs and Religious Beliefs." *Royal Society of Queensland Proceedings* 22:23–30.

Somerville, Boyle T. (1897). "Ethnographical Notes on New Georgia, Solomon Islands." *Journal of the Royal Anthropological Institute of Great Britain and Ireland* 26:357–412.

Ngatatjara

ETHNONYMS: Ngaayatjara, Ngadadjara, Pitjantjatjara, Western Desert Aborigines

Orientation

Identification. The Ngatatjara speak the Warburton Ranges dialect of the Western Desert Language Group (Pitjantjatjara) in Western Australia and adjacent southwestern Northern Territory and northwestern South Australia. Their name for themselves, which means "those who have the word *ngaata,*" which in turn means "middle distance," identifies the Warburton Ranges group in contrast with other, similarly identified dialect groups around them and does not imply any kind of tribal identity.

Location. The Warburton Ranges region is located at approximately 26° S and 127° E. The Warburton region includes rocky hills rising to an elevation of 700 meters above sea level and 300 meters above the surrounding terrain. Most of the region around these ranges consists of sandhills, sandplains, and low knolls of laterite. There is no permanent surface water, although some relatively dependable water can be obtained by digging into dry creek beds and at other special localities. Weather records indicate that drought or semidrought conditions prevail throughout this region about 50 percent of the time, making it unsuitable for sustained, European-introduced agriculture or pastoralism.

Demography. In 1981 the Aboriginal population of Western Australia was estimated at 31,351, but no accurate count is available for the Ngatatjara as a separate group within this total. Even if one includes people who are only part Aborigine, the total for the Warburton Ranges people and related groups nearby stands at less than 2,000, with high mobility as a further complicating factor in achieving an accurate enumeration. Before resettlement by the government in the late 1950s and early 1960s, many of these people followed a traditional, nomadic hunting-and-gathering way of life that dispersed them widely over the landscape. By 1970, the resident population at the Warburton Ranges Mission stood at around 400, and many Warburton people had already moved to other locations.

Linguistic Affiliation. The Ngatatjara dialect belongs to the Pitjantjatjara language, which is spoken over a wide area ranging from Kalgoorlie and Cundeelee, Western Australia, to the south and west; Ernabella and Musgrave Park, South

Australia, to the east; and Papunya and Areyonga, Northern Territory, to the north. Currently accepted linguistic classifications place Pitjantjatjara within the Wati Subgroup of the South-West Group in the Pama-Nyungan (also called the Western Desert) Family. Most Ngatatjara are multilingual, at least at the dialect level, and they often switch dialects when residing in new areas. The Western Desert linguistic family shares many features in common with other native Australian languages, which, with the sole exception of a group in northern Australia, are believed by linguists to be closely cognate and to have diverged from a single, ancestral language within the last 10,000 years. The separation of these languages from their Asian antecedents occurred so long ago, however, that no clear genetic connections have been detected with languages in Asia today.

History and Cultural Relations

Archaeology at Puntutjarpa RockShelter, close to the Warburton Ranges, demonstrates continuous use of this area for foraging and habitation for at least the last 10,000 years by Aboriginal people whose technology and economy closely resembled those of the traditional Ngatatjara at the time of European contact. Some changes are noted, such as a shift toward greater dependence upon edible grass seeds and the addition of small, geometric flaked-stone artifacts to the tool kit. But the economy remained oriented toward hunting and gathering wild foods that occur naturally in this area today. Recent archaeology to the west of Alice Springs, Northern Territory, has produced a sequence of Aboriginal occupation extending back 22,000 years, so the possibility exists that ancient ancestors of the present-day Western Desert Aborigines exploited Pleistocene species that are now extinct. European-Australian explorers first entered this region in 1873, but permanent settlement based upon water from a drilled well at the Warburton Ranges Mission did not occur until 1934. What followed was a period during which increasing numbers of nomadic desert people settled at the mission. Although the population at the mission grew as a result of in-migration, periodic epidemics severely reduced the number of inhabitants from time to time. By 1970 the mission was a settlement with government services that included a school, clinic, and a small store but with no self-sustaining economy. The Warburton population has remained primarily dependent upon outside support in the form of mission donations and government aid, although resident Aborigines are now becoming increasingly involved in decisions about their community, and there are indications, such as those shown by the movement by some Aborigines to outstations during the 1970s, that the period of colonial dependency at Warburton and elsewhere in this region is ending.

Settlements

Prior to 1934, all Ngatatjara were highly mobile and relatively opportunistic in their settlement pattern. During periods of sustained rains in particular parts of the desert, families congregated to take advantage of the water and to hunt game attracted by improved vegetation growth produced by such rains. Such maximal groups are estimated to have been as large as 150 individuals, but the duration of such aggregations was limited by the amount of game and water available and tended to be only a few weeks. These were major social events, when ceremonies and initiations occurred along with betrothals and curing activities. As drought conditions worsened, extended families departed in search of better hunting, with even smaller family groups setting out for more reliable water sources as drought stress increased. In extreme cases of long-term drought, families would leave their home area altogether and take up temporary residence with related families in areas as far as 500 kilometers away. Particular campsites might not be visited for several years in succession, or they might be visited several times in the same year, depending upon rains and associated plant and animal resources. There was no bounded territory within which such groups confined their foraging, nor were their social groups fixed in size or composition. Minimal social groups consisting of members of related families and totaling about ten to fifteen individuals could be found residing and foraging together around more or less dependable water sources during droughts. Domestic architecture consisted of conical or semicircular bough shelters during the summer, mainly to provide shade, and open-air campsites with linear or semicircular bough windbreaks during winter. Each family campsite had a central hearth that served as the focus for its social activities along with subsidiary hearths for warmth while sleeping. There were also task-specific sites that included quarries, hunting blinds, woodworking localities, and ceremonial and rock-art sites.

Economy

Subsistence and Commercial Activities. The traditional economy prior to 1934 and among isolated and uncontacted groups after 1934 was based primarily upon a limited number of edible wild plant foods that were harvested according to the particular conditions of rainfall and geography rather than on an annual seasonal basis. On most occasions, from day to day, women obtained the bulk of the diet, which consisted of plant staples and small animals, mainly lizards. Even before 1934, feral species introduced in other areas by European-Australians had spread to the Western Desert and had become an important part of the Ngatatjara diet. These animals included rabbits, feral cats, and, occasionally, camels and goats. Aboriginal men expended considerable time and energy in hunting but with generally poor returns. The principal kinds of game sought by hunters included kangaroos, wallabies, and emus. Allocation of all food supplies, including plant foods as well as large and small game, was structured by kin-based rules of sharing that resulted in an egalitarian distribution of food within the camp.

Industrial Arts. Subsistence technology was characterized by different technological responses to the requirements of mobility. These alternatives included multi-purpose tools like the spear thrower, which could also be used for lighting fires and mixing tobacco and pigments and as a percussion instrument to accompany songs and dances; appliances like heavy stone seed grinders, which were left at the campsite as permanent fixtures to be used whenever the family returned; and instant tools consisting of materials collected at the spot and fashioned as needed for a particular task. Despite the strictly utilitarian nature of most Ngatatjara technology, spear throwers were often decorated with complex incised designs that served a maplike function to aid men and their families in pinpointing geographical landmarks.

Trade. Long-distance transport and exchange of materials and artifacts occurred throughout the Western Desert. But this took place mainly within the context of the ceremonial life, often between individuals with a mutual affiliation to the same mythical ancestors and places where those ancestors traveled in the mythical past. Ceremonial exchange networks covered vast areas of the Western Desert, with the result that exotic items, such as incised pearl shells from the northwest coast of Australia and incised sacred stones from central Australia, circulated within these networks, either between individuals or between patrilineages.

Division of Labor. Division of labor or activity by sex was more pronounced in the domain of ritual and sacred affairs than in daily life. Under conditions of desert living, there was a general tendency in domestic activities for the women to focus on foraging for plant foods and small game, such as grubs and lizards. Males concentrated on hunting, with the corollary that women generally did not handle hunting equipment like spears and spear throwers. Women generally performed food-processing activities such as seed grinding as well as certain technological activities like the collection and production of spinifex resin adhesive. Men, on the other hand, were usually involved in stone artifact production and use. However, exceptions occurred in all of these activities under conditions of desert living, and new trends have arisen due to changes in the context of settlement near European-Australians. For example, in the 1960s women began taking a more active role in hunting large animals, using special dogs. Ritual activities, however, involved strict exclusion, mainly of women from male ceremonies but of men from female rituals as well. While some ceremonies were conducted jointly, by both sexes, the rules of participation by sex are more defined and strictly enforced than was the case for domestic activities.

Land Tenure. Concepts of tenure over land are dominated by the principle of joint affiliation and control by corporate groups, primarily patrilineages in which the members claim descent from a common, mythical ancestor. Such ancestors are believed to have lived and traveled in a mythical past called "the Dreaming" (*tjukurpa*), and the places where they lived, traveled, and had their adventures are also referred to by this term. These places are regarded as sacred sites that currently contain the spirit of the particular ancestor. Tenure applies specifically to these sites rather than to the control of territories, but the related idea of trespass ensures that the territory surrounding such sacred sites is also under a kind of de facto control of these patrilineages. Danger of trespass, whether intentional or accidental, is taken seriously by visitors who know that the patrilineage that "owns" the sacred sites within a particular area will punish such trespass. People do not venture into unfamiliar territory until shown the location of sacred sites within the area by members of the local patrilineage, and then only if they have established social relationships with members of the patrilineage, usually through marriage, that qualify them for access. This system of tenure is threatened today by relatively unrestricted movement by European-Australians who seek to establish mines and other kinds of development at or near such sacred sites. Legal arguments about "land claims" over Aboriginal sacred sites are a dominant theme in current Australian domestic politics.

Kinship

Kin Groups and Descent. Patrilineal descent is an important principle in structuring group affiliation, especially to the patrilineages that claim descent from a common, mythical ancestor and to the specific places where that ancestor lived and performed important acts in the mythical past. Another form of social classification in Ngatatjara society has to do with the dual division of kin into readily identifiable groups, referred to by anthropologists as sections and subsections, to simplify and facilitate expectations regarding whom one may marry or with whom one may expect to share food and access to resources. Aborigines who had resided at the Warburton Mission and at Laverton (and other settlements like Mount Margaret and Cosmo Newberry) tended to group themselves into four sections, correlated with a preference for first cross-cousin marriage. Historically during the period of European contact, different Aboriginal families coming together at such settlements adjusted their section terminology to produce a hybrid "six-section" system that appears to be unique to this area, although it is just as symmetric as its four-section antecedents. However, families arriving from the desert for the first time during the mid-1960s and early 1970s tended to use an eight-subsection mode of classification, correlated with second cross-cousin marriage. During this period such newly arrived desert people at the Warburton Ranges were making rapid adjustments to the "section" system in general use by the mission population.

Kinship Terminology. Classificatory rules of kinship permit extension of kin terms normally used between blood relatives (consanguines) to other individuals of the same sex and generation level. Such categories subsume basic expectations about behavior, such as with whom one may share food or access to resources or whom one may address directly or not, regardless of how one may feel about a particular individual.

Marriage and Family

Marriage. Polygynous marriage is preferred, although monogamous marriages continue to be common. Residential rules favor patrilocality, but in actual cases residence is often determined by movement in response to drought and other local factors. Strong obligations of both avoidance and sharing behavior exist between in-laws of similar and different generations. Divorce, however, can occur by mutual consent and without formality.

Domestic Unit. People who habitually camp and sleep together, mainly spouses and their offspring, are considered a family and constitute the minimal social unit. Related family units sometimes group themselves in clusters within the overall campsite when conditions of rainfall and hunting permit.

Inheritance. Affiliation for purposes of ceremonial and land-tenure group membership are inherited patrilineally, but portable property is not considered important enough to warrant special rules of inheritance.

Socialization. Infants are closely nurtured until weaning, after which they rapidly assert their independence by forming play groups consisting of children of mixed ages that sometimes establish separate, temporary campsites of their own and can even travel cross-country and feed themselves by means of their own foraging. Child rearing is benign, and physical punishment is rare.

Sociopolitical Organization

Social Organization. No corporate groups exist above the level of patrilineages, and these operate primarily in the domain of sacred and ceremonial affairs. In such patrilineages, age and subgroupings into alternating generations are sometimes important, expecially in the conduct of ritual activities.

Political Organization. In matters of daily life, Ngatatjara society is essentially egalitarian. Joint decisions involving several families are reached only after considerable argument, and the parties may exhibit reluctance to impose or accept decisions. Matters involving sacred affairs present indications of a more coherent leadership structure based upon relative age and sacred knowledge.

Conflict. Conflicts between individuals and individual families are fairly common and can result in personal violence. Disputes over marriages and sexual affairs are frequent, with some disputes over control of sacred sites and other sacred information as well. Cases of this latter kind of dispute became more common as European-Australian mining exploration extended deeply into the Western Desert during the 1960s and later.

Social Control. Individuals who are aggrieved in some way may call upon their kin to support them against whoever may have offended them. In serious cases this can result in spearing directed at the thighs of males representing their respective kin groups. There are no courts or officials to settle matters at a higher level. Patrilineages can apply sanctions to anyone who trespasses or commits a sacrilege on a sacred Dreaming site under their control. Informal mechanisms like gossip are often effective for social control at the domestic level.

Religion and Expressive Culture

Religious Beliefs. The Ngatatjara identify a range of ancestral beings, mainly animals and other natural species, that performed creative acts during the Dreaming that have led to their present sacred geography. Patrilineages affiliated with these different ancestors are responsible for instructing male initiates in these sacred traditions and for maintaining the sacred sites under their care as a way of increasing the abundance of the ancestral species. Dances and songs reenacting the myths of the Dreaming are performed in connection with these two kinds of duties. Traditionally, initiations most often occurred during maximal social aggregations when local conditions of water and food resources were favorable. Novices were "saved up" for such occasions and put through initiations together. Under more sedentary circumstances at the mission, novices are initiated when they are deemed to be old enough, with the result that ceremonies occur more often but with fewer novices at any one time. A similar increase in ceremonial activity at the mission and other settlements is evident with regard to ceremonies involving the "increase" of the ancestral species, either by revisiting the sacred sites or, if these are too far away, by performing such ceremonies in absentia at the mission.

Arts. Decorative body painting, ceremonial paraphernalia, cave and rock painting, and a rich variety of songs and oral narratives characterize the sacred life of the Ngatatjara on ceremonial occasions. The Ngatatjara were among the few people anywhere in the world in the 1960s and 1970s who still practiced cave and rock painting as a regular form of artistic expression. All Ngatatjara visual art, oral tradition, and singing are expressions of jointly held values and beliefs, mainly regarding the Dreaming, and are not generally seen as opportunities for individual artistic expression. Western Desert Aborigine painting, with modern acrylics, is presently undergoing rapid development in the context of a European-Australian demand for this type of art, but Ngatatjara participation in this trend is still somewhat marginal.

Medicine. In addition to individual sorcerers who can perform cures and an array of herbal and common remedies, the Ngatatjara have developed a perception of illness and death as willed by someone else, usually in a distant area. Such a belief may prompt an inquest by a sorcerer to locate the source and/or direction of the malevolent force and to carry out "countersorcery" against it.

Death and Afterlife. The traditional belief is that the soul divides into two parts after death. One part becomes a ghost that hovers around camp and serves as a sort of bogey to keep people (especially children) from wandering at night. The other part is the actual soul substance of an individual's ancestral Dreaming, which, after death, is believed to return to the sacred Dreaming site and rejoin a kind of undifferentiated pool of spirit ancestors—later to reemerge as part of the soul substance of another living person affiliated with that particular Dreaming. When a person dies, the campsite is changed to avoid the ghost, and the body is interred without ceremony. Later, when the group returns to the same area, the remains are reburied in a more elaborate ceremony.

See also Aranda, Mardudjara, Pintupi, Warlpiri

Bibliography

Berndt, R. M. (1959). "The Concept of 'the Tribe' in the Western Desert of Australia." *Oceania* 30:81–107.

Berndt, R. M., and Berndt, C. H. (1964). *The World of the First Australians.* Sydney: Angus & Robertson.

Berndt, R. M., and Berndt, C. H., eds. (1979). *Aborigines of the West.* Nedlands: University of Western Australia Press.

Gould, Richard A. (1969). "Subsistence Behaviour among the Western Desert Aborigines of Australia." *Oceania* 39:253–274.

Gould, Richard A. (1969). *Yiwara: Foragers of the Australian Desert.* New York: Scribners.

Peterson, Nicolas, and Jeremy Long (1986). *Australian Territorial Organization.* Oceania Monograph no. 30. Sydney: Oceania Publications.

Sutton, Peter, ed. (1988). *Dreamings: The Art of Aboriginal Australia.* New York: Braziller.

RICHARD A. GOULD

Nguna

ETHNONYMS: Efate, Ngunese, Sesake

Orientation

Identification. "Ngunese" is the name for the inhabitants of the island of Nguna, Vanuatu (formerly the New Hebrides).

Location. Nguna is in the central region of Vanuatu, lying approximately 7 kilometers off the north coast of the major island of Efate, where the country's national capital, Port Vila (Vila), is located, at about 17°30' S, 168° E. Nguna is a volcanic island with several prominent cones, although they are all inactive and grass-covered. The central part of the island is hilly, with a narrow fringe of coastal plain on the south shore and a smaller one on the north end. The climate is tropical, with distinct dry and hot (September–April) and rainy and cool (May–August) seasons. Neither electricity nor running water is available on the island, the latter representing a serious problem in times of drought, there being but one or two fresh springs to supply drinking water.

Demography. With measurements of approximately 5 by 10 kilometers, Nguna supports an ethnically homogeneous Melanesian population of close to 2,000 people, a figure which has almost doubled over the last decade.

Linguistic Affiliation. Most Ngunese are trilingual. They learn either English or French at school and acquire the nation's lingua franca, Bislama, through traveling to or working in other parts of the country or through listening to the national radio station and visitors from other islands. Their first language, however, is Ngunese, which is actually one of several dialects spoken in central Vanuatu and collectively referred to as "the Efate dialects." The language itself has not as yet been unambiguously named, being variously known as Nguna, Efate, North Efate, or Sesake, and classified in the Central Vanuatu Subgroup of Austronesian languages.

History and Cultural Relations

Nguna's first mention by Europeans came with a brief landing by Captain Cook in 1774. Another visit, by the H.M.S. *Pearl* in 1875, provided us with a freehand drawing of ritual carvings (slit drums) from the northern end of the island. Between these two events were many other contacts, most of which left no record. It is known, however, that beginning in the 1860s, young Ngunese men began joining ships (sometimes willingly, sometimes not) bound for the sugarcane plantations of Fiji and Queensland, Australia. Missionization, too, had begun on Nguna with the arrival of the Scot, Rev. Peter Milne, in 1870. His 54-year-long stay was unprecedented in the archipelago in terms of its length, the lasting success he had in "eradicating heathenism," and the installation of Milne's own son as his successor. Between Reverend Milne's heavy influence, reprisals launched by the colonial government against any unrest on the island, and various epidemics during the 1890s, the turn of the century saw a radically changed society and culture on Nguna. Upon becoming Christians of a strict Presbyterian denomination, the Ngunese forsook many aspects of their lives, including kava drinking, intervillage feuding, cannibalism, and competitive displays of wealth and slaughtering of pigs. Broader historical developments, of course, left indelible marks on Nguna as well. With the signing of an agreement between Britain and France in 1906, the archipelago became the New Hebrides/Les Nouvelles Hébrides under what was termed a "condominium government." This was a unique, joint-rule arrangement, some of the complications of which remain even after the country's attainment of independent nationhood, as Vanuatu, in 1980. For example, many duplicated essential services and institutions—such as two school systems, one English-speaking, one French-speaking—are still in place.

Settlements

There are approximately thirteen villages on Nguna. While all are clean and compact in design, village size varies from a dozen inhabitants to over 200, with the majority having 60–70 people. Housing itself varies in terms of style and materials, most being a combination of traditional and European. The traditional house form has been described as being like an upturned boat, having rounded, closed ends, a low crawl-through entrance, and no windows. The largest remaining example of this type of structure (some 20 by 8 meters in dimensions) is the village meeting house (*varea*) in Nguna's largest village. Houses made in this way, though on a much smaller scale, were relatively easy to heat (though smoky) and resistant to hurricanes, but the wood and thatch would rot within a few years, making attractive (though expensive) the more durable Western materials, such as corrugated iron roofing sheets and concrete blocks. In terms of village location, historically government officials and missionaries encouraged people to move down to the coast, but recently that trend has begun to reverse. As the population has risen people have increasingly sought less crowded, cooler, and airier sites for their homes on the bluffs above and behind the coastal villages. In a few cases long-deserted inland village sites are beginning to be reoccupied.

Economy

Subsistence and Commercial Activities. Ngunese horticultural production focuses on manioc and numerous varieties of taro and yams, although imported foods such as rice, sugar, and tea may also be considered staples. Seasonal supplements to these staples are: fish and other seafoods; and fruits and nuts, including papayas, oranges, bananas, *Canarium* almonds, mangoes, pineapples, and breadfruit. In addition, small numbers of livestock—chickens, pigs, and cattle—are raised. These animals are rarely consumed, however, outside of special events such as weddings. The universal primary source of cash is the cutting and drying of ripe coconuts, producing copra to be marketed through local cooperatives, each of which employs a "secretary" to oversee the sale of the copra and run a general store owned by the members. A few individuals—or, more often, a group of kin (a "company")—make a portion of their cash income through "taxi" work (i.e., running a transportation service by launch or truck) or through opening a small store in their home. Many engage in part-time work that entails many labor hours but little, if any, cash outlay (e.g., baking bread, sewing, weaving, and carving).

Industrial Arts. Many women are expert weavers of various types of pandanus mats and baskets for use by themselves and their families, as well as for giving as gifts on special occasions or for sale. While men generally do not weave, some carve such articles as souvenir war clubs, bows and arrows, and outrigger canoes for sale. A small handful of people engage in more substantial craft production (e.g., building launches, which take several months to complete but net a very large cash income).

Trade. There is evidence for the existence of an extensive trade network involving Nguna in precontact times. Today, Vila is the hub: the primary trade activity is that of taking produce, in both raw and cooked forms, and products of the arts and crafts industry to the Vila market for sale to urbanites and tourists. While labor-intensive, this enterprise yields a substantial profit and constitutes a pleasant day's outing as well, especially for women who, traveling cheaply and safely in groups of six to ten, often take the opportunity to visit relatives, especially grown children who live in Vila or surrounding areas.

Division of Labor. In terms of garden work, male and female tasks are differentiated: males do the jobs entailed in field preparation that require greater muscular strength, such as felling and clearing trees; females do those jobs requiring more time and care, such as the cleanup that follows burning off vegetation. Planting is often engaged in by both sexes. Once established, fields and crops are largely maintained and harvested by women, although gardening trips are often conducted in tandem by wife and husband. These divisions and similar ones in other contexts—such as women being the primary cooks in the home—are generally, but not strictly, observed, and they are not backed by any strong convictions such as the "female pollution" beliefs found in other parts of Melanesia.

Land Tenure. Communal ownership of land is vested in matriclans. The pattern of actual land use, however, is a matter of individuals' pressing claims through diverse lines of connection. The strongest claim is through one's father's having worked the land previously. But claims through one's mother or other relatives may also be made. Several factors make rival land claims difficult to resolve in the contemporary situation: a growing population; absenteeism of young Ngunese employed off-island; and more land given over to coconuts. Together these have put the land tenure system under considerable stress and rendered land distribution less flexible.

Kinship

Kin Groups and Descent. There are some twenty-two matriclans (*nakainaga*) recognized on Nguna; these are totemic, exogamous, matrilineal descent groups named for various objects, such as fish, types of trees, food plants, etc. Of these a small handful can be considered "extinct," as they have no living members. Others, on the brink of disappearing, have undertaken to preserve themselves by "adopting" adult females who already have daughters themselves. Ties to the matriclan of one's father are also recognized and maintained with care.

Kinship Terminology. The Ngunese have a Crow-type kinship terminology.

Marriage and Family

Marriage. In the past most marriages were arranged, uniting couples in a reciprocal system of sister exchange, the preferential spouse being a cross cousin. While there still may be some pressure to marry in particular ways, especially where the groom is expected to succeed to a high chiefly position, people assert that today they "marry for love." The past custom of polygamy, of course, was terminated with the adoption of Christianity. Nonetheless, weddings, following which the couple resides patrilocally, are one of the major social activities with which people concern themselves today, with substantial resources being amassed by the groom's relatives to provide a bride-price. For the Ngunese this does not constitute a payment for the woman; rather, the money and other valuables are gifts expressing gratitude and commitment to the relatives of the new bride on the part of the groom and his relatives. It is also true, however, that the size of the monetary portion of the bride-price, set at a very low figure by Reverend Milne, has escalated dramatically in recent years. Moreover, this sum varies substantially depending on the natal origin of the bride-to-be and the existing relationship that pertains between the families concerned.

Domestic Unit. The nuclear or extended family is the basic residential unit. Villages tend to be subdivided by the use of hedges, low fences, or stone borders to demarcate separate compounds, each of which is comprised of a couple's home and those of their married sons. This agnatic cluster supplies most labor required by any of the householders within it, beyond that which wife and husband can do together.

Inheritance. Land rights and personal possessions are inherited by both females and males; the latter, however, typically inherit substantially more land rights than do the former. In addition, a son (especially the firstborn) will more often inherit his parents' home since daughters usually leave their natal village upon marrying. Use rights regarding trees belong to the person who plants the tree without regard to who owns the land beneath it, and so these rights are inherited in the same way as are personal possessions. Coconut trees, however, being slow to mature but generating cash for decades thereafter, stimulate people to make longer-term claims to ownership of the land beneath them.

Socialization. Child-rearing practices shift as children age, becoming more demanding and likely to involve both verbal ridicule and mild physical punishment after a child reaches school age. Until then few behaviors elicit a strong response from adults, with the exception of a child's stinginess or refusal to share food or toys with other children. Intellectual and moral maturation are taken to be natural processes that develop with age and cannot be taught or instilled.

Sociopolitical Organization

Social Organization. The essential bases of social organization on modern Nguna are agnation and matriliny. With the matriclans dispersed widely across the island's villages, preferential male agnatic coresidence results in small aggregations of male matrikin in each village. Village membership itself is also a powerful force, uniting the different sets of kinfolk and clanfolk under the village high chief, in whose name villagers act collectively on certain significant occasions, such as planting yam gardens.

Political Organization. During the late nineteenth century, the precontact system of ranked, hereditary titles underwent a series of changes, becoming more rigid and less based on competition. With conversion to Christianity around 1900, the traditional economic base—pigs—was replaced by copra. Simultaneously, the titles ceased being transmitted matrilineally in favor of the patriline (i.e., sons rather than sisters' sons became the usual successors). Yet, since these changes did not entail a restructuring of the distribution of wealth nor of the power relations that it supported, most of the men who had dominated in the previous system continued to do so. Today, a few chiefs still retain disproportionate control over land (including large coconut stands) as a result of the attachment of rights over certain plots of land to their chiefly titles. Even after tremendous historical upheavals and alterations, bearers of the highest titles continue to inherit the associated lands and to dominate the other two power structures that govern island life: the local "session" of church elders and the pastor; and the village councils, some of which are more formally organized bodies while others merely constitute the adult membership of the village as a whole.

Social Control. This is largely under the authority of both village councils and the council of chiefs, whose memberships overlap to a significant degree, as mentioned above. A sliding scale of fines in cash, mats, pigs, and community labor (e.g., road maintenance) is applied to various misdemeanors such as swearing, theft, adultery, minor fights, and destruction of property. The central government has jurisdiction over all crimes of violence via an appointed local intermediary, the "Government Assessor."

Conflict. Land claims are a major source of conflict, for reasons discussed above. Village councils tend to have difficulty putting such arguments to rest permanently. Where these or other interpersonal conflicts end in destructive behavior or violent confrontation, alcohol abuse is usually a factor.

Religion and Expressive Culture

Religious Beliefs. Formerly the Ngunese, like people throughout the central part of the archipelago, believed that the god Mauitikitiki had pulled the islands up out of the sea with a rope. Apart from that, he played no known role in relation to everyday life. Numerous lesser spirits were thought to inhabit particular caves, trees, or rocks in the sea, and they could be influenced by a chief or, at his bidding, his religious specialist. In the present, the Ngunese continue to follow Presbyterian Christianity. There are challenges, of course, in the form of minor inroads made by other denominations and, to a degree, by a secular trend in modern ni-Vanuatu society in general. There have also been cargo-cult ideas abroad at different times, but they have never developed into any coherent movement on Nguna.

Religious Practitioners. While sorcery is said to have been rife on Nguna in the past, and some fear remains that it could be revitalized, there is no concrete evidence of such practices today. High chiefs, however, are still believed to be possessed bodily of spiritual powers: for example, it is believed that neither they nor their belongings can be touched safely by people other than their spouses or close family members.

Ceremonies. In the past the *naleoana* and *natamate* were the focal ritual activities, the first entailing pig sacrifice and gift exchange, the second centering on dancing before an orchestra of slit gongs, which are hollowed-out logs carved in the image of powerful ancestors and erected on a flat, ceremonial clearing. Today a first-yams ceremony, annual prestations to high chiefs and the pastor (at least in some villages), investitures of chiefs, and other such ceremonies occur, but they are divested of traditional religious content.

Arts. While pre-Christian ritual dances have disappeared, having been replaced by secular string bands and Westernized dances for young people, what is apparently a traditional form of oral performance (including four different genres of story text) is still widely engaged in and enjoyed.

Medicine. The "diviner" is a shamanic type of healer who uses herbal cures and supernatural messages, which may involve spirit travel during sleep to divine the cause of illness or misfortune. Many Ngunese consult such specialists in addition to making use of the services of a paramedic in the local clinic or traveling to one of Vila's hospitals for more serious matters.

Death and Afterlife. Although now looking toward Heaven as conceptualized in Presbyterian doctrine, the Ngunese once saw death as the beginning of a journey to the spirit world, which began with one's passage under the sea to emerge at Point Tukituki, on the southwest corner of Efate. Leaping from the cliffs into the sea, the spirit had a number of encounters with dangerous spirit beings as it passed through three different worlds, each stage being less familiar and less comfortable than the preceding one. Upon reaching the last, the person lost all contact with the living, in so doing completing his or her descent into nothingness.

Bibliography

Clark, Ross (1985). "The Efate Dialects." *Te Reo* 28:3–35.

Facey, Ellen E. (1981). "Hereditary Chiefship in Nguna." In *Vanuatu: Politics, Economics and Ritual in Island Melanesia,* edited by Michael R. Allen, 295–313. Sydney: Academic Press.

Facey, Ellen E. (1988). *Nguna Voices: Text and Culture from Central Vanuatu.* Calgary: University of Calgary Press.

Guiart, J., J. J. Espirat, M.-S. Lagrange, and M. Renaud (1973). Système *des titres, électifs ou héréditaires, dans les Nouvelles-Hébrides centrales d'Efate aux Iles Shepherd.* Paris: Institut d'Ethnologie, Musée de l'Homme.

Schütz, Albert J. (1969). *Nguna Grammar.* Oceanic Linguistics Special Publication no. 5. Honolulu: University of Hawaii Press.

ELLEN E. FACEY

Ningerum

ETHNONYMS: Kai, Ninggiroem, Ninggirum

Orientation

Identification. "Ningerum" is the name for the people living to the northeast of Ningerum Station (Kiunga District of Western Province, Papua New Guinea). They are one of the ethnic groups whose customary lands straddled the international border that separates Papua New Guinea from Irian Jaya. At contact with Westerners they had no common name for themselves; individual groups identified themselves according to their local clan names. The name of Ningerum appears to have been adopted in the 1950s by Dutch colonial administrators from the Muyu name (Ninggiroem or Ninggirum) for these closely related peoples who speak mutually intelligible dialects of the same language.

Location. The Ningerum inhabit the rain-forested ridge country that forms the southern foothills of the Star Mountains. Their territory lies primarily between the Ok Tedi (or Alice) River and the Ok Birim at 140°45' to 141°20' E and 5°15' to 5°35' S. The Ok Mani (just south of the Ok Tedi copper mine) and the rugged country south of the Ok Kawol are the customary northern limits of their territory. Except when under cultivation, this interior lowlands region is everywhere covered by dense rain forest. Elevation varies from about 100 meters in the south to over 1,000 meters at the summits of the highest hills in the north. The majority of the territory, however, is under 500 meters and consists of ridges running north to south, divided by steep, V-shaped valleys formed by many rivers and streams. Swampy areas are found in most of the valleys, especially in the south where the terrain is less rugged. The main walking tracks follow the major ridge tops and spurs. The climate is humid and tropical, characterized by very heavy rainfall (in excess of 250 centimeters annually) and warm temperatures (with a range of 20° C to 33° C in the south but somewhat cooler in the north). There are pronounced wet and dry seasons.

Demography. There are about 4,500 Ningerum people today. Over 3,300 live in Kiunga District (Papua New Guinea) and it is estimated that over 1,000 live in Kecamatan Mindiptana (Irian Jaya). Smaller numbers have migrated to Daru, Port Moresby, Merauke, and other urban centers. Population density ranges from 7 persons per square kilometer in the south of their territory to less than 2 in the north. At the time of Western contact, the population may have reached 6,000, but the region suffered population decline following numerous influenza epidemics in the 1950s and 1960s.

Linguistic Affiliation. Ningerum, with at least four dialects, is classified as a member of the Lowland Ok Subfamily of the Ok Family of Non-Austronesian languages. Its closest links are with the languages spoken by the Muyu and Yonggom peoples (North and South Kati languages), although these languages are unintelligible to monolingual Ningerum speakers. Besides phonological and traditional vocabulary differences in these dialects, the contemporary linguistic pattern is influenced by recent borrowings from the three contact languages (Motu, Tok Pisin, and Malay) that are used in the southern, northern, and western parts of Ningerum, respectively.

History and Cultural Relations

Ningerum were first contacted early in the century by Indonesian bird-of-paradise hunters and later by Dutch and Australian administrative patrols. For fifty years, outside contacts were few and left little impact, but in the 1950s Dutch and Australian government patrols began to visit Ningerum settlements on a regular basis. The government appointed village constables who were expected to keep order and represent the government's rule of law. Dutch colonial officers administered several villages along the border. After international border agreements between the Dutch and Australian governments, boundary markers were erected in four Ningerum villages in 1962. Not long afterwards, inhabitants of these villages were compelled to move their houses away from the border and choose residence in Irian Barat (now under Indonesian control) or Papua (under the Australians). The Ningerum Patrol Post was opened in 1964, and regular patrols were established two or three times a year. But despite increasing contact with the government for a few years, people on both sides of the border felt neglected once the frequency of patrols began to decline in the mid-1970s. Mining exploration and test drilling in the nearby Star Mountains brought several periods of intense activity, followed by relative neglect. With the construction of the Ok Tedi Mine in the 1980s, large townships have been established in Tabubil and Kiunga. The mine has brought a dramatic increase in contact with expatriates, environmental degradation in several rivers, and a great deal of commerce to the region. The long-term impact of the mine on Ningerum life and relations with outsiders is still uncertain.

Settlements

Customary settlements were small hamlets located on clan territories near gardens, sago swamps, and hunting lands. Most hamlets consisted of a single extended-family dwelling (*am* or *hanua*) built as a tree house 5 meters or more above the ground. Houses were rectangular, with separate sections for women and men. Each section contained two or more hearths. About every five years, houses were rebuilt near new gardens. Beginning about 1950, Ningerum began forming villages (*kampong*) at the encouragement of Dutch missionaries. At first these villages comprised only a few houses, but they gradually increased in size with the encouragement of Australian officials. In the 1980s there were thirty-two Ningerum villages in Papua New Guinea, ranging in size from 29 people (in two houses) to 350 (in more than fifty houses). Like customary hamlets, most villages have periodically moved following epidemics or intravillage conflict. In Irian Jaya, the Indonesian government encouraged even larger villages (*desa*). Village formation has not led Ningerum to abandon their customary residences; most families have both an isolated bush house, near their gardens, and a village house. Individuals and their nuclear families continue to reside with extended families, but they may live with different sets of relatives in their village and bush houses. Most Ningerum consider their bush house as their primary residence but spend two to three days in the village each week.

Economy

Subsistence and Commercial Activities. The extended family household was traditionally the basic unit of both production and consumption. Sago and bananas are the major staples eaten every day. These foods are supplemented by sweet potatoes, taro, yams, breadfruit, *okari* and *galip* nuts, greens, sugarcane, *pitpit*, pineapples, and local fruits. There are two kinds of gardens in the south: extensive banana gardens (up to 2 hectares) and small, mixed gardens, fenced to keep pigs out. Banana gardens require little tending aside from felling trees and planting suckers around the fallen trunks. Mixed gardens require considerable time for fencing, ground preparation, weeding, and tending. Gardens produce for about two years, after which they should lie fallow for fifteen or more years. Sago is abundant in the south, but it is planted and managed by weeding and cutting selected trees to increase productivity. In the north, sago is less common and monocropping of taro is important. Domesticated pigs run wild in most villages and forage for most of their diet. They are given some food in the evening to keep them from joining the feral herd. Domesticated boars are gelded, and sows are serviced by feral boars. Pork is an important part of the diet; in the dry season it is frequently eaten at pig feasts and other ceremonies, while in the wet season pigs are easily tracked and hunted with shotguns or bows and arrows. Hunting for marsupials and birds is of relatively minor importance, while small fish and crayfish are often caught in large numbers. Sago grubs, frogs, bush eggs, ant larvae, and other foods foraged in the forest are delicacies, but they are of minor importance in the daily diet. Until construction of the Ok Tedi copper mine began, small red chili peppers (*lombok*) were the only cash crop, and they were cultivated on a very small scale. With the coming of the mine, economic opportunities have diversified and expanded into wage employment and vegetable production for cash sale.

Industrial Arts. Crafts include string bags, skirts from rushes, bows, and arrows. Other household utensils are of simple manufacture, using bush materials. Men occasionally make dugout canoes, used only for crossing major rivers. Houses are built high up on tree trunks or on shorter house posts in villages. Floors are of narrow palm slats, roofs are of sago-leaf thatch sewn in panels, and walls are made from the stems of sago fronds.

Trade. Considerable trade was conducted at large pig feasts, which brought together Ningerum, Yonggom, and Muyu from a wide area. This trade consisted of many small transactions involving manufactured goods (string bags and bows), raw materials (rushes for skirts, red ocher), dogs, piglets, cassowary chicks, and magic or other ritual knowledge. Money cowries, nassa shells, and dogs' teeth were the standard mediums of exchange throughout the region. Men also occasionally went on long-distance trading expeditions as far as Mount Koreom in the west and up into the Star Mountains in the north. There was little product specialization in the lowlands; individuals sold what they had in excess of their needs and bought things that they might need but that they could ordinarily make themselves or get from close relatives. Trade with Star Mountains people was more specialized: Ningerum black-palm bows and shells were traded to Wopkaimin people for tobacco and hand drums, which were obtained from the Tifalmin people farther north.

Division of Labor. Most gardening is a cooperative effort involving a husband and his wife (or wives), often assisted by coresident kin. Women process sago in small groups after a tree has been cut down and opened by men. For tasks that require a great deal of labor—such as house building or clearing and fencing gardens—families often invite twenty to thirty relatives and neighbors to help, reciprocating with an elaborate meal. Only men hunt with bows and arrows or shotguns, usually by themselves. Both women and men go diving for fish in streams (using fishing arrows and goggles) in small groups. Women do most of the cooking, child tending, and firewood gathering, although men often assist when women are busy with other work. The only cooperative subsistence activity involving large groups (up to 100 men, women, and children) is the occasional use of derris root to poison large numbers of fish when streams are low. Major feasts involve the cooperative effort of two or more local clan segments—occasionally a village—but most construction and food production for these events is done by a small group of closely related men and women, respectively. Up to 1980, few Ningerum were regularly earning cash wages, and this was almost exclusively a male domain that usually required moving to an urban center or plantation (up to about 1970).

Land Tenure. All land is associated with a named, patrilineal clan segment and, in theory, owned by this group of individuals. Fallow garden lands are usually considered owned by the male heirs of the last man to have cultivated the property. Usually these rights are held in common by a group of brothers or cousins, but where land is scarce, men may divide their holdings among their sons. Daughters retain rights of usufruct and may cultivate the land with their husbands if they live nearby. Usufruct rights to garden land may be allocated to friends or kin as a way of recruiting nonagnates into the local clan segment. After a generation such land becomes more closely associated with the family of the most recent cultivator than with the original owner. Less commonly, parcels of garden land have been alienated from their original clan segment through purchase by an individual for shell money. Rivers, ritual sites, and hunting lands—as well as the rights to their flora and fauna—are owned in common by the clan segment, whose interests are managed by the clan segment's elders. Land belonging to moribund clan segments can be expropriated by anyone who can make use of the resources and claim usufructuary rights through nonagnatic kin ties, through previous residence, or through former residence on the land of a parent or grandparent.

Kinship

Kin Groups and Descent. Each person is born into the named patrilineal clan (*kawatom*) of his or her father. Clans are associated with identifiable territories and one or more men's cult ritual sites situated in the bush away from the view of women and children. There are more than 200 local clans, and only the smallest clans are exogamous. Several clan segments may share myths about their origin from a single (usually unnamed) ancestor. As corporate groups, local clan segments include many nonagnates—mainly wives and a variety of coresident kinsmen from other clans. Coresidence is far more important in defining rights and membership in the corporate group than formal clan membership according to birth.

Kinship Terminology. Kinship terminology is of the Omaha type.

Marriage and Family

Marriage. Marriage with a matrilateral cross cousin is preferred, but only a few marriages are contracted between actual cross cousins. Most spouses are understood to be classificatory cross cousins, but a lack of detailed knowledge about relationships in the second and third ascending generations allows considerable flexibility. Of more importance in arranging marriages is a preference to marry into nearby households. Such marriages consolidate land holdings and existing alliances. Polygyny is accepted but was more common in the past. The most influential men had four or five wives at one time. Divorce is possible but extremely rare. In most marriages there are strong emotional bonds between husbands and wives. Large bride-price payments are required. After a substantial initial payment, continuing bride-price installments are usually paid for the life of the marriage.

Domestic Unit. Traditionally, an extended family of up to thirty people lived as a cooperative domestic group. A household usually consisted of 2 or 3 brothers together with their wives and children and a handful of other relatives. With the cessation of intergroup raids and with the formation of villages, these extended family units are now smaller, often only a nuclear family and a few other individuals (e.g., a grandmother, foster children, and unmarried siblings). Increasingly, the nuclear family is the key domestic group, although there is always room to incorporate otherwise unattached kin, particularly orphans and young single adults.

Inheritance. Children inherit land primarily from their father, but they retain some rights through their mother. Sago, breadfruit, and nut trees are usually divided up among the children by their owner before death or can be distributed among the heirs in the absence of oral instructions. Portable wealth is nearly always insufficient to cover death payments to the deceased's matrikin and creditors. Such debts are inherited jointly by the deceased's adult sons and sometimes brothers (or husband if the deceased is a woman).

Socialization. Parents are generally permissive, scolding and occasionally threatening children who misbehave. Ghosts, spirits, and sorcerers are often mentioned to frighten young children. Up to the opening of the Ok Tedi copper mine there were few opportunities for public education.

Sociopolitical Organization

Social Organization. Ningerum social relations are centered on maintaining a network of alliances between a local clan segment and surrounding clan segments. Before pacification, such positive relations created a security circle for each isolated household. Such ties consolidated land rights and minimized resource scarcities for local groups. A complex set of social obligations consisting of ongoing bride-price, child-price, widow-price, death payments, burial payments, and other personal debts ensured continuing positive relations between neighboring allied families, as long as token payments were made from time to time. Today, allied families cooperate for feasting, ritual activities, house building, and fence building. Formerly, they also supported one another in defense and raiding.

Political Organization. Traditionally there was no form of central authority or hereditary leadership whose authority extended beyond the extended family household. Often political authority was only nominal within a large household. Influential men (*kaa horen*), elder members of the local clan segment, attempted to exert authority over their families through exhortations to action and proper behavior, but they had few other ways to influence their kin. Today, a man of influence is often able to attract support from clan segments whose members are related to him through blood or marriage. Such ties, however, offer a very weak source of political cohesion and relatives often ignore exhortations. In the 1950s, village constables (*mamus*) were appointed in most villages by the Australian administration. Although most of these men were chosen because they were prominent, even the government's backing did little to augment their authority or expand political cohesion within the region. The Ningerum Local Government Council was established in 1971 with councillors elected to represent two or three villages.

Social Control. In principle, conflict should not exist within a local clan segment, but disagreements leading to sorcery accusations among close relatives are not uncommon. There are no formal courts to air disputes and in the past a household or clan segment (together with allied individuals) would attack another household to defend their rights. Today, fear of sorcery and government intervention serve as the only mechanisms for maintaining cohesion within the villages.

Conflict. Before pacification in the 1950s, raids by small groups of warriors were a constant threat. Conflict typically arose as the result of sorcery suspicions following an unexpected death. Usually a single individual was the chosen victim in a raid. Since government control was established, traditional tensions have not abated and traditional forms of conflict have been rechannelled into heightened sorcery fears and frequent accusations of assault sorcery. In recent times, sorcery accusations have often been leveled against very close relatives, especially brothers and parallel cousins.

Religion and Expressive Culture

Religious Beliefs. Religious beliefs center on men's cult ritual, which concerns itself with celebrating the ghosts of dead male relatives. Ningerum also believe in a variety of culture heroes (called "ahwaman"), bush spirits, and powerful essences, all of which are felt to have power (for good or bad) over human endeavors. They also believe in manipulation of the natural world through magic for both positive ends (success in hunting, gardening, and feasting) and for destructive ends (sorcery). The Montfort Catholic Mission has had catechists in a few villages since the late 1960s and the Evangelical Church of Papua has sponsored a few teachers since the late 1970s. Missionization has proceeded slowly and has had little impact on Ningerum religious beliefs.

Religious Practitioners. Men's cult leaders officiate over rites to celebrate the exhumed bones of the dead and release their spirits. Ningerum also have a variety of different kinds of healers. There are no shamans or general-purpose "medicine men." Typically each healer knows only one or two different ritual therapies, each suitable for specific problems.

Ceremonies. The most important ceremonies are the major pig feasts and the men's cult feasts that often accompany them. Public feasts are held in specially constructed feast compounds, containing a large feast house and a long plaza flanked by sleeping quarters for as many as 700 guests. Feasts may take more than six months to prepare and are held by a clan segment about once a decade. The public purpose of these feasts is to redistribute pork, but for the host families these events are an opportunity to celebrate the dead and to promote the host group's prosperity. Men's cult feasts resemble the public feasts in form, but they are also associated with male initiation in addition to pork redistribution and celebrating the dead.

Arts. Ningerum art is focused on decorating the human face and body for a variety of dances and ceremonies. They have few carvings or plastic arts, although formerly they carved and painted hand drums and probably had large painted shields. They have a variety of traditional songs and dances, many of which use drums or other simple percussion instruments.

Medicine. Traditional medicine includes a variety of ritual treatments aimed at attacks by ghosts, spirits, and sorcery. Assault sorcery is believed to be incurable, but projection sorcery is cured by removing substances that have been magically projected into the body. Curing rituals aimed at ghost attack often promote community cohesion. Few treatments involve herbal remedies. Government-sponsored aid posts have been available since the late 1960s and are regularly used by Ningerum people when sick, but they are often used in conjunction with traditional treatments.

Death and Afterlife. Ningerum believe that at death the soul leaves the body and stays near its living relatives, whose lives it continues to influence for many years. Ghosts punish harmful action toward their living kin with sickness and can punish their living relatives if the ghosts are neglected. Death is never attributed to the work of ghosts. Deaths of the very young, the old, and the infirm are explained as due to weak physiology; for those in the prime of life, death is always considered to be the work of various kinds of assault sorcery.

See also Muyu

Bibliography

Austen, Leo (1925). "Report of a Patrol from Wukpit Camp (Tedi River) to Star Mountains." *Papua Annual Report for 1922–23, 27–37. Melbourne: Government Printer.*

Jackson, Richard (1982). *Ok Tedi: The Pot of Gold.* Waigani: University of Papua New Guinea.

Welsch, Robert L. (1983). "Traditional Medicine and Western Medical Options among the Ningerum of Papua New Guinea." In *The Anthropology of Medicine: From Culture to Method,* edited by L. Romanucci-Ross, D. Moerman, and L. Tancredi, 32–53. New York: Praeger.

Welsch, Robert L. (1985). "The Distribution of Therapeutic Knowledge in Ningerum: Implications for Primary Health Care and the Use of Aid Posts." *Papua New Guinea Medical Journal* 28:67–72.

Welsch, Robert L. (1987). "Multinational Development and Customary Land Tenure: The Ok Tedi Project of Papua New Guinea." *The Journal of Anthropology* no. 6, pt. 2, 109–132.

ROBERT L. WELSCH

Nissan

ETHNONYM: Green Island

Orientation

Identification. The Nissan Islanders live on Nissan Atoll and Pinipel Atoll, which together form the Nissan or Green Island Group in the North Solomons Province of Papua New Guinea.

Location. Nissan lies at 154°10' E and 4°27' S. Located 64 kilometers northwest of Buka and 110 kilometers east of New Ireland, Nissan links the Bismarck Archipelago to the Solomon Islands. Nissan Atoll is elliptically shaped, measuring 15 kilometers on its longitudinal axis with a maximum width of 7 kilometers. A land rim, nowhere wider than 2 kilometers and broken by three passages on the northwest side, encloses a large, picturesque lagoon. Two and a half kilometers to the northwest of Nissan, Pinipel—locally known as "Pinipir" (the name used in this discussion)—consists of a narrow island less than 10 kilometers long and a tiny uninhabited islet. The islands have a wet tropical climate with a year-round average daily temperature in the 20s. Seasonal monsoon and trade winds visit Nissan, and there is considerable rain (320 centimeters in 1971).

Demography. Early European visitors to Nissan estimated the population to be 1,500 or less. A 1940 census estimated the population at 1,427. In 1971, Nissan had a population of 3,094 (including absentees): 2,551 on Nissan Atoll and 543 on Pinipir. Almost half of these people were born after 1955, the population having doubled since World War II.

Linguistic Affiliation. Islanders speak a Non-Austronesian language including two major dialects, spoken respectively on Nissan Atoll and Pinipir; linguistically, Nissan is closest to Buka. Islanders also speak Melanesian Pidgin (Neo-Melanesian).

History and Cultural Relations

Most scholars agree that the Nissan people are Melanesians of Bukan origin, some believing that Nissan was first occupied by Polynesians and later overrun by Bukans. New Ireland cultural influence is also evident on Nissan. The Dutch explorers Jacob Le Maire and Willem Schouten were the first Europeans to sight Nissan in 1616. Abel Tasman again sighted the group in 1643 and Philip Carteret in 1767. By the

1870s European recruiters were taking islanders to work on plantations in Queensland, Fiji, and Samoa. After 1885, the Forsayth Company based in New Britain established a coconut plantation on Nissan. In 1890, Georg Schmiele, an official with the German colonial government, also based in New Britain, visited Nissan to investigate the murder of the resident Forsayth trader. He recorded local customs, mapped the atoll group, and identified it by what he assumed to be the islanders' own name for it, Nissan. Australia took over New Guinea in 1914, and Nissan eventually became part of the Bougainville District. In 1926 Catholic missionaries from the Society of Mary extended their influence to Nissan, the first priest being stationed there in 1939. In 1942 the Japanese forcibly occupied Nissan, remaining there until a joint American–New Zealand force expelled them. The Allies built a base on Nissan, relocating most islanders for the duration of the war to Aola on Guadalcanal, where many died of malaria. After the war a civilian Australian administration reestablished control; it was replaced in 1975 by the government of Papua New Guinea. Also, after the war, mission-run grade schools opened, and high school and trade schools exist there now as well.

Settlements

There are fifteen villages on Nissan Atoll and three on Pinipir with populations in 1971 ranging from 80 to 337 persons. Most villages consist of one or two hamlets and houses scattered individually or in clusters in the bush. In precontact times, settlements were smaller and, because of endemic warfare, were located strategically in the bush. Consisting of a single or double row of houses, the hamlets were originally created by colonial officials as convenient administrative units. Some villagers maintain residences both in the hamlet and near their gardens in the bush to protect them against marauding pigs. The central feature of a settlement is its men's house (*iabas*), where in the past all unmarried males over the age of 9 slept. Other men sometimes slept in the house as did male visitors to the village. Although many iabas customs are disappearing, it still serves as a clubhouse exclusively for men; in it they plan activities and gossip. Contemporary residences of traditional construction are single-room, windowless, rectangular structures with ridged, steeply sloping roofs. They are built on the ground with walls of areca-palm bark and sago-thatch roofs. Nowadays, islanders often build houses on piles and incorporate introduced materials such as plywood, sawed timbers, concrete, and galvanized iron roofing.

Economy

Subsistence and Commercial Activities. Islanders are slash-and-burn subsistence horticulturalists. After a post–World War II taro blight, yams replaced taro as the major crop. Islanders also grow sweet potatoes (introduced in German times), tobacco, sugarcane, and minor foods introduced with sweet potatoes (cassava, pumpkins, corn, beans, watermelons, tomatoes, and cabbages). Garden land lies fallow for years between plantings. Tree crops—some grown in gardens, others partially cultivated in the bush—include coconuts, plantains, bananas, papayas, breadfruit, *Barringtonia, Canarium indicum,* and *Areca catechu,* whose nut is an ingredient in a betel mixture (consumed as a stimulant). On Pinipir, which has extensive mangrove swamps, mangrove fruit is a local staple. Islanders also fish in the lagoon and sea using purchased lines and hooks, locally made spears and spear guns, nets, baskets, scoops, a stunning agent made of *Pongamia pinnata* leaves, and dynamite. Sea resources include fish, crabs, lobsters, shellfish, *palolo* worms, and giant sea turtles. Domestic animals include chickens, dogs (eaten in some villages), cats, and, most importantly, pigs. Consumed mostly on ceremonial occasions, pigs, together with large manufactured rings of *Tridacna* shell, are the major form of traditional island wealth. Claiming that the activities of pigs interfere with copra production, some villages have eliminated their pigs in recent years. Although a few pigs are raised in villages, most are semidomesticated and approach humans only to be fed. Other pigs have become feral. Islanders hunt these pigs as well as the brown cuscus and, occasionally, birds and flying foxes. Purchased foods, such as coffee and tinned fish and meat, are also popular. Since German days islanders have raised coconuts for copra, deriving a small cash income; recently islanders have also started producing cocoa. Since German times, islanders have left Nissan to find employment in other parts of the country on plantations, in towns (as domestics), and on boats. Beginning in the 1970s, many have gone to work for a multinational copper-mining company on Bougainville. A few send money to relatives at home; others start new families outside Nissan.

Industrial Arts. Nissan men construct houses and single-outrigger dugout canoes (replacing traditional double-outrigger canoes and seagoing plank canoes without outriggers). Men also manufacture masks and other dance objects. Specialists make the large wooden slit gongs found in men's houses. Women plait coconut-frond leaflets into a variety of baskets and mats; they sew pandanus-leaf hoods and carrying straps. Islanders no longer manufacture stone axheads, *Tridacna* shell arm rings, and tools of war (bows and arrows, spears, clubs, slings, arm guards). Most technology currently used is of Western manufacture.

Trade. The people of Nissan Atoll once exchanged trading visits with the coastal villagers of northern Buka; those of Pinipir traded with the villagers of Anir off New Ireland. The major Nissan contribution to interisland trade was pigs. Bukans contributed clay pots, pipes, and bows and arrows; Anir gave shell rings, red ocher, tobacco, and riverine stones. Minor trade in foods between villages and districts on Nissan continues today. Exchanges of goods and services are particularly common within villages. Some islanders also engage in entrepreneurial activities associated with coconut and cocoa production or operate small trade stores on Nissan.

Division of Labor. Women undertake most domestic and child-care activities. Men take the lead in subsistence activities requiring strength, such as certain stages of gardening. Men are the primary actors at ceremonies, the women working mainly behind the scenes under male direction. Persons with special ritual or technological expertise assist others on a part-time basis. Various church and government employees on Nissan receive salaries.

Land Tenure. All land is divided into named sections. Each section, including settlement sites and stretches of beach, belongs to an individual or small group. Men inherit land and movable property from their fathers, sons inheriting land jointly but eventually dividing it among themselves. The men's sisters and their children have defined usufructuary rights to that land. Recent population growth and the diversion of garden land to coconut production mean that the size of cultivable properties is diminishing, a factor encouraging emigration.

Kinship

Kinship Groups and Descent. Matrilineal descent groups crosscut village and district boundaries. These groups include moieties—"Eat the Dog" and "Eat the Pigeon"—that are divided into sibs named after major dietary restrictions (*tobu*) imposed upon members. Sibs may contain partially localized subgroups, sometimes named after specific land areas. Descent groups own no property although they may once have done so. Primarily they regulate marriage and breach the political autonomy of once-warring villages and districts.

Kinship Terminology. A person distinguishes consanguineal relatives within his genealogical generation by sex only. Islanders believe the relationship between brothers and sisters to be the most important of all relationships, a basis, indeed, of Nissan society and morality. It is characterized by formal avoidances known as *walatur* (literal meaning: "causing to stand up"), including the rule—still observed to varying degrees—that a brother may not remain seated while his sister stands in his presence. In the parental generation, all females, including the mother, are identified by a common term; two other terms distinguish the father and his male kin from the mother's male kin, such as the mother's brother. Kinship terminology could be described as a variant of the Hawaiian system, but unlike the ideal Hawaiian system the Nissan terminology distinguishes one's mother's brother from other male relatives of one's parental generation.

Marriage and the Family

Marriage. Marriages within moieties are allowed, although not preferred; but marriages within sibs are discouraged. Islanders tend to marry within their own villages and districts, but they also often marry outside. Traditionally, parents and other relatives of the couple arranged the marriage. Nowadays the couples themselves often take the initiative, seeking family approval afterwards. Brother-sister exchange is the ideal; at the least, the sib giving a woman in marriage should eventually receive one in return. Relatives still exercise some control over a couple's marriage by contributing to the payment of bride-wealth in cash, shell rings, and store goods. A traditional "giving" of the bride accompanies a church wedding. Upon marriage, the couple establishes a new household, usually near the households of the man's father and brothers. Although infrequent today, polygamous unions were once common. Nowadays islanders working or studying elsewhere in Papua New Guinea also marry people of other islands. Because of Catholic strictures, divorce on Nissan is uncommon, as it was traditionally.

Domestic Unit. The nuclear family is the household unit, often combining for economic activities with other units related through the male heads of household.

Inheritance. On Nissan, men own land and movable wealth (shell rings and pigs). In some cases, a man will indicate during his lifetime the desired disposition of land and wealth upon his death. In most instances, a man's sons inherit equally and divide the property and wealth among themselves. If a man has no sons, his brothers and brothers' sons—or, in the absence of these persons, his sisters' sons—inherit his property and wealth.

Socialization. Parents allow children to mature at their own pace. They show affection for small children primarily by physical means. Adults inculcate in children a sense of shame, considered a vital aspect of Nissan character. Preferred punishments are scolding and teasing. When not in school, children are expected to assist in the household. However, they often engage in unorganized, desultory play among themselves.

Sociopolitical Organization

Social Organization. Islanders boast that their society is egalitarian. Major differences in wealth and power are uncommon. Nonetheless, sex, age, family name, personal character, and achievement affect social status. The system of ranking that sets big-men apart from ordinary men allows individuals to draw distinctions of rank among these men as well, but it does not provide a basis for consensus on rank order.

Political Organization. Nissan has a local government, including elected officials, administered under the North Solomons Province of Papua New Guinea. Nissan villages and sometimes hamlets also have traditional leaders, "big [important] persons." Such big-men inherit their claims to leadership from their fathers, sometimes also inheriting the land on which their hamlets are located. But big-men must validate and maintain their positions by demonstrating interpersonal and leadership skills—coordinating work efforts, settling disputes, and demonstrating generosity—and by organizing mortuary feasts. Given islanders' egalitarian sentiments, big-men adopt various strategies of indirect leadership, and followers, because they are not the equals of leaders, practice formal avoidances of them. It is possible that competition for the position of big-man was once more common than it is today. Another leader similar to the big-man existed in the past, the *toia,* who was surrounded by formal avoidances.

Social Control. Nowadays the provincial government and its local representatives have assumed many of the formal functions of social control. Big-men and other elders also resolve disputes within and between villages. A traditional form of mediated dispute settlement, *poluk,* involving the exchange of pigs and shell rings between disputants, is uncommon today.

Conflict. The major causes of disputes are marital infidelity, contested land rights and boundaries, the marauding of pigs, and misdirected gossip. Thefts, unsolicited borrowings, unpaid debts, suspicions of sorcery, and fights between children also cause disputes between people. Intervillage rivalries are common. Once these resulted in warfare (and cannibalism), and even nowadays they lead to occasional fights between groups.

Religion and Expressive Culture

Religious Beliefs. Islanders are Catholics who regularly attend church and village chapel services. Many also believe in and ritually interact with various local supernatural entities including spirits of the dead and nonhuman bush spirits. Dangerous supernatural power (*barang*) is associated with women's menstrual blood and with several societies of magicians who derive barang from the spirits of the bush. Islanders consider bush spirits to be malicious, especially when not under human control. A pantheon of these and other nonhuman spirits associated with dance magic (*buai*) and masked dance performances (*dukduk* and *tubuan* spirits) are the center of much attention in the context of dance competition at mortuary feasts. Although not malicious, spirits of the dead sometimes interfere in human activities. People also invoke the dead in rituals of divination and in magical rituals as former experts who assist the living magician.

Religious Practitioners. Practitioners of Catholicism include foreign-born priests and sisters as well as local catechists. Many adults also practice magical rituals in which they manipulate words and objects symbolizing desired ends. Magical knowledge is widespread on Nissan and is associated with virtually every important activity or event. Certain bodies of magical ritual belong to trained specialists. They are members of village-based male societies of weather magicians and also of dance magicians. These latter perform the buai rituals introduced after World War II from New Ireland and the Gazelle Peninsula of New Britain. In the past, societies of grand sorcerers also existed.

Ceremonies. The most elaborate ceremonies on Nissan are associated with pig feasts that villages or hamlets stage under the direction of their big-men. At these feasts the hosts feed visitors pork and other delicacies; big-men make speeches; and villagers exchange large sections of pork with one another in order to discharge obligations arising out of the deaths of close relatives and in so doing validate inheritance claims, including ones to headmanship itself. Feasts are scenes of ritual competition between villages. Weather magicians of the host group work publicly to guarantee a sunny day for the feast, while the magicians of rival villages, including the guest villages, surreptitiously summon rain clouds. Host and guest villages also perform choral line dances; in preparation for these performances, magicians act to ensure the success of their own dances at the expense of those of rival teams.

Arts. Traditional songs and stories continue to be important to islanders. Contemporary art focuses on dances introduced from New Ireland and New Britain. Islanders adopt or create their own versions of foreign dance songs, dance movements (accompanied by the beating of hourglass drums), and dance costumes (masks, wooden dance sticks, and wooden headpieces).

Medicine. Islanders attribute illness to natural causes as well as to sorcery or malicious spirits. Numerous magical cures exist to treat illnesses as do corresponding rituals of sorcery to cause them. Islanders also use Western biomedicine; they consult local medical orderlies.

Death and Afterlife. Islanders once dropped the weighted bodies of their dead into the sea. Nowadays, the dead receive Catholic burial in village cemeteries. A series of ceremonies once followed a death in order to effect the transition of the deceased to the afterworld. The final mortuary feast and minor celebrations preliminary to it continue to be held primarily to honor the dead and to dismiss formally their claims upon village society.

See also Kurtatchi, Lak

Bibliography

Krause, Fritz (1907). "Zur Ethnographie der Insel Nissan." *Jahrbuch des Staedtischen Museums fuer Voelkerkunde zu Leipzig* 1:44–159.

Nachman, Steven R. (1981). "Buai: Expressions of Sorcery in the Dance." *Social Analysis* 8:42–57.

Nachman, Steven R. (1982). "Anti-Humor: Why the Grand Sorcerer Wags His Penis." *Ethos* 10:117–135.

Nachman, Steven R. (1982). "The Validation of Leadership on Nissan." *Oceania* 52:199–220.

Nachman, Steven R. (1984). "Shame and Moral Aggression on a Melanesian Atoll." *Journal of Psychoanalytic Anthropology* 7:335–365.

STEVEN R. NACHMAN

Niue

ETHNONYMS: Niuean, Niuefekai

Niue is a 260-square-kilometer raised coral atoll. Culturally and linguistically it is very similar to Tonga. Niue is located at 19° S and 169°50' W, 385 kilometers east of Vavau, Tonga. There were 6,000 people on Niue and about 5,500 Niueans in New Zealand in the early 1980s. Niuean is part of the Tongic group of Austronesian languages. At present, only the narrow coastal fringe is inhabited and exploited; formerly, the island was more evenly settled.

Subsistence is based on marine exploitation, taro, arrowroot, coconuts, yams, and bananas; breadfruit is a relatively recent introduction. Fishing is difficult and catches are poor, due to the limited reef around the island. Chickens were raised in the past, but they have been replaced by wild rats and fish as the main sources of protein. There is a tendency toward a reliance on fishing on the coast and taro farming farther inland. Ramages are the landholding groups.

Kin groups include the Motu and Tafiti moieties, general bilateral kin groups, ramages, and extended families. Descent is ambilineal, with a patrilineal bias. Marriages are often arranged. Polygyny was common among chiefs in the past. Both moieties are endogamous. Households were very flexible in their membership, but they usually contained a core group of siblings or parents and children. In addition to the kin groups, Niuean society was stratified into three classes: the warriors, the warriors' retainers, and low people. A paramount chief (*patuiki*) formerly ruled over the entire island,

and he could be ceremonially killed during drought or famine for what was considered neglect of duty. The Niueans were politically subordinate to the Tongans, whose leader evidently had a hand in the selection of their paramount chief.

The concepts of mana and *tapu* were primary among aboriginal religious beliefs. Nearly all Niueans are now Christian. The Niueans had many gods, organized into a hierarchical pantheon.

See also Tonga

Bibliography

Crocombe, Ron, ed. (1971). *Land Tenure in the Pacific.* Oxford: Oxford University Press.

Loeb, Edwin M. (1926). *History and Traditions of Niue.* Bernice P. Bishop Museum Bulletin no. 32. Honolulu.

Nomoi

ETHNONYM: Mortlock Islands

Nomoi includes the cluster of Etal, Lukunor, and Satawan atolls in the Mortlocks and the lone Namoluk Atoll 56 kilometers to the northwest. Nomoi is located in the central Carolines at approximately 5° N and 153° E. The population of Nomoi has gone through several crashes and recoveries. In 1968 there were some 6,000 inhabitants in Nomoi, and many "official" residents actually live away from their home island. Mortlockese is classified in the Micronesian Family of Oceanic Austronesian languages. Settlements are nearly always on the lagoon side of islets, and they may be either discrete or contiguous. Some inhabited islets also have garden islets where supplemental cultigens are grown, especially swamp taro. Traditional dwellings had cleared courtyards and were mainly used as sleeping quarters, with a floor of breadfruit planks raised up from the ground. Most houses are now of "European" style, made of corrugated metal.

The Nomoi diet includes coconut, breadfruit (fresh and preserved), taro, swamp taro, rice, flour, bananas, pandanus, papayas, limes, sour oranges, squashes, fish (canned and fresh), shellfish, octopuses, turtles, wild fowls, chickens, and pigs. Taro is the staple. Both island-grown and imported foods are eaten. Men generally fish and do the gardening, and they bring the food to the cook house for the women to cook. In precontact times regular trading and visiting voyages were made to all of the islands of Truk and to several islands in Ponape (Ponape, Ngatik, Nukuoro, and Kapingamarangi). Today both men and women travel to Moen, Truk, to earn cash through wage labor. Copra is widely grown as a cash crop. Food exchanges among the islets' inhabitants serve to terminate mourning and resource taboos. Formerly, all land was held in full title by the sibs, but individual land tenure was instituted in the 1930s. Clans were also important in the organization of group tasks, such as house building, fishing, gardening, canoe construction, etc.

The people of Nomoi are organized into several named, exogamous corporate matrilineal sibs. The sibs are ranked based on the sequence of their initial arrival on the islands. The matrisibs of Namoluk and Etal are thought to be especially closely related. Some writers refer to the presence of two primary sibs in Nomoi as a loose moiety organization. The sibs, in turn, are organized into subsibs and lineages. Adoption is very common in Nomoi. A rule of sib exogamy is observed, and marriages tend to be arranged by the couple's parents. Bilateral cross-cousin and sibling-set marriage is the ideal. Interatoll marriages are quite common, with most spouses coming from other parts of Nomoi and from Truk. Residence tends to be matrilocal. The sororate and levirate are also practiced. Households consist of the women of a matrilineage, their children, and their resident husbands. The household is headed by the husband of the oldest woman in the lineage. Nuclear families are discernible within the household, but the latter is the real economic and social unit of importance. Members of a household share a cook house, and many households have adopted members. Households, then, are localized lineages. Matrilineages are hierarchically arranged into matrisibs, which are also hierarchically ordered in their relationship to the two primary matrisibs. Lineages were formerly the property-owning group. The sibs were cooperative and mutually supportive bodies whose members aided one another in economic activities, child rearing, litigation, warfare, etc. Today, sibs serve mainly to regulate marriage.

Beyond kinship ties, there are formal friendships (*pwiipwii*) between two nonkin, which extend incest and exogamy restrictions to these two individuals and their children. The traditional leader of each sib was the chief, who was the oldest brother or son of the oldest female clan member most closely related to the founding ancestress. The chief controlled land use and usufruct, organized work groups, approved marriages, settled disputes, oversaw rituals, organized clan contributions to ceremonial exchanges, and trained and readied men for combat, among other duties. Clans were ranked hierarchically, and on some islets there was a paramount chief, who was also the leader of the senior clan. Political positions were formerly kin-based, but they are now elective offices. Island leaders cannot force their wishes on followers; they must govern by influence and persuasion. Nomoi was formerly divided into two military alliances, with Etal, Namoluk, and part of Lukunor and Satawan allied against the remainder of Lukunor and Satawan.

Today, nearly all of the people of Nomoi are Catholics or Protestants. The conversion was nearly complete by the early years of the twentieth century. Shortly after the missionaries' arrival, in 1905 and 1906, a nativistic movement involving dancing and shamanism sprang up. The Nomoi people originally believed the world to be flat, and they referred to it as "inside heaven." In the "above heaven" were winds and gods. Also included in the latter were the sib heavens, which were located above certain parts of various islands. The ancestors were worshipped and charged with both the protection and the punishment of living people. The natural and supernatural worlds were thought to be directly connected and correlated with the Nomoi social structure. Shamans were the intermediaries between the natural and supernatural worlds.

The hypnotic trances into which the shamans fell were thought to be spirit possession. During a trance the spirit would express its wishes and would provide information and divinations through the shaman. Breadfruit and other natural products were believed to be possessed of a soul or spirit. Each person was thought to have two souls, with the primary soul (*ngun*) going to its sib heaven at death. The souls of stronger individuals could elect to undergo a series of trials and become sib heroes.

See also Kapingamarangi, Pohnpei, Truk

Bibliography

Marshall, Mac (1975). "Changing Patterns of Marriage and Migration on Namoluk Atoll." In *Pacific Atoll Populations*, edited by Vern Carroll, 160–211. ASAO Monograph no. 3. Honolulu: University Press of Hawaii.

Nason, James D. (1974). "Political Change: An Outer Island Perspective." In *Political Development in Micronesia*, edited by Daniel T. Hughes and Sherwood G. Lingenfelter, 119–142. Columbus: Ohio State University Press.

Tolerton, Burt, and Jerome Rauch (1949). *Social Organization, Land Tenure, and Subsistence Economy of Lukunor, Nomoi Islands*. Coordinated Investigation of Micronesian Anthropology, Report no. 26. Washington, D.C.: Pacific Science Board.

Ontong Java

ETHNONYMS: Lord Howe, Lord Howe's Group, Luangiua

Orientation

Identification. Ontong Java is a coral atoll in the Solomon Islands and is one of the so-called Polynesian outliers, a number of islands and atolls located outside of the Polynesian triangle that are inhabited by people who are Polynesian in their language and culture. The name "Ontong Java" was bestowed in 1643 by the Dutch explorer Abel Tasman, who apparently was reminded of Java. In 1791, Captain Hunter of the *Waaksamhey'd* named it "Lord Howe's Group." In official publications of the Solomon Islands government it is listed as "Ontong Java," although some Solomon Islanders continue to refer to it by the name of "Lord Howe." Most of what is known about traditional life on Ontong Java is based on the anthropological research of Ernst Sarfert in 1910 and Ian Hogbin in 1927–1928. Much has changed since then and more recent information is derived from research by Timothy Bayliss-Smith and the author's conversations with Ontong Java people while doing research on neighboring islands.

Location. Ontong Java is located at 5°30' S, 160° E. The atoll, one of the largest in the world, is 72 kilometers across at its greatest length and its width varies from 11 to 26 kilometers. It has 23 passages into the lagoon and more than 100 islets. The climate is tropical.

Demography. Ontong Java suffered a severe population decline in the early twentieth century. Some estimates place its nineteenth-century population as high as 5,000 inhabitants, but it is more likely that it was about 2,000. It dropped to fewer than 600 in the 1930s. Since then the population has stabilized and begun increasing; it had reached at least 1,400 in 1986. In addition, in recent years, people have migrated away from the atoll and reside in other parts of the Solomon Islands.

Linguistic Affiliation. Linguists place the language within the Samoic-Outlier Group of Polynesian languages in the Oceanic Branch of Austronesian languages.

History and Cultural Relations

According to a local legend, the ancestors of the present population arrived from the overpopulated island of "Ngiua" (which cannot be identified) and named their new home "Lua Ngiua," literally "Second Ngiua." Other legends refer to immigrants who arrived from the north and "Ko'olau," which could be Kiribati or Tuvalu. Comparative studies of language and material culture indicate strong affinities with Samoa and Tuvalu and probable contacts with Micronesia. The atoll was first sighted by Europeans in 1616 and occasionally visited during the following two centuries. In the nineteenth century the atoll's inhabitants were hostile toward foreign traders and whalers. The British bombarded the atoll in 1875 in retaliation for the slaughter of the crew of a trading ship. Afterward, traders established permanent businesses there. Germany administered Ontong Java from 1893 until 1900, when it was turned over to Great Britain, which placed it within the British Solomon Islands Protectorate. In the twentieth century the atoll adopted and incorporated many Western institutions and practices including Christianity, formal education, labor for wages, and governmental administrative services. When the Solomon Islands became an independent nation in 1978, Ontong Java was administratively incorporated into Malaita Province.

Settlements

Luangiua, in the southeast, and Pelau, in the northeast, are among the few islets containing swamps suitable for the cultivation of taro, a major staple in the diet. Throughout the history of Ontong Java, these two villages have been the centers of economic, political, and ceremonial life. Almost everyone maintains permanent residences in one of these two villages, although people leave them to stay on smaller islets when collecting coconuts, trochus shell, and bêche-de-mer (trepang). At present, there is a large settlement of Ontong Java migrants residing at the mouth of the Matanikau River in Honiara, the capital of the Solomon Islands.

Economy

Subsistence and Commercial Activities. The main indigenous foods are fish, coconuts, and taro (*Cyrtosperma chamissonis* and *Colocasia esculenta*); other local food includes bananas, sweet potatoes, shellfish, turtles, chickens, and pigs. At present, imported foods such as rice, flour, sugar, and canned products are purchased at one of several small stores in each village and make up approximately 50 percent of the total diet. With its long reef and large number of islets, Ontong Java has very valuable resources for trade, especially copra and bêche-de-mer. The money earned from selling these goods is used to purchase a variety of commodities including imported food, tools, clothing, gasoline, outboard engines, and fiberglass boats.

Industrial Arts and Division of Labor. The main division of labor on the atoll is based upon sex. Men fish and dive; women care for young children, tend gardens, and plait. Traditionally men made clothing out of hibiscus fibers on a backstrap loom, but at present clothing material is usually purchased in stores. Many Ontong Java people, especially male migrants living away from the atoll, also participate in the Westernized economic system in the Solomon Islands. They work as teachers, businesspeople, laborers, church officials, and medical workers and in other occupations and professions.

Land Tenure. The land-tenure system must be understood in terms of the settlement patterns and kinship groups. Patrilineal descent groups ("joint families") have rights to most land where coconut trees are planted, including most of the islets other than Pelau and Luangiua. On the latter, rights to house sites and taro gardens are inherited through women.

Kinship

Kin Groups and Descent. Kinship-based groups include the family, the household, the house-owning group, the garden-owning group, the cooperating or fishing group, and the joint family. With regard to those groups beyond the family and household, rights to house sites on Luangiua and Pelau are held by house-owning groups that trace their ancestry through females. Men, as sons and brothers of these women, also have interests in the house sites. The garden-owning group is also formed around females: daughters inherit their rights to taro gardens from their mothers, and they may decide to divide their garden land. The cooperating or fishing group is an informal group of closely related males, often brothers and their sons, who fish together and cooperate informally in other activities. The members of a joint family usually are related through patrilineal descent from an ancestor who lived about six generations earlier. In some cases, nonagnates (e.g., the offspring of a member's sister) can be incorporated into the joint family. Members of the joint family share rights to land planted with coconut trees, most notably the islets others than Luangiua and Pelau. Joint families have leaders, usually the oldest males. The patrilineal principles followed with regard to joint families apparently developed in response to the increased importance of the copra trade in the late nineteenth century. There are many land disputes in present-day Ontong Java, and tracing genealogies is important in litigating and adjudicating them.

Kinship Terminology. Ontong Java uses a Hawaiian-type, or generational, kinship terminology system, with one notable exception: the mother's brother and his sister's children address one another by a reciprocal term, *lamoku*, and their relationship entails special obligations.

Marriage and Family

Marriage. In traditional times, some marriages were arranged although it is also clear that sometimes such arrangements could be avoided. Early sources also indicate that some women were prostitutes and some men transvestites. Residence in the villages of Pelau and Luangiua is normally uxorilocal, at the house site of the wife. When residing on the islets away from these villages, the couple usually lives on land controlled by the husband's joint family. Traditionally, divorce could arise from adultery by either husband or wife, laziness on the part of either, ill treatment by the husband, or incompatibility. The couple would simply stop cooperating and live in separate places, sometimes to reunite later. Currently, divorce is affected by Christian beliefs about marriage and it is subject to the laws of the Solomon Islands.

Domestic Unit. The family consists of a husband, wife, and their offspring. A household includes those families (or people) who are residing together.

Inheritance. Rights to land for coconut groves are held by joint families, which are formed through patrilineal descent, while rights to taro gardens are inherited from a mother by her daughters; rights to house sites are inherited through females, passing from mothers to their offspring. Personal property is inherited according to sex: a woman's property goes to her daughters, and a man's to his sons; the oldest offspring sometimes have a larger share.

Socialization. Children of both sexes are primarily cared for by their mothers until about the age of three. As they mature, boys generally associate with older males, including those from outside their household. Girls associate with older females but not so often with people from outside the household as boys do. Formerly, there were numerous behavioral avoidances between brothers and sisters that derived from incest prohibitions. In adolescence, both sexes are influenced by their peer groups.

Sociopolitical Organization

Political Organization. Before 1800, there was no centralized political authority within either village. During the nineteenth century, however, there were rivalries between the leaders of prominent joint families for dominance and certain individuals emerged, especially in Luangiua, who held considerable power. During the protectorate period the British established Western political institutions. At the time of national independence in 1978, Pelau and Luangiua were separate wards with local administrative services. Each village sends an elected representative to the Malaita Provincial Assembly. Ontong Java and Sikaiana together elect one representative to the national parliament.

Social Control. Informal sanctions, such as public opinion, are important mechanisms for social control. Also, in their traditional religion the Ontong Java people believed that the spirits of the deceased, *kipua,* took an interest in human affairs and could punish with sickness and death offenses such as incest, adultery, or failure to fulfill social obligations. More formally, a leader of a joint family could temporarily bar a disobedient member from using land. At present, Ontong Java is part of a court system established by the British and now administered by their provincial and national governments.

Conflict. In the nineteenth century, there was constant feuding as various leaders tried to consolidate their power. By the end of the century each village had one ruler who was able to settle some disputes and punish people. At present, land disputes are a major source of tension and conflict.

Religion and Expressive Culture

Religious Beliefs. The traditional ritual system centered on the *sanga* ceremony, which was performed to honor the island's legendary founders and to ensure that taro, coconuts, and fish would be plentiful. It was also believed that the spirits of deceased ancestors, kipua, were aware of all human events and could interfere in them. By 1927, the traditional religious system was disintegrating as a result of culture contact, and at present most people are members of the Church of Melanesia, which was originally established by Anglican missionaries.

Religious Practitioners. Formerly, the *maakua,* who were the leaders of certain joint families, supervised the performance of the sanga ceremony. In times of famine or pestilence, the maakua were held responsible for the community's misfortune and were either put to death or asked to resign their positions. Other traditional beliefs centered on spirit mediums who were able to contact the spirits of deceased ancestors (kipua) to learn of their intentions and enlist their aid. At present, people participate in various Christian offices and organizations.

Ceremonies. Apart from the church calendar, there are frequent occasions for dances and song performances in the present-day life of Ontong Java. These performances include traditional musical, dance, and song genres. In addition there are new genres, such as guitar music and songs that derive from culture contact.

Arts. Men formerly wore nose ornaments and even now some people are tattooed, although not as extensively as in former times. Women still cover themselves with turmeric when dancing.

Medicine. In traditional times, most sickness and death were attributed to the actions of kipua (ancestor spirits).

Death and Afterlife. When people died, their relatives stopped most work activities and mourned the deceased by weeping and singing dirges. The Ontong Java buried their dead in a cemetery with slabs of coral rock for grave markers. Upon death, a person became a kipua. Nowadays, Christian beliefs are prevalent.

See also Malaita, Samoa, Tuvalu

Bibliography

Bayliss-Smith, Timothy (1986). *Ontong Java Atoll: Population Economy and Society, 1970–1986.* South Pacific Smallholder Project Occasional Paper no. 9. Armidale, N.S.W., Australia: University of New England.

Friedlander, Jonathan S., et al. (1987). *The Solomon Islands Project: A Long-Term Study of Health, Human Biology, and Culture Change.* New York: Oxford University Press.

Hogbin, H. Ian (1931). "The Social Organization of Ontong Java." *Oceania* 1:399–425.

Hogbin, H. Ian (1934). *Law and Order in Polynesia: A Study of Primitive Legal Institutions.* London: Christophers. Reprint. 1961. Hamden, Conn.: Shoe String Press.

Keopo, John, comp. (1981). *Kelaungiu: Ngakakala, Ngalue, Nga'ai: Stories from Luangiua, Ontong Java.* In *Journal of Oral Tradition and Contemporary History.* Vol. 1. Honiara: National Museum of the Solomon Islands.

Sarfert, Ernst, and Hans Damm (1931). *"Luangiua und Nukumanu."* In *Ergebnisse der Südsee Expedition, 1908-1910,* edited by Georg Thilenius. II. Ethnographie; B. Mikronesien, vol. 12. Hamburg: Friedrichsen.

WILLIAM W. DONNER

Orokaiva

ETHNONYMS: Aiga, Binandele, Hunjara, Mambare, Wasida

Orientation

Identification. "Orokaiva" is the name for a number of culturally similar tribes in Papua New Guinea who speak mutually intelligible dialects. Although the tribes did not have an inclusive name for themselves until "Orokaiva" was introduced by Westerners, they generally distinguished among themselves as the river people (*umo-ke*), saltwater people (*eva'embo*), and inland people (*periho*).

Location. The Orokaiva reside in the Oro Province of Papua New Guinea and are concentrated in the Popondetta district in an area reaching from the coast at Buna Island to the northern slopes of Mount Lamington and in the regions to the north of this general line. This area is a humid tropical lowland, and uniformly high temperatures and rainfall provide a year-round growing season. The wet season, from December to March, is characterized by northeasterly or northwesterly winds, high temperatures and humidity, and late-afternoon thunderstorms, while the dry season, from May to October, produces northeasterly winds, lower temperatures, less cloud cover, and less-predictable rainfall.

Demography. The indigenous population of the Popondetta district totals some 36,500, of whom 26,500 are Orokaiva in the central lowland area. The number of Orokaiva at the time of Western contact is not known.

Linguistic Affiliation. Orokaiva is classified in the Binandere (or Binandele) Family of eight languages spoken in most of the more densely populated parts of Oro Province. Orokaiva is spoken by about half of the population in the Orokaiva-Binandere area. Dialect divisions within the Orokaiva language area are minor; the boundaries of the area coincide with those of the region administered by the Higaturu Local Government Council, which covers the Saiho and most of the Sohe-Popondetta census divisions. While there are considerable vocabulary differences between the Binandere languages, there is a close resemblance in grammar and enough similarity in vocabulary to make a limited degree of communication possible.

History and Cultural Relations

In response to Australian pressure, the British government annexed Papua in 1888. Gold was discovered shortly thereafter, resulting in a major movement of prospectors and miners to what was then the Northern District. Relations with the Papuans were bad from the start, and there were numerous killings on both sides. The Protectorate of British New Guinea became Australian territory by the passing of the Papua Act of 1905 by the Commonwealth Government of Australia. The new administration adopted a policy of peaceful penetration, and many measures of social and economic national development were introduced. Local control was in the hands of village constables, paid servants of the Crown. Chosen by European officers, they were intermediaries between the government and the people. In 1951 an eruption occurred on Mount Lamington, completely devastating a large part of the area occupied by the Orokaiva. Survivors were provided with food, medicine, and other relief by the government and were maintained in evacuation camps. Large-scale, expertly planned social, economic, and political development began in Papua around 1960 with the introduction of cash crops, agricultural extension work, land-title improvement, road improvement, and educational development.

Settlements

Small villages with populations not exceeding 720 are the typical units of settlement, with houses dispersed in a more or less rectangular form around a central earth or grass "square." Villages are in flat clearings where the grass is scrupulously cut and kept free of rubbish. Houses are built by the men, each house normally being occupied by one nuclear family. Bachelors' houses, of the same size and construction, are also built.

Economy

Subsistence and Commercial Activities. The household is the basic unit of production and consumption, with swidden horticulture as the subsistence base. The main crop is taro, which occupies about 90 percent of the cultivated land. A variety of other plants are grown as well, including bananas, sugarcane, edible *pitpit,* and a few introduced cultigens such as pineapples, tomatoes, beans, and sweet potatoes. Although the Orokaiva traditionally tended coconut, sago, betel-nut, and a few other varieties of trees in gardens, villages, and in the bush, their arboriculture was rudimentary in comparison to their precise and detailed attention to tubers, especially taro. In response to Australian pressure during the colonial period, rubber, coffee, and coconut palms for copra have been planted, providing the Orokaiva with a reliable and substantial cash income in recent years. A good deal of plant and animal food is obtained by foraging, especially in the tropical rain forest that covers most of the Northern District. Foraged animal foods include grubs, frogs, snails, rats, and bush eggs. Foraged plant foods are valued during the dry season, when roots, leaves, and fern fronds make up part of a meal. Fish are an important resource, being used not only for consumption but for trade. Hunting is less important; the usual quarry consists of small marsupials, birds, and pigs. Pigs, dogs, and fowl have been domesticated and each man has one or more small dogs that he uses for hunting but that are ultimately destined for the pot. Fowl are a useful source of meat, eggs, and feathers for decoration on headdresses, spears, etc. Domestic pigs are slowly disappearing from the villages, due to a government campaign to eliminate pig husbandry in an attempt to improve village hygiene.

Industrial Arts. Items produced include rafts and canoes, pottery, bark cloth (tapa) from the paper mulberry, mats and baskets of coconut and pandanus leaves, wooden bowls, various musical instruments, and weapons.

Trade. Intertribal trade was mainly in animal products, betel-nut products, feathers, and certain artifacts known to be of high quality in particular districts. Although small in volume, trade was politically important in providing a motive for terminating warlike disputes.

Division of Labor. Cooperation among men is common during hunting and house-building. Cooperation of a total village is rare, but there are cooperative hunting and fishing expeditions. There is also a sharp sexual division of labor. Men hunt; prepare tools and equipment; make sago; plant all crops, both traditional (taro, yams, sweet potatoes) and introduced (rubber, coffee); maintain the yams and rubber; harvest rubber; and market coffee. Women cook, care for the sick, maintain the taro and sweet potatoes, harvest taro, and market root crops. Men and women both fish, build fences, collect firewood, maintain and harvest the coffee crop, and market rubber.

Land Tenure. Various land rights may be given to the clan branch, the lineage, or an individual, the relative significance of each varying with the locality and population density. More than one descent group may have rights in a single piece of land. In many instances, the clan branch functions as a reference group, with all land being associated with it. However, it may also function as a primary right-holding group for those hunting areas distinct from current garden land, typically the grasslands. Primary rights to garden land are normally vested in the lineage. Nevertheless, all such land is ultimately identifiable with individuals who may distribute land (and property) prior to their death not only to their immediate family but also to more distant kin. Traditional tree crops are not planted in stands or groups like cash-crop trees but are widely scattered and are as likely to be planted on patrimonial land as on the land of affines or matrilateral kin. Inheritance of rights to trees usually does not bring rights to the land on which they stand.

Kinship

Kin Groups and Descent. Every Orokaiva is recruited by birth into the clan of his or her father. All members of a clan claim, but cannot necessarily trace, common descent from a usually eponymous ancestor. Each clan is subdivided into named subgroups or lineages that trace their origin to a named ancestor.

Kinship Terminology. Kinship terminology is of the Iroquois type.

Marriage and Family

Marriage. Polygyny among the Orokaiva is accepted but rare. Clan exogamy is preferred, but not strictly enforced. Villages are not exogamous. A large bride-price is required for arranged marriages, although in the past wives were also obtained through capture. Postmarital residence is ideally patrilocal, but in practice people have a wide choice between the villages of patrilateral or matrilateral kin or of affines, and residence may be changed at any time. The distribution of clan branches through a number of villages is closely related to access to the group's land, hence the initial motivation for a long-term change in residence may be influenced by proximity to land intended to be brought into cultivation. Divorce is allowed, with custody of minor children going to the father, except for infants.

Domestic Unit. The basic domestic and economic unit is the household, composed of either a nuclear or extended family.

Inheritance. Inheritance is usually patrilineal.

Socialization. Errant children are subject to beating and especially to scolding. Education is predominantly through a system of mission schools, partly financed by the government's department of education.

Sociopolitical Organization

Social Organization. The social system is characterized by flexibility in arrangements for group membership and for transmission of rights to land. A village normally contains more than one clan branch and consequently is not necessarily a landholding unit. Residents may have closer kinship ties to residents of other villages than with some of their coresidents. Nevertheless, common residence implies some community of interest and a degree of group solidarity that is reinforced by government policy, which recognizes villages rather than descent groups as functional entities. Marriages between members of different clan branches within the village also reinforce this solidarity, which is expressed in ways such as daily food gifts, cooperation in certain tasks, and joint ceremonial activities. On the average, a lineage comprises three households. Usually, several clans are represented in a village, with members of a single clan (clan branches) being scattered among a number of neighboring villages. Lineages are more localized in character, frequently being confined to a single village and tending to occupy one section of it.

Political Organization. Political organization incorporates no central authority or hereditary leadership. Instead, it is characterized by big-men (*embo dambo*) and an ascendancy of elders who have proved themselves equal to the task. Such men command the respect of the village, based upon observed qualities of generosity, diligence, wealth, ability to make wise decisions, and skill in arranging ceremonial activities. This status confers no sanctioning authority, however. The Orokaiva tribes, around twelve in number, are very loose units politically and recognize no single leader. The largest unit is the tribe, which has a common territory usually demarcated from neighboring tribal territories by a belt of uninhabited land.

Social Control. There are customary restrictions upon feuding within the tribe, which exist in sharp contrast to the standard acceptance and formalization of hostility between tribes. Formerly, official legal penalties, generally violent, were meted out to criminals. Fear of the ancestors and desire to avoid unfavorable public opinion remain the major mechanisms of social control.

Conflict. Prior to European contact, aggression against the members of another tribe took the form of organized, often cannibalistic raids.

Religion and Expressive Culture

Religious Beliefs. The traditional beliefs of the Orokaiva, though in many respects vague and locally variable, focused primarily on the "spirits of the dead" and their influence on the living. The Orokaiva had no high god. Formerly, they were animists, believing in the existence of souls (*asisi*) in humans, plants, and animals. The taro spirit was of particular importance and was the inspiration and foundation of the Taro Cult. The Orokaiva have been swept recently by a series of new cults, indicative of their religious adaptability in the face of fresh experience. Mission influence is strong in the Northern District. Religious training is provided almost exclusively by the Anglican church, although mission influence has not totally eradicated traditional beliefs, producing an air of mysticism about the resultant religious system.

Religious Practitioners. Orokaiva shamans, or "taro men" serve as healers, weather magicians, and sorcerers.

Ceremonies. Dances are held often, sometimes accompanied by music, singing, and drums. From time to time, big-men sponsor large redistributive feasts, featuring pig sacrifices and food distribution. Activities associated with the taro cult (the "Kava Keva" cult) are the major ritual activity. The Taro Cult began about 1915 and soon evolved into ritual practices meant to placate the spirits of the dead (*sovai*) who control the taro crop. Thus, it is both a fertility cult and a cult of the dead. Taro men lead the ritual which includes choral singing, drumming, feasting, and violent shaking movements.

Arts. The Orokaiva decorate all manner of artifacts with abstract and representational figures. They are especially fond of music and in the past produced wooden drums and pipes, conch and wooden trumpets, and Jew's harps of bamboo.

Medicine. Illness and misfortune are attributed to the sprits of the dead, to the actions of sorcerers, or to natural causes such as an accident or the weather. Since illness is generally seen as caused by a foreign element entering the body, most cures used by curers (those who have *sivo,* or special power and knowledge) are designed to extract the foreign element. These methods include producing noxious odors, rubbing the affected area, and extracting a foreign object by sucking.

Death and Afterlife. The Orokaiva believe that upon death the human soul is released and becomes a sovai. Initially, the sovai roam the village, but they ultimately depart to special places of the dead, such as rock outcroppings and stagnant pools of water. Sovai often chastise errant kin by bringing upon them misfortune, illness, and even death. Death is appraised with particular realism, although it is still considered to be ultimately the result of supernatural causes.

Bibliography

Keesing, Felix M. (1952). "The Papuan Orokaiva vs. Mount Lamington: Cultural Shock and Its Aftermath." *Human Organization* 11:16–22.

New Guinea Research Unit (1966). *Orokaiva Papers.* New Guinea Research Bulletin no. 13. Canberra: Australian National University Press.

Oostermeyer, W. J., and Joanne Gray, eds. (1967). *Papuan Entrepreneurs.* Canberra: Australian National University, New Guinea Research Unit.

Schwimmer, Erik G. (1973). *Exchange in the Social Structure of the Orokaiva.* New York: St. Martin's Press.

Schwimmer, Erik G. (1979). "Reciprocity and Structure: A Semiotic Analysis of Some Orokaiva Exchange Data." *Man* 14:271–285.

Williams, Francis Edgar (1930). *Orokaiva Society.* London: Oxford University Press.

CHRISTOPHER S. LATHAM

Orokolo

ETHNONYMS: Elema, Ipi, Western Elema

Orientation

Identification. The term "Orokolo" generally refers to all of the Western Elema people living around Orokolo Bay in Papua New Guinea, although the name also refers to one of the five languages in the Eleman Language Family, to the major dialect of this language, and also to one of the five major Orokolo villages (Arihava, Yogu, Orokolo, Auma, and Vailala). The Orokolo are similar to the Eastern Elema people (sometimes called Toaripi) in both language and culture.

Location. The Orokolo live in the Gulf Province of Papua New Guinea, between the mouths of the Vailala River (to the east) and the Aivei River (to the west) at 8° S and 145° E. Their villages are located along the beaches of the 20-mile-wide Orokolo Bay in the Gulf of Papua. Orokolo territory consists of a wide coastal strip, fringed by coconut palms, behind which lie the sago swamps that provide much of the people's food. The area is tropical, but, due to an unusual local pattern, the monsoon rainfall patterns are the reverse of those generally prevalent in New Guinea. Hence the northwest monsoon, from October to April, brings a comparatively pleasant, drier season of relative calm, whereas the normally mild southeast trade winds blow directly into the gulf, bringing heavy rains and restless surf for the balance of the year.

Demography. In 1937, the ethnographic present for this report (when F. E. Williams concluded his major monograph on the Orokolo), the population was 4,500. Today it is in excess of 7,500.

Linguistic Affiliation. Orokolo is a member of the Eleman Language Family, a group of about five closely related, mutually intelligible Non-Austronesian languages generally placed within the Purari-Eleman Stock. The Eleman Family has about eight different dialects. The major Eleman linguistic distinction, like the major cultural division, is between the Eastern Eleman and Western Eleman groups of languages, which are bisected by an only distantly related language called Raepa Tati, spoken near the provincial headquarters at Kerema.

History and Cultural Relations

European contact along the Gulf of Papua began well before the turn of the century and was quite extensive. Missionaries and labor recruiters were active, and the entire area was considered "controlled" before 1912. By 1919, there were reports of the "Vailala Madness"—one of the first recorded manifestations of a Melanesian cargo cult—among the Orokolo. These cargo cults are generally thought to be linked to mental confusion surrounding rapid sociocultural change associated with European contact and to a breakdown of traditional culture. "Vailala Madness" involved mass hysteria, in which large numbers of people became giddy, appeared to lose control of their limbs, and reeled about. This condition was known locally as *haro heraipe,* meaning "one's head is turning around." These psychosomatic symptoms were associated with teachings that the spirits of the dead would return and that the old ceremonies and cultural practices should be eliminated. In Eastern Orokolo villages, bullroarers and masks associated with sacred ceremonies were taken from men's houses and burned in front of women and uninitiated boys. After several years, however, traditional practices were resumed in this area on a more limited basis.

Settlements

Villages, perhaps 800 meters in length but only about 54 meters in width, stretch out along the beach. Large areas are fenced to keep pigs either in or out. There are some vacant spaces, however, so that the entire village resembles a series of very elongated rectangles. Inside the rectangles lie the houses, built in several alternative styles but generally on piles, with veranda platforms and small entrances. Dominating the ordinary dwellings are the large men's houses, called *eravo,* some 30 meters long and 15 meters tall, accompanied by one or two smaller versions, nominally for boys. The rectangular enclosures are generally kept meticulously clean of weeds and debris.

Economy

Subsistence and Commercial Activities. The Orokolo are predominantly dependent on the sago palm for their livelihood. Sago grows in such profusion that there is no need to tend trees or plant suckers. The other main sources of staples are gardens that are communally fenced and divided into individually tended lateral strips. Main garden crops are yams, taro, and bananas. Coconuts and domestic pigs are also eaten. Hunting—generally with bows and arrows, sometimes with spears, and often aided by dogs—is practiced. Larger quarry include wild pigs and cassowaries, while smaller prey include marsupials and birds. Orokolo also fish, employing a variety of techniques: most commonly they use nets or fish with bows and arrows or spears from pedestals in the water. However, considering the Orokolo's proximity to the sea, maritime produce contributes relatively little to their diets.

Industrial Arts. Orokolo adults are generalists, commonly producing nearly all of the art, craft objects, tools, and clothing used in their daily lives. There are different individuals who are acknowledged experts in making dugout canoes, drums, ceremonial masks, and carvings, but these crafts are not in any sense commercial activities.

Trade. Orokolo engage in utilitarian barter among themselves and in some rather limited trade for ornamental shells with groups to the east, but historically their most important intertribal exchange is the anthropologically well-known *hiri* trade with the Motu people of the Central Province. Because of prolonged dry spells and resultant food shortages in their territory, the Motu made annual voyages to the eastern Gulf of Papua to exchange clay pots, shell ornaments, and stone blades for gulf sago. The Orokolo obtained their cooking pots in this fashion. The medium of communication between the tribes that developed through this trade was a pidginized form of Motu, combining a limited Motu vocabulary with a structure grammatically and syntactically similar to Toaripi (and Orokolo). This language, called "Police Motu" or "Hiri Motu," subsequently became the lingua franca of all Papua and is today one of Papua New Guinea's three official languages.

Division of Labor. As in most tribal societies, division of labor is primarily based on age and sex. Orokolo often say that women's work is in the village and men's work is abroad, although this description is not entirely accurate. Women tend to the children, cook, clean the house and grounds, feed the pigs, provide the water and firewood, and do skilled-craftwork, including the making of nets. Another important part of their work is making sago, a task shared with men. Men fell the trees, split the trunks, and scrape out the pith, while women wash and beat the sago and carry it home. Men do virtually all of the gardening, hunting, fishing, and building.

Land Tenure. Land is not in particularly short supply, and land tenure and ownership are quite flexible. Ownership of land is nominally vested in the *bira'ipi,* a rather fluid group based on both residence and descent. In actuality, it is subdivided among *larava,* patrilineal kinship groups that might best be termed lineages. The senior male of the lineage (based on principles of descent) is the "controller" of the land. In practice, however, permission to use land is freely given, and sometimes an entire village segment will garden on land technically belonging to just one of its constituent lineages.

Kinship

Kin Groups and Descent. Orokolo have a series of about ten named, totemic, exogamous patrilineal clans subdivided into patrilineal lineages. Each clan has an extensive mythology, including art forms associated with the myths, that relates to the clan ancestors and totems.

Kinship Terminology. Kinship terminology is of the Iroquois type.

Marriage and Family

Marriage. Marriage rules, like many other rules among the Orokolo, are flexible. Most marriages are monogamous, but polygyny is permitted. Traditionally, young men generally married immediately after emerging from the age-grade seclusion associated with male initiation; there was thus a marriage "season." Young women generally married one of their age mates at this time. It is preferred that women marry outside their lineages but within their villages. Bride-price, in the form of shell ornaments and a live pig, is paid to the wife's family by the husband's, and the two families also exchange shell valuables. After marriage, the bride generally lives with the husband's family, although matrilocal postmarital residence is not uncommon. Marriages are mostly permanent, although they may be severed by the restitution of shell ornaments.

Domestic Unit. The basic domestic unit is the household, generally consisting of a married couple and their children. In polygynous marriages, both wives live together in the same household. Households often include related individuals, such as widowed parents, unmarried or newly married siblings, or orphaned children, on a temporary or permanent basis.

Inheritance. Inheritance is normally patrilineal.

Socialization. Among the Orokolo, direct coercion of any individual, and most particularly physical coercion, is considered inappropriate behavior. Children are no exception, and, by Western standards, children are indulged. Parents frequently play with children, and they do not order them about; even small children enjoy a considerable freedom of will and action. Children learn by watching and imitating the actions of their elders. They have very few "duties." Young men pass through a series of age grades that traditionally included a period of seclusion lasting some six to twelve months at about the age of 14 or 15. Each age grade was associated with a particular costume. Women have no such age grades, but they do have a recognized age-group membership corresponding to that of men.

Sociopolitical Organization

Social Organization. Social organization is very complex, consisting of a great many crosscutting units, primarily based on residence, descent, and age affiliation. In terms of residence, the Elema people are divided into tribes, of which the Orokolo is one, and subdivided into village groups, villages, and units called *karigara,* or village segments. Each village segment is normally associated with a men's house or eravo. These eravo communities are further subdivided into bira'ipi, units that combine descent and residence principles. In terms of descent, Orokolo have the previously described patrilineal clans and lineages. They also recognize a variety of fictive friendship relationships, as well as numerous named age groups that pass through a series of eight age grades.

Political Organization. The Orokolo are fundamentally an egalitarian culture, and influential people typically achieve their status through a combination of individual competence, force of personality, age, and experience. Each eravo or men's house community has a dual division, with each half technically headed by a "chief." The entire group also has a "village chief," a descendant of one of the original settlers who owned and controlled village land, although this chief is often one of the eravo chiefs. In practice, these chiefs cannot command action and have very little power, since decisions are usually reached through group consensus.

Social Control. In the absence of a coercive tradition, social control within the group is maintained largely through the strength of public opinion and the fear of supernatural retribution. Since reciprocity is so important in Orokolo activities, individuals who do not meet their social obligations soon have problems. Sexual infidelities and perceived inequalities in exchange are common causes of conflict within the village. Cases are usually settled in group meetings with the aid of influential men who act as mediators. Traditionally, each clan had a "chief" (*bukari*) with particular legitimacy to stop conflicts and achieve settlement by virtue of his control over the clan bullroarer.

Conflict. Before European contact, warfare between tribes was not uncommon, though it was very rare within the tribe.

Religion and Expressive Culture

Religious Beliefs. Traditional Orokolo have no belief in a high god or gods, and, in some sense, the exact nature of their beliefs is rather vague. There is a fundamental animistic notion of a sort of mana or impersonal force present in certain objects. However, the most important aspects of their religion involve two categories of spirits: spirits of the dead, or ghosts; and spirits of the natural environment. While both groups are considered to be capable of affecting human affairs, the latter spirits—who once lived, whose exploits are told of in myth, and who now haunt parts of the natural environment—are the focus of most religious magic. Individuals seek to control events through partial reenactments of mythological episodes.

Religious Practitioners. While all people practice magic, there are part-time specialists who are acknowledged as particularly proficient in garden magic, in diagnosing and in treating sicknesses, and in sorcery.

Ceremonies. Traditional Orokolo ceremonial life is extremely rich and varied. Like all of the Elema people, Orokolo have a bullroarer cult and a series of elaborate ceremonies characterized by distinctive and ornate masks. For the Orokolo, the most important masked ceremonies are the *kovave* and *hevehe.* The latter ceremony involves a series of stages linked in a ritual cycle taking as long as twenty years to complete.

Arts. All sorts of mundane and ritual objects are elaborately decorated by the Orokolo. Wooden objects, including musical instruments (especially bullroarers and drums), are often carved with stylistic designs. By far the most spectacular of the Orokolo decorative arts involves the large (9- or 10-foot) elaborately constructed and decorated hevehe masks.

Medicine. Traditional notions of medicine are related to the belief in sorcery. Medical practitioners are of two broad types: diagnosticians (locally known as "men who see sickness with their eyes") and actual practitioners (referred to as "men who treat sickness"). Treatments frequently involve "blood sucking" (removing surplus blood from areas where it is thought to cause pain and sickness), "phlegm sucking" (doctors spitting out mouthfuls of phlegm as if it had been drawn from the patient's body), and extraction of miscellaneous objects (like crocodile teeth or glass fragments) thought to have been introduced by a sorcerer.

Death and Afterlife. A death in the village generally results in the suspension of all but the most essential activities. Bodies are shallowly interred, traditionally within the village compound but now outside it, with feet facing the sea. Deaths are accompanied by considerable public mourning and a series of mortuary feasts. Spirits of the dead are thought to hover about their homes for a time, able to influence human affairs, before departing for a vague "land of the dead."

See also Motu

Bibliography

Brown, Herbert A. (1973). "The Eleman Language Family." In *The Linguistic Situation in the Gulf District and Adjacent Areas, Papua New Guinea,* edited by K. Franklin, 279–376. Pacific Linguistics, Series C, no. 26, Canberra: Australian National University.

Holmes, John Henry (1924). *In Primitive New Guinea.* London: Seely Service.

Williams, Francis Edgar (1923). *The Vailala Madness and the Destruction of Native Ceremonies in the Gulf Division.* Territory of Papua Anthropology Report no. 4. Port Moresby: Government Printer.

Williams, Francis Edgar (1932–1933). "Trading Voyages from the Gulf of Papua." *Oceania* 3:139–166.

Williams, Francis Edgar (1936). *Bull-roarers in the Papuan Gulf.* Territory of Papua Anthropology Report no. 17. Port Moresby: Government Printer.

Williams, Francis Edgar (1940). *Drama of Orokolo: The Social and Ceremonial Life of the Elema.* Territory of Papua Anthropology Report no. 18. Oxford: Clarendon Press.

RICHARD SCAGLION

Pentecost

ETHNONYMS: Bunlap, Pornowol, Sa, South Ragans

Orientation

Identification. The Sa, who are the focus of this summary, live on the southern part of Pentecost Island in northern Vanuatu. Pentecost was so called by the French explorer Louis Antoine de Bougainville, who sighted it on Whitsunday in 1768. "Sa" means "what" in the language spoken by the people, who themselves call the language "Lokit," which means "the inside of us all." The Sa have previously been called the Pornowol tribe, and the region has been known as South Raga as well as South Pentecost.

Location. Pentecost is an island 60 kilometers long by 12 kilometers wide, located at 15°30' to 16° S and 168°30' E. The landmass is predominantly basaltic, with a few limestone ridges formed by the uplifting of coral reefs. The eastern coast is precipitous, fringed by extensive coral reefs, and windward, with few safe anchorages. The western coast is flat and leeward, with coral reefs, extensive sandy beaches, and good anchorages. The central part of the island is mountainous and covered with dense primary rain forest. Many rivers and streams flow from the mountains to the coast, especially on the western side, and they are the primary sources of fresh water. Temperatures range between 22° and 30° C, and about 400 centimeters of rain falls in an average year. It is typically cooler and drier May–October and hotter and wetter November–April when tropical cyclones occur. Southern Pentecost experiences occasional falls of volcanic ash from Benbow Crater on nearby Ambrym Island.

Demography. In 1979 the population of Pentecost was 9,361, about 1,700 of whom were Sa speakers. Most Sa are resident locally, although young men in particular are involved in circular labor migration to the towns of Santo and Port Vila as well as plantations elsewhere. A few Sa have become permanent migrants to towns or other rural centers to work for churches, the government, or private companies or to pursue higher education.

Linguistic Affiliation. Sa is classified in the North and Central Vanuatu Group of Austronesian languages. Although it had no script prior to colonization, it has now been written down through the work of mission linguists and local cultural workers. Most speakers of Sa are also fluent in Bislama, the lingua franca of Vanuatu, and increasingly younger Sa attain verbal and written fluency in English or French, taught in church and state schools.

History and Cultural Relations

The first contacts between ni-Vanuatu and Europeans took place in the seventeenth and eighteenth centuries, but there was initial reluctance to trade with European navigators. From the early nineteenth century, Europeans sought whales, sandalwood, and bêche-de-mer in the islands with more success. In 1839 the London Missionary Society, and later the Presbyterians, set up missions in the southern islands and were followed by Anglicans, Marists, and, in the twentieth century, Seventh-Day Adventists and the Church of Christ.

From 1857 thousands of men and some women were recruited as laborers to work on plantations in New Caledonia, Queensland, Fiji, and islands in Vanuatu. In 1906 the rivalry between British and French influences was resolved by the creation of the Condominium of the New Hebrides. Indigenous cash cropping of copra started in the late 1920s, and during World War II the island of Santo was a major staging base for American forces. Beginning in the late 1960s anticolonial and nationalist sentiments crystallized, and in 1980 Vanuatu achieved political independence.

Settlements

The pattern of settlement in South Pentecost includes both nucleated villages and dispersed homestead patterns. In the traditionalist or *kastom* villages, such as Bunlap in the southeast, the predominant pattern is nucleated, with houses strung out down a ridge and communal men's houses and dancing grounds at the highest elevation. In traditionalist villages the preferred materials and house designs are indigenous: earth floors, bamboo-pole walls, and sago-palm thatch roofs on a rectangular frame. Each of these dwellings typically contains a single room, but within this room a transverse log divides the cooking fires of women and children at the front from men at the back. The men's houses are of the same materials and design, but they are much larger and have a series of fires for men of different rank. These traditional structures are complemented by more novel sleeping houses that are raised on stilts, with woven bamboo floors and walls and thatch roofs. This is the usual style of houses in Christian settlements; today, however, they are sometimes made of concrete and corrugated iron with several rooms. Most villages are connected by paths, although between coastal settlements, especially in the west, people may travel by sea in outrigger canoes, dinghies with outboard motors, or occasionally motorized launches. On the level western coast there is a vehicular road stretching from Lonoror to Wanur.

Economy

Subsistence and Commercial Activities. The Sa speakers subsisted precolonially by swidden horticulture, fishing, and forest foraging. The main crops are still taro and yams, although these are complemented by sweet potatoes, manioc, arrowroot, sago, and breadfruit. Some leafy green vegetables, sugarcane, squashes, melons, and tomatoes are grown. They fish extensively in the coastal waters off the fringing reefs and in freshwater streams for fish, lobsters, shrimps, crabs, eels, and octopuses. They have extensive groves of fruit and nut trees and they also forage for wild greens, ferns, algae, and mushrooms in the forest, where they hunt birds, flying foxes, snakes, and stick insects. They herd pigs, which are consumed on ritual occasions only. Kava is cultivated; only men may drink kava in the traditionalist villages, where it tends to be reserved for hospitality and ritual occasions. In some Anglican and Catholic communities women may drink kava, but they do not do so as routinely as men; in Church of Christ villages its use is totally proscribed. Traditionalist and Christian communities diverge greatly in their links to the cash economy. The latter have converted far more land to copra, cacao, and coffee and are more dependent on introduced foods such as rice, tinned fish, meat, biscuits, and tea. Some cattle are being raised commercially, but most are killed for local feast consumption.

Industrial Arts. Apart from indigenous architecture, a range of tools, weapons, and ritual artifacts are produced. The precolonial tool kit included wooden and stone axes, adzes, shell scrapers, digging sticks, clubs, bows and arrows, and fishing spears, but these items mainly have been supplanted by modern steel implements purchased from local or urban stores. The old digging stick persists, however, and in traditionalist villages people still use bamboo vessels for cooking and carrying water and carved wooden food platters lined with banana leaves for eating. But even there cans, plastic buckets, kettles, pots, and pans are becoming more common. Outrigger canoes are still fashioned by hollowing out tree trunks and lashing them with lianas. Slit gongs, spears, clubs, and shelters are still produced for ceremonial purposes. An ensemble of ceremonial masks and headdresses made in the past are today rarely made for use but more often for purchase by museums, art collectors, or tourists. In addition to these wooden crafts made by men, women soften and weave pandanus and bark to fashion clothing and mats for sleeping and exchange at birth, marriage, circumcision, and death. In traditionalist villages women wear fiber skirts made of pandanus or banana spathes and men wear woven pandanus penis wrappers and bark belts. Elsewhere, women's attire is typically a Mother Hubbard (a loose dress) of skirt and blouse, while men typically wear shirts and shorts or trousers or, more rarely, wraparound skirts.

Trade. In precolonial times Pentecost was part of an intensive regional trade system with the neighboring islands of Ambrym, Malekula, and Ambae. Items traded included yams, pigs, mats, ochers for body painting and sculpture, and ritual forms such as dances and chants. Modern trade is focused on the purchase of imported commodities at small local stores with money derived from cash cropping or wage labor. There are no local markets such as those in the towns of Port Vila and Santo.

Division of Labor. The sexual division of labor is pronounced. Men exclusively hunt and fish from canoes, while women engage only in reef and river fishing. Men carve wooden artifacts; women weave pandanus and palm leaves. Men construct house frames; women make thatch battens for roofs. Women look after small pigs and sows, while men nurture highly valued tusked boars. Agricultural work is shared, although men do more of the fencing and clearing and women more of the weeding and harvesting; however, regarding yams, men alone can plant the seed yams and women alone can mound the topsoil. Household maintenance and child care are fairly evenly divided between the sexes. There are also divisions of ritual labor, with part-time practitioners that include male priests (who initiate agricultural cycles), medical diviners, midwives, sorcerers, and, in the past, warriors and war diviners.

Land Tenure. Primary rights derive from agnatic relationship with a founding ancestor who claimed prior occupation, although secondary rights are granted to agnatic descendants of later arrivals, who were given land by the original occupants. Land, like fruit and nut trees, is inherited patrilineally and shared between sons and daughters. Rights are held in perpetuity by male agnatic descendants and for their lifetimes by females. Women cannot pass on natal land to their children. Land rights may also pass matrilaterally if payments in pigs and mats are not made at death by the agnates to the matrilateral kin of the deceased. Temporary rights of usufruct may be granted to affines or those without locally available land. Retaining ownership of land depends on continual use and thus continual residence. Control over the distribution of land is ultimately vested in the senior male of a descent category called *buluhim*.

Kinship

Kin Groups and Descent. The major kin category is buluhim, which is best translated as "house" rather than "clan." These houses are geographically dispersed, but there are also localized patrilineages. The major emphasis in descent is patrilineal, but there are crucial debts to matrilateral kin that cycle over generations.

Kinship Terminology. A Crow-type system is employed, which is predicated on two basic rules: the equivalence of agnates of alternate generations and the equivalence of same-sex siblings. For a male, all agnates of his father's father's generation are thus "brother."

Marriage and Family

Marriage. From the viewpoint of the male, marriage is ideally with the same "house" from which the father's mother came; marriage between agnates should be avoided. The mothers of spouses should be agnates of adjacent and not alternate generations. Marriages have always been primarily effected through the formal exchange of bride-wealth, but the alternatives of elopement or infant betrothal were more prevalent in the past. Bride-wealth is now predominantly paid in cash, with token payments of pigs and mats, the traditional components. Only Church of Christ converts totally outlaw bride-wealth. Although marriages in both traditionalist and Christian villages are to some extent "arranged," the desires of prospective spouses are also crucial. Most adults are now in monogamous marriages, but a third of all adult men in traditionalist villages have at some time been polygynous. Monogamy is mandatory for Christian converts. On marriage the couple typically (85 percent) live patrilocally, with about 10 percent living neolocally. Because marriages are often contracted within a village, women often remain close to their natal kin. Divorce is rare, constituting only 5 percent of all unions contracted.

Domestic Unit. The domestic unit is typically an elementary family, with a minority being patrilaterally extended and a tiny percentage consisting of a sole parent with children. Where a man is polygynous, his wives usually maintain separate dwellings. Now men sleep and eat more routinely in the domestic dwelling, using the male clubhouse as a refectory and dormitory on rare ritual occasions. Such exclusivist male clubhouses no longer exist in Christian communities, and there husbands and wives eat and sleep together rather than separately.

Inheritance. Inheritance of house sites and household effects is predominantly patrilineal, with a greater share going to the eldest son. Pigs, however, are not inherited but are killed at the deaths of their owners. Land, fishing grounds, and fruit groves are patrilineally inherited. Ritual powers of priests and diviners are typically inherited patrilineally by males, but the spiritual skills of sorcery, weather magic, love magic, and war magic may be purchased, though often by close male kin.

Socialization. Although children are primarily nurtured by their parents, elder siblings, and grandparents, there is much communal socialization and interhousehold visiting. The primary values imparted are those of respect for rank and age, the centrality of hard work, cooperation, and consensus. Most children in Christian villages, and some in traditionalist ones, are currently in school.

Sociopolitical Organization

Social Organization. Social organization is based on the intersection of the traditional hierarchical principles of rank, seniority, and gender. These principles are being transformed by the impact of the commodity economy, so that class differences are emerging. Such distinctions are most pronounced in urban centers, but they are also apparent in rural regions, although these novel inequalities interpenetrate indigenous patterns of rank.

Political Organization. Precolonial politics were based on achieved rank in an institution called "the graded society." Through the exchange and sacrifice of pigs (including tusked boars), mats, and other valuables, men (and in some places women) assumed titles in a hierarchically ordered series. This arrangement conferred on men more than women sacred powers enhancing their capacity to grow crops, nurture tusked boars, control the weather, and perform rituals controlling human sexuality, health, and fecundity. But such powers were also considered to be dangerous and potentially destructive. This belief necessitated segregated commensality, whereby men ate separately from women and children, and high-ranking men from those of low rank. High-ranking men exerted greater political influence without having assured authority. In the modern state of Vanuatu, the symbolism of the graded society is still employed in the imagery of the state, and the importance of high rank permeates to the national level through the institution of the National Council of Chiefs, which gives advice on matters of kastom (traditional culture). The chiefs in this council are, however, those created and recognized by the state, rather than necessarily those with locally recognized high rank.

Social Control. Although there are official courts and asssessors that are part of the national legal stucture, disputes—which arise most frequently over land, marriage, and pigs—are in fact usually resolved in informal village courts. These courts are protracted meetings that try to effect consensus. Men rather than women are vocal in such meetings, and those who speak most and exert most influence tend to be older and high-ranking. Decisions at such meetings are thought to be binding on all in the community and may occasion the payment of fines.

Conflict. Violent conflict is rare, and domestic violence is almost nonexistent. Only on very rare occasions do people resort to outside agencies of police, prisons, or asylums to control offenders. This current state of affairs is a major departure from precolonial practice, when warfare was endemic between villages and violent resolutions of conflict were frequent.

Religion and Expressive Culture

Religious Beliefs. The vast majority of ni-Vanuatu today are Christians affiliated with Protestant and Catholic denominations, although beliefs and practices involve novel reworkings of both Christianity and ancestral religion. In the past, religion centered on the sacred character of ancestors. The Sa speakers thought their ancestors were primordial creator beings responsible for the natural and the social world. There was no easy translation of these beliefs into monotheistic Christianity. The ancestors are thought still to exert a continual influence in the world of the living, and the living are often engaged in attempts to please or placate remote or recent ancestors. The graded society is predicated on a desire to approach a state of ancestral power. As well as the supernatural powers credited to the dead and the living, other supernatural entities are thought to exist. In south Pentecost, these include the spirits of uncultivated ancestral groves, spirits of the men's houses, dwarf spirits inhabiting the forest and riverbeds, and a kind of ogre with a special appetite for young children.

Religious Practitioners. Ancestral religion employed some part-time specialists, including priests of agricultural fertility, weather, and war, as well as sorcerers and diviners. Despite the influence of Christianity, priests and sorcerers are still identified, even in Christian communities. They have been complemented by Christian ritual specialists—priests, ministers, and deacons, who are for the most part also men.

Ceremonies. The major traditional ceremonies are birth, circumcision, marriage, grade taking, and death. Of these circumcision and grade taking are by far the most spectacular and protracted. In addition there is the unique rite of land diving, performed annually at the time of the yam harvest. This has become a major tourist spectacle. In popular representation the athletic aspect of diving from a 100-foot tower is emphasized, but the religous aspect is paramount for the Sa speakers, and there is thought to be a direct link between the success of the dive and the quality of the yam harvest. Young men who so desire do the diving, from platforms at increasing heights with lianas tied to their ankles to arrest their fall. The construction and ritual supervision involves older men. Women are not allowed to observe the tower until they dance underneath it on the day of the diving, although myth credits a woman with being the first to devise the practice.

Arts. The major artistic expressions are woven mats and baskets, body decoration, ephemeral ceremonial structures, and, in the past, masks. Musical instruments include plain slit gongs, reed panpipes, and bamboo flutes. Guitars and ukuleles are also played, and local compositions are much influenced by the string-band music heard on radio and cassettes. Music and dance are central to most ceremonies and are constantly being composed and reinterpreted. There is also a huge corpus of myths that are a source of aesthetic delight and are often accompanied by songs.

Medicine. In the past many illnesses were seen as ancestral vengeance for the breaking of rules of sexual and rank segregation. This sometimes took the form of spirit possession requiring exorcism. Other remedies included curative spells, amulets, and the use of a wide pharmacopoeia of herbs and clays. Medicine was often administered within the household, but if the treatment was unsuccessful the help of diviners might be sought. People are eclectic in integrating traditional and Western medicine, and they will typically try both. There are local dispensaries and some health centers run by missions or the state, and increasingly women are giving birth there. Chronic or serious illness requires removal to a hospital in Santo or Port Vila.

Death and Afterlife. Death is usually seen as the result of attack by ancestors or sorcerers. Close kin cluster in the house of the dying person and stroke him or her, wailing the mourning chant. The body of the deceased is wrapped in ritual finery and mats and then buried (previously below the house but now outside the village). At death crucial prestations are made to the mother's brother and other matrilateral kin. Mourning consists of dress and food restrictions, which are progressively relaxed until a feast is held on the hundredth day. On the twentieth day the spirit of the dead person is thought to run down the mountain range in the middle of the island and jump through a black cave into Lonwe, the subterranean village of the dead. There all is heavenly: food comes without work, there are constant beautiful melodies to dance to, and sweet perfumes fill the air.

See also Ambae, Malekula

Bibliography

Jolly, Margaret (1981). "People and Their Products in South Pentecost." In *Vanuatu: Politics, Economics, and Ritual in Island Melanesia,* edited by Michael Allen, 269–293. Sydney: Academic Press.

Jolly, Margaret (1991). "Soaring Hawks and Grounded Persons: The Politics of Rank and Gender in North Vanuatu." In *Big Men and Great Men: Personifications of Power in Melanesia,* edited by Maurice Godelier and Marilyn Strathern. Cambridge: Cambridge University Press.

Van Trease, Howard (1987). *The Politics of Land in Vanuatu: From Colony to Independence.* Suva, Fiji: University of the South Pacific, Institute of Pacific Studies.

MARGARET JOLLY

Pintupi

ETHNONYM: Pintubi

Orientation

Identification. The term "Pintupi" refers to a group of Australian Aboriginal hunting and gathering people originally from the Western Desert region of Australia. Their shared social identity derives not so much from linguistic or cultural practice but from common experience, destination, and settlement during successive waves of eastward migrations out of their traditional homelands to the outskirts of White settlements. Pintupi is not an indigenous term for a particular dialect nor for any sort of closed or autonomous community.

Location. The traditional territory of the Pintupi is in the Gibson Desert, in Australia's western territory. This territory is bounded by the Ehrenberg and Walter James ranges in the east and south, respectively, by the plains to the west of Jupiter Wells in the west, and by Lake Mackay to the north. These areas are predominantly sandy desert lands, interspersed with gravelly plain and a few hills. The climate is arid, rainfall averages only 20 centimeters annually, and in some years there is no rainfall at all. Daytime temperatures in summer reach about 50° C and nights are warm, while in winter the days are milder but nights may be cold enough for frost to form. Water is scarce here, and vegetation is limited. The desert dunes support spinifex and a few mulga trees, and on the gravel plains there are occasional stands of desert oaks. Faunal resources, too, are limited—large game animals include kangaroos, emus, and wallabies; smaller animals include feral cats and rabbits. Water is only periodically available on the ground surface after rains; the people rely on rock and claypan caches in the hills and underground soakages and wells in the gravel pan and sandy dunes.

Demography. Population figures for the Western Desert peoples as a whole are difficult to obtain. The sparsely populated Pintupi region was estimated to support one person per 520 square kilometers, but given the highly mobile, flexible, and circumstance-dependent nature of the designation "Pintupi," it is difficult to come up with absolute numbers. The people suffered a population loss during the years of settlement in the east due to the unaccustomed overcrowding and to violence that arose between the Pintupi and White settlers and other Aboriginal groups.

Linguistic Affiliation. Pintupi is a member of the Pama-Nyungan Language Family, also called the Western Desert Language Family.

History and Cultural Relations

The Pintupi were among the last of the Western Desert peoples to experience the effects of contact with Whites—prior to the early 1900s, most of their contacts were with other peoples of similar culture who lived in adjacent territories of the desert. With the establishment of White settlements in the areas to the north, east, and west of Pintupi territory, Pintupi began to migrate to settlement outskirts, attracted by the availability of water and food during times of drought. In the early days of this migration, Pintupi tended to settle in camps separate from those of other migrants such as the Aranda and Walpiri, but as these communities grew in response to further droughts in the desert, the government began to establish permanent camps. Pintupi resisted integration into the broader population of the camps, attempting to maintain their own separate settlements apart from the rest and participating minimally in the affairs of the larger settlement. The trend since the late 1970s has been for the Pintupi to move back toward their traditional Gibson Desert territory, a process that has been facilitated by the drilling of new bore holes at outstations so that access to permanent water sources may be achieved.

Settlements

Pintupi traditional life is highly mobile for most of the year, so encampments are only temporary, sometimes simply overnight. Such camps are segregated by gender and marital status: unmarried men and youths live in one camp, with single women in another nearby; each husband-wife pair and their young children camp together. These camps tend to be quite small. Larger aggregates of people occur at permanent water holes after periods of heavy rains. Camp shelter is a simple windbreak made of brush or, more recently, corrugated iron. The more sedentary settlements around bore holes are quite large—as many as 300 to 350 people—but the spatial deployment of individuals and family groups follows the pattern of traditional encampments.

Economy

Subsistence and Commercial Activities. The Pintupi were traditionally a hunting and gathering people. Australian Aboriginal policy included attempts to introduce the concept of working for a wage, and Pintupi who came to settlements were largely employed on cattle stations, working with the stock. At present, most Pintupi are dependent upon assistance payments from the Australian government.

Industrial Arts. Tools and implements of traditional manufacture include digging sticks and stone-cutting tools, boomerangs, spears, and spear throwers. Shelters used to be made of local materials, but now they are constructed from canvas or corrugated iron. Most manufactured items are of a ritual nature.

Division of Labor. For communal use, men hunt kangaroos, wallabies, and emus when such are available; they hunt feral cats, smaller marsupials, and rabbits at other times. Women gather what plant food can be found, honey ants, grubs, and lizards. Food so obtained is shared throughout the residential group. Food preparation is considered to be a woman's task, although men are capable of it; likewise, the preparation and maintenance of the tools necessary for food gathering and hunting is a man's job, but women can do such tasks if necessary.

Land Tenure. Rights in land refer to Dreamtime associations: that is, one has a right to live in and use the resources of areas to which one can trace ties of family or friendship (the latter most often being treated in kinship terms). One's own place of birth, or the places where one's parents were born, establish claims—but not claims to the land per se, simply to rights of association with others who also use that land.

Kinship

Kin Groups and Descent. The Pintupi recognize two endogamous patrilineal moieties, which are crosscut by generational moieties, themselves consisting of eight paired (as wife-giving/wife-taking) patrilineally defined subsections. These distinctions of relatedness do not translate into rigid, on-the-ground groupings of individuals but rather provide the terms according to which people may forge ties with one another, make claims for hospitality, or be initiated into Dreaming lore.

Kinship Terminology. Terminologically, Pintupi differentiate initially according to subsection membership and further according to gender; that is, members of a single subsection are styled as siblings, but within a subsection the children of the set of "brothers" are understood to belong to a different category than the children of the set of "sisters."

Marriage and Family

Marriage. First marriages are generally arranged by the parents, rather than according to the preferences of the prospective spouses. A man approaching marriageable age will begin to travel with the camp of his prospective in-laws, contributing his hunting skills to their support. Upon marriage, the husband joins the camp of the wife's parents until the birth of the first child or children, while the wife begins instruction in her domestic responsibilities and in women's ritual lore. Once children are born, however, the couple will set up their own distinct camp. Polygyny is common.

Domestic Unit. The Pintupi domestic unit minimally consists of a man, his wife or wives, and their children. However, it is usual that there may also be one or more other dependents—one or more of the husband's or wife's parents or a widowed sibling.

Inheritance. For the Pintupi, ritual associations with Dreaming sites, which also imply rights to resource usage in the associated territory, are the principle benefits of the concept of inheritance. Such associations and rights are normatively passed down patrilineally. Portable personal property is negligible among the Pintupi and its distribution is not normatively prescribed, except that it be given to "distant" kin because it is felt that "near" kin would be reminded of their grief by personal effects of the deceased.

Socialization. Child rearing is the province of the mother during the early years, but it tends to be shared by cowives and other female kin in the camp. At this early stage, children are treated with great indulgence, but they are taught early on that principles of sharing and cooperation are important. Both male and female children are granted a great deal of freedom. Male initiation, by which young boys begin their transformation to manhood, involves introduction into ritual lore and circumcision, after which point they embark upon a period of their lives when it is expected that they will travel widely. In such a way young men develop broader social ties and are exposed to greater amounts of ritual lore. It is only after marriage that women begin to be educated into "women's business," the ritual lore held exclusively by women. There is no female counterpart to the traveling period of male youths.

Sociopolitical Organization

Social Organization. The patrilineage is the largest unit of organization of functional significance for the Pintupi, and it is invoked primarily in the context of ritual life, in justifying one's presence in a place (through reference to the Dreaming), and in marking the intermarriageability of members of one group with another.

Political Organization. Pintupi egalitarianism militates against formal leadership to any great degree. Leaders are elders who are schooled in ritual lore and whose skill in achieving consensus in any gathering has been acknowledged. Since few decisions in Pintupi traditional life require the involvement of large numbers of people, the role of a leader is primarily to mediate disputes. In the mission-based settlements, councillors also serve to keep the peace and to allocate government-provided resources, but the concept of hierarchically organized authority is neither customary nor particularly comfortable for Pintupi.

Social Control. Most social control is effected through the mediation of friends or kin, but there are some circumstances requiring the application of collective sanctions—primarily in the case of violations of sacred tradition, such as the giving away of ritual secrets.

Conflict. Disputes between individuals can erupt at any time over any number of disagreements, but they tend to be most common during times when large numbers of people are gathered together. At such times, fighting can break out and may result in injury or even death. Disputes over women are common. In disputes occurring between individuals, it is common that the aggrieved party will seek out his opponent to spear him in the thigh, and he may commonly attempt to secure the support of his kin in this effort to seek revenge. Acts of "sacrilege" are the single most likely cause for larger-scale hostile action. In the sedentary communities near mission stations, the possibility of conflict, exacerbated by the availability of alcohol, is dramatically higher than it is in traditional Pintupi life.

Religion and Expressive Culture

Religious Beliefs. Central to Pintupi beliefs is the Dreaming (*tjukurrpa*), according to which the world was created and continues to be ordered. The Dreaming is both past and present. In its unfolding—that is, through the activities of the ancestral heroes—not only were the physical features of the world created but also the social order according to which Pintupi life is conducted. Particular geologic features of the terrain are understood to be the direct result of specific deeds of these heroes. Yet the Dreaming is also ongoing, providing the force that animates and maintains life and the rituals that are required to renew or enrich that force.

Religious Practitioners. Religious practitioners are patrilineage elders, whose depth of knowledge of the sacred traditions of their patriline and its totems qualifies them for the instruction of younger and less knowledgeable initiates. The accumulation of ritual knowledge is something that occurs over time, as an individual is gradually led deeper and deeper into the secrets of ritual life. Practitioners are responsible not only for transmitting this ritual knowledge to younger generations but also for maintaining the sacred sites and the spirits associated with them.

Ceremonies. Both men and women have a rich store of ritual lore, linked to the Dreaming, with attendant ceremonies that are performed in the context of initiations and as a part of the process by which sacred sites may be maintained. As with other Western Desert peoples, ceremonial occasions are tied to times and places where large numbers of people can congregate—at water-hole encampments during periods of heavy rains, for example. During these ceremonies there is singing, chanting, and the reenactment of myths appropriate to the specific occasion.

Arts. Pintupi visual art, bodily adornment, and songs are tied to ritual practice, specifically to the Dreaming, and each myth has specific signs and chants associated with it, as well as dramatic reenactments that must be performed. There has been some Pintupi participation in the production and sale of acrylic paintings of Western Desert themes to Australians and Europeans interested in local art.

Medicine. Traditional curing involved sorcery and the use of herbal remedies. The Pintupi today avail themselves of medical care provided through the Australian government health services.

Death and Afterlife. Behavior after the death of a loved one focuses on the grief of the deceased's survivors: people abandon the site at which the death occurred; close kin distribute the belongings of the deceased to more distant kin (whose grief will ostensibly be much less); the bereaved physically harm themselves as an expression of grief; and "sorry fights"—ritual attacks by relatives upon the deceased's coresidents for their failure to prevent the death—also occur. Actual interment of the body is done by the more distant relatives, for close kin are thought to be too grief-stricken to carry out the necessary work. The spirit is thought to survive the body and to remain in the area of this first burial, only departing after a second ceremony is held months later. Where the spirit ultimately goes is vaguely described as somewhere "up in the sky."

See also: Aranda, Mardudjara, Ngatatjara, Warlpiri

Bibliography

Hansen, K., and L. Hansen (1974). *Pintupi Kinship*. Alice Springs: Institute for Aboriginal Development.

Myers, Fred R. (1980). "The Cultural Basis of Pintupi Politics." *Mankind* 12:197–213.

Myers, Fred R. (1986). *Pintupi Country, Pintupi Self: Settlement, Place, and Politics among Western Desert Aborigines*. Washington, D.C.: Smithsonian Institution Press.

NANCY E. GRATTON

Pohnpei

ETHNONYM: Ponape

Orientation

Identification. Pohnpei is a high island in the Eastern Caroline island group of Micronesia. The name "Pohnpei" means "upon a stone altar"; the people refer to themselves as "Mehn Pohnpei" or "of Pohnpei." Throughout the nineteenth and most of the twentieth centuries, the island was known to the outside world as "Ponape." In modern political terms, Pohnpei Island and the neighboring atolls of Mokil, Pingelap, Sapwuafik (formerly Ngatik), Nukuoro, and Kapingamarangi constitute the State of Pohnpei, one of the four Caroline island groups that make up the Federated States of Micronesia.

Location. Pohnpei, lying at 6°57' N, 158°14' E, is an exposed tip of a submerged volcanic mountain. A protective barrier reef surrounds Pohnpei and creates a lagoon of varying width that covers an area of roughly 207 square kilometers. A total of forty small islands of volcanic and coral origin rest on or within the reef. The landmass of Pohnpei proper is 336.7 square kilometers. The interior is covered by dense rain forests and rugged mountains, the highest of which is 778 meters, running west and northwest. A coastal plain, marked by ridges and various rivers and streams, is found to the south and east. This plain gradually gives way to mangrove swamps that hide the shoreline. To the north is a wide valley that runs toward the interior. Pohnpei is visited by heavy northeast trade winds between January and March. The island is subject to heavy rainfall throughout the remainder of the year. Precipitation along the coast averages 482 centimeters a year; the interior receives considerably more. The low-lying clouds that sit atop the mountains after a heavy rain create a majestic sight that has impressed many a visitor.

Demography. Contact with Europeans brought many new diseases to Pohnpei with profound consequences (e.g., a smallpox epidemic in 1854 reduced the population from about 10,000 to fewer than 5,000). The past century has seen steady growth, however, and in 1988 the population of Pohnpei Island was estimated at 27,719, about 6,000 of whom live in Kolonia town, the center of government and commerce for the island. Most of the residents of Kolonia are from the neighboring atolls of Pohnpei State or from other areas within the larger Federated States of Micronesia, of which Pohnpei is the capital. Outside of Kolonia, the overwhelming majority of the population is ethnically Pohnpeian.

Linguistic Affiliation. Pohnpeian, of which there are two principal dialects, is classified as a Nuclear Micronesian language within the Eastern Oceanic Subgroup of Austronesian languages.

History and Cultural Relations

Oral traditions and scientific evidence indicate Pohnpei to have been settled from areas to the east, south, and west. Archaeological evidence dates the earliest human activity at roughly the beginning of the Christian era. Of particular note is the megalithic site of Nan Madol, located just off the southeastern shore of Pohnpei. Archaeologists estimate that construction began sometime during the thirteenth century A.D. and continued for a period of approximately five centuries. Local histories speak of a line of rulers, the Saudeleurs, who attempted to dominate the island from Nan Madol. Following the fall of the Saudeleurs, there developed a more decentralized system of chieftainship. By the end of the nineteenth century, there were five chiefdoms coexisting with several smaller, autonomous regions that possessed a less stratified system of political organization. Intensified contact with the European-American world in the nineteenth century brought trade, Christianity, new diseases, and social disruption. One of the major patterns of the Pohnpeian past, however, has been a pronounced ability to adapt constructively to forces of change. Resistance to foreign domination has been another strong characteristic of this culture. Pohnpeians resorted to violent resistance against both Spanish (1886–1899) and German (1899–1914) colonial rule. Pohnpeian resistance to later Japanese (1914–1945) and American (1945–1983) colonialism has involved less violent and more subtle cultural forms.

Settlements

Outside of Kolonia town, Pohnpeian settlement patterns remain dispersed, with the majority of the population living within half a mile of the shore. With the exception of population concentrations in the Awak and Wone areas, there are no hamlets or villages. Households are scattered and relatively distant from one another. Formerly, individual dwellings were rectangular in shape with thatched roofs, reed walls, dirt floors, and raised stone foundations. The *nahs* or community meetinghouse, with its pitched roof, open sides, and raised seating platforms on three sides, persists as a major architectural form on the island. Imported lumber, cement, and tin have become the preferred building materials in recent years.

Economy

Subsistence and Commercial Activities. The generally rugged topography of the island, combined with the heavy rainfall, works against large-scale agriculture, and a system of cultural values that places greater emphasis on social relationships than on productivity inhibits general economic development; in addition, the infusion of large amounts of American aid has caused problems. Although purchasing increasing amounts of imported foods, Pohnpeians still depend on their lush gardens and surrounding waters for daily sustenance. Breadfruit, yams, taro, cassava, and sweet potatoes are the most common food plants cultivated on the island. These starchy foods are supplemented with fruit plants such as coconuts, bananas, mangoes, papayas, mountain apples, avocados, and various kinds of citrus. Dogs, pigs, and chickens are domestic animals that provide a source of protein for the local diet. There are also smaller numbers of deer, cows, and goats. More than 120 kinds of fish inhabit the waters off Pohnpei; almost all are considered edible. Pohnpeians usually fish within the lagoon and at night, using a variety of fishing techniques including nets, spears, hooks and lines, and local poisons. Much of Pohnpei's subsistence activity centers on an elaborate system of feasting. There exist different feasts for almost all of life's major events; there are also feasts to honor chiefs and family heads. Pigs, yams, and kava (*sakau*) remain the three principal feasting foods. While there have been various attempts to establish small industries, most commercial enterprise centers on small stores in Kolonia and the rural areas that sell imported foods and merchandise. There are also markets that sell local produce.

Industrial Arts. Traditionally, each household produced its own clothing and implements as well as its food. This arrangement is much less common today, as the people increasingly rely on manufactured goods.

Trade. In the past there was no trade as such among Pohnpeians but rather an emphasis on gift exchanges at once determined by and expressive of social rank. In the mid-nineteenth century, European beachcombers and traders established a thriving trade in such goods as tortoiseshells, for which Pohnpeians received muskets, gunpowder, steel tools, and tobacco.

Division of Labor. Men hunt, fish, build houses, hold jobs, and perform the heavier agricultural work involved in the raising of such prestige crops as yams and sakau. Women have the prime responsibility for raising children, taking care of domestic animals, washing and sewing clothes, and carrying out the lighter gardening chores. Women also work in the modern economic sector primarily as secretaries or shopkeepers. Both sexes cook, although men are charged with preparing the rock oven for feasts. Men and women each possess specialized—sometimes even sex-specific—knowledge concerning songs, dances, chants, medicines, and traditional lore.

Land Tenure. In earliest times, land was controlled by matrilineal descent groups or clans that resided in specific locales. With the establishment of a system of chieftainship, all land in a given chiefdom theoretically came under the jurisdiction of the paramount chief. Individuals occupied small farmsteads as tenants. The planting of crops on the farmstead earned tenure and security for the land's occupants as any crops were considered the property of the person or persons who planted them. An offering of first fruits to the local and paramount chiefs was required. In 1907, the German colonial administration removed all land from the jurisdiction of the chiefs and deeded it to the actual occupants. The German reforms further specified that inheritance was to be patrilineal with all wealth and property going to the eldest surviving son. Later, Japanese administrators revised the German system, permitting the division of parcels of land among a number of heirs that could include female relatives. These reforms provide the basis for the modern land tenure system. Competing land claims within family groups are a major source of friction.

Kinship

Kin Groups and Descent. While the immediate family has become the basic social unit, Pohnpeians remain members of clans that are named, matrilineally organized, exogamous, and nonlocalized. Most clans are divided into subclans that claim descent from different female deities of the mother clan. Pressures brought on by modernization have diminished the role of clans as a source of solidarity and support.

Kinship Terminology. The cousin terminology used is a modified Crow type that reflects Pohnpeian society's emphasis on matrilineal rather than generational relationships.

Marriage and Family

Marriage. There are two forms of marriage on Pohnpei today. Common marriage is accomplished simply by a couple's decision to live together. A real or legal marriage usually consists of a feast and a church service at which a man and a woman receive recognition and gifts from parents, chiefs, members of the extended families, friends, and fellow clanmembers. Modern marriages are monogamous; divorce is rare. In the past, the chiefly clans encouraged cross-cousin marriages in which a young man or young woman married a member of the father's clan. This practice helped ensure that both parental clans benefited from a division of property in a society where descent was matrilineal and inheritance patrilineal. High-titled chiefs often took more than one wife. The nobility also practiced infant betrothal.

Domestic Unit. The immediate family is the basic domestic unit on Pohnpei. An average household consists of a man, his wife, their children, and their children's offspring. Residence is usually patrilocal. The notion of extended family is also quite strong.

Inheritance. Inheritance is patrilineal. Current practice permits the division of property among all surviving heirs.

Socialization. Children are raised by both parents and older siblings. Adoption is quite common, especially arrangements involving childless couples who desire an heir for their property and a source of labor and support in their old age. The practice of adoption also provides an inheritance to younger children who, as members of a large immediate family, would otherwise receive only a small portion of the father's inheritable wealth. Children are usually adopted by members of their parents' immediate families. Despite modern economic pressures, Pohnpeians still consider children to be a source of wealth and security; large families are desired.

Sociopolitical Organization

Social Organization. Pohnpeian society is ordered by consideration of rank and status, which derive from clan membership and from individual merit. The traditional distinction betwen noble and commoner has been softened. Education, employment, travel, and material wealth have become increasingly important determinants of modern status.

Political Organization. Although it is a member of the Federated States of Micronesia and has a modern local government that includes an elected governor, his administration, and a popularly chosen state legislature, Pohnpei retains its indigenous system of political organization. The island is divided into five separate chiefdoms that also serve as municipalities for modern governmental purposes; each is governed by two distinct chiefly lines. At the head of the primary ruling line of titles is the *nahnmwarki* or paramount chief. The *nahnken,* a "talking" or administrative chief, leads the second line of ruling titles. Different clans control the two title lines in each of the five chiefdoms. In theory, the senior male members of the ruling clans succeed to the titles of nahnmwarki and nahnken. In actuality, political maneuvering, circumstance, and personal skills affect succession. Each chiefdom or *wehi* is composed of smaller administrative sections called *kousapw.* Each kousapw is governed by two lines of title holders that, in effect, mirror those of the larger chiefdom. A kousapw is, in turn, divided into smaller farmsteads known as *peliensapw.* Traditionally, the chiefs' most direct source of power was their claim to jurisdiction over all land contained within their chiefdom. More than a century and a half of intensified contact with the larger world has worked to diminish the actual power of the island's chiefly system.

Social Control. On Pohnpei, social control is maintained through subscription to cultural values and practices that stress deference, reserve, and accommodation. *Wahu,* or respect, is a fundamental value that characterizes personal relationships today. A fear of social embarrassment leads Pohnpeians to behave with a reserve known as *mahk.* In times of stress, Pohnpeians are expected to evidence a patience called *kanengamah.* When grievous offense is given, Pohnpeians seek reconciliation through a ceremony called a *tohmw.* This ceremony usually includes formal apologies and offerings of sakau to the offended parties and their chiefs, family heads, and clan leaders. Pohnpeians also honor, somewhat selectively, a Western system of courts and laws.

Conflict. Warfare did occur between different chiefdoms or regions. Pitched battles, however, were rare; casualties tended to be light. Raids into enemy territory constituted the most common form of overt hostility. Causes of warfare included disputes over access to resources, competition over the acquisition of chiefly titles, or affronts to chiefly honor or clan dignity. What crime there is today tends to be petty in nature.

Religion and Expressive Culture

Religious Beliefs. Prior to the arrival of foreign missionaries, there existed an elaborate system of religious beliefs. Beneath an order of paramount deities, there were lesser spirits called *eniwohs* that directed the movements of the land, sky, and sea. The spirits of the deceased, especially chiefs, were thought to involve themselves in the affairs of the living. Varying beliefs in different areas added to the complexity of Pohnpei's religious system. Nowadays, the island is divided equally between Roman Catholicism and a number of Protestant denominations, the largest of which is the Congregational church. While Christianity has displaced much of this system of indigenous beliefs, most Pohnpeians today still admit to the existence of local spirits and to the efficacy of sorcery.

Religious Practitioners. In the past, priests called *samworo* mediated between men and gods through a complex collection of rituals and prayers. Sorcery for both constructive and harmful purposes was practiced. Today, American Jesuit missionaries, with the help of local deacons, direct the affairs of the Catholic church. Most Protestant churches are headed by Pohnpeian pastors.

Ceremonies. Pohnpeians today follow the Christian religious calendar. Formerly, there were religious ceremonies at sacred spots about the island to worship local deities, to secure the bounty of the land and sea, and to ensure success for a variety of human endeavors. These ceremonies often were conducted upon stone altars called *pei.*

Arts. Many of Pohnpei's unique forms of artistic expression have been lost as a result of contact with the West. Previously, men carved fine canoes and built large, attractive meetinghouses, while women wove fine mats, chiefly belts, and decorative headbands. Tattooing was a highly refined art entrusted to women that served to record individual lineages and clan histories. Musical instruments included the drum and nose flute. Pohnpeian dance survives. These dances, in which men stand and women sit, tend to be largely stationary and emphasize head and hand movements.

Medicine. Pohnpeians rely upon a combination of Western medicine and local herbal remedies. Massage is also believed to have curative powers. While acknowledging many Western medical practices and beliefs, Pohnpeians still see much disease as caused by sorcery or the violation of cultural taboos.

Death and Afterlife. Pohnpeians possess a stoic, accepting attitude toward death. The funeral feast is the largest and most important form of feast held on the island today. Interment usually takes place within twenty-four hours of death. The funeral feast lasts for four days. Family members, fellow clanmembers, and close friends remain together for an additional three days of feasting. A commemorative feast on the one-year anniversary of the person's death marks the formal end of all mourning. Christianity has changed Pohnpeian beliefs regarding the nature of life after death and the dwelling places of departed souls.

See also Kapingamarangi, Nomoi, Truk

Bibliography

Bascom, William R. (1965). *Ponape: A Pacific Economy in Transition.* Anthropological Records, no. 22. Berkeley: University of California.

Hanlon, David (1988). *Upon a Stone Altar: A History of the Island of Pohnpei to 1980.* Pacific Islands Monograph Series, no. 5. Honolulu: University of Hawaii Press.

Petersen, Glenn (1982). *One Man Cannot Rule a Thousand: Fission in a Pohnpeian Chiefdom.* Studies in Pacific Anthropology. Ann Arbor: University of Michigan Press.

Riesenberg, Saul H. (1968). *The Native Polity of Ponape.* Smithsonian Contributions to Anthropology, vol. 10. Washington, D.C.: Smithsonian Institution.

DAVID HANLON

Pukapuka

ETHNONYMS: none

Orientation

Identification. Pukapuka is a small Polynesian atoll located among the northern atolls of the Cook Islands. Today, dwellers on the atoll refer to themselves as "Pukapukan," though the name appears to lack a specific meaning in the indigenous language. The traditional name for the atoll is "Te Ulu o te Watu," which means "the head of the rock."

Location. Pukapuka is located at 165°50' W by 11°55' S, which makes it roughly 640 kilometers northeast of Samoa and 1120 kilometers northwest of Rarotonga. The total land area of the atoll is approximately 500 hectares; its highest point is 12 meters. The tropical climate has an average mean temperature of 27.9° C and an annual rainfall of 284.1 centimeters. Prevailing winds are from the east and southeast during May through October, from the north and northwest during November through April. The island technically lies outside the "hurricane belt." But it has been ravaged several times by hurricanes in its history. Consisting of a relatively poor soil of sand and coral gravel, vegetation is somewhat limited compared to higher Polynesian islands. Tropical plants and trees do, however, grow in reasonable abundance in the middle of the island. To facilitate growth, banana trees and taro plants need to be fertilized with leaves usually twice a year. A considerable variety of fish exist—in the lagoon, near the reef, and in open water—but the atoll seems to lack the large supply reported for certain northern Cook Islands such as Manihiki. While Pukapukans report that no dogs previously existed on the island (and indeed, there is no traditional word for them), archaeologists discovered dog bones from a site on the atoll dated at 2310 B.P.

Demography. The 1976 Cook Islands census lists the atoll's total population as 785 with an additional 123 Pukapukans living on Nassau (a nearby island owned by Pukapuka). In 1974, Julia Hecht counted approximately 600 Pukapukans in New Zealand (mostly in the Auckland area) and another 200 in Rarotonga. Decimated by a hurricane roughly 400 years ago, the atoll's population reputedly dropped to less than 50 individuals. It subsequently rebuilt itself, but following raids by blackbirders and an epidemic during the latter half of the nineteenth century, the population again dropped, this time to around 300. Since then, it has increased steadily, reaching 505 in 1902, 651 in 1936, and 732 in 1971.

Linguistic Affiliation. Pukapukan is classified within the Samoic-Outlier category of Polynesian languages. While its closest relations are with Tokelauan and Samoan, it also shares linguistic features with languages of Eastern Polynesia.

History and Cultural Relations

From genealogical information, anthropologists Ernest and Pearl Beaglehole deduced that the island was settled around 1300. More recent archeological data (Chikamori and Yoshida) suggest the atoll was settled perhaps during the third century B.C. Traditional accounts indicate that prior to Western contact immigrants came from two sources: Yayake and Manihiki. Reports also describe voyages by Pukapukans to other Polynesian islands, mostly to the west of the atoll, such as the Tokelaus, Samoa, and Tonga. Pukapuka was formally "discovered" by the West when Spanish explorers Alvaro de Mendaña and Pedro Quiros sighted the atoll in 1595. Byron sighted it again in 1765. Because the rocks surrounding the atoll made a landing dangerous, Byron called the atoll's three islets "islands of danger," a phrase from which the name "Danger Island," still used on certain maps, derives. In 1857 native missionaries from the London Missionary Society landed on the island. Pukapuka became a British protectorate in 1892 and in 1901 New Zealand took over its administration. It was incorporated into the Cook Islands in 1915. The Cook Islands became self-governing in internal matters in 1965. The Beagleholes suggest Pukapukan culture shows strong affinities with both eastern and western Polynesia but, overall, is not part of the western Polynesian core.

Settlements

The atoll consists of three major islets. Permanent settlement is allowed only on one of these. During the copra season, many Pukapukans live on the other islets, but when copra production is finished people are required to return to the main islet, Wale. The atoll's three villages are located here, spread out in ribbon fashion along the inner lagoon. In 1976, 219 people lived within the geographic boundaries of Ngake village, 274 within Loto village, and 292 within Yato village. It is important to note that social membership in a village overlaps but is not coterminous with geographic residence. People may reside in one village but belong—in terms of social membership—to another. Each village possesses its own large area of reserved land. A meetinghouse is centrally located within each village. Previously, most houses were constructed of pandanus and coconut materials. Today, cement-walled homes with galvanized tin roofs are the norm. The Beagleholes discuss traditional house types at some length.

Economy

Subsistence and Commercial Activities. Fish and taro were the traditional mainstays of the Pukapukan diet prior to Western contact. According to the Beagleholes, pigs and chickens became regular parts of the diet subsequent to contact. Today, despite its isolation, the island is very much tied into a wider economic system. It imports large amounts of sugar, rice, flour, and canned meat as well as a host of other products such as building materials, outboard motors, and benzine lanterns. Still, despite its poor atoll environment, the island could in theory be nutritionally self-sufficient. The island possesses roughly 15.2 hectares of taro swamps, more than 280 hectares of coconut palms, reasonable marine resources, and some papaya, banana, and breadfruit trees. As elsewhere in Polynesia, domesticated pigs and chickens supplement the regular diet. A number of privately owned trade stores exist on the atoll. These stores produce a limited income at best. Ships call at the atoll three to five times a year with supplies.

Trade. The atoll's major exports are copra and people. Copra exports vary widely. During the 1970s they annually ranged from under 100 to a little over 200 metric tons. The income from copra production and remittances can be considerable, but the mainstay of the economy is government salaries and grants. On the atoll, sharing—of both a formal and an informal nature—is pervasive. While some food resources are shared by the island as a whole, most sharing occurs on a formal basis among village members and on an informal basis among friends and relatives. Copra income as well as food resources within a village's reserve, for instance, are shared out by village food-sharing units (*tuanga kai*). Individual shares vary. But men and women usually possess equal shares, children somewhat smaller ones.

Division of Labor. Division of labor is based on sex and age. Although flexibility exists, men tend to fish (inside and outside the lagoon), build canoes, gather coconuts, prepare pigs for cooking, conduct food divisions, and carry out major political responsibilities. Women tend to fish near the shore (or on the reef), plait mats, work in the taro swamp, cook, and carry out domestic chores. Young men climb coconut trees and do much of the heavy labor. With symbolic implication, Hecht suggests women tend to work in the wet center and men on the dry periphery of the atoll. Elderly men and women are both viewed as important sources of traditional knowledge.

Land Tenure. In modern Pukapuka, two alternative patterns of land tenure coexist. Village reserves (*motu*) are owned by the village as a whole. They are located on the northern portion of Wale (for Loto) and on the other islets (for Ngake and Yato). They involve more than half of the atoll's landmass. Traditionally, each patrilineage used a particular section of a reserve. But today only a slight tendency to continue this practice exists—primarily within Loto and secondarily within Ngake. Village-owned taro swamps are divided annually among members for their personal use during the year. The second pattern of tenure involves cognatic groups termed *koputangata.* Their land is located mostly in the nonreserve portion of Wale. (Certain taro swamps in Loto and Ngake reserves, however, are also owned by koputangata.) While one must have genealogical ties to a particular ancestor (or ancestress) in order to claim land tenure, a host of other factors—including residential proximity to a site, need, and personality—also play a role. Importantly, a person usually belongs to a number of koputangata at the same time; considerable ambiguity surrounds the delineation of koputangata membership and ownership. From an anthropological perspective, such ambiguity provides a degree of flexibility in adjusting land/population ratios to meet various contingencies.

Kinship

Kin Groups and Descent. The Beagleholes describe traditional Pukapukan kinship as a case of double descent. Matrilineal groupings were subsumed under two overarching moieties (*wua*). Major subdivisions (*keinanga* or *momo*) existed within these. None of the units were localized. In contrast, patrilineages (*po*) were localized. Ngake had two patrilineages, Loto three, and Yato three. An individual's burial site—a status marker with important symbolic significance—was traditionally traced patrilineally. Recent studies (Borofsky and Hecht) question the degree to which Pukapukan kinship actually constituted a case of double descent. Both suggest traditional kinship groupings involved a more fluid situation than described by the Beagleholes, with cognatic ties playing a significant role. Modern groupings are now cognatic. Today burial-site affiliation is based on cognatic ties to a deceased relation. Still, while a person may in principle join any village, a patrilineal bias remains regarding who actually becomes a member of which village. A patrilineal bias also remains in the selection of chiefs.

Kinship Terminology. Hecht suggests Pukapuka has an Iroquois-type cousin terminology for opposite-sex cousins; the Beagleholes report an Eskimo-type cousin terminology. Terminology for same-sex cousins and siblings involves a simple Hawaiian-type pattern.

Marriage and Family

Marriage. Reflecting a relaxed attitude toward sex, it is not uncommon for couples to live together in informal unions, though if these unions endure formal marriage usually occurs eventually. Monogamy was and is the rule. Other than restrictions on marrying a relative three generations removed and, in earlier times, on marrying within the smallest matrilineal unit, no formal prescriptions or proscriptions exist regarding marriage choice. Hecht intriguingly observes, however, that more than half of all marriages appear to be endogamous within a five-generation span of a cognatic descent group, and about a quarter are endogamous in respect to village membership. Initial postmarital residence follows a bilateral pattern with a patrilocal bias. Later choice of house sites is flexible depending on the options open to the couple.

Domestic Unit. The immediate nuclear family constitutes the basic household unit, though it is also common to have an extended family share the same household. Formal adoption (*tama kokoti*) involves about 20 percent of the population; fosterage (*tama wangai*) involves 8 percent.

Inheritance. According to the Beagleholes, the traditional system of double descent involved children inheriting land, sections of smaller taro swamps, and burial sites through their fathers and sections of larger taro swamps through their mothers. Today inheritance is cognatic, with all children—in principle, at least—receiving equal shares.

Socialization. Multiparenting—involving a number of adults and older siblings—is common on the atoll. The general Polynesian pattern exists in which an indulgent, nurturing period is followed by a separation from the parents and the child's increasing affiliation with his or her peer group. The learning of everyday activities is mostly done informally, through observation rather than direct instruction. In learning, both cooperation and competition play important roles. Other themes include repetition, ridiculing mistakes rather than praising successes, and learning through performance. While parents beat their children for a variety of offenses, this practice rarely manifests itself in later adult violence. Violent crimes are extremely rare on the island.

Sociopolitical Organization

Social Organization. The most prominent element of modern Pukapukan social organization—other than the above-cited social units relating to land tenure—is a pattern of crosscutting ties that binds individuals of different groups together. As noted, a single individual may well belong to a number of koputangata at the same time. Also, residence within a village does not necessarily coincide with membership (especially in Ngake village). The traditional matrilineal units also provided crosscutting ties for the localized patrilineages. Such ties fit with a general pattern among Polynesian atolls: group boundaries are not demarcated to the extent that individuals cannot readily cross them in time of need. Today, the production of copra and sport competitions are organized on a village basis.

Political Organization. Like other Polynesian islands, Pukapuka traditionally possessed a number of chiefs. Paramount among these was the chief associated with the i Tua (the founding ancestor) patrilineage. But like other atolls, egalitarian orientations were also emphasized and chiefly status did not have the markers or privileges common on higher islands. Today the overall allocation of funding for the atoll is made by the Cook Islands' parliament in Rarotonga to which Pukapuka elects one member. On the island itself, a government-appointed chief administration officer wields considerable power in interpreting and carrying out the national government's orders. An island council with two representatives from each village conducts much of the islandwide business. Along with a more traditional "Council of Important People" (in native terms, "Kau Wowolo"), it represents the central law-making body on the island. At a lower level, villages hold meetings every fortnight in which all adult members participate.

Social Control. There are relatively few formal criminal violations on the island. The rare occurrences are handled by the government's single police officer. Each village has its own *pule,* or council of elders, that enforces village decisions. Being reduced to a child's share in village food divisions (*wakatamaliki*) is perhaps the most serious punishment outside of the rare jail sentence.

Conflict. Armed conflict occurred between various groups in precontact times, though not on a continuing basis. Today, competition in the form of status rivalries pervades the island. It finds its most prominent expression in sports. Winners proudly display themselves before losers, ridiculing them in victory speeches. But very rarely does such verbal humor lead to physical conflict.

Religion and Expressive Culture

Religious Beliefs and Practitioners. According to the 1976 Cook Islands census, 76 percent of the population were Cook Islands Congregationalist (derived from the former London Missionary Society), 14 percent Catholic, and 10 percent Seventh-Day Adventist. All three groups practice a conservative form of Christianity in which the Sabbath is strictly observed. In recent times, the Congregationalist and Adventist ministers have been Cook Islanders, the Catholic priest European. Along with traditional Christian beliefs, there exists a belief in ghosts who are perceived as causing a variety of maladies. In the atoll's traditional religion, a god was associated with each patrilineage. Just as the head of the i Tua lineage was the dominant chief of the atoll, Mataaliki (the main god of the i Tua lineage) constituted the principal god of the atoll. Communication with these gods was usually through a priest. Major religious structures involved both a god house (*wale atua*) and a sacred enclosure (*awanga ya*).

Ceremonies. The most significant islandwide ceremony today is Christmas. All men of a village travel to another village where they partake in a feast prepared by that village's women. Dancing follows. (The following year roles are reversed—the women visit, and the men act as hosts.) The sports competitions surrounding the holiday last well into January. At various times villages may decide to hold other feasts. (Although the food is gathered collectively, each family usually eats it separately.)

Arts. The major art forms today are chanting, dancing, building canoes, plaiting, and singing. Most chants possess a traditional aura and are sung on special occasions. Dancing, especially line dancing, occurs at victory celebrations. New dance steps are often created for special events. Pukapukan women plait pandanus into a variety of products, especially mats. The singing of modern songs is common among the younger generation.

Medicine. According to the Beagleholes, sickness in precontact times had a strong moral component in which diseases were related to moral infractions and antisocial behavior. Responsibility for such infractions extended beyond the individual to other members of the individual's family. Sickness might be sent by gods, a malicious spirit, or a spirit from a foreign land. Treatment involved communication through a seer with one or more gods who would indicate the cause and treatment for the malady. Pukapukans had (and still practice) a number of folk remedies and physical therapy techniques, most prominent being deep-pressure massage.

Death and Afterlife. Today Pukapukans mostly follow Christian doctrine regarding life after death though, as noted, a belief in ghosts also exists. Prior to missionization, the Beagleholes report a belief existed that a person died when the soul permanently left the individual's body. The soul then journeyed to the underworld (*po*) where it took up residence enjoying various pleasures denied it in the upper world.

See also Cook Islands, Manihiki

Bibliography

Beaglehole, Ernest, and Pearl Beaglehole (1938). *Ethnology of Pukapuka.* Bernice P. Bishop Museum Bulletin no. 150. Honolulu.

Borofsky, Robert (1987). *Making History: Pukapukan and Anthropological Constructions of Knowledge.* Cambridge: Cambridge University Press.

Frisbie, Robert (1930). *The Book of Pukapuka.* New York: Century.

Hecht, Julia (1977). "The Culture of Gender in Pukapuka: Male, Female, and the *Mayakitanga* 'Sacred Maid.'" *Journal of the Polynesian Society* 86:183–206.

Hecht, Julia (1981). "The Cultural Context of Siblingship in Pukapuka." In *Siblingship in Oceania,* edited by Mac Marshall, 53–77. Landham, Md.: University Press of America.

ROBERT BOROFSKY

Rapa

ETHNONYMS: Austral Islands, Oparo, Rapa-Iti, Tubuai Archipelago

Orientation

Identification. Rapa is the southernmost island in the Austral Archipelago. Its name is often given as "Rapa-Iti" ("Little Rapa") to distinguish it from the distant Easter Island, which is commonly known as "Rapa-Nui" ("Big Rapa"). On Rapa itself, however, "Rapa-Iti" refers to a small islet off the east coast of the main island. Early European visitors frequently identified the island as "Oparo," but the source of that name is not clear.

Location. The Austral Islands, occasionally known also as the Tubuai Archipelago, straddle the Tropic of Capricorn in the South Pacific. They form part of French Polynesia and lie to the south of the Society Islands and east of the Cook Islands. The four islands in the group in addition to Rapa are Rimatara, Rurutu, Tubuai, and Ra'ivavae. With coordinates of 27°37' S, 144°20' W, Rapa is located some 420 kilometers south-southwest of Tahiti and 180 kilometers southeast of Ra'ivavae, its nearest inhabited neighbor. Rapa is a small island of some 39 square kilometers. It is a high island, the cone of a long-extinct volcano. The highest of the peaks exceeds 600 meters. The east side of the cone has been breached by the sea so that the island has the form of a large bay (the volcanic crater) encircled by a ring of mountains. The coast is indented by several bays, each watered by one or more streams. High mountain ridges between the bays, often meeting the sea in precipitous cliffs, make inland travel difficult. Skies are often overcast and rainfall is abundant (slightly over 254 centimeters annually). Rapa becomes noticeably chilly in the winter months and average monthly temperatures range from 17° C in August to 24° C in February.

Demography. When first sighted by Europeans in 1791, Rapa reportedly had 1,500–2,000 inhabitants, but largely because of introduced diseases the population declined to a low point of only 120 in 1867. In 1964 Rapans numbered only 360, and recent estimates indicate only 400 speakers of the Rapa language.

Linguistic Affiliation. Rapa is grouped with numerous others, including Tahitian, Tongareva, and Cook Islands Maori, in the Eastern Polynesian Subcluster of the Nuclear Polynesian Subgroup of Austronesian languages, though it has virtually disappeared as a distinct language. Tahitian is currently spoken on Rapa as it is in most parts of French Polynesia.

History and Cultural Relations

The first settlement of Rapa has been estimated at about A.D. 950 from genealogical evidence, and the earliest radiocarbon date from the island is A.D. 1,337, plus or minus 200 years. The first European to visit the islands was George Vancouver, in 1791. At that time the population lived in fortified mountain villages. Remains of at least fifteen of these still prominently mark Rapa's landscape; they are among the largest handmade structures in ancient Polynesia. Apparently population pressure forced the construction of these mountain villages to free scarce arable land for cultivation and for security in a time of frequent warfare. The prospect of the Panama Canal stirred the interest of Britain and France in the 1860s and again in the 1880s, for Rapa was ideally located on the route between Panama and Australia and New Zealand. The British established a coaling station on Rapa in late 1867 and it served monthly steamers until it was abandoned in early 1869. Meanwhile Rapa's strategic location moved the French to establish political power over the island. Rapa was made a French protectorate in 1867 and became a French possession twenty years later. The interest in Rapa as a coaling station was sporadic and short-lived and the island slipped into international insignificance. As late as 1964 three months might pass without a visit from the outside. In that year, however, a weather station was established on Rapa and this gave the island some importance in the context of the French nuclear weapons testing program.

Settlements

Sometime prior to 1830 internal warfare ceased, probably because massive depopulation ended the keen competition for arable land, and the people abandoned the fortified mountain villages in favor of lowland villages on the various bays, which offered easier access to the sea and to cultivation areas. With further depopulation villages in the outer bays were gradually abandoned and the village of Ha'urei became Rapa's major population center. In 1964 Rapa's population resided in two villages located on opposite sides of Ha'urei Bay (the large, central bay, crater of the ancient volcano).

Economy

Subsistence and Commercial Activities. For the most part, Rapans support themselves by farming and fishing. Taro (*Colocasia esculenta*) is the staple, and is eaten at every meal. It is grown in irrigated terraces located in level areas adjacent to the village of Ha'urei, at the head of Ha'urei Bay, and on the outer bays. Rapans sometimes reach their taro terraces on the outer bays on foot, but the rugged terrain makes this difficult and they often travel by water in locally made canoes or whaleboats. These vessels are also used for fishing, which is done with spear guns or hooks and lines in the bays and (in whaleboats only) offshore. Oranges and watermelons are grown for local consumption. The main cash crop is coffee, although in 1964 potatoes were introduced for export to Tahiti. Some pigs are tethered on the outskirts of the villages, and goats, cattle, and a few sheep roam unattended in the hills. Goats are eaten when inclement weather prevents fishing; pork and beef are served at special feasts. Occasionally some goats or cattle are captured and shipped to Tahiti for sale. Goats are owned privately, but cattle belong to the Cooperative Society, an organization of shareholders that also oversees coffee exports and operates a small store on the island.

Industrial Arts. Rapan men make wicker baskets in many sizes and often fanciful shapes. Some are used locally, but the more elaborate ones are made for export to Tahiti or for sale to passengers on ocean liners that pass close enough to the island for whaleboats to go out to them. Some of the locally made whaleboats—graceful, narrow, and highly seaworthy—are themselves works of high artisanry.

Division of Labor. Men are charged with boat construction, most aspects of house construction, and fishing from boats and canoes. Women gather shellfish from the shore, prepare food, do laundry, and take care of small children. Both sexes pick coffee and engage in taro cultivation, although the men build and maintain the irrigation ditches and turn the soil in a terrace prior to flooding. Labor is divided at least as significantly by age as by sex. The heaviest work (boat rowing, turning soil, carrying heavy bags of harvested taro) is done by youths and young adults. After about the age of 40, people begin to leave these jobs to younger members of the household.

Land Tenure. Essential to the Rapan system of land tenure is the proposition that improvements (gardens, groves of trees, and houses) may be and usually are owned separately from the land on which they are located. Both territory and improvements are owned by ramages, known as *'opu*.

Kinship

Kin Groups and Descent. The modern ramage or 'opu is a nonexclusive cognatic descent group; that is, it is composed of all legitimate descendants of its founder, counted through both male and female links. So far as territory is concerned, ramage founders were individuals to whom land was awarded in a general land distribution in 1889. Founders of improvement-owning ramages are individuals who create the improvement: who make the taro terraces, build the houses, or plant the coffee groves. Depending on the activity of the founder, then, the ramage composed of his or her descendants may own one or more parcels of territory, taro terraces, coffee groves, houses, or any combination of these. The property of a ramage may be widely dispersed over the island. Because ramage membership passes through both males and females, the various ramages overlap in membership. Membership in some is counted through one's father, and others through one's mother. Most Rapans belong to eight to ten (or more) ramages. A ramage has no function beyond the ownership of property. Its limited affairs are handled by a manager, who is usually the senior male of the group.

Kinship Terminology. Kin terms are of the Hawaiian or generational type, with terms that mark the relative age of same-sex siblings and cousins.

Marriage and Family

Marriage. Marriage is monogamous. Rapans express a slight preference for virilocality, but in actuality virilocal and uxorilocal residence occur with equal frequency. Cohabiting couples are often reluctant to marry formally, as this is a sign that they are shifting from the carefree life of youth to the sober responsibilities of adulthood. The decision to marry is frequently made upon the application of pressure by lay officials of the church. Divorce is rare. Should a spouse die, the preferred remarriage is with the brother or sister of the decedent.

Domestic Unit. Households range from 2 to 15 members, with an average of 6.7. Rapans express a preference for extended family households because of greater sociability and economic efficiency. Largely because of interpersonal tensions that develop between constituent families in extended family households, however, the majority of households on the island consist of an elementary family. To improve their economic efficiency and enhance sociability, many elementary family households have formed themselves into work groups, each of which is composed of four to five households. One or two individuals from each household participate in the group, and the group as a whole works on a rotating schedule, devoting a day to each of its member households in turn. Some work groups are composed of neighboring households regardless of kin ties between them, while others are based on kinship.

Inheritance. Property passes from both parents to all children. Some gardens may be willed to individual children or foster children, but the usual pattern is to leave property jointly to children according to the rules of descent.

Socialization. Children are raised by their own or foster parents. In fosterage, a child ideally acquires the obligation to support his or her foster parents in their old age. The strength of this obligation depends on how much of a person's childhood was actually spent in the foster parents' home. From the age of 4 or 5 children make their own decisions as to where they will live, and often they move between the homes of their biological and foster parents. In any event, a person's legal status and inheritance rights continue to be reckoned through the biological parents. Couples with few or no biological offspring usually foster children of their more prolific close relatives.

Sociopolitical Organization

Social Organization. Class distinctions are not visible in Rapan society. Some persons are more active in church, political, and other affairs than are others, but such involvement depends upon individual leadership qualities. Voluntary associations are organized along village lines. Both villages have funeral clubs, which manage the feast and other practical matters connected with the funeral at the death of someone from a member household, and youth clubs, which form soccer teams, organize entertainment for the 14 July Bastille Day celebration, and undertake other projects for the benefit of the village.

Political Organization. In 1964, the Austral Islands formed one of the five administrative divisions of French Polynesia. Local government on Rapa at that time was vested in a district council, consisting of seven members elected at large for five-year terms. After their election the new council selected from its number a chief and assistant chief. The district council had relatively little power, and the role of chief was largely ceremonial, but it was coveted nonetheless for its salary. In recent years the government has been reorganized in French Polynesia, giving the territory more internal autonomy from France and increasing the power of local councils.

Social Control. In 1964 Rapa fell under the jurisdiction of a French gendarme stationed on Ra'ivavae, some 180 kilometers to the north. Since then, one Rapan has held the position of local police officer. Social control is provided for the most part, however, by the church. Nearly all Rapans are affiliated with the Protestant church, and one of the primary responsibilities of the elected deacons and their wives is to visit and admonish those whose behavior is not satisfactory. Rapans believe, furthermore, than one should not take communion while harboring ill will toward others, so they often make efforts to resolve their disputes prior to the communion service on the first Sunday of every month. Finally, in this small society there are few secrets and a good measure of social control is achieved by gossip or the fear of it.

Conflict. Disputes occasionally erupt over accusations of petty theft, hostilities between stepparents and stepchildren, or the location of boundaries between coffee groves. These seldom go beyond shouting matches, which usually take place around mealtimes when many people are in the village and which invariably and instantly draw large crowds. More permanent factionalism exists between the two villages and between vaguely defined and shifting groups of families. Issues at stake usually involve the distribution of benefits received from the French government. The head schoolteacher, an official appointed from Tahiti and the individual with whom visiting officials interact most frequently, is a center of factionalism for she is in a good position to steer government jobs and other benefits toward those Rapans who get along with her and away from those who do not. The pastor, probably the most powerful person on the island, may also become a center of dissension if it is sensed that he does not treat his parishioners equally. Factionalism is fueled by a contradiction in the Rapan value system. Those who have nothing special to expect from an individual in a public position trumpet the ideal that such a person is bound to act in the interests of all, while relatives and others with special ties to him or her operate under the expectation that a person's first obligations are to kin and allies. Both of these values are honored in Rapa, and anyone in a position of authority finds it difficult to walk a line between them.

Religion and Expressive Culture

Religious Beliefs. Rapa was converted to Protestant Christianity soon after the arrival in 1826 of Tahitian teachers representing the London Missionary Society. With the exception of a few Roman Catholics, the entire population of Rapa is Protestant. In addition to Biblical supernaturals, most Rapans believe in the existence of ghosts, normally of persons who have died relatively recently, called *tupapa'u*. They may cause sickness among the living, either out of anger or from a powerful desire to draw a dearly beloved spouse or child to them. If other means fail, a tupapa'u can be stopped by exhuming and destroying the corpse, a practice probably encouraged by Dracula films, which are very popular in Tahiti.

Religious Practitioners. One pastor (a Rapan who was elected as a young man by the church members and sent to Tahiti for seminary training) divides his Sundays between the two villages. In addition to the pastor, a chief deacon serves both villages, and each village has two deacons and an assistant deacon. To the assistant deacon falls the tasks of ringing the church bell and prowling the aisle during services with a long bamboo pole to prod dozing parishioners. All of these officials are elected by the communicant members, who essentially are the married adults.

Ceremonies. Physically, the church in each village consists of a church proper, a meetinghouse, and an eating house. The church is immensely important in Rapan society, with no fewer than eleven church functions each week. Although scarcely anyone attends all of these events, one can easily appreciate the joking remark made by one man that "in Rapa, we spend more time discussing the Bible than cultivating taro!"

Medicine. Some illnesses are thought to be caused by ghosts, but most are attributed to natural causes. Rapans affirm a hot-cold system of illness, whereby an upset of the body's proper temperature equilibrium brings on disease. Medicines are herbal and each one is accompanied by a special massage. Medicines are private property, and nearly every adult woman on the island owns one or more of them. Thus instead of a few practitioners who treat many different sorts of illness, the Rapan system of medicine has a great many practitioners, each of whom specializes in one or a few disorders. Although others may know the herbal recipe for a certain medicine, it is ineffective unless applied by, or with the express permission of, its owner. No charge is ever assessed for administering medicines, but patients do reciprocate with gifts. Medicines originate in dreams. Someone is sick, no treatment is effective, and then a woman of the household sees, in a dream, her deceased mother or grandmother preparing and administering a hitherto unknown medical concoction of various leaves, water, etc. Upon awakening, the woman prepares the medicine just as she dreamed it. She gives it to the patient, who rapidly recovers. The woman who dreamed it is the owner of the new medicine, and others with the same symptoms come to her to be cured. When she gets old she gives the medicine, and others she may have dreamed or inherited, to individual heirs—usually her daughters—and thus medicines pass through the generations.

Death and Afterlife. The deceased are thought to enter the Christian heaven. A funeral service and burial is followed by a large feast. People congregate at the house of the deceased for several evenings after the funeral for Bible discussion and hymn singing, to support the surviving loved ones, and to reintegrate them gently into society.

See also Raroia, Tahiti

Bibliography

Caillot, A.-C. Eugene (1932). *Histoire de l'île Oparo or Rapa.* Paris: Leroux.

Hanson, F. Allan (1970). *Rapan Lifeways: Society and History on a Polynesian Island.* Boston: Little, Brown. Reprint. 1983. Prospect Heights, Ill.: Waveland Press.

Hanson, F. Allan, and Patrick O'Reilly (1973). *Bibliographie de Rapa.* Paris: Société des Océanistes.

F. ALLAN HANSON

Raroia

ETHNONYMS: Dangerous Islands, Paumotu, Poumot, Tuamotu

Raroia is an atoll in the Tuamotu-Gambier Archipelago in Polynesia. The archipelago consists of seventy-eight atolls located between 135° and 149° W and 14° and 23° S. Raroia is located at about 142° W and 16° S. As are all the atolls except Makatea, Raroia is a low atoll with a land area of 21 square kilometers and a lagoon of 240 square kilometers. The land is mostly sand and gravel. There are 30 species of plants and 19 species of birds indigenous to the atoll and numerous fish and shellfish in the lagoon and sea. The western atolls were settled by people migrating east from Tahiti, the other atolls by people from the Marquesas and Mangareva. Since the time of first settlement there has been regular contact with Tahiti. The population of the Tuamotus was 6,588 in 1863 and it subsequently decreased by nearly a third until it began increasing in the 1920s. In 1987, the number of people claiming Tuamotu identity was estimated at 14,400, with about 7,000 in the Tuamotus and a sizable population in Tahiti. In 1897, Raroians numbered 260, by 1926 the population had decreased to 60, and then it slowly increased to 120 by 1950.

First contact with Europeans was in 1606, which was followed by only occasional contact with explorers and traders from various European nations for the next two hundred years or so. From 1817 to 1945 the Tuamotus were under the control of Tahiti, with Tahitian influence greatest in the western atolls. However, by the end of the period, Tahitian influence had reached the eastern atolls and Raroians were involved in the mother-of-pearl trade network. In 1845 the Tuamotus came under French control and offical French rule began in 1880. Roman Catholic missionaries entered the atolls in the 1860s and the population was quickly converted to Catholicism.

Prior to European contact, Raroia was politically linked to the neighboring atoll of Tukume. Atoll land was divided into districts with the land owned by a combination of lineally and laterally extended kin groups. Descent was bilateral, with Hawaiian-type cousin terms. Leadership rested with extended household heads, with the head of one household serving as the atoll leader and the ruler of Tahiti serving as the head chief of the Tuamotus. The subsistence economy was based on fishing in the lagoon and sea and the gathering of shellfish, supplemented by pandanus nuts and taro. Raroians were skilled canoe builders and sailors. The traditional religion focused on various gods, spirits, ghosts, and associated cults.

Contact with traders, French officials, and missionaries for more than 100 years effectively destroyed the traditional culture and replaced it with a Western economic and social system. The subsistence economy has been replaced by a cash economy, with the collection of pearls and pearl shells and copra production being the primary economic pursuits at various times. Both activities have now declined in importance as sources of income. Tourism is now a major source of income on some atolls, though not on Raroia. Leadership now rests with elected representatives, the wealthy, and missionaries. Families are now smaller and nuclear in form, with an emphasis on individual ownership of property. About 98 percent of Raroians are now Roman Catholics.

See also Mangareva, Rapa, Tahiti

Bibliography

Danielsson, Bengt (1956). *Work and Life on Raroia.* London: George Allen & Unwin.

Emory, Kenneth P. (1975). *Material Culture of the Tuamotu Archipelago.* Honolulu: Bernice P. Bishop Museum.

Rennell Island

ETHNONYMS: Mugaba, Munggava, Rennellese

Both Rennell and its twin island Bellona (Munggiki) are Polynesian outliers in the central Solomon Islands. Rennell is a raised coral atoll, with a large lake in its southeastern end, located between 11°34' and 11°47' S and 159°54' and 160°37' E. In 1976 there were 1,945 inhabitants of Rennell Island. Rennellese is part of the West Polynesian Group of Austronesian languages. Rennellese settlements tend not to be nucleated into villages but rather are scattered throughout the island. They consist of one or more dwellings and a cook house around an open clearing off the main path.

Food is obtained mainly through horticulture and fishing, supplemented by hunting and collecting. Yams, taro, and bananas are very important cultigens. The coconut is tremendously important as a source of food and raw material. Various birds, flying foxes, and sharks are also eaten. In general, women cook, garden, collect fruits and herbs, fish inshore, plait, make nets, and take care of the children. Men do the heavy gardening, hunt, fish, make tapa and sennit, and are responsible for wood carving, canoe making, and house building. Elaborate feasts effect the distribution of agricultural, sea, and forest products among the descent groups. Land is held individually by the men of a lineage. The profession of expert carpenter (*mataisau*) is a highly respected one.

Important kin groups include clans, subclans, and patrilineages. The Rennellese view marriage as a means of creating alliances (*hepotu'akinga*) and as a way to continue a man's lineage. One's mother's brother's daughter is the preferred mate, and this tradition leads at times to conflict between parents and child in the choice of spouse. Polygyny was traditionally approved but was not very common. Residence is nearly always patrilocal, although after a divorce a woman returns with her infant children to her father. The core of the domestic unit (*manaha*) is a nuclear family, often supplemented with various relatives, both natural and adopted.

The *kakai'anga* was the largest politically integrated unit. Primary authority was vested in the landholding males and in the senior men of senior lineages in each generation. In addition to these leaders Rennell had a paramount chief (*angiki*) who was descended from the leader of the first immigrants. The angiki could communicate with and influence the gods during trances. He was also the judicial authority and could have criminals beaten or put to death or have their crops destroyed. In spite of the overwhelming patrilineal emphasis of Rennellese society, a person maintains close ties with the members of his or her matriline as well.

Rennellese religion had little to say about eschatology or cosmology; its major concern was life and the fertility of humans and of the plants and animals they depended on. Today, nearly all of the people are Christians. All adult males officiated at the various rituals, which were directed by priest-chiefs (*tunihenua*). The most important rituals were associated with the harvest and distribution of yams. Mediums possessed by supernatural forces could convey the latter's messages and wishes. Each kakai'anga had its own set of ancestors, who were worshiped as gods. In addition, there were two high gods: Tehainga'atna, the fierce god of nature; and Tehu'aigabenga, the god of culture, society, and cultivated plants.

Bibliography

Birket-Smith, Kaj (1956). *An Ethnological Sketch of Rennell Island: A Polynesian Outlier in Melanesia.* Det Kongelige Danske Videnskabernes Selskab, Historiskfilologiske Meddelelser Bind 35, no. 3. Copenhagen: Danish Natural Museum.

Birket-Smith, Kaj (1966). *Language and Culture of Rennell and Bellona Islands.* Copenhagen: Danish Natural Museum.

Rossel Island

ETHNONYMS: Duba, Rova, Yela

Orientation

Identification. The Rossel Islanders live on the easternmost island of the Louisiade Archipelago in the Massim culture region (Milne Bay Province) at the east end of New Guinea. They speak "Yelatnye," meaning "language of Yela," and their name for themselves is "Yelatpi," meaning "Rossel people."

Location. Rossel Island is located at about 11° S and 154° E. The island is 34 kilometers long and 14 kilometers across, being approximately 290 square kilometers in area. It is very mountainous, with the highest peak, Mount Rossel (also known locally as "Mbgö"), reaching 800 meters. The coast is highly indented and mainly fringed by mangrove swamp. The island is covered in tropical rain forest. It is surrounded by a coral reef extending 12 kilometers east and 40 kilometers west of the island forming two lagoons. The distance from Rossel to the nearest westward island of Sudest (Vanatinai) is 33 kilometers. The trade wind blows from the southeast from

May to October, the more irregular northwest monsoon from January to March, both bringing rain.

Demography. In 1979 the population of Rossel Island was about 3,000 persons, with 800 being away from the island working or studying. The population density averages 8 persons per square kilometer and the population is growing at the rate of 3 percent per year. Before 1950 it was declining.

Linguistic Affiliation. Yelatnye is a Non-Austronesian language whose affiliation to other "Papuan" languages of New Guinea and Melanesian islands has not yet been established. Rossel Islanders are the only people in the region who speak a Non-Austronesian language. The number of cognates with the language of the nearest island, Sudest, is only 6 percent. Yelatnye has a very complex phonology and grammar and is regarded as extremely difficult by outsiders.

History and Cultural Relations

The Rossel Islanders probably represent the last remnants of an original population of the region, which on the other islands has been superseded by, probably, several waves of Austronesian-speaking immigrants. In one of these pottery, derived from the Lapita culture, spread through the Massim about 2,000 B.P. It is probable that a stratified social system was introduced at the same time, linking island populations to political centers. Although Rossel preserved its Non-Austronesian language, the culture is much affected by its Austronesian neighbors. The first historical contact gave Rossel an ill repute: 316 Chinese coolies, bound for Australia, were reported massacred and eaten after a shipwreck in 1858. Rossel became a part of the British (later Australian) protectorate of Papua in 1884. During the next decades the island was "pacified" by government patrols. In 1903 an enterprising family of traders established a plantation that became the economic center of the island for the next fifty years and deeply transformed the socioeconomic relations of the people. Rossel is now more involved in the cash economy than its nearest neighbors to the west. The plantation is now worked by local people. Missions were established starting in 1930; the first was the Methodist (now United Church) mission, followed in 1947 by the Catholic. Now, roughly the western half of the island is United Church, while the eastern half is Catholic.

Settlements

Earlier the settlement pattern was one of hamlets scattered along the coast and in the interior. A census in 1919 showed 145 villages with an average of ten inhabitants. During World War II the population was concentrated in about 10 villages on the coast. Most of these settlements broke up into hamlets or hamlet clusters after the war, but people did not return to the interior. Although there is no standard site plan, hamlets often feature a carefully weeded square or street surrounded by living houses and with one or two stone sitting circles, common in the southern Massim. In "traditional" hamlets, a seclusion house for menstruating and postpartum women is built behind the house line. Hamlets are surrounded by banana trees, coconut palms, and other fruit trees. Early house types included a barrel-roofed ground house and a pile house entered through a trapdoor in the floor. Today, living houses are regularly built on posts with a roof of sago-palm leaves and walls of sago-leaf sheaths. Cooking takes place under the house or on a clay hearth on the kitchen floor.

Economy

Subsistence and Commercial Activities. Basic subsistence is by swidden horticulture, gardens being used for two or more plantings and left fallow or, near the coast, being often used for small coconut plantations. Crops are tubers such as taro, yams, sweet potatoes, and cassava, as well as bananas and sugarcane. Sago flour is prepared from the pith of the sago palm. Tree crops are coconuts and breadfruit. Wild nuts and fruits are collected, as well as shellfish. Feral pigs and opossums are hunted and fish are caught by line, spear, or net or by means of dams. A plant poison is also sometimes used for fishing. Cooking methods include boiling with cream of coconut, roasting in embers, and baking in hot stones. Commercial crops are mainly coconut (for copra) and some coffee. Other important sources of cash income are the manufacture of shell necklaces and labor migration.

Industrial Arts. Rossel is well known for its high-quality red-shell necklaces made from the mollusk *Chama,* which is common in the lagoon along the western half of the island. This traditional craft was expanded and managed by the traders in the early decades of this century. Imported grinding blocks are now used. The necklaces are of the type that move in the *kula* ring. The islanders build their own houses, canoes, and dinghies. A few larger boats have been built during recent years. Basketwork, made by women, is of high quality.

Trade. The dominant trade store is run by the Catholic mission but small stores are found in many hamlets. Otherwise there is no market on Rossel. Through a traditional visiting trade with Sudest Rossel exported shell necklaces and imported clay pots, pigs, and stone axes. This trade connection is now much weakened. Internal noncommercial exchanges by means of a complex system of shell valuables—the famous "Rossel Island money"—are important and include payments for pigs, houses, canoes, garden crops, and some forms of labor service. There are two kinds of shell money. *Ndap* are flat pieces of *Spondylus, kö* are sets of 10 disks of *Chama* on a string. Both are ranked into many classes. Higher-ranking ndap are rare treasures believed to have been made by deities and, like kula shells, individually named. They are now out of open circulation and change ownership through inheritance. Kö and low-ranking ndap still circulate and are still made. Women own shell money and participate in exchange but they rarely sponsor payments. Exchange rules are very complex. Wallace Armstrong, who first described this monetary system, explained it by supposing lending at compound interest. This interpretation was based on misunderstandings of the operation of the system. Other valuables are ceremonial stone axes and shell necklaces. Cash now enters into some payments.

Division of Labor. The main division of labor is by sex. Men fell large trees for gardens, build houses and canoes, hunt, and fish; women collect most shellfish and dominate in domestic tasks, such as cooking and child care. Both sexes plant, weed, and harvest crops. They combine work in sago preparation.

Land Tenure. With a fairly small population land pressure is slight. The tenure practices are flexible and disputes over land infrequent. Areas of land are associated with matrilineal subclans, but stewards of land often belong to different clans. Use rights are frequently based on descent from bilateral grandparents. Mortuary payments of traditional valuables from the deceased's spouse's relatives to the deceased's relatives confirm such land rights.

Kinship

Kin Groups and Descent. There are some fifteen totemic, matrilineal, and dispersed clans (*pũ*). Subclans (*pũghi*) share exogamy with one or more linked subclans of different clans. The members of subclans do not all reside in the same area but there are local subclan sections. A more loose cognatic category (*yo*) denotes the bilateral descendants of an ancestor or the bilateral kindred of a person.

Kinship Terminology. The terminology system is classificatory and of the Crow type, with alternate-generation terminology in one's own (male speaking) and one's father's line (both sexes speaking).

Marriage and Family

Marriage. Marriage within most clans, between one's own and linked subclans, between children of men of the above categories, and between first cousins is proscribed. Marriage with a classificatory mother's brother's daughter is discouraged while marriage with a classificatory father's sister or father's sister's daughter is preferred. Actually, only 46 percent of a small sample had actually married according to this preference. There is a tendency toward local endogamy. Many marriages are still arranged by elderly relatives. A considerable bride-wealth is paid in shell money, no cash being allowed. Due to mission pressure polygynous marriages are now infrequent. Residence is predominantly patrivirilocal. Divorce is rare.

Domestic Unit. The nuclear family is the primary domestic unit (the people who pool food resources and eat together), with the addition of occasional unmarried young or old enfeebled relatives. This unit conducts daily food production but is assisted by bilateral kin and affines for larger tasks such as forest clearing or house building.

Inheritance. The main significant property is fruit trees and ceremonial stone and shell valuables. Sons tend to inherit from their fathers and daughters from their mothers. The person who takes main responsibility for taking care of a close relative in old age receives the major share.

Socialization. Infants and children are raised by members of the domestic unit and by grandparents and other elderly relatives. Socialization practice varies between families. Generally sharing and cooperation is emphasized and, although self-assertion is discouraged, autonomy of the individual is valued.

Sociopolitical Organization

Rossel Island is part of Papua New Guinea, a sovereign state in the British Commonwealth. Rossel elects one member to the Provincial Assembly of the Milne Bay Province. With the East Calvados chain and Sudest Rossel forms the Yelayamba Local Government Council and elects seven of the sixteen councillors.

Social Organization. There is no descent group rank on Rossel. Inequality is manifested in the greater influence and prestige of elders in relation to the young and men in relation to women. A "financial aristocracy" of exchange experts and owners of high-rank shell money form the dominating stratum of the population.

Political Organization. The island is divided into ten census "villages" that, in combinations, elect the seven local government councillors. A lower-lever functionary is the *komiti*. Precolonial leaders were warriors, ritual experts, and powerful big-men. The last category had attached henchmen and controlled high-rank shell money used in payments for cannibal victims. Pacification and mission influence weakened the power of indigenous leaders but elderly males with financial expertise still command some local influence. Councillors are younger men with outside experience and language ability. The government provides primary-school education, a hospital, medical aid posts, and other services, such as an airstrip, a minor wharf, and water-supply facilities.

Social Control and Conflict. Pacification and mission influence have produced a very peaceful society on Rossel Island. Conflicts and disputes are remarkably rare. A major deterrent from offending others is fear of sorcery retaliation. Dominance over the young is supported by the control of the elders of supernatural knowledge and of the intricate system of exchange of indigenous valuables. While villagers attempt to settle minor offenses informally, major delicts are prosecuted by the government, represented on the island by a patrol post.

Religion and Expressive Culture

Religious Beliefs. The religious system is a combination of Christianity and traditional beliefs. Although two Christian denominations (United Church and Catholic) divide the island, the relations between them are harmonious. The islanders have adopted Christianity as a means of acquiring a link to forces of the greater world, spiritually as well as in terms of health-care, education, and cash opportunities. The government has taken over hospitals and schools, but these services are still located at the missions. Apart from Christian beliefs the islanders still hold beliefs in local supernatural beings and ways of communicating with them by means of incantation and sacrifice. Deities (*woyili*) are believed to have lived on the island before, when they brought or created natural and cultural features such as landscape forms, food plants, sorcery, etc. Some are regarded as ancestors of subclans. Later they disappeared into the underworld (*teme*) at the sacred places. They may appear as snakes, crocodiles, or dugongs. Armstrong's report of a hierarchy of gods cannot be supported. The power of the deities can cause blessings, such as crop fertility, or misfortune, such as sickness. Each sacred place is associated with only one or two effects. Formerly, they were avoided, except by the knowledgeable custodians. Now some have fallen into disuse and are not respected any more. Other supernaturals were ogres (*podyem*), with white skin and long hair, and gnomes (*kömba*) living in hollow trees. They are rarely, if ever, reported now.

Religious Practitioners. Christian practitioners are United Church pastors—largely from neighboring islands—and Catholic catechists. Some men, who have inherited spells and ritual knowledge associated with sacred places (*yopo*), still perform rites there. Because of mission aversion such practices tend to be secret.

Ceremonies. The guardians of sacred places are supposed to keep them clean and at certain times of the year, or when needed, perform rites such as libations and reciting of spells in the presence of other men. Other ceremonies connected to the deities are nocturnal singing of sacred songs (*ndamö*). This worship is a male cult. Women have won a legitimate place in religious worship only with Christianity.

Arts. Traditional Rossel carving style, for example on canoes and lime spatulas, is plain, usually nonfigurative, and symmetric. It has largely been supplanted by the Massim style characterized by the use of spirals and scrolls. A number of types of baskets are woven, from large food containers to fine baskets for shell money. There are no traditional musical instruments but drumming on canoe hulls may take place in connection with the singing of ndamö. There are several types of traditional dance and song performances. The most common is the *tpilöve,* in which men appear in dancing skirts.

Medicine. Illness is traditionally mainly attributed to sorcery and infringement of sacred places. Curing practices include countermagic, sacrifices at sacred places, traditional medicines, and healing.

Death and Afterlife. Burial takes place in an L-shaped grave, usually in a common cemetery for a number of hamlets. Formerly, the body was placed in a shallow grave in the house and later exhumed. The skull was exposed in the hamlet and later deposited in a shelter in the bush. At the death of an important person in-laws were usually accused of sorcery and had to atone by supplying a cannibal victim for a special feast (*kannö*). Now, a week after the death the mortuary feast (*kpakpa*) is held. Here, the burial services are rewarded and donations of traditional valuables are presented to various categories of relatives of the deceased. When the spirit (*ghötmi*) leaves the body at death it travels to Yeme, the mountain of the dead, at the western end of Rossel. According to another belief the dead go to the underworld. Formerly, the spirits of victims of cannibalism were believed to go to Tpi, a mountain on the south side of Rossel. Ordinary ghosts (*mbwe*) are not greatly feared, unlike the ghosts of cannibal victims. In contrast to beliefs in Sudest, in Rossel culture the dead are not supposed to interfere much in the life of the living.

Bibliography

Armstrong, Wallace E. (1928). *Rossel Island: An Ethnological Study.* Cambridge: Cambridge University Press.

Liep, John (1983). "Ranked Exchange in Yela (Rossel Island)." In *The Kula: New Perspectives on Massim Exchange,* edited by J. W. Leach and E. Leach, 503–525. Cambridge: Cambridge University Press.

Liep, John (1983). "'This Civilising Influence': The Colonial Transformation of Rossel Island Society." *The Journal of Pacific History* 18:113–131.

Liep, John (1989). "The Day of Reckoning on Rossel Island." In *Death and Life Rituals in the Societies of the Kula Ring,* edited by F. Damon and R. Wagner, 230–253. DeKalb: Northern Illinois University Press.

JOHN LIEP

Rotuma

ETHNONYMS: none

Orientation

Identification. Rotuma lies approximately 480 kilometers north of Fiji, on the western fringe of Polynesia. The island is very near the intersection of the conventional boundaries of Micronesia, Melanesia, and Polynesia, and traces of influence from each of these areas can be found in the physical composition, language, and culture of the island's inhabitants. Although Rotuma has been politically associated with Fiji since 1881, when the chiefs ceded the island to Great Britain, the Rotuman people are unique, forming a distinctive enclave within the Republic.

Location. Rotuma is located at 12°30' S and 177°40' E. The island is of volcanic origin, with the highest craters rising to heights of 260 meters. It is divided into two main parts joined by an isthmus of sand, forming a total configuration about 13 kilometers long and, at its widest, nearly 5 kilometers wide. The land area is approximately 44 square kilometers. April through November the prevailing winds are from east to south, December through March from north to west. Rainfall averages about 350 centimeters per year.

Demography. The first census of Rotuma was taken in 1881, the year of its cession to Great Britain. The population was reported as 2,452. Following a devastating measles epidemic in 1911, it declined to under 2,000, then began to increase gradually. As the total approached 3,000 in the late 1930s, out-migration to Fiji became an important means of alleviating population pressure. According to Fiji census records, in 1936 91.3 percent of Rotumans were living on their home island. By 1956 the percentage had decreased to 67.7 percent, and by 1976 it had declined to 37.1 percent. In recent years out-migration has accelerated, not only to Fiji but to New Zealand, Australia, and the United States. As a result, the population of the island has declined to around 2,500, representing less than 25 percent of the total number of Rotumans.

Linguistic Affiliation. Linguistic evidence suggests that Rotuman belongs in a subgrouping (Central Pacific) that includes Fijian and the Polynesian languages; within this group there appears to be a special relationship between Rotuman and the languages of western Fiji. The vocabulary shows a considerable degree of borrowing from Tongan and Samoan.

History and Cultural Relations

Until the archaeology of Rotuma is done, the origins of its population will remain clouded. There is, however, solid evidence that migrations from Samoa and Tonga occurred after initial settlement, and other data suggest Rotumans were in contact with Tuvalu (Ellice Islands) to the north, Kiribati (Gilbert Islands) to the northwest, Futuna and Uvea to the east, and Fiji to the south. The first recorded European contact was in 1791 with Captain Edwards in H.M.S. *Pandora,* while he was searching for the mutineers of the *Bounty*. The first half of the nineteenth century was a time of increasing contact, as Rotuma became a favorite place for whalers to replenish their provisions. A substantial number of sailors jumped ship there, and the beachcomber population was estimated at times to be more than 100. In addition to whalers were labor recruiters, who found Rotumans quite willing to sign on. By the mid-nineteenth century many Rotuman men had been abroad, and some had visited the centers of European civilization before returning home. In the 1860s European missionaries from the Wesleyan and Roman Catholic churches established themselves on Rotuma, and the island was divided between them. Antagonisms between converts to each faith mounted until 1878, when they culminated in a war won by the numerically superior Wesleyans. The unrest that followed led the chiefs of Rotuma's seven districts to petition Queen Victoria for annexation, and in 1881 the island was officially ceded to Great Britain. Rotuma was governed as part of the Colony of Fiji until 1970, when Fiji gained its independence. Since then it has been an integral part of that island nation.

Settlements

A packed-sand road encircles the perimeter of the eastern part of the island and extends to the northern and southern sides of the western part. Since colonial times, at least, almost all settlement has been on the coastal areas along this road. Although the island is divided into districts and the districts into villages, settlement along the road is nearly continuous, and it is often difficult to determine boundaries. In recent years bush paths have been widened, and though still quite rough, they make it possible to traverse the interior of the island by motor vehicle. Traditional Rotuman houses were made of thatch, but over time limestone, cut lumber, and corrugated iron replaced much of the thatching. In 1972 Hurricane Bebe destroyed most of the remaining native-style houses. A relief team from New Zealand organized the construction of over 300 cement and iron structures. Most households also maintain a thatched cooking house, and some have separate toilets and wash houses. There are no freshwater streams on Rotuma, and until recently rainwater stored in cement or iron tanks was the main source of water for drinking and bathing. During the 1970s, however, a freshwater underground lens was tapped and now most households have access to piped water. Income from salaries and remittances are often used to improve houses, and a number of two-story structures have been built over the past few years.

Economy

Subsistence and Commercial Activities. The vast majority of households in Rotuma maintain gardens that supply their staples (taro, yams, tapioca, breadfruit, and bananas). Pineapples, papayas, mangoes, watermelons, and oranges are also grown in abundance to supplement the diet. Soil type varies from sandy to loam, and the soil is quite deep. While the entire island is exceptionally fertile, the eastern side is covered with stones and boulders, making it more difficult to work. The main implements in gardening are the bush knife, for clearing land, and the dibble stick, which is used to make holes in the earth for planting root crops. Rotation of crops is the common pattern; typically yams are planted the first season, followed by taro and then by tapioca and banana trees. Although only a few men engage in deep-sea fishing, the fringing reef that surrounds the island is widely exploited for a variety of fish, octopuses, crustaceans, and edible seaweed. Chicken, canned corned beef, and canned mackerel supplement the daily diet, while cattle, goats, and pigs are consumed on special occasions such as weddings, funerals, and welcoming ceremonies. The main export product is copra. It is marketed by the Rotuma Cooperative Association, which dominates the commercial life of the island.

Industrial Arts. The main Rotuman handicrafts are pandanus mats and baskets. Mats, particularly fine white ones, are central to Rotuman ceremonies, and they were traditionally considered to be the main form of wealth. Canoe making still occurs on a small scale, but aside from foods made in two bakeries, Rotumans do not produce any goods for commercial markets.

Trade. An airstrip was opened on Rotuma in 1981, but few goods are transported by air. Shipping by sea is irregular, aggravating the problem of Rotuma's isolation from potential markets. This isolation has especially inhibited the development of agricultural exports. Rotuman oranges, for example, are famous for their quality and are extremely abundant, but as yet they have not been commercially exploited because of difficulties with storage and transportation.

Division of Labor. In general, Rotumans follow the general Polynesian pattern of women's work being close to home while men's labor takes them farther afield. Women are exclusively responsible for mat making, and they take major responsibility for child care, washing clothes, cleaning the household compound, and the preparation and serving of family meals. They also harvest marine resources on the reef. Men take primary responsibility for gardening, animal husbandry, cooking in earthen ovens, and house construction. The division of labor is not rigid, however, and couples generally help each other when required.

Land Tenure. Land is important to Rotumans for its symbolic significance as well as for its subsistence value. The main landholding unit is the *kainaga,* a bilateral group based upon common descent from ancestors who resided at, and held rights in, a named house site (*fuaq ri*). Each person is considered to have rights in the fuaq ri of his eight great-grandparents, although typically rights are exercised selectively. Associated with each fuaq ri are sections of bush land, and membership in a given kainaga entitles one to rights in this land. The person who lives on the fuaq ri acts as steward of the land and controls access. He, or she, is obligated to grant usufructuary rights to kainaga members for any reasonable request. At times land has been sold or given for services to specific individuals, but over generations it becomes kainaga land again. When the population of the island approached its highest levels, during the 1950s and 1960s, land disputes intensified and access was generally restricted to close relatives. In recent years, however, out-migration has relieved tensions and the main problem now is often to determine which of a set of siblings will remain behind to steward the land and care for aging parents.

Kinship

Kin Groups and Descent. Descent is bilateral. The term kainaga, in its most general sense, denotes common membership in a class. It is used to describe animal and plant species as well as human kinship, and it applies to personal kin who function during life-crisis ceremonies (e.g., the bride's relatives), as well as to descent-based landholding units (see section on land tenure).

Kinship Terminology. Kin terms are essentially of the Hawaiian type. Within ego's generation, cross-sex siblings are distinguished from those of the same sex.

Marriage and Family

Marriage. Traditionally, Rotuman marriages were arranged by parents, although generally with the prior consent of the partners. Public courtship displays were frowned upon, so liaisons had to be formed surreptitiously. Courtship rules have been relaxed in recent years, but a strong concern remains for the decorum of unmarried youths. Marriages with second cousins are allowed. Postmarital residence with the wife's family is preferred, although movement between husband's and wife's natal homes is common over the span of a lifetime. Marriages are quite stable; the great majority are terminated only by the death of a spouse. Divorce is under the jurisdiction of Fijian courts, which are modeled on British law. Property is rarely involved, and young children are distributed by mutual agreement.

Domestic Unit. Households are defined in terms of sharing a common hearth and eating together. Household size has declined in response to out-migration, from an average of about 7.5 in 1960 to about 4.5 in 1988. Most consist of a nuclear family, extended by relatives of either the husband or wife. Children are often left with grandparents when married couples emigrate, so three- and four-generation households are common. Since maintaining a household requires the labor of both men and women, single persons are often invited to become de facto members of a neighbor's household.

Inheritance. Each surviving child inherits an equal share in rights over family landholdings, although traditionally the senior male is favored in succession to stewardship. Today, however, it is often one of the younger siblings who remains behind to look after the family estate while elder siblings emigrate.

Socialization. Infants and children are cared for by both parents, by grandparents, and by elder siblings. Physical punishment is rare, and children's autonomy is respected. Children circulate freely between households in the vicinity of their household, and they are never excluded from adult-centered events. Value emphases are placed on sharing, cooperation, and respecting the autonomy of others.

Sociopolitical Organization

Rotuma was governed as an integral part of the Colony of Fiji after cession to Great Britain in 1881. Following Fiji's independence in 1970 and the military coups of 1987, Rotuma remained with Fiji.

Social Organization. Rotuma is divided into seven autonomous districts, each with its own headman (*gagaj 'es itu'u*). The districts are divided into subgroupings of households (*ho'aga*) that function as work groups under the leadership of a subchief (*gagaj 'es ho'aga*). All district headmen and the majority of ho'aga headmen are titled. In addition, some men hold titles without headship, although they are expected to exercise leadership roles in support of the district headman. Titles, which are held for life, belong to specified house sites (fuaq ri). All the descendents of previous occupants of a fuaq ri have a right to participate in the selection of successors to titles. On formal occasions titled men and dignitaries such as ministers and priests, government officials, and distinguished visitors occupy a place of honor. They are ceremonially served food from special baskets and kava. In the daily routine of village life, however, they are not especially privileged. As yet no significant class distinctions based on wealth or control of resources have emerged, but investments in elaborate housing and motor vehicles by a few families have led to visible differences in standard of living.

Political Organization. At the time of discovery by Europeans there were three pan-Rotuman political positions: the *fakpure,* the *sau,* and the *mua.* The fakpure acted as convener and presiding officer over the council of district headmen and was responsible for appointing the sau and ensuring that he was cared for properly. The fakpure was headman of the district that headed the alliance that had won the last war. The sau's role was to take part in the ritual cycle, oriented toward ensuring prosperity, as an object of veneration. Early European visitors referred to the sau as "king," but he actually had no secular power. The position of sau was supposed to rotate between districts, and a breach of this custom was considered to be incitement to war. The role of mua is more obscure, but like the sau, he was an active participant in the ritual cycle. According to some accounts the mua acted as a kind of high priest. Following Christianization in the 1860s, the offices of sau and mua were terminated. Colonial administration involved the appointment by the governor of Fiji of a Resident Commissioner (after 1935, a District Officer) to Rotuma. He was advised by a council composed of the district headmen. In 1940 the council was expanded to include an elected representative from each district and the Assistant Medical Practitioner. Following Fiji's independence in 1970, the council assumed responsibility for the internal governance of Rotuma, with the District Officer assigned to an advisory role. Up until the first coup, Rotuma was represented in the Fiji legislature by a single senator.

Social Control. The basis for social control is a strong socialization emphasis on social responsibility and a sensitivity to shaming. Gossip serves as a mechanism for sanctioning deviation, but the most powerful deterrent to antisocial behavior is an abiding belief in immanent justice, that supernatural forces will punish wrongdoing. Rotumans are a gentle people; violence is extremely rare and serious crimes nearly nonexistent.

Conflict. Prior to cession, warfare, though conducted on a modest scale, was endemic in Rotuma. During the colonial era political rivalries were muted, since power was concentrated in the offices of Resident Commissioner and District Officer. Following Fiji's independence, however, interdistrict rivalries were again given expression, now in the form of political contention. Following the second coup, when Fiji left the British Commonwealth of Nations, a segment of the Rotuman population rejected the council's decision to remain with the newly declared republic. Arguing that Rotuma had been ceded to Great Britain and not to Fiji, these rebels declared Rotuma independent and were charged with sedition. Majority opinion appears to favor remaining with Fiji, but rumblings of discontent remain.

Religion and Expressive Culture

Religious Beliefs. The precontact religion involved a combination of animism, ancestor worship, and pantheism. The pre-Christian religion of Rotuma included several types of supernatural beings, including high gods, ancestral ghosts, and local spirits. The high gods, of whom Tagaroa was the most noteworthy, were the source of sustenance. They were prayed to for rain, for fruitful land, and for success in islandwide efforts. Tagaroa was the god of human fertility and the deity of the sau and mua. His son, Tairagoni, was personified by a turtle and was considered to be able to render the sea fruitful and safe. Ancestral ghosts were presumed to occupy the localities where they lived and to require propitiation. The good or bad fortune of individuals, families, and local groups were attributed to them. In addition, a number of free-roaming, largely malevolent spirits, who sometimes appeared in the form of anomalous creatures, were believed to inhabit the land.

Rotuma was converted to Christianity in the 1860s by English Wesleyans and French Catholics. The Catholics, who compose approximately one-third of the population, are concentrated on the south side of the island. In recent years a Seventh-Day Adventist church has been built and serves a number of families, and a small group of Jehovah's Witnesses meet together regularly. The churches play a vital role in the lives of most people and are centers for many communal activities.

Religious Practitioners. The sau and mua were traditionally responsible for attending to ritual activities propitiating the high gods to ensure the prosperity of the island. At the local level, certain individuals were designated to channel the powers of the spirits to ensure success and to heal sickness. Following missionization these activities were curtailed and now are viewed by most Rotumans as examples of devil worship. Today a significant number of Rotumans hold offices in the Christian churches as ministers, lay preachers, stewards, and the like.

Ceremonies. Ceremonial events play a major role in the social life of the island. Key elements in every ceremony are formal presentations of kava and food to the chiefs by men, the giving of mats by women, a feast, and formal speeches. Group dances are also often performed as entertainment. Ceremonial occasions include: life-crisis events, such as weddings, firstborn children's first birthdays, funerals, and the unveiling of headstones a year after death; welcoming ceremonies for Rotumans who have been away or for first visits of outside dignitaries; the anniversaries of historic occasions such as cession and the coming of the missionaries; and various church events.

Arts. At the time of contact the main forms of artistic expression included tattooing, personal ornaments such as breastplates and necklaces, and the manufacture of fine mats and tapa. Dancing and oratory were also well developed. Today, singing, dancing, and oratory (including preaching) are the dominant art forms. Fine mats are still produced by women, along with such handicrafts as fans, purses, and crocheted items. Although such items are sold on occasion at island events, they are not marketed overseas.

Medicine. Traditionally, therapeutic practices included cutting and burning and massage. Coconut oil, cold water, and purgatives were important items in purification rituals. Poultices were made with various leaves, mixed with turmeric, and applied to sores and inflammations. Healers derived their curative efficacy from ancestral spirits who guided their actions during possession episodes. The ability to heal was thought to be transmitted within families or directly from a practitioner to a chosen apprentice. Western medicine has largely replaced these folk practices, although massage remains popular as an alternative form of treatment.

Death and Afterlife. A person's soul was believed to wander during sleep, and if it did not return to the body before wakening or if it was carried off by a spirit, the person would sicken and die. When a person was seriously ill and apparently dying, it was presumed that his or her soul was wandering, and efforts were made to coax it to return. The ghost of a recently deceased relative was often implored to assist in such circumstances. At death the soul migrated to "the unseen world," said to be under the sea. This realm was divided into regions corresponding to places on the island. The final resting place of souls was off the western end of the island, where the sun sets. The ancient Rotumans buried their dignitaries under large basaltic stones, which sometimes weighed several tons and were transported over considerable distances. Following contact, cannons obtained from European vessels were sometimes used as grave markers. Cemeteries are usually on hills or promontories, and they are well cared for by the communities that use them.

See also Futuna, Kiribati, Samoa, Tonga, Tuvalu, Uvea

Bibliography

Howard, Alan (1970). *Learning to Be Rotuman.* New York: Columbia Teachers College Press.

Gardiner, J. Stanley (1898). "The Natives of Rotuma." *Journal of the Royal Anthropological Institute* 27:396–435, 457–524.

Plant, Chris, ed. (1977). *Rotuma: Split Island.* Suva: Institute of Pacific Studies.

ALAN HOWARD

Sambia

ETHNONYMS: None

Orientation

Identification. The Sambia, a congeries of historically and socially integrated phratries that speak the Sambia language, live in the fringe areas of the Eastern Highlands Province of Papua New Guinea. They are tribal, animistic, and primarily pagan. The name Sambia derives from the Sambia clan, an original pioneer people that settled the central Sambia region in the Puruya River Valley, and is mainly used by Westerners. The term "Kukukuku" (derogatory) was generically applied to Sambia and their neighbors until the 1970s; "Anga" (which means "house") is now more frequently used as an ethnic term to embrace Sambia and related societies.

Location. The Sambia are located in the rugged Kratke Mountains bounded by the Lamari River, the alluvial Papuan lowlands, and adjacent river valleys of the Eastern Highland Province, Marawaka District. Virgin rain forest covers approximately two-thirds of their territory. Settlements and gardens are located at elevations of 1,000 to 2,000 meters, and hunting territories extend up to elevations of 3,000 meters.

Demography. In 1989 the population of Sambia was estimated at 2,700, including absentee coastal workers. The population density averages 1.5 persons per square kilometer, though settlement areas are much higher. The population growth rate is about 5 percent per year. Sambia-speaking people constitute 95 percent of its resident population. Scattered, in-marrying speakers of the Fore and Baruya languages are present, and about 3 percent Tok Pisin speakers of other New Guinea languages reside there, mainly in government or mission jobs.

Linguistic Affiliation. Sambia is considered one of several languages belonging to the Non-Austronesian Angan Language Family of the Papuan Gulf. Sambia and the neighboring Baruya tribe share 60 percent of their cognate terms, for example, although a majority of speakers from both groups cannot speak the other group's language. There are at least two dialects of Sambia, represented in the northern and southern parts of central Sambia. They are mutually intelligible, with minor lexical and vocabulary variations and tonal differences.

History and Cultural Relations

The precise derivation of Sambia and related Angan peoples is unknown, but they are believed to have migrated south to the Papuan Gulf and later, perhaps as recently as A.D. 1700, to their present territory. Their mythological place of origin is located near the area of Menyamya. Legend and recent historical material suggests endemic warfare and raiding between Sambia and neighboring tribes, especially the Fore and Baruya. Initial contact with Europeans, at first Australian government patrols, began about 1956. The Australian colonial regime, operating under a mandate from the United Nations, entered and gradually enforced pacification around 1963. Warfare was halted in 1967, and in 1968 the Sambia area was "derestricted" and opened to Western missionaries and traders. Coffee was introduced as a cash crop about 1970. An abortive head-man system (modeled after African colonial regimes) was replaced in 1973, with *komiti* and *kaunsal* (councillors) being freely elected to a government council in the district. Papua New Guinea achieved independence in 1975; modernization efforts have followed rapidly.

Settlements

Villages range in size from approximately 40 to 250 persons. All villages are spatially distinct. There are two village types: pioneering and consolidated. The pioneering type is built on a steep mountain ridge, fortified by palisades and fences to prevent attack. A pioneer village contains a great clan and component clans, with surrounding gardens, and a common hunting and gathering territory. The consolidated type is the result of two previously distinct villages uniting into a larger, somewhat less clustered settlement. Houses are built in a neat line pattern atop the ridges. Footpaths connect houses with gardens above and streams and rivers below. Each nuclear family lives in a hut, though other extended family members may at times sleep there. The house is gabled, thatched, and small, with a hearth and no windows. There are two other types of dwellings. One is a menstrual hut built slightly below the village, wherein birth and menstrual events occur and women's ceremonies are held. The other is a men's house, where all males dwell after initiation (at age 7–10) until marriage (in the late teens to early 20s), when a separate residence is built. Military and secret male ritual activities occur in that clubhouse. The menstrual and men's houses are taboo to the opposite sex. Casual shelters are placed in gardens as necessary. Pig-herding and hunting lodges of more permanent construction are built in distant gardens and the forest, and certain nuclear families or extended clan families reside in them, sometimes for several months.

Economy

Subsistence and Commercial Activities. Sedentary gardening dominates the Sambia economy, supplemented by modest pig herding, and, traditionally, extensive hunting for game by men. Sweet potatoes are the main staple. Taro is also significant. Yams are a seasonal and largely ceremonial crop. All planting and harvesting is done by hand, predominantly by women. Men, however, slash-and-burn the land first and participate in harvesting. Additional indigenous crops include sugarcane, pandanus fruit and nuts, wild taro and yams, and a variety of local greens, palms, and bamboo hearts. European kitchen vegetables are today plentiful, especially green beans, corn, and tapioca, supplemented by potatoes, tomatoes, and peanuts. Commercial crops include coffee, which is now predominant, as well as chilies. Traditional hunting was mainly for opossums and native marsupials, birds, and cassowaries. Fishing for freshwater carp and eels was traditional but sporadic. All meats were on occasion smoked for preservation and eventual consumption or trade. In addition to pigs, domestic animals include dogs and chickens.

Industrial Arts. There are specialists in a few native crafts, but not industrial arts, in villages. Weaving of grass skirts and string bags is done by women; armbands, headbands, arrows, bows, and all military gear are made by men. Sacred art is rare, and masks and carvings are not made.

Trade. Vegetable salt bars, bark capes, feather headdresses, and dried meats and fish were all traded traditionally with the neighboring Wantukiu and Usurumpia tribes and as far south as the Purari Delta. Women today bring homegrown produce to local markets.

Division of Labor. The sexual division of labor is striking and rigid among the Sambia. Women do most of the gardening, weaving, cooking, and child care. Men hunt, fish, and are responsible for war and public affairs. Most household chores, except house construction itself, are female activities. Men and women share the harvesting of feast crops and nowadays of coffee gardens.

Land Tenure. All land and watercourses are owned by individuals and clans as corporate groups. Fishing, hunting, gardening, and foraging rights are inviolable, and use rights may be extended to distant kin, in-laws, or trade partners. Landlessness is nonexistent.

Kinship

Kin Groups and Descent. Three levels of kin grouping are found. The clan, linked by patrilineal descent, is exogamous. The "great clan" is formed from two or more clans that trace descent to a real ancestor. The phratry is constituted of many clans and great clans, whose putative ancestors are regarded as "brothers," making inclusive members related. They also share adjacent territories, certain identity markers such as dress, and ritual customs. They intermarry. In times of war they usually support each other, and for ritual initiation, they conduct joint ceremonies for their sons.

Kinship Terminology. Sambia kin terms are essentially of the Omaha type, with marked generational skewing. Age grading in the initiation system also creates putative kin relations for males (brothers) and females (sisters).

Marriage and Family

Marriage. There are four types of marriage: infant betrothal (delayed exchange), sister exchange (direct exchange), and bride-service (delayed exchange), which are traditional; and bride-wealth marriage, which has been introduced since 1973. Marriage is primarily arranged by parents and clan elders. Because of exogamy, intravillage marriage in pioneer villages is absent, but it does occur in consolidated villages. Infant betrothal and sister-exchange marriage accounted for 90 percent of all marriage transactions traditionally. Father's sister's daughter marriage is approved. Newlyweds establish patrilocal residence soon after marriage in a new hut household. Divorce is rare. Polygyny is ideally preferred but is infrequent.

Domestic Unit. The nuclear family is the minimal domestic unit. They eat and sleep together. Sons remain domiciled there until initiation, and daughters ideally remain as well until marriage. The extended family of familiarity includes grandparents, grandchildren, aunts, uncles, and cousins, usually within the same village. All active adults contribute to domestic labor and children also help. Cowives may reside together, but typically they have separate residences.

Inheritance. Property is inherited mainly by males, although daughters have use rights to certain garden land. Status and offices are not inherited but achieved, except for mystical powers of shamans.

Socialization. Early infant care is exclusively done by women. Older children are cared for by both parents and older siblings. Independence and autonomy are stressed, but more for males than females. Gender and sexual socialization are accomplished mainly through rituals.

Sociopolitical Organization

Sambia was traditionally an acephalous tribe. Today it is an encapsulated semiautonomous tribal group within the bureaucratic administration of a parliamentary democracy, with the English monarch as its putative head of state.

Social Organization. The tribe is hierarchically organized on the basis of age and sex. Older people are higher than younger people. Clan elders, warriors, and ritual specialists hold the highest status. Men are higher than women. Social class is absent. However, modernization and mobility based upon wealth and education are currently introducing class status differences.

Political Organization. Political control by the state operates from the provincial district levels. Sambia is divided into census divisions with a head tax for adult men. The village operates as the most powerful political unit in daily public affairs. However, administrative and dispute settlement tasks are overseen by local councillors. Warfare was organized primarily at the village level. The dance ground confederacy is of special importance. Villages that initiate together on the same dance ground usually defend each other's territory and intermarry. Confederacies are usually constituted by one phratry; however, interphratry confederacies exist in central Sambia. The Papua New Guinea government provides school, court, and health services.

Social Control. Most features of social control devolve from clan hamlet elders. War leaders are crucial. Ritual initiation instills values of conformity and loyalty in individuals. Dance ground confederacies exert control in intertribal relations.

Conflict. Minor disputes in villages are handled through moots. Traditional warfare between villages usually occurred over adultery, sorcery accusations, ritual violations or theft of ritual customs, and destruction of gardens by pigs. Councillors and district courts handle conflicts today.

Religion and Expressive Culture

Ritual and the men's secret society are the key cultural forces in Sambia. Initiations occur on a grand scale every three or four years and are mandatory for all males. Female initiations occur later, at marriage, menarche, and first birth. Initiation for males also involved military training in the warriorhood.

Religious Beliefs. Sambia are animistic and believe that all forces and events have life. Men are superior and women inferior. Female menstrual and birth pollution are abhorred. Male maturation requires homoerotic insemination to attain biological competence. Initiation rituals thus involve complex homosexual contact from late childhood until marriage, when it stops. Female homosexual activity is believed to be absent. Men's ritual cult ceremonies centrally involve flute spirits (female). Other forms of supernatural entities include ghosts, forest spirits (male), and nature sprites. Bogs, for example, are inhabited by ghosts and sprites. Contemporary mission activities center primarily on the local Seventh-Day Adventist church. Daily and Saturday services are held. Baptisms and marriages are performed. Missionized Sambia are largely nominal converts.

Religious Practitioners. Each village has at least one senior ritual specialist who officiates at initiation. Shamans are the main religious specialists, however; they may be male or female, though traditionally males were more frequent and critical. They divine, exorcise, and sorcerize. They are believed to retrieve souls of the sick through magical flight. There are strong and weak shamans. Shamans organize events in ritual and funeral ceremonies.

Ceremonies. The seasonal calendar is based on a cyclical sense of time, with ritual events and feast gardens synergistic with dry season and early monsoon periods (May–September).

Arts. The greatest decorative architecture is the ritual cult house, which is not maintained following initiation. Carving is limited to daily utensils and weapons. Body painting is elaborate in ritual and warfare. Feather headdresses are especially admired. Traditional musical instruments include ritual flutes and bullroarers and the Jew's harp. Dancing is extensive but simple and is part of all initiations.

Medicine. Illness is attributed to ghosts and sorcery. Possession is usually believed to be by ghosts or forest spirits. Local healing and spells are common. Herbal medicines are widely used, especially ginger and local salt. Shamans are the main healers.

Death and Afterlife. Funerals were traditionally shallow ceremonial events. The corpse was placed on a platform until its bones were exposed. The bones were retained by close kin for their sorcery power. The soul is believed to survive death and is seen in dreams. The widow observes a year or two of mourning. Today the corpse is buried. A name taboo is still observed for the dead for several years.

See also Fore

Bibliography

Godelier, Maurice (1986). *The Making of Great Men.* Cambridge: Cambridge University Press.

Herdt, Gilbert (1981). *Guardians of the Flutes.* New York: McGraw-Hill.

Herdt, Gilbert (1987). *The Sambia: Ritual and Gender in New Guinea.* New York: Holt, Rinehart & Winston.

Herdt, Gilbert (1989). "Spirit Familiars in the Religious Imagination of Sambia." In *The Religious Imagination in New Guinea,* edited by G. Herdt and M. Stephen, 99–121. New Brunswick, N.J.: Rutgers University Press.

Lloyd, Richard G. (1973). "The Angan Language Family." In *The Linguistic Situation in the Gulf District and Adjacent Areas, Papua New Guinea,* edited by K. Franklin, 31–111. Pacific Linguistics, Series C. no. 26. Canberra: Australian National University.

GILBERT HERDT

Samoa

ETHNONYMS: Tagata Sāmoa

Orientation

Identification. There is no generally agreed upon explanation of the meaning of the name "Samoa." According to one Samoan version, the name is compounded of "Sā," meaning "tribe, people of," and "Moa," which means "chicken," referring to the "family" of the Tui Manu'a, the highest-ranking titleholder of eastern (American) Samoa. Another proposal suggests that linguistic evidence points to the meaning of Samoa as "people of the ocean or deep sea."

Location. The Samoan Archipelago (about 3,000 square kilometers in land area) lies in western Polynesia in the central Pacific, from 13° to 15°S to 173°W. The Manu'a group (Ta'ū, Ofu, and Olosega), Tutuila, and 'Aunu'u comprise the Territory of American Samoa; 'Upolu, Manono, Apolima, and Savai'i make up the Independent State of Western Samoa. The islands are of volcanic origin. Beyond the coastal plains, the mountain ranges rise steeply to a maximum of 1,859 meters on Savai'i. The climate is tropical with abundant rainfall. Humidity averages 80 percent. The average monthly temperature ranges from 22° to 30° C.

Demography. In 1980, the Samoan population was about 188,000 (American Samoa: 32,000; Western Samoa: 156,000). In the middle of the nineteenth century, the aboriginal population of Western Samoa was estimated at 35,000; the aboriginal population of Tutuila was estimated at 3,900 in 1865. The Samoan Islands are the home of the largest concentration of full-blooded Polynesians in the world. Today, many Samoans live and work abroad, mainly in New Zealand, Australia, Hawaii, and California.

Linguistic Affiliation. The Samoan language belongs to the Polynesian Group of Austronesian languages. There are no dialects; except for minor local variants the same language is spoken on all the Samoan Islands.

History and Cultural Relations

Settlement of the Fiji-Tonga-Samoa area by people belonging to the prehistoric Melanesian Lapita culture took place between about 1500 and 1000 B.C. Genealogical, mythological, and linguistic evidence suggests that relations with both Tonga and Fiji were maintained throughout the prehistoric period, with intermarriage occurring among the upper classes especially of the Samoan and Tongan population. The first European to sight the Samoan Islands in 1722 was the Dutch explorer Jacob Roggeveen, though he did not land there. In about 1800 some isolated European sailors and escaped convicts settled on Samoa, bringing with them the first notion of Christianity. In 1830, the missionary John Williams of the London Missionary Society (LMS) landed in Savai'i during a power struggle among factions, bringing with him native Polynesian missionaries from Tahiti and the Cook Islands. The first permanent European missionaries arrived in 1835 (LMS and Methodists), followed by Roman Catholic priests in 1845. During the nineteenth century, Germany, Great Britain, and the United States strove for influence among the diverse Samoan factions. In 1900, Western Samoa became a German colony (until 1914) and Eastern Samoa was claimed by the United States. From 1914 to 1962, New Zealand administered Western Samoa, which became an independent state in 1962, with kings Malietoa Tanumafili II and Tupua Tamasese Mea'ole serving as joint heads of state. Before World War II, administrative policies by the New Zealand administration led to the "Mau," a resistance movement (1926–1936) that mustered the support of about 90 percent of the Samoan population at its height. American Samoa remains a United States territory. After constitutional changes, Peter Tali Coleman became the first elected native Samoan governor in 1977.

Settlements

The Samoans have been mainly a coast-dwelling people living in self-governing, autonomous towns (*nu'u*) linked by political and ceremonial alliances. Households center on the sacred central place (*malae*) of each nu'u where the ranking high chief's assembly house is also situated. Town populations range between 300 and 1,200 persons and average 450 to 600 persons. In the middle of the last century, town populations averaged 200 to 500 persons. However, a census taken of twenty-two towns in the district of Aana, Western Upolu, Manono, and Apolima in 1867 shows that town populations ranged between 40 and 310 persons only, the mean being 164 persons. In the nineteenth century, there were a few inland settlements, too. In recent years, there has been a tendency to give up settlements along the coast and to shift towns to newly built roads farther inland.

Economy

Subsistence and Commercial Activities. The Samoans are horticulturalists, raising tubers (taro and yams) on a swidden basis. They also grow bananas, breadfruit, and coconuts and supplement their diet through fishing. They raise chickens and pigs, too, but pork is reserved as a special food for ceremonial occasions. Hunting for runaway pigs is still practiced with the help of dogs, but it's probably done more for sport than for food. Pigeon snaring also formerly served as an entertainment and as a sporting event. Terracing and irrigation are not practiced. There are small house gardens for raising staple foods in the back of the households, but the main taro gardens often lie 3–4 kilometers farther inland. The primary cultigens are taro and breadfruit. Contact with Europeans resulted in the addition of new sorts of bananas and vegetables, which are grown today mainly by the small Chinese population for consumption and sale. Many Samoan families earn a small income by selling coconuts to the Western Samoan Trust Estate Corporation, which does the processing. There are many small family businesses, shops, and guest houses, the majority of them in Apia, the capital of Western Samoa. In many local communities there is a small shop where locals can buy a limited range of products, many of them imported.

Industrial Arts. Aboriginal crafts included the making of bark cloth, house building, boat building, and tattooing. House builders, boat builders, and tattooers were organized in guilds. They met the demands of prestige consumption, since small boats and houses were and are built by the male members of each household. Mat weaving is practiced by women.

Trade. There was only a limited amount of interregional trade in precontact times. Samoan fine mats (*'ie tōga*) were exchanged for parrots and red parrot feathers from Tonga and sometimes from Fiji. Intraregional trade, too, was limited. Some regions and places were noted for their products, such as nets, which are said to have been made mostly by towns in the interior. Some places were noted for their boats, adzes, and kava bowls. After contact with the Europeans, trade of coconut products (oil and copra) was encouraged by the missionaries, but it became a regular and important activity only after the German firm of Godeffroy and Son from Hamburg founded a branch in Apia, Western Samoa, in 1857. Traders were stationed in Samoa and on other Pacific islands, but there was also direct trading with the Samoans. In 1865, the firm established its first coconut plantations. Today, Western Samoa is dependent on the world market, its three most important export items being copra, cocoa, and bananas. Western Samoan governments seek to promote tourism, and beer brewing may develop into a profitable enterprise, at least for the regional market.

Division of Labor. Men do the more strenuous agricultural work, such as clearing and planting with a pointed hardwood digging stick, while women may weed and help in harvest activities. Men are responsible for fishing beyond the reef and for cooking; they engage in toolmaking, house and boat building, and ornament making. Women look after the household, raise the children, and plait mats and fans; formerly they also made bark cloth. They collect edible wild plants to supplement the diet and they forage in the lagoon and reef for small sea animals.

Land Tenure. Aboriginally, the widest social unit for landownership was the community (nu'u). Its domain included all the territory from the central mountain ridge to the reef. The heads (*matai*) of the different descent groups (*'āiga*) of the community were entitled to claim blocks of land for themselves and their dependents. Overall authority over lands, however, was vested in the council of matai (*fono*), whose members could revoke ownership of the respective 'āiga. Individuals had the right to occupy and cultivate the land of the descent group to which they belonged. When Western Samoa became independent, 80.5 percent of its territory was still considered customary land, administered outside the statute law in accordance with traditional principles of tenure; 3.7 percent of the land was freehold; 11.3 percent was government land; and the Western Samoan Trust Estate Corporation owned 4.5 percent. American Samoa, too, has provisions that restrict ownership of land to Samoans.

Kinship

Kin Groups and Descent. In Samoa there are overlapping cognatic descent groups ('āiga) with an emphasis on agnation. Each descent group has a localized section in a community where its lands and chiefly (matai) titles traditionally belong; other members live in other communities on the lands of other 'āiga. Localized sections hold and allocate land to their members, regulate marriage, and control conflict among members. Between the descent groups there exist multifarious relationships that are genealogically explained, forming ramified descent structures, both at the community and at the supracommunity level. Not all of these structures are descent groups in the strict anthropological sense of the term, however, since in some of them only matai are members. These structures are 'āiga in a metaphorical sense only. They play an important part in supracommunity territorial integration.

Kinship Terminology. Kin terms follow a Hawaiian-type system.

Marriage and the Family

Marriage. Members of the father's and mother's descent groups are forbidden as marriage partners, and community endogamy is also discouraged. Bride and groom should be of similar rank. Today, a church wedding is an important and costly affair, but many marriages are still customary ones, man and wife living together with their parents' consent after the appropriate exchange of goods. Premarital virginity is highly valued and a girl's moral code prohibits sexual relations with a man unless she is recognized as his wife. Customary marriages among younger people frequently end in divorce, however, and the partners may have undergone several such marriages before eventually contracting a church wedding. Residence tends to be virilocal, but during the early stages of married life a couple frequently resides with the wife's family. In pre-Christian times, polygyny was practiced, although probably only by matai of high rank.

Domestic Unit. The localized section of a descent group, forming an extended family and living in a group of houses clustered around a common hearth, is the customary domestic unit. In modern times, the nuclear family has become more frequent.

Inheritance. Members of the descent group retain rights to use and control of customary land occupied and cultivated by their 'āiga, regardless of where they live. The same applies to matai titles that are not subject to any automatic inheritance rule. A family council will decide to confer a vacant title upon a member—usually male—whom they consider to be the best choice. Especially with regard to high titles, however, agnatic succession is preferred.

Socialization. Starting at about 1½ years of age, children become subject to an education Europeans would label as "authoritarian." They are expected to obey their parents and elders at once, without hesitation and without asking questions. Overt and direct expressions of hostility and aggression are discouraged, but *musu,* the state of sullen unwillingness to comply with orders, is a culturally tolerated outlet. Much of the actual education work takes place in the peer groups where older brothers and especially sisters are made responsible for the behavior of their younger siblings. Formal education in schools is considered essential for the well-being of the entire family today and parents usually encourage some of their children to remain in high school.

Sociopolitical Organization

Social Organization. Rank goes with age and the position a matai title holds within the complicated title structure. An older sister ranks higher than her brother. The descendants of a sister still enjoy a special respected status within the descent group. Christianity has emphasized the status of the wife, however, and the sister's position is not as pronounced today as it once was. Within most descent groups, there are two sets of matai: aristocrats (*ali'i*), who embody the group's dignity; and orators (*tulāfale*), who take a more official role when they speak on behalf of the ali'i at certain formal public events. Each matai supervises and looks after the family under his immediate control and is responsible for it vis-à-vis the community.

Political Organization. Communities (nu'u) are politically independent but are organized into districts and subdistricts for ceremonial purposes. Aboriginally, war, too, was a supracommunity concern. Ceremonies on a supracommunity level often focus on the life-crisis rites of certain very high-ranking titleholders, the *tama-a-'āiga,* which are not to be confused with matai and should rather be called kings. Formal political control within the community is exercised by the council of matai (fono) with the *'aumaga* (the untitled men's organization) serving as executive body. Women's committees exist today in all communities, playing an important role in community affairs as an unofficial arm of local government. They replace or complement the *aualuma,* the group made up of the sisters and daughters of the community, which played an important ceremonial role in former times.

Social Control. Informal social control is exercised through gossip and was formerly aided by the open Samoan houses, which prevented privacy. Formal control is exercised through the fono, which retains the right to expel individuals and, in rare cases, entire 'āiga from the community and its lands.

Conflict. In aboriginal times and throughout the nineteenth century, conflicts over titles and lands often resulted in wars. Such cases are adjudicated today by special law courts. Competitiveness—such as evidenced in, for instance, the zeal of untitled men to distinguish themselves as good servants to their matai, in oratory, in donations to the church, etc.—adds areas of conflict to social life.

Religion and Expressive Culture

Religious Beliefs. Today, Samoans are devout Christians, following diverse Protestant denominations, as well as the Roman Catholic church. Pre-Christian beliefs in ancestor-spirits (*aitu*) are still widespread, but they are not openly confessed vis-à-vis Europeans. Aitu formerly were family gods, and they have retained their character as locally associated and kinship-bound deified ancestors. There was a belief in a supreme being, Tangaloa, but Samoa probably never developed a national cult like that of the Society Islands or Hawaii. Tangaloa was a *deus otiosus* who withdrew after having caused the emergence of the islands and set in motion the process which led to the evolution of natural phenomena and, ultimately, humans. Aitu were the active numinous beings who interfered directly in everyday life.

Religious Practitioners. In aboriginal times, each matai was a religious practitioner responsible for the worship of the family aitu. Some matai played paramount roles as oracles of particular aitu of supralocal importance. Today, matai continue to lead family prayers (to the Christian God), but there are also native pastors, trained in local theological seminaries, and priests who conduct formal church services.

Ceremonies. Many native ceremonies focus on life-cycle rites. Attendance is an expression of the rank of the persons involved. The kava ceremony, in which a beverage prepared from the *'ava* root (*Piper methysticum*) was consumed in ceremonial style, was performed to honor important guests and to mark important social events, such as the deliberations of the fono.

Arts. Oratory, dancing, singing, and tattooing continue to be means of aesthetic expression. Today, hymns for church services are an important outlet for expressive needs. The traditional art of bark-cloth (*siapo*) making and printing is not very widespread today.

Medicine. In aboriginal times, disease was supposed to be caused by the wrath of some particular aitu. Treatment was sought with the aid of the special matai, Taulāitu (whose name means "anchor of the Aitu"). They were asked to intercede with the aitu they represented. Various herbs and plants were administered and massage was also applied.

Death and Afterlife. Samoans believe in the dichotomous character of human nature. The separation of the "soul" (*agāga*) and body (*tino*) is tantamount to death. That the agāga continued to live after death as an aitu was the focal topic of the pre-Christian religion. There are various accounts of an afterworld, but no uniform picture of its nature can be gleaned from the historical and ethnographic sources.

See also Ontong Java, Rotuma, Tokelau, Tonga

Bibliography

Cain, Horst (1979). *Aitu. Eine Untersuchung zur Autochthonen Religion der Samoaner.* Wiesbaden: Franz Steiner Verlag.

Finney, Joseph C. (1973). "The Meaning of the Name Sāmoa." *Journal of the Polynesian Society* 82:301–303.

Gilson, R. P. (1970). *Samoa 1830 to 1900. The Politics of a Multi-Cultural Community.* Melbourne: Oxford University Press.

Holmes, Lowell D. (1974). *Samoan Village.* Case Studies in Cultural Anthropology. New York: Holt, Rinehart & Winston.

THOMAS BARGATZKY

San Cristobal

ETHNONYM: Makira

Four groups totaling about 10,000 individuals live on the high volcanic island of Makira or San Cristobal: the Arosi, Bauro, Kahua, and Tawarafa. San Cristobal is located in the southeastern Solomon Islands at approximately 10° S and 160° E. The languages of the island are classified in the Eastern Oceanic Group of the Oceanic Branch of Austronesian languages. Most settlements are on the coast, though they extend inland several thousand feet. The settlements are organized into hamlets consisting of a cluster of houses irregularly situated around a central place. Houses are of pole and thatch, and they are often decorated with paintings and statues.

The diet is based on coconuts, which are the specialty of the coastal areas, and root crops (mainly yams and taro), which are the specialty of the inland areas. Sago is also harvested along the coastal marshes. Other trees of importance are breadfruit, *Canarium* almond, and various fruit trees. Domesticated pigs and hunting are complemented by fishing in the deep sea (for bonito) and along the shore. The seasonal exploitation of the sea worm is an important source of protein. Land is owned by the resident extended family. Canoe building was formerly a highly specialized and respected craft. In the past, shell money, consisting of shell rings and strings of shell-disk beads, was used in interisland trading expeditions.

The most important kin groups are bilateral extended families. Bride-price payments are required and are generally collected from the members of a man's entire domestic group. Residence is patrilocal, descent is patrilineal, and polygyny is common among the wealthier men. The primary domestic group is a bilateral extended family; these families are organized into larger patrilineal descent groups, each of which traditionally had a hereditary line of chiefs. Big-men also exist on San Cristobal, and they are generally the wealthiest and most influential men in the community.

In the past, human sacrifice was practiced to propitiate the ancestors. Mana, or supernatural power, is greatly revered and believed to be possessed by certain persons, ghosts, and certain objects. Ancestor worship is a major part of the indigenous religion, with ghosts of ancestors considered to be the most important supernaturals.

See also Guadalcanal, Malaita

Bibliography

Ivens, W. G. (1927). *Melanesians of the South-East Solomon Islands.* London: Kegan Paul.

Verguet, T. (1885). "Arossi ou San Christoval est ses habitants." *Revue d'Ethnographie* 4:193–232.

Santa Cruz

ETHNONYM: Nendö

Orientation

Identification. The Santa Cruz Islanders are Melanesians who are in most respects fully integrated, as a constituent ethnic society, into the national political and economic system of the Solomon Islands.

Location. Santa Cruz Island, or Nendö (Nidu, Ndeni, Nende, Nitende; 10°45' S, 166°00' E) is the largest island of an archipelago, called the Santa Cruz Islands. Nendö consists of a mountainous spine of volcanic rock, surrounded by extensive terraces of uplifted reef limestones. From October to May the climate is dominated by the Australian-Asian monsoon system; from June through September, the southeastern trade wind system prevails.

Demography. In the late nineteenth and early twentieth century Nendö and the other Santa Cruz Islands suffered severe depopulation, due to introduced diseases. The population of Nendö between 1929 and 1931 is estimated to have been about 1,800 persons, which was probably half the predepopulation number. In 1960 the population (by census) was 2,516; by 1970 it had increased to 3,126, and in 1976 it had reached 4,620, of which 273 were Polynesian-speaking immigrants.

Linguistic Affiliation. Santa Cruz Islanders speak three closely related Non-Austronesian languages, of which two are single-dialect languages and one is a dialect chain. A small minority of Polynesian speakers have recently migrated to Nendö from islands immediately to the north.

History and Cultural Relations

Archaeological research reveals that Nendö was inhabited by people with the Lapita culture as early as 1200 B.C. European contact commenced in A.D. 1595 with the arrival of Alvaro de Mendaña's second expedition. This Mendaña expedition, which gave the island the name "Santa Cruz," tried to establish a colony at Graciosa Bay, Nendö, but the settlement failed because of poor relations with the inhabitants, diseases, and the death of Mendaña. For the next 250 years the Santa Cruz Islands were seldom visited by European ships, but during the last decades of the nineteenth century European contacts increased when the Anglican mission ship *Southern Cross* began making regular pastoral calls there and when blackbirders started abducting men from the group. During this period relationships with Europeans were poor and there were violent incidents. In 1898 the Santa Cruz Islands were incorporated into the British Solomon Islands Protectorate, but effective administration of them did not commence until the 1920s and the "Pax Britannica" was not fully established on Nendö for another decade. Colonial development proceeded very slowly during the 1930s and proselytizing by the Anglicans was largely ineffectual. Suddenly, in 1942, British authority was withdrawn when Japanese military forces invaded the Solomon Islands. The Japanese did not occupy the Santa Cruz Islands, but during the fighting to retake the Solomon Islands, there were skirmishes and one great battle in the area between Japanese and U.S. naval forces. Following hostilities, some Santa Cruz Islanders were recruited by the United States to work at military bases in the Central Solomon Islands, and what they saw there was a revelation. After World War II the British returned with an increasingly vigorous social development policy. Likewise, the Anglican mission came back with determination to complete the conversion of the Santa Cruz people. During the next twenty years, native councils, native courts, health and medical programs, churches, and local schools were established. An administrative center with an airfield was build at Graciosa Bay, Nendö, just before political independence was granted the Solomon Islands in 1978. The Santa Cruz Islands (including Tikopia and Anuta) now constitute the province called Temotu, with its administrative center on Nendö. The culture of Nendö extends northward, with minor ecological adaptations, to the Reef Islands and Taumako. The language of the Main Reef Islands is Non-Austronesian and related to the languages of Nendö, but the language of the Outer Reef Islands (Nifiloli, Pileni, Nukapu, Nupani, Matema) and Taumako is Polynesian. The cultures of Utupua and Vanikoro in the south, while resembling Nendö culture in some respects, are sufficiently different to constitute a southern subcultural area. Also, the languages of Upupua and Vanikoro (three on each island) are Austronesian. Until the 1930s, all the Santa Cruz Islands were involved in a complex network of commercial trade, carried on by large sailing canoes that cruised the entire archipelago and sometimes beyond. There were occasional contacts outside the Santa Cruz Islands with Tikopia to the east, the Torres and Banks Islands (part of Vanuatu) to the south, and with Santa Ana/Catalina and San Cristobal (Solomon Islands) to the west.

Settlements

All the people of Nendö live in compact villages with populations that usually number less than 200 persons. Most villages are now located along the coast, but before the severe depopulation and imposition of colonial rule, settlements were smaller and more dispersed, and many were located at inland sites. Until peace was established, each village was surrounded by a protective stone wall, and many dwellings within settlements were also walled.

Economy

Subsistence and Commercial Activities. All Nendö communities are intensely agricultural, employing a combination of swidden (bush fallow or slash-and-burn) cultivation of gardens and arboriculture. The most important traditional crops are yams, taro, sweet potatoes, bananas, breadfruit, coconuts, and *Canarium* almonds. There is also a large variety of secondary crops, some of which are post-European introductions. Both fishing and marine collecting are important, and much attention is given to raising pigs. There is some hunting (of feral pigs and fowl, bats, and birds) and gathering of forest products. Since 1960, much effort has been directed toward increasing coconut plantings for copra, which is also sold for cash.

Industrial Arts. The most distinctive Nendö manufactures were outrigger canoes, loom-woven fabrics of banana fibers, bark cloth, a currency made of fibers and red feathers, and personal ornaments made from a variety of materials. Since World War II the manufacture of local products has rapidly declined, as goods imported from the industrial world, and cash to purchase them, have become increasingly available.

Trade. As mentioned, the most conspicuous feature of traditional Nendö economy was intra- and interisland trade, in which profit and the amassing of wealth were the main objectives. Since the trade concerned the distribution of locally produced commodities, it has all but disappeared as imported, industrially produced goods have displaced local products. Feather currency, the former medium of exchange for trade, has also nearly disappeared.

Division of Labor. Women do most of the gardening and collecting of reef products; men look after orchards, fish, hunt, and collect in the forests; both sexes tend pigs. Until the 1930s there was much specialization of labor with respect to the production of commodities and performance of skilled services. Every mature man was expected to have an economic specialty, by means of which he earned wealth that could be accumulated and stored in feather currency. Women could also have economic specialties. Such specialization has all but disappeared. Men leave the island to work for wages and process copra for cash.

Land Tenure. Land that has been improved and used "belongs" to the user. Such use rights can be loaned, rented, given away, and transmitted by inheritance, but only recently could they be sold for monetary gain to another individual. Land rights that have lapsed by failure to exercise them revert to corporate ownership by a district. With district consent, an individual may convert corporate ownership of designated plots to exclusive personal use rights by improving or using the land. Rights over reefs and lagoons are corporately held by districts; men's associations control the canoe passages that serve their club houses.

Kinship

Kin Groups and Descent. There are three kinds of kin groups on Nendö: domestic groups; dispersed descent groups (sibs); and men's associations. A men's association can be started by any adult man who wishes to form one for his sons and, often, his brothers and their sons. Some associations flourish and grow; some do not. In time, those that flourish will include distant agnates, affines, and even nonkin, but the consanguineal ideology remains. Over most of Nendö, individuals are affiliated with nonlocalized, exogamous, usually totemic, matrilineal descent groups (sibs). In some areas sibs are arranged into matrimoieties. In several districts around Graciosa Bay, the descent principle is patrilineal, but individuals are often unsure of their affiliations. In one district on the south coast descent is not recognized, although it is believed that matriliny was formerly the rule.

Kinship Terminology. Kin terms vary between special versions of Hawaiian and Iroquois types. All terminologies distinguish the relation of mother's brother to sister's child from other avuncular relationships. In some localities the term for "sister" (as used by a male speaker) is applied to father's sister and father's father's sister with the logical consequences.

Marriage and Family

Marriage. Traditionally, all first cousins were marriageable, marriages were usually monogamous, and a large brideprice was, and still is, required. Nendö men often import wives from the Reef Islands, especially from the poorer Polynesian-speaking communities there. Sororal and nonsororal polygyny were permitted; polygynous unions rarely involved more than two wives. Polygyny is not practiced now. Formerly, too, there was a pattern of collective concubinage, which was also a form of female slavery, in which a group of men jointly purchased a woman as a sex partner and prostitute. The protectorate government banned this concubinage pattern in the late 1920s. Initial postmarital residence is usually viripatrilocal, only occasionally uxorimatrilocal, but after children are born residence often becomes neolocal. Marital separations are frequent; divorce has always been difficult, except in cases of severe abuse and continued adultery.

Domestic Unit. The most common domestic group is a nuclear family, often augmented by elder dependent relatives of either the husband or wife. Small patrilocal extended families exist for a short period when a son marries. Joint families, consisting of the domestic units of brothers and/or close male agnates, are common. Women of these joint families assist each other with their domestic responsibilities.

Inheritance. Garden and orchard plots are usually not partible, and they can be passed on to either male or female heirs, but most real property goes to males. Personal property, especially heirlooms and valuables, are inherited along gender lines: mothers to daughters, fathers to sons.

Socialization. Boys and girls are socialized separately and quite differently. From an early age, girls are rigorously trained at their mother's side to master gardening and domestic skills as soon as they can. At a young age boys move away from their dwellings and into dormitories or men's association houses, and an avoidance of their sisters and other females is invoked. There are no initiation rites for either sex, but at marriage women undergo a formal transition from minor to adult social status.

Sociopolitical Organization

Social Organization. Formerly, there was a marked social dichotomy and separation between men's and women's spheres of life. Women were focused on their gardens and households, men on their specialized skills and men's associations. Under attack from mission and government alike, this division by gender, which amounted to a generalized avoidance, has greatly lessened over the past few decades.

Political Organization. Traditionally, the basic political unit was the set of households (one to twenty or more) whose male heads belonged to the same men's association. One or more men's associations, in a loose confederation, formed a village, and most villages, over time, became incorporated to the extent that they controlled and defended a bounded territory. Such was the corporate district. Most districts were hostile to each other, but alliances between men's associations of different districts made it possible for men to cross the boundaries. Trade moved along these lines of men's association alliances, each association agreeing to purchase and redistribute locally all the goods offered by an allied association. There were no political offices. Each men's association was governed, autocratically, by its most influential senior men (big-men); district policies and interdistrict relations were handled by informal groups of senior men. Personal rivalries among senior men were common, and this constant tension led to divisiveness and fighting at each political level.

Social Control and Conflict. Interpersonal social control is greatly enforced by fears of sorcery and male witchcraft. Before peace was established, the ultimate secular coercive threat was fighting with bows and arrows; interpersonal violence and feuds were commonplace. Feuds could be ended by offering the unavenged side a victim to kill. Serious disputes could escalate into wars between districts, but large-scale violence could be avoided by resorting to competitive exchanges that were continued until one side went bankrupt.

Religion and Expressive Culture

Religious Beliefs. The most significant beliefs are that Nendö culture was given by supernatural beings; these beings continue to control human events for good and bad; each adult male, and some women, must have a personal supernatural tutelary to protect and promote his or her general welfare. However, not all tutelaries are equal; some have more influence over events than others. Individuals who have attentive tutelaries will succeed; those who succeed the most have the most powerful tutelaries. Misfortune is believed to be caused by supernatural influences. Initially, Christian beliefs were grafted onto these traditional beliefs, so that God was the most powerful of tutelary deities.

Religious Practitioners. The only religious practitioners are female mediums who are called upon to determine the causes of misfortune. Otherwise, each adult performs or sponsors propitiatory rites to his or her tutelary deity.

Ceremonies. The preeminent ceremony is an extended series, lasting several years, of invitational feasts and dances sponsored by a small group of men to propitiate their tutelary deities. As well as being costly religious rituals, these were, and still are, the most enjoyed social events, and they are the occasions at which much of Nendö aesthetic and expressive culture is displayed. These ceremonies are still celebrated, but in abbreviated forms.

Arts. The most distinctive arts include religious sculpture, lyric poetry, costumery and dramatizations, precision dancing, and personal ornamentation. This ornamentation is associated with hierarchical position among senior persons; the other arts are mostly associated with propitiating tutelary deities. Many traditional arts have declined or disappeared in recent decades.

Medicine. For minor and acute disorders there are specialized practitioners and nonreligious remedies, but treatments of severe and chronic illnesses must be accomplished through tutelary deities.

Death and Afterlife. For socially unimportant persons, funerals are perfunctory, but for personages they can be major observances, including extended viewing of the corpse and a postburial feast. Formerly, burial was in the earthen floor of the deceased's dwelling, but it is now done in cemeteries. Traditional ideas about the aferlife are not elaborate: the soul goes to the western extremity of Nendö where it resides with other souls and supernaturals.

See also Anuta

Bibliography

Davenport, William H. (1962). "Red-Feather Money." *Scientific American* 206:94–104.

Davenport, William H. (1964). "Social Structure of Santa Cruz Island." In *Explorations in Cultural Anthropology*, edited by Ward H. Goodenough, 57–93. New York: McGraw-Hill.

Davenport, William H. (1975). "Lyric Verse in the Santa Cruz Islands." *Expedition* 18:32–47.

Davenport, William H. (1985). "A Miniature Figure from Santa Cruz Island." Bulletin no. 25 of the Musée Barbier-Müller. Geneva.

Koch, Gerd (1971). *Materielle Kultur der Santa Cruz-Iseln.* Berlin: Museum für Völkerkunde.

WILLIAM H. DAVENPORT

Selepet

ETHNONYMS: None

Orientation

Identification. The name "Selepet" is derived from the sentence "Selep pekyap," meaning "The house collapsed," an event recounted in the story of the people's dispersal from their primordial residential site.

Location. The people live in the Valley of the Pumune River, a tributary of the Kwama River, and along the windward slopes of a low coastal range to the north, located on the Huon Peninsula, Morobe Province, Papua New Guinea, around 6° S and 147° E, mainly at altitudes of 900 to 1,800 meters. They are bounded to the east and west by the more numerous Komba and Timbe peoples. Together these three peoples are separated from the other mountain peoples of the Huon Peninsula by a natural barrier formed by the 3,000–3,900-meter Saruwaged and Cromwell ranges.

Demography. The 1980 census states that 3,600 persons speak the Northern Selepet dialect and 2,700 speak the Southern. The mountain population is relatively dense: 19.6 persons per square kilometer as compared to a national average of 4.6.

Linguistic Affiliation. The language is a member of the Western Huon Family, Finisterre-Huon Stock, Trans–New Guinea Phylum of Papuan languages. It has two major dialects: the Northern, spoken along the coastal slopes and the

Lower Pumune Valley; and the Southern, spoken in the Upper Pumune Valley.

History and Cultural Relations

The central location of the Selepet among the mountain peoples has been very fortuitous. The Selepet people have continually benefited by the expatriates' choosing their location as the point of entry for developing the interior. Lutheran missionaries opened a station on Selepet land overlooking the coast in 1928. They also built a school, a hospital, and a trade store, and they connected these by road to the coast, thereby creating a route for channeling European goods to the interior peoples. Fortuitously, there already existed a trade system stretching throughout the Huon Peninsula, and the Selepet people were pivotal to it. Thus they gained a commercial advantage over all the other peoples. After World War II the Australian administration established a station on the coast and later moved it near the mission station. In 1960, in order to facilitate the administration of the interior peoples, the government built a central airstrip, a subdistrict office, an agricultural station, and an English language school at Kabwum in the heart of the Selepet country. An expatriate missionary and trade stores followed. As roads were built from Kabwum into the adjacent valleys, the Selepet people benefited because they could more readily market their coffee beans, purchase expatriate goods, and supply the growing expatriate community with produce than could the neighboring peoples. The net result, however, was that by the 1970s they were generally characterized as lethargic because they did not have to work as hard as other peoples to gain prosperity. Such lethargy, however, is consistent with their belief that fertility and prosperity are gained by asking for a blessing from one's ancestors, rather than by strenuous personal effort.

Settlements

In aboriginal times the people lived in clusters of related hamlets, each hamlet typically consisting of a patrilineal clan centered on a men's house. When the missionaries arrived they encouraged the people to build central villages revolving around churches. The Australian administration also encouraged the building of central villages, but subsequent overcrowding led to a decline in village hygiene that contributed to the spread of disease. It also led to a shortage of arable land near the villages with resultant intravillage feuding and the destruction of gardens. Life in the village became undesirable, and large numbers of people now live in shelters in their gardens and return to the villages primarily to meet with administrative officers or to attend church. Some larger villages have subdivided, and some leaders have talked of relocating whole villages across the coastal ridge in the unclaimed territory overlooking the coast. Since the 1960s, 60 percent of the population have lived in seven villages within an hour's walk of Kabwum.

Economy

Subsistence and Commercial Activities. The people practice horticulture, with the main crops being varieties of sweet potatoes, taro, yams, and pandanus. They also grow coconut palms and sago near the coast. Wild pigs and wallabies are hunted in the coastal grasslands and smaller marsupials in the mountain forests. Pig husbandry has been practiced from aboriginal times, and more recently the missionaries have introduced cattle. They also introduced many European vegetables and other tropical fruits, so that today the people supplement their diet with maize, cabbages, European potatoes, tomatoes, pineapples, oranges, and papayas. The main cash crops are copra along the coast and coffee at the higher altitudes.

Industrial Arts. There never has been a specialization of labor, so that every person can produce the necessities of life from local resources, though with differing degrees of skill and success. By knocking out all but the last node in a length of bamboo they make containers for carrying water or tubes for baking food in the open fire. Men use adzes to make wooden basins and they carve bows from black palm. Lengths of wild cane are used for arrow shafts, and points are crafted from bamboo, black palm, or animal bones. The lack of feathers and of weighted arrow points contributes to poor accuracy, but points made of bone are reputed to be more accurate because the bones of the quarry attract the bone arrow point. Women weave string bags from twine rolled from hemp, make skirts from a long-bladed indigenous grass, and plait armbands from rattan.

Trade. The Selepet people were pivotal to the trade routes connecting the hinterland and coastal peoples. In exchange for tobacco, taro, bows and arrows, dogs, and pigs, they received fish, coconuts, seashells, lime, wooden bowls, clay pots, obsidian, and boars' tusks.

Division of Labor. Traditionally, members of each sex manufactured the artifacts concerned with their roles. Men made the loincloths and cloaks of armor from the bark of an indigenous tree, items for hunting and warfare, lime gourds, and spatulas. Women made grass skirts and string bags. Today, the men clear the land and dig the soil, and the women break up the clods of soil and prepare the garden for planting. Men build the garden fences to keep out the wild pigs and generally care for the domestic pigs and cattle. Women draw water and carry anything that fits into a string bag, such as infants, piglets, and garden produce. Men carry the heavier items such as beams, planks, and grown pigs.

Land Tenure. With the exception of land purchased by the government or the mission, all land is owned by the patrilineal clans. If a man's clan lacks sufficient arable land, he and his wife often prepare their gardens on land belonging to her clan.

Kinship

Kin Groups and Descent. Selepet villages consist of one or more exogamous, patrilineal clans centered on men's houses and organized into localized, agamous phratries. When membership increases, the members subdivide along lineage or sublineage lines and build a new house. The men's houses were the context for the cultic religious activities, and women were forbidden entry. Although Christianization has transferred the religious activities to the church, women still do not enter men's houses. Loyalty is primarily to one's own lineage, then to the other lineages (if any) affiliated with the same men's house, and last to the phratry. Phratry loyalty is manifested by the exclusive patronage of the businesses of one's own phratry. Members of a phratry combine their resources to build trade stores and participate in other joint ventures such as taxi trucks.

Kinship Terminology. The system is characterized by bifurcate-collateral terms for uncles and bifurcate-merging terms for aunts. Cousin terms are of the Iroquois type. The avunculate is strongly developed. In aboriginal times a boy's maternal uncle was responsible for initiating him and teaching him the secrets of the cultic religion. All affinal relationships are characterized by some measure of avoidance.

Marriage and the Family

Marriage. Marriages are generally arranged between patrilineal clans with a goal of maintaining a balance in the exchange of women. Formerly the preferred exchange was that of men exchanging sisters. Marriage has been considered final at pregnancy, and today marriage ceremonies in the church are sometimes combined with the baptism of the first-born. With the coming of peace and greater mobility exchanges now take place without respect for phratry membership, and in some cases they occur between villages, even between people from different linguistic groups. Arranged marriages are less frequent today, because the young men meet potential mates at school or in the cities, and they are able to earn their own bride-payment through outside employment. Such independence has led to an increase in divorce. Polygamy used to be common, and the number of a man's children were considered to be a direct reflection of his strength. One man with three wives produced a progeny of more than 250 great-grandchildren. The missionaries prohibited polygamy, but with the arrival of nationhood and the nationalization of ecclesiastical authority, some men have ignored the ban.

Domestic Unit. The men and the initiated male youth used to live together in the men's houses, while the married women and children lived in separate residences. Men who were polygamous maintained separate houses for each of their wives with their daughters and uninitiated sons. The trend to monogamy has not significantly influenced this residential pattern, although a married man does sleep more frequently in the home of his wife.

Inheritance. In aboriginal times there was little for one to inherit because the people did not produce durable goods, and the land belonged to the patrilineal clans. What was inheritable were personal adornments such as pigs' tusks, dogs'-teeth headbands, and shell money that figured in the trade system. These items also had the potential of embodying the power of previous owners. The introduction of European commodities has not significantly altered this pattern, because individually purchased items such as radios have a short life span, and larger items such as motor vehicles belong to large social units.

Socialization. Responsibility for raising children is shared by the children's parents, aunts, and uncles. Generally greater permissiveness is common in the raising of young boys. Children learn their roles by working with their parents and, in the case of initiated males, also with their paternal uncles. Young men help in building homes and fences, and they participate in marsupial hunts during times of full moon, when the forest canopy is illuminated. Girls help their mother with gardening, child care, and domestic chores. Male initiation was traditionally the most complex rite of passage; at this time the young men were circumcised, had their earlobes pierced, endured various ordeals such as prolonged fasting, and were shown the religious artifacts. Their maternal uncles also explained the secrets of the male cultic religion. When Christianity was introduced, the initiation ceremonies were replaced with confirmation classes taught by pastors who were not Selepet, thereby weakening the role of the maternal uncle as well as the societal constraints of religion. Today maternal uncles often provide for the educational expenses of their sororal nephews and nieces.

Sociopolitical Organization

Social Organization. Kinship responsibilities require that material goods be shared, so that Selepet society has never had class distinctions. Persons who leave the Selepet area for employment and do not send funds back to their relatives generally do not return.

Political Organization. Although villages often consist of several clans, the clan remains the largest stable political unit, so that within a village there is no certainty of interclan cooperation. A clan was generally led by the man who was most recognized as a religious practitioner. When the missionaries appointed non-Selepet pastors to exercise religious authority, men with other qualities (e.g., medical knowledge) became leaders. Political control in villages is exercised by committees composed of the clan leaders. Marital connections between clans, however, entail mutual support in times of conflict.

Social Control. The responsibilities of kin relationships and the dependency of members upon their clan for support entails an acceptance of the clan's values. Men have traditionally regarded women as inferior, and in aboriginal times they maintained control by keeping their cultic rituals secret and threatening the women with supernatural harm.

Conflict. Traditionally, loyalty was primarily to one's clan, so that aboriginal Selepet society was highly fragmented into warring factions. With the arrival of Europeans came peace, a greater freedom of movement, and an increased awareness of other peoples, so that loyalty has been extended to increasingly inclusive sociopolitical groups. Today the people seek to negotiate rather than resort to violence.

Religion and Expressive Culture

Religious Beliefs. The central concepts of Selepet religion were power and control, and these ideas were the exclusive concern of men. Power existed apart from men, so that they continually sought to increase their power, either supernaturally from snakes or by keeping artifacts formerly belonging to powerful ancestors. Men maintained control over people through the exchange system, since every gift put the recipient under an obligation to reciprocate when called upon. This obligation was true of the dead as well as the living. The body of a deceased man was buried vertically under the men's house with the top of the head exposed. This enabled people to rub his skull, remind him of his kinship obligations, and ask for prosperity. Eventually two very powerful men died, and their survivors carved wooden statues to represent them. Food was placed at the feet of the statues and the ancestors were implored to bless the living with fertility and prosperity. This custom became ritualized and spread throughout the

Selepet villages. When the missionaries arrived with a superior material culture, the people assumed that they too obtained their prosperity from ancestors by the correct manipulation of secret ritual. This belief was confirmed by the reference in the New Testament book of Colossians to the secret that God kept hidden through the ages and only recently revealed to his people, which the Selepet people understood to be the missionaries. The discovery of that secret became life's greatest concern. Culture heroes supplied the people with their material culture and all the requisite knowledge. When they died, various useful plants grew from their bodies. Malevolent spirits inhabit springs, deep pools, caves, cliffs, and other unusual land formations. When encountered or offended, they cause psychological disorders and unusual diseases. Because the Christian God is a spirit, people assume that when he is offended he too causes psychological disorders and serious diseases.

Religious Practitioners. All men performed rituals, but only the most successful became recognized practitioners. In addition to serving the community by performing rites ensuring fertility, they also practiced curative rites, divination, and sorcery. Thus they were both feared and respected. When the Lutheran missionaries arrived in Papua New Guinea, they faced scores of hostile peoples speaking mutually unintelligible languages. Therefore, they attempted to unify all the hinterland peoples by teaching them a common language; the language they chose was Kotte (Kâte), one of two languages they first encountered. Since the women were automatically excluded from significant participation in the religious rites, only the men received education in Kotte to perform the new rituals and learn the secrets. This process resulted in Christianity being regarded as having a secret knowledge parallel to that of the traditional religion.

Ceremonies. The practitioners used to lead in the performance of numerous ceremonies to increase fertility. Today pastors lead in Christian ceremonies based upon the New Testament verses concerning God blessing his people. Elaborate dances used to be held to increase fertility or to celebrate a victory, but today dances are primarily social events.

Arts. There was little art apart from the highly decorated headdresses worn by the men during the ritual dances.

Medicine. Illness was thought to be caused by malevolent spirits or sorcery. Although the malevolent spirits could be tricked and eluded, people who were harmed by them were considered to be incurable. Sorcery, however, could be rendered harmless by the practitioner performing the appropriate ritual.

Death and Afterlife. Death enhances a person's function in society. Initially, a person's ghost carries out vengeance upon those who have not fulfilled their kinship obligations, but eventually the deceased are able to aid their survivors by providing fertility and prosperity.

See also Sio

Bibliography

McElhanon, Kenneth A. (1968). "Selepet Social Organization and Kinship." *Ethnology* 7:296–304.

McElhanon, Kenneth A. (1969). "Current Cargo Beliefs in the Kabwum Sub-District." *Oceania* 39:174–186.

KENNETH MCELHANON

Sengseng

ETHNONYMS: Arawe, Asengseng

Orientation

Identification. To outsiders, the Sengseng tend to identify themselves simply as "Arawe," a term designating all the people of southwest New Britain, including Arawe Islanders, who practice artificial deformation of the skull.

Location. Scattered through a region that extends from approximately 149°52' E and from 6° to 6°17' S, the Sengseng live on either side of the Andru River on the southern side of the island of New Britain, in the state of Papua New Guinea. A few live directly on the coast, in villages that also contain speakers of neighboring languages, but most are located in the interior, up to a height of about 424 meters in the foothills of the Whiteman Range. The country is limestone karst broken by many small streams that can turn into flash floods during the frequent heavy rains. This is one of the wettest parts of Papua New Guinea, averaging about 635 centimeters annually, with the heaviest falls concentrated from June to September. It is warm during the day but, particularly at the higher altitudes, very cool at night.

Demography. The population in 1980 was probably just under 1,000. There is no evidence of overall increase since the early 1960s. Accurate figures are impossible to obtain because so many villages now contain speakers of other languages. Earlier census material indicated a considerable excess of adult males, but this does not appear in the 1980 census (which may not be accurate).

Linguistic Affiliation. Sengseng is one of several closely related languages spoken along the southern and eastern side of the Whiteman Range. These languages include Kaulong, with the largest group of speakers, and Miu, to the west, and Karore and Psohoh to the east. Linguists disagree about which languages are the closest relatives of this group, which has been called Pasismanua after the name of a government census division in which most of the Kaulong and Sengseng speakers live. Pasismanua are generally agreed to be Oceanic (Austronesian), but several linguists have argued that they show influences from Non-Austronesian (Papuan) languages once spoken in this region.

History and Cultural Relations

Culturally, the Sengseng are almost identical to speakers of other Pasismanua languages, but they also have much in common with speakers of other southwest New Britain languages, particularly Arawe and Lamogai (Bibling). The difficult terrain and sparse population isolated many interior Sengseng from direct contact with the Australian government until the mid-1950s, though villagers nearer the coast came under government influence earlier. Followers of a cargo cult centered outside Sengseng territory persuaded a number of interior people to move nearer the coast in the late 1950s, and these villagers were converted to Roman Catholicism. Since that time they also have belonged to the system of local government councils, whereas interior villages still had a system of government-appointed headmen in 1981. Missionaries began to work in the interior about 1984.

Settlements

Settlements are tiny, usually containing no more than a dozen people and often fewer. The Australian government established official consolidated villages for census purposes but these places are rarely inhabited. A settlement contains a men's house, one or more family houses, and a few trees such as coconut and betel palms. Until warfare was forbidden, each settlement was located on a hilltop, which ideally featured a large strangler fig that could be climbed if enemies attacked. Women use shelters built in the bush outside the settlement while menstruating and giving birth.

Economy

Subsistence and Commercial Activities. The starch staple is taro, but because it has been affected by a blight since about 1960, manioc has become increasingly important. Other cultigens include bananas, various greens (especially *Hibiscus manihot*), yams, sugarcane, and, near the coast, sweet potatoes. Because of a traditional pattern of planting a single large garden in one day, often no taro is available for long periods. Then the Sengseng rely on wild foods, particularly wild yams (*Dioscorea* spp.) and, in season, breadfruit. Year-round, perhaps 50 percent of their calories come from wild foods. Coconuts do not grow well in the interior and are reserved for feasts. Domestic animals are limited to pigs and dogs. When a pig's upper canines are removed, the lower ones eventually grow in a complete circle, and the killing of such a tusker is a major event. Domestic pork is eaten only at feasts; most protein comes from wild sources. Birds, bats, and arboreal marsupials are hunted with long blowguns, and wild pigs with dogs and spears. Other creatures are collected when encountered. They include pythons, bandicoots, frogs, and insects, especially the grubs of longicorn beetles and tent caterpillars, supplemented by an occasional wallaby or cassowary. Eels are highly prized, and during dry weather streams are dammed and bailed dry so as to obtain large supplies of shrimp and other crustaceans. Many wild fruits and nuts supplement the diet. Men go away to work to obtain money and particularly to buy cheaply elsewhere in Papua New Guinea one of the main forms of wealth in Sengseng, gold-lip pearl shells. Locally the Sengseng earn money by selling shells to foreigners, who use them to manufacture their own money.

Industrial Arts. Technology includes wooden spears, shields, hourglass drums, flutes, panpipes, bark cloth, and bags made of vine. The most important wealth items—pierced, polished disks of black and white stone, called *niklak*—are of unknown origin. Ornaments are made of plaited vines, dogs' teeth, shells, and cassowary pinions, as well as circular pigs' tusks.

Trade. Tobacco and betel nuts grow particularly well in the interior and are traded towards the coast in exchange for coconuts, lizard skins for drumheads, and bivalves. Prepared salt and wood for spears are received from the Miu to the west. Local trade includes pigments such as manganese for blackening teeth and red minerals for painting shields. Now that they are no longer made on the coast, shields and bark cloth manufactured in the interior are sold to coastal Sengseng, the shields being used in dancing.

Division of Labor. The planting of a new garden is the main communal task, being carried out by a group of men. Men also may cooperate in building a men's house and in hunting wild pigs. Family houses are usually built by husband and wife. Because men believe that taro will not grow well if planted by a woman, and unmarried men also fear being "poisoned" if they eat food cooked near where women sleep, Sengseng men do many tasks that, in other societies, are carried out by women. Women prepare food for themselves and their children, and men for themselves. Purely masculine jobs are usually the heaviest: cutting down trees, damming streams, fencing gardens against pigs, and hunting, as well as butchering and cooking domestic pigs. Men also manufacture weapons, drums, and bark cloth. Particularly female tasks are the weeding of gardens, the manufacture of bags and baskets, the rearing of domestic pigs, and the care of young babies.

Land Tenure. Surprisingly for horticulturalists, gardening land is not owned, though the site of a men's house and the trees planted nearby are. It is believed that taro grows best near where an ancestor is buried, but any descendant of a person who once lived in a settlement can make a garden in the vicinity. There is no shortage of land.

Kinship

Kin Groups and Descent. Each Sengseng traces membership in several cognatic descent categories, composed of all those who share a named, remote, common ancestor, who may be a bird or a supernatural being. Sometimes a food taboo is associated with the category, but the members do not constitute any sort of social group. A settlement is composed of some of the descendants, through both men and women, of the founder, and though in theory descendants through men have authority over descendants through women and can expel them if a quarrel arises, in practice this rarely happens. Sengseng genealogies are long and enable people to trace connections with all those with whom they normally interact. A strong preference is expressed for marriage between certain categories of kin, particularly, for a man, with a daughter of a woman called *taso*, "father's sister." Most feel, however, that first cross cousins are too closely related to marry; if they do, they have to pay off any aggrieved kin. Marriage between first parallel cousins is forbidden, and sexual relations between them are considered incestuous. Kin ties are extended by adoption; the traditional pattern of killing widows left many children parentless, and even an unmarried man might adopt a child old enough to be weaned.

Kinship Terminology. This does not fit any usual classification. Cousin terminology is of the Hawaiian type, so that distinctions between various kinds of cousin rest on description of the links. Mother and mother's sister are called by the same term, with a separate term for father's sister, but there are separate terms for father, father's brother, and mother's brother.

Marriage and Family

Marriage. All women marry, but a number of men do not, fearing the physical weakening thought to afflict men who engage in sexual intercourse. Ideally, the woman chooses her own husband, singling out a man in the most approved kinship category (classificatory, not true, mother's brother or mother's brother's son) at a dance and physically attacking him. He gives her a gift that indicates their betrothal. If her family members agree to the marriage, they deliver her to him with payments in shells and pigs. The payments from the man's side are larger and entitle his kin to expect that when the husband dies, the wife will be killed by her own closest male kin. Today, widow killing has been forbidden by the successive governments of Australia and Papua New Guinea, but remarriage for widows is still disapproved. Because marriage is for eternity, there is no divorce, but men are permitted to take more than one wife, who may be sisters. Relations between affines include many taboos on disrespectful or antagonistic behavior; fines in shells are demanded for any breach of these restrictions, and misfortune befalls the perpetrator. Most conspicuously, it is taboo to say any word that resembles the name of an affine of senior generation, and a special "married" vocabulary exists to deal with this problem. A great social divide separates the married and unmarried; it is improper for the unmarried, especially men, to show any interest in such matters as the pregnancy of a married woman, and an unmarried man should not approach the house of a married man other than his own father.

Domestic Unit. Newlyweds usually live apart from others, largely because of sexual jealousy on the man's part. Those couples who have been married longer may join a settlement, but they almost always have their own house. The father moves permanently to the men's house once a daughter approaches adolescence. Boys sleep in the men's house from the age of about 7, but they may still come home to eat. Some older, unmarried men live alone or join forces with each other, calling on female kin for help with such tasks as weeding their gardens. Married couples with their older children work together in gardens.

Inheritance. The major wealth items, niklak and gold-lip pearl shells, are often buried to avoid theft, and they may be lost forever if the owner dies unexpectedly. In theory, niklak are inherited only by men, but a woman may receive small ones if she has no brothers, whereas larger ones go to a nephew. In general, the oldest man in a sibling set holds the valuables inherited from a father; when he dies, the next brother takes them over. The same rule applies to such male goods as spears, shields, and hourglass drums. Girls inherit any personal goods from the mother, with the eldest daughter usually taking precedence. All descendants of the planter can take fruit from his trees.

Socialization. In line with eventual courtship patterns, baby girls are encouraged to be physically aggressive as soon as they can toddle. Boys may fight with each other but should tolerate blows from girls. Both sexes are warned against engaging in any kind of premarital sexual behavior and must observe taboos on acts that might stunt their growth or, in the case of girls, affect eventual childbearing. Children are not held responsible for their actions until they are adolescent, and they enjoy considerable freedom, though little girls are expected to baby-sit and to help care for piglets. Almost from birth, babies are constantly sung to and bounced in rhythm, and many learn to carry a tune before they can talk.

Sociopolitical Organization

Social Organization. The Sengseng believe that association with others is likely to lead to quarrels, and quarreling is in fact frequent between coresidents, though they try to avoid killing. Settlements constantly split up; it is always possible to join cognatic kin elsewhere. Links between settlements are maintained by marriage, attendance at dances, trade, and the practice of giving a visitor a pearl shell on departure, leading to return visits to settle the debt with an identical shell. With the establishment of official villages, however, coresidents often act as a unit in confronting other villages, but internal harmony remains minimal except when a resident is planning a ceremony and makes a special effort to gain cooperation from others.

Political Organization. The Sengseng identify themselves as speaking a common language, but they have never been united politically. Leadership depends on a combination of ability as a warrior and as an organizer of feasts in which domestic pigs are killed, and the possession of wealth in niklak and pearl shells. A leader need not be married, but he must be willing to travel widely, to trade and collect debts, and to attend ceremonies at which pork is distributed together with pearl shells.

Social Control. The older men of a settlement punished certain offenses, such as public use of sexual terms, by spearing the offender. Most quarrels result from failure to pay debts on demand. Ending a quarrel requires an exchange of matched pearl shells, even in villages near the coast, where village officials and elders of both sexes try to settle disputes.

Conflict. In the past, warfare might erupt at any time. A man shamed in his own village, as by falling down in the presence of women, would relieve his feelings by spearing the first outsider he encountered, and any hapless traveler might be speared by a man wishing to enhance his own reputation as a warrior. Dances still often lead to brawls and occasionally to killing, if any offense such as an insult is remembered. All killings demand a return death, but then peace is likely to be restored, with payments exchanged. Victims of warfare should not include a child, an important man, or more than one victim at a time; breach of these rules would provoke uncontrolled retaliation.

Religion and Expressive Culture

Religious Beliefs. Apart from the period immediately after a death, ghosts have little to do with the living, but the landscape, including all deep pools, is inhabited by a variety of spirits of other sorts (called *masalai* in Pidgin English) who threaten but occasionally help people. The most important are invoked in garden magic to make the crops bear. Numerous taboos surround everyday life. The breach of some is punished by spirits, but often the consequences simply follow automatically. Much apparently religious behavior, such as the treatment of bones of the dead, is only vaguely and inconsistently explained in terms of spiritual beings. Characteristic of all southwest New Britain is the sacralization of fire, which, because it enables people to cook food, is considered to be the basis of human survival. Oaths are sworn on it, it is used to break up fights and to make sites taboo, and it must be treated with respect; serious burns follow breaches of taboo.

Religious Practitioners. Specialists practice garden magic, magic to control the weather, and many types of curing, for which they are paid if they are not working for close kin. A few men claim to be able to injure and kill through sorcery, but most sorcerers are thought to be anonymous foreigners, especially Kaulong speakers. Most men know some love magic, minor garden spells, and magic to induce debtors to pay up.

Ceremonies. The most important center on blackening the teeth of adolescent boys (to make them look attractive), the killing of pigs with circular tusks, funerals, and the decoration and honoring of the skulls of dead men. In some villages, masked figures appear periodically: formerly, they chased and beat women and children, but today, now that violence has been forbidden by the government, they simply collect fines for offenses.

Art. Music, especially song, is the major art form, loved and constantly indulged in by everyone. Decorative arts are minimal; one kind of design is carved on all shields, and another is painted on all bark cloth. At dances, men simply sing, drum, and beat spears against their shields; only women actually dance.

Medicine. All respiratory disease in men is blamed on pollution by females: the people believe that girls and women should never be physically higher than men (i.e., they should never stand over or sit above men). Special cures exist for respiratory conditions and are used by both sexes. Other ailments are blamed on sorcery, breach of a taboo, and soul loss, the last especially if a sleeper is startled awake. Nonmagical cures are used for minor ailments. Western medicine is much desired but usually only available at a distant aid post staffed by a medical orderly paid by the government.

Death and Afterlife. Traditionally, a woman was strangled and buried with her husband in order to accompany him to the afterlife. Occasionally, a woman was killed to accompany a dead child. Burial was under the floor of the men's house, which continued to be occupied (still the case in interior villages in 1981). Near the coast, the dead are buried in separate cemeteries, but pigs are still killed, growing taro is cut up, and one or more fruit trees are cut down, all to supply the dead in the afterlife. Most argue that after the ghost, accompanied by other ghosts, reaches the land of the dead in the interior, it shows no further interest in the living, though it may attack and eat any human beings met on the way. But there are contradictory beliefs in ghosts that live in certain places, especially caves, near villages, where they duplicate the activities of the living. Ghosts may also be summoned by rituals, especially one type of garden magic. Sometimes an aspiring leader exhumes a man's skull and holds ceremonies over it. These rituals bring good luck to the people of the settlement, but Sengseng disagree as to whether the ghost is attached to the skull.

Bibliography

Chinnery, E. W. P. (1928). *Certain Natives in South New Britain and Dampier Straights.* Territory of New Guinea Anthropological Report no. 3. Port Moresby: Government Printer.

Chowning, Ann (1974). "Disputing in Two West New Britain Societies." In *Contention and Dispute: Aspects of Law and Social Control in Melanesia,* edited by A. L. Epstein. Canberra: Australian National University Press.

Chowning, Ann (1978). "Changes in West New Britain Trading Systems in the Twentieth Century." *Mankind* 11:296–307.

Chowning, Ann (1980). "Culture and Biology among the Sengseng." *Journal of the Polynesian Society* 89:7–31.

Chowning, Ann, and Jane C. Goodale (1965). "The Passismanua Census Division, West New Britain Open Electorate." In *The Papua-New Guinea Elections, 1964,* edited by D. G. Bettison, C. A. Hughes, and P. W. van der Veur, 264–279. Canberra: Australian National University Press.

ANN CHOWNING

Siane

ETHNONYMS: None

Siane refers to a number of ethnic groups located in the highlands of Eastern Highlands Province, Goroka Subprovince, Papua New Guinea. In 1975 the Siane numbered some 18,000. Siane is a Papuan language with five dialects in the East-Central Family of the East New Guinea Highlands Stock. Settlements are situated along minor ridges of mountains, at an elevation of about 2,000 meters. A central path runs the length of each village, with the large, oval men's houses and women's and children's dwellings built at intervals along the path. A typical village has 200 to 250 inhabitants.

Swidden gardens are planted with several crops, including sweet potatoes, taro, yams, maize, green vegetables, bananas and sugarcane. Men are responsible for clearing garden sites, and building fences and support poles for various cultigens. Women plant, weed, harvest, and cook the crops. Women also tend the pigs and collect straw, firewood, and water. Men build houses and beat out bark for women's clothing. Big-men stage competitive dance feasts, contributed to by their followers, thereby gaining prestige. Items contributed include pork, various shells, bird of paradise feathers, and bark strips with small shells attached. The big-man represents his entire clan in these events.

Important kin groups are phratries, localized patrilineal

clans, patrilineages, and nuclear and extended families. Clans and phratries are exogamous. Residence is nearly always patrilocal. Polygyny is the ideal marriage form. The members of a domestic unit are not coresident; a husband and his older sons live in the men's house (often comprising a descent group of related males), while their immediate female relatives live in a separate dwelling. The basic economic unit, however, is a man with his wives and children.

The Siane consist of sixteen "tribes" which are culturally and linguistically similar but not politically integrated. The primary social unit is the clan village, several of which comprise a phratry. The clan is the most inclusive politically integrated unit, and, formerly, it was also the military unit. The patrilineage is the landholding unit. There is a keen sense of competitiveness between nonrelated clans, which is manifested in affinal relations, competitive feasts, alliances, and, formerly, warfare.

The Siane have animatistic beliefs about "spirit," which is a nonmaterial, nondiscrete supernatural essence associated with living things. An individual has a uniquely constituted spirit (*oinya*) throughout his or her lifetime. At death the oinya becomes a ghost (*korova*), which is eventually reabsorbed into the undifferentiated "pool" of spirit, from which subsequent oinya are constituted. Persons can be possessed by korova, which must then be exorcised from the individual. Birth and initiation ceremonies are the occasions of large pig feasts, during which many swine are slaughtered and the ancestors appeased. A major god, Oma Rumufa or "Black Way," is recognized to have existed before the creation of humans but is not worshiped or revered. The ghosts of the ancestors are the object of worship and propitiation, as they are thought to be interested and influential in the affairs of humans.

See also Chimbu, Gahuku-Gama, Gururumba

Bibliography

Dwyer, Peter D. (1974). "The Price of Protein: 500 Hours of Hunting in the New Guinea Highlands." *Oceania* 44:278–293.

Salisbury, Richard F. (1962). *From Stone to Steel: Economic Consequences of a Technological Change in New Guinea.* London: Cambridge University Press.

Salisbury, Richard F. (1965). "The Siane of the Eastern Highlands." In *Gods, Ghosts, and Men in Melanesia,* edited by Peter Lawrence and Mervyn J. Meggitt, 50–77. New York: Oxford University Press.

Sio

ETHNONYMS: Sigaba, Sigawa

Orientation

Identification. "Sio" is the name of a Papua New Guinea people, of their group of four villages, and of their language (also spoken in Nambariwa, a small coastal village to the east). The word means "they put, take up position," and was adopted by the people themselves, in place of their traditional name "Sigaba," less than a century ago.

Location. The Sio inhabit tropical savanna situated on the north coast of the Huon Peninsula in Morobe Province. They are located at 147°20' E and 6°50' S. Although predominantly grassland, the area includes extensive tracts of rain forest, and Sio territory also includes several miles of fringing reef, a large lagoon, and a small offshore island where, prior to World War II, most of the Sio-speaking people resided. Precipitation is markedly seasonal, with only a fifth or less of the annual rainfall occurring during the southeast trade wind season from May to October. Drought years and poor harvests occur, but with varying severity.

Demography. At the time of initial European contact in the late nineteenth century, the Sio numbered about 700. The population had increased to 1,500 by the mid-1960s, and in the generation since it has doubled once again.

Linguistic Affiliation. Sio is an Austronesian language that lacks "close relatives" among the dozens of Austronesian languages spoken by the coastal and island peoples of the region. Beginning before 1920, a written form of the language, for liturgical purposes, was produced by German missionaries and Sio catechists. Currently, with the help of missionary linguists, the people are recording traditional myths and folktales.

History and Cultural Relations

A Sio youth, abducted by German officials and introduced to the governor of the colony, played a key role in establishing peaceful relations between the Sio and Whites during the German colonial period (1884–1914). A Lutheran mission station was established at Sio in 1910, and the same youth, now grown and an appointed village headman, helped lead the people toward mass conversion to Christianity in 1919. Since then a succession of leaders have conducted Sio's relations with outside agencies, drawing to the community varied benefits while insisting that land and resources remain under local control. In 1959, a government primary school opened and a regional service cooperative for marketing the copra and coffee of village producers was inaugurated. Both the school and the co-op owed much to Sio initiative. In the mid-1960s, Sio was incorporated in a local government council. Developments of the 1980s included cattle ranching, the formation of a Sio company engaged in logging of hardwoods in conjunction with an Asian firm, and, to compensate for the decline of the copra market—copra having been the principal cash crop—the extensive planting of cocoa.

Settlements

For two to three centuries the Sio lived on a tiny offshore island (later known as the "Dorfinsel" to the German colonists). The island village was divided into residential wards, each of them densely packed with houses that were typically occupied by two or three nuclear families. Each ward also had a men's ceremonial house. The island village was destroyed during World War II and was not rebuilt. Instead, the people established four villages on the opposite mainland, all of them near the sites of prehistoric Sio villages. The houses are rectangular pile dwellings roofed with sago-leaf thatch. Men's clubhouses, of similar design, were not built in the postwar villages, and this signaled the demise of the traditional men's organization together with male initiation.

Economy

Subsistence and Commercial Activities. Shifting cultivation, mainly of yams in fenced grassland plantations divided into household plots, absorbs the largest share of domestic labor and is the basis of subsistence. Subsidiary crops include bananas, taro, sweet potatoes, edible *pitpit,* sugarcane, and introduced cultigens such as squash, manioc, and corn. Economic trees include coconut, sago, betel nut, and pandanus. Cattle have been added to the traditional domestic animals: pigs, dogs, and chickens. Fishing by a variety of techniques and reef collecting contribute significantly to the food supply. Feral-pig hunting by means of fire, dogs, and bows and arrows, a ritual associated with the annual burning of the grassland in preparation for cultivation, is the only productive form of hunting. Over the years, coconut plantings that were greatly extended beginning in the late 1930s have been a principal source of cash income. Attempts at cultivating dry rice, peanuts, and coffee failed. Current efforts and plans focus on timber, cocoa, cattle, and wet rice cultivation on cut-over hillsides.

Industrial Arts. Principal crafts are pottery—cooking pots made by women by means of the paddle-and-anvil technique—and outrigger canoes. Many objects in daily or frequent use—stone axes, mats, wooden bowls, bark cloth, bows and arrows, and drums—were imported.

Trade. External trade helped to alleviate seasonal food shortages and also brought a variety of goods, some of which were retraded. Pots, fish, and coconuts were traded for taro and sweet potatoes from the interior. In the Sio view, pottery was the basis of their trading, not only with the interior peoples but also with neighboring coastal peoples and the Siassi Island seaborne traders who visited them twice annually.

Division of Labor. Pig hunting and most of the work in yam cultivation, canoe and house building, and festive cooking are done by men. Pot making, weaving net bags, daily cooking, and much of the work in pig tending are done by women. Both men and women fish, though by different methods, and both prepare and sell copra. Cooperation beyond the household is at its widest in the annual pig hunts and in building houses and canoes. Traditionally, digging-stick teams of three to six men did the heavy work of tilling the ground for planting; aside from that work, the labor of members of a household was sufficient.

Land Tenure. Ownership of estates consisting of scattered and named tracts of land is vested in patrilineal lineages. Each lineage is headed by a senior male who is styled "father of the land" (*tono tama*) and whose superior knowledge of genealogy and histories of landholdings is brought to bear in the event of disputes. Gardening land, however, is not scarce and disputes are rare. Moreover, since tillage teams whose members are frequently affines or maternal relatives garden together, people regularly enjoy temporary use rights to land that belongs to lineages other than their own.

Kinship

Kin Groups and Descent. Every Sio is a member by birth of a patrilineal descent group (lineage). There is no term for "lineage," nor are the various lineages named. Rather they are known by the names of their heads, who tend to be firstborn sons. The lineage is principally a custodial landholding group and rarely assembles as an action group. Male members of the lineage, however, tend to live in residential clusters and frequently combine in gardening associations and for house building and other tasks.

Kinship Terminology. Cousin terms are of the generational or Hawaiian type. Avuncular terms are of the bifurcate-merging or Iroquois type.

Marriage and Family

Marriage. Sio as a whole, including the outlying village of Nambariwa, tended to be an endogamous unit. People with common great-grandparents are not supposed to marry. Lineages are exogamous and people whose fathers or grandfathers were associated in the same men's house, whatever their genealogical connections, were likewise forbidden to marry. Postmarital residence tends to be patrilocal, but exceptions are frequent. Bride-wealth payments of pigs and valuables are assembled from a variety of kinsmen and in local theory are a mark of respect for the bride. The status of women is high and marriage resembles the egalitarian, companionate form of the West. The levirate and sororate are not practiced. Polygyny was approved but tended to be confined to big-men. Divorce under traditional conditions is said to have been rare.

Domestic Unit. The household comprised of a nuclear family is the basic domestic unit.

Inheritance. Inheritance is patrilineal, though inter vivos gifts of pigs, valuables, and economic trees from men to their sisters' sons are common. Pot-making skills, implements, and decorative designs pass from mother to daughter.

Socialization. Traditional male initiation ceremonies, in which the youths' maternal uncles had a prominent role in instructing them in "the laws," lapsed in the 1920s. Mission schools since then, but mainly a government school since 1959, have provided primary education.

Sociopolitical Organization

Social Organization. People regard their society as a body of kin who share a common language, culture, and territory and who are sharply set off from neighboring peoples. Dividing the body politic roughly in half are residential moieties, whose members maintain a friendly rivalry. The population is further subdivided into landowning patrilineages; the men of these groups formerly comprised men's clubhouses, whose activities included ancestral cult ritual and the not-so-friendly rivalries entailed in the competitive distribution of yams and pigs and exacting vengeance—or compensation—for death or injury inflicted by another group. Much of Sio social life, however, consists in participating in those relationships that serve to bind members of these groups together, namely, those between affines, maternal uncles and nephews, and age mates (formerly, men who had undergone initiation together as youths).

Political Organization. Traditional leaders combined a number of ascribed and achieved roles. First, they were first-born sons, clubhouse leaders, and lineage heads. Second, they were expected to demonstrate superior performance in gardening, artisanship, trade, oratory, diplomacy, fighting skill, competitive feasting, and learning. Those who were pre-eminently successful in these varied activities, helped of course by their wives and supporters, were true big-men who wielded influence in the community at large.

Social Control. Antisocial and violent behaviors were dealt with by: the disposition to demand and accept compensation rather than to fight with weapons; the weight of public opinion, especially as articulated by influential leaders; and the fear of punishment by ancestral ghosts.

Conflict. The interior peoples were the traditional enemies in contrast to island and coastal neighbors with whom Sio had mainly peaceful dealings in trade. Their military posture was primarily defensive; the island village provided a natural defense and remote gardens were worked by associations that were large enough to cope with parties of raiders.

Religion and Expressive Culture

Religious Beliefs. Ancestral ghosts who served as patron deities of the men's clubhouses and forest-dwelling spirits figured prominently in traditional beliefs. The ghosts were vengeful beings who, although they could be placated by the sacrifice of pigs, inflicted illness and death for transgressions of social rules. Spirits, whose usual form was that of hairy dwarfs but who also manifested themselves as animals or inanimate objects, were capricious in their behavior toward humans. Sometimes malevolent, causing mishaps, they might also reveal themselves to humans, in dreams for example, and offer magical knowledge in return for the observance of certain taboos. An otiose creator deity named Kindaeni is said to have created the universe. Magical knowledge and techniques were brought to bear in all areas of life, whether in growing crops, conducting a love affair, trading, healing, controlling the weather, or protecting against theft.

Religious Practitioners. Esoteric knowledge of myths, particular magical and divinatory techniques, and the like was highly valued, and many men possessed exclusive knowledge that they had inherited or sometimes purchased. Generally, the big-men who headed the clubhouse groups were specialists in yam magic, and their wealth in valuables allowed them to hire sorcerers.

Ceremonies. The rainy season of the northwest monsoon heralded the major ceremonies that were associated with male initiation and the large-scale distribution of food and pigs by which big-men (male clubhouse leaders) competed for status.

Arts. Dances performed on all major ceremonial occasions incorporate drums, singing, and elaborate headdresses and body ornamentation. Carving and painting skills are most notably demonstrated on the prows and planks of canoes, but most artifacts are decorated in some fashion. Musical instruments and noisemakers include wooden hand drums, conch trumpets, and bullroarers.

Death and Afterlife. The souls of people recently deceased were believed to remain in the village where they could cause accident and injury. Some months after burial, the souls were ceremonially induced to depart for the abode of the dead, a series of coastal bluffs several miles to the southeast. Supernatural causation was considered to be a factor in all deaths. If sorcery was suspected, as it often was, divination was used to identify the community of the sorcerer.

See also Selepet

Bibliography

Groves, W. C. (1934). "The Natives of Sio Island, South-Eastern New Guinea." *Oceania* 5:43–63.

Harding, Thomas G. (1967). "Ecological and Technical Factors in a Melanesian Gardening Cycle." *Mankind* 6:403-408.

Harding, Thomas G. (1967). "A History of Cargoism in Sio, Northeast New Guinea." *Oceania* 38:1–23.

Harding, Thomas G. (1967). "Money, Kinship, and Change in a New Guinea Economy." *Southwestern Journal of Anthropology* 23:209–233.

Harding, Thomas G. (1967). *Voyagers of the Vitiaz Strait.* Seattle and London: University of Washington Press.

Harding, Thomas G. (1985). *Kunai Men: Horticultural Systems of a Papua New Guinea Society.* University of California Publications in Anthropology, vol. 16. Berkeley: University of California Press.

THOMAS G. HARDING

Siwai

ETHNONYM: Siuai

Orientation

Identification. The word "Siuai" originally applied to a cape on the southern coast of Bougainville, but it later came to identify a wider area of the coast, its hinterland, and the people who lived there.

Location. The Siwai occupy the center of the Buin Plain of southern Bougainville, North Solomons Province, Papua

New Guinea. The area, which is 7°S and 155° W, is in the humid tropical lowlands, almost all of the population living below 200 meters above sea level. Some Siwais now live in urban areas in other parts of Papua New Guinea.

Demography. In prewar years, the Siwai population was around 4,500; by the mid-1970s it had grown to about 9,000 and by the late 1980s was probably about 13,000.

Linguistic Affiliation. The Siwai (or Motuna) language is a Non-Austronesian (Papuan) language similar to other inland South Bougainvillean languages such as Buin, Nagovisi, and Nasioi. There are trivial differences in language within the Siwai area.

History and Cultural Relations

Linguistic, archaeological, and mythological evidence indicates that Siwais migrated to Bougainville from New Guinea and have lived in and around their present location for at least 2,000 years and probably very much longer. They have close linguistic relations with Buin people to the south and, to a lesser extent, with Nagovisi people to the north. In precontact times contact with other linguistic groups was not great, though there was some intermarriage, trade (especially with the Alu and Mono islands in the Solomon Islands), and occasional warfare. Europeans traded intermittently and indirectly with the Siwai coast in the last two decades of the nineteenth century, but beyond steel tools there was minimal trade until well into the twentieth century. Around the turn of the century, a small number of men worked on distant plantations and brought back new plants; others were introduced in the period of German administration. Colonial administration effectively reached Siwai after 1919 when an Australian administration post was set up on the Buin coast. In the early 1920s, both the Catholic and Methodist missions set up stations in Siwai and in the years before World War II there was a small amount of trade in copra, most people were converted to Christianity, monetization followed the imposition of taxation, and most adult men were employed for substantial periods as plantation laborers, mainly on the east coast of the island. Cultural change was more rapid in the postwar years: cash cropping, especially of cocoa, became important; education became almost universal and continued to the tertiary level; traditions were transformed; a massive copper mine (Panguna) was constructed 50 kilometers away, introducing new forms of employment; alien political institutions were introduced; and Siwai became part of an independent Papua New Guinea in 1975.

Settlements

In precontact times Siwais lived in small, dispersed hamlets scattered throughout the region. Most such hamlets had between one and ten houses and were located on the garden land of the matrilineage. The houses were built directly on the ground. In the 1920s the Australian administration imposed a policy consolidating the scattered hamlets into about sixty line villages in order to simplify control and improve public health. Each married man was required to build a house on piles and the new villages were located on ridges, near springs (for drinking water) and large streams (for bathing and sanitation). Many families retained their hamlet, or garden, houses and spent periods of time in both. Following the independence of Papua New Guinea and considerable pressure on resources there has been some movement away from line villages to the original hamlet sites on traditionally owned land. In most villages there was at least one men's clubhouse (*kaposo*), a much larger building where men met to talk, beat slit gongs, and organize and hold feasts. A century ago some men's houses were well decorated. Traditionally, houses have been simply made of wood, woven bamboo walls, and sago-leaf roofs. From the 1970s onward some more permanent houses have been constructed, a few with electrical generators, water supplies, or even solar power. Villages, and the population as a whole, have remained in much the same locations in historic times. New developments, including mission stations, schools, and administrative buildings, have been built outside villages and have not grown into settlements.

Economy

Subsistence and Commercial Activities. The Siwai have long been horticulturalists. Until World War II the horticultural system was dominated in every way by taro (*Colocasia esculenta*) of which there were more than fifty different kinds. Other root crops such as yams and sweet potatoes were also grown, alongside sugarcane, bananas, and various green vegetables. Tree crops, including coconuts, breadfruit, sago, and almonds, were important, pigs were of major significance (for exchange and feasting), and fish and prawns were taken from small streams. Taro constituted about 80 percent of the diet. Taro blight (*Phytopthora colocasiae*) wiped out taro in the early 1940s and, despite constant attempts to regenerate taro, sweet potatoes now dominate the horticultural system as taro previously did. In the postwar years, Siwais attempted to withdraw from plantation labor and establish their own commercial agricultural system. Rice, always a prestigious food, was widely grown; peanuts, corn, and coffee were also tried but a lack of access to markets prevented commercial success. Cocoa was introduced at the end of the 1950s. Construction of roads to the Buin coast in the 1960s and across the mountains to the east coast in the 1970s enabled cocoa marketing to become increasingly successful. After experiments with other forms of commercial agriculture, mainly cattle farming, cocoa is now the sole commercial crop and is planted and marketed by almost all households. Cash income is primarily generated from cocoa sales, vegetable sales in markets within Siwai, some local wage and salary employment, and the remittances and expenditure of Siwais working at Panguna and elsewhere.

Industrial Arts. Few artifacts are currently produced in Siwai. Pottery manufacture effectively ended not long after World War II. Finely woven baskets of different kinds—known as "Buka baskets," though almost all are made in Siwai—are produced on a significant scale by several village households and sold extensively in Bougainville and beyond.

Trade. In the nineteenth century there was considerable precontact trade and intermarriage with the nearby Solomon Islands. One significant traded item was shell money, brought from Malaita in the Central Solomon Islands. Trade with European traders began before the end of the nineteenth century, and it increased in the 1920s and 1930s, with monetization and missionization. European trade largely replaced trade with other Melanesians, though shell money continued to be traded until recent years. In 1956, a Siwai Rural Progress Society was established to market cocoa, copra, and other local commodities; the society grew rapidly in the 1960s and 1970s but collapsed as individual producers traded directly with east coast wholesalers. Most villages have at least one trade store.

Division of Labor. Horticulture was and is women's work, and women worked in the gardens four times as much as men in the early decades of this century. Men spent some time in the gardens, undertook arduous clearing activities, hunted, were responsible for garden magic, and organized ceremonial activities. The introduction of sweet potatoes reduced the necessity for long hours of horticultural work for the women. Cash crops became male activities, garden magic disappeared, and time spent on ceremonial activities declined. Many men and some women are now employed inside Siwai, but even more of the people work outside Siwai at the mine and in the towns.

Land Tenure. Throughout Siwai, land is owned by matrilineages. Every matrilineage owns full or residual rights to tracts of garden land or potential garden land and most matrilineages claim ownership of more distant hunting areas or fishing streams. Land was sold in certain exceptional circumstances, and some rare tracts of land are now individually owned. Men conducted agricultural activities on their wives' land, and high levels of cross-cousin marriage previously ensured the integrity of tracts of matrilineage land. High population densities, nontraditional marriage, and cocoa cultivation have increased the complexity of land tenure and inheritance.

Kinship

Kin Groups and Descent. Siwai society is divided into many matrilineages, but most villages are primarily composed of two matrilineages whose members have been marrying each other for generations. Such intermarrying matrilineages become local descent groups. Most matrilineages produce their own stores of wealth and their own particular tracts of land. There is regular interaction between matrilineage members.

Kinship Terminology. Siwai kinship terminology is similar to other terminologies that have been labeled Dravidian, characterized as two-section systems, and associated with bilateral cross-cousin marriage and sister exchange. Genealogical knowledge is very shallow. There are few strictly affinal terms.

Marriage and Family

Marriage. In the traditional marriage system, matrilineages were often paired and both matrilateral and patrilateral cross-cousin marriage were strongly favored. Marriages to members of the same matrilineage were forbidden and have not occurred. In the past, polygyny was not uncommon and leaders occasionally had several wives. It is rare in contemporary Siwai. Divorce was common and widows and widowers normally remarried. Although cross-cousin marriages within villages remain common, many marriages are now contracted between Siwais and members of other linguistic groups from other parts of the country or even beyond. Postmarital residence was initially virilocal, but later it often shifted to avunculocal or uxorilocal.

Domestic Unit. Most households are nuclear families; extended households are very rare. Youths often sleep in separate houses from their parents.

Inheritance. Personal effects are usually inherited by the oldest son. Until very recently such goods have been few and inconsequential.

Socialization. Children are normally treated with affectionate indulgence by their parents and disciplining is often ineffective. Punishment and rewards are normally verbal. Conflicts between children, especially brothers, are more common than disputes and conflicts with parents, who are accorded considerable respect. Primary school education is now effectively universal and many children go on to secondary and tertiary education.

Sociopolitical Organization

Social Organization. In precontact times age carried some status but the greatest status was held by traditional leaders or big-men (*mumi*), the greatest of whom in the present century was Soni of Tutuguan village. Leadership was achieved through acquiring wealth and renown, which resulted from industriousness, charisma, acumen, diplomacy, and kinship support. Leaders normally acquired wealth in pigs, land, and also wives, through various exchanges, and through forms of redistribution, usually in association with funerary feasts. Other men had various degrees of renown and prestige, but there was no formal ranking system. Women had substantial authority principally in their own productive and ritual areas; women were not recognized as traditional leaders in their own right. In the postwar years, though some men are still recognized as traditional leaders, leadership itself has taken on new forms, as businessmen and politicians have acquired different spheres of operation and feasting has become generally less substantial and significant in everyday life. Many men are often absent from the villages for long periods of time. The economic independence of women has lessened as the cash economy has become more important.

Political Organization. In precontact time Siwai was not a tribal group in any sense other than linguistically. In the prewar years, the administration appointed individuals in each village to liaise with administration officials, but Siwai only became an effective political unit in the 1960s with the establishment of a local government council. Otherwise, Siwai was still divided into seven districts, and it effectively reverted to its former decentralized political organization in the 1970s with the establishment of community governments to replace the local government council. Most villages now have their own councils. Siwai elects two members of the North Solomons Provincial Government and is part of the national South Bougainville constituency.

Social Control. In earlier times, leaders were the principal means of social control and acquired renown partly through their ability to achieve this. In the 1920s, the administration appointed village headmen to assist the administration in achieving law and order; however, except for new offenses, their authority was less than that of traditional leaders. A more modern court system evolved alongside the local government council but was replaced by more traditional village courts working with community governments. Serious offenses are considered at the provincial level. Traditional leaders now have less ability to achieve social control. Social control was also achieved by avoidance behavior. Sorcerers also had considerable authority, which is now more often wielded by church leaders.

Conflict. Before the twentieth century there was intermittent feuding and localized warfare within Siwai, and probably occasionally with neighboring language groups. Wars were organized by mumis, but they rarely involved many people, lasted long, caused much loss of life, or covered a wide area. Individual disputes rarely led to open hostility. In the present century, such warfare has ended. There remain divisions within Siwai, marked by the adherence of different districts to the Catholic or the United church, which have occasionally sparked conflicts. More recently, there have been disputes over political issues such as secession and over the closure of the Panguna mine that have led to conflict.

Religion and Expressive Culture

Religious Beliefs. Creation myths surround the great historic spirits, primarily "the Maker" ("Tartanu") who brought life to earth. There are many spirits (*mara*) associated with particular areas, kin groups, or men's houses, which are believed to have positive and negative qualities, but no systematic religious behavior related people to these spirits. Although mara are still feared, Christianity has generally replaced traditional beliefs and most Siwai are at least nominal adherents of either the Catholic or the United church. In the last two decades there have also been some revival movements.

Religious Practitioners. There was no set of ritual practices or priesthood, though both mumis and sorcerers (*mikai*) were believed to have some ability to control the spirit world.

Ceremonies. A ceremonial cycle marked most significant stages in the life cycle. Betrothal was marked by the exchange of strings of shell money and marriage by magical rites to ensure the well-being of the couple. Baptisms were held four or five weeks after the birth of a child. Little if any ceremony marked the achievement of adulthood. The most elaborate ceremonies accompanied cremations and ceremonies to mark the end of mourning periods, which were accompanied by the exchange of pigs, shell money, and other goods.

Arts. Singing and dancing mark memorial ceremonies especially. Women's songs and dances are distinct and performed separately from those of men. Large slit gongs in men's houses are beaten in unison at various stages in the preparation of ceremonies. Men's dances are accompanied by panpipes and wooden trumpets and women's dances by a wooden sounding board.

Medicine. Diseases were attributed to a number of sources but usually to the action of malevolent spirits or the breaking of taboos. Curing techniques consisted of ritual precautions and the use of herbal medicines of many kinds. Both women and men might have knowledge of medical skills, and there were specialists in areas such as bone surgery. Sorcerers would ward off or drive out evil spirits and cause them to avenge particular incidents. Western medicine is now sought, especially for more recently introduced diseases, but traditional herbal medicines remain in use.

Death and Afterlife. In exceptional cases death was also attributed to sorcery or mara, but, especially for the old, it was usually considered to be quite normal. At death the soul was traditionally believed to leave the body and set out for one of three abodes: "Paradise," a lake in northeast Siwai, the abode of fortunate ghosts; or "Kaopiri," a legendary lake in the north for those who have not been adequately mourned; or "Blood Place," for those who died in fighting. Such beliefs have been largely replaced by Christian beliefs concerning Heaven and Hell.

See also Nasioi

Bibliography

Oliver, Douglas L. (1955). *A Solomon Island Society: Kinship and Leadership among the Siuai of Bougainville.* Cambridge, Mass.: Harvard University Press.

Connell, John (1978). *Taim Bilong Mari: The Evolution of Agriculture in a Solomon Island Society*. Canberra: Australian National University Development Studies Centre.

JOHN CONNELL

Tahiti

ETHNONYM: Society Islands

Orientation

Identification. The name "Tahiti"—or, as Bougainville first wrote it in 1768, "Taiti," and Cook in 1769, "Otaheite"—was the name the natives gave their island and which Europeans came to apply to the indigenes. If the Tahitians had a name specifically identifying themselves, it is not known. What is known is that all of those living in the Society Archipelago, including Tahiti, referred to themselves as "Maohi."

Location. The island of Tahiti upon which the Tahitians lived is the largest of the Society Islands and is located in the windward segment of that group at 149°30' W and 17°30' S. It is a high island of volcanic origin with peaks rising above 1,500 meters. The mountainous interior is covered with forest and ferns while the lower slopes, especially on the leeward side, are brush and reed covered. In the inhabited valleys and coastal plains open stands of indigenous trees and tall grasses were scattered between the cultivated fields of the Tahitians. Wild fowl were said to have been relatively scarce and limited to a few species, pigeons and ducks being specifically mentioned. Wild four-legged creatures were limited to a few small lizards and the Polynesian rat, the latter probably brought by Polynesians.

Linguistic Affiliation. The Tahitic language of the Tahitians belongs to the Eastern Polynesian Subgroup of the Malayo-Polynesian Subdivision of the Austronesian languages.

Demography. Estimates of Tahiti's population in the later years of the eighteenth century varied from as few as 16,050 to approximately 30,000 persons, and thus these estimates are of little factual value. A nineteenth-century decline in population due to wars and diseases is known to have occurred. However, by 1907, after which it was no longer possible to segregate indigenous totals from those of foreigners and immigrant Polynesians from other islands, the number of Tahitians was said to number 11,691.

History and Cultural Relations

Present archaeological evidence supports the view that the Society Islands, of which Tahiti is a part, were the first to be populated in eastern Polynesia from an eastern Polynesia dispersal center in the Marquesas, perhaps as early as A.D. 850. Whether later prehistoric migrants ever reached the Society Islands is an open question. Limited archaeological data and tradition suggest the occurrence of prehistoric Society Island emigrations to New Zealand and Hawaii. However, by contact times Tahitian voyaging, primarily for political and trade purposes, was limited to the islands of the archipelago and the atolls of the western Tuamotus. In contrast to prehistoric culture change on Tahiti, which had occurred in small increments, the discovery of the island by Wallis in 1767 marked the beginning of strong European acculturative forces impacting on the traditional life-ways of Tahitians. Except for material goods, the most notable changes occurred with the arrival of Protestant missionaries in 1797. Within several years after their arrival a number of Tahitians, including the paramount chief, Pomare II, had been taught to read and write, and the Christian faith and mores had begun to be accepted. However, objections by more conservative members of the society resulted in a series of internecine wars and it was not until 1815 that Pomare II crushed his opponents and, with the aid of the missionaries, successfully guided a religious and political modification of the older traditional order. With the development of American and European whaling and sealing activities Tahiti became a prime distribution center for goods. By 1840 South American currencies had come to be accepted as a substitute for the old trading techniques. At the same time, foreign immigrants and investments on the island produced a variety of problems for which the Tahitians were ill prepared. Foreign government overtures to Queen Pomare to establish a protectorate resulted in the French moving quickly to annex the island in 1842 and thus dissolving Tahitian native rule.

Settlements

Prior to European intervention, Tahitians followed a pattern of dispersed settlements, dwellings being scattered along the coastal plain and up the broader valleys. By the nineteenth century missionary activities and the use by European vessels of safe harbors on the island resulted in the formation of villages near these locations. The Tahitian house resembled a flattened oval inground plan, the long sides being parallel and the two ends rounded. The thatched roof extended down on all sides from a central ridgepole extending lengthwise along the house. Most dwellings were enclosed by a wall of vertically lashed bamboo poles, a space being left open in the middle of one long side to serve as a doorway. Such structures averaged about 6 meters in length with a width of 3.6 meters and a ridge height of 2.7 meters. However, important chiefs might have buildings measuring as much as 91 meters in length and proportionately wide, with a ridgepole resting some 9 meters above the tamped earthen floor.

Economy

Subsistence and Commercial Activities. Tahitians were horticulturalists raising a variety of tree and tuberous crops as well as plantains, all of which, except sweet potatoes, originated in southeast Asia or Melanesia. Domesticated animals included pigs, dogs, and chickens. Fish, caught by a variety of techniques, were a dominant source of protein. Contact with Europeans resulted in the addition of several American and Old World plants and domesticated animals. During the early nineteenth century a successful pork trade with New South Wales was carried on and this was followed later by exports of coconut oil, sugarcane, and arrowroot. Provisioning of European ships became a major nineteenth-century source of income.

Industrial Arts. Decorated bark cloth was a major aboriginal industrial art created by women and used as clothing, as formal gifts, and for export trade. Bark-cloth production continued into the twentieth century, but such cloth is no longer manufactured.

Trade. Regular aboriginal trading was carried on with the leeward islands of the Society Archipelago and the western atolls of the Tuamotus. The principal item for exchange was bark cloth, to which was added provisions in the case of the Tuamotu atolls. With the arrival of Europeans, iron became the dominant item traded to those atolls. In exchange, Tahitians obtained dog hair, pearls, and pearl shells from the Tuamotus and coconut oil and canoes from the leeward islands.

Division of Labor. Traditionally, general construction work and manufacturing of tools, weapons, canoes, and fishing gear was men's work, as was fishing, major ritualism, and warfare. Women created bark cloth, wove mats, and fashioned clothing from both materials. Farming was shared by both sexes.

Land Tenure. At the time of contact landownership with the right of inheritance was recognized for those of the chiefly and commoner classes, with only the lower class, known as *teuteu*, being excluded. Such lands were subject to taxation in kind by the ruling chiefs who could banish an owner if such taxes were not forthcoming. Missionary activity in the nineteenth century seems to have resulted in at least some of the teuteu class obtaining land rights.

Kinship

Kin Groups and Descent. Descent was bilateral with social weight tending to favor patrilateral ties. Consanguineal and, perhaps, affinal kin were grouped in what have been referred to as kin congregations who worshiped their own tutelar deity at their group religious structure, referred to as a *marae*. Primogeniture was important in ranking within the kin congregation. While women were excluded from the marae of the large kin congregations, that was not always true for marae of smaller kin congregations.

Kinship Terminology. The term *matahiapo* was applied to firstborn as well as all representatives of a family stock descended in the line of the firstborn. *Teina* was used to distinguish younger brothers, sisters, and cousins who were not matahiapo; otherwise, the Hawaiian type of kinship terminology was used.

Marriage and Family

Marriage. Tahitians disapproved of marriage between close consanguineal kin, but how close was never made clear. However, marriage was not permitted between those of differing social classes. Therefore, children resulting from a sexual relationship between partners of differing classes were killed upon birth. In the eighteenth century young couples were required to obtain the permission of their parents before marriage, and among the chiefly class early betrothal was said to be the norm and concubinage was common. Marriage ceremonies, when present, consisted of prayers at a marae. There appeared to be no fixed residency requirement and divorce was by common consent.

Domestic Unit. The nuclear family was the dominant unit.

Inheritance. The firstborn son became the head of the family at birth and succeeded to his father's name, lands, and title, if any. The father then served as the child's regent until he became of age. In the event of the firstborn dying, the next son succeeded him. There is some indication that in the absence of male offspring, an oldest daughter might be the inheritor.

Socialization. Children were raised permissively by their parents, although those of the chiefly class were given a degree of education through teachers of that class. Men and women ate separately, and there was a variety of restrictions regarding who might prepare another's meal.

Sociopolitical Organization

Social Organization. During the eighteenth century, there were basically three social classes: the *ari'i*, or chiefs; the commoners, variously known as *manahuni* or *ra'atira*; and the laboring and servant class known as teuteu. Only the last group could not own land. By the beginning of the nineteenth century, perhaps because of European influence, a fourth class called *titi*, consisting of slaves derived from warfare, had been added.

Political Organization. In the early years of European contact Tahitian tribes were grouped into two major territorial units. One constituted the larger northwestern portion of the island and was known as Tahiti Nui, while the other consisted of the southeastern Taiarapu Peninsula and was known as Tahiti Iti. Each maintained a paramount chief of socioreligious power. Below this highest position were chiefs who ruled over what may be likened to districts. These were divided into smaller units and managed by inferior ranked chiefs. A paramount chief's power was not unlimited, since important matters affecting most or all of his region were decided by a council of high-ranking chiefs. Paramountcy was not totally preordained, as wars and kinship alliances served to maintain such a status. It was with European aid and combinations of these factors that the Pomare paramountcy was maintained well into the nineteenth century.

Social Control. Fear of divine retribution was a major control, while human sacrifice and a variety of corporal punishments for secular antisocial behavior were also used as sanctions. Justice in the latter cases was determined by a district chief, and the right to appeal to one's paramount chief was available.

Conflict. Confusion regarding tribal territories and overindulgence of chiefly demands for products and services were sources of irritation. At the time of European contact, warfare for chiefly aggrandizement, rather than territorial acquisition, was dominant. By the close of the eighteenth century the European tradition of warfare for territorial gain had been added to the traditional theme of warfare. Minor interpersonal conflicts were resolved by each antagonist being allowed to exhibit publicly his strong resentment of whatever indiscretion had caused the conflict, after which both parties soon reconciled. However, more important conflicts were settled by a district chief, the antagonists having the right to appeal his decision to the paramount chief if not satisfied.

Religion and Expressive Culture

Religious Beliefs. Just as with Tahitian society, native religion recognized a ranked series of gods starting with one supreme deity and passing down through lesser gods and subordinates to individual family spirits of departed relatives. Religion was centered on regional, tribal, and kin tutelar deities, although a few of the gods transcended such limitations and were, in effect, supratribal deities. Gods required a wide variety of appeasements in order to ensure the continued welfare of the individual as well as the tribe. Early nineteenth century missionary activity successfully substituted Christian beliefs for the earlier traditional ones.

Religious Practitioners. Aboriginally, priests were of the chiefly class and were of two kinds. There were those who conducted formal rituals during which the gods were prayed to and appeased by gifts in order to gain their favor. Others were inspirational priests through whom particular gods spoke and offered oracular advice. All priests received some sort of payment for their activities and many were believed to have powers of sorcery. With the nineteenth-century acceptance of Christianity, various Tahitians, not all necessarily of the chiefly class, were trained by the missionaries to become lay preachers.

Ceremonies. Religious ceremonies were carried out in marae, most of which were tabooed to women. Some ceremonies were seasonal affairs, while others pertained to war and peace, thanksgiving, atonement, and critical life-cycle events of chiefs. The degree of ceremonialism was dependent upon the deity and the importance of the marae, those for commoners in districts and smaller land divisions being the least elaborate.

Arts. Drums—and, in the early nineteenth century, shell trumpets—were the only musical instruments used during ceremonies. The raised platforms of certain marae were decorated with carved boards, while the god, Oro, was personified by a wickerwork cylinder enclosing sacred feathers. The culture-hero god, Maui, was represented by a large humanoid wicker figure covered with patterns of feathers. Plaited masks were worn during certain ceremonies on the Taiarapu Peninsula.

Medicine. Obvious ailments such as sores and open wounds were treated with herbal medicines and poultices, and splints were applied to broken bones. Less obvious illnesses were thought to occur as a result of sorcery, contact with a sacred individual or object, or the anger of one's god. Curing was attempted through priestly prayers and offerings. Among the chiefly class, these cures were performed at the patient's marae and might include human sacrifices.

Death and Afterlife. Untimely death was thought to be because of the anger of one's god, while death through aging was regarded as a natural process. Rank determined the extent of expressions of mourning and the length of time the corpse was exposed on a platform before burial. In the case of high-ranking members of the chiefly class, this time factor was greatly extended by evisceration and oiling of the body. Simple burial, secretive for those of high rank, was customary. There is some indication that cremation was employed for certain individuals on the Taiarapu Peninsula. Among the upper classes human relics were preserved. For some, the afterlife was seen as a state of nothingness, but for others it was believed to be a happy life, for rank in the spirit world remained the same as in life.

See also Hawaiians, Marquesas, Rapa, Raroia

Bibliography

Ferdon, Edwin N. (1981). *Early Tahiti as the Explorers Saw It.* Tucson: University of Arizona Press.

Newbury, Colin (1980). *Tahiti Nui: Change and Survival in French Polynesia, 1767–1945.* Honolulu: University Press of Hawaii.

Oliver, Douglas L. (1974). *Ancient Tahitian Society.* 3 vols. Honolulu: University Press of Hawaii.

EDWIN N. FERDON

Tairora

ETHNONYMS: Kainantu, Ndumba, Ommura, Taiora

Orientation

Identification. The Tairora live in the Kainantu District of the Eastern Highlands Province of Papua New Guinea. Group names and place names are usually the same; for example, "Tairora" (or "Tai-ora") is the name of a phratry, settlement, and creek near the present-day town of Kainantu. This designation was generalized by Europeans in the 1920s to include all of the much larger ethnolinguistic group.

Location. Tairora speakers occupy about 1,035 square kilometers of the region south and east of Kainantu, at 145°45' to 146°15' E and 6°15' to 6°45' S. With annual rainfall of 220–250 centimeters, the region is a catchment area for the Ramu and Lamari River headwaters. The terrain is highly diverse, with large, open grassland dominating the northern basins at elevations of 1,625 to 1,880 meters above sea level, and steeply incised forest- or grass-covered ridges in the south, where the Kratke Range culminates in Mount Piora, at 3,450 meters. The climate is fairly uniform throughout the region, with cool nights, warm days, and relatively wet and dry seasons that alternate with the southeast and northwest monsoons, respectively.

Demography. Current estimates for Tairora speakers place the population at about 14,000, reflecting a steady, if slight, rate of increase since European contact. Nowadays, sizable numbers of Tairora, especially from northern settlements, emigrate to the towns of Kainantu, Goroka, and Lae.

Linguistic Affiliation. Tairora, with at least five dialects, is a member of the Eastern Family of Non-Austronesian languages in the East New Guinea Highlands Stock. Many Tairora are bilingual with neighboring languages (Agarabi, Auyana, Binumarien, Gadsup, and Kamano in the north; Awa and Waffa in the south) and currently most males and younger women are fluent in Tok Pisin. Summer Institute of Linguistics translators have produced a considerable amount of religious and educational material in Tairora, but the number of people who are literate in their own language is still fairly small.

History and Cultural Relations

People, perhaps ancestral to Tairora, have occupied the region for at least 18,000 years. The earliest-known era archaeologically, the Mamu Phase, appears to have been a period of continuous growth and development, with subsistence based in hunting and collecting. After 3,000 B.P., in the Tentika Phase, evidence for sedentarism occurs, as do other suggestions of the adoption of horticulture. In general, oral traditions point to Tairora homelands to the west and southwest, but groups' origin myths tend to be highly localized. Tairora territory abuts those of other language groups on all sides, and many different sources have contributed to the linguistic and cultural diversity of the region. Since earliest contact with European missionaries, gold prospectors, and administrators (beginning in the 1920s in the north and 1950s in the south), the Tairora social universe has expanded considerably. The establishment of the Upper Ramu Patrol Post (now Kainantu) in 1932 and the Aiyura Agricultural Experimental Station in 1937—both in the north—were notable events, beginning the processes of pacification and economic development leading to the current situation, in which Tairora play a prominent role in provincial government.

Settlements

Settlements in northern Tairora are generally closer together and more nucleated than in the south, where they tend to be hamlet clusters about a half day's walk apart. Most settlements are found at elevations between 1,500 and 1,900 meters, and typically they each had 200–250 residents until recent population surges. Traditionally, wherever allowed by the terrain, ridge-top locations were preferred for defensive purposes; also for defense, except for a few groups living in the open grasslands of the north, settlements were surrounded with high palisades. In an arrangement used until the 1960s in the north, and still used in much of the south, Tairora settlements focused on one or more large, separately palisaded men's houses, with women's houses clustered below (where slope permitted) and with seclusion houses—used by women during menstruation and childbirth and sometimes for sanctuary—separated from living areas and usually surrounded by their own fences. The traditional style for all houses is circular, with low grass and timber walls and conical thatched roofs, windowless and tightly insulated against the night cold. Increasingly nowadays, Tairora have adopted rectangular house styles with walls of woven bamboo.

Economy

Subsistence and Commercial Activities. Tairora derive most of their subsistence from a wide variety of gardens. Sweet potatoes are the dominant root crop, although yams and taro are also major sources of carbohydrates, especially in the south. Tairora are sophisticated horticulturalists, employing fallowing, mounding of sweet potatoes, and ditching of gardens; in the south, elaborate systems of bamboo pipes are used to irrigate taro gardens. Other important crops include legumes, maize, bananas, sugarcane, and leafy greens; tree crops include pandanus nuts and, in some areas, betel nuts. Domestic pigs are a major source of protein, but they are generally killed and the pork exchanged only on ceremonial occasions. Hunting and collecting also yield food, especially in the more heavily forested south where both game and wild plant foods are more abundant; everywhere, however, game has special salience in rituals and ceremonial prestations. The forests, and to a lesser extent the grasslands, also serve as the source of countless raw materials for manufacture, medicines, and ornamentation. In recent decades various cash crops have been tried by Tairora, with coffee being the most successful; in the north, cattle raising has also become an important source of monetary income.

Industrial Arts. Apart from structures, such as palisades, fences, bridges, and houses, a partial inventory of locally produced goods includes weapons (bows, arrows, clubs, spears [in the north], and shields); implements (digging sticks, wooden spades [in the north], adzes, knives, and daggers); and string bags, pandanus sleeping mats, and bamboo cooking tubes (with wooden cooking cylinders also manufactured in the north). Locally made traditional clothing for both sexes includes skirts or sporrans made of pounded bark strips or rushes and, in the north, wooden "codpieces" for men.

Trade. From neighbors at lower elevations to the east, Tairora obtain black palm for arrow shafts and bow, adze, and axe staves; bark cloth for capes worn by both sexes; and shells for ornamentation. Stone adze blades were traded in from any sources available and, in the south, Tairora were important distributors in the Baruya salt trade. Major export items include rush skirts, string bags, and plumes. By the 1980s, many of these items had been replaced by Western goods that were now available in indigenously owned trade stores.

Division of Labor. Except for modern skills such as auto mechanics or carpentry that are known only to a few, there is no occupational specialization, although some individuals are renowned as exceptionally good weavers of string bags or arrow makers. Each man is able to build houses and fences, clear garden land, hunt, and fashion his own weapons and implements, just as all women are gardeners and skilled in making string bags, sleeping mats, and items of clothing for both sexes. Construction tasks are male responsibilities, as are clearing garden land, fencing, and ditching; women are charged with planting, weeding, and harvesting of crops, with the exception of tree crops, bananas, sugarcane, yams, and taro, which are the province of males. Both sexes collect wild plant foods opportunistically. Cooking of vegetable foods is largely a female task, while men generally both butcher and cook domestic and wild meats.

Land Tenure. In principle, all land, whether for gardening or forest resources, is held by patrilineal descent groups, though residence in itself usually confers rights of usufruct. However, when land disputes arise, claims to land associated with either one's father's or mother's clan are usually stronger than those based solely on residence, with elders called upon to authenticate both genealogy and history of use. Watercourses, paths, fences, and hamlets or village open areas are generally considered the common property of all who live in a settlement.

Kinship

Kin Groups and Descent. A patrilineal ideology ascribes at birth membership in one's father's lineage and clan, although residence in itself can blur such distinctions, especially in the north, where immigrants (such as refugees in time of war) acquire the status of "quasiagnates." Patriclans are named and exogamous but not localized; while land in any settlement is associated with particular clans, clan segments may reside (and claim land) in a number of neighboring settlements. Clan members seldom act as a unit in ceremonies, exchange, or war.

Kinship Terminology. In the north, kin terms are of a modified Iroquois type, with collaterals in Ego's generation other than mother's brother's children, and all collaterals in the first descending generation other than sister's children, being terminologically equivalent to a man's own children. Farther south, terms for mother's kin show Omaha-type tendencies; however, choices of terms are complicated by bridewealth exchange.

Marriage and Family

Marriage. Pairs of clans often have long-standing patterns of intermarriage, with adult males negotiating complex bridewealth payments. Settlements have high rates of endogamy, but this practice is not an explicit preference; substantial numbers of women in-marry from enemy groups, with marriages in the past sometimes incorporated into peace-making ceremonies. Individuals of both sexes typically are assigned likely spouses while still in childhood, with formal betrothal deferred until young adulthood. Virilocality is the norm, with a new bride usually moving into the house of her groom's mother, but exceptions can occur. Polygyny is allowed, though few men have more than one wife; cowives typically live in different hamlets and usually object strongly to their husbands' polygyny. Divorce or extended separation is not unusual, but they are formal options only for men; traditionally, a married woman's only alternatives to an unhappy marriage were running away or suicide. Remarriage for both divorcées and widows is usual; there are very few permanent bachelors and virtually no women (apart from albinos and lepers) who go through life unmarried.

Domestic Unit. Traditionally, out of concern for the supposed debilitating effects of contact with women, all males past the age of 10–12 lived in men's houses; a family household would include one or more adult women (sometimes a mother and daughter, or sisters), their uninitiated sons, and unmarried daughters. Variants include households of several nubile young women or young bachelors. Increasingly, especially in the north, Tairora are adopting the practice of nuclear families residing in a single household. Husbands and wives seldom form a work unit, except in early stages of garden preparation.

Inheritance. Upon death, gardens and movable property ideally are claimed by adult unmarried children; otherwise they are divided among married sons.

Socialization. Responsibility for nurturing and socializing young children primarily falls on the women and older girls of a household; once male children are initiated and move into their fathers' men's houses, their socialization is largely taken over by adult males. Girls work side by side with their mothers from an early age, while boys are allowed to roam freely with age mates until adolescence. Distraction and oral admonishments are used rather than corporal punishment for young children, but older boys are sometimes disciplined severely in the men's house. Nowadays, and especially in the north, sizable numbers of children attend mission- or government-run schools, where parental supervision is limited.

Sociopolitical Organization

Social Organization. Especially in the north, Tairora extend genealogical metaphors widely, qualifying strict reckoning of descent and kinship as social identities are based more importantly in residence. Also in the north, clans are linked in phratries, forming near-connubia within which warfare is disallowed; in the south, clans may be joined in exogamous, nonwarring pairs. Coresidents of a settlement act as a unit more often than do kin groups in warfare, ceremonies, and intercommunity exchanges. An egalitarian ethos pervades social life, with an emphasis on individualism, though associations are strong among age mates of either sex.

Political Organization. Traditional leadership was of a big-man or "strong-man" type, with individuals attaining stature through warfare and management of affairs between communities. In recent decades, officials appointed by the Australian administration have been replaced with elected members of the provincial government.

Social Control. Disputes arise most commonly over sorcery accusations, failures to meet compensation and bridewealth obligations, marriage arrangements, land, depredations of pigs, and, nowadays, coffee theft. Parties are usually supported by kin and age mates in informal moots. Increasingly, disputes unresolved through informal means are referred to elected officials or formal courts in Kainantu.

Conflict. Physical violence is strongly discouraged within one's clan, but otherwise it is not infrequent, with domestic violence being especially common. Traditionally, warfare was endemic throughout Tairora, and it has seen a resurgence in the 1980s. Each settlement has "traditional enemies" among its immediate neighbors, though enmity/amity relations are subject to alternation over time, with periods of peace effected through formal ceremonies that often include intermarriage. Competing claims to land are less often the source of intercommunity conflict than are murder and purported sorcery attacks.

Religion and Expressive Culture

Religious Beliefs. The Tairora cosmos is filled with supernatural beings of a wide variety, including ghosts, monstrous anthropomorphs, localized nature spirits, and zoomorphic forest spirits. Men's house rites draw on a generalized force available through ancestors, and diverse types of magic are employed by individuals. Since 1940 in the north and the 1960s in the south, a variety of Christian missions have operated, with a decreasing north-south gradient in numbers of converts.

Religious Practitioners. Most adult Tairora have knowledge of spells and magic to meet their individual needs. Knowledgeable elders of both sexes conduct rituals and ceremonies at the hamlet or settlement level, and some individuals are noted diviners and shamans. Nowadays, too, many settlements have resident mission catechists.

Ceremonies. Life-cycle ceremonies include feasts for babies after they emerge from seclusion houses; septum- and ear-piercing (for both sexes, traditionally); first-menstruation and nubility rites; a two-stage sequence of male initiation; weddings; and funerals. Seasonal yam and winged-bean festivals and peacemaking ceremonies draw communities together, as did periodic renewal ceremonies in the north. Recently in the north, public community dance festivals have become a source of income, with outsiders being charged admission.

Arts. As with other New Guinea highlanders, plastic arts play a limited role in Tairora artistic life; apart from individual costuming and ornamentation on ceremonial occasions, decoration is largely restricted to string bags, arrows, and shields, though in the north men wore wooden frames with painted bark panels on occasions of public dancing. Jew's harps are played occasionally as private entertainment; otherwise only hour-glass drums supplement the human voice. Several genres of oral literature provide evening household entertainment and instruction during ceremonies.

Medicine. Their natural environment supplies the Tairora with an extensive range of medicines, which most individuals obtain and administer themselves. Some individuals of both sexes are renowned diagnosticians and curers. Nowadays, most settlements have or are near a mission- or government-run medical aid post.

Death and Afterlife. Wakes are held for several days, at the conclusion of which the ghost possesses a local resident who transports it out of the settlement to begin its journey to the land of the dead, located to the northeast in the Markham Valley. There it will live a life that replicates the ordinary world, complete with gardens and pigs. The corpse left behind is traditionally buried in a grave with its individual fence on clan land.

See also Fore, Gahuku-Gama, Gururumba

Bibliography

Grossman, Lawrence S. (1984). *Peasants, Subsistence Ecology, and Development in the Highlands of Papua New Guinea.* Princeton: Princeton University Press.

Hays, Terence E., and Patricia H. Hays (1982). "Opposition and Complementarity of the Sexes in Ndumba Initiation." In *Rituals of Manhood: Male Initiation in Papua New Guinea,* edited by Gilbert Herdt, 201–238. Berkeley: University of California Press.

Johnson, S. Ragnar (1982). "Food, Other Valuables, Payment, and the Relative Scale of Ommura Ceremonies (New Guinea)." *Anthropos* 77:509–523.

Pataki-Schweizer, K. J. (1980). *A New Guinea Landscape: Community, Space, and Time in the Eastern Highlands.* Seattle: University of Washington Press.

Radford, Robin (1987). *Highlanders and Foreigners in the Upper Ramu: The Kainantu Area, 1919–1942.* Melbourne: Melbourne University Press.

Watson, James B. (1983). *Tairora Culture: Contingency and Pragmatism.* Seattle: University of Washington Press.

Watson, Virginia Drew, and J. David Cole (1977). *Prehistory of the Eastern Highlands of New Guinea.* Seattle: University of Washington Press.

TERENCE E. HAYS

Tangu

ETHNONYMS: None

Orientation

Identification. The term "Tangu" generally refers to one of several culturally similar communities living in the Bogia region of the Madang Province of Papua New Guinea. The name also refers to the language spoken by both the Tangu "proper" and certain other related groups.

Location. Tangu live on a series of steep, forested ridges about 24 kilometers inland from Bogia Bay in the northern coastal area of Papua New Guinea, at about 4°25' S by 144°55' E.

Demography. In 1951–1952, the ethnographic present for this report, Kenelm Burridge estimated the Tangu population at roughly 2,000, distributed throughout about thirty settlements of varying size. The population is now approaching 3,000.

Linguistic Affiliation. Tangu is a Non-Austronesian language in the Ataitan Language Family.

History and Cultural Relations

While the Tangu are ethnographically quite similar to their neighbors, they consider themselves to be a distinct polity, tied closely together by kinship, trading, and exchange relationships. Perhaps the most distinctive feature setting them apart from their neighbors is their participation in a disputing activity known as *br'ngun'guni,* in which grievances are aired at public assemblies. European contact with Tangu was first made by German administrative officials shortly before World War I, although the event had relatively little effect on traditional life. Effective "control" was established by the Australians in the 1920s, at which time a Society of the Divine Word mission was also founded. Tangu have been known for participation in cargo cults or millenarian movements under the influence of two messianic leaders: first Mambu, in the 1930s and 1940s, and later Yali, in the 1950s.

Settlements

The Tangu population is roughly grouped into four named neighborhoods. Each neighborhood contains one or more large settlements of some twenty or more houses and several smaller settlements, some comprised of only a few homesteads. Settlements are strung out along a series of steep, interconnected ridges. Garden sites are scattered around the surrounding countryside. Tangu usually have temporary bush settlements associated with hunting and gardening areas far from the main village, and they may live in them for several weeks at a time.

Economy

Subsistence and Commercial Activities. The Tangu are primarily subsistence farmers who practice swidden or slash-and-burn horticulture. Their staple crops include numerous varieties of yams, taro, and bananas, planted in rotation and supplemented with sago and breadfruit, especially during December and January, which are months of relative scarcity of the primary foods. These main crops are supported by sugarcane, coconuts, *pitpit,* gourds, beans, squashes, and greens. Maize, tapioca, sweet potatoes, melons, pumpkins, tomatoes, and other vegetables have been recently introduced. Pigs and chickens are kept domestically, the latter mainly for their feathers. Tangu forage in the forest, and they also hunt wild pigs, cassowaries, lizards, possums, cuscus, wallabies and other small marsupials, and birds. Land animals are usually tracked with the aid of dogs, or caught in snares or traps. Birds are usually shot with bows and arrows. Fish were traditionally netted with hand nets by women, speared by men, or stunned in pools by using poison roots. This life-style of basic subsistence farming, supplemented by some hunting and gathering, is also augmented by migrant or occasional labor for cash.

Industrial Arts. Tangu produce a variety of utilitarian objects used in their everyday lives, including banana-fiber underskirts, pandanus-fiber skirts, woven-cane bands and personal adornments, and pandanus-fiber cord, from which they fashion string bags and fishing nets. They manufacture slit gongs, used for signaling public announcements, and traditional musical instruments including hand drums and Jew's harps. Their only commercial manufactures are clay pots, made with the coil technique, and string bags. These are traded within Tangu and also sold for cash.

Trade. Tangu have extensive trading relations, both among themselves and with neighboring people. Two of the four Tangu neighborhoods specialize in clay-pot making and two specialize in string bag and sago production. These items are traded within Tangu and are also sold to outsiders. The string bags and sago are sold mainly to people from the coast, while the clay pots are sold both to coastal inhabitants and to people from the hinterland. Other traditional items of exchange include hunting dogs, tobacco, and betel nuts. More recently, the mission trade store stocks goods of European manufacture, which are sold or exchanged for local products and services. These items are often exchanged again, typically with hinterland neighbors.

Division of Labor. As in most tribal societies, Tangu division of labor is based on age and sex. Women cook, weed, look after young children, and do certain craftswork, such as making string bags. Men hunt, build houses and shelters, and do other craftswork, such as wood carving. Garden work is carried on by both sexes, although the sexes once again perform slightly different tasks, with men doing most of the heavy felling, clearing, and digging and women doing most of the daily carrying, weeding, and cleaning.

Land Tenure. Land can be "inherited" through either male or female relatives, but the practices governing the actual transfer of land are extremely flexible. Each individual has "claims" on land belonging to his or her relatives, depending on the closeness of those relatives, and the strengths of the competing claims of others. Such "claims," recognized to a greater or lesser extent by the community, are always greater when actually exercised. Particularly strong structural claims can be made by sons on their father's claims, by nephews on their mother's brother's claims, and by husbands and wives on each other's claims. In general, the Tangu have ample land, and they tend to gravitate toward those areas where their claims are most easily exercised and their personal prospects best.

Kinship

Kin Groups and Descent. Perhaps because individual Tangu can choose to exercise their "claims" in a variety of ways, Tangu have no named lineal descent groups. Kinship is based on mutual relationships between people rather than on corporate groups defined by categories of parentage or quasi-parentage. The most important interrelationships are between brothers, sisters, brothers and sisters, friends, siblings-in-law, cross cousins not intending to marry, betrothed couples, and spouses.

Kinship Terminology. Kinship terminology is of the Iroquois type.

Marriage and Family

Marriage. Because of the sexual division of labor in Tangu, there are few unmarried adults. Marriages bring about cooperative exchange relationships between the families of the husband and wife. Ideally, marriages are arranged between the children of people who are already friends or between certain cross cousins. There is a period of formal betrothal lasting for several years, marked by the groom's family presenting a pig, chaplets of dogs' teeth, and other valuables to the wife's family. At first the engaged pair practice avoidance behavior, but later they exchange labor in one another's households. At the wedding itself, the wife's brothers host the husband's family. This practice not only clears the debt created by the betrothal pig and valuables, but it also sets up the exchange relationship between husband and wife's brothers that continues through the life of the marriage. Either partner is free to break off the marriage at will, but the close ties between their families make it difficult to do so without good cause. Men may often seek a second wife, commonly a sister of the first wife, or sometimes a divorced woman. These second marriages are accompanied by relatively little ceremony: a payment to the woman's brothers usually contracts the marriage. Later, a return payment to the husband sets up the exchange relationship and frees the woman to divorce the man if she wishes.

Domestic Unit. The basic and most permanent cooperative work group is the household, generally consisting of a man, his wife or wives, and their natural and adopted children. Occasionally an aging parent of either spouse may reside with them, but households are typically small and simply constituted.

Inheritance. Among the most important things that can be inherited are land claims and friendship relationships. These pass from parents of either sex to all of their children. People of the same sex, whose parents were friends, are expected to be friends. Land claims and personal relationships can also be inherited from other close relatives. As with land claims, people usually inherit more friendship relations than they can actually use, and they choose to activate those they find most congenial or most useful.

Socialization. Young children spend most of their time with their mothers and mother's sisters for the first few years of their lives. For girls, the natal household is the focus of their lives. They follow a fairly tranquil transition to adulthood, practicing the skills of Tangu womanhood from an early age. They learn the skills and crafts of women from their mothers and aunts: how to cook, carry, collect water, clear brush, and weed; how to make string, skirts, and string bags; how to gather and use wild plants; and how to care for younger siblings. For boys, the path to adulthood is less smooth. When a boy is about 6, he leaves his mother and begins to spend more time with his father, for whom he performs small services, and is taught a variety of skills. He learns about household lands and his father's special talents, such as curing, painting, carving, drumming, dancing, plaiting, building, trapping, or fishing. At the same time, he becomes involved with his mother's brothers, from whom he learns of their land claims and their special skills. Traditionally, at adolescence, boys entered a clubhouse, to be secluded, circumcised, and initiated. With the breakdown of this system, adolescent boys have some difficulties handling the authority of their fathers and mothers' brothers as they come of age, and a period of contract labor is common before marriage. Socialization in sexual matters is provided in part by the *gangaringniengi* or "sweetheart" relationship with a particular cross cousin who, although in a marriageable category, is forbidden as a marriage partner. "Sweethearts" dance, sit together, flirt, and fondle and stroke one another, engaging in love play. Breast and penis stimulation are common, but coitus is formally prohibited.

Sociopolitical Organization

Social Organization. Traditionally, local communities were comprised of two exogamous intermarrying groups called *gagawa.* Households would establish exchange relationships with other households in the opposite group. Ideally, these exchange relationships would continue through time as parents transmitted them to their children. Today, exchange relationships are still of major importance. Through marriage and formal friendships, individuals in different communities are also linked. Thus Tangu society is integrated through mutual relationships between individuals and between families.

Political Organization. Tangu have no chiefs. Instead, groups of households tend to be held together by *wunika ruma,* dynamic and hardworking big-men, who have no specific authority but lead by example and through respect gained in production and oratory.

Social Control. Social control within the group is maintained largely through the institution of br'ngun'guni: debating, talking, and disputing in public assembly. Matters of public concern are brought up and discussed on frequent occasions, and the weight of public opinion is usually enough to make people conform to collective norms of behavior.

Conflict. Conflict within the group often arises out of competition for status. Grievances may relate to competing claims on fishing, hunting and gardening resources, kinship matters, exchange obligations, or allegations of sorcery or trespass. Traditionally, when grievances arose between people whose groups were not sufficiently close to engage in br'ngun'guni, feuds and warfare generally resulted. Warfare with outsiders, such as the Diawat people, who were trying to expand their territory at the expense of the Tangu, was also common.

Religion and Expressive Culture

Religious Beliefs. Tangu believe in a group of divine beings called *puoker,* water beings called *pap'ta,* and ghosts of the dead, who ultimately become ancestral beings. Spirit beings of all sorts are thought to be capable of affecting human affairs, but they are somewhat capricious and difficult to placate.

Religious Practitioners. The nature of Tangu religious practitioners is linked to the belief in *ranguova,* men who practice a combination of sorcery and witchcraft. Ranguova are responsible for inflicting many types of illness and death. Their identity can be determined by dreamer-diviners, and they can be killed by a different sort of specialist.

Ceremonies. Dances and feasts are held frequently to mark a variety of social occasions. Formerly, elaborate ritual accompanied boys' circumcision and also the manufacture and positioning of wooden slit gongs, but these rites are no longer practiced.

Arts. While goods of European manufacture are increasingly taking the place of certain traditional arts, finely produced personal accessories are still made, including banana-fiber underskirts and pandanus-fiber overskirts, bark-cloth breechclouts, woven-cane ornaments and waistbands, and string bags. Slit gongs and hand drums are made, but without the carving, incising, pigmentation, and decoration that they formerly carried.

Medicine. Tangu recognize certain types of sicknesses as physiological and treat them with a variety of medicines. Other illnesses are linked with the activities of ranguova (sorcerers). Such illnesses are "treated" by determining the identity of the sorcerer, exposing him, and forcing him to cease his harmful activities.

Death and Afterlife. In Tangu, death is matter-of-fact, and deceased are buried quickly, often within an hour or two of dying. Traditionally, personal valuables were buried with the corpse. People mourn individually, on slit gongs, when they think of deceased loved ones from time to time. Each individual is thought to have a "soul" or "mind" called *gnek.*

After death, this soul becomes a ghost temporarily, then finally becomes an ancestral spirit.

Bibliography

Burridge, Kenelm (1960). *Mambu: A Melanesian Millennium.* London: Methuen.

Burridge, Kenelm (1969). *Tangu Traditions: A Study of the Way of Life, Mythology, and Developing Experience of a New Guinea People.* London: Oxford University Press.

RICHARD SCAGLION

Tanna

ETHNONYMS: Ipare, Tana, Tannese

Orientation

Identification. Tanna Island is part of the Southern District of Vanuatu, a southwestern Pacific archipelago once called the New Hebrides. James Cook, the first European to visit this part of Melanesia, gave Tanna its name in 1774. "Tanna," in many of the island's languages, actually means "ground" or "land." Cook, pointing downward, no doubt asked "What do you call this [place]?" The Tannese mistook his question just as he mistook their answer. This cross-cultural misunderstanding was the first of many to follow.

Location. Tanna is located at 19° S and 169° E. The island is 40 kilometers long by 27 kilometers wide at its broadest point, with a total area of 561 square kilometers. A well-populated central plateau (Middle Bush) rises in the south to mountains more than 1,000 meters high. The island is mostly tropical forest, except for a grassy plain in the northwest that lies in the rain shadow of the mountains. In the east, a small but continuously eruptive cinder-cone volcano coughs up lava bombs and spreads volcanic ash across the island.

Demography. There are about 20,000 Tannese, 10 percent of whom have left home to work in Port Vila or Luganville, Vanuatu's two towns, and in New Caledonia. The island's population density is around 32.3 persons per square kilometer; the population is growing at a rate of 3.2 percent per year.

Linguistic Affiliation. The Tannese speak five related languages that are syntactically and semantically very similar, differing mostly in phonology and lexicon. They are part of the Southern Vanuatu Subbranch of the Oceanic Branch of Austronesian languages. Most Tannese also speak Bislama (Vanuatu Pidgin English), and some are schooled in English or French as well.

History and Cultural Relations

Although the archaeological record has yet to be fully explored, it is thought that oceangoing Melanesians first landed on Tanna about 3,500 years ago. The island has also experienced considerable Polynesian influence. In fact, Tanna's two nearest neighbors, Aniwa and Futuna, are Polynesian outliers. From the 1860s through 1900, labor recruiters removed more than 5,000 Tannese men to work on plantations in Queensland and Fiji. During these years, too, Presbyterian missionaries opened stations on the island. In mission literature, Tanna was infamous for its resistance to Christianity, but by 1910 the missionaries had succeeded in converting about two-thirds of the population. Mission success correlated with the establishment of joint British and French colonial rule over the archipelago in 1906. Vanuatu remained under this unusual "condominium" form of colonial administration until its independence in 1980. Starting in the late 1930s, a number of island social movements emerged in reaction to foreign rule, and many people quit the missions. The John Frum movement, much influenced by World War II, is the best known of these. A spirit figure, John Frum, counseled people to return to traditional practices and to seek help from American troops. This movement, once a cargo cult, remains an important religious group and political party. Other national political parties are also active on the island. In general, Presbyterians support the Vanuaaku party, while John Frum and "Custom" people (traditionalists) and French-educated Catholics support its rival, the Union of Moderate Parties. This contemporary political opposition reflects an enduring traditional dualism in island culture.

Settlements

The most salient feature in the cultural landscape is the kava-drinking ground. These are forest clearings, shaded by magnificent banyan trees. Men convene there daily to prepare and drink kava (*Piper methysticum*). People also meet there to dance, to exchange goods, and to resolve disputes. Nucleated villages or scattered hamlets are located along the periphery of these circular clearings. At the last official census in 1979, Tanna had ninety-two villages that included 370 hamlets. Most villages are small, averaging about sixty residents. Most families possess one or more sleeping houses, plus a cook house. The traditional thatched house is still common, although many people now also build with corrugated aluminum and cement brick.

Economy

Subsistence and Commercial Activities. The Tannese are swidden horticulturalists. Using hand tools, they clear and burn off plots for yams and taro, ritually the two most important staples. They also grow manioc, sweet potatoes, bananas, and a range of other fruits and vegetables. Thanks to fertilizing ash falls from Iasur volcano, garden-plot fallow time is quite short. Domestic animals include pigs, dogs, fowl, and also introduced cattle and horses. Coastal villagers fish and gather reef products, although the Tannese are indifferent fishers. People are engaged primarily in subsistence production, although they also plant cash crops, especially coconuts, coffee, and vegetables. The average family's annual cash income, however, is less than $500 [U.S.].

Industrial Arts. Traditionally, island industrial arts were quite simple, consisting of stone tool making, the weaving of pandanus mats and baskets, and the manufacture of women's bark skirts and tapa belts that once held up men's penis wrappers. Today, a few men earn a little money in cement brick manufacture, automobile repair, etc.

Trade. The island's principal exports are copra and coffee. Its imports include Japanese vehicles, fuel, tools, processed foods, and clothing. Cooperatives and small-business owners operate a handful of trade stores, and women sell produce at several roadside markets. Rudimentary tourism, focused on the volcano, also brings some money into the island.

Division of Labor. Islanders practice a muted division of labor. Men do heavy garden clearing, plant yams, erect house frames, fish beyond the reef, and drive trucks. Women perform day-to-day garden work, cook, wash clothes, and weave baskets and mats. Men, however, also cook, weed gardens, and may wash their own clothes in a pinch. Both sexes, moreover, care for children.

Land Tenure. Every Tannese boy receives a personal name that entitles him to several plots of land near a kava-drinking ground. Women's names have no land entitlements. A name also may entitle a male bearer to perform various ritual acts, to control a section of traditional road, and so on. Every family possesses a limited number of names that are used each generation. If a man has no sons, he adopts boys (or other grown men) by giving them one of his names. In actual practice, the exact connection between a particular personal name and its associated lands is often disputed. Garden land, however, is plentiful, except in a few locales. Moreover, most people neither live nor garden upon their own lands; permission to use another's land is usually readily obtained.

Kinship

Kin Groups and Descent. The most important kin group is the nuclear family. People have a notion of patrilineal descent, and families group into something like patrilineages, localized at kava-drinking grounds. These larger groups, however, are perhaps better called "name sets" rather than lineages inasmuch as new members are recruited by receiving personal names rather than by being born into the groups. A man only becomes a member of his father's lineage if he receives one of its names. Up to half of all men receive names from someone other than their fathers, and thus they may belong to a different name set. Single lineage/name sets are joined into larger groupings, associated with particular places or regions. Finally, each lineage/name set belongs to one or two moieties, Numrukwen and Kaviameta, though today these have only occasional ritual importance.

Kinship Terminology. The terminological system is of the Dravidian type in which every person of one's generation falls into one of four categories: brother, sister, spouse, and brother/sister-in-law.

Marriage and Family

Marriage. Kin terminology reflects the island practice of sister-exchange, bilateral cross-cousin marriage. The ideal marriage partner is a child of one's mother's brother, or father's sister, although many people marry less closely related classificatory cross cousins. The ideal marriage also consists of a sister exchange between two men. Many marriages, in actuality, involve complex transactions in which women are "swapped" among three or more families. Many men obtain a wife by exchanging a classificatory sister or some other female relative. Some promise a firstborn daughter in return for her mother. A concern for balance governs marriage, as it does all other forms of exchange. With sister exchange, every marriage entails another, and divorce is very uncommon. Should a marriage fail, the wife's family must provide the husband's family with another woman in order to maintain the exchange balance.

Domestic Unit. A nuclear family is the basic domestic group that produces and consumes food and other goods. Residence is virilocal. As boys get older, many build their own sleeping houses, although they continue to eat with their parents until they marry.

Inheritance. There are few material goods on Tanna that survive more than one generation. Women inherit little. Men inherit land as well as rights to ritual and medical knowledge from the men who named them, most often their fathers. Men also succeed to the social positions of older namesakes.

Socialization. A child is raised by both parents and, importantly, by older siblings. Disciplining is rarely physical, but rather takes the form of teasing and shaming. Boys are circumcised between 5 and 10 years of age; their emergence from about six weeks of social seclusion is an important ceremonial occasion. Girls' first menstruation is sometimes marked by the gift of pig and kava from their fathers to their mothers' brothers.

Sociopolitical Organization

Social Organization. Two or more lineages/name sets are localized at each kava drinking ground. The men of several neighboring kava-drinking grounds together belong to a named, regional group, of which there are about 115. Kava-drinking grounds across the island are linked by a complex system of traditional "roads" along which men exchange messages, goods, and spouses. This road network, by which each Tannese village is linked to all others, has produced cultural homogeneity across the island, despite linguistic diversity.

Political Organization. Tannese society is hierarchically organized on the basis of sex and age. There are also two chiefly positions at most kava-drinking grounds: the *ianiniteta* ("spokesman of the canoe") and the *ierumanu* ("ruler"). These today have only occasional ritual importance. Among adult men a principle of egalitarianism governs social interaction. A few men, however, enjoy more influence and prestige than others. In the main, these *iema asori,* big-men, are unlike those found elsewhere in Melanesia whose positions depend on economic ability. On Tanna, a village leader owes his status to his age, his ritual and other local knowledge, and to the size of his name set. A second kind of "ideological" big-men are the leaders of the various island-wide political and religious organizations, such as the John Frum and Custom movements.

Social Control. Although national police and island courts operate on Tanna, most disputes are handled unofficially. Avoidance is a common tactic. When people must resolve their differences, they convene a dispute-settlement meeting at a local kava-drinking ground. Here, big-men and involved third parties attempt to establish a social consensus that at least temporarily resolves the problem and ends avoidance between disputants. Resolution is signified by the exchange of pigs and kava between the two sides. Although traditional sorcery is today uncommon, islanders believe that ancestors displeased with conflict may make them sick. A serious illness thus induces people to attempt to resolve outstanding disputes.

Conflict. The root of most conflict is exchange imbalance, particularly within sister-exchange agreements. People also dispute land ownership and boundaries, and disagreements sometimes occur between husbands and wives. Traditional raiding and cannibalism ceased in the early 1900s. In the period leading up to independence considerable social disruption took place but today, aside from occasional fights during dispute-settlement meetings gone awry, the island is remarkably peaceful.

Religion and Expressive Culture

Religious Beliefs. Christianity has merged with—not replaced—the traditional concern with ancestors and spirits. Missionaries proscribed a number of customary practices, including dancing and kava drinking, and reworked local political and economic structures. The John Frum and other movements, drawing upon both custom and Christianity, have added further, syncretic elements to Tanna's religious life. In addition to ancestors, people recognize various spirits associated with particular places, such as the reefs and mountain peaks. The Polynesian Mauitikitiki (Mwatiktiki on Tanna) is also a popular culture hero. John Frum continues his work as a spiritual mediator to the outside world, particularly to America. The John Frum–Custom people of the southwest claim a special relationship with Prince Philip of Britain who is, they maintain, a son of the mountain spirit Kalpwapen.

Religious Practitioners. All men are in contact with their own ancestors. Kava drinkers, spitting out their last mouthful of the drug, utter prayers to surrounding ancestors buried on the kava-drinking ground. A few men and women are known to have particularly good contacts with the supernatural world by way of dreams and various ritual devices. These "clevers" diagnose illness, find lost objects, and so on. Most of the Christian denominations have ordained local pastors. The successful prophets of John Frum and other notable spirits also serve as religious officiants.

Ceremonies. All Tannese ceremonies consist of exchange (of pigs, food, kava, woven goods, and lengths of cloth), kava drinking, and dancing that lasts through the night. Most of them are associated with important events in the life cycle of individuals. The family of the person involved gathers goods to present to his or her mother's brothers, with an equal amount of goods returned when the exchange is later reversed. Two ceremonies, not tied to individual life cycles, function to maintain regional relations. In *nieri,* people of two kava-drinking grounds exchange different kinds of food such as yams for taro. The *nakwiari,* involving several thousand people, is the island's most spectacular ceremony and involves exchange of pigs and kava between two regions, after a night and day of song and dance.

Arts. There is little material art on Tanna. Island aesthetics focus instead on singing, dancing, and body decoration. Although people make panpipes and bamboo flutes, they use no musical instruments to accompany song or dance that, for rhythm, relies instead upon hand clapping and foot stomping. Women paint their faces in mosaics of color that reflect the decorative dyed patterns on the bark skirts they wear to dance.

Medicine. Island etiology cites maleficent spirits and ancestral displeasure to explain many illnesses. Also, an imbalance of body elements may cause disease. Everyone knows at least one or more secret herbal cures for specific ailments, and a few men and women are renowned as particularly astute curers or bone setters.

Death and Afterlife. Important men are buried on the kava-drinking ground; other people are buried in the village. Christian pastors typically officiate at burial. The traditional funeral, however, that takes place a month or so after death is the final exchange between a person's family and that of his or her mother's brothers. Ancestral ghosts go off to a land called "Ipai"; they may also remain close to their old homes, and they are often seen in gardens and the forest.

Bibliography

Adams, R. (1984). *In the Land of Strangers: A Century of European Contact with Tanna, 1774–1874.* Canberra: Australian National University.

Allen, M. R., ed. (1981). *Vanuatu: Politics, Economics, and Ritual in Island Melanesia.* Sydney: Academic Press.

Bonnemaison, J. (1987). *La dernière ile.* Paris: ORSTOM/Plon.

Guiart, Jean (1956). *Un siècle et demi de contacts culturels à Tanna, Nouvelles-Hébrides.* Paris: Musée de l'Homme.

LAMONT LINDSTROM

Tasmanians

ETHNONYMS: None

Orientation

Identification. The term "Tasmanians" refers to the native inhabitants of the island of Tasmania. These inhabitants formed a number of societies and communities, all of which had disappeared as distinct cultural groups by the twentieth century. What is known of the Aboriginal culture is largely the result of archaeological research and reconstructions based on the reports of early European visitors and settlers. The name of the island and its inhabitants is taken from the Dutch navigator, Abel Tasman, who discovered the island in 1642. Despite being extinct, the Tasmanians have continued to draw scholarly and public attention, caused in part by their isolation from other cultures for thousands of years and the Stone Age technology they used when first discovered by Europeans.

Location. Tasmania is an island of some 67,000 square kilometers located about 240 kilometers southeast of mainland Australia, with the two land masses separated by the rough waters of the Bass Strait. Tasmania is a state of Australia. At one time a peninsula of Australia, Tasmania was cut off by rising waters about 7,000 to 8,000 years ago. It is a mountainous island, with a variety of ecological zones, considerable rainfall, and a generally mild climate. Land mammals such as kangaroos, wallabies, and native dogs are relatively abundant as are seals, shellfish, and birds.

Demography. Estimates place the precontact population at from 2,000 to 5,000 individuals.

Linguistic Affiliation. Experts guess that from five to twelve different languages, with some grammatical, phonological, and lexical similarities between them, were spoken by Aboriginal Tasmanians. What relationship those languages had to other Papuan or Australian languages is unknown.

History and Cultural Relations

The Tasmanian peninsula of Australia has been occupied for some 23,000 years. Since the islands separated from the mainland some 7,000 or so years ago, there is little evidence of contact between mainland peoples and the Tasmanians. In fact, it is likely that the Tasmanians were largely isolated until contact with the Dutch in 1642, the French in 1772, and settlement by the English in 1803. The English regarded the Tasmanians as subhuman and hunted them down; the Tasmanians responded by both fighting back and retreating farther and farther inland. In 1835, after repeated attempts by the English to round them up, the 203 surviving Tasmanians were gathered together and resettled on Flinders Island in Bass Strait. Although treated more kindly, their numbers continued to decrease and in 1847 the 40 survivors were again resettled, this time on a reserve near Hobart. The last "full-blood" Tasmanian died there in 1876. While the native languages and culture have disappeared, there are still some few dozen individuals who claim biological links to the indigenous population.

Settlements

It is not clear whether the Tasmanians were nomadic, moving to new encampments every day or two, or transhumant, moving inland in the warm months and to the sea in the colder months. There is some evidence of regional variation in settlement patterns, with groups in the west being more settled than those in the east. In either case, the location of settlements was determined largely by the availability of food. Tasmanian societies were territorial, and trespass into another group's territory usually led to warfare. Shelters for nomadic groups were windbreaks made from bark, while more settled groups lived in communities of beehive-shaped shelters located along the banks of rivers or lagoons.

Economy

Subsistence Activities. The Tasmanians were hunters and gatherers who had no agriculture and no domesticated animals but exploited nearly all animal and plant foodstuffs available to them. Kangaroos, wallabies, wombats, and seals were speared; snakes, lizards, snails, insects, eggs, scallops, and other mollusks were gathered; and root, fungus, berries, and native root crops were picked and dug. There is some evidence of communal hunting of kangaroos and birds and gathering of plant foods. For the most part, however, food acquisition was a matter for the household unit of a man, a woman, and their children. The most interesting and perplexing aspect of Tasmanian subsistence practices was the absence (during the last 4,000 years of their existence) of fishing and consumption of scaly fish. Why they gave up fish is not clear, and a variety of explanations citing religious factors, isolation from the mainland, and the difficulty of catching fish have been suggested.

Industrial Arts. The Tasmanian tool kit was limited largely to objects made from wood, stone, and shell. Wooden spears and throwing sticks were the main weapons, and flaked stone knives and scrapers were used for shellfish gathering and food preparation. Shellfish shells served as cooking vessels, along with kelp baskets and baskets and nets twined from grass, reeds, and bark.

Trade. There is no record of trade between Tasmanian societies nor between Tasmanians and peoples of Australia or other Pacific islands.

Division of Labor. Men made the wood and stone tools, hunted for large animals, and fought in wars with other island societies. Women did most everything else, including building the windbreaks and huts, gathering water, and hunting possums by scaling trees.

Land Tenure. Weapons, ornaments, and other objects could be owned individually, though there was no individual ownership of land. Evidence suggests that each community in each society controlled access to a 300- to 5,600-square-kilometer territory. Use of another community's land without permission was the primary cause of war, particularly between communities from different societies.

Kinship, Marriage and Family

Little is known about Tasmanian kinship and kinship terminology.

Marriage. Marriage was evidently community exogamous and many men captured wives from other communities. Arranged marriages are also reported. Most marriages were monogamous, although older men might have more than one wife. Divorce was allowed, and widows were considered the property of the society into which they married, suggesting the generally lower status afforded women than men.

Domestic Unit. The monogamous or polygynous family (perhaps with an additional relative) was the basic residential, production, and consumption unit. Early reports suggest large families, with later accounts noting frequent abortion and infanticide after contact with Europeans.

Socialization. Children were cared for primarily by their mothers. Both parents were indulgent and physical punishment was not used. The major childhood task for boys and girls was to master the hunting, collecting, climbing, building, and manufacturing skills they would need as adults. At puberty, boys were initiated through a ceremony involving scarification, naming, and the presentation of a fetish stone. There evidently was no comparable ceremony for girls.

Sociopolitical Organization

As noted above, the term "Tasmanians" refers to an unknown number of groups or societies. The societies had no formal leaders nor were they landholding or war-making units. Each society was composed of a number of named communities which were further subdivided into households. Each society had from five to fifteen communities (with from thirty to eighty related members in each), which were the basic landholding and war-making units and were led by an older man renowned for his hunting ability, although he probably had little authority except during warfare. Community affiliation was expressed through shared myths, dances, songs, and hair style. Affiliation with other communities within the society was weak, even though it was expressed by a reluctance to fight against affiliated communities and a greater willingness to allow those communities access to community land. The aged were afforded some prestige, and there is some evidence of three age grades for males, with ceremonial marking of passage into a new age grade.

Social Control. In the absence of centralized leadership, social order was maintained by the community. Individual disputes were often settled by throwing-stick duels and violations of customs were punished by group ridicule. Transgressions against the community were punished by hurling spears at the stationary offender who could try to dodge them only by twisting his body out of the way.

Conflict. War between communities from different societies is reported to have been common, although this may reflect only the postcontact situation. Trespassing and stealing a woman were the major reasons for war, which consisted mostly of surprise attacks and skirmishes and rarely produced more than one death.

Religion and Expressive Culture

Religious Beliefs. Tasmanian religious beliefs focused on ghosts and their influence on the affairs of the living. While they might occasionally be considered beneficial, spirits of the dead were mostly feared and thought to be the source of much harm and suffering. Consequently, burial spots were avoided and the names of the dead tabooed. They also believed in categories of spirits more powerful than ghosts, including a thunder demon, a moon spirit, and harmful spirits who occupied dark places such as caves and tree trunks. Magic and witchcraft were important and death and sickness were always attributed to the action of evil spirits or witchcraft. The bones of the dead and certain stones were believed to be imbued with protective, curative, or malevolent powers.

Ceremonies. Community dances were an important form of social, religious and artistic expression. Men danced until collapse, while women kept time with sticks and rolled-bark drums. Religious dances were open only to the men; women evidently had secret dances of their own emphasizing women's activities such as digging roots or nursing infants. The initiation ceremony for boys and the age-grade ceremonies were of considerable social importance. Ceremonies marking birth and marriage are unreported, although death was marked as discussed below.

Religious Practitioners. Part-time shamans used bleeding, sucking, baths, massage, and vegetal remedies to cure illness or treat injuries. They also relied on the supernatural, which they reached through possession trance and a rattle made from a dead man's bones.

Arts. In addition to dances, the Tasmanians decorated trees and their huts with charcoal figures of people and objects and sang of the heroic deeds of the singers and their ancestors. The most elaborate form of artistic expression was reserved for body adornment. Men colored their hair and skin with charcoal, clay, and grease and both sexes wore colored feathers and flowers in their hair. Both sexes also scarified their extremities and rubbed charcoal in to produce rows of dark scars.

Death and Afterlife. The deceased was disposed of as quickly as possible, usually by cremation and then burial of the bones and ashes, although some bones might be retained to be worn by relatives. During the night of the burial, the entire community assembled around the grave, where they sat and wailed until dawn. Widows cut and burned their bodies and cut off their hair and placed it on the grave. Each person was believed to have a soul which lived on after death as a ghost. The afterworld was though to be much like the real world, except for the absence of evil.

Bibliography

Jones, Rhys (1974). "Tasmanian Tribes." In *Aboriginal Tribes of Australia,* edited by N. B. Tindale. Berkeley: University of California Press.

Roth, Henry L. (1890). *The Aborigines of Tasmania.* London: Kegan Paul, Trench, Trübner.

Tauade

ETHNONYMS: Goilala, Tauata

Orientation

Identification. Tauata is one of a number of closely related dialects, and the name "Tauatade," which is used by the neighboring Fuyughe to designate the speakers of all these dialects, passed—slightly modified—into official usage as "Tauade."

Location. The Tauade live in the Goilala Subprovince of the Central Province of Papua New Guinea, mainly in the valley of the Aibala River, at 8° S, 147° E. The elevations of this valley range from 600 to 3,000 meters; the lower slopes are grassland, produced by prolonged burning, and the upper slopes are forested. Rainfall averages 254 centimeters per year, humidity is seldom below 75 percent, and the yearly average temperature at 2,100 meters 18° C. The main rainy season lasts from the beginning of December until the end of

May, and the months of June to September tend to be the driest.

Demography. In 1966, the population of the Tauade census districts was 8,661. The precontact population was probably smaller. A number of Tauade have migrated to Port Moresby in recent years.

Linguistic Affiliation. The Tauade language is a member of the Goilalan Family of Papuan languages.

History and Cultural Relations

The first recorded European visitor was Fr. V. M. Egidi of the Sacred Heart Mission in about 1906, and the first patrol by the Australian government was in 1911. Pacification of the area was a very slow process and was not fully accomplished until after World War II. The Sacred Heart Mission came to the area in the 1930s and established a school at Kerau in 1939. The government established a school at Tapini, the Subprovince headquarters, in 1962. Graded tracks, constructed under the supervision of the mission, extend throughout the Subprovince, but there is no vehicular road link with the coast. An airstrip was built at Tapini in 1938 and another at Kerau in 1967; they provide the main access to Port Moresby, approximately 50 kilometers away. There has been considerable labor migration and an influx of trade goods, notably steel axes and other tools, and alternative sources of food, such as rice. Government incentives to raise cattle as a form of income have generally been unsuccessful. Local councils were established in 1963, and in the following year elections were held for the national House of Assembly. Papua New Guinea received its independence in 1975.

Settlements

The typical settlement pattern is one of scattered hamlets with an average population of forty-five and about fifteen houses (fewer today), often located on the crests of ridges near the forest line. The houses, arranged in two parallel rows, accommodate the women and children, while married men and bachelors occupy the men's house at the head of the two rows. In modern times, men's houses have mostly fallen into disuse. In precolonial days, each hamlet was surrounded by a stockade. The space between the houses is used for feasts and dances. The houses are often protected by windbreaks of *Cordyline terminalis.* Hamlets are only occupied for a few years in succession, though the sites themselves are often reoccupied periodically for a long time. Large villages with seventy or more houses are built for ceremonial purposes, but they are only occupied for a few months.

Economy

Subsistence and Commercial Activities. The Tauade are swidden horticulturalists whose main source of food is the sweet potato, of which they grow at least twenty-two varieties. They also grow bananas, sugarcane, some yams, and a little taro. Pandanus nuts, however, are a very important supplement to their diet, since they can be preserved by smoking. Pigs are kept, roaming in the forest and bush, often destroying gardens, and returning to their owners' homes at night for a meal of sweet potatoes. Gardens are prepared when the rains cease, and strong fences are constructed around them to keep out the pigs. The ground for gardens is cleared by fire and, nowadays, with steel axes. In the past, stone adzes and wooden digging sticks were the only tools. The preferred area for gardens is the secondary rather than the primary forest, but grassland is seldom used. There is an ample supply of land, the population density being approximately 7.7 persons per square kilometer. The pandanus tree is the main source of house-building materials: its outer bark is easily stripped off for planks; its leaves, when dry, are an ideal roofing material; and its aerial roots supply tough bindings for the framework of the house. It is likely that hunting—for small animals, cassowaries, and pigs—and collecting were much more important in the past than they are today.

Industrial Arts. In the past, stone was used to make adzes and bark-cloth beaters. Stone has been replaced by steel, and bark cloth by imported textiles. String bags are still made from local plant fibers. No pottery was made, and green bamboo tubes were the only cooking vessels. Bows were made from black palm, while bamboo is used for tobacco pipes and as a simple drum, sounded by dropping the end of the tube on the ground. In general, the traditional material culture was extremely simple.

Trade. There was little or no contact with the tribes on the south coast of Papua, but feathers were traded for various shells—and, later, steel—along a route through Fuyughe country that ended at the upper reaches of the Waria River in New Guinea. Steel tools were already being used in the Aibala Valley at the time of Egidi's visit in 1906.

Division of Labor. Men are responsible for felling trees, clearing land for gardens, erecting fences, climbing the pandanus trees to cut down the nuts, and house building. Men plant taro, yams, sugarcane, bananas, and tobacco. Women plant sweet potatoes, and most of the work in the gardens is done by women, who also carry the harvested pandanus nuts home in their string bags and collect dried pandanus leaves to bring to a hamlet where a new house is being built. Women also care for the pigs.

Land Tenure. There are roughly demarcated areas of land belonging to each clan, and it is said that the clan ancestors who first cleared the forest thereby established their ownership of the land and passed on these rights to their descendants. But permission to use clan land has been given to many cognates, affines, and friends over the course of time, and this practice has thus also established inheritable rights of use. Customary rights to make gardens on the land of a clan that is not one's own need to be exercised from time to time if they are to be respected. In practice, therefore, since there is an abundance of land and since use rights have been so diffused, people are able to make gardens with considerable freedom. Gardens are made by groups of friends, and often different groups will be involved in making gardens simultaneously. There are no clearly bounded plots of land owned by individuals that can be inherited. Rights of use in land are also transmitted through women, so that men may make use of the land rights of their wives and mothers. Pandanus trees are owned and inherited in a totally different manner from land. Here the laws of ownership hold—as opposed to rights of use—and the model of hereditary, clearly demarcated plots of land can be applied quite realistically. The pandanus forests are composed of many named areas, and within these areas are the plots of the owners marked by *Cordyline* at strategic intervals.

Kinship

Kin Groups and Descent. There is no word in the Tauade language to denote "kin" as distinct from affine or cognate. Nor are there generic terms for "clan" or "lineage," but there are named groups of kin, traditionally descended from a founding group of ancestors, that it is appropriate to call clans, and the reckoning of descent is patrilineal. This is not, however, a strict, jural principle, but rather it seems to be a result of the fact that influence and cooperation are organized in terms of social relationships between people. So it is possible for a person to claim membership in more than one clan. Clans not only claim tracts of land; each clan has a cave in which the bones of ancestors were deposited. (Today, burial in cemeteries is compulsory.) Very few marriages take place within clans, and homicide within clans seems not to occur. Clans are not formally subdivided into lineages, although important ancestors within the clan are genealogical reference points for their descendants.

Kinship Terminology. The terminology is of the Iroquois type.

Marriage and Family

Marriage. About 10 percent of men have more than one wife; relations between cowives are frequently hostile, and only men of high status succeed in maintaining stable, polygynous unions. By far the greatest proportion of divorces occur as the result of men taking second wives. First marriages are arranged by the woman's father or brother, and the ideal form of marriage is sister exchange, though this ideal is uncommon in practice. Infant betrothal was customary and the marriage was completed when the girl attained maturity. Bride-wealth was paid at this time and continues to be an important feature of marriage. Adultery is extremely common, and compensation is often offered and accepted by the husband, but some men attack adulterers if they catch them in the act. Patrilocality is the dominant form of marital residence, but it is normal for a man to live with his wife's relatives for several years to establish good relations with them. Only about 20 percent of marriages are within the "tribe" (see the section on social organization), and while some of these marriages are between members of fairly hostile tribes, intermarriage tends to be inhibited by a high level of hostility.

Domestic Unit. The basic unit of production and cooperation is the nuclear family.

Inheritance. There are no bounded plots of land that can be treated as private property; houses are impermanent; and a man's pigs are slaughtered at his funeral feast. Pandanus trees are the only real property of any significance that can be inherited. Normally this inheritance is through the male line—though men may also inherit use rights through their mothers—but if a man has no sons, his trees may be inherited by a daughter.

Socialization. Parents are kind and indulgent to their children, and relations within the family are close and affectionate. In the traditional society, boys at puberty were subject to seclusion for a few months, during which they were beaten to make them fierce. Some children now attend the mission or government schools.

Sociopolitical Organization

Social Organization. The Tauade are divided into a number of autonomous named groups inhabiting the spurs between major streams on the side of the valleys. It is convenient to refer to these groups as "tribes," and their average population is about 200. Tribes are divided into several named clans, who live dispersed in hamlets—usually about five or six in each tribe. Hamlets comprise groups of brothers, often with their fathers and mothers if these are still alive, and these groups are linked by cognatic and affinal ties or by friendship alone. Men frequently move from one hamlet to another and to other tribes, but there are norms of cooperation between hamlet members and fighting is rare. Relations between members of different hamlets are frequently hostile.

Political Organization. In each hamlet there is at least one big-man with his supporters, who may include agnates, cognates, affines, and friends. The functions of the big-man are to coordinate ceremonies, to make speeches, and to give generously, and in each tribe there is a senior clan whose leading big-man traditionally was responsible for conducting peace negotiations with other tribes when warfare occurred. While the status of big-man is not inherited and depends on personal qualities, it has a strong hereditary component, and in many cases big-men are the sons, grandsons, or nephews of former big-men, whose places they are said to take. Ceremonial exchange of pork is very important in Tauade society, and big-men take a leading part in this practice, but they are not the managerial figures described in the ethnography of highland New Guinea. Some of them were war leaders, but this position was not essential to becoming a big-man. At the other end of the social scale are "rubbish men," who are usually bachelors (because they are unable to attract wives), poor, and regarded as mean and useless members of society. In traditional times, they were killed with relative impunity, unlike the big-men whose deaths always produced large-scale vengeance.

Social Control. Big-men have no judicial authority, and while they may be able to persuade a supporter to pay compensation, they have no authority to settle disputes. Disagreements are extremely frequent, since the Tauade are very sensitive to insult, and there was a high level of violence in the traditional society over pigs, women, theft, and other provocations. In the case of disputes within the family, the relatives of the husband and wife may try to make peace, and residence in the same hamlet restrains disputes fairly effectively. A man's fellow residents will support him if he has a dispute with someone of another hamlet or of a different tribe, and they may even accompany him if he goes to get redress for a stolen wife or pig. They will also put pressure on him to pay compensation if he is the guilty party in a dispute, and they do not feel obliged to risk a fight to defend him in such cases. If a man is injured in some way, he may take immediate physical revenge, delay retribution for years, or ask for compensation. In the case of adultery, such compensation is often paid, but there is no way of legally enforcing claims to compensation except through government courts. Those who are on bad terms avoid one another and live in different hamlets, and these hostilities are often long-standing, so that when the Tauade are asked why they do not live in a single village—which would be quite practicable—they reply "because of our ancestors." In the case of homicide, the murderer often flees to his wife's or mother's tribe and stays there until tempers cool, at which time he offers compensation; if this restitution is accepted he may return to his own tribe.

Conflict. In the traditional society, the murder rate was approximately 1 in 200 per year or even higher, and there was almost as much killing, violence, and theft within the tribes as there was between them. Proximity was the principal cause of this: adjacent tribes on the same side of a river fought most often; tribes on opposite sides of a river fought less; and tribes on opposite sides of the forested mountain ridges fought least. A man who had killed another was entitled to wear a shell homicide emblem on his forehead, and this medal was much admired by women. A man might take vengeance against any member of a tribe that had killed a member of his own tribe (or one of his friends or relatives in any other tribe) so that there were many occasions for vengeance. Those selected as victims were usually weak or insignificant persons whose killing could be readily settled by an offer of compensation; grudges were remembered for many years. The killing of a big-man could start full-scale war between tribes, in which hamlets were burned, gardens destroyed, and many deaths inflicted. Members of a tribe that was losing such a war might disperse to live with their relatives in neighboring tribes, and it was common to show hospitality to those driven out of their tribal land. But tribes usually returned to their land after a year or two, and land conquest was not a feature of Tauade warfare. The bodies of slain enemies from other tribes were often eaten, or they were mutilated to cause distress to their relatives.

Religion and Expressive Culture

Religious Beliefs. The relationship between the "wild" (*kariari*), and the "tame" or domesticated (*vala*), is fundamental to the worldview of the Tauade. The forest is represented in myth as the antisocial opposite to village life, but it is not merely the destructive alternative to the social order—and it is the source of life and of creativity in general. The Tauade have no beliefs in any kind of god, but their elaborate mythology is concerned with the culture heroes, *agotevaun*, who are supposed to have inhabited the country and carved out the valleys before the first human emerged from a rock. The agotevaun were preeminently figures belonging to the wild, with superhuman powers which they used to kill and torment humans, but they also instructed humans in ceremonies, customs, and the making of artifacts. In Tauade myths, women are portrayed as the inventors and sustainers of culture through fire, cooking, betel nuts, string bags, and the useful arts, while men are portrayed as basically destructive. Each natural species of plant and animal is sustained by a supernatural prototype, often in the form of a rock, and if this prototype were destroyed the species would die out. The big-men are thought to partake in some aspects of this power, which emerges in generation after generation to sustain the people. In traditional times, when a big-man died his body was placed in a sacred enclosure, hidden from women, in which a bullroarer was swung. The same enclosure was also used for the initiation of boys, if suitable numbers were ready for it. Seclusion lasted for three or four months; the boys were fed special food to make them tough. They danced inside the enclosure and were beaten with nettles to make them fierce. The cult of the dead was extremely important. Bodies of big-men were placed in elevated baskets within the hamlets to rot, while the bodies of ordinary people were buried. When decomposition was complete and the bones and skulls were collected, a great feast and dance was organized and the bones of the dead were carried in the dance to honor the ghosts. The bones of big-men were then deposited in the branches of oak trees and those of ordinary people in one of the clan bone caves. The Tauade also believe in a number of spirits, almost all of which are malevolent and which inhabit streams, rocks, trees, and other natural features.

Religious Practitioners. Some men are supposed to be powerful sorcerers, but there is no social category of sorcerer or diviner. Some use is made of magical substances and spells, but the practice of magic is not an important aspect of Tauade life.

Ceremonies. The elements of Tauade ceremonies include: the killing of pigs; the distribution of pork and garden produce, especially yams, taro, and pandanus nuts; speeches; and dancing (when guests from other tribes are invited). Small ceremonies are held within the tribe for various rites of passage, especially at death, but the largest and most important ceremonies are the large pig killings organized by the whole tribe to honor their dead. These rituals are arranged by the big-men, who invite many other tribes (often hostile). Thus there is a strongly agonistic quality in these occasions, as the hosts try to impress their guests by their generosity, the splendor of the dance village and men's house, and the speeches of the big-men (in the native language, "to make a speech" is literally "to boast"). Dancing that lasts all night is a feature of such occasions, as a means by which hosts and guests compete in displays of stamina, and the ceremony concludes with the slaughter of large numbers of pigs. Elaborate platforms are built for the speeches, and the dance villages for these occasions may have more than seventy houses, with a very large and decorated men's house.

Arts. The use of feather ornaments in dances is the only significant expression of visual art among the Tauade. Singing is also a prominent feature of dances. They are familiar with a large variety of string figures, which are a very popular form of amusement.

Medicine. Traditionally, plants were used as abortifacients and for the treatment of some diseases, and there were also a number of magical remedies.

Death and Afterlife. Tauade believe that a person consists of flesh, energy or strength, and a soul, which becomes a ghost after death, while flesh rots and energy disappears. The world of the ghosts in some accounts is a reversal of the world of the living. Their food stinks, they sleep in the day and wake up at night, and so on. Ghosts are encountered in dreams but not apparently in waking life. There is no belief that the ghosts of big-men and rubbish men go to different places after death.

See also Mafulu, Mekeo

Bibliography

Egidi, V. M. (1907). "La Tribù di Tauata." *Anthropos* 2:675–681, 1009–1021.

Hallpike, C. R. (1977). *Bloodshed and Vengeance in the Papuan Mountains: The Generation of Conflict in Tauade Society.* Oxford: Clarendon Press.

C. R. HALIPIKE

Telefolmin

ETHNONYMS: Kelefomin, Kelefoten, Telefol, Telefomin

Orientation

Identification. Telefolmin are one of a group of related peoples known as the Mountain Ok or "Min" (after the common suffix for group names). Popular traditions derive the name from Telefolip, the ancestral village of all Telefolmin, which was founded by the culture heroine Afek.

Location. Telefolmin live in the southern portion of the Sandaun (or West Sepik) Province of Papua New Guinea atut 141°30' E, 5° S. There are two main subgroupings of Telefolmin in the Upper Sepik and Donner (or Elip) river valleys, with a small outlying group along the Nena (or Upper Frieda) River.

Demography. The total population is about 4,000, concentrated in the Upper Sepik and Donner river valleys. Since 1982 much of the adult male population has been working at the Ok Tedi mining project in the Western Province.

Linguistic Affiliation. Telefol belongs to the Mountain Ok Subfamily of the Ok Family of Non-Austronesian languages.

History and Cultural Relations

Warfare with neighboring peoples was often intense, and in the nineteenth century the Telefolmin waged a successful campaign of annihilation against the Iligimin, whose lands they settled. Contacts with Europeans date from the early part of this century but only became significant after the U.S. Army Air Force built an emergency airstrip in Ifitaman during World War II. The postwar administration established a patrol post at this site, with the first mission following in the early 1950s. By 1953 an accumulation of grievances led to an attempted rebellion, which resulted in the deaths of some government personnel and the imprisonment of a number of local men. Telefolmin entered the cash economy through participation in plantation labor. Mineral exploration in the early 1970s gave rise to hopes for prosperity that grew with national independence in 1975. In 1974–1975 a new form of spirit mediumship emerged, culminating in the Ok Bembem cult aimed at reestablishing contact with the dead. Ok Bembem subsided, but it was followed in 1978–1979 by the Rebaibal, an evangelistic movement inspired by female mediums possessed by the Holy Spirit. Rebaibal resulted in the destruction of men's cult houses (with the significant exception of Telefolip). Rebaibal's goals included conversion to Christianity, closer ties between men and women, the abrogation of traditional cult practices, and the legitimation of the sale of pork for cash. This movement coincided with the introduction of cash crops and the announcement of plans to go ahead with large-scale mining in the area. With the inauguration of the Ok Tedi project in the early 1980s, large numbers of men left their villages for the high wages offered at the mine site.

Settlements

Permanent villages range in size from about 60 to 300 persons, with an average of just over 200. These villages coexist with a pattern of widely dispersed and shifting garden houses. The system is thus two-tiered, with a constant circulation of people between isolated domestic units and central village sites. Traditionally each village had its own men's-house complex as part of a regional ritual system. Churches now provide a community focus for many villages, while Telefolip retains its traditional cult-house complex. With the mining boom of the 1980s a small but growing "town" has emerged along a roadside strip near the government station.

Economy

Subsistence and Commercial Activities. Swidden cultivation of taro and a number of subsidiary crops (including bananas, sweet potatoes, pandanus, and cassava) provide the basis of subsistence, supplemented by pig husbandry, hunting, and casual collecting. An important feature of the traditional economy was a series of taboos prescribing differential patterns of food distribution. These taboos were abrogated in the Rebaibal movement—a response, in part, to dilemmas posed by the anticipated influx of cash associated with copper mining. Traditional shell valuables tended to circulate mainly in bride-wealth and mortuary payments or in interethnic trade. Results of cash cropping (coffee and chilies) have been disappointing, largely because of poor market access (there are no road links to the outside). The chief source of cash for Telefolmin has been migratory labor, whether on plantations in other parts of the country or, more recently, at the Ok Tedi mine. Nowadays, village people (including women) raise cash through the sale of pork. Small trade stores are common, but only a few local entrepreneurs have had success in business.

Industrial Arts. Traditional industrial arts involve house building and carving. The houses are built on slender piles with elevated floors and thatched roofs, normally with a pair of baked clay hearths set in the floor. Techniques for fence building and house building are similar (walls are fences). Men make arrows that are carved and painted, as are war shields and door boards. In the past, men made woven cane cuirasses, as found in other parts of New Guinea. Most villages have at least one or two returned mine employees who are skilled in carpentry, and many of these men earn supplementary cash by building new-style houses.

Trade. Most Telefol trade was conducted with the Faiwolmin (Fegolmin) to the south and the Atbalmin to the west, with the former playing a larger role. There was occasional trade with the Wopkaimin to the southwest, but only if Telefol traders first passed through Faiwol territory, since the direct route towards Wopkaimin country was blocked by the Tifalmin, enemies of the Telefolmin. For the Telefolmin, trade and warfare were generally incompatible, so there was virtually no exchange between Telefolmin and their enemies (Miyanmin, Tifalmin, Falamin, Enkayaakmin, etc.). After the cessation of warfare, Telefolmin began intensive trade with the Tifalmin and Wopkaimin, since the latter were on a direct route to the path of shells making their way into the interior from the south coast via Ningerum.

Division of Labor. Both sexes participate in gardening, though to differing extents. Men are traditionally responsible for forest clearance and fencing, while women and children bear the major burden of weeding. Planting and harvesting are done by both sexes and by young and old alike. Pig rearing is primarily a woman's task, as is the collection of frogs and other small fauna; hunting is a male occupation. With the advent of Ok Tedi, however, hunting has virtually lapsed as a subsistence pursuit, while pig rearing has been dramatically intensified with the sale of pork for cash. Given the high level of male absenteeism, many previously masculine tasks are either being abandoned or are now taken up by women. Thus it has become common for women to clear their own gardens without male assistance, and gardens are only rarely fenced. Older people and women gain access to cash through pork sales, bride-wealth payments, and remittances from mine workers.

Land Tenure. Rights to garden land in named tracts of bush are conferred either by first clearance or bilateral inheritance. Both men and women have independent land rights that must be maintained by repeated clearance and cultivation. These rights are individualized, and there are no collective blocks of land, although full siblings have similar patterns of holdings. Because Telefol agriculture puts a premium on cultivation in different altitudinal zones, most people have claims scattered in several different locations. Claims to land in respect to hunting are much more diffuse and apply to large stretches of bush vaguely associated with villages or clusters of villages. Disputes over hunting rights were traditionally a source of tension between Telefolmin and neighboring peoples.

Kinship

Kin Groups and Descent. There are named and overlapping cognatic stocks; these stocks are nonlocalized and nonexogamous and have no corporate features apart from a common tale of origin. Although village endogamy produces inwardly reticulating kin networks, there are no formal kin groupings as such. Male action sets are referred to as *niinggil,* notionally "brothers." Incest regulations are defined with reference to the bilateral kindred within first-cousin range. There are ritual moieties associated with the men's cult, but they operate independently of kinship.

Kinship Terminology. Telefol kin terminology is a variant of the Iroquoian type in that it departs from usual forms by differentiating patrilateral from matrilateral parallel cousins. Terms for the first ascending generation are bifurcate-collateral, with parents' same-sex siblings differentiated by seniority. Siblings are differentiated by sex and seniority and are distinguished from cousins. There are separate terms for three types of cousin: patrilateral parallel cousins, matrilateral parallel cousins, and cross cousins. All kin of descending generations are designated by a single term, though optional distinctions can be made. In addition to these terms, Telefolmin also employ more complex terms for varying combinations of individual kin.

Marriage and Family

Marriage. Traditionally, marriage was by sister exchange accompanied by a small bride-wealth of shells matched by a return payment of pork. Marriages were ideally between fellow villagers, though intervillage marriages sometimes occurred. Divorce was relatively easy and frequent, with an attempt to allocate children equally to the mother and father after separation. There has been a progressive trend towards monetization of bride-wealth, while government policies forbidding coercion of brides have made sister exchange difficult to enforce. Contemporary marriages are less likely to have been arranged than in the past, often take place between villages (with virilocal residence), and almost always include a bride-wealth ranging from several hundred to several thousand kina (one kina-approximately $1.50 U.S.) in value.

Domestic Unit. The domestic unit is a two-generation nuclear family, usually allied with another such family to form a joint household; dwelling houses normally have two hearths, one for each family. The component families of a joint household are most often related through brother-sister or brother-brother links. Despite common residence, the families of a joint household have separate sets of land rights and form independent productive units.

Inheritance. Rights to garden sites are bilaterally inherited, with an equal division between siblings of both sexes. Children may in principle inherit shell valuables and pigs, but these items tend to be dispersed to more distantly related claimants in the course of mortuary rites. No clear precedent has emerged for the inheritance of modern houses built of permanent materials.

Socialization. Early socialization is in the hands of mothers, although fathers and elder siblings (especially sisters) also play a role in caring for small children. Girls grow into adult roles early. Traditionally, boys underwent a series of initiations from the age of about 7 until their late twenties; these initiations had been discontinued for some time, but they were revived in the late 1980s. Since the 1970s a number of children attend public schools, and there are signs of increasing differentiation between school-educated Telefolmin and others.

Sociopolitical Organization

Papua New Guinea is an independent country with a Westminster form of government. Telefolmin and their neighbors are represented by elected members at national and provincial levels.

Social Organization. The endogamous village is the basic unit of social organization and was traditionally tied to the men's cult, which was structured in terms of initiation levels and ritual moieties. In contrast to other New Guinea societies, exchange traditionally played a minor role in intergroup relations, which were instead organized through male initiations centered on Telefolip. Today, church groups are important at the village and intervillage level. Traditional social organization emphasized egalitarian values associated with a community differentiated by ritual knowledge rather than wealth, and one issue now facing Telefol society is the accommodation of wealth differences within small communities. At present, the general tendency seems to be to emphasize conjugal ties and the nuclear family while restricting the claims of less closely related kin.

Political Organization. There are no formal political offices at the local level apart from elected village councillors and ward committee members, who have only marginal influence on village affairs. In the past prominent men (*kamookim*) held some sway, particularly in fights with enemies, but even their influence was minimal. Despite this, Telefolmin displayed a remarkable degree of unity, which is largely attributable to common ritual ties to Telefolip. Telefolmin were unusual among New Guinea peoples for forbidding warfare within their ethnic group; however, they often combined en masse against outside enemies, as in the case of the extermination of the Iligimin. More recently, Telefolmin have spearheaded movements toward the creation of a "pan-Min" political identity in negotiations with the central government concerning the Ok Tedi mine.

Social Control. There is little exercise of authority, even on the part of parents over children, and social control is for the most part informally managed through shame and withdrawal of reciprocity. Tact is highly prized, and people avoid giving offense for fear of sorcery. Intravillage disputes generally go unaired; the parties merely avoid each other until matters cool down.

Conflict. Traditionally, warfare only took place between Telefolmin and other ethnic groups (especially Falamin, Tifalmin, Miyanmin, and the now-defunct Iligimin). Tensions between Telefol villages sometimes erupted into brawling, but more often it surfaced in sorcery suspicions. Violence between fellow villagers was and is rare. The government holds village councillors responsible for reporting trouble cases, but such reports are made only when all else fails.

Religion and Expressive Culture

Since the late 1970s the majority of Telefolmin practice a local version of Baptist Christianity. Some older men, and especially the villagers of Telefolip, however, adhere to traditional religious practices.

Religious Beliefs. Traditional ritual knowledge is partitioned along lines of sex, age, and ritual moiety affiliation; cult secrecy is highly developed, with the result that there is great variation in belief. The division in cult lore parallels a ritual division of labor, with the Taro moiety responsible for life promoting (gardening, pig rearing) while the Arrow moiety is responsible for life taking (warfare and hunting). The two most important cosmological figures are Afek and Magalim, the Bush Spirit. Afek founded Telefol culture and the men's cult, and she left a legacy of myths and rituals. She is closely identified with the central cult house at Telefolip, which is held to govern the fertility of taro gardens throughout the region. But while Afek died long ago, Magalim continues to play an active role in Telefol life by disrupting the expected pattern of things. Christians espouse belief in God the Father, Jesus, and the Holy Spirit, who intervenes in human affairs through mediums. Although many beliefs surrounding Afek seem to have been relegated to the past, Magalim remains active in Telefol thought. He is capable of assuming many forms, including posing as the Holy Spirit, and he is often interpreted by Christians as a manifestation of the devil.

Religious Practitioners. Ritual experts officiated in the men's cult on the basis of esoteric knowledge; outside of the cult, seers or diviners diagnosed illness and sorcery. Nowadays village churches are presided over by pastors, and a number of women act as diviners and mediums for the Holy Spirit. Sorcerers are feared, are almost always unidentified, and are generally thought to belong to other Telefol villages.

Ceremonies. Traditional religion revolves around a complex series of male initiations. Senior rites were performed at Telefolip, where they have recently been revived after a long hiatus. All Telefolmin, pagan or Christian, also celebrate Christmas, which coincides with the return of mine workers to their home villages for the holidays.

Arts. Carved and painted shields and house boards are the most prominent forms of visual art. Men's arrow shafts are often intricately carved and sometimes painted, and women's net bags are locally renowned for their quality. Although some individuals are better at these things than others, no craft specialization exists apart from the sexual division of labor.

Medicine. Minor ailments are treated by heating the body with warm stones, rubbing with nettles, and avoiding foods thought responsible for a particular complaint. More serious illnesses are attributed to sorcery, violation of food taboos, cult spirits punishing misconduct, attacks by the Bush Spirit (Magalim) or, nowadays, the Holy Spirit. Such matters were usually determined by diviners; since the Rebaibal, female mediums also diagnose illness and often prescribe a course of treatment involving prayer and changes in the patient's pattern of activities. Most villages are also in close proximity to rural aid posts where routine problems are dealt with. More difficult cases are brought to the government hospital or the Baptist maternity clinic.

Death and Afterlife. Burial was by exposure on a raised platform, often in or near a garden of the deceased. Traditional ideas hold that ghosts depart for an underground land of the dead, where they have no further contact with the living. Those killed in warfare, however, were inimical to the living and returned as fruit bats to raid gardens. In addition, the bones of noted warriors, gardeners, and pig rearers were retrieved as men's cult relics. These relics were the locus of the spirits who voluntarily remained among the living to promote village welfare in return for pig sacrifices and the observance of food taboos. The Australian administration prohibited exposure burial in the 1950s, and since then Telefolmin have buried their dead in village cemeteries. Contemporary beliefs assign the souls of pagans to the traditional land of the dead, while Christians go to heaven.

See also Miyanmin

Bibliography

Craig, B., and D. Hyndman, editors (1990). *The Children of Afek: Tradition, Place and Change among the Mountain Ok of Central New Guinea*. Oceania Monograph no. 40. Sydney: Oceania Publications.

Jorgensen, Dan (1980). "What's in a Name: The Meaning of Meaninglessness in Telefolmin." *Ethos* 8:349–366.

Jorgensen, Dan (1981). "Life on the Fringe: History and Society in Telefolmin." In *The Plight of Peripheral People in Papua New Guinea,* edited by R. Gordon, 59–79. Cultural Survival Occasional Paper no. 7. Cambridge, Mass.

Jorgensen, Dan (1983). "Mirroring Nature? Men's and Women's Models of Conception in Telefolmin." *Mankind* 14:57–65.

Jorgensen, Dan (1985). "Femsep's Last Garden: A Telefol Response to Mortality." In *Aging and Its Transformations: Moving toward Death in Pacific Societies,* edited by D. A. Counts and D. Counts, 203–221. Lanham: University Press of America.

DAN JORGENSEN

Tikopia

ETHNONYM: Nga Tikopia.

Orientation

Identification. The name "Tikopia" (sometimes written "Tucopia" by early European voyagers), given to a small island in the Solomon group, is also applied by the inhabitants to themselves. The expression, glossed as "we, the Tikopia," is commonly used to differentiate themselves from the people of other islands in the Solomons and elsewhere.

Location. Tikopia is a little, isolated, high island, primarily an extinct volcano with fringing coral reef, rising to a peak of 350 meters but extending only 4.6 square kilometers. It is in the southeast of the Solomons, at 168°50' E and 12°18' S. Historically, until the mid-1950s, the Tikopia people occupied only this island. But then, stimulated by the pressure of the population on the food supply and by a desire for experience of the outside world, Tikopia people began to settle in groups elsewhere in the Solomons. Now the substantial settlements abroad include Nukufero in the Russell Islands, Nukukaisi (Waimasi) in San Cristobal, and Murivai in Vanikoro. All Tikopia live in a tropical climate, with alternating trade-wind and monsoon seasons; during the latter their homes are subject to periodic hurricanes (tropical cyclones).

Demography. About half a century ago Tikopia had a dense population, about 300 persons per square kilometer. This density caused anxiety among the people's leaders, who feared food shortages. (In 1952–1953 a famine occurred as a result of a tropical cyclone.) In 1929 the population was about 1,270; by 1952 it had risen to about 1,750. But by about 1980, through emigration, the population on Tikopia Island had been reduced to about 1,100, while another 1,200 or so Tikopia lived in the external settlements and around Honiara, the capital of the Solomons. There is much interchange of population between the settlements and Tikopia Island.

Linguistic Affiliation. The Tikopia are Polynesian in language and culture, their language being assigned to a Western Polynesian grouping. But from neighboring peoples they have acquired some Melanesian loan words as well as other cultural items. Tikopia has no dialects. But as a result of external contact many Tikopia now speak English and all can use "pijin."

History and Cultural Relations

From recent archaeological research it appears that Tikopia has been occupied for about 3,000 years. Three phases of traditional culture have been distinguished. The earliest (c. 900 to 100 B.C.) used locally made sand-tempered earthenware of Lapitoid type; the second (c. 100 B.C. to A.D. 1200) probably imported its pottery, of more elaborate style, from the New Hebrides (Vanuatu) to the south. In the latter part of the third phase (c. A.D. 1200 to 1800) no pottery was used at all. Diet changes were marked. In the first two phases pigs, fruit bats, and eels were eaten. By the end of the last phase, into the historical period (c. A.D. 1800 to present) no pigs were kept and bats and eels were regarded with aversion as food. The third traditional phase was seemingly the result of a separate immigration and bore a more markedly Polynesian character. It is clear that over the whole period of occupation Tikopia people have had irregular, infrequent, but sustained cultural relations with Polynesian and Melanesian peoples in other islands around, by arduous, often dangerous canoe voyages. European contact began with a sighting of the island by Spanish voyagers in 1606, and was renewed in the early nineteenth century by visits of Peter Dillon and Dumont d'Urville and by later calls of labor recruiters and missionaries. Only toward the end of the century did the British government claim control over Tikopia; this control was exercised only rarely until after World War II, during which Tikopia remained undisturbed. Since then both mission and government contacts have been fairly regular, though often interrupted by poor sea communication.

Settlements

The population is distributed in more than twenty nucleated villages, situated around the sandy coastal strip at the base of the hills; there is no settlement on the rocky northern coast. Houses are still of traditional pattern, built directly on the ground in rectangular shapes, with low palm-leaf thatched roofs on a timber frame, and doorways to be entered only on hands and knees. Earth floors are covered with plaited coconut-palm-leaf mats. Houses in a village are set irregularly, in no formal pattern, with canoe sheds adjacent, giving easy access to the sea. In the settlements abroad, housing is often of traditional style, but modern types also occur.

Economy

Subsistence and Commercial Activities. On the island, Tikopia are primarily agriculturalists and fishers. Crops include taro (*Colocasia*), manioc (cassava, *Manihot*), giant taro (*Alocasia*), and sago (*Metroxylon*). In the settlements abroad their occupations include agriculture, plantation labor, police and hospital work, and schoolteaching. Several Tikopia men have become priests in the Church of Melanesia, and one has become bishop in the diocese of Temotu, in the eastern Solomons. In general, Tikopia have not engaged in commerce.

Industrial Arts. Traditionally, Tikopia men practiced crafts of canoe building and other woodwork, net making, and extraction of turmeric pigment, while women wove mats of coconut-palm leaf and pandanus leaf and beat out from the inner bark of a tree (*Antiaris toxicaria*) the bark-cloth garments and blankets used by both sexes. A few such objects are now made for sale to tourists who travel on the rare vessels that call at the island, but there are no industrial arts of significance.

Trade. Archaeological and ethnographic records indicate that since archaic times Tikopia residents have engaged in sporadic trade with neighboring island communities, receiving items such as arrows and shell ornaments from Melanesian sources and fine pandanus mats from the closely related Polynesian people of Anuta in return for turmeric pigment. Trade with Western visitors was historically by barter—steel tools, fishhooks, calico, and tobacco being sought in return for local artifacts and food. But nowadays money is used freely, even in transactions among Tikopia themselves.

Division of Labor. Men do woodwork and go sea fishing in canoes. Women do domestic work, but both sexes tend the earth ovens for cooking. Both men and women fish the reef, men with spears and seine nets, women with hand nets. In agriculture, men do the heavy work of breaking up the soil, both men and women plant, but women do most of the weeding. Specialization was recognised particularly among men (e.g., in canoe building). Men alone could be priests in the traditional religion.

Land Tenure. All the land of Tikopia is divided into orchards (*tofi*) of palms and fruit trees and into open gardens (*vao*), marked off into plots for annual cropping. Every orchard and garden plot is owned as of ancestral right by a distinct lineage group, with titular supreme rights exercised by the clan chief. (A similar system operates in overseas Tikopia settlements that have agricultural lands.) Within the lineage land, rights to produce are held by individual cultivators. By ancient custom, vacant garden land may be used for a season by other than its owners, on payment of a proportion of the crop. Permanent transfers of land from one group to another were rare, but historically transfers sometimes occurred when a chief gave some land to a daughter on her marriage. Sale of land is unknown. No land on Tikopia is held by other than Tikopia people.

Kinship

Kin Groups and Descent. Tikopia society has been divided into a large number of unilineal named descent groups, determined genealogically and tracing ancestry back for up to ten generations. These groups are termed *paito*, a word with a wide range of meanings including "house" and "household." They can be conveniently called lineages. Over time, segmentation can lead to the formation of new lineages, while failure of male heirs leads to lineage extinction. For corporate kin group membership as regards land rights, marriage arrangements, and funeral rites, the principle of transmission is rigidly patrilineal. But the kin bond with mother and mother's lineage is also very strongly held, represented by formal and informal support in a variety of social situations. The importance of this bond is indicated by the term *tama tapu* (literally, "sacred child") applied formally to a child of any woman of a lineage. Members of a mother's lineage rally round their nephew or niece at birth, initiation, illness, or death.

Kinship Terminology. Tikopia kinship terminology is relatively simple with cousin terms of the Hawaiian type. Generation differences are marked: grandparent (*puna*); parent (mātua); father (*tamana*); mother (*nana*); sibling (*taina*, of same sex; *kave*, of opposite sex); child (*tama*); grandchild (*makopuna*). In general the system is "classificatory," putting all kin of the same general type under one term. But distinct terms exist for father's sister (*masikitanga*) and mother's brother (*tuatina*), who have special social roles.

Marriage and Family

Marriage. Modern Tikopia marriage is solemnized by a religious service in a Christian church. But traditionally it was initiated by elopement or abduction of a woman from her father's house to that of her chosen or self-elected husband. Nowadays, as formerly, the crux of the marriage arrangement is an elaborate series of exchanges of food and other property between the lineages of bride and groom, occupying several days. The bride commonly goes to live with her husband, either in his parents' house or in a new dwelling adjacent to theirs. Entry into the married state is marked by assumption of a new name, often that of the dwelling where they live. So if they reside in the house "Nukuora," the husband is known as Pa (Mr.) Nukuora, the wife as Nau (Mrs.) Nukuora. Traditionally, polygyny was permissible, and men of rank did often have more than one wife. No woman could have more than one husband, however. Marriages seem to have been fairly stable. Divorce was rare and adultery by married women was not common, in contrast to the sexual freedom of both sexes before marriage. Infidelity by married men did occur, but if it came to the wife's notice it often seems to have elicited a violent reaction from her.

Domestic Unit. The core of a Tikopia domestic unit is a husband, wife, and children, but ordinarily a household is apt to contain additional kin—an elderly widowed mother, an unmarried sister or brother, a youth or girl fostered from an allied kin group. Occasionally two brothers and their families share accommodations, forming a multiple-family household. Adjacent, kin-related domestic units may share in the preparation of meals, using a common oven house.

Inheritance. Major property (e.g., land, canoes, houses, and house sites) is inherited patrilineally, with the eldest son acting as the main controller and his siblings sharing in rights of use and residence. But sometimes after a man's death his sons may dispute and decide to split the landed property. Smaller items, such as a wooden headrest or shell ornament, may be allocated personally to specific kin by a man before his death.

Socialization. Social control by public opinion has been strong in Tikopia. Although raised permissively, children are very aware of the discipline of their parents and are also trained much by other kin and by peer-group association. Formerly, the educational process was smooth and uninterrupted from birth to maturity; nowadays many children go abroad to school for a period and are exposed to a range of alien influences.

Sociopolitical Organization

Social Organization. A major social division in Tikopia is into four *kainanga* (clans), each an aggregate of half a dozen or so paito (lineages). Each clan is headed by a hereditary chief, with an order of precedence based upon former religious ritual: Kafika, Tafua, Taumako, Fangarere. Crosscutting the clan organization is a local grouping into residential districts. Between the two largest of these, Ravenga on the east side of the island and Faea on the west, there is traditional rivalry, most notably in dancing and political prestige. The Tikopia social system has been asymmetrical in the relative status of men and women. Men have held all positions of political and ritual power, though the influence of women has been strong domestically and in general social affairs. Modern developments, especially in the overseas settlements, have tended to modify, and not necessarily improve, these relations.

Political Organization. Traditionally, Tikopia chiefs held absolute power in extremity over their people, especially over their own clanmembers, though this power could be modified by conventional methods of constraining a chief to respond to public opinion. Chiefs were and still are *tapu* (sacred) and treated with great respect. Formerly, chiefly families tended to form an intermarrying class, but nowadays unions between commoners and the children of chiefs are frequent.

Conflict and Social Control. According to tradition, conflict between individuals and between groups has been common in Tikopia in struggles for land and power, resulting in slaughter or expulsion of sections of the population. Nowadays external government sanctions and the influence of Christianity make such extreme solutions most improbable, and social friction seems to be held in check by a sense of common purpose in the advancement of Tikopia against the outside world. Internally, chiefs exercise their control through executives (*maru*), their brothers or cousins in the male line who act in the chief's name to keep public order. In overseas settlements, men appointed by the chiefs serve as leaders and advisers. In modern times especially, public assemblies (*fono*) are called by maru to hear the instructions of chiefs.

Religion and Expressive Culture

Religious Beliefs. Until the early present century all Tikopia were pagan, practicing a polytheistic religion. They believed in spirit beings called *atua,* a term including ghosts of the dead, ancestors, and spirit powers that had never assumed human form. (These last beings were sometimes termed *tupua,* a word now applied mainly to the Christian God.)

Religious Practitioners. The major practitioners in rites, as priests, were the chiefs of the four clans, assisted by ritual elders who were the heads of the most important lineages. By about 1923 about half the Tikopia population became Christian, under the aegis of the Melanesian mission of the Anglican communion (now the Church of Melanesia). This conversion led to friction in the Tikopia community, but the new religion gained ground till in 1956 the last pagans, led by their chiefs, joined the church, thus radically changing ceremonies and practitioners.

Ceremonies. The major spirit beings were worshipped in elaborate rites, with offerings of food and bark cloth. The validating feature of every rite was the pouring of libations of kava, a liquid formed by chewing up the root or stem of a pepper plant (*Piper methysticum*). Every six months ceremonies were performed in which canoes, crops, temples, and people were rededicated to gods and ancestors for protection and prosperity.

Arts. The Tikopia traditionally have had little competence in graphic arts. Their sculpture consisted of simple geometrical forms applied to woodwork. Their great performing art has been dancing, which has inspired a profusion of songs and which is of great social and (formerly) religious importance.

Medicine. Tikopia medical practices were rudimentary, consisting of massage and external application of coconut oil and leaf infusions. These practices were linked with appeals to spirit forces, usually held responsible for illness. The trance—in which a medium, man or woman, explored the cause of illness and suggested remedy, in alleged spirit guise—was a common mode of treatment. Such practices still persist, but modern Tikopia rely largely on Western medicine and hospital treatment.

Death and Afterlife. A death is an occasion for great mourning. Tikopia funeral ceremonies continue after burial of the body with periodic wailing and massive exchanges of food and other goods between the kin groups concerned. Traditional conceptions of the afterlife were vague but involved a notion of a series of heavens on different levels or in different wind points (sources of prevailing winds), each controlled by a major god. There was also an image of a "rubbish pool," into which would be thrown the souls of those who had consistently misbehaved on earth. Life in the afterworld followed much the same pattern as on earth, but with dancing as the main activity. Nowadays,conceptions of the afterlife follow a Christian model, but elements of traditional belief may still persist.

See also Anuta

Bibliography

Firth, Raymond (1936). *We, The Tikopia: A Sociological Study of Kinship in Primitive Polynesia.* London: Allen & Unwin.

Firth, Raymond (1939). *Primitive Polynesian Economy.* London: Routledge.

Firth, Raymond (1970). *Rank and Religion in Tikopia.* London: Allen & Unwin.

Firth, Raymond (1985). *Tikopia-English Dictionary.* Auckland: Auckland University Press.

Kirch, Patrick V., and D. E. Yen (1982). *Tikopia: The Prehistory and Ecology of a Polynesian Outlier.* Bernice P. Bishop Museum Bulletin no. 238. Honolulu.

RAYMOND FIRTH

Tiwi

ETHNONYMS: Bathurst Islanders, Melville Islanders

Orientation

Identification. The word "Tiwi" means "people" in the language of the Aboriginal inhabitants and owners of Melville and Bathurst islands of north Australia.

Location. Melville and Bathurst islands are located 40 kilometers north of Darwin at 11°30' S and 131°15' E. The land (approximately 7,500 square kilometers) is relatively flat with a low central ridge on Melville Island running west to east. Running south to north from this ridge are nine rivers. On Bathurst there is less elevation and draining rivers are small and largely tidal. Along the tidal reaches of rivers and smaller streams are mangrove forests, while mixed eucalyptus and cypress forests characterize much of the uplands. At the freshwater headlands of the larger rivers are small areas of true rain-forest vegetation and along the coast are areas of sandy beach and rocky reef. This varied environment makes for a varied and rich diet for the Tiwi today as in the past. The rainfall is monsoonal, with heavy rains occurring between November and March. Almost no rain falls from June to September; the nights are cool and the air is filled with smoke from the fires of hunting parties. The range of temperatures is only a few degrees during the monsoon season, averaging about 27° C, while during the dry season the range is greater.

Demography. In 1986 the Tiwi population of the islands was about 2,000, divided between the Bathhurst Island township Nguiu with 1,300 and the two Melville Island townships of Parlingimpi and Milikapiti with 300 and 400, respectively.

Linguistic Affiliation. The Tiwi speak a distinctive language, distantly related to other Aboriginal languages. At Nguiu there is a bilingual literature center producing texts in Tiwi language for use in the local primary school. At the Parlingimpi and Milikapiti primary schools education is in English. Both Tiwi and English are used by nearly everyone. However, elders bemoan the loss of fluency in Tiwi among the younger generations. In the past, fluency in Tiwi was an important marker of full adult status, enabling both men and women to participate fully in the important ceremonial activity of composing and singing songs.

History and Cultural Relations

The prehistory of the Tiwi is related to that of other Aboriginal Australians. Recently calculated (1981) dates for earliest signs of human cultural activity are approximately forty thousand years ago. The Tiwi themselves are mentioned in historic records from the early eighteenth century, when they came in contact with Dutch, Portuguese, and British explorers. Prior to these recorded contacts by Europeans, there is evidence for early Chinese and Indonesian contact but no sustained settlement. The first foreign settlement on the islands occurred in 1824, when the British established Fort Dundas near the contemporary Parlingimpi township. After five years of hardship the settlement was abandoned and it was nearly seventy-five years before European settlement was again attempted early in the twentieth century. In 1911, Father Gsell, M.S.C., established a Catholic mission at Nguiu on the southeastern coast of Bathurst Island, and following this development there was a significantly increased amount of contact with White Australians. The township of Parlingimpi, located near the ruins of Fort Dundas at Garden Point, was first established as a government settlement in 1939. In the late 1940s the government settlement was moved from Garden Point to Snake Bay (Milikapiti). Milikapiti continued as a government settlement until the late 1970s, when it became the first of three communities to incorporate as a township.

Settlements

The Tiwi today live in housing largely built by outside contractors during the past ten to fifteen years, each with two to four bedrooms, kitchen and bath, electricity, and plumbing. Some families have built housing for themselves outside of the townships on their own local groups' land. What they gain in "rural" peace and quiet they lose in proximity to school, store, and clinic—all of which are located in each township. Many families own private vehicles or boats and leave their home township frequently to hunt, visit, attend ceremonies, or fly to Darwin for shopping and visiting. Perhaps the most important recent event in the history of the Tiwi was the granting back to the traditional Tiwi owners of all their original tribal lands (both Bathurst and Melville islands) under the Land Rights Bill (Northern Territory) of 1976.

Economy

Subsistence and Commercial Activities. Prior to European settlement on the islands, the Tiwi had an abundant subsistence economy of hunting, fishing, and foraging in the bush, sea, and along the shore. Increasingly after European settlement, Tiwi became employed in a variety of jobs related to settlement life, including education, health, community service, and government. While each community has a shop where food and other material goods may be purchased, the majority of Tiwi are concerned with the maintenance of hunting and foraging skills among the young. With a preference for "bush" over "store-bought" foods, Tiwi make up much of their weekly diet with native foods.

Industrial Arts. A number of local industries have had commercial success: silk-screened textiles; clothing manufacturing; pottery; and, more recently, a large pine (timber) plantation—a legacy of the Australian government—and several tourist facilities.

Trade. External trade with the mainland peoples did not exist prior to the early twentieth century and the arrival of European settlers on the islands.

Division of Labor. In the precolonial subsistence economy the division of labor was such that hunting in the sea or air was the exclusive domain of men, while extracting roots, seeds, fruits, etc. from plants rooted in the ground was the exclusive domain of women. However, aside from these particular exclusions, both men and women hunted and gathered ground- or tree-dwelling animals, shellfish, turtle eggs, and the like from the shore, and both sexes contributed equally to the daily diet. There were no full- or part-time specialists.

Land Tenure. There are a number of named local groups that hold exclusive responsibility for geographically distinct areas (*murukupupuni,* or "countries") on the two islands. The number and boundaries of these countries are known to have fluctuated over the nearly one hundred years of recorded Tiwi history. Currently there are seven countries and each of these is represented by delegates to the Tiwi Land Council, which came into existence in 1976 when the islands were deeded back to the Tiwi under the Land Rights Bill. Currently one is considered an owner of one's father's country although in the presettlement days one was an owner of the country in which one's father was buried. Owners of a country are collectively held responsible for maintaining that country (and its natural and spiritual resources) and for transmitting the knowledge of and responsibility for that country to the next generation.

Kinship

Kin Groups and Descent. The matrilineal clan is a group whose members assume common descent from an ancestrally conceived group of unborn spirit beings located in clan-specific localities in or near a body of water. In the precolonial belief system, conception is accomplished when a father locates one of these unborn spirits and sends it to his wife, who must be of the same clan origin. Each clan is named and members of a clan provide physical, moral, and emotional support to fellow clan members in numerous and diverse situations. These clans are further grouped into four larger and exogamous groups. For each individual, two clans are significant: his or her own clan; and his or her father's clan. It is among the latter clan group that one should seek a spouse. One's father's clan and the natural species with which it is affiliated is also considered to be one's "Dreaming." One's Dreaming serves as inspiration for expressive ceremonial dances, songs, and art. In the social world of the Tiwi everyone is related.

Kinship Terminology. In the first ascending generation, one's parent's siblings of the same sex are classified with the parent, and their children (one's parallel cousins) are classed with one and one's siblings. One's parent's opposite-sex siblings are distinguished from each other, as are their children (one's cross cousins and potential spouses). One's siblings are distinguished in several ways: first by gender and then by relative age. Further distinction is made for siblings who have the same father but whose mothers are of different clans. There are two further distinctions that are behaviorally significant although unmarked by terminology. *Aminiyati* siblings are those who have the same (named) father's father, and "one-granny" siblings are those who have the same (named) mother's mother. Among the latter group there is strict avoidance between siblings of the opposite sex once sexual maturity is imminent, while the potentially much larger group, those who acknowledge a common grandfather, was in precolonial days the group of siblings that was largely responsible for the integrity of the countries.

Marriage and Family

Marriage. In precontact times—and in some cases today—marriages were arranged by a system of selecting a son-in-law for a young woman at the conclusion of her first-menstruation celebration. The young woman (who, in the past, would already have been married by this time) and her son-in-law are in a reciprocal relationship in which the son-in-law is obliged to "feed" his potential wife's mother, providing her not only food but any goods and services she demands. In return he will receive as wives all daughters born to his mother-in-law prior to their sexual maturity. For each woman, this kind of marriage arrangement generally characterized her first marriage and also often her secondary marriages to a deceased husband's brother(s) through the levirate. For the male, this form of marriage was often contracted for well past middle age, as it was the most prestigious and required considerable political acumen and accomplishment. Earlier marriages for men (after the age of 30 or more years) were most frequently to older women, widows of older brothers. Because a woman was usually married to a series of younger men, divorce rarely took place. Changes in the regulation of marriage have occurred since contact. While the actual cohabitation of a young girl with her promised husband is more frequently not taking place, such marriage contracts are still being made. In many of these cases the mother-in-law/son-in-law relationship still follows the traditional pattern, and the marriage usually conforms to the societal preference for marrying someone in one's father's matrilineal clan—someone who falls into the category of acceptable potential spouses yet who is, at the same time, someone closer in age. There are, however, an increasing number of marriages of Tiwi to non-Tiwi Aboriginals of mixed (Asian or European) background.

Domestic Unit. The precontact domestic unit—a woman, her daughters, her daughters' husbands, and her grandchildren—remains today a viable domestic unit, although monogamy is almost universal. Within the townships there are groups of houses in close proximity to each other that operate as economic units. The modern domestic unit is often under the "direction" of a senior woman as in the past, and all members contribute differentially, from wages, pensions, and foraging activities. Ceremonial activities (dancing and carving) are now monetized, as is gambling (a redistributive institution).

Socialization. The socialization of children is carried out by the entire domestic unit today as in the past. All children attend elementary school in their home community until the sixth grade. Some may continue their schooling at Nguiu, in Darwin, or even farther away from home in Brisbane, Sydney, Melbourne, or Alice Springs. A few Tiwi have gone beyond high school, and in each community there are women and men who have been trained as educators, health workers, or office managers. The annual *kulama* yam ceremony was the event at which initiation of males and females was finalized. Initiates traditionally participated in six such annual ceremonies, advancing in rank in each and ultimately reaching senior status as a full initiate between ages 40 and 50. Today, initiation is more often for males (though women attend and participate) and involves only one or two participations. In contrast to practices on the mainland, there is no body scarification or mutilation (circumcision or subincision) in Tiwi male initiation. There is, however, a ritual sequence of body painting and decoration, heavily imbued with symbolic meaning.

Sociopolitical Organization

Social Organization. The precontact social organization was characterized by the matrilineal clans and by the local groups affiliated with each country. In matrilineal clans, leadership was largely ceremonial and was conferred according to seniority and competence among the males. Under the country system of organization, some leaders in the past were men who achieved great prominence through arranging multiple (reportedly sometimes as many as a hundred) marriage contracts for themselves; they also were men whose domestic groups were very large and regionally influential. Such men also gained notoriety as ceremonial leaders in song, dance, and art.

Political Organization. Today, imposed upon the kinship, kin group, and local group organizations are (in ascending order) the township council, the Tiwi Land Council, and the Northern Territory and Australian Commonwealth governments. In each of the three communities an elected township council is empowered to impose bylaws regulating community affairs and is responsible for budgeting and for maintaining township services. The council hires a town clerk (a manager) and other personnel to manage and oversee the various operations of the township. Both men and women serve on the town council.

Social Control. The Tiwi Land Council meets once a month to decide issues that concern matters outside of those of individual townships. While most of these have to do with land and its use, some are concerned with matters of law and its enforcement. Who or what body is concerned with social control and conflict resolution is sometimes problematic. Clan members are often the proper ones to resolve domestic and intradomestic conflict. However, the territory government maintains a two-person police station at Parlingimpi and one or two police aides in each township to handle internal disputes.

Conflict. Conflicts occurred between matrilineal clans and patrifocal local groups and mainly concerned rights to women as wives, almost never other resources. Today, such conflicts are still settled by localized close cognatic and/or matrilineal kin groups or, if this fails, by affiliated matrilineal clans that consider that their close relationship requires their involvement on behalf of their kin. A very few interregional conflicts are part of the oral history of contemporary Tiwi and were resolved by holding a "war" at a designated place and time, during which the opposite sides took turns throwing and dodging spears and throwing clubs. Interpersonal conflicts were often settled by sneak attacks and ambushes.

Religion and Expressive Culture

Religious Beliefs. Tiwi religion focuses on ancestral spirits of those who have lived in the recent past and including those who, in "the Dreamtime," created the land, sea, and all that is found within. The Catholic church is a strong and consistent element of daily life in Nguiu and Parlingimpi and to a lesser extent in Milikapiti. At the present time there is open acceptance of Tiwi ceremonial life by the church and church members, although in the past this was not so.

Ceremonies. The annual kulama yam ceremony is held near the end of the wet season (November–March). The three-day ritual involves the digging, preparation, cooking, and eating of the kulama type of wild yam. The yam symbolizes reproduction and maintenance of life, both human and nonhuman. Participants must, in addition to carrying out the preparation and cooking of the yams, compose and sing more than a dozen new songs throughout the three days. Other major ceremonies include the celebration of the transition of the living to the world of the dead. In connection with funeral rituals, elaborately carved and painted poles are commissioned and paid for by the close kin of the deceased, and for related activities painted bark baskets and spears are also manufactured. In the songs and dances of these ceremonies, historic and mythological events as well as contemporary events and problems (complaints or explanations) are remembered and marked. To both compose and understand the sung metaphoric poetic allusions to significant elements in Tiwi culture requires an extremely high level of verbal skill in the Tiwi language.

Arts. With the slow erosion of Tiwi language in favor of fluency in English in postcontact times, the verbal arts are in danger of substantial loss, whereas the visual arts (painting, sculpture, and dance) are being maintained, as they not only are an essential part of the ceremonial life (reinforcing the Tiwi worldview) but also are being translated to the commercial production of wood sculpture, textiles, clothing and pottery design, and other related enterprises.

Medicine. Traditionally, good commonsense medical knowledge among the Tiwi utilized the curative values of the island environment. Although some men and women were said to have greater knowledge of particular plants, animal parts, and other curative items, there were no full-time or even part-time curers. Magical death, sorcery, bone pointing, and kidney-fat theft are considered to be illnesses caused by mainlanders and are believed to be cured only by mainland curers. The spread of these illnesses is a feature of contemporary Tiwi life, and the people seek cures from non-Tiwi specialists on the mainland.

Death and Afterlife. The most important myth of the Tiwi deals with the permanence of death, after the death-by-neglect of Purukupali's son. This culture hero walked into the sea with his son's body, declaring that henceforth all Tiwi shall die and never return to life. The spirits of the deceased reside in the country where they are buried, although to accommodate the increased mobility of Tiwi (over to the mainland and overseas) the spirits are said to be able to travel back to their "homeland" as well. The life in this spirit world mirrors that of the living, in that the dead hunt, fish, and hold parallel ceremonies with the living.

Bibliography

Goodale, Jane C. (1971). *Tiwi Wives: A Study of the Women of Melville Island, North Australia.* Seattle: University of Washington Press.

Hart, C. W. M., Arnold R. Pilling, and Jane C. Goodale (1988). *The Tiwi of North Australia.* 3rd ed. New York: Holt, Rinehart & Winston.

JANE C. GOODALE

Tokelau

ETHNONYM: Union Islands

Orientation

Identification. "Tokelau" (Anglicized as "Tokelauan") refers both to the people and to their distinctive Polynesian language, as well as to their homeland which consists of three atolls: Atafu, Nukunonu, and Fakaofo. "Tokelau" means "north" or "northeast" in many Polynesian languages, including their own, but it was also the name of the preeminent god of the atolls, Tui Tokelau. The name "Union Islands" was coined in 1841 to label collectively the three atolls then known to outsiders as Duke of York (Atafu), Duke of Clarence (Nukunonu), and D'Wolf or Bowditch (Fakaofo). These names were never used by Tokelauans but were "official" for over a hundred years until the three islands, with their local names, were collectively designated Tokelau Islands in 1948 and in 1976 simply Tokelau.

Location. The atolls lie along a northwest-southeast axis of about 150 kilometers between 8° and 10° S and 171° and 173° W. The closest islands of any size are those of Western Samoa, about 480 kilometers to the south. Together the atolls have a total land area of only about 12 square kilometers and are separated from each other by 60 to 90 kilometers of open sea. They are all true atolls: they have central lagoons completely enclosed by coral reef, which forms the base of islets of sand and coral detritus. Although rainfall is 250 to 280 centimeters annually, rain is apt to be scarce between April and September, causing drought, and tropical cyclones or the swells generated by them at a distance are a hazard between December and March.

Demography. Contact estimates of the population varied widely (500–1,000). Even the lowest figure was more than halved in the 1860s by the advent of slavers and dysentery. From that time the population of the atolls gradually and then rapidly increased, reaching a high of 1,900 persons in the mid-1960s. Thereafter it dropped and stabilized at around 1,600 in the 1970s–1980s following relatively heavy migration to New Zealand, where the population identified as Tokelau numbered about 3,400 in 1986. Although Tokelau people count among their more recent ancestors some other Polynesians and European-derived foreigners, only persons with (or married to people with) Tokelau ancestry are permanent residents of the atolls.

Linguistic Affiliation. The Tokelau language is a member of the Samoic Subgroup of Polynesian languages and is probably most closely related to dialects of Tuvalu (Ellice). Until very recently, all Tokelauans were bilingual in Samoan, the language of Christianity and literacy, from which their own language has borrowed heavily for over a hundred years while still retaining its own distinctive features.

History and Cultural Relations

Tokelau traditions assert autochthonous origins; provisional archaeological evidence shows people residing in the atolls one thousand years ago with Samoan and Tuvalu cultural affinities. Oral narratives tell of hostilities among the three atolls which ended when Fakaofo gained ascendancy by conquering Nukunonu and driving off the people of Atafu; until the nineteenth century, explorers found Atafu uninhabited, Nukunonu lightly peopled, and Fakaofo clearly preeminent as the place of the highest chief and the shrine of Tui Tokelau. Christian conversion and depopulation in the 1860s brought an end to Fakaofo domination, and each atoll became a tiny theocratic polity. Mission dominance was marginally compromised at the end of the century when the atolls were declared British protectorates. For a brief period (1910–1914) protectorate officials were assigned to the atolls, and in 1916 Tokelau was added to the Gilbert and Ellice Island Colony, then removed when New Zealand assumed responsibility for the atolls on Britain's behalf in 1926. Despite these arrangements, the administration of Tokelau is best characterized as benign neglect until after World War II. Tokelauans received New Zealand citizenship in 1948, but they did not begin to emigrate there until the 1960s, some on government schemes of various kinds. Aid and development programs escalated in the mid-1970s, accompanied by increasing involvement of Tokelauans in administrative and decision-making roles. This trend continued in the 1980s, yet Tokelau remains a New Zealand dependency at its inhabitants' expressed and reiterated wish.

Settlements

On one leeward islet of each atoll is a clearly bounded village. Rectangular houses, until recently of thatch construction, are more or less aligned to well-defined paths. The villages are densely settled yet the open houses give a sense of spaciousness. At the lagoon shore, reclamations faced with coral boulders—from which extend over-water latrines—alternate with natural shores where vessels are beached. The ocean or back of the village is the preferred location for cook houses. Here the prevailing winds carry smoke out to sea. Village amenities—church, meetinghouse, and cricket pitch—tend to be clustered in the center, while recently constructed public structures—copra sheds, hospitals, and schools—are located at the peripheries.

Economy

Subsistence and Commercial Activities. The Tokelau have always had coconuts and fish in abundance. Fishing is strictly a subsistence pursuit and the catches are widely distributed by both formal and informal means. Fishing techniques are ingenious and various, and knowledge of them and of the sea and its denizens is extensive and highly valued. Coconuts are harvested both for subsistence and for sale in the form of copra. Indeed, until the recent development of an extensively subsidized public-service sector, copra was the main source of cash with which to purchase imported essentials, such as kerosene, soap, tobacco, cloth, flour, rice, and sugar. With more cash from wages there are now more imports, which are purchased from a cooperative village store rather than from trading ships. For subsistence, aside from fish, coconuts, and imports, there are breadfruit, pandanus fruit, and swamp taro (*pulaka*). For cash there has always been some handicraft production, primarily plaited mats, hats, fans, and baskets made by women.

Industrial Arts. Until the early 1970s, both canoes and houses were made almost exclusively of local materials. Early European accounts describe double-hulled, oceangoing sailing canoes and an extensive range of nets, lines, hooks, and other fishing equipment, including watertight wooden boxes (*tuluma*), as well as matting and other plaited wares. Imported substitutes are now widely used, although a number of traditional items are produced for sale.

Trade. There is no internal market for local products. People request what they need from others and give to neighbors and kin. A formal and versatile system of absolutely equal sharing, both in receiving and providing, operates in the village. Since the latter part of the nineteenth century, copra has been the major export crop of the atolls.

Division of Labor. What is regularly done by men or women, young or old, is clear. Men fish and harvest, doing most of their work outside; women process and allocate food and oversee the home and family. Children fetch and carry; young adults undertake the most arduous tasks; elders are managers.

Land Tenure. Aside from land vested in the village or one of the churches, all land in Tokelau is controlled by recognized cognatic kin groups who jointly tend and harvest its resources and share its produce. Their land includes one or more house sites within the village, where mature female members of the group normally reside. Everyone in Tokelau has rights to land (or has a spouse with such rights) and thus shares the produce from one or more joint holdings. Since all offspring receive rights from both parents, a person's joint holdings are multiple and the people with rights to any one holding may be many. Such holdings are eventually divided and combined with others likewise divided, thus reducing people's multiple rights and the number of right holders.

Kinship

Kin Groups and Descent. Descent is thoroughly cognatic both in principle and practice, and the sister-brother relationship is central. Landholding kin groups are composed of anyone who can trace descent by any route from their founders, and they are internally divided into "sons and their issue" and "daughters and their issue" with reference to the sons and daughters of the founding ancestor or ancestral couple. From the side of the "sons" the head of the "family" is selected. He represents the group in villagewide matters and has authority over the productive property of the group. The "daughters" side provides the woman known as the "foundation" of the family. She resides in the ancestral home and allocates produce from family property among its members.

Kinship Terminology. A Hawaiian-type system is modified by the same-sex or opposite-sex distinction in sibling terms so that there are three such terms: sibling of own sex, male or female; sibling of opposite sex, male; and sibling of opposite sex, female. Correspondingly, "mother's brother" and "sister's child" are marked terms, as is "father's sister."

Marriage and Family

Marriage. Postmarital residence is uxorilocal or, as Tokelauans phrase it, "women stay and men go." Tokelauans assert that second cousins cannot marry, though in fact some have done so. The rule is that people who hold common rights to property do not marry. Since second cousins tend to belong to a common kin group, they are thus usually unmarriageable, as third or fourth cousins may also be. If such cousins do marry, then the property held in common is divided, and the rule is upheld: They are no longer kin. De facto unions are not tolerated in the villages and the majority of marriages are village-endogamous.

Domestic Unit. The nature and composition of domestic units is not easy to define. Each focuses on a mature woman, married or widowed, who runs the household by directing the activities of others, especially younger women and children. It is not an exclusive production and consumption unit because its members work with various kin groups and receive goods and produce from several kin groups. It is the regular sleeping place of some members, but grown boys rarely sleep at home, children frequently sleep with other close kin, and visitors or a birth within the given household or a related one may precipitate a major shift. Households thus are variable and flexible in their composition, but because of the dense, open village settlement it is well known where any person is at any given time.

Inheritance. When property is divided within a kin group it is divided in the names of the founders' children, either living or dead, in equitable shares. The actual division may entail considerable negotiation among spokespersons of the recipient groups, and once the initial division is made it is possible for recipients to redivide the property at the level of the subsequent generation.

Socialization. Infants are much indulged. They are weaned at about a year and a half, or as soon as the mother becomes pregnant again, and they take second place when a new infant appears. The interval between births is properly two years or longer, so each child has at least two years of indulgence. From an early age, children are directed to fetch and carry. The increasing range of these directed activities depends on their verbal skills, for messages accompany goods and must be transmitted accurately. Children are closely disciplined to do as they are told and follow instructions precisely. Misbehavior may be punished by any adult and punishment may be severe.

Sociopolitical Organization

Tokelau is a dependency of New Zealand. Its administrator, based in New Zealand, is appointed by the governor-general on the recommendation of the ministry of foreign affairs. The administrator delegates normal administrative responsibility to the official secretary, since 1987 a Tokelauan, who is head of the Tokelau Public Service and based in Western Samoa. General meetings of elected officials and representatives in the atolls are held twice yearly. Real governance is at the village level.

Social Organization. Tokelau villages are very tightly controlled and basically egalitarian. This order is achieved by a dominating age hierarchy based on the precept that wisdom is acquired with years and therefore elderly people should decide, direct, and supervise. In short, authority comes with age, and in principle anyone will have authority in due course, if he or she lives long enough. Men ultimately have a wider sphere of authority than women, controlling the affairs of the village as a whole. But Tokelau matrons can be very domineering and are not easily dismissed by their male counterparts.

Political Organization. Each village has a ruling council made up of male elders and/or heads of recognized kin groups. Two elected officials are part of this body: a political representative of the village to the administration and the mayor or manager of village activities. In the villages, the council has very considerable authority—making local regulations and enforcing them and deciding, directing, and regulating all village activities. Numerous other groups operate in the village context under the direction of the council. The male work force, made up of all able adult men, maintains and improves village amenities, provides food for the village and/or its guests, etc., at the direction of the elders or at their own initiative. The women of the village complement the male work force, undertaking tasks and projects in the female domain such as mat plaiting and village housekeeping under the direction of the elderly matrons. For other purposes, each village is divided into two competing sides. Organized groups within the churches partially replicate the secular organization (e.g., deacons or elders and women's committees). More ephemeral groups are organized from time to time and are recognized by the elders as "clubs" of one kind or another. This scheme of village organization applies to all three villages, but it takes particular forms in each. Interatoll political organization was virtually nonexistent until the 1970s. Gatherings at one village traditionally included ceremonial events such as church openings and cricket matches, and though these had political undercurrents arising from historical antagonisms, the antagonisms were muted by many specific loyalties based on kinship links between villages. Now that Tokelau has more say in running its own affairs, each village is watchful that another does not get more than its share of jobs, aid funds, etc. The twice-yearly general meetings rotate between the atolls, are chaired by the hosting village, and are true forums where the interests of the three villages are intensely negotiated. It is notable that atoll parochialism is just as intense, if not more so, in the New Zealand Tokelau communities.

Social Control. It is impossible in a small atoll village for any person's comings and goings to be unobserved. Everyone knows what everyone else is doing and speculates about what they are going to do. People's activities are programmed and closely monitored by the elders of the village and their elder kin. Self-serving and aggressive behavior is socially condemned, and public disputes bring immediate intervention.

Conflict. Since the establishment of the hegemony of Fakaofo in "ancient times," there has been little conflict between the atolls. Tokelau has no hostile neighbors. Internal conflicts are mediated effectively by the village councils. Conflict is also channeled into competition between the two village sides in various entertainments, including ongoing cricket matches and song-dance exchanges. When on occasion this competition becomes too intense and threatens to disrupt the peace, the competing sides are simply revised, so that enemies and allies are scrambled.

Religion and Expressive Culture

Religious Beliefs. Since the latter half of the nineteenth century, Christianity has been a central part of Tokelau life. Of the gods and spirits of the past little is known. Tui Tokelau was preeminent, had no visible being, and was represented by a huge mat-wrapped pillar in front of his shrine in Fakaofo. Here annual rites were held appealing to the god for continued abundance and fertility. Other gods or spirits were associated with particular places or kin groups. Catholic and Protestant proselytizers competed for Tokelau souls in the 1850s–1860s. Their successes were initially in Atafu, which became and remains wholly Protestant, and Nukunonu, which became and remains wholly Catholic. Fakaofo ended up with adherents of both denominations and decades of veiled antagonism, if not open hostility, between them. However, a true ecumenical spirit came to prevail there and has become part of general Tokelau morality. Whether Protestant or Catholic, Tokelau Christianity is of a fundamentalist, puritanical bent. Christian morality is preached in support of Tokelau precepts: respect for elders, obedience to parents, unity of community, equality of all, etc.

Religious Practitioners. Protestant congregations have pastors, until recently Samoan ones, who have been "invited" by the congregation to "serve." The governance of each parish is in the hands of local deacons and lay preachers, upstanding male members of the congregation. Catholic congregations have catechists, always Tokelauans, and sometimes host a resident, non-Tokelauan priest.

Ceremonies. Celebrations, whether of Christian derivation or Tokelau origin, have both Christian and local components. Significant days of the Christian calendar, days set aside for local groups (often marking their founding), and events of moment to the community (such as weddings) invariably include four features: prayer, food, games, and entertainment (i.e., a church service, a feast, a cricket match, and a song-dance evening). Other features may be added, such as a parade, and the basic ones may be elaborated and modified in innumerable ways.

Arts. The performing arts are the most developed and creative Tokelau arts. The song-dance repertoire is huge, and new performances are continually being created. Equally creative, but more individual, are comic skits and routines devised and repeated by recognized clowns and comedians, many of whom are older women.

Medicine. Hospitals with Western-trained Tokelau doctors and nurses are long-standing village institutions. When they are ill or injured most people go to the hospital for attention. Certain local people are recognized masseurs whose skills are sought to relieve or correct various conditions. Although herbal remedies and other "medicines" are used, there are few specialist healers of this sort.

Death and Afterlife. A death in the village is signaled by the tolling of the church bell, and from then until burial all other activity is in abeyance. The body is laid out in the appropriate family home. Women of the immediate family remain in attendance, their wailing broken by speeches, hymns, and prayers of visitors. Before the body is placed in its coffin, people gather at the house of mourning to take part in final farewells. Following a Christian service, the coffin is transported to the burial ground and placed in a deeply dug grave. After the last rites, all men present give a hand in filling the grave. A period of postburial mourning ends with a feast. The influence of the dead is often remarked on soon after burial: the deceased may bring an abundance of fish, or the deceased's ghost may be encountered, or the ghost may bring misfortune to kin who do not follow specified instructions. Mainly, however, the dead are considered to be remote, though they are fondly remembered.

See also Samoa, Tuvalu

Bibliography

Hooper, A. (1985). "Tokelau Fishing in Traditional and Modern Contexts." In *The Traditional Knowledge and Management of Coastal Systems in Asia and the Pacific,* edited by K. Ruddle and R. E. Johannes. Jakarta: UNESCO.

Hooper, A., and J. Huntsman (1973). "A Demographic History of the Tokelau Islands." *Journal of the Polynesian Society* 82:366–411.

Huntsman, J. (1971). "Concepts of Kinship and Categories of Kinsmen in the Tokelau Islands." *Journal of the Polynesian Society* 80:317–354.

Huntsman, J., and A. Hooper (1975). "Male and Female in Tokelau Culture." *Journal of the Polynesian Society* 84:415–430.

Huntsman, J., and A. Hooper (1985). "Structures of Tokelau History." In *Transformations of Polynesian Culture,* edited by A. Hooper and J. Huntsman. Auckland: The Polynesian Society.

Macgregor, G. (1937). *Ethnology of Tokelau Islands.* Bernice P. Bishop Museum Bulletin no. 146. Honolulu.

JUDITH HUNTSMAN AND ANTONY HOOPER

Tolai

ETHNONYMS: None

Orientation

Identification. "Tolai" is the modern name for the indigenous people who live within a radius of about 32 kilometers of the port town of Rabaul in the northeast corner of New Britain known as the Gazelle Peninsula. In the past they had no inclusive name for themselves, and early Roman Catholic missionaries introduced the name "Gunantuna" (meaning the "true land" or the "proper land"), a usage that is no longer followed. "Tolai" itself (from a local greeting akin to "mate," "buddy," and the like) appears to date back to the 1930s.

Location. The Tolai live at 151°30' E and 4°30' S on the Gazelle Peninsula. The peninsula was in the past effectively cut off from the rest of New Britain by the Baining Mountains. It is a highly tectonic area, its chief physical landmarks being the volcanic craters that ring Rabaul Harbor. A major eruption in 1937 brought massive loss of life and virtually destroyed Rabaul. The volcanic ash deposited for centuries across the land has given the soils an unusual fertility. The year falls into two seasons: the *taubar,* the time of the southeast trade winds (roughly May to October); and the *labur,* the northwest monsoon or rainy season.

Demography. Estimates place the population at contact at about 30,000. This is one of the most densely populated areas of Melanesia—over a hundred people per square kilometer at first contact. Over the past twenty-five years the population has been growing at an explosive rate—in some communities at about 4.5 percent per annum. Tolai are presently estimated to number about 120,000. Given an area of some 910 square kilometers, population density is exceedingly high, creating many social problems.

Linguistic Affiliation. Tolai call their language *tinata tuna,* meaning the "true word" or the "proper word." It is also known as "Kuanua," or nowadays simply "Tolai." As an Austronesian language, it is more closely related to the languages of southern New Ireland than to those of other parts of New Britain. Formerly dialectical differences were important, but missionary influence has encouraged the present homogeneity as well as its spread to the Duke of York Islands, New Ireland, and elsewhere.

History and Cultural Relations

Traders, missionaries, and others began to converge on the Gazelle Peninsula in the 1870s, and in 1884 it was annexed to form part of the German empire in New Guinea. Climate, soils, and the magnificent natural harbor offered by Blanche Bay combined to make it ideally suited for the establishment of a colony built around a plantation economy. By 1914 the Tolai had come to experience great changes in their way of life. Much of their land had been expropriated, but they had also prospered through the sale of copra and other produce as well as the provision of schooling that had opened up to some Tolai a range of occupations outside the village. After World War I the area came under Australian rule by mandate of the League of Nations. The period between the wars was characterized by much stagnation, though in the later 1930s there were signs of economic recovery and improved standards of living for those Tolai in villages close to Rabaul. During World War II the Gazelle Peninsula became in effect a vast Japanese garrison, and when their supply lines were cut as a result of U.S. naval victories, life became increasingly harsh for the Tolai: many died from maltreatment, malnutrition, and lack of medicines. The Australian administration was restored after the war, but quite a different approach was now adopted leading to major developments in the fields of local government, the economy, health, and education. Yet, through the 1960s, despite the evidence of growing affluence, there were also clear signs of mounting social tensions at work. These tensions were to culminate in the emergence of the Mataungan movement, which came to play a prominent part in bringing about self-government and a little later national independence for Papua New Guinea.

Settlements

Local communities, referred to as villages, with populations about 300, are the typical units of settlement. Villages, in the past the main territorial units, were and still are divided into tiny hamlets each consisting of a few households. In the more remote rural parts, houses are more likely to be built of traditional materials, but nearer Rabaul they are often costly two-story structures with copper roofs, louvered glass windows, and their own water tanks. Many villages have their own churches and schools, sometimes very substantial buildings, designed and built by the villagers themselves.

Economy

Subsistence and Commercial Activities. The household is the basic unit of production and consumption, with swidden horticulture as the subsistence base. Fertile soils encourage the growing of a wide range of crops. In inland communities taro, yams, and sweet potatoes are all grown in abundance; bananas, reported to be known in seventy varieties, are grown everywhere as another major staple. In coastal communities there are also seine and basket fishing, depending on the season. The bush turkey deposits its eggs in the warm soil close to the base of the volcanic craters, and these are a particularly prized item of the local diet. Above all there is the coconut palm, serving a variety of needs: the nut itself is food and drink as well as a basic ingredient in cooking, while husks can be used for fuel, and fronds for shelter and the weaving of mats. Very quickly too, following the arrival of the first European traders, the palm became the prime source of a new cash income through the sale of copra. In the 1950s cocoa was introduced and soon came to rival copra as a source of revenue. In addition to horticulture, Tolai have also been engaged in wage labor for many years. In the immediate post–World War II period, Tolai emerged as an occupational elite. They served as teachers, worked in administrative offices, and worked at carpentry and other trades in many parts of the country materially much less developed than their own. Nowadays many have received higher education and have earned professional qualifications as doctors, lawyers, architects, and the like; others serve in senior posts in the administration in Port Moresby, the nation's capital, or other urban centers.

Industrial Arts. Items produced include canoes and the huge basketlike fish traps known as *a wup,* as well as a wide variety of mats and baskets of coconut and pandanus leaves. Finely carved and painted staves and specially designed masks are made for particular dances.

Trade. Despite its tiny size, the Gazelle Peninsula is marked by a high degree of ecological diversity. Production is thus often highly localized. This combination of diversity and specialization has provided the basis for a complex system of internal trade. Even in precontact times a series of markets crisscrossed the area, goods passing by way of intermediaries from the coast to inland villages and vice versa. The economy, moreover, was highly monetized: all transactions were conducted through the medium of a shell currency called *tambu.* Nowadays the main markets are at Rabaul and the other township in the area, Kokopo: the Rabaul market is now open daily, offering a colorful and varied array of produce to a cosmopolitan clientele. Most market transactions are for cash, but tambu is still legal tender.

Division of Labor. The pattern of cooperation varies with the task. In general, however, where men cooperate, as in housebuilding or helping to launch a fish basket, those assisting have to be rewarded either by payment in shell money or by a small feast given by the person who has called them together. There is a fairly clear-cut division of labor along sexual lines. Broadly speaking, the heavy work of preparing a new garden falls to the men, with women following later to do the weeding and collecting. But husbands and wives are often seen working together in their gardens. Only men fish—the beaches set aside for activities connected with fishing are taboo to women—but women quickly gather when a catch is landed in order to buy: they cook the fish and sell it at the market. Women also accompany men when they go digging for megapode eggs: they sell snacks to the men and also buy eggs, again for sale at market.

Land Tenure. In theory all land is "owned"—that is, it is vested in perpetuity in the group called a *vunatarai,* a matrilineal clan whose members may be dispersed through many villages. In practice, effective control vests in a local segment of the clan or local matrilineage also called vunatarai. The estate is owned jointly, but the leader of the group may subdivide or grant rights of use to individual members of the lineage. In fulfilling his duty to care properly for his children, a man is also entitled to make a gift of matrilineal land to a son. The land is supposed to revert to the matrilineage on the father's death, but it frequently happens that with the passage of time details of the arrangement are forgotten and heated disputes are commonly generated in this way.

Kinship

Kin Groups and Descent. The dual division is the pivot of Tolai social organization. Every Tolai belongs to one of two matrimoieties, the chief function of which is the regulation of marriage. Sexual relations within the moiety constitute the most heinous of offenses, which in the past called for the death of the guilty parties. By birth every Tolai is also affiliated with the clan of the mother. The clan is a dispersed unit, associated with a place (or places) of origin, from which members scattered over the course of time to form separate branches or local matrilineages elsewhere within the area.

The clan (or segments of it) provides an elaborate network of kin relations covering many different local communities, and to this day it continues to provide a basis for cooperation in a variety of economic activities and above all in ceremonial affairs.

Kinship Terminology. Kinship terminology is of the Iroquois type. In the context of everyday social interaction, personal names are generally used and kinship terms are rarely heard save in dealing with affines.

Marriage and Family

Marriage. Traditionally polygyny was an important feature of Tolai marriage, but it is only rarely encountered nowadays. A proper marriage has always required bride-price in the form of payment in tambu, and this practice continues even today. Postmarital residence is expected to be virilocal, but there is no strict rule in the matter and a certain proportion of unions will be uxorilocal or involve some other arrangement. In legal terms, divorce in the case of customary marriage is easy; in practice marriages are very stable, though recent evidence suggests things may now be changing in this regard.

Domestic Unit. The basic domestic and economic unit is the household, ordinarily composed of a nuclear family.

Inheritance. Inheritance is in the matriline, but nowadays there is increasing pressure to recognize the claims of a man's wife and children in respect to personal property and money.

Socialization. In the upbringing of children Tolai lay great stress on obedience, and those who disobey are punished in a variety of ways. Schooling is another major concern of parents. Large numbers of Tolai children have received their education away from home, thus affecting their knowledge of village ways and local culture.

Sociopolitical Organization

Social Organization. Social relations are highly localized and most everyday interaction takes place within the hamlet or in some larger communities within the village section. However, through the clan system each hamlet in a village maintains friendly relations with hamlets in other villages. These links are maintained and perpetuated through intermarriage, trade, and ceremonial activities. Today, because of the large number of motor vehicles owned by Tolai and the fact that surfaced roads run throughout the Gazelle, this aspect of traditional social organization has been buttressed, rather than undermined, by modern conditions.

Political Organization. There was no central authority or hereditary leadership in the traditional system. Within local communities certain big-men were acknowledged as leaders. A big-man achieved his position by entrepreneurial flair. This flair was demonstrated in his ability to command considerable resources in the form of shell money—resources he put to use in organizing large-scale ceremonies or, in the modern context, in running a business enterprise. Since the 1950s the Tolai have been organized within local government councils, which continue to be based to a considerable degree on earlier local divisions.

Social Control and Conflict. Through their command of wealth in the form of tambu, big-men wielded considerable authority within their own communities. In the past the *tubuan*, a central figure in the male cult, was said to act as an agent of social control. Disputes between members of the local community were brought before the village assembly or moot; fines might be imposed or compensation awarded, in either case to be paid in tambu. In the past conflicts between different Tolai groups were also compounded by the payment of tambu. Until recently arranging for the hearing of disputes was a primary responsibility of the village councillor, but the village moot or *varkurai* has now given way to hearings before village courts, while disputes over land are heard by newly appointed land mediators.

Religion and Expressive Culture

Religious Beliefs. Tolai cosmology includes a vast assortment of spirits usually referred to collectively by the term *tabaran*. "Spirits of the air" are benign and their help is sought by those seeking inspiration in the composition of a new song, the design of costumes, or the choreography for a dance to be performed at a ceremony. Others, denizens of the bush and sometimes of grotesque form, are malevolent and much feared. The spirit of the tubuan lies at the heart of their religious system. The tubuan is "raised" to dance at a variety of festivals or *balaguan*, but the great climactic rite is the *matamatam*, a ceremony to honor all the deceased of the clan, when the masked figures of tubuan and *dukduk* (a central spirit figure of the secret male cult) both appear.

Religious Practitioners. Experts, or *melem*, are still required for the "raising" of the tubuan, but knowledge relating to garden and fishing magic and the like seems to have disappeared and the rites are now rarely, if ever, performed. By contrast, the reality of sorcery is still almost universally acknowledged.

Ceremonies. Despite the efforts of the earlier missionaries, the balaguan and matamatam continue to be performed very much as Richard Parkinson, an early planter in New Britain, observed them a century ago. At the same time, the vast majority of Tolai acknowledge a profound commitment to Christianity, and congregational matters are intimately woven into the daily life of the village. In addition to the ceremonies associated with the tubuan and those that follow a death, Tolai nowadays also celebrate with ceremonies to mark the completion of a new house, the installation of a new water tank, or even a birthday. However, all of these take a traditional form in that they involve exchanges of tambu.

Arts. Ceremonies are occasions of great pageantry, and much of Tolai artistry is invested in these events. Dancers wear colorful, specially designed costumes, and some of them carry carved and ornamented staves prepared for that particular occasion. The artist, whether carver or composer, enjoys very high prestige.

Medicine. Individuals with a knowledge of the properties of particular plants may be consulted as healers for particular complaints. But healing is another area in which the indigenous culture has been much eroded. Nowadays, Tolai regularly consult Western-trained practitioners, some of whom are themselves Tolai.

Death and Afterlife. In former times, coils of tambu had to be cut up and distributed so that the deceased would be able to enter the "Abode of the Spirits." To die without having tambu "cut" for one was not only shameful for the surviving members of lineage and clan, but it also condemned the deceased to an existence of everlasting misery in the land of IaKupia. Such a set of ideas underlay the whole tambu complex. After more than a century of Christianity, much of the traditional ideology touching these matters has been lost, but tambu has retained its ritual and symbolic significance, providing the link between present and past generations.

See also Lak, Lakalai

Bibliography

Epstein, A. L. (1969). *Matupit: Land Politics and Change among the Tolai of New Britain.* Berkeley: University of California Press.

Epstein, A. L. (1979). "Tambu: The Shell-Money of the Tolai." In *Fantasy and Symbol,* edited by R. H. Hook. London: Academic Press.

Epstein, A. L. (1988). "Matupit Revisited: Social Change, Local Organization, and the Sense of Place." *Journal de la Société des Océanistes* 86: 21–40.

Epstein, T. S. (1968). *Capitalism, Primitive and Modern: Some Aspects of Tolai Economic Growth.* Canberra: Australian National University.

Parkinson, R. (1907). *Dreissig Jahre in der Südsee.* Stuttgart: Strecker und Schroder.

Salisbury, R. F. (1970). *Vunamami: Economic Transformation in a Traditional Society.* Berkeley: University of California Press.

A. L. EPSTEIN

Tonga

ETHNONYMS: None

Orientation

Identification. The Kingdom of Tonga, located in the South Pacific Ocean, was under the protection of Great Britain from 1900 to 1970. Tongans have had a constitutional monarchy since 1875 and in 1970 Tonga became an independent country, joining the British Commonwealth of Nations. The islands of Tonga (known to eighteenth-century Europeans as the "Friendly Islands" because of the friendly reception given to explorers) have a total area of approximately 646 square kilometers. The word *tonga* means "south" in many Polynesian languages.

Location. In 1887, the territorial boundaries of the kingdom were established to encompass an ocean area from 15° to 23° S by 173° to 177° W. The islands fall within a rectangle some 959 kilometers from north to south and 425 kilometers from east to west. The three principal island groups, from north to south, are: the Tongatapu group (*tapu* means "sacred"); the Ha'apai group; and the Yava'u group. Tongatapu Island, the largest island in the kingdom, is the seat of Tongan government. The Tongan Islands are the low coral type, with some volcanic formations. The highest point in the Kingdom of Tonga is 1,030 meters on the uninhabited volcanic island of Kao. Tongatapu Island has a maximum elevation of 82 meters along the southern coast and the island of Yava'u reaches to the height of 305 meters. Average temperature in the Kingdom of Tonga in the winter months of June–July is 16–21° C and in the summer months of December–January it is about 27° C. The island chain of Tonga is classified as semitropical even though in the northern islands there is a true tropical climate and rainfall on Yava'u can be as much as 221 centimeters per year. Rainfall on Tongatapu averages 160 centimeters per year, with November to March being the local hurricane season. Because of the destructive powers of hurricanes striking mainly in the northern Tongan Islands, the southern island of Tongatapu became the place where Tongan culture was established with relative permanency.

Demography. It has been estimated that in the year 1800 there were approximately 15,000 to 20,000 Tongans residing throughout the islands. In 1989 the resident population of the Kingdom of Tonga was estimated to be 108,000, with Tongans comprising 98 percent of the population and the remainder being other islanders or foreign nationals. The capital and principal city of the kingdom is Nuku'alofa, with an estimated population of 30,000, located on Tongatapu Island. Tongatapu Island itself has an estimated island population of 64,000. There are 48,000 Tongans who are ages of 0–14 (45 percent); 54,000 ages 15–59 (50 percent); and 6,000 (5 percent) over the age of 60. There are also approximately 40,000 to 50,000 Tongan nationals residing in Australia, New Zealand, and the United States of America.

Linguistic Affiliation. The Tongan language is derived from a proto–Fijian-Polynesian language originally spoken by Fiji islanders about 1500 B.C. Linguistic and archaeological evidence points to the migration of people into Tonga from locations north and west of the islands.

History and Cultural Relations

Through the use of carbon-14 dating techniques, a date of 1140 B.C. is the given date for the beginning of human occupation of Tongatapu. The first Europeans to visit the Tongan Islands were Dutch navigators in 1616 (Willem Schouten and Jacob LeMaire) and additional contacts occurred as other Europeans explored the Pacific throughout the seventeenth and eighteenth centuries. Contacts between Europeans and Tongans lasted for periods of a few days to several weeks. Publications by Europeans about Pacific Islanders placed Tonga firmly on the map of the world. These published accounts, coupled with the great evangelical revival that swept Europe in the nineteenth century, caused organizations to send individuals to convert the peoples of the Pacific. Tonga, along with the South Pacific islands of Tahiti, was one of the first island groups to receive European missionaries specifically for the purpose of converting the native inhabitants to Christianity. After European missionaries landed in Tahiti in 1797, additional missionaries continued on to Tongatapu. Other missionaries also arrived in Tonga in 1822 and in 1826 two Tahitians who had converted to Christianity in their native islands arrived on Tongatapu while en route to Fiji and began their Christian work among the Tongan natives. There is no indication that Tongans had extensive trading voyages with other Polynesian island groups. Modern Tonga, an ethnically homogeneous Polynesian kingdom, is attempting to find its way into the twenty-first century. Tongans in the islands are extremely dependent upon relatives living overseas who send money back to family members. In recent years, funds sent back to Tonga from relatives living abroad amounted to ten times the amount of income the kingdom generated from the export of agricultural products such as copra, vanilla, and bananas. Attempts at solving the inherent economic problems of the kingdom have included oil exploration since the 1960s, foreign aid, and increased tourism ventures. As of this publication, however, no oil has been discovered, foreign aid continues, and the tourism industry is much too fragile and dependent upon variables beyond the control of Tongans. Late in 1989, individuals in Tonga began discussing the possibility of a casino for tourists that would be open only to foreign-passport holders in the kingdom.

Settlements

Prior to European missionaries, Tongans lived in dispersed settlement patterns that were kin-based and kin-related territorial units. A typical Tongan residential site included a home (*fale*), with a thatched roof and sides made from woven coconut-palm fronds, as well as a separate area for cooking purposes that would have an earthen oven (*'umu*). Today, in addition to some traditional thatched homes, numerous nontraditional or European-American homes (made of wood, concrete, and metal) are located throughout the islands.

Economy

Subsistence and Commercial Activities. Prior to the establishment of a market economy, Tongans were subsistence farmers and fishers who had adapted to the environment of their relatively small groups of islands. Because of the relatively low population density of the islands in traditional times, Tongans were essentially self-sufficient horticulturalists and fishers who traded for foodstuffs and material goods among themselves. In the late 1980s, earnings from the tourism industry, accompanied by funds received from Tongans living abroad, accounted for the majority of all personal income in the Kingdom of Tonga. In traditional Tonga, tropical products such as yams, breadfruit, taro, and coconuts were all cultivated on small farms. Tongans fished the surrounding waters by spear fishing, by net fishing, and by hand. In recent years the pressures of population growth and tourism have forced Tongans to import much of their foodstuffs, including canned meats and fish.

Industrial Arts. Contemporary Tongans are small-scale handicraft manufacturers for the tourist industry and there are still independent artisans, manufacturers of basketry and wood carvings, on the islands. In traditional times, Tongans carved small statues and bowls and manufactured other items, such as baskets, mats, and sails, from tropical materials.

Trade. Evidence indicates that, in traditional times, Tongans had large double-hulled canoes called *kalia* that could carry provisions for up to 200 people, and in them Tongans made extensive trading voyages between Fiji and Samoa.

Division of Labor. Young males in traditional Tonga followed their father's occupation, with the eldest son receiving the title to the trade. Hereditary occupations included canoe building, fishing, and cooking; some trades could be hereditary or not, such as tattooing and barbering. Both men and women could be priests, and women also gathered reef fishes and fished with nets in the lagoon. Women manufactured valuable items (*koloa*), such as basketry, mats, and tapa, and women prepared kava. Kava, the nonnarcotic drink made from the roots of the *Piper methysticum* plant, continues to be an important social and ceremonial drink and elaborate rituals involving kava drinking exist for various ceremonial occasions such as marriages and funerals. Tapa, a clothlike material made from the bark of the paper mulberry tree (*Broussonetia papyrifera*), is still widely manufactured today for sale to tourists. Mats in traditional Tonga, woven for floors and walls, could also be worn as waist garments (*ta'ovala*) or used as sails for canoes. With a cash economy and increased sales of female-produced items for the tourist market, certain women now make more money than men, and tensions between the sexes have increased in contemporary Tonga.

Land Tenure. Current Tongan law guarantees that every male over the age of 16 should receive an allotment of land: an *'api* of 3.3 hectares for agricultural purposes and 0.16 of a hectare as a site for a home. Because of population growth and limited natural resources, however, thousands of Tongan males are landless today. Prior to the Tongan constitution, established in 1875 by King George Tupou I (1797–1893), land rights in Tonga were vested with an extended kinship group, the *ha'a*, a corporate landholding and property-sharing descent group. The leadership of the ha'a distributed resources to members. In 1875, however, all land was acquired by the Crown for redistribution to a newly created class of hereditary nobles (*nopele*) for eventual redistribution to the people.

Kinship

Kin Groups and Descent. Divided into various ha'a, traditional Tongan society had a patrilineal descent system, yet matrilineal lines were also taken into consideration for decisions involving chiefs. Tongan society was—and continues to be—an extremely rank-conscious society, with rank being based on age or birth order, gender, and kinship affiliation. There was a great deal of mobility in traditional Tongan society, and the rank of an individual on any given occasion was relative to the other individuals present at that occasion.

Kinship Terminology. Kinship terminology was extended to collateral relatives, though to a lesser degree than in the Hawaiian system.

Marriage and the Family

Marriage. Monogamy was and is the norm in Tonga, but in traditional times multiple marriages were not uncommon and marriage dissolutions and subsequent remarriages often occurred.

Domestic Unit. Traditionally, a wife became part of her husband's lineage upon marriage and set up residence in the territory of her husband's ha'a or in the area of a smaller kindred group (*kainga*). Large families were the rule in Tonga, and children were frequently adopted by individuals. The extended family was—and continues to be—an important organizing group in Tonga.

Inheritance. Currently there are strict rules of male primogeniture in Tonga, but in traditional times adopted and fictive kin could inherit various titles and possessions. Much of traditional Tongan consensus and flexibility was eliminated with the introduction of Tongan law codes and the constitution of 1875.

Socialization. That which occurs in Tonga in day-to-day existence is *fakatonga,* or the Tongan way of life or doing things; Tongans have continuously adapted to changing environmental situations to the best of their abilities. The most important agents of socialization in traditional Tonga were members within the immediate family and then individuals of the ha'a: parents, siblings, and near relations were key. In contemporary Tonga, in addition to family relations, criteria such as religious affiliation, educational background, and whether one is of the nopele class or "commoner" class contribute to day-to-day socialization activities. Perhaps the most important expression of Tongan reality is the concept of *'ofa,* literally "to love" or have a fondness towards an individual; the phrase *'ofa atu* (literally, "love to you") can be heard on many important ceremonial occasions.

Sociopolitical Organization

Social Organization. Tongan society was and is hierarchical in nature. There is an administrative class consisting of the agreed-upon titleholders or rulers, currently personified by the nobles (nopele) and the reigning monarch. Experts in traditions or spokespersons (*matapule*) are next, followed by the bulk of the populace, the commoners. Before the Europeans arrived in Tonga, the embodiment of all that was sacred and secular (and leader of all Tongans) was the individual designated as the "Tu'i Tonga." In approximately the fifteenth century, as Tongan society expanded in size, a division was made between the sacred and secular aspects of managing the islands. An individual who was the brother of the Tu'i Tonga was designated the "Tu'i Ha'a Takalaua," the administrator of the secular aspects of Tongan society. Approximately 200 years later, the Tu'i Ha'a Takalaua delegated some of his secular authority to his son and created the lineage known as the "Tu'i Kanokupolu." In traditional times, the fourth major Tongan individual was the sister of the Tu'i Tonga, designated the "Tu'i Tonga Fefine," given the title of "Tamaha." All Tongans, including the reigning monarch of the modern Kingdom of Tonga, theoretically trace their kinship affiliations, and hence their rank relative to one another, from these four chiefly titleholders. In traditional Tonga, succession to a title and chieftainship depended upon a variety of factors, especially the decision of the corporate land-holding and property-sharing descent group. Any individual who had a position of authority in traditional Tongan society and had a title as evidence of rank did not have the title because of any inherent rights but only because he or she had the consensus of the governed group. The titleholder operated within a system of checks and balances that ensured that the governed were willing to be influenced and led by these individuals.

Political Organization. Tongan culture began to change in the seventeenth century, when the first European explorers landed in the islands. The culmination of these changes took place in 1875 when the Tongan constitution was introduced. By the nineteenth century, a traditional and flexible system of titles and inheritance, which had been in operation for hundreds of years, passed out of existence. In 1875, a rigid father-to-son inheritance system was instituted and the inherent consensus and flexibility concerning the rights of leadership or chieftainship passed out of existence.

Social Control. Informal social control could take the form of gossip when there was inadequate social reciprocity on various occasions. Tonga operates under a constitutional monarchy and in addition to the current reigning monarch there is an executive branch (consisting of the prime minister and a cabinet appointed by the king) as well as the legislative and judicial branches. The twenty-nine-member Legislative Assembly or parliament consists of the governors of Ha'apai and Yava'u, nine cabinet ministers, nine nobles, and nine commoners. Tonga also maintains the Tonga Defense School of 400 individuals, charged with maintaining public order, patrolling coastal waters, and engaging in various Kingdom of Tonga projects.

Conflict. Although Tongan oral histories report some traditional conflicts relating to political situations, Tongans were essentially peaceful islanders prior to the coming of European missionaries. In early nineteenth-century Tonga, the Christian missionaries made numerous efforts to convert the chiefs to the new religion, since if the chiefs converted, their people would follow. As word of missionary successes in the islands spread, other missionaries arrived and religious wars of intense fury began in 1826. Although it may not have been a deliberate nineteenth-century missionary plan, a divide-and-conquer policy saw non-Christian Tongans fighting against Christian Tongans, and there were additional conflicts in 1837, 1840, and 1852. With the aid of missionaries, three Tongan law codes were introduced to Tongans in 1839, 1850, and 1862. The culmination of all missionary involvement was the Tongan constitution of 1875. Tonga continues to have problems: its economy remains unsound and the lack of serious planning for its improvement may lead to political unrest in the future.

Religion and Expressive Culture

Religious Beliefs. Traditional Tongans believed in a multideity world including Tangaloa, who pulled up certain islands from the sea. There were traditional gods of various trades (such as fishers or artisans) and gods of various ha'a. In observance of the strictures of fundamentalist Christianity, it is written into the Tongan constitution that the Sabbath is a legal day of rest in the Kingdom of Tonga, and no commercial activities or entertainment are officially allowed.

It should be pointed out, however, that these legal regulations do not coincide with actual activities.

Arts. In traditional Tonga, tattooing was an important form of ornamentation, but with European contact this traditional art has all but vanished. One of the highest forms of traditional arts that has survived into the twentieth century is tapa artistry. Tapa continues to play an important role in gift giving, being redistributed among Tongans on important occasions. Other forms of the expressive arts in Tonga surviving into the twentieth century include dances and kava preparation.

Medicine. Tongans practiced traditional medicinal techniques, utilizing local products and the assistance of Tongan specialists who interceded with the deities for good health. Today there are modern hospital facilities on Tongatapu.

Death and Afterlife. In traditional times, after a Tongan titleholder died the body would be interred in a royal tomb (*langi*) on Tongatapu Island, and the soul was believed to go to Pulotu, the home of Tongan deities and the location where Tongans were thought to reside with their principal gods in the afterlife. Prior to the introduction of Christianity, commoners were believed not to have souls, but this way of thinking appears to have changed. Tongan kinship ties are truly demonstrated at times of death, and each individual who is related to the deceased has a specific task to perform during the funeral activities. Black is the color of mourning in Tonga.

See also Anuta, Futuna, Lau, Niue, Rotuma, Samoa, Uvea

Bibliography

Connelly-Kirch, Debra (1982). "Economic and Social Correlates of Handicraft Sellers in Tonga." *Annals of Tourism Research.* 9:383–402.

Ferdon, Edwin N. (1987). *Early Tonga: As the Explorers Saw It, 1616–1810.* Tucson: University of Arizona Press.

Gifford, Edward W. (1929). *Tongan Society.* Bernice P. Bishop Museum Bulletin no. 61. Honolulu.

Tanham, George K. (1988). *The Kingdom of Tonga.* [RAND: N-2799-OSD, prepared for the Office of the United States Secretary of Defense.] Santa Monica, Calif. Rand Corporation.

Urbanowicz, C. F. (1977). "Motives and Methods: Missionaries in Tonga in the Early Nineteenth Century." *Journal of the Polynesian Society.* 86:245–263.

Urbanowicz, C. F. (1979). "Changes in Rank and Status in the Polynesian Kingdom of Tonga." In *Political Anthropology: The State of the Art,* edited by S. L. Seaton and H. J. M. Claessen, 224–242. The Hague: Mouton.

Urbanowicz, C. F. (1989). "Tourism in Tonga Revisited: Continued Troubled Times?" In *Hosts and Guests: The Anthropology of Tourism,* 2nd ed., edited by Valene Smith, 105–117. Philadelphia: University of Pennsylvania Press.

CHARLES F. URBANOWICZ

Tongareva

ETHNONYM: Penrhyn Islanders

Orientation

Identification. In 1853, the brig *Chatham* ran aground on a reef off the southwest coast of Tongareva (Penrhyn Island), marooning fourteen crew members and passengers, some for more than a year. This event heralded dramatic and traumatic changes in the island's demography and culture, and it marks what commonly is considered the contact era. Its single virtue was the account of atoll life written by one of the castaways, E. H. Lamont, that quite properly has been described as "one of the best narratives of first-hand contact with a group of Polynesian people before they were influenced by Western culture" and forms the basis of the contact-era ethnography that follows.

Location. Tongareva, lying at 8°59'45" S and 157°58'50" W, is a rhomboid-shaped atoll of more than 100 islets, with a total land area of 9.73 square kilometers. Annual rainfall is 195.5 centimeters. The atoll is subjected to occasional droughts and hurricanes, often with disastrous effects on subsistence.

Demography. Tongareva's contact-era population was between 1,500 and 2,500, giving a contact-era population density somewhere between about 150 and 250 persons per square kilometer, one of the highest on any atoll in the Pacific. One early visitor commented that the population appeared "so numerous, in proportion to the island, that I cannot, even now, think how so many can find subsistence."

Linguistic Affiliation. Beyond the fact that Tongarevan is a Nuclear Polynesian language, a lack of data coupled with several idiosyncratic linguistic features leave its precise affiliation unclear.

History and Cultural Relations

A tentative prehistory of Tongareva suggests that the atoll was first settled in the thirteenth century or earlier, possibly from Samoa, with later arrivals from Aitutaki and Tahiti (via Rakahanga). Later still, there seems to have been contact with the Line Islands. The first recorded European sighting of the island occurred in 1788, and during the next sixty years traders, whalers, and explorers made at least nine further contacts. Prior to the wreck of the *Chatham* in 1853, however, the islanders' (mistaken) reputation as cannibals kept these foreign contacts to a matter of hours. Sadly, within a decade of the *Chatham's* demise, introduced diseases, labor migration, and the depredations of Peruvian slave ships had reduced the population to about a third of its contact-era level.

Settlements

With the exception of some small unpopulated cays, a few depopulated islets in the northeast, and several strips of unclaimed land, the population in 1853 was distributed fairly evenly around the atoll. In times of peace, family-based settlements of a few houses, sometimes set around a plaza or public place, were dispersed across the land, a pattern that may have developed to protect the food supply from raiders. When war threatened, however, the islanders commonly clustered their houses into villages for mutual protection and rapid mobilization against enemy attacks. There were at least two styles of housing. The most common kind of house was about 2 meters wide, 2.5 meters long, and 1.8 meters high; it featured a roof of plaited coconut fronds with the eaves resting on the ground and the front and back enclosed by more plaited fronds. On some islets, though, there were also larger houses, probably belonging to people of eminence. These dwellings were about 3 or 4 meters square and 1.8 meters at the ridgepole, with their eaves supported on 30-centimeter stakes. Although they had no walls beneath the eaves, matting often was used against the wind. Houses of both types commonly rested on rectangular stone floors, strewn with coral gravel and curbed with thin slabs of coral that jutted 10–30 centimeters above the ground. Pandanus-leaf mats sometimes covered the floors.

Economy.

Subsistence and Commercial Activities. The coconut—its flesh, fluid, embryo, certain types of husk, and (in famine) bud—was the staple of Tongarevan existence. In the absence of domesticated animals and all but a few game animals, marine resources were the principal source of protein. Reef fish were the most favored, but shellfish, flying fish, porpoises, and sharks also were taken. Dietary supplements included the aerial root tips and soft inner kernels of the pandanus.

Industrial Arts. The islanders manufactured baskets, cooking and eating utensils, backrests, sitting and sleeping mats, loincloths and skirts, canoes (including large war canoes), shell axes, nets, fishing lines, hooks, spears, and clubs.

Trade. There was no trade to speak of, either within the atoll or beyond it.

Division of Labor. There was some division of labor by age and sex. Young men and boys gathered and husked coconuts. Both men and women participated in fishing, but only men went turtling and deep-sea diving. While these folk were away at their daily tasks, children and old women remained at home, watching for raids on the coconut supply. At home, women did most of the portering and cooking, though men lit the fires, cooked turtles, and sometimes scraped coconuts. Women plaited mats, while men made canoes and weaponry. Both men and women participated in battle, though women—whose main task was deflecting and breaking incoming spears—were seldom deliberately harmed. Women seem to have done much of the child rearing.

Land Tenure. Palms and land were vested in individuals rather than groups, and, perhaps because of the atoll's population density, they were highly valued and a major source of conflict. The ocean and lagoon apparently were common property resources, though reefs, shellfish grounds, and other submarine beds were exploited only by adjacent inhabitants.

Kinship

Kin Groups and Descent. The principal kin group and basic economic and residential unit was a first-order ramage known as the *haanau,* a patrilineal extended family of up to four generations of agnates. The chief's haanau into which Lamont was adopted comprised about fifteen people and occupied a single settlement of three sleeping houses and a common cook house. Recruitment to the haanau was by birth or adoption, the latter being a very common practice, possibly a consequence of the extreme resource pressure. Sets of haanau tracing descent from a common ancestor and inhabiting part or all of an islet were united into a second-order ramage that may have been called the *huaanga.*

Kinship Terminology. The Tongarevan kin terminology was used for reference rather than address. Like other Polynesian societies, it was Hawaiian, but relative seniority was marked between ego and same-sex relatives of his or her generation. It was atypical and Eskimo-like, however, in having additional descriptive terms for "father," "mother," "uncle," "aunt," "nephew," and "niece." With the exception of "husband" and "wife," in-law terms were collaterally extended within a generation.

Marriage and Family

Marriage. Women apparently could be betrothed before puberty and seem commonly to have married in their mid-teens. Husbands were probably older. "Chiefs" excepted, marriage to second cousins and closer was proscribed; beyond these limits, members of the same huaanga were encouraged to marry to maintain its solidarity and limit the fragmentation of its land. Marriage ceremonies varied in elaboration, the more complex involving the bride's seclusion in mats and self-mutilation by relatives; neither dowry nor bride-wealth was paid. Polygyny principally was restricted to "chiefs." Divorce seems to have been quite common, and postmarital residence was usually virilocal.

Domestic Unit. It is unclear whether the basic domestic unit was the haanau—the patrilineal extended family—or a subsection of it. To judge by the communal cook house in Lamont's settlement, though, it was the haanau.

Inheritance. Land and palms were inherited individually, at the will of the owner, by real and adopted children, nieces, and nephews. At the time of a 1929 study, sons were favored over daughters and elder brothers over younger, but it is unclear if these preferences also were true of the contact era. Spouses might extend usufruct rights to one another. Nothing is known concerning inheritance of movable property.

Socialization. Apart from the fact that many children were adopted or fostered out to consanguineal relatives for greater or lesser periods of time, little is known of Tongarevan socialization.

Sociopolitical Organization

Social Organization. The basic social divisions of Tongareva society were by sex and age. Adult men were the principal authorities within the family, though it appears that women enjoyed considerable autonomy.

Political Organization. The huaanga was the basic political unit, its members united under an *ariki* or "chief" and attending the same *marae* (ritual place); there were about thirteen huaanga in 1853, averaging about 150 members each. The relationships among huaanga were marked by varying degrees of mutual suspicion and hostility, dominance and submission. Groups of four or five adjacent huaanga were united by kinship, realpolitik, or conquest into one of three largely endogamous *hititangata*, which acted primarily as war confederacies. Occasionally, two hititangata would ally against the third. Normatively, ariki were men chosen by primogeniture in a chiefly line, though sometimes at least succession was the subject of competition and decision by council. Although ariki had some ritual authority—imposing taboos and performing rituals to incorporate strangers, for example—their influence rested largely on control of property and networks of kin and allies. The more powerful among them had others do much of their manual labor; Lamont regarded their long thumbnails as "testimony of their privileged idleness." They acted as spokespersons, managers of communal work, arbitrators in serious disputes, and war officials.

Social Control. Taboos imposed by individuals or ariki on use of property were an important means of social control. In 1929, Peter H. Buck reported the importance also of public opinion, vilification, and beating, and it seems probable that these sanctions were employed in the contact era as well. Disputes and other matters of moment commonly were discussed in open-air councils that might involve a haanau alone, one or two huaanga, or even occasionally a whole hititangata.

Conflict. In 1853, Tongareva was divided by warfare among the three hititangata. This conflict was somewhat atypical, however, since the *Chatham* castaways fomented several of the engagements. The usual causes of fighting were coconut shortages, political machination, and revenge. At the first sign of trouble, the elderly would take the very young into hiding. Confrontations occurred both on land and sea. Land engagements frequently involved amphibious landings in large war canoes and often were preceded by ceremonial speeches that might result in conciliation; sometimes, however, Tongarevans launched surprise attacks. Engagements seldom turned into blood baths, possibly because—on land at least—warriors usually were separated by their women, who were considered inviolable.

Religion and Expressive Culture

Religious Beliefs. According to oral tradition, the first Tongarevan humans were the autochthons, Atea and his wife Hakahotu. Several generations later, after a brief stay by the settler Taruia, the great chief Mahuta and his wife, Ocura, arrived from the "land beyond the sky" bringing "cocoa-nuts and other plants for the earth, fish for the sea, and birds for the air." There were four principal gods, incarnated in feather, wood, and hair images but otherwise invisible to all but the *taura* (high priests). Their ritual loci were twenty-nine or so marae scattered around the atoll. Two of the gods gave life and everything necessary to its preservation; another was supplicated to weaken enemies; and the fourth also was malevolent. In addition, the Tongarevans believed in and feared spirits of the dead and the force of taboos.

Religious Practitioners. Although ariki performed certain ritual functions, the principal practitioners were the taura. Invested at, and associated with, specific marae, they acted as mediums for the gods and ancestral spirits, invoking them for assistance in sickness, war, and other troubles. Taura could travel through enemy territory with impunity, and their "spirit houses" were places of refuge; some taura seem to have possessed secular influence to rival that of the more powerful arikis. There may also have been seers.

Ceremonies. Birth was minimally ritualized, but more extensive rites involving genital operations, sexual initiation, and investiture with loincloths or skirts were performed at puberty for both males and females. Marriage ceremonies varied in complexity. There were quite elaborate greeting and welcoming ceremonies, as well as celebratory dances and turtle-eating ceremonies. Mortuary rites, however, were the most involved rituals.

Arts. The contact-era record mentions very little material art beyond the images of the gods, minor embellishments of weaponry, black-feather headdresses worn by an undetermined class of men (probably ariki), and necklets of human hair and fingernails. The more common arts seem to have been ephemeral: songs, dances, pageants, and the recitation of legends.

Medicine. Beyond the fact that the gods frequently were implicated, it is unclear to what causes illness was attributed. Bathing was a very common therapy, occasionally attended, according to Lamont, with (unspecified) "superstitious forms." A coconut-based purgative allegedly was the only medicine they knew. Otherwise, most treatment was in the hands of the taura, aided in the case of eminent patients by the images of the gods.

Death and Afterlife. For some time after death, it was believed, the spirit of the deceased might be seen haunting its familiar grounds. After interment of its bones, it then left for a distant realm, then becoming visible only as stars. At death, the body was washed, anointed with coconut oil, and, along with its spouse or another close relative, covered with a mat. After dirges, dances, self-laceration, and rites to exorcise its spirit, the corpse and some of its utensils and tools were sewn in the mat and hung from the roof of a sleeping house under the observance of a chief mourner. If the deceased were eminent, this vigil might last as long as six months; afterwards, the bones were buried and a funeral feast celebrated.

See also Cook Islands

Bibliography

Bellwood, Peter S. (1978). *Archaeological Research in the Cook Islands.* Pacific Anthropological Records, no. 27. Honolulu: Bernice P. Biship Museum, Department of Anthropology.

Buck, P. H. (1932). *Ethnology of Tongareva.* Bernice P. Bishop Museum Bulletin no. 92. Honolulu.

Campbell, Andrew R. T. (1985). *Social Relations in Ancient Tongareva.* Pacific Anthropological Records, no. 36. Honolulu: Bernice P. Bishop Museum, Department of Anthropology.

Lamont, E. H. (1867). *Wild Life among the Pacific Islanders.* London: Hurst & Blackett.

Roscoe, Paul B. (1987). "Of Canoes and Castaways: Reassessing the Population of Tongareva (Penrhyn Island) at Contact." *Pacific Studies* 11:43–61.

PAUL B. ROSCOE

Tor

ETHNONYMS: Berik, Bonerif, Kaowerawedj, Kwerba, Mander, Soromaja

Orientation

Identification. The Tor River (as it is called in the Berik language) promotes a sense of cultural if not linguistic unity, with the groups living along its banks conscious of being "People of the Tor," or "Torangwa." The term "Tor" will be used here to refer mainly to the Berik, Bonerif, and Mander peoples and, to a lesser extent, their Kwerba neighbors on the Apauwar and Mamberamo rivers to the west.

Location. The Tor River arises in the Gauttier Mountains of the Sarmi Subdivision of Jayapura Division in northern Irian Jaya, and it empties into the Pacific Ocean about 25 kilometers east of the town of Sarmi, at about 1°50' S, 139° E. The Upper Tor is a region of foothills, plains, and tropical rain forest, where the river is too braided and filled with debris for canoe travel. Farther downstream, the Middle Tor is a rugged region giving way to the Lower Tor, where the river meanders through sago swamps. In these lower regions people can use canoes for transport, but in the Upper Tor watercourses are used whenever possible as footpaths. Large areas of this region of about 2,200 square kilometers are never visited by the widely dispersed and seminomadic populations.

Demography. In the late 1950s, the Tor Basin was estimated to be home to about 1,000 people, with perhaps twice as many Kwerba living immediately to the west. While reliable figures are not currently available, recent estimates suggest small if any increases since then. Indeed, one of the striking features of the Tor populations is that between the 1930s and 1960 a very low birth rate combined with 35–40 percent infant mortality to produce a serious depopulation problem, which was compounded by extremely high ratios of males to females in all tribes of the region and which threatened extinction for many groups. There is still no explanation for the high degree of masculinization of the population.

Linguistic Affiliation. Most of the languages spoken in the region constitute the Tor Family of Non-Austronesian languages, with Kwerba a member of its own separate family. Throughout the area Berik is used most and has become a lingua franca of the district.

History and Cultural Relations

Nothing is known of the prehistory of the Tor peoples apart from oral traditions that indicate that many of the people have immigrated there during the twentieth century from the Lake Plains area of the Idenburg River to the southeast. The combination of a very difficult physical environment and depredations by the Wares and other groups to the east and south have resulted in continual fissioning, extinctions, and migrations. The Tor groups had almost no contact with the Western world until the Dutch administration and missionaries began development and conversion attempts after World War II. Since Irian Jaya became a province of Indonesia, almost no new information about the Tor has become available; the description provided here is based almost entirely on the situation in the late 1950s.

Settlements

All of the Tor peoples are seminomadic, but villages are maintained as semipermanent residences and are the centers of social and religious life. Usually a village consists of eight to twelve houses built on piles, with a cult house in the center of the settlement. The houses are arranged in a straight line if located on rivers or ridge tops, or in a circle if in a forest clearing. In addition, branch villages, containing about four houses, are found all over the territory; these are used for sexual intercourse (which is forbidden in the main village), as refuges from sorcery fears, and as temporary residences during sago processing.

Economy

Subsistence and Commercial Activities. More than 90 percent of the Tor diet consists of sago, which is never planted but grows wild in extensive groves in the Middle and Lower Tor. The ideal meal consists of sago and fish, with the latter obtained by bow and arrow or through damming and poisoning of rivulets (not the Tor itself). Collecting of shellfish, larvae, worms, slugs, eggs, greens, wild fruits, and breadfruit is very important, whereas hunting of wild pigs, cassowaries, lizards, rats, opossums, and birds makes little contribution to the larder. Pigs are raised from wild piglets caught in the forest; though they are hand-fed sago, they forage freely for most of their food and when fully grown are killed for feasts. Some rudimentary gardens are made near rivers but they are widely dispersed; bananas and pawpaws are grown but, with no fences, are subject to the depredations of pigs. Recently corn, yams, and beans have been introduced and are grown in gardens around mission settlements and schools. The only potential cash crop is dammar, a resin collected from the foot of *Agathis* trees. The Tor peoples use dammar for illumination at night, and the Dutch government encouraged its production as a source of cash in the 1950s. The Mander people are the main producers of dammar, which is then transported to the Lower Tor and coast by Berik people for sale to Chinese and coastal traders. The dammar, which is used in the West for varnish and other products, has been virtually the only source of money and Western goods for the Tor.

Industrial Arts. Apart from canoes, which are made and used only on the Middle and Lower Tor, houses are the only large objects manufactured. Clothing for both sexes consists of crushed-bark aprons, supplemented with fern-fiber abdomen shields for men. Knotted net bags, rattan headdresses, and ceremonial figures are also made, and men carve arrows as a group project on a fixed schedule. Tor sago spoons and forks are regarded as models of wood carving.

Trade. Barter is conducted only between tribes with close social relations, and even then it is largely a matter of individual ties. "Silent trade" is also engaged in between enemy groups. Products circulating in the region include dogs, arrows, pork, drums, cassowary quills, shells, and charms, with poultry entering the trade system in recent decades.

Division of Labor. No occupational specialization exists, with the division of labor based simply on sex. Men engage in trade, wood carving, house building, hunting, and fishing, and they also conduct religious ceremonies. Both sexes collect wild foods, but this is mainly a task assigned to women, who also tend the pigs. When gardens are made, it is the man's job to clear the forest and both husband and wife may share the planting tasks, although this would be true mostly for older men. Women have primary responsibility for the food supply, and sago processing is exclusively a female task, beginning at about the age of 8. Sago processing is always done by groups of women while men hunt in the forest, usually alone but sometimes in groups of bachelors.

Land Tenure. Except in sago groves (which are exclusively allocated to women) all members of a tribe, irrespective of age or sex, have equal rights to collect, hunt, fish, garden, and live on its territory. These rights are permanent as long as one visits the territory. Usufruct rights may be granted to people outside the tribe only if all agree to the extension. Planted fruit trees or gardens, however, belong to the individuals responsible, though rights in them are usually shared with siblings and spouses. Again, usufruct rights may be given to friends, kin, or visitors.

Kinship

Kin Groups and Descent. Kinship is all-important to the Tor. They feel safe only among kin, because kin are believed never to perform sorcery against relatives and also cannot refuse to share food. Descent is traced bilaterally (though in Kwerba communities patriclans can be found), and, in the small populations characteristic of the region, virtually everyone is related to everyone else in the tribal community.

Kinship Terminology. At least three distinct types of kinship terminology systems are found in the region, though kin terms are typically extended to friends and the situation is complicated by the existence of many different paths by which kin connections may be traced. The most widespread system is that of the Berik, who do not mark sex but attend principally to relative age except in the case of mother's brother; they also employ Hawaiian-type cousin terms. The Mander do not extend parent or child terms, and they use Iroquois-type cousin terms. The latter are also used by Kwerba, who otherwise show a strong tendency toward a generational system and distinguish between the sexes.

Marriage and Family

Marriage. Marriage, viewed as an economic institution, is indispensable to the status and very survival of a male. By the time he is considered marriageable, at about age 23, his mother is usually dead and his sisters are married; without a wife he has no source of sago, for which he is expected to reciprocate fish and pork. Young women generally marry when they are age 17 to 22 after complex negotiations, especially involving the elder brothers of the pair. The ideal arrangement is sister exchange (although the "sister" may be any kinswoman younger than the male giver), and in principle all four parties must agree to the union, with the potential bride being free to refuse. Especially given the demographic situation in recent decades, the exchange is not usually immediate and simultaneous, but if it is not the groom must periodically give gifts to his wife's elder brothers. In contrast to the ideal, however, elopement and "love marriages" based on personal attraction are frequent; elopement with a wife deserting one man for another is the only way, apart from death, by which a marriage may be dissolved. Again because of the masculinization of the population, about 30 percent of the men are unable to marry and become permanent bachelors. Despite this fact, polyandry is not allowed (although any woman may have sexual intercourse with her husband's brothers), but about 20 percent of the men are polygynous. These, however, are nearly always older men with old wives, who would be destitute without viable sources of sago; indeed, polygyny is regarded as a sign of weakness on the part of a man. A strong preference for tribal endogamy (marrying classificatory siblings and cousins) results in about 90 percent of marriages taking place between members of the same community. In cases of village exogamy, the ideal is for the couple to reside virilocally, but given the need for access to sago, uxorilocality is about equal in frequency.

Domestic Unit. The nuclear family is clearly distinguishable throughout the region, but two main forms of household are found. Among the Mander the nuclear family forms an independent unit, with its members residing all in one house (including older cowives, though usually not younger ones) and sharing gardening and child-care tasks. In the other groups, the "domestic family" or "fraternal joint family" is the domestic and economic unit, usually with brothers and their families sharing a house and gardens and moving together in the nomadic food quest.

Inheritance. A person inherits rights to territory from both father and mother, and usually before death rights to sago or fruit trees are bequeathed to one's children or siblings and dogs are given to the sons or younger brothers of their male owners. Otherwise, at death all of a person's possessions are destroyed: a man's arrows are broken and burned; pigs are killed and the meat fed to dogs; and fruit trees are cut down.

Socialization. Among the Mander, who have access to the most sago, children are looked after by men while their wives are off processing sago. Elsewhere, women who are currently in the village look after all of the children while some of the working women are working in sago groves and men are hunting in the forest.

Sociopolitical Organization

Social Organization. The village is the largest and most important social group and is virtually synonymous with the tribe: it is a named territorial group with fixed boundaries, which acts as a political unit and, despite its small size (seldom more than eighty-five people), usually consists of all of the speakers of a given language; given its strong tendency towards endogamy, it may also be considered a deme. There is considerable rivalry among all Tor tribes, with each thinking itself superior to all others. In recent decades, bachelors have emerged as a distinct social grouping, living together in their own house in the village or wandering together in the forest. New functions of the bachelors' group include conducting barter across tribal boundaries and organizing festivities. Increasingly bachelors have been attracted to European centers in search of work.

Political Organization. Territorial groups (tribes) are autonomous, though usually they are on either friendly or enemy terms with others. Tor communities are egalitarian, with no hereditary leadership; men achieve status and influence through their demonstrated economic skills or cleverness, traits that are more important than age in the power structure. The Dutch administration appointed headmen of villages, and recently in mission settlements non-Tor teachers have become community leaders. Perhaps because of their overwhelming importance in the food quest, women are the main determiners of public opinion; it is common for a wife to threaten to desert her husband if her wishes are not heeded.

Social Control. Community opinion is the only real form of social control. If ridicule and physical conflict prove to be insufficient sanctions, ostracism may lead to voluntary or involuntary banishment.

Conflict. Nearly all quarrels occur in the context of disputes over women. While they may begin between individuals, obligations of kin to assist each other soon turn them into conflicts between villages. If conflict is not resolved through ritual purification or gift exchange, it can be a main source of community fission.

Religion and Expressive Culture

Religious Beliefs. Apart from ghosts, the Tor cosmos includes two main types of supernatural beings: those who were never human; and those who were but who have gone to Heaven without dying first. Among the former are personifications of the sun and moon, and Oetantifie, the omnipresent, omniscient originator of world order. In the view of the ethnographer Gottfried Oosterwal, he is the "power in the background" for the Tor, ever threatening to punish human beings, especially by causing floods and reducing the world to chaos. The other beings are culture heroes, usually localized by tribe, who live in the sky and are mainly friendly and benevolent, assisting people in fishing, hunting, and healing, though there are also malevolent demons.

Religious Practitioners. Apart from healers, the only practitioners are adult men who conduct ceremonies and, increasingly, bachelors who play major roles in organizing and carrying out feasts.

Ceremonies. Life-cycle ceremonies are held for females only at birth and death; for males, these two rituals are supplemented by initiation into the men's cult and a "coming to manhood" rite. Male initiation occurs at about the age of 14, when youths are forcibly taken to a specially constructed house deep in the forest and secluded for several months. There they are taught the secret of the growth- and prosperity-inducing sacred flutes of the men's cult and instructed in the ways of the forest. Following this seclusion the boys move from their family houses into the bachelors' house to await coming to manhood and marriageability at age 18 to 23. The major ceremony for the community as a whole involves building and inaugurating a new cult house. Over a period of months, each stage in its construction is marked by feasting and dancing. Upon completion, the inauguration ceremony draws people from far and wide who feast together to consolidate and restore friendship bonds. At a special flute feast, the men's secret flutes are fed with pork from a pig especially killed for the occasion, and thus the strength, growing power, and good order of the community are renewed and reassured.

Arts. Rattan figures of fruit bats and the moon are hung in the community cult house, as are carved wooden phalluses intended to arouse women while they dance during associated ceremonies. Both sexes engage in tattooing through burning, and large repertoires of songs and dances are performed during feasts. Each tribe has its distinctive styles of decoration of arrows, sago spatulas, and sago forks.

Medicine. Malaria is endemic in most of the Tor, and pneumonia, filariasis, and yaws are common health problems. In response, bush medicines are used, and mothers commonly rub their children with saliva as a treatment procedure. Most disease and all accidents are attributed ultimately to sorcery, which is a constant concern leading to fear of any nonkin. Healing specialists have some sex-specific methods: only men engage in bloodletting—and that only with male patients—while women healers suck out "bad blood" from people of both sexes.

Death and Afterlife. Except in cases involving the very old, sorcery is the first explanation offered for a death. Traditionally, the corpse was wrapped in sago leaves and either exposed on a scaffold or in a tree or buried under its house; after that procedure, all of the deceased's possessions were destroyed and the village abandoned. The shade remaining after decomposition of the physical remains is believed to float in space, with some body parts being luminous. Shades are believed to live together in villages in well-identified locations that are avoided by all people. Life after death is regarded as torture, with constant food scarcity (because sago cannot grow in their areas) driving the shades to prowl in human villages seeking food.

Bibliography

DeVries, Jim (1988). "Kwerba View of the Supernatural World." *Irian* 16:1–16.

Eechoud, J. P. K. van (1962). *Etnografie van de Kaowerawedj (Centraal Nieuw-Guinea)*. The Hague: Martinus Nijhoff.

Oosterwal, Gottfried (1959). "The Position of the Bachelor in the Upper Tor Territory." *American Anthropologist* 61:829–839.

Oosterwal, Gottfried (1961). *People of the Tor: A Cultural-Anthropological Study on the Tribes of the Tor Territory (Northern Netherlands New Guinea)*. Assen: Royal Van Gorcum.

Oosterwal, Gottfried (1967). "Muremarew: A Dual Organized Village on the Mamberamo, West Irian." In *Villages in*

Indonesia, edited by Koentjaraningrat, 157–188. Ithaca: Cornell University Press.

Oosterwal, Gottfried (1976). "The Role of Women in the Male Cults of the Soromaja in New Guinea." In *The Realm of the Extra-Human: Agents and Audiences,* edited by Agehananda Bharati, 323–334. The Hague: Mouton.

TERENCE E. HAYS

Torres Strait Islanders

ETHNONYMS: None

Orientation

Identification. The Torres Strait Islanders are a Melanesian group who live on the islands of Torres Strait and in coastal communities of Queensland, Australia. The strait is named for its Spanish discoverer, Captain Luis Baez de Torres, who first explored the region in 1606. The islands and their inhabitants are among the most famous of ethnographic subjects as a result of the Cambridge University expedition of 1898, organized and led by A. C. Haddon.

Location. Torres Strait, which connects the Coral and Arafura seas, lies between the southwestern coast of Papua New Guinea and Australia's Cape York. Out of the more than 100 islands in the strait, only about 20 were or are inhabited—the rest being too small or too lacking in resources to support a full-time population. The inhabited islands are of four basic physical types. The Western Islands are large high islands, well-watered and fringed by mangrove swamps; the Central Islands are sand cays on coral reefs; the Eastern Islands are small, volcanic formations with fertile soil; and, to the north, near the coast of Papua New Guinea, there are large, low islands frequently subject to flooding, whose predominant vegetation is mangrove swamps.

Demography. At the time of European contact the population of the islands was estimated at between 4,000 and 5,000, living in communities that varied in size from less than 100 people to more than 800. By the end of the 1800s, the population had dropped to about 3,000, largely as a result of the depredations of introduced disease and of overwork and ill-treatment by the European-controlled trepang and pearling industries. The first official population count, in 1913, showed 2,368 islanders. Figures for more recent times are rather questionable, because of methodological problems in ethnic identification, but a 1981 commonwealth census puts the figure at 15,232, about half of whom live and work in communities on the Australian mainland.

Linguistic Affiliation. Meriam Mir (or Miriam), the language of the Eastern Torres Strait Islands, is a member of the Eastern Trans-Fly Family. On the other islands the language spoken (Mabuiag) betrays a mix of Melanesian and Aboriginal linguistic elements.

History and Cultural Relations

Traditional history holds that the current Torres Strait Islands were originally settled by people from Papua, and linguistic and material cultural evidence suggests ties to Australian Aboriginal peoples as well. What is certain is that there was trade between the islanders and both Papuan and Aboriginal peoples long before contact with Europeans, and the influences of these trading partners are apparent in a wide range of material and cultural elements of Torres Strait society even today. The islands were first sighted by Europeans in the early 1600s but were largely ignored until the 1770 voyage of Captain Cook, shortly after which the straits became regularly traveled. These early contacts were largely incidental to the European use of the straits en route elsewhere, such as the British colony of New South Wales. By the middle of the 1800s, however, the straits attracted trepangers and pearlers whose impact upon island life was rather more dramatic: islanders were forced to work, and women were often abducted. By 1863, Queensland had established a colonial post in the islands, and in 1871 the London Missionary Society landed teachers on Darnley Island. Conversion of the islanders to Christianity and to participation in the pearling industry was swift. The conflicting goals and aims of the colonial administration vis-à-vis those of the society resulted in the withdrawal of the society and the entry of the Anglican church. Pentecostalism, introduced by islanders who had worked on the mainland, began attracting a strong following in the islands by the late 1930s. The annexation of the islands by Queensland was completed by 1879. In 1898, elected councils were established, but economic control of island life remained, and still largely remains, in outsiders' hands. Islanders participated in World War II, and memories of those "army days" inspired islanders to the effort of gaining full citizenship and civil rights—an effort that continues to this day.

Settlements

Settlement types varied in the islands. On those islands capable of supporting gardening to any great extent, villages consisted of a collection of huts grouped together along the shore, with a cult shrine and associated garden plots. Permanent shelters varied in construction type throughout the islands: the eastern islanders favored a cone-shaped hut of reeds and grasses, while the northern islanders built long huts elevated on stilts. On the smaller or less fertile islands, only temporary structures were established, as might be expected for people depending primarily upon hunting and gathering for their subsistence. Traditionally, men and initiated boys slept in one hut or portion of camp, separate from the dwellings or camping grounds of the women and children. With Christianity, settlements were established in clusters around the church mission and schools, and the separation of men's and women's housing was replaced by the nuclear-family household.

Economy

Subsistence and Commercial Activities. The principal protein sources for islanders are turtles, dugongs, fish, and shellfish. Most of the Torres Strait Islands are not particularly suited to cultivation to any great extent, because of their small tillable areas and low soil fertility. The larger northern and eastern islands support swidden horticulture, but elsewhere in the strait most vegetable matter is gathered in the wild. Vegetable staples include yams, edible mangrove fruits, beans, and a variety of fruits and nuts. On those islands capable of supporting cultivation, the primary crop is yams, but other crops include bananas, taro, sugarcane, sweet potatoes, tobacco, and coconuts. Harvesting the products of the sea was always a major portion of the islanders' subsistence economy, but this took on a more commercial aspect with the European introduction of the trepang and pearling industries. In the 1950s, the development of plastics disrupted the islander economy by undercutting the market for pearl shells, and this in turn precipitated a major labor migration to the Australian mainland and prompted islander youths to seek cash-based employment.

Industrial Arts. Until recent times, many items of daily use, such as spears, stone clubs, canoe hulls, bows, and arrows, were acquired through trade, for the islands do not provide suitable timber or hard stone for their manufacture. But Torres Straits Islanders made their own shell hoes and digging sticks, as well as adzes and axes that were constructed from the shells of the giant clams. Other tools and implements were fashioned from turtleshells. Mats, used in the construction of temporary shelters, as canoe sails, and for sitting or sleeping on, were woven from pandanus or coconut leaves. While canoe hulls were imported from Papua New Guinea, the construction of a finished Torres Strait canoe involved a great deal of additional work: to the dug-out hull would be attached outrigger poles and floats; masts and paddles; a platform; and storage "lockers" for food and trade items. Other manufactured goods included: masks; items of personal adornment made of shell, tooth, bone, and imported feathers; and net bags.

Trade. Traditionally, the most important trade was with the peoples of Papua New Guinea: the islanders traded items made of pearl shells, turtleshells, and conus shells—as well as trading human heads—in return for canoes, drums, cassowary and bird-of-paradise feathers, and weapons. A lesser—but nonetheless important—trade network existed between the islanders and the Aboriginal peoples of Australia, who provided spears, spear throwers, and red and white ocher. Trade also occurred among the Torres Strait Islands themselves, primarily involving foodstuffs and tobacco but also permitting the circulation of finished ear ornaments, pendants, hair combs, necklets, armbands, and the like.

Division of Labor. Men hunt sea turtles with harpoons or, more commonly, simply by slipping a rope around the front flippers and towing them back to land. Dugongs are harpooned. Fish are caught with multipronged, thrusting spears, with hooks and lines of turtleshell, or with the use of spear throwers. On some islands bamboo scoops or stone fish traps are used. Men also collect crustaceans and shellfish from the reefs and atolls. Women collect wild vegetables, fruit, and nuts in net bags that they weave from pandanus leaves, grass, rattan, and rushes. Women also provide most of the labor for weeding and harvesting on those islands supporting horticulture, while men on such islands do the heavy work of clearing gardens and burning off the ground cover in preparing the gardens. Garden magic is men's work, while cooking and food processing is routinely done by women. Both men and women participated in the early days of the trepanging and pearling, but once the shallower coastal beds were worked out it became a predominantly male enterprise.

Kinship

Kin Groups and Descent. Throughout the islands there is a patrilineal bias to the reckoning of kinship, but maternal kin are recognized as well. Community groups tend to be predominantly made up of patrilaterally related men, their spouses, and their children, but descent is not reckoned very deeply. The concept of "family" is now strongly "privatized" in accordance with the majority practice of Australian society.

Marriage and Family

Marriage. Courtship was traditionally initiated by the prospective wife, who expressed her interest in a young man by sending him a small gift—usually through his sister. Should the boy be interested, the girl's parents would eventually involve themselves in negotiations with the boy's family to set the bride-price. Upon the payment of the bride-price, the bride would simply be brought to the camp of her new husband where she would build a fire and begin the responsibilities of wifehood. While there appears to have been no formal ceremony, a community feast and dance such as generally accompanied all major life-cycle events would be held. Island custom permitted polygyny, but it was generally only the most successful of leading men who were able to afford the multiple bride-prices that polygynous marriages required, and with Christianity the practice was ended. Postmarital residence was initially with the family of the groom, but after the birth of children the young family would generally establish their own household and were free to live wherever they chose. Divorce was and is frowned upon, but it did and does occur.

Domestic Unit. The traditional domestic unit minimally consisted of a nuclear family plus one or more dependent relatives of the grandparental generation, and this pattern constitutes the general rule on the islands.

Inheritance. Traditionally, land rights, magic spells, and fetishes were inherited by sons for the most part, although a daughter might be permitted a small plot of land upon her marriage or might even inherit the whole plot in the absence of brothers. Women's lore passed from mother to daughter.

Socialization. In earlier times, mothers taught their daughters their future roles and responsibilities as wives and mothers by the simple expedient of enlisting the girls' help as the mothers went about their daily tasks. Young boys were largely free of such responsibilities. Female initiation occurred at puberty, and involved seclusion with a paternal aunt who provided assistance and instruction. Male initiation ritual was more elaborate—boys were secluded in pairs under the tutelage of a maternal uncle for up to three months during which time they underwent dietary taboos and were instructed in proper adult male behavior, as well as undergoing physical ordeals that were intended to transform them into men. A central feature of male initiation was the introduction of the boys to the chants, lore, fetishes, and sacred masks of the culture heroes. For both boys and girls, initiation rites marked the transition from childhood to adult status.

Sociopolitical Organization

Social Organization. Kinship, bilaterally reckoned, is invoked as the organizing principle in island life, be it in putting together a work crew, justifying the establishment of residence in a community, or cooperating in throwing a feast.

Political Organization. Torres Strait leadership was traditionally achieved rather than ascribed, and it was largely based upon a reputation for generosity and a willingness to help one's fellows. But the egalitarian nature of traditional society, and the relatively autonomous nature of households meant that there were limited occasions wherein leadership was required on a communitywide basis. Warfare was one such enterprise, as was land allocation and dispute settlement, and community elders provided the means for achieving consensus in such circumstances. With the establishment of island councils, communities elected representatives (councillors) to serve the traditional functions of elders and to mediate islanders and the government.

Social Control. Traditional mechanisms of social control were largely informal and mainly consisted of public censure or disapproval. But with the advent of the missionaries, social control often came under the auspices of the church and its representatives, and the threat of expulsion from the church provided an institutionalized means of securing individual compliance with social norms.

Conflict. All small communities give rise to interpersonal frictions, and the Torres Strait Islanders were not exempt from this. But friends or kin were always ready to mediate when possible, and if they failed, the community elders would attempt to reconcile disputants before hostilities could get out of hand. Conflicts between individuals of different communities were commonly expressed in accusations of witchcraft or sorcery; within the community antagonisms found release in arguments or, more rarely, brawls.

Warfare and raiding was common throughout the Torres Strait, encouraged by traditional beliefs that the taking of a human head marked a boy's attainment of full manhood. Stated reasons for a particular raiding expedition usually included revenge for perceived insult to one's group. Over time, relations of enmity between two islands or communities assumed the character of tradition. Wars were fought with bows and arrows and stone clubs, and members of war parties carried braided cane shields and wore distinctive feather headdresses and shell ornaments. Prior to a raid, warriors sought out the offices of medicine men for magic to secure a successful outcome, and dances and chants were composed to celebrate victory. With the advent of colonialism and the influence of missionaries, a policy of pacification brought an end to warfare and head-hunting in the region.

Religion and Expressive Culture

Religious Beliefs. Indigenous religion in the Torres Strait fell victim to Christianity early and thoroughly in the years of European contact, and few traces of it remain. It appears that beliefs focused upon a cast of culture heroes whose travels throughout the region were recounted in creation myths. Through the exploits of these mythological beings the physical features of the islands and many of the social and cultural practices of the islanders were brought into being. Principal among these culture heroes, at least in the Western Islands, was Kwoiam, said to have come from the Aboriginal peoples of Cape York, whose deeds were recounted on important ceremonial occasions. Culture heroes, the things they used, and the places with which they were associated assumed a totemic character in the beliefs of the islanders, and a variety of hero cults existed throughout the islands. There is some evidence to suggest that the hero cults are an importation from Aboriginal and Papuan sources and that they were grafted onto an earlier belief system, which itself was totemic in nature. Christianity was first introduced through the efforts of the London Missionary Society in the late 1700s; this creed was replaced by Anglicanism when the society withdrew from the strait in 1914. In the 1930s, Pentecostalism was introduced by islanders returning from Queensland communities and established a rivalry with Anglicanism for island followers. Island Christianity today incorporates much precontact religious practice, and recourse to magic (for gardening, fishing, revenge, and curing) still occurs.

Religious Practitioners. Traditionally medicine men, or magicians, began training in their early teens by becoming apprenticed to an established practitioner. Training involved direct teaching, practice, and submission to trials by ritual ordeal. The apprentice attained full practitioner status when he successfully cast a "hostile" spell—that is, when he succeeded in causing the death of an intended victim through magic. Traditional officiants at ceremonial occasions are elder men of high repute and esteem within their villages, for these are the people in whom resides the greatest knowledge of and experience in cult lore, practice, and magic. Islander men have been trained to the ministry and priesthood since the early days of proselytizing in the region.

Ceremonies. The principal island ritual occasion is the "tombstone opening," wherein the grave marker is formally revealed to all kin and friends of the deceased; this ceremony may take place many years after the actual death. This ritual is an occasion of feasting and dancing and may bring in celebrants from throughout the strait as well as from the mainland. Other major ceremonial occasions follow the Christian calendar and include Christmas and Lent. Of particular importance is the 1 July celebration, commemorating the date of the arrival of "The Light"—that is, the arrival of the first mission teachers sent by the London Missionary Society. Celebrations involve feasting, dancing, and singing. Traditional hero-cult ceremonials occurred in the context of initiation rites and involved the reenactment of important events in the hero myths. Ceremonial costume included elaborate sacred masks.

Arts. In traditional times, masks, headdresses, and articles of personal adornment attained a high degree of decorative elaboration. Islander canoes were highly carved. Current musical instruments include drums, panpipes, whistles, flutes, and rattles, and the composition and performance of songs for festive occasions is still a highly valued skill. Island dance is a dramatic, coordinated series of stamping and leaps performed by troupes of young men, often in competition with one another.

Medicine. Traditional medicine involved the use of magic, either alone or in conjunction with herbal remedies or bloodletting. The type of cure employed was dependent upon diagnosis of visible symptoms. Today, islanders may make use of Western medicine but still respect traditional curing practices.

Death and Afterlife. Traditional beliefs held that the spirit of the deceased was capable of bringing harm to the community, and funerary ritual was intended to avert such danger through appeasing the spirit and freeing it to make the journey to an "Isle of the Dead" somewhere in the west. When a man died, the village members marked the occurrence with loud wailing and crying, then abandoned the village site to the corpse and the male kin of the widow, who built a platform upon which the body was placed. At a later date, the head of the corpse would be removed for use in ritual divination to learn if sorcery was the cause of death and thus to determine the necessity of mounting a revenge party. The widow kept the skull to carry about with her throughout her mourning period, but the remainder of the corpse would be interred. Current funerary practice follows customary Western standards, although a tombstone-opening festival, featuring traditional feasting and dancing, is later held.

See also Kiwai

Bibliography

Beckett, Jeremy (1987). *Torres Strait Islanders: Custom and Colonialism.* New York: Cambridge University Press.

Haddon, A., ed. (1901–1935). *Reports of the Cambridge Anthropological Expedition to Torres Strait.* 6 vols. Cambridge: Cambridge University Press.

Singe, J. (1979). *The Torres Strait Islanders.* St. Lucia: Queensland University Press.

NANCY E. GRATTON

Trobriand Islands

ETHNONYMS: Kaileuna, Kilivila, Kiriwina, Kitava, Vakuta

Orientation

Identification. The Trobriand Islands were named for Denis de Trobriand, the first lieutenant in one of D'Entrecasteaux's frigates when this group of populated atolls and hundreds of islets was sighted in 1793. Traditionally, Kiriwina—the largest and most heavily populated island—and three other neighboring islands—Kaileuna, Kitava, and Vakuta—were each divided into discrete, named political districts. Although these divisions still exist, the islands now form a more unified political unit as parts of Milne Bay Province, Papua New Guinea.

Location. The Trobriands (approximately 8°30' S, 151° E) are situated about 384 km by sea from Port Moresby, the capital of Papua New Guinea, in the northern tip of the Massim. Kiriwina is 40 kilometers long but only 3.2 to 12.8 kilometers wide, and the other islands are much smaller. Except for Kitava, where cliffs rise sheer for 90 meters, the islands are relatively flat, crosscut by swampy areas, tidal creeks, and rich garden lands that abut rough coral outcroppings. Reefs may extend up to 10 kilometers offshore; anchorage is often dependent upon high tides and careful navigation. Temperatures and humidity are uniformly high. Rain showers, heavy but usually of short duration, average from 25 to 38 centimeters each month. Yet unexpected droughts can occur, causing severe food shortages.

Demography. At the beginning of this century, the population in the Trobriands was about 8,000, but by 1990 it had increased to approximately 20,000. Although many young people leave the islands to find wage labor or to attend technical schools or the University of Papua New Guinea, a large percentage of them eventually return to resume village life.

Linguistic Affiliation. The Kilivila language belongs to the Milne Bay Family of Austronesian languages. Although Kilivila is spoken on a few other Massim islands, the major speakers are Trobrianders. Mutually understandable local dialects are used in which different phonological rules are employed without affecting the syntax. Since the time of first contact, many English words have been incorporated into the Kilivila lexicon. Tok Pisin is rarely heard, although, along with Motu, it is often learned by Trobrianders who have resided elsewhere in Papua New Guinea. English is taught in the local grammar schools as well as the high school on Kiriwina, but less than half of the young population attend school.

History and Cultural Relations

The origin stories for each matrilineage describe how different groups arrived in the Trobriands from under the ground or by canoe and claimed garden and hamlet lands as their own. These claims were often contested by others who arrived later, so that subdivisions of matrilineages occurred. American whalers were in the northern Massim during the 1840s, and twenty years later Queensland's blackbirding ships made frequent kidnapping excursions to other islands in the vicinity. In the 1890s, Germans periodically sailed from New Britain to purchase tons of Trobriand yams, while wood carvings, decorated shells, and canoe prows were already becoming part of museum collections. The turn of the century marked the establishment of the Methodist Overseas Mission (now the United Church Mission) on Kiriwina, followed in 1905 by the arrival of Dr. Rayner Bellamy, the first Australian resident government officer. Bellamy spent ten years in charge of the government station on Kiriwina and assisted C. G. Seligman with ethnographic information during Seligman's Massim research. Following his mentor, Bronislaw Malinowski stopped on Kiriwina and then stayed for two years between 1915 and 1918. The Sacred Heart Catholic Mission arrived in the 1930s but during World War II all resident Europeans were evacuated. Australian and U.S. troops set up a hospital and two airstrips on Kiriwina. Although no battles were fought the area served as a staging ground for planes en route to Rabaul and the Coral Sea. In 1950, when Harry Powell arrived to undertake ethnographic research, surprisingly few fundamental cultural changes had occurred. Even in

1990, *kula*, the interisland exchange of arm shells and necklaces, was as intense as ever, while yam harvests and women's mortuary distributions remain as politically dynamic.

Settlements

Trobrianders live in named hamlets associated with specific garden, bush, and beach lands. Usually, from four to six hamlets are grouped together to form a discrete village with populations ranging from 200 to 500. Yam houses stand prominently around a central clearing, dwarfing the individual dwellings built behind this plaza. Chiefs may decorate their houses and their yam houses with ancestral designs and hang cowrie shells indicating differences in ranking. If a chief is polygynous, each wife will have her own separate house. In all other cases, husbands and wives live together with their young children while adolescent boys, and sometimes girls, have their own small sleeping houses close by their parents' living quarters. These are the houses widows and widowers retire to when they are too old to remarry. Hamlets look much as they did in Bronislaw Malinowski's photographs. Roofs are still thatched (although some metal roofs are in evidence) and the walls are made from plaited coconut-palm fronds. The interior of the house is private, with a fireplace and sleeping areas, while most social life takes place on the verandas. Burial plots are at the edge of the hamlet. From there footpaths provide quick communication between villages. On Kiriwina, only one vehicular road (with several spurs) bisects the island.

Economy

Subsistence and Commercial Activities. Trobrianders are yam growers par excellence. Through slash-and-burn technology, large yam harvests are produced once a year. Taro, sweet potatoes, bananas, sugarcane, leafy greens, beans, tapioca, squashes, coconuts, and areca palms are also grown. The pig population is small; pork is usually eaten only at special feasts. Few chickens are raised and fish provides the major protein source. There is almost no game, except for birds that are sometimes hunted; children catch and eat frogs, grubs, insect eggs, as well as mollusks they collect along the reefs. Since colonization, government attempts at developing cash crops have failed (except for a period of copra production) and only within the past few years has a local market run by women been installed on Kiriwina. Fishing provides many coastal men with cash incomes and a fishing cooperative has been successful on Vakuta Island. In the 1970s, weekend tourist charters resulted in increasing carving sales, but over the past decade tourism has declined dramatically. Ebony wood, once prized for fine carvings, is depleted and must be imported from other islands. A few Kiriwinans own successful trade stores; a guest lodge and two other trade stores are owned and run by expatriates. Today, remittances from children working elsewhere in the country provide villagers with their main source of cash. Women's bundles of dried banana leaves act as a limited currency when villagers buy trade-store foods, tobacco, kerosene, or cloth and sell such things to other villagers for payment in bundles. In this way, those without cash can purchase Western merchandise.

Industrial Arts. Most garden and other tools are metal. Canoes still are built in the traditional way, with their elaborately carved prows. Pandanus sleeping and floor mats, baskets, and armbands are woven; so are traditional women's skirts, which, although only worn on special occasions, are considered as wealth and are vital for mortuary exchanges. Bundles of dried banana leaves are also produced by women and as wealth are necessary for mortuary distributions. A few men still make arm shells for kula exchanges as well as decorations, such as *Spondylus* earrings and necklaces.

Trade. Stone axe blades are men's wealth; in the last century the stones were traded in from Muyua Island and polished in the Trobriands. Large cooking pots, also used in local exchanges, come from the Amphlett Islands. Canoes from Normanby and Goodenough islands arrive periodically with sacks of betel nuts that are sold at the Kiriwina wharf. Kula voyaging also enables partners to bring back exotic goods from other islands.

Division of Labor. Women and men work together in clearing new garden land. Men tend to planting yams and staking up the vines, as well as building garden fences and harvesting. Women produce other garden foods, although occasionally a woman decides to make her own yam garden. Men fish and butcher pigs. Women attend to the daily cooking, while men prepare pork and cook taro pudding for feasts. Men and women weave mats but only women make skirts and the banana-leaf bundles that are women's wealth.

Land Tenure. Provisionally, hamlet, garden, bush, and beach lands are owned by a founding matrilineage and are under the control of the lineage's chief or hamlet leader. Rights to residence and the use of land are given by these men to others, such as their sons, who are not members of the matrilineage. Land disputes are frequent and, because the court cases are public, they are fraught with tensions that sometimes lead to fighting. Knowledge of the history of the land from the time of the first ancestors legitimates a person's claim, but competing stories make the arbitrating chiefs' decisions difficult.

Kinship

Kin Groups and Descent. The strength of matrilineal identity is embodied in the belief that conception occurs when an ancestral spirit child enters a woman's body. All members of the matrilineage are believed to have the "same blood" and also to have rights to the "same land." Land, ancestral names, body and house decorations, magic spells, dances, and taboos are all owned by members of individual matrilineages. Although men may lend the use of land and names to their children, they must be reclaimed by men's sisters at a later time. From birth, Trobrianders belong to one of four exogamous matriclans that are not corporate groups. Clan membership determines marriage categories, bringing together in alternating generations members of different matrilineages within the same clan who view themselves as close kin. These are the people who support each other in important exchange events.

Kinship Terminology. Kin terms are a modified Crow type with a number of atypical features. For example, the same term is used for ego's mother and mother's brother's wife and the terms for parallel siblings-in-law are merged with parallel siblings.

Marriage and Family

Marriage. Most marriages occur between young people living in different hamlets within the same or neighboring villages. By marrying a father's sister's daughter—usually three generations removed—a man marries someone from another matrilineage within his father's clan. Endogamous clan marriages sometimes occur but they are regarded as incestuous and are not discussed openly. Only when a young man may inherit the leadership of the matrilineage will he live avunculocally in his mother's brother's hamlet. Other married couples usually reside virilocally in the young man's father's hamlet. The major commitment that follows each marriage is the annual yam harvest produced by the woman's father and eventually by her brother in the woman's name. These yams obligate her husband to obtain many bundles of banana leaves for her when she participates in a mortuary distribution. Divorce has few obstacles and although the couple's kin may seek to prevent the dissolution of the marriage there is little they can do if either spouse is adamant about their separation. If a divorced man wants one of his children to remain with him, he must give his wife's kin valuables. Remarriage is usual for both spouses. There are a few permanent bachelors but women do not go through life unmarried.

Domestic Unit. Nuclear families live together in one household. Older people usually take one of their grandchildren to live with them.

Inheritance. A villager's personal property, including magic spells, are given to those who have helped him or her by making yam gardens and assisting with other food. This is the way sons inherit from their fathers. Matrilineal property, such as land and decorations, is given to a man's sister's son, while a woman may inherit banana trees, coconut or areca palms, magic spells, and banana-leaf wealth from her mother. Among kula men, shells and partners are inherited either by a son or a sister's son. When a man dies, his house and yam house are destroyed and his wife usually returns to her natal hamlet.

Socialization. Young children are cared for by both parents. Because marriages often take place among people living in the same village, grandparents also provide child care. A man's sister performs beauty magic for his children and acts as a confidant when they reach puberty and seek out sexual liaisons. Children who attend the Kiriwina high school board during the week, while others who go to high schools on the mainland only return for holidays.

Sociopolitical Organization

Social Organization. Trobrianders are divided between those born into chiefly and commoner matrilineages. Chiefly matrilineages, ranked among themselves, own rights to special prerogatives surrounding food prohibitions and taboos that mark spatial and physical separation as well as rights to wear particular feather and shell decorations and to decorate houses with ancestral designs and cowrie shells. For all villagers including chiefs, the locus of social organization is the hamlet with networks of social relations through affinal and patrilateral ties to those living in other hamlets within the same village. Women and men also consider themselves kin to those whose ancestors came from the same place of origin. Traditionally, only members of chiefly lineages and their sons participated in kula, but now many more villagers (although by no means all) engage in kula. Chiefs remain the most important kula players.

Political Organization. Each ranking matrilineage is controlled by a chief but the highest-ranking chief is a member of the *tabalu* matrilineage and resides in Omarakana village. The most important chiefly prerogative is the entitlement to many wives. At least four of each wife's relatives make huge yam gardens for her and this is the way a chief achieves great power. But if a chief is weak, he will have difficulty finding women to marry. The villagers of all the islands elect councillors who are members of the Kiriwina Local Government Council. Chiefs sit at the Council of Chiefs, and the Omarakana chief presides over both councils. Chiefs' kula partners are the most important players in other kula communities, and chiefs have the potential to gain the highest-ranking shells.

Social Control. Disputes most often arise over land tenure, usually before the time of planting new yam gardens. Other causes of conflict concern cases of adultery, thefts, physical violence and, more rarely, sorcery accusations. The Council of Chiefs arbitrates most problems but some cases are referred to formal courts.

Conflict. Because of the many intermarriages that occur within a village, conflicts are quickly resolved by public debate. Warfare between village districts was a common occurrence prior to colonization. Such fighting, undertaken by chiefs, most often took place during the harvest season when political power or its absence was exposed. Today, fights sometimes erupt for the same reasons, but the presence of government officials usually holds these incidents in check. The most dangerous conflict is the traditional yam competition where the members of one matrilineage line up their largest and longest yams to be measured against the yams brought together by the members of a rival matrilineage. Lengthy speeches made by intervening kin or affines will usually stop the competition from proceeding. Once a winner is declared, the losers become the most dangerous enemies of the winning matrilineage for generations.

Religion and Expressive Culture

Religious Beliefs. Trobrianders believe in spirits who reside in the bush who cause illness and death, but their greatest fear is sorcery. Only some people are believed to have the knowledge of spells that will "poison" a person and such experts can be petitioned to exercise their power for others. Counterspells are also known; chemical poisons obtained from elsewhere are thought to be prevalent. In addition, magic spells are chanted for many other desires, such as control over the weather, love, beauty, carving expertise, yam gardening, and sailing. Mission teachers have not disrupted the strong beliefs in and practice of magic. Recently, villagers from two hamlets have introduced a new fundamentalist religion whose tenets negate the practice of magic.

Religious Practitioners. Most villagers own some magic spells, but only certain women and men are known to have the most sought after and powerful spells for gardening, weather, and sorcery. The most powerful spells are owned by the Omarakana chief. Some villages have resident mission catechists who conduct Sunday church services.

Ceremonies. A series of rituals are performed for a pregnant woman, and for several months after birth the mother and infant remain secluded. Their emergence is marked by a feast. The largest festivities occur during the annual harvest season after the yams are brought from the garden and loaded into yam houses. Led by a chief or hamlet leader, a village may also host cricket matches, dancing, or competitive yam exchanges, all of which culminate in a huge feast for participants. Kula activities are surrounded by many rituals and feasts.

Arts. Dances first brought by the original ancestors are still owned by the members of individual matrilineages. Drums are the only traditional musical instruments for these dances. Jew's harps or flutes made from bush materials are played for personal enjoyment. String bands are now common. Traditional songs are still sung when someone dies. Traditionally, only certain special people had the magical knowledge necessary to make them expert carvers of canoe prows, war shields, dancing paddles, large bowls, and betel chewing implements. Today, many other villagers carve tourist items.

Medicine. Some women and men are renowned curers, depending upon plants and herbs from the bush that they use with magic spells. A small hospital is located near the government station on Kiriwina, and medical aid posts (usually poorly stocked) are within walking distance of most villages. Adequate medical care is still a grave problem.

Death and Afterlife. When a person dies, the spirit goes to live on the distant island of Tuma where the ancestors continue their existence. At the end of the harvest period, the ancestors of a matrilineage return to the Trobriands to examine the well-being of their kin. The mourning and exchanges following a death are the most lengthy and costly of all ritual events. When a person dies, an all-night vigil takes place in which men sing traditional songs and the spouse and children of the deceased cry over the body. A series of food and women's wealth distributions takes place after the burial, and then the close relatives of the spouse and father of the dead person shave their hair and/or blacken their bodies while the spouse remains secluded. On Kiriwina, about six months later, women of the deceased's matrilineage host a huge distribution of skirts and banana-leaf bundles to repay the hundreds of people who have been in mourning. (On Vakuta Island, only skirts are exchanged.) The woman who distributes more wealth than anyone else is a big-woman. Today, trade-store cloth is sometimes used in place of bundles, and such cloth is central when a women's distribution is held in the capital by Trobrianders living there. Annual distributions of yams, pork, taro pudding, sugarcane, or betel nuts take place each year after an important person dies. When a harvest is especially large, a villagewide distribution is held that honors all the recently deceased from one clan.

See also Dobu, Goodenough Island

Bibliography

Leach, Jerry W., and Edmund Leach, eds. (1983). *The Kula: New Perspectives on Massim Exchange.* Cambridge: Cambridge University Press.

Malinowski, Bronislaw (1922). *Argonauts of the Western Pacific.* London: Routledge & Kegan Paul.

Munn, Nancy (1986). *The Fame of Gawa: A Symbolic Study of Value Transformation in a Massim (Papua New Guinea) Society.* Cambridge: Cambridge University Press.

Scoditti, Giancarlo M. G. (1990). *Kitawa: A Linguistic and Aesthetic Analysis of Visual Art in Melanesia.* Berlin: Mouton de Gruyter.

Seligman, C. G. (1910). *The Melanesians of British New Guinea.* Cambridge: Cambridge University Press.

Weiner, Annette B. (1976). *Women of Value, Men of Renown: New Perspectives in Trobriand Exchange.* Austin: University of Texas Press.

Weiner, Annette B. (1988). *The Trobrianders of Papua New Guinea.* New York: Holt, Rinehart & Winston.

ANNETTE B. WEINER

Truk

ETHNONYM: Aramasen Chuuk

Orientation

Identification. Truk is in the Caroline Islands of Micronesia. Along with the surrounding atolls, it forms one of the four states of the Federated States of Micronesia, which were part of the U.S. Trust Territory of the Pacific Islands.

Location. Lying between 7°7' and 7°14' N and 151°22' and 152°4' E, Truk is a complex atoll composed of a circle of reefs and about forty low coral islets enclosing a lagoon of 48 to 64 kilometers in diameter and, within it, seventeen high islands of volcanic origin, with a total land area of 86 square kilometers. There are two major seasons, a dry one with northeast trade winds from November to June and a wet one with light winds from the south and southwest.

Demography. In 1947 Truk's population was about 9,200. By 1988 it was more than 35,000 with a density of about 385 persons per square kilometer.

Linguistic Affiliation. The Trukese language is one of many members of the Micronesian Family of Oceanic Austronesian languages.

History and Cultural Relations

Truk was settled by the first century A.D. In the fourteenth century, a cult center was established on Moen Island. It was abandoned in the eighteenth century following a fresh immigration from neighboring atolls. Japan replaced Germany as the ruling power in World War I and was in turn replaced by the United States under United Nations trusteeship in 1945. In 1986 Truk and its surrounding atolls became a state within the newly independent Federated States of Micronesia. Protestant missionaries and traders came in the 1880s and Roman Catholic missionaries after 1900. Japan sought to develop Truk economically and introduce elementary education in Japanese. Education was much expanded under American administration, and many Trukese learned English. Some went to college in Guam, Hawaii, and the United States mainland. The American administration introduced representative government.

Settlements

Truk was divided into small districts, each consisting of a small island or a wedge-shaped segment of a larger one. Not clustered into villages, households were scattered on rising land back from the shore. With population growth many of the once looser neighborhoods have become more densely settled villages. Landholdings were scattered.

Economy

Subsistence and Commercial Activities. In the past, swidden gardens with dry taro, turmeric, and sugarcane were few and small. Breadfruit, supplemented by wet taro, was the staple. Being seasonal, breadfruit was preserved by fermenting in pits. Copra has become the only export. Fishing was important. Okinawans developed commercial fishing during Japanese rule; and some commercial fishing on a small scale was continued by the Trukese after World War II. Under American rule, the principal source of cash income was government employment as teachers and program administrators. Tourism was unimportant.

Industrial Arts. Traditional crafts included: making outrigger paddle canoes; building houses; woodworking (to make bowls, storage chests, spears); gardening; cordage (to make rope, string, slings); working stone (for sling stones), shell (for adz blades), and coral (for breadfruit pounders); preparing medicines; loom weaving with hibiscus and banana fibers (to make loin clothes, wraparound skirts, shirts, mosquito canopies); plaiting (of baskets, mats); and other leaf working (for thatch, sun hats). Sewing arts and dressmaking have replaced weaving. New arts include: motor maintenance (of cars and outboards); boat building; bookkeeping; school teaching; government administration; and nursing and medical practice.

Trade. In traditional times, the atoll people around Truk traded with Pohnpei, Yap, and the Mariana Islands. The major export from Truk to the atolls was processed turmeric in the form of sticks that were used as a cosmetic. The major imports were woven pandanus mats and sennit cord, both of which were also produced on Truk. Sometimes, important men on Truk would trade for outrigger canoes or contract with men on atolls to make the canoes for them. Men from the atolls were also sometimes retained to sail the canoes of Trukese men.

Division of Labor. Traditionally, men gardened, cooked and processed food in bulk (in the earth oven), did deep-water fishing, engaged in war and public affairs, and practiced the arts of canoe and house building and of wood, shell, and stone working. Women wove, plaited mats, prepared meals (as distinct from food in bulk), did inshore fishing, and took main responsibility for child care. Men and women have both entered into school teaching, clerical work, and administration.

Land Tenure. Land was held privately both by individuals and matrilineal, corporate descent groups. Rights in undeveloped space, productive soil, trees, and gardens were separable. When soil and breadfruit trees were given in grant, the grantor retained residual rights and the grantee acquired provisional rights. Grantors and grantees could be either individuals or corporations. Full rights went to the survivor on the death or extinction of the other.

Kinship

Kin Groups and Descent. Truk's population is divided into a number of dispersed, matrilineal clans. Within any one district the several lineages are usually but not always of different clans. There are also personal kindreds. As a principle of clan and lineage membership, descent is matrilineal, but otherwise kinship is reckoned bilaterally.

Kinship Terminology. Kinship terms are few. A generation mode of reckoning is skewed in a Crow manner so that all members of one's father's lineage are in a senior generation, children of men of that lineage are in one's own generation, and children of men of one's own lineage are in a junior generation.

Marriage and Family

Marriage. Marriage took place for women a bit before and for men a bit after the age of 20. Premarital courtship was covert and included sexual relations. Residence was usually matrilocal. Divorce, common before the birth of children, was rare thereafter. It could be initiated by either spouse and was often instigated by the wife's brothers. Levirate and sororate remarriages were valued. To keep soil and trees that had been granted to the children of a lineage's men circulating back, marriage preferences with one or another kind of cousin, varying from locality to locality, were widespread.

Domestic Unit. The domestic unit was an extended family, based on the women of a lineage or sublineage. It consisted of at least one experienced older woman and two or more younger women of childbearing age together with their husbands. Unmarried sons and brothers slept apart in their lineage's meetinghouse. Extended family households continued through the periods of foreign administration.

Inheritance. Individually owned property was inherited by the owner's children. Corporately owned property was inherited by the corporation's "children" (the children of its men) when the corporation's membership died out.

Socialization. Small children were much held, fed on demand, and never left alone. They slept on the same mat with their mothers. By age 3 they were expected to begin to look after themselves. Children were lectured on correct social behavior, but they were not held fully accountable for it until they became junior adults. Parents used switches to punish their children. Often persuaded to do what others wanted with promises that were broken afterwards, children learned to be wary of the intentions of others. They enjoyed much freedom to play, sharpening their physical skills. Transmission of special lore and knowledge became increasingly important as children grew to be young adults. The eldest son and eldest daughter were treated differently from other children. Their persons were inviolate, their wishes were honored, and they were not liable to physical punishment.

Sociopolitical Organization

Social Organization. In each district the lineage with title to its space held the chiefship. The several lineages with full or residual titles to plots of soil had full residential rights. Lineages with only provisional titles to plots of soil in grant from other lineages had only conditional residential rights. Lineages with full residential rights maintained symbolic hearths where, with their client lineages, they prepared food to present to the chief in recognition of his lineage's ownership of the space.

Political Organization. A district chiefship was divided between the oldest man in the senior female line in the chiefly lineage and the oldest man in the lineage generally. The latter was executive chief, or "chief of talk," and the former was symbolic chief, or "chief of food." Food presentations were made to the symbolic chief. Sometimes the symbolic and executive functions fell to the same individual; often they did not. The symbolic chief was surrounded by his lineage brothers and by his sons, who acted as his agents. These followers and his sisters and daughters were of chiefly rank, distinct from commoners. Through conquest, a lineage might gain the chiefship in more than one district and establish a junior branch as the chiefly lineage in the conquered district. The now subordinate district rendered food presentations to the superordinate one. Most districts were linked in two rival leagues based on competing schools of magic and ritual relating to war, politics, and rhetoric. A chief's authority derived from two things. His lineage's ownership of the district's space entitled him to presentations of first fruits at stated times of the year. More importantly, it gave him authority over the conservation and use of the district's food resources. His authority also derived from his connection with the sky world, its gods, and their superhuman power to accomplish purposes. There was, therefore, a degree of sacredness associated with chiefs.

Social Control. There were no police. A chief's brothers or sons might act on his behalf to intimidate or attack someone who had offended him. But it was control of magical power, either by the chief or one his brothers or sons, that made improper conduct liable to punishment. Major craft specialists could also make ill those who violated the taboos of their craft. Finally, members of chiefly lineages and their close associates were likely to have knowledge of sorcery. All such knowledge gave punitive power to chiefs and important specialists. People stressed maintaining the appearance of propriety in behavior so as not to give just cause for offense.

Conflict. Within districts, conflict arose over land, succession to chiefship, theft, adultery, and avenging homicide. Between districts, it arose over attentions to local women by outside men, the status of one district as subordinate to another, and rights of access to fishing areas. Formal procedures for terminating conflict between districts involved payments of valuables and land by the losing side to the winning side. Fighting involved surprise raids and prearranged meetings on a field of battle. The principal weapons were slings, spears, and clubs. Firearms, introduced late in the nineteenth century, were confiscated by German authorities in 1903. Martial arts included an elaborate system of throws and holds by which an unarmed man could kill, maim, or disarm an armed opponent.

Religion and Expressive Culture

Religious Beliefs. In traditional belief, spirit beings were widely distributed in the sky, under the sea, and on land. The important places among spirit lands in the sky were: a region under the dome of Heaven, home of the gods who could take human form; a region in the south from which came all the plant and marine life that gave people food; and a region named "Achaw" or "Kachaw," abode of the ancestors of many Trukese clans and particularly of the clans associated with the chiefship and the special bodies of magical lore from which chiefly power derived. Spirits could accomplish their intentions at will and were thus the source of all that was *manaman* (mana), such as efficacious spells, medicines, and rituals. Good souls of the dead were consulted through mediums. The Trukese also invoked in spells the spirits inhabiting the dome of Heaven, presided over by "Great Spirit," and the spirits associated with particular crafts and major bodies of lore.

Religious Practitioners. Ritual practices were conducted by their own specialists. Such specialists included spirit mediums, breadfruit summoners, fish summoners, healers, masters of spells, masters of sorcery, builders, navigators, diviners, and most importantly the masters of magic and ritual relating to war and politics. Their knowledge was private property passed down to their children and junior lineage mates.

Ceremonies. Major ceremonies were those associated with death, communicating with good souls of the dead, summoning breadfruit, and making food presentations to chiefs. Ritual was also associated with divination, curing, warfare, political meetings, house building, and courtship.

Arts. Performing arts included dancing, storytelling, playing the noseflute and the bamboo Jew's harp (in courtship serenading), singing, poetry, and rhetoric. Other arts were associated with tattooing, woodworking, weaving, and warfare.

Medicine. Sickness was believed to result from the "bite" of a malevolent spirit or of any other spirit one had offended or that was controlled by a ritual specialist one had offended or by a sorcerer. Sickness might also result from soul loss. In all but the latter case, treatment involved the use of medicines to be applied externally, to be drunk, or to be inhaled. For soul loss, a spirit medium was consulted to help find and restore the soul. Divination was used as a diagnostic aid in cases of severe or prolonged illness. Massage was used to treat bruises, local infections, and muscle ailments.

Death and Afterlife. As soon as a person died, female kin wailed and other relatives came bringing gifts of woven fabrics, turmeric, and perfume. Burial might be in the ground or in a mat bundle at sea (since Christianity, in a wooden coffin). After burial, the grave was watched by close kin for four nights to see if the good soul would possess one of them as its future medium. On the fourth day after burial, the deceased's immediate effects were burned and the good soul ascended to Heaven in the smoke. Everyone had two souls, one "good" and one "bad." The good soul came from the sky world and returned there after death. The bad soul became a ghost that might be dangerous and cause illness. By the middle of the twentieth century all of Truk's people were at least nominally Christian, either Protestant or Catholic, and Christianity had become the focus of religious life.

See also Nomoi, Pohnpei, Ulithi, Woleai, Yap

Bibliography

Bollig, P. Laurentius (1927). *Die Bewohner der Truk Inseln.* Anthropos ethnologische Bibliothek 3, no. 1. Münster i.W.: Aschendorffsche Verlagsbuchhandlung.

Gladwin, Thomas, and Seymour B. Sarason (1953). *Truk: Man in Paradise.* Viking Fund Publications in Anthropology, no. 20. New York: Wenner-Gren Foundation for Anthropological Research.

Goodenough, Ward H. (1978). *Property, Kin, and Community on Truk.* 2nd ed. Hamden, Conn.: Archon Books.

Käser, Lothar (1977). "Der Begriff Seele bei den Insulanern von Truk." Ph.D. dissertation, Albert-Ludwigs-Universität, Freiburg i.Br.

Krämer, Augustin (1932). "Truk." In *Ergebnisse der Südsee-Expedition 1908–1910,* edited by Georg Thilenius. II. Ethnographie; B., Mikronesien, vol. 5. Hamburg: Friederichsen, De Gruyter.

LeBar, Frank M. (1964). *The Material Culture of Truk.* Yale University Publications in Anthropology, no. 68. New Haven: Human Relations Area Files.

Parker, Patricia L. (1985). *Land Law in Trukese Society: 1850–1980.* Ann Arbor: University Microfilms.

WARD H. GOODENOUGH

Tuvalu

ETHNONYMS: Ellice Islands, Lagoon Islands

Orientation

Identification. The name "Tuvalu" is apparently traditional and refers to the original "cluster of eight" islands. It was adopted as the national name when the group achieved self-governing status in 1975, after breaking away from the Gilbert Islands with which it had been administered by Britain since 1892. The name "Ellice Islands" was initially given only to Funafuti in 1819 by Captain de Peyster of the *Rebecca* in honor of the owner of his cargo, Edward Ellice, an English member of Parliament.

Location. Tuvalu is an archipelago of nine small islands lying in a northwest-southeast chain stretching over 640 kilometers of ocean between 176° and 180° E and between 5° and 11° S. Closest to the equator is Nanumea, followed southwards by Niutao, Nanumaga, Nui, Vaitupu, Nukufetau, Funafuti, Nukulaelae, and Niulakita. The first three constitute the northern geographical subgroup proper, with Nui occupying an ambiguous position between them and the more widely scattered southern grouping. The environment is tropical maritime (with the average daily maximum temperature ranging from about 24° to 30° C) and there is no distinct dry season, though December, January, and February are normally the wettest (and stormiest) months. Strong westerlies are a common occurrence at this time but for most of the year easterly trade winds predominate. Rainfall is generally adequate (about 300 to 350 centimeters per year) though limited water storage capacity means that rationing may be imposed after a relatively short dry spell. The northern islands tend to be the driest.

Demography. It is now generally acknowledged that early estimates of a precontact Tuvaluan population of 20,000 were grossly in error and that the total actually fluctuated around 3,000 people. After European contact, Tuvalu generally escaped the depredations wrought by epidemic diseases in other parts of the Pacific, but two of the islands (Nukulaelae and Funafuti) suffered huge population losses in 1863 when blackbirders (Peruvians operating a form of labor trade akin to slavery) kidnapped hundreds of people. The population has more than recovered since then. The 1979 census enumerated 7,349 persons but the total population of Tuvaluans was estimated at about 10,000, including all those living in Kiribati, Nauru, Fiji, New Zealand, and other parts of the Pacific. A 1989 estimate of the de facto population in the group itself was 8,619, and no doubt considerable numbers of Tuvaluans continue to dwell outside the home group. The population is presently growing at a rate of 1.9 percent per year and has an average density of 332 persons per square kilometer, though the latter varies greatly from Funafuti (highest) to Vaitupu (lowest). The absolute size of each community also shows considerable range, from the 50 persons or so on Niulakita to the more than 2,000 on Funafuti, the capital and main communication center. The vast majority of this population is of Tuvaluan ethnic origin, though some inhabitants belong to other Pacific ethnic groups and there is a sizable cadre of expatriate (mainly White) advisers, officials, development workers, and volunteers, especially on Funafuti.

Linguistic Affiliation. The majority of people speak Tuvaluan, a Polynesian language, although the inhabitants of one island, Nui, speak a mainly Gilbertese (Micronesian) dialect. Although all varieties of Tuvaluan are mutually intelligible, a clear dialectal difference exists between the northern and southern clusters of islands, and within those groupings each island has its own distinctive communalect. Tuvaluan is one language of the relatively nonhomogeneous Samoic-Outlier Subgroup of Nuclear Polynesian languages; the subgroup's other major component is Eastern Polynesian. Samoan used to be the dominant language of literacy but has since been supplanted by Tuvaluan for Christian scriptures, church and government publications, and personal letter writing. Samoan is being replaced by English as the main second language.

History and Cultural Relations

Tuvalu was probably settled as part of the backwash by which the outliers were populated after the main eastward historical wave of Polynesian migration. Prehistoric Samoan cultural influence was undoubtedly strong, as the linguistic affiliation suggests, but this influence also may have been retrospectively enhanced by religious and administrative links in the modern era. Precontact history is difficult to reconstruct, since there has been very little archaeological investigation. Moreover, local traditions, while essential for a proper historical understanding, often contradict each other as political charters for descent groups within local status hierarchies. Different island communities claim different founding ancestors, some autochthonous and some hailing from Samoa, Tonga, East Uvea, and/or Kiribati. Funafuti is also cited as the immediate homeland of some of the other islands. Evidence from material culture, comparative linguistics, and culture history all indicate relatively recent settlement dates from the fourteenth to the eighteenth centuries. Skeletal remains from Vaitupu, however, may point to a slightly longer time scale of 500 to 800 years. The first sighting of a Tuvaluan island (Nui) by a Westerner (*ppaalagi*) was probably made by the Spanish explorer Mendaña, in 1568, but it was not until the early nineteenth century that real contact began. Explorers, traders, and whalers charted the group and, as the century wore on, White traders and beachcombers settled on some of the islands. The most intensive phase of contact began in 1865 with the arrival of (mainly) Samoan teachers and pastors sent by the London Missionary Society. Their version of evangelical and congregationalist Protestantism continues to be a major sociocultural influence to the present day, though the Tuvalu church is now autonomous. Other churches and religions have obtained footholds but remain minorities in a society that emphasizes individual conformity with communal ideology. In 1892, Great Britain declared a protectorate over what were then called the Ellice Islands, which was administered jointly with the Gilbert Islands (as a colony after 1916) until 1975. While the Gilberts were occupied by Japanese troops during World War II, Tuvalu became a forward base for U.S. forces. It largely escaped the direct effects of battle but the presence of large numbers of servicemen on Nanumea, Nukufatau, and Funafuti had a substantial impact. As Great Britain moved to divest itself of its Pacific possessions in the 1960s, Tuvaluans decided against remaining tied to the Gilbertese (who were culturally different, negatively stereotyped, and much more numerous). They seceded in 1975 and became fully independent in 1978, retaining ties to Great Britain through membership in the Commonwealth.

Settlements

Most scholars accept that, prior to Western contact, each island probably had a fairly scattered distribution of subcommunities based on core kin groups. Centralized habitation complexes (one village or two contiguous ones) were established either late last century by the London Missionary Society or early this century by the British administration—or possibly by the combined efforts of both. It appears, for example, that large centralized meetinghouses (*maneapa*) did not exist on the southern islands before the late nineteenth century, despite the fact that these structures have become symbols of traditional culture and Tuvaluan identity.

Economy

Subsistence and Commercial Activities. The most important cultigens are coconut palms (used for the collection of *kaleve* "toddy" as well as for the nuts), pandanus, bananas, breadfruit, and *pulaka* (swamp taro). The latter is grown in large pits dug into the top layer of a freshwater lens. Its great value stems from its ability to withstand both drought and flooding by seawater. Fish, mollusks, and birds were traditionally the main sources of dietary protein. It is not clear whether pigs, like chickens, were a postcontact introduction. As a major component of ceremonial meals, they are the principal focus of animal husbandry.

Industrial Arts. The main traditional craft activity of women is the weaving of pandanus mats, which are important items in gift exchange (for example, at weddings). Women also sew clothes, usually with imported machines and using imported materials. Men's crafts include canoe and house building, tackle making, and wood carving (which may be combined with any of the others). The technology of fishing—hooks, lures, canoes, nets, traps, and the techniques for their use—was and is highly elaborated. Traditional forms are now supplemented or supplanted by imported boats, engines, hooks, lines, and nets. Today, clothing is almost all made of imported fabrics, but some dance skirts are made from traditional materials. Items for the small tourist traffic such as shell necklaces, fans, and wooden artifacts are also made.

Trade. It is unlikely that the separate islands were involved in significant trade networks before Western contact, though there was interisland voyaging and visiting that may have been accompanied by exchanges, marriages, and political tribute. Foreign traders were originally interested in coconut oil and subsequently in copra (dried coconut flesh for the food and cosmetics industries). Copra is still exported but has declined in importance, owing to inefficiencies of scale, difficulties of transport, and fluctuating prices on the world market.

Division of Labor. At the ideological level, though perhaps less assiduously in practice, there was and is a general sexual division of labor, in which men engage in pelagic and lagoon fishing from canoes as well as the gathering of coconuts and palm toddy and the more strenuous forms of cultivation. Women share the activity of reef fishing and collecting and take responsibility for weaving and infant care, as well as harvesting some crops and preparing food. This division is less clear-cut in the modern occupational fields opened up by Western-style education. Women, however, are still underrepresented in positions of authority in government, civil service, and the church. Traditionally, there was little full-time specialization, though certain men were acknowledged experts at fishing, navigation, defense, canoe making, house building, and gardening. Both men and women were able to inherit or acquire skills as curers and diviners. On at least some of the islands, this division was formalized into bodies of knowledge (*poto*) or tasks (*pologa*) pertaining to and jealously guarded by separate descent groups. Traditional chiefs do not seem to have been exempt from working at the common range of pursuits. It was with introduced models of organization in the church and in government that specialization really took hold. Fishing, however, remains a valued activity for many men who are otherwise full-time waged workers.

Land Tenure. Reconstruction of fully traditional forms is speculative. It is possible that the original form of tenure was communal, as this arrangement still exists and is accorded symbolic priority. From a system in which chiefs probably allocated land rights on a usufruct basis, more complex forms of title have evolved. Land may now be held privately, either by individuals or by groups—though this distinction is blurred by the developmental cycle of groups with rights in estates. Landholding groups go by different names on different islands: *puikaaiga* (most southern islands), *kopiti* (Nanumea), etc.

Kinship

Kin Groups, Descent, and Inheritance. Kinship is cognatic, with important links being traced through both parents in the construction of ego-centered kindreds. Descent, however, has an agnatic bias, as shown in the calculation of genealogical links and in property inheritance, title succession, and postmarital residence patterns (virilocal). Thus, while the apex of a descent group was and is typically a founding set of siblings, and the estates that accrued to them could be inherited by males and females alike, eldest sons inherited most. Genealogical knowledge is shallow by Polynesian standards.

Kinship Terminology. Despite variation from one island to another (and within communities), kinship terminology can be summarized as a modified version of the Hawaiian or generational type. Probably the most marked relationship is that between "brother" and "sister" since cross-sex relations produce terms for "father's sister" and "mother's brother" in the parental generation (even though their children are not marked in the same way). Most of these terms are capable of wide genealogical extension, including to affines, and many of them are reciprocal. Given the multiplicity of genealogical paths in a cognatic system, choice of kinship terms is often a matter of choice, rhetoric, and pragmatic advantage.

Marriage and Family

Marriage. Polygyny was suppressed by missionization, and present-day attitudes concerning marriage, sexuality, and family obligation are heavily influenced by Christianity. Marriage is one of the most important rites of passage in Tuvaluan culture, since it legitimizes children and establishes links of kinship in relation to land rights. Divorce is comparatively rare. All those who descend from a recognized ancestral sibling set and have rights in its estate are obliged to provide food and labor for each other's marriage celebrations. Not to do so is tantamount to a rupture of relations. Hence, contributions come from the cognatic kindreds of all four parents of the marrying couple, in the form of appropriate kinds of labor, the provision of food at specific times, and the exchange of gifts (especially pandanus mats, clothes, and tobacco). Such reciprocity often acquires a competitive edge.

Domestic Unit. Marriage is seen as establishing a new economic unit—a nuclear family usually living virilocally (though sometimes with the bride's parents until after the first child is born). It is this group that provides the core of any domestic unit. Extended families are not commonly residential units. Children are often redistributed among related families by different levels of adoption. In this way, grandparents or childless siblings may maintain multigenerational domestic units.

Socialization. Mothers are infants' primary care givers, but a wide range of kin may be mobilized if necessary. Children, especially girls, are involved in the rearing of younger siblings. Physical punishment is used but it is rarely severe, with amicable relations restored almost immediately. Shaming and peer pressure generally prove more potent sanctions.

Sociopolitical Organization

Social Organization. Apart from the primary dimension of kinship, many other social identities and collectivities are important. Individuals identify strongly with their natal island (*fenua*). Most of the centralized villages are divided into two "sides" (and on some islands there are four sections). These have competitive functions in games, gift exchanges, and certain kinds of fishing and communal projects. Class formation is incipient in Tuvaluan society, with the growth of specialized occupations, the cash economy, and business development. Chiefly status is more salient, however, with a few descent lines acknowledged as meriting traditional respect. High status can also be achieved through the Tuvalu church, with pastors commanding great prestige but less political power than before, since their tours of duty are now limited and they cannot be posted to their natal village. Consequently, deacons and lay preachers probably wield more long-term influence in the village. In comparison to the complex quasi state forms of some larger Polynesian societies, Tuvalu has always been fairly egalitarian.

Political Organization. Traditionally, each island was politically self-sufficient, though a wider grouping based on common ancestor worship and ritual hierarchy seems to have connected Funafuti to Vaitupu, Nukufetau, and Nukulaelae. Chiefs (*aliki*) headed the major descent groups and on most islands they deferred to one or two paramount chiefs (often termed "kings" in early accounts). The chiefs seem to have been as much religious leaders as political ones, though there were also religious specialists (spirit mediums, diviners, etc.). While the latter were suppressed by missionaries, the chiefly system survived. Its political clout was greatly reduced under missionary and colonial hegemony but has never disappeared and it is occasionally revived as a source of local prestige. Nowadays, elected island councils exercise direct political control over local affairs with advice from central government, including island executive officers. There are no organized political parties, however, and much of the requisite upper-level administrative expertise is provided by expatriates on short-term contracts.

Social Control and Conflict. A good deal of control is effected by such social sanctions as gossip, shaming, and public admonition. Tuvaluans try to avoid direct confrontation, placing emphasis on maintaining smooth and harmonious interpersonal relations. By reputation—and probably in fact—the society has lower levels of violence and crime than many others in the Pacific, even in the relatively urbanized capital. Nevertheless, serious fights did take place occasionally in the precolonial era. More frequent was low-intensity warfare between different islands in the group in which various male warriors (*toa*) took part. There are also oral accounts of invasions from Kiribati and Tonga, most of which were successfully repulsed.

Religion and Expressive Culture

Religious Beliefs. Tuvalu is a solidly Protestant society, with other sects and religions still having only minor significance. Beliefs and practices associated with ancestor worship and animism began to crumble even before the arrival of missionaries, though some of the northern islands, where visitors were subjected to rigorous "quarantine ceremonies," initially proved recalcitrant. Nevertheless, some syncretic beliefs in magic and sorcery remain. The Christian deity, known to Tuvaluans as "Te Atua Ieova," is universally acknowledged, with the Tuvalu church (unlike some of the more fundamentalist sects) giving equal prominence to Jesus, known as "Iesu, Te Aliki." In pre-Christian times, supernaturals included worshiped ancestors, culture heroes, and some natural phenomena. It is also possible that some pan-Polynesian deities were recognized (e.g., Tagaloa).

Religious Practitioners. Missionary accounts never specified whether pre-Christian priests were chiefs as well as religious specialists. Their roles and powers are extremely difficult to reconstruct, though it seems clear that chiefs themselves had important ritual duties and were hedged in by taboo. For several decades after missionization, great power was wielded by (predominantly Samoan) pastors of the London Missionary Society, and the role became a prestigious career choice for Tuvaluan males as well, a number of whom were appointed to other parts of the Pacific. Locally, deacons (men and women) and lay preachers (men only) play important parts in religious affairs.

Ceremonies. Apart from regular Christian holidays and days of worship, Tuvaluans celebrate islandwide festivities held to commemorate a variety of significant events and people (founding ancestors, arrival of missionaries, deliverance from human or natural disaster, etc.) Ceremonies are also held in conjunction with communal activities. Some rites of passage are also held on a communal basis (e.g., multiple-village-sponsored wedding ceremonies), but the preference is for nuptials to be organized by the families concerned. Next to weddings, funerals are the most important life-cycle rituals.

Arts. The major artistic traditions are performance-oriented—oratory, plays composed for specific occasions, and, above all, the action songs known as *faatele*. These songs take the form of seated singers and standing dancers singing and acting out the repeated verses of a song faster and faster until they reach a crescendo. Faatele may involve competition between different sides, be an adjunct to other festivities, or be an end in themselves at family gatherings. Tuvaluans also enjoy other kinds of musical activity: hymn singing (often on a competitive basis between choirs as well as in church), Western-style dances, and pop music, among others.

Medicine. Western medicine is practiced by trained doctors and nurses, but it is variably available throughout the archipelago. Local curing practices are a syncretic combination of traditional, Christian, and scientific ideas; massage; herbal and other medicines; special foods or food prohibitions; faith healing; prayer; and other methods.

Death and Afterlife. In contemporary Tuvalu, Christian ideology proclaims the existence of Heaven and Hell as the destinations of souls. Alternative views, if they exist, are not officially condoned, though the spirits of the dead are believed to have the power of action under certain circumstances (lack of filial piety, bad relations between kin, etc.).

See also Anuta, Kiribati, Nauru, Ontong Java, Rotuma, Tokelau

Bibliography

Chambers, Anne (1984). *Nanumea.*Canberra: Australian National University Development Studies Centre.

Brady, Ivan A. (1975). "Christians, Pagans, and Government Men: Culture Change in the Ellice Islands." In *A Reader in Culture Change, Vol. 2,* edited by I. Brady and B. Isaac. New York: Shenkman.

Goldsmith, Michael (1985). "Transformations of the Meeting-House in Tuvalu." In *Transformations of Polynesian Culture,* edited by A. Hooper and J. Huntsman. Auckland: Polynesian Society.

Laracy, Hugh, ed. (1983). *Tuvalu: A History.* Suva: University of the South Pacific; Funafuti: Government of Tuvalu.

Noricks, Jay Smith (1983). "Unrestricted Cognatic Descent and Corporateness on Niutao, a Polynesian Island of Tuvalu." *American Ethnologist* 10:571–584.

MICHAEL GOLDSMITH

Ulithi

ETHNONYM: Re Ulithi

Orientation

Identification. Ulithians are Micronesians living on an atoll in the west-central Caroline Islands. While the natives refer to their land as "Ma Ulithi," Europeans have applied other names to their islands: Isles de Sequeira, Los Dolores, Los Garbanzos, Mackenzie, and Mogmog. The Japanese call them "Ulissi" and "Urishi." Their culture has undergone strong change since the atoll came under U.S. control in 1944 and can best be described in terms of its traditional culture, with observations as to current modifications.

Location. The atoll, which is not really one entity but is made of four geologic units, is located at about 10° N and 140° E. Its closest neighbors are Yap and Ngulu to the west and Fais to the east. Guam is about 640 kilometers to the northeast. The climate is that of the doldrums belt, with much rainfall and high humidity.

Demography. In 1731 Father Cantova reported a population of 592, in 1870 Tetens and Kubary counted about 700, and in 1903 District Officer Senfft reported 797, after which there was a steady decline, with a census by Lessa showing only 421 in 1949. Then, as the result of U.S. medical and public health measures, there was an upswing, with a census by Lessa showing 514 people in 1960.

Linguistic Affiliation. The language is a dialect of Trukese, a subdivision of the far-flung Austronesian languages.

History and Cultural Relations

Most likely Ulithi was discovered in 1525 by Portuguese who had been blown there from the Celebes and remained for several weeks in great harmony with the people while rebuilding their small vessel. The Spaniards in the Philippines often encountered Carolinians marooned there, some of them apparently being Ulithians. Missionaries were inspired to convert the natives of the Carolines, but they did not succeed in establishing a mission until 1731. It was headed by Father Cantova and was in Ulithi, but very soon afterwards he and his party were murdered by the people. Between the time of the Cantova episode and the stopovers of British, French, and Russian explorers, however, Ulithi did not live entirely in a world isolated from foreign influences. The people were in continual indirect contact with Spaniards through the sustained trade being carried on by Carolinians sailing to the Marianas. These native traders would return home with iron implements, cloth, and glass beads. In the nineteenth century two large-scale traders worked throughout the Carolines. One was a German, Alfred Tetens; the other was the Irish-American David O'Keefe. German interest in the region grew strong and in 1899 after much dispute Germany acquired all of the Carolines from Spain. Japan took over the area in 1914 and in 1920 was given a class C mandate by the League of Nations. Two Spanish missionaries were permitted to begin conversion of Ulithi to Catholicism. The United States seized the atoll in 1944 and immediately converted it into a huge naval base for the invasion of Okinawa and the Philippines. In 1947 the United Nations gave the United States a trusteeship over most of Micronesia, after which intensive educational activity took place and very large payments and subsidies were given to the Ulithian people, resulting in a rapid deterioration of the traditional culture. In 1986 Ulithi became part of the newly established group of Caroline Islands known as the Federated States of Micronesia, independent but in "free association" with the United States.

Settlements

The settlement pattern is that of small, highly nucleated villages, although it has been speculated that formerly it was that of neighborhoods, each of which had a strip of land extending from the sea to the interior, with a house, cook hut, and canoe shed, surrounded by garden areas. Each village has its large men's council house, used not only as a meetingplace but also as a dormitory for unmarried men and a clubhouse for all males. At the time of maximum population in 1903 the average number of inhabitants per village was 88. All dwellings are on the lagoon side of an islet. Houses are built on platforms made of slabs of coral, and they are characterized by sharply pitched roofs made of plaited palm leaves and walls of paneled wood. Such traditional houses have now been replaced by boxlike wooden ones or concrete-block structures useful to withstand typhoons. In the interior of the isles of Mogmog and Falalop are artificially constructed gardens, used principally for growing taro. The vast lagoon serves not only as a fishing ground but also as a highway for the extremely fast lateen-sailed outrigger canoes used to transport people and goods.

Economy

Subsistence and Commercial Activities. Simple horticulture dominates subsistence activities, although fish and other sea foods are more highly prized in the diet. The chief plant food is the coconut, consumed in many forms, followed by breadfruit, true taro and pseudotaro, bananas, and from time to time squashes and sweet potatoes. There is some gathering, especially of wild berries and other fruits. Pigs are valued but are few because of the scarcity of suitable feed. Chickens are more abundant, being the predominant domestic animal. Birds are occasionally trapped for consumption. Highly desirable but limited by religious and political taboos is the giant sea turtle, *Chelonia mydas*. With the rise of a cash economy, originally instigated by the manufacture of copra and then enormously expanded by U.S. welfare allotments and other grants, the traditional economy has been reduced to a shambles.

Industrial Arts. There are part-time specialists, especially canoe and house carpenters, who are exclusively men. Women weave garments on a true loom, probably introduced long ago from Indonesia. Weaving materials are made of banana fiber, hibiscus fiber, or a combination of the two, although these textiles have largely been supplanted by commercial cloth. There is no pottery making, due to the absence of clay, but some pottery is imported from nearby Yap. Prior to the introduction of iron tools, such tools as adzes, knives, and scrapers were made from shells or coral. Since the advent of traders the chief commercial activity has been the manufacture of copra, with some seasonal gathering of trochus shells for the foreign market.

Trade. While there is some internal trade between individuals, most of it is external and somewhat ritualistic, being carried on in a complex system involving exchange with Yap and the islands of the Woleai, almost as far east as Truk. Although Ulithians are regarded as being of low caste by Yapese, because they live on out-lying islands, Ulithi receives more from Yap than it gives, especially in the form of foodstuffs and large timber for constructing canoes. A common form of exchange, largely political, is the giving of fine mats used as men's and women's clothing.

Division of Labor. Sex plays a part in dividing household and village activities: men mainly do the fishing and carpentry, while women cultivate gardens, harvest wild plants and shore fish, weave, and almost exclusively raise children and perform most domestic work, including cooking.

Land Tenure. Land is held in various ways. In theory the six landownership chiefs of the atoll have the right of eminent domain. In practice land is owned by lineages in a fee-simple system, which is administered by the lineage's chief. It is broken up into plots that are worked by family groups with usufruct rights that are tantamount to ownership.

Kinship

Kin Groups and Descent. In addition to the nuclear family there are the extended family, the composite family, and the all-important corporate lineage. Lineages are matrilineal. Even though adoption is extremely common, in theory the adoptee retains membership in his natural mother's lineage.

Kinship Terminology. Kin terms are a slight variation of the Crow type, which reflects unilineal descent by "overriding" generations. A kin term always embraces secondary and tertiary relatives in addition to primary ones. The system of nomenclature serves both for purposes of reference and of address.

Marriage and Family

Marriage. Marriage is monogamous. Residence is patrilocal, but the residence rule is somewhat elastic, especially because a husband spends long stretches of time helping in his wife's gardens if the land assigned for her use by the prevailing system of land tenure is on another islet. In actuality there is some matrilocal, avunculocal, and neolocal residence. Until the advent of Catholicism divorce was very common and easily accomplished by mutual agreement.

Domestic Unit. While the nuclear family is the basis of the domestic unit, in actuality households consist less of a husband and wife and their offspring than they do of either extended families, composite families, or units not involving a marital pair. Although members of a nuclear family may live under one roof, for purposes of eating they may be scattered among commensal units.

Inheritance. Individual inheritance is greatly restricted by the rights of the matrilineal corporate group, which has its traditional lands, traditional house, common hearth, canoes, and canoe sheds. Individuals acquire usufruct tenure to a plot of land in three ways: intralineally, by matrilineal inheritance through another member; extralineally, as a result of patrilineal inheritance of usufruct tenure originally acquired by gift exchange or purchase; and, last, life usufruct tenure, which is held only for the lifetime of the individual or for even less time. The system of land tenure is basically a matter of lineage "ownership" and the granting of rights to individuals either matrilineally or patrilineally.

Socialization. The social personalities of infants and children are shaped mostly by their mothers, but other kin are very crucial. These include their fathers, older siblings, lineage mates, and also members of the kindred, or *iermat,* who are all the people who are their cognates. When children are adopted, which is always before they are born, they continue to be domiciled with their real parents until the ages of 5 to 10, because these years are considered to be the most crucial formative years of their lives. Much permissiveness characterizes child rearing, which involves a minimum of corporal punishment and an abundance of scolding and ridicule. Affection is lavished on children by all those around them, giving them a strong sense of security.

Sociopolitical Organization

Kinship factors dominate the whole sociopolitical organization.

Social Organization. Although certain lineages outrank others, there is virtually no social stratification. Such ranking seems to be lost in historical factors. Individuals may rise to a favorable position by virtue of the acquisition of certain specialties and skills, none of which are hereditary.

Political Organization. The basic unit of government is the village council, made up of all elderly men except for outright incompetents. The head chief and district chiefs are hereditary. These chiefs each succeed to their positions by virtue of their status as the oldest male member of certain lineages, which being matrilineal do not allow a man to succeed his father. Complicating what is otherwise a simple local system is a highly complex arrangement superimposed on Ulithi by its "owners" in the Gagil district of the Yap Islands to the west. Gagil extends its dominance also to all the islands east of Ulithi as far as Truk. Yap's caste system is applied to all of these islands.

Social Control. Pressure to conform to social norms comes not from law, which is only rudimentary at best, but from the fear of criticism, public contempt, ridicule, and ostracism, as well as the utter need for cooperation in a small society dependent on mutual assistance for its very existence. Litigation is suppressed. The gods and the ancestral ghosts are major influences in controlling social behavior. With the advent of foreign control some law has been introduced and traditional restraints that were operative under the old religion have been weakened.

Conflict. Warfare internally and externally ceased long ago because of its suppression by foreign powers, but oral tradition proves conclusively that it was not uncommon in the past.

Religion and Expressive Culture

Religious Beliefs. Since the 1930s Ulithians have gradually been converted to Roman Catholicism. But the old beliefs and practices persist in the minds of the elderly. There is a mélange of many diverse elements: celestial and terrestrial deities, nature spirits, demons, and ancestral ghosts, supplemented by magic, divination, and taboos. The gods of heaven, earth, and sea are lofty, but they are really more the objects of mythology than participants in everyday life, a sphere that is dominated by the ancestral ghosts. Nature spirits are characterized as being either malevolent or benevolent and are thought to be active in human endeavors and conditions.

Religious Practitioners. Lineage ghosts are the object of ritual attention through mediums, who transmit advice through them. Four major part-time magical practitioners are recognized—in navigation, typhoon control, community fishing, and palm-leaf divination, with medicine not far behind. There are also sorcerers and countersorcerers.

Ceremonies. A rite of passage is important for girls but less so for boys. One major ritual, prolonged for weeks, is designed to promote an abundance of fish for the community. Other rituals are political, magical, and religious.

Arts. Artistic expression occurs mostly in song and dance. The graphic and plastic arts are minimal.

Medicine. Illness is believed to be essentially supernatural rather than natural in origin. Healers may be either specialized or domestic.

Death and Afterlife. According to traditional beliefs, death is the result of sorcery, taboo violation, or the hostility of spirits, except when the deceased has reached old age and succumbed to natural causes. After burial the soul lingers for four days on earth and then journeys to Lang, the sky world, where a god assigns the soul to either a paradisal or a tortured afterlife, depending on the person's behavior while alive. A period of mourning lasting for four lunar months is ended when a large feast, called "pay stone," is given for those who washed the corpse or dug the grave. The numerous taboos imposed on the living are then lifted. The dead often visit their relatives and communicate with them through mediums.

See also Truk, Woleai, Yap

Bibliography

Lessa, William A. (1966). *Ulithi: A Micronesian Design for Living.* New York: Holt, Rinehart & Winston. Reprint. 1980. Prospect Heights, Ill.: Waveland Press.

Lessa, William A. (1980). *More Tales from Ulithi Atoll: A Content Analysis.* University of California Publications: Folklore and Mythology Studies, no. 32. Berkeley and Los Angeles.

Lessa, William A. (1987). "Micronesian Religion: An Overview." In *The Encyclopedia of Religion,* edited by Mircea Eliade et al., vol. 9, 498–505. New York: Macmillan.

WILLIAM A. LESSA

Usino

ETHNONYM: Tariba

Orientation

Identification. The name "Usino" refers to the inhabitants of four lowland social and territorial units (parishes), each corresponding to a dialect of the Usino language. Although all speakers of the language are known to the Usino people as "Tariba," they distinguish between mountain and lowland speakers. This summary focuses on the lowlanders, who call themselves "Usino folovo" or "Usino men," because Usino is the name of the central village of the lowland region. Prior to contact, these parishes rarely united as a single sociopolitical unit and had no collective name for themselves, despite intensive social and linguistic alliance.

Location. The Usino people live in Madang Province of Papua New Guinea in three major villages and seven hamlets, all of which are centered in the Ramu River Valley near Usino Patrol Post, just east of the Ramu River. To the west rise the Bismarck Mountains and to the east the Finisterre Mountains rise to about 1200 meters. The area is steamy tropical rain forest, characterized by rich biotic resources and two climatic seasons, a wet season from December to May and a dry season from May to November. Located 60 meters above sea level, the dense rain forest is crisscrossed by numerous streams and rivers utilized for canoe travel and fishing. Because yearly rainfall approximates 508 centimeters, these waterways flood, turning the rain forest into swamp during the wet season.

Demography. The land is sparsely populated with about 2.7 persons per square kilometer. In 1974, 250 Usino people resided in three centralized villages, but since then the population has increased to about 400, owing in part to a rise in the birth rate and the return of wage laborers and their families.

Linguistic Affiliation. The term "Usino people" refers to inhabitants of a geographic region, near Usino village in the lowlands, rather than to a linguistic isolate. The Usino language also encompasses groups in several mountain villages. It appears to be closely related to Sumau (or Garia) in the Finisterre Mountains and to Danaru and Urugina in the Upper Ramu Valley. These four languages comprise the Peka Family of the Rai Coast Stock of Non-Austronesian languages. Most Usino people can understand at least one or two neighboring languages, and all except the oldest Usino women now speak Tok Pisin as well.

History and Cultural Relations

Little is known about the origins of the Usino people; linguistic evidence suggests that they may derive from the Madang coastal area to the east. Usino people date first European contact in the late 1920s when the German Lutheran mission first settled in the Finisterre Mountains. Apparently, indigenous missionaries from the coast were the only source of regular foreign influence, while European government and mission patrols from Madang and Bundi made frequent visits until the 1960s. During World War II, German and indigenous missionaries returned to their homes while Usino people scattered to the bush during the fighting between Americans and Japanese in the region. When the missionaries returned in the late 1940s and 1950s, Christianity had been eclipsed by cargo cults, which flourished until the mid-1960s. Although an indigenous Lutheran missionary settled in Usino village in 1980, traditional beliefs remain strong. Prior to the establishment of Usino Patrol Post and airstrip in 1967, access to the port town of Madang entailed a four-day trek. In 1974, a feeder road from the Lae-Madang Highway connected Usino Patrol Post with the coast and the highlands. In 1981, when Walium supplanted Usino Patrol Post as the Upper Ramu District headquarters, the airstrip and health center closed, and Usino people were alienated from their primary source of cash income. Usino responded to these recidivistic trends in the mid-1970s to mid-1980s with a sense of increased relative isolation.

Settlements

Until mission contact in the 1930s, Usino resided in scattered homesteads, gardening and hunting within their traditional parish territories. Afterward they formed one large village in accord with government policy. The site of this village changed several times and fission occurred about 1967, creating two major villages, the largest of which is Usino. Each village and hamlet is in a constant state of internal flux with regard to residence patterns and household membership. Houses are built year-round as extended families outgrow their homes or as families nucleate. Rectangular houses, made of bush materials, encircle a central common. In the past, initiated men usually resided in one house that doubled as a male cult house, but they could live with their families if they wished. Until recently, residential patterns reflected traditional beliefs about ritual pollution; if men and women shared a house, they partitioned their sleeping areas, and women had isolated menstrual huts on the edge of the village. In 1974, women observed menstrual seclusion in the backs of their houses, with separate back doors for their exclusive use. Since 1981, there are no more back doors, although women still observe menstrual seclusion.

Economy

Subsistence and Commercial Activities. The Usino subsistence base has changed little in the past four generations. The production of taro, bananas, pumpkins, sweet potatoes, tapioca, and yams characterizes the swidden horticultural economy. Coconuts, betel nuts, papayas, and tobacco are also cultivated in village plots. Garden produce is supplemented by bush foraging, fishing, and the hunting of wild pigs, cassowaries, bandicoots and other small marsupials, birds, lizards, snakes, crocodiles, and insects. Pig husbandry is practiced to a lesser extent than in the highlands. Although most Usino men have engaged in contractual labor on the coast for a year or two, at present Usino access to wage labor is minimal. Until the late 1980s, attempts at commercial production of coffee, rice, and peanuts were unsuccessful, and cattle projects have engendered few profits.

Industrial Arts. Usino people traditionally manufactured carved wooden bowls, one of their major items of exchange. Additional handicrafts include canoes, drums, bark cloth from the paper mulberry tree, woven bamboo mats for house walls, pandanus baskets, spears, bows, and woven-fiber net bags.

Trade. Usino is an entrepreneurial community, economically and geographically intermediate in several important trade networks extending across the Ramu Valley. Unlike neighboring highland areas, the Usino bush abounds with wildlife and is a source of feral pigs, cassowaries, bird of paradise plumes, Victoria pigeon and hornbill feathers, lizards, opossum meat and fur, and mussel shells for lime. In addition to being richer in natural resources than the bordering mountain groups, Usino produces wooden bowls, betel nuts, tobacco, taro, and coconuts—lowland products highly valued by upland groups. Usino's location, intermediate between two mountain ranges, ensures its entrepreneurial role as goods from the Bismarck Mountains flow through Usino to the Finisterres and vice versa. Usino's position as a trading center allows it to survive as an in-marrying group, maintaining exchange relationships with outside groups by means other than marriage.

Division of Labor. A relatively sharp sexual division of labor characterizes Usino life. Men work collectively at hunting, carving canoes, building garden fences and houses, planning and conducting exchange ceremonies, and performing harvest and initiation rituals. They also perform planting and hunting rituals and magic, curing, manufacture of tools and weapons, and public oratory. Women are primarily responsible for child care, cooking, collecting firewood, weaving net bags, and weeding and harvesting gardens. Girls begin these tasks at about age 5, while boys are relatively free to play until adolescence. Women cooperate with men in several tasks, collecting grass for thatch, hunting small rodents and carrying home the meat, clearing the undergrowth in new gardens as men fell the large trees, making lime, planting gardens, preparing sago, and preparing vegetables while men undertake the cooking at public feasts. Both men and women fish, but by different methods. Recently women have joined their husbands in the production of cash crops.

Land Tenure. Parish membership entails hereditary land rights to a particular associated terrritory, collectively owned by a group of patrilineal kin. Usufruct is usually transmitted according to patrilineal inheritance rules, but cognatic principles play a large part in determining land-use alternatives. Despite the patrilineal ideal, a majority of men actually utilize land obtained through affiliation with mothers or wives. Although a person relinquishes ownership rights to his natal territory if he leaves and his children become members of another parish, most people maintain limited hunting and fishing rights in their native parish by virtue of strong family ties and continuity of use. Because no discernible population pressure yet exists, borrowing land is relatively easy; a man and his children can eventually gain rights to land of another Usino parish by helping the owners cultivate the land. Ideally, children inherit land from their father if he has paid bride-price and child-price. Otherwise, children remain members of their maternal parish, and they inherit land accordingly.

Kinship

Kin Groups and Descent. The largest local group in Usino is the parish, a named social and territorial unit. A parish is composed of persons associated with a certain tract of land, bearing a distinct name, and forming a political unit. There are four such traditional units, and members have grouped along kinship lines into three villages. At present each Usino parish is divided into two social and territorial subunits, or "carpels." A carpel is an exogamous unilinear group, or patrilineage, which has its social center within a parish territory. Descent is patrilineal; by making a payment for his wife and each child, a father attains rights to his children and thereby establishes claims to his daughter's bride-price as well as to child-price for his daughter's children. Despite the patrilineal ideal, however, a child will remain a member of the mother's patrilineage unless bought by the father. Although child-price is functionally an autonomous payment, it is seen by most as an extension of the bride-price.

Kinship Terminology. Deviating from standard systems, in Usino paternal parallel cousins are merged with siblings while cross cousins are distinguished from maternal parallel cousins. The distinction between cross and parallel cousins is important, and matrikin play an important social role for each individual. Relative age is an important marker; parents' younger siblings are lumped with parents, but parents' older siblings are called "grandmother" and "grandfather." There is also terminological merging between grandparents and grandchildren, distinguished by sex. Great-grandparents and great-grandchildren call one another "husband" or "wife." Affinal kin are distinguished from consanguineal kin. Intracommunity marriage results in many overlapping kin categories.

Marriage and Family

Marriage. Polygyny in Usino is accepted but not preferred, and it is practiced by only about 18 percent of the families. Successful polygynous unions are initiated by the cowives themselves. Preferential intraparish marriage and sister exchange characterize Usino, and if suitable mates are not available within the opposite carpel, spouses are selected from other Usino parishes. Consequently, a multiplicity of affinal and cognatic ties connect Usino parishes. Intergroup alliances are maintained through trade partnerships rather than marriage. Divorces do not threaten the system of alliance and exchange, and they are accomplished with relative ease. Low population density and minimal cash income limit access to wealth and goods, prohibiting large bride-price prestations, and there are no marriage-payment negotiations. Partners are officially betrothed by their parents, sometimes as children, but in practice young people often choose their own mates. Women generally choose their second husbands. Postmarital residence is usually virilocal, but most parish members live their entire lives within Usino territory, if not in the same village.

Domestic Unit. The basic domestic and economic unit is the household, composed of either a nuclear or extended family.

Inheritance. Inheritance is patrilineal, once bride-price and child-price are paid by the husband to his affines.

Socialization. Education is primarily informal, through observation and imitation; relatively few children attend the primary school 6.4 kilometers away, and only a few Usino men have attended high school. Scolding and physical punishment are frequently used to impress upon children their responsibilities.

Sociopolitical Organization

Social Organization. The cultural-linguistic unit that includes the mountain speakers of Usino is called a "phyle" since the word "tribe" is inappropriate for a group which lacks corporate existence. The phyle is divided into smaller units, based on slight differences in culture. The lowland Usino subphyle is divided into four "parishes," political units associated with defined tracts of land. Members of these parishes have grouped along kinship lines into villages and hamlets, but members of extraphyle parishes are also incorporated into the villages. Each Usino parish is subdivided into two smaller social and territorial subunits called carpels, the exogamous patrilineal groups (discussed previously) that have their social centers within parish territory. The Usino social structure is one of discrete multicarpellary parishes, because each parish has a set of unilinear kinship groups that belong to it and to it alone. Parishes in this system may be self-sufficient, and in precontact times they always were. Unlike the neighboring mountain-dwelling Garia, Usino people have definite territorial groups with fixed boundaries.

Political Organization. Each patrilineage, or carpel, has a patriarch who oversees land and ritual that is patrilineally inherited, but for the most part he is a figurehead for the descent group. Actual leadership depends on a combination of personal qualities. The vernacular term for big-man (*namagem*) means "good man" and can refer to any man who excels in some way. Almost all men over age 40 are considered namagem in some capacity, but leaders are those who excel in activities such as accumulating pigs, wealth, or trade partners and who demonstrate skill at initiating and directing communal activities. There are no distinctive visual symbols of economic differentiation and no obvious differences in standard of living, consumption, or material wealth. What little status differentiation exists is based on acquired trade ties, the possession of powerful ritual names and secrets, or access to cash.

Social Control. Internal hostilities are managed through informal mechanisms such as gossip, physical confrontation, threat of sorcery, and health beliefs that attribute illness to unresolved grievances, disharmony, and intervention by ancestral spirits. Pigs destroying gardens, bride-price and child-price, marital disputes, and trespass on hunting rights are primary sources of interpersonal conflict. In a washing ceremony, disputants absolve one another of transgression. Village moots or courts consider those cases that defy informal settlement, and government courts are used as a last resort.

Conflict. Extraphyle raiding characterized external conflict until the 1920s and 1930s, when Usino voluntarily accepted pacification. Relations with other groups are generally amicable, but issues over exchange, land use, and sorcery occasionally require traditional methods of dispute settlement—that is, a moot or court in which the contending parties air their differences and seek consensus. If consensus is not attained, sorcery or appeal to government courts may follow.

Religion and Expressive Culture

Religious Beliefs. The secret ritual names of the mythological culture heroes and heroines are owned by patrilineages and are used in ritual for warfare, hunting, planting, harvesting, feasts, and magic: these secret names give rituals their power. Ownership of these names is the most valuable kind of ritual knowledge, but secret names of bush spirits—those who protect parish land as well as the mischievous and dangerous wild men and women spirits—may also be invoked by patrilineages for protection and healing. Access to spiritual power is unequal; early missionaries burned some of the sacred names, rendering them ineffective, so some lineages lost this powerful knowledge. Additional secret names were lost when elders died before passing the names on to younger members. Also, some people have greater success in attracting the favor of spirits. Although Usino cargo cults ended in the 1970s, a strong cargo bias still underlies relationships with Europeans. Lutheran concepts of God have been added by some to the spiritual belief system, but traditional belief in spirits remains universal.

Religious Practitioners. Any man who seeks success in planting, hunting, and exchange must attempt to control the spirit world by giving gifts to the spirits and invoking their ritual names. Most men inherit or buy a few names and rituals and occasionally observe taboos, in order to achieve material well-being, but there are also several kinds of ritual specialists in Usino. One or two specialize in dance ritual, making the dances ritually powerful so as to enhance intergroup exchange and to attract potential mates. Two other men control rituals for planting and harvesting. Other men control rituals for male initiation, but female initiation, last conducted in 1975, was performed by specialists from outside Usino because that ritual knowledge had been lost.

Ceremonies. Rituals are associated with nearly all activities: dances, initiations, warfare, hunting, curing, gardening, rainmaking, love magic, canoe and wooden bowl making, slit gong and drum making, feasts and exchanges, weddings, deaths, and births. Dance ceremonies, with singing and drumming, accompany most weddings and formal redistributive feasts. Public oratory and exchange of food and valued trade items mark most exchange ceremonies. Funerals are characterized by the ritual drinking of kava. Most sacred are the male cult ceremonies, including male initiations—which involve seclusion of initiates, physical trials, and dancing—from which women are excluded. Female initiation follows first menstruation, just prior to marriage. Male initiations are performed every few years. Hand-washing ceremonies end ritual seclusion for mourners and cleanse them of ritual pollution.

Arts. Artistic endeavors include the carving of plain wooden bowls and drums, with minimal decoration. Some spears are decorated and net bags are dyed with simple designs. Dancing and ceremonial body decorations exhibit the most artistic elaboration.

Medicine. Minor illness is often traced to intragroup conflict and supernatural intervention (such as attacks by ghosts), but serious illness and death are generally attributed to sorcery from the mountains. Many illnesses are explained by soul loss, and curers are called upon to locate and retrieve the soul. In the past, two curers divined the causes of illnesses and treated them, but both men died without passing on their knowledge. Usino people now rely on a Garia healer, related by marriage, and the government health center.

Death and Afterlife. Ghosts of the deceased (*gob*) are said to roam the village and, if offended, cause illness. A hand-washing ceremony following the mourning period ritually buries the ghost. The ghosts of those who die violently, *kenaime,* may be especially dangerous, so control of them through spells and secret names is important for healers and big-men. Eventually gob disappear, some say to a mountain village. Traditionally the spirits of the dead offered no assistance to the living, but during the cargo cults of the 1950s and 1960s people went to their parents' graves and asked for their assistance in acquiring material goods.

See also Garia

Bibliography

Conton, Leslie (1977). "Women's Roles in a Man's World: Appearance and Reality in a Lowland New Guinea Village." Ph.D. dissertation, University of Oregon, Eugene.

Conton, Leslie (1985). "Reproductive Decision-Making in the Upper Ramu District, Papua New Guinea: Cognitive Aspects of Adaptive Problem-Solving." *Papua New Guinea Medical Journal* 28:163–176.

Conton, Leslie (1985). "Social, Economic, and Ecological Paramaters of Infant Feeding in Usino, Papua New Guinea." *Ecology of Food and Nutrition* 16:39–54.

Conton, Leslie, and David Eisler (1976). "The Ecology of Exchange in the Upper Ramu Valley." *Oceania* 47:134–143.

Eisler, David (1979). *Continuity and Change in a Lowland Political System in Papua New Guinea.* Ph.D. dissertation, University of Oregon, Eugene.

LESLIE CONTON

Uvea

ETHNONYMS: East Uvean, Uvean, Wallis Island

Uvea, like its twin island Futuna, is culturally and linguistically closely related to Tonga. Uvea is a volcanic high island located 180 kilometers northeast of Futuna at 13° S and 176° W. There are close to 6,000 people in Uvea and Futuna. In 1982 there were 12,000 migrant workers from these islands in Nouméa, New Caledonia. Uvean is classified in the Eastern Polynesian Group of Austronesian languages. Settlements are now mainly along the coast. In the past, wetland taro cultivators were nucleated along coastal areas while the settlements were scattered in the more arid uplands.

Uvea is a well-watered, fertile island. Yams, taro, and breadfruit were the traditional staples, complemented by fish, pigs and chickens. Sea turtles were eaten only by the chiefs, who could also place conservation taboos on certain crops. There were irrigation works for taro in the lowlands. Artisans specialized in the three respected trades of canoe making, house building, and dye preparation. Households and lineages engaged in ritual feasting and property exchanges with each other.

Important kin groups included patrilineages, ramages, and broad bilateral kin groups. Individuals had some freedom in the choice of a spouse. Residence was usually patrilocal, but could have been matrilocal if specific advantages warranted the deviation. Chiefs were formerly polygynous. The people of a common residence group (*api*) occupied several dwellings and shared a single cook house. Uvean families were ranked according to genealogical prestige. Both noble and commoner ramages held land and comprised several households. The chiefs tended not to play a central role in either economy or ritual. The first paramount chief (*aliki*) was evidently installed by the Tui Tonga of Tonga. Succession to this office was from oldest to younger brothers and then to the son of the oldest (deceased) brother. Great deference was shown the paramount chief, who was very powerful and could put his subjects to death.

Uvean religious beliefs centered on the concept of *tapu* or sacredness, a quality greatly revered and feared. There were originally three types of gods, hierarchically ordered by degrees of power. The more important deities had associated *maraes,* which were administered by the priests.

See also Futuna, Rotuma, Tonga

Bibliography

Burrows, E. G. (1937). *The Ethnology of Uvea.* Bernice P. Bishop Museum Bulletin no. 145. Honolulu.

Wamira

ETHNONYMS: Bartle Bay, Wedau

Orientation

Identification. "Wamira" is the name for both the village and its residents, and it is used by Wamirans as well as by outsiders.

Location. Wamira lies in Milne Bay Province, the most southeastern province of Papua New Guinea, at 10°1' S and 150°2' E. The village is located directly on the southern shore of Goodenough Bay, midway between the rounded mouth of the bay at Sirisiri and the long spindly tip of East Cape. The residential area stretches along the shore for about 2.5 kilometers between the Uruam and Wamira rivers. A large alluvial plain with fertile garden land lies behind the hamlets and extends into the foothills that rise farther inland to become the Owen Stanley peaks. These massive mountains create a rain shadow, and Wamira—like the 30 kilometers of coastal land to its west—is uncharacteristically dry and savannalike for a tropical lowland environment. The region receives an average of only 140 centimeters of rainfall a year. Seasonal extremes in rainfall create a dry and a wet season. The dry season is unusually long, lasting from approximately April to December. During this time it is not unusual for three months to pass with uninterrupted, scorching sun. The temperature remains fairly constant during both seasons. The mean annual temperature is 27° C; the lowest temperature at night is about 17° C, and the highest, around noon, is 35° C.

Demography. The population, although large compared to the surrounding villages, is moderate in size. From 1896, when the earliest population figures were recorded, until today, the population within the village has remained relatively constant, hovering around 400. Since contact and the first recording of population figures, however, there has been a threefold increase in total Wamiran population. The excess population, which has increased exponentially, is drained off by out-migration from Wamira. Thus the total Wamiran population in Papua New Guinea today is about 1,200, only one-third of whom live in the village. The remainder of the Wamirans live in other villages and many now live in towns. Due to the attraction of town life and its employment opportunities for young people, both men and women in the 20–30 age bracket are poorly represented within the village.

Linguistic Affiliation. The language, which is Austronesian, was given the name "Wedau" by early missionaries. Wedau is the native language of the people who live in the neighboring coastal villages of Wedau, Wamira, Divari, and Lavora. Wedau language belongs to the larger Taupota Family of languages, which includes the three languages of Taupota, Tawara, and Garuai spoken along the coast to the east of Wamira. As one moves east within the Taupota Language Family, one encounters gradual shifts in vocabulary due to phonological and morphological changes between neighboring villages. In classic dialect-chain fashion, although intermediate forms differ only by small steps, the farther away one moves, the more unintelligible in relation to Wedau the languages become. The missionaries mastered Wedau within a few years of their arrival in 1891. They then taught the local people to read and write, so that today nearly all Wedau speakers are literate in their own tongue. Because Wedau was the language learned by the missionaries and was used to preach in church and teach in school, it soon became the lingua franca of the larger geographical area that extends along the coast and into the mountains. Today, Wamiran schoolchildren are taught in English by teachers from other regions of Papua New Guinea. Most younger Wamirans are fairly fluent in English, although they are often too shy to speak it.

History and Cultural Relations

The region in which Wamira lies has had a long history of contact with Europeans. In 1888, Britain annexed the southeastern portion of New Guinea, which became the Protectorate of British New Guinea. With the passing of the Papua Act of 1905, the Protectorate of British New Guinea became the Australian Territory of Papua. First missionary contact with Wamirans occurred in 1891 when two Anglican missionaries, Albert Maclaren and Copland King, landed on the shore between the villages of Wamira and Wedau. Soon thereafter, the mission station of Dogura was built on the plateau above Wedau. Dominating Dogura Plateau, as a majestic landmark visible from great distances, is the monumental white-walled, red-roofed Cathedral of St. Peter and St. Paul which, when completed in 1936, was the largest cathedral in the Southern Hemisphere. The Anglican mission has had a major effect on the villages in the immediate area. Most Wamirans express positive feelings toward the mission and demonstrate respect for most of the changes it has brought: cessation of village warfare, improved health care, and formal education. Since 1975, when Papua New Guinea gained independence from Australia, however, Wamirans have expressed regret that formerly the mission, and now the government, have not brought more in the way of development. The area has neither roads, electricity, running water, nor any means of earning cash.

Settlements

Wamira is bounded on all sides. To the west and east lie the Wamira and Uruam rivers. To the north and south are the sea and mountains. Wamiran land, thus circumscribed, comprises a total of about 5 square kilometers and is roughly square in shape. The village is divided into two wards: the original old village at the western end called Damaladona or Wadubo (*wadubo* meaning "old"); and Rumaruma on the eastern fringe. Rumaruma originated several generations ago when the growing population of Damaladona spread out and settled land that formerly had been used for banana gardens. Damaladona has about one-third of the population, and Rumaruma the remaining two-thirds. Within each ward, settlements are scattered into seaside hamlets, of which there are a total of eighteen. The larger hamlets are further divided into named sections. Within these, people live in households of nuclear, and occasionally extended, families. House construction was traditionally of woven coconut-frond walls and thatched roofs, although many roofs are being replaced by corrugated sheets of tin. Tin roofs are valued because, coupled with gutters and water tanks, they allow for the collection of rainwater.

Economy

Subsistence and Commercial Activities. The household is the main unit of production and consumption, with swidden horticulture as the subsistence base. Wamirans divide their food world into two categories: *tia* (animal foods) and *lam* (vegetable foods). Although seasonal differences exist in the food supply, there is no annual "lean" time. The category of tia, which constitutes about 3 percent of the total calories consumed, has fish as its most stable ingredient. This term includes saltwater fish, freshwater fish, and shellfish. Wild animals, which used to be caught by communal fire drives, trapping, and spearing, are now primarily hunted with shotguns. Although fishing is still practiced extensively, hunting is dwindling in importance. The main domesticated animals are pigs, of which there are about 200 in the village. Every major feast includes pork. Two government cattle projects were established in Wamira in the early 1970s, and beef is also prized now. Lam make up about 97 percent of the total calories in the Wamiran diet. There are numerous wild vegetable foods, such as wild yams, arrowroot, pandanus fruit, licorice root, *Cycas* palm fruit, wild chestnuts, and numerous varieties of green leaves and seaweed. Many large leafy trees stand within the village and produce coconuts, breadfruit, chestnuts, Java almonds, Malay apples, and mangoes. All other fruit and vegetable crops are cultivated in one of two types of family gardens: banana gardens or taro gardens. The most common garden foods include bananas, plantains, taro, yams, sweet potatoes, tapioca, *pitpit,* sugarcane, squashes, corn, papayas, and numerous varieties of beans, peas, and greens. Taro predominates as the staple crop of ritual significance. To enable the year-round cultivation of taro, which requires much water, the Wamirans, as well as the people in several of the neighboring coastal villages to the west, devised a means of irrigating their taro. The Wamiran irrigation system consists of some 12 kilometers of unlined earth canals and subsidiary canals. At the sites of the canal sources (one at the Wamira River and two at the Uruam River), stone dams approximately 15 meters long and 1 meter high are packed across the river to direct the water into the canals. Moreover, in precontact times, the Wamirans alone created a hollowed-log aqueduct as part of their irrigation system to transport river water from the Uruam River across a dry riverbed and onto the plain behind the village. Each aqueduct is used for only four to five years, by which time it breaks and lies dormant until another one is constructed. In the past century, new aqueducts were built in 1892, 1904, 1914, 1928, 1948, and 1977. The 1977 aqueduct was financed by the Papua New Guinean government and constructed of metal pipe. In addition to the traditional foods mentioned above, introduced foods, such as oranges, lemons, limes, pineapples, watermelons, tomatoes, scallions, and peanuts, are grown now as well and are usually sold in the market. Due to the dry climate, the introduction of cash crops has been unsuccessful.

Industrial Arts. Utilitarian goods produced by Wamirans include houses, canoes, clothing, mats, wooden bowls, coconut-shell drinking cups, lime spatulas, baskets, fish nets, net bags, drums, rattles, headdresses, various dance paraphernalia, and weapons. The aqueduct, of course, is a major technological accomplishment and a distinguishing feature of the village. It is flanked by carved wooden figures who are said to be its guardians.

Trade. In the past, intervillage trade was common. Coastal goods such as coconuts and fish moved inland, while areca nuts and certain hardwoods used for digging sticks moved to the coast. Trade also occurred along the coast, where items such as pottery, bark cloth, and food were exchanged among villages. Today, the main form of exchange occurs between Wamira and towns like Alotau, Lae, and Port Moresby. Wamirans send people to work in towns. In return, money and purchased goods, such as food, tools, clothing, and construction materials for houses, enter the village. The money is used to purchase kerosene, matches, tobacco, and food from the trade stores in Wamira and Dogura.

Division of Labor. The village as a whole unites to work for only one activity, the erection and maintenance of the aqueduct that feeds the large, fertile plot of land behind the hamlets. This event occurs every ten to twenty years, and it results in suspicion and antagonism when men from the two wards work side by side. Within each ward, people cooperate for women's communal riverine fishing and men's hunting of wild animals. Hamlet members cooperate on a number of activities. Residents of each hamlet garden adjacent taro plots and cooperation exists among the men when they repair the irrigation canals and turn the sod to make new gardens. The women of each hamlet work together to maintain the taro gardens, digging hollows around the plants to allow the irrigation water to seep in and weeding around the young shoots. Otherwise, people work cooperatively mainly by household, with sex defining who does which task. Men build houses, hunt, make gardens and tools, and climb coconut trees. Women carry foods to the market at Dogura, collect firewood, cook, clean the house, wash dishes, wash clothes, and sweep the hamlet area. Both men and women fish, although only women do so communally. Nowadays, women's clubs are active and each ward has its own club that works on various income-generating projects. These projects include making sweet potato gardens, sewing uniforms for the hospital, and baking and selling bread.

Land Tenure. Rights to both residential and horticultural land are passed down from father to son. Although certain food trees are owned by individuals, anyone who walks by may pick fruit from the tree. Rights to trees do not include rights to the land on which they stand.

Kinship

Kin Groups and Descent. A Wamiran is born into his or her mother's lineage. All members of a lineage claim common descent from an ancestor, although they cannot necessarily trace the links. There are twenty named lineages, each distinguishing itself from the others by its geographical place of origin. Each matrilineage has its own group of animals, usually birds, lizards, snakes, or fish, which are taboo to its members. In the past, each had its prescribed exchange partner at revenge-death feasts, but these feasts have not been practiced for decades.

Kinship Terminology. Kinship terminology is of the Iroquois type.

Marriage and Family

Marriage. Lineage exogamy is prescribed. Because women move to their husband's land after marriage, matrilineal groups are geographically dispersed throughout the village. Marriage ceremonies now often consist of two events—a traditional wedding, with the appropriate exchange of taro and pork, and a church ceremony followed by a European-style feast that includes such things as bread, butter, and jam. Adultery was, and still is, fairly common. Divorce may be initiated by either spouse and usually occurs when one simply moves away from the other.

Domestic Unit. The domestic unit usually consists of a husband and wife with their offspring. Occasionally an elderly parent or an unmarried sibling of the husband or wife lives with the nuclear family.

Inheritance. Inheritance is through the father and the mother. Residential and horticultural land and some types of garden magic are passed from father to son. Other forms of magic are passed down from mother to daughter.

Socialization. Cultural virtues valued by Wamirans include empathy, respect, politeness, and generosity, all of which are taught to children at an early age. From the turn of the century until the 1960s, schooling was through the mission, but it is now run by the government. It is not uncommon for large families to keep one or two children out of school to teach them "village ways."

Sociopolitical Organization

Social Organization. Marriage and matrilineal affiliation are the only social links that crosscut the geographically separate units of patrilocal residence and horticultural production and patrilineal political organization. Although lineage affiliation is the primary link across these otherwise separate and often antagonistic units, the links formed at marriages, which are rekindled and redefined at death, are neither strong nor numerous enough to bond the village together permanently as one unit. This is for two reasons. First, once a woman marries, she severs most ties to her natal family, including those to residential and horticultural land. She remains on her husband's land even after his death, returning to her natal land after his death only if she bore no sons to anchor her to her husband's land. The second reason is that about 82 percent of Wamiran women marry within their ward. Thus, even marriages and deaths, with their accompanying rituals, exchanges, and feasts, fail to bring together people of the two wards very often.

Political Organization. Leadership is hereditary, passing from a man to his firstborn son. Leaders command the respect of Wamirans based upon observed qualities of wisdom, diligence, generosity, horticultural prowess, ceremonial skill, and their ability to organize their group to work. There is one traditional leader for the village as a whole, as well as one in each ward. Each of the eighteen patrilocal hamlets also has one acknowledged leader. The hamlet leader's primary power, which rests in (but is not guaranteed by) his genealogical status of patrilineal primogeniture, must be continually reconfirmed. He achieves respect through his ability to organize and unify his groups and expresses his leadership through the manipulation of food at feasts. His group consists of smaller antagonistic hamlet sections, each of which also has its own genealogically ascribed leader of slightly lesser status than the hamlet leader. The presence of these aspiring competitors challenges a leader's powers and makes his task of unifying the group difficult. Rivalries and conflicts among minor leaders usually threaten to erupt during the process of taro cultivation and harvest, when male powers are especially at stake.

Social Control. Laughter at an individual's nonconformity and ostracism for more serious breaches of conduct function as the main forms of social control. In extreme cases, an individual may be banished to his or her banana garden because of misconduct. Since 1964, local government councils have been established, which also settle major disputes.

Conflict. Prior to contact with Europeans and the cessation of village warfare, intervillage fights often resulted in cannibal raids. Today, conflict and competition surface mainly during horticultural activities, feasts, dances, and organized sports competitions.

Religion and Expressive Culture

Religious Beliefs. Indigenous religious tenets are rooted in animism and beliefs in spirits and spiritlike beings. These spirits reside in numerous forms: human beings, plants, animals, rocks, rivers, etc. Since contact and exposure to the Anglican mission, many Wamirans have become Christian. They are now baptized, take Christian names, and regularly go to church in the village or at the mission station. The two types of beliefs, animism and Christianity, today exist side by side.

Religious Practitioners. Traditional village healers perform magic to help the sick, bring rain, and entice taro to grow. Black magic is practiced in the form of sorcery and witchcraft. Men perform sorcery against one another, usually in their taro gardens. Women practice witchcraft, usually aiming it at members of their own matrilineage such as siblings or children.

Ceremonies. Feasts are held to celebrate marriages, deaths, and various stages of the cultivation of taro. Nowadays, celebrations for club birthdays (women's clubs, men's clubs, boys' clubs, etc.) are also common.

Arts. In the past, utilitarian objects, such as wooden bowls, coconut-shell drinking cups, lime spatulas, and drums, were embellished with carvings. The figures flanking the aqueduct are elaborately carved and decorated with shells. Wamirans engage in competitive dancing and perform buffoonery.

Medicine. Traditional medicines were made from plants. Many villagers go to St. Barnabas Hospital at Dogura for medications. The most common illness for which medicine is sought is malaria. Other commonly occurring illnesses are respiratory infections and infected wounds.

Death and Afterlife. Wamirans believe that upon death the human soul is released, crosses a body of water, and becomes a spirit of the dead. Initially, these spirits roam the village, but ultimately they depart to special places of the dead. They return to advise and haunt the living, chastising errant kin by bringing misfortune, illness, and even death upon them. Death is usually believed to be the result of supernatural causes.

Bibliography

Kahn, Miriam (1986). *Always Hungry, Never Greedy: Food and the Expression of Gender in a Melanesian Society.* Cambridge: Cambridge University Press.

Ker, Annie (1910). *Papuan Fairy Tales.* London: Macmillan.

King, Copland (1899). *A History of the New Guinea Mission.* Sydney: W. A. Pepperday.

Newton, Henry (1914). *In Far New Guinea.* Philadelphia, Pa.: J. B. Lippincott.

Seligmann, Carl G. (1910). *The Melanesians of British New Guinea.* Cambridge: Cambridge University Press.

Wetherell, David (1977). *Reluctant Mission: The Anglican Church in Papua New Guinea, 1891–1942.* St. Lucia: University of Queensland Press.

MIRIAM KAHN

Wantoat

ETHNONYMS: Awara, Wapu, Wopu

Orientation

Identification. Like many ethnic groups in Papua New Guinea the people of the Wantoat Valley had no need to name themselves. They knew their territorial boundaries and who were their enemies. Expatriates named them after their principal locality, the valley of the Wantoat River, a tributary of the Leron River which flows into the Markham River.

Location. The people live along the rugged, southern foothills of the Finisterre Mountains in the Morobe Province of Papua New Guinea, around 6° S and 146°30' E at altitudes from 360 to 1,800 meters. As the altitude increases the climate becomes more temperate.

Demography. In 1980 the population was estimated at 5,500 for the Central dialect, 1,500 for Awara, and 300 for Wapu.

Linguistic Affiliation. The language is a member of the Wantoat Family, Finisterre–Huon Stock, Trans-New Guinea Phylum of Papuan languages. It has three dialects: the Central; the Awara in the west; and the Wapu in the south.

History and Cultural Relations

The Wantoat homeland is in what was originally the German colony of Kaiser Wilhelmsland. Although Australia was given the administration of the area by the League of Nations following World War I, the people were first contacted in 1927 by a patrol led by German missionaries. In 1929 the missionaries began evangelization with national evangelists using the

Kotte (Kâte) language as a church lingua franca. Rival evangelists from the nearby Kaiapit mission station in the Markham Valley to the south charged them with encroachment, and clashes followed. Subsequently the Wantoat people were divided into two circuits, one having Kotte (Kate) and the other having the Yabem language as the lingua franca. The results of the Australian administration establishing control and bringing peace to the area following World War II were increased mobility, marriage between people of more distant villages, the blending of minor dialectal differences, greater longevity for men, and less polygamy. Administrative control also allowed for the introduction of a limited cash economy and for the young men to leave for employment in towns and plantations. These trends were accelerated with the completion of the central Wantoat airstrip in 1956, the opening of a government patrol post with an English-language school, the arrival of trading companies, and the residency of an expatriate Lutheran missionary in 1960. With the connection of the Wantoat station to the national road system via the Leron Valley in 1985, one can expect ever greater changes.

Settlements

In precontact times the people lived in small, relatively isolated hamlets of thirty to eighty persons located in defensible positions, usually on mountain ridges. Generally, several related hamlets were located within two to three hours walking time of one another, but it often took a day to walk to the next complex of related hamlets. Mutual hostility between these groups led to considerable linguistic variation; more than twenty-five minor dialects have been reported. To aid in administration the government required related hamlets to combine into larger villages, thereby reducing the number of settlements substantially. This policy, however, caused the garden areas to be situated farther from the village and hence more vulnerable to destruction by enemies; it also overloaded the capacity for village hygiene, thereby contributing to the more rapid spread of disease; and it renewed latent antagonisms so that village life generally became undesirable. Consequently, many people live in shelters in the gardens and return to the villages to meet governmental officers and attend church. Currently there are about sixty settlements with an average population of 120, but ranging from 43 to 318.

Economy

Subsistence and Commercial Activities. The people are horticulturalists, with the main crops being varieties of sweet potatoes, taro, yams, pandanus, sugarcane, and bananas. Traditionally, a deficiency in animal protein was partially offset by hunting marsupials in the forest; today, canned fish and meat are purchased. There were few wild pigs in the area, and the people practiced little pig husbandry. Consequently, both the Lutheran missionaries and the government agricultural workers had limited success in introducing European pigs for breeding. Attempts to introduce sheep and donkeys also met with little interest. The introduction of European vegetables for cash cropping failed because of the inaccessibility of markets. Some of the vegetables, such as maize, tomatoes, and cabbages, are still grown for local consumption. More successful was the introduction of the Singapore (Chinese) taro, which is now preferred over local varieties. The government introduced the cultivation of coffee, and with the construction of airstrips in the Wantoat and Awara valleys, coffee has become a viable cash crop. The recently completed road link to the coast should increase the marketability of all locally grown produce.

Industrial Arts. For the most part, each local group of people was self-sufficient and able to produce all the necessary tools and utensils from local resources. From bamboo they made containers for carrying water and baking by knocking out all but the last node. Men carved basins and war shields from wood, used the inner bark of a tree for loincloths and protective cloaks, carved bows of black palm, and used cane for arrow shafts with points made of bamboo, black palm, or animal bones. Women wove string bags from twine rolled from the leaves of an indigenous shrub. They made skirts from the fibers found on the inside of banana plants and plaited armbands from rattan.

Trade. What was not available from local resources was imported through trade contacts. Shells and other sea products came from the Rai coast to the north via the neighboring Nankina and Yupna peoples. Pandanus leaf mats came either from the coast or from the Atzera people of the Markham Valley to the south.

Division of Labor. Members of each sex manufacture the artifacts concerned with their roles. Men make the loincloths, drums, ornamental frames for the dances, items for hunting and warfare, lime gourds, and spatulas. Women make grass skirts and string bags. Whereas the men clear the land, the women prepare the gardens and care for most crops except bananas, sugarcane, pandanus, and yams. Women carry food, firewood, babies, and almost anything that can fit in a string bag. Men carry the heavier items such as beams and planks. The introduction of European material culture has not affected this dichotomy of sex roles.

Land Tenure. There is no concept of private landownership, and apart from the limited amount of land purchased by the government to establish offices and schools, all land in the Wantoat area belongs to patrilineal clans.

Kinship

Kin Groups and Descent. The largest functioning unit in Wantoat society is the patrilineal, exogamous clan, whose members claim descent from a common mythical founder. The clan was the context for religious activities. In times of conflict or stress the individual turned to the clan for refuge and support. Today the clan still functions in this way, although increased individualism has weakened the authority of the elders.

Kinship Terminology. The system is characterized by bifurcate-merging terms for aunts and uncles and Iroquois terms for cousins.

Marriage and the Family

Marriage. Marriages are generally arranged between participating clans to maintain a balance in the exchange of women. The preferred exchange was by men exchanging sisters. Although marriages were often arranged prior to the girl reaching puberty, the pattern was for postpubescent girls to marry men who were several years older. If a period of premarital residence of the woman with the man's clan proved her acceptability, the families exchanged gifts. Then the couple entered a new house, ceremonially rekindled a fire, and the wife cooked her first meal for her husband. Divorce was rare. Polygamy used to be common, but with the increase of available men due to the cessation of warfare and the prohibition of polygamy by the missionaries, it has largely given way to monogamy. Arranged marriages are less frequent because the youth meet potential mates at school, and the young men are able to earn their own bride-payment through outside employment. Such independence has resulted in an increase in divorce.

Domestic Unit. The men and the initiated male youth used to live together in a men's house, while the women and children lived in separate residences. Men who were polygamous maintained separate houses for their wives, daughters, and uninitiated sons. When not staying with one of their wives, they would join the initiated young men in the men's house. With the trend to monogamy the primary unit has become the nuclear family, and the married men only infrequently move in with the young men.

Inheritance. Since land rights belonged to the clan and the people did not manufacture durable goods, there was little personal inheritance. Shells, pig tusks, and other personal adornments and utensils, however, did have the potential of embodying the power of previous owners. As such these heirlooms were inherited by a man's offspring, primarily his sons.

Socialization. Parents were permissive in raising their children, particular in the case of boys. Children learned their roles by working with their parents. Girls helped their mothers with gardening, child care, and domestic chores. Of all the rites of passage, the most complex was that of male initiation. Boys were initiated by their maternal uncles who explained the religious beliefs and gave them their first taste of yams and pandanus. Thereafter they worked with the men in clearing brush, building structures, and hunting. Adulthood came with marriage. When the missionaries arrived, the initiation ceremonies were replaced with confirmation classes, and the responsibility of teaching was transferred to pastors from outside the Wantoat area. In modern times the maternal uncles often provide for the educational expenses of their sororal nephews and nieces.

Sociopolitical Organization

Social Organization. Prior to European contact Wantoat society had no class distinctions, although the most successful warrior was the most influential person. A man's strength was considered to be evident in the number of his children, so nearly one-third of the households were polygamous. With European influence and the growth of individualism, a person's status is frequently determined by material possessions, particularly motor vehicles.

Political Organization. The clans are the largest political units, each led by an elder who, in the past, demonstrated prowess in battle and successfully performed the religious rites. Marital connections between clans entailed mutual support in times of conflict. Prior to European contact, villages were small with clan members generally living in more than one village. As a result, there were occasional alliances between villages for ceremonial purposes or for battle. With the trend to larger settlements, modern villages usually consist of two such clans that cooperate in economic ventures. Political control is exercised by a committee of the most respected clan elders.

Social Control. The responsibilities of kin relationships and the dependence of members upon their clan for support entailed an acceptance of the clan's values and social constraints. Men traditionally kept their cultic ritual secret, and today men readily admit that by this secrecy they were able to control the women. With the arrival of the Europeans came the cessation of hostilities, greater mobility, private wage earnings, and the demise of the cultic religion—changes that have made individuals more independent and less responsive to the wishes of other clan members.

Conflict. Loyalty was primarily to one's clan, so that Wantoat society was heavily fragmented. An externally imposed peace has resulted in much latent hostility, particularly in matters of landownership.

Religion and Expressive Culture

Religious Beliefs. A complex mythology, comprised of three major tenets, accounts for the origin of the people and their culture. First, the center of creation for all the peoples of the world, including the more recently encountered Europeans and Japanese, is the Wantoat Valley. Second, at the time of creation the gods provided the people with all the necessary plant and animal life, all the elements of culture, and, most importantly, all the knowledge necessary for their use. No cultural trait or artifact, or the knowledge of its use, has a human origin. Included were sacred stones from which one could through ritual draw power for fertility, healing, and success. Third, because all the other peoples migrated out of the valley, the Wantoat people alone became the chosen people and the repository of the knowledge and rituals by which one maintained life and enjoyed its material benefits. This belief system, however, was somewhat shaken by contact with Western peoples. When the Europeans arrived with an obviously superior material culture, the Wantoat people wished to acquire the knowledge by which they could enjoy the same material culture and standard of living. When they failed to grasp the concepts that the Europeans attempted to teach them, they assumed that the Europeans were withholding knowledge of the secret rituals that accounted for their wealth. Life became centered on the quest for these secrets. A creator god retreated to the sun and maintained contact via insects. Yam gardens were dedicated to it and rats were sacrificed. Culture heroes supplied the people with their culture, and when they died, various useful and edible plants grew from their bodies. Today malevolent spirits inhabit springs, deep pools, and other unusual physical features.

Religious Practitioners. The men formed a male cult from which the women were excluded. Ritual knowledge was relegated to the men, and the more successful cult members became the practitioners who performed sorcery as well as fertility and curative rites. When missionaries introduced the Christian religion, it was readily assumed that it would be the men who would be educated to perform the new rituals and learn the secrets.

Ceremonies. Many ceremonies related to the productivity of the gardens which were planted on steeply terraced slopes and so were always in danger of being washed away by heavy rains. Every few years, as many as 3,000 people would gather to witness a distinctive Wantoat ceremony, the breaching of the dams. The men would build more than thirty shallow dams along an ascending mountain ridge for several hundred feet, and with precise timing they would breach the dams in sequence to form a cascade of water. Other fertility ceremonies involving the use of sacred stones and the reenactment of creation legends were performed when the gardens were planted.

Arts. Traditionally, there was little art apart from the elaborately painted bark-covered bamboo frames carried on the backs of men in the cultic dances. These works of art either decayed or were destroyed when the ceremonies were over, so that new ones had to be built each year. Today, musical instruments are few. The cadence for the dances is maintained by the men with hand-held drums. Panpipes used to be blown during the horticultural rituals.

Medicine. Major illness was thought to be caused by either sorcery or by offended malevolent spirits. Sorcery was rendered harmless by the practitioner performing the appropriate ritual. Evil spirits could be either tricked or placated. When Christianity was introduced, people often regarded illness as punishment by God.

Death and Afterlife. According to traditional beliefs, at birth every person receives as his or her personality a particle of creative force from a general reservoir. After death, this particle becomes an ancestral spirit, then a spirit of the dead, and then it returns to the reservoir to be directed to another person as another personality. To increase the potency of their own particles, a person's surviving relatives used to exhume the skull of the deceased and keep it on a shelf at the back of the house. Under the influence of Christianity, the people now bury their dead in cemeteries.

Bibliography

Schmitz, Carl A. (1955). "Zur Ethnographie der Huon-Halbinsel, Nordost Neuguinea." *Zeitschrift für Ethnologie* 80:298–312.

Schmitz, Carl A. (1960). *Beiträge zur Ethnographie des Wantoat Tales, Nordost Neuguinea.* Kolner ethnologische Mitteilungen. Köln: Kölner Universitäts Verlag.

Schmitz, Carl A. (1963). *Wantoat: Art and Religion of the northeast New Guinea Papuans.* Den Haag: Mouton. Reprint. 1967. Melbourne: Paul Flesch.

KENNETH A. MCELHANON

Wape

ETHNONYMS: Olo, Wapei, Wapë, Wapi

Orientation

Identification. "Wape" is a designation given by Westerners to the culturally similar Olo-speaking people on the inland side of the Torricelli Mountains of Papua New Guinea. The term is derived from *metene wape,* which means a human being in contrast to a spirit being.

Location. The Wape are located at 142°3' E and 3°30' S, in the northwestern section of Papua New Guinea in Sandaun (or West Sepik) Province on the leeward side of the Torricelli Mountains in the Lumi Local, Somoro, and West Wape census divisions. They live in fifty-five villages between 390 to about 840 meters above sea level. The terrain, broken and rugged, is covered with tropical rain forests drained by many streams and small rivers. Earth tremors are commonplace. The humidity is high, there is little change in temperatures throughout the year, and rainfall is generally heavy, with an intense wet season occurring between October and April.

Demography. The Wape number about 10,000 with approximately 19 people per square kilometer. There are no reliable early population estimates.

Linguistic Affiliation. Olo, the Wape language, is one of the forty-seven languages of the Torricelli Phylum. These languages are divided into thirteen families and seven stocks, with Olo classified as being in the Wapei family (23,378 speakers) and the Wapei-Palei Stock (31,770 speakers). It is a complex language with six vowels, seven diphthongs, twelve consonants, six classes of nouns, four classes of verbs, and two tenses. Tok Pisin, the lingua franca, is spoken by most of the men, many children, and some of the women. Rudimentary English is spoken by those attending grammar school, while high school students are more fluent.

History and Cultural Relations

The linguistic and limited cultural data suggest that the Wape migrated from the north coast over the Torricelli Mountains to their present inland home several thousand years ago. The area was first claimed in 1885 by the Germans who were very active on the coast, but there is no evidence that they visited the Wape. After World War II, the Wape area became a part of the League of Nations Mandated Territory of New Guinea administered by Australia; the first government patrols into the area were probably in the early 1920s. The first known material on the Wape was collected in 1926 by E. A. Briggs, a zoologist from the University of Sidney. In the late 1920s and 1930s, labor recruiters and explorers for oil and gold also visited the Wape, who received them peacefully. The Wape were relatively undisturbed by Western intervention until World War II when a small military airstrip and base were established near Lumi village. This post was abandoned after the war; then, in 1947, two Franciscan priests opened a mission station by the Lumi airstrip, and shortly afterward the government established a patrol station nearby. Christian Brethren missionaries also have been active in the area and in the 1980s an indigenous evangelical church began winning some adherents. Nevertheless, most Wape continue to follow the rituals of the ancestors. Although various small-scale developmental schemes have been attempted by the missions and government, none have been very successful and the people remain subsistence farmers. To obtain cash to buy Western commodities, Wape men have relied on work as indentured laborers in other parts of the country. With this source of work no longer available, some Wape villages are being depopulated as families move to coastal towns to find work. In the 1980s an unpaved road reached Lumi from the coastal town of Wewak, but heavy rains and occasional blockades erected by angry landowners along the route make its use problematical.

Settlements

Villages are usually situated on ridges and before contact were stockaded. Villages are comprised of two or more hamlets and clans with an overall population of several hundred. Houses are still made of forest materials and are either situated on the ground as traditionally or elevated a few feet on posts. The interior of the house is restricted to family and close relatives while the veranda is used to socialize with neighbors and friends. Each house contains several small fires with sleeping benches on either side. Babies and toddlers sleep with their parents and sexual intercourse usually occurs in the garden areas. Menstruating family members remain within the house but sleep at a separate fire. If a man continues to eat his wife's cooking while she is menstruating, he will not hunt. In the center of the village is a dirt plaza where children play and villagers assemble for ritual dancing and ceremonials. Each village also has a men's house for sacred objects and one or two other houses where unmarried males live. Traditionally, Wape men were naked and women wore a string skirt fore and aft; today men wear shorts and shirts and women skirts and blouses purchased from the mission and private trade stores.

Economy

Subsistence and Commercial Activities. Although the sago palm is not indigenous to the Torricelli Mountains, the Wape plant it in wet areas and process the pith of the trunk into a starch that is their major staple. Sago is extremely low in nutritional value and is eaten with various greens from their slash-and-burn gardens in which root crops like sweet potatoes and yam are also grown as well as bananas, coconuts, sugarcane, and tobacco. The Wape also forage for grubs, mushrooms, frogs, and bush eggs. Small fish are occasionally speared by youths but are insignificant in the Wape diet. A few domesticated pigs are kept for ceremonial purposes and, increasingly, a few chickens. Hunting for wild pigs, cassowaries, marsupials, and birds is of great ritual and social importance to men. Unfortunately, the introduction of the shotgun has further decimated the animal breeding populations, and so most Wape meals are very low in protein; this diet has adversely affected their rate of maturation and size. Most villages now have indigenously run trade stores but they are usually padlocked and contain little or no stock.

Industrial Arts. Wape men traditionally made wooden shields painted black with carved designs, wooden bowls, and shell decorations; they still make large wooden slit gongs, small dance drums, and bows and arrows. Women traditionally made their string skirts and still make string.

Trade. Traditional trade was primarily with the coastal people on the other side of the Torricelli Mountains, with imported and exported items usually being passed through nearby villages. The Wape traded sago, black-palm bows, and bird feathers, including those of the bird of paradise, for pottery and the shells that Wape men then fabricated into ornaments used as bride-wealth and as personal and mask decorations in their large curing festivals. This trade has ceased and today the Wape are part of the international commodities market using scarce cash to purchase essentials.

Division of Labor. Men hunt, prepare gardens for planting, cut down the sago palms, build houses, perform curing rituals, and make their tools, ceremonial ornaments, and drums. Women forage, fetch water and firewood, make string, sell produce at the government market in Lumi, and cook. Men and women both participate in child care, garden weeding, and harvesting.

Land Tenure. Land is identified with lineages and transmitted patrilineally with the eldest brother generally having the most authority. The right to use garden land is sometimes given to others who come to live in the village. Men often plant a few food trees on another person's land, especially that of their mothers' brothers, and these trees are inherited patrilineally.

Kinship

Kin Groups and Descent. Every Wape child is born into a named patrilineage that is identified by a special slit-gong signal. Its members usually live in a single village. These lineages are the most important economic and social units in Wape society. Patrilineages are combined into much larger named patriclans whose members reside in a number of different villages. These clan ties provide access to others in time of hardship, although fellow clan members are not bound to assist as lineage mates are.

Kinship Terminology. Kin terms are of the Omaha type.

Marriage and Family

Marriage. A person never marries a member of his or her patrilineage. Although marriage within the patriclan also is not allowed, this restriction is sometimes violated. Even traditionally, women usually were given some say in their marriage choice. Bride-wealth is still required, but money is now used instead of shell wealth. Plural marriages are permitted but unusual. Postmarital residence is virilocal. Most marriages are amicable and wife abuse is very rare. In the unlikely event of divorce, the woman returns to her village while the children stay with the father's kin. If a woman's husband dies, she usually remarries a man of his lineage.

Domestic Unit. A husband and wife live in a separate house with their children. At or near puberty, boys move to a separate dwelling but usually take their meals with the family. Because the majority of men and women die of disease in their forties, it is unusual for a child to know her or his grandparents.

Inheritance. Inheritance of land and food trees planted elsewhere is patrilineal.

Socialization. Children are gently scolded and rarely struck. A temper tantrum is simply ignored. Today most children have access to government primary schools with instruction in English but, as the tuition is expensive by Wape standards, some children—especially girls—do not attend.

Sociopolitical Organization

Social Organization. The visible social units are the nuclear family and the village. Kinship ties to a father's and mother's lineages and clans—and, by marriage, to those of one's spouse and one's children's spouses—are still of paramount importance in terms of mutual obligations throughout one's life. The strict exchange obligations of these relationships, supplemented by a general passion for gambling among men, make it almost impossible for a man, even today, to amass wealth and power over others.

Political Organization. Traditionally, each village was a minination composed of a number of patrilineages belonging to several different clans and, although some men were more influential than others, there was no custom of a village headman or chief. Ties to other villages were via these clan ties and the kinship ties of in-marrying women. These ties continue to be important although today the nation has imposed other political institutions including elected regional councils, the police, and courts. The Wape also participate in elections to send representatives to the House of Assembly, the nation's highest law-making body.

Social Control. Ancestral ghosts and the demons resident on one's land are perceived as being very active forces in everyday life. Since these spirits are omniscient, a person offends them at her or his peril. Lineage mates also keep close track of one another and any social infractions are met with disapproval. Fear of sorcery as a reprisal for offending others is also still an active concern.

Conflict. The Wape generally are a pacific people who dislike conflict and work hard to prevent it. When a villager is deeply offended they go to the offender's house and, standing outside, give a haranguing lecture. If a problem escalates, the village is called together to hash out the dispute and reach a consensus decision. Villagers generally avoid using the courts for recourse when possible. Traditionally, pay-back killings with enemy villages did occur, but sometimes there were intervals of several years between killings. Some villages had abandoned feuding even before visitations by government patrols.

Religion and Expressive Culture

Religious Beliefs. All things are believed to have a spirit. When in distress, one calls to a strong ancestor, often a dead father, for help. The spirits of the recently dead and demons are especially dangerous. The introduced Western religions have many nominal adherents but, because the indigenous religious beliefs are anchored in an extensive exchange system that establishes one's worth, the two belief systems comfortably coexist in the thinking of most Wape. While belief in an omnipotent Christian God might be acknowledged, he seems far removed and irrelevant to most Wape crises.

Religious Practitioners. Indigenous curers are known as *numoin* and *wobif.* The former is a feared shaman-witch with magical powers to both kill and cure, who is said also to have the power to become invisible and to fly. Although no longer trained by the Wape, the numoin sometimes uses the services of those who live in the societies south of the Wape. The wobif, whose powers are more benign, is expert at massage and sucking out bad blood and bits of tabooed food that cause illness. The *glasman,* a Tok Pisin word, is a more recent type of practitioner who is clairvoyant, a diagnostician with second sight but with no curing skills. All three types of practitioners receive nominal payments.

Ceremonies. There are no important puberty or marital rites but curing festivals are of great social significance, sometimes bringing together many hundreds of people from diverse villages. The spirit fish-curing festival is the largest and most important of these. It is held in stages by each village every few years and involves an extensive network of economic exchanges among the relatives of the host village. The *mani* festival is second in social importance and is held either to treat disease or to promote successful hunting.

Arts. Dancing and most music are associated with curing festivals. Dancing, restricted to females and youths, is mostly a shuffling step circling the dance plaza to the beat of the booming slit gongs and hand-held dance drums. Chants are melodically restricted to a few notes and sung by both sexes at the curing festivals and by men at hunting festivals. Masks of various shapes are constructed and painted with designs for curing and hunting festivals. Women also compose words to a traditional chant lamenting their departure from their natal village at marriage, and these songs are later sung by both men and women when they are relaxing or at work.

Medicine. Various plants—for example, ginger and stinging nettles—are used in the Wape pharmacopoeia; however, as all serious illness has a supernatural cause—frequently, the intrusion of demons—exorcism is of greater importance in effecting a cure. Western medicine and procedures administered at medical aide posts and the hospital in Lumi also are popular as treatments, but they are mostly utilized after indigenous exorcisms or other procedures have been performed and are rarely given credit for a cure.

Death and Afterlife. At death, the spirit leaves the body via the anus and becomes a rapacious ghost who eventually retires to his lineage lands as a protective vengeful spirit. Traditionally the body was smoked in the village for many days while attended by mourners night and day, then finally buried. Today, by government law, the body is buried the day of the death but relatives still come from surrounding villages to mourn.

See also Gnau

Bibliography

McGregor, Donald E. (1982). *The Fish and the Cross.* Goroko: Melanesian Institute.

McGregor, Donald E., and Aileen R. F. McGregor (1982). *Olo Language Materials.* Pacific Linguistics, Series D, no. 42. Canberra: Australian National University.

Mitchell, William E. Mitchell (1973). "A New Weapon Stirs Up Old Ghosts." *Natural History* 82:74–84.

Mitchell, William E. Mitchell (1987). *The Bamboo Fire: Field Work with the New Guinea Wape*. 2nd ed. Prospect Heights, Ill.: Waveland Press.

Mitchell, William E. Mitchell (1988). "The Defeat of Hierarchy: Gambling as Exchange in a Sepik Society." *American Ethnologist* 15:638–657.

Wark, Lynette, and L. A. Malcolm (1969). "Growth and Development of the Lumi Child in the Sepik District of New Guinea." *Medical Journal of Australia* 2:129–136.

WILLIAM E. MITCHELL

Warlpiri

ETHNONYMS: Ilpirra, Wailpiri, Walbiri, Walpiri

Orientation

Identification. Warlpiri country lies in central Australia, with its center about 180 kilometers northwest of Alice Springs.

Location. Traditionally the Warlpiri-speaking people occupied the Tanami Desert; today they live mainly in various towns and on the Aboriginally-owned cattle station of Willowra. A number of Warlpiri live in Alice Springs and others can be found scattered across the top of northern Australia and the Kimberly region.

Demography. Prior to colonization, it is estimated that there were around 1,200 Warlpiri. By 1976 the estimated number was put at 2,700, perhaps somewhat generously, but it can confidently be assumed that there are upwards of 2,500 speakers today. These people all have Warlpiri as their first language and English as only their second, third, or even fourth language.

Linguistic Affiliation. Warlpiri belongs to the Pama Nyungan Language Family, which includes the languages of Cape York and the southern three-quarters of the continent. As with all other Australian languages, the genetic relationship with languages outside the continent is now lost. Because widows had to observe a one-to-two-year speech taboo following the death of a husband, the Warlpiri women have developed a highly elaborated sign language still in use among the older people.

History and Cultural Relations

There is no archaeological evidence indicating when the area the Warlpiri inhabited at first contact was originally occupied. Other parts of central Australia were, however, sparsely occupied 22,000 years ago and parts of Australia for at least 40,000 years. European explorers began passing through their country from 1862 onward, but it was the development of the pastoral industry in the Victoria River District to the north in the 1880s, and a gold rush at the same period in the Halls Creek region, that initiated sustained contact for some Warlpiri. In 1910 and again in 1930 there were short-lived gold rushes in the Tanami Desert; like the pastoral industry, gold mines utilized Aboriginal people for labor but, unlike the pastoral industry, only briefly. Both industries brought conflict and displacement for those nearest to them. From the 1920s onward pastoral settlement in the area northwest of Alice Springs impinged more directly on Warlpiri resulting in, among other things, the 1928 killing of a station hand at Coniston Station. This led to major reprisal expeditions in which police and station workers admitted to killing thirty-one people, although they probably killed many more. This outbreak of violence scattered the Warlpiri in the area, some of whom retreated to other cattle stations for protection. In 1946 the government established the settlement of Yuendumu, to which it moved many Warlpiri in the region, thus ending the period in which any Warlpiri were living a completely independent life in the bush. Today, with government assistance, a number of small groups have set up outstations or homeland centers in the area of their traditional land interests, leading to a limited recolonization of the remoter desert regions, supported by modern technology.

Settlements

Traditionally, shelter was provided mainly in the form of low windbreaks, but in rainy periods more substantial domed huts with spinifex thatch were used. Nowadays, most Warlpiri live in towns ranging in size from 300 to 1,200 people, most of whom are Warlpiri speakers. The core of each town includes a store from which all day-to-day nutritional and material requirements are bought, a clinic, a primary school, a municipal office, a workshop, usually a church and a police station, and a number of European-style houses. The professional staff are nearly all non-Aborigines; all of them are assisted by Warlpiri coworkers and occupy the European houses along with a limited number of Warlpiri. The remainder of the Warlpiri population live in a wide variety of housing, ranging from "humpies" (sheets of corrugated iron arranged in a tentlike structure), through one- and two-room huts, to various kinds of more substantial housing. Access to immediately located water and electricity is poor for all but those in good housing; the situation is, however, slowly improving.

Economy

Subsistence and Commercial Activities. Until settlement, the Warlpiri lived by hunting and gathering on a diet of roots, fruits, grass and tree seeds, lizards, and small marsupials, supplemented from time to time by large game in the form of kangaroos and emus. Until the 1960s, a number of Warlpiri men worked for substantial portions of the year as stockmen on neighboring cattle stations and a few Warlpiri women worked as domestics in the station homesteads. Those remaining in the settlements performed community maintenance and small jobs in return for rations and limited amounts of cash. Following the introduction of equal pay in the cattle industry in 1968, most Aboriginal people were laid off, and the majority of Warlpiri are now unemployed and living on transfer payments. A few work in the schools, hospitals, and municipal offices, and some are involved in running their own cattle station. Within the last five years the main commercial activity has been painting of traditionally derived designs for the local—and, increasingly, the international—art market.

Industrial Arts. Traditional technology included a small range of versatile artifacts, such as spears, spear throwers, digging sticks, dishes, stone-cutting and maintenance tools, and hair string. The greatest variety of objects made were religious, to be used in men's and women's public and secret ceremonies. These items included sacred boards, poles and crosses, hats, and ground paintings, often combined in complex ways with mounds, pits, and colored decoration made of plant or feather down and ochers.

Trade. There was extensive exchange of items of material culture in the past, but it was mainly in the nature of gift exchange rather than economic necessity. Much prized, both locally and beyond, was the red ocher from a mine at Mount Stanley. It was exchanged for balls of hair string, spear shafts, or shields. Incised pearl shells and dentalia were exchanged into the Warlpiri area from the Kimberly range. Such exchanges continue today as do the exchanges of ceremonies with members of other linguistic groups in the region.

Division of Labor. Tasks are organized along sex and age lines within the household. Women gather vegetable foods and small game, while the men concentrate on hunting small and large game.

Land Tenure. Rights in places and tracts of land (estates) are acquired from one's father or mother but also on the basis of one's place of conception, the burial place of a parent, or a shared ceremonial interest as a result of having interests on the track of an ancestral hero who traveled widely. The Warlpiri have an ideology of patrilineal descent that gives primacy to rights inherited from the father, which confer an absolute right to use the everyday resources of the tract of land or estate with which it is associated. These tracts are not well defined, but they tend to fócus on a cluster of sites and lines of ancestral travel (also called mythical, ancestral, or dreaming tracks) linking important places. Being linked to a place or estate by an interest raises the expectation that one will be consulted on matters relating to it; the importance given to one's opinions will vary with the kind of rights held and, more importantly, the depth of ritual knowledge associated with the place or estate. As a person with a patrilineal interest, one has the right to expect to be taught the corpus of religious knowledge associated with the estate. A maternal interest is of considerable importance, too, for when people with such an interest reach middle age they may be the custodians of their mother's and mother's brother's patrimony. They play a crucial role in the organization of their ceremonial life, which cannot be accomplished without participation from some people with this kind of interest. Since the passing of the Aboriginal Land Rights (Northern Territory) Act in 1976 and subsequent land claims, the Warlpiri now collectively own most of their traditional lands in inalienable freehold and receive royalty payments from mining activity on their lands.

Kinship

Kin Groups and Descent. The Warlpiri have an Arandic system of kinship with four terminological lines of descent but no named patrilineal or matrilineal descent groups. They also have patrilineal, matrilineal, and generational moieties, semimoieties, and subsections. The subsection system divides the population into eight named categories and provides for a distinction between female and male members of each. These named categories are much used in day-to-day speech and in talking to Europeans, but they are not the persuasive organizers of activity they appear to be; instead, they are a shorthand way of referring to matters organized by genealogy, land, religious interests, and other factors.

Kinship Terminology. The kinship terminology system is of the bifurcate-merging type, recognizing sex differences among primary relatives but ignoring collaterality among most categories of kin.

Marriage and Family

Marriage. In the past all first marriages were arranged, often when the girl was young or even before she was born. The average age difference at first marriage was 21 years, with a girl of about 10 marrying a man in his thirties. These age differences are now in sharp decline as are the numbers of arranged marriages. Middle-aged men at present can still expect to have two or three wives in the normal course of events, which is made possible by the delay in men's first marriage, but this is changing rapidly. Permanent, stable unions were the ideal and separation and divorce were comparatively rare; however, because of the age differences between husbands and wives, most women could and can expect to have several husbands over a lifetime and to have more say in whom they marry as they get older. Preferred marriage partners in the past were classificatory second cousins, but more people are now marrying first cousins, and a few are marrying classificatory mother's mother's daughter's sons. In the past, intertribal marriages could result in the couple's living in the wife's tribal territory, but eventually at least the children would be taken back by the father to Warlpiri country.

Domestic Unit. The domestic unit is composed of a man, his wife or wives, their unmarried children, and often some elderly dependent, usually one of the couple's parents. Today and in the past, the widowed members of the household will usually sleep in a widows' camp, while the boys age 10 or older will sleep in a single men's camp.

Inheritance. There is little material property to inherit. The senior mother's brother supervises the distribution of his nephews' possessions among his own brothers and of his nieces' possessions among his sisters. He also takes steps to arrange the avenging of the death.

Socialization. While primary socialization takes place in the domestic unit, mothers spend much of their time with co-wives and close female kin, all of whom may act as care givers. All children are indulged; male children in particular have a great deal of freedom. The freedom ends with marriage for girls and at initiation for boys, which involves seclusion and circumcision at about 11–13 years of age.

Sociopolitical Organization

Social Organization. Minor dialect variations among northern, southern, and eastern Warlpiri reflect loose regional kin networks sometimes called "communities" in the scholarly literature, but these networks have no corporate political or territorial significance. Today as in the past, life is based on an economy of knowledge that confers respect and authority on middle-aged and older men and women.

Political Organization. There are no institutionalized leadership roles or communitywide political structures, but senior members of a patriline have considerable authority in religious affairs. Today there are also town council chairmen and councillors who control large sums of money and resources, which can make them quite influential—but usually only temporarily, as they eventually succumb to pervasive egalitarian pressures.

Social Control. Control was, and is, exercised largely informally and on the basis of public opinion, fear of sorcery, or supernatural sanctions for the breach of religious taboos. Older siblings exercise limited authority over their younger siblings. In the contemporary context the lack of broad-based community political structures poses problems in dealing with issues such as alcohol and vandalism, now usually handled by non-Aboriginal police.

Conflict. Most conflict in the past arose out of disputes concerning deaths (almost all of which were related to sorcery), women, or perceived breaches of ritual rights. Conflict today is aggravated by the availability of alcohol, which can make people more combative and reduce the effectiveness of traditional dispute-settling procedures, which included formalized dueling and dispute-settling ceremonies. In the past, deaths were sometimes avenged by small parties of closely related kin pursuing the killer.

Religion and Expressive Culture

Religious Beliefs. The central concept in Warlpiri religious beliefs is *jukurrpa,* usually translated as "the Dreaming." This term refers to the period when the world was created, the features of the landscape made, and the pre-European rules for conduct laid down, all by the ancestral heroes. These beings, at once both human and nonhuman, emerged from the subterranean ancestral spirit world and led a life much like that of traditional Warlpiri, only on a grander scale. The land surface was transformed into its present-day features by their activity. At each point where they engaged in creative acts are sources of water, and at some other places they left behind life force in the form of spirit children, which are responsible for new human and nonhuman life. The ancestral heroes had designs on their bodies, which carried the life force and which are the designs that men and women reproduce in ceremony today to renew the life force by recreating the founding dramas of their world. In addition to the ancestral beings, mildly malevolent spirits called *gugu* are often invoked to keep children close to adults at night or away from areas where men are holding ceremonies. *Mungamunga,* female ancestral spirits, may appear to either men or women in dreams with new songs, dances, or designs. Large or permanent bodies of water are thought to harbor rainbow serpents that can be offended if proper precautions are not taken.

Religious Practitioners. There is no separate class of religious practitioners since all adults play an active part in religious life. Nevertheless, some people are regarded as particularly knowledgeable about specific bodies of religious knowledge, usually manifested in the mastery of a large repertoire of songs relating to the deeds of particular ancestors.

Ceremonies. The Warlpiri have a rich religious life with a wide variety of ceremonies. These include: secular *purlapa,* based on songs and dance steps brought to people in dreams by ancestral spirits and then fashioned into performances; maturation ceremonies, principally for males; women's *yawulyu* and men's *panpa* ceremonies, which are separately held rites for paternal ancestral dreamings; community-based ceremonies to resolve conflicts and to celebrate the winter solstice; important religious festivals; and magical and sorcery rites performed by an individual or small group for immediate personal ends. Settlement life has removed many logistic problems formerly associated with holding ceremonies, leading to an efflorescence of ritual and a greatly increased catchment area for participation in and exchange of ceremonies.

Arts. Art is central to Warlpiri religious life. The designs given to the people by the ancestors are principal elements of religious property, important in substantiating rights to land and essential to the reproduction of people and nature. Even more important than the designs are the songs commemorating the deeds of the heroic ancestors, which often run into the hundreds for particular lines of travel. Singing is essential for turning boys into men, curing the sick, easing childbirth, attacking enemies, ensuring fertility, and tapping the powers of the Dreaming. In addition to various styles of dancing, there is a huge range of religious sculpture that is dismantled immediately following the ceremony for which it was constructed.

Medicine. A number of older people, almost all of whom are men, are thought to have healing powers and are called upon to treat the sick, especially when the major problem is internal and has no obvious immediate cause. A wide range of herbal medicines is known to people throughout the community and still used from time to time.

Death and Afterlife. The individual personality dissolves with death but the spirit returns to the ancestral spirit world. Traditional practices surrounding death and disposal of the body have been modified more than most aspects of Warlpiri life. At death the house of the deceased, if of a temporary nature, is vacated and destroyed. In the past there was platform burial with disposal of the recovered bones in a termite mound. Nowadays people are buried in cemeteries, although recently some people have been buried back in their own home territories.

See also Aranda, Mardudjara, Ngatatjara, Pintupi

Bibliography

Dussart, F. (1989). "Warlpiri Women's Yawalyu Ceremonies." Ph.D. dissertation, Australian National University, Canberra.

Meggitt, Mervyn J. (1952). *Desert People: A Study of the Walbiri Aborigines of Central Australia.* Sydney: Angus & Robertson.

Meggitt, Mervyn J. (1966). *Gadjari among the Australian Aborigines of Central Australia.* Oceania Monograph no. 14. Sydney: Oceania Publications.

Munn, Nancy (1973). *Walbiri Iconography: Graphic Representation and Cultural Symbolism in a Central Australian Society.* Ithaca: Cornell University Press.

NICOLAS PETERSON

Waropen

ETHNONYMS: Wonti, Worpen

The Waropen are an Austronesian group in the Vogelkop of Irian Jaya, New Guinea. They numbered some 6,000 in 1982 and are located along the eastern part of Geelvink Bay, on the south coast of Yapen Island, and on the mainland from the Kerome River, south of the Mamberamo, to the mouth of the Woisimi River at Wandamen Bay. Waropen is classified as part of the Geelvink Bay Subgroup of Austronesian languages. The people live in some fourteen villages along various watercourses, just inland from Geelvink Bay. Houses are built in the tidal forest, on stilts over the water. Most dwellings are large multifamily buildings, each with several apartments for couples and children. There is also a young men's house for boys and unmarried men.

Subsistence is based on the cultivation of sago and coconuts, fishing, and swine herding. Hunting is much less important. The women typically collect firewood, carry water, gather mollusks, and produce sago. Men generally build canoes and houses, hunt, and fish (with lines and hooks, nets, spears and arrows, poison, and traps). Formerly, a large trading network extended over all of Geelvink Bay, and pottery was an important import item for the Waropen. Travel was most often by sea.

The Waropen are organized into clans, which are localized, nonexogamous kin groups, and localized patrilineages, which are exogamous. The preferred marriage partner for a man is a mother's brother's daughter. For each patrilineage, some lineages are considered wife givers and others wife takers. At the wedding, marriage gifts are exchanged by both parties and bride-price is required. Polygyny is quite common, and children are greatly desired. Divorce is somewhat unusual and can only be concluded after the bride-price and all wedding gifts have been returned. A group of related brothers lives in one longhouse (*ruma*). There is an apartment for each of the resident males' wives. It also happens that some families live alone, away from their affiliated longhouse.

Several lineages are affiliated with a particular clan. Certain clans and lineages are recognized as senior to the others and so are more influential and respected. Many lineages are also linked through patterned marriage exchanges. Each lineage has a headman; and the oldest male descendant of the oldest lineage in a clan is recognized as a chief (*sera*). Both of these leaders are respected and quite influential. Personal distinction and influence are acquired by virtue of age or by possessing the quality of being *kako* (rough, hard, cruel). The Waropen also formerly had many honorific titles, acquired mainly through acts of warfare (i.e., killing people and taking slaves). Finally, there were non-kin-based leaders, or chiefs (*serabawa*), who were mainly from the senior lineages of their clan. The serabawa were primarily military leaders, and most acted in consultation with other influential men.

The Waropen worldview is dualistic, dividing the world into sacred versus profane things and situations. Ancestor worship is also an important part of Waropen religion. Initiation ceremonies exist for both sexes, involving piercing of the ears and septum. Sorcery can be practiced by anyone, and all of the men of a patrilineage are responsible for the worship of their ancestors. Shamans (*ghasaiwin*) are most often old women, and one of their primary responsibilities is the recovery of stolen souls; the theft of a soul is believed to be the primary cause of sickness.

Bibliography

Held, Gerrit Jan (1951). *The Papuas of Waropen.* Koninklijk Instituut voor Taal-, Land- en Volkenkunde. Translation Series 2. The Hague: M. Nijhoff.

Wik Mungkan

ETHNONYMS: Munggan, Wik, Wikmunkan

Orientation

Identification. In early ethnographies of the area, "Wik Mungkan" has been used both for the particular language and for the "tribe" nominally speaking it. In fact, dialect names throughout this region are commonly prefixed by a term meaning "language" (i.e., "Wik–") together with a lexical item that typifies the particular dialect. Thus, "Wik Mungkan" refers to "those who say *mungkan* to mean 'eating.'"

Location. The various Wik-speaking peoples occupied an extensive zone on western Cape York Peninsula in northern Queensland between roughly 13 and 14° S along the rivers of the area, in the sclerophyll forests between them, and in the coastal floodplains bounding the Gulf of Carpentaria to the west. Particularly on the coast, the region was one of great ecological diversity and marked seasonal variations, with an annual intense monsoon period over two or three months and an extended dry season.

Demography. Population estimates for the region before European settlement are difficult to make with any degree of accuracy. There could have been some 2,000 Wik in the less ecologically diverse inland sclerophyll-forest zone, and at least as many could have lived in the much richer coastal zone. There was rapid depopulation beginning in the latter part of the nineteenth century from such factors as measles and influenza epidemics, punitive expeditions by cattlemen, and forced labor on pearling and fishing vessels. Today, there would be some 1,200 or so Wik people in the settlements of the region, with a high birth rate in recent years.

Linguistic Affiliation. There were a great variety of dialects referred to by their speakers as "Wik Mungkan." With dialect exogamy being the dominant pattern, particularly in the coastal zone, people were commonly multilingual. For complex social and political reasons, in the contemporary settlements Wik Mungkan and Aboriginal English have become the lingua francas for most people and there are no extant speakers for many of the original dialects.

History And Cultural Relations

While the Cape York region could originally have been a major route along which migration into the Australian landmass occurred, little detailed archaeological or prehistoric research has been conducted in the area occupied by the Wik. Linguistic and other evidence demonstrates the existence of links between various Wik groups and their neighbors on the coasts and inland. Direct contact with Macassan fishermen or with Torres Strait Islanders appears to have been minimal on the west coast of Cape York. The first Europeans known to have contacted Wik people were the Dutch, early in the seventeenth century. Pressures from the outside world began in earnest for the inland Wik with the encroachment of cattlemen in the latter part of the nineteenth century and a consequent history of dispossession from lands and punitive expeditions that continued well into the present century, in living memory of some of the older Wik. Along the coasts, there has been intermittent contact with itinerant timber cutters for many years, but it was the bêche-de-mer fishermen working in the Torres Strait and looking for labor who caused the greatest depredations. Partly in response to public disquiet about the situation, missions were established in the remote areas of Cape York from the early 1900s, operating under the assimilationist policies and legislative framework of the Queensland government. These saw the gradual sedentarization of the Wik, with systematic attempts to inculcate a social, political, and economic regime based on settled village life rather than the precontact pattern of dispersed seminomadic groups. A fundamental set of changes was set in train in 1978 with the institution of a secular administration under the state local-government model and by a concomitant massive increase in funding, capital development, and bureaucratic involvement—all of which have led to severe pressures on Wik internal social mechanisms.

Settlements

Traditionally, people had a more restricted range of movement during the wet season, when they were generally confined to camps, typically centered on a focal male in his clan estate, on higher ground. In the dry season, groups dispersed more widely, with base camps typically being made near lagoons and lakes. People moved over the country for other than strictly economic reasons (e.g., to meet for ritual occasions and for social intercourse after living in the small and confined wet-season camps). Nowadays, most Wik people live in three small townships and settlements situated on the fringes of what once were their traditional lands.

Economy

Subsistence and Commercial Activities. The Wik were hunters and gatherers, constrained by the generally flat terrain and seasonal variations. Food resources were scarcest at the height of the wet season when people also had a more restricted range; in the dry season, groups camped near lagoons and lakes to exploit such resources as fish, swamp tortoises, birds, and water-lily roots. Yams were taken in large quantities from sand-ridge country, and fish and crustaceans from estuarine waters. The forms of economic life have changed radically in the contemporary settlements, particularly with the large-scale introduction of a cash economy in the late 1960s. Some of the Wik still spend periods on or near their traditional lands, supplementing their cash incomes with hunting and fishing. However, government transfer payments are the main source of income for the Wik, and almost all of the various attempts to institute economically viable industries, such as beef-cattle raising, have failed.

Industrial Arts. Wik technology was relatively complex by Aboriginal Australian standards, and there are a variety of distinctive items (e.g., spears and spear throwers, woven bags, and fishing nets) that today form the basis for a small handicraft industry selling mainly to urban centers elsewhere in Australia.

Trade. There is evidence of trade in material items such as pearl shells, originating in the Torres Strait and most likely being traded down by northern and eastern neighbors, with stone axes and stingray barbs being traded out. Internal trade in the region also existed, as it still does to some extent, in spear handles, ochers, and resins. However, trade was, and is, rarely a purely economic activity, serving social, political, and ritual ends rather than formal economic ones.

Division of Labor. While the general picture is one where women and children gathered and men hunted, the fine-grained picture is more complex. Culturally appropriate tasks varied through the life cycle of individuals, and they also depended to some extent on the composition of the particular exploiting party. Men and women both fish, although women rarely do so with spears. Women never hunt game with rifles or spears. The material items associated with each sex's roles were in general manufactured by members of that sex, although certain women made spears on occasion. The food gathered or hunted was usually prepared by the person obtaining it; thus men cooked game and women prepared vegetable foods. It is fairly common today, however, to see men preparing bread baked in ashes. Indigenous models of the division of labor in the contemporary settlements have been influenced profoundly by those of the cattle stations, missionaries, and European settlement staff. Only Wik men work at cattle mustering or as mechanics or operators of heavy equipment. Nurses' aides and health workers are all female. Some men have recently become involved as teachers' aides and clerical staff.

Land Tenure. The model of the Wik presented by early ethnographers was essentially one of patrilineal landowning clans that combined to form dialectal tribes, with territories containing sites relating to species or phenomena that were the totems of the particular clans. There is evidence that along the Archer River and in the sclerophyll-forest country there was some degree of isomorphic mapping of landholding clan estates and sites relating to their own totems and a lower degree of linguistic diversity than along the coast. In coastal areas, and most probably in the inland zones as well, the ideological native model is indeed that of patrilineal totemic clans with unique bounded estates (although it is a form of custodianship rather than of ownership). But the actual picture is considerably more complex, with crosscutting land tenure, clan totems, totemic ritual cults, and linguistic affiliations. This model has been rendered even more complex where landholding groups have died out and estates are now vacant. Furthermore, claims to land and to sites through the mother's side and into the grandparental generation can in certain circumstances be legitimate, and a further complication is added by the necessity to consider the difference between tenure of land and access to it.

Kinship

Kin Groups and Descent. It is necessary to distinguish between actual social groups formed for a specific purpose—such as residence or fighting—and clan membership, even though to some extent the latter provides the benchmark against which the former are conceptualized by the Wik. Residential groups in the bush, for example, may be comprised of members of several clans, including spouses of core clan members, visitors from neighboring estates, and those whose kin ties to the core residence group give them legitimate rights to be there. Clans are patrilineal, exogamous, landholding units, with shallow genealogical connections that are rarely traced beyond the second or third ascending generation. Clan membership itself, however, may vary over time, with schism being a common feature, resulting from conflict and, in the past, possibly environmental and demographic pressures. The web of kin ties, traced bilaterally, is much more important in mundane life, however, than is clan solidarity, which is realized mainly in events such as major conflicts and mortuary rituals.

Kinship Terminology. Essentially, terminology is of a simple Dravidian type, with grandparents divided into parallel and cross varieties.

Marriage and Family

Marriage. The preferred marriage type was between classificatory cross cousins. However, at least one group of Wik Mungkan speakers has shown a strong preference for actual cross-cousin marriages and liaisons, and there were numbers of marriages predating major European influence that did not conform to either of these types and were termed "wronghead." In coastal regions there was a strong tendency for dialect exogamy and for marriages to form relatively endogamous regional clusters defined by the sclerophyll-forest/coastal distinction and totemic ritual cult membership.

Domestic Unit. Within local groups there would normally be a number of "households," generally made up of a focal male and his wife or wives, their offspring, and perhaps inlaws and aging parents. Residential groups also commonly would include a single men's camp. In the contemporary settlements there is if anything even more fluidity, with a continual flux in household compositions. A household, as a basic unit involving resource exploitation, distribution, and consumption, care of children, and so on, is not necessarily confined to one particular dwelling.

Inheritance. Land, its sites, its associated ritual and mythology, its totems, and the rights to the pool of clan names that are oblique references to the totems, as well as totemic ritual cult affiliation, are all patrilineally inherited. There are, however, rights of access to land and certain sites that may be realized through such factors as marriage or residential association with the landowning group.

Socialization. While the daily minutiae of child rearing may be the province of women, men—older siblings, fathers, and uncles—take part in playing with and caring for young children. Children are indulged, and once weaned they spend a great deal of their time playing with siblings and age mates from compatible kin groups. Learning rarely took place in formal contexts, with the exception of male initiations. The missions severely disrupted many aspects of family life and child socialization, with children being brought up in dormitories until their abolition in 1966. Of great concern to many of the older Wik today is the perceived lack of social control over children and young people, a matter about which they feel powerless.

Sociopolitical Organization

Social Organization. The kinship system formed a basic matrix by which social relations and organization were interpreted, but other forms of association included the basic inland/coastal dichotomy, regional marriage clusters, loose areal associations, short-term collectivities for certain seasonal economic pursuits and the ceremonies surrounding initiation, and the over-arching regional totemic ritual cults. While clan and family structures have been undergoing major changes in the settlements over many years now, and many of the precontact regional and ritual associations are severely attenuated or no longer exist, kinship is still the basic idiom of everyday interactions. New forms of group and corporate structures are emerging, centered on such activities as work, alcohol consumption, and on the governing and administrative bodies instituted in the settlements.

Political Organization. A primary feature of the coastal Wik, but apparently less important inland, is the concept of "bosses"—men who are knowledgeable in terms of country and ritual; who are politically astute leaders, skilled fighters, and commanding public orators; and who can mobilize large numbers of kin. Women can be leaders, especially as they get older, but in general they command a more restricted influence. Clans would normally have a senior man or woman who is a recognized "boss," and there are regional leaders drawn from the ranks of these clan spokespersons. While the bosses may have had major roles in decisions regarding ceremonies, alliances, camp locations, etc., there was and is a strong resistance to hierarchical authority and an emphasis on personal autonomy in much of everyday life. The dominant contemporary settlement political organization consists of elected councils, set up under local-government models that, while nominally encouraging self-determination, are run very much according to European agendas and priorities. Almost all service and administrative staff are White Australians or other non-Wik. The locus of control of Wik affairs is firmly in the hands of the state.

Social Control and Conflict. Conflict was an ever-present factor in the precontact society as well as today, but there were mechanisms to resolve or contain it—in particular, what has been called "the resolution of conflict by fission." This option of moving away from potential or actual conflict is severely compromised in the settlements, built on European models of small compact townships for administrative and service convenience. The parental and grandparental generations no longer have control of the sexuality of young people, and much conflict arises from unsanctioned sexual relations. Older men no longer control crucial aspects of the socialization of younger ones through initiations, which have not been held for some twenty years. Large-scale alcohol consumption has further compromised the Wik's own conflict-resolution mechanisms, and there are very high levels of interpersonal violence that ultimately lead to further bureaucratic intervention in Wik affairs.

Religion and Expressive Culture

Religious Beliefs. Culture in its broadest sense—land and its sacred sites, languages, totems, rituals, and body-paint designs; technology; and the fundamentals of social relations—is not the work of creative human agents in the Wik view but was "left" by culture heroes. In the coastal regions, these heroes are two brothers, whose exploits form the basis of ritual cults that over-arch clan totemism and bind clans in regional associations. For the inland Wik, the clans' founding heroes are as a rule also their major totemic species. This creation time of heroic exploits is represented as being just beyond living memory of the oldest people, but its power is brought into the present through the performance of the various rituals. Also populating the Wik cosmos are spirits of the dead and various other nonhuman beings and spirits, some of whom are malevolent. Like people, however, they have language and are territorial. Many Wik are nominally Christian today, but beliefs and their modes of expression show strong elements of syncretism with traditional Wik ones.

Religious Practitioners. As in the past, there are ritual specialists, although their numbers are now few and the knowledge of many of the ritual and initiatory cycles is greatly attenuated. Ritual leaders are not necessarily secular ones, especially in the settlements.

Ceremonies. Minor ceremonies included those performed at totemic increase sites, but the major ones were those surrounding birth, male initiation, and the complex cycle of mortuary practices. The totemic ritual cult cycles figured prominently in the latter two. Land and its sites, along with individual and corporate-group relationships to them, were at the core of ceremony and other social practices. Many rituals were and are relatively public and had both men and women taking part in specific roles, while others traditionally were restricted, though this is seldom the case today. Women had their own specific rituals in the mortuary cycles, as well as in certain increase ceremonies at particular clan totemic sites, but there was no autonomous domain of women's ritual life as such, apart from certain ceremonies surrounding birth. Mortuary rituals, transformed to a degree from precontact forms, continue to be major features of settlement life, but initiation and formal birth rituals are no longer practiced.

Arts. From the 1950s on, carved and painted ceremonial objects relating to totemic figures of the major ritual cults have been produced by the Wik for use in public and semi-public ceremonies. Prior to this time, they were evidently much simpler, more abstract in form, and used for secret rituals. There are various body-paint designs that are a form of clan corporate property and today are seen only in mortuary rites. There have been some small-scale art workshops developed over the past few years, producing screen-printed cards and clothing.

Medicine. Sickness and misfortune are assigned ultimately to human causality through the medium of (always male) sorcery, or they are attributed to ritual infringements of various kinds, such as approaching a ritually dangerous site to which the individual did not have the right of access. Healers, who counteract the sorcerers' work through their own ritual interventions, are referred to today as "*murri* doctors." Remedies such as bark poultices and infusions are used for such conditions as wounds or diarrhea, but these treatments are not just the province of the healers and hence their application is somewhat idiosyncratic.

Death and Afterlife. For the coastal Wik, there are at least two spiritual constituents of a person. Immediately after death, what could be regarded as the "life essence" goes west, over the sea. The "earthly shadow" of the deceased remains, infusing the places and objects owned and used by him or her, and purification rites are performed over time to resocialize them. The totemic spirit is dispatched to the clan spirit-sending center a few days after death (though inland Wik do not perform this particular ritual). Since mission times, burial has replaced cremation and a Christian service is used for this segment of the mortuary ceremonies.

Bibliography

McConnel, U. (1930). "The Wik-Munkan Tribe of Cape York Peninsula." *Oceania* 1:97–104.

Sutton, P. J. (1978). "Wik: Aboriginal Society, Territory, and Language at Cape Keerweer, Cape York Peninsula, Australia." Ph.D. dissertation, University of Queensland, Brisbane.

Thomson, D. F. (1939). "The Seasonal Factor in Human Culture: Illustrated from the Life of a Contemporary Nomadic Group." *Proceedings of the Prehistoric Society* 5:209–221.

Thomson, D. F. (1972). *Kinship and Behaviour in North Queensland: A Preliminary Account of Kinship and Social Organization on Cape York Peninsula.* Canberra: Australian Institute of Aboriginal Studies.

von Sturmer, J. (1978). "The Wik Region: Economy, Territoriality, and Totemism in Western Cape York Peninsula, North Queensland." Ph.D. dissertation, University of Queensland, Brisbane.

DAVID F. MARTIN

Wogeo

ETHNONYMS: Roissy, Vokeo, Wageva

Orientation

Identification. The Wogeo, who call themselves Wageva, are the Melanesian inhabitants of the island of Wogeo off the north coast of Papua New Guinea. Wogeo is well described for the period from 1934 to 1948, but it has not been studied closely before or since that time. The description here focuses on the traditional culture, although large political, social, and economic changes have probably taken place during the last forty years. The contemporary Wogeo probably closely resemble the neighboring Manam.

Location. Wogeo is located near the intersection of 3° S and 144° E and is one of the Schouten Islands, which include Manam and Kairiru, among others. About 24 kilometers in circumference, Wogeo is a mountainous island of volcanic origin with two peaks reaching about 600 meters above sea level. There are two major seasons: June to September is governed by the southeast trade winds, and the monsoon season lasts from November to April. Rainfall is plentiful and ranges from 228 to 508 centimeters per year. The topography is a mix of rocky outcroppings, beaches, tropical forests, and hilly slopes.

Demography. The population at contact is unknown. In 1934 there were 929 Wogeo on the island, 839 in 1948, and 1,237 in 1981. Despite a smallpox epidemic following first contact, the Wogeo evidently escaped any serious depopulation caused by European contact.

Linguistic Affiliation. Wogeo is a member of the Manam Subfamily of the Siassi Family of Austronesian languages. There are slight dialect differences between villages.

History and Cultural Relations

Wogeo was discovered by the Dutch navigators Jacob Le Maire and Willem Schouten in 1616. Regular contact with Europeans did not begin until the late 1800s through traders, plantation labor recruiters, and government agents from New Guinea. In 1905 routine recruiting of plantation workers began; most men served for three to four years off the island. In 1934 a Roman Catholic mission was established. Contact with neighboring groups such as the Manam mostly involved organized trading expeditions every two or three years.

Settlements

Wogeo is divided into five districts: Wonevaro, Takul, Bukdi, Ga, and Bagiau. Each district has a number of villages of about sixty persons, each of which is located along the coast. In most villages the largest structure is the men's house (*niabwa*) located in the center of the village, with dwellings clustered in groups of two or three to the right and left of the niabwa. The sizable village gardens are generally cleared out of the forest behind the village or on not-too-distant mountain slopes. Dwellings are of different sizes, although all are much the same in appearance—raised on piles 0.9 to 1.5 meters off the ground and featuring a palm-thatch roof, veranda, and palm-wood floor.

Economy

Subsistence and Commercial Activities. The Wogeo subsist through a combination of slash-and-burn horticulture, fruit and nut collecting, fishing, and shellfish collecting. The primary foods are taro, bananas, coconuts, yams, breadfruit, sago, pawpaw fruit, and almonds. Wild pigs are hunted and domesticated pigs slaughtered and eaten, as are lizards and dogs. The climate is such that the horticultural cycle runs at a leisurely pace year-round, with little concern about food shortages. About 40 percent of the gardens are planted near the villages in the coastal belt that circles the island, with the other 60 percent planted farther inland on hilly slopes.

Industrial Arts. The Wogeo make dugout canoes, baskets, drums, bamboo flutes, fish nets, and various other tools, utensils, and ceremonial objects. Most notable are the large seagoing canoes made from whole tree trunks and decorated with carved figureheads.

Trade. Trade is primarily with neighboring island societies and societies on the mainland of Papua New Guinea. Every five or six years about six Wogeo canoes head out on extended trading expeditions loaded with almonds and other nuts, fishing nets, and small, woven baskets. They return with clay pots, produce bags, bamboo for flutes, and ornaments such as shell rings and pigeon feathers. In between the Wogeo expeditions, other island groups launch similar trips, which include stops at Wogeo. These trading expeditions are an important activity on Wogeo and involve communal building of large seagoing canoes, accumulation of the trade goods, magical ceremonies, and gift exchanges between trading partners.

Division of Labor. Division of labor is mainly by sex, although some men enjoy increased status because they are better craftsmen or manifest better control of magical forces. Women care for the children (men have almost no contact with infants), keep house, cook, plant taro, make their clothes, and collect shellfish. Men do the heavy gardening work, gather nuts, build houses, make most tools and utensils, catch fish, and make their own clothes. Despite the task segregation, men and women cooperate closely in the planning and working of the gardens, although their lives are mostly separate otherwise.

Land Tenure. Each district controls the forest area in its boundaries with all district residents having equal access to the forest and its products. Entry by a nonresident into the forest often leads to suspicion of adultery or sorcery and to vengeance raids. Rights to marshland are shared by village residents and rights to the beach are divided among the two or three clans in each village. Every man has the right to build a house in the village nearest the gardens he has a right to cultivate. This village is usually his father's, as gardens are usually inherited patrilineally. Gardens are allotted to villages and clans, although once a man works a plot he "owns" it. Men generally "own" between ten and twenty garden plots. Ownership of a plot rests as much on paying tribute to the headman and clan inheritance rules as on individual claims based on use. All objects are owned by individuals and it is considered a serious breach of etiquette to use someone else's property without their permission.

Kinship

Kin Groups and Descent. Wogeo society is divided into two exogamous moieties, associated with the bat and the hawk. Beyond providing marriage partners, moieties play a major ceremonial role, with mutual ceremonial obligations existing between members of each moiety. Wogeo is described as having a double descent system, as the matrilineal moieties are accompanied by primarily patrilineal rules of descent, inheritance, and political succession. Each village population is aggregated into two or sometimes three clans. While mostly patrilineal, clan membership really rests on ties (not always through descent) to the clan headman.

Kinship Terminology. Kin terms follow the Iroquois system.

Marriage and Family

Marriage. Marriages are made through betrothal, elopement, bride capture, or simply setting up a household. Elopement is most common, except for firstborn boys and girls, whose marriages are arranged by their parents. Marriages are prohibited with members of one's moiety, one's clan, and cross cousins. About one-third of all marriages are polygynous, although few men have more than two wives. These marriages, effected mostly by older, wealthier men, are described as considerably more contentious than monogamous ones. Postmarital residence is typically patrilocal—to be near the husband's father's gardens—but after two years most couples form their own households. In the early years of marriage, separation and divorce are common, but after the birth of the first child divorce is discouraged. However, adultery by the husband, which is quite common, is seen as a reasonable ground for divorce for wives.

Domestic Unit. The basic residential unit is the husband, the wife, and their children, although other relatives may also be present. In polygynous families, each wife has her own dwelling.

Inheritance. Sons generally inherit land from their fathers, with decisions about the size of the inheritance made when the sons are still children. Eldest sons generally inherit the most land. When there are no sons, land is left to the daughters, who in turn leave it to their sons. Succession to clan leadership and family magic are also inherited by sons.

Socialization. Infants are raised by their mothers, with fathers having little to do with their offspring until the children can walk. The mother's and father's sisters have a special relationship with their siblings' children, and grandmothers and unmarried girls often help care for children. Children are indulged until about age 3, after which much of their time is spent in play and assisting adults. Boys' initiation begins with piercing of their ears during infancy, followed by residence in the men's house during childhood, scarification of the tongue at puberty, the first self-incision of the penis after puberty, and finally the wearing of the adult headdress. A girl's first menstruation is often marked by body ornamentation, feasting, and the planting of extra gardens. Adoption of children is quite common.

Sociopolitical Organization

Social and Political Organization. As described above, Wogeo society is organized into residential districts, villages, and clans with an overlay of the two exogamous moieties. Wealth and status differences are reflected in the number of garden plots "owned" by a man and in polygynous marriage. The village is the primary sociopolitical unit, with much contact and cooperation occurring between residents of the same village. Each clan has a headman (*kokwal*) who adjudicates disputes and controls magic; the most respected clan headman serves as the village leader. Headman succession usually, though not always, is to the oldest son.

Social Control and Conflict. Violation of marriage and incest rules, the stealing of pigs, and adultery are serious offenses. Sanctions include supernatural punishments achieved through sorcery, individual retribution, payment of compensation, change of residence, shunning, and gossip. Which method is used depends on the seriousness of the offense, the reputation of the offender, and the relationship between the offender and the victim. District rivalries are intense and short-lived battles often occur over charges of adultery and theft.

Religion and Expressive Culture

Religious Beliefs. Like many Oceanic groups, the Wogeo distinguish between those things that can be handled rationally—the secular—and those things that must be approached with caution because of their religious nature. Three categories of supernaturals are found among the Wogeo: the culture heroes (*nanarang*)—the creators and shapers of the world and the ultimate arbitrators of the rules of daily conduct; the spirit monsters—*lewa,* whose power is called upon during district food distributions, and *nibek,* who is called upon during interdistrict festivals; and the souls of the dead (*mariap*), who actually play little part in the affairs of the living. Magic plays a central role in daily affairs, and it is used by headmen to prevent misfortune and bring good luck. Additionally, there is a strong belief in sorcery as a major cause of illness and death.

Religious Practitioners. Headmen are the key religious practitioners and lead the local, distict, and interdistrict ceremonies, using flutes to call the power of the lewa. The headman's power comes from his proven ability to use magic to provide favorable results for the clan or village, and thus he often has a monopoly on magic used for group activities—such as trading, planting, raiding, etc.—which is passed on to his sons.

Ceremonies. Religious practices focus on the ritual involved in the use of magic. Considerable mystery surrounds the use of sorcery. Much attention has been given to the practice of "male menstruation" in which men cut their penises to make them bleed or "menstruate."

Arts. Music, especially singing and the playing of flutes, drums, and slit gongs, is of ceremonial and recreational importance. Costumed dancing is an important component of rituals. Bamboo flutes of various lengths made from imported bamboo are the primary musical instruments.

Medicine. Illness is generally attributed to sorcery or, less often, to having trespassed on another's property or having failed to incise one's penis recently. In the latter cases, an apology to the property owner or an immediate incision should cure the illness. Each illness is associated with a specific magical system and at least one person in each community knows the rites for that illness. Thus, people generally know whom to blame for their ailments and from whom to seek relief.

Death and Afterlife. Death is almost always ascribed to *yabou* sorcery (intended to be lethal rather than simply cause illness or misfortune), and the relatives of the deceased demand an inquest to identify and punish the culprit. However, these demands are short-lived, and in most cases death is ultimately blamed instead on some violation of incest or menstrual taboos by the deceased. When a person dies, the event is announced to the community and spread to other communities by tolling a slit gong. The length and elaboration of ceremonies depend on the status of the deceased, with ceremonies for a headman being the most elaborate. Gift giving, displays of anger, taboos on touching the corpse and eating, and ritualized wailing all lead up to the actual burial, which is followed by various purification rituals for the relatives of the deceased. While there is the notion of an afterlife, it is not particularly important, as reflected in the little influence ascribed to the spirits of the dead.

See also Manam, Murik

Bibliography

Hogbin, H. Ian (1970). *The Island of Menstruating Men: Religion in Wogeo, New Guinea.* Scranton: Chandler Publishing Company.

Hogbin, H. Ian (1978). *The Leaders and the Led: Social Control in Wogeo.* Carlton: Melbourne University Press.

Woleai

ETHNONYMS: Anangai, Mereyon, Oleai, Olnea, Thirteen Island, Uleai, Weleya

Orientation

Identification. Woleai is the largest of a group of closely related atolls in the central and west-central Caroline Islands of Micronesia that also includes Eauripik, Ifaluk, Faraulep, Elato, and Lamotrek. Collectively, they are sometimes called "the Woleai." Residents, however, label themselves by means of a nominal prefixed to their particular island name, as in *reweleya,* which means "person of Woleai [nationality]."

Location. Woleai is located at 7°21' N and 143°52' E. Eauripik lies 111 kilometers southwest, Ifaluk 55 kilometers east, Faraulep 150 kilometers north-northeast, Elato 250 kilometers east, and Lamotrek 280 kilometers east of Woleai. Each atoll consists of a reef-enclosed lagoon with a number of islets distributed along that reef. These average 1 or 2 meters above sea level with a maximum elevation of 7 to 8 meters. At Woleai there are twenty islets, totaling 3.9 square kilometers in area. Eauripik's five islets only total 0.23 square kilometer, Ifaluk's four islets have 1.5 square kilometers, Faraulep's four islets equal 0.41 square kilometer, Elato's four islets total 0.31 square kilometer, and Lamotrek has three islets equaling 0.96 square kilometer. The year has two seasons—that of the trade winds (November to May) and the other of variable westerly winds (June to October). All of these atolls lie within a region where tropical storms and typhoons are near-constant threats. Rainfall is high (250 to 300 centimeters) and relatively evenly distributed throughout the year, but the coralline soils are poor. Each atoll, therefore, supports fewer than 200 plant species. Terrestrial fauna are also limited, composed primarily of domesticated dogs, pigs, chickens, cats, wild lizards, rats, crabs, and a variety of tropical marine birds.

Demography. In 1980 Woleai had 638 inhabitants settled on five of its islets; Eauripik, 121, all on one islet; Ifaluk, 389 on two; Faraulep, 132 on two; Elato, 51 on one; and Lamotrek, 242 on one islet. The region's population density is a relatively high 600 persons per square kilometer. The population throughout the region is growing at a rate of 2 to 3 percent per annum.

Linguistic Affiliation. The peoples of these islands all speak dialects of Woleaian, a Micronesian language of the Eastern Oceanic Branch of Austronesian. This language is part of a linguistic chain that includes Ulithian and Sonsorolese to the west and Satawalese and Trukese to the east. They are only distantly related to the Non-Oceanic Austronesian Western Micronesian languages of Yap and Palau.

History and Cultural Relations

No firm dates for the first settlement of these islands have been established, although it is possible that migrants from the east (possibly Truk) arrived between A.D. 300 and A.D. 1000. Once settled, the residents of each atoll continued wide-ranging interisland voyages as far as Truk, Yap, Palau, and the Marianas. European explorers found the islands in the late 1700s and early 1800s. These islands were claimed by Spain in 1885, and subsequently they have been administered by Germany (1898), Japan (1914), and the United States (1945). Since 1986 they have been part of the state of Yap in the Federated States of Micronesia, which maintains a treaty of "free association" with the United States but is largely self-governing.

Settlements

Lineal villages (*gapilamw*) are found along the lagoon shore of each inhabited islet. Most islands are divided into two or three districts (*tabw*). A village and its district usually share the same name, which is often descriptive of the village's location on the islet, such as, "Ifang," meaning "North," and "Tabwogap," meaning "West District." Some of the larger and more populous districts may have more than one village. Dwellings are located 30 or more meters inland from the lagoon shore. They are one-room rectangular or hexagonal structures, twice as long as they are wide, with mat-covered earthen floors, plank or plaited-mat walls, and thatched roofs. In some cases (especially on Eauripik and Faraulep) they are built on raised stone platforms up to 1 meter above the surrounding ground. Several such houses may be found on a single named plot or estate (*bwogot*). Each estate has a separate cook house. A main path parallels the lagoon and separates the dwellings from the canoe houses that are located nearer the lagoon. The village or island menstrual house is also located near the beach, but it is removed from the canoe houses. Early in the century each island had a centrally located men's house. Only Ifaluk and Eauripik retain such structures today.

Economy

Subsistence and Commercial Activities. The economy is primarily subsistence-oriented, although it has been linked to the outside world for at least a century through the sale of copra. The interiors of the larger islets are devoted to taro (*Cyrtosperma* and *Colocasia*) and breadfruit cultivation, while coconut palms and bananas are grown elsewhere. Pigs, dogs, and chickens are eaten. A wide variety of reef and pelagic fish are exploited. Green sea turtles are hunted and provide an important part of the diet on Lamotrek and Elato. In recent years some residents have become dependent on money they earn as employees of the state government (as teachers and medical services personnel) and money earned by emigrants who work on Yap and elsewhere.

Industrial Arts. Canoes, woven loincloths and skirts, and shell belts and necklaces are manufactured primarily for local use rather than export.

Trade. These islands have long participated in a number of interisland trading networks. A formal exchange and redistribution system (*chülifeimag*) links the eastern with the western islets of Woleai atoll. Elato is tied to Lamotrek by another system called the "fishhook" (*hü*), and all of these islands (as well as others) were once linked to Yap in a "tribute" exchange system called the *sawei*. These systems permit easy transfer of surpluses to alleviate shortages when an island in the network is damaged by storms or drought.

Division of Labor. Men are primarily fishermen and women are gardeners. Only men are permitted to fish from canoes or along distant reefs. Women can fish reefs adjacent to an island with nets if they can reach the area by walking and wading, but their primary activities are to cultivate taro, weave, and cook. Men tend coconut and breadfruit trees, build houses and canoes, and occupy themselves with tasks centered at the canoe houses, such as repair and manufacture of cordage, rope, nets, and other fishing equipment.

Land Tenure. Control of land is in the hands of the senior women of matrilineal subclans and lineages. These women assign plots for cultivation to their "sisters and daughters" and those rights are defended by their "brothers," the men of the lineage. At marriage a man gains some exploitation rights to the tree crops of his wife's lineage. Land can be gift-transferred between lineages, but it is not sold. Reef and lagoon areas are also owned by subclans, clans, or entire islets. Each lineage owns parcels of land along the lagoon and ocean shore and in the interior; this distribution ensures that each lineage has access to all environmental zones on an island. However, those lineages or subclans with the longest settlement histories usually control the largest number of parcels.

Kinship

Kin Groups and Descent. From four to twelve matrilineal clans (*gailang*) are found on each island. Each is divided into subclans, lineages, and descent lines.

Kinship Terminology. Woleai kinship terminology has a generation emphasis with Hawaiian cousin terminology. Kin terms are referential as individuals always address each other by personal name. The matrilineal emphasis of the society is reflected in separate terms for mother's brother and sister's children. Terms can be compounded to guarantee clarity of meaning. That is, although one's mother's sister is formally *silei*, meaning "my mother," she may be more descriptively identified as *bwisilisilei*, meaning "sister of my mother."

Marriage and Family

Marriage. Today monogamy is the most common form of marriage, although traditionally polygamy was permitted. One's mother's brother arranges or has the power to veto a first marriage. Ritually, only a small exchange of food between the lineages marks the occasion. Clan exogamy is preferred and subclan exogamy enforced. Postmarital residence is matrilocal. Divorce and remarriage were very common until conversion to Christianity in the 1950s.

Domestic Unit. Households average six to eight members. Residents share meals within or near the estate's cookhouse. The typical estate group includes an old woman (or set of sisters), her/their daughters, unmarried sons, and in-marrying husbands. Unmarried adult males do not sleep at the estate but in the men's house or one of the canoe houses.

Inheritance. Since land, canoes, and houses are collectively owned by lineages, issues of inheritance seldom arise. When they do, property is transmitted matrilineally first within the lineage, then within the subclan, and finally within the clan. Gender-specific personal possessions such as female weaving and gardening tools or male fishing equipment are usually passed from mother to daughter or father to son.

Socialization. All members of a household have responsibilities for the care of infants and young children. Adoption is extremely common, not only by childless couples but also by those with their own children. Children have great freedom to move about the island and between households. Only rarely are they punished, most usually if caught fighting with other children. For that purpose a mother's brother may be called to lecture them or administer some form of mild physical punishment, such as ear flicking. As they approach puberty socialization emphasizes conduct considered appropriate to each sex. Boys are encouraged to spend more time in the canoe house while girls are told to remain in the vicinity of the dwellings and interior gardens. Puberty ceremonies are held for girls at first menses and involve isolation in the village menstrual house for several weeks and a shift in dress to an adult woman's woven skirt.

Sociopolitical Organization

Each island is largely self-governing but linked to others through intermarriage and exchange networks of varying size.

Social Organization. The matrilineal clans on each island are ranked according to seniority of settlement and control of land. Genealogy, gender, age, and specialized knowledge determine an individual's rank within the community. Men outrank women in public affairs and older residents have priority over younger. Men who have mastered certain traditional domains of knowledge such as navigation, divination, and canoe building are respected and formerly were referred to as "taboo men."

Political Organization. Each district of an island has a chief, usually the senior man (sometimes woman) of the clan that first settled or conquered it. These chiefs are ranked and constitute the island's governing council along with a senior man from every other clan on the island. Some islands have a paramount chief. The Lamotrek paramount chief also has authority over Elato. A chief's authority permits him (or her) to receive first fruits from all other clans and subclans that reside in the district or (in the case of a paramount chief) on the island, to command and schedule community labor and rituals, and to invoke taboos. The chief does not have the right to dispossess lower-ranking individuals or kin groups. Today, Woleai elects three representatives by precinct to the Yap state legislature and, along with the other outer islands of Yap, one senator to the FSM national congress. Traditional chiefs hold membership on a council that advises and oversees the activities of the state legislature.

Social Control. The senior members of lineages and clans have the responsibility to maintain peace and harmony among members. Chiefs can fine malefactors if they break the peace or taboos. The offender's kin group is held responsible for paying such fines, which are usually levied in traditional goods. Fines are not kept by the chief(s) but redistributed within the community. In extreme cases a troublemaker may be denied harvesting rights by his or her kin group and thereby forced into exile on a neighboring island.

Conflict. Warfare between islands, which occurred in precontact times, ceased about 100 years ago. The presence of interisland exchange and trading networks probably has served to harmonize interaction.

Religion and Expressive Culture

Religious Beliefs. Nearly all residents are Roman Catholic. Each island has a church tended by a lay deacon. Each island is visited four or five times a year by a priest from the mission on Ulithi. Perhaps no more than a dozen non-Christian residents remain. The traditional religion was animistic and ancestor-focused. Many Christians retain some degree of belief in various elements of the traditional system. *Yalus* is a term applied to all gods, spirits, and ghosts. A number of gods (who were also patrons of important crafts) existed beyond the island. Malevolent and benevolent spirits inhabited the sea, sky, and land. Ancestral spirits and ghosts might remain on estate lands to aid their descendants or to punish them if taboos were broken.

Religious Practitioners. Traditional specialists included diviners, curers, navigators, mediums, and weather, crop, and fishing magicians.

Ceremonies. The main house of each lineage had an altar dedicated to ancestral spirits where offerings were periodically renewed. Rituals were held when deemed appropriate by the chiefs, as before overseas voyages, or to ward off typhoons or guard against illness. Church services and processions are now held on important Catholic holidays.

Arts. Women have an inventory of complex weaving designs and men carve images or paint designs on canoe-house lintels. Both sexes tattooed themselves in traditional times with an extensive set of elaborate designs. Song and dance are the most developed of the arts. Songs are composed by women and both sexes have separate inventories of standing and sitting dances.

Medicine. Most illnesses are diagnosed by a diviner and thought caused by malevolent spirits. Medicines are prepared by curers from land and sea ingredients that frequently have some homologous association with the illness. Massage is also a highly developed curing technique.

Death and Afterlife. A period of mourning may last for several months, but the first four days are the most restrictive. Dirges are sung from the time of death until burial on land or at sea the next day. Today most bodies are buried in the church graveyard. Taboos are placed on harvesting coconuts for a period of several weeks to several months, depending on the rank of the deceased. Similar restrictions are placed on reef fishing if a chief or his sister or mother dies. People who die in accidents or during pregnancy or childbirth may be captured by evil spirits and haunt the living. Others may help the living by communicating through mediums.

See also Belau, Kapingamarangi, Truk, Ulithi, Yap

Bibliography

Alkire, William H. (1965). *Lamotrek Atoll and Inter-island Socioeconomic Ties.* Urbana: University of Illinois Press.

Alkire, William H. (1970). "Systems of Measurement on Woleai Atoll, Caroline Islands." *Anthropos* 65:1–73.

Alkire, William H. (1974). "Land Tenure in the Woleai." In *Land Tenure in Oceania,* edited by H. Lundsgaarde, 39–69. Honolulu: University of Hawaii Press.

Burrows, E. G., and M. E. Spiro (1953). *An Atoll Culture: Ethnography of Ifaluk in the Central Carolines.* New Haven, Conn.: Human Relations Area Files Press.

Krämer, Augustin (1937). "Zentral-Karolinen." In *Ergebnisse der Südsee Expedition, 1908–1910,* edited by Georg Thilenius. II. Ethnographie; B. Mikronesien, vol. 10, pt. 1. Hamburg: De Gruyter.

WILLIAM H. ALKIRE

Wongaibon

ETHNONYMS: Wombunger, Wongai-bun, Wonghi, Wonghibon

The Wongaibon are an extinct Australian Aboriginal group who ranged over an area of some 70,000 square kilometers in New South Wales. Their territory was centered at 146°30' E and 32° S at the headwaters of Bogan Creek and on Tigers Camp and Boggy Cowal creeks. They used more of the territory and sometimes moved into the territory of adjacent groups during dry periods when food was scarce.

Bibliography

Cameron, A. L. P. (1985). "Notes on Some Tribes of New South Wales." *Journal of the Royal Anthropological Institute of Great Britain and Ireland* 14:344–370.

Woods, J. D., ed. (1879). *The Native Tribes of South Australia.* Adelaide: E. S. Wigg & Son.

Wovan

ETHNONYMS: Haruai, Waibuk, Wiyaw

Orientation

Identification. The name "Wovan," applied to a small, culturally distinct population in Papua New Guinea, is derived from the label that the people themselves apply to their language (*wovan a mona,* or "Wovan talk"). It is quite possibly an adaptation or corruption of the term "Kopon" (Kobon) applied to the larger ethnic group to the east.

Location. The majority of Wovan live in the Arame River Valley in the Schrader Range of Madang Province, located at about 5°10' to 5°15' S and 144°14' to 144°18' E. The Arame is a southerly flowing tributary of the Jimi River, and most of their dwellings are located on the southern fall of the range. However, the Wovan claim ownership of and control large hunting and gardening territories on the northern fall of the range extending almost to the Sepik lowlands. The area is ruggedly mountainous, with steep valleys cut by swift rivers. Wovan territory varies in altitude from about 2,100 meters above sea level at the top of the range to scarcely 200 meters above sea level at the confluence of the Jimi and Arame rivers. It thus provides the Wovan with a variety of ecological zones from which subsistence may be extracted. Rainfall is distributed throughout the year but a wetter season may be discerned from December through February and a relatively dry season from June through August.

Demography. The total Wovan population as of 1980 was approximately 700 persons. About 53 percent of these were male and approximately 50 percent of the total population were under 20 years of age. The population appears to be relatively stable.

Linguistic Affiliation. Wovan is a Non-Austronesian language and is classified in the Waibuk or Piawi Family, which also includes the Aramo, Pinai, and Wapi languages. It is still not certain whether or how this language family is related to already established, larger linguistic groups in New Guinea. While there is a great deal of language borrowing from Kopon into Wovan, it is uncertain if these languages are related at some more inclusive level. The closest linguistic neighbors of the Wovan are the Aramo people.

History and Cultural Relations

Cut off by a mountain spur that ran parallel to the Jimi River, the Wovan remained undisturbed by European-Australian contact until 1962, when a patrol led by J. A. Johnston, out of Tabibuga, in the Western Highlands Province, entered Wovan territory. While the Wovan treated the outsiders with considerable suspicion and caution, no hostilities were reported. For many years large segments of the population simply avoided the yearly government patrols when they passed through the territory. Only 161 persons presented themselves at the first census in 1968. Village leaders (*luluai, tultul*) were appointed by the patrol officers to act as intermediaries between the people and the government. Government health and agricultural officers visited Wovan territory on a regular basis, encouraging changes in burial practices, improved hygiene, and the adoption of coffee as a cash crop. A government-sponsored medical aid post, staffed by a medical orderly, was established at Fitako in the mid-1970s. The Anglican church established a mission station, staffed by members of the Melanesian Brotherhood, at Aradip in 1977. The Church of the Nazarene, a fundamentalist sect, established outlier mission churches at Funkafunk and on the fringe of Wovan territory near Aradip. The conflict in religious messages has engendered considerable confusion among the Wovan, leading a number of them simply to avoid the missionaries.

Settlements

Despite government and mission pressure to relocate into convenient hamlets, the majority of the people still reside in the scattered homesteads that formed their traditional residence pattern. The small hamlets (Aradip, Fitako, and Funkafunk) developed in the postcontact period. Homesteads were constructed on ridge spurs, giving residents control of the valleys below. Ideally, a homestead consisted of a set of married male siblings, their in-married wives, their married sons and their wives, and all their unmarried children. Homestead populations ranged in size from a single nuclear family of three persons to a large extended family of thirty-seven. Each house is internally divided into a male and female side with married couples residing in rooms located at each end of the main structure.

Economy

Subsistence and Commercial Activities. The homestead (*hram diib,* or "big house") is the basic unit of production and consumption. Swidden horticulture and pig herding, supplemented by hunting, form the basis of Wovan subsistence. Taro and sweet potatoes are the major crops but bananas, edible *pitpit*, sugarcane, beans, maize, and a variety of greens are also important in the diet. Tobacco is grown in almost all gardens. A wide range of "wild" crops are harvested. Among the most important of these are betel nuts, *marita* pandanus, pandanus nuts, and a wide range of fungi. Recently coffee has been planted, but it has not yet yielded significant harvests. The Wovan keep domesticated pigs, dogs, and fowl. Pigs are of central import both in terms of their contribution to the diet and in terms of their value as items of exchange. Dogs are used in hunting and are generally treated well. Recently introduced domestic fowl are proliferating but neither they nor their eggs are considered desirable food by the Wovan. Animal protein supplied by hunting or foraging is obtained from cassowaries, wild pigs, many varieties of birds and marsupials, frogs, various rodents, grubs, and megapode eggs. Eels are important both ceremonially and in terms of their contribution to the overall diet. Sago is obtained in trade from the Sepik River area but does not contribute substantially to the diet.

Industrial Arts. The most significant items produced include black-palm bows, arrows, net bags, pandanus-leaf mats, and elaborately carved bamboo combs. Wovan men invest considerable energy in producing elaborate dancing finery. This decoration includes large "busby" hats decorated with beetle shards, opossum fur, and, nowadays, cloth. These hats are crowned with rings of eagle feathers, cassowary plumes, and bird of paradise plumes. The Wovan produce *kundu* drums, small panpipes, and bamboo Jew's harps.

Trade. Trade has always been important both to provide access to desired goods and to solidify friendships and alliances. As well as trading items of their own manufacture, the Wovan acted as intermediaries in the long-distance trade networks that extended from the Sepik River area into the central highlands. Wovan black-palm bows and net bags, as well as ax heads that the Wovan had obtained from their central highlands trading partners, were highly valued among lowlanders to the north. They, in turn, supplied the Wovan with tobacco and shell valuables. These shells and a wide range of marsupial pelts and bird of paradise plumes were traded to the highlanders to the south for ax heads, for salt, and, increasingly in the postcontact era, for cash.

Division of Labor. A division of labor is evidenced in most activities, but, as in many areas, the Wovan tolerate considerable overlap. Men and women cooperate in gardening. Men fell the trees and build fences to prepare the plots. Men and women both plant crops. Women do the daily harvesting and garden maintenance. Coffee is almost exclusively a male-controlled crop. While men are the nominal owners of pigs, women tend them on a daily basis and no man would kill a pig for exchange without obtaining his wife's agreement. Females are more likely than males to be accused of witchcraft but both males and females may act as shamans.

Land Tenure. Theoretically, land is owned by corporate patrilineal descent groups. An individual's rights to both gardening and hunting land are derived from membership in these patrilineages. Parallel-cousin marriage and flexibility in affiliation, however, allow the Wovan considerable room to maneuver. Actual gardening and hunting decisions are made at the level of the homestead rather than the patrilineage.

Kinship

Kin Groups and Descent. The term *yam* is applied to all social groups, irrespective of whether these groups are based on recognized genealogical relationships or not. When qualified by the name of a senior male, the term designates a nuclear or extended family. When qualified by the name of a place, it designates a coresidential or local group or a group of people who believe themselves to be derived from a particular locale. Despite an ideology of patrilineal descent, group affiliation is flexible. Fulfillment of the obligations of kinship is frequently of greater importance than actual genealogical relatedness in establishing and maintaining kinship.

Kinship Terminology. Kinship terminology is basically of the Iroquois type, with generational skewing of both the paternal and maternal same-sex senior sibling.

Marriage and Family

Marriage. The Wovan are monogamous by rule, although a few isolated instances of polygyny do occur. They state a rule of preferential parallel-cousin marriage with sister exchange, but genealogical manipulation to achieve the desired relationship status after the fact is common. The majority of marriages are the products of elopement rather than arrangement, with women taking an active role in initiating marital transactions. While fathers play a prominent role in disputes over their daughters' marriages, brothers (whose own marital futures are dependent on their sisters) take the leading role in all marital arrangements. Bride-prices are small and men boast of not paying. Postmarital residence is patrilocal (both ideally and statistically). Wovan marriages are remarkably stable. In the first month following elopement, relationships are very unstable, but once a domicile has been established, one can expect a permanent relationship. Normatively, divorce is impossible; even infertility is not considered grounds for divorce.

Domestic Unit. The household— consisting of an extended family (or minimal lineage) of brothers, their wives, and unmarried children—forms the basic domestic unit.

Inheritance. Inheritance of land rights is through the patriline, and, theoretically this is immutable. Numerous cases of affiliation through matrilateral connections can be demonstrated. Individually owned wealth is also inherited in the patriline.

Socialization. The arrival of the Anglican church in 1977 introduced a mission school for the first time. Prior to that, socialization was accomplished by the explicit teachings of parents and elder siblings, as well as the imitative strategies of children. Children may occasionally be reprimanded verbally and even more occasionally be subjected to a cuffing, but physical punishment of children is rare.

Sociopolitical Organization

Social Organization. The social system is characterized by a great deal of flexibility despite an ideology of patrilineal descent. The rule of parallel-cousin ("sister") marriage provides added flexibility in terms of landownership and access to forest resources. Homesteads in many, though not all, cases recognize their membership in larger landholding units and their consequent kinship with members of other homesteads with whom they co-own hunting and gardening lands. Genealogical depth is shallow, with only six of forty-eight "big houses" claiming relatedness through connections as distant as or more distant than father's father's father. Kinship and social relations are forged by a continuous flow of gifts and counter gifts, by cooperative gardening relationships, and by the construction of ties of partnership either through ritual or exchange.

Political Organization. The Wovan lack the big-man phenomenon so prominent in the central highlands. To them, all men (especially those who have completed their initiation cycle) are big-men (*numbe diib*). Despite the fact that some men are recognized as better hunters, some as better traders, and some as better orators, shared initiation and other experiences are used to ensure that men continue to regard each other, and behave in relation to each other, as equals. Elders have authority over juniors and males in general have authority over females, but the dominant character of the political organization is egalitarian. The homestead (hram diib, or "big house") group was the only unit over which any particular individual could claim authority.

Social Control. While it was expected that members of the same minimal lineage would not normally use violence to solve disputes, traditionally there were never any restrictions that extended the peace community to the whole Wovan people. Disputes could be solved peacefully by public moots wherein anyone might express an opinion. Restitution payments were offered after public opinion had been heard and evaluated. In cases where the defendant suspected that the punishment would be violent, he or she could choose flight and take up residence with kin among the Kopon or Aramo people.

Conflict. Internal and external conflict took the form of small-scale ambushes and retaliatory raids. Permanent relations of enmity existed between particular Wovan kin groups and some Wovan would align themselves with non-Wovan against their Wovan enemies if the opportunity arose. Raiding ceased immediately after contact. The Wovan assisted both Kopon and Aramo neighbors in conflicts against more distant people.

Religion and Expressive Culture

Religious Beliefs. Wovan religious life, as one finds generally on the northern fringe of the highlands, focuses on the spirits of the dead. The spirits (souls) of deceased relatives are rarely far away. These spirits inhabit stagnant water pools and large trees but venture into the village during the ceremonies surrounding initiation. Animal and forest spirits also affect the fortunes of humans, particularly in relation to the hunt.

Religious Practitioners. The Wovan do not appear to be overly concerned with the supernatural on a daily basis. They lack religious specialists and concede that the Kopon to the east possess more powerful sorcery than they do. A few men are regarded as having influence over the weather. Most, if not all, adult men are familiar with spells and incantations that protect them and their children from attack by malicious ghosts. Men's most important religious and ritual obligations revolve around the initiation of young men.

Ceremonies. The Wovan have an elaborate set of initiation rites through which all males must pass. The first of these takes place when the boy is about 5–7 years old and the last may occur when he is already in his forties. Adolescent (*hamo*) rites are the most elaborate in this ritual calendar and take several days to complete. All such rituals are accompanied by the ceremonial distribution of pork and by dancing.

Arts. Arrows, drums, combs, and Jew's harps are decorated by abstract designs. Considerable energy is devoted to body decoration during festivals and dancing celebrations. All dancing is accompanied by singing and drumming and some Wovan men have gained reputations as being particularly inventive songwriters.

Medicine. Witchcraft and sorcery are pervasive as sources of illness and other misfortunes, though the Wovan deny that they are particularly adept sorcerers or shamans. The use of stinging nettles, medicinal herbs, and tobacco are important among Wovan shamans, who are able to treat some illnesses effectively. Serious illnesses require the intervention of specialists from among the Kopon people to the east.

Death and Afterlife. The Wovan conception of the soul is complex, consisting of both a shadow and a life force. These things have very different careers after death. The shadow departs to life in the land of the dead—a place of uncertain location accessed through pools of water and in which the order of the world is largely inverted. The life force remains close by and continues to have an impact on the lives of living human beings. It is these spirits who are placated by the performance of male initiation rituals that form the core of Wovan religious life. These spirits also assist men in hunting. Death, except in the case of the elderly or in the case of violence, is never accepted as the result of anything other than supernatural forces.

Bibliography

Comrie, Bernard (1988). "Haruai Verb Structure and Language Classification in the Upper Yuat." *Language and Linguistics in Melanesia* 17:140–160.

Davies, John, and Bernard Comrie (1984). "A Linguistic Survey of the Upper Yuat." *Papers in New Guinea Linguistics* 22:275–312.

Flanagan, James G. (1983). "Wovan Social Organization." Ph.D. dissertation, University of Michigan, Ann Arbor.

Flanagan, James G. (1987). "Temporary Out-Migration and the Disruption of Indigenous Law and Order." *Journal of Anthropology* 61:25–49.

Flanagan, J. G. (1988). "The Cultural Construction of Equality on the New Guinea Highlands' Fringe." In *Rules, Decisions, and Inequality in Egalitarian Societies,* edited by J. G. Flanagan and Steve Rayner, 164–180. London: Gower.

Jenkins, Carol, M. Dimitrakakis, I. Cook, R. Sanders, and N. Stallman (1989). "Culture Change and Epidemiological Patterns among the Hagahai, Papua New Guinea." *Human Ecology* 17:27–57.

JAMES G. FLANAGAN

Yangoru Boiken

ETHNONYMS: Nugum, Wianu, Yangoru

Orientation

Identification. The Boiken people of the East Sepik Province, Papua New Guinea, occupy one of the most extensive and ecologically heterogeneous territories in New Guinea. Their boundaries encompass the islands of Walis, Tarawai, and Muschu in the Bismarck Sea and cut a broad swathe inland across the coastal Prince Alexander range before descending through fertile foothills into the rolling grassland north of the Sepik River. Coupled with their complex migrational prehistory, this ecological heterogeneity has conferred an extreme linguistic and cultural diversity on the Boiken, and consequently only one dialect group, the Yangoru Boiken, is described here. The Yangoru Boiken speak five distinct subdialects, each of which exhibits distinct subcultural variations; the data to follow are most representative of the north central subdialect speakers in the villagers of Sima, Kambelyi, and Kworabri. "Boiken" is the name of the coastal village where the first missionaries lived; "Yangoru" is the local name of the area in which Yangoru Patrol Post was located. Until European contact, the Yangoru Boiken had no conception of themselves as a single unit; local polities referred to themselves only as *nina*, which means "we all," or *tua*, which means "people."

Location. The Yangoru Boiken live between 3°36' and 3°45' S and 143°14' and 143°22' E, around Yangoru government station in the southern foothills of the Prince Alexander range. Annual rainfall is about 175 centimeters.

Demography. In 1980, the Boiken numbered some 40,000 people. Of these, about 13,300 were Yangoru Boiken, though only about 9,600 were resident in Yangoru; the rest were living elsewhere in Papua New Guinea. This total represents a considerable increase over the 4,000 to 5,000 Yangoru Boiken estimated at the beginning of significant European contact in the 1920s. In 1980, overall density in Yangoru averaged about 51 persons per square kilometer; within the main population belt, however, it averaged 66 persons per square kilometer. The population growth rate is about 2.5 to 3 percent.

Linguistic Affiliation. The Yangoru Boiken have been classified as one of seven dialect groups of the Boiken language, Ndu Family, Middle Sepik Stock, of the Sepik-Ramu Phylum. The Boiken language is perhaps more accurately characterized, however, as two or more linguistically chained languages, with the Yangoru Boiken located toward the middle of the chain.

History and Cultural Relations

Thousands of years ago, Boiken territory was occupied by speakers of Torricelli Phylum languages. Subsequently, a large body of Ndu speakers from the Koiwat region north of the Sepik River infiltrated what is now southeast Boiken territory and spread northward to the offshore islands, linguistically assimilating the Torricelli residents as they moved. In consequence, the Yangoru Boiken appear to have a dual ancestry, Ndu and Torricelli, which may explain their close cultural affinities to the Torricelli-speaking Mountain Arapesh. First contact occurred around the turn of the century, but it was 1930 before missionaries, labor recruiters, and patrol officers began to have a significant influence on Yangoru Boiken culture. By then, steel had largely displaced stone, and warfare was in decline. By 1980, male initiation, all but the first stage of female initiation, and most traditional arts were defunct, currency had largely displaced shell wealth, and aluminum utensils had replaced clay pots and wooden plates.

Settlement

The Yangoru Boiken live in villages of about fifteen to thirty-five hamlets, located mainly on the leveled crests of densely forested ridges. Most villages have between 150 and 400 people. In 1980, Sima village comprised twenty-eight inhabited hamlets—each with an average of three dwelling houses and two food houses—and 275 residents, with another 57 being absent in towns. Each hamlet is home to one or two patrilineagelike units called *hring*. Each village has several *mandawia* ("big places"), hamlets that clanlike congeries of related hring claim as the homes of their apical ancestors; here they build their spirit houses, conduct their exchange ceremonies, and hold major moots. There are two basic house structures: the pile house, which is raised a meter or so off the ground on stilts and is particularly common in the higher foothills; and the ground house, which is built directly on the earth and is more common in the lower foothills. Both are thatched with coconut-palm fronds or tiles of sago leaflets; they are walled with sago-bark shingles or sago-frond stems, and floored with *limbum* palm planks or cane.

Economy

Subsistence and Commercial Activities. The staples of Yangoru Boiken subsistence are yams and taro, cultivated separately under slash-and-burn horticulture, and a feast-or-famine dependence on the sago palm. Supplements include bananas, coconuts, breadfruit, greens, sugarcane, bamboo sprouts, and a wide variety of game, including pigs, cassowaries, a range of smaller ground and arboreal mammals, birds, grubs, and fish. During the Japanese occupation in World War II, game and fish supplies were seriously depleted and, following the introduction of shotguns and nylon netting, they remain depressed. In consequence, dependence on game and fish has decreased, while reliance on store-bought meat, fish, and rice has increased.

Industrial Arts. In the past, villagers manufactured stone adzes, bamboo knives, carved plates, ceramic pots and bowls, wooden eating utensils, spears, war clubs, shields, slit gongs, and certain items of shell wealth. Nowadays, almost all industrial products are bought in shops.

Trade. Traditionally, the high foothill villages of Yangoru were linked in trade to coastal Boiken villages on the far side of the mountains. They exported smoked pork, tobacco, net bags, and clay pots and imported piglets, salt, and *Turbo* clamshells. Fashions, songs, and dances seem to have passed both ways. From the high foothills, salt, pottery, and *Turbo*-based shell wealth were traded to the low foothills in exchange for net bags and shell wealth. By the late 1960s, however, these networks were largely defunct.

Division of Labor. There is a distinct division of labor by sex. Men hunt and fish, clear and fence gardens, plant and harvest yams and sago, process sago, cook ceremonial foods, and build houses. In earlier days, they also conducted the fighting, made pots and plates, and created most of the artwork. Women rear pigs; plant, weed, and harvest the taro, bananas, and greens; help with weeding and harvesting the yams; do the daily cooking and most of the portering; fetch water; forage for firewood and bush foods; and do most of the child care. Both sexes manufacture ornaments, clothing, bags, and baskets. In modern times, this division has begun to crumble, partly under the influence of Western values and partly because the frequent absence of young men in urban centers forces wives to do their husbands' work.

Land Tenure. Land and domesticated trees are vested in the hring. The most influential man in the hring, its "father" (*yaba*), nominally controls the disposal of its resources, but it would be unusual for him to dispute the wishes of his agnates concerning the resources they farm.

Kinship

Kin Groups and Descent. The principal kin groups, known as hring, are patrilineagelike segments averaging about ten to fourteen members. Hring are usually linked by stipulated patrilineal descent into totemic, quasisubclan and quasiclan groups (also known as hring), and they sustain alliances to yet other hring based on affinal links, legendary connections, friendship, or common political interests. Recruitment to a hring is by birth to the wife of a male member or by use of its resources, the latter way being legitimized by assisting the group in its wealth, food, and pig exchange obligations. Wives become members of their husbands' hring at marriage. It is not uncommon for a man to belong to two or even three different hring; accordingly, kinship relations are often multiplex.

Kinship Terminology. There are two kinship terminologies. The first and more salient is employed principally in public and formal discourse and is essentially of the Omaha type. The second is used in private, informal discourse and, with due regard to age and sex, extends nuclear kin terms bilaterally, with the exception that maternal brothers are called "mother" and paternal sisters "father."

Marriage and Family

Marriage. Although formal betrothal may occur during a girl's initiation at first menses, nowadays it is often omitted. There always has been considerable freedom of choice in marriage partners, and young people typically enter several "trial" marriages that dissolve before consummation. Once a wife has borne her husband a child, however, divorce is extremely rare. Ideally, a man should marry his father's mother's brother's sister's daughter or, failing that, his mother's mother's brother's sister's daughter, but such marriages are uncommon in practice. Marriage is proscribed with members of one's own hring, most more-distant agnates, and close maternal and affinal relatives. Marriage involves bride-wealth and initiates a flow of shell valuables from wife-receiving to wife-giving hring that is reciprocated with food, labor, and protection. The wealth is said to "buy" the "skins" or "bodies" of the woman's children; the food, labor, and protection reflect the "maternal" obligations of her natal hring toward her children. These exchanges continue until the woman's death. Marriage is usually virilocal, though uxorilocal residence occurs quite frequently. Since the early years of this century, the endogamy rate within Sima village has fluctuated between 38 and 56 percent of all marriages. Polygyny is less common now than in the past: in 1980 only 13 percent of Sima marriages were polygynous.

Domestic Unit. The basic domestic unit is a nuclear family, with the common additions of the father's parents and unmarried siblings. It occupies anywhere from one to all of the dwelling houses in a hamlet. Usually, the nuclear family shares a house, but the father and older sons sometimes live in a small dwelling separate from the mother and the other children.

Inheritance. As each son comes of age, his father usually confers on him an exchange partner together with land and domesticated trees sufficient to support his future family. Pressure on resources is sufficiently high, however, that the father's holdings commonly are exhausted by the time younger sons reach maturity. Consequently, these young men must seek resources elsewhere—usually from a classificatory brother, a mother's brother, or a wife's brother. Shell wealth, utensils, sacred relics, and ritual knowledge are inherited patrilineally by men and from mothers-in-law by women.

Socialization. Children are raised primarily by their mothers. From an early age, girls are taught the virtues of hard work, nurturance, and the care and protection of the hring's children. Boys lead a rather carefree life until their early teens, when their male elders begin to recruit them to men's work and start to inculcate the virtues of energy, strength, calculation, and controlled minacity esteemed in an adult male.

Sociopolitical Organization

Social Organization. The basic social divisions in Yangoru society are by sex and age. Men command the formal political arena, and middle-aged men are the major political players. By the time a man reaches his sixties, he usually has retired from active political life, but his counsel still may be very influential.

Political Organization. The basic political unit is the hring. The modern village, which comprises between ten and forty hring—Sima had about twenty-seven—constitutes the basic political unit of the nation-state as it impinges on Yangoru. Nowadays, village boundaries are territorial; in precontact days, however, they were more socially and situationally defined. Depending on their location, precontact villages also belonged to one or other of Yangoru's two great war confederacies, "Samawung," or "Dark Pig" and "Lebuging," or "Light Pig." The members of most villages are divided between two moieties, also called Samawung and Lebuging. Adult males inherit an exchange partner (*urli* or *gurli*) from the opposite moiety with whom they exchange pigs and yams on a competitive basis into their late middle age. In north-central Yangoru, a phratry organization crosscuts village and moiety lines, organized under the totems "Homung," or "Hawk," and "Sengi," or "Parrot." Groups of hring descended from a common ancestor recognize a *hwapomia,* an elder ideally descended by primogeniture who is their ceremonial leader in pig exchanges and, in earlier days, was the ceremonial master of their military actions. In other respects, however, the Yangoru Boiken represent a typical Melanesian big-man political system: men achieve renown principally by the number and size of the pigs they give to their exchange partners and by the promptness and generosity with which they meet financial obligations to maternal and affinal kin. These capabilities, in turn, stem from the skillful manipulation of social relationships aided by oratorical, histrionic, and affective ability. Although women are disenfranchised from formal political life, there exist big-women who build influence and reputation among other women by their eminence in small-scale wealth exchanges and their energy and ability in women's tasks—in particular, food production, cooking, and child rearing. Through other women and through their male relatives, such women also exert some influence over the community's formal politics.

Social Control. The formal means of social control is the moot, in which parties to a dispute meet to talk out their differences. Frequently, issues remain unsettled through several moots, and a significant number of disputes peter out unresolved. Informal means of conflict resolution include gossip, sorcery threats, and even flight.

Conflict. Until the mid-1930s, warfare was endemic, common causes being land, the abduction of women, and revenge. War was waged primarily against villages in the opposite confederacy, as either ambushes or confrontations across traditional battlefields located on confederacy frontiers. Neither men, women, nor children were spared. Although fights often broke out within a confederacy, murder was proscribed. By clandestine subterfuge, nonetheless, a rival within a person's confederacy frequently could be delivered into the hands of enemies beyond. In north-central Yangoru, the Homung/Sengi phratry organization complicated matters, and frequently hring from the same village would face one another across the battleground; in these confrontations, however, weapons were used in a manner that would inflict injury but avoid death.

Religion and Expressive Culture

Religious Beliefs. The constituents of the Yangoru Boiken universe are viewed either as "given" or as the creations of the culture heroes; they are believed to be influenced by ancestral spirits and *wala* spirits but most of all by magical forces. The principal supernaturals are human fiends that stalk lone villagers at certain seasons, the spirits of the ancestors, and the wala spirits. The last include the great culture heroes of time past, some of them nowadays incarnated as local mountains; the others are male and female spirits of the bush and stream. All wala are believed to be formed by the mystical union of ancestral shades, and each hring is associated with a male wala of the stream, where the ancestral shades of its male members are believed to congregate and unite as the wala. There is some difference of opinion over whether a woman's spirit goes to her husband's or her brother's wala.

Religious Practitioners. Knowledge of many magical and ritual practices is diffused widely through the community so that a hring usually can call on a member or close relative for most services. Nowadays, the main practitioners hired from beyond this circle are sorcerers, including earth and rain magicians, and those whose magic combats these powers. In traditional times, the hring also would have to cast beyond close relatives for specialists in carving and various ritual services associated with male initiation.

Ceremonies. The main ceremonies are associated with the life cycle, spirit houses, the wala, and the pig exchange. Birth, initiation, marriage, and death are, or were, observed for both sexes, with women also observing a few simple menstrual taboos to avoid polluting men. Traditionally, initiations were the most elaborate ceremonies, celebrated around puberty, again in the late twenties, and finally in the early to mid-forties; nowadays, however, only the first stage of female initiation endures. In western Yangoru, initiations were conducted in and around elaborately decorated spirit houses (*ka nimbia*); in north-central Yangoru, however, ka nimbia were divorced from initiation and constructed instead as a statement of political strength. In bygone days, if the wife of an important man insulted the sexuality of her husband, she would be disciplined by "the wala," a group of men swinging a bullroarer who would destroy her and her husband's belongings. Nowadays, the most elaborate ceremonies are the pig exchange festivals in which one moiety en masse confers pigs on exchange partners in the opposite moiety. (In western Yangoru, some villages recently have adopted the long-yam cult of the Abelam and the Kaboibus or "Plains" Arapesh.) Since contact, the Yangoru Boiken have earned considerable notoriety for their millenarian movements.

Arts. Traditional graphic and plastic art included wooden initiation statues; the painted facades, carved crosspieces, and other ornaments of spirit houses; shell-wealth basketry masks; plaited armlets; ornamented spinning tops; and dogs'-teeth and shell necklaces and headpieces. Items such as bullroarers, weaponry, and cooking and dining utensils were sometimes incised with abstract designs, often said to be the "face of the wala." Some productions, such as spirit dance masks, were only temporary, constructed for a specific ceremony and then dismantled. The main musical instruments were hand drums and monotone flutes. Nowadays, hardly any of this art is still produced. Songs and oratory were and still are the major ephemeral productions.

Medicine. Illness is attributed to ancestral spirits, wala spirits, human fiends, pollution by females or younger adults, infractions of ritual and taboo, protective magic on property, and in particular sorcery. Some epidemic diseases supposedly were decreed by the culture heroes.

Death and Afterlife. The deaths of all but the very old are attributed to sorcery. There is considerable doubt about the afterlife, but normatively the spirit of the deceased spends the first days of its existence around its hamlet before departing to its hring's wala pool. Spirits from throughout Yangoru are also said to go to Mount Hurun, the peak overlooking Yangoru, where they become Walarurun, the great culture hero associated with the mountain. Nowadays, countries such as Australia, America, and England are also variously identified as the place of the dead. At death, relatives are summoned on the slit gong, and the deceased is mourned with funeral dirges for a day or two. In the past, the corpses of eminent men were sliced and placed in trees to decay; others were buried in or under houses. The bones, especially the jawbones, later were retrieved for use in garden magic and occasionally sorcery. Nowadays, the deceased are buried in graveyards adjacent to the main ceremonial hamlets, and their bones are no longer retrieved—though graves are still opened after about six months to diagnose the perpetrators of the death.

See also Abelam, Mountain Arapesh

Bibliography

Gesch, Patrick F. (1985). *Initiative and Initiation: A Cargo Cult–Type Movement in the Sepik against Its Background in Traditional Village Religion.* St. Augustin, Germany: Anthropos-Institut.

Roscoe, Paul B. (1988). "The Far Side of Hurun: The Management of Melanesian Millenarian Movements." *American Ethnologist* 15:515–529.

Roscoe, Paul B. (1989). "The Pig and the Long Yam: The Expansion of a Sepik Symbol Complex." *Ethnology* 28:219–231.

Roscoe, Paul B. (1989). "The Flight from the Fen: The Prehistoric Migrations of the Boiken of the East Sepik Province, Papua New Guinea." *Oceania* 60:139–154.

PAUL B. ROSCOE

Yap

ETHNONYM: Uap

Orientation

Identification. Yap is one of four states in the Federated States of Micronesia, which were part of the U.S. Trust Territory of the Pacific Islands. The Yap State includes Yap proper, Ulithi, Woleai, and other atolls east of Yap, in what was once the Yap District of the Trust Territory. The Yapese language, culture, and people are distinct in Yap State from the inhabitants of the atolls (Carolinians). The Yapese people are only those who are born in the Yap Islands and who speak the Yapese language.

Location. The islands of Yap are located approximately 720 kilometers southwest of Guam and approximately 480 kilometers northeast of Palau, in the Western Caroline Islands. Yap proper is comprised of four contiguous high islands inside a fringing reef. The land area is approximately 100 square kilometers, much of which is rugged, infertile grassy hills and forest. The climate is tropical, subject to easterly trade winds, typhoons, and a monsoon rainy season from May to October.

Demography. Yap suffered critical depopulation, caused by European diseases and aided by cultural practices of abortion. Since World War II the use of antibiotics has controlled venereal diseases and the islands are currently experiencing a population explosion. The population has recovered from a low point of 2,582 in 1946 to more than 7,000 people in the 1980s.

Linguistic Affiliation. Yapese is an Austronesian language, but it is distinct from the nearby Palauan and the Carolinian languages. Some linguists regard Yapese as closer to Austronesian languages of Vanuatu (New Hebrides).

History and Cultural Relations

In the period prior to European contact, the Yapese had extensive relationships with the other island groups in the region. Yapese sailors traveled from Yap to Palau where courageous men quarried stones in the Rock Islands to be carted back to Yap and utilized for ceremonial exchanges. People in the eastern villages in Gagil had extensive relationships with Carolinean sailors from Ulithi, Fais and other atolls to the east. These sailors came to Yap particularly during times of food shortage and typhoon crises in the atolls and Yapese often sailed with them back to their home islands. With the entrance of European traders into the area as early as 1526, Yapese continued their exploration of the surrounding islands in the company of European sailors. It was in this early period that European diseases spread from Guam, resulting in devastating epidemics. In 1872, David O'Keefe arrived in a Chinese junk and immediately set up a copra and trepang trade. He transported large Yapese stones from Palau in exchange for payment in copra and trepang. Yap was officially colonized by both Spain and Germany in 1885. Carrying their dispute to the pope, Germany achieved sovereignty over the island, and the Spanish were allowed to continue their religious work to convert the Yapese to Christianity. The German era ended in 1914 when the Japanese navy seized control of Yap. Japanese development projects on Yap proved to be of little economic value, but as World War II neared, they constructed military bases, including troop garrisons and two airfields. During this period, the Yapese attended a five-year school in Japanese language and culture; the most promising students were sent to craft schools on Palau where they studied agriculture, carpentry, nursing, mechanics and other practical occupations. In 1944, the United States bombed Yap, and at the end of World War II the U.S. Navy set up an occupation government that lasted until June 1951. The United States Trust Territory of the Pacific Islands was formally established in 1951, and Yap was one of six districts in the trust territory. During this era, the U.S. government emphasized education and political development among the islanders. The Yap Islands Congress first convened in May 1959 and established the foundation for Yap State, which was formally organized in 1978. In 1964, the Yap High School was opened and American contract teachers were hired to staff it. By 1980, Yapese fully controlled the state and local governments and administered their schools and churches. Many Yapese men and women today are graduates of colleges and universities in the United States and hold positions of leadership in the economic, educational, and political life of the islands. Yap State is now part of the Federated States of Micronesia, which also includes the states of Truk, Pohnpei, and Kosrae.

Settlements

During the periods of heaviest population, the Yapese recognized over 180 separate villages. In recent years 91 of those villages contain at least one resident household, and the largest villages have forty to fifty households with up to 300 people in residence. Most of the inhabited villages lie in close proximity to the sea, and households are dispersed over a fairly large area along the shoreline. Since the construction of roads in the late 1960s and the extension of electricity along these roads in the late 1970s, many people are now building houses on the roads for accessibility to the town and to electricity. The largest villages are located in the administrative town of Colonia. These villages include inhabitants from all areas of the island. Rural villages are inhabited predominantly by people who are born or marry into them. Traditional Yapese villages are a marvel of stonework. Yapese houses are surrounded by stone platforms and are constructed on a coral stone foundation. Stone pathways connect houses in one section of the village to another. In the center of each village, a public meeting area and community house are marked by extensive, wide stone platforms for seating guests at public ceremonies and the large stone foundations for the traditional community house. Each village also has constructed taro patches, usually bounded by stone paths and stone retaining walls to contain the water for irrigating these swamp gardens. On the shoreline of many villages, men have built stone piers out into the water and the very large stone platforms on which men's houses have been traditionally constructed. The contemporary Yapese house is generally made of plywood and corrugated metal with a planked or cement floor. Some of the more prosperous Yapese are building concrete-block or poured-concrete houses today because of the extensive termite damage to wooden structures. In sandy beach areas and in the urban center, many people build houses on posts, raised off the ground, closed in with bamboo or plywood, and covered with corrugated iron.

Economy

Subsistence and Commercial Activities. Most Yapese today combine some wage work activities with subsistence farming. Many Yapese are employed by the government, and private trading companies and service industries provide additional jobs, so that more than half of the adult male population—and up to 20 percent of the adult female population—earn wages. In addition to wage employment, nearly all Yapese engage in some subsistence food production. Swamp taro is the primary staple crop of the Yapese, and most villages have large taro swamps that have been constructed as village projects in the past. Individual families own parcels of the village taro patches and also have garden plots in the surrounding hills on which they produce yams, bananas, breadfruit, and other supplementary fruits and crops. A few farmers produce copra as a cash crop, and a handful of entrepreneurs raise chickens, pigs, and other cash items for the domestic market.

Industrial Arts. The primary tools for traditional Yapese production included the shell adz, bamboo knives, and digging sticks made of mangrove. Steel adzes and knives have replaced their traditional counterparts, and contemporary Yapese continue to use these tools in their daily subsistence activities. Sennit made from the coconut husk is used for nearly every type of construction task. The blades of the adzes, the beams of the houses, the outriggers on the canoes, the bamboo of the fish traps, and the thatch of the roofs are all tied together with this coconut sennit. Skilled artisans include canoe builders and house builders. Canoe building has nearly disappeared in contemporary Yapese culture, but the experts in house construction continue to play an important role in Yapese villages.

Trade. Two eastern villages in Yap, Gachpar and Wonyan, hold traditional trading rights to the atoll groups in the central Carolines, including Ulithi and Woleai. For the atoll dwellers, trade with Yap provided a source of lumber and food not available to them in their restricted environments. The Yapese in these two villages gained supplies of sennit, valuable woven mats, fiber loincloths, and shell valuables that were important for ceremonial exchanges and political prestige and power in Yap. Yapese sailors often made extended trips to Palau and to Guam where they quarried stone disks, which also were of value in the ceremonial exchanges of Yap. These stones were not technically items of trade since they had no value in Palau or in Guam where they were quarried. Yet, as a special-purpose money, they were very important in the internal relationships and political struggles in Yap.

Division of Labor. In the subsistence economy, Yapese women care for the swamp taro patches and the yam gardens. Men aid their wives and sisters in the clearing of fields and in heavy agricultural work, but the primary subsistence role of men is in fishing. Reef fish, caught with spear guns, nets, and fish traps, are the predominant source of protein for Yapese families. Men who engage in regular wage labor buy canned fish and canned meats to provide their portion of their subsistence diet for the family.

Land Tenure. Rights to land, lagoon, other fishing and agricultural resources, and village authority are held corporately by the patrilineal estate group. The heads of estates in consultation with their junior members exercise authority over these rights on behalf of the members. Male members have use rights to estate resources with which they may support a wife and children. Succession to headship is based upon generation and seniority.

Kinship

Kin Groups and Descent. The concept of *tabinaw* governs Yapese thinking about family, kinship, and social organization. In its primary reference, tabinaw refers to the household or nuclear family. However, each nuclear family is part of an estate group, comprised of adult men and women who hold common rights to land and who share resources and labor in reference to exploitation of this land. An estate group may include three or four generations of men with their wives and children. Each married couple will have a separate household located on estate land. Yapese practice a variation of double descent. Every individual has a matrilineal kinship affiliation, termed *genung,* which plays a predominant role in the definition of sibling relationships and the identification of kin ties for mutual support and assistance. In Yapese thought, one obtains one's blood relationship through one's mother. In addition to this matrilineal principle, Yapese trace their spiritual and subsistence relationships to the land through their fathers. Each Yapese receives a name from one of his or her patrilineally related ancestors who have occupied the land estate upon which he or she is born and nurtured. The ancestral line of land and nurture comes through the patrilineally inherited estate. The matrilineal principle does not define significant descent groups on Yap, but only an affiliation of kin to whom one relates to serve significant individual interests. The estate group is formed more appropriately in terms of relationship to land than in terms of patrilineal descent. With these qualifications we may speak of double descent on Yap.

Kinship Terminology. Traditionally Yapese have a Crow-type pattern of cousin terminology. In the present younger generation, a Hawaiian-type pattern is emerging as the dominant pattern of kinship classification, complicated further by the introduction of English cousin terminology in schools.

Marriage and Family

Marriage. Yapese consider it improper to marry anyone who may be kin. Yapese young people generally select their own mates, and most have one or two trial marriages before they establish a permanent relationship that results in children. Yapese parents prefer that their children marry in the same village or among similar ranking villages. However, today with the central high school on the island and young people commuting by bus, many Yapese are marrying people from other villages and other districts of the island. Generally, a Yapese couple resides initially with the husband's family and establishes permanent residence on the husband's land in the husband's village. Divorce among the Yapese is common and is effected by mutual agreement. The young woman returns to her household of birth, leaving the children and property with her husband.

Domestic Unit. People who eat together constitute the tabinaw. This household is usually a nuclear family in which a husband and wife work according to a complementary division of labor and responsibility for their subsistence and children. A newly married couple may join the husband's father's household for a temporary period until they establish their own gardens and build a sleeping and cooking house.

Inheritance. Fathers distribute land to their sons according to need and age. The oldest son receives the rights to titled parts of the estate and will assume the father's leadership role among his siblings upon his father's death and in his younger brothers' families upon and their deaths. Younger sons receive an appropriate portion of the estate to support their families. Daughters do not inherit land, but they may be given a gift of a small parcel to provide support in case of divorce. Parents provide support for their adult unmarried or divorced daughters.

Socialization. Yapese parents and siblings share responsibilities for care and upbringing of children. Yapese emphasize generosity and sharing, and they give elder siblings the primary responsibility for the protection and care of the younger. This pattern is carried into adult life and characterizes the relationship between siblings until death.

Sociopolitical Organization

Yapese say the land is chief. It is their primary focus on land that organizes the social and political aspects of Yapese life.

Social Organization. The estate group and the village are the primary units organizing the social life of Yap. Within each village, family estates place individuals in a hierarchy of relationships within the community. Particular estates own titles that confer authority and prestige upon the members of that estate group. Villages in Yap are also ranked to include two major divisions: "Pilung," or "autonomous villages"; and "Pimilngay," or "serf villages." The autonomous villages are further ranked in three divisions: chief villages, noble villages, and commoner villages. The serf villages are ranked in two divisions: chief's servants and serfs. All the inhabitants born in a particular village automatically carry the rank of that village. One may marry people from other ranks, but one can never change the rank of birth. Within each village people are also ranked according to relative age, sex, and title from one's estate.

Political Organization. Each village in Yap is led by at least three titled estates: village chief; chief of young men; and chief of ritual. The men who speak for these titled estates oversee a council made up of men who represent lesser titles in the village. To hold political authority one must be the eldest living member of the family estate and be capable of speaking articulately for its interest in public. Decision making on Yap is characterized by indirect communication and consensus. The village chief articulates for the public the decision that has been made by consensus of the group. Prior to American administration, the government of the Yap Islands was organized by the chiefs of the paramount villages scattered around Yap. Three paramount villages located in Gagil, Tamil, and Rull provided the locus of power from which were formed two major alliances of villages and chiefs. These leaders maintained power primarily by controlling communication through legitimate channels connecting villages and estates and by planning punitive wars against those individuals who violated the decisions and expectations of the majority in an alliance. Today the Yap state government has supplanted the traditional system of alliances and governs through the legislative, administrative, and judicial branches. While contemporary Yapese officials are elected to their positions, many hold traditional titles and traditional bases of support. However, in the situation of contemporary politics, education and expertise in the functions of modern government are essential to political success.

Social Control. In the traditional village setting, the council of elders maintains social control through a system of punitive fines and mediation by the chiefs between families in conflict. In the contemporary setting the state court plays a major role in the adjudication of disputes among Yapese. The court has effectively replaced village elders as the arena and process for the resolution of contemporary disputes.

Conflict. Excessive consumption of alcohol and limited opportunities for employment following graduation from high school create an atmosphere in which young men on Yap have little to challenge their ambitions and interests. Village divisions and hostilities that characterized the precontact period have reemerged in the 1980s as a basis for gangs and for intervillage and interregional conflicts. Gangs of youths in each of the major regions of Yap stake out their territory and threaten violence to those who dare enter. Incidents of violence usually end in a court case in which the injured parties seek punitive action against those responsible.

Religion and Expressive Culture

Catholic Christianity is the central and unifying belief system in Yapese society today. People attend Catholic churches in every major district on the islands, and the first Yapese Catholic priest was ordained in the mid-1980s. Deacons in each area organize local church activities and support. Protestant and other Christian sects have small congregations scattered through the islands.

Religious Beliefs. Animistic beliefs in spirits and magic persist in Yapese culture in spite of nearly a century of Christianity. Most Yapese fear ghosts and many use magic for health or protection from spirits who may threaten their enterprises. The Yapese divided their traditional world into domains of spirits and humans. Female spirits inhabited the sea and threatened the lives and work of fishermen. Male spirits inhabited the land, threatening the livelihood and produce of the women gardening. Some Yapese still follow customs of abstention and rituals of protection in fishing and gardening activities.

Religious Practitioners. In traditional Yapese villages, specialist magicians addressed the uncertainties of house building, fishing, gardening, and warfare. Today most of these specialties have been forgotten and people turn to the local deacons or the priest of the Catholic church for assistance in these uncertainties of life. Whereas once priests and magicians mediated between humans and the spirit world, now these tensions are addressed by the leaders of the church and by psychiatric doctors in the local hospital. Folk medicine has a limited following, and Yapese rely almost exclusively on the hospital for health care.

Ceremonies. Prior to their conversion to Christianity, Yapese prayed to ancestors, breaking segments of mother-of-pearl shells as offerings. The welfare of all Yapese was thought to reside in several sacred places for which particular families had responsibility and from which they derived power. The traditional priest cared for the sacred place and organized the sacred calendar, which included rebuilding the sacred house, making annual offerings to the spirits of these places, and divining the future of warfare and politics in Yap. The eating-class initiation, still observed by a few contemporary Yapese, involved periods of isolation, preparation of new loincloths and personal items, fasting, and ceremonial feasting at the end of the isolation period. Individuals who observed this ritual moved into a higher-ranking eating class and gained political and social influence in their villages. Traditional Yapese ceremonies have been all but forgotten by Yapese people. The only persisting forms of traditional ceremonies are the sitting dances, which provide a public drama of storytelling and recounting of myth. People have also borrowed standing and stick dances from other Micronesians. The religious calendar today includes Christmas, Easter, strict observance of Sunday as a day of rest and worship, and large public funerals.

Arts. Items of great value to the Yapese included the white coral disks known as Yap stone money, mother-of-pearl shells that were collected and exchanged in village ceremonies, and long necklaces of red shells and bracelets of white shells made famous by Bronislaw Malinowski in his description of the *kula* in the Trobriand Islands. Yapese also make ceremonial betel pounders and decorate their houses with unique patterns of rope tying.

Medicine. In traditional times, the Yapese people did not have specialized medical practitioners. In every family the members who had knowledge of magic associated with controlling weather, warfare, or fishing also had knowledge with regard to health and disease. These magicians gained prestige based upon the effectiveness of their knowledge in curing those who were ill or in aborting or controlling potential disasters in nature. Today, few Yapese use herbal medicines; most rely on the local hospital.

Death and Afterlife. The funeral is the most important life-cycle event in Yap. Even for an ordinary family member, it is a time to gather the most distant relations from various parts of the islands. Everyone who comes brings gifts of cigarettes, food, money, or liquor in support of the mourning family. Members of the family prepare the body and wait for the guests for three days. The funeral concludes with a Christian service and the deceased is buried in either a church burial ground or an ancestral plot. About one month after the burial, the members of the family repay their guests by sponsoring a large party. The funeral and the following party reestablish kinship connections among dispersed relations.

See also Kosrae, Pohnpei, Truk, Ulithi, Woleai

Bibliography

Labby, David (1976). *The Demystification of Yap: Dialectics of Culture on a Micronesian Island.* Chicago: University of Chicago Press.

Lingenfelter, Sherwood Galen (1975). *Yap: Political Leadership and Cultural Change in an Island Society.* Honolulu: University Press of Hawaii.

Lingenfelter, Sherwood Galen (1977). "Emic Structure and Decision-Making in Yap." *Ethnology* 16:331–352.

Lingenfelter, Sherwood Galen (1979). "Yap Eating Classes: A Study of Structure and Communities." *The Journal of the Polynesian Society* 88:415–432.

Müller, Wilhelm (1917). "Yap." In *Ergenbnisse der Südsee Expedition, 1908–1910,* edited by Georg Thilenius. II. Ethnographie; B. Mikronesien. Hamburg: Friedenchsen.

SHERWOOD GALEN LINGENFELTER

Yir Yoront

ETHNONYMS: Jirjoront, Koko Manjoen, Kokomindjan, Koka-mungin

The Yir Yoront (Yir-Yoront) are an Australian Aboriginal people whose traditional territory and current reserve are centered at 141°45' E and 15°20' S along the Gulf of Carpentaria coast of the Cape York Peninsula in Queensland. The territory encompasses about 1,300 square kilometers and runs along the coast from the mouth of the Coleman River south through the three mouths of the Mitchell River. First contact with Europeans was evidently with Dutch explorers in 1623. The second and more significant contact was with a party of cattle herders in 1864, an encounter now known as the "Battle of Mitchell River." Acculturation into European-Australian society began after 1900 with settlement of the lower Cape York Peninsula and the establishment of an Anglican mission station just south of Yir Yoront territory in 1915. The Yir Yoront were, however, shielded from encroachment on their land when the Australian government established the reserve along the coast. Although some Yir Yoront moved south and settled at the mission, and various products of European manufacture were used by all Yir Yoront, much of the traditional culture survived into the 1940s.

The Yir Yoront speak a "Yir-" language related to the "Wik-" and "Koko-" Aboriginal languages of Australia. The Yir Yoront subsisted by hunting, fishing, and gathering shellfish and plant foods. Men hunted and fished, often in groups, while women gathered and maintained the camp. The Yir Yoront also maintained trade relations with groups to the north and south. Spears made from stingray spines were the major export, while stone from tribes to the south for stone ax heads was the major import. Trading often took place at the annual intertribal ceremonies, with male trading partners often having the status of fictive brothers. Yir Yoront trade, however, was less elaborated and of less economic importance than that of many other Queensland Aboriginal groups. The introduction of European goods such as tools, cloth, and tobacco and the establishment of the reserve have altered the traditional hunting and gathering economy.

Traditional Yir Yoront society was divided into patrilineal, totemic clans and two exogamous moieties. A distinction was also made, apart from kinship organization, between "coastal people" and "inland people." The nuclear family was the basic residential and economic unit. Traditionally, social relations were based on superordinate and subordinate status, with men dominant over women and older people dominant over younger people. Leadership rested with the clan leaders. While individuals displaying superior knowledge or skill might enjoy personal prestige, there was no formal status system. The day-to-day world of the Yir Yoront was seen by them as a reflection of the world of their ancestors, with all new developments accounted for by myths and totems. With the recent acceleration of acculturation into White Australian society, many traditional beliefs and practices have disappeared and have been replaced by involvement in the cash economy and more permanent settlement near cattle ranches and small towns.

Bibliography

Sharp, Lauriston (1934). "Ritual Life and Economics of the Yir-Yoront of Cape York Peninsula." *Oceania* 5:19–42.

Sharp, Lauriston (1968). "Steel Axes for Stone Age Australians." In *Man in Adaptation: The Cultural Present,* edited by Yehudi A. Cohen, 82–93. Chicago: Aldine.

Yungar

The name given to a number of closely related and affiliated Aboriginal groups who lived in the deserts of western Australia. Known groups included the Koreng, Minang, Pibelman, Pindjarup, Wardardi, and Wheelman. All of the Yungar groups are either totally or nearly extinct.

Bibliography

Hassell, Ethel, and D. S. Davidson (1936). "Notes on the Ethnology of the Wheelman Tribe of South-western Australia." *Anthropos* 31:679–711.

Glossary

aborigine. *See* autochthones

affine A relative by marriage.

agamy Absence of a marriage rule; neither endogamy nor exogamy.

age grade A social category composed of persons who fall within a culturally defined age range.

agnatic descent. *See* patrilineal descent

ambilineal descent The practice of tracing kinship affiliation through either the male or the female line.

ancestor spirits Ghosts of deceased relatives who are believed to have supernatural powers that can influence the lives of the living.

animism A belief in spiritual beings.

ariki (ali'i, aliki, ari'i) A hereditary chief in Polynesia.

atoll An island consisting of a coral reef surrounding a lagoon.

Austronesian languages A large group of languages (formerly called "Malayo-Polynesian") including about 450 in Oceania. They are found mostly on the coasts in Melanesia and New Guinea, but otherwise throughout Polynesia and Micronesia.

autochthones The indigenous inhabitants of a region. Often used to refer to the native inhabitants encountered by European explorers or settlers.

avunculocal residence The practice of a newly married couple residing in the community or household of the husband's mother's brother.

bark cloth. *See* tapa

bêche-de-mer A sea slug found in shallow tropical waters. It was gathered in large quantities in the nineteenth century by Europeans (and earlier by Chinese and Japanese traders) for export to Asia for use in soups.

betel nut A nicotinelike stimulant used in western Melanesia and Micronesia as well as in Asia. A "betel quid" is formed of the nut of the *Areca catechu* palm and the leaf, bean, or stem of the *Piper betle* vine, then chewed with slaked lime from shells or coral and expectorated.

big man A political leader whose influence is based on personal prestige or qualities rather than formal authority. Such influence often is achieved through factional politics or the manipulation of exchange relationships.

bilateral descent The practice of tracing kinship affiliation more or less equally through both the male and the female line.

blackbirding A form of labor recruiting, often involving coercion or deception. From the 1840s to the end of the nineteenth century thousands of male Pacific islanders were taken to Australia or South America as laborers to be returned home (though many were not) after a period of years in service.

breadfruit A fruiting tree (*Artocarpus altilis*) that is usually seasonal and cultivated mainly in Micronesia and Polynesia, but also in some parts of Melanesia. The fruit's starchy pulp is either cooked or fermented in pits as a staple or important standby food.

bride-price, bride-wealth The practice of a groom or his kin giving substantial property or wealth to the bride's kin before, at the time of, or after marriage.

bride-service The practice of a groom performing work for his wife's kin for a set period of time either before or after marriage.

bullroarer A sacred oval-shaped object, usually wooden, that is swung on a cord to make a buzzing sound representing the voices of ancestors or other spirits. In Australia, New Guinea, and Melanesia revelation of the bullroarer was often an important part of male initiation ceremonies.

cargo cult A millenarian or nativistic movement, found mostly in Melanesia and New Guinea during the first half of the twentieth century in the context of colonialism and World War II. The cults usually focused on the prophesied arrival of trade goods ("cargo") heralding a new era of material plenty and native control.

cassava A starchy root crop (*Manihot esculenta*), also called manioc or tapioca, that was introduced to Oceania following the arrival of Europeans.

cassowary A large, flightless bird with three species endemic to New Guinea and New Britain. The bird is locally prized for its flesh, plumes, and bones.

caste An endogamous hereditary group, usually with a distinct hereditary occupation, who has a virtually immutable position in a hierarchy. Although the caste system is most elaborated throughout South Asia, castes have also been reported in Tibet, Japan, Burundi, and the American South.

churinga (tjuringa, tjurunga) A term from the Aranda language applied generally by various Australian Aboriginal desert groups to stone or wooden sacred objects (including bullroarers) symbolizing culture heroes or ancestral figures.

clan, sib A group of unilineally affiliated kin who usually reside in the same community and share common property.

classificatory kin terms Kinship terms, such as aunt, that designate several categories of distinct relatives, such as mother's sister and father's sister.

cognates Words that belong to different languages but have similar sounds and meanings.

collaterals A person's relatives not related to him or her as ascendants or descendants; one's uncle, aunt, cousin, brother, sister, nephew, niece.

consanguine A relative by blood (birth).

continental islands Islands formed from the portions of the Continental Australasiatic Platform that are currently above sea level.

copra The dried flesh of the coconut used as the basis of oils, soaps, cosmetics, and dried coconut. Beginning in the 1860s copra became the chief commercial export in most Pacific islands.

coral islands Islands, including atolls, formed of the exoskeleton created by the excretion of lime from sea water by tiny marine animals.

Cordyline An ornamental or ritually important shrub (*Cordyline terminalis*) planted widely in Oceania; in some places the tuber is sometimes eaten.

cousin, cross Children of one's parent's siblings of the opposite sex—one's father's sisters' and mother's brothers' children.

cousin, parallel Children of one's parent's siblings of the same sex—one's father's brothers' and mother's sisters' children.

creole A general, inconsistently used term usually applied to a spoken language or dialect that is based on grammatical and lexical features combined from two or more natural languages. It is a first language, distinct from a pidgin.

cross cousin. *See* cousin, cross

cult The beliefs, ideas, and activities associated with the worship of a supernatural force or its representations, such as an ancestor cult or a bear cult.

culture hero A mythical bird, animal, or person who is believed to be the group's protector.

cuscus A type of marsupial found in New Guinea and highly prized for its meat and fur.

deme A group based on the merging of locality, descent, and in-marriage.

descriptive kin terms Kinship terms that are used to distinguish different categories of relatives such as *mother* or *father.*

Dreaming, The (Dreamtime, The) A sacred time in the Australian Aboriginal mythological past when culture heroes and totemic ancestors created many of the physical features of the land and established traditional customs.

Ego In kinship studies ego is a male or female whom the anthropologist arbitrarily designates as the reference point for a particular kinship diagram or discussion of kinship terminology.

endogamy Marriage within a specific group or social category of which the person is a member, such as one's caste or community.

exogamy Marriage outside a specific group or social category of which the person is a member, such as one's clan or community.

extensive cultivation A form of horticulture in which plots of land are cleared and planted for a few years and then left to fallow for a number of years while other plots are used. Also called swidden, shifting, or slash-and-burn cultivation.

fictive kin Individuals referred to or addressed with kin terms and treated as kin, although they are neither affines nor consanguines.

horticulture Plant cultivation carried out by relatively simple means, usually without permanent fields, artificial fertilizers, or plowing.

initiation, or puberty, rites Ceremonies and related activities that mark the transition from childhood to adulthood or from secular status to being a cult-member.

kava A fermented beverage traditionally consumed ritually or ceremonially (though sometimes merely for its euphoric and soporific effects) in Melanesia, New Guinea, and Polynesia. The drink is made from the dried and ground root of the *kava* plant (*Piper methysticum*) mixed in water.

kin terms, bifurcate-collateral A system of kinship terminology in which all collaterals in the parental generation are referred to by different kin terms.

kin terms, bifurcate-merging A system of kinship terminology in which members of the two descent groups in the parental generation are referred to by different kin terms.

kin terms, Crow A system of kinship terminology in which matrilateral cross cousins are distinguished from each other and from parallel cousins and siblings, but patrilateral cross cousins are referred to by the same terms used for father or father's sister.

kin terms, Dravidian. *See* kin terms, Iroquois

kin terms, Eskimo A system of kinship terminology in which cousins are distinguished from brothers and sisters, but no distinction is made between cross and parallel cousins.

kin terms, generational A system of kinship terminology in which all kin of the same sex in the parental generation are referred to by the same term.

kin terms, Hawaiian A system of kinship terminology in which all male cousins are referred to by the same term used for *brother,* and all female cousins are referred to by the same term used for *sister.*

kin terms, Iroquois A system of kinship terminology in which parallel cousins are referred to by the same terms used for brothers and sisters but cross cousins are identified by different terms.

kin terms, lineal A system of kinship terminology in which direct descendants or ascendants are distinguished from collateral kin.

kin terms, Omaha A system of kinship terminology in which female matrilateral cross cousins are referred to by the same term used for one's mother, and female patrilateral cross cousins are referred to by the same term used for one's sister's daughter.

kin terms, Sudanese A system of kinship terminology in which there are distinct terms for each category of cousin and sibling, and for aunts, uncles, nieces, and nephews.

kindred The bilateral kin group of near kinsmen who may be expected to be present and participant on important ceremonial occasions, usually in the absence of unilineal descent.

kinship Family relationship, whether traced through marital ties or through blood and descent.

kula ring A system of ceremonial exchange in the Massim area and southeastern tip of New Guinea characterized by the circulation of shell necklaces and shell armbands in opposite directions, hence the "ring" of islands linked by the system.

kunai The Tok Pisin term for the tall swordgrass (*Imperata cylindrica*) that typically covers drier regions in New Guinea and Melanesia that have been cleared of forest by burning. The grass is commonly used for housing and thatching material.

kundu The Tok Pisin term for the hourglass-shaped drum used in many New Guinea and Melanesian societies.

lagoon A sheltered body of sea water encircled by a coral reef.

Lapita Culture A hypothesized culture that flourished from about 4,000 to 2,500 B.P., characterized by a distinctive type of pottery with dentate impressed designs and associated with a widely distributed seafaring people and Austronesian languages.

levirate The practice of requiring a man to marry his brother's widow.

lineage A unilineal (whether patrilineal or matrilineal) kin group that traces kinship affiliation from a common, known ancestor and extends through a number of generations.

longhouse A large, rectangular-shaped dwelling with a wood frame covered by planks, bark, mats, or other siding and usually housing a number of related families.

luluai The Tok Pisin term for village leaders appointed by the government in New Guinea and Melanesia during the colonial period.

magic Beliefs and ritual practices designed to harness supernatural forces to achieve the goals of the magician.

mana A term with cognates in numerous Melanesian and Polynesian languages for a type of spiritual power, energy, or energizing capability believed to be physically resident in objects, persons, or places.

marae A stone plaza, platform, or walls regarded throughout Polynesia as a sacred enclosure. Traditionally a *marae* was a center of ceremonial rituals and the focal point of community life.

Massim A region consisting of islands and island groups off the southeastern tip of New Guinea characterized by distinctive art styles and interisland exchange links, especially the kula system.

matrilineal descent, uterine descent The practice of tracing kinship affiliation only through the female line.

matrilocal residence, uxorilocal residence The practice of a newly married couple residing in the community of the wife's kin. *Uxorilocal* is sometimes used in a more restrictive sense to indicate residence in the household of the wife's family.

Melanesia A general term (derived from the Greek for "black islands") for New Guinea, the Bismarck Archipelago, the Solomon Islands, Vanuatu (New Hebrides), and New Caledonia.

men's house A structure, common in New Guinea and Melanesia, usually housing the young adult males and adult men of a community. A men's house typically serves as both a residence and ceremonial center.

Micronesia A general term (from the Greek for "tiny islands") for the Mariana, Caroline, Marshall, and Gilbert island groups in the north Pacific.

moiety A form of social organization in which an entire cultural group is made up of two social groups. Each moiety is often composed of a number of interrelated clans, sibs, or phratries.

monogamy Marriage between one man and one woman at a time.

nativism A movement often with social, religious, or political components that centers on the rebirth of the native culture and the demise of the colonizers.

Near Oceania A general term for the islands of the western and southwestern Pacific nearest to Asia, including Australia, New Guinea, and Melanesia east to the Solomon Islands.

neolocal residence The practice of a newly-married couple living apart from the immediate kin of either party.

Neo-Melanesian. *See* Tok Pisin

net bag An expandable string bag hand-made from local materials throughout New Guinea and Melanesia. Net bags are used to carry garden produce, infants, and piglets.

Non-Austronesian languages. *See* Papuan languages

pandanus A general term for numerous species of the *Pandanus* palm that grow wild or are cultivated throughout the Pacific. The oily kernels or nuts of some species are eaten, and the long leaves are commonly used for thatching and for wrapping material.

Papuan languages Also called Non-Austronesian languages, these number over 700 and are found mostly in New Guinea, the Bismarck Archipelago, and Bougainville.

parallel cousin. *See* cousin, parallel

patois A dialect of a language spoken by a specific social or occupational group in a multi-cultural environment.

patrilineal descent, agnatic descent The practice of tracing kinship affiliation only through the male line.

patrilocal residence, virilocal residence The practice of a newly married couple residing in the community of the husband's kin. *Virilocal* is sometimes used in a more restrictive sense to indicate residence in the household of the husband's family.

pearlshell Also called "mother-of-pearl," the shells of *Pinctada* spp. are found on many of the coral reefs of the southern Pacific and traditionally were widely traded, especially in New Guinea and Melanesia, for use in body decoration and ceremonial exchange systems.

phratry A social group consisting of two or more clans joined by some common bond and standing in opposition to other phratries in the society.

pidgin A second language very often made up of words and grammatical features from several languages and used as the medium of communication between speakers of different languages.

pitpit A Tok Pisin term generally applied to a type of wild sugar cane (*Saccharum spontaneum*) and other cane grasses. In New Guinea and Melanesia, *pitpit* is commonly used for house walls and fencing material. The term also refers to the plant *Setaria palmifolia,* a common garden plant in New Guinea. The edible heart of the stem is cooked in earth ovens or steam-cooked in bamboo tubes.

polyandry The marriage of one woman to more than one man at a time.

polygyny The marriage of one man to more than one woman at a time.

Polynesia A general term (from Greek for "many islands") for the islands located within the huge triangle formed by the Hawaiian Islands, New Zealand, and Easter Island.

Polynesian Outlier An island located in Melanesia or Micronesia but whose inhabitants speak Polynesian languages and whose cultures resemble those found on Polynesian islands.

prestation A form of reciprocal gift-giving, often associated with marriage negotiations and ceremonial exchange.

puberty rites. *See* initiation rites

ramage An ancestor-focused bilateral descent group consisting of an entire community whose descent is traced from a common ancestor, with graded ranks based on closeness to the senior line of descent.

Remote Oceania A general term for all of the islands of the Pacific located east and north of the Solomon Islands.

sago A large palm (*Metroxylon* spp.) found widely in the western Pacific in natural stands or cultivated in swampy areas. Sago is an important source of starch in lowland areas and a staple food in much of New Guinea; its fronds are typically used as thatching material.

Sahul A prehistoric land mass, connecting Australia with New Guinea, that emerged during worldwide lowerings of sea levels.

sennit Fibers from the husk of the coconut made into string and widely used for cordage in Micronesia, Polynesia, and parts of Melanesia.

shaman A religious practitioner who receives his or her power directly from supernatural forces.

shifting cultivation. *See* extensive cultivation

sib. *See* clan

sister exchange A form of arranged marriage in which two brothers exchange their sisters as wives.

slash-and-burn horticulture A system of food production that involves burning trees and brush to clear and fertilize a garden plot, and then planting crops. The plot is used for a few years and then left to fallow while other plots are similarly used.

slit gong (slit drum) A large drum made of a hollowed-out tree trunk, used as a signaling device or for ceremonial purposes.

sorcery The use of supernatural forces to further the interests of the sorcerer, primarily through formulae and the ritual manipulation of material objects.

sororal polygyny The marriage of one man to two or more sisters at the same time.

sororate The practice of a woman being required to marry her deceased sister's husband.

sucking cure A curing technique often used by shamans which involved sucking out a foreign object from the patient's body through an implement such as a bone tube. The foreign object, a piece of bone or stone, was viewed as the cause of the malady and the sucking out the cure.

sugar cane The grass *Saccharum officinarum,* indigenous to Melanesia but now cultivated widely in the Pacific. The juicy pith is sucked or chewed for its sweet moisture.

Sunda A prehistoric land mass, connecting mainland Asia with much of Malaysia and Indonesia, that emerged during worldwide lowerings of sea levels.

sweet potato The New World plant *Ipomoea batatas,* established in parts of Polynesia prior to the arrival of Europeans and subsequently introduced to the western Pacific. It is a major source of carbohydrates and often used as pig fodder in much of the Pacific.

swidden The field or garden plot resulting from slash-and-burn field preparation.

Tambaran cult A general term applied to male cults widespread in the Sepik and northern regions of New Guinea, focused on ancestral spirits (or *tambaran* in Tok Pisin) and usually associated with large ceremonial structures, or *haus tambaran.*

tapa A fabric (or bark cloth) made by soaking and beating the inner bark of trees, especially the paper mulberry (*Broussonetia papyrifera*), *Ficus* spp., or *Hibiscus* spp. *Tapa* was traditionally used in much of Oceania for protective cloaks or clothing.

tapu A Polynesian term (from which the word "taboo" is derived) for a sacred quality combining ritual power and ritual danger; the term may apply to objects, places, or people.

taro A starchy root crop cultivated throughout Oceania. When "true taro" is intended, the term applies to *Colocasia esculenta,* but recent usages extend it to other aroids such as *Alocasia macrorrhiza, Cyrtosperma chamissonis,* and *Xanthosoma* spp.

teknonymy The practice of addressing a person after the name of his wife or his or her child rather than by the individual name. For example, "Bill" is called "Father of John."

Tok Pisin A lingua franca (sometimes called Neo-Melanesian Pidgin) that is now one of the official languages of Papua New Guinea.

totem A plant or animal emblematic of a clan that usually has special meaning to the group.

trepang. *See* bêche-de-mer

tribe Although there is some variation in use, the term usually applies to a distinct people who view themselves and are recognized by outsiders as being a distinct culture. The tribal society has its own name, territory, customs, subsistence activities, and often its own language.

unilineal descent The practice of tracing kinship affiliation through only one line, either the matriline or the patriline.

unilocal residence The general term for matrilocal, patrilocal, or avunculocal postmarital residence.

usufruct The right to use land or property without actually owning it.

uterine descent. *See* matrilineal descent

uxorilocal residence. *See* matrilocal residence

virilocal residence. *See* patrilocal residence

volcanic islands Islands (often called "high islands") formed through volcanic intrusion from the Australasiatic Continental Platform or directly from the ocean floor.

weir A wall of sticks or rocks placed in a body of water, river, or stream to prevent fish from passing.

witchcraft The use of supernatural forces to control or harm another person. Unlike sorcery, witchcraft does not require the use of special rituals, formulae, or ritual objects.

yam A term applied to various species of *Dioscorea,* a cultivated plant whose vines are usually trained to climb up sticks or poles. The starchy root is eaten and often is the basis of competitive exchanges in Oceania.

Filmography

Following is a list of films and videos on cultures in Oceania. Except for those that cover Oceania in general, the subject of each is indicated following the title. This list is not meant to be complete; rather it is a sampling of videos and films available from many distributors. Listing a film or video here does not constitute an endorsement by the volume editor or the summary authors, nor does the absence of a film represent a nonendorsement. Abbreviations for names of distributors are provided at the end of each citation. The full name and address may be found in the directory of distributors that follows the filmography. Many of these films are also available through the Extension Media Center of the University of California at Berkeley and/or the Audio-Visual Services of the Pennsylvania State University, indicated by (EMC) or (PS) at the end of the citation.

Aborigines of the Seacoast. (Australian Aborigines) 1973. Color, 20 minutes, 16mm. (PS).

American Samoa: Paradise Lost? (Samoa) 1969. Color, 55 minutes, 16mm. (EMC).

Ancestors: The Last Tasmanian. (Tasmanians) 1980. Color, 12 minutes, 16mm. McG-H (EMC).

Angels of War: World War II in Papua New Guinea. (Papua New Guinea) 1983. Andrew Pike, Hank Nelson, and Gavan Daws. Color, 54 minutes or 30 minutes, 16mm, VHS. FL.

Asmat: Cannibal Craftsmen of New Guinea. (Asmat) 1977. William Leimbach, Jean-Pierre Dutilleux, and Peter Van Arsdale. Color, 60 minutes, 16mm. MAC.

Atoll Life on Kiribati. (Kiribati) 1987. Human Face of the Pacific Series. Color, 28 minutes, VHS. FIV.

Axes and Aré: Stone Tools of the Duna. (Papua New Guinea) 1977. J. Peter White. Color, 41 minutes, 16mm, VHS, U-mat. (EMC).

Bathing Babies in Three Cultures. (Iatmul) 1954. Gregory Bateson and Margaret Mead. B&W, 11 minutes, 16mm. NYU (EMC).

Becoming Aboriginal. (Australian Aborigines) 1978. Color, 10 minutes, 16mm. (PS).

Bougainville Copper Project. (Nasioi) 1972. Color, 28 minutes, 16mm. (EMC).

Cannibal Tours. (Papua New Guinea, Sepik) 1987. Dennis O'Rourke. Color, 70 minutes, 16mm, VHS. DCL.

Childhood Rivalry in Bali and New Guinea. (Iatmul) 1952. Gregory Bateson and Margaret Mead. B&W, 17 minutes, 16mm. NYU (EMC).

Collum Calling Canberra. (Australian Aborigines) 1984. David MacDougall and Judith MacDougall. Color, 58 minutes, 16mm. (EMC).

Coniston Muster. (Australian Aborigines) 1976. Roger Sandall. Australian Institute of Aboriginal Studies Series. Color, 29 minutes, 16mm, VHS, U-mat. (EMC).

Dani Houses. (Dani) 1974. Karl G. Heider. Color, 16 minutes, 16mm, VHS, U-mat. (EMC) (PS).

Dani Sweet Potatoes. (Dani) 1974. Karl G. Heider. Color, 19 minutes, 16mm, VHS, U-mat. (EMC) (PS).

Dead Birds. (Dani) 1963. Robert Gardner. Color, 82 minutes, 16mm, VHS, U-mat. PHENIX (EMC).

Desert People, The. (Mardudjara) 1968. Ian Dunlop and Robert Tonkinson. B&W, 51 minutes, 16mm. CRM, McG-H (EMC) (PS).

Dingari Ceremonies at Papunya—June 1972. (Pintupi) 1977. Color, 15 minutes, 16mm. (EMC).

Easter Island: Puzzle of the Pacific. (Easter Island) 1970. William Mulloy and Peter Jennings. Color, 28 minutes, 16mm. MAC (EMC).

Echoes of War. 1987. The New Pacific Series. Color, 50 minutes, VHS. FIV.

Emu Ritual at Ruguri. (Warlbiri) 1969. Australian Institute of Aboriginal Studies Series. Color, 33 minutes, 16mm. (PS).

Extinction: The Last Tasmanian. (Tasmanians) 1980. Color, 60 minutes, 16mm. McG-H (EMC).

Familiar Places. (Australian Aborigines) 1981. David MacDougall. Color, 53 minutes, 16mm, VHS, U-mat. (EMC).

Fifty Ways to Get Enlightened. 1987. The New Pacific Series. Color, 50 minutes, VHS. FIV.

Fiji: Legacies of Empire. (Fiji) 1987. Human Face of the Pacific Series. Color, 28 minutes, VHS. FIV.

First Contact. (Papua New Guinea) 1982. Bob Connolly and Robin Anderson. Color, 54 minutes, 16mm. FL (EMC) (PS).

First Days in the Life of a New Guinea Baby. (Iatmul) 1951. Gregory Bateson and Margaret Mead. B&W, 19 minutes, 16mm. NYU (EMC).

For Richer, for Poorer. 1987. The New Pacific Series. Color, 50 minutes, VHS. FIV.

Gogodala: A Cultural Revival? (Gogodala) 1982. Chris Owen. Color, 58 minutes, 16mm. DER.

Goodbye, Old Man. (Tiwi) 1979. David MacDougall. Color, 70 minutes, 16mm, VHS, U-mat. (EMC).

House-Opening, The. (Australian Aborigines) 1980. Judith MacDougall. Color, 45 minutes, 16mm, VHS, U-mat. (EMC).

Island of the Red Prawns. (Fiji) 1978. William R. Geddes. Color, 52 minutes, 16mm, VHS, U-mat. (EMC).

Jugs to Be Filled or Candles to Be Lit. 1987. The New Pacific Series. Color, 50 minutes, VHS. FIV.

Kawelka: Ongka's Big Moka. (Melpa) 1989. Disappearing World Series. Color, 52 minutes, VHS. FIV.

Kerepe's House: A House Building in New Guinea. (Maring)

1966. Allison Jablonko and Marek Jablonko. Color, 50 minutes, 16mm, U-mat. PSUPCR (PS).

Kula: Argonauts of the Western Pacific. (Trobriand Islands) 1971. Color, 60 minutes, 16mm. (EMC).

Land Divers of Melanesia. (Pentecost) 1973. Kal Muller. Color, 31 minutes, 16mm. PHENIX (PS).

Lau of Malaita, The. (Malaita) 1989. Disappearing World Series. Color, 53 minutes, VHS. FIV.

Malbangka Country. (Australian Aborigines) 1979. Australian Institute of Aboriginal Studies Series. Color, 30 minutes, 16mm, VHS, U-mat. (EMC).

Man Blong Custom. (Guadalcanal, Vanuatu) 1975. Tribal Eye Series. Color, 52 minutes, 16mm. T-L (EMC).

Margaret Mead's New Guinea Journal. (Manus) 1969. Color, 90 minutes, 16mm. (EMC) (PS).

Maring in Motion. (Maring) 1968. Allison Jablonko and Marek Jablonko. Color, 16 minutes, 16mm, U-mat. PSUPCR (PS).

Marshall Islands: Living with the Bomb. (Bikini) 1987. Human Face of the Pacific Series. Color, 28 minutes, VHS. FIV.

Matjemosh. (Asmat) 1964. Color, 27 minutes, 16mm. (EMC).

Mendi, The. (Mendi) n.d. Color, 57 minutes, 16mm. CBC.

Moana Roa. (Cook Islands) n.d. Color, 32 minutes, 16mm. NZNFU, IU.

Mokil. (Marshall Islands) 1950. Conrad Bentzen. B&W, 58 minutes, 16mm. (EMC).

Mourning for Mangatopi. (Tiwi) 1977. Curtis Levy. Australian Institute of Aboriginal Studies Series. Color, 25 minutes, 16mm, VHS, U-mat. (EMC).

Mulga Seed Ceremony, The. (Australian Aborigines) 1968. Australian Institute of Aboriginal Studies Series. Color, 25 minutes, 16mm. (EMC) (PS).

Navigators, The. (Polynesia) 1983. Color, 60 minutes, 16mm. T-L (EMC).

New Caledonia: A Land in Search of Itself. (Ajië) 1987. Human Face of the Pacific Series. Color, 28 minutes, VHS. FIV.

New Lives for Old. (Manus) 1959. Horizons of Science Series. Color, 20 minutes, 16mm. (PS).

New Rangers, The. (Australian Aborigines) 1980. Color, 31 minutes, 16mm. (PS).

Not to Lose You, My Language: Bilingual Education in the Northern Territory. (Australian Aborigines) 1974. Color, 27 minutes, 16mm. (PS).

Over Rich, Over Sexed, and Over Here. 1987. The New Pacific Series. Color, 50 minutes, VHS. FIV.

Pacific Age, The. 1987. The New Pacific Series. Color, 50 minutes, VHS. FIV.

Pacific Island. (Marshall Islands) 1949. B&W, 18 minutes, 16mm. IFF (PS).

Papua New Guinea: Anthropology on Trial. (Melpa, Maisin Manus) 1983. Nova Series. Color, 57 minutes, 16mm. T-L (EMC) (PS).

People of the Free Train. (Fiji) n.d. Color, 14 minutes, 16mm. IU.

Place of Power in French Polynesia. (Tahiti) 1987. Human Face of the Pacific Series. Color, 28 minutes, VHS. FIV.

Quest for the Killers: The Kuru Mystery. (Fore) 1984. Color, 60 minutes, VHS. (PS).

Red Bowmen, The. (Papua New Guinea) 1982. Chris Owen. Color, 58 minutes, 16mm. DER.

Return to Paradise. 1987. The New Pacific Series. Color, 50 minutes, VHS. FIV.

Rock Engravings. (Australian Aborigines) 1969. Australian Museum Series. Color, 7 minutes, 16mm. (EMC) (PS).

Secrets of Easter Island. (Easter Island) 1988. Nova Series. Color, 58 minutes, VHS. (PS).

Shadow of the Rising Sun. 1987. The New Pacific Series. Color, 50 minutes, VHS. FIV.

Shark Callers of Kontu, The. (New Ireland) 1986. Dennis O'Rourke. Color, 54 minutes, 16mm, VHS. DCL.

Sons of Namatjira. (Australian Aborigines) 1982. Color, 50 minutes, 16mm. (EMC).

Spear in the Stone. (Australian Aborigines) 1983. Color, 35 minutes, 16mm. (EMC).

Stockman's Strategy. (Australian Aborigines) 1984. David MacDougall and Judith MacDougall. Color, 54 minutes, 16mm. (EMC).

Takeover. (Australian Aborigines) 1981. David MacDougall and Judith MacDougall. Color, 90 minutes, 16mm. (EMC).

Three Horsemen. (Australian Aborigines) 1983. David MacDougall and Judith MacDougall. Color, 55 minutes, 16mm, VHS, U-mat. (EMC).

Tidikawa and Friends. (Gebusi) 1973. Jef Doring and Su Doring. Color, 82 minutes, 16mm. DER (EMC) (PS).

Tighten the Drums: Self-Decoration among the Enga. (Mae Enga) 1982. Chris Owen. Color, 58 minutes, 16mm. DER.

Trobriand Cricket: An Ingenious Response to Colonialism. (Trobriand Islands) 1976. Jerry W. Leach. Color, 54 minutes, 16mm. (EMC) (PS).

Waiting for Harry. (Australian Aborigines) 1981. Kim McKenzie. Color, 57 minutes, 16mm. (EMC).

Walbiri Fire Ceremony: Ngatjakula. (Warlbiri) 1979. Roger Sandall. Australian Institute of Aboriginal Studies Series. Color, 21 minutes, 16mm. (EMC).

Walkabout (Revised Version). (Australian Aborigines) 1974. C. P. Mountford. (Original version 1946.) Color, 25 minutes, 16mm. (PS).

Western Samoa: I Can Get Another Wife but I Can't Get Parents. (Samoa) 1987. Human Face of the Pacific Series. Color, 28 minutes, VHS. FIV.

White Clay and Ochre. (Australian Aborigines) 1969. Australian Museum Series. Color, 15 minutes, 16mm. (EMC) (PS).

Yap: How Did You Know We'd Like TV? (Yap) 1987. Dennis O'Rourke. Color, 54 minutes, 16mm, VHS. DCL.

Yumi Yet. (Papua New Guinea) 1987. Dennis O'Rourke. Color, 54 minutes, 16mm, VHS. DCL.

Directory of Distributors

CBC	Canadian Broadcasting Corporation, CBC Educational Films, English Services Division, P.O. Box 500, Terminal A, Toronto, ON M5W 1E6 (245 Park Avenue, New York, NY 10017)
CRM	CRM/McGraw-Hill Films, 674 Via de la Valle, P.O. Box 641, Del Mar, CA 92014
DCL	Direct Cinema Limited Library, P.O. Box 315, Franklin Lakes, NJ 07417
DER	Documentary Educational Resources, 101 Morse Street, Watertown, MA 02172
EMC	University of California Extension Media Center, 2176 Shattuck Avenue, Berkeley, CA 94704
FIV	Films Incorporated Video, 5547 North Ravenswood Avenue, Chicago, IL 60640-1199
FL	Filmakers Library, Inc., 124 East Fortieth Street, New York, NY 10016
IFF	International Film Foundation, 155 West Seventy-Second Street, Room 306, New York, NY 10023
IU	Indiana University, Audio-Visual Center, Bloomington, IN 47405
MAC	Macmillan Films, 34 MacQuesten Parkway South, Mount Vernon, NY 10550
McG-H	McGraw-Hill Films, 11 West Nineteenth Street, New York, NY 10011
NYU	New York University, Films Division, Division of Center for Media Services, 26 Washington Place, New York, NY 10003
NZNFU	New Zealand National Film Unit, Fairway Drive, Avalon, Lower Hutt, New Zealand
PHENIX	Phoenix/BFA Films and Video, Inc., 468 Park Avenue South, New York, NY 10016
PS	Pennsylvania State University, Audio-Visual Services, Special Services Building, University Park, PA 16802
PSUPCR	Pennsylvania State University, Psych Cinema Register, 6 Willard Building, University Park, PA 16802
T-L	Time-Life Multimedia, 100 Eisenhower Drive, P.O. Box 644, Paramus, NJ 07653

Ethnonym Index

This index provides some of the alternative names and the names of major subgroups for cultures covered in this volume. The culture names that are entry titles are in boldface.